The Family and Local History Handbook

incorporating
The Genealogical Services Directory

8th Edition

In collaboration with

BRITISH ASSOCIATION FOR LOCAL HISTORY
www.balh.co.uk

Edited & Compiled

by

Robert Blatchford

Contents

265   Local History

315   Military History

361   The Genealogical Services Directory

443   Index to Advertisers, Index & Miscellaneous Information

Editorial

Welcome to the 8th Edition of the Handbook. During the time since the 7th Edition was published in February 2003 we will have lived through some memorable times both in our personal lives and in historical terms. Family events that have taken place have continued to build on our personal family histories. Events will have been happy and in some instances sad but they all help to create the rich tapestry of family and local history. These past twelve months have seen the war in Iraq with the tragic loss of life; in the United Kingdom one of the hottest summers for many years; and the exhilaration for the English of England winning the Rugby World Cup. In our personal lives weddings, births and deaths. should all be recorded for future generations.

Our own family has witnessed the wedding of our son, a family holiday in the Dordogne and the anticipation of a new member joining our daughter's two sons as this book is published. I organised The Great North Fair in September and then Elizabeth and I visited New England for the 'fall' colours and for research. On our return the production was progressing well until the postal strike held up much material for this Edition.

Again all design, layout and preparation is done in house on Apple Macintosh computers, a G4 Desktop and a G3 Power Book,using Quark Xpress 5, Adobe Photoshop 7 and Adobe Acrobat 5. The *Handbook* is produced electronically and is transferred to paper only when it is printed.

It may seem repetitive but I must acknowledge all the many people, too numerous to name individually who have helped me in so many ways. I am especially grateful to my wife, Elizabeth, who now must be regarded as one of the Editors, and the family for their patience and forbearance. Once again the technical help and advice from my printers Alan and Sandra Williamson has been invaluable, as is the support from the BALH.

Michael Cowan, the General Secretary of the BALH, retired in March 2003. I cannot let that event pass without acknowledging his help, advice and contribution over the previous seven editions for which I am very grateful.

Last but not least I am grateful once again to Nancy Redpath for her work in the final stages of preparation before the book goes to the printer.

Please support our advertisers as their contribution to the production of the *Handbook* is essential. If you do contact any of the advertisers please tell them that you saw their advertisement in *The Family and Local History Handbook*.

Suggestions from our readers are always welcome and where possible they are implemented in the next edition.We hope that you, our readers, enjoy this 8th edition as much as the previous ones.

Robert Blatchford

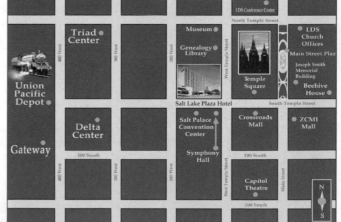

Feature Articles

"When I was a Boy"

Starting Out
A Beginners Guide to Family History
Doreen Hopwood
guides you through the early stages

Every family has its own, unique history, and our ancestors have helped to make us what we are today. For those of you about to embark on the ancestral trail, here are some basic guidelines to help you to proceed effectively and efficiently.

Until recently, it was the families of the rich and famous (or infamous!) whose histories were researched, but the same investigative techniques must be applied whatever the status of the family in order to produce a family tree. Patience and perseverance are two 'musts' for the prospective family historian, along with a 'sense of the past'. As research takes you back in time, be prepared for surprises – and maybe the odd shock! We need to step back into the contemporary world of our forebears to understand their daily lives and you'll soon find yourselves delving into local and social history to find out more. What did a puddler do for a living? Court Heneage in Aston Manor may sound like a very grand address, but was a set of back- to-back houses in Victorian Birmingham!

Success with research may also depend on the survival of records, whether your family moved frequently, their status and even the popularity of the surname being studied. Perhaps you have an unusual surname and want to find out more - but be aware that in the nineteenth century many of our ancestors were illiterate and you may well encounter changes in spelling as they were written down as they sounded. On the plus side, however, names like Jones aren't prone to this problem!

Whilst this directory contains information about all of the major repositories in the United Kingdom – the Public Record Office, the Family Records Centre, county record offices and libraries – these are NOT the places to start your research. Your first steps should be to talk to members of your family and gather together as much information as you can. In addition to 'official' documents such as birth, death and marriage certificates, wills etc, the following may provide valuable information to aid research:

A family bible – a great find, as it usually records dates of events as they happened.

Memorial cards, obituaries and grave papers.

School reports, apprenticeship papers, graduation certificates, occupational pensions.

Military service records, medals or other awards.

Society/club membership cards or trade union subscription cards.

Diaries, scrapbooks, letters, newspaper cuttings, old address or birthday books.

Photograph albums are particularly helpful as 'memory joggers' when talking to older members of the family, and if possible, make a recording of any interviews. Whilst there are certain questions you need to ask, take care not to be too demanding - several short interviews may be more productive than one long one. This is also a good time to ensure that you have recorded on your own photos 'who, when and where'. Future generations will thank you for it!

Don't discount the family myth or legend – every family has at least one. They are usually firmly based on the truth, but like Chinese whispers, they tend to become embellished or distorted as they are passed on from generation to generation. Set out to verify the information with documentary evidence and share your findings with other family members. You may find out that someone is already researching your family's history, or is interested in joining in with you. This is an excellent way of sharing the workload – and the costs. There are numerous books about genealogical research available – and you may be able to borrow some of these from your library. Monthly family history magazines usually contain a 'Readers Interests' section in which people submit details of the surname, period, and area of their research, and you may find a possible entry for your family. If you do respond to any of these, please remember to enclose a stamped address envelope or international reply coupon.

Joining your local family history society will bring you into contact with individuals with the same interest – the addresses of members of the Federation of Family History Societies can be found on the Internet at www.ffhs.org.uk As well as regular meetings, you'll receive newsletters containing details of their publications and a 'members interest' section. As you progress with your research, you may also want to join the society covering the area where your ancestors lived.

Attend a family history class. There is a whole range available, ranging from one-off workshops to academic courses leading to formal qualifications. Your local Education Authority will be able to advise you of locally run courses and look out for information at libraries and in family history journals.

In this electronic age, more and more information is becoming available through the Internet. This is a great way of finding out about resources held in the area you are interested in and there are some excellent genealogical websites. However, don't expect to be able to compile your family tree solely from the World Wide Web. Whilst there are many indexes and resources accessible in this way, you will need to carry out research in numerous repositories – and this is part of the fun of family history. Nothing is more rewarding than seeing a 150-year old signature of one of your ancestors in a parish register, or visiting the church where family events were celebrated!

YOU are the most important person in your family tree, because you must always work from the known back to the unknown, generation by generation - yourself, parents, grandparents, great grandparents and so on. Never try to come forwards with your research – you may end up with an impressive family tree, but not necessarily your own. For most of us the first major national source we encounter is the General Register Office (GRO) Index, which includes every birth, death and marriage registered in England and Wales since the introduction of civil registration on 1 July 1837. Scotland and Ireland have their own registration systems, which commenced in 1855 and 1864 respectively. The index has separate volumes for birth, death and marriage and until 1984, when it became an annual cumulative index, it is split into four quarters:

March:
events registered in January, February and March
June:
events registered in April, May and June
September:
events registered in July, August and September
December:
events registered in October, November and December
Each index is arranged alphabetically by surname, then by forename(s) and shows the district where the event was registered, the volume and page number. As a period of up to 42 days is allowed between the birth and its registration, check the quarter following the birth.

Your birth certificate shows your parents names and mothers maiden name   THEN
Your parents marriage certificate shows the names of both grandfathers THEN
Your parents birth certificates show your grandparents names and grandmothers maiden name   THEN
Your grandparents marriage certificates show the names of both greatgrandfathers.......and so on.......

The General Register Office Index is now available in many libraries and other repositories. The Office of National Statistics (ONS) at Smedley Hydro, Trafalgar Road, Birkdale, Southport, Merseyside, PR8 2HH can provide details of local holdings. Once you have traced the entry you require, the full copy certificate can be purchased by post from the above address, from the register office at which the event was registered or by personal visit to the Family Records Centre at Myddleton Place, Myddleton

Street, London EC1R 1UW. In the latter case, the certificate can either be collected a few days later or posted to you.

Before the establishment of civil registration, it was the responsibility of the Church to record baptisms, marriages and burials, and in order to utilise the church registers, you will need to know the parish where the events took place. A census – a count of the population – has been taken every 10 years since 1801 with the exception of 1941. The census of 1841 is the earliest to contain information about individuals and as there is a 100-year closure on public access to the census enumerator's books, the latest that is currently available (for England and Wales) is the 1901 census. For the first time this has now become available online and has a full name index, so you do not need to have an address in order to trace individuals. There are also facilities to search by area.

Census returns contain lists of all inhabited buildings, showing the names, ages, occupations, marital status, birth places and relationship to the head of household of everyone resident on the night the census was taken – but with less detail on the 1841 return. It is usually necessary to know an address – or at least a street to 'find' a household as the returns are arranged by enumeration district, but there is a surname index to the 1881 census of the whole of England and Wales. Many local family history societies have produced indices for their own locality in respect of other returns. The census enumerators books for the whole of England and Wales are available at the Family Records Centre, whilst county record offices and main libraries usually hold copies covering their locality.

The Church of Jesus Christ of Latter Day Saints (the Mormon Church) has produced the International Genealogical Index (IGI), which is a worldwide resource and regularly expanded in its on-line form as FamilySearch on the Internet. Much of the information has been taken from original parish registers and complemented by family histories submitted by Church members. In its microfiche format, it is arranged by country then region/county and within these, alphabetically by surname, then forename and chronologically by event. For England and Wales, the majority of entries cover baptisms and marriages in the Established Church and may go back to the introduction of parish registers in the mid sixteenth century. The IGI can be found at major libraries, county record offices and at Church of Jesus

Christ of Latter Day Saints Family History Centres. Their addresses can be found in telephone directories. Once an entry has been found on the IGI/FamilySearch always obtain a copy of the entry from the relevant repository as this will, in most cases, provide additional information, including the signatures of the bride groom and witnesses at marriages. Whilst some churches still hold their parish registers, the majority will be found in the Diocesan Record Office – which is often based at the County Record Office. As well as registers of baptism, marriage and burial, the 'Parish Chest' contains numerous other records relating to the Church, its officers and its parishioners. You may find that one of your ancestors was a prominent member of the church and appears as a Churchwarden or other parish official. Alternatively, an ancestor may have hit hard times and appear in the Overseers of the Poor's accounts as being in receipt of parish relief.

More and more 'finding aids' and indexes are being produced for family history. Such as the National

Burials Index available on CD, and complements the published books of monumental inscriptions transcribed from (legible) gravestones in church burial grounds. You can "browse" the catalogue of the Public Record Office (PRO) on-line prior to paying a visit and so organise your time effectively. The series of information leaflets is also available on the Internet at www.pro.gov.uk, and these cover a wide range of topics for family history. Servicemen who died during the First and Second World Wars can be traced on the Commonwealth War Graves Commission website at www.cwgc.org.uk

Since 1858 it has been the responsibility of the Government to administer wills and grant probates. The national, annual indexes (Index of Wills and Letters of Administration) can be found in major libraries and other record offices and the extracts include sufficient information to enable a full copy will to be purchased. They are arranged in alphabetical order by surname, then forename, and appear in the index covering the year in which the probate was granted - which may be several years after the date of death. Don't assume that only the rich or gentry left wills – a glance at the above indexes shows how many 'ordinary' people made wills – and whilst the monetary value may be negligible, the amount of genealogical information can be enormous.

Do keep an open mind as you carry out research – whilst official documents provide evidence of names, dates, occupations and addresses, there are many other sources that will help to put your ancestors in their contemporary setting. Maps and photographs of the area in which the family lived will show how much (or how little) it has changed over time, whilst local newspapers give an account of what was going on in the area. National and global events – such as the world wars of the twentieth century – affected our families and the demise of a local industry/employer might have instigated migration or a complete change of occupation for family members.

You may have thought that your family was 'Brummie born and bred' but as you progress back in time, you will probably find that your ancestors came from all over the British Isles – and maybe beyond. The search will take you far afield in geographical terms as well as in time, adding to the fascination that is family history.

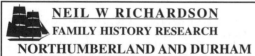

Making sense of certificates - reading between the lines!
Doreen Hopwood

From 1538 to 1837, the government of England (and Wales) relied on the church to record the population by the keeping of registers of baptism, marriage, and burial. This system was by no means comprehensive, and there was no central register of events.

The introduction of civil registration on 1st July 1837 in England and Wales rectified this by the keeping of records locally (at the relevant register office) and centrally (by the Register General Office). The certificates of birth, marriage and death are one of the main sources used by family historians, but, as well as the information they are designed to give, they also contain 'pointers' for further research.

Birth certificates

If a time of birth is given on a birth certificate, this usually indicates a multiple live birth. However, in the early day of civil registration, some registrars include this information as a matter of course. Twins (or other multiple births) can generally be identified on the General Register Office Index because they either have the same or consecutive GRO reference number.

It did not become compulsory to register births until 1875, so you may find that the person you are seeking was simply not registered. In these cases, it may be necessary to purchase the birth certificate of a sibling in order to establish the mother's maiden name.

A period of 42 days (six weeks) is given in which to register a birth. Occasionally, the parents did not get round to registering within this timescale, so you may find that a birth date has been 'adjusted' to fall within six weeks of the date of registration. This accounts for some baptismal entries which seem to suggest that the child was baptised before he/she was born.

Before the Registration Act of 1874 came into effect, the mother of an illegitimate child could have the name of the putative father put on the birth certificate. Since then, in cases where the parents are not married to one another, both mother and father must be present at the registration of the birth to enable both their names to be on the certificate. When a married woman registers the birth of her child, it is assumed that the child is that of her husband and will be registered as such, unless the mother states otherwise.

A person may not be known by the name on his/her birth certificate. Sometimes forenames

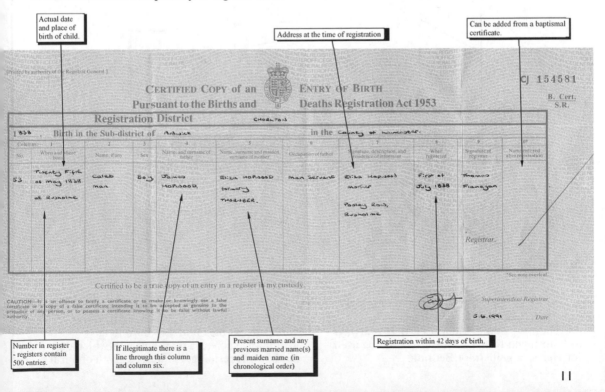

Actual date and place of birth of child.

Address at the time of registration

Can be added from a baptismal certificate.

Number in register - registers contain 500 entries.

If illegitimate there is a line through this column and column six.

Present surname and any previous married name(s) and maiden name (in chronological order)

Registration within 42 days of birth.

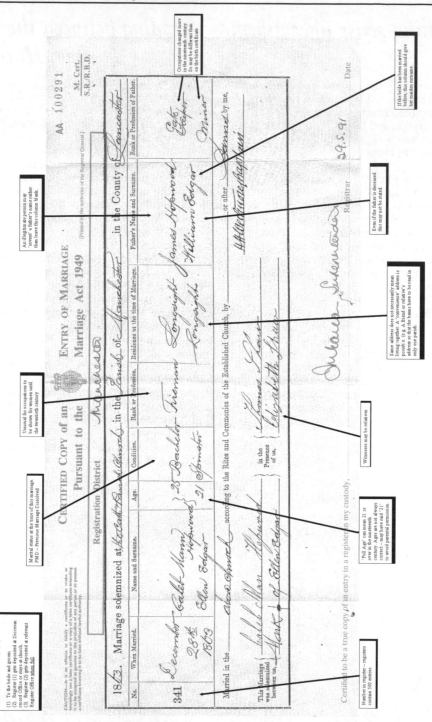

become transposed, or one may be dropped altogether. Names which are popular today, such as Jack, Millie etc., would probably have been registered as John and Millicent until the early twentieth century. Abbreviations can be misleading – don't assume that Bert is always the shortened form of Albert, it could be used for Herbert, Hubert, or Bertram.

The address at which the child was born may be a hospital or nursing home, or the home of another family member. The address shown at the time of registration is usually the family home, unless the child was born in an institution, such as a workhouse in which the mother was residing. Addresses given on birth certificates do not always tally with those given on census returns, so it is worthwhile examining a contemporary map if possible. Frustratingly, only the name of the street or village may be shown on the certificate, which can involve a lengthy search of the relevant census.

Occupations of fathers may differ from the birth registration of one child to that of the next. This may simply be that the registrars used different terminology for the same type of work – such as 'tinsmith' and 'metalworker'. Workers had to be flexible to meet the demands of industry and the decline of agriculture, so the rural 'Ag/lab' of 1845 may appear as a 'general labourer' in an urban environment ten years later.

Marriage Certificates
The format of these certificates has not changed since the introduction of civil registration in 1837, unlike those of birth and death, which were radically altered in 1969. Whilst birth and death certificates can only be obtained from the register office where the event took place, or through the General Register Office, it may be possible to obtain a copy of a marriage certificate from the church or the Diocesan Record Office covering the parish. At a church wedding, the bride and groom sign their names three times:
1.   On the certificate, which is issued to them, and in two registers:
2.   Register One – when full is sent to the Register Office in which the parish is located. Register Two – when full either stays at the Church, or is deposited in the relevant Diocesan Record Office.

In some small parishes, the register that was started on 1 July 1837 may still not be full, so the only way of obtaining a marriage certificate in these instances is from the incumbent of the Church.

Many certificates describe the bride and groom as 'full age', which means 21 years of age before 1969 and 18 years after that date. In the nineteenth century neither party would have had to present their birth certificates to the registrar, so, even where ages are shown, they are not always correct. There was a great movement from rural areas into the growing towns and so the bride and groom may well not have been known by the vicar who married them, making it easier to give false ages.

Although register offices were established on 1st July 1837, these accounted for only a small proportion of marriages in the early days – possibly because of their close association to the local workhouse – in many cases the

Superintendent Registrar was one of the Guardians of the Poor.

If you are able to examine the actual parish register, or view it on microfilm, it is worth having a look at entries either side of the one you require, especially if the names of the witnesses do not appear to be relatives of the bride or groom. In some parishes it was the practice for a member of the parish council to be a witness at all weddings.

Although Hardwicke's Marriage Act of 1754 removed the legality of marriages other than in the Church of England, Jews, and members of the Society of Friends (Quaker), were the exception and could still be married within their faith. Quaker marriage certificates generally include the signatures of all members present at the marriage as witnesses.

The absence of a father's name on the certificate usually denotes illegitimacy, but some incumbents were in the habit of leaving this column blank. Isaac Spooner was the vicar of Edgbaston Parish Church in Birmingham during the mid nineteenth century, and, according to the entries he made, it would be easy to assume that all the marriage parties were over 21, lived in Birmingham, and had no fathers.

Death Certificates
After the June quarter of 1969, these become more helpful for the family historian because they give the date and place of birth of the deceased person, and the maiden name of a married woman. However, the information on certificates is not always accurate, especially concerning the 'age at death'. The person who attended the register office to register the death may not have known the true age of the deceased person, so this may be a 'guesstimate'. There is no linkage between the death registration and the burial/cremation, but, by the twentieth century, announcements of deaths generally appeared in the 'Family Announcements' sections of local newspapers, and these provide details of the funeral arrangements.

It is also worth looking for a will/letters of administration for the deceased, as this should provide additional biographical information about the family. The National Index of Wills and Letters of Administration can be found in major repositories from 1858. Before this wills were proved in the ecclesiastical courts, and many wills proved at the Prerogative Court of Canterbury can be found at www.documentsonline.gov.uk

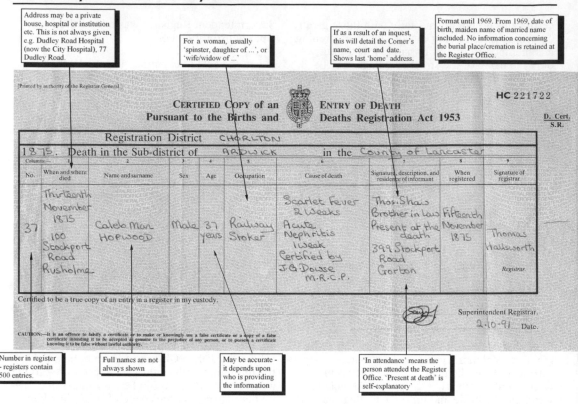

Address may be a private house, hospital or institution etc. This is not always given, e.g. Dudley Road Hospital (now the City Hospital), 77 Dudley Road.

For a woman, usually 'spinster, daughter of ...', or 'wife/widow of ...'

If as a result of an inquest, this will detail the Corner's name, court and date. Shows last 'home' address.

Format until 1969. From 1969, date of birth, maiden name of married name included. No information concerning the burial place/cremation is retained at the Register Office.

[Printed by authority of the Registrar General.]

CERTIFIED COPY of an ENTRY of DEATH
Pursuant to the Births and Deaths Registration Act 1953

HC 221722

D. Cert.
S.R.

Registration District CHORLTON

1875. Death in the Sub-district of ARDWICK in the County of Lancaster

No.	When and where died	Name and surname	Sex	Age	Occupation	Cause of death	Signature, description, and residence of informant	When registered	Signature of registrar
37	Thirteenth November 1875 100 Stockport Road Rusholme	Caleb Man Hopwood	Male	37 years	Railway Stoker	Scarlet Fever 2 Weeks Acute Nephritis 1 week Certified by J.G. Dowse M.R.C.P.	Thos. Shaw Brother in Law Present at the death 399 Stockport Road Gorton	Fifteenth November 1875	Thomas Hallsworth Registrar.

Certified to be a true copy of an entry in a register in my custody.

Superintendent Registrar.
2·10·91 Date.

CAUTION:—It is an offence to falsify a certificate or to make or knowingly use a false certificate or a copy of a false certificate intending it to be accepted as genuine to the prejudice of any person, or to possess a certificate knowing it to be false without lawful authority.

Number in register - registers contain 500 entries.

Full names are not always shown

May be accurate - it depends upon who is providing the information

'In attendance' means the person attended the Register Office. 'Present at death' is self-explanatory'

Causes of death are sometimes vague, especially in early death certificates, and can be shown as 'old age', 'syncope' etc. Old medical dictionaries provide details of terms used and their modern day equivalents.

Where there was a coroner's inquest, the coroner is shown as the informant on the death certificate, along with the date of the inquest. Coroner's records are closed for a period of 75 years following the date of the inquest, and are usually deposited at the local or county record office. If the event occurred less than 75 years ago, it is likely that there was a report in the local newspaper, and many libraries have produced files of coroner's news cuttings – usually catalogued according to the date of the inquest.

The Register of Stillbirths (and the Adopted Children's Register) came into effect in 1927 – prior to this date, stillbirths were not registered. However, it may be possible to find adoption documents in solicitors' deposits preceding 1927 if a formal arrangement had been made between the natural and adoptive parents. There is no linkage between the 'natural' birth registration and the adopted register entry. The former is simply endorsed 'adopted'

As well as providing the key to the next stage of research, civil registration certificates give us a greater insight into our ancestors' lives – did

they sign the marriage certificate or mark it with an 'X'? What kind of work did a puddler do? Their movements can be charted by reference to certificates issued during their lifetimes, and their last address, taken from the death certificate, will help us to find their final resting places.

County & Country Codes (Pre 1974 counties)

England

All Counties	ALL
Bedfordshire	BDF
Berkshire	BRK
Buckinghamshire	BKM
Cambridgeshire	CAM
Cheshire	CHS
Cornwall	CON
Cumberland	CUL
Derbyshire	DBY
Devonshire	DEV
Dorsetshire	DOR
Durham	DUR
Essex	ESS
Gloucestershire	GLS
Hampshire	HAM
Herefordshire	HEF
Hertfordshire	HRT
Huntingdonshire	HUN
Isle of Wight	IOW
Kent	KEN
Lancashire	LAN
Leicestershire	LEI
Lincolnshire	LIN
London (city)	LND
Middlesex	MDX
Norfolk	NFK
Northamptonshire	NTH
Northumberland	NBL
Nottinghamshire	NTT
Oxfordshire	OXF
Rutland	RUT
Shropshire	SAL
Somerset	SOM
Staffordshire	STS
Suffolk	SFK
Surrey	SRY
Sussex	SSX
Warwickshire	WAR
Westmorland	WES
Wiltshire	WIL
Worcestershire	WOR
Yorkshire	YKS
YKS E Riding	ERY
YKS N Riding	NRY
YKS W Riding	WRY

Wales — **WLS**

Anglesey	AGY
Brecknockshire	BRE
Caernarvonshire	CAE
Cardiganshire	CGN
Carmarthenshire	CMN
Denbighshire	DEN
Flintshire	FLN
Glamorgan	GLA
Merionethshire	MER
Monmouthshire	MON
Montgomeryshire	MGY
Pembrokeshire	PEM
Radnorshire	RAD

Scotland — **SCT**

Aberdeenshire	ABD
Angus	ANS
Argyllshire	ARL
Ayrshire	AYR
Banffshire	BAN
Berwickshire	BEW
Bute	BUT
Caithness-shire	CAI
Clackmannanshire	CLK
Dumfriesshire	DFS
Dunbartonshire	DNB
East Lothian	ELN
Fifeshire	FIF
Forfarshire	ANS
Invernessshire	INV
Kincardineshire	KCD
Kinrossshire	KRS
Kirkcudbrightshire	KKD
Lanarkshire	LKS
Midlothian	MLN
Moray	MOR
Nairnshire	NAI
Orkney Isles	OKI
Peeblesshire	PEE
Perthshire	PER
Renfrewshire	RFW
Ross & cromarty	ROC
Roxburghshire	ROX
Selkirkshire	SEL
Shetland Isles	SHI
Stirlingshire	STI
Sutherland	SUT
West Lothian	WLN
Wigtownshire	WIG

Ireland (Eire) — **IRL**

Antrim	ANT
Armagh	ARM
Carlow	CAR
Cavan	CAV
Clare	CLA
Cork	COR
Donegal	DON
Down	DOW
Dublin	DUB
Fermanagh	FER
Galway	GAL
Kerry	KER
Kildare	KID
Kilkenny	KIK
Leitrim	LEI
Leix(Queens)	LEX
Limerick	LIM
Londonderry	LDY
Longford	LOG
Louth	LOU
Mayo	MAY
Meath	MEA
Monaghan	MOG
Offaly(Kings)	OFF
Roscommon	ROS
Sligo	SLI
Tipperary	TIP
Tyrone	TYR
Waterford	WAT
Westmeath	WES
Wexford	WEX
Wicklow	WIC

Channel Islands — **CHI**

Alderney	ALD
Guernsey	GSY
Jersey	JSY
Sark	SRK

Isle of Man — **IOM**

Australia — **AUS**

Capital Territory	ACT
New South Wales	NSW
Northern Territory	NT
Queensland	QLD
South Australia	SA
Tasmania	TAS
Victoria	VIC
Western Australia	WA

Canada — **CAN**

Alberta	ALB
British Columbia	BC
Manitoba	MAN
New Brunswick	NB
Newfoundland	NFD
North West Terr	NWT
Nova Scotia	NS
Ontario	ONT
Prince Edward Is	PEI
Quebec	QUE
Saskatchewan	SAS
Yukon Territory	YUK

Europe

Austria	OES
Belarus	BRS
Belgium	BEL
Croatia	CRO
Czechoslovakia	CS
Czech Republic	CZR
Denmark	DEN
Estonia	EST
Finland	FIN
France	FRA
Germany (1991)	BRD
German Old Emp	GER
Greece	GR
Hungary	HU
Italy	ITL
Latvia	LAT
Liechtenstein	LIE
Lithguania	LIT
Luxembourg	LUX
Netherlands	NL
New Zealand	NZ
Norway	NOR
Poland	POL
Romania	RO
Russia	RUS
Slovakia	SLK
Slovinia	SLO
Spain (Espagne)	ESP
Sweden	SWE
Switzerland	CH
Ukraine	UKR
United Kingdom	UK
United States	USA
USSR	SU
Yugoslavia	YU
Papua New Guinea	PNG
Rep South Africa	RSA

These codes are used to avoid confusion in the use of abbreviations for countries and counties. Created by Dr Colin Chapman they are universally recognised and should always be used.

Lochin Publishing 6 Holywell Road, Dursley GL11 5RS England

Census Returns

A Census has been taken every 10 years since 1801 except in 1941 during the Second World War.
The census returns for 1801, 1811, 1821, 1831 were not preserved.
However there are some areas where returns for these years have been found.
The first census that is useful to researchers is the one taken in 1841.
The Census returns were taken on:

1841	7th June 1841	1851	30th March 1851	1861	7th April 1861
1871	2nd April 1871	1881	3rd April 1881	1891	5th April 1891
		1901	31st March 1901		

These census returns can be consulted. They were subject to public closure for 100 years because of the sensitive personal information they contained.

WE'LL HELP YOU TRACE YOUR FAMILY HISTORY

Your FamilyTree

THE BEST MAGAZINE FOR GENEALOGY

YES! I would like to subscribe to 6 issues of Your Family Tree

SUBSCRIBE! (I understand that I will receive the next 6 issues)

☐ Direct Debit – (UK only) I would like to pay £20.96 by Direct Debit

ALTERNATIVE METHODS

UK Credit Card
☐ £20.96 – save 30%

North America/Europe
☐ £22.99

Rest of World
☐ £24.99

PAYEE'S DETAILS

Title ....Initials .... Surname ....

Address ....

.... Postcode .... Country........................

Tel no. (inc. STD) .... Email address...

Your subscription will start with the next available issue

METHOD OF PAYMENT

☐ Cheque ☐ Switch ☐ Mastercard ☐ Visa ☐ American Express

(£ sterling cheque drawn on a UK bank account payable to Future Publishing Ltd)

Card no.

☐☐☐☐ ☐☐☐☐ ☐☐☐☐ ☐☐☐☐ ☐☐☐☐ ☐☐☐☐

Expiry date ☐☐ / ☐☐   Switch only: issue no. ☐☐   valid date ☐☐ / ☐☐

Signature .... Date...............................

☐ Please tick here if you do not wish to receive mail from Future Publishing and other carefully selected companies

Send to: **Your Family Tree, Subscriptions**
UK: Future Publishing, FREEPOST BS4900, Somerton, Somerset, TA11 6BR
Overseas: Future Publishing, Cary Court, Somerton, Somerset TA11 6TB, UK

You may photocopy this blank form and then complete it. You cannot fax or email Direct Debit forms

---

Instruction to your Bank or Building Society to pay Direct Debits.

future publishing

1. Name and full postal address of your Bank or Building Society branch

To: The Manager

....Bank/Building Society

Address ....

....

.........................Postcode ....

2. Name(s) of account holder(s)

3. Branch sort code
(from the top right hand corner of your cheque)
☐☐ ☐☐ ☐☐

Originator's Identification Number

7 6 8 1 9 5

Media with passion
Future Publishing Ltd,
Cary Court, Somerton,
Somerset, TA11 6BR

DIRECT Debit

4. Bank or Building Society account number
☐☐☐☐☐☐☐☐

5. Instruction to your bank or building society
Please pay Future Publishing Direct Debits from the account detailed on this Instruction subject to the safeguards assured by the Direct Debit Guarantee. I understand that this instruction may remain with Future Publishing and if so, details will be passed electronically to my bank or building society.

Signature(s)_____
Date_____

Ref No (Office use only)
Banks and Building Societies may not accept Direct Debit Instructions for some types of account.

OFFER ENDS 31 December 2004

ORDER CODE: YFTLFH

The National British Fair
for Family and Local History

The Great North Fair

Gateshead International Stadium
Neilson Road Gateshead NE10 0EF

Saturday 11th September 2004
10.00a.m. - 4.30.p.m.

Admission £2.50
Accompanied Children under 15 Free

The *NEW* National Fair for Family and Local History

Major exhibitors from England, Wales, Scotland and Ireland and from Overseas

Easy Access by Air, Rail, Metro and Motorway

Free Parking

Refreshments

Free Advice

www.GreatNorthFair.com

2005 - Saturday 10th September 2005

Poor & Destitute Children and the Law
Jean Cole

Family history has always been a matter of dogged detective work but to trace the history of some of our ancestors when they were children, especially if they came from poor families in large towns and cities, may have been more than difficult. There are so many ways but here I suggest a few sources that may not have been tapped.

Not the least amongst the following records are those of crimes and prisons. For some poor children crime was a way of life - neglect being one of the major factors. In London, alone, it was estimated there were 30,000 poor and lawless children committing 95% of crimes and in Manchester an 1865 Survey showed that out of every 15 children aged between 2 and 12 years of age, eight were neglected.

Calendars of Prisoners and cases heard in Petty, Quarter Sessions and the Assize Courts reveal endless young folk being held in custody for a diversity of misdemeanours. The Home Office records at *The National Archives* (PRO) reveal a wealth of information concerning young boys from the ages of 8 and 9 being convicted of various crimes, being sent to gaol and then transferred to prison hulks ready for transportation and, in some cases, being apprenticed to one of HM's colonies overseas (New Zealand and Australia). It was obvious, too, that some of these children would not survive into adulthood. Edward Darmeday, 10, convicted of stealing a bundle of paper at London Sessions in October 1823, sentenced to seven years, died in March 1826 and John Clough, 14, convicted of felony at Preston Sessions, sentenced to 7 years in 1824, had been sent to one of the prison hulks but, on becoming sick, was transferred to the 'Canada Hospital Ship' in 1826 where he died. Descriptions of the boys were often supplied such as that of 9 year old Francis Hayden, in 1842, born at Westminster, mother, Mary Hayden, 22 Nottingham Street, Brighton. He was convicted of larceny and according to the gaoler's report was 'bad and disorderly.' Francis was C of E, had brown hair, blue eyes, fair complexion, round visage, small made, single, 4ft 1in, able to read and write. Distinguishing marks, large scar near corner of left eye, face freckled, small scar on left thumb. He was transferred from Parkhurst Prison, Isle of Wight to the York hulk at Chatham on 15 September 1842. Other boys such as William Tuck, aged 8 years, who was convicted of stealing bottles at Norwich Assizes in January 1839 was sentenced to 7 years

transportation and eventually was apprenticed to New Zealand. Gaoler's report of 31 May 1842 revealed that William was single, unable to read or write but was 'quick'. One could only feel compassion for Isaac Burnand, 12 years, convicted of burglary at Northallerton Assizes, April 1839, sentenced to 10 years transportation. In May 1842 he was apprenticed to New Zealand and was described as single, unable to read or write, had been an errand boy. Behaviour - poor and destitute, turned out by his parents. The list of such boys being convicted for so many years was seemingly endless.

In 1876 James Cogan of Great Bedwin, a widower with seven children, applied to the Marlborough magistrates in Petty Sessions, under Section 16 of the Industrial Schools Act 1866, for his uncontrollable daughter, Julia aged 12, to be placed in an Industrial School. His eldest daughter Ann, who had been brought back from her position in service to look after the children after her mother's death, stated Julia was sulky, in mischief every day, had been stealing money and kept running away. Even after being chastised she ran away again the same day and had been found on the railway station at Hungerford. She affirmed Julia had been brought up in the traditions of the Church of England. After further enquiries the magistrates ordered that Julia was to be taken by Ann to the Dorset Home Certified School for Girls at Poole to be detained there for four years. Records of this school may reveal whether Julia had become a reformed character by the time of her release.

John Pounds, a poor crippled shoemaker of Portsmouth, was just an ordinary man who had been instrumental in leading children into more useful lives and was the originator of the Ragged Schools. By 1844 the Ragged School Union was founded by Lord Shaftesbury and ragged schools were set up around the country in crowded towns and cities in an endeavour to teach poor children the 3 R's to enable them to obtain employment and so avoid a life of crime. School log books and records of various institutions can yield fertile results and, into the bargain, these types of sources can furnish a vast cornucopia of social history as it actually happened.

There were other men who brought to the fore the plight of poor children, men such as Charles Dickens, Henry Mayhew, Angus Bethune Reach and John Hollingshead to name but a few.

In the late 1840's Mayhew interviewed a poor little watercress seller who, aged only 8 years, spent from 4 in the morning to late at night selling her watercress to scrape a living. It was inevitable that many such poor young children would eventually be enticed into a life of crime and prostitution. For instance, under the auspices of Sir John Fielding, the Female Orphan Asylum was opened to rescue vagrant girls from the streets of London who were in imminent danger of being forced into prostitution. Here they were trained in the domestic arts and places found for them in domestic service. Eventually, the Government, aware of prostitution being rife, set up a Parliamentary Select Committee in 1881 to investigate cases of young girls who had been enticed into this trade for French and Belgian brothels. To read the results of this enquiry is chilling to say the least.

Illegitimate babies and very young children would often be abandoned by their parents who were unable to take care of them and some of the more fortunate ones ended up in various institutions such as the Foundling Hospital, Barnardo's, Shaftesbury Homes and other philanthropic societies such as the Waifs and Strays Society and the Marine Society.

Average life expectancy in the northern industrial areas during the late 18th and early 19th centuries were, I have to say, quite shocking, for Manchester workers life expectancy was 17 yrs, Liverpool 15 yrs, Leeds 19 yrs, Bolton 18 yrs although life expectancy for the gentry in these areas were approximately double those of workers - Manchester 38 yrs, Liverpool 35 yrs, Leeds 44 yrs and Bolton 34 yrs.

Statistics for England and Wales in 1880, 1881 and 1882 revealed the following information. 1880 - 42,542 illegitimate births out of 881,643

total births registered: 1881 - 43,120 illegitimate births out of 883,642 total births registered: 1882 - 43,155 illegitimate births out of 889,014 total births registered.

'The Poor Law Unions' Gazette' copies of which are held in the British Library Newspaper Library at Colindale, reveals many an advertisement from Poor Law Union Clerks for mothers of abandoned children to be found and to pay the consequences of deserting their children. Correspondence between Poor Law Unions Boards of Guardians and the Poor Law Commissioners can be found in the records of the Ministry of Health (MH) in *The National Archives* (PRO) (see Reading and Sources list)

The Parish of St James, Clerkenwell, London in 1859 inserted the following advertisement.

> Harriet Matilda Purchase, aged 24 years, 5ft 8 ins, fair complexion, hazel eyes and dark hair, left her illegitimate child, Thomas Bullen Gill at the surgery of Mr Gill, White Lion Street, Pentonville. She formerly lived as a servant in the neighbourhood of Duncan Terrace, City Road, afterwards at Mr Goodyears, Aldersgate Street - last heard of in Ramsgate.

One can imagine the consternation of Mr Gill, the dentist, being dumped with a small, squalling baby. To me, Mr Gill was probably the father of young Thomas!

Pauper apprenticeships are another invaluable source for tracing the whereabouts of some of our poorer ancestors. Many city, town and parish records include these documents which inform us to whom and where a poor child was apprenticed and with some good fortune, what happened to them eventually when their extremely long apprenticeship was completed. The Duke of Somerset's Charity in Salisbury placed pauper children all over the country, even overseas, into various trades. From the numerous settlement certificates I have transcribed and indexed over the years, it was noticeable that many young folk did not remain in the places where they had been born or apprenticed and recourse to settlement records may reveal more information. Between 1700 and 1708 the Master of the Salisbury Workhouse, apprenticed four workhouse boys, Thomas Mann, John Bishop, Moses Clarke and Peter Hobbs to Commander Peter Chamberlaine of HMS Advice - records of the Admiralty (ADM) in the National Archives (PRO) for the 'Advice' may reveal more information about these boys, their naval careers and whether they survived the harsh life at sea. Other poor children from this workhouse such as the unfortunate orphan or abandoned child, John Grist of St Edmund's, Salisbury, was apprenticed to Thomas Woodford, chimney sweeper. One can only hazard a guess at the terrible life this poor child was forced to lead as little chimney sweep. Joseph Hibberd, son of Elizabeth Hibberd, widow, was apprenticed in 1742 to Richard Dennis of Portsea, Hampshire, master attendant at HM Dockyard as a seaman, to prepare and fit rigging for ships, again his career should be traceable.

In the Marlborough St Peter's pauper apprenticeship indentures it was shown that about nine small children were offloaded from the parish on 8 May 1745 to Benjamin Cowley of Wolverhampton, locksmith, to be apprenticed to that trade for varying terms. John, Mary and Jane May were apprenticed by the Bradford on Avon overseers to Joseph Buckley of Ashton under Lyne in 1802 as 'fine drawers' which was not a particularly wonderful occupation for young folk as this involved making wire by drawing pieces of ductile metal through a series of holes decreasing in diameter, through a steel plate! Where else, though, would a genealogist discover seemingly firm ancestry in the areas of Wolverhampton and Ashton under Lyne and their environments to be really that of Wiltshire origin?

The 'Bristol Mirror' dated 15 February 1812 published the following advertisement: 'Wanted: 50 female children to be apprenticed to cotton weavers in Derby - ages 9 to 16.' Certainly this was an excellent way for a parish to offload their unwanted poor children and to hope they were off their hands forever. In 1817 the Vicar of

Congleton, Cheshire, full of Christian spirit, wrote to Samuel Greg of Styal Mill 'the thought had occurred to me that some of the younger branches of the poor of this parish might be useful to you as apprentices in your factory at Quarry Bank. If you are in want of any of the above, we could readily furnish you with ten or more at from nine to twelve years of age, of both sexes...' Samuel Greg replied that he wanted about twelve young girls aged from ten to twelve years and that he required two guineas each from the parish plus specified clothing. Children, then it seemed, were so much unwanted liabilities to be sent away with no thought as to their future welfare. Records of Styal Mill may well provide information about these children from Congleton and what happened to them, eventually.

Parliamentary Commission Enquiries into the various living and working conditions of men, women and children are what I term 'on the spot' interviews with workers who informed the Commissioners and were recorded in their own words just how they lived and worked. To me these can be the most marvellous sources of social history and, who knows, an ancestor may have even been interviewed and his or her words then recorded for posterity. Nineteenth century Parliamentary Commission enquiries into working conditions in mines, factories, lacemaking, chimney sweeps, agricultural labourers, boarding out of workhouse orphans etc can be invaluable in its historical and genealogical content.

Obviously there are so many other sources, other than the brief ones outlined here, to discover more about some of our poorer ancestors when they were children which could be investigated during our genealogical work. The following Reading List provides just some of those available.

Reading and Sources.
Bennett A. *A Working Life: Child Labour through the Nineteenth Century* (Waterfront Publications, Dorset. 1991)
Bevan A. *Tracing Your Ancestors in the Public Record Office* (6th ed)
Memoirs of Robert Blincoe (reprint Caliban Books)
'*Charities Digest*' published since 1882.
Cunnington P & Lucas C - *Charity Costumes* (Black 1978)
Ford P&G. *Hansard's Breviate of British Parliamentary Papers to 1833*
Select List of British Parliamentary Papers 1833-1890.
Gibson Guide to Poor Law Union Records (4 Vols) (FFHS)
Johnson W Branch. *The English Prison Hulks* (Phillimore 1957: revised 1970)

Lowe's Handbook to the Charities of London (1867) recorded many charitable societies including some outside London such as the Welsh Society, Somerset Society etc.
Mayhew H. London *Life and the Labouring Poor* (ed P. Quennell) (Spring Books)
Mayhew H. *Mayhew's Characters* (ed P.Quennell) (Spring Books).
Pinchbeck I & Hewitt M. *Children in English Society* (2 Vols RKP 1969)
Reese RA. *Britain 1815-1851* (Longman History Studies in Depth 1990)
Rimmer J. *Yesterday's Naughty Children: Training Ship, Girls' Reformatory and Farm School: A History of the Liverpool Reformatory Association founded 1855* (N. Richardson 1986)
Rose L. *Young Offenders and the Law* (Batsford 1984)
Bradford on Avon, Marlborough and Salisbury Records are held at the Wiltshire and Swindon Record Office, Bythesea Road, Trowbridge.
Records of the Marine Society and the Worcester Training Ships are held at the National Maritime Museum, Greenwich.
Ragged School Museum, 46-50 Copperfield Road, Bow, London. Es 4RR

Small Beginnings

Dr Barnardo's early work described by
Professor Blaikie in "The Quiver" 1887.

A CANDIDATE :
ENTERING PARTICULARS.

Somewhere near Houndsditch they came upon an empty shed, but no boys lay there – it was too much under the observation of the police. Scrambling up a wall without any help from a ladder, they reached the roof of the shed, and there, beyond all doubt, lay eleven boys in miserable rags and without other covering of any description – some coiled up like dogs, others huddled two or three together, others more apart. The average age was from nine to fourteen. In the severity of a winter night they lay asleep, their faces pale with cold and hunger. And this was only one little colony of a much larger community. "There's lots more", said the poor boy; but Dr Barnardo has seen enough to set his heart in motion, and his brains too, for he must find some way of saving them.

It is now some four or five and twenty years since a young medical student attached to the London Hospital, in the White-chapel Road who had been conducting a voluntary night-school among rough boys and girls, the children of the neighbourhood, found himself confronted with a pupil not to be easily got quit of.

After the class had been dismissed, a little ragged boy remained standing near the large fire at the end of the room, as if decidedly of the opinion that it would be more comfortable to spend the bitter wintry night there than in any of the wretched hiding holes to which fear of the police compelled a homeless child to resort. At first, Dr Barnardo would not believe the boy when, in answer to the question where he lived, he doggedly replied, "Don't live nowhere". But when the boy solemnly assured him that many other boys were in the like predicament, and when he offered to take him along and show him the open-air hiding places where they would be spending that very night, it seemed reasonable to put his story to the test. So, fortified with a cup of hot coffee, he and Dr Barnardo at length sallied forth, the boy telling his own miserable tale, and the kindly medical student slipping in a word respecting Him who came to save.

Dr Barnardo decided to open a little house in Stepney with accommodation for five and twenty which was occupied from the beginning with poor homeless boys, gathered by him from such places as we have described, glad indeed of the shelter that enabled them to spend their nights to very differently from the time when they lived 'nowhere'. A man that had five and twenty boys on his hands would probably be inclined to think that these hands were pretty full. But during the two dozen years that have intervened, Dr Barnardo's hands have been undergoing a very wonderful expansion. His family, at the present moment amounts to some two thousand. In all, some ten thousand children have passed under his care, most of whom have had to be set out in the world, and furnished with ways of living creditably. It goes without saying that the little fellow who had lived nowhere has turned the whole current of Dr Barnardo's life. Instead of devoting himself to curing diseased bodies, he has devoted himself to save soul and body together, and that on a scale so great as to seem incredible.

It would occupy many pages to enumerate the various steps by which Dr Barnardo advanced from his 'small beginnings' to the vast ramifications of benevolence by which he is now caring for two thousand children. When

25

COMING BY TRAIN.

and body, the grand object of his operations remained unfulfilled.

It is only recently that Dr Barnardo has added an Emigration Home to his operations. The first, by whom the idea of emigration as a great means of saving destitute British children, was turned into a reality by Miss Macpherson. It was fit that a lady should take the lead in a plan which lays so much stress on family life, and is so successful in bringing its sunny influence to bear on our poor city waifs. Miss Macpherson's work began in the East End and she had little idea of how her labours there were to grow. Her first care was for 'the little matchmakers', the poor mites of humanity that were turned into infant slaves to make boxes for Lucifer matches. In 1869 she gained possession of the building now so well known as the 'Home of Industry' which has become the centre of such varied work – this set among 130,000 of the poorest of the poor, amid thieves' kitchens, tramps' lodging houses, costermongers' dens, and the vilest haunts of iniquity!

one begins to work among neglected children, one finds that many different contrivances have to be resorted to to meet the case. What is suitable for boys may not be well adapted for girls. Some are more advanced in years and more civilised in habits than the 'green' material that is constantly being added to the stock. Many of the children are diseased and must be separated from the healthy, and cared for in hospitals. So Dr Barnardo was not content merely to extend his Stepney Home for Boys. When he began to take charge of girls he soon discovered that it is far better to rear them in homes where there is a real family life, than in barracks, which he still considers to be fairly adapted for boys. Village homes in Essex, in Jersey and in other places were soon added. Then accommodation had to be provided for the 'Shoeblack Brigade'; a Labour House had to be found for destitute youths, where they might get training for work; a Free Registry for girls in search of situations; an All-night Refuge to receive destitute children; and, when Dr Barnardo added an emigration scheme to his other projects, depots and distributing homes had to be found at Peterborough and Toronto in Canada. The great motive that compelled him was that they were God's creatures, and until God's image should be restored both to soul

Two years before she had accompanied a sister with her family to New York, to help them get settled, but the family had returned to England. They did not return without ideas. Miss Macpherson had got a new view in New York of what faith and courage could enable Christian women to do for their Lord. The first emigration projects were of a more general kind - mixed parties of men, women, and children. The scheme with which her name is more specially identified, the emigration of children, began in 1870.

It needed some courage for a lady to go on board the 'Peruvian' on the 12th may 1870, with one hundred boys rescued from crime and misery in the lowest haunts of London, to settle them in a colony where she was a complete stranger, and get for them engagements in agricultural work, for which they had had no training! However, it was known that their rawness in agriculture would be no obstacle to their engagement by the farmers who were keen for assistance. At Quebec she might have disposed of all one hundred boys; she left eleven. At Montreal, the same: she left twenty-three: at Belleville eight: the rest at Toronto. In June 1870 it was my good fortune to meet Miss Macpherson at the home of the late George Brown, afterwards Prime minister of Canada. She had just placed at his farm the last two boys of the hundred and was happy at her highly successful achievement.

The council of the County of Hastings presented her with a house at Belleville capable of containing two hundred boys, and her friend and companion, Miss Bilbrough agreed to furnish and take charge of it as a home for future emigrants. Her brother-in-law, Mr Merry brought out another seventy boys, while Miss Macpherson hastened home, and before autumn came out with another hundred needy children. Every year the same work has gone on and hundreds more emigrants have been taken out. And very happy have the results usually been. Only two or three per cent have turned out 'good-for-nothing'.

When we say that Miss Macpherson has taken to Canada 4,600 destitute children, and placed them in situations of comfort and promise, we tell but a fraction of her work, for it would never do to send to another land the reclaimed waifs of East London without training and preparation. The Home of Industry receives the raw material, an English country 'Home' works it up and a Reception Home in Canada takes in the emigrants upon arrival. Various operations connected with the Home of Industry embrace a widows' sewing class, mothers' meetings, factory girls' classes, evening school for young men and boys, Gospel meetings and Bands of Hope, lodging-house visitation, and Bible flower mission.

Bottling Mineral Waters

The sum needed to carry it on, under the most economical management, and with a vast amount of volunteer labour averages £5000 per year. The emigration of each child costs about £10. The condition of the children in Canada often seems almost too good to be true. I can say this from personal observation as my wife has been connected with the work. I have also seen a number of cases where children have been rescued from the worst conditions in Edinburgh who have gone to Canada – clothed, civilised, bright and happy and serving God and benefiting their fellow-men.

But it is not Edinburgh, but Glasgow that furnishes the great record connected with Scotland of progress from 'Small Beginnings'. The name of William Quarrier is now a household name for faith, hope and charity. At the age of eight, Quarrier once stood in the High Street in Glasgow – bareheaded, barefooted, cold and hungry, having tasted no food for a day and a half; and as he gazed at one person after another passing along, and none noticing him – he thought that if he were like them he would make provision for

Brush Making

addition to what is needed for buildings. All this money has come to Mr Quarrier unasked.

Take the railway from Glasgow to Greenock, leave at Bridge of Weir station, and drive on a couple of miles. That fresh, neat, bright settlement you come to is Mr Quarrier's village. Scattered over an undulating park of forty acres, sloping down to the river Gryfe, you find about a dozen villas, each a cottage home, named after some conspicuous giver, presided over by a cottage mother, and, where there are boys – a cottage father - Storehouse, infirmary, school, and church vary the aspect of the settlement. Inside all is fresh and bright, for Mr Quarrier believes in beauty of form and colour and hates the poorhouse dinginess. And that strange phenomenon near the river is actually a ship, although fixed on solid mother earth, the gift of a lady friend, and designed as a training ship to prepare for a seafaring life such boys as desire it. And Mr Quarrier goes on toiling and rejoicing, untroubled by fear of failure or of being left high and dry as the ship.

poor children. A Dr Guthrie's efforts benefited him greatly. Quarrier noticed a shoeblack who had been robbed of his stock-in-trade. Mr Quarrier tried to soothe him and gave him what he needed to resume business. He went home and wrote a letter to the newspapers on the necessity of organising the shoeblacks into a brigade. Some agreed, but some argued that Glasgow was so rainy a place and the streets so muddy that there was no use in getting one's boots brushed. Mr Quarrier realised that if anything were to be done, he would have to take the burden of it himself. Soon after, he met Miss Macpherson in Glasgow – heard of her work at home and in Canada, and was so stirred in spirit as to resolve that if the Lord sent him £1000 to begin with, he would start a Home and care for the destitute of Glasgow. On the 1st September 1871 he published a letter in the Glasgow newspapers showing the urgent need for such a Home. On the 13th September, he got a letter from a gentleman in London promising £2000.

By the 18th November he had opened a workshop in Renfrew Lane rudely fitted up for a Home. The first boy, though he came in dripping rags, was rather put out to find he had no comrade; but he stayed; and the next night he brought another, and so the ball began to roll. And thus from this small beginning, began the work which has now advanced to so gigantic a scale, carried on in the City Homes which cost £12,000, and the Homes at Bridge of Weir, on which there has already been an outlay of £50,000. In these, about five hundred destitute children are cared for, of whom between three and four hundred are sent yearly to Canada. To carry on the work requires about £10,000 per year in

Thus our British orphan homes, the number of which might easily be multiplied tenfold if the space available allowed, have reached their great dimensions through faith and prayer.

Victorian childhood: a period of endurance or enjoyment?
Doreen Hopwood

The type of childhood experience by those born during the reign of Queen Victoria depended considerably on where the child grew up, as well as the class of society into which he or she was born.

When Queen Victoria was crowned in 1837 the landscape of Britain was very different from that of 1901 when she died. By the mid-nineteenth century urbanisation was rapidly increasing as the population moved from the countryside to the growing towns and cities. The 1831 census of Middlesborough enumerated only 338 persons, but, by 1901, it had a population of almost 40,000. Throughout Victoria's reign, one in three of the population was aged under 15 years, most of whom lived in an urban environment.

Experiences did not only vary between town and country, but within the towns and cities themselves. Children growing up in leafy, middle class Edgbaston in Birmingham were geographically only a mile or so away from the overcrowded working class district of Ladywood, but socially they were a million miles apart.

Sexual stereotyping came into play from an early age amongst all classes and continued to be reinforced throughout childhood. Molly Hughes grew up in London in the 1870s and lamented "My father's slogan was that boys should go everywhere and know everything, and that girls should stay at home and know nothing". Advice for mothers concerning their children (especially daughters) was plentiful and reinforced the separate female and male spheres of adult life. In 'Womankind' by Charlotte Yonge, published in 1876, she stated

> "... the instinct of the boy is to drum and strike in a way that never seems to occur to his sister ... while she almost as certainly cuddles even the semblance of a child."

The type of education received by Victorian children reflected gender and class too. It was not until the 1870s that education became compulsory, and, for working class children and their rural counterparts, it was very much an *adhoc* arrangement until then. Schools (before the ubiquitous Board Schools) were very rarely purpose built, and country children attended classes in cottages, barns, rectories and even haylofts. The rudimentary schooling provided by the Dame Schools came in for criticism by the Inspector for Berkshire, Hampshire and Wiltshire in 1858 where the children "... spend a great part of their school hours sitting on forms while the 'schoolmistress' is engaged in sewing, washing or cooking".

Whilst boys received vocational training in carpentry, husbandry and shoemaking, the only practical classes offered to female working class scholars were in laundry-work and cookery. Few of the girls would be able to make use of the skills they acquired in their own homes because they either had no oven or could not afford the cost of the ingredients. One girl spent hours labouring over the starching of white collars, but none of the menfolk in her family possessed such luxuries! Attendance at school was a problem in town and countryside alike. Girls would be kept away whenever their help was needed at home – usually to look after younger (or new) siblings, or to help with the 'cottage' industries. In some areas, domestic (home-based) industries such as nail/chain making, straw-plaiting and lace making continued throughout the Victorian period, and children formed an important (or even vital) part of the family workforce. Out workers in towns where pin/button carding, matchbox making or pen handle varnishing were common 'home industries' also depended upon the help of children.

Visiting a sick child

the sons of the professional classes, and aimed to form 'valuable social qualities and manly virtues'. For local gentry and middle classes, Grammar Schools provided the type of education needed to ensure 'a good position' in life.

Whilst the sons of the upper-middle classes went out to school each day, or were boarders, their sisters were generally educated at home by a governess, a series of teachers, or, in some households, the mother took on the education of her daughters. The maternal influence was seen as being very important, and emphasis was made on the duties of being a wife and a mother. At the end of the nineteenth century, the Cornhill Magazine recommended that parents should save £300 per year from birth to send a son to Eton, but that 'a girl can be kept through those twenty years for rather over £100 a year'. In 1850, Miss Buss established the North London Collegiate School for Girls incorporating more intellectual subjects into the curriculum. Despite encouraging academic ambition in her students, a girl was, on leaving the school, advised to 'take up all domestic duties ... be ready to help her mother, and not be a burden to her'. One mid-Victorian commentator remarked that on average, a privately educated schoolgirl spent 640 hours of her school life studying arithmetic and devoted some 5,000 hours to musical studies.

In the countryside, the annual hiring of farm servants took place at Michaelmass, just as the Autumn school term commenced. This, together with seasonal work, disrupted schooling causing a Lincolnshire Inspector in the 1870s to complain "The children are pretty regular in winter and early spring, but when summer comes, the fields claim their presence and the schools are half-emptied".

Even after the introduction of the Education Act it was not unusual to find country children working on the family's smallholding rather than in the classroom. The possibility of a five shillings (25 pence) fine was deemed worth the risk in view of the two shillings (10 pence) that could be saved each day – the cost of adult labour.

For wealthy parents, the choice of school was important, and there were plenty to choose from —especially for the boys. At the top were the major public schools such as Eton, Rugby, Harrow and Winchester, followed by the newer 'public schools' such as Cheltenham, Marlborough and Wellington. These catered for

As Victoria's reign progressed, concern about the employment of children grew. The Factory Act of 1833 had excluded children aged under nine years from working in factories, and Acts passed in 1842 and 1843 banned the employment of children in mines, and as chimney sweeps. In 1864, Emma Lane, aged 16 years, appeared before the Children's Employment Commission. She told the Commissioners she had been working in the button trade since she was ten, earning 2s. 6d. (12p pence) a week by the time she was 12 years old.

The extended family was common in Victorian Britain; especially if a parent died. Widows with

a young family needed a breadwinner, and widowers required a new wife, housekeeper, or mother for his family. This would create a new family made up of step- and half-siblings. In Victorian times, the term 'in-law' was taken to mean 'step', and this can sometimes cause confusion in the interpretation of census entries. Children often lived with grandparents or uncles and aunts if space in the family home was at a premium, and Victorian households often included boarders or lodgers whose contributions were needed to pay the rent.

Children accepted their role as helper in the family. Joseph Ashby of Tysoe grew up in Warwickshire in the 1870s, and recalled "To 'help' was the price of contact with beloved and adored parents; even tiny ones understood that our parents could not 'manage' without us". Boys helped with the livestock and jobs on the farm, while girls were left to mind their younger siblings and carry out household chores.

Town dwelling children performed similar tasks, causing one social commentator (George Simms) to remark of the little girls he saw in the East End of London "By the time she marries and has had children of her own, she will be a woman weary of motherhood".

Victorian children grew up with an understanding of the fragility of life. By the time they had reached their teens, most would have experience the loss of at least one sibling, or even a parent. They were taught that God and parents (especially fathers) were to be loved and feared.

Mortality rates for infants and children under five years of age continued to be high throughout Victoria's reign, although figures were better for rural districts than those for towns and cities. Illegitimate babies were at an even higher risk – it was estimated that the death rate of illegitimate infants in London was twice as high as that of babies born to married couples. At a time when most of the population could not afford the services of a doctor, those of a local woman would be called upon. She would bring babies into the world, lay out the dead and provide 'remedies' for a whole range of illnesses and afflictions. Her services would be augmented by quack doctors and herbalists who would sell their 'cure-alls' at local fairs and markets. In the country most cottages would have a section of the garden set aside for herbs ready to use for medicinal concoctions. Old wives tales and folklore continued to form the basis of the recipes – a small shallot was heated and placed in the ear to cure earache, whilst diarrhoea was treated with dried and ground acorns. One of Manchester's registrars suggested that as many as 25% of infant deaths in a given three-month period could be attributed to 'advice' given by these 'incompetent and unqualified practitioners'.

By the late nineteenth century, the manufacture of children's toys was becoming a lucrative business, and many of the board games still played today, such as 'snakes and ladders', 'Ludo' and 'draughts' were invented during the Victorian period.

Middle class children were encouraged to read edifying literature and play instructive games.

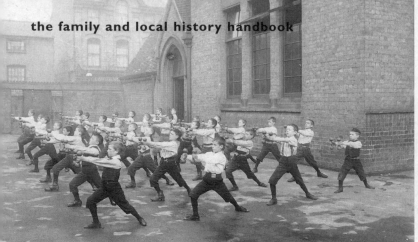

village pond or urban canal, provided a skating rink in the winter, and in the summer they were used for fishing and swimming in. Seasons of the year, and special days dotted the calendar of Victorian children, and May Days were enjoyed by all. The Oxford Chronicle on 7 May 1870 reported that '… the town was alive with children carrying garlands'. They would collect coppers, which were used to buy sweets. Local delicacies called 'suckballs' were sold on May Day – just as treacle toffee became associated with Bonfire Night.

Their choice of toys was restricted on Sundays, and the famous Hamley's Toy Shop in London became known as 'Noah's Ark'. This was one of its best selling toys because, being based upon the Bible, it could legitimately be played with on Sundays.

The streets of the cities were full of amusements for children, and Molly Hughes took delight in "… the hawkers cries of "Flowers a-blowing and a-growing", the barrel organs, the calls of the 'hokeypokey' [ice-cream] sellers, as well as the myriad delivery services required to bring the daily requisites, the black-dressed coal men and chimney sweeps, the butcher's and baker's boys on their bicycles".

The street was an urban playground for working class children, just as their rural contemporaries found amusement in the countryside. The frozen

Unlike the exquisite dolls and mechanical toys and games owned by middle class children, those of the working classes played games which needed no equipment, or items which could be obtained free of charge. A piece of slate was all that was needed for a game of 'hopscotch', and a length of old rope attached to a lampost made a swing or it could be used for all kinds of skipping games.

In the nineteenth century, fairy stories and boys adventure stories started to appear. There was still a market for 'moral' tales – often portraying the virtuous young slum-dwellers who 'made the best of everything without complaint'.

Upper class school clothing

Children, too, had their share of 'penny dreadfuls', such as The Boys of England' (1866), which advertised itself as 'wild and wonderful but healthy fiction'. This was counter balanced in 1879 by the 'Boys Own Paper' – published by the Religious Tract Society. The 'Girls Own Paper' was first published in 1880. In 1887 the recorder of the City of London claimed that it was the "effects of unwholesome literature on his mind that brought virtually every boy before the court".

The Sunday School Movement played a wide social role by providing outings and processions. In 1844, 4,000 children and teachers of the Wigan Sunday School Union took the train for a day's outing to Bootle.

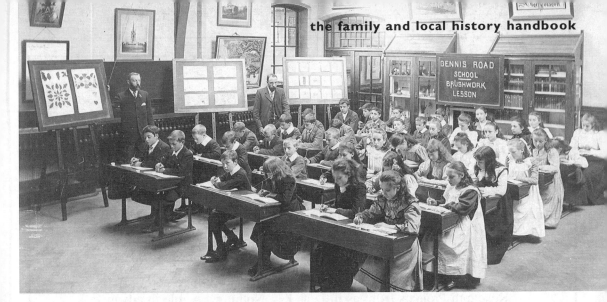

Punishment for crimes was harsh, and the Parliamentary Papers of 1852 (Select Committee on Criminal and Destitute Juveniles) reported 'The scourge of juvenile delinquency affects very little the agricultural districts – it is chiefly confined to towns of large population'. Most rural crimes committed by children under 16 years of age were concerned with theft – usually of goods of low value (under a pound), and often of food items as a result of hunger. Punishment could be severe, even in respect of petty offences. At Henley in Oxfordshire in the 1880s two brothers aged 12 and 15 years of age were each imprisoned for a month (with hard labour), and then sentenced to a Reformatory for four years – their crime was to steal a bag containing bread and butter valued at 6d (2? pence).

Reformatories were established in 1854 for 'the better care and reformation of Youthful Offenders in Great Britain' (for those aged 16 years of age and under). The duration of their stay was between two and five years. Here they received industrial or agricultural training for the boys and domestic or laundry work for the girls. These were aimed to provide them with training

for farm work or for service if the young people chose a 'new life' in the colonies.

The colonies, especially Canada, were seen as places of opportunity for orphaned and abandoned children, and, by the late nineteenth century, there were numerous emigration homes sending children to Canada to start a new life. Between 1870 and 1882, Dr Barnardo sent 1,000 children, and Boards of Guardians across the country followed suit. Testimonials from children settled in their new homes were often printed in the annual reports of the Homes or Institutions who had organised their emigration.

Children were dressed as miniature adults, and clothing did little to accommodate childhood activity, as can be seen from the example (taken from the advertisement of a children's outfitter-*above*). In 1880, Richard Jefferies described a young Wiltshire lad's clothing "His hat, an old one of his father's, a mile too big, … a pair of stumping boots, heeled and tipped with iron. His naked legs red with cold, but thick and strong". Many Victorian babies started their life in borrowed clothing – thanks to 'lying-in Societies' and charities, which loaned these to families to save the expense of a layette. Clothes were returned when the bay was a few weeks old and ready to wear the cut-down clothes of older siblings – town and country alike. However poor the family, each member would have their 'Sunday Best', much of which spent the greater part of the week in the pawnbrokers.

Nineteenth century children experienced a very different childhood from those born in the late twentieth century, but continuity can be found in the playground games which are still enjoyed today. It was during the Victorian times that Christmas celebrations as we now know them were introduced.

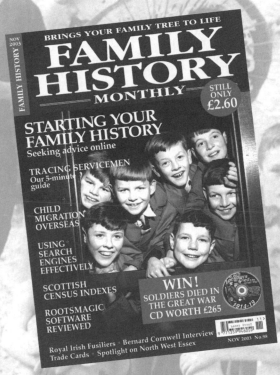
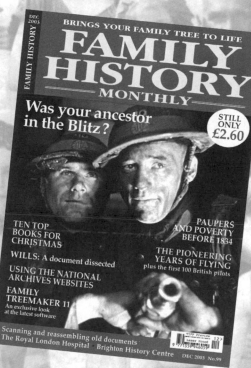

Family Records Centre

1 Myddelton Street, London, EC1R 1UW
www.familyrecords.gov.uk
A service provided by The Public Record Office &
The Office for National Statistics (General Register Office)

The Family Records Centre

The Family Records Centre provides access to the following:

Ground Floor
• Indexes of births, marriages and deaths in England and Wales from 1837
• Indexes of legal adoptions in England and Wales from 1927
• Indexes of some births, marriages and deaths of British nationals and British Armed Forces, which took place abroad, from the late 18th Century including both World Wars

Certificates can be purchased of any entry in the above. Please note that the certificates are not produced on the same day. If you need a certificate but cannot visit the Family Records Centre in person, you can place an order by post, fax or telephone. Please ring 0870 243 7788 for further information and details of fees.

First Floor
• Census returns for England and Wales
  1841-1901)
• Wills and administrations from the PCC up to
  1858
• Death Duty registers (1796-1858) and indexes
  (1796-1903)
• Records of nonconformist births, baptisms and burials (mainly pre-1837) and marriages (mainly pre-1754)
• Miscellaneous foreign returns of births, deaths and marriages from 1627 to 1960
• Family History Databases providing access to
  the International Genealogical Index,
  1901 Census Online, Documents
  Online and a collection of census
  surname indexes and trade directories

The Family Records Centre also offers the following services:
• Advice on family and local history research
• Family history reference area, including books, magazines and maps
• Bookshop, selling publications on family and local history
• Exhibitions, lectures and other events
• Self-service or staffed photocopying service on the first floor
• Regular user's consultations
• Quarterly newsletter – The Family Record
• Adoption counselling service (by appointment only)
• Good facilities for customers with special needs
• Refreshment area with vending machines
• Baby changing room

Contact Details
Births, Marriages, Deaths, Adoptions and Overseas enquiries
Telephone: 0870 243 7788
Fax: 01704 550013
Email: certificate.services@ons.gov.uk
Census and general enquiries
Telephone: 020 8392 5300
Fax: 020 8392 5307
Email: frc@nationalarchives.gov.uk

Planning your visit
Opening hours
Monday 9:00 am – 5:00 pm, Tuesday 10:00 am – 7:00 pm
Wednesday 9:00 am – 5:00 pm Thursday 9:00 am – 7:00 pm
Friday 9:00 am – 5:00 pm Saturday 9:30 am – 5:00 pm

The Centre is closed on Sundays and Public Holidays. Closure dates for Easter and Christmas are publicised in advance.

Group Visits
You are welcome to bring a group or coach party to the FRC at any time during our normal opening hours. However, we would advise you to plan your visits to avoid our busiest times. On our busy days the lockers are often all in use so try to bring no more than you need for your research. Please let us know if you are planning to bring a large group to the FRC.

How to get here
• *By rail*
Angel – Northern Line (City Branch)
Farringdon – Hammersmith & City,
Metropolitan, Circle Lines and Thameslink
King's Cross – Victoria, Northern, Piccadilly,
Circle, Metropolitan, Hammersmith & City
Lines and mainline services
• *By bus*
19, 38 and 341 along Rosebery Avenue
63 along Farringdon Road
• *By car*
There are NCP car parks in Bowling Green Lane (off Farringdon Road) and Skinner Street, both of which are within easy walking distance of the Centre. There is limited Pay & Display parking in the surrounding streets. **The FRC is located within the London Congestion Charging Zone.** *There is reserved parking for visitors with disabilities at the Centre, but spaces must be booked in advance. Please ring 020 7533 6436 before you visit.*

General Register Office - Certificate Services
Melanie Lee
Communications Manager

The General Register Office is part of the Office for National Statistics and is the central source of certified copies of register entries (certificates) in England and Wales. Since 1837 each entry made in a register of births, marriages or deaths in England and Wales has been copied to the centrally held national record maintained by General Register Office. Certificate Services is the name given to the arm of the General Register Office (GRO) that deals with applications for copies from this record of births, marriages and deaths and is based in Southport, Merseyside.

Many customers who apply to Certificate Services for a certificate do so for legal or administrative purposes such as applying for a passport or pension but increasingly a large proportion of applications are from family historians and professional genealogists. In 2002/2003 we received over 950,000 certificate applications. This is an increase of 42% over the past six years, and interest in family history accounts for most of that increase. GRO also has separate sections that deal with adoption certificates and certain overseas records.

Family Records Centre. Many of you will be familiar with the "public face" of Certificate Services, the Family Records Centre (FRC) at 1 Myddelton Street London EC1R 1UW. The FRC is run in partnership with The National Archives *formally The Public Record Office* and aims to provide a one-stop shop for family history research. The Family Record Centre provides access to:

Paper indexes of births, marriages and deaths registered in England and Wales from 1st July 1837. Indexes of legal adoptions in England and Wales from 1927.
Indexes of births, marriages and deaths of some British citizen's abroad and those relating to British Armed Forces, posted overseas from the late 18th century. These include: Consular and High Commission returns since 1849; Marine births and deaths since 1837; aircraft births, deaths and missing persons from 1947; Army returns from 1881; Regimental registers 1761-1924; (these cover the UK, Ireland and abroad (including India) Army Chaplains returns 1796-1880; deaths in World Wars I and II and the Boer War; Ionic Islands and Indian State deaths. A CD-ROM index of births which have taken place in Northern Ireland from 1922-1993.

How to go about finding a register entry
It is not possible for applicants to search through copies of the actual register entries themselves. However the indexes may be searched to identify the entry you seek. The indexes are arranged by year and then alphabetically by surname. Before 1983 the indexes are also split into the quarter of the year in which the event was registered e.g. events registered in January, February or March are indexed in the March quarter for the relevant year.

To apply for a certificate of the entry you can choose which method best suits you:
Application in person via the FRC
The Family Records Centre is open to the public at the following times: Monday, Wednesday, Thursday, Friday:9am-5pm Tuesday: 10am-7pm Saturday: 9.30am-5pm

Once you have searched the indexes and identified an entry you simply complete an application form, including the GRO Reference Number listed in the index and take it to the cashiers for payment. The fee for each certificate is £7.00.

Smedley Hydro
All applications made at the FRC are transported overnight to Certificate Services at Smedley Hydro, Southport, Merseyside. Many people have asked about the unusual name of the office where their certificates are produced. Smedley Hydro was build in early Victorian times and known as the Birkdale College for the education of young gentlemen. It then became a Hydropathic Hotel whose electro-chemical baths where extremely popular "in restoring the work-weary, the enfeebled and those of a naturally delicate organisation". With the outbreak of the Second World War the building was requisitioned by His Majesty's government for the purpose of National Registration and there are now 750 people working at the Southport Office with over 300 of them employed within Certificate Services.

Production Process
Once your application is received at Smedley Hydro the race then begins to have the applications sorted ready for the staff to retrieve the relevant microfilm, load the film onto a reader, find the entry, scan the image and produce the certificate ready for either posting out on the fourth working day or returning to the FRC for collection on the fourth working day. This is no mean feat when you consider that around ten thousand applications are received via the FRC every week.

Application direct to GRO Southport
If it is not convenient for you to go to central London and visit the FRC, you can apply directly to GRO Southport for your certificates. It would, of course, help us to have the index reference for the entry you want, so you may wish to look this up at one of the many centres around the country which hold copies of the national GRO index on microfiche. There are over 100 such locations including libraries, County Records Offices and Family History Centres within the UK and overseas. To find out the nearest one to you telephone Certificate Services on 0870 243 7788.

Alternatively you may wish to view the indexes on line. Recent changes to the conditions of sale of the GRO Indexes now mean that some organisations have made Index information available on the Internet.

Smedley Hydro, Southport
Reproduced with the permission of Martin Perry, Southport Civic Society

Please note that it is not possible for members of the public to search the indexes at our Southport office itself. Personal callers are welcome to leave certificate applications between the hours of 9am – 5pm, Monday – Friday at GRO, Smedley Hydro, Trafalgar Rd, Birkdale, Southport.

Most applicants to GRO Southport prefer to apply by one of the following methods:

By telephone:
Our call centre may be reached by dialling 0870 243 7788. You will hear a menu selection before being transferred to an operator who can take the details of the GRO reference number(s) you want and then arrange for your certificate(s) to be posted out to you within 5 working days. The fee for this service is £8.50, and payment can be made by Visa, Master or Switch. Please note we do not accept Electron or American Express Cards. The Call Centre is available 6 days a week (Monday – Friday 8am-8pm and Saturday 9am – 4pm) .

Our Call Centre deals with a variety of enquires relating to certificate services and each week a team of 25 staff deal with over four and a half thousand telephone calls.

By fax or post:
You may wish to fax your certificate application to 01704 550013. Alternatively you can post in your application enclosing a cheque or postal order payable to **ONS** to :
The General Register Office
PO Box 2, Southport, Merseyside PR8 2JD

On Line:
This is a secure website that can be used to place orders using the GRO Index reference number and for certificates in the twentieth century where the exact details are known. For further information visit our website at: www.statisitcs.gov.uk/registration

How to contact our office by email
As the e-revolution continues certificate services increasingly deal with a large number of enquiries from people who have visited our website. If you wish to contact us by email our address is certificate.services@ons.gov.uk

What if you do not know the GRO reference number of the entry you want?
If you do not wish to conduct you own search of the indexes we are happy to do this for you. For a fee of £11.50 we will undertake a search of the indexes for the year in which you tell us the event concerned occurred, and if necessary a year either side as well if it cannot be found in that year. Due to the additional searches involved this service takes a little longer. Once the application is received the certificate is posted out within 15 working days. Should we be unable to find the entry, we will refund your fee minus a search fee of £4.50

To assist us in the search you will need to provide as much information as possible about the person on the certificate you are trying to obtain. For a birth – full name, date of birth, place of birth and if known the parents names including the mothers maiden name. For a marriage, you will need to supply the names of both the bride and groom, date of marriage, place of marriage and if known, the fathers name for both bride and groom. For a death you will need to supply a full name, date of death, place of death and if a female their marital status. The occupation of the deceased is also helpful.

Application to a local Register Office
If you know exactly where the birth, marriage or death that you are looking for took place you may also apply to the local Register Office covering that area. The Superintendent Registrar will be able to provide you with a certificate from his or her records. Please note that the GRO reference number does not refer to these local records, and will unfortunately be of no use to them in finding the entry for you. You will be asked to provide details similar to those listed in the paragraphs above so that they can locate the entry for you.

Other services provided by GRO:
Commemorative Certificates. Something that people may be unaware of is our Commemorative Certificate Section. For a cost of £40 they can provide a commemorative marriage certificate to mark silver, ruby, gold or diamond anniversaries. These certificates are colour printed on high quality paper and come mounted in frame within a presentation box, they do make an unusual and attractive gift. For further information call 0151 471 4256.

Overseas Section. GRO also holds Overseas Records. They have records of the births, marriages and deaths of British Citizens overseas that have been registered with the British Registering authorities e.g. British Consuls, High Commissions, HM Forces, the Civil Aviation Authority and the Registrar General of Shipping and Seamen.

national
STaTiSTiCS

Overseas certificates can be applied for in person at the FRC or alternatively, by post, on line or by telephone at the General Register Office, Southport. They will usually be produced within 5 working days. Please telephone 0151 471 4801 or email overseas.gro@ons.gov.uk for further information.

Adoption Branch.
The General Register Office also maintains the Adopted Children Register (ACR). This register contains particulars of adoptions authorised by order of a court in England and Wales since 1st January 1927.

An entry in the ACR replaces the original birth record and should be used for all legal purposes. An index is available at the FRC for applications for adoption certificates. Certificate applications can also be made by post - to Southport, on line or by telephone - normal processing times are within 5 working days. For further information please contact 0151 471 4830. Once adopted children reach the age of eighteen they are entitled to apply for access to their original birth record. If they were adopted before 12 November 1975 they are required to attend an interview with an Adoption Counsellor before information about original birth records can be obtained. Anybody adopted after this date has the choice of either receiving this information directly or via an adoption

counsellor. This facility is also available to people who have been adopted in England and Wales and are now living outside the UK. The General Register Office provides a counselling service at Southport, which supplements that provided by local authorities.

Adoptions Branch also maintains an Adoption Contact Register. This is a facility for both adopted adults and birth relatives to register an interest in contacting one another. A "link" is made when both parties register but the onus on whether contact is followed up lies with the adopted person. Since the register was established in 1991 there have been over 750 links. For more information on the services provided by Adoptions Branch please email adoptions@ons.gov.uk or telephone 0151 471 4830.

New legislation, The Adoption and Children Act 2002, proposes an additional service for birth relatives to gain access to adoptive details, however, secondary legislation needs to be drafted for public consultation before the act is implemented, currently scheduled for September 2005.

Certificate Services welcomes Feedback: We welcome feedback and customer input on the level and quality of service currently being provided. If you have any comments about our services please write to - Customer Service Unit Manager, PO Box 2, Southport, Merseyside, PR8 2JD or email certificate.services@ons.gov.uk

Frederick Matthias Alexander and his Ancestors

Jacqueline Evans provides a fascinating insight into the family history of the developer of The Alexander Technique

Life in rural England was always difficult and harsh but it changed dramatically between the middle of the 18th and 19th centuries. Firstly, the population increased significantly from 7.74 million in 1791 to 13.2 million in 1831.[1] Secondly, as a result of the Enclosure Acts, between 1750 and 1850, well over 6 million acres, or something like one quarter of the cultivated acreage, changed from open field, common land, meadow or waste into private fields. The increase in grain production was dramatic. In the 1830s, it is estimated that production covered 98 per cent of British consumption; this shows that cereal output kept pace with the population increase and nearly doubled in 40 years. This increase was not the result of mechanisation but the change from family enterprises to larger commercially-based farming units employing labour.[2] This increase in the number of landless farm labourers combined with the effects of the Enclosure Acts was devastating. Prior to the enclosures even the lowest labourer did not depend on his wages alone. He took his wood for fuel from the waste land, he had a cow or a pig that could wander and feed on the common pasture and he probably raised some crops on a strip of the common land. Suddenly, these sources of income were denied to him and he was dependent on his wages. Thus he was reliant on his farmer boss who, over the years, became a more and more remote figure.[3] The rural poor were emerging as a significant and now more obvious group of people. There were food riots; these took place in periods of harvest failure and high prices, in 1795/6, 1800/1, 1810-13 and 1816-1818. The Game laws were enhanced making poaching to supplement the meagre diet more hazardous; these laws created an even greater divide between the landowners and the villagers. In 1803, resistance to arrest was made punishable by death and, in 1817, a punishment of seven years transportation was introduced for armed poachers caught at night.[4]

The poverty and the desperation of the rural poor increased as the 19th century progressed. By 1815/16 many of the men had returned from the Napoleonic wars unemployed, underfed and itinerant. It is estimated that approximately 250,000 men appeared over a short period and totally swamped the rural labour market.[5] The situation continued to deteriorate and the bad harvests of 1828 and 1829 together with outbreaks of disease among the livestock were almost the final straw.[6] However, it was the invention and introduction of the threshing machine that was the catalyst to the extensive rioting, which took place in the latter part of 1830. Traditionally, labourers had worked in the fields for much of the year and threshed the corn through the winter months. The machine replaced most of the men and left them out of work for almost six months of the year. People's patience became exhausted and on 1 June 1830, with the destruction of farmer Mosyer's ricks and barn at Orpington in Kent, began the Swing Riots. These riots spread across the country but, within six months, would produce savage retribution from a frightened government and a more terrified landowning community.

The Alexander family lived in the village of Ramsbury in Wiltshire and this was where Edward and Jane brought up their 11 children, the first child being born in 1804 and the last in 1828. The oldest son was Joseph, who became a wheelwright and the next son, Matthias, was a carpenter. By 19 November 1830, the riots had reached many counties in England including Wiltshire. In Ramsbury and the immediate vicinity during 22 and 23 November 1830 some 17 threshing machines were smashed, together with two other agricultural machines; there were 8-recorded riots and four cases of robbery with menaces. In Wiltshire alone, in those two days, according to Hobsbawn and Rudé, 64 machines were demolished; a further 26 were broken over the next 2 days, a total of 90 machines. It shows how quickly the insurrection was quelled when one learns that the

Port Arthur, Tasmania

total number of machines destroyed throughout the Swing Riot period in Wiltshire was 101.[7]

On 22 November 1830, Matthias and Joseph Alexander were part of the Ramsbury gang that visited John Sheppard's mill and allegedly smashed a threshing machine. There were a number of witnesses to this event and so Matthias and his brother were soon arrested and charged with this offence and then taken to the Bridewell in Marlborough. Their father, Edward and a cousin, Ambrose, were also arrested and taken to Marlborough. Subsequently, Edward was released without charge and Ambrose was released when the Jury decided that there was insufficient evidence to convict. Matthias and Joseph were not so fortunate and on 4 January 1831 they appeared before the Special Assizes and were found guilty.[8] The next day they were brought before the court again for sentencing and *The Times* reporter eloquently described events:

> "Matthias Alexander, Joseph Alexander and Joseph Liddiard, were put to the bar, having been convicted of a like offence. Mr. Justice Alderson said the case of these prisoners was very different. They belonged to a class of persons who had not even the vain pretence that these machines could affect them in any manner. One was a carpenter, the other a blacksmith, and the third a woodman. Such outrages by any party must be put down: but the law would visit with the strictest severity, such persons as the prisoners, when proved to have taken part in them which they were proved to have done. The sentence of the Court on each of the prisoners was that they should be transported to such place beyond the seas as His Majesty should direct for the term of seven years."[9]

So ended the short hearings of Joseph, aged 24 married with three small children and Matthias aged 20 years, the results of which would completely change their lives. They were taken to Fisherton Anger Gaol, Salisbury and this was vividly described in the *Devizes and Wiltshire Gazette*. The article stated,

> "On leaving the court, we mixed amongst the crowd who were waiting to see the prisoners

leave. The scene here was heart-breaking beyond everything, a mass of women were standing bathed in tears, supported by men who looked as having hearts which nothing could daunt, but which had given way to feelings better nature, and, in endeavouring to support the weaker sex, they themselves could not but betray their grief and were actually shedding the tears of pity and affliction." The article went on to describe how as the convicts came out "their wives, their mothers, their sisters and their children, clasped them in their arms with an agonising grip. The convicts, whose hearts had not been hardened by having been before incarcerated in a goal, gave way. They wept like children." The report ended "We left the scene with a hope that it would have the effect desired, accompanied with a prayer that we might be spared from again being witness of such dreadful distress."[10]

About three weeks later the Alexander brothers were transferred to the hulk *York* but their stay on the hulk was short as they were soon embarked on the *Eliza* and on 6 February 1831 they sailed with 222 other Swing Rioters from Portsmouth for Van Diemen's Land.[11] They all arrived safely in Hobart on 29 May 1831 and were greeted by the Lieutenant Governor, Colonel Arthur, who was pleased to see "these men with trades, possessing strength, shrewdness and simplicity to help build the Colony".[12] Clearly, Matthias and Joseph had skills that were much in demand. Joseph was employed in a government department and Matthias was sent to the Van Diemen's Land Establishment, commonly known as the Cressy Company. Matthias was granted his Ticket of Leave on 1 June 1835 and Joseph a few weeks later on 26 August.[13] A few months later on 5 February 1836, along with most of the other

ESPLANADE AND WARSHIPS HOBART.

Swing Rioters, Matthias and Joseph were granted an absolute pardon by the British Parliament.[14] Matthias and Joseph stayed in the Longford area of Tasmania where Matthias married, working at an estate called Wickford. Matthias and his wife, Mary Reading, an Irish girl who was transported, at the age of 16 years, for stealing a dress in London, had six children who reached adulthood. Mary died of consumption in 1850 at the approximate age of 34 years leaving Matthias with six children aged between 11 years and 18 months.

Shortly after this tragedy, Matthias moved to the Deloraine area where he acquired 500 acres of farm land.[15] In 1852, Matthias moved to Table Cape near Wynyard on the North West Coast of Tasmania, where another brother, John, had bought a considerable amount of land.[16] Matthias rented his land at Deloraine to a number of farmers. At Table Cape the Alexander brothers established a township called Alexandria, opened a number of little shops and an Inn, began to farm some of the land on the Cape which at that time was thick forest and ship some of the timber to the gold fields in Victoria. They were pioneers of the area. Matthias remarried and fathered a further seven children. He continued to hold the licence of the Inn and farm an extensive area of land until his death. His brother, Joseph, went from the Longford area initially to Circular Head, now known as Stanley, where he bought a number of properties. After a few years he joined his brothers in the Table Cape area.

Frederick Matthias
Alexander
New York
1907

Matthias died at Table Cape on 31 October 1865 just a few years before his famous grandson, my great uncle was born. This grandson, my grandmother's oldest brother, was Frederick Matthias Alexander, who bequeathed to the world the Alexander Technique that is now taught around the globe to thousands of people. The Technique has been the subject of

dozens of books and numerous articles in medical journals. Alexander was born near Table Cape on 20 January 1869, all his grand parents were convicts, and he is listed as one of the 200 men who made Australia great.

He was the oldest of 10 children born to John, a blacksmith, and Betsy Alexander and he spent his formative years in Wynyard. In 1885, he obtained his first job as a clerk with the Mount Bischoff Tin Mining Company in the then booming mining town of Waratah, some three years later moving to Melbourne where again he undertook clerical work. By now he was an accomplished amateur reciter but he discovered that when he gave a recitation that he lost his voice. After many visits to doctors including months of resting his voice the problem remained and so Alexander decided that he must be doing something that was causing his difficulty. By watching his actions in mirrors that he set up in his room he discovered that when he was reciting amongst other things, he threw his head back, this was something he did not do when he was speaking normally. Thus he decided that if he could inhibit this action he would retain his voice while he recited.[17] This proved to be the case and he began to recite again successfully. He went on a recital tour of Tasmania and New Zealand with a view to becoming a professional reciter. Although his recitals were popular and well attended, he discovered that people were particularly interested in his method of voice production and so he began to teach his ideas. He taught first in Melbourne and then in Sydney developing his theories all the time. This was to be a lifetime task and, as time progressed, he discovered that he could help people with all manner of difficulties not just speaking.

In 1904, he came to London and for the next 50 years he taught his ideas in London, Kent and America. During the First World War, which had a great impact on his thinking, he crossed the Atlantic every six months dividing his teaching time between London and New York. During the 1920s and 1930s large numbers of people came to his teaching rooms in Ashley Place, London, and many famous people became devotees of the Technique including George Bernard Shaw, Paul Nash, Aldous Huxley, the Earl of Lytton, one time Viceroy of India, Robert Donat and Stafford Cripps. He established a three-year training course for student teachers and a school at his country house at Penhill in Kent for hyperactive children. After the Dunkirk evacuation and the fall of France, he was persuaded to take some of these children to the safety of America. He was reluctant to leave his family and friends to the wrath of Hitler and the

Germans but with an invasion expected within days he was urged to leave England with the children. Soon this 72-year-old man, his party of children and four ladies sailed on the *Monarch of Bermuda* from George V dock at Greenock on the Clyde and they arrived in Halifax, Canada on 11 July 1940.[18] It was six months before the party was installed at a homestead in Stow, Massachusetts and Alexander was able to teach in New York, Boston and at Stow.

Alexander was most concerned about events in England and was very unhappy about his sisters and friends living in London and Kent subjected, as they were, to terrible bombing. Fortunately, none of his family died as a result but there was damage to his teaching rooms in Ashley Place and at Penhill. One night his sister, Amy, my grandmother, was on her own in a large house in Sidcup, Kent. She listened, watched and waited as 250 incendiaries landed, most of them within a quarter of a mile of her, in the space of 20 minutes. The area was reported as looking like a 'Brock's benefit' with flares all over the place, in front and back gardens, on the roads, in open spaces and in houses. [19] Alexander was most anxious to return but he was unable to obtain a passage until the summer of 1943. Then he was able continue teaching in London and living at Penhill at the weekends. He arranged for his rooms in Ashley Place and the house at Penhill to be repaired but this was a little premature as both buildings received further damage during the V1 and V2 bombing raids in 1944 and early 1945. The last

years of his life were marred by a court case for libel in South Africa, which he won, fortunately for the future of his work.

The Alexander Technique lives on and has literally thousands of devotees. There are teachers' associations in many countries around the world including Great Britain, America, Australia, Brazil, Canada, Israel, New Zealand, South Africa and most Western European countries. The Technique has found particular favour with actors and people in the performing arts. It is taught in most of the leading academies and conservatoires in the English-speaking world and beyond. Without doubt the Alexander Technique can and does help thousands of people around the globe. In summary, it is a better and more relaxed way of using oneself, as the saying goes, it is not what you do that does the damage it is the way the you do it.

Further information on the history of Frederick Matthias Alexander, his convict ancestry, transportation of all his grand parents to Tasmania and an account of Alexander's life can be found in a book, Frederick Matthias Alexander A Family History, written by Jackie Evans and published by Phillimore & Co. Ltd of Chichester on www.phillimore.co.uk or in Australia the book is available at Einstein's Moon Bookshop, 336 Clarendon Street, South Melbourne, Victoria 3205, Australia.

Frederick Matthias Alexander 1947

Notes:
1.Wrigley, E.A. and Schofield, R.S., *The Population History of England 1541-1871 A Reconstruction* (London: Edward Arnold (Publishers Ltd., 1981) p.529.
2.Hobsbawn, E.J. and Rudé, George, *Captain Swing* (London: Lawrence and Wishart (1969), 1970), pp.23-31.
3.Hammond J.L. and Barbara, *The Village Labour* (London: Longmans, Green and Co. (1911) 1966,pp. 93 and 102.
4.Mingay, G.A., (ed), *The Unquiet Countryside*, pp. 28 & 40.
5.Hobsbawn, E.J. and Rudé, *Captain Swing*, p. 72.
6.Mingay, *The Unquiet Countryside*, p. 43.
7.Hobsbawn, E.J. and Rudé, *Captain Swing*, Appendix I, p. 305 and Appendix III, pp. 329-36.
8.P.R.O., ASSI 24/18/3 and HO 27/42.
9.*The Times*, 7 January 1831.
10.Devizes *and Wiltshire Gazette*, 13 and 20 January 1831.
11.P.R.O., H.O. 8/27, H.O. 11/8 and Hobsbawn, E.J. and Rudé, George, *Captain Swing* (London: Lawrence and Wishart (1969), 1970), p.263.
12.Bateson, Charles, *The Convict Ships 1787-1868*, (Glasgow: Brown, Son & Ferguson Ltd.), pp.360, 361 and 386 and Robson, L.L., *A History of Tasmania, Vol. 1*, (Melbourne: Oxford University Press, 1983), p. 166.
13.P.R.O., CO 283/6.
14.P.R.O., CO 283/7.
15.P.R.O., CO 283/26, pp. 317, 318 and 320, CO 283/31, pp. 2033-5 and 2037, CO 283/50, pp. 339-42.
16.P.R.O., CO 283/22, pp. 304 and 529.
17.Alexander, F.M., *The Use of The Self*, (London: Methuen & Co. Ltd., 1932), pp. 3-36.
18.P.R.O., ADM 199/2208.
19.Bexley Local Studies and Archive Centre, Post 22 Log Book of Air Raid Incidents in Birchwood Ward (Area 4), Official Record for Major H. Allen: List of Incidents up to December 1943, dated January 1944, including cuttings from *Kentish Times*.

Was your ancestor a Grave Robber?
Fred Feather
Chairman of the Essex Society for Family History

A stream of family research, which often translates into booklets, starts with the premise or title "Was your ancestor a........"

There has always been also the possibility that the legal opening of graves would provide serious research for scholars on how their forebears had lived and died, witness the following paragraph which appeared in the Chelmsford Chronicle for Friday 22nd October 1779. "On Monday last as some workmen were sinking a grave in the north aisle of the parish church of Danbury, Essex, they discovered a leaden coffin, which inclosed a stout Elm coffin, about one inch and quarter thick, in which was a shell of about half that thickness, containing the body of a Knight Templar, supposed to be of the family of the Sancto Claro's or St.Cleres, who were eminent in this parish in the beginning of the reign of Edward 1; the body was found entire, being embalmed in a liquor or pickle, of which the coffin was half full; the linen in which the body was interred was of a fine texture and quite perfect. An effigy in wood of the above Knight Templar and two others, are placed in niches in the wall of the said church, which are still entire, and accounted by the curious as valuable monuments of antiquity,

being from the best accounts at least 500 years old."

But what about the illegal activity undertaken by entrepreneurs? We hear little of the work of the Resurrection men, or "Grave robbers" as they were known at the lower end of the market, but without them would medical science have advanced at the pace it did? Scotland was often at the forefront of medical research and the case of "Burke and Hare" is a better known example of the genre. According to a Glaswegian source, one Wm. Divan, Devan or Devine was executed in that city on 23rd July 1824 and his body handed over to the surgeons. In a lengthy report it was said that, with a bellows, they attempted to reflate the lungs, then by use of shock tactics on nerves, to get limbs to move. This was not a pleasant end to the career of someone's ancestor. Were such occurrences not to have the effect of causing serious fear in the minds of even our innocent nearest and dearest forebears, who could not tranquilly look upon death without consideration of the possibilities of such "resurrection." However, someone's ancestors were involved.

An outrage
A report of 20th June 1823 named Wm.Thompson, Thomas Thompson, John Hicks and Thomas Wells, who were together charged at Bow Street before Sir Richard Birnie, with being ringleaders in "an outrage." "Lushy Tom," or "Brandy Tom," were the nicknames of Thomas Baskerville who had lived in Turnham Green for many years. It is clear that he had a drink problem and the usual consequences of his life style occurred. His "friends" declared that they would obey a drunken wish he had expressed to "Christen his grave" with gin. Between his death and funeral a man named Cotton, owner of a Chiswick errand-cart, disgraced himself by offering the widow £2 for her husband's body, his intention was to sell it to a surgeon. The old lady refused despite Cotton's warning that Tom Baskerville had better be buried deep as he would be taken up within 5 hours of interment. As this threat became widely known Baskerville's friends arranged that his grave would be dug to a depth of 18 feet.

On Sunday 14th June 1823 about 300 people accompanied the corpse to Chiswick Burial Ground, and when the body was deposited and some earth thrown around, the Turnham Green men formed a ring around the grave. They threw

a quart of liquor on the grave and uttered oaths that it should not be taken up. Mr Wright the Sexton and his assistants tried to stop this behaviour when there was a general cry of "shove the ...... into the grave and bury them." The Rector Mr Blowerbank was abused and the village was in uproar. Wright was thrown in and the crowd started to throw earth upon him. He was immersed up to his waist, at which moment a party of Constables arrived, and with great spirit (sic) attacked the crowd, dispersed the mob and took the prisoners into custody. Thomas Thompson was given bail, the others were remanded in custody. The widow applied to Sir R. Birnie to know what steps she should take to prevent further outrage and her husband's body being stolen. Sir Richard said that he knew of no other course than watching the grave and the poor old woman said she would do so.

A ghostly and much taller tale
In January 1784 Colonel Simeon Thompson of Kerry in Ireland wrote to his friend George Barry Douglas, of Fowey in Cornwall, but currently lodging in London. He described his shooting rights on a piece of land he called "Do as you please" and that he had men sinking a well therein. Two labourers were down about 60 feet and, not finding water, they delved down another 48 feet. A sort of vapour or smoke then appeared and they were taken up by basket to the surface whilst it evaporated. They dug another 3 feet, then, in the north-west corner found a curious passage, arched over with sticks and clay. They were able to walk inside, almost upright, when, about 10 yards from the shaft, they heard a noise like the chattering of a number of jays. This frightened the two workman and they were again drawn up. The Colonel and his brother Stephen descended in their place and found themselves in a chamber. They were unable to discover the source of the noise that their workmen heard, except it was what their fears created, but then found an enormous stone coffin. With some difficulty they prized off the lid and there discovered a human form. They measured it as a fraction short of 13 feet long, all but the head and neck swathed in the skin of an animal. On touching the face, parts of it fell into yellow powder and the head separated from the body. They went up in the basket to the surface and made arrangements for the entrance to be enlarged to take 7 men, and with this stratagem the workforce brought the coffin to the surface. When it was exposed to daylight and air the animal skin turned, by degrees, from black to pure white. They opened the skin and the body and arms of a woman appeared quite perfect and formed. On the thumb of the right hand was a

very curious cornelian in the form of a ring and on it, as well as inside the lid of the coffin, were these cyphers o-o-o-l-o-x-x-x. They put the body into spirits of wine intending to send it to Dublin as a present for the university. There had been many traditional stories of giants in that part of Ireland and this discovery made them seem all fact to the credulous common folk locally, who spent each day ascending and descending the well from sunrise to sunset.

Parricide
Should anyone be researching the name Smith and trace an ancestor to the ranks of the Bow Street Runners, then they will want to know what happened to him on the night of Tuesday 24th June 1824. The two patrolmen covering that night could not have expected that at 6am they would be approached by Hansom Cab driver William Chiswick (badge number 841). Chiswick took officer Smith to his cab, where he found a body wrapped in matting. This cadaver exactly resembled that described in the newspaper reports that they could have been reading. Chiswick said that he had been hailed by a man in Oxford Street, then told to drive towards St. Giles (eastwards). Two other men got in and he was re-directed to Eaton Street, Pimlico. There, whilst he waited, they dug up the body, covered his number plates with paper then ordered him to Foley Place. There they decamped and the terrified coachman, frightened that he would be caught with the body in his

cab, drove to Bow Street. A crowd gathered, and Officer Smith told Chiswick to take the body to St. Martin's Work House, but thoughtlessly did not accompany him. The doorkeeper at the workhouse refused the body entry on the grounds that it had been interred in the parish of St.George, Hanover Square. It was eventually taken to the work house at Grosvenor Square. Chiswick was brought in to Queen's Square police office by officer Banks but could not add anything to his previous testimony. Perusal of other reports made it clear that the deceased was a parricide, 23 year old Abel Griffiths, of a Southampton family. He had shot to death his father Thomas Howard Griffiths, a wealthy Barbados planter who lodged at 4, Maddox Street. The son was a trainee lawyer, suffering from scrofula and rheumatism and was in dispute with his father over his allowance. A coroner's Jury at the Green Dragon Inn in Maddox Street, Hanover Square, brought in a verdict of murder against the son, and in the circumstances of felo-de-se Coroner Thomas Higgs issued for a warrant for the felon to be buried at a cross-road. The body born by four men, slowly proceeded up Mount Street, South Audley Street, Stanhope Street and Hyde Park Corner to Grosvenor Place. It was followed by watchmen and constables and the procession increased in number as it arrived at the chosen cross-road, where Grosvenor Place meets Eaton Street and the Kings Road. About 200 people were present and constables held them back whilst the body was wrapped in Russian matting and dropped into a hole about 5 feet deep. The reporter was grateful that the usual disgusting practice of throwing lime on the body and driving a stake through it had been dispensed with. It was from this fate that the body had been recovered, though the motives of those who did so have, to my knowledge, never been ascertained. Friends of the deceased purchased a coffin and that night the body was re-interred in the burial ground for the poor in the parish of St.George's, the coffin borne by four paupers.

Ale and toast
It was the second day of the New Year 1824 when Samuel Clark stood before the Chelmsford Magistrates to be examined for "an offence." To prevent this offence, the burial grounds of London were now being so well protected, that the purveyors of human flesh had turned to the countryside for their supplies. This proclivity had been made a capital crime in France, to which country numerous skeletons were now being exported. Clark's unhealthy pallid hangdog look caused the reporter to declaim that "his avocations called him abroad at a time when church yards yawn and graves give up their dead." On Boxing Day Friday 26th

December 1823 Charles Rogers of Fairstead found a horse and cart in a field near the Mr Redwood's Turnpike at Little Leighs, close to where a footpath leads to Felsted. Unable to find an owner he left it with the landlord at the Castle (now St. Anne's Castle) from where it was reclaimed by the prisoner, who said that he left it because he had "got tipsy overnight through drinking ale and eating toast." The open cart had a special compartment ("For inside passengers") and a foetid smell. Robert Broomfield, a blacksmith, was suspicious and began looking into Mr Richardson and Mr Simon's fields at the spot near where the cart had been found. He found a shovel, pistols and, later, body parts. A full description of Clark, the cart and the horse was circulated as he had been seen drinking in the Castle on a previous occasion, together with a companion. They aroused suspicion as they spent much money but drank little. The body parts were identified as belonging to Joanna the wife of James Chennery, buried in Little Leighs churchyard the previous Sunday 21st December 1823. She was described as a fine young woman and a professional man estimated that her body would have been worth sixteen guineas to a surgeon in London. He added that she was better value than the live women the Blacksmith at Ongar had recently purchased for ten shillings. Further enquiries indicated that Joanna's half sister, a 33 year old married woman called Knight had been buried in that yard on 4th December 1823, as had Abraham Leader, a labouring man of similar age. The reporter was not kind to the memory of the late Mrs Knight, describing her as "a woman of but indifferent character, and who was known to be connected with much vice in this parish, and therefore met a premature death." On Wednesday 28th December 1823 both their graves were opened and found to contain only shrouds. On Friday 2nd January 1824 the Magistrates committed Clark to the next Quarter Sessions for trial.

A happy ending or Neighbourhood Watch

Grave robbing had its own inherent dangers. At about 4am on the morning of the Saturday nearest 25th January 1817 a party of men scaled the wall of St. Martin's burying ground, situated in a field at the back of Camden Town Their purpose, as it was supposed, was to steal the body of a grenadier, nearly 7 feet tall, who had died in the poor house of the parish and been buried there. The sexton, had, more ingeniously than lawfully, put together a number of gun barrels, so as to form them into a magazine, that they might all be discharged together. After burying the bodies of the paupers he made it a practice to direct the muzzle of this formidable engine towards the mound of earth, which was the general receptacle for the dead parochial poor, and having fixed a string around the trigger, he fastened it round a large piece of wood which he buried in the grave about a foot below the surface, so that should anyone attempt to dig, they must necessarily remove the wood, the string would pull the trigger and a volley of bullets would immediately sweep that corner of the burying ground. On the morning in question, at about half past four, he heard a tremendous report, and concluding it was his new piece of ordnance he went out as soon as possible. At the guarded spot, he found some spades, shovels, pick-axes and other resurrection paraphernalia. Among other things there was a man's hat, through one side of which a bullet had obviously passed; but from there being no mark upon the other side of it, it is concluded the bullet had lodged in the head of the owner, and killed him, and that he had been carried off by his associates.

The conclusion that I have drawn from putting these diverse events into a single heading is that their sheer variety of modus operandi and motives must have been a nightmare for the variety of pre-police enforcement officers to report and detect.

The National Archives
John Wood
Public Services Development Team

the national archives

The National Archives is the new name for the former Public Record Office. Formed in April 2003, when the PRO joined together with the Historical Manuscripts Commission, The National Archives (TNA) is the national treasure trove for all interested in genealogy as well as local, national or international history.

Housed in impressive facilities near Richmond in Surrey is one of the definitive archive collections in the world. The collection, available to all, represents the events and people of the past thousand years that helped form the nation we know today. Although the TNA is recognised as a major international research institution in fact around 75% of the online and onsite visitors are researching their family, community or local history.

The TNA truly has something for everyone. The gateway to the TNA is it's website at www.nationalarchives.gov.uk/ The website portal allows you to search our online catalogue of over 8 million documents, plan your visit and pre register for a readers ticket as well as download an extensive range of information leaflets covering nearly 200 topics of interest to genealogists and historians. This means that you can effectively plan your research and get a flavour of the material available before you visit. Planned for 2004 is the launch of an online virtual tour, allowing you to see the research trail and orientate yourselves before you visit.

A few good reasons
Why all those interested in family history should visit TNA…over 3million records of soldiers up

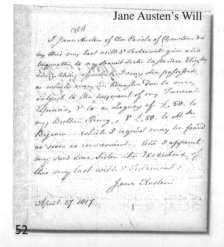

Jane Austen's Will

to the end World War 1, over a million merchant seamen's records, ships passenger lists, naturalisation records, railway staff records, over a million royal navy service records, RAF (RFC) WRAF, WRENS, Royal Marines, Tithe and Valuation plus over 2 million more maps, divorce, change of name, court records, transportation to the colonies……….the list of sources available is endless.

Onsite Facilities
The modern reception area is located within the main entrance to TNA. The ground floor houses:
An extensive modern bookshop
The free Museum featuring the treasures of TNA
Comprehensive restaurant facilities
Free cyber café
Cloakroom and locker facilities

Admission is free and, other than for coach parties and large groups, no advance booking is required. Researchers need to obtain a readers ticket at Reception to gain admission to the reading rooms. The website has full details on the registration process and an advance registration facility or you can call the contact centre for individual information.

The newly refurbished first floor facilities incorporate an information kiosk, specialist advice desks, library and extensive browsery area. The main document reading room is also located on the first floor. The most popular records have been made available in the self-service Microfilm Reading Room. There are always staff on hand to help you make the most of your research and to advise on the different avenues that you can follow.

TNA is online
Now you can carry out many preliminary searches and locate advance information online

On Date of Disembarkation.		NAME.		Date of Dis-embarkation.	REMARKS. (a) If non-effective :—Cause, etc. (b) If transferred :—Present Regtl. No., Rank and Unit. (c) If forfeited ;—Cause.
Regtl. No.	Rank.				
3/243	Pte	MONK	A.R.	1-6-15(1)	D. pres. 30-11-17.
SR/10771	"	MONK	W.G.	18-9-15(1)	K in A. 29-12-15.
3/128	L/Sgt	MONRO	John.	1-6-15(1)	" " 13-10-15.
1480	Pte	MOODY	B.G.	5-8-15(5c)	Disembd. 8-4-19.
3/8317	Cpl	MOON	A.E.	17-1-15(1)	Dis.para.392.XVI. 24-4-16.
3/7982	Pte	MOON	Alfred.	30-12-15(1)	K in A. 11-3-16.
SR/10041	Sgt	MOON	George.	17-8-15(1)	Dis.para.392XVI. 8-6-18.
3/2134	Pte	MOON	G.W.	28-7-15(1)	A.R. "Z". 2-4-19.
3/4181	"	MOON	L.G.	2-9-15(1)	D of W. 23-7-17.
3/745	"	MOOR	William.	1-6-15(1)	K in A. 13-10-15.
3/3109	"	MOOR	William.	1-6-15(1)	A.R. "Z". 14-3-19.
3/1349	Sgt	MOORCOCK	F.C.	28-7-15(1)	A.R. "Z". 9-3-19.

From 2004 you will be able to search the medal rolls at the TNA Documents Online service

regiment, rank and regimental number. It is planned to make available the names on the medal roll in batches according to surname.

Coach parties and groups

Coach parties are welcome to visit the PRO. As space is limited for coaches all parties must be pre-booked. Bookings are taken up to 18 months in advance. All coach parties receive a dedicated orientation tour for newcomers in their party and are provided with an advance reader ticket registration service. To enquire about available dates and reserve your coach group booking telephone the coach party booking number or use the email facility listed below. NB: there is no access to the site for coaches that have not pre - booked.

at the TNA portal - **www.nationalarchives.gov.uk** where you will find
The complete PRO catalogue online including a keyword search
Hundreds of information leaflets on the PRO's holdings
Advance order service
Document copying ordering facility
Online bookshop and ordering service
Award winning interactive education and museum galleries.
Details of all the PRO services and events and Documents online

The acclaimed online catalogue has been enhanced to make searching for relevant items in the catalogue far easier. Taken in tandem with the information leaflets the online catalogue allows name searches amongst some popular records such as soldiers discharged to pension before 1854 and merchant seamen's records.

Documents online, accessed via www.nationalarchives.gov.uk is the exciting new development for family historians. This, the digital image document delivery arm of the TNA, has a free name index search that allows you to

Search over 1 million wills from the Prerogative Court of Canterbury covering nearly 500 years
Discover new records recently opened to the public and Access the 1901 census.
Due to go online in late 2004 is the 1st World War campaign medal index. This exciting development means that you will be able to name search any of the millions of soldiers, officers and women awarded campaign medals in that conflict. As well as a name search you will be able to search by

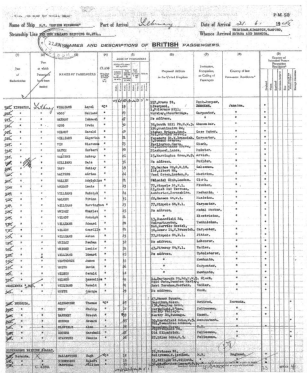

The Passenger list of the Empire Windrush from the West Indies in 1948

Opening hours

The TNA is open 6 days a week throughout the year except bank and public holiday weekends and the annual stocktaking week - usually in late November or early December. Up to date details of opening times and closure dates are on the website or can be checked through the Contact Centre. It is always advisable to call the us before visiting for the latest information on opening times, records availability, travel conditions and events.

Transport and Access

The PRO is 200 yards level walk from Kew Gardens station, served by the District underground line and the Silverlink Metro rail service. Kew Bridge station is half a mile away. Local bus services run nearby. Road access to the motorway system is good. Free parking is available on site. Easy access facilities for those with disabilities, including a lift to all floors.

Essential contacts and information

The National Archives Kew
Richmond, Surrey, TW9 4DU United Kingdom
Website: www.nationalarchives.gov.uk
Contact :020 8392 5200 Fax: 020 8392 5286
Email: enquiry@nationalarchives.gov.uk
Coach party bookings: 020 8392 5393
Or email: coaches@nationalarchives.gov.uk
Events: 020 8392 5202
Publications or bookshop enquiries: 020 8392 5271

Title Deed Treasures
Arthur Percival

Honorary Director
Fleur de Lis Heritage Centre, Faversham

When we buy a car, we look for its service history. When we consider candidates for a job, we set store by their track record. When we buy a thoroughbred, we expect to see its pedigree. When we buy a house ... we commission a survey, but the last thing we are usually told is anything about its past, except in the most general terms - 'Edwardian', 'Georgian', 'former coach-house', or whatever.

Even dating can be untrustworthy. Helpfully, the Dutch and Flemish Belgians used to say on their buildings, by way of date-stones or numerical tie-bars, when they originated. So did they if they settled in this country as refugees or traders in the 16th and 17th centuries. The native British seldom followed suit. So here homes which are palpably early Victorian become 'Georgian'; and an oak-framed building is 'Tudor' when as often as not it is Elizabethan, Jacobean or even Carolean.

Strange. In many cases we could be so much better-informed. Though title deeds are no longer required as proof of ownership - the simple Land Certificate suffices - they tell us much about a property's past.

Better still, from the family or local historian's point of view, they are often vivid reflections of social and economic history, telling us about figures in a community's past and how they contributed to its life and development. They can be of priceless importance, sometimes helping to unravel seemingly insoluble mysteries.

Don't be downcast if your house was 'only' built in (say) the 1930s or the 1900s. The earliest conveyance may be only be 70 or 100 years old; but, because of the need, before compulsory land registration, to establish reliable title (lineage in genealogical terms) it will probably include near the start a 'recital' of earlier transactions which authenticate the vendor's ownership and right to sell. Alternatively the conveyance may be accompanied by an 'abstract of title' which fulfils the same function.

In their clients' interest, solicitors and their clerks are cautious by nature, so they often went to great lengths to ensure that recitals and abstracts were legally watertight. The more cautious they were, the fuller the recital or abstract will be. In some cases, where there appears to be room for doubt about a particular stage in the 'descent' of a property, there may be an affidavit sworn by a third party to testify to its validity. This may well include informative extra background details of one of the parties involved.

Deeds relate to land as well as to whatever buildings stand on it, so the recital or abstract will take the story of the site back at least a few years, sometimes many more, to its rural past, affording a picture of the farming scene which the property replaced. In some cases, though, even 70 or 100 years ago, a new house may have been built on what would now be known as a 'brownfield' site - one vacated by industry, perhaps water-powered. Either way, the deeds will shed light on how the local economy has changed.

But, though you are the owner, you haven't got the title deeds of your house? As already noted, you no longer need them as proof of ownership, this duty now being done by the simple Land Certificate. However compulsory land registration is a relatively recent phenomenon, and the chances are that your deeds survive, and that you have deposited them with your bank or solicitor, or that, if you have a mortgage, they have been retained with the Land Certificate by your building society or other lender.

Herein lies a possible disappointment, though. Lenders only have limited space for the storage of securities and they no longer need deeds as evidence of title. If an earlier owner has mortgaged the property they may have been asked by the lender if they wanted to retain the deeds. On being told they are no longer needed as evidence of ownership, they may well have agreed to their disposal - in which case heaven knows what will have happened to them. Strictly speaking they should have been shredded, and probably they have been, but it is not unknown for stray deeds, or even bundles of deeds, to appear in antique shops, or even at boot fairs, as curios. They then get dispersed to the four corners, if not of the earth, at least of Britain. Some even get cut up for trendy lampshades. Either way you are never likely to see the ones which belonged to your property.

Let's look on the bright side now, and assume that either you have your property's deeds already, or that you have retrieved them from your solicitor, bank or lender. Naturally you would like to make sense of them. This may not be as easy as you might expect, and, particularly with older deeds, mistakes can be made if you try just a cursory inspection.

Just as there are professional family historians, there will probably emerge a band of property historians. Indeed there are some already, but they perhaps tend to interpret more the physical attributes of a property than the documents which belong to it. Full marks to them, though: they are contributing much to our understanding of the evolution of vernacular building design and technology.

If you have no access to a suitably qualified property historian, or the cash is not available to pay them, what to do? Title deeds can be intimidating documents, full of traps for the unwary and inexperienced. Before the advent of the typewriter, they were beautifully hand-written, usually on vellum. However before 1800 the hand may be hard to read and - what is worse - many documents were written on sheets so wide that at the end of one line it is all too easy not to move down to the next but to start reading the same line again. The fact that the vellum has been rigidly folded does not help, as it may be difficult to keep flat.

Vellum is robust and long-lasting, but, like paper, is all too easily damaged by damp. Some deeds have been stored for long periods in cellars or attics where they have suffered prolonged exposure to moisture. They will have probably become mouldy and will certainly be fragile. No attempt should be made to refer to them until they have been restored by a professional repairer. The nearest official record office may be able to suggest one. The wax seals which feature on many deeds may also be fragile and require attention. In any event, they should be handled very carefully.

Even if the deeds are in sound condition, there is another problem. They are written in stylised legal English. There is a lot of jargon, and also repetition, again because of solicitors' need to protect their clients' interests by eliminating any possible doubt or ambiguity. As late as the 18th century some documents ('fines', usually on small slips of paper) will be in Latin, and in a special hand which bears little relationship to conventional handwriting, copperplate or otherwise, or even to 16th-century 'court hand' - which is much easier to read.

If all this puts you off the job of 'decoding' your title deeds, you might be lucky enough to find someone in your area's local history society who is experienced enough to summarise them for you free of charge or in return for a contribution to the society. If so, you will be getting a bargain. A bundle of deeds 9" thick (by no means uncommon) can take a solid week to summarise - at £20 an hour, that's £800-worth of work.

What's the catch? There isn't one, because the local history society will use the information gleaned from your deeds to add to its understanding of the area's development, and the figures involved in it. The information may also turn out to be of vital importance in solving a problem posed by a family history enquirer who has sought its help.

But - no luck with the local history society? Then you are on your own, but don't give up! With a bit of application, and help from reference books, you should be able to decode your deeds yourself. Not all the books are still in print, but you may be able to borrow these through your local library, or from a lawyer acquaintance.

Some basic points first. Use pencil for your note - you don't want to get stray ink on old documents. If you are any kind of typist and are lucky enough to own a Psion or other PDA with a QWERTY keyboard, you may be able to enjoy the luxury of sitting in an armchair with a tray on your lap to get to work - a laptop, ironically, will probably be too heavy and take up too much room. You'll also need a lined pad to make written notes.

Now sort the documents into chronological order, starting with the earliest. Then look for any abstracts. These will probably be on paper and much easier to handle than original deeds, because the lay-out is conventional 'portrait', rather than the 'landscape' of deeds. These are your 'short-cuts' and if you have them you should start by summarising these.

Yes, they are summaries themselves, but you can still extract the information in them more concisely and systematically. They will describe a number of events in succession - not just conveyances or mortgages of title, but also other relevant events like marriages, deaths and the making and probate of wills. The best course is to give each a serial number as you summarise them in date order. You will then have a framework to which you can add extra information as you tackle the deeds themselves.

If there are no abstracts, then you start with the first deed. In fact if this records a conveyance before the early 19th century, there will probably be two deeds, one tucked inside the other - a 'lease and release', signed by the parties on successive days. You need only look at the release, which is usually a little longer than the lease and may contain more information.

With any luck soon after the beginning it will contain a magic section beginning 'Whereas ..' and tracing the earlier ownership of the property. This is the 'recital' and serves much the same purpose as an abstract: it validates the vendor's ownership of the property. Therefore you begin by summarising this and then at the end add details of the sale recorded in the release. This will record the occupation or other status of the vendor and purchaser, and so begin to give you a picture of the social and family history attaching to the property.

The vendor may be 'late of Casterbridge but now of Melchester', letting you know that he has interests in both places, and has moved from one to the other. Or he may be of 'the parish of Marlott in the town of Shaston', telling you that he lived in the town concerned but in an enclave within it which was a detached part of a rural parish just outside it. This could be important if later you needed to look for the baptism of his children: you would probably find the record in the register of the rural parish rather than the town. These detached portions of parishes are not at all uncommon, and often survived till the early 20th century.

In many towns and villages property numbers were not assigned till the 19th or even 20th centuries. This means that in deeds properties had to be defined by their 'abutments', or by a plan, or both - but in towns usually only by their abutments. These help local historians by recording the names of owners, and often also of occupiers, of adjacent properties. This is particularly helpful if their own deeds have not survived. Three abutments, described by compass-point, will usually be identified, the fourth being the street concerned, or 'the King's highway', meaning simply the public thoroughfare where the property stands. There will be more than three if more than one property is adjacent on one side.

You then continue to summarise the other deeds in sequence, right up to the present day, or at least until the date of the first Land Certificate included with the deeds. Some deeds will include details of occupiers, as well as owners, but they seldom include a complete chronological list, because the

details needed recording only when the property changed hands.

It is worth remembering that till relatively recently most people with money to invest put it into 'bricks and mortar', rather than gilts or equities, so before the middle of the 20th century many more dwellings were tenanted. Equally before the development of bank and building society mortgages, most money for property purchases was lent by well-off individuals. Often, too, it was understood that borrowers had no intention of repaying the capital sum: they were content to repay the interest. This provided the lender with regular income, and for borrowers amounted virtually to a form of rent.

Because they relate primarily to land and only secondarily to the structures on it, deeds do not always record explicitly when a property was built or rebuilt. However they often contain useful 'implicit' evidence. A particular deed may refer to 'that late built tenement' which, taken in conjunction with an earlier deed, gives a timespan within which it was built, or rebuilt.

Wills, or extracts from wills, are often included in title deeds. Though these may be accessible elsewhere, it is very handy to have them where they are most relevant, and they help to flesh out our pictures of owners.

At the end of a deed come the witnessed signatures of the parties involved. As well as being informative in themselves, these help with background details useful to the local historian. If a party signed with a cross (X), then clearly they were illiterate - though this should not necessarily lead to the conclusion that they were poor or of low standing. Successful businesspeople were often illiterate - all they needed was a literate clerk. The witnesses were usually solicitors, or their clerks, and by collating information from different sets of deeds it is possible to trace the development of their practices and personnel.

Owners of properties in historic towns can sometimes be disappointed because though theirs dates from (say) the 16th century, or at least occupies a site known to have been built-up for centuries, the deeds start only in (say) the early 19th century. One possibility is that earlier deeds have been lost or discarded. More likely their property once formed part of a portfolio of properties, and the earlier deeds survive with the 'head' property. There is no easy way of tracing which this may have been - it could have been miles away - but it may well have been an adjacent, or near-adjacent, property - so it may be worth asking neighbours if they have their deeds, and then asking to see them. Of course should yours turn out to be a 'head' property, it will include much invaluable information about other properties as well as your own, and your deeds will be even more valuable to local and family

historians.

Once your summary has been completed, you can then extract lists of owners and occupiers, and list them in chronological order. This is your property's 'pedigree'. You can add similar lists for adjacent properties, where the information is available from the 'abutments'. To round your work off, bring it to life, and make it more useful to local and family historians, you can compile in alphabetical order a list of dramatis personae, annotating it with information culled from local histories and other reference sources, like directories.

You may find that one 19th-century owner - a draper, let us say - was a town councillor, churchwarden and director of the local water company - a prominent local figure, evidently, and probably the very person who had the money to install the elaborate Victorian fireplaces of which you are so proud. You may even find significant links with the history of the nation and the Empire. The deeds of one early 18th-century house in Faversham showed a millwright, William Smith, as its occupier in the 1750s. It was he, it emerged, from other sources, who was later head-hunted by the East India Company to pioneer gunpowder manufacture in Bengal. He sailed on the Lord Anson in 1760, accompanied by scale-models of works machinery.

Two other local illustrations, finally, of the value of deeds to local and family historians. For the past

thirty years or so, and not just to comply with legislation, the big brewers have been disposing of pubs which no longer yield the return they expect. They may not always hand over the title deeds, but when they do these can be most informative.

The Faversham Arms, sold off about 10 years ago, was built on a greenfield site about 160 years ago to serve a developing part of the town. Its deeds go back 160 years further, to 1686, when they tell us that another millwright, William Homersham, was the owner of the site. This was Gallows Hole Field, in fact a corruption of Gallows Sole Field, sole being a Kentish word for a muddy pond. Picture perhaps weary farm workers looking the other way when an execution took place.

By the mid 18th-century, the deeds record, part of the site belonged to Thomas Fuller, a man of means who lived near Sandwich. He was keen to find a good husband for his young daughter Jane. At the same time William Boys, a young Sandwich GP, was looking for a wife who would bring him a handy dowry. QED. They married, and the deeds show that through Jane William became part-owner of Gallows Hole Field - and doubtless other property besides. Nobody could accuse of William being simply 'on the make'. He served Sandwich twice as Mayor, wrote its first comprehensive history, and was elected a Fellow of the Society of Antiquaries in 1776.

Another recent phenomenon has been the creation of retirement housing complexes. An attractive one was built on backland in the centre of Faversham about 15 years ago. Another delicensed pub, the Star, stood on the street nearby and was converted to form part of the development. Its deeds went back further than most - to 1659 - and the recital in the first took the story of the site back to 1577, when it was owned by a wealthy Londoner, Martin James, and leased to a local councillor, Thomas Belke. It was then, a bit surprisingly, considering its position close to the Market Place, a greenfield site. Perhaps it had formed part of the garden of an adjacent property.

Belke or one of his successors built a house on it - so we know the building dates from between 1577 and 1659. This went by the name of The Chequer. At a time when so many people were illiterate, not only inns but also private houses were sometimes known by their signs. The name, and use, soon changed, however. The local militia practised on open ground at the end of its curtilage. It was thirsty work, and the house became a pub, astutely named The Gun.

By 1784 it belonged to Charlotte Corne, a young spinster. More, she was something of an heiress, owning no less than 19 other properties within a 15-mile radius of the town. There are details of all of them in the deeds, so there is useful information here for local historians in villages like Hothfield, Selling and Sheldwich. The pub, now re-named The Star, was leased to Faversham brewer, Julius Shepherd. He cannot have been best pleased when a year later Charlotte, now married, sold it to his arch-rival John Rigden. He would have been a happier man now: the old Rigden brewery was closed by Whitbread in 1990, while his business, now Shepherd Neame, thrives as never before, with its popular Spitfire bitter exported worldwide. And finally, unless you feel there is a skeleton in the property cupboard, do let the local reference library and local and family history societies have copies of your summary. It could be so useful to them.

Further reading:
The standard layman's guide is N W Alcock's excellent *Old Title Deeds* (2nd edition, Phillimore, 2001). A helpful booklet is also published by *The Historical Association*. In second-hand bookshops it is worth looking out for relevant legal textbooks. Even if they are out-of-date they will still be useful for the interpretation of older documents - and if they are out-of-date, they will probably be cheap.
These titles include Michael Harwood's *English Land Law* (Sweet & Maxwell, 1975), A H Cosway's *Abstracting and Deducing Title* (Pitman, 1931) and Francis R Stead's *Title Deeds, Old and New* (Pitman, 1928).

Genealogy, family history or history?

Dr Andrew Gritt

Director Institute of Local and Family History

For too long there has been a widespread mutual mistrust between academic historians and genealogists – a divide caused by academic snobbery on the one hand and on the other by a perception of history derived from school history lessons and the popular media. Despite the valiant efforts of some, 'proper' history is still perceived by the many to be the history of nations, empires, politicians, monarchs, wars and dictators. True, these areas of history remain popular and provide the mainstay of the history national curriculum and many history degrees in British Universities. But that is not the end of the story.

Since the 1950s, and increasingly since the 1980s, the 'ordinary' lives of 'ordinary' people have been the subject of extensive academic study. Historians now know far more about the social history of the British people than ever before. Studies of poverty, for instance, are now much more dominated by the experience of poverty and coping strategies deployed by the poor, rather than the legislative history of poor law policy. Studies of industrialisation are now far less likely to be concerned with economic output and the technological advances developed by the engineers and inventors, and more likely to consider the effects on kinship, families, domestic life and standards of living. In short, a great deal of academic history is now much less concerned with key dates and major historical figures, and more focused on the daily experiences of men, women and children.

In contrast, many genealogists have remained faithful to the old-fashioned definition of history, being dominated by the pursuit of names, dates and 'key' events such as births, marriages and deaths. This perhaps explains why so many family history courses are dominated by developing an intimate knowledge of archival sources, where to find them, and how to use them for the purposes of identifying ancestors. There is an undoubted need for this level of knowledge and instruction, but the endless pursuit of names and dates, nurturing the sapling into a full-grown tree with innumerable branches, too often omits the detail waiting to be discovered through carefully targeted, yet imaginative, research.

Needles and haystacks

The 1851 census for Altcar, a small rural community north of Liverpool, contains the household of Richard Goore Balshaw, who, at the age of 70 lived with his daughter, two grandchildren and two servants on a farm of 190 acres. The genealogist might be content to turn to the Altcar parish registers, where his baptism is easily found on 3 December 1780. From this information, and using simple genealogical techniques, the maternal ancestors of Richard Goore Balshaw can be traced to Altcar in the early eighteenth century and his paternal ancestors to a neighbouring parish. The registers also allow the identification of his wider family of brothers, sisters and cousins.

The eager genealogist might painstakingly pursue the gaps in the Balshaw family tree, desperately trying to make sense of the defective Altcar registers, seeking out Roman Catholic registers or other local records to augment the Anglican registers of baptisms, marriages and burials in this area that largely remained faithful to the old religion. Such a search may well be fruitful, but the needles are very small and the haystack in which they are buried is very large. However, there is much more that can be done with the Balshaw family without the need to plug the gaps left by the registers in the family tree.

Reconstructing lives

Many family historians profess an interest not just in recording names and dates, but in actually reconstructing people's lives. Such apparently impossible questions as an individual's mental outlook, attitudes, decisions made, behaviour and other personal qualities are goals which, for many, remain unanswerable. However, this is just the kind of approach to family history adopted by the Institute of Local and Family History. When Richard Goore Balshaw died in 1854, he was worth around £4,000; when his grandfather died in 1798 he was worth just £10. In the intervening years Richard Goore Balshaw's father and uncles had died, each of whom were worth several hundred or even several thousand pounds. How had the family achieved this economic success so quickly? Were the Balshaw's 'typical'? How can we begin to reconstruct the attitudes and behaviour of the Balshaw clan that enabled them to experience their financial success?

By looking more widely at the testamentary behaviour, patterns of landholding of the Balshaws and other local farmers, the attitudes of the local aristocracy and gentry towards the Balshaws through manorial records, the marriage 'policy' adopted by the Balshaw family and the aggressive way in which they behaved towards many of their neighbours each help to build a picture of a single minded family with a long-term vision. Locally, they made their mark on their own time and had a part to play in the transformation of the English agrarian economy during the agricultural revolution. They were recognised as innovators by the local agricultural society, and some of the houses that they built still stand as monuments to their success. With the right approach family history can bring people to life, and rescue them from their lifeless position hanging on the branches of the family tree.

The Guildhall, Preston 1882

Institute of Local and Family History
This is the approach of the Institute of Local and Family History at the University of Central Lancashire. Founded in January 2001, the Institute's main objective is to bridge the gap between family history and academic history for the mutual benefit of both. The Institute runs regular conferences, day schools, evening lectures and training days specifically designed for local and family historians. The Institute has very close links with local archives in the North West and is involved in a number of ongoing projects developing indexes of archival holdings. Members of the Institute receive discounts on events and publications and a new members' area of the website is to be launched in the Spring of 2004 which will include discussion boards, previews of publications, limited access to research indexes, and an archive of Institute newsletters.

Online courses in family history
The Institute offers award-bearing courses in family history which are currently taught on campus. However, after a grant of £15,500 was awarded to the Institute these courses are now being developed for delivery online. Online delivery of courses offers many advantages – not least of which is the ability to study in the comfort of your own home at a time convenient to you.

University Certificate in Family History
This is a twelve-week course aimed at genealogists who want to develop an understanding of the sources and methods of family history research, and some of the problems of using certain sources. Students will benefit from the knowledge derived from large-scale academic projects that have tested the reliability and accuracy of the sources and developed methods for maximising the information they can glean from their research. Students are introduced to the techniques needed to begin to reconstruct the life-time experiences and behaviour patterns of ancestors.

University Advanced Certificate in Family History
This is a twenty-four week course which is aimed at the more experienced genealogist who wants to

develop their research skills and their knowledge of family history in the past. Students are guided through some key academic literature that opens up new lines of enquiry and sheds light on issues that often relate to their own families. Issues such as child labour, old age, migration, work, poverty and illegitimacy are common to most families, and the family historian can benefit enormously from the academic work undertaken in these areas. Students are also guided through the research process that academics use, and in the process are exposed to a very wide range of archival and library resources. Through a series of case studies, students are enabled to undertake detailed family history research and discover for themselves the hidden depths of even the most ordinary source.

Further Information
We would very much like you to get involved in the broad range of Institute activities and help us to forge beneficial links between the academic community and the global network of family historians. If you would like to know more then please contact us by phone or email. Further information is available on the Website.
Tel: 01772-893053
Email: locfamhistory@uclan.ac.uk
Web: www.localandfamilyhistory.com

Finding out more about gas workers
Simon Fowler

A major development during the 19th century was the increasing use of coal gas for lighting streets and houses. This led to a flourishing new industry producing and supplying gas to consumers in factories and at home. It employed tens of thousands of men and, increasingly, women.

In 1730, Cumbrian mine owner James Lowther brought fire-damp from his coal seams to the surface in a pipe and burnt it. He also collected the gas in bladders and demonstrated its properties to the Royal Society in London. However, a subsequent proposal to light the town of Whitehaven with the gas was rejected by the magistrates.

At about the same time chemists discovered that by heating coal it was possible to produce a flammable gas. The first house to be lit by gas was that of the engineer William Murdock in Redruth, Cornwall in 1792. The first serious application, however, was to light factories. William Murdock fitted out the mill of Messrs Phillips and Lee in Salford with its own gas plant and more than 900 burners. The citizens of Manchester flocked to gaze over the River Irwell at this great illumination and Murdock was awarded the Rumford Gold Medal by the Royal Society of Arts in 1809.

Gas plants were installed in a number of factories. However, the future however lay in public gasworks supplying customers through a network of pipes laid beneath the streets. The first person to suggest this was Frederic Albert Winsor, who demonstrated his gaslights in theatres and, in 1807, on the walls of Carlton House, the home of the Prince of Wales. His claims for the benefits of gas, and the returns which would be available to investors in his Universal Gas Light Company, were wildly exaggerated. It did not help that his plans were also ridiculed by many people, including Sir Walter Scott who laughed at the "madman who proposed to light London with - what do you think? Why, with smoke".

In 1812, however, under parliamentary authority, the Chartered Gas Light and Coke Company was established to supply gas to London, Westminster and Southwark. Slowly the lighting of the streets of the metropolis was transformed as the company's mains spread out from its works near Westminster Abbey. By 1815, there were 30 miles of gas mains under the streets of London. The demand was so great that rival companies soon competed for contracts to light streets and public buildings within London.

It is little wonder that the new lighting was popular: it was eighteen-times as bright as the oil lamps previously used. Hester Thrale wrote in 1817 that "such a glare is cast by the gas lights I know not where I am after sunset". Not everybody was pleased, a cartoon by Rowlandson had a prostitute grumble: "If this light is not put a stop to - we must give up our business", to which her client adds: "True my dear, not a dark corner to be got for love or money."

The first provincial town to adopt the new method of lighting was Preston in 1816. Gas lighting soon spread to Edinburgh, Glasgow, Liverpool, Bristol and Leeds. By 1829 there were over 200 companies producing and selling gas across Britain.

Shops and pubs were quick to install gas lighting, as a way of enticing customers into their premises. In 1840 Flora Tristan wrote of London at night that it was: 'magically lit by its millions of gas

Gas Lighting,
Carlton House
1823

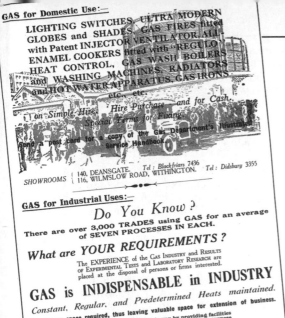
lights and is resplendent! Its broad streets
disappearing into the distance; its shops, where
floods of light reveal the myriad sparking
colours of all the masterpieces conceived by
human industry.'

The introduction of gas for domestic uses
however was very slow. Although George IV
had gas installed in the Royal Pavilion at
Brighton in 1821, it took another 20 years for it
to arrive at Buckingham Palace. In 1823 the
Reverend Sidney Smith visited Lambton Hall in
Durham and wrote to the *Morning Post* its
'splendour and glow make all other houses
mean. How pitiful to submit to farthing-candle
existence when science puts such intense
gratification within your reach. It is surely better
to eat dry bread by the splendour of gas than to
dine on beef and wax candles.'

An early problem was finding an effective way
to measure the gas used by consumers. Gas
companies initially charged according to the
number of mantles and the amount of time they
were in use, rather than by volume, a system
which was open to abuse. By the 1830s
companies were encouraging the use of gas
meters, offering discounts for people who used
them. The Gas Light and Coke Company made
their use compulsory in 1840 and other
undertakings followed suit. Early meters could
be large - the one supplied to the Houses of
Parliament in 1846 was in a hexagonal case, ten

feet high and finished in gothic style.

It was not until the 1880s that gas became
widely available in working class homes. New
mantles provided bright light with the minimum
of attention. They also used less gas, which
helped reduce bills. Another important
development was the pre-payment coin-operated
meter, which allowed families to purchase small
amounts of fuel. By the 1930s nearly two-thirds
of customers paid for their gas in this way.

The supply of gas depended on the adequate
supply of coal. In the late 1830s the Gas Light
and Coke Company was using 60,000 tons of
coal every year. The gas itself had to be cleansed
of impurities. Initially, this was done by being
passed through slaked lime, although from the
1850s iron oxide was increasingly used. An
most important by-product, however, was coke,
which was sold to iron manufacturers and
householders as a smokeless fuel.

Through mergers and takeovers, by the end of
the 19th century the Gas Light and Coke
Company had become the largest company in
Britain. It supplied gas to much of London north
of the Thames. In 1868, it had begun building
the biggest gas works in the world on 540 acres
of land adjacent to Barking Creek in East
London. The area was named Beckton after the
Company's chairman Simon Adams Beck. The
aim was to concentrate production there and
close smaller plants elsewhere in the metropolis.
A reporter from the *Illustrated London News*
who visited the works in 1878 found: "vast piles
of building, with a stately monumental clock
tower in the spacious front lawn with seven or
eight gas holders - cylindrical iron structures
painted bright red, supported by lofty iron pillars
- rise near the water's edge. The persons
employed here is nearly 2,000, of whom about
1,200 work in the retort houses." The company
provided a church on the site, a school and
housing for its workers.
Gas companies were known for a paternal
relationship towards their staff. The Gas Light
and Coke Company provided workmen's benefit
and pension schemes and a company doctor,
long before this became normal practice.
However, this disguised the fact that conditions
were often poor, particularly for men who
worked in the retort houses. It also was usual to
work 12 hours a day, seven days a week with
perhaps just one or two days off a month.

By the First World War, many gas companies
were operating performance schemes - known as
co-partnerships - which allowed employees to
buy shares in the firm. The idea was pioneered
by the South Metropolitan Gas Company in

1889 and it quickly spread. Apart from giving a substantial pay bonus - perhaps as much as 10 per cent in good years - it helped fostered better relations between management and the workers.

From the 1880s the gas industry faced increasing competition from electricity. The response was to find new customers by cutting the cost of gas and providing new services. By the end of the century, gas-fired heaters, boilers and cookers were all on sale, often available on a hire-purchase scheme. Although, gas cooking was nothing new - the Reform Club in London had been cooking with gas as early as 1841.

Efforts were made to persuade customers, particularly women, to buy cookers and other gas appliances. A Miss Edden was appointed by the Gas Light and Coke Company as: "a lady to visit consumers in their homes and instruct them in the use of gas cooking stoves". Showrooms were also opened in most town centres to sell appliances and deal with customers.

Between the wars, gas was gradually replaced by electricity as a means of lighting, although in many households it remained the fuel of choice for heating and cooking. In the 1930s it was increasingly clear that having a large number of small companies was not an economic way to run the industry. Matters were made worse during the Second World War. In London there were 20,500 incidents involving damage to 6,000 mains and 65,000 service pipes. Liverpool was raided 68 times, and in all but three raids, mains and services were hit: all at a time of unprecedented demand.

A report in 1944 in effect recommended

nationalisation. The proposal met with little opposition from within the gas industry. Twelve area boards (including ones for Scotland and Wales) were set up, with a Gas Council to co-ordinate their work. The companies and the gas council were subsequently merged to form British Gas in 1972, which in turn was privatised in 1986.

A programme of modernisation was set in motion. The number of gas works fell by half between 1948 and 1958, with a slight increase in productivity. Unfortunately gas was largely out of favour with the consumer, who increasingly preferred electricity with its clean contemporary image.

The fortunes of the industry were transformed during the late 1960s and 1970s, firstly with the 'High Speed Gas' advertising campaign, but more importantly with the introduction of natural gas from the North Sea. Within a decade of taking the decision to use this new resource, every appliance in Britain (nearly 30 million) had been converted in an operation of remarkable smoothness.

Thanks to Elaine Brison of the National Gas Archive and Terry Mitchell for their help with this article.

Finding Out More
Until well into the 20th century the gas industry was characterised by the large number of undertakings which operated. Every town had its own gasworks, and large cities may have had several competing firms. In 1912, there were nearly 1,500 such firms throughout the British Isles, a quarter of whom were controlled by local authorities - the rest were privately owned companies. A few villages, like Debenham in Suffolk, Wedmore, Somerset and Rhayader, even had their own companies distributing gas to local people. The industry as a whole employed nearly a quarter of a million people.

It was an industry with strong family ties. It was not uncommon for three or four generations of the same family to work for one company. There are many sources of information, if you know where to look. Even if it is not possible to trace a particular person, you can often find something about the place in which they worked and the conditions they endured.

Gas Showroom, Deansgate, Manchester 1932

The major source of archives for the gas industry is the: *National Gas Archive*, Common Lane, Partington, Manchester M31 4BR. Tel. (0161) 777 7193. The Archive holds records relating to the gas industry from 1812 to the present day, including site plans of local gas works and associated property records, minute books of many of the early gas companies, an extensive photographic collection, with more than 500,000 images, and a good library. Enquiries should be made in writing and an appointment has to be made before visiting the Archive. They have recently published a free leaflet for family historians.

Records of many gas companies, or undertakings, have been deposited with local record offices. Many Gas Light and Coke Company documents, for example, are held by the London Metropolitan Archives. The National Register of Archives, which is part of the National Archives, can tell you which records for individual companies survive and where they are stored. This information can be found on the web site *www.hmc.gov.uk* or by calling (020) 8392 5200.

Personnel records of individual workers are likely to be closed for 75 years or longer. There are other series of records that may provide additional information, including apprenticeship records, wage books and accident registers. Another useful source is company magazines and trade journals, which often mention individuals and include illustrations. The most important was the weekly *Gas Journal*, published from 1849. The oldest company magazine was the South Metropolitan Gas Company's *Co-partnership Journal*, first published in 1903.

Terry Mitchell maintains the Gas Industry Genealogical Index, (GIGI) which includes some 250,000 names. He is willing to search it, for a small fee, as well as provide other help for people who had ancestors in the industry. His address is Old Barnshaw Cottage, Pepper St, Moberley, Cheshire WA16

6JH, or e-mail: tmm@tinyworld.co.uk.

Further Reading
There is no modern history about the gas industry and people who worked in it. There are however several books that may provide some background information:
Dean Chandler and A. Douglas Lacy, *The Rise of the Gas Industry in Great Britain* (Gas Council, 1949)
Maureen Dillon, *Artificial Sunshine: A Social History of Domestic Lighting* (National Trust, 2001)
Mary Mills, *Places and People in the Early East London Gas Industry*, available at £25 from M. Wright, 24 Hyde Road, London SE3 7LT.
Trevor I. Williams, *A History of the British Gas Industry* (Oxford University Press, 1981)
Hugh Barty-King, *New Flame: A History of Piped Gas, 1783-1984* (Graphmitre,1984)
The *Historic Gas Times* is a quarterly journal published by the Institute of Gas Engineers Panel for the History of the Industry. For details contact the Institute of Gas Engineers, 21 Portland Place, London W1B 1PY, *www.igasebg.com*.

Museums
There are several museums either devoted to the gas industry:
National Gas Museum, Aylestone Rd, Leicester LE2 7QH, tel. (0116) 250 3190, *www.gasmuseum.co.uk*. Claims to be the largest museum devoted to the gas industry in the world, but holds few archives.
Fakenham Museum of Gas and Local History, Hempton Rd, Fakenham NR21 9EP, tel. (01328) 855579, *www.fakenham.org. uk/gasmus1.htm* The Museum looks after the only surviving town gas production plant in Britain.
Biggar Gas Works, Biggar Museum Trust, Moat Park, Biggar ML12 6BT, tel. (01899) 221050 *http://www.redfern83.freeserve.co.uk/coal_gas_manufactur e/ia_003_biggar_gasworks.html*. The gasworks is the only remaining gas production plant in Scotland.
Societies
The North West Gas History Society produces an informative newsletter and organises meetings and visits. Despite the name, members are interested in the gas industry throughout England. The Society can be contacted via the treasurer Brian Bingham, 24 Greenhill, Timperley, Cheshire WA15 7BQ.

Normal Early Morning Load of Gas Appliances - Manchester 1932

Sheffield and District Family History Society

Our area: The ancient townships of Sheffield, Ecclesall Bierlow, Brightside Bierlow, Nether Hallam, Upper Hallam, now the modern Metropolitan District of Sheffield

Society Publications:
• 1861 census index for Sheffield and Rotherham
• 1891 census transcription for Sheffield
  (on-going project)
• Burial transcriptions and indexes for over 250,000 burials in the Sheffield area
Other local and family history publications available by post or via http://www.genfair.com

Quarterly journal
For Membership details please contact:
Mrs J. Pitchforth, 10 Hallam Grange Road, Sheffield S10 4BJ (enclosing an sae please)

For all other details including publications information, please contact the Hon Secretary, Mrs D. Maskell, 5 Old Houses, Piccadilly Road, Chesterfield, Derbys S41 0EH (enclosing an sae please), quoting GSD

Email: secretary@sheffieldfhs.org.uk
Web page: http://www.sheffieldfhs.org.uk

WAKEFIELD & DISTRICT
FAMILY HISTORY SOCIETY

We cover the parishes of : Ackworth, Badsworth, Castleford, Crofton, Darrington, Featherstone, Ferry Fryston, Hemsworth, Horbury, Knottingley, Normanton, Ossett, Pontefract, Sandal Magna, South Kirkby, Wakefield, Warmfield, West Bretton, Woolley, Wragby, and parts of the parishes of Dewsbury, Felkirk, Royston & Thornhill.

Our meetings are on the first Saturday of each month except August, from 10.00 am at St. John's Parish Centre, Wentworth Street, Wakefield : speakers, bookstalls, library, fiche and computer searches. Members receive a quarterly journal.

Our publications include the 1851 Census Index, 1813-1837 Marriage Indexes, Bishop's Transcripts, various church and newspaper indexes, and Monumental Inscriptions. We offer a range of search services, and our website carries useful resources and information.

CONTACT : Mrs. D. Shackleton, 18 Rosedale Avenue, Sandal, Wakefield, WF2 6EP
email : membership@wdfhs.co.uk
website : www.wdfhs.co.uk

Huddersfield & District
Family History Society
Registered Charity No. 702199

The Huddersfield & District Family History Society caters for those researching and with interests in the Kirklees Metropolitan area which covers about 160 square miles. Within our boundaries lie the ancient parishes of Almondbury, Batley, Birstall, Dewsbury, Emley, Hartshead, Huddersfield, Kirkburton, Kirkheaton, Mirfield and Thornhill.

We have a research room and library at Meltham, which houses our transcriptions of the 1841 & 1851 census for our area, the 1881 census for England & Wales plus the 1992 edition of the IGI for the whole of Britain and the National Probate Calenders 1858 - 1943.

The Society has about 300 publications for sale of Parish Registers and the 1841 and 1851 censuses. We are also participating in the National Burial Index. Search Services on these and other databases are also available.

For further details please contact our
Secretary at
15 Market Place, Meltham, West Yorkshire HD9 4NJ
or visit
our website at www.hdfhs.org.uk

Doncaster and District Family History Society

The Society meets on the last Wednesday of each month (except December)
at 7 pm for 7.30 pm at Doncaster College for the Deaf, Leger Way, Doncaster

Palgrave Research Room
Our Research Room at Doncaster Archives, King Edward Road, Balby, Doncaster
Open Monday, Tuesday, Wednesday and Friday 10 am to 4 pm and Saturday 10 am to 2 pm

Find your ancestors with our numerous fiches, publications and CDs in our Research Room:

Fiche: GRO Indexes 1837-1950, IGI, 1901 Census for Whole of Yorkshire
1891 Census for all parishes covered by the Society, Cemetery Registers,
Monumental Inscriptions, Doncaster Health Authority Death Registers,
Parish Registers 1754 to 1950 for Archdeaconry of Doncaster,
Also Non-Conformist and Catholic Registers

Books: Burial Indexes from commencement of parish registers to at least 1900
1851 Census Index and Marriage Indexes for all parishes covered by the Society

CDs: 1881 Census for whole country, Austerfield – Its People

Computer: 1871 and 1891 Census for Archdeaconry of Doncaster and much more

Annual Family History Day
Held on 6 November 2004r. Three speakers, optional lunch, bookstalls from visiting societies,
access to computer databases, help tables, free parking, disabled facilities

Secretary: Mrs June Staniforth, 125 The Grove, Wheatley Hills, Doncaster, DN2 5SN
Tel: 01302 326695 Email: marton-house@blueyonder.co.uk
Website: http://www.doncasterfhs.freeserve.co.uk

Drama in Regency Yorkshire 1811 - 1820
Prudence Bebb

An Itinerant Theatrical Sketch

London Published by Allen & Co. 15 Paternoster Row February 25, 1797.

Was your Regency ancestor an actor? Probably not. Did your ancestor go to the theatre? Very likely. You may think, "But my ancestor was in service; he or she hadn't much chance of visiting a theatre." Actually they did have a good chance. When people paid for a seat at the playhouse, they were not given a numbered ticket. All they were guaranteed was <u>a</u> seat. However, if someone wanted a good view, they were allowed to send a servant early to sit exactly where the employer wanted to be. After a couple of hours sitting in the auditorium, the poor servant had to vacate the place for the arrival of sir or madam.

Even if you secured a good seat, you might not be able to hear very well because audiences were not so quiet as they should be. If two people sitting next to you kept exchanging remarks, they would certainly impede your hearing - the more so because there was no amplifying system. This, of course, meant that actors had to declaim their lines loudly whether that seemed appropriate or not. Romeo didn't

exactly shout at Juliet but he had to make himself audible to the gentlemen at the back.

Unfortunately, it was fashionable to wear feathers in the hair in the evening. This was not just unfortunate for the birds, it was a disadvantage to anyone sitting behind a nodding plume as it could interrupt one's view of the stage.

And the stage was worth viewing. Scenery had become more realistic than in past years. Indeed, the scene was sometimes better than the thespians. In 1819 Henry Crabb Robinson wrote in his diary: "Went to the theatre.. .the acting is very bad but the show and scenery tolerable enough - I saw a spectacle - exhibiting the wretchedness of a family on the coast of Labrador and left there by pirates - The scenery was imposing and that was all, of course."

In March 1815 The Theatre Royal, York, advertised a performance in which: "The wall of the Cottage is struck with lightning, and falls.

MRS SIDDONS,
as Constance *in* King John.

The River is seen through the Opening." That may not have been as hazardous as it seems. The rolling of wooden balls above the stage ceiling simulated thunder and coloured glass could imitate lightning.

Worse effects were sometimes produced and it is not surprising that some Regency theatres literally went up in smoke. To add to the hazard, the auditorium was lit by wax candles in brass chandeliers which guttered and dripped dangerously above the feathered and bald heads beneath them. A man was employed who carried a long pole with a cone - shaped snuffer on the end. When anyone noticed melting wax, they probably ducked their head but they also called out: "Snuffer!" It didn't matter if Lady Macbeth was seeing a dagger at the time, the snuffer was more important. No one could forget that, when Drury Lane had been burnt down in 1809, the conflagration was enough to illuminate the Thames and nearby buildings.

Regency people were able to see the actors wearing costumes suitable for the parts they were to play. It had been different in Papa and Mama's day when Romeo might appear in a Cavalier hat with feathers, lace and seventeenth century boots. By 1811 Shakespeare's medieval characters wore medieval costume. Indeed York's wardrobe master, Johnny Winters, found historical accuracy a great nuisance, especially when Mrs Siddon's brother was performing. Johnny complained: "That John Kemble and

Shakespeare have given me more trouble than all the other people in the world put together, and my spouse into t'bargain."

The Bard was frequently performed but he took his place in a three - part evening's entertainment. It was usual to have a tragedy and a farce with a gap, during which an acrobat or singer performed. Yorkshire people got plenty for their shilling.

In August 1814 York Theatre Royal presented The Merchant of Venice, followed by the singing of Hark the Lark, and subsequently the pantomime Don Juan. Pantomimes became very popular, especially Harlequin and Mother Goose. The short performance between the two dramatic productions could create its own drama. Sieur Sanches was in York during 1814 when he walked upside down above the stage, probably using magnets on his boots. His advertisement foretold that he "..... will balance four Chairs with a Person in each, One of which he will hold in his mouth while suspended from the Rope, and will take up a Person with his Teeth while on the Rope".

Theatres were often closed. In many places people eagerly waited for the arrival of the actors, a travelling company who worked on a circuit of theatres. A waggon rolled into the town carrying scenery, costumes, and other props. Poor actors might travel on the stage - coach; those who commanded higher wages were sent on a post - chaise so they arrived in style.

Samuel Butler was a well - known actor - manager who supplied the theatres in Beverley, Harrogate, Kendal, Ripon, Whitby and York. This would have been an impossible job if they had all been open at the same time. In fact, Mr Butler led his troupe of actors on a circuit of these theatres, opening them at the most lucrative times - Race Weeks for York and Beverley, the Season for Spa drinkers in Harrogate. In 1812 they were billed to perform in Beverley during the June races. Everything started well then, suddenly, on the 15th Samuel Butler died. His memorial is in St Mary's Church at Beverley; his widow took his place in charge of the company of actors.

Tate Wilkinson lived beside York's theatre. He had raised its status (at a cost of £500) by getting it a royal patent. As a result famous players were willing to act there. The great tragedian, Sarah Siddons, performed in York

Theatre Royal on a number of occasions. By Regency days she was on the verge of retirement but couldn't quite give up. In 1812 she was back again and Mr Wilkinson advertised in The York Chronicle: "Mr Wilkinson most respectfully acquaints his friends and the public that in consequence of the earnest solicitations of many of the First Families, he has engaged
MRS SIDDONS.
(this being positively the last year of her appearing on the stage) for TWO NIGHTS, Tomorrow (Friday) the Tragedy DOUGLAS
Lady Randolph - Mrs Siddons
Saturday, a play, in which Mrs Siddons will act a principal character. Being the last night of the company's performing till Easter".
Sarah Siddons had been a Miss Kemble before her marriage and her brothers were also famous actors. Stephen Kemble was a great favourite with the audience in Scarborough. His son, Henry, leased its theatre and, besides providing other actors, performed there himself.
Everybody loved to see him as Falstaff: he was the only actor who did not need to be padded in order to play Shakespeare's fat fellow. Henry Kemble's theatre was in the road we call St Thomas Street, formerly Tanner Street. There they put on a special performance to raise money for the Waterloo Fund, a charity to help the widows and orphans of men killed in the victory of 1815.

The attractive, dark - eyed Dorothy Jordan acted in several Yorkshire theatres and wrote home, describing them to her partner who was a Royal Duke, the future William IV. She was the mother of his ten children and whilst in York decided to be known as Mrs Jordan which sounded very respectable.

Whilst in Leeds, Dorothy wrote to her duke that she had got a sore throat which did not surprise her because the theatre was so damp. "Half the upper part of it admitting the wind and rain", she said and, as for her dressing - room, it was "running down with wet. . .I was obliged to stand on my great coat to keep my feet from wet." However, the audience listened intently to her and applauded heartily, a courtesy which not many actors received from them.
In Hull the audience was busy cracking and eating nuts during the performance and even throwing some empty shells onto the stage. Actors worked hard for they often performed in both the tragedy and the farce on the same night. They attended rehearsals, learnt parts and stayed in lodgings. Life was not comfortable but they could become popular.

Sometimes a wealthy patron might request and pay for the performance of a particular play, This happened in York when the judge came for the Assizes. It happened in Harrogate when affluent and aristocratic people stayed for the Season. The theatre was opposite to the Granby

A 'Fancy Sketch, to the Memory of Shakespeare.

London Pub⁰. by Allen & C⁰ 15. Paternoster Row. February.18, 1797 —

Hotel where Harrogate's richest visitors stayed; the guests there and those at the Green Dragon, the Queen's Head and the Crown all contributed to offer Dorothy Jordan a lucrative inducement to break her journey from London to Edinburgh and spend four nights in Harrogate.

Probably the gouty gentleman at the Spa in 1817, drinking sulphur water which smelt of bad eggs, consoled himself with the thought that he would spend the evening in the theatre at High Harrogate watching Othello and the farce Love and the Toothache. Between these plays Miss Stoker would dance and Mr Jefferson would sing a comic song. As he sat on the low wall beside the well, holding his stomach and trying not to feel sick, the gentleman felt that two shillings to sit in the pit or even three shillings to hire a box was money well spent.

Visitors to the sea at Bridlington enjoyed going to the theatre which was managed by Mr Smedley who brought a company from Lincolnshire to act there. His own family acted and parts were taken by his "three or four fine daughters with whose charms the young sparks were much bewitched." So wrote an old gentleman remembering Bridlington as it had been in his youth during the Regency. The young men were not the only supporters of Mr Smedley's troupe. In 1813 the newspaper recorded that "The Duchess of Leeds bespoke a play on Wednesday night, which was well attended. Amongst the fashionables there we noticed: The Duchess of Leeds, Lady Anne Hudson and family; the Countess of Erne, Mr and Lady Caroline Wortley, Sir Edward and Lady Smith. . .Lady Boynton, Mr Packhurst and his two lovely daughters who still continue to grace Bridlington - Quay by their appearance. .".

Some scenery painters became well - known. Young Mr Gill painted very successful backdrops for Henry Kemble in Scarborough. By Regency days audiences had a natural - looking scene to view such as a panelled room with a picture hanging over a fireplace. You could feel as if you were in the scene because they had recently learnt to use flats at the side of the stage. This gave more impression of distance.

The oldest scenery in England is at Richmond in North Yorkshire where the small theatre used a woodland scene with trees painted on canvas flats. This charming theatre even started a fashion which London copied. In 1813 an actor actually pushed a wheelbarrow along a tightrope from the gallery to the stage. This idea was copied at Covent Garden in 1816.

Actors certainly earned the wages which the managers paid them. Some were allowed a benefit performance when the ticket money was given to a particular actor who was allowed to choose who would perform with them. Naturally a good supporting cast helped to increase the audience. Unfortunately, if your benefit night turned out to be wet, fewer people came.

As so often, the British weather played its own part.

Life in REGENCY BEVERLEY

Prudence Bebb

Prudence Bebb's latest book, *Life in Regency Beverley*, was published by Sessions of York in 2003.

This is another very welcome book from the pen (and camera) of this talented author in which she tells us about the fascinating way people went about their everyday lives in the historic Yorkshire town of Beverley.
As with her previous books in the series the author takes us through many aspects of life in the period - from the poor to the prosperous and the good and the bad, indeed one chapter is entitled The Good, The Guilty and The Gallows. Buy this book and be transported back through time and judge for yourself whether these really were 'the good old days' or is the expression a merely a myth?

ISBN 1 85072 303 6 Size A5 88 pages
Contains many illustrations Price £6.50 UK
p & p £1.50 Overseas p & p £2.50 (surface mail)

Not as daft as they look?
John Titford

says that unusual surnames
can be a source of great delight...

I try to make it a rule never to let an interesting
or unusual surname pass me by. How is it that
some people can merrily go about their
everyday lives bearing names like **Earwig**,
Headache or **Lickorish**? How might such
names have originated - and where?

There's a lifetime's enjoyment to be had from
collecting and analysing surnames. Refer to one
or more surname dictionaries to establish
meanings and origins if you like; failing that,
use your imagination backed up by a certain
amount of background reading - or, if I can
suggest this with all due modesty - take a look
at my book, Searching for surnames
(Countryside Books, 2002), which suggests
strategies for teasing out the meaning of a name
from first principles.

Perhaps Frederick **Conker** (born in Liverpool in
1829) had the right idea: born with one unusual
surname, he changed it to another when he
enlisted in the army, claiming that he was
Frederick **Whirlpool**. Under this extraordinary
name he won the Victoria Cross on 3 April
1858, though later in life, when he was living as
a hermit in Australia, he used a deed poll to
make a further change, becoming Frederick
Humphrey **James**. Yet the wheel would come
full circle, after all: when he died in 1899 and
was laid to rest in the General Presbyterian
Cemetery, McGarth's Hill, Windsor, New South
Wales, the burial record calls him Frederick
Whirlpool once more.

A fascination with surnames is nothing new. A
book called *Memorials of St.John at Hackney* by
R.Simpson (Part Two, 1882) reproduces a little
ditty (originally featured in the *Hackney
Magazine*) which celebrates the range of
surnames in evidence in the district:

If the Surnames in Hackney be read through with care,
There are certainly some will be found very rare:
Such as Bull, and Buck, and Peacock, a Bond and a Freeman,
A Hogg and a Lyon, a Land-on and Seaman;
A Hawke and a Partridge, a Swan and a Jay,
White, Callow, and Brown, Black, Green, and a Gray;
A Monk and a Prior, a Pope and a King,
Some Bells and some Bowes, an Offor and Ring;
A Grounds and an Arewater, Frost, Snow, and Hale,
Greenwood and Woodifield, Montaigne and Vale.
A Man and a Child, a Knight and a Day,
A Farmer and Squires, Heath, Oldfield and May;
A Jackson, a Johnson, a Long and a Longman,

Jolly Jack Tar

A Large and a Little, a Short and a Shortman.
An Archer and Bowman, a Shepherd and Crook,
A Fountain and Bowerbank, Arber and Brook;
A Temple, a Hovell, a Street and a Church,
Thorowgood, Masters, Young, Children, and Birch.
A Dean and a Bishop, a Fox and a Guy,
Goode, Hogsflesh and Salmon, Dabbs, Bacon and Fry;
Fatt, Cook, and a Kitching, a Gosling and Drake,
Keyes, Lock and Wards; Flint, Steel and a Rake.
Cave, Pitts, and a Hole, Wells, Bridges and Ford,
A Penny and Argent, and Riches and Ord;
A Sargant and Banner, a Cannon and Major,—
That these names may be found we would bet any Wager.

Bill Lloyd of Chapel Books, Chapel Centre,
Llanishen, Chepstow, Mon. NP6 6QT.
(www.chapelbooks.co.uk), who specialises in
the sale of manuscript material of interest to
family historians and others, is well-placed to
unearth examples of distinctive or amusing
surnames, and has very kindly provided me with
some examples:

Anger (Lancs. 20th century); **Bytheway**
(Worcs./Warwicks. 19th century); **Drinkmilk**
(Suffolk, 19th century); **Household** (Suffolk,
19th century); **Hundlebee** (Middlesex, 18th
century); **Lard** (Notts. 18th century); **Martyr**
(Surrey 19th century); **Oppy** (Cornwall 19th
century); **Prettejohn** (Devon 19th century);
Stonehewer (Lancs./Chesh. 18th century);
Twallin (Chesh. 17th century).

Bill tells me that he is always fascinated to
come across so many documents for people with
what appear at first sight to be animal names:

**Badger; Bear; Beetle; Beever; Bird; Brock;
Buck; Bullock; Cockerell; Crane; Crow; Doe;
Dolphin; Drake; Duck; Eeles; Finch; Fish;
Fox; Goose; Gosling; Haddock; Herring;
Hogg; Lamb; Lamprey; Leech; Moles; Pigg;
Rook; Salmon; Sparrow; Stagg; Swann;
Whale.**

Robert Shortshanks,
Duke of Normandy
from Mr Punch's
Collection of Historical
Portraits

A search on the Internet using the words 'Unusual surnames' throws up a surprising number of web-sites devoted to this subject. One such, compiled by Sheila Francis, can be found at: (http://freepages.genealogy.rootsweb.com/~sheilafrancis/ unusualp1.htm).

Sheila's site is great fun; names are arranged alphabetically under the following headings: Name; Reference; Details. So a typical entry reads like this: `Pelican, Margaret; Quarter Sessions Book, Glamorgan, 1847-1852; 13, of Merthyr Tydfil, 3 months hard labour, 30.4.1859'. Sheila has written to tell me that she set up the site in 2001 with the help of her daughter, and that her favourite names so far are **Pine Coffin, Kindlysides, Knoo, Nightscales, Proverbs, Pyfinch, Shavegrass, Silversides, Tongue, Toes, Turnip, Twiddle, Littleboy** and **Horsenail**. There are plenty more such gems on her web-site!

My own favourites, I must say, include: Private William **Tellogram** (awarded the Naval General Service Medal for having served at battles in Martinique [1809] and Guadaloupe [1810]); Captain William **Chatterbox** of the twenty-seventh foot regiment (married Miss Gilman at Limerick in Ireland in November 1798); Marg' **Doredraught** (Poll Tax returns for Tilney, Norfolk, 1381); Ann **Pancak** (a legatee named in the will of Isabella Morice of Ottryden, Kent, widow, proved on 20th.June 1531) - and even I suppose, **Birdseye**. Oddly enough, the well-known frozen food company Bird's Eye took its name from the surname of its founder, Clarence (Bob) Birdseye (1886-1956) of Brooklyn, New York. No-one seems to be certain just where the name comes from, though early examples of its use may be found in Bedfordshire in particular. C.W.Bardsley, in his Dictionary of English and Welsh surnames (first published in 1901) says: " .. of Birdsey, I cannot find the place...But the meaning seems clear: the 'Birdseye', i.e., the

islet or eyot in the stream frequented by birds'. Alternative spellings include **Birdsey, Budsey, Berdsay, Birdesey, Birdsaie** and **Birdsay(e)**.

To round off Searching for surnames, I compiled a section entitled 'Not as daft as they look', devoted to surnames which are simply not what they appear to be. This may be because they have become corrupted and unrecognisable over the years, or because the language has moved on, introducing new words and meanings whilst abandoning the old, occasionally turning formerly innocent words into guilty ones or vice versa. There are no rules to follow when trying to understand names such as these; it's largely a matter of gleaning information from existing published material, include surname dictionaries, language dictionaries and the like.

Here, then, are some examples:
• **Anger**. From a Germanic personal name, *Ansger*.
• **Arbuckle**. No connexion with *buckles*, but from a place of this name in Lanarkshire, Scotland.
• **Bannister**. A basket weaver, a maker of what were known as *banastres*. The use of the word *bannister* for a stair-rail dates only from the seventeenth century.
• **Belcher**. Originally *bel chere (fair face)*, and later confused with a form of address such as *bel sire (fair sir)*, though we can't discount the possibility that in some cases the name might have been imposed upon a person who was inordinately fond of belching.
• **Blackadder**. This has nothing to do with poisonous snakes, but is a name derived from an estate and a river called *Blackadder* (presumed to be a corruption of *Blackwater*) in Berwickshire, Scotland.
• **Boosey**. Nothing to do with heavy drinking, but a name used for someone who lived near a cattle stall, or was a cowherd. Scottish **Booseys** may have come from *Balhousie* in Fife.
• **Brolly**. Long before the umbrella had been invented, and was referred to colloquially as a brolly, there were individuals bearing the surname *Brolly*, an anglicized form of the Irish *O'Brolaigh* (descendant of *Brolach*).
• **Coffee**. An anglicised form of the Irish name **O'Cobhthaigh**.
• **Coffin**. An occupational name for a basket-maker. This is a surname well-known in Devon, where Rev.John **Pine** of East Down assumed the additional surname and arms of **Coffin** by Royal Licence in 1797, thus establishing the well-known family of **Pine-Coffin**.
• **Colledge**. From *Colwich* in Staffordshire or *Colwick* in Nottinghamshire.
• **Crapper** A variation of **Cropper**, a person who cropped (cloth). There is a long-standing

The original Mr.Belcher may have been fair of face, not troubled with excess wind...
This is the bookplate of William Belcher of Savannah, Georgia, U.S.A.

William Belcher

SAVANNAH.

urban myth that it was the surname of the Yorkshire-born Thomas **Crapper** (1836-1910), a famous English sanitary engineer, which gave the English language the word crap. The full story is more complex than that (see *Searching for surnames*). Some Crappers have been keen to leave their surname behind as soon as possible; so once Lynda **Crapper** entered the entertainment busines, she lost no time in adopting the stage name of '*Marti Caine*'.

• **Cushion**. cousin, relation.

• **Custard**. The derivation here is from a costard apple, though *Costard* is known to have been used as a personal name before it became a surname.

• **Daft**. **Daft** was once a not-uncommon name in the counties of Leicestershire and Nottinghamshire, where examples of it can be found as early as the thirteenth century. Long before the word meant *crazy* or *foolish*, it was applied to a person who was humble and meek; these once being regarded as principally female qualities, some men may have been called **Daft** because they were considered to be effeminate.

• **Eatwell**. From *Etwall*, Derbyshire.

• **Fake**. This is a variation on **Faulkes**, being derived from a Norman personal name, *Fau(l)ques* (from a Germanic byname meaning *falcon*).

• **Fidget**. A diminutive of the name **Fitch**, the meaning of which is uncertain. A polecat? Someone who worked with an iron-pointed implement?.

• **Freak**. A topographical surname from the word *frith*, referring to woodland or scrub.

• **Fridge**. A surname which long pre-dates the invention of the refrigerator. Cornish, from *fry, fridge*, meaning a promontory - literally a *nose*.

• **Funnell**. Someone who grew or sold the herb *fennel*.

• **Goosey**. From *Goosey* in Berkshire.

• **Grumble**. From a Norman personal name, *Grimbald*.

• **Gumboil**. Not as painful as it seems, but a corruption of the personal name *Grimbold*.

• **Hooker**. There might have been many *Happy Hookers* in times past - but they wouldn't have been ladies of easy virtue, simply makers or sellers of *hooks*, or people who lived near a *hook* of land.

• **Kiss/Kisser**. A maker of leg armour.

• **Lavender**. A washer of wool, from Anglo-Norman French (compare the Modern French verb *laver*, to wash).

• **Maggot**. A diminutive of *Margaret*.

• **Nutter**. In modern slang a *nutter* is someone who is *nuts*, meaning crazy. The surname **Nutter** has an altogether different origin: it could refer to a scribe (compare the word *notary*) or to a keeper of oxen.

• **Oddie**. There is nothing necessarily strange or peculiar about people with the surname **Oddie** or **Oddy**, which comes from a Scandinavian personal name, *Oddi*. The surname's origins would appear to lie firmly in the West Riding of Yorkshire, though the well-known actor, writer and ornithologist Bill **Oddie** hails from Rochdale in Lancashire.

• **Onions**. This can be a name applied to a grower or seller of onions, but it can equally be a Welsh surname, a corruption of the personal name *Einion*.

• **Pharaoh**. Thus the surname **Farrar** (occupational term for a smith) has been

William Rufus returning from a day's sport in The New Forest from Mr Punch's Collection of Historical Portraits

elevated to the giddy heights of ancient Egyptian civilisation, thanks to the workings of folk etymology.

• **Phoenix**. This is the surname **Fenwick** (from one of a number of place-names in England and Scotland) dressed up in unfamiliar garb.

• **Pinch**. From a Middle English word for a chaffinch; so, like the surname **Pink**, it originally referred to a chirpy person.

• **Quarrell** A maker of crossbow bolts - or a nickname for a short man.

• **Rabbitt**. Pet-form of Robert, or from a Norman personal name, *Radbode/Rabbode*.

• **Rainbow**. From an Old French personal name, *Rainbaut*.

• **Ramsbottom**. Mercifully, a place-name in Lancashire - *the valley where wild garlic grows* - is the origin here.

• **Raper**. A northern form of **Roper**, a maker or seller of rope.

• **Silly**. A variant of **Sealey**, used for a cheerful person (from the Middle English *seely*, meaning happy). *Silly* in its modern sense of *stupid* only dates back to the fifteenth century.

• **Stammers**. There's no connexion here with any speech defect; **Stammers** is derived from the Old English personal name *Stanmoer*.

• **Tickle**. From the Old English personal name *Tica*, or from *Tickhill* in Yorkshire.

• **Tipple**. Not referring to a boozer, but a surname derived from the personal name *Theobald*.

• **Totty**. These days this is a rather tasteless term referring to a desirable young lady (originally used of a high-class prostitute). The surname **Totty** is quite different, being a pet form of the Old English name *Tota* or *Totta*.

• **Tremble**. From an Old English personal name *Trumbeald*, with variants **Trumble, Trumbull** and **Trimble** (Northern Ireland). There may also be a connexion with the surname **Turnbull**, and

also possibly a Cornish origin (with variants **Trebell/Treble**) from places called *Trebell* in Lanivet or *Trebila* near Boscastle.

• **Trollope**. The novelist Anthony **Trollope** had ancestors who came from *Troughburn* in Northumberland, which was once known as *Trollope*. The first known example of the word trollop being used for a slattern or a slut dates from as recently as 1615.

• **Truebody**. A Cornish surname, from *Tre-bude* (dwelling near a haven) or from *Tre-body* (the town of Body).

• **Twatt**. A Scottish surname with a place-name origin; the **Twatts** of Orkney may derive their surname from *Twatt* in Birsay, and the **Twatt** family of Shetland from *Twatt* in the parish of Aithsting.

• **Ugly**. From *Ugley* in Essex or *Ughill* in Yorkshire.

• **Wedlock**. A Cornish surname, possibly a variant on **Vallack** [from *vallack, vallick*, meaning walled or fenced].

• **Wildsmith**. Not all **Wildsmiths** were wild in character; they were originally wheel-makers.

If you intend to start collecting surnames, let me wish you all good luck - and do try never to let a good one pass you by...

John Titford is a professional genealogist and writer, author of *The Titford family 1547-1947* (1989), *Writing and Publishing your Family History* (2nd edition, 2003), *Succeeding in family history* (2001) *Searching for surnames* (2002), and co-author, with Jean Cole, of *Tracing your Family Tree* (4th edition, 2003).

William "Longsword' Duke of Salisbury from Mr Punch's Collection of Historical Portraits

Sarah's Journals
Pauline Litton

Sarah's Journals - two large, handwritten, leather-bound volumes, profusely illustrated with contemporary prints, many of buildings and scenes which have long since vanished - came into my possession some years ago. They cover two journeys in 1815 and 1818. They were shown on the *Antiques Road Show* in 2002 and excited much interest from a wide range of people. The Journals provide not only an insight into some aspects of how a young lady of Sarah's class lived but also snapshots into the living and working conditions of the working classes who, for most of us, constitute our ancestors. What follows is a small selection from the Journals, giving a flavour of life at the end of the Napoleonic Wars.

On 23 July 1815, a week after Napoleon had surrendered to a British naval captain, Sarah Mayo Parkes left London, with her father, on a five month journey which would take them to the north of England and the lowlands of Scotland. She had just turned 18 years of age and was accompanying her father on a lengthy "business trip". Samuel Parkes was a well-known manufacturing chemist and author of a number of manuals of chemistry, including a *Chemical Catechism* written for Sarah's education. He was a zealous Unitarian, and a collector of prints, autographs, coins and minerals - interests which his daughter shared. Sarah was the only child of Samuel and of his wife, Sarah Twamley, who had died in 1813; both parents were descended from long-established Nonconformist families in Worcestershire but Sarah was born in Stoke on Trent and spent much of her early life in London. From a comment in the second Journal, kept during the 1818 journey,

> Mrs Horne pointed out to me the village of Bootle [near Liverpool], so frequented as a sea-bathing place, and where my father tells me I first learnt to walk, being there with my mother on account of her health

it would seem that her mother was not robust and Sarah appears to have been raised, and educated, as the son her father never had.

Her journeys coincide with the years of publication of several of Jane Austen's novels and, on occasion, particularly when visiting her friends and relations in Worcestershire and Birmingham, her journal reads almost like an extract from one of them

> Thursday 4th [January 1816] This morning I was accompanied by some of my Cousins in a ramble to the Castle-

hill [Dudley], where after a long and diligent search I found a few petrifations ... Friday 5th We went again to the Castle but were not successful in finding many petrifations ... Saturday 6th We spent our morning in calling upon some friends in the Town ... Sunday 7th This proved an agreeable and pleasant day to me. We attended divine service twice ... Our whole party dined at Mr Joseph Hodgett's ... Monday 8th This day we spent at Mr Priestley's near Tipton.

What distinguishes Sarah's Journals from similar ones kept by her contemporaries is the fact that what she saw, and recorded, on her travels in England and Scotland, goes far beyond the social scene as experienced by the young ladies in Jane Austen's novels. There is no mention of money or dowries; of clothes (except for the occasional reference to drying them - the Autumn of 1815 sounds to have been a wet one!); of young men in a romantic sense; of music, drawing or embroidery; of amateur theatricals or of petty jealousies. The only criticisms she makes are of the quality of some of the sermons which she sits

LE PORT DE SCARBOROUGH
Vu du côté du Sud

LUSS, Dunbartonshire.

through - and she attended Noncomformist chapels at least twice, often three times, every Sunday - and the standard of some of the accommodation and food she encounters.

Their means of transport varied. For long journeys they tended to travel by 'the Mail', often travelling through the night, and arriving early in the morning ready to undertake a full day's business or pleasure. They also used coaches, chaises (often hired for day excursions), and frequently rode on horseback, with Sarah riding side-saddle. They took a regular Packet boat from Glasgow to Paisley; the Steam Boat from Glasgow to Dumbarton (which ran aground and they had to wait several hours

until the tide served to take us off, which it did about ten o'clock... Finding ourselves cold, we went down to the engine fire, and upon the whole we did very well, but were not sorry to get to our inn) and were ferried *over the river Tummel with our chaise and horses at the same time; the boatman was assisted in his labours by a woman, the most robust athletic looking creature I ever saw; we would have conversed with her but she spoke only Gaelic.*

They also walked a great deal and Sarah appears to have spent a lot of time, when she had no acquaintances in the area, wandering around towns on her own.

They stayed at inns, a hotel in Edinburgh, with friends and, in Scarborough, at Hodgens' Boarding-house where, on their first evening, in August 1818, they *joined the party at the public table at supper.* They spent several days there and Sarah thoroughly enjoyed herself:

Monday 17th. I rode on horseback with my father and Mr Jenner and Miss Midwood (two of the party at our house) to a very high hill called Oliver's Mount ... In the evening we formed a party with Mr and Miss Jenner to the play, where we saw **Rob Roy** *and* No song, no supper*; the Actors were some of them very good, and for a country performance it was admirable.*

Thursday 20th This evening we had a ball at the house, which was extremely well conducted, and I enjoyed it much.

Friday 21st I rode on the sands with Miss Jenner and Mrs Rogers, in that lady's carriage,

and I think never saw the sea finer; it was rather rough and its dashing against the rocks at Filey Bridge was very beautiful... Saturday 22nd Rode on the sands again with Miss Milner and a party. I find many of the inmates of the house very pleasant people, particularly Mrs and Miss Milner, Mr and Miss Jenner of York, Captain & Mrs Priestley, Miss Cartledge, Major Oakes, and Captain Mason; we usually set down about 40 to dinner.

Some inns found less favour. The one at Luss *was most intolerably bad ... The provisions at this Inn are extremely bad and dirty.* They were rowed on Loch Lomond and afterwards *As we could not obtain any thing fit to eat at the inn we went with the poor boatman to his cottage, where we had some eggs and bread and butter and milk.* That at Callendar was *dirty, the people uncivil, and nothing comfortable; however we procured tea and beds, and having previously determined to be content with all we met with, retired to rest ...* next day they were off in a chaise by 5.30am! Booking in advance was not an option and at Kenmore *we had some difficulty in being admitted, as the house was quite full; however between scolding and coaxing we were at last accommodated ... my father had a bed in a room with another gentleman, while I took up my lodging upon a bed made on six chairs in the parlour.* Sarah spent quite a lot of her time in inns - when the weather was bad and when her father was out on business appointments - but she never complains of being bored and filled her time writing her journal or *occupying myself the best way I could.*

Her father had strong connections with the scientific, literary, and business worlds. They visited *Mr Wordsworth the poet* and met John Dalton on several occasions as he and Sarah's father *made some chemical experiments* together. Sarah accompanied her father on visits to manufactories (never 'factories'), mines, alum works, print fields, paper-making works and many more. Her descriptions of the mills and manufactories of the West Riding are included in the 2003 Miscellany volume published by the Thoresby Society (of Leeds). She was particularly impressed in 1815 by the Middleton Railway and by the Pottery in Leeds and made return visits to both in 1818.

TO
PUDSEY DAWSON, ESQ,
THIS VIEW OF THE SCHOOL FOR THE BLIND,
with the intended Additional Building,
IS RESPECTFULLY INSCRIBED, BY HIS OBEDIENT SERVANT,
T. TROUGHTON.

Her descriptions are not always very technical but they give a good idea of the processes involved and of the conditions in which people worked. Only occasionally is there a hint that what she is experiencing is out of the ordinary for a girl of her age and upbringing. She says, after describing what went on in the Tilting Mill in Sheffield *I was sorry I could not stay to see more ... but the noise and the heat of the place prevented me* and in Borrowdale, having climbed on foot a thousand feet up the Black Mountain to the plumbago (lead) mine, she comments *I did not enter the mine, as I should have found it very dirty, and as the men were not then at work, there was not much to see. I saw them dressing the plumbago ... .*

Her account of the making of red lead in Newcastle upon Tyne serves as an example of her prose.

A great number of pigs of lead are put into a reverberatory furnace and melted. When the metal is in a fluid state it soon becomes covered with a coat of oxide which is removed by an iron rake, another coat then forms which is removed in like manner, and so on until the whole of the fliud lead is converted into a metalic oxide.
As the metal is thus scummed the oxide is pushed to the further part of the furnace, and when the whole is formed into an oxide the entire bottom of the furnace is covered with it, and it is suffered to remain in that state for 30 hours more, a workman turning it occasionally that every portion may be exposed to the fire and the influence of the atmospheric air. After this, the whole of the oxide which is then of a yellow colour, is raked out of the furnace, and cooled by water being thrown on it, it is then ground to an impalpable powder and again submitted to the action of the fire till it becomes of a brilliant red colour, and this finishes the process.

Some of what she saw has a curiously modern ring to it.

After dinner [lunch] *and while my Father was engaged in business I went with Mrs Scott to see what is considered to be a great curiosity at Glasgow, Mr Harleigh's Cowhouse. This is a receptacle for nearly 200 Cows, which are kept there for supplying the City with milk. What renders this place worth visiting, is the cleanliness with which the animals are kept, and the contrivances for supplying them with food and water; as they are never allowed to go out of the house from the time they are first put in, until the time they are disposed of. This man generally has every beast fit for the butcher in twelve months, so that his whole stock is renewed once a year.*

As well as industrial premises, visits were made to private museums and collections, libraries, schools, prisons and asylums. Among the museums and collections, principally dealing with minerals, were those of Mr Todhunter at Kendal, Mr Hutton and Mr Crosthwait at Keswick (the latter *a pretty good one*), the Hunterian Museum in Glasgow, Mr Brown and Mr Allan in Edinburgh (*a most splendid collection*), Mr Mawe in Matlock, Mr

Hinderwell in Scarborough, the Rev. Mr Young and Mr Bird, both in Whitby. Mr Hinderwell had written the *History of Scarborough* and Rev. Young the *History of Whitby* as well as a history of the mineralogy of Yorkshire.

The Minster Library at York was much admired. *We were told that in the early part of the 17th century Mrs Matthews relict of Archbishop Matthews presented her husbands valuable collection of books consisting of more than three thousand volumes to this church and this appears to be the foundation of the first library they had. Since then it has been enlarged by the addition of the Revd. Marmaduke Fothergill's books and now it is become a very valuable collection, as they have a great many curious old and scarce books, amongst which are many rare manuscripts and some of Caxton's early printed books. Some time ago when Mr Dibden the Author of Bibliomania was at this library he was much enraptured at seeing so many rare old books and when one particular book of Caxtons was shewn him he took it up and kissed it.*
The room in which the books are kept is of a very pretty and light construction, and the gallery is very beautiful, it is of oak, supported by light iron rings.

The school for the Blind in Edinburgh did not find favour, and Sarah considered it *greatly inferior to the one at Norwich* (which she had evidently visited). *It is kept dirty and does not appear to me well managed* but she was *wonderfully pleased* with the Blind Asylum in Liverpool, which surpassed Norwich.

There are 107 patients now in the house beside a great many more that only attend in the working hours. Their chief employments are basket making, knitting, rope making, and some of the most expert work well with their needle (on a return visit in 1818 she saw *some shirts and sheets of their making, which were certainly very neat*); *the work is all sold for the support of the Charity ... we observed the pupils in deep conversation and some of them were teaching each other their prayers and catechism. Never in my life did I see people who had more the appearance of being happy ... .*

The Deaf and Dumb Asylum in Edinburgh, however, earned high praise. Whilst there they *met Miss Hall, daughter of Mr Hall of Thorney bank, who is one of the most pleasing girls I ever saw. In*

Lord Nelson's Monument,
ERECTED IN THE AREA OF THE LIVERPOOL EXCHANGE BUILDINGS:
COMPLETED OCTOBER XXI. MDCCCXIII.

the school room there were about 40 children all of them deaf and dumb. The first thing they did to show their acquirements was to explain various designs engraved on copper and printed on pasteboards for their use. They are figures of different things similar to the small prints sold to amuse children. The visitors are requested to point out any of these figures to the pupils who instantly write on their slates what they are. The quickness with which they write is truly surprising. Some of them are also taught to draw, and considering their very great disadvantages, they succeed admirably.

My Father and I held a long conversation with Miss Hall who answered all our questions with great quickness on her slate. The pupils are all made to articulate, but it is difficult at all times to understand them, they converse with each other by their fingers, and by signs. I was more pleased with this institution than by any Charity I ever saw.

The prisons visited varied greatly and some of Sarah's comments sound surprisingly modern for an 18 year old writing nearly two hundred years ago.

At Perth, *the Depot which has been erected within the last five years for the purpose of holding the French prisoners taken during the last war, is an immense pile of building, and what is curious, it was begun and finished within a year. Each of the prisons usually contained 400 prisoners and the hammocks on which they slept were suspended above each other. There are three of these prisons, and a hospital, the latter is fitted up with iron bedsteads to prevent infection. In the kitchen I observed two immense iron boilers which were used for making the soup. This building is now only used for holding stores, as all the prisoners were set at liberty at the late peace.*

This is the only direct reference anywhere in the Journals to the Napoleonic Wars. There are mentions of several memorials to Lord Nelson but nothing about his exploits.

In Edinburgh, she went to *the new Bridewell or house of Correction for culprits who are kept to hard labour. This is an excellent institution and is kept as clean as possible. It was only finished in 1796. The night cells are very well arranged as each has a window, that the prisoner can open and shut at pleasure. The bedsteads are all of iron. There were in this place three times as many women as men, and they appeared so very comfortable that there may be a danger of their not sufficiently fearing a repetition of their imprisonment.*

At Lancaster Castle she went into *the Court yard where we saw a vast number of Debtors of all ranks; how melancholy that such persons must associate with the very lowest of mankind; and as long as this plan continues, there can I fear be little hope of a suppression of vice; for in these places, those who enter the prison gates for trifling offences, and are comparatively virtuous, often by this indiscriminate treatment become contaminated, and as depraved as their wretched companions, and thus originates much of the guilt and misery we daily see and deplore.*

Sarah in her journals sounds sometimes like an excited 18 year old, at others like a prig, but she clearly enjoyed her expeditions with her father. She was born in 1797 and died at St Bees in Cumberland in July 1890, having outlived her husband (her father's partner; killed in a chemical explosion in 1851) and all her children. Did she re-read her journals in her old age and remember when she was young, full of life and fascinated by the world around her?

Pauline points out that all spelling, punctuation etc. within italics is as it was written in the original.

EDINBURGH BRIDEWELL, from the NORTH WEST.

Wesleyan Methodist Historic Roll

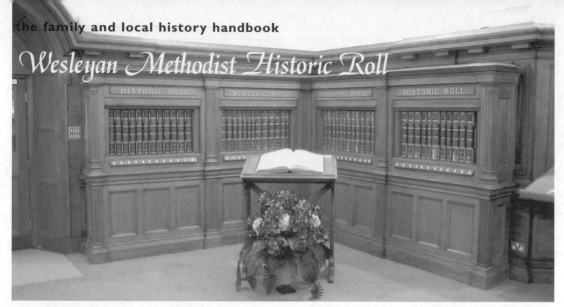

To commemorate the Centenary of the death of John Wesley, the Wesleyan Methodist Conference of 1897 decided to launch an Appeal to raise One Million Guineas to purchase a suitable site in London, erect a Church and World Headquarters for Wesleyan Methodists and develop the mission of the Wesleyan Methodist Church at home and overseas.
The Appeal was launched in 1898 and eventually closed in 1908. By then it had raised £1,073,682.

The site of the Royal Aquarium opposite the West Door of Westminster Abbey was purchased and a competition inviting architects to design a suitable building attracted 126 entries. The design submitted by the architects Rickards and Lanchester was adjudged the winner and the work of constructing the Central Hall started in 1909. The building was completed in 1912 and the Grand Opening celebrations began on October 2nd, 1912.

When the Appeal was launched in 1898, the Fund Raising Committee decided to keep a record of the names of all contributors. Special pages were sent to every Wesleyan Methodist Circuit in England, Wales and Scotland and to circuits overseas. Contributors were invited to write their own names and addresses on these pages which were eventually returned to the Wesleyan Methodist Church Conference Office where they were bound into 50 volumes called the Historic Roll and placed in a specially constructed bookcase in Westminster Methodist Central Hall where they have been available for inspection ever since.

However the condition of this unique set of books has begun to deteriorate and the Trustees took the decision in 2002 to have the volumes microfilmed and allow researchers to use microfiche copies instead of handling the original volumes. The 50 volumes take up 1646 microfiche and researchers visiting Westminster Methodist Central Hall can easily find the fiche of the District or Circuit or

Church from the master index which has been compiled by the Central Hall Archivist, Richard Ratcliffe. Researchers can now obtain instant print outs of pages from the Historic Roll instead of waiting up to 4 weeks for a photograph of a requested page. It is also now possible for researchers to order sets of microfiche for a District, a Circuit or for individual Churches, although some Circuits did not list their individual Churches.

Many pages of the Historic Roll show donations given "In Memoriam" with the name and dates of birth and/or death written along side. It is estimated that the Historic Roll contains the names of 1,025,000 contributors, including a considerable number of Sunday School scholars who donated one shilling each.

For more information about the Historic Roll and how you can obtain copies of microfiche or photocopies of the names of contributors from a particular District, Circuit or Church please contact Westminster Methodist Central Hall Visitor Services Manager, Central Hall Westminster, Storey's Gate, Westminster, London SW1H 9NH www.events@c-h-w.co.uk

B&B Accommodation Central London

London School of Economics Residences available for Easter, Summer and Christmas Breaks

Easter 20 March to 24 April
Summer 17 August to 29 September
Christmas 11 December to 8 January

**Singles from £25 per night
twins from £40 per night**

Tel: 020 7955 7575
Fax: 020 7955 7676

Email:vacations@lse.ac.uk
Web:www.lsevacations.co.uk

LSE THE **LONDON SCHOOL**
OF **ECONOMICS** AND
POLITICAL SCIENCE ∎

Devon Family History Society

Like many Family History Societies, we have celebrated our Silver Anniversary and are looking forward to our Pearl celebration! Such a lot has happened in the Family History world in the last few years, so in Devon we have kept up to date with new developments and technology. We have published a CD of the Tamerton Deanery, an index of baptisms, marriages and burials in 12 parishes, with photographs of the churches and extracts from White,s Directory of 1850. A similar CD is planned for the three towns: Plymouth, Stoke Damerel (Devonport) and East Stonehouse. A full Index of Devon FHS Members' Interests was issued on CD-rom, free to all members in 2003, and it is also available for sale to non-members.

The Society was formed in Plymouth in the second half of 1976, with aims which included promoting the study of genealogy and history and encouraging the preservation and transcription of relevant documents and records. The pages of the first magazine, The Devon Family Historian, rolled off the roneo machine in January 1977, listing 110 members. Devon Family History Society was on its way and we joined the newly established Federation of Family History Societies.

Those were early non-index days for members. The first finding aid appeared at about the same time. The IGI was held (and still is in some quarters) to be the fount of all wisdom, despite the fact that the entries for Devon were extracted from transcriptions of the bishops transcripts carried out for the Devon and Cornwall Record Society and only cover about 60% of the county. Our second chairman and founder member number 1, Miss Joy Beer, had two great visions: to set up groups in the county and to establish a research centre and office. Her first was realised when groups were set up in North Devon in 1981, Torbay in 1982 and Exeter in 1983. Her second took a little longer. Not bothered about the rather silly rivalry between Plymouth and Exeter, it was obvious that Exeter was the place for our centre, as it is comparatively easy to reach by road and rail.

Our research centre was opened in Wynards on 2nd April 1991 and Joy Beer, who had campaigned so tirelessly, was there to cut the tape at the official opening. Wynards was an interesting old listed building. William Wynard was Recorder for Exeter between 1418 and 1442 and Wynards was built in 1430. The buildings, damaged during the civil war, were restored in 1856, and really appealed to our sense of history,

but with four very small rooms, very uneven floors and ceilings, as well as a weight-bearing limit, we were only able to allow four members in at a time! The adrenaline flowed and the pulse quickened when the bell went and the odd person popped in to see what was on offer.

It was soon realised that, picturesque as Wynards might be, the Society was running out of space and more members wanted to visit. In January 1994 we settled into an inauspicious Victorian warehouse building in King Street, off Fore Street, next door to a Wesleyan School dating from 1862. Perhaps it is more allied to the Victorian 'ag.labs' that most of us claim in our family trees than the splendour of Wynards. So Tree House was established. We received donated fiche readers and inherited pieces of furniture and bookcases, suitable for housing booklets etc with other stock in the cupboards beneath. Our biggest expense at that time was a Canon microfiche reader-printer costing several thousand pounds. It is still in use and is treated with care as befits an "old lady" but now computers and the GRO indexes have become our largest expense.

We have become victims of our own success! In 1994 -1995 our visitors totalled 1144, in 2002 - 2003 we welcomed 3680 visitors. Our most popular holding is the GRO fiche and issues have topped 100,000. We have a wonderful cheerful bunch of volunteers and an enthusiastic administrator working for the Society at Tree House and they cope with around 40 people on a busy day. We seldom run out of fiche readers and can always find room for one more visitor. Tree House is situated within walking distance of the city centre, check out the map on our website and on the Devon Family Historian cover. Opening times are Tuesday, Wednesday, Thursday 10.30am - 4pm. It is free for members to use, and temporary membership is available to other visitors.

The Society welcomes new members, who receive a member's pack, which contains details on Devon research, information about our indexes, a publications list, and where to find genealogical and historical records in Devon and other parts of the country. Because of good housekeeping, the Devon Family History Society has been able to peg its subscription for many years at £10, (£12 overseas), which covers two people at the same address receiving one magazine. DFHS will provide any enquirer with a list of its members who are willing to carry out research on agreed terms. The Society it is itself unable to undertake extended research, however a loyal and experienced volunteer offers a small amount of free assistance to get members onto the lower branches of their family trees

All members receive the quarterly journal, The Devon Family Historian, and the latest new members' interests list. These publications enable members to make their queries and interests known to others and to see what research lines other members are following. Articles in the journal are full of background information about the lives and times of Devon families, and others help members to keep themselves well informed about developments in family history in Devon, throughout this country and abroad. Coloured photos of Devon are a well-received addition to the journal.

Members and other friends have helped to compile information from primary sources - the parish registers - and this is available in booklet form. Devon has over 500 parishes, so we have published several thousand books containing baptisms, marriages and burials. We are also building up a selection of finding aids on topics which include Union Workhouses, Hospitals & Asylums, Epidemics and Diseases, Bastardy Quarter Sessions Returns, all relating to Devon. Some of these are joint projects with the county's record offices. All production is done 'in house' on an 'all singing all dancing' copier.

Ongoing indexing projects include Baptisms 1813-39, Burials 1813-37, Memorial Inscriptions, Strays, Plymouth Ford Park Cemetery Burials and the Devon 1861 census. Our computerised indexes include these, plus all

available Devon Marriages 1754-1812 and 1813-1837 and Plymouth Marriages post 1837. Full details are available on our website. Plymouth and District Marriages post 1837 and Tamerton Deanery Baptisms, Marriages and Burials have been issued on CD-roms and more Devon Deanery CDs are planned.

We have an excellent Librarian at Tree House who buys books and accepts donations, which get reviewed in the Historian. She produces and regularly updates "Tree House Resources Part 1 - Books" and "Tree House Resources Part 2 - Documents and Microfiche."

Keeping up to date with technology is high on our list of priorities. Our Website is ably managed and regularly updated by our Webmaster and we have submitted it for the FFHS's website award. Our message board, WWWboard, is well used and orders for indexes and publications are taken by e-mail as well as snail mail. We are not able to offer a 24-hour service, although at times our hardworking and overstretched volunteers feel like they do! The Society is a co-sponsor of DEVON-L, the internet mailing list for the exchange of messages relating to Devon genealogy, with over 1400 listers regularly dropping in to request and offer advice.

The originally established groups still meet regularly and numbers continue to grow, especially those who meet in an online computer suite to wrestle with the WWW and share computing problems and successes. Trips to the National Archives and Family Records Centre are well supported and our stall can be seen at several fairs and conferences. We try to encourage local interest in family history, with the chairman broadcasting on Radio Devon phone-ins, whilst another member starred in a television programme on the 1887 Exeter Theatre Fire, following our publication of her

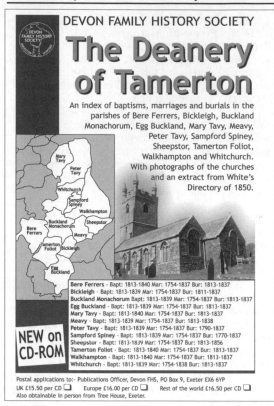

DEVON FAMILY HISTORY SOCIETY

The Deanery of Tamerton

An index of baptisms, marriages and burials in the parishes of Bere Ferrers, Bickleigh, Buckland Monachorum, Egg Buckland, Mary Tavy, Meavy, Peter Tavy, Sampford Spiney, Sheepstor, Tamerton Foliot, Walkhampton and Whitchurch. With photographs of the churches and an extract from White's Directory of 1850.

Bere Ferrers - Bapt: 1813-1840 Mar: 1754-1837 Bur: 1813-1837
Bickleigh - Bapt: 1813-1839 Mar: 1754-1837 Bur: 1811-1837
Buckland Monachorum Bapt: 1813-1839 Mar: 1754-1837 Bur: 1813-1837
Egg Buckland - Bapt: 1813-1839 Mar: 1754-1837 Bur: 1813-1837
Mary Tavy - Bapt: 1813-1840 Mar: 1754-1837 Bur: 1813-1837
Meavy - Bapt: 1813-1839 Mar: 1754-1837 Bur: 1813-1838
Peter Tavy - Bapt: 1813-1839 Mar: 1754-1837 Bur: 1790-1837
Sampford Spiney - Bapt: 1813-1839 Mar: 1754-1837 Bur: 1770-1837
Sheepstor - Bapt: 1813-1839 Mar: 1754-1837 Bur: 1813-1856
Tamerton Foliot - Bapt: 1813-1840 Mar: 1754-1837 Bur: 1813-1837
Walkhampton - Bapt: 1813-1840 Mar: 1754-1837 Bur: 1813-1837
Whitchurch - Bapt: 1813-1839 Mar: 1754-1838 Bur: 1813-1837

NEW on CD-ROM

Postal applications to:- Publications Officer, Devon FHS, PO Box 9, Exeter EX6 6YP
UK £15.50 per CD ☐   Europe £16.00 per CD ☐   Rest of the world £16.50 per CD ☐
Also obtainable in person from Tree Home, Exeter.

booklets about those people involved in the disaster.

Like most Societies, although we are volunteers, we do our very best to satisfy the needs of those who share in this fascinating and frustrating hobby. Devon is one of the larger counties and also had an adventurous population with families migrating worldwide, so it is likely that at some time you will come across a Devon ancestor. If we can help with any Devon related queries, let us know, either by letter or drop in on our website. Good luck with your research and if you are in Devon - come and see us.

Useful addresses:
Devon Family History Society, PO Box 9, Exeter EX2 6YP
Website http://www.devonfhs.org.uk/
email secretary@devonfhs.org.uk
Devon FHS web site at http://www.devonfhs.org.uk and the **Genuki (Genealogy in UK and Ireland) website** at http://www.cs.ncl.ac.uk/genuki/DEV/ provide links to the various repositories with maps of their locations.

Devon Record Office Castle Street, Exeter, Devon EX4 3PU. Telephone: 01392 384253   Email: devrec@devon.gov.uk   website http://www.devon.gov.uk/dro/
There is a daily charge to view documents, or a yearly reader's ticket may be purchased. Readers' tickets are valid in all three Devon Record Offices. A professional research service is available. The new Devon Record Office building at Great Moor House, Sowton, Exeter, is due for completion in summer 2004. Castle Street will close to the public at that time, while the documents, equipment, and staff relocate, and will reopen sometime in the autumn. During this period microfiche and microfilm will continue to be available at the Castle Street office. Microform copies of many records are also available at the North Devon Record Office, which will remain open throughout, and at the Plymouth and West Devon Record Office.
If you are considering a visit in 2004, ring 01392 384253 or see
http://www.devon.gov.uk/dro/
West Country Studies Library Castle Street, Exeter, Devon EX4 3PQ
Telephone: 01392 384216 Email: imaxted@devon.gov.uk

Web site: http://www.devon.gov.uk/library/locstudy/wsl.html
Devon and Cornwall Record Society The Society's holdings are housed at the West Country Studies Library. The collection includes the D&CR Society's own publications, parish register transcriptions, files on a large number of individual parishes and families.
Web site:
http://www.devon.gov.uk/library/locstudy/dcrs.html.
Family History Centre
Church of Jesus Christ of Latter Day Saints Exeter Chapel, Wonford Road, Exeter, Devon. Tel: 01392 250723. By appointment only.
Wills
Exeter Probate Sub Registry Finance House, Barnfield Road, Exeter, Devon EX1 1QR.
For post-1858 wills only. Tel: 01392 274515.
North Devon Record Office 1 Tuly Street, Barnstaple, Devon EX31 1EL. Tel: 01271 388607/388608 Email: ndevrec@devon.gov.uk
Web site: http://www.devon.gov.uk/dro/ndhomep1.html
The Record Office makes a daily charge to view documents, or a reader's ticket may be purchased.
North Devon Local Studies Centre 1 Tuly Street, Barnstaple, Devon EX31 1EL.
Web site:
http://www.devon.gov.uk/library/locstudy/barnstap.html
Plymouth and West Devon Record Office 3 Clare Place, Coxside, Plymouth, Devon PL4 0JW Telephone: 01752 305940 Fax: 01752 223939   Email: pwdro@plymouth.gov.uk
http://www.plymouth.gov.uk/main.asp?page=1262
There is a daily charge to view documents, or a yearly reader's ticket may be purchased.

Plymouth Central Reference Library Drake Circus, Plymouth Devon PL4 8AL Telephone: 01752 305907 01752 305908
Email: ref@plymouth.gov.uk   Web site:
http://www.plymouth.gov.uk/content-702
Plymouth Local Studies and Naval History Libraries Drake Circus, Plymouth, Devon PL4 8AL Telephone: 01752 305909 Email: localstudies@plymouth.gov.uk
Web site: http://www.plymouth.gov.uk/content-695
Family History Centre
Church of Jesus Christ of Latter Day Saints Plymouth Chapel, Mannamead Road, Plymouth, Devon. Telephone: 01752 668666 By appointment only.
Many more links may be found on the Devon Family History Society's web site at http://www.devonfhs.org.uk

The Manby-Colegrave Coat of Arms – A signpost to the past
Anthony Adolph

Genealogists are immensely fortunate in having an armory of different tools at their disposal when it comes to tracing family trees. Besides the rich stores of written records with which Britain is more than usually blessed, a lot can be told about families simply by studying their surnames. In recent years, DNA technology has also appeared, enabling researchers to test the theories they have formed from written records, sometimes confirming old hypotheses, and in other cases overturning them altogether. As those people who have seen my TV series Antiques Ghostshow will know, I have also been investigating the use of psychics in family history- and who knows what other disciplines will contribute themselves to this ever–evolving subject. But of all the extra tools we have, one of the best remains the oldest of all- heraldry.

Heraldry often receives a bad press in genealogical publications. Many people still regard it with fear and suspicion, protesting that their ancestors were all agricultural labourers and quite unconnected with the lofty heights of society where coats of arms were sported about as emblems of snobbery and élitism.

The system was evolved in the Middle Ages as a means of identifying knights on the battlefield, both in the heat of combat and also in the bloody aftermath when corpses might be too badly mangled to be told one from another. At that stage, certainly, heraldry was the preserve of the warrior élite, but as centuries passed many non-noble families of merchants, lawyers, farmers and clergy, having made some money by means fair or foul, sought to take on the trappings of nobility by acquiring coats of arms. Often, you do not have to go very far up the social scale to find an ancestor with a coat of arms, and it is also worth bearing in mind the extent to which families could slide down the social scale very quickly indeed. The head of a family of landed gentry family, with his coat of arms engraved proudly over the fireplace, might not be nearly so prosperous as he might seem, and often the acquisition and maintenance of the many essential trappings of gentility were enough to lead to the debtor's prison. And even if the head of the family was doing very comfortably on his estate, his younger brothers' sons were unlikely to be familiar with the taste of silver spoons, whilst the younger sons of the younger sons could expect either to work for their bread or starve. It is therefore not at all unusual to find families of agricultural labourers who can be traced back to such younger sons of younger sons- and thus to an ancestral coat of arms.

Heraldry helps genealogists and indeed, heralds- the men delegated by the monarch to the task of regulating and overseeing the use of coats of arms- were amongst the first people to start recording family trees. The pedigree collections of the College of Arms in London are amongst the best in the world and contain information on many more of their ancestors than most people probably realise. But it also has other uses. Because it is possible to identify coats of arms in their own right, portraits, china-and silver-ware and a host of other antiques and artifacts decorated with heraldry can be dated and connected with their original owners on that basis alone. And, in many cases, arms can be the key to unravelling the story of a whole family. In the case of the coat of arms illustrated here, heraldry went one step further, shedding considerable light on not only a family, but also the land the family owned, land which was once picturesque farmland but which is now subsumed beneath the fumy arteries and pealing

edifices of part of East London.

The arms were found, painted on a piece of almost crumbling yellow paper in a ramshackle frame, in a junk shop in Canterbury, by a long-deceased heraldry enthusiast called Noël Hatcher. Coats of arms are usually shown individually on shields. Sometimes, however, the heir of one armigerous family marries the heiress of another. The eldest son of the marriage therefore inherits and represents not one but two families' homes (or living quarters) and thus quarters both coats of arms on his shield. If successive heirs marry further heiresses, the number of quarters they are entitled to place on their shield increases, especially if the heiresses' families themselves used several quarters. In this case, the full achievements of arms included a remarkable twenty quarterings.

If identified correctly, such quartered coats of arms may unravel the story of a family and its different lines of ancestry. Arms are identified by describing them in correct heraldic language-blazonry, derived from Norman French-breaking them down into their constituent parts and then looking up the main charges in ordinaries, the main one being Papworth's Ordinary of British Armorials. For example, the arms of the main family, in the top left-hand corner of our quartered shield, are blazoned Argent, on two bars Gules four crescents between three pheons Or. Under 'two bars' Papworth gives the correct identification-Colegrave, and further study reveals the family to have lived at Cann Hall, Leytonstone, Essex.

The other arms, working from top left to bottom right, are blazoned below. Most of the blazons are straightforward enough to understand when compared to the pictures- and the colours are also quite easy to remember:

Or   = gold or yellow (interchangeable)
Argent   = silver or white (interchangeable)
Gules   = red
Azure   = blue
Vert   = green
Sable   = black
Ermine   = white with black spots, supposed to resemble the white pelts of ermines (stoats) with the little black-tipped tails hanging down.

The arms are:
2. Manby; Argent, a lion rampant Sable within an orle of ten escalops Gules.
3. Malcake; Vert, a saltire lozengy Or.
4. Arkybus; Ermine, on a fess engrailed Sable three mascles Or.
5. Maunsell; Sable, a chevron between three mullets of six points pierced Argent.
6. Gibthorpe; Quarterly Ermine and checky Or and Gules.
7. Thorpe; Argent, two bars Gules within a bordure Sable.
8. Lindsey; Or, a bend compony Gules and Sable on an eagle displayed of the last.
9. Kyme; Gules, a chevron between ten crosses crosslet Or.
10. Caldwell; Azure, a cross formy fitchy within an orle of ten estolies Or.
11. Selby; Barry of ten Or and Sable.
12. Fenwick; Per fess Gules and Argent six martlets counterchanged.
13. Hoidon; Or, between three birds (larks?) Vert, a fess Vair counter-vair.

14. Essenden; Gules, on a cross Argent five crosses crosslet of the field. 15. Camhow; Gules, on a bend Argent three (roses or mullets) Vert.
16. Barrett; Argent, between three mullets a fess Sable.
17. Norton; Vert, a lion rampant within a bordure Or.
18. Baxter; Argent, a wyvern displayed Vert.
19. Wallington; Argent, a chevron between three martlets Gules.
20. Fraser; Quarterly, Azure and Argent, 1 and 4 three frases Or, 2 and 3 three antique crowns Gules.

The crests, which are descended from the ornaments which knights wore on top of their helmets, tied on by a twisted cloth tort of the main colour and metal of the principal shield, ie silver and red, are:

Manby; An arm couped at the elbow erect, vested per pale crenelly Or and Argent holding in the gauntlet a sword of the first.
Colegrave; An ostrich feather erect and two arrows in saltire, points in base Or, banded by a mural crown Gules.
Selby; A saracen's proper couped at the chest, clothed Gules trimmed Or, wreathed about the temples Or and Argent.

Mottoes tend to be a later development: in this case, the Selbys did not have one. Fidei constans was the motto of the Colegraves, and Pro patria mori was that of the Manbys. The mantling, which follows the same colouring rules as the tort, derives from the cloth draped over the helmet, especially during the Crusades, to stop knights' head from boiling in the sun, was red and silver.

When I first encountered them, in the course of a heraldry exhibition I was asked to organise, the arms fascinated me in their own right, but they were of especial interest because I knew that a cousin of mine, the late Phillip Coverdale of the Essex Recusant Society, had studied the Colegrave-Manby's family papers at the Essex Record Office in Chelmsford, and traced their remarkable history. His researches explained how the quarterings had arisen and, in turn, why some of the names I have listed above- and others which I have underlined in the following story- became transmogrified into the names of streets in modern Leytonstone.

The story starts in 1670 with a property speculator called William Colegrave of St Botolph-without-Aldgate, London, who married Frances, granddaughter of Thomas Bourne, a prominent London bookseller whose shop near the Bethlehem Hospital had narrowly escaped destruction in the Great Fire of 1666. He already owned the Norfolk manor of Little Ellingham, but a condition of the dowry was that Colegrave

should spend it on a country estate for his bride nearer London. Later that year, he bought Cann Hall, a Tudor mansion house with an estate of fertile farmland near the village of Leytonstone, for £2,750.

William was a Catholic at a time when the Catholic minority was regarded (sometimes correctly) as being dangerously subversive. In 1715 there was an uprising against George I in favour of the Catholic James Stuart, the 'Old Pretender'. William's cousin Sir George Colegrave and son-in-law Thomas Walmesley both joined the doomed rebellion- the latter was outlawed for High Treason.

By keeping his head down and disguising his ownership of the estate behind a web of legal complexities, William survived the anti-Catholic backlash and saved Cann Hall from confiscation. William and Mary's son William Colegrave married the outlawed Thomas Walmesley's sister Mary. Their son William (1727-1793) inherited the estate and married Mary Manby. Mary's family, which was also Catholic, owned Downsells Hall in South Weald, Essex and also had estates at Wragby and Elsham, Lincolnshire, and they were descended from a number of Lincolnshire families including the Thorpes.

Mary's grandfather, Sir Thomas Manby (1654-1729), had served as Lord Lieutenant of Essex during the brief reign of the Old Pretender's Catholic father, James II (1685-1688). Sir Thomas, whose mother was the heraldic heiress of Daniel Caldwell of Horndon on the Hill, married twice, first Elizabeth Cary of Torr Abbey, Devon and secondly Juliana Selby, also an heraldic heiress.

When William Colegrave died in 1793, he left no children. His brother Merry Colegrave, a wine merchant, inherited the estates, but also died childless. The estates then passed to their sister Mary who by a strange twist of fate had married Mary Manby's brother Thomas. Their son John Manby (1763-1819) therefore inherited both the Colegrave and Manby estates. He was a member of the successful campaign to have the repressive anti-Catholic laws repealed. Once this had happened, he was able to serve as a captain in the Essex militia during the Napoleonic wars.

John's sister Frances Manby was a remarkable woman. At the Reformation Anthony, 1st Viscount Montagu was granted Battle Abbey in Sussex. The dispossessed monks cursed his family to perish by water. In 1793, in eerie fulfillment of the curse, George, 8th Viscount Montagu attempted to shoot the

Schauffenhausen Falls, Switzerland, in a flat-bottomed boat and was dashed to pieces. Unfortunately his brother Mark Anthony, the very last male member of the family, was a monk at Fountainbleau. Desperate to keep the family title alive, his sisters pursuaded the Pope to dispense Mark's vows and forced the poor man to marry young Frances Manby. Force could only extend so far, however, and when the 9th Viscount died nine months later Frances was still decidedly virginal. Retaining her courtesy title of Viscountess Montagu, Frances went on to have a happy and fruitful marriage to Dr Henry Slaughter, who lived at Fryerning near Ingatestone.

Back at Cann Hall, John Manby died childless in 1819, leaving the estates to his nephew William Manby. William's father (who was a brother of John Manby and the Viscountess Montagu) had been a wine merchant at Merquette, France. When the Revolution broke out, he was forced to flee with his family to Lille, Belgium, where he died in 1794. Little William, aged only six, then came to Essex. When he inherited the family's estates he changed his name to Colegrave. The family subsequently called itself, variously, Manby-Colegrave and Colegrave-Manby. William joined the British army and became Master of the Board of Ordnance of Waltham Abbey Gunpowder Mills. He married Catherine,

daughter and heraldic heiress of Sir John Fraser in Gibraltar in 1810. Their third son was William Manby junior, who married Miss Chichester of Arlington, Sussex, whilst their eldest son John (1811-1879) married Louise Matcham Isaac.

The nineteenth century saw a vast influx of North American corn which pushed down domestic grain prices and ruined many farmers and estate owners, especially in East Anglia. John, who became an army officer, had to sell Downsells Hall and lease out Cann Hall. His son Thomas (1841-1898), who married Alice Cayley-Worsley, saw the value of the Cann Hall estate plummet from £30,000 to £14,000 in twenty years. His grandson Gerald had to sell up in 1935, bringing two and a half centuries of history to a close.

This brief history shows how some of the quarterings came into the family coat of arms. The last one was Fraser which, combined with the artistic style, enables us to date the painting to about 1810. The other quarterings are derived through ancestors of the Manbys including the Kymes, of whom Robin de Kyme is thought by some researchers to have been the real Robin Hood.

After Gerald Manby-Colegrave sold the Cann Hall estate, the property developers moved in. The Hall was demolished and the area was swallowed up by the expanding East End. The family were gone, but its legacy lived on in the names of some of Leytonstone's new streets. The main road connecting Leytonstone High Road (the A11) with Wanstead Flats was named Cann Hall Road. The names underlined in this article also appear as road names in the area, thus connecting noisy modern Leytonstone with an ancient coat of arms and a family of Catholics who owned the area when the roads were lined with primroses and the air smelt sweet.

WHERE CAN YOU

- Access over 100,000 items on local & family history?
- Use the largest collection of parish register & census index copies in Britain?
- Get immediate, valuable advice from experienced genealogists?
- Attend informative lectures presented by experts?
- Browse our great range of publications?
- Surf a growing range of online records?

YOU WILL GET ALL THESE AND MORE FROM

THE SOCIETY OF GENEALOGISTS
the one-stop resource for everyone in family & local history

Take advantage of our unique, newly refurbished **LIBRARY** with over 9,000 Parish Register copies and wide-ranging material on Civil Registration, Censuses, County Records, Poll Books, Heraldry & Family Histories - on microfilm, fiche and PC.

Visit our online sales ordering system at www.sog.org.uk for details of society **PUBLICATIONS** – over 150 titles containing valuable information on where to find source material. Titles include My Ancestor was a Merchant Seaman, My Ancestor was a Coalminer, National Index Parish Register (by county)

Join the Society – **MEMBERSHIP** gives you:

- FREE access to the library & borrowing rights
- A 20% discount on all Society publications, lectures & courses
- FREE copies of the highly respected Genealogists' Magazine
- FREE access to an increasing range of online records

all for **just £40 a year!***

For an **INFORMATION PACK**, simply email the Membership Secretary on:
membership@sog.org.uk   OR   Tel: 020 7553 3291

MAKE THE MOST OF YOUR RESEARCH WITH:
SOCIETY OF GENEALOGISTS, 14 Charterhouse Buildings, Goswell Road, London EC1M 7BA
Tel: 020 7251 8799   Fax: 020 7250 1800   Web: www.sog.org.uk

* Special Direct Debit offer plus Initial Joining Fee £10.00

Registered Charity No. 233701. Company limited by guarantee. Registered No. 115703. Registered office, 14 Charterhouse Buildings, London, EC1M 7BA

They paid the Ultimate Price – Police Officers murdered in Britain
Paul Williams
discusses another aspect of *Murder Files*

MURDER *files*

I'd been working in Scotland Yard's Criminal Record Office for about 3 years. It was early 1960s: the days when the criminal records were kept in tin cans in the basement of the old New Scotland Yard building situated on London's Embankment; the indexes were on card systems and major crimes were solved by the old time detective who knew all the villains on his patch. There were no computers or DNA and officers spent hours pouring through paper records trying to link the information they had with known criminals.

Records held details of criminals who had committed all sorts of crime: theft, receiving, assaults of all kinds, robberies and of course murders and manslaughters. People who had killed on the spur of the moment and regretted their actions immediately thereafter; others who had committed cold blooded murder intentionally, planned and premeditated. It was the latter type of murder that on the 12 August 1966 caused everyone in CRO initially to go into shock but then, remembering their professionalism, to work in 'overdrive' to find clues to the murders of three of their London police colleagues at the same incident. The incident – to become known as the Shepherds Bush police murders - was more poignant in that one of the officers killed had only recently transferred from CRO and was known to so many.

Needless to say the incident was headlined in all the national papers and remained so up to the trial in December 1966 when the three

murderers -
Harry Roberts, John Duddy and John Witney – each received life imprisonment with a recommendation of serving a minimum of 30 years. Only Harry Roberts is still alive and currently is trying to gain his release.

I suspect many of the 'older' generation will remember the Shepherds Bush case. They will probably remember also the murder of WPC Yvonne Fletcher on 17 April 1984 whilst on crowd control at a demonstration outside the Libyan People's Bureau in London's St James's Square. Her murder was to cause a diplomatic incident lasting years.

Yet, in the last 300 years, over 200 peace (as they were once called) or police officers around the Country have been murdered in the execution of their duty. Tragically very few of them will now readily come to mind. They have been forgotten. And it was for this very reason that for 5 years I contacted police forces, historians, libraries, relatives of murdered officers and record and newspaper offices gathering details of their deaths. The resultant information has now been put into two CD Roms. The cases referred to in the article below are just some of those recorded in *The Ultimate Price, Part 1* (1700 – 1899) *and Part 2* (1900 – 2000).

The murder of Bow Street Runner Smithers 1820
In the early 1800's many people in the lower classes of Britain were experiencing extreme

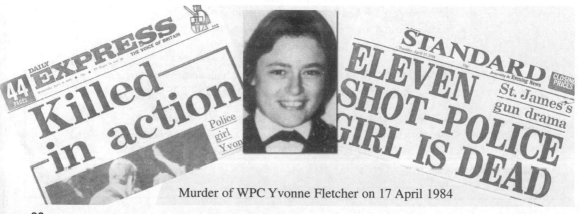
Murder of WPC Yvonne Fletcher on 17 April 1984

Arthur Thistlewood

poverty and hunger despite the Industrial Revolution which was starting to put the Country on its feet. It was natural, therefore, that most of the opposition to the Government would come from this area.

Arthur Thistlewood came from a lower class background and set himself the task in life of bringing down the Government. In February 1820 he decided on a way to achieve his aim and form a new Government with himself as its Head. Thistlewood's determination was such that he had already previously been charged with High Treason, had stood trial, but been acquitted.

Thistlewood discovered that on 23 February 1820 the entire Cabinet had been invited to dinner with Lord Harrowby at his home in Grosvenor Square, London. This was his theme, therefore, for him to kill them all in one go. His plan was that, during the dinner, one of his thirsty accomplices would deliver a parcel to the main door of Lord Harrowby's home. As soon as the door opened his gang would burst in, make their way to the dining room and murder them all. If that was not bad enough in itself Thistlewood had also given them a bag in which to put the heads of Lord Casterleigh and Lord Sidmouth, Home Secretary.

Had it not been for a man named Edwards informing on the gang, Thistlewood might well have succeeded with his plan. Possibly it was the horrendous outcry that such action would have brought that made Edwards tell the Bow Street Runners, London's forerunner to the present Metropolitan Police. Immediately Sir Richard Binnie, the Magistrate, together with the Bow Street Patrol and some Guards went to Cato Street where it was known the conspirators

were meeting prior to their attack. As the Guards broke down the main doors the Runners gained entry to a hayloft above a disused stable, via a narrow trap door. Runner Rutheven was the first to reach the loft, followed immediately by Runner Smithers. Smithers rushed forward to arrest Thistlewood but as he did so the latter drew his sword and plunged it into Smithers' chest. Smithers fell to his knees clutching his wound and was dead within seconds.

As more Guards arrived on the scene, Thistlewood ordered his colleagues to dowse the lights. In the darkness the Runners and conspirators clashed. Nine of the gang were arrested but Thistlewood, Edwards and several others managed to escape.

The following day Edwards was able to tell the Runners that Thistlewood was at No. 8, White Street, Moorsfield. A large group of Runners went to the address where he was arrested without too much of a struggle and imprisoned in the Tower of London. On Monday 17 April 1820 he was found guilty of High Treason and to murdering Runner Smithers. He and four of his fellow conspirators were executed at the Old Bailey on Monday 1 May 1820.

Sergeant Adam Eves

The murder of Sergeant Eves in 1893
Sergeant Eves (35) called into the Oak Public House at Purleigh to deliver a message, just after 10 o'clock on the Saturday night of 15 April 1893. It was to be the last time he was seen alive. Sergeant Eve's body was found at about 3 pm the following day by a carpenter named Herbert Patten as he left Hazeleigh Hall Farm near Maldon in Essex.

Patten had noticed splashes of blood on the gravel at a spot near Bill Rope Gate. He thought an animal may have injured itself so when he followed the trail which led into a ditch at the side of the lane he must have had the shock of his life. Lying in about six inches of water was the body of a police sergeant. As Patten approached nearer to the body he could see several wounds on the left hand side of the head and the officer's throat had been cut from ear to ear.

Police were called and Superintendent Halsey, who was already investigating the theft of some corn from Hall Farm, arrived to take charge of the enquiry together with an Inspector Pryke. When they searched the area they found the dead officer's helmet lying a few yards from the body and three sticks, one of which was completely broken. Inspector Pryke also found three sacks containing wheat which, enquiries later showed, had been stolen from the nearby farm. Three more sacks were found concealed at the side of the pond.

As the officers pieced together the evidence it became clear that the victim, Sergeant Eves, had come across his murderer or murderers that night whilst they were in possession of wheat. He had stopped them, there had been a brief struggle during which he was hit over the head and his throat was cut before his body was thrown into the ditch.

Enquiries led to the arrest of six men, Richard Davies (30) and his brother John (34), Charles Sale (47), John Bateman (37), James Ramsey and his son, similarly named James. All lived at Purleigh and had been working with the threshing machines at Hall Farm the day of the murder.

The two Davis brothers and Bateman were eventually charged with the officer's murder. When the charge against Bateman was later withdrawn he was called as a witness and said that John Davis had confided that he was going to kill Sergeant Eves. At the Essex Assizes the Jury took just on an hour to find the two brothers guilty and both were sentenced to death. After appealing only Richard had his death sentence changed to one of penal servitude for life. John Davis was executed at Chelmsford on 16 August 1893.

Sergeant Eves had been in the Force since 1877. He left a widow who received a pension of £38.17s.3d. There were no children. The officer was buried in Purleigh Churchyard.

Murder of Sergeant Purdy in 1959
The trial of Guenther Fritz Erwin Podola for the murder of Sergeant Purdy was unique in English legal history. It was the first time a prisoner had

3 a.m. West End hunt for killer of C.I.D. sergeant

EXPRESS CRIME REPORTERS

A KILLER who knows he must die was on the run early today, probably still in London, after shooting a detective in South Kensington's fashionable Onslow-square.

The man, a blackmailer in dark glasses, brutally shot down Detective Sergeant Ray-

Newspaper Headline reporting the murder of Sergeant Purdy in 1959

pleaded amnesia following a murder. If the amnesia was genuine he could not be found guilty of the crime.

30 year old Podola lived mainly from the proceeds of housebreaking and blackmail. Born in Berlin, he had been deported from Canada in 1958 because of convictions for theft and burglary. He returned to Germany but after a short time came to England and continued a life of crime.

It was a burglary in July 1959 that was to lead to his downfall and end in his execution. He had stolen jewellery and furs from a luxury flat in South Kensington belonging to Mrs Verne Schiffman. Not content with his proceeds he then tried to blackmail her four days later by saying he was a private detective named Levine and that he had incriminating photographs and tape recordings of her. Mrs Schiffman immediately informed the police and arrangements were made for her telephone to be tapped.
At about 3.45 pm on 13 July a further telephone call by the blackmailer was to send DS Raymond Purdy and DS John Sandford rushing to the telephone box in South Kensington Underground Station. Podola was still in the telephone box when they arrived. On their way to Chelsea Police Station he succeeded in breaking away from the two officers but was soon caught again in the entrance hall of some flats at 105 Onslow Square, Chelsea.

Whilst Ds Sandford tried to raise the porter of the flats to help look after the prisoner whilst he went for police transport, Sergeant Purdy told Podola to sit on the window sill. The prisoner, doing as he was told, put his hands on the marble ledge and eased himself up. Sergeant Sandford meanwhile was not having much luck. As Purdy turned towards his colleague Podola took immediate advantage of the distraction.

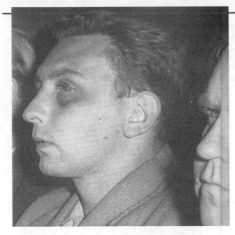

Guenther Fritz Erwin Podola

2 women, however decided that Podola was not suffering from a genuine loss of memory and was fit for trial.

The actual murder trial lasted only 1 day. The Jury took just 37 minutes to find Podola guilty. Guentha Podola was hanged at 9.45 am on 5 November at Wandsworth Prison. He was the last man to be executed for murdering a policeman.

Ds Purdy had been in the Force for 19 years. He was married with three children, sons aged 18 and 13 and a daughter of 12. His funeral took place at St Matthew's, Surbiton, Surrey. He was buried at Surbiton cemetery.

Pulling a gun out of his pocket he shot the officer through the heart at point blank range. As the officer slid to the floor, Podola ran off towards Sumner Place. Sandford raced after him but he escaped.

A palm print found on the window ledge identified the gunman. He was soon traced to Room 105 of Claremont House Hotel at 95 Queen's Gate, Kensington where he had registered in the name of Paul Camay.

When police broke into his room the door, which was unlocked, hit Podola over the left eye sending him sprawling across the floor. He ended up with his head in the fireplace. Believing him to be armed, police jumped on him and restrained him. He was taken to Chelsea Police Station where he appeared to the police surgeon who examined him to be dazed and frightened and suffering from muscular tremors. The surgeon then transferred him to St Stephen's Hospital. During his time there he started to recover but said he could not remember any events prior to the time of his arrest. After four days he was taken back to Chelsea and charged with Sergeant Purdy's murder.

At his trial the Judge ruled that it was first necessary to establish whether the prisoner was genuinely suffering from amnesia. He was examined by six doctors, four of whom believed he was genuine, the other two saying it was only feigned. The Jury also heard that Podola had given himself away in a letter which he had written from his cell to a man named Starkey, Starkey was produced in Court and told how he had met Podola three times and that Podola had also stayed with him once. Podola told the Court he had only replied to Starkey's letter so he would have a visitor and hopefully receive some cigarettes. He could not recall who Starkey was. The jury, consisting of 10 men and

Murder of WPC Fletcher in 1984

Yvonne Fletcher (25) had wanted to be a policewoman since the age of three. She was only 5'2" tall when she joined the Metropolitan Police at the age of 18 and was probably one of the smallest police women in Britain. Attached to Bow Street Police Station she was unofficially engaged to a policeman at the same Station and they planned to marry during 1984. Yet a routine duty for her on 17 April of that year was to bring an abrupt end to her young life, a life she had dedicated to helping others.

On that day, she and her fiancé had been detailed with 21 other officers for duty at one of nearly 400 demonstrations held each year in London. About 70 Libyan Protesters, some of them wearing masks, were demonstrating against Colonel Gaddafi's regime outside the Libyan People's Bureau in St James's Square. The chanting demonstrators were basically well behaved but at about ten minutes past ten that morning about 40 pro-Gaddafi supporters arrived and commenced a counter demonstration on each side of the main demonstration but opposite to it.

Wpc Fletcher was standing about 25 yards from the anti-Gaddafi demonstrators with her back to the Libyan People's Bureau. What happened next was to appal the people of Britain; lead to the British Government breaking off diplomatic relations with Libya and withdrawing the British Ambassador; and convince everyone that diplomatic immunity needed urgent reform. Several witnesses saw a man looking out of one of the first floor windows. Then a barrel of a gun appeared followed by a number of shots from possibly one or two automatic weapons. Constable Fletcher collapsed to the ground. She had been shot in the back. Her colleagues, initially stunned, ran to her aid. She was immediately taken to the Westminster Hospital where she died about an hour later. Eleven of the demonstrators were also injured on that fateful morning.

Within minutes police had surrounded the Libyan People's Bureau. Because the building held diplomatic status police were unable to enter it without the Libyan's authority and this naturally, they were not going to give. As a result the Bureau was cordoned off for 10 days at the end of which the 30 occupants, who included the murderer, all claiming diplomatic immunity were escorted to Heathrow Airport and flew back to a heroes welcome in Tripoli.

A total of 12 bullet fragments were found; ten from St James's Square, one from a wounded demonstrator and the other was found in the ambulance which had taken WPC Fletcher to hospital. All were of 9mm calibre. Fire arms experts later stated at the Coroner's Inquest that they were satisfied that 9 of the bullets had come from one gun, the remaining three from another.

With the departure of the Libyans, the Bureau was sealed by police and forensic experts. They found a cache of arms and ammunition as well as ballistic residues under two of the windows indicating that a weapon had been fired from those windows of the first floor. But the murder weapon was never found and it is probably safe to assume that it was taken out of the Country in a Diplomatic bag.

The Prime Minister, Home Secretary and Commissioner of Police were among the thousands who attended the funeral service at Salisbury Cathedral and the memorial service held in St James's Square.

Diplomatic relations with Libya were not reinstated until July 1999 when Colonel Gaddafi's regime admitted "general responsibility" for the shooting.

Police murders form just a small part of the information held by **Murderfiles**.
Murderfiles is a private collection of information on murders that have occurred in Britain over the last 300 years. Information from this collection is available to serious enquirers and details of cost involved are available on request.

Genealogists may have information that an ancestor was either the victim of murder or the murderer. **Murderfiles** may be able to tell what happened and details about either party. Information is also available on the British hangmen and those they 'switched off'.

Should you wish to know whether any information is stored on a particular case please do not hesitate to write or email giving as much information as possible. A stamped addressed envelope (if you are located in the UK) for your reply or an International Reply Coupon if enquiring from outside the UK, would be appreciated.

If you need to know more about any 'skeletons' in your cupboard I can be emailed on enquiry@murderfiles.com or written to at Dommett Hill Farm, Hare Lane, Buckland St Mary, Chard, Somerset, TA20 3JS.
Paul Williams

Biography:
Paul Williams worked for the Metropolitan Police in London for 26 years during which time he not only spent several years in their Criminal Record Office but was for over 8 years responsible for their Force Museums. One of these Museums was the world famous Black Museum which holds crime exhibits from notorious criminal cases. Whilst there he lectured, with the Curator, to police officers, members of the Judiciary and eminent people including members of the British and foreign Royal families. Amongst the many interesting visitors he met were Albert Pierrepoint, the last British Hangman and Professor Sir Bernard Spilsby, the pathologist.

As well as running Murder Files, Paul Williams, who is also a Winston Churchill Fellow, writes articles for books, magazines and CD-Roms as well as providing storylines for TV documentaries and dramas.

My Great-Great Grandmother Was Murdered!

Richard Ratcliffe FSG

Christmas Eve 1998.
The post included a large brown envelope postmarked Southport. I knew it contained a copy of the Death Certificate of my Great-Great Grandmother, Ann Tennant, which I had ordered at the Family Records Centre a week earlier. I needed this certificate to complete my collection of death certificates of my 16 great-great grandparents.

My great-great grandmother was born Ann Smith. She was baptised in Long Compton Parish Church, Warwickshire in 1794 and was the daughter of Edward Smith and his wife Elizabeth. Ann married John Tennant, formerly of Spelsbury, Oxfordshire at Long Compton, after Banns on April 12th, 1819. Between 1822 and 1836 they had 7 children, 5 sons and 2 daughters, all of whom were baptised in Long Compton Parish Church.

In the 1841 Census, all 7 children were living at home with John and Ann. In 1851, only William, John and James were living at home

Joseph [bap January 28th, 1825]
    who married Elizabeth Clifton at Brailes on October 28th, 1842.
Elizabeth [bap February 11th, 1827]
    who married William Hughes at Long Compton on December 25th, 1843.
Charles [bap February 11th, 1827]
    who married Elizabeth Rose at Whichford on December 23rd, 1848.
William [bap February 11th, 1827]
    who married Leah Bishop at Long Compton on June 26th, 1852.
John [bap December 14th, 1828]
    who married Mary Ann Woolam at Whichford on March 4th, 1854.
Sarah [bap June 26th, 1831]
    who married Richard Coleman at Long Compton Independent Chapel on November 12th, 1850.
James [bap June 19th,1837]
    my great grandfather, who married Ann Dyer at Barton on the Heath on July 10th, 1862
    because Long Compton Church was under repair.

with John and Ann. In 1861, only James was still at home with his parents. John was the described as a butcher, having previously been described as an Agricultural Labourer. In 1871, John and Ann were on their own but John was now described as a Shoemaker. In 1881, John then aged 84, a Pauper, was living at home with his wife Elizabeth aged 78 whose place of birth was given as Salford, Oxfordshire.

I knew that Ann had died having found her burial recorded in the Long Compton Burials Register on September 19th, 1875 aged 79 years, with no additional comment against the entry. I thought that I was getting a fairly straight forward Death Certificate. So when I opened the big brown envelope I was totally unprepared for the cause of death, " Wilful murder, deliberately stabbed to death by James [Hayward] with a fork under a delusion of witchcraft." Certificate

received from J B Couchman, Coroner for Warwickshire. Inquest held September 17th, 1875.

My immediate reaction was to visit the British Library Newspaper Library at Colindale and see how the murder and subsequent events were reported as the report in the *Warwickshire Advertiser* of 25th September, 1875 quoted in Edward Rainsberry's history of Long Compton *"Through the Lych Gate"* [Roundwood Press,1969] gave no clue that the victim was my great, great grandmother.

"A weak minded agricultural labourer named James assaulted an old woman of 80, believing her to be a witch. She was on her way back to her cottage from the baker's shop and he was returning from the harvest field. The old lady was knocked down and later died from shock

CERTIFIED COPY OF AN ENTRY OF DEATH GIVEN AT THE GENERAL REGISTER OFFICE

Application Number GO1O35O

REGISTRATION DISTRICT Chipping Norton

1875. DEATH in the Sub-district of Chipping Norton in the Counties of Oxford and Warwick

No.	When and where died	Name and surname	Sex	Age	Occupation	Cause of death	Signature, description and residence of informant	When registered	Signature of registrar
	15th September 1875 Long Compton	Ann Tennant	Female	80 Years	Wife of John Tennant agricultural Labourer	Wilful Murder deliberately Stabbed to death by James with a fork under a delusion of Witchcraft	Certificate received from JB Couchman Coroner for Warwickshire Inquest held Seventeenth September 1875	Twentieth September 1875	H Hartley Registrar

CERTIFIED to be a true copy of an entry in the certified copy of a Register of Deaths in the District above mentioned.

Given at the GENERAL REGISTER OFFICE, under the Seal of the said Office, the 23rd day of December 1998

DAZ 036445 CAUTION:- It is an offence to falsify a certificate or to make or knowingly use a false certificate or a copy of a false certificate intending it to be accepted as genuine to the prejudice of any person or to possess a certificate knowing it to be false without lawful authority.

of December 17th, 1875 describes his appearance in court.

"He was placed in the dock where his appearance created much sympathy. He is evidently a very simple minded and superstitious man. He is about 5 feet 4 inches in height, with a low, receding forehead and an almost idiotic expression of countenance, his awkwardness being increased by his great deafness. He stared wildly about the court and seemed quite unable to give a direct answer to the single question put to him. "Are you guilty or not guilty?" As he could not hear what the Judge said to him, one of the gaol porters shouted in his ear the question put by the court. The nature of his answer showed that he was still labouring under the hallucination that his victim had bewitched him. To the first question addressed to him, he replied, "I be sorry I hurt the woman, but she tormented me for a long time in witchcraft."

His Lordship Baron Bramwell: "Do you plead guilty or not guilty?"
Hayward: "I hurt the woman."
His Lordship: "He has to plead now and make his defence afterwards."
Hayward: "I did not kill the woman."
His Lordship: "Then you are not guilty?"
Hayward: "I did not kill the person."
His Lordship: "Do you say not guilty?"
Hayward: "No, I say not guilty."
The plea of not guilty was then recorded.
Baron Bramwell then asked Hayward if he wished to be defended by Counsel.
Hayward: " Yes, but I can't pay him."
Baron Bramwell then asked Hayward if he should request a barrister to conduct his defence without a fee.
Hayward: "Yes."
Mr Buzzard was then asked to undertake Hayward's defence and the case was adjourned to the following day.

and injuries received. The accused was arrested and declared that he had been bewitched and prevented from working properly by witches' spells, and that there were sixteen others in the village that deserved similar treatment."

The murder was reported in all the local papers covering South Warwickshire, North Oxfordshire and nearby Worcestershire and Gloucestershire, as was the Inquest. Evidence was given at the Inquest by my great, great grandfather, John Tennant who identified the murdered woman, John Henry Ivens , a16 year old labourer who had been working in the harvest field all day with James Hayward, John Taylor, a farmer who stopped Hayward inflicting further injuries to my great, great grandmother, Elizabeth Hughes, one of John and Ann Tennant's daughters who rendered first aid and took her mother into her cottage pending the arrival of a doctor, P.C. John Simpson, the Long Compton village policeman who arrested Hayward, Police Superintendent James Thompson who had charged Hayward with murder after he had been taken to the lock-up at Shipston on Stour and Dr George Wright Hutchinson who had travelled from Chipping Norton to attend my great, great grandmother.

Summing up the evidence, the Coroner told the jury that if Ann Tennant had died from wounds inflicted on her by Hayward, they should return a verdict of wilful murder, leaving his state of mind to be inquired onto at the Assizes.

The trial of James Hayward began at Warwick Assizes on Tuesday, December 14th, 1875 with Hayward being arraigned to see if he wished to be defended. "The Stratford upon Avon Herald"

On Wednesday, December 15th, 1875 the trial of James Hayward took place with Mr J Stratford Dugdale and Mr Chamberlain prosecuting and Mr Buzzard defending. After hearing the evidence, the jury who consulted together in their box for a few moments only, returned a

Date of Information	Name & surname of Deceased	Rank or profession	Age	Date & place of death	Cause of death	Date of Inquest, when and where held	Verdict	Miles Travelled	Hours Expend	Expenses £ s d
						Brought forward		34	9	6 15 8
17 August 1875.	Robert Salmon of Armscott		58 Years	18th August 1875 Armscott	Died suddenly	18 Augt 1875 at Mode Heath Fenleylor, at Lr Brayton	asphyxia caused by accidental choking	32	6	3 9 6
15th Sept 1875.	Harriet Collins of Shatford on Stour	Domestic Servant	15 Years	13 Sept 1875 Shatford on Stour	Found drowned in River Stour	17th Sept 1875 at Shatford Shatford on Stour at 12 oClock Noon	Found Drowned		16	4 18 6
16th Sept 1875.	Ann Tennant of Long Compton	Wife of John Tennant Farm Labourer	80 77 Years	15 Sept 1875 at Long Compton	Killed by James Haywood with a Hay fork	17 Sept 1875 at Red Lion Long Compton at 4 oClock pm	Wilful Murder	12 Noons 50		3 4 6
4th Octbr 1875.	Maria Court of Alcester	Wife of Thos Court Innkeeper	51 Years	2nd October 1875 at Alcester	Fall down stairs	5th Oct 1875 at Swan Inn Alcester at 11 oClock am	Accidentally Killed	16	4	2 19 9
5th Octbr 1875.	Ann Clarke of Coughton	Wife of William Clarke, Labourer	28 Years	2nd October 1875	Died suddenly after eating Mushrooms	6th Octbr 1875 at Throckmorton Arms Coughton at 2 oClock	Natural Causes	18	5	3 18 .
14th October 1875. Quarterly Return sent with Vouchers to Finance Committee, Warwick.						Recognizance to prosecute & c - James Haywood				2 6
						to prosecute Niches				6 .
						Total		166	36	£26 6 11

EXTRACT TAKEN FROM CORONERS RECORD OF DATE AND PLACE OF INQUEST OF THE MURDER OF ANN TENNANT.

verdict of "Not guilty on the grounds of insanity."

His Lordship ordered Hayward to be confined during Her Majesty's Pleasure. Hayward died in Warwick Gaol a few months later.

I am still trying to locate descendants of John and Ann Tennant. Their seven children produced a large number of grandchildren many of whom sought employment away from Long Compton mainly in the North Warwickshire coalfield or on the railways in the Greater Birmingham area although I have tracked one line of descent to Queensland, Australia.

A Tale of Two Foundlings

Doreen Berger

It was May 1869. In Fountain Court, Cheapside, London an abandoned child was found. The child was taken to the City Union Workhouse, and there named Samuel Fountain by the officers of the Workhouse.

In November of that year Mr. J.M. Johnson, a Jewish gentleman and a member of the City of London Board of Guardians, wrote unofficially to a member of the Jewish Board of Guardians, saying that he considered the child had been circumcised as a Jewish child. Samuel was examined a few days later in the presence of the Medical Officer of the City Union Workhouse, and this opinion was confirmed. This was reported back to the Executive Committee of the Jewish Board of Guardians, but they resolved they could not interfere, as at that time there was no Jewish certified institution in which to place such a young child. In December 1871 Samuel was moved to Hanwell Schools.

It was the summer of 1876 when the case of the foundling, Samuel Fountain, was again brought to the attention of the Jewish Board of Guardians, after notice had been drawn to the child by a Jewish visitor to the institution, The Chief Rabbi was consulted. After all, Samuel's parentage was unknown and he was, therefore, considered not totally deserving. To be a recipient of charity, the Victorians considered one ought to be 'deserving'. The 'deserving poor' were regarded very differently from the 'undeserving poor', Unfortunately, Samuel fell into the latter category. However, the Chief Rabbi assured the Jewish Board of Guardians that Samuel would suffer no religious disqualification by reason of his parentage being unknown. As a result, the Jewish Board of Guardians decided to apply to the City Board of Guardians for the order of removal to a certified Jewish School under the Pauper Removal Act.

In September 1876 a deputation waited upon the City Board of Guardians. The Jewish Board of Guardians now had two certified institutions in which Samuel could be maintained at their own cost, and they considered that he was a Jewish child. They were listened to politely and then the deputation withdrew. The City Board of Guardians earnestly discussed the matter. They voted by thirty four to twenty two not to give the child up to the Jewish Board of Guardians.

This issue was by now a matter of great interest in the national press. The Daily Telegraph published a leader on the subject and the City Press reported on it. A letter even appeared in the Daily Telegraph in defence of the City Board of Guardians.

At a meeting of the City Board of Guardians in October, 1876 a letter was read from the Jewish Board of Guardians, stating they had determined to submit the question to the Local Government Board. They would like three representatives to confer with representatives of the City Guardians to prepare a statement of facts for submission to the Local Government Board. A motion was carried that the Jewish Board should be informed they could not assist.

In early 1877, adoption of a report from the General Purposes Committee in reference to the case of Samuel Fountain was moved by the City Board of Guardians, after hearing from the Local Government Board. Samuel had now been baptised. Mr. Solomons, a Jewish member, said "Circumcision" was entered in a register, and showed that rite had been performed prior to baptism. Mr. Bloor said that answer was evasive. There were two books. In one both the words 'Hebrew' and 'Ditto', under 'Church of England', had been entered. In the other book, only the word 'Hebrew' had been entered. The report was adopted and the City Board of Guardians decided that the Local Government Board should be informed the decision had been arrived at after full consideration and according to the legal aspect of the case.

We do not know the fate of Samuel Fountain, but undoubtedly he grew up without any knowledge of his Jewish heritage.

At about this time, the fate of another child was engaging the correspondence pages of the Jewish newspapers.

John Nunez was the illegitimate offspring of a Jewish mother and non-Jewish father. In Jewish religious law he was considered to be a Jewish child, as the matriarchal lineage is the deciding factor. In addition, he came under the auspices of the ancient Spanish and Portuguese Jewish congregation, as his mother belonged to this community.

The matter of the child, John Nunez, was brought before the Board of Elders of the congregation. It was unanimously decided congregational funds could not fairly be appropriated for adopting unfortunate children of this class, It was considered by countenancing such a case they would be assisting to perpetuate the evil, if it was understood they were ready to assume not only pecuniary but moral charge of bastard children when abandoned by their parents. It was pointed out that if the mother had been married to a non-member of the congregation, her children would have no claim upon them.

There were many letters of protest and sarcasm in the Jewish press on the treatment of John Nunez. The mother was dead and the child was at the moment with the Forest and District Parochial School. Finally, the Ecclesiastical Chief of the Spanish and Portuguese Congregation successfully interposed. In 1878 the child was placed with one of its relatives. As the relative was in humble circumstances, a private subscription was raised for the maintenance of John Nunez. In this particular case, the child Nunez remained in the Jewish community.

The British Jewish community was established in 1656, when Oliver Cromwell agreed to the re-admission of the Jews, which had been brought to an end by Edward I in the year 1290.

In the years which have elapsed since the Re-

Settlement, many are the conversions and intermarriage that have taken place. There were people who found it more convenient not to identify themselves with the Jewish community. They may have wanted to make a complete break with the past, They may have drifted apart from their family. There may have been a family quarrel in the dim and distant past, leaving bitterness in its wake, and the result may have been a deliberate cutting off on either side. As time has passed, all knowledge of Jewish family connections may have been lost.

For these reasons, it sometimes happens that people researching their genealogical background are surprised to find that they have a Jewish ancestor. This is even more likely if the family has lived for many years in London, where the largest Jewish community has traditionally been established.

If you number among your ancestors a Jewish link, The Jewish Genealogical Society of Great Britain could be of interest to you. The Society now has over a thousand members, some of them based overseas. If you are interested in membership, please contact the Secretary at PO Box 2508, Maidenhead SL6 8WS.

The following books would be helpful for those wishing to research their Jewish background:
Jewish Ancestors? A Beginner's Guide to Jewish Genealogy in Great Britain Available from The Jewish Genealogical Society of Great Britain. (80 pages)
My Ancestors were Jewish. By Dr. Anthony Joseph. Available from the Society of Genealogists Enterprises Ltd. (60 pages)
The Jewish Victorian: Genealogical Information from the Jewish Newspapers 1871-80 by Doreen Berger (600 pages)
The Jewish Victorian: Genealogical Information from the Jewish Newspapers 1861-70 by Doreen Berger
Both available from Robert Boyd Publications, 260 Colwell Drive, Witney, Oxfordshire OX8 7LW Email: BOYDPUBS@aol.com

The Barnbow Canaries

Anne Batchelor

It was just a casual conversation in a taxi, but it led me on yet another "Miss Marple" adventure. I was chatting with the driver, Bob, about my love of the detective work involved in family history research - coming across a mystery, following clues, finding lost infomation and solving the mystery. What a wonderful moment it is when, after months of false leads and frustration, you uncover the solution and want to punch the air and shout, "YES!"

"I've a mystery for you," said Bob. He told me how, as a young boy, he had been told about a massive explosion at the Barnbow Munitions Factory, Crossgates, during W.W.I. It was said that over thirty women and girls were killed and, because it was wartime, the event was hushed up and never reported in the local newspaper, for fear of affecting public morale. Bob was told that all the girls were buried together in an unmarked grave.

It seemed to him so sad. Could "Miss Marple", perhaps, find out where they were buried? It would be nice to take them some flowers. A man after my own heart! The purpose which drives the family historian on is that our people of the past should not be forgotten. "NOT FORGOTTEN" are the words I had carved on my maternal grandparents' gravestone, though I had never met them. The same words were on the posy of poppies placed on the war - grave of my mother's beloved brother, Will, who is "asleep in Italy".

So at once I agreed to look for the Barnbow girls for Bob. I explained that it could take ages and there was no guarantee that I would find them, but I would do my level best. Like Bob I felt that they had given their lives for their country and their sacrifice should not be forgotten.

My first move was to read all I could about Barnbow. The National Shell Filling Factory, one of the largest in the country, was built in 1915 on the outskirts of Leeds, some distance beyond the village of Crossgates. This was so that, in the event of an explosion, there would be no damage or loss of life in homes surrounding the factory. By 1916 sixteen thousand workers were employed in three daily shifts, producing 6,000 shells per day. Typical wages were £3 per week, workers in the danger/powder room being paid extra.

Barnbow was like a small town covering 400 acres. It had its own farm, producing 300 gallons of fresh milk per day, to counteract the effect of cordite on the health of the workers. Potatoes were grown and a slaughterhouse and butcher's shop were set up to provide fresh meat for the three massive canteens.

Inside the factory, heavy loads were transported on a 2ft gauge track in tubs pulled by ponies. There was a fully equipped garage, and Barnbow even had its own railway station where workers were brought in daily on thirty - eight special trains from as far away as Wakefield, Harrogate and York.

There was a team of welfare workers, two dentists, a resident doctor and a staff of nurses. Those employed in danger zones had regular health checks. Barnbow even had its own fire - brigade. By the end of the war, in 1918, an amazing total of 24,750,000 shells had been filled and over 19,000,000 were fused and packed.

All very impressive, but what I now craved was the personal stories of the Barnbow girls. I believe that the more people you tell about your research, the more likely you are to be successful, so I now embarked on a mission to

Loading Shells

had expected but the very graphic "Shock due to injuries to vital organs caused accidentally by explosion at a shell factory". Poor Mary Jane. Far better to be killed outright than to linger into the next day.

This was my first inkling that Bob's story of a mass grave might not be true. Possibly the poor souls right at the centre of the explosion would have been just a mass of body parts, identifiable only by their security dog - tags. They might have been buried together. Others who, like Mary Jane, died from their injuries would surely have been returned to their families for burial? That means that I could be looking for up to thirty different burial sites!

Now material was coming in thick and fast. I had a note from Raymond Earnshaw telling me that his mother, from Sharleston Common, near Wakefield, had worked at Barnbow during World War I. I rang him and had a fascinating chat. He sent me a photograph of his mother with two of her Barnbow friends, in their overalls and unflattering mob - caps. He also sent me a photocopy of her Barnbow badge, and a document certifying that she "worked at Barnbow during the Great War, 1914 - 1918 - For King and Country."

Most wonderful of all was a note she had written in July,1939, when she was trying to make contact with some of her old Barnbow friends. She writes, "I remember one night when all the nightworkers were out all night because the Germans were at York dropping bombs. We had a night all in darkness. Nobody allowed through the barriers. Police telling us not to speak. Then, when all was safe, we were

tell everyone I could the story of my search.

I started with the local newspaper and John Thorpe's "Old Yorkshire Diary". Was there anyone out there whose mother, aunt or grandmother had worked at Barnbow? I mentioned my quest on my frequent phone - ins on John Boyd's programme on Radio Leeds. Within a few days I received a magazine article from an old friend, Ron Taylor. Written by Adrian Budge of the Royal Armouries, it gave lots of detail of the factory, including "my" explosion on 5 December 1916, caused by a fuse exploding as it was being fitted in a shell. He gave a list of the women and girls killed.

Another magazine article, from the Barwick Historical society, had a copy of the official Roll of Honour bearing the girls' names. At last they had become named individuals rather than an anonymous group. They were now Emmie and Martha, Polly and Agnes - real people. I was now totally committed to telling their story and finding their last resting place.

As there had been a total press blackout covering up the story I wondered what had been given as cause of death on the girls' certificates. I picked out Mary Jane Blackstone form the Roll of Honour and bought her death certificate.

She was thirty - five years old, a young married woman, the wife of Arthur, an iron moulder. I wondered whether she had left any children? She died, not in the initial explosion, but the next day in the Leeds General Infirmary. Cause of death was not a vague "accidental death" as I

Moving Shells

The Factory after the explosion

allowed to the canteen for milk.

I worked at Barnbow in C.Factory, known as "Canary Factory", from 1915 to 1918. You may wonder why we called it "Canary Factory". - because are (sic) feet and hands and hair went yellow. I've seen when I have been yellow up to the elbows when weighing up TNT. Signed Mrs. Earnshaw neé Lucy Lackenby One of Sharleston Barnbow girls".

Now I understood why the girls were often referred to as the Barnbow Canaries. Lucy came to no harm in the explosion nor in the unhealthy working conditions, for she lived to the age of ninety - five. However it had been a hard life. If she was on the early shift (6am to 2pm) she had to be up at 2.3O .a.m. and, running down a lonely snicket to the station, catch the special train at 3.15am. She would not get home until tea - time.

Many of the Barnbow girls had husbands, sons or brothers serving in France, so they felt that providing shells for the war effort was a way in which they could help to hasten the end of hostilities and the return home of their loved ones. I was told that often the unattached girls would chalk their names and addresses on the shells in the hope that some lonely soldier might get in touch. I'd love to think that this might have happened. I'm an old romantic at heart!

Next my friend, local historian John Gilleghan, sent me a magazine article about the explosion by a lady called Irene Burton. Irene told me of her mother's work at Barnbow. "She had the job of packing shells into tubs on wheels which were drawn by ponies whose hooves were rubbershod to prevent sparks. The women and girls had to harness them and hers was a stubborn and at times vicious animal named Jacky. He was difficult to handle and, although Mum was quite sturdy, he was very strong and muscular. She had two deep scars where he had kicked her, regarded with fascination by her children and later her grandchildren. Nevertheless, she grew very fond of him, and they eventually reached an understanding."

She described a gruesome incident - "My mother was working on the shift the night the explosion occured and was standing next to a girl who had her head blown clean off, my mother being very lucky to escape alive." Irene told me that the girl's head had been stuck to the ceiling. However did the other girls live with that kind of memory?

In a Yorkshire Evening Post account, published in 1973, an eyewitness descibes surviving girls rushing, crying, out of the factory, with their faces bright yellow from the explosion. One girl had a miraculous escape, having been blown out of her shoes. She had to be restrained by the security guards because she was frantic to go back inside – "If I go home without my shoes, Mother will be furious!.

Derek Naylor, in his 1973 article, gives a graphic description of the explosion –

"Machine 2, where the explosion had occurred, was completely wrecked. Steam pipes burst and the floor was a mixture of blood and water. Ignoring the danger, men and women alike hurried into the room to drag the injured to safety. Mr William Parkin performed heroic deeds. So much so that the girls later presented him with an inscribed silver watch for his bravery in bringing out a dozen girls. Within a few hours of the bodies having been taken out, girls were volunteering to work in the same room, and production was only briefly halted."

What courage! My Barnbow Canaries were proving to be very special ladies. Still I was greedy for more information. Surely someone must know where my girls were buried?

I wrote to the PRO (The National Archives) to see what they had. They found some records and if I would send a cheque. I sent it First Class! Then I pestered my postie for weeks until he brought me a huge envelope containing details of compensation awarded to the families of some of my girls. Some of the documents gave details of their home life.

"Edith Sykes aged $15^3/_4$, Father earning 30/ - to 35/ - a week. Eight children left in family, aged 21,19,13,11,9,7,5,2. Deceased is said to have contributed £1 a week."

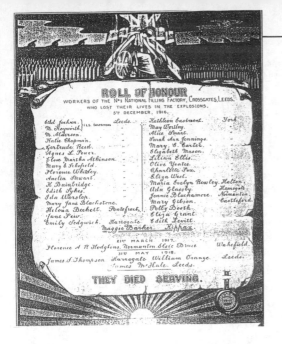

Edith's father was awarded £100 because her £1 per week helped to maintain the large family. Nineteen year old Janet Few's wounded soldier husband, on the other hand, was only allowed up to £10 to cover burial fees. Olive Yeats of Harrogate was aged seventeen and had only worked at Barnbow for two weeks. Her family received a mere £1.2.11d. How sad that she died in the service of her country but her life was valued so cheaply.

Now I decided to contact Adrian Budge at the Royal Armouries, whose article had given me so much help in the early days. He told me that even though the Leeds newspapers didn't report the explosion, the York papers had reported the funerals of the girls from York. I sent for copies from the York Reference Library and they arrived bearing photographs of four of my girls. My cup runneth over!

There I was, face to face with Mary Carter aged 22 who left her soldier husband to bring up her 2yr. old child; Elizabeth Mason, who left a husband and five children, four of whom were under the age of fourteen; Gertrude Reed, whose husband was a prisoner of war in Germany, and the sweetfaced Mary Elizabeth Wortley, nine of whose children attended her funeral - Kezia (aged 22), Charles William (16), Eleanor (13), Gladys (12), Ronald (11), Stanley (10), George (7), Leslie (6), and little Mary (4). No wonder the headline was, "Pathetic Scenes at York Cemetery" and many of the crowd were moved to tears. The funerals took place at the old York Cemetery - one of my favourite places. There old Theophilus Batchelor is buried - the first of my Hertfordshire family to come to Yorkshire.

So are George and Eliza, my great - grandparents, and under the big tree by the gate, my dear father and sweet mother. I have booked my place there, too, when my time comes and I hand in my notebook and pencil. (Or perhaps I should take them with me?) How strange that my girls were in my cemetery and I never knew.

So one beautiful afternoon, armed with their plot number and accompanied by David Poole, an enthusiastic volunteer guide, wielding his spade for the brambles, I eventually stood at the last resting place of some of my girls. They were buried together in a public grave but not unmarked. The late Fred Emmerson, stonemason, a dear and kindly man, had noticed some time ago that they had no memorial, so at his own expense he made one! So Mary Elizabeth Wortley, Mary Carter, Elizabeth West and Lilian Ellis will be remembered. I left my tribute at the foot of their stone - some yellow and white flowers for my Barnbow Canaries.

What about the other girls? Will they be forgotten? No, because in York Minster I found a special memorial to women who gave their lives for their country. Listed there, under "Munition Workers" are all my Barnbow girls. Wonderful! And the famous Five Sisters window nearby was beautifully restored and then rededicated by the Duchess of York in 1925, in memory of 1,400 women who gave their lives during World War I.

So was my search fruitless? Instead of finding a mass grave to which my taxi driver, Bob, could take his flowers, I had found that most of our girls were buried privately by their families, in Leeds, York, Kippax, Pontefract, Harrogate and Normanton. A waste of time then? Certainly not. Owing I hope in part to the interest I had stirred

up in the press, on radio and elsewhere, something wonderful happened.

On Remembrance Day, in November 2002, the Royal Armouries at Leeds held a special service for my Barnbow Canaries. Two young girls in Barnbow overalls and mobcaps laid a wreath of yellow and white flowers in the shape of the Barnbow badge. I stood, with a lump in my throat, with Bob and his wife beside me, as the familiar names of my girls were read out and poppies fell at each name.

Then came the almost unbearable 11th hour silence as more poppies fell, followed by the haunting notes of the Last Post. I gave a tremulous but contented sigh. My girls had been honoured at last, and the sacrifice they had made, for King and Country, had been recognised .

In the words of the Archbishop of York at the dedication of their window in York Minster in

1925, I prayed, "Grant them, 0 Lord, eternal rest, and let perpetual light shine upon them."

Anne's three books are still available from 34 Bancroft Heights Leeds LS14 1HP
A Batchelor's Delight £9.10 inc p & p
My Gallant Hussar £4.25 inc p&p
My Name is Frances £10.10 inc p&p

Children of the Hulks
Jill Chambers

In 1823 all the adult prisoners on the Bellerophon were transferred to other hulks, and the ship, which lay in the harbour at Sheerness, was to be used exclusively for boy convicts. Until that time boys had been housed along with the adult prisoners on board the hulks. The Bellerophon was the 74-gun man-of-war in which Napoleon was brought to England after his defeat at Waterloo, and had been remodelled by the Navy for use as a prison hulk. The Bellerophon was equipped with forty separate housing bays in her under decks, each suitable for eight or ten prisoners. There were secure central corridors for patrol by the one guard assigned below decks duty during the night. It would appear that there was no attempt made to classify the boys, the smaller, weaker boys living alongside the stronger, more aggressive boys. All the boys were assigned to work on board. John Steadman was assigned as overseer of the hulk and the Reverend Edward Edwards was the Chaplain.

On the 19th February 1823 16 boys were received on board the Bellerophon from the Justitia hulk. The youngest was ten year old William Murphy who had been found guilty of Felony at Salford on the 22nd October 1821, and sentenced to seven years transportation. Twelve year old William Donald was tried at Middlesex on the 11th April 1821, also for Felony, and sentenced to transportation for life. A note next to his name says that he was discharged 2nd March 1823 per Countess Harcourt to New South Wales.

On the 14th April 1823 fifty six boys from the Retribution hulk were received on board, they included fifteen year old James Brown who had been found guilty of Mobbing & Rioting at Glasgow on 25th April 1822 and sentenced to 14 years transportation. He did not stay long on the Bellerophon as in the 'How & When Disposed of' column it says he was discharged 23rd July 1823 per the Sir Godfrey Webster, NSW.

Over the following months boys continued to be transferred from other hulks, Newgate, and Horsemonger Lane to the Bellerophon. On the 9th November three boys arrived from Ilchester Gaol in Somerset. They were James Carter, age 12, Charles Haines age 16 and 15 year old Charles Old. All three had been tried for Grand Larceny at Taunton on the 13th October 1823, and sentenced to 7 years transportation. A little less than two years later Charles Haines was on board the Medway on his way to Van Diemans Land.

In his report, dated 24th July 1823, John Capper stated,

"In obedience to your command and in reference to my former Report upon the subject of Juvenile Offenders, I have now to observe, that the whole of the Boys have been brought from the several Depots to the Bellerophon, where they are fully occupied in carrying on various branches of trades; and I have the satisfaction to report, that the arrangements which I had the honour to submit to you for their future government and employment, have been effectively carried into execution."

In the same Report, dated 22nd January 1824 he adds, "Since my former Report upon the measures which I have taken in obedience to your orders for appropriating the Bellerophon Hulk into a Prison Ship, exclusively for the Boys under sentence of Transportation, they were collected together from the other Depots, and have for the last eight months been employed in making clothing, and various other articles for the Convict Establishment.

The number of Boys at present confined in that ship, amounts to 320, the greater part of whom are under fourteen years of age; they naturally require strict attention; but by keeping them fully occupied little opportunity has offered from them to depart from regulations laid down for their government; and considering them as Boys left in early infancy to pursue the most vicious courses. I may safely state that their behaviour has been much better than I had anticipated."

On the 1st July 1824, the hulk Chaplain, the Reverend Edward Edwards, had reported to Mr Capper that,

"The boys on board this Ship have, generally, made a considerable progress in their several Trades;

their propensity to lying is, however, I am sorry to say, such, that scarce any confidence can be placed in any thing they say. From the first day of the passing of the year to the present, seven hundred and eighty-five chapters of Holy Writ, averaging about twenty-three verses, have been committed to memory. Out of the three hundred and fifty (the number now on board), a hundred and forty-four repeat the Church Catechism from time to time; thirty-one, the Thirty-nine Articles of Religion; very many of the remainder are yet incapable of reading, not knowing the alphabet when they were brought here. Amongst these are many who are very dull, and others are reluctant. During Devine Service, owing to very strict vigilance kept up, they conduct themselves very well. Thanks are due and are hereby given to the Commanding Officer, and others acting under his express directions, for constant co-operation."

By the end of 1825 the boys on the Bellerophon had been transferred to a new addition to the hulk fleet, the Euryalus, a smaller vessel that had been "specially fitted for them" and situated at Chatham, ten miles up the River Medway, and the Reverend Thomas Price was appointed Chaplain.

The quarterly hulk register for the quarter covering the 1st October and 1st of December 1825 is signed by Samuel Owen.

"I Samuel Owen, late Overseer of the Bellerophon Hulk at Sheerness, now of the Euryalus, Chatham, make Oath, that the above Return contains the name of every person now confined on board the said Hulk, Euryalus, the Offence of which he was guilty, the Court before which he was Convicted & the Sentence of such Court, together with his age & bodily state, his behaviour whilst in Custody, & of such Offenders as had died whilst in Custody, or have escaped, or have been lawfully discharged from the said Hulks, between the first of October & thirty first of December 1825, both inclusive."

At this time we learn that were 11 adults on board, ranging in age from 49 year old William Wright, sentenced to seven years for Grand Larceny at Sandwich on 27th December 1821, and 'lent to the Dolphin 3rd Oct & discharged therefrom 26th November 1825 per Free Pardon', and 17 year old George James, sentenced to transportation for life for Highway Robbery at Shrewsbury 20th March 1822, who was discharged 23rd November 1825 per Woodman, NSW. The names of 410 boys are listed - the youngest appear to be eight and the oldest 17. During this period a number of the older boys were removed to other hulks, some were sent to New South Wales on board the Woodman, at least two were discharged with a Free Pardon and a similar number had their sentence mitigated to a short term of imprisonment. Only one death is reported, that of 13 year old Thomas Beeching, sentenced to seven years for Felony at Maidstone on the 29th March 1825, and 'Died 23rd Dec 1825 at 4 a.m. on board the Canada Hospital Ship'. We also learn that 9 year old John Scott is a very good little Boy, 14 year old Edward Partridge is rather idle and very little improved, and 12 year old James Knox is noisy & artful.

On 26th July 1826, the Reverend Price submitted his first Report, after taking over as Chaplain on the Euryalus.

"In consequence of my removal from the Retribution, Adult Convict Ship, at Sheerness, to the Euryalus of this place, my services are transferred to the exclusive charge of Juvenile Convicts. Upon entering this new scene of labour, it was represented to me, that whatever might be effected with adult Prisoners, yet such was the depravity of the Boys, that every attempt to moralize them would only terminate in disappointment. I found much reason for the remark. My confidence, however, was not to be overcome, and the last six months attention to them has fully convinced me, that by the removal of some impediments great good might here also be effected.

It must be borne in remembrance, that these poor children are taken out of our streets, not only deplorably ignorant of all religious knowledge, but with habits opposed to every moral and social restraint; and nothing can operate so sufficiently as an auxiliary to my instructions in correcting this evil, as a careful separation, and the adoption of an effective classification, which, I lament to state, cannot possibly be accomplished, on account of the inadequate size of the ship for so great a number of delinquents.

There can be no question but that this branch of the Convict Department is of paramount importance, as the hopes of the future generation depend upon the care and culture of the present."

In the same Report, dated 26th July 1826, John Henry Capper said, "The Boys confined in the Euryalus Hulk at Chatham have been employed on board in making clothing and other articles for the Service. Scurvy and Opthalmia prevailed among them for a short time. But both of those disorders have been subdued."

The following January Mr Capper reported that there has been some trouble from the boys of the Euryalus and put it down to the size of the ship. "The Boys confined in the Euryalus Hulk have, upon two or three occasions, been refractory, and committed outrages on the persons of some of the Officers. The Ship in which they are confined is found too small to effect a proper classification, - a measure which is absolutely required for keeping them in a proper state of discipline."

In his reports the following year Chaplain Price continued to urge separation and classification if any sort of reform was to take place.

"To effect something more than an external decency of behaviour it is my most serious conviction that it is absolutely necessary not only that a plan of separation and classification should be adopted . . . but that these unfortunately neglected boys should be governed by persons competent to so highly important a charge; and in venturing to give this opinion I feel I am only discharging a duty I owe to the Government and the country. It is true that the exercise of power may restrain unruly dispositions, and the operation of sinister motives may produce a degree of obedience; but no permanent and radical reformation can ever be expected where the nature of mental and moral discipline is not understood, and as such, cannot possibly be adequately conducted."

Six months later he reported, "I feel I am under the necessity of further pressing upon your notice the subject of my last report, in which I expressed it as my full conviction that no permanent reformation can be effected among the juvenile prisoners confined on board the Euryalus but by their being separated and classified . . . and besides, that a more efficient system than at present be adopted for the better ensuring the improvement of their morals and furthering the object the Government had in view in placing them here. The great importance of the subject will, I trust, be duly considered and meet the attention it

deserves."

Shortly after this the Reverend Price was transferred to the Retribution at Sheerness, and his place taken by the Reverend Henry John Dawes.

It was reported in 1828 that the behaviour of the boys had improved after a substantial number of the more recalcitrant boys had been shipped out to Australia. Mr Capper made the same observation again in his Report dated 10th July 1834. "Since the reduction of the number of the Convict Boys, by Transportation of the elder ones, considerable improvement has manifested itself in the behaviour of the younger ones."

In 1835 a Select Committee was appointed to inquire into the 'Present State of Gaols and Houses of Correction in England and Wales.' The results of this inquiry give an insight into what life was like for the boys on the hulks in 1835, as the following extract shows.

"At Five o'clock in the Morning All Hands are called. Ports opened, Hammocks lowered and lashed up, the Boys washed and examined. At Half past Five a Signal is given to prepare for Chapel, when the Boys stand round in their respective Wards, after which they go in, headed by the older Boys of the Ward, who place them in their respective Seats with profound Silence: the Morning Hymn is sung, and Prayers read by the Schoolmaster; the Officers and a Portion of the Guards being present. After Prayers they return to their respective Wards and still in Ranks till the Breakfast is served down at Six o'clock, equally divided and examined by the Steward and others; he then desires the Boys on One Side of the Deck at a Time to go to their Table, hold up their Bread, give Thanks, and sit down. At half past Six the Boys commence coming on Deck, each elder Boy heading his Division, and his Deputy bringing up

the Rear. Hammocks stowed, Boys filed up into their respective Divisions by the elder Boy of their Ward, after which the Officer orders all elder Boys on the Quarter Deck for the Purpose of making known anything that might have occurred since their last Report, when each of their Complaints are noted down in order that they may be inquired into. The Boys return below, in a single File, to clean their respective Wards, with the exception of those who are appointed to wash the Main and Quarter Deck. At Eight o'clock the Boys are set to their respective Work, when Silence is observed. At Nine the elder Boys, accompanied by those of whom they complain, state their complaints to the Commander, when each correction is awarded as the Nature of their Offence deserves, i.e. by stopping their Dinners, or correcting them moderately with the Cane, or by Solitary Confinement on Bread and Water, not exceeding Seven Days; but should anything of Consequence occur during the Day it is immediately inquired into. At Twelve the Dinners are served down, under the inspection of the Steward; all Quarter-masters and Guard are in Attendance, for the Purpose of seeing that each Boy eats his proper Allowance. At Half past Twelve Boys sent on Deck for Air and Exercise, but not permitted to make the least Noise. At Half past One Boys filed up as in the Morning, and sent below to their respective Work. At Two a Division consisting of One Third of the Boys sent into the Chapel for the Afternoon, when they are taught reading and writing. At Five the Boys leave off Work, clean their Wards, and wash themselves. At Half past Five Supper is served down, after which the Boys come on Deck for Air and Exercise. At Half past Six the Boys file up as usual, and take their Hammocks down. At Seven the Signal is given to prepare for Chapel, when they proceed in, as in the Morning; after which a Portion of the Boys are catechised, the Evening Hymn sung, and Prayers read by the Schoolmaster. The Boys return to their respective Wards. At Eight the Signal is given to prepare for Muster, when each Boy stands with his Hammock placed before him, till the whole of them are mustered; the Signal is then given for them to hang up their Hammocks. At Nine profound Silence throughout the Ship; Boats secured, Fires extinguished, Locks examined by the Officer, and the Keys delivered up for the Night. The Watch, consisting of Two Guards, one of which is placed below, and the other on Deck, relieved every Three Hours and a Half, the Bell struck, and Alls well called every Half Hour through the Night. On Saturday the Boys are washed all over in tepid Water and Soap."

Although the House of Lords Committee recommended a reduction of the number of boys on the Euryalus and the eventual deactivation of the hulk it was a long time in coming. By July 1836 the number on board was down to 160, as priority had been given for a shipment of the older boys to Australia. By the July of 1839 the number had risen again, up to 190 and John Capper again asked for a vessel to be chartered for the transportation of the older boys. His request was granted. Over the next three years

between six and eight hundred boys left the Euryalus for Australia and around the same number were transferred to Parkhurst Prison, on the Isle of Wight. The last Quarterly Return for the Euryalus was for the Quarter ending 31st December 1843, during which time only 42 boys remained on the hulk. Most of the boys were transferred to the Fortitude Hulk during October, the last seven boys being transferred on the 7th November. Three boys John Edwards, George Long and Frederick Dell were sent to Millbank on the 29th October, and four boys, David Field, William Martin, William A Grantham and George Eade, were Pardoned between the 26th and the 31st October.

By the end of 1843 the Euryalus had been decommissioned and sent to the breakers yard. This did not mean an end to the transportation of young boys, but now many of them spent the first part of their sentence at Parkhurst, before being sent to Tasmania, Western Australia and New Zealand, as either an apprentice, emigrant, or in the case of the former places a transported convict.

References:
PRO HO9/7; HO8/7; HO8/78
Parliamentary Papers - Vol. XIX pages 137, 139, 143, 183, 185; Vol. XLX page 1
The Intolerable Hulks - Charles Cambell
The English Prison Hulks - W Branch Johnson
Artful Dodgers - Heather Shore

The House of Gournay
Gabriel Alington

The Record of the House of Gournay is the title of a book, an impressive title for a book of impressive length and weight: it takes strength to so much as lift it from the shelf. The Record, compiled in the 19th century by Daniel Gurney, tells the history of the Gournay family, or Gurney as the name became, from many centuries before the Norman Conquest to 1848 when it was printed.

The earliest known traceable Gournay ancestor is a warrior by the name of Eudes, either a Norman or a Dane, who acquired territory in Normandy. The land was a reward from his chieftain, Rollo, who having siezed the whole duchy of Normandy, divided his spoils between his followers. Eudes' share included Gournay en Bray, a small town between Rouen and Beauvais, as well as the Norman region of the Pays de Bray. This is fertile land threaded with rivers which, having been cleared and cultivated, would have provided a good living for Eudes and his kinsmen. Certainly they appear to have prospered so that in time, as the family grew, they were able to extend their territory. By the 11th century the descendants of Eudes were prominent among the landowning families of Normandy..

In 1066 Hugh de Gournay fought alongside Duke William at the Battle of Hastings. Like the early warlord, Rollo, Duke William rewarded his comrades with newly captured land. For Hugh de Gournay there were extensive areas of Norfolk and Suffolk with a number of castles and manors; there was also the honour of a barony. It was recognition well merited for Hugh de Gournay was no longer young and, though accompanied by his son and a party of kinsmen, the ordeal of battle must have been hard for an older man. Now, as the first Baron de Gournay, Hugh owned considerable territory on both sides of the Channel.

The East Anglian country, like the Pays de Bray, was ideal farming land so that, as in Normandy, the de Gournays thrived. The middle Ages was a time when agriculture expanded both in crop cultivation and husbandry, notably the farming of sheep and the production of wool. The wool trade brought great wealth to landowners in many parts of England but the Wool Fairs of East Anglia were major events attracting merchants from all over Europe. It would therefore be surprising if the de Gournays had not been part of this lucrative trade.

At the end of the 12th century the de Gurneys were united in marriage to another of landowning

families of Norman descent. Millicent, a daughter of the then Baron de Gournay, married William Cantilupe, who was seneschal, or steward, to the royal court. Their third son, Thomas, grew up to be one of the outstanding figures of his day. Thomas, a highly intelligent and studious boy, was destined for the church. As a priest he spent many years studying law and theology, became Chancellor of Oxford and then, increasingly involved in the government of the country, was appointed Chancellor of England. It was a controversial time when Simon de Montfort was leading the barons in their claim to take part in government, a rebellion culminating in the Baron's War against the all powerful monarchy. Although Thomas, who believed passionately in social justice was a Montfortian, his proven integrity, honesty and fairness meant that he was trusted by both sides. In 1275, ten years after the brief but bitter civil war, Thomas was elected Bishop of Hereford. His attempts to root out corruption from the church provoked fierce opposition, ill feeling, and rows. Worst were his relations with the Archbishop of Canterbury, a fiery character who, after increasingly acrimonious disputes, pronounced Thomas excommunicate. Devastated, Thomas travelled all the way to Italy to appeal to the Pope. While the case was being heard by the Curia, Thomas, already in poor health, became seriously ill; soon afterwards he died. But some 30 years later Thomas's reputation was redeemed for, after a long and detailed enquiry, Thomas was officially canonized. In 1320 Thomas Cantilupe was claimed as Saint Thomas of Hereford.

How proud his mother, Millicent would have been.

In 1204 King John who had ascended the English throne in 1199, lost the Duchy of Normandy to Philip Augustus. The 5th Baron de Gournay, also Hugh, was in a difficult position. With property in two kingdoms to which monarch should he swear allegiance?
For a time he wavered, switching at intervals from king to king till eventually he made up his mind and retired to East Anglia. Sadly his only

King John

surviving son left no heirs. And so, with the death of the 6th Baron de Gournay, the line became extinct.

Meanwhile a younger branch of the family who had inherited manors in Norfolk at Hardingham and Hingham from the elder line, still held fiefdoms (a feudal term denoting tenancy) in Normandy. What's more since Henry II's reign they had been gradually adding to their estates in both Norfolk and Suffolk through a number of judiciously arranged marriages. Then in 1661, as had happened in the early 13th century, the head of the family, Henry Gurney, died without a son. Nonetheless there were daughters to inherit the estates; there were also cousins.

One of them, John Gournay, born in 1655, earned his living as a cordwainer, or leather merchant, in Norwich, where, as the Record tells us, he realised a considerable fortune. It goes on to relate that John Gurney was 'so learned in the law as to be a provincial oracle to whom law questions were frequently submitted by members of Norwich Corporation.'

More controversially John was a Quaker. He had been converted in his youth at a time when the Society of Friends, founded in the 1640s, was denounced by the established church. Despite being imprisoned for three years, John remained faithful to his belief and married a Suffolk girl, Elizabeth Swanton, in a strictly Quaker marriage service. When he died, in 1721, he left a sizable fortune. Elizabeth died six years later.

John and Elizabeth's second son, also John, born in 1692, invested a large amount of his inherited wealth in a property that remained in the Gurney family for many generations. John was well into middle age when, in 1747, he bought Keswick near Norwich. He had married Hannah Middleton 34 years earlier so that by the time they and their family moved into their new home, there were grandchildren as well to fill the imposing red brick mansion and play in the gardens. It seems that John and Hannah were happy at Keswick for the Record tells as that in 1760 John died there 'in great peace', whether still in the Quaker faith of his parents is not clear. A grandson, Richard Gurney, added to the Keswick estate but then the upkeep of the

house became too much. The whole estate was sold. Today, sadly, Keswick is no longer a family home.

The Quaker connection crops up again in the succeeding generation. John Gurney, a wealthy banker who settled in Essex, was a member of the Society of Friends. Of his family, brought up in the same tradition, two became prominent among the Quaker reformers of the early 19th century. His daughter, Elizabeth, born in 1780, was married at twenty to a Quaker merchant; his name was Joseph Fry. While still young Elizabeth was taken to Newgate prison where she saw three hundred women, many with young children, crowded together in dreadful squalour. Appalled, she vowed to do her utmost to reform conditions for women prisoners. In 1817 she formed an association to promote this cause and with her brother, Joseph Gurney, complied a report setting out their ideas for prison reform. Though in 1828 her husband was declared bankrupt, Elizabeth worked on, travelling round Europe to study the treatment and conditions of women, not only in prison, and to campaign for their rights. The image of Elizabeth Fry, the Quaker lady in her plain grey dress and white cap became, justifiably, well known.

In Hannah's case it was through her husband that she played a part in social reform. Unlike her elder sister and brother, Joseph, Harriet Gurney's involvement in reform was through her husband, Thomas Fowell Buxton. Thomas Buxton, whose mother was a Quaker, was a brewer by trade. In 1818 he became MP for Weymouth, a seat he held until 1837. His main aim in life was, however, the abolition of slavery and in 1822 he joined William Wilberforce in campaigning towards that end. Two years later the elderly Wilberforce

retired as leader of the Anti-Slavery Campaign appointing Buxton in his place. Buxton went on to work for the freeing of slaves in the colonies, eventually persuading his fellow campaigners that the only fair way to achieve this was by paying the slave owners compensation.

Thomas Buxton died in 1845 and was buried in Overstrand church close to his Norfolk home. Later he was honoured with a memorial statue in Westminster Abbey. His only surviving son, Charles, wrote a biography of his distinguished father who, within the family, was known as the Liberator or the Emancipator. His grandson, Sydney, nicknamed him the Slave Driver.

Sydney Buxton's youngest daughter, Alethea, is the eldest surviving Gurney descendant. Born in 1910, Lady Alethea Eliot, as she now is, has clear memories of her childhood, of growing up in Sussex, of her countless relations and particularly of her father who was Governor General of South Africa during the First World War. As a small girl Alethea was bridesmaid to her two half sisters, Phyllis and Doreen. When planning her wedding to the Reverend Maurice Ponsonby, Phyllis decided that Alethea should represent the family link with the Society of Friends. So instead of the pretty bridesmaid's gown she had dreamed of, Alethea found herself wearing a Quaker dress, plain and grey, and a demure white cap. She was very disappointed, also very cross.

However when Doreen, married Charles Fitzroy, Alethea, to her great delight, wore the costume of a cavalier. Charles Fitzroy was descended from Charles II so for Alethea to resemble a Van Dyk portrait, seemed appropriate. It certainly suited the small cavalier.

Alethea married Peter Eliot, a solicitor who later joined the army and was then ordained. He became Archdeacon of Worcester and, having lived in the area for many years, Alethea and Peter decided to retire to nearby Herefordshire. And so they did in 1975 having four years earlier found a delightful house in a village in the north of the county.

From the beginning Alethea and Peter took an active part in village life and their appearance in the annual village pantomime, a highly entertaining song and dance act, became the star attraction. After Peter died in 1995, Alethea made a final appearance as the dowager empress in Aladdin. It was a swan song that raised the roof.

Alethea is proud of her Gurney ancestry and it delights her to know that she shares the family link with another special Herefordian. He was the son of Millicent de Gournay, Thomas Cantilupe, Saint Thomas of Hereford.

And what of the place where it all began, Gournay en Bray in Normandy? Today Gournay en Bray is a lively town with a flourishing dairy industry. For more than a century it supplied most of the cheese to the Paris and though today there is competition Gournay still produces an important share. It is particularly proud of its own speciality first made by a local farmer's wife in 1850. One day she tried mixing fresh cream with curds before it had been beaten rather than afterwards as was usual. The result, 'Petit Suisse' has been widely popular ever since. Indeed altogether the produce of Gournay en Bray has a fine record.

The same could be said of the family of that name.

Remote Access to the
Society of Genealogists Collections
Else Churchill

It very clear that not everyone finds it convenient to visit the Society's Library in Central London. Although situated in what Islington now likes to call its Genealogy Quarter near to the Family Record Centre and the London Metropolitan Archives only twenty percent of our members ever visit the Society of Genealogists each year and about 2,500 non members come to use the collections as temporary day searchers. The Society has always had a very limited postal search/copy service. The number of staff in the Library is very small and it relies heavily on volunteer members to help with much of the donkey-work involved in looking at indexes and finding aids and copying information. The Library will charge a fee for this, enabling the income to be ploughed back into creating yet more indexes and finding aids. This means that the Society is unable to look at un-indexed

materials such as the many original parish registers on fiche or film in the collection but if a particular collection is indexed, for example the Trinity House Petitions for aid made by the families of mariners or the Teachers Registration Council Indexes, then the Society of Genealogists has always been happy to examine the indexes and post on copies of relevant entries in the records (if found). However the postal search service itself isn't that heavily used and it is still quite time consuming at the Library end. The Society of Genealogists would find it difficult to service if even more people wanted to use it.

So the Society of Genealogists started thinking how it could make some of its unique collections and resources available to those who couldn't visit in person, but who could use the Internet. We know that over seventy five percent of our members have access to the Internet although not all of them use it for their genealogical research. Most were using their computers to look at data published on CD ROMs. Throughout the early nineties various companies had been making information available on electronic form, usually selling indexes or facsimiles of out of print but useful books in electronic form. The Society started thinking about access to its collections at the end of the 1990s when most people were trying to convince us that Internet was going to be the cure for every business's problems.

We certainly knew that the Internet had become a very popular tool used by genealogists but we felt that the reason our members were telling us that they weren't using it for their research was because they weren't finding much information on it. The Internet was becoming a great means of communicating with other family historians via email and to see who might be researching the same name or family as you. It could be used as a reference source to see where information and records might be found as all the record repositories launched web sites to describe their collections, to explain what they held and how the records might be accessed, giving details of opening times etc. Some record offices even made their catalogues available on line.

Gradually more and more useful data was being put in the web and this was well received by family historians. The Commonwealth Wargraves Commission and LDS Church launched their tremendous data bases on the Internet (with some technical problems I remember). The Pubic

Marriage Licence Allegation issued 11 September 1846 by the Archbishop of Canterbury's Faculty Office for the Marriage of Robert Browning to Elizabeth Barrett. The couple applied for a licence to marry at either St Paul Deptford or St Mary le Bone. The marriage actually took place at St Marylebone. Elizabeth returned home to Wimpole Street and left with her husband some weeks later.

Record Office (as it was then) announced it was going to make the images of the forthcoming 1901 census available on the Internet and provide a name index for the whole of England and Wales from January 2nd 2002! It was certainly becoming clearer that the Internet was one possible way of providing quality genealogical information. Perhaps, more significantly we had seen how the General Register Office for Scotland published its indexes of births, marriages and death and immediately made it easier for anyone to obtain copies of certificates away from Edinburgh. Significantly the GROS had provided a pay-per-view model that was reasonably inexpensive (especially when compared with the cost of travelling to Edinburgh) and quicker than the postal system. More importantly this system didn't seem to topple over with too many people using it from day one. So with only about 20 million records which would be added to as the system increased and a pay-per-view system that gave access to the index entries during a specified period, this model illustrated how the Society of Genealogists might approach putting some of its indexes on line.

There weren't that many companies who were working in the genealogical field at the time. Some were based in America but they hadn't been dealing with much British material.. Also the payment model was slightly different and it seemed unlikely that many British people would pay annual or quarterly subscriptions to a service where British data might be overwhelmed by all the American sources.

So this is how the situation looked in 1999 when the Society of Genealogists was looking for a partner who could help it take the first tentative steps to make some of its material available on-line. The Society had been using computers to generate some of its indexing projects and hence had some data in electronic form already that could go onto a web site. However most of the unique indexes had been collated and typed up well before the electronic age and these would need to be captured somehow. The Society of Genealogists cast about its library to decide which

were the indexes that would prove most popular and which could be the easiest to transfer onto a web site. Having made that decision it talked to various potential partners and decided that Origins.net, the company that had had a track record with British material and had developed the GROS site, would offer the best potential for the Society. So after a couple of years work finding a partner and preparing the indexes for publication in electronic form (which took a surprising amount of time) the Society of Genealogists launched its first Internet publishing venture in January 2000.

What's on Line?
The site www.englishorigins.net now contains over seven million names from some of the most significant finding aids held in the Society of Genealogists' Library. The indexes are known as

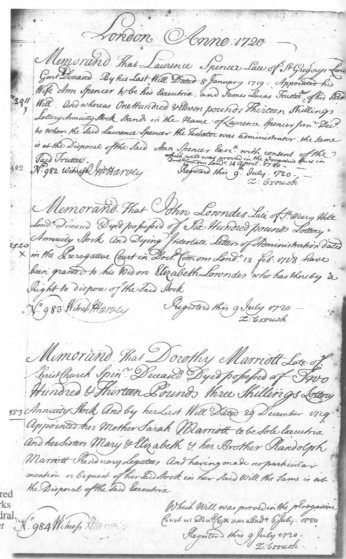

Bank of England Will Abstract relating to £111 13 shillings worth of annuity stock held by Lawrence Spencer as noted in his PCC will of 1719 and registered by the Bank in 1720. Lawrence was the Clerk of Works for Christopher Wren's rebuilding of St Paul's Cathedral. His family grave was excavated on the BBC tvs' *Meet the Ancestors* programme.

data sets and at the time of writing the site contains seven separate datasets as follows:

Boyd's Marriage 1538-1840 with over 6.4 million names
Marriage Licence Allegation Index 1694-1850 with 670,000
London City Apprenticeships Abstracts with over 300,000 names
Bank of England Wills Extracts 1717-1845 with 61,000 names
Prerogative Court of Canterbury Wills Index 1750-1800, 208,000 names
Archdeaconry of London Wills Index 1700-1807, 5000 names
London Consistory Court Depositions Index 1700-1713, 3,200 names

Work is ongoing to add more information, not only to the above data sets but to include other indexes. The London Apprentices include records from some 40 separate guilds and livery companies but now work has started on some of the larger companies with many thousands of records. To supplement this database we hope to shortly add the Society's Apprentices of Great Britain Index that includes details of the apprenticeships that were subject to tax for the period 1772-1774.

The Society of Genealogists has always intended to make records easier to use by producing name indexes and indeed has rescued records from destruction. The Bank of England collection of abstracts of wills that relate to the testator's possession of government stock would have been destroyed had the Society of Genealogists not taken them in. The original registers were housed and indexed over a very long period and eventually the full index covering the years 1717-1845 was produced on the website. The index entries on the data base provide enough information to obtain a copy of the will abstract which are on film at the Society of Genealogists' Library or if you can't get to London, you can order a copy of the abstract on-line via the website.

Boyd's Marriage is clearly well known, being the first attempt to index millions of marriages. Perhaps lesser known are his notes on over 60,000 London families called The Inhabitants of London which we hope to index and scan onto the website soon.

The Society had the opportunity to index the marriage licence allegations issued by the Archbishop of Canterbury's London Courts in Doctors Commons known as the Faculty Office and Vicar General. While there were strict rules that should have governed when a licence was to be issued by either court, in practice many Londoners went straight to these courts to obtain a licence and hence the Society's Marriage

Licence database has become an important source of information on London marriages. Again the index should give enough information to locate a copy of the allegation either at Lambeth Palace where the originals are held or from the films in the SoG's Library. However if you can't get to London then a copy can ordered via the website.

Work continues to capture more of the Society's unique indexes electronically so they can be accessed on line. The index to the Trinity House Petitions from families of mariners who were applying for alms, usually after the death of the mariner has been re-keyed and once checked should be available on the data base along with the chance to order copies of the petitions themselves.

How to access the data
The index entries have always been available on the site on pay per view basis. Significant improvements have been made to www.englishorigins.net, since it was launched. Anyone can check, free of charge, to see if the name they are interested in appears in anyone of the data sets. This will tell you how many times and name appears and in which indexes. Once you have established this you can then register to view the full entries. No charge is made until you actually select the entries you want to view and you only pay once however many times you look at a particular entry. Now anyone wanting to look at the entries on line can view up to 300 index entries within the seven-day viewing period on payment of £6. Origins are also introducing different access periods for subscribers who want to view more records over a longer period. We expect the new £10 rate for 14 days and 600 entries will prove very popular. The site itself is being redesigned and will be easier to use as more data sets are added. Occasionally you might wish to see the original record which may be fuller than the index entry. Hard copies of some of documents can be ordered via the website on payment of an extra copy/search fee of £10 per document. This means you can obtain a copy of the Bank of England Will Abstract, or Marriage Licence Allegation without travelling to London.

Members of the Society of Genealogists have the extra benefit of a free session on the database four times a year (once each calendar quarter). However any visitor to the Society's Library can, of course, view as many entries as they like, completely free of charge at the Society's Library. For as much as we want to make our collections available to as many people as possible who can't come to the library, we wouldn't want to drive anyone away!

$\mathcal{A}$ stitch in time saves nine:
the sampler as a record of family history
Dr Jane Batchelor

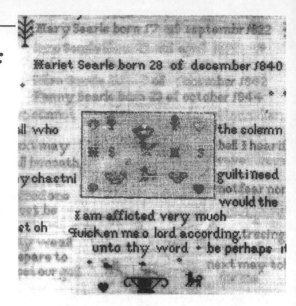

By this may I remembered be
When I should be forgotten
– Sampler, 1736 (Llewellyn, p.9).
The popularity of samplers today is most explained
by the fact that they make attractive pictures to
hang on people's wall. Samplers have long been
used for this purpose, but for the local and family
historian they can be much more than this;
samplers are pictures of the past, and looking at
them can tell us a lot about local and family
history. In this article I will be telling the story of
one sampler and what it can tell us about the
family to which it belonged. First of all however it
is useful to understand a bit more about why
samplers came about, and what they can tell us.

The History of the sampler in England
1 Convents and samplers
The word "sampler" is related to "sample" and this
is indeed what samplers originally were. On a
sampler women and young girls preparing for
adulthood would practice the sewing stitches that
they needed for marriage and for running a
household. In medieval times it was customary for
young noblewomen especially to be sent to
convents, where they would practice their
needlework skills with nuns skilled in
embroidering vestments (Toller, p. 11), and it
seems likely that the sampler originally arose out
of this practice.

2 The sixteenth-seventeenth centuries: samplers grow in popularity
To Thomas Fische for an elle of lynnyn (linen) cloth
For a sampler for the Queen. (Toller, p.11).
This early reference to a sampler shows the
importance that was attached to the sampler as a
means of practicing the desirable domestic skill of
needlework. By the mid sixteenth century however
it was not only queens and noblewomen who
understood the value of this skill. The new social
mobility meant that not only courtiers but
merchants could display their wealth on their
person, and in their house. Embroidery was in
demand for embroidered bed hangings, for
curtains, for gloves, scarves and hats – all of which
required a skilled needlewoman. It was usual for
each woman to make a pattern book filled with
stitches from family and friends, and using the
sampler, to sample these stitches by stitching them
on to linen. Again, not only women but young girls
would practice this skill. By the seventeenth
century samplers had become increasingly ornate
display items, incorporating flowers, animals, birds
and geometric designs, reflecting the status of the
family in which they were made.(Toller, pp 12-15).

3 The eighteenth century
Education
Youth like softened wax with ease will take
Those Images that first impressions make.
Mary Ferry, sampler, 1796 (Walker, p.10).
By the eighteenth century the idea of the sampler
as a means of educating "Youth" that is young
girls was well established. It became usual to
incorporate alphabets and improving moral verses
(Milne, p.15). Sometimes the name and age of the
needle-worker was included, but only if there was
room, as the improving nature of the work was
much more important that authorship (Toller,
p.16). It was also common to use the sampler to
record family events such as deaths and births.

4 Nineteenth century to present
Table napkins should not be marked in ink, but the
monograph worked in raised embroidery – Mrs
Beeton (1836 – 1865),
Every Day Cookery, p. 568.
The nineteenth century saw continued emphasis on
the educative value of the sampler as practicing
embroidery skills. 1820 – 1830 saw the decline of
the pictorial sampler, replaced by wordier versions
incorporating religious texts such as the Lord's
Prayer (Toller, p.31). The map sampler was
popular as it combined sewing and geography
together and so was very instructive; an attractive
version of a map sampler is reproduced in Milne's
Samplers. The advent of the sewing machine
however meant that hand sewing became less
important, which led to a decline in sampler
making. It would be a mistake however to assume
that the sampler's legacy, the legacy of women
doing needlework for the home has completely
disappeared. On the contrary, the ready availability
of designs in women's magazines such as the
napkin with stitched sequin strips (*Essentials*,
2001) and cross-stitched lavender bags (cross stitch
being a favoured filler stitch for samplers) (*Make
it*, Nov/Dec 2001), shows that this tradition is still
very much with us.

The rhyme on the sampler is typical of the moral theme which samplers tend to display. Whereas the list of the family evokes birth, the rhyme evokes death as an ever present cyclical event. Every family member is born; every family member must die, united in death as in birth, for this is God's will "We cannot tell who next may fall", "One must be first so may we all prepare to meet our god". A sampler is a personal thing, and death affects the maker of the sampler personally, whence the move away from "we" to the first person "I" – "I am afflicted very much". "Afflicted" is an ambiguous phrase, it could suggest that the maker of the sampler is grief-stricken, or it could suggest that she is sick, and may "Quicken" to death; for in God's world paradoxically death is life, as it symbolises rebirth, saving her from life's sins "I need not fear." Yet death is an ever present fact from which she cannot escape; now she hears the solemn bell, but later the bell may toll for her The words she quickly sews are the evidence of her skill, her life, her family's life and her inexorable progress towards death, the afterlife.

In fact, by listing her family's name the needle-worker literally brings her family to life again. This is because it is not often that the family historian has a chance to see a whole family listed together. Usually the problem is that you may start with one name or two names and then have to go and connect them with other names. Maybe Sarah Brown and Mary Brown are connected but there are hundreds of people with the same name; even if you do have a date of birth the connection is a tenuous one. However, if Sarah and Mary appear on the same sampler there is something to connect them together, and if you have their dates of birth as well you have the makings of a family tree.

Tracing a family through a sampler

Samplers may have followed traditional patterns or moral themes, but they were also very individual. Since they often give the age of the person doing the work or commemorate family members they can be used to trace what has happened to that person or that family. If for example you know a girl is ten in 1770 then her birth date must be 1760, and you can search for her birth certificate. Equally birth dates, marriage dates and death dates are sometimes given in samplers.

The Searle sampler:
a mid nineteenth century sampler

The sampler reproduced in the photograph has been done by a member of the Searle family and lists the dates of birth of all the family members:

Henary Searle born 26 of december 1818
Mary Searle born 17 of september 1822
Jane Searle born 28 of april 1839
Harriet Searle born 28 december 1840
Ellen Searle born 2 december 1842
Fanny Searle born 23 of October 1844

The names Henary Searle and Harriet Searle are picked out in darker stitch, possibly highlighting on this relationship. Underneath the names is a sober moral rhyme:

We cannot tell who next may fall
Beneath thy chastening rod.
One must be first so may we all prepare to meet our god.
I am afflicted very much
Quicken me o lord unto thy word
Then when the solemn bell I hear, if saved from guilt, I need not fear.
Would the thought distressing be perhaps it next may Toll for me.

What I did with the Searle family is to look up their details on the British Isles Vital Records CD-Rom which is held at the Public Records Office at Kew. I searched for their names and produced the following results:

Henry (Henary) Searle

Henry Searle married Mary Ann Aptead (the Mary Searle on the sampler) on 12 February 1839, when he was twenty and she was seventeen. His father's name was Henry Searle, so it is probable that he was named after him.

Mary Anne (Ann) Searle (maiden name Aptead)

Mary Anne was christened on the 13 October 1822, a month after the date given on the sampler as her birth date. Her father's name was William, and her mother's name was Ellen.

Harriet Searle

Eliza Harriet Searle was christened on 24 January 1841, about a month after the birthdate given on the sampler. Her father is listed as Henry and her mother as Mary Ann, so she is clearly their daughter.

Searle Family Tree

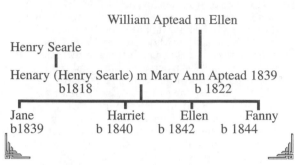

William Aptead m Ellen

Henry Searle

Henary (Henry Searle) m Mary Ann Aptead 1839
b1818   b 1822

Jane   Harriet   Ellen   Fanny
b1839   b 1840   b 1842   b 1844

Eleanor Mary Ann (Ellen) Searle
Eleanor Mary Ann Searle was christened on 8 January 1843, about a month after the birthdate given on the sampler. Her father is Henry and her mother is Mary Ann, so she is clearly their daughter and, in all likelihood, the younger sister of Harriet Searle. The fact that the sampler lists her name as Ellen suggests she was named after her grandmother Ellen.

Fanny Searle
Fanny was christened on 24 November 1844, a month after the birthdate given on the sampler. She too is Henry and Mary's daughter, and appears to be the youngest child.

Jane Searle
I do not have a record for Jane at present. As the sampler is accurate in other respects it seems reasonable to assume that Jane was indeed born in April 1839. Her age tallies with her sisters, and she appears to be the eldest child.

To sum up, from following the clues given in the sampler I have managed to confirm that the names listed there most probably consist of a father, a mother and four daughters. Thus, the dark stitching of Henry and Harriet Searle could be specifically emphasising this father/daughter relationship. It seems possible that the sampler is commemorating a family event, but it is not clear whether it is a birth or a death. The lists of names being born suggests a birth, but the sober text could suggest a death, whether of Henry or the impending death of a daughter (Harriet?). As stated earlier this confusion could be deliberate, in a world that did not make the modern day distinction between birth and death, but saw both more as part of God's cycle of creation, destruction and rebirth. Whatever the case, the lists of births on the sampler gives extra credence to the historical records that all these people were related, while the repetition of names emphasises the close family ties which the sampler presents.

This is as far as I have gone with the research on this sampler, however the next stage would be to visit the church or record office listed on the CD to confirm the information, and obtain Parish Registry certificates, which might tell me more about the family, where they lived and what they did. In the case of the Searle family all the records are listed at Sussex which suggests that they may have some connection with this area, so it would be necessary to visit Sussex records centre. Since I know now the names of Mary's mother and Henry's father it would be possible to trace the family back even further. The marriage certificate of Mary and Henry is likely to list his occupation, which could tell me more about the life which they led.

All this from a piece of decorative needlework which is much more than it seems.

In conclusion, today in the age of the sewing machine the decorative needlework which the sampler represents is often seen as simply a relaxing hobby. However, this is to deny the crucial importance that the sampler had as a way of displaying the skill and provenance of those who were involved in creating it. The sampler for women historically was as much a display of skill as writing a sonnet was for a Renaissance courtier, displaying the education and family connections of the creator, signalling her status in a socially acceptable way.

As much as a family bible in which family history was traditionally written a sampler frequently provides a tangible written record, a snapshot if you like, of a particular family at a particular time. Samplers are not just pretty things to hang on our walls; they are, quite literally, the fabric of our past lives, and any local or family researcher neglects them at his or her peril.

Select Bibliography
Mrs Beeton, *Every Day Cookery* (2[nd]edn, Ward, Lock & Co Ltd, London and Melbourne [n.d.]) the household section provides an interesting glimpse into the importance of domestic needlework.
Nigel Llewellyn, *The Art of Death: Visual Culture in the English Death Ritual c.1500 – c. 1800* (Victoria and Albert Museum, London, 1991) a fascinating work on the depiction of death through the ages, which makes mention of the sampler as emphasising death as an ever present theme in life and art (pp. 9 – 12).
Julia Milne, *Samplers How to Create Your Own Designs* (Quintet Publishing, London, 1989) – a book about creating your own traditional sampler. History of sampler at front and some striking pictures of map samplers.
Jane Toller, *British Samplers: A Concise History* (Phillimore, Sussex, 1980) – a comprehensive history of the sampler in England, also contains information on American and Welsh Samplers.
Jeannie Walker, *Creative Embroidery* – a lively modern embroidery book. There are some nice illustrations of traditional samplers at the front. (New Holland, London, 1989).

YORKSHIRE ANCESTORS.COM

Visit the Yorkshire Family History Research Centre with Accommodation

Located in the pretty village of Ebberston, with its stone cottages and running stream, between Pickering and Scarborough, North Yorkshire, England. Studley House Farm is an ideal location for a vacation—with easy access to York, the moors, the wolds and the coast

Stay for the day, overnight or longer

We offer en-suite Bed & Breakfast in our lovely Victorian farmhouse,
self-catering in Cow Pasture Cottage or wheelchair friendly Swallowtail Cottage
and facilities for 8 caravans, motorhomes or tents in the old apple orchard.

Day visitors welcome, by appointment

Our new, purpose built, Yorkshire Family History Research Library is small but very well equipped and is equally useful to the newly addicted researcher or experienced genealogist

We have a very good coverage of 1841-1901 census for Yorkshire, National 1881 census, hundreds of Yorkshire census indexes for 1851, 1861, 1891 & 1901. £5 Vouchers for 1901 census online on sale here. Marriages, M.I.'s, Hearth Tax, Burials, Wills indexes. A huge collection of Trade Directories, Parish Registers, Local Histories, Specialist books for Family Historians, Internet access & much, much more.

Many of the Trade Directories, Parish Registers & other useful books from our library have been put on CD and are now available for purchase.

Some of the books available on CD-Rom:

Criminal Chronology of York Castle, Yorkshire Place Names in Domesday Book 1086, Scarborough Guides, Hovingham Parish Magazines, York Municipal Records 14th—16th Centuries, Bridlington Charters, Flamborough Parish Magazines, Yorkshire Wit & Character, 1838 Guide to the City of York, Admissions Book of Leeds Grammar School 1820-1900, Rural Economy of Yorkshire, Historia Rievallensis, 1829 History of Scalby, Burniston & Cloughton, Whitby & It's Shipping 1717-1900, Yorkshire Landowners 1871, Parish Registers of Calverley, Topcliffe & Morley, Whitkirk, Ingleby Greenhow, Adel, Lost Towns of the Yorkshire Coast, 1904 Phone Book Northern Section, Poll Books of West Yorkshire 1848, East Yorkshire (Beverley) 1868-9, Leeds & Borough 1868, A List of Roman Catholics in the County of York in 1604, Biographies of John Richardson 1666–1753 — Quaker of North Yorkshire, Thomas Langton - 19th Century Evangelist, a selection of Trade & Post Office Directories from 1798 to 1909 and more. See our website for new titles.

Contact Brenda Green for brochure

Studley House Farm, Main Street, Ebberston, SCARBOROUGH, YO13 9NR
Phone: 01723 859285, Email: brenda@yorkshireancestors.com or
VISIT OUR WEBSITE: www.yorkshireancestors.com

Two Master Mariners in the Family
A Work in Progress
Len Barnett

"Pressganged"

As a freelance maritime researcher I am not infrequently contacted by potential clients convinced that their forebears were not only 'master mariners', but also great adventurers. Unfortunately, in a significant percentage of cases the mariners prove not to have been masters at all, or if they were, that family stories cannot be confirmed in any way. It was in this manner that I approached one past commission. The initial information was sketchy, but concerned two men, father and son who were said to have both been master mariners. While there was no trace of the father in the surviving records pertaining directly to mercantile service, the son was found easily enough: though there was a particularly significant gap in information recorded on him. Some missing elements have subsequently been found purely by expending considerable time and effort in careful examination of documents; through the kind aid of one expert known to me in the United States of America; and also, happily by artefacts uncovered within this client's family. Apart from his naval service during the Napoleonic Wars, most of the elder man's time at sea is still unknown and in all likelihood will remain so. However, the family stories about the son can now be seen, at least in part, as grounded in hard fact.

This article outlines their interesting careers as far as is currently known, mentioning classes of records that may not necessarily normally be drawn on by those researching merchant mariners. Although tackled in a very different order, this is related chronologically.

The Father
Bristol born Robert Roche was pressed into the

naval service of King George III on 8th September 1808. Very briefly aboard a 'slops' (clothes) vessel named *Ceres*, then permanently anchored in the Great Nore, on the 13th he began his time on His Majesty's gun-brig *Gallant*. He remained one of her company for almost seven years.

When *Gallant* was ready to engage in warlike operations soon after, these included convoying merchantmen to and from the Baltic Sea and in support of the trade blockade through stopping and searching freighters. At times there were large numbers of 'supernumeraries' onboard, including prisoners, which would seem to indicate other roles also.

Immediately rated able seaman, the twenty-two year old must have had previous maritime experience: though whether aboard merchantmen or other men-o-war cannot be ascertained. Most of the crew had similarly been newly pressed and in the following months there was a steady trickle that ran (deserted). When she began operating from Leith, on the Forth, a significantly higher number disappeared. In turn Scots replacements came and went.

Young Robert Roach (as incorrectly entered into muster books) was obviously regarded as reliable. A year later he was rated the captain of the foretop, giving him a slightly increased pay (as of a quartermaster's mate). In August 1810 he was made the quartermaster. This was a petty officer's rate and on such a small vessel was a responsible position. Among his duties would have been directing *Gallant*'s steerage; and stowage of ballast and provisions (relating to her trim). After almost four years of this he became a midshipman. This was also a petty officer's rate and although many were by this era 'young gentlemen', many others were not. This was a stepping stone, either to a commission, or, alternatively to some warranted ranks. Whether a lieutenancy was his aim, or not, on 17th May 1815 he was appointed *Gallant*'s acting master. He remained in this capacity, as a warrant officer until she paid off at Woolwich on the 11th September that same year. As master he was the navigator and though not necessarily regarded as a gentleman, in a small vessel was second only in status and pay to the commander: who was a lieutenant. In this case there were only three officers on the ship's book. The third, also holding a warrant, was the surgeon.

There is little doubt that Robert Roach's wartime promotion was more than respectable, possibly in part due to the nature of life onboard 'small ships'. Post war, he was part of the ninety percent of the Monarch's Navy demobilised and his experience should have stood him in good stead in getting mercantile work. It is thought he was the master of a brig named the *Packet of Hull* in 1824, but this cannot be verified. (Unlike in the Royal Navy, masters in merchant service were and remain those in command and not just responsible for navigation.) In 1832 he began an association with the Trinity House, as a pilot for the Humber. In the mid 1840s he was a steward, though apparently went no further.

Entries in *Gallant*'s muster books gave the bones of Mr. Roach's naval time above and there is much fascinating information that can be gleaned from this class of records. As an example, it would seem that Robert Roach paid for his midshipman's uniform over a six-month period. Incidentally, only commissioned officers and midshipmen then wore uniforms, though as

master he would have been required to furnish his own charts and navigating instruments. Rather than Admiralty editions, in all likelihood these charts would have been commercially produced, either as atlases, or the new 'bluebacks'.

Even for minor vessels such as *Gallant*, captains' and masters' logs can be very detailed, giving lots of operational and navigational information, though a good knowledge of seamanship is needed to get the best out of these records. And, with the Royal Navy even then being greatly bureaucratic, all sorts of other lists, accounts and registers survive, allowing potentially for considerable research possibilities. Again a wider understanding of naval administration helps study of these documents.

But, there is an inherent weakness inasmuch as service sheets in the modern sense did not then exist: although certificates of service were put together in some circumstances as of 1802. Of course, the careers of commissioned officers and some warrant officers can be traced easily enough, via *Steel's Original and Correct List of the Royal Navy and Honourable East-India Company's Shipping*, but for the majority who formed 'the people' if one does not have ships' names and approximate dates onboard, investigation is simply not a realistic proposition. All these above mentioned naval records are to be found as part of the National Archives, formerly the Public Records Office, at Kew, Surrey.

The Son
Anyway, retaining the changed surname Roach, his son also named Robert went to sea in 1857 as a fourteen-year-old apprentice. Trading to the Baltic and Burma on the Hull registered barque

Hull Docks

Indian, he only completed three years eight months of his five years apprenticeship. Instead, he became mate on another barque, the *Free Trader*, for a return voyage from Burma to the United Kingdom. Excepting a few months as second mate of a coastal schooner named the *Albatross*, the next few years were to form the beginning of a long association with Hull steamship owners named Brownlow and Lumsden. Initially there was a year as second mate on the *Nautilus*, latterly with ten days as mate of the *Falcon* in November 1862.

The above has been drawn from the normally used Board of Trade and associated documents, in this case largely Mr. Roach's application forms for professional certification. When later applying for examination as master there was a gap in his service from January 1863 (when he qualified for mate) until February 1865. But, there was an accompanying letter whereby he maintained that his certificate had been 'destroyed by Rats' on a vessel travelling from London to Bermuda. Initially the vessel's name was not entirely clear, but was subsequently identified as the *Don*. She was a London-built fast steamship, constructed specifically to run the blockade imposed by the United States Government on rebelling southern states, during the American Civil War. Sailing in July 1863 for Nassau, New Providence, the 'office' copy of her articles show Mr. Roach had signed on as her second mate.

As she never returned to British waters other sources were required to take this further. A massive undertaking known as the *Official Records of the Union and Confederate Navies in the War of the Rebellion* was checked. This gave particularly good information on the runner's capture by Northern forces in March 1864. Incidentally, this publication can be found in

facsimile form in the 'making of America' section of Cornwell University's website (at http://cdl.library.cornell.edu/moa/). Next British Foreign Office records, in the National Archives at Kew, were consulted and proved of considerable use. This showed that there were *very* high level diplomatic exchanges over this and other similar affairs concerning British subjects. Not only was the Foreign Secretary, Lord Russell, personally involved, Queen Victoria also saw some of these papers. From photographic evidence Mr. Roach is thought still to have been onboard in December 1863 and it is highly probable that he remained as her second officer with two changes of command. As U.S. sources have maintained that these particular officers used false names on capture, at the stage of writing it has not yet been established conclusively whether he was one of her number briefly imprisoned in Fort Warren, Boston: before ejection from the United States as undesirable aliens later in the month. However, this would seem to be unlikely and probably was released very soon after capture (though when and where is not yet clear).

Until recently this still left an eight-month gap. It was assumed that he returned to Nassau, but in spite of some Bahamian newspapers (at the National Newspaper Library, Colindale) giving details of passengers landed, no comment was apparently made for men late of the *Don*: though there was an interesting editorial on her capture. However, an obituary found elsewhere gave another hint. This told a tale of derring-do, in almost escaping from the Yankees after detention, but this simply did not fit with the known information on the *Don*. But, another vessel was mentioned - the *Alliance*. Although this cannot be confirmed as yet, it would seem that on return to Nassau, our man took command of this brand new steamer, which had been built locally. It may be that he had a financial interest in her, but the obituary claim of being her owner would seem to be dubious. One contemporaneous study reckoned that the average building costs of such blockade-running steamers were around $100,000 per vessel. Anyway, attempting to run into Wilmington, she went aground during the night of 11th April 1864, was captured the following day and sent off as a prize to Boston. This vessel certainly did *not* make a profit for her owners.

1860 Barque Merchantman

By late November Robert Roach was back in the United Kingdom, as he applied for a replacement first mate's certificate at Hull.

Bearing in mind his exploits I had not taken seriously the claim that his 'ticket' had been a meal for rats. However, found recently among family papers was this very document - badly gnawed.

That was not the end of his involvement in blockade running either. The relevant crew list for the *Louisa Ann Fanny* confirmed him as mate, joining in February 1865 in London. Correspondence in more British Foreign Office files (again at Kew) show that she was the subject of U.S. diplomatic petitions. Although not a privateer, as claimed by Washington's diplomats in London, she was another newly built fast steamer, of considerable size and as such not liable to any constraint by the British authorities. Nevertheless, on instructions from Whitehall the British governors at Bermuda and the Bahamas kept a watch on her activities. With the war going so badly for the Confederacy, it would seem from the few details to hand that the *Louisa Ann Fanny* did not attempt to run into Charleston: the last port open after the fall of Wilmington. Instead, and particularly because of her large size, she may well have transported considerable quantities of goods including arms to neutral Matamoros, just over the Mexican border. Although adding greatly to the distance, this became an important and increasingly essential link in the Confederacy's supply chain. Anyway, with the South's final surrender in April 1865 the *Louisa Ann Fanny* returned to Liverpool in May, via Bermuda.

It is said that Robert Roach made two fortunes and lost them both. Certainly there was adequate scope for making fabulous sums of money in blockade running. While shipowners, managers and brokers undoubtedly made the *real* money, one source reckoned at the height of these activities that a mate could make $1,250 (in gold or U.S. dollars) per successful trip. Not bad for an average of about ten days from start to finish. Masters apparently did *even* better, at a cool $5,000 per undertaking. As officers were also allowed limited space for cotton bales on their own personal accounts, they would have earned

more still. With such profits, mariners would have had stakes for others' speculative ventures, although there was the very real risk of losing such money gambled: especially as the Northern naval blockade became far more effective as the war went on. And, perhaps not unnaturally, there were also *very* expensive diversions for the mariners to squander their earnings on: both within the Confederacy and also at the *entrepôts*.

Less than a month and a half after arriving back at Liverpool, Mr. Roach became mate of a Hull registered coaster named the *Prince* for a few months. This alone would appear to indicate that he had not returned a rich man. After a further half year on the *Falcon* once again, he passed for master mariner: though on his second attempt.

His subsequent career until 1888 was closely related to the steamer lines of Hull. A whole series of commands followed and while there were a few minor scrapes, he managed to shrug these off. The shipowner Lumsden disappeared off the scene (since he died), while another named Marsdin as partner of Brownlow replaced him. In turn they were taken over by the famous Wilson Line. Most of Mr. Roach's voyages were either coastal (across to Belgium and western Germany), or short-sea (to the Baltic or the Mediterranean). However, there were occasional trips further afield.

Like his father, he also had links with Trinity House, becoming a pilot in 1866. He progressed much further, becoming the Commodore for the Humber in 1889. (While the main Trinity House collection is held at the Guildhall Library, in the City of London, two outports' records are held locally. One of these is the Humber, the other being that of the Tyne.)

Then there were other adventures. Recently, through *Lloyd's Register of Shipping*, the command of two steam-yachts named the *Argonaut* and the *Ceylon* for a decade between the mid 1890s and 1900s has just been substantiated. With such a full life, apparently there was also a fruit-growing experiment in

California and this can only have been fitted in either in the early 1890s, or in the last ten years or so of his life. (He died in 1916.) As well as this, it may be that Captain Roach had an association with Sir Donald Currie (of the well-known Castle Line) in his early dealings in South Africa. It is thought that this was in the 1870s, while in command of the *Marsdin*. His obituary stated he was also a freemason.

So much for past research, potentially there is much more to be found. The British Foreign Office records so far examined have been specific cases related to the American Civil War and these are filed as one single class (FO 5). But the normal official correspondence, in this case to and from Bermuda and Nassau, *may* well hold more information. There was much routine contact between British merchant ships' masters and their nation's official representatives abroad though. Surviving Colonial and Foreign Office records not infrequently contain mentions of freighters and men: often relating to disputes.

Investigation of the United States' National Archives may, or may not, be realistic from the eastern side of the Atlantic Ocean. This is something the author is presently making forays into. Potentially Boston's Prize Court records for the cases of the *Don* and the *Alliance* could yield useful results. It would be interesting to know whether Robert Roach was in the infamous Fort Warren, as claimed in his obituary. Certainly there are listings of thousands of official records pertaining to naval aspects of this conflict on the U.S. government's national archives' website.

Similarly, looking into the potential links with Sir Donald Currie may, or may not prove possible. Judging from initial searches few corporate papers appear to exist, though there are some at the National Maritime Museum, Greenwich and the British Library, London. However, it is sometimes surprising where documents can be found, so more may well turn up out of the blue elsewhere. The ownership of the two as yet un-researched yachts may also prove interesting.

I would welcome any authoritative information from readers, especially on the detailed workings of the particular civil war blockade-runners mentioned. Incidentally there is a little information on Robert Roach and his association with the *Don* within my guide on researching merchant mariners at http://www.barnettresearch.freeserve.co.uk on the page dealing with crew lists. And, I can be contacted by e-mail at lenny@barnettresearch.freeserve.co.uk .
© Len Barnett 2003

Leases and Rental Surveys ~ Their Relevance to Family Historians
Jill Groves

This article uses three-life leases and rental surveys from Northenden and Etchells in North-east Cheshire.

Introduction
The estate records of Northenden and Etchells from 1648 to 1760 are very complete and give a detailed picture of tenants and tenancies. In fact, the evidence is such that it is possible to trace the history of over 120 tenements from 1648 to 1733 and a further fifteen of these to 1820, through changes of tenant families, changes in ownership and even changes in size.[1]

Three-lives leases or customary leases were the most common type of lease until the eighteenth century. Tenants had virtual ownership of the land they tenanted, could farm it how they liked within reason and within the customs of the village, town or manor, i.e. growing the same crop on their lount (local name for a 'strip') within a 'shut' or 'furlong' (local names for a division of an open field).

However, they had obligations to the landlord, to pay suite to his mill and court, and to provide services or boons, either in kind or in money. One of the many services could be sheaving on the lord's demesne at harvest-time and the boons providing hens or capons for the lord at particular times of the year.

In addition to this the tenants had to keep their buildings in good repair and plant a certain number of trees, ash oak and elm, in their hedgerows every year (this was a time when wood for building was becoming scarce and half-timber buildings were still the norm). There were sometimes other obligations. In five leases from the manors of Northenden and Etchells the obligation to plant trees was negated in favour of supplying arms and armour (muskets, half-corsletts and full corslets) to the lord of the manor. Whether or not they had to supply a man was not specified in the leases.

The rents were small when compared with the economic rents charged on short-term leases because they had been frozen in the late fifteenth/early sixteenth century. For example, an economic short-term lease rent would be £1 per Cheshire measure acre in the seventeenth century (Cheshire measure - 2.1 statute acres) but a three-lives lease rent of £1 would be for a farm of 20 Cheshire measure acres.

Entry fines (i.e. fines paid by tenants on entry

into new leases - not always after the death of the third life, but often to add a member of the same family, son or daughter or widow) were even higher. The national average was fifteen times the rent and usually fixed (i.e. the entry fine was paid on the same farm or tenement every time a new lease was entered into).[2]

The chief use to family historians of three life leases is that the three lives were often mentioned, often with their relationship to each other. The rental surveys may also have details of the lives in a lease and if the rental surveys have been used as working estate documents for many years, they will also have details of the deaths of the 'lives' or even where other 'lives' had moved to. The 1670 Rental Survey of Northenden and Etchells is especially good for the amount of detail it gives for each tenement, including 'lives' and their relationships, rent, boons and services and heriots paid on the death of each life.

Understanding Three Life Leases and Other Post-Medieval Deeds: A Practical Guide for Family Historians. by Mike Brown is an excellent booklet on how to read and interpret life leases and other documents

The Northenden and Etchells sequence of rental surveys and leases found in the Tatton Family Muniments, John Rylands Library, starts with a few leases from the 1630s, a rental survey for 1648 (drawn up because Robert Tatton, the lord of the two manors, needed money and needed something to show the potential mortgager, Humphrey Chetham, what surety he was putting his £3,000 into),[3] 1657 Schedule for Northenden (drawn up to show another potential mortgager - the Schedule for Etchells was either never drawn up or has since disappeared), 1670 Rental Survey (drawn up for a new lord of the manor and used as a working estate document for thirty-fifty years), a number of leases from 1673/74 (again the Tattons were trying to re-mortgage the estate), 1699 Rental Survey (another mortgager), a lot of leases from 1700-1720 - most of which were granting the tenements to their tenants forever - more or less selling them, and the Account Books 1748-1763. There is also an undated Rental Survey from c.1730s.

Sources used
1648 Rental Survey
This is a list of named tenants, the acreage of the tenements, annual rents, a list of freeholders and accumulated totals of boons and services. The acreages used in this rental survey are Cheshire Measure.

Chamber Hall –
Rear of Chamber Hall, showing the bell used
when the hall was a Presbyterian meeting place.

1657 Northenden Schedule

This details for every tenement the current tenant, the size of his house and outbuildings (given in bays), details of the outbuildings, the acreage of the tenement, details of the boons and services owed, the number of lives left in the lease, the rent and the yearly value of the tenement. A comment was made by one of Robert Tatton's mortgage brokers, his brother-in-law, Peter Brereton, that these values were too high. The acreages in this rental survey are statute.

1670 Rental Survey

This details the tenants and lives in every tenement, with the rents, boons and services. Occasionally, if a tenement was out of lease the fields where the tenement lands were situated were listed. Because this rental survey was used as a working estate document for over thirty years, there were often notes of the deaths of lives.

1699 Rental Survey

This listed the current tenants, acreage of the tenement, the yearly value of the tenement, the number of years left in lease, the numbers of boons and services, the value of the boons and services, the number of lives in lease, and the ages of the lives left in lease - a possible guide to when people were born, but not guaranteed. For example, Richard Goulden said he was eighty in 1699. He was actually born in 1629 and so was only seventy. He wasn't the only suspect octogenarian in this rental survey. The acreages in this rental survey are Cheshire Measure.

Undated Rental Survey (C.1728-1735)

This is just a list of the people paying 'Free Rent' or ground rent. It is not as useful as the previous rental surveys and it is difficult to tie in tenants with their tenements, since a certain amount of

change in the rents paid and also amalgamation of tenements had taken place between 1700 and 1730s.

Account Book 1748-1763

This was kept by William Tatton to detail the lands he bought and the rents paid by his tenants; it is possible to follow some tenements from 1699 to this account book. The acreages here are probably statute.

Together with the leases, it is possible to use all these rental surveys and account book to compile tenement histories for the nearly 180 tenements in Northenden and Etchells and to know quite a lot of the family history of the tenants from 1648 to 1763 in some cases. What follows are some examples of what the history of tenements can tell you about a family in the seventeenth and early eighteenth centuries.

Northenden Moorside Tenement and Northenden Town End Tenement

These two tenements were on what is now the western edge of the town of Northenden, just outside of the centre towards the Post House Hotel and the M56. They were run by members of the same family until the 1730s, when Moorside was in the hands of one branch of the family and Town End tenanted by another branch.

In 1648 it was held by Widow Royle and was 5.75 Cheshire measure acres or about 11.5 statute acres. By 1657 the tenement was in the hands of Henry Royle, probably the son of Widow Royle. The acreage was reckoned to be 10.5 statute acres and the rent 9s 4d. The value of the tenement was £5 17s 6d. The boons and services included:
2 hens or 1s
1 day ploughing or 2s
1 day mucking or 2s
4 loads of turves or 1s 4d
2 days leading weirwood - taking wood that was trapped behind a weir
2 days sheaving or 6d - helping with the corn and hay harvest on the lord's lands
weir money - 1s - money for the upkeep of the weir at Northenden
The heriot was best goods or £3 6s 8d. There was one life (Henry Royle) left in the lease.
Henry Ryle also had another tenement at Northenden Town End, which was where the farmhouse stood. The farmhouse was three bays in length (about 27 feet) and probably two-storey - larger than a modern semi. The outbuildings included a barn, stable, shippon and other outhouses. The Town End farm included an orchard garden, fold, common pasture and rights to take turves off Northern Moor. The rent was £1 3s 11d. The house and land around it was worth £10 13s 4d a year. Henry Royle had a third lease of 16 statute acres rented for £1 3s 11d. It was worth £1 16s 3d a year. The boons and

Chamber Hall –
Front of Chamber Hall,
showing the two cross wing
and central original hall.
In 1703 the whole building
was encased in brick.

services were worth 11s 4d and included 1 (cart) load of coal dug out from Northern Moor coal pit - there were also at least a couple of bell pits on Shadow Moss digging coal from just below the surface turf - or 2s 6d. These coal pits were communal ones, used by everyone to supplement the turves out from the moor. Both turf cutting and coal mining were summer jobs, done during dry weather, before the main corn harvest got underway. There were two lives left in the lease on this farm.

Between 1657 and 1670 the 10.5 acre tenement had been lease again. However, by 1670 two of the three lives in the lease were dead before this survey was made. According to Northenden Parish Registers Henry was buried on 26 November 1664 and his wife Elizabeth four days later. Arnold, the third life and the son, continued to farm until at least 1706. The number of loads of turves had increased to eight or 2s 8d but the heriot had decreased to £3.

The second tenement held by Henry Royle was also leased again by 1670. This time the three lives in the lease were Henry, John his son and Jane Ryle, who was probably a daughter. Jane, as well as Henry, was dead by 1670, but John continued to farm the tenement until his own death, noted in the Rental Survey as being 8 February 1690.
In 1699 Henry Royle was the tenant of the Moorside tenement. He was aged thirty according to the Rental Survey and a son of Arnold. Henry was baptised on 27 August 1671. He was the only life in lease.

On the 16 acre Town End tenement John Royle was the tenant, aged sixty, son of Thomas. He ran it with one of his nephews, aged thirty-five.

The Town End farm was leased on 10 October 1674 to Thomas Royle, tailor. The lives in lease were Thomas's brother John and his sons John and Isaac. Which begs the question which John

Royle died in February 1690? Or was '90 written down instead of '98 or '99. The boons and services were still the same as in 1657. The entry fine was £54. The Royles had liberty to cut wood to repair the hedges, the farmhouse and outbuildings, the ploughs, the carts, and cut wood for fuel (listed in a lease as hedgebote, housebote, ploughbote, cartbote and firebote). The woods and underwoods were reserved to the lord of the manor. Thomas Royle also had to plant six trees a year of oak, ash or elm. This was a common requirement of the time. Timber for building and general repairs on farms were needed. Also the newly re-established Royal Navy needed wood for its ships. So wood was becoming a valuable and increasingly rarer commodity. By the 1730s the tenement was in the hands of John Royle.

The Moorside farm was leased on 14 April 1706 to Arnold Ryle, father of Henry who was counted as the tenant in 1699. The lives were Arnold, Henry and Arnold's wife Mary. The amount of loads of turves had decreased to just two or 8d. The entry fine was £35. Arnold had the same right and liberties to cut wood as his cousin Thomas. The lord of the manor retained the right to the woods, underwoods, fishing, mines and quarries - there were no quarries in Northenden but the Tattons put that it in case. Arnold also had to plant trees - five oaks, ashes and elms.

Henry's parents had died so he now took out a lease on 24 June 1710. The rent was increased to 10s 4d and the entry fine increased to £54. The lease lists the cottage held by Henry's father Arnold. At this time a tenement of half an acre and a cottage in Northenden, formerly held by William Ryle, was added, a small parcel of newly enclosed common land, a marl pit and a right to the warrens on Northen Moor for when he and his family fancied rabbit pie. In fact, Henry Royle was one of a number of tenants given the right to use and manage the warrens as a food resource. The farm was granted forever and so the rent was now a chief or 'free' rent.

Chamber Hall
Interior of hall of
Chamber Hall,
showing the solid
seventeenth century door
and the deeply
recessed windows.

Henry Royle, yeoman, was the tenant still at the Town End farm in the 1720s and the rent had been increased to £1 2s 4d. Henry died in 1725.

Northenden Boat or Ferry Tenement
This was a tenement or smallholding near the River Mersey on or near the Victorian Tatton Arms on Boat Lane/Mill Lane.

James Dean was the tenant and ferryman in 17648. Because he had served Robert Tatton in the Royalist Garrison at Wythenshawe Hall and Parliamentarian soldiers had occupied his ferry house and probably damaged it, his rent was abated to 5s instead of the 7s 8d it should have been. With the ferry went a house, and one acre of land. 5s was a high rent for just an acre, even a Cheshire measure acre, but the Boat House or Northenden Boat as it was known was also a pub and James Dean charged people to take them and their horses even across the Mersey. However, part of this ferry money may have been given to the lord of the manor. The ferry was a very necessary part of local life before the bridge was built at Northenden in the early twentieth century. The Mersey in winter spate had been known to drown people. The ferry was probably a flat bottomed open boat, worked with chains slung across the river, as was the ferry at Sale (Jackson's Boat).

James Dean was still the tenant in 1657. The Boat House was three bays of building (c.27 feet), a cowhouse, stable (for customers'/passengers' horses), orchard, garden and back garden, with two statute acres. James Dean, like all the tenants, had rights to the common pasture and to take turves off Northen Moor. The rent had increased to 7s 8d. The boons and services were money to repair the weir 1s. The heriot was best goods or 10s. The nine-year value was £12. There were three lives in the lease, but James died and was buried on 13 August 1661.

After the death of James Dean, John his son took it over. In 1670 the lives in lease were John, his mother Mary and Elizabeth Dean (sister?). The heriot was now £2. The Court Leet Records for Northenden show that John was running an alehouse at Northenden Boat from at least 1667.

John renewed the lease with himself, his mother and his wife Jane as the lives in 1673. The entry fine was just £2. All three lives died thirteen years later in 1685 and 1686. Richard, John's brother, was entered as the next tenant in the Court Leet Records in 1686.

Richard Dean was still the tenant in 1699. The yearly value was £1 10s. Some time between 1699 and 1749 the Boat House turned from a customary three-life lease to being a short-term tenancy. The rent was now £10 15s a year and the Boat House was a pub mainly, possibly with a ferry attached rather than the other way about. Northenden Court Leet met at the Boat House four times a year. Unfortunately, the 1748-1764 Accounts do not mention the name of the tenant, but the Court Leet Records name him as Nathaniel Jenkinson.

Renshaw Tenement, Northenden
The Renshaw family who tenanted this farm can be traced back to the earliest dates of the Northenden Parish Registers Book 1, to the time of the father of James Renshaw, the earliest known tenant.

In 1648 James Renshaw tenanted 9 Cheshire measure acres in Northenden and 5 acres of the Sheep Heyes in Etchells on which the rent was abated. This was in recognition that James Renshaw and his two sons Robert and Henry had served in the Royalist garrison of Wythenshawe Hall under the lord of the manor, Robert Tatton, then when the hall surrendered to the Parliamentarians Robert had gone with Mr Tatton to Chester as one of two bodyguards and soldiers.

The rent was 11s 2d

After the death of James Renshaw, Robert and his wife Joan took out another lease in 1650. No entry fine was charged

'in considerac[i]on of Service all ready due him [Robert Tatton] by the said Robert Rainshaw'.

A £1 released was paid to Mrs Nicholls (Robert Tatton's mother) for the Sheep Heyes. In total the acreage was 14 statute acres in Northenden and 5 statute acres in Etchells. The rent had risen to 18s 4d and there were thirteen boons and services worth 11s 4d. The heriot was £4.

Seven years later, in 1657, Robert Renshaw was still the tenant. The rent had decreased to 11s 2d, just for the Northenden part of the farm, which was now 18 statute acres. The farmhouse was large at four bays (36 feet long), with barn, stables, cowhouse, orchard, garden, fold and hempyard. The herior had reduced to £3 6s 8d and the ten year value was £100.

The tenant in 1670 was now Edmund Sumner, yeoman, aged sixty and the farm was 10 Cheshire measure acres. However, Edmund may have been a brother-in-law to the Renshaws, as a lease of 1700 lists the lives as Henry and Thomas, sons of Henry Renshaw, and John Sumner, son of Edmund. The rent, boons and heriot were unchanged and the entry fine only £12.

Sumner Tenement, Gatley

In 1648 Widow Sumner was the tenant of a half acre (statute) smallholding/garden and cottage in Gatley. Twenty-two years later in 1670 her son Reginald was the tenant. The lives in lease were Reginald, Jane his wife and Edward his son. The rent was 2s, the boons and services worth 1s and the heriot just 10s. In 1699 the tenant was Peter Sumner, aged thirty-five, another son of Reginald and Jane. The yearly value was 15s.

Nearly fifty years later, in 1747, another Peter Sumner (possibly a son or grandson of Peter) took out a lease. This tiny smallholding was one of the few tenements still with a three-life lease. Other lives in the lease were Peter's daughter Jane, aged seven, and his son Thomas, aged three. The rent had increased to 3s and the entry fine was 310 10s.

Gretrax Cottage, 4 Lane Ends, Gatley-Sharston

This smallholding shows how a three-life tenancy could move to another family but then return to the original family. In 1648 William Gretrax was the tenant of this half acre smallholding. Edward Gratrax, possible a son of William, held it in 1670, with his son John and John's wife Ellen as the other lives in the lease. According to the 1670

Rental Surey, John Gretrax didn't die until 1734. Since he was fifty-eight years old in 1699 (born c.1637), he was ninety-seven at the time of his death, a very great age for that date. In 1699 the smallholding was three-quarters of an acre with a cottage.

Two years later John Gretrax, husbandman, took out a new lease. The lives in the lease were himself, his wife Ellen and his son John and the entry fine was £1 10s. Three years after Old John's death another new lease was taken by the Wainwright family, Humphrey Wainwright and his sons Richard and Robert. The rent had decreased to 1s, but the entry fine was £4.

The last three-life lease for this smallholding was taken out just nineteenth years later - by a member of the Gretrax family. In the meantime Humphrey Wainwright had drowned only three years after taking out the 1737 lease and possibly at least one of his sons had died.

James Gretrax, the new tenant, was probably a grandson of Old John. The lives in lease were James himself, Sarah his wife and James his son. The entry fine had risen over three-fold to £12 12s.

Chamber Hall Farm, Shadow Moss

Chamber Hall was the court house for the manor of Etchells until probably the mid-sixteenth century. By 1648 it was in the hands of Mr Edmund Joydrell of Yeardsley, near Macclesfield. However, by 1670 the Tattons had brought it from the Joydrell family and the tenant was Francis Shelmerdine, ex-Puritan curate of Cheadle, ex-vicar of Mottram-in-Longdendale, weaver, and later Presbyterian minister. Other documents from the Tatton Family Muniments show that Francis Shelmerdine and his family were the tenants in the days of Edmund Joydrell in the 1640s.

In 1670 the lives in lease were Francis Shelmerdine, William his eldest son and a cousin, John Shelmerdine of Northenden. Three years later Francis took out a new lease with himself, his wife Elizabeth and his son William as the lives in lease. The rent was £1 3s, boons and services 9s 8d and the heriot £4.

By 1699, Matthew the second son was the tenant. After Francis's death in 1674, William took over the farm, but on his death in 1681 Matthew was the tenant. Matthew was a woollendraper with business interests in Stockport. Chamber Hall farm was 17.5 statute acres.

Matthew married Mary Bainbridge by licence at Chester on 12 July 1697, a possible second marriage. He took a new lease in 1700 and paid an entry fine of £90. The lease was granted forever. When Matthew died in 1711, his son, also Matthew took over Chamber Hall. Matthew the son took out a mortgage on Chamber Hall. On his death in 1733, Chamber Hall had to be sold off to pay the mortgage. It was brought by the trustees of Didsbury parish church. But in 1751 Chamber Hall was again sold - this time to William Tatton of Wythenshawe Hall. At the time Thomas Walker was the short term tenant, paying an annual rent of £26, probably for 26 acres.

The 1748-1763 Accounts show that £4 10s, £3 2s 9d, over £13 a year in 1755 was spent on Chamber Hall Farm, possibly a sign that the farm needed a lot of work on it. Then in 1757 Chamber Hall was leased to Henry Meyers at an annual rent of £80. Land from Peel Hall farm was added at that time to Chamber Hall farm, making it at 70 acres the second largest farm on the estate. The farm remained at this size until at least 1826 when it was tenanted by Joseph Simpson.

Chamber Hall farm remained in the hands of the Simpson family and their relations until it was sold (minus its dwindling farmland) by its then landlord, Manchester City Council in the early 1990s.

Shadow Moss Farm, Shadow Moss
This farm was originally tenanted by the Downes family. In 1648 Richard Davies was the tenant of 6 Cheshire measure acres. By 1670 the tenant was John Downes, with his son John the shoemaker and sister Martha Downes as the other two lives in lease. The rent was 6s 8d, boons and services of nine worth 3s 5d and the heriot £3.

In 1699 Ebenezer Downes, probably another son of John the elder, was the tenant. He was born c.1636. The smallholding was 5 Cheshire measure acres and the yearly value £6. Two years later Shadow Moss Farm passed to the Torkington family. Thomas Torkington of Wythenshawe, yeoman, took out a new lease, granted forever, for an entry fine of £30. Henry Bailey was the subtenant. The farm was probably only a means of gaining surety for a large mortgage, because within the year Thomas Torkington had mortgaged it to Hannah Hughson for £160.

Thomas Torkington moved up in the world in the next ten years. By 1713 he was a gentleman living at Ashley, a small village some 5-6 miles to the south. In that year he leased Shadow Moss Farm to a relative, perhaps even a son, Samuel Torkington of Easingwold, Yorkshire. The entry fine was £100 £70 up on the 1701 lease. The lease was bought back a day later by Thomas Torkington and Henry Bailey, so perhaps the

lease was only a device to remortgage the farm.

In 1753, Samuel Torkington, now the full owner, leased the farm to Peter Wood for a rent of £10 10s on a short term lease of seven years. Three years later the farm was sold to William Tatton and records of its rent and tenants were entered in the Accounts Book. Peter Wood continued as tenant until his death in 1766, when his widow took over. In 1763, the rent was £11.

The farmhouse of Shadow Moss farm still exists, although all of its land is now under the car parks, terminals and hotels of Manchester International Airport.

Notes
1. Much of the Introduction to this article has been taken from the chapter on Land Tenure in my book *Piggins, Husslements and Desperate Debts*, originally published in 1995.

2. John Bannister junior, like many other tenants in Northenden and Etchells, bought Cooke's Croft in 1710 for a fine of £6 and a chief rent of 4s. In 1736 he sold the cottage and half acre croft to Benjamin Irlam for £100, a high price. The average price for land in Northenden and Etchells in the mid-eighteenth century was £30 per acre.

3. For more detail on this episode in the history of Northenden, Etchells and the Tattons see *The Impact of Civil War on a Community: Northenden and Etchells, 1642-1660* by Jill Groves, 2nd revised edition (published 2002).

References
J. Littler, *The Protector of Dunham Massey*, p.82.
R.N. Dore, *A History of Hale* pp.152-3;
Inventory of James Leicester of Halelow, gentleman, 1635 (Cheshire Archives)
Inventory of Edward Worsley, yeoman, 1642 (CCRO).
Tatton Family Muniments, John Rylands Library, University of Manchester
Leases 959, 965, 979, 1035, 1051, 1056, 1057, 1058, 1091, 1098, 1302, 1363
Lease for Chamber Hall
1648 Rental Survey
1656 Schedule of Northenden
1670 Rental Survey
1699 Rental Survey
Accounts Book, 1748-1763
Northenden Parish Registers, Book 1, 1560-1640, Book 2, 1640-1680, Stockport Local Studies Library.
Understanding Three Life Leases and Other Post-Medieval Deeds: A Practical Guide for Family Historians by Mike Brown, Dartmoor Press, PO Box 132, Plymouth PL4 7YL (published 1998).
Chester Marriage Indexes, 1690-1700, Part 8.
The Impact of Civil War on a Community: Northenden and Etchells, Cheshire, 1642-1660

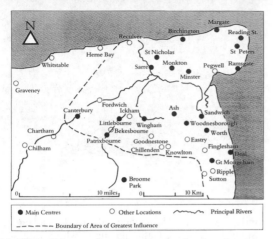

● Main Centres ○ Other Locations ∿ Principal Rivers
– – – – Boundary of Area of Greatest Influence

A Taste of Holland:
Dutch Influences on Kentish Architecture
Arthur Percival

Of all English counties Kent lies by far the closest to the Continent, and places like Faversham, Canterbury and Ashford are nearer to France (at least as the crow flies) than they are to London.

Yet it is among the most English of counties. There's less sense of being close to a frontier than there is in Shropshire, Cumbria or Northumbria. No Man or Maid of Kent has a faint French accent, and the only traditional dishes are English ones which owe nothing to French cuisine. 'This fortress built by Nature for herself' (as Shakespeare put it) has served Kent well, not only 'against infection and the hand of war' but also against alien influences of every kind. Somehow it seems entirely appropriate that the greatest English composer, whose music epitomises the national character, bears a Kentish surname – Elgar.

This is no coincidence, for his father was born and bred in Dover, a border-town and a front-line one in time of war, but as English as they come. Calais may be only 22 miles away but if language, way of life and appearance are anything to go by, it might just as well be 220.

The architectural contrast could hardly be greater, and much the same goes for Folkestone and Boulogne, just 30 miles apart. The truth, it seems, is that in cultural and architectural terms Kent has vastly more in common with New Zealand than it has with France. The Victorian and Edwardian buildings of Auckland and Wellington would look perfectly at home in Dover or Folkestone – and utterly out of place in Calais or Boulogne. They drive on the left, there, too, and chance meetings are quite likely to be with people of Kentish extraction – there was a lot of emigration in the 19th century.

However, superficial appearances, as ever, can be deceptive. At least in terms of building design, the people of Kent have become more, and not less, insular as time

has gone on and communications have improved. There was evidently a time, in the sixteenth, seventeenth and early eighteenth centuries, when East Kent, at least, moved close to the mainstream of Continental building tradition. Why it then moved out, and back into the English tradition, in the later eighteenth century, no-one can be quite sure. However until decent turnpike roads and then railways were built, travel and trade links with London and beyond were more of a challenge than the Channel crossings to ports such as Calais, Dunkirk (an English possession from 1658 to 1662) and Ostend.

Dutch Gables
East Kent's sixteenth, seventeenth and early eighteenth century 'Continental' buildings have attracted less attention than they deserve, perhaps because their numbers have slowly dwindled and, as towns and villages have grown, they have become less conspicuous. However in rural areas they remain very prominent, and most East Kent readers must know of at least one or two – like School Farm, Guilton on the main road through Ash from Canterbury to Sandwich, Chilton Farm near Pegwell (Ramsgate) and Maison Dieu House in Dover.

What these three, and most of the others, have in common are showy curvilinear 'Dutch' gables. That they were a key element in East Kent's distinctive heritage was first recognised over a hundred years ago, when observant architects began sketching and even imitating them. They were also pinpointed by Sir Patrick Abercrombie,

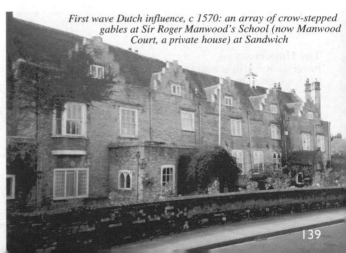

First wave Dutch influence, c 1570: an array of crow-stepped gables at Sir Roger Manwood's School (now Manwood Court, a private house) at Sandwich

in his great pioneering planning study of East Kent undertaken when it seemed the coalfield would be more intensively exploited than, in the event, it was. But though the contributor of this article has undertaken some research, much more is needed to establish precisely why the style took root. There are probably several reasons.

Some of the earlier examples, with crow-stepped gables rather than curvilinear, must be the result of Dutch immigration. Protestant refugees from Holland settled in Sandwich and formed their own church there in 1562; two years later a new grammar school (now a private house) was built very much in Dutch style.

Most of East Kent's 'Continental' buildings are a good bit later, however. They tend to fall within the period 1650-1725, by which time Holland's

Typical decorative tie-bar and blind oval recess at School Farm (1691

Two-storey porches with curvilinear gables were sometimes grafted onto medieval buildings. This is at Oare, near Faversham – the western limit of the Dutch influence in East Kent

United Provinces had thrown off Spain's Catholic yoke – and were indeed so prosperous that their trading interests led to war with England in 1652-4, 1664-7 and 1672-4. There must be some other explanation for the popularity of the 'Dutch' style at this time.

The Huguenots
Immigration still seems the most likely explanation. The style of building design we tend to call 'Dutch' was in fact popular throughout all 17 provinces of the Netherlands, which originally included as well as present-day Holland the whole of Belgium and part of north-eastern France, including Arras, Lille and Dunkirk. Calais and Boulogne were just outside this area, but close enough for a few residual signs of the 'Dutch' idiom to survive today.

For most of the period 1650-1725 Belgium (an

independent kingdom since only 1831) was under Spanish rule – the Catholics, upon whom England had turned its back, were on East Kent's doorstep and any remaining Protestants wanting to escape their hostility would look for sanctuary to England in general and East Kent in particular.

Perhaps more significant for the East Kent scene was the revocation, in 1685, of the Edict of Nantes. A flood of Huguenots who could no longer practice their Protestant religion in France settled in England, where they enriched our culture and technology, as have later waves of immigrants.

We tend to think of them all, quite reasonably, as 'French'. But some in fact were Netherlanders from the provinces of French Flanders, French Hainaut and Artois, which had only been annexed by France 36 years previously. They came from places whose names were not French but Flemish or Anglo-Saxon, their language was probably Flemish (little different from Dutch) and their building style was what we call 'Dutch'.

Where they settled in East Kent, and when they could afford to build new houses of their own, they must, sometimes at least, have tried to adopt their

Apogee of Dutch influence: showy gable, with pilasters, added to earlier building at Wingham Well. The unusual double pediment is necessary to conceal the apex of the steep-pitched roof

The classic 'East Kent Dutch' house, with curvilinear gables at both ends and over the porch: School Farm, Guilton, Ash-next-Sandwich (1691)

own idiom. 'Tried to', only, because English bricks were larger, and not so capable of the fine effects you see in (say) Bruges in Belgium; and the Kentish brickie, reliable craftsman though he was, may not have been able to cope with the intricacies of 'Dutch' design. So, with a few exceptions, the 'Dutch' houses of East Kent, though they certainly look pleasantly exotic, are never quite like the 'real thing'.

Examples
If you have a bit of time and a camera, it's well worth 'collecting' 'Dutch' houses in East Kent and other places in England where they can be seen. In East Kent Almost all of them are east of a line drawn from Faversham through Ashford to Dover. Curly gables don't weather terribly well and may have been rather brutally shaved down – but if there is decorative brickwork elsewhere on the building, there may have been a gable.

Many of the buildings bear their dates (usually on tie-bars that also serve to brace the roofs) and this in itself is a clue – since Netherlanders almost always dated their buildings and native Kentish

people hardly ever did. (What a pity. Every building ought to bear its date, anyway.) You'll find some gables squeezed into positions (notably in Deal) where they're almost invisible and you wonder why anyone took the trouble; and you'll find them prominently added onto 'old-fashioned' timber-framed farmhouses to give them a fashionable new look.

Outside Kent you'll find plenty – sometimes in seemingly the oddest places, though invariably there'll be a logical reason. It's perhaps no surprise that there should be lots in Norfolk and Suffolk, and one or two in Hull and Newcastle upon Tyne. But what about that tiny town of Cawood, near York, where the gables could have stepped straight out of East Kent, or Topsham in Devon, where the Strand is majestically lined with them? Trade with Holland in both cases is almost certainly the answer.

One final point. The Netherlanders have never suffered as badly from architectural hiccoughs as the English. Regardless of Gothic Revivals, Modern Movements or other ephemeral fashions, they have gone on building in traditional style if this was right for the site. You can see newspaper offices, chainstores, even service stations done this way, and without looking self-conscious or Disneyesque. In East Kent, by contrast, this continuity has been lost, and almost the last significant contribution to the 'Dutch' scene here was a house built at Sandwich Bay about 70 years ago – but in fact in 'Cape Dutch' style, and that's a different story.

Inspiration
There are plenty of gifted and enterprising architects. Isn't it about time that in East Kent and other areas with old 'Dutch' buildings more of them looked for inspiration, as Anthony Swaine did a few years ago in Canterbury, at the area's handsome 'Dutch' heritage? They and their clients and contractors would be doing everyone a favour.

Arthur Percival MBE MA DLitt FSA FAHI is Honorary Director of the Fleur de Lis Heritage Centre, Faversham, and a lecturer and author on environmental matters and Faversham's social history.

Curvilinear gables wather badly if not properly maintained, so were sometimes shaved down. Only the pediment survives at Letterbox Cottages, Staple Road, Wingham

Life in the Workhouse

Simon Fowler

Even though the last workhouse disappeared nearly seventy years ago they still exert a powerful fascination on the popular imagination. Many readers may remember hearing about workhouses from parents or grandparents or perhaps were cared for in hospitals which formerly housed paupers. The reopening as a museum of the old Southwell workhouse in Nottinghamshire by the National Trust made front-page news in April 2002. Many of the issues relating to the poor and how to deal with their problems, which the poor law guardians and the overseers of the poor had to tackle in the 18th and 19th centuries, may have different name but still remain high up on the political agenda today.

The workhouse has almost disappeared from the landscape. Most have been pulled down or converted to other uses, particularly hospital wards. The one in Richmond, Surrey ironically has become luxury flats; it is a fair bet that the present residents have not given a thought to the poor people who once struggled to survive there.

Workhouses existed to house the poor of the community, either those who could not work – the senile and bastard children -or those who would not – vagrants and the so-called 'able-bodied poor'. In return for basic board and lodging inmates were set to work, where ever possible, breaking stones and picking oakum (that is unpicking tarred rope). Conditions in the workhouse were designed to be a deterrent encouraging the poor to fend for themselves rather than become a burden on the rates.
The first workhouse opened in Bristol in 1698 and the idea gradually spread. At Beverley, near Hull, a local resident recorded in 1728 how: "on opening the workhouse notice was given to the poor that the weekly pension was to cease and that such as were not able to maintain themselves might apply to the governors of the workhouse. The result of

this was that though before the opening of the house 116 persons received the parish allowance, not above eight came in first and the subsequent winter the number in the house never exceeded 26, although all kinds of provisions were very dear and the season was sickly."

This success in cutting the numbers of paupers, naturally, had an immediate appeal to the richer inhabitants, whose rates supported the poor. By the 1830s most parishes provided one or more workhouses, or House of Industry as they were sometimes called. Although conditions varied most residents (normally the elderly or chronically ill) were reasonably well treated. In Reading, for example, the beer brewed at the workhouse had a very high reputation.

However it was becoming increasingly clear that the old system of poor relief, which had its origins in the reign of Elizabeth I was breaking down. It could not cope with the rapid growth in the population which was taking place as the result of the industrial revolution or the economic dislocation caused by the slump that followed the end of the Napoleonic Wars. At the same time there was an almost universal belief amongst the middle classes that the poor should be self-sufficient when ever possible. Samuel Smiles, the greatest exponent of self-help (the phrase comes from a title of one of this books), argued that 'any class of men that lives from hand to mouth will ever be an inferior class. They will necessarily remain, impotent and helpless, hanging onto the skirts of society, the sport of time and season.'

The effects of local workhouses in cutting pauper numbers did not go unnoticed by the members of the Royal Commission set up in 1832 to investigate the old poor law and suggestions improvements. It recommended the setting up of 636 Poor Law Unions in England and Wales. Each Union had to establish a workhouse where the poor of the parish would reside. Those who refused to enter the workhouse would loose their right to assistance. The conditions inside the house would be such as to deter all but the most desperate. Thus, at a stroke, the problem of rising rates and the temptation to rely on handouts rather than work for a living were solved at one stroke.

By the end of the 1830s most parishes had been combined into unions and had established a local workhouse. This was achieved relatively peacefully in southern England, but in the industrial areas of the north, and rural East Anglia,

paupers outside the workhouse, continued. In 1849 nearly 90% of paupers received out-relief, although the proportion fell by the end of the nineteenth century. The reasons were simple. Out-relief cost less and was more humane. As most paupers receiving out-relief were elderly they could expect to be cared for by relations and friends, further saving the expense of nursing.

there were considerable protests. Richard Oastler, a well known radical, for example wrote in the Northern Star in March 1838 that: "The real object of [the New Poor Law]…is to lower wages and punish poverty as a crime. Remember also that children and parents are lying frequently in the same Bastille without seeing one another or knowing the other's fate."

Where the new system had been peacefully established the benefits, to the taxpayer at least, was immediately apparent. The Poor Law Guardians of Richmond, Surrey petitioned to Parliament in 1841 that they had: "No hesitation in stating it is the result of their experience in this union, that it has been eminently beneficial as a means of reclaiming many of the labouring classes from indolent and vicious habits, encouraging industry and forethought and restoring that independence of character which the old Poor Law was rapidly destroying." Few paupers would have agreed with these sentiments.

The workhouses, under the direction of poor law guardians, soon acquired the reputation, which haunts them even today, of being cruel and heartless places. During the 1840s, there were a number of scandals which rather reinforced this view. The worst was at Andover, where conditions were so bad that the paupers were reduced to eat the marrow from the bones for sustenance they were supposed to be crushing. In the official enquiry one witness reported on the behaviour of the inmates of the house: "They said that when they found… a fresh bone, one that appeared a little moist, that were almost ready to fight over it, and that the man who was fortunate to get it was obliged to hide it that he might eat it when he was alone."

The enquiry found that Andover was a special case where the Guardians, responsible for the poor law locally, were unusually mean, and the workhouse master, responsible for running the house, particularly dishonest and sadistic towards the men, women and children in his charge.

Despite the Act of 1834, which outlawed it, the old system of out-relief, that is paying pensions to

The workhouses were originally set up to house the 'able-bodied' poor who theorists argued need the constant reminder of the workhouse as an incentive to find work. During the economic depression of the 1830s and 1840s work was hard to come by so the workhouse was no real deterrent. Men, women, and families fleeing the famine in Ireland made matters worse. No amount of moralising could overturn the iron laws of economics.

One aspect of the problem was the waves of vagrants moving from town to town in search of work or, as the authorities feared, mischief. Workhouses established casual wards to provide a night's rest for men on the tramp, in return for an hour or two's hard labour. Word soon got around about which workhouse offered the best accommodation or food. In a report of 1850 the Master of the Worksop Workhouse wrote: "We are mostly annoyed with vagrants ... and a great many Irish. This is an increasing evil, we had 148 last week, 20 more applied who we were not able to lodge. I do not think the greater part of these men are in search of work, they are people who make a tradition of tramping and begging; they beg and steal and they know that they have always the Union Workhouse to fall back upon."

The Guardians responded with new regulations which effectively cutting the relief offered to vagrants. Undoubtedly the horde moved onto a neighbouring and more hospitable workhouse, where eventually the same measures were adopted forcing the vagrants elsewhere. Responses such as these by individual guardians were symptomatic of a piecemeal approach to the unemployed.

Over the sixty years between the end of the great mid-Victorian slump and the outbreak of the First World War the role of the workhouse and the poor law guardians changed. The reason for the change is simple. Many workers experienced a rise in their living standards between 1850 and 1900, so for the first time the better off members of the working classes could now afford to save for periods of unemployment with friendly societies, the Post Office Saving Bank, or the insurance company. This meant that they were not forced to rely on the poor law in times of hardship.

This was coupled with a deep and abiding fear of the workhouse and the humiliation it reputedly meted out daily to the paupers by the authorities. If people got into trouble sought assistance from neighbours or friends and in some cases charities. The stigma, for example, against pauper funerals was so great amongst the poor of Lambeth, that Mrs Pember Reeve a social researcher, found in 1912 they would go to great lengths to avoid it: "The pauper funeral carries with the pauperisation of the father of the child – a humiliation which adds disgrace to the natural grief of the parents. More than that they declare that the pauper family is wanting in dignity and in respect to their dead. One woman expressed the feeling of many more when she said she would soon have the dust-cart call for the body of her child than 'that there Black Maria'."

Workhouses increasingly became the refugee of outcasts from society: the elderly, orphans, nursing mothers with bastard children, and the insane. A survey in 1897 found that a third of old people over seventy were helped in some way by the poor law authorities.

Despite fears that any softening of the regime would encourage people to seek relief the workhouse slowly changed to meet the new needs. Whitehall cautiously encouraged these changes. Guardians became increasingly responsive to the needs of the workhouse inmates. This responsiveness was helped first by the election of women as guardians and secondly by the election of working class men in a few areas who were determined to improve conditions. Guardians were particularly aware of the need to educate children in their care and many unions set up successful schemes to foster orphans.

Despite improvements conditions varied considerably between individual workhouses. One observer found that in Chelmsford the old people were, after 1901, allowed to walk in the garden to 5pm, but they still had to go to bed by 7pm, and garden seats were not provided until 1905. In Bradford, however, the position was rather different aged paupers were provided with separate day rooms equipped with armchairs, cushions, curtains, and coloured tablecloths.

For most paupers and their masters a crucial matter was food and drink. The Poor Law Commissioners in Whitehall (and their successors) laid down menus, known as dietaries, which workhouses had to follow, although there was some local discretion permitted. For example, it recommended in 1869 that able-bodied paupers had for breakfast 7ounces of bread, and 1.5 pints of porridge. The diet was filling but dull, but it was probably better than what the poorest of the working class ate outside the workhouse. At Christmas and national celebrations, such as Queen Victoria's diamond jubilee in 1897, inmates of the house might be treated to roast beef. Whether however they were allowed a glass of beer with their Christmas meal was often a matter of great debate locally with advocates of temperance strongly against this little luxury.

Despite these changes the workhouse seemed increasingly outdated by the beginning of the twentieth century. The government set up a royal commission in November1905 to investigate the poor law and it make recommendations for its reform. When the Commission finally reported in 1909 it was split. Both reports however recommended the abolition of the Boards of Guardians and the workhouse and the assumption of their work by local government. It wasn't until 1930, however, that the system was finally dismantled.

What eventually forced the government to act was the slump of the 1920s which placed disproportionate burdens on certain Unions. In West Ham for example one in ten was on relief. In Bedwellty in South Wales the Poor Law Union had run up a debt of £1m helping unemployed miners. Added to this, working class guardians in places such as Poplar were increasing payments made to pensioners and financing improvements to the workhouse to which local ratepayers had great objections. It was clear that assistance to the unemployed had to be a national responsibility, rather than left to the well meaning if often limited guardians and poor law officials.

How successful were the workhouses? In the long term they did little to curb the 'able-bodied pauper' that so excised social thinkers of the 1830s and 1840s. Better economic prospects and fuller employment from the 1850s did more than any deterrent to empty the workhouse wards of healthy young men and women. The workhouse then housed those in society who could not be cared for in other way – this increasingly meant the elderly poor who had nobody to look after them, orphans and the insane. With increasing encouragement from Whitehall poor law guardians and workhouse officials endeavoured to improve conditions from the 1840s on. Guardians became more than just grinders of the poor.

In the end it did not matter how good the workhouse was and its services became. What mattered was the perception amongst the politicians and the public that the poor law unions were narrow-minded and penny-pinching. Amongst the working classes there grew up a loathing for the workhouse and all it stood for which has remained to this day.

Further Reading
The most readable book about workhouses is

Norman Longmate, *The Workhouse* (Temple Smith, 1974). M.A. Crowther, *The Workhouse System 1834-1929* (Batsford, 1981) is a more academic approach.

The Records
Extensive poor law records survive, many of which contain information about individual paupers. Most workhouse material is at county record offices. There is a clear divide between records created before 1834 and those afterwards. Before 1834 you are likely to use parish records such as vestry minute books and overseers of the poor accounts. These records are described in more detail in Anne Cole, *Poor Law Documents Before 1834* (Federation of Family History Societies, 2000)

After 1834 there is considerable more choice. You may find admission and discharge registers, registers of births and deaths in the workhouse, case papers, and references to the fate of individual paupers in the minutes of the boards of guardians. These records are described in more details in Jeremy Gibson, *Poor Law Union Records* (4 vols, Federation of Family History Societies, 2000).

In Whitehall, the Poor Law Commissioners (later the Local Government Board) kept a close eye on individual unions. Voluminous correspondence can be found in series MH 12 at the National Archives (TNA), although it is rare to find mention of individual paupers. However there is often correspondence about the appointment (and dismissal) of individual people who worked at the workhouse. The Office also has registers of paid offices in MH 9 between 1837 and 1921, although more comprehensive from the 1870s onwards. These records are described in more detail in Simon Fowler, *Using Poor Law Records* (Public Record Office Pocket Guide, 2001).

Web sites
A superb site on workhouses and the resources which are available for their study is
www.workhouses.org.uk
See for your self
Several workhouses are now museums. They include:
Ripon Workhouse, with restored vagrants' wards from 1877 showing the treatment of paupers in Yorkshire workhouses and includes a Victorian Hard Times Gallery. Address: Allhallowgate, Ripon, North Yorkshire, HG4 1LE, Tel: 01765 690799
www.ripon.co.uk/museums
Norfolk Museum of Rural Life, Gressenhall, Dereham, Norfolk, NR20 4DR, Tel: 01362 860563
www.norfolk.gov.uk/tourism/museums/nrlm.htm The museum's collections of rural and Norfolk life are housed in Georgian workhouse buildings dating back to 1777. There is also a display about life in the workhouse.
Southwell Workhouse, Upton Road, Southwell, NG25 0PT, Tel: 01636 817250
www.nationaltrust.org.uk/places/theworkhouse The Workhouse at Southwell is a formidable 19th-century brick institution. The revolutionary but harsh 'welfare' system introduced here in 1824 was adopted nation-wide in the New Poor Law. The building is the least altered workhouse in existence today, a survivor from the hundreds that once covered the country. You can find out about the people who lived and worked here, what life was like and how things have changed in the care of the poor.

Medical Officer of Health Reports
Doreen Hopwood
asks How healthy (or unhealthy) was the area
where your ancestors lived?

Public health and sanitary reform were two
topics high on the agenda in Victorian Britain.
Together they were seen as the universal panacea
for improving the living and working
environment for the population of England and
Wales.

The publication of Edward Chadwick's 'Report
of the Sanitary Condition of the Labouring
Classes of Great Britain' in 1842 highlighted the
insanitary conditions of working class dwellings,
their place of work and the domestic habits
which affected the lives of most of the country's
population. His report demonstrated the need for
national action and was instrumental in forcing
questions of public health into the political
arena. The 1848 Public Health Act was one of a
series of measures effected during the latter half
of the nineteenth century in an attempt to
improve the mortality rates across the country,
but even at the beginning of the twentieth
century there were still vast differences, not only
between town and country, but within towns and
cities themselves.

When Queen Victoria came to the throne in
1837, epidemics of
diseases such as
cholera, typhoid and
smallpox swept
across the United
Kingdom, leaving
behind high
numbers of fatalities
and permanently
disabled survivors.
Preventive medicine
was in its infancy,
but when an
effective vaccine to
combat smallpox
was developed, the
Vaccination Act of
1861significantly
reduced the numbers
of deaths from this
disease.

Increased activity
within the sphere of
public health created
new demands and
responsibilities for

local government. The Public Health Act of
1872 required all urban sanitary districts
(USD's) with a population of over 250,000 to
appoint a full-time Medical Officer of Health.
Prior to this date, sanitary reform had been
piecemeal with no national guidelines and the
introduction of the post of Medical Officer of
Health was a step towards monitoring the health
of towns, cities and rural districts on a regular
basis. Three-monthly reports were compiled,
together with an annual cumulative report, and
these were sent to the government who then
compiled national statistics based upon them.
The Registrar General used the figures (together
with population statistics from the ten-yearly
census reports) to forecast the future needs in
respect of housing, schools etc., and to monitor
where mortality (death) rates were the highest.
Towns and cities which returned high mortality
rates were exhorted to improve them by more
(and better) public health reforms.

Many of the newly appointed Medical Officers
of Health were already involved in public health.
Dr Alfred Hill was the Public Analyst prior to
his appointment in Birmingham in 1872, where

TYPICAL COURT-YARD HOUSES BEFORE IMPROVEMENT AND
RECONSTRUCTION.

DEATH-RATES IN TOWNS (FROM ANNUAL SUMMARY OF REGISTRAR-GENERAL).

	1901.	1902.	19.3.	1904.	Mean.
London	17·6	17·7	15·7	16·6	16·9
Liverpool	22·3	22·5	20·5	22·6	22·0
Manchester	22·1	20·0	19·7	21·3	20·8
Birmingham	20·5	18·6	17·8	19·9	19·2
Leeds	19·3	17·6	16·6	18·0	17·9
Sheffield	20·4	17·1	18·6	16·8	18·2
Bristol	16·0	17·4	14·3	15·6	15·8
Bradford	16·8	15·8	16·4	17·6	16·6
West Ham	17·9	17·1	15·3	16·5	16·7
Hull	18·7	17·2	16·9	18·6	17·8
Nottingham	18·5	16·7	16·9	17·7	17·4
Salford	21·7	19·3	19·0	21·2	20.3
Newcastle	21·9	19·9	19·2	194	20·1
Leicester	15·9	14·9	14 2	14·5	14·9
Portsmouth	17·9	16·8	14·7	16·9	16·6
Cardiff	15·8	16·8	14·0	14·8	15·3
Bolton	18·2	16·9	17·5	16·9	17·4
Sunderland	21·4	19·5	19·9	19·5	20·1
Croydon	12·9	14·0	11·8	13·8	13·1
Oldham	19·6	19 1	18·6	18·2	18·9

he remained as Medical Officer of Health until 1903. The duties and responsibilities of the Medical Officer of Health were varied and involved working closely with local organisations and individuals. These included Council Committees for Health and Housing (and later education), Coroner's, Sanitary Inspectors, Vaccinating Officers, Registrars of Birth and Death, and, from the beginning of the twentieth century, Health Visitors and Midwives.

As well as reporting on the vital statistics of the area for which they were responsible – the population, birth, death and marriage rate, each Medical Officer of Health was required to produce an analysis of the numbers of deaths from certain diseases which occurred within the period covered by the report. Statistics for a city were further broken down and analysed at ward/district level. From the latter it is easy to see which areas had the highest population density and were therefore likely to be the least healthy places to live. The Medical Officer of Health Report for Birmingham in 1903 showed that in the central, working class ward, of St George's, there were 170.1 persons per acre, whilst the leafy middle/upper class wards of Edgbaston and Harborne returned a density of just 9.2 persons per acre.

The Medical Officer of Health collected data from a whole range of sources and committees, each of which appeared in his annual report. It was hoped that, by studying statistics taken over a period of time, it would be possible to identify mortality trends and overcome the problems. However, it soon became apparent that although problems were clearly identified by the Medical Officer of Health, he was not always able to effect action.

Following the passing of the Housing of the

Working Classes Act (Artisans' Dwelling Act) of 1875, Medical Officers of Health were empowered to 'close' houses deemed unfit for habitation. The houses would then either be renovated or demolished. This caused a dilemma for the Medical Officer of Health because it meant that occupiers would be rendered homeless and, as most cities already had an insufficient number of affordable houses, they would be forced to live in already overcrowded properties in the vicinity. Vigorous campaigns by local councillors, press and churchmen often succeeded in instigating reforms, especially where the Medical Officer of Health had brought the problem out into the open. At the beginning of the twentieth century these pressures helped to bring about improvements to existing properties as shown in the photographs, taken from the 1904 Medical Officer of Health's report for Birmingham. By the early 1900s, there were numerous officers who were required to report to the Medical Officer of Health directly. Veterinary Inspectors were responsible for ensuring that healthy conditions prevailed in cow sheds and stables, for both cows and horses could be found living in areas close to the city centre, and a high proportion of the city's milk supply was produced locally. At 31st December 1903, Birmingham had 24 licensed cow-keepers who had over 600 cows between them. A Milkshop Inspector devoted his working day to the examining the conditions under which milk was stored and sold, whilst the Public Analyst was required to examine the milk itself for impurities or adulteration. In addition to these, an inspector appointed by the Markets and Fairs Committee inspected all shops which stored and sold food, as well as slaughter-houses. During 1904, 10,102 visits were paid to the latter alone – all of which were found to be 'in a clean condition'.

With 7,121 workshops and 639 bakehouses registered under the Factory and Workshops Act (1901), the three Workshops Inspectors, who had to examine these premises at least twice a year, certainly had their hands full. The trades covered included almost 1,700 dressmakers and tailors down to three safe-makers.

Meteorological observations were deemed of high importance as these could be used to gauge the effect of climate on certain diseases, especially those of the respiratory system such as bronchitis or pneumonia in the winter months, and the widespread epidemic diarrhoea which prevailed in the third quarter of each year. This became known as 'summer diarrhoea' and by 1904 it was accounting for such a high proportion of deaths, especially amongst infants and the elderly,. Medical Officers of Health across the country were required to effect even more rigorous data-collection. This included the numbers of flies caught on special fly papers distributed across the cities. The collation of data provided by individual Medical Officers of Health did much to help doctors understand the underlying causes of disease and mortality tables were produced by the Registrar General on an annual basis. These took the form of league tables, from which it was easy to define how healthy (or unhealthy) it was in any of the towns/cities listed. This was usually made up of about 20 towns and, as can be seen from the table, taken from the 1904 report, Liverpool had the highest death rate (at 22.6% per thousand) and Croydon the lowest (at 13.8% per thousand).

COURT-YARD AFTER IMPROVEMENT AND RECONSTRUCTION.

Infant mortality was probably the most contentious issue from the last quarter of the nineteenth century to the outbreak of the First World War. Whilst mortality rates at all ages over one year were falling quite dramatically, the infant mortality rate remained unchanged, or had increased. This had a knock on effect in the data given for the average age at death, reducing it to 27 years at the turn of the twentieth century. From the start, Medical Officers of Health had been acutely aware of the causes of high mortality rates – poverty combined with insanitary living conditions and probably the poor health of the mother. However, the cost of overcoming such problems was deemed too high and often the blame was passed back to the mother. Working mothers were condemned for leaving their babies with minders, those who did not (or could not) breast-feed and were labelled 'neglectful' and mothers who did not provide adequate food were deemed 'careless'. In his letter to the Health Committee, accompanying the report for 1904, John Robertson, Birmingham's Medical Officer of Health stressed 'the necessity for concerted action in dealing with the ignorance and carelessness which is everywhere prevalent in the feeding and rearing of infants'.

The figures supplied by Medical Officers of Health confirmed that, by the beginning of the twentieth century, the birth rate was declining, whilst the infant mortality rates were still rising. This came at a time when the eugenics debate

about the physique and health of the population was a burning issue. In some areas as many as 60% of recruits for the South African War were rejected because of their poor physical condition. An Inter-departmental Committee was set up to investigate the extent of the physical deterioration of the population. The findings confirmed what the Medical Officers of Health had been saying for some thirty years – that overcrowding, insanitary living conditions, ignorance and unhealthy factory environments were all responsible. This did go some way to acknowledging that maternal health and family diet were vital issues, and, soon after, Medical Officers of Health were including reports on the establishment of milk depots, meals for pregnant women and nursing mothers, and the provision of school meals. Special investigations were regularly carried out, and such reports can be found in the appendices to the Medical Officer of Health annual reports.

Whilst the documents will not help you get any further back with your family history research, Medical Officer of Health reports provide a keen insight into the prevalent conditions of a town, city or rural district at quarterly intervals from 1872 onwards. Surviving Medical Officer of Health reports can be found in county record offices or major libraries, and the Report of the Chief Medical Officer of the Department of Health for 1907 can be viewed at the Department of Health website. This under-utilised source of information can help to place your ancestors in their contemporary setting, linking together elements of social and local history to complement your family history research findings.

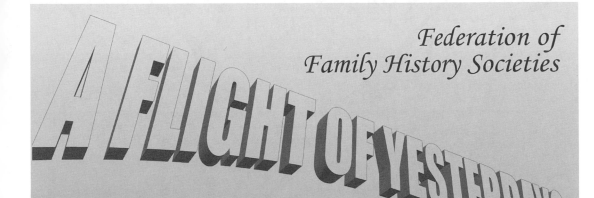

Federation of
Family History Societies

A five-day international conference to celebrate the thirtieth anniversary of the Federation of Family History Societies

Loughborough University, Leicestershire
Thursday 26 to Monday 30 August 2004

A five-day celebration of local and family history with lectures given by highly respected speakers from around the world, a series of workshops, debates, and many other attractions. This is going to be the event in 2004's history calendar. As part of the event there will be a major one-day Local History and Family History Fair that will be open to the general public as well as conference delegates.

The conference has no one theme but will cover a broad spectrum of subjects of interest to the family and local historian, including those that will be increasingly topical during 2004. Streams of lectures will cover: the British overseas; crime and punishment; house history and vernacular architecture; poor relief; local history; Internet resources; surname studies; and much, much more.

Make your 2004 a memorable year by participating in this major genealogy event.

Full programme details and booking form are available from
Bernard Amps
100 Lynwood Drive, Romford, Essex RM5 2QT, England
tel: +44 (0) 1708 761125   email: society.liaison@ffhs.org.uk
or visit our website   www.flightofyesterdays.co.uk

Conference supported by:
The Family and Local History Handbook,
Ancestry.co.uk, Hague-Lambert, The Halstead Trust, The National Archives,
FFHS (Publications) Ltd, English Heritage

Registered Charity No. 1038721   Company No. 2930189 (England)

KSG promotions

THE SCOTTISH NATIONAL

FAMILY HISTORY

FAIR

JULY 10 2004

CONCERT HALL MOTHERWELL

10AM - 4PM   ADMISSION £2.00
ACCOMPANIED CHILDREN FREE

My Nan told me I was going to live with another lady
Robert Blatchford

Sogar Farm 1920s

Nearly two years ago I heard the story of Joan's *adoption* from John, a family history tutor, who had had Joan join his class as one of his students. She was eighty years of age and wanted to discover more about her father. It transpired that Joan had been adopted in very unusual circumstances when she was four.

Apart from her quest for knowledge about her family I soon discovered that not only was Joan's adoption unusual, she had lived a very eventful life. In April 2003 I met Joan and she told me her story. The following is a short account, some of it in her own words.

Joan's mother and father lived in London at 176 Putney Bridge Road. Her mother, Annie – originally from Pembroke Dock, was in Domestic Service and her father Augustus Hazlewood was a Gramaphone Record Maker. The house was a shared house. The Hazlewoods lived on the upper floor. Downstairs lived another family the Hills. Mrs Hill had a son and daughter. Joan was born at 176 Putney Bridge Road and during the birth or shortly afterwards Joan's mother died. Augustus Hazlewood registered the birth and according to Joan abandoned her to Mrs Hill. Joan says, 'She was very kind to me and took me everywhere.' Joan had been living with the Hills for nearly four years when Mrs Hill's husband and son contracted Tubercolosis. Showing concern for such a young child and not having heard from Augustus Hazlewood for several years Mrs Hill decided to take Joan to her grandmother's home in Pembrokeshire. 'She took me shopping before she went. And she told me I could pick

anything I wanted in the shop. So I picked this sailor suit with a little skirt. I wore it down to Pembroke Dock. Oh! I was very fond of that suit!'

Travelling from London to Pembroke Dock in Wales Joan then met her grandparents. Living with 'lots of children' 'six girls and one boy younger than me' at 42 King Street Joan can

Annie Sophia
Hazlewood née Laffan
Joan's mother

Joan's Birth Certificate

remember very little about the house but remembers being 'given a penny for the collection to go to Sunday school.'

Joan had only lived with her grandmother, Mrs Laffan, for a few weeks when, Mrs Laffan went to the local market in Pembroke Dock. One trader was selling 'little girls' dresses from the back of a lorry.' One lady seeing the dresses said, 'Oh I wish I had a little girl but I only had boys! At that Mrs Laffan who was standing beside her said, 'Do you still want a little girl?' The lady replied, 'Oh I'm too old now.' Mrs Laffan said, 'No you are not. What time train are you going back on?' Somehow Mrs Laffan realised the lady, who was a Mrs Thomas, was not from Pembroke Dock. Mrs Thomas said, 'Twenty past four.' and 'never thought any more about it.' 'My nan came home from the market and told me I was going to live with another lady.' Mrs Laffan did not know Mrs Thomas but 'she packed up my clothes in a brown paper parcel. I kept saying 'is my sailor suit in there?' and Nan kept telling me it was. I was very fond of that sailor suit. It was all I could remember of the Hills.'

When Mrs Thomas came back to the Railway Station 'in all innocence I was waiting there with my Nan and was just handed over! I can remember there were two ladies in the compartment and looking from one to the other wondering who I was going to live with.' At Manorbier station Stanley, my older (adoptive) brother was waiting there with the pony and trap.' Taken to her new home Joan 'felt like royalty in the pony and trap because she had never ridden in anything like that before.'

Joan discovered that she had three new brothers – Sid 15 years of age, Reg 17 years old and Stanley who was nineteen. Her new 'father' Jack worked in the dockyard at Pembroke Dock and the farm – Rose Cottage was run by her new 'mother' Sarah. Most of the work on the farm was done by her brothers and a man employed by Mrs Thomas. On an adjoining farm, Sogar, lived Mrs Thomas' sister, Joan's new 'aunt.'

When Joan opened her parcel of clothes she discovered that the sailor suit was missing. 'I think Joey got it – my uncle who was younger

Joan (on the left)
at her adoptive brother
Reg's Wedding

than me- I was so disappointed!' Joan, however, was 'spoilt rotten' by her new brothers and whenever her mother bought her a dress she got another one from her aunt.

In September of that year, 1925, Joan's grandfather, Mr Laffan, drew up an 'adoption agreement' between himself and Mrs Thomas transferring the care of Joan to Mrs Thomas with the proviso that 'I or my wife can see her when ever we like.' They never did visit.

Some two years later Joan remembers her

Joan in her WAAF uniform

grandfather, Mr Laffan, arriving by train at the Sogar, where the Thomas's had moved from Rose Cottage. Mr Laffan told them that his wife had died and he was moving to Bedwelty, Monmouthshire with his family to be near his sister. 'Joey would only have been about six. So his sisters would have helped bring up the kids.' Her grandfather had brought Joan a photograph of her mother, her parents' marriage certificate and Joan's birth certificate.

Joan spent 15 happy years living with the Thomas family.

In 1940 Mrs Thomas, the person who Joan knew and loved as her mother, died, and Joan, at 19 years of age, decided to join the WAAF, where she served for five years until the end of the war. During her war service, Joan moved several times, ending up working at the Air Ministry, Whitehall.

Joan is now trying to trace information on her father Augustus Hazlewood ; whether he re-married; if she has any half-brothers or half-sisters ; and details of any surviving members of the Laffan family, who she believes now live in Bedwellty.

Interviews as One Source in
Genealogy and Local History
Len Barnett

'Old Uncle Charlie there, he'll tell you some stories'! Sure enough, he can. But are they accurate? And, did they happen to him?

Interviewing people involved in past and current events is a commonly used technique, seen everywhere from television and news reporting, through to heavy academic treatise and much more besides. This is a powerful tool in the hands of skilled exponents: often imperceptibly, but effectively, shaping understandings of the intended audience, or readership.

Not surprisingly then, verbal testimonies can also be employed by genealogists, local historians and also others, such as military specialists. But, there are many potential pitfalls for the unwary. So, it may be helpful to outline both the pros and cons, taking good note especially of the latter.

There are, of course, many ways to interview and there is little point in prescribing techniques if they are not necessarily appropriate. So, sense, experience and perhaps even intuition should be used to taste.

For genealogists, family members will obviously be the likely interviewees. Already knowing relatives may be seen as advantageous, but it should be borne in mind that this may actually be a hindrance to gaining meaningful information. Family relations are frequently far from harmonious and unfortunately, it is not unknown for testimonies to be heavily tainted by agendas and animosities.

Taking an optimistic tone though, if one has the luxury of extensive contact with interviewees, such as with kinsfolk, it is perfectly possible to build a good investigative relationship over time. Whether this is based on a series of formal interviews, or questions in normal conversation is obviously down to personal situations and the temperaments of both, or indeed all, parties concerned.

With family members it is often simply not possible to construct such associations because of age and distance in time. Nevertheless, some useful information can still frequently be gleaned, even from apparently unpromising material.

Asked to look into some military connections in my own family by my mother, she said that she remembered a photograph of her grandfather in a white uniform, including a white 'spiked helmet'. Subsequent research proved that he had been a private soldier in the Highland Light Infantry and had taken part in operations on the Northwest Frontier of India (now Afghanistan) in the late 1890s. However, 'expert' opinion, including that of a major from the relevant unit museum, maintains that this regiment never wore tropical versions of the then militarily fashionable Pickelhaube. In total contradiction though the regimental journal (copies of which are held at the National Army Museum, Chelsea) shows line drawings of soldiers of the other regular battalion (then at Malta) clearly wearing white helmets - complete with spikes. So, sometimes it can be worthwhile not dismissing apparently flawed memories and detail. (Whether these were cloth covers of some variety, or actual helmets I have still to resolve.)

Moving on, local historians may theoretically have a larger pool of potential interviewees to draw on. Those studying particular professions, trades, crafts and industries may too be viewed in this light. And, military historians (at least of conflicts from the 1940s onwards) potentially still have considerable scope for interviewing veterans. But, in practice, in all three of these types of study finding useful interviewees alone can be problematical and even once solved, there can be additional hurdles in breaking down barriers and gaining trust.

Whether one is face to face with one's interviewees; using the telephone; or even through the written word, it is well to have made preparations beforehand. Apart from determining the most suitable manner for recording information; such as by tape-recorder, laptop computer, shorthand, scribbled cryptic notes, or relying on one's short-term memory; an idea of what is wanted should be kept in mind.

Often first, or only, interviews are purely experimental. In such cases intended questions often need to be scrapped, but just occasionally, going off at tangents can prove highly informative. I once interviewed an elderly lady whose civilian father had been interned in Germany during the First World War. My principal aim was to get a thumbnail sketch of the man, but this rapidly proved unrealistic for reasons that I need not go into here. In some respects still bright as a pin, instead within long and slightly rambling reminiscences she told me about other male relations: all seafaring men that I was also interested in. One particular piece of information was invaluable, as it was of a variety that just would not show up in documentary evidence. These snippets, however, had to be disentangled from copious dollops of 'ancient' village gossip - some of which was clearly libellous!

Initial, or one off, interviews in particular can also pose problems in determining the veracity of information gained. One way of gauging this is to ask a few key questions where one is already absolutely certain of the facts: such as relating to well-documented family links. This can also be a good way of being seen not to know very much, which can sometimes be useful. Nevertheless, there are circumstances when this can be less than predictable. In one case of mine, where a master mariner was married twice, it became obvious even all these years later that there was lasting friction between the families concerned. Even the simplest of questions resulted in contradictory answers.

Sometimes, with the best will in the world, the information gained is limited. An example in my own experience related to a merchant seaman who spent twenty-five years with the same company. Even if the descriptions of him after retirement were highly atmospheric and the artefacts shown to me fascinating, there simply was not enough information (from documentary sources) to conduct any further meaningful research on him.

Occasionally, with prior research, interviewers can supply information unknown to the interviewees. This should obviously be done with tact and caution. On one particular occasion I was able to tell the son of a master mariner the probable nature of his father's death. Prior to the meeting I had severe reservations about dealing with this in more than the most general terms. But I need not have worried. I was rewarded with personal, poignant remembrances of the way he learned the initial news and then the anguished pain as it slowly dawned, over the next year or so, that his father had not survived after all.

Even potentially uplifting information can cause unforeseen difficulties. Although not in an interview as such, I had dealings with a near descendent of one merchant officer. It was 'known' locally that this mariner had been aboard a vessel lost with all hands in a storm. However, through reliable documentary records I had conclusively proved that he had left her immediately prior to sailing and was most definitely still alive some years later. I have not even been able to get an acknowledgement from the descendent of having ever received this information, never mind comment on my findings.

When research relates to the workings of professions, trades and industries; or alternatively to historical events; there are yet more potential snags. This can be particularly so when naval and military history is concerned.
Often interviewees will open up to interviewers, who even if they do not have direct experience of a way of life, do at least have a good appreciation of the subject being covered. Contrary to the view of propagandists, 'What did you do in the war Daddy?' cannot be regarded as an effective question in most cases. If they were involved in traumatic events it may be that the interviewees will simply not speak of these, even decades later, though they just might if they think the interviewer might understand the realities. Even if the interviewee does react positively to such general questions, without background knowledge even terminology used might make such interviews all but useless. (This can frequently be seen in current media reporting from war zones, by way of example where designations of units such as companies, battalions and divisions are used interchangeably. In reality these all have specific meanings and there is a very real difference between assaults at company and divisional levels: a company numbers around 100 men and a division traditionally in the British army as approximately 12,000!)

If one does have a good knowledge of the subject in hand (and also a not dissimilar experience to draw on), it can be possible to draw out all sorts of extra detail from co-operative interviewees. As an example, while onboard a Second World War Liberty ship on a visit to Britain some years ago, I was speaking to a chap who had served on similar vessels. With a little prompting he gave me some very interesting insights into life onboard British operated 'Liberties'. When his explanations became too technical for me to completely grasp, as in the action taken immediately after propeller shafts broke at sea, I quietly reminded him that I was not an engineer and he gladly restated his point in words that I understood.

On the other hand one can often detect failures, through interviewers' lack of wider, practical experience. In one published example drawn to my attention, a First World War veteran had mentioned wearing a gas mask. Perhaps if the interviewer had worn even a modern anti-gas respirator (thereby experiencing the still considerable discomforts in these contrivances) he, or she, would have thought to get some more detail on suffering the earliest versions in combat.

Again direct, or even good indirect, knowledge can be a defence against some spurious stories. In a biography of a colourful and adventurous merchant navy officer is a supposed wartime account of a gunnery shoot on an armed-merchant cruiser that went awry, with the towing tug coming under fire rather than the target. Apart from operational documentary sources proving without a doubt that this incident could not have happened, this is a sailors' 'ditty' and surfaces with each generation slightly differently.

(In my day it was elderly Hawker Hunter aircraft almost getting shot out of the sky by ships' anti-aircraft missiles! I have no doubt that there will be a current version.)

Even when anecdotes are essentially true, over time and many retellings they may well have become polished and embellished. Sometimes gentle questioning of such stories can bring out further details, which are helpful in either confirming, or throwing doubt on the anecdotes. On one occasion in my experience this surprisingly opened a vast gulf between the statements made and what was actually remembered though. By letter I had asked some very general questions of a chap who had been a merchant officer during the First World War. I received long tape recordings back by post that were most interesting, though slightly confusing in places. Where I asked for limited clarification, I received answers. However, subsequent questions were never answered. Years later another contact sent me photocopies of religious pamphlets from the 1920s. It turned out that this officer had left the sea soon after the war and become a preacher. The tape recordings I had been sent were his sermons, almost word for word of those in the pamphlets!

While the immediately above-related experience can be regarded as an extreme example, some understanding as to how memory works should also be taken into consideration. Even at the time, people involved in events may hold highly discrepant assessments: even of relatively simple cases such as road traffic accidents. In larger and more complex happenings, especially when highly stressful, in close proximity people will almost always see events differently. And, even where social origins and considerations such as education and upbringing are similar, differing characters will register some pieces, or classes, of information and discard others in ways that are not entirely clear. Documentary sources of debriefing interviews frequently show this trait well and sometimes inherent contradictions just cannot be resolved.

The passing of time brings yet more complications. Even if individuals actually

want to remember and often they do not, some details apparently become lost, while others seem to surface: if only briefly. Attitudes are oft to change, both in a social context and personally: whether recognised and acknowledged, or not. With further experience the human mind has a habit of re-editing memory, a concept that must be borne in mind when dealing in verbal testimonies.

Subsequent knowledge can also cloud realistic renderings of memories. Some people retain professional interests, whether through continued physical contact with 'the regiment' or 'the company' and serious study at one end of the scale, or merely by reading occasional books at the other. Some individuals return to long past events and experiences in their minds for different reasons, including belated attempts to make sense of these.

The membership of old comrades associations should be seen fundamentally as having gained 'additional' knowledge then. The reasons for veterans joining such organisations are known to range widely from a complete alienation towards civil society post conflict through to a need, or want of a continued shared sense of past identity. Through these associations common understandings have naturally enough been fostered, as information and perspectives have flowed through their numbers.

With this in mind, the end result of verbal consultations with veterans, far from being accurate may actually be severely contaminated

by other inputs. Dates and places may well have not been particularly noteworthy to many at the time, but have subsequently taken on great importance. Likewise, details of strategy, planning and tactics, all of which would have generally been unknown to all but senior officers and immediate staffs, have become mixed in veterans' minds. Also, events originally barely known about, in telling and re-telling have unknowingly taken on lives of their own. Also, rumours have a habit of resurfacing as 'fact', again perhaps unknowingly. Ironically, genuine events can become lost.

There is another complication that interviewers (and researchers in general) should be on their guard against - that is the deliberately falsified statement. This is particularly problematical when it is mixed with accuracy and delivered convincingly. Motives can be varied, from people talking up their personal importance, to others diverting attention from their own shortcomings. In my experience where I have realised false testimony, it has not necessarily been until later that disparities have become apparent. If realised at the time, I would suggest as full a record as possible should be kept. Expert knowledge and careful checking of other sources (such as service sheets and operational records) may subsequently identify suspect testimony, but this is not always possible.

Similarly, it would seem from some evidence that there are times when interviewees wish to please the interviewer, the former giving the latter what is thought is wanted: degenerating from remembrance to performance. And, there is the question of whether particular individuals' accounts reflect common, or exceptional, experience.

So much for all the downsides. Much can also be gained, especially with a little practice. Anyway, not everyone is interested in the supposedly glorious martial exploits of forebears, or great exploits in the Empire. Instead, working conditions down mines, in factories, shops, offices, or on the land can perfectly legitimately be regarded as just as interesting. General social attitudes have definitely changed over the last half dozen decades in the 'developed world' (though some of the more negative ideas unfortunately tend to remain). Even in terms of changing technology, life even forty or so years ago can be regarded as significantly different. The sum total of humankind's experience in any one age must be staggering. So I am sure that interviews will remain one technique for gathering and recording information.
© Len Barnett 2003

Capt: James Cook of the Endeavour.

Captain Cook in Whitby
Dr Sophie Forgan
Chairman Cook Museum Trust

In a narrow lane, Grape Lane, alongside Whitby harbour on Yorkshire's dangerous North East coast, is a substantial 17th century red-brick house. It is the Captain Cook Memorial Museum. It has been known as "Captain Cook's House", which it wasn't - at least not in the sense that it had been his! But "John Walker's House" it undoubtedly was. Traditionally it is the house to which the young James Cook came in 1746 to be apprenticed to the Whitby shipowner Captain John Walker, and to which he returned on a visit in the winter of 1771/2 after the momentous First Voyage.

There is a huge amount of original material about Cook - numerous accounts by contemporaries and not least the fat volumes of his own Journals. But why should anyone have given a thought to his early life until that moment twenty years on when he returned to Whitby to visit his former master John Walker? At that moment, on New Year's Day 1772, he stood a celebrated naval officer, the successful commander of a three year scientific expedition to the South Seas, explorer, circumnavigator, discoverer of new lands, and recently introduced to the highest in the land, the King. The Walker household was lined up to receive him, the elderly housekeeper told to mind her Ps and Qs, and the story goes that she so far forgot herself that she flung her arms around Cook exclaiming: "Oh honey James, how glad I'se to see thee!"

It may have been then that folks started to recollect the young James as he was when he first came to Whitby. Not until his death did anyone try to set it down.

The gist was that he was the son of a farm labourer who became bailiff on a property near Great Ayton in Yorkshire. There Cook received a village education. It got him a job in a shop in a nearby fishing village, Staithes. The job did not particularly suit him, and he was apprenticed to Captain John Walker in Whitby as a "three year servant", and then spent a further six years serving in Walker's ships, rising to master's mate. He was on the point of promotion to master, when he threw it all up and left Whitby in 1756 to join the Royal Navy and start all over again.

On many points the original sources, written thirty or more years later, disagree with each other. Was he actually an apprentice at Staithes? Was there a dispute about money? Was he apprenticed to John Walker, or to both John and his brother Henry? However by far the most reliable of the early accounts is that of the pastor and antiquarian, the Rev. George Young, who worked in Whitby in the early 1800s. Young comes across as a careful historian, all the more so in Cook's case because he names his sources as two sons of Captain John Walker, both of them master mariners. They were born around the time of James' apprenticeship and were young men at the time of the 1772 visit. Young firmly places Cook's lodging as Walker's House in Grape Lane, with its large attic where the Walkers' many apprentices slept, and where Mary Prowd gave him candles for his studies. From our knowledge of the house, and from the muster rolls and records of Whitby we can piece together Cook's Whitby years and their context.

When Cook arrived in 1746 the house was owned by Captain John Walker and his elder brother Henry. They had inherited it three years earlier from their father, the founder of the family shipping business. At his death - the original of his will confirms it - he divided his ships between his sons, but left the house in Grape Lane jointly to the two. The sons each had their own smaller establishment elsewhere in Whitby. Their mother continued to live in an upstairs 'chamber' and paid the rates as occupier. At that time houses served both business and domestic purposes and Whitby wives are known to have played a major part in the business, often keeping the accounts and sometimes even sailing with their husbands. We do not know what role Esther Walker had, but it is likely that she continued to help with the business. Indeed, the disposition of the house in the will, and the recent discovery of a slipway three feet below the surface of the present day yard is consistent with the view that the house was the centre of the family shipping business in the father's time and continued to be so after his death - including lodging the apprentices when not at sea.

long period in which the house was a hospital before reverting to use as a dwelling. In the 1980's the last owner sold it to the Cook Museum Trust so that the house could be preserved for the people of Whitby as a Museum to celebrate the life of Captain Cook.

Readers of this Handbook may be familiar with Walker's House in Whitby's Grape Lane, and with the Captain Cook Memorial Museum. Many will have visited the Museum during the fifteen years since it was opened in 1987. Fewer will perhaps have been in since it was re-opened last year after significant extension and refurbishment.

When the Cook Museum Trust bought Walker's House, it was agreed that the former owner, Canon Morris should continue to live in the 'cottage' which adjoins the main house. In the fullness of years the Canon died and the cottage became available.

The Museum's new wing has been a major project. At a cost of £464,000, financed by a grant of £347,000 from the Heritage Lottery Fund, and grants from other charitable Trusts, it took all of three years, culminating in major building works, reconstruction and refurbishment. A huge thank-you is owed to donors, suppliers, volunteers and staff. A project like this does not happen without its local Council. They helped in innumerable ways, signage, public art, crumbling walls - theirs! - all sorts of permissions, and constant service to us and encouragement.

Nothing really prepares one for the enormity of taking an old building apart and putting it together again, all in a Whitby winter. No matter that the surveyors surveyed and the archaeologist dug his holes, it wasn't till the builders opened it up, that it became clear the extent to which the cottage was "held together by its roof trusses"!

The archaeologist, Colin Briden, made two important discoveries which contributed greatly to our understanding. Three feet below the surface of the flag-stoned yard between the house and the sea wall, under a layer of sand, was a sloping stone slipway dating from the first half of the eighteenth century. The house and the harbour were directly linked, consistent with combined domestic and business use as one would expect in the period of Cook's apprenticeship in the late 1740s.

John Walker did not move in until 1755 after the deaths of his mother and elder brother - after Cook had completed his three year apprenticeship. It is out of a realisation of that circumstance that doubt arose in the 1890s as to whether Cook had actually lodged in Grape Lane. We are sure that he did because of the location of the house and the nature of the business, as argued above, and all possible local avenues of research have been exhaustively examined! The visitor may choose between an 1890's doubt and the Walker family tradition recorded 70 years closer to the events it describes.

It was a Quaker household. Cook married into a Quaker family. Some attribute Cook's application, modesty, humanity, and general restraint to Quaker influence. It must also have been a very crowded household at times. The muster rolls show that half the crew of a Whitby collier might be apprentices. John Walker himself had up to seventeen at times. What the attic was like when they were all at home at once may be imagined - seventeen sweaty, salt-stained youngsters all in one large room!

The house evokes the world in which Cook lived and the people who trained him, the busy shipyards, and above all the ships in which he sailed, the flat-bottomed colliers that plied between Newcastle and London. By the time he left Whitby, Cook was a highly competent ship's officer, experienced in the handling of crews and in practical navigation, with wide knowledge of the North Sea and the Baltic, the ports and their approaches.

The house remained in the Walker family until well into the 19th century. It assumed a more domestic appearance as the Walkers moved from being owners of ships and farms, through the financing and insurance of shipping, into banking. In the twentieth century there was a

There was a dispute in the 1750s in the Walker family over the father's will. An inventory, room by room, was taken of the contents of the house. We still have it and it was the basis of the restoration and period re-furnishing of the ground floor rooms - they are now much as they were in 1750. However the inventory referred to a "Brick floored room" which from its contents appeared to be the kitchen. But where was it? There seemed to be no space for it in Walker's House as it is today. Colin dug a hole in the floor of the cottage closest to the main house, and there two feet down, at a similar level to the top of the slipway, was a herringbone patterned brick floor - we had found the kitchen! The brick floor remains exposed for the visitor to imagine the domain of Mary Prowd, the housekeeper who befriended the young Cook.

Pausing first in the yard, looking out over Whitby harbour, the visitor now finds the Museum's entrance through a doorway into the cottage wing. The enlarged building provides much needed exhibition space, allowing us to tell more of the Cook story, and an education room for school parties. Themed rooms introduce Cook and the history of the house. The visitor then enters Walker's House at ground floor level. There has been some rearrangement of displays, but it remains with period rooms on the ground floor according to the inventory, in the simple Quaker style Cook knew while serving the Walkers in Whitby. Above are the Whitby, London, Voyages, Scientists and Artists rooms, together with the attic where Cook lodged with

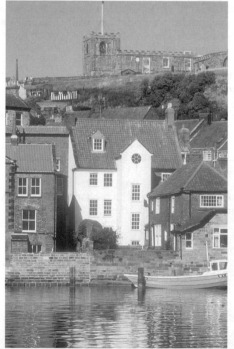

the other apprentices when ashore. The visitor returns to the entrance at first floor level: the final room is devoted to Cook and his Antarctic exploration.

Much of the displays consist of original material, important manuscripts, letters in Cook's hand, models, prints and paintings, including recent acquisitions by Gainsborough, John Russell and William Hodges - of Lord Sandwich, William Bligh and his wife Elizabeth, and of the island of Madeira.

Our latest acquisition links Cook, Whitby and the far reaches of the Pacific. During the Second Voyage a Polynesian islander, Omai, came to Britain in Cook's sister ship the Adventure. He was taken under the wing of Joseph Banks, the botanist on the First Voyage, who brought him to visit Yorkshire. They went to the races in York, and then on to Scarborough, where Omai (picturesquely described as "a specimen of pale moving mahogany tattooed from the hips down with arches)"swam in the sea. Given a gun at Mulgrave Castle near Whitby, he popped away at game and farmyard fowls with equal abandon! He also had his portrait painted in company with Banks and Dr Solander. It is this portrait by the Welsh artist William Parry, historically though not artistically more important than the better known Reynolds painting of Omai, that this small museum has just acquired in a most unusual three way partnership with London's National Portrait Gallery, and the National Museums and Galleries of Wales. Next year, 2004, Omai will be ready to greet you in Grape Lane at the Captain Cook Memorial Museum.

Whitby may be reached by the A169 from York and by the A171 from Scarborough and Teesside and by rail from Teesside on the Esk valley line from Middlesborough. Railway enthusiasts use the North York Moors steam railway from Pickering changing at Grosmont. The Museum is in the town centre on the east side of the harbour in Grape Lane, to the right of the swing bridge below the Abbey. It is open weekends in March, 11am to 3.00pm and for the rest of the year to the end of October every day, 9.45am to 5pm.

The Museum is a charity dependent for its running costs on entry charges and donations from the public. Entry for adults is £3.00 with appropriate concessions for senior citizens, families, children and school parties. There is wheelchair access for the disabled to the first floor and a DVD to cover the two upper floors.

Tel/fax 01947 601900
E:captcookmuseumwhitby@ukgateway.net.
Website:cookmuseumwhitby.co.uk. Administrator: Mick Green
© CCMM Illustrations - Graham Smith, The Works, Leeds.

FEDERATION OF FAMILY HISTORY SOCIETIES (PUBLICATIONS) LIMITED

*Publishers and Suppliers of a wide range of books on
Family History (and related subjects) to
Family History Societies, individual Family Historians,
Libraries, Record Offices and Booksellers, etc.*

- *Well over 100 titles commissioned by the Federation of Family Historians and produced at attractive prices, plus a fine selection of titles from other publishers.*

- *A wide range of **'Basic Series'** and **'Introduction to'** books with detailed guidance on most aspects of family history research.*

- ***Gibson Guides** giving explicit advice on the precise extent and whereabouts of major record sources*

- ***Stuart Raymond's** extensive listings of published family history reference material at national and local level*

- ***Web Directories***

*Titles available from your local Family History Society
and by post from:-*

**FFHS (Publications) Limited,
Units 15 and 16 Chesham Industrial Centre,
Oram Street, Bury, Lancashire, BL9 6EN**

Visit our 'On-line bookshop' and Catalogue at

www.familyhistorybooks.co.uk
Tel: 0161 797 3843 Fax: 0161 797 3846
Email enquiries to: sales@ffhs.co.uk

Research your Family History On-Line

We publish on-line records compiled by Family History Societies and others - quality data from experienced researchers with local knowledge, providing accurate details at fees that give real value for money.

Visit our 'pay per view' site at:
www.familyhistoryonline.net <http://www.familyhistoryonline.net/>

110 Naughty Ladies Transported to a Land beyond the Seas
Jackie Evans

Some years ago, I investigated the cases of women who committed offences in London, were tried at the Old Bailey Sessions during the Mayoralty of Sir Peter Laurie, November 1832 and October 1833, and were sentenced totransportation to Australia.

The 1831 Census shows that the population in London at that time was large. In the City of London both within and without the walls, the population was 123,683; in the Hundred of Ossulstone, Holborn Division, which included St Andrews, Holborn, Paddington, St Pancras and St Clement Danes, it was 346,255 and in Ossulstone, Tower Division, which covered the East End including Bethnal Green and Wapping it was 359,864.[1] Many of these people were housed in overcrowded conditions; those who had money moved out to the surrounding areas, while the poor gravitated to the ccntre. The "Rookeries" of London developed, accommodating hundreds of people who had little, if any means of support. These areas were disease ridden and insanitary. The conditions, poverty and hardship in the centre of London caused many people both young and old to turn to crime. Henry Mayhew decided that there were two kinds of London criminal, one group who were professionals and who objected to working for a living, the second category were people who committed "accidental" crimes through force of Circumstance. In his extensive wanderings around London during the 1840s he interviewed many people involved in criminal activities. His description of female pickpockets who he recorded dressed in "fashionable attire" was interesting. "They were often superior in intellect to the men and more orderly in their habits. They seldom married but cohabited with pickpockets, burglars and other infamous characters."[2] The crowded conditions of London and the difficulties of sheer survival made the City of London and the adjacent areas a centre for beggars, thieves and destitute people.

The law for many people in London was synonymous with the Old Bailey. In this street a Sessions Hall had stood for many years where trials were heard for both the City of London and the Shire of Middlesex. In 1824, a second Sessions house was built so by 1832 trials were heard in both the Old and New Sessions Houses.[3] The majority of these cases were for stealing and associated crimes, although there were some for rape, bigamy, forgery and coining. The adjacent Newgate prison had existed for hundreds of years and also came under the jurisdiction of the City of London.

Over the years, Newgate prison was destroyed a number of times. It was burnt to the ground during the Gordon Riots of 1780 and again rebuilt but within a few years suffered from severe overcrowding. In the main gaol there were female criminals of four different types; those awaiting trial; those under sentence of imprisonment; those awaiting transportation; and those awaiting execution. All these women were herded together and by 1813 some 300 women and their children were contained in two wards and two cells, a total area of 192 square yards.[4] The conditions were appalling, most of the prisoners were clad in rags, they had to sleep on the floor, they were desperate for food and drink and the whole area was filthy beyond description. The Quaker, Stephen Grellet, visited the women in January 1813 and was so disturbed that he inspired Elizabeth Fry to visit the prison.[5] By 1817, Elizabeth Fry had formed a school at Newgate for the children and with eleven members of the Society of Friends had formed an association for the improvement of female prisoners at Newgate. This committee existed until 1878.[6] At least one of the

Newgate Prison

Committee visited the prison daily, a matron was employed, clothes were provided for the women and they were given work materials. In addition, the women were introduced to the Holy Scriptures which the Committee believed produced "habits of order, sobriety and industry". Rules of behaviour were established within the female prison and the female workshop produced clothes for the convict settlements in Australia. A careful system of supervision was established. Over every twelve or thirteen women, a matron was placed, who was answerable for their work and kept an account of their conduct.[7] A yardwoman maintained good order in the yard and the sickroom was ruled by a nurse and an assistant. These managers were all prisoners.

In 1818 Mrs Fry faced a potential riot at Newgate with a group of prisoners about to be transported. The night before their departure, they broke up the furniture, smashed the windows and generally caused chaos within the prison. The following morning, they were put in irons, loaded onto open wagons and driven to the river for embarkation through jeering crowds. Mrs Fry persuaded Governor Newman to permit the women to travel in closed hackney-coaches with the turnkeys escorting them. She joined the end of the procession in her own carriage. When the party arrived at Deptford the women were herded on to the Maria. The women from other gaols who arrived in irons, with hoops around their waists, clambered awkwardly aboard. Mrs Fry was deeply distressed by the cramped conditions and, so, she divided the 128 convicts into classes of twelve based on the Newgate system. A small space in the stern of the ship was set aside for the schoolroom for the fourteen prisoners' children who were old enough to read and sew. A school mistress was appointed and if she worked well the Captain would pay her at the end of the trip. The Ladies Association

bought material from which the women could make patchwork quilts during the journey for sale on arrival in Australia. Before the ship sailed Mrs Fry went on board to read the Bible to the assembled gathering of convicts. For the next 20 years, whenever she could, Mrs Fry personally inspected female convict ships before they left London to ensure that the women would live decently and piously during the voyage.[8]

During the period that Sir Peter Laurie was Lord Mayor of London commencing in November 1832, there were eight Sessions at the Old Bailey. I estimated that 1401 men and 342 women were tried during this time. What did surprise me was how quickly these cases were heard after the offence was committed. In most instances the cases were heard at the next available Session which was often a few days later. Although the Session Papers are indexed, some people were not included in the index, others were shown under their own names and their alias and others were charged with a number of offences and appear separately listed in the index. I found that of the men 102 were found guilty of capital offences and sentenced to death; 605 were sentenced to transportation; seven were fined; 33 had their judgements respited; 292 were found not guilty; and 14 were shown as guilty but no sentence was recorded. In addition, 28 boys were sentenced to be whipped. By comparison, among the women, I found that four were guilty of capital offences, of whom three were sentenced to death and one was awarded 14 years transportation; a further 124 were sentenced to transportation; 97 were imprisoned; five were fined; five had their judgements respited; 100 were found not guilty; and seven were found guilty but no sentence was recorded.[9]

The judgements made against the women showed that nearly one third were found not guilty or had judgements respited, nearly one third were imprisoned, often for only a few weeks although there was one case of 18 months, and just over a third were sentenced to transportation. In comparison with the men very few women were tried for capital offences; during the year there was a total of seven women, three of whom were found not guilty. Three of these guilty women were sentenced to death but the sentence in all cases was reduced to transportation for life.

The majority of the women sentenced to transportation, 116, were found guilty of non capital offences and charged with stealing, four were charged with making and counterfeiting coins and four were charged with receiving. Nearly half these women, 59, were aged between 20 and 29 years but 32 were under the age of 20, including one, Mary Roberts, who was 11 years old. She was born in Bristol and charged with stealing various goods from Charles Terry of Aldergate Street on 6 March 1833. She was found guilty and sentenced to 7 years transportation. Although the Old Bailey Session papers recorded that judgement was respited, this was not recorded on the prison records and, certainly, she travelled as a convict on the William Bryan.[10] The oldest woman was a 60 year widow who was charged with receiving stolen goods valued at 3s. She was sentenced to fourteen transportation but she was removed from Newgate prison and sent to the Penitentiary in January 1833 and did not travel to Australia. A further 11 women were sent to the Penitentiary and two to the House of Correction and, therefore, were not transported and four women were pardoned. This left 106 who were transported in accordance with their sentences and the four who were guilty of capital offences making a total of 110 ladies who were sent to Australia.

It is perhaps interesting to note that of the original 128 women sentenced to transportation many of them were migrants to London. Clearly, all were living in London at the time of their offence but I found that while 54 were Londoners by birth, 39 came from other parts of England, 28 came from Ireland, 2 from Scotland and one each from Wales, France and Germany. I was unable to find the place of birth of 2 of the women.[11]

So what was to become of these women? During the period of transportation, 1787 to 1868, many hundreds of ships left the United Kingdom carrying some 150,000 individuals who had been sentenced to a life in a land beyond the seas. Of these nearly 25,000 were women about 15% of the total.[12] In the early days men and women were transported together on ships but, by 1806, the perhaps obvious decision was taken that men and women should be transported on different ships. However, some ships continued to take men and women convicts for the next few years. The last such ship to sail was the Francis and Eliza, she left England in 1815 with 54 men and 69 women convicts on board.

The ships used throughout the

transportation period varied considerably but no vessel was specifically designed or built as a convict ship, though many made numerous journeys. The crew usually consisted of a master and 3 officers, a few carried a fourth mate, and a crew of between 25 and 40 men. Although the naval authorities could do little to ensure high standards amongst the officers and men, they could and did make sure that only the better class of vessel was hired for convict service. Their examinations were thorough and they insisted on a reasonable standard of seaworthiness. No convict ship foundered on the passage to Australia although losses in other trades were heavy. However, the journey to Australia was long and tedious and the ships were generally small. It defies the imagination to contemplate the conditions below deck in temperatures of 90oF to 100oF. Many medical officers reported that the stench of the prison, crowded with perspiring humanity, was indescribable. The sleeping berths were doubled bunked, each berth was 6 feet square and accommodated 4 convicts, this provided each individual with 18 inches of sleeping space![13] It says much for the surgeons who looked after the prisoners that there were so few deaths on the voyages. Fortunately, many of the Surgeons' Journals survive and it is these documents which provide the best insight into life on board the convict ships.

The women that I investigated were transported remarkably quickly after sentence was passed, normally on the next available ship. The 110 female prisoners boarded seven different ships, the Jane, HMS Buffalo, the William Bryan, the Amphitrite, the Numa, the Edward and the George Hibbert.[14] The first four women travelled on the Jane; they embarked at Woolwich and sailed on 22 February 1833. The trip that took 128 days reached Tasmania on 30 June 1833. The next ship to sail was the rather larger 600 ton HMS Buffalo. She carried 179 female convicts including 38 from the London

group and 25 children. The journey from Woolwich via Spithead, Rio de Janeiro and King George's Sound took 146 days to reach New South Wales.[15] The surgeon on this ship kept very good records. He listed all the female convicts by name, their place of birth, their education and whether they could read or write. He declared that 48 were able to read and write, 87 were able to read but not write but 44 could not achieve either skill. Of the London group of 38, 31 were from England, two had attended Sunday School, 16 had attended 'other' schools and 13 were uneducated, the one Welsh girl had attended an 'other' school. Of the 5 Irish women, two had attended 'other' schools and three were uneducated and the French woman had attended an 'other' school.[16] All 38 women arrived safely in Sydney but one was taken to hospital where shortly afterwards she died. Another had a young child with her and she was sent to the Parramatta Female Factory, the prison near Sydney. Of the remaining 36, four were sent by steamer to Newcastle and the remainder were disembarked in Sydney.

The third ship to sail was the William Bryan. The prisoners began embarkation at Woolwich on 10 May 1833 and this continued until 10 June by which time some 100 women had boarded the ship including 18 from the London group. The convicts suffered from a number of ailments prior to sailing, 29 suffered from diarrhoea and by 11 June two had died of cholera. A further six died by the end of June. Eventually, the William Bryan sailed on 4 July and took 111 days to reach Tasmania arriving in Hobart on 23 October. During the voyage one female died and she was from the London group but the other 17 arrived safely.[17]

Sadly the success of the previous voyages was not reflected in the case of the fourth ship the Amphitrite. On 13 August 1833, 17 of the women convicts from London embarked at Woolwich. In all 106 convicts and 12 of their children sailed for New South Wales on 25 August under the Master John Hunter who had commanded the ship for 8 years. As the Amphitrite sailed passed Dungeness she met a violent storm and on the morning of 30 August she hove to and by noon she was lying about three miles east of Boulogne Harbour. During the afternoon, in strong winds, poor visibility and mountainous seas an attempt was made to keep her off land. Hunter set the fore and main top sails, but she continued to drift towards the coast and by 3 o'clock was in sight of Boulogne. An hour and a half later the tide had carried her into the harbour and she grounded on the sands. Her plight was observed by thousands of people who rushed on to the beach to watch the stricken vessel. Immediately, a pilot boat was launched and was alongside the Amphitrite by 5 o'clock. However, Hunter refused offers of help and he and the surgeon insisted that the women should not be landed as they might escape. An hour later a sailor swam to the Amphitrite and persuaded the crew to throw a line, again Hunter and the surgeon refused to abandon ship and ordered that the line be cast away in a most positive manner. It was reported that Hunter had a pistol in each hand.

One can only imagine the chaos and fear below decks in the convict areas. Suffice to say the women broke down the half deck hatch sometime during the evening and rushed frantically on deck. Their piteous cries carried clearly on the rising wind to the shore. When the flood tide began the Amphitrite was pounded heavily against the sand and about 11pm she broke in two amid ships. She went to pieces in a few minutes. Only three sailors reached the shore, the remainder including all the prisoners drowned. The accounts in The Times expressed horror that such an accident should have occurred. The reporters were most indignant that the Captain had not accepted assistance when it was offered by the French seamen.[18] There was an official inquiry which concluded that the Amphitrite had undergone repairs at Deptford some five months earlier under the supervision of the Naval authorities and that the Naval examination had found her sea-worthy and well found. Furthermore, it was established that if Hunter had accepted the pilot boat's offer of help, or that of the sailor, passengers and crew might have been saved. All 17 London women perished and it is perhaps ironic that two of them had been sentenced to death but had their sentences remitted to life transportation.

The next to sail was the Numa. There were 140 women prisoners on board including 31 of the London women. They embarked at Woolwich on 18 November 1833 and the Numa set sail on 29 January 1834. She sailed via the Cape of Good Hope arriving in new South Wales 135 days later on 13 June. Two of the London women died on the journey, another fell and broke her arm and two others were ill for part of the journey. By the end of 1833, there were only two of the London women left in Newgate. One travelled on the Edward and the other on the George Hibbert. The Edward sailed on 5 May 1834 and arrived in Hobart on 5 September. This was a very long journey via the Cape of Good Hope but by careful distribution of prison meats and lemon juice the surgeon managed to get all the prisoners safely to Tasmania. The last ship the George Hibbert sailed on 27 July and took 127 days to reach Sydney. There were 144 female convicts, 11 free women and 64 children on board and although the surgeon treated 92 people during the journey all arrived safely in Australia.[19]

In summary, of the 110 women who were finally sentenced to transportation, 17 were drowned on the Aphitrite, three died on the journey and one shortly after arrival in Australia. The 89 others started out on their new lives at the other end of the world. For the record one of these was Mary Reading my great, great, grandmother. She was 15 years old when she committed her offence, stealing a dress worth 5s, and 16 years old when she sailed for Australia leaving behind her parents and siblings.

Notes:
1. Census of Great Britain, Enumeration Abstract, (Printed by order of the House of Commons, 2 April 1833, 3 Vols.), Vol. 1 pp. 365-376.
2. H.Mayhew, London Labour and the London Poor, (New York: 4 Vols, Dover Publication, 1968), Vol. IV pp. 29 and 308.
3. Albert Crew, The Old Bailey, (London: Ivor, Nicholson & Watson, 1933), p.13.
4. Arthur Griffiths, The Chronicles of Newgate, (London: Bracken Books, 1987), pp. 287-289 & 376.
5. June Rose, Elizabeth Fry, (London: Macmillan, 1980), p. 69.
6. Griffiths, The Chronicles, pp. 376-379.
7. Rose, Elizabeth Fry, pp. 84-89.
8. Ibid, pp. 98-100.
9. The Old Bailey Session Papers, November 1832 to October 1833.
10. Session Papers, case 784; National Archives, P.C.O.M. 2/202; H.O. 77/40; H.O. 11/9.
11. National Archives, P.C.O.M. 2/202.
12. L.L.Robson, The Convict Settlers of Australia, (Hong Kong: Melbourne University Press, 1879), pp. 3 & 74.
13. Charles Bateson, The Convict Ships 1787-1868, (Hong Kong: A.H. & A.W. Reed, 1974) pp. 69, 83 & 87.
14. National Archives, H.O. 11/9.
15. Bateson, The Convict Ships 1787-1868, pp. 352-353 & 388.
16. National Archives, A.D.M. 101 13/9.
17. National Archives, A.D.M. 101 74/6.
18. The Times 3, 4 & 8 September 1833.
19. Bateson, The Convict Ships 1787-1868, pp. 352-353 & 362-363, National Archives, A.D.M. 101 57/7, 29/3 & 22/8.

Jackie Evans is the author of Frederick Matthias Alexander, A Family History. The book gives a detailed account of the Alexander family, transportation to Australia and life in the early days of Tasmania. The publishers are Phillimore & Co. Ltd of Chichester on www.phillimore.co.uk or in Australia the book is available at Einstein's Moon Bookshop, 336 Clarendon Street, South Melbourne, Victoria

I had a very happy childhood!
Richard Heylings
tells us about finding his brothers and sisters

When I was about eight years old I was told by Mum and Dad that I had been adopted!. I cannot remember my exact feelings that day, BUT, it was something that was always on my mind .I was told that my parents were Scottish and that my Father was a Doctor. Nothing more. Nothing less. I never broached the subject with Mum or Dad. I thought that the subject was a secret and that it should not be discussed.

It was not until much later in life that I found out just how many people knew that I had been adopted. It had not been a secret after all. Anyway as time went on I got married and started a family of my own.

In the 1980s the adoption laws were more relaxed and one day whilst visiting Mum and Dad they approached the subject of adoption and asked me if I wanted anymore information about my adoption. I was embarrassed and uncomfortable so I said. "No". However, at the back of my mind I always had this yearning to find out more about my real family. In 1987 Mum died and a couple of years later Dad had a heart attack and before going to Hospital he handed me some keys to a bureau telling me to open the bureau if he died but only in the presence of my brother. My dad said there were some papers in the top right hand drawer for me, and top left hand drawer for my brother, Jonathan, who had also been adopted. The temptation to look in the bureau was great but without looking I gave the keys back to Dad the following day.

The subject of our adoption was never discussed again even when a few years later my brother and I were given Power of Attorney when Dad was diagnosed with a terminal illness. Dad died in March 1994. My brother and I opened the bureaua couple of days later but there was no information about our adoptions. A few weeks later after locking Dad's house up one night my wife told me she had something to show me and suggested that I sit down. She gave me a brown envelope with " Richard's details" written on the front. I opened it and pulled out the contents.

The envelope contained official adoption papers and a letter from my natural Father giving a brief family history which was written in a most formal fashion. I was forty-six years old and only now had details of my birth parents. Pauline, my wife, asked me if I wanted to do anything with the paperwork. I was stunned I did not know whether to say 'yes' or 'no'. I just kept on reading the various documents. My head was spinning, I had just started a new job, my father had died and I now had my adoption papers.

What do I do? I had always had a desire to find out about my past. I now had the documentation and the chance to find out. Pauline said I could have a brother or sister. We agreed that we would find out more. We did not discuss it for several days especially with a complete career change and a lot to learn. About a week later we had checked Dad's house Pauline reminded me of our conversation a few days earlier that I might have a brother or sister. She had been making some enquiries and had discovered that I had two brothers and five sisters!

I was utterly amazed, my head was spinning! I asked Pauline how she had got the information so quickly. The questions tumbled out of me – 'Where do they live?' 'Are they older than I am?' (That

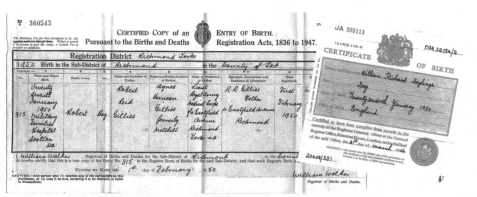

Richard's Original Full Birth Certificate
and the Short Birth Certificate issued on adoption

would perhaps explain my adoption) 'Just a minute, brothers, sisters, what about my Mother and Father?' Pauline told me that both my mother and father had died. (I was stunned, shocked, gob smacked!) 'How have you found out such detailed information in only a few days?'

When we had read the details from my adoption papers it had been evident that my father had been a medical Doctor. Following this, Pauline, had gone to the local library in Richmond to see if they had a Register for Doctors - Medical Practitioners. Redirected to the larger County Library at Northallerton and after a short car journey, Pauline went to the reference library and searhed the Medical Practitioners Register. Searching through the pages for the name Gillies, which was my birth surname, she found twenty one! Photocopying the list Pauline drove home to continue the search. It did not take long. After checking several of the entries Pauline telephoned Queens University Belfast although she did not know what she was going to say. The number was dialed and after a couple of rings Pauline asked to be put through to Professor Gillies department when she was informed that Professor Gillies had died in 1983. Pauline found out that the Professor's wife lived in Bangor.

Telephoning Mrs Gillies Pauline explained that following the death of Dr. Heylings, my adoptive father, some paper work had come to light relating to her late husband, Mrs Gillies told Pauline that she was not Agnes Gillies who had died a few years previously. Pauline said she a letter outlining the details in the papers. The letter was written and posted. The

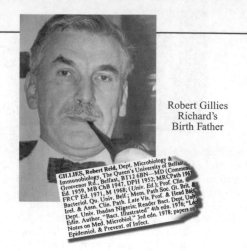

Robert Gillies
Richard's
Birth Father

following day Pauline received a telephone call.

Mrs Gillies was ringing to discuss the contents of Pauline's letter. She wanted to meet Pauline and me but needed time to tell my newly found brother and sisters that they had an older Brother.

Within a couple of weeks Mrs Gillies had told all of my Brothers and Sisters about me. They could not understand why I had been adopted. The only conclusion we can reach is that my parents were married in August 1949 and I was born the following January. Apparently the families of my natural parents were staunch churchgoers. Times were different then with different moral codes. A child conceived before marriage would have created a family rift and shame. Some time later when one of my sisters told my birth mother's sister of my existence my aunt said she had been told that her elder sister had a miscarriage in January 1950. My birth mother and her sister had been very close but shehad been totally unaware aware of my existence. Both my birth mother and father had taken their secret with them to their graves.

It was in 1994 that I met all my brothers and sisters. A very emotional year! I still find it very difficult to try and describe my emotions and feelings. We have had many meetings over the past eight years and I still get a special buzz. Blood is definitely thicker than water!

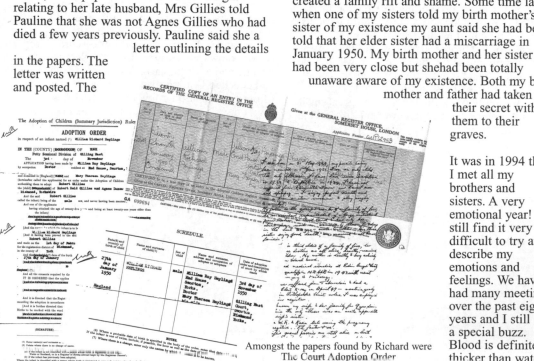

Amongst the papers found by Richard were
The Court Adoption Order
Adoption Schedule
Adoption Certificate
Robert Gillies' letter

A Floating Population – Tracing canal-faring ancestors
Doreen Hopwood

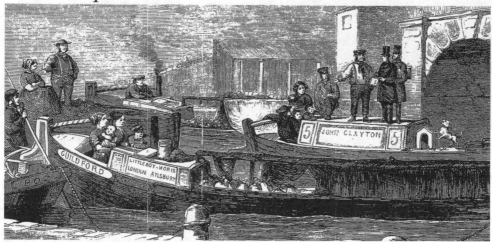

Anyone finding an ancestor described as a 'boatman' automatically believes that it will be difficult, if not impossible, to get further back with family history research. This is not necessarily the case, and the fact that the canal farers often married within their own community can actually make research easier. Even though their lives were lived only a few yards away from 'dry land', the canal-faring community spent little time with the sedentary population, so both their social and working lives were inextricably mixed.

Folklore often labels these people as ungodly – not attending church regularly, not having their children baptised, and not bothering to get married. They were also accused of being uneducated, dirty and unlawful – always by people who lived outside of the community! For many, the largest crime that they committed was

their failure to register the births of their children. However, given the circumstances, this was not always possible for families 'on the move', and especially for those on working boats which travelled some distances along the canals. Births had to be registered at the Register Office covering the location of the birth, and, in many cases, this was some distance from the Register Office. If the boat was travelling at the time it may well have been more than 42 days (the time allowed to register a birth) before it was back in the area, and so, rather than have to pay a penalty for late registration (after 1875), the birth simply remained unregistered.

Having no parish of their own, the canal-faring community tended to use certain churches along their canal routes where they knew they would be welcome. Initially, this involved a few Church of England Churches, such as Braunston Parish Church in Northamptonshire, but, generally, the non-conformist churches were chosen for baptisms and also marriages after 1837 (when marriages could take place outside the Church of England). It is not unusual to find several children of one marriage baptised together, as families would wait until they were within reach of a welcoming church

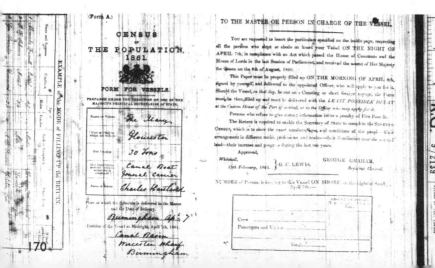

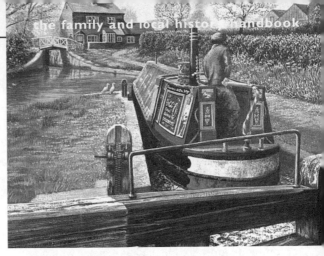

before having the children baptised. Later in the nineteenth century other religious organisations, such as the Salvation Army, became heavily involved with the canal-farers, and missions were set up alongside some of the canals. The Incorporated Seamen and Boatmen's Friendly Society was established in the 1860s, and its main aim was to 'promote the moral and religious welfare of Sailors, Bargemen, Fishermen, Canal Boatmen, and their families'. Amongst their activities were open-air services – on boats and quaysides, providing winter clothing and comforts, and the provision of mission halls, institutes, coffee rooms and reading/recreation rooms. They also offered a letter-writing service for the illiterate, and held Sabbath Schools for the children of boatmen. Annual reports of organisations such as these can generally be found in local record offices or libraries.

Illiteracy was commonplace amongst the canal-faring community as they had little opportunity for any formal education. However, most of the men were brilliant arithmeticians, ably reckoning up the weights of their boatloads and payment due. You are, therefore, likely to find most birth and marriage certificate marked with a cross rather than a signature, but, in respect of marriages, it is likely that the witnesses were also members of the canal-faring community, and possibly related to the bride and/or the groom. From the last quarter of the nineteenth century children of canal-farers were required to attend school when the boats were moored for a period of time. This was generally during the wintertime, and can be verified by reference to school logbooks and admission registers. As with churches, certain schools were more receptive than others to the children of canal-workers, and, in Birmingham, there was a large influx to Floodgate Street School, which was located close to a wharf on the Fazeley Canal.

Narrow-boats, barges and carriers have always been the subject of paintings and photographs, sometimes capturing the grimy reality of the working barges and sometimes depicting the romantic idyll of a life spent on the waterways. Boatmen often worked for a specific company, such as Cadbury's, and the company name as well as the name of the vessel were painted on the sides, often in a prominent position. There is a vast collection of photographs at the British Waterways Archive at Gloucester, and many local repositories hold photographs relating to their locality. It is unlikely that any images will be indexed under an individual person's name, but you may find the name of the vessel listed. In many instances, the catalogue may simply describe the photograph as 'Worcester Wharf', or 'Gas Street Basin'. It's well worth browsing these as many will include people as well as craft, and you may find your ancestor in the picture.

Standard genealogical sources, such as the General Record Office Index, parish registers, register offices and the census records, include canal-farers but, there are other types of records which are applicable to this group of people.

As far as the census returns are concerned, arrangements up to and including 1861 were ad hoc. The enumerator was required to find a 'trustworthy person' to ascertain the whereabouts of any vessels in his enumeration district. The person in charge of the vessel was then given a ship's schedule for completion. The information

TO THE MASTER OR PERSON IN CHARGE OF THE VESSEL.

You are requested to insert the particulars specified on the inside page, respecting all the persons who slept or abode on board your Vessel ON THE NIGHT OF APRIL 7th, in compliance with an Act which passed the House of Commons and the House of Lords in the last Session of Parliament, and received the assent of Her Majesty the Queen on the 6th of August, 1860.

This Paper must be properly filled up ON THE MORNING OF APRIL 8th, signed by yourself, and delivered to the appointed Officer, who will apply to you for it. Should the Vessel, on that day, be out on a Coasting or short foreign voyage, the Form must be then filled up and must be delivered with the *LEAST POSSIBLE DELAY* at the Custom House of the Port of arrival, or to the Officer who may apply for it.

Persons who refuse to give correct information incur a penalty of Five Pounds.

The Return is required to enable the Secretary of State to complete the SEVENTH CENSUS, which is to show the exact numbers, ages, and conditions of the people—their arrangement in different ranks, professions and trades—their distribution over the surface of the land—their increase and progress during the last ten years.

Approved,

Whitehall, 13th February, 1861. } G. C. LEWIS.

GEORGE GRAHAM, *Registrar General.*

NUMBER of Persons belonging to this Vessel ON SHORE on the night of Sunday, April 7th :—

Crew		
Passengers and Visitors		
Total		

is listed in the census enumerator's book after those of 'normal' households. After 1881, vessels arriving in the district on a census date were also enumerated there – which occasionally leads to double enumeration! The Registrar General reported that, in 1871, 29,500 workers were enumerated on the waterways.

Various Canal Boat Acts were passed between 1877 and 1884 with the aim of improving living standards. As with the settled population, overcrowding was a problem, and under these acts inspectors were required to ensure that there was sufficient space for the number of persons living on board. All the vessels with living accommodation were required to register with a local authority, and these Public Health Registers contain details about the size/weight of the vessel, as well as the owner/master. Each boat was allocated a number which, along with the registration number of the town where it was registered was painted on the side of the cabin.

The Medical Officer of Health's annual reports from 1875 include a summary of the work of the sanitary inspectors, but this does not usually contain the names of individuals/vessels. During 1904, the canal inspector for Birmingham made 1,182 visits, and in only four circumstances did he find 'Want of cleanliness', indicating that the canal-farers did not deserved to be labelled 'unclean'. Neither could they have been called unlawful, because for every breach regulation a notice was issued, but all were complied with without recourse to legal proceedings'.

From 1795, all inland waterways craft were required to be registered in the name of the owner with the local Clerk of the Peace. These Registers of Boats and Barges can usually be found in local record offices.

Gauge Books, or Gauging Tables, are deposited at the British Waterways Archive at Gloucester, and are indexed in the name of the vessel. They include the carrying capacity of the vessel (to determine the tolls payable), the date and place of registration, and the owner's name and address. Sometimes the name of the master is listed.

Whilst toll-tickets do not have a good survival rate they provide detailed information about the routes taken by vessels, as well as the name of the steerer, details of what was being carried, and the name of the company.

If your ancestor worked for one of these companies you may find information with company records – such as account books, engineer's reports etc., and these will probably be held locally.

In the nineteenth century many individuals came together to form companies for the building of canal boats or for the carrying of goods, and most records will be found in the local record office. In November 1838 about thirty men formed the Birmingham Boat Company, and the occupations of the shareholders include coal dealers, boat builders, tarpaulin makers, carpenters, timber merchants, as well as boatmen. Various other deeds/agreements may include the name of an ancestor if he was involved with the formation of any such company. The cutting of new canals involved the passing of an Act of Parliament and the drawing up of maps to show their route. These can be found at the Public Record Office at Kew.

Most canal-farers worked specific routes/canals and there is a range of maps showing the canal-networks, both nationally and locally. These should be available in main libraries, but some can be found on the Internet. The canal-network around Birmingham and the Black Country is at www.upthecut.co.uk .
The Waterways Trust is responsible for the museums, each of which can be visited to gain a greater insight into the local waterways, the boats and the people who worked on them. Their addresses are:
The National Waterways Museum, Llanthony Warehouse, Gloucester Docks, Gloucester, GL1 2EH www.nwm.org.co.uk
The Boat Museum, South Pier Road, Ellesmere Port, Cheshire, CH65 4EH www.boatmuseum.org.uk
The Canal Museum, Stoke Bruerne, Northamptonshire www.canaljunction.com
The Waterway Trust at www.thewaterwaystrust.com/archives has excellent links to other organisations and societies connected with canals, as does www.canaljunction.com

YORKSHIRE FAMILY HISTORY FAIR

KNAVESMIRE EXHIBITION CENTRE
YORK RACECOURSE

SATURDAY 26TH JUNE 2004
10.00.a.m. to 4.30.p.m.

Many Stalls including:
Society of Genealogists, Federation Publications
The Family & Local History Handbook
(The Genealogical Services Directory)
Family Tree Magazine, Local Archives,
Family History Societies from all over Great Britain
Maps, Postcards, Printouts,
New & Second-hand Microfiche Readers
Genealogy Computer Programs
Advice Table

224 Tables in 2003

FREE CAR PARKING
ADMISSION £3.00

Further Details from:
Mr A Sampson
1 Oxgang Close, Redcar TS10 4ND
Tel: 01642 486615

NOTE FOR YOUR DIARY:
YEAR 2005 - YORKSHIRE FAMILY HISTORY FAIR
SATURDAY 25TH JUNE 2005
YEAR 2006 - YORKSHIRE FAMILY HISTORY FAIR
SATURDAY 24TH JUNE 2006
YEAR 2007 - YORKSHIRE FAMILY HISTORY FAIR
SATURDAY 23rd JUNE 2007

City of York & District Family History Society

(Registered Charity No. 1085228)

The City of York & District Family History Society was founded 1975 and covers the modern Archdeaconry of York, which stretches from Coxwold in the North, to Ledsham and Selby in the South, and from Bramham and Sherburn in Elmet in the West, to Huggate and Bubwith in the East. The Society's area overlaps parishes covered by the Yorkshire Archaeological Society, and The East Yorkshire Family History Society. The Society is affiliated to the Federation of Family History Societies and is also involved with the North East group of Family History Societies. With the Society's Study Centre and repositories such as the York Minster Library, the City Archives and the Borthwick Institute for Historical Research, York is an ideal base for research into one's Yorkshire roots and local history.

The Society is very privileged to have as its president Dame Judi Dench, DBE, OBE. The famous actress was born in York.

Members and visitors are welcomed to the regular meetings on the first Wednesday of each Month (except August) at 7:00pm for 7:30pm at The Priory Street Centre, Priory Street, York with access to the library, bookstall, help desk and sales of Society publications, as well as offering opportunities to listen to interesting speakers. The talks have brought variety, entertained and given practical help with family history research.

The Society's Journal is published three times per year. The Society is active in publishing indexes of the 1851 and 1891 censuses for the Society's area: Burial Indexes, which also appear as part of the National Burial Index: Parish Registers for York churches, and specialised lists, such as the 1914-18 Roll of Honour for employees of the North Eastern Railway. The publication medium has changed with the years from paper to microfiche and then to CD-ROM and Website.

Each March the work of the Society is put on show at its annual Family History Fair, which provides access to other local family history societies, and local and national organisations supplying products and services for the genealogist. In addition to holding its own fair, the Society attends other local and family history events across the North of England.

The Society's website www.yorkfamilyhistory.org.uk publicises its activities and publications; but it does more than that, sharing meeting reports, providing for on-line sales, and free downloads of useful local research. Members are encouraged to join the Society's 'eGroup'or bulletin board, which allows members from around the world to be actively involved in the Society and to exchange information and helpful tips. Members' research interests are held on a database and can be accessed via the website. It is also possible to join the Society on-line.

The Society had long had the vision of providing a research room in the city for use of members and visitors alike. That vision was realised in 2002 with the opening of its first Study Centre, but as the amount of resources available to researchers multiplied, it was obvious that more space was required, and new premises were found and the centre transferred to the current site at 10 Priory Street, York, a stone's throw from the regular meeting venue. Society volunteers man the centre on Tuesdays and Thursdays from 10 to 4, and it is also open before Society meetings. Resources available include the staples of parish registers and census returns (1841 to 1901), plus directories, and the more unusual lists such as York Merchant Adventurers (1560 to 1835), and York Freemen (1680 to 1986). Research at the Study centre can be fruitful and none more so than when a member could report that he had been sworn in as a Freeman of York, which to quote "…all came about from my family history research at the study centre. I am now in the market for a herd of cattle to put on Knavesmire."

Like the proverbial woman a family history society's work is never done, and current projects include the continuing work of indexing Census records and mental hospital patient lists, contributing to the National Burials' Index and recording memorial inscriptions; with possibilities for the future in extracting names from nearly three centuries worth of local newspapers. The City of York & District Family History Society is not content to rest on its laurels, but looks forward to providing an improving service to its members and all family historians in York, and those with links to the city and its environs.

The Study Centre

The
City of York & District
Family History Society

Since our formation in 1975, we have been working hard to preserve our genealogical heritage, encouraging people far and near to discover their roots and, at the same time, learn more about our area.

We cover a large area of Yorkshire... check our website for full details:

www.yorkfamilyhistory.org.uk.

Wherever you are, if you have ancestors from our area, or even if you live locally and are researching elsewhere come and join us!

We meet on the first Wednesday of each month (excl. Aug) at:
The Priory Centre, Priory Street, York at 7pm for 7.30pm

Where you will find …..
- Guest Speaker   • Help Desk   • Burial Index Database   • Extensive Library   • Bookstall
- Membership enrolment (all members receive a journal three times a year)
  Local, national & international members welcomed
- Our own publications on sale (monumental inscriptions, burial indexes, census indexes and much more !!)
- Friendly, helpful and knowledgeable members

NEW!! Our STUDY CENTRE in the Heart of York HAS MOVED
to larger premises at 10 Priory Street, Micklegate, York
Tel: 01904 652363
Call for details, bookings, opening times etc., or see our website

FAMILY HISTORY DAY
YORK FAMILY HISTORY FAIR
Held every year on a Saturday in March

For any Society details see our web-site or contact the
Secretary enclosing a s.a.e.
Mrs Dorothy Croft, 140 Shipton Road, York YO30 5RU

Registered Charity No. 1085228

Twentieth Century Research
Stuart A. Raymond

In theory, it should be easy to trace families in the twentieth century. If the procedures of civil registration were properly followed, and none of the family were born, married, or died overseas, then the construction of a family tree from birth, marriage and death certificates should be simple. Unfortunately, however, the records of the Registrar General are not always straightforward or correctly indexed, and many of our forebears did travel. Consequently, it may be the case that you will need to consult sources other than the civil registers. If you want to compile a family history, rather than just a pedigree, then you will certainly need to do so.

Apart from the civil registers, the 1901 census is almost certainly the source most consulted by genealogists. It is, again, in theory, a complete listing of the population in 1901, and has the great advantage of having been indexed on the web. A great deal of ink has been spilt in discussing its idiosyncracies; there is therefore, no point in adding anything here. The point of this article is to draw to your attention the many other readily available sources for twentieth century research, some of which are grossly neglected by family historians.

Civil registration replaced parish registers. Or did it? Most family historians act as if they believe this, although there may be a dim awareness that in fact parish registers have continued to be kept to this day. Indeed, the marriage register used by all denominations today is a duplicate of the register sent to the registrar and subsequently indexed with the civil registers by the Registrar General. If your 20th century

ancestors were married in church, you do not need to pay for a marriage certificate if you can find the relevant parish register.

Registers of baptisms and burials have also continued to be kept. Baptism registers are quite distinct from the civil birth registers, but certificates of burials do have to be made to the registrar. By law a register must be kept for every burial ground.

The records of non-conformists are in some respects identical to those of the Church of England: they too keep a duplicate marriage register and send a copy to the registrar; they too are required to maintain burial registers for their cemeteries. In other respects, however, they diverge from the Church of England pattern; each denomination, and, in some denominations, each church, has its own pattern of record keeping, dependent upon both the structure of each denomination, and on their beliefs. Baptist registers of baptism, for example, if kept at all, record the baptism of adults, not of infants. Quakers do not practice baptism at all; however, all births were recorded in a digest of births, maintained centrally at Friend's House Library until 1959. Similar

digests of Quaker marriages (still continuing) and deaths (until 1961) are also available.

The keeping of registers by the Methodists was similarly dependent on their denominational structure. Methodist ministers are appointed by the Circuit, rather than by individual chapels, and Methodist records reflect that fact. The Salvation Army has a different structure again; each 'corps' maintains its own dedication, marriage and promotion to glory' registers for its soldiers (i.e. ordinary members); officers records are maintained centrally.

Birth, marriage and death notices in newspapers may also prove useful, although lack of indexing may mean that these are difficult to find, unless you already have dates. If you do find a notice, or if you have death dates anyway, then it should be easy to check further for newspaper obituaries and accounts of funerals, which may reveal a great deal of information, especially if your ancestor was active in the church, a profession, or public life. Other family events may also have attracted notice in the newspapers - accidents, bankruptcies, war service, advertisements, even passing examinations. If you have dates for particular events, then it is easy to search newspapers held at the British Library's Newspaper Library and in local studies libraries.

In order to identify the dates of events that are worth researching, you need to talk to your older relatives and family friends. Indeed, that is the most obvious way to begin researching your family history. I correct myself. You need to get them to talk to you! You can obtain a great deal of basic information from archival records and printed sources, but if you seek an appreciation of the inner dynamics of your family, then oral evidence from those who experienced them is vital. Who ruled his family with a rod of iron? Who were the favourite sons, the drunkards, the ones who could never do anything right? The answers to questions such as these are unlikely to be written down. But they may be stored in the memory of an older generation.

There are, of course, many problems in collecting and using oral evidence. Memory often plays tricks; relatives may not want to reveal certain information, and what they do tell you is necessarily a partial account; it is their memory of how they participated in, or heard about, particular events. Wherever possible, you should check oral evidence against other sources, and not simply assume the veracity of what you are told.

There are a wide range of both published and archived sources that can be checked. Some of these are well known and heavily used - army records, trade directories, monumental inscriptions. In the rest of this article, I want to concentrate attention on some of the lesser used sources for twentieth century family history.

There were two major surveys of land-holdings in the twentieth century, both of which led to the creation of huge archives which are now available for research. Lloyd George's famous 'People's Budget' of 1910 proposed a tax on the value of land which necessitated the valuation of every land-holding in the country. There are 95,000 valuation books in the National Archives, and similar numbers of field books in local record offices. These name owners and occupiers, and provide detailed descriptions of the land and property valued. They enable us to see inside our ancestors houses, and to examine the conditions in which they lived and worked.

The national farm survey of 1941-3 was not quite as wide-ranging as Lloyd George's survey: it was confined to agricultural land. It stemmed from the fact that Britain's overseas food supplies were cut off during the war; the government needed to ensure that as much food as possible was produced at home. The survey was intended to produce the data needed for long-term planning of food production.

The National Archives now holds extensive records produced by the survey. These records provide detailed descriptions of every farm in the country, including names of farmers, comments on their abilities, the general condition of the farm, details of the crops they had planted and the livestock they kept, information on their labour force, their length of tenancy, etc. etc. Again, these returns provide us with a detailed snapshot of the world in which our parents and grandparents lived.

These are perhaps the two most detailed and broad-ranging official sources of information for the twentieth century. There are however, numerous other sources with less detail, but which may nevertheless provide invaluable clues. Lists of names are the life-blood of the genealogist, and a wide variety of official lists are available. Apart from the census, the most comprehensive such lists are the electoral registers, likely to be available in both local studies libraries and in the British Library. These registers reflect the history of the franchise in England, hence prior to 1918 they only record about 60% of the adult male population. Franchise reform in that year extended the vote to almost all adult males, and to women over 30; subsequent reforms gave women equality with men, abolished the university constituency and the property qualification, and reduced the age of voting from 21 to 18. These changes are reflected in the names listed in electoral registers. Mention should also be made of the absent voters registers, compiled from 1918 for a number of years, which list soldiers absent from their homes but entitled to vote in their home constituencies.

The prime use of electoral registers to the family historian is to establish the place of residence of ancestors. The fact that they were annual compilations means that it is possible to identify when particular names first appeared in them, and when they disappeared. It is also possible to use them to trace the distribution of surnames at particular dates.

Rate books provide similar information, but list fewer people, and may not survive to the same extent as electoral registers. Records of the land tax may also provide vital clues, although the process of commutation means that assessments list increasingly fewer taxpayers, and become increasingly less useful, as the century progresses. The tax was finally abolished in 1963.

One of the major new taxes of the twentieth century was that imposed on motor vehicles in 1903. Until 1969, this tax was administered by local authorities, and some of their registers survive in local record offices - although there are no name indexes; arrangement is by car registration number. If your ancestor owned a car in the early part of the century, this is a source which may be worth checking, especially if you have a registration number.

The government - both national and local - required licences for a wide range of activities. Pubs, tobacconists, entertainment, taxis, peddlars, gamekeepers, etc., etc., have all required licences, and it may be worth searching in local record offices for records of such licences. Government has also increasingly regulated a variety of professions - company directors, doctors and nurses, and seamen are just three of the occupations whose practitioners require government approval. The London gazette (now available on the inter-net at www.gazettes-online.co.uk) often carried lists of those whose qualifications are recognized; in some instances, entire registers are published regularly e.g. the Medical register, issued annually since 1859.

Many lists of other professions are available

- job applications, apprenticeship records, pay lists, pension records, etc., etc. A few large employers maintain their own archives, e.g. the Post Office; many records of smaller employers, and of local government as an employer, may be found in local record offices; the National Archives houses many records of civil servants, and of the armed forces.

It is not possible in an article of this length to do more than skim through a selection of twentieth century records that are available to the family historian. Many sources have not even been mentioned - wills, school registers, divorce records, court archives, to mention but a few. There are also many records which are not yet open to the public, for example, those relating to hospital patients, to World War II conscription, to soldiers post-1920. Many records are closed for privacy reasons. The quantity of records available for the twentieth century is far greater than for any previous century, and most family historians could probably find out a great deal more about their twentieth century family than they realise.

This article in based on the author's recently published *Tracing your Twentieth Century Family History*, F.F.H.S., 2003. The book provides much more detailed information, and is available from S.A. & M.J. Raymond, P.O.Box 35, Exeter, EX4 5EF, price £5.95 + 65p postage.

from non-governmental sources. Professional organizations frequently publish lists of their members: for example, the Library Association yearbook, giving details of librarians and their employers, has been published annually since 1891. Entry to most professions was by examination, and the records of such examinations will have been retained by the relevant bodies and may be accessible.

There are many other records relating to particular occupations. Personnel records, if they survive, may provide a great deal of information

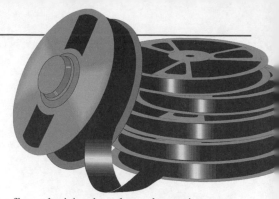

Film and Sound Archives
Simon Fowler

Film and sound recordings exist from the 1890s. Surviving material is stored in a network of film and sound archives, which may provide footage of relations or radio interviews as well as provide information about individuals who worked in the industry. They are likely to be very different from any other archive repository you may have used. In particular you will need to make an appointment perhaps two or three weeks away to view a particular film or hear a tape. There may well also be a charge. And lastly they may be unused to dealing with amateur family and local historians. However, on the positive side, they are likely to have detailed catalogues so it should be easy to track down a particular individual or event. In addition these catalogues and perhaps some clips may have been placed on the internet.

If you have old film shot by family members or recordings of interviews with elderly relations you might consider depositing them with the appropriate archive.

The BBC

Sound – radio – and film – television – in Britain is closely linked to the BBC, which has been the dominant broadcaster since the early 1920s. The British Broadcasting Corporation (BBC) was formed as the British Broadcasting Company in 1922, receiving its charter (and change of name) in 1927. It had a monopoly over radio broadcasting until 1972 (with the setting up of the London Broadcasting Company and Capital Radio in 1973) and television (with ITV on 22nd September 1955 – the first advertisement was for SR toothpaste).

By 1939 the BBC had a national wireless station National (now Radio 4), plus regional stations. The Light Programme (Radio 2) originally began in 1940 as the Forces Programme. Both stations had a profound effect on raising the nation's morale and keeping it informed on the progress of the war. The Third Programme (Radio3) was established in 1947, and Radio 1 was set up in 1967 in competition to pirate radio stations which were broadcasting from ships in the North Sea.

The first television broadcasts began in November 1936, from a studio at Alexandria Palace in North London, but ceased on the declaration of war in September 1939. Programmes resumed in June 1946, with the completion of a broadcast of the Walter Disney cartoon which had been abruptly taken off the air nearly seven years earlier. Television really only took off with the broadcasting of the Queen's coronation in June 1955. The arrival of commercial broadcasting (ITV) in September 1955 brought with it more popular programmes, such as soap operas and quiz shows. However the tone generally remained respectful. One American writer commented that: 'The British have decided to paint the gaudy thing a sombre grey to blend with the general fog.' BBC 2 arrived in 1964 and after many years of debate Channel 4 in 1982. With the 1960s came more controversial programmes as well as sex and swearing.

All this has needed large numbers of staff, not just the broadcasters and announcers, but sound engineers, cameramen, production assistants and security guards. Some staff records are held by the BBC Written Archives Centre, Caversham Park, Reading RG4 8TZ, *www.bbc.co.uk/thenandnow*. The Centre holds thousands of files, scripts and other working papers of the BBC from its formation in 1922 to the 1980s. It also has information about past programmes (which were broadcast more than three years ago) and about broadcasting history. The Centre however does not have any sound or television recordings – sound recordings are with the National Sound Archive and old television programmes are with the National Film and TV Archives which is part of the British Film Institute. In addition they are not really geared up to cater for family historians. If you think an ancestor worked for the BBC you will need to approach them in writing for assistance. If they have material

Anna Neagle

which might be of use then you will need to make an appointment, at least three weeks in advance, to see it.

Film Archives
There are a dozen or so public film archives in Britain and Ireland, which collect film, television programmes and videos. England also has a number of regional film archives that collect local material. The archives are open to the public, although it is essential that you make an appointment before you turn up. If you want to see a specific film it may take a few days as they are usually kept off-site in special storage areas. There should be a comprehensive catalogue of the films, which can help locate material relating to people and places. You can get a flavour of what is available and advice about how to use this material on the Moving History website *www.movinghistory.ac.uk*, which also includes a 100 or so historic clips. These archives, particularly the regional ones, are often very glad to receive donations of films made by amateur film-makers. Naturally they are more interested in older material.

British Film Institute
21 Stephen St, London W1T 1LN Tel. (020) 7957 4824 *www.bfi.org.uk* The library has a selection of the most commonly used books on open access, various databases to holdings of film archives and other resources. The Institute's Special Collections include personal and working papers of individuals and organisations

in film and television, ephemera including cinema programmes, tickets and promotional material and press cuttings. The BFI also acts as the regional film archive for London. A day pass to use the library currently costs £6. You will, however, have to make a separate appointment to see a particular film, and pay a £40 viewing fee.

British Universities Film and Video Council
77 Wells Street , London W1T 3QJ Tel: (020) 7393 1500 *www.bufvc.ac.uk* For family historians the most important resource the Council offers is an on-line database of the people who worked in newsreels between 1910 and 1979, including cameramen, editors, sound recordists. There is also a database to all the newsreels and the stories they contained. Unfortunately they make a charge for non-academics. The web site also features a history of the newsreel, reading lists and other useful information.

Imperial War Museum Film and Video Archive
Lambeth Rd, London, SE1 6HZ Tel. (020) 7416 5291 *www.iwm.org.uk/collections/film.htm* The IWM has films, both official and unofficial, for the two world wars and other conflicts of the 20th century. They range from the famous WW1 film *Battle of the Somme* to *Elworth School Presents School Life in Wartime* made by a Cheshire primary school during the Second World War. At least a week's notice is required to see a specific film. It is possible to have copies made on VHS videocassette. They also have some oral history interviews with cameramen and others who helped film the Second World War.

Northern Ireland Film Commission
21 Ormeau Avenue, Belfast, BT2 8HD
www.nifc.co.uk

Scottish Screen Archive
Scottish Screen, 1 Bowmont Gardens, Glasgow G12 9LR Tel. (0141) 337 7400
www.scottishscreen.com

National Screen and Sound Archive of Wales
Unit 1 Science Park, Aberystwyth SY23 3AH
Tel. (01970) 626007
http://screenandsound.llgc.org.uk

Film Institute of Ireland
6 Eustace St, Dublin 2 Tel. (01) 679 5744
www.fli.ie

Regional Film Archives
East Anglian Film Archive
Norfolk Record Office, The Archive Centre, Martineau Lane, Norwich NR1 2DQ Tel:

Jimmy Hanley

South West Film and Television Archive
New Cooperage, Royal William Yard ,
Stonehouse, Plymouth PL1 3RP Tel. (01752)
202650 *www.tswfta.co.uk*

Wessex Film and Sound Archive
Hampshire Record Office, Sussex St,
Winchester SO23 8TH Tel. (01962) 847742
www.hants.gov.uk/record-office/film.html

Yorkshire Film Archive
York St John College, Lord Mayor's Walk, York
YO31 7EX Tel. (01904) 716 550
*www.movinghistory.ac.uk/archives/ya/collection.
html*

Other useful addresses
Bill Douglas Centre for the History of Cinema
and Popular Culture
University of Exeter, Queen's Building, Queen's
Drive Exeter EX4 4QH
Tel. (01392) 264321 *www.ex.ac.uk/bill.douglas*
The Centre houses an enormous collection
(18,000 books and 50,000 other items) relating
to film and visual media. Visitors are welcome
and access is free, although you will need to
provide two passport photographs and proof
of identity. There is a museum in the
University's Old Library, which is open
between 10am and 4pm Monday to Friday.

National Museum of Photography, Film and
Television
Manchester Road, Bradford BD1 1NQ Tel.
(01274) 202030 *www.nmpgt.org.uk*
Among many other artefacts the Museum has
the first example of a moving picture — Louis
Le Prince's 1888 film of Leeds Bridge, examples
of equipment used in British film making,
thousands of photographs of movie stars, and
considerable collections of films made by
amateur film makers.

In addition the former newsreel companies keep
their own film archives. Indexes to the stories
covered can be found on each of their web sites.
Unfortunately they do not normally sell copies
of newsreels to the general public:
Movietone: *www.movietone.com*
Universal, British Gaumont, British Paramount:
www.itnarchives.com

The exception to this is British Pathe who have
made the bulk of their archive available online
for free. This amazing resource is extensively
indexed and is a joy to use.
www.britishpathe.com,

Sound Archives
As the name suggests sound archives hold sound
recordings. Family and local historians are most

(01603) 222599. *www.uea.ac.uk/eafa*

Media Archive for Central England
Institute of Film Studies, School of American
and Canadian Studies, University of
Nottingham, University Park Nottingham, NG7
2RD *www.nottingham.ac.uk/film/mace*

Northern Region Film and Television Centre
School of Law, Arts and Humanities, Room
M616, Middlesbrough Tower, University of
Teesside, Middlesbrough TS1 3BA
www.nrfta.org.uk/

North West Film Archive
Manchester Metropolitan University, Minshull
House, 47-49 Chorlton, St Manchester M1 3EU
Tel. (0161) 247 3097 *www.nwfa.mmu.ac.uk* The
Archive is the largest regional film archive and
houses some newsreels made specifically to be
shown in the North West.

South East Film and Video Archive
Brighton History Centre, Pavilion Gardens,
Brighton BN1 2EE Tel. (01273) 643213
*www.movinghistory.ac.uk/archives/se/collection.
html*

DAVID NIVEN   UNITED ARTISTS

likely to be interested in the collections of oral history recordings. Oral history is a fairly recent development. It captures the diversity of ordinary people's experiences at home, at work and at leisure and will provide future generations with a unique insight into how life was first lived. One of the earliest practitioners was George Ewart Evans, who interviewed Suffolk farmer labourers and other groups of workers in the 1950s: the resulting books are a fascinating account of how life was lived by ordinary people before the First World War. Various projects have been undertaken, by academics, and amateur groups, to interview particular groups of people. I was involved with the Labour Oral History Project, where a hundred Labour Party members across the country were interviewed about their involvement with political and social activities. The tapes with deposited with the National Sound Archive and the results edited and published in an entertaining book called *Generating Socialism* by Dan Weinbren (Sutton, 1997).

Many local archives, museums and libraries have small collections of tapes usually interviews with local people. If the national and regional bodies listed below can't help it is worth asking locally.

National Sound Archive
British Library, 96 Euston Road, London NW1 2DB Tel: (020) 7412 7440
www.bl.uk/collections/sound-archive/nsa.html
Founded in 1955 the NSA is one of the largest sound archives in the world, with over a million discs, 185,000 tapes, and many other sound and video recordings. The collections come from all over the world and cover the entire range of recorded sound from music, drama and literature, to oral history and wildlife sounds. They range from cylinders made in the late 19th century to the latest CD, DVD and minidisc recordings. They hold copies of commercial recordings issued in the United Kingdom, together with radio broadcasts and many privately-made recordings. All this has been catalogued which is available online. There are also links to oral history societies and groups across the country.

East Midlands Oral History Archive
Centre for Urban History, University of Leicester LE1 7RH Tel: (0116) 252 5065
www.le.ac.uk/emoha
North West Sound Archive
Old Steward's Office, Clitheroe Castle, Clitheroe, Lancashire BB7 1AZ Tel: (01200) 427897
www.lancashire.gov.uk/education/d_lif/ro/content/sound/nwsound.asp With 110,000 recordings the Sound Archive is probably the largest outside London. Among the tapes can found the memories of cotton mill workers, engineers, canal workers, railway workers, colliers and even conversations with prisoners in Strangeways Prison.

The National Screen and Sound Archive of Wales
National Library of Wales, Aberystwyth, Ceredigion SY23 3BU Tel: (01970) 632828
http://screenandsound.llgc.org.uk/ Established in April 2001,the archive collects material relating to Wales and the Welsh.

Wessex Film and Sound Archive
Hampshire Record Office, Sussex St, Winchester, SO23 8TH Tel. (01962) 847742
www.hants.gov.uk/record-office/film.html Has collections relating to Hampshire, Dorset, Berkshire, Wiltshire and the Isle of Wight

National Coal Mining Museum for England

NATIONAL COAL MINING MUSEUM

for England

Alison Henesey Museum Librarian

The National Coal Mining Museum for England, originally the Yorkshire Coal Mining Museum, opened in 1988, on the site of Caphouse Colliery, near Wakefield. It acquired its national status in 1995, and a successful lottery bid in 2002 enabled new galleries, visitor centre, education block, large object store and library to be built. The Museum aims to provide an insight into coal mining and the lives of coal miners in England through the ages.

The highlight of any visit is the underground tour, which lasts approximately one hour. Experienced local miners guide parties around the underground workings, which portray the development of mining from the early nineteenth century to modern times. Above ground there are genuine pit ponies, a train ride, machinery displays, steam winder, pithead baths and the 17-acre rural site with its nature trail to be enjoyed. The visitor centre has a licensed cafe and well-stocked shop.

Restoration of the adjacent Hope Pit site is underway, which will provide access to a small, early nineteenth-century colliery, which was linked to the Caphouse workings underground.

The Collections
The collections at the Museum cover the whole of England. They consist of mining machinery and tools, social-history items from mining communities, photographs and videos, printed ephemera and art, primarily from the nineteenth and twentieth centuries, although there is some material from earlier periods. There is a small, but growing, collection of oral-history material. The strength of the collection lies in its comprehensive cover of the latter half of the twentieth century. The significant lamp collection and the art

collection, which includes miners' own work, is unique.

The Museum's Library
The library moved into its present accommodation in Spring 2002, and opened in the autumn. The main collection is housed in an environmentally controlled and secure room, on moveable racking. A smaller collection of duplicate titles is on display for visitors in the study room. This accommodates about a dozen people, is light and comfortable, with spectacular views across the valley.

Scope of the Collection
There are about 5,000 items in the collection at the moment, although the library continues to grow through donations and purchases. The collection is primarily of printed items, mostly books, reports and journals. Archives, except those relating to Caphouse or specific objects, are not collected, as these are kept by local record offices. The Museum's large photographic collection is accessible via the computer catalogue in the library. Ephemeral items such as posters, serviettes, and newspaper cuttings are available to researchers as part of the Museum collection but, where possible, are replicated for use in the library.

Content
The core collection is coal mining in England. Both Scotland and Wales have their own national coal-mining collections. The Museum began as a Yorkshire-based collection and so the history of coal mining in different regions of England is less well represented than in Yorkshire, but this is being addressed through the current acquisition programme.

The Lamp Collection. National Coal Mining Museum for England

Within the core subject, there are many aspects to the industry. One of the most used sections is that of the social history of mining, including politics and economics. The most comprehensive section is the collection on the technical aspects of coal mining, which contains for example, books on surveying, shaft sinking, supports, ventilation, haulage, working methods and mechanisation and lighting.

The library has a special collection of fiction, songs, poetry and plays, biography and autobiography, either by miners or about miners. There is

The library study. National Coal Mining Museum for England

also a selection of books on miners as artists to support the Museum's art collection.

Source books
There are a number of sources which are unique to coal mining history and provide a good starting point for any research.

A Colliery Guardian and Journal of the Coal and Iron Trades.
This journal began in 1858.
> 'The objects of this Journal will be to afford interesting and useful information, in connection with current events, to all engaged in the management of Collieries, or concerned in the operations of the Coal and Iron Trades; and to vindicate their interests, so far as these may be affected by social or legislative arrangements'
> (*Colliery Guardian* 231 (4) April1983 p.142)

In his report of 1858, Mr H. S. Tremenheere showed his appreciation that such a journal had been produced by saying the establishment of the *Colliery Guardian* was 'a fortunate circumstance,' and one 'of much promise for the future prosperity and welfare, material and intellectual, of the mining districts'. He added that 'the existence of a weekly periodical of the above character makes the gratuitous circulation of my reports no longer necessary'.
(*Report of the Commissioner appointed...in the Mining Districts* 1858 p. 35)

The periodical was founded by Mr William Hutchins and was produced regularly for the first year. There followed a two-year period when it was not published, but then issues appeared regularly from January 1861. The periodical continues today, although in 1997 it was retitled *Coal International* to reflect a wider audience.

The periodical is an excellent source of information on all manner of topics for example on individual mines, miners, the coal trade, legislation, patents, advertisements, mining abroad, events, statistics, disasters, new publications, editorial comments, and obituaries.

The *Colliery Guardian* was used to answer an enquiry about a cargo of briquettes, which was found on a ship, wrecked in 1914. The enquirer

wanted to know where the briquettes, marked with a crown and the word Cardiff, had come from and where they might have been going. By using the *Colliery Guardian*, it was possible to trace the rise and fall in trading of the Crown Company in Cardiff, and the impact that the war was having on the South Wales coalfield. It even recorded the weather at the time, which may have caused the ship to sink!

Although missing the earlier volumes, the library has an almost complete run from 1878.

The Guide to the Coalfields
This annual publication was produced for the National Coal Board by the *Colliery Guardian*. The first volume appeared in 1948 and it listed all the mines managed by the NCB after nationalisation. It continues to be published today, now the *International Guide to the Coalfields*, and the list of working UK mines now only takes a page or two, graphically illustrating the decline of the coal industry in Britain. It also lists the licensed mines, those which the National Coal Board took over and then leased out.

For each mine, the *Guide* listed the NCB area under which it was managed, the contact details, the type of mineral mined, the names of the seams, and the number of men working above and below ground. It also gives the names of the agent, manager and undermanager of the colliery in that particular year. Another useful feature of the *Guide* are the pages of Ordnance Survey maps showing the precise location of each mine. The personal name index for each volume is useful, as are the advertisements and buyers' guide information.

The *Guides* can be used in a number of ways, for example to see when a pit closed, to trace the history of a particular pit, or as a means of identification of a particular pit. It is of course limited to 1947 onwards, but serves as a useful starting point. The library has a full set of these *Guides*, except for the 1950 volume.

For pre-1947 lists of mines there is the *Colliery Yearbook and Coal Trades Directory*. This was produced from 1923 to 1964. As well as an index to mines, the Directory lists the different colliery companies that were operating in that year, giving details of the mines, seams worked, number of men employed, type of coal produced and other minerals worked. A very useful section is the Colliery Who's Who, which gives brief biographical details of notable people in the industry. Each volume also provides a brief summary of current regulations and statistics.

The 1872 Act required inspectors to produce a list of mines in each area. These were published as separate volumes. Early mines can be located by using archives, maps, the *Victoria County Histories* and local directories. The Coal Authority in Mansfeld has a large collection of old mine maps.

The Inspectors' Reports
In 1850 the Act for the Inspection of Coal Mines in Great Britain empowered the Secretary of State to appoint Inspectors of Mines to go underground. Four were appointed, which increased to six, and then to twelve in 1855. In 1908, R.A. Redmayne was appointed the first Chief Inspector.

At first the reports reflected the individual inspector's own view of what it was his duty to report, but by 1862, the annual reports assumed a more common form. From the 1880s, the Secretary of State ordered special inquiries into major incidents, which were then published as separate Command Papers.

During World War I, only a *General Report* by the Chief Inspector was published, with brief Divisional Reports. In 1920, the responsibility of the inspections transferred to the Board of Trade, which set up a new Mines Department. An annual report from the Secretary of Mines was published, together with that of the Chief Inspector, between 1921 and 1938. A brief report was issued to cover the years of World War II, which gives the basic statistics, but very little detail on individuals killed in the mines for this period.

Latterly, the Health and Safety Executive have taken responsibility for reporting on accidents in mines. Fortunately, there are few men killed now as a result of accidents each year, but surprisingly, no details of the fatalities are given.

The Inspectors' reports are rich sources of information. The earlier reports give very detailed accounts of the accidents, and up until World War I, the names of individuals who were killed were included. Non-fatal injuries were not recorded, and if as a result of an accident, death occurred after a year and a day, this was not counted as a fatality. As well as giving statistics on the number of accidents, where they took place, and what the outcome was, the reports also include, for instance, the number of pit ponies underground, awards of bravery medals, and details of prosecutions for misdemeanors. Glancing through some of these reports graphically illustrates how dangerous and how cheap life was in the mines:
The library has an extensive collection of the Inspectors' *Reports* from the 1870s. It also has a good collection of disaster reports, those in which more than ten people were killed in one incident. These reports appear as Command Papers and

contain a wealth of detail, often accompanied by maps and illustrations.

The Mining Journal
The first edition of the *Mining Journal and Commercial Gazette* appeared in 1835. Three years later, in his preface, the editor was able to reflect:

On the commencement of this Publication there was much to contend with, more especially from a prevailing opinion which at the time existed, that success could not be expected, the subject being supposed to be too confined to allow of support to a Weekly Journal exclusively devoted to its consideration. This prejudice existed merely from the circumstance of the attempt being the first to furnish information on a Science not only interesting in itself, but of indefinite importance, from the large sums of money which have been embarked in Mining Companies. That the view we took at the time was a correct one, the proud position in which we now stand affords the best evidence, by the INCREASING CIRCULATION, and increasing interest which each successive number creates, arising, as we are induced to believe, from the value and importance of the articles inserted, either furnished by Correspondents or selected from works of acknowledged value.(from the Preface to third volume 1838)

How much more self-congratulatory would the editors have been knowing that the journal would continue to be published, and prove useful, well into the twenty-first century!

In 1844 the publication was retitled the *Mining Journal Railway and Commercial Gazette*, but is generally referred to as the *Mining Journal*. From its inception, the *Journal* has taken as its brief all types of mining across the world. It focuses on trade and new developments in the industry. The library has a substantial run of early volumes up to the 1930s. As these are now rare, work is in progress to rebind and conserve the older volumes, befitting the role of a national collection. However, as each volume can cost several hundred pounds to restore, progress is inevitably slow.

Transactions of the Proceedings of the Institute of Mining Engineers
It had been realized early on that there was a need to exchange views and information on how to solve some of the problems facing a rapidly

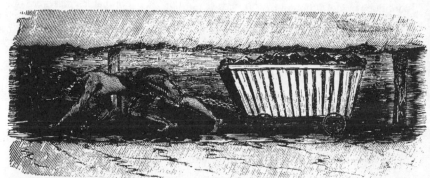

Date.	No. of Accident.	Name of the Mine or Colliery.	Where situate.	Owner's or Company's Name.	Persons killed.	Occupation.	Reputed Age.	Cause of Death, and Remarks.	Explosions of Fire-damp.	Falls of Roof and Sides.	In Shafts.	Miscellaneous Underground.	Above Ground.	Total.
1878. Oct. 1	52	Hoyland Silkstone.	Barnsley -	Wells, Birch, Ryde, & Co.	Jas. Kilcullan	- - -	28	Fall of roof - - -	-	1	-	-	-	1
„ 11	53	Car House -	Rotherham	John Brown & Co.	Oliver Fowler -	Trammer	51	Crushed by corves -	-	-	-	1	-	1
„ 14	54	Haigh -	Barnsley	Geo. Fountain & Son -	Jas. Wakefield	Hurrier	48	Fall of roof -	-	1	-	-	-	1
„ 18	55	Park Liversedge	Dewsbury	Park Coal Co. -	David Wood	Collier	27	Ditto -	-	1	-	-	-	1
„ 18	56	Smithies	Barnsley	C. Marsden & Son	Joseph Hunt	Ditto	28	Explosion of gas; died 22nd Oct.	1	-	-	-	-	1
„ 25	57	Featherstone Main.	Pontefract	Featherstone Main Coal Co.	John Hunter	Driver	14	Run over by corves -	-	-	-	1	-	1
„ 29	58	Wheldale -	Ditto	Wheldale Coal Co.	Stephen Gover -	Collier	18	Fall of coal and roof -	-	1	-	-	-	1
								Total—October	1	4	-	2	-	7
Nov. 4	59	Glass Houghton	Pontefract	J. D. Thorp's Exors.	J. Mattison -	Driver	63	Crushed by corves -	-	-	-	-	1	1
„ 8	60	Waterloo Woodlesford.	Leeds -	Waterloo Woodsford Coal Co.	Solomon Butterworth. / Robert Inman	Colliers	33 / 31	Fell with cage down shaft after safety hook disengaged.	-	-	2	-	-	2
„ 13	61	Rawmarsh -	Rotherham	J. & J. Charlesworth	Geo. Shaw -	Packer	53	Fall of roof -	-	1	-	-	-	1
„ 13	62	Wooley	Barnsley	Wooley Coal Co.	Wm. Staley -	Collier	50	Fall of roof; died 14th November	-	1	-	-	-	1
„ 13	63	Dungworth -	Sheffield	Ibbotson & Hague	Thos. Hawksworth	Hurrier	14	Fell down shaft -	-	-	1	-	-	1
„ 15	64	Edmunds Main	Barnsley	Edmunds and Swaithe Main Co.	Chas. Harper -	Screenman	56	Crushed by waggons; died 16th Nov.	-	-	-	-	1	1
„ 18	65	Morley Main -	Leeds -	W. Ackroyd & Bros.	Thos. Herald -	Collier	29	Fall of coal and roof -	-	1	-	-	-	1
„ 18	66	Micklefield -	Ditto -	Cliff & Sons -	Jas. Heelegrave -	Hanger-on	24	Piece of coal fell down shaft	-	-	1	-	-	1
„ 20	67	Rothwell Haigh	Ditto -	J. & J. Charlesworth	T. W. Rawling -	Dayman	16	Fall of roof -	-	1	-	-	-	1
„ 21	68	Helm -	Huddersfield	Chas. Wheatley -	Wm. Charlesworth	Deputy	48	Crushed by corves; died 27th Nov.	-	-	-	1	-	1
„ 22	69	Stanley Ferry -	Wakefield	R. Hudson & Co.	Wm. Read	Hurrier	25	Crushed by corves -	-	-	-	1	-	1
„ 23	70	High Elsecar -	Barnsley -	Earl Fitzwilliam -	Richard White	Corf repairer	50	Crushed by machinery -	-	-	-	-	1	1
								Total—November	-	4	4	2	3	13

M m 4

Page from
the
*Report of the
Inspector of Mines
for
Yorkshire
1878*

expanding mining industry. For example the North of England Institute of Mining and Mechanical Engineers was established in 1852 and the Midland Institute in 1869.

In 1890 the existing regional institutions came together as the Federated Institution of Mining Engineers. Although each still published their own papers, the Federated Institution published volumes of selected papers from each of the regions.

Over the years, various other societies and institutions have amalgamated with the Institution as the industry contracted, for example the Institution of Mining and Metallurgy. In 2002, the organisation became the Institute of Materials, Minerals and Mining (IOM3) and like other publications, their serials now reflect the international mining industry.

The papers that these institutions published represent an extensive body of scientific knowledge. Topics cover, for example, mining overseas and the opening up of mineral fields abroad, and the appraisal of new technology. The list of members and the obituaries are also very useful.

An enquirer requested information on her relative, Frank, who, she knew from entries in a family Bible, had been out to Africa four times, the last being in 1912. He had been working at Hucknall Colliery. She wanted to know why he had gone and what did he do there. By using the *Transactions* and the *Colliery Guardian*, it was possible to describe the likely scenario.

There was a lot of unrest in the Nottinghamshire area at this time between the managers and the new trades unions. The Boer War has ended in 1902, and opportunities were again opening up in Africa. The Middelburg coalfield was just being discovered. The coal seams lay adjacent to gold

and it is possible that Frank had gone out to Africa, initially to mine coal but saw a better opportunity in gold. It was probable that Frank was an overseer rather than a miner, and the membership list in the Transactions listed a Philip Francis, who was Surveyor-General for the Orange River Colony at the time. It seems likely that this Philip Francis was indeed the Frank recorded in the family Bible, and in fact he had gone out to Africa in a senior position to help oversee the mining developments taking place. His last trip was in 1912, and he died of emphysema in 1915.

Reports of the Select Committees
The most influential and oft-quoted report is that of 1842, which inquired into the working conditions of children in employment. The evidence, much of it collected from young women and children working in the mines, produced a harrowing picture. It was described by Royston Pike as: a masterly document, clear in expression, sober in presentation, and most comprehensive. (R. Pike *Human Documents of the Industrial Revolution in Britain*, (1966) Allen & Unwin, p.156)

Dr Southwood Smith, one of the Commissioners, had suggested that pictures should be included in the Report, '…as members of Parliament were busy people and could not have been expected to read through the mass of evidence' (Pike 1966, p156). As he had shrewdly anticipated, these were strikingly successful in arousing public interest, and have continued to be so even today.

As a result of this inquiry, women, girls, and boys below the age of ten were prohibited from working underground.

Reports from the Select Committees are an excellent source for researchers, as they contain verbatim records of interviews with different kinds of people. For example, the 1842 report has accounts given by children, miners, mine owners, and managers. Here are two examples:

No. 262 David Hewitt, examined in Messrs.
Ackeroyd's Colliery, Birtenshaw, May 26 1841:
I am 11 years old. I come down at 6 and go up at 5. I
come out at 12 and 3 on Saturdays. I hurry all day. I
stop a quarter of an hour to get my dinner, and then I go
and bare [i.e. cut away the bottom of the seam of coal].
I generally hurry with naked feet like I am now; it hurts
my feet to wear clogs. My work tires me a good deal; it
tires my legs. I get a little sometimes; and have to fill
after the getter is gone one corf perhaps. I go to
Sunday-school. I read in Reading made Easy. [to hurry
–to pull carts of coal; to get - to mine the coal; getter –
miner; corf – basket]

No. 107 Joseph Dawson [South Durham Coalfield]
…I get up at two or half past two. Some pits are farther
off than others. The men get up sufficiently soon as to
be at the pit by four, but some come in at two. It is half
an hour before we get all down; in some pits it is much
longer. I take a bit of meat, and bread, and water, when
I have a mind; there is no regular time. I take six, seven
or eight hours at my work; some will take 12 hours to
do the same quantity of work. Sometimes coal varies,
and sometimes there is difficulty in getting the coal
taken away, which causes delay. I come up about 11 or
12; I go home and get myself washed, and take my
dinner, and go to bed an hour or two: I get up then and
have a walk about for an hour or two; it is then tea time.
I go to bed at 10 and get up at half past two…
(Extracts from the *Children's Employment
Commission*, 1842 volume 7 of the Irish University
Press series of British Parliamentary papers, p. 291
and p.158)

The library has a good collection of reports from
Select Committees from 1810 and this forms part
of a larger collection of government publications on
coal mining in England.

The Coal Magazine
Coal was first produced in 1947 as the industry
was nationalised. It became *Coal News* in 1961
and then *RJB News* in1995. In 2002 it became the
UK Coal Newscene. Although the later issues
concentrate more on the achievements at the work
place, the earlier volumes contain articles on
holidays, pastimes, fashion, housekeeping, short
stories and competitions. It was aimed at the miner
and his family, and provides a rich source of
information on the social history of the 1940s and
50s.

Special collections in the library
The Eastwood collection was part of the National
Coal Board library and contains some very early
publications on coal mining, for example *The
Compleat Collier* of 1708. Others are beautifully
illustrated publications, for example Hair's *A series
of views of* the *collieries in the counties of
Northumberland and Durham* (1844). Others are
unusual for example *The mineralogy of Derbyshire:
with a description of the most interesting mines in
the North of England, in Scotland, and in
Wales;…subjoined is a gloffary of the terms and
phrafes ufed by miners in Derbyshire* (1802).

The library also has an extensive collection of trade
catalogues. From these publications it is possible
to trace not only new products, but also the history
of companies involved in their manufacture.

Another special collection in the library is the radio
and television transcripts and press cuttings, which
provide useful contemporary information on such
major events as the Miners' Strike of 1984/5.

Users
The library welcomes all who would like to find
out more about coal mining in England. Records
show that researchers, family historians, students
and staff are the main users, although the library
opening hours have been extended in the hope that
visitors to the Museum will be encouraged to
browse in the library after their visit around the
site.

Page from *Coal* volume 12, 1958

Miners underground- *Coal* - volume 12,1958

already afoot to encourage people to write their own stories using the library collection, and to actively support groups and individuals in their research.

As the industry declines, it is imperative that those who worked in the industry and their families record what it was like for future generations. As the evidence in the landscape disappears through regeneration, and coal is no longer burned in homes, this, and similar museums, will become vital to understanding the coal mining industry in the future.

Access
The Museum is open every day from 10am until 5pm. The library is open by appointment. It is also open the first full weekend of each month, on Saturdays and Sundays from 10am until 4pm without the need to book. There is full disability access to the study and photocopying facilities are available on site. Items are available to read in the study only.

The future
Now that the library has reestablished itself in new premises and as a national collection, it is hoped to continue to develop the collection through purchase and donations, and to continue to conserve the more precious items. Plans are

Tyne and Wear Archives Service
Carolyn Ball
Archives and Record Services Manager

Tyne and Wear Archives Service was established in 1974 following the creation of Tyne and Wear County Council. The service took over responsibility for the records previously held by Newcastle City Archives (which ceased to exist), as well as certain collections relating to the newly created county previously held in either the Northumberland or Durham Record Offices, for example, records of some predecessor local authorities, poor law unions and schools. The Archives Service survived the abolition of the metropolitan councils in 1986 and is now is a joint local authority record office supported by the five districts formerly part of Tyne & Wear county - Gateshead (the lead authority for archives), Newcastle, North Tyneside, South Tyneside and Sunderland.

Despite the fact that Tyne and Wear county technically does not exist any more, the Archives Service itself is very much alive and well. We are one of the largest local authority offices in the country: over twenty staff look after somewhere in the region of 12 miles of shelving in our five storage areas – and offer a full range of services to our users. Our supervised public search room is open to anyone who wants to consult the documents in our care and our Education Officer works closely with schools, colleges, family and local history groups. The expertise within our conservation unit helps to ensure the continued preservation of the documents in our care while skilled cataloguers produce detailed finding aids for collections. Our touring exhibitions are extremely popular and are always well received while our experienced staff are always on hand to provide expert advice on the history of the area and on the documents in our care.

We share a listed building, Blandford House, with the Newcastle Discovery Museum. Built in 1899, Blandford House was formerly a Co-operative Wholesale Society office and warehouse. Many features, such as stained glass windows, wood panelling and art deco lighting, survive, adding great character to the Archives Service accommodation. Our search room was at one time the Directors' Dining Room and we still use the Dumb Waiter – not for serving elaborate business lunches – but to transfer documents between the search room and the storage areas on the third floor!

Lunch is no longer served in the search room but the Discovery Museum Café does offer a wide selection of refreshments and an opportunity to relax with a dramatic view of some of the museum galleries. Indeed, some of the objects on display around the museum are equally well represented by documents in our archive collections. The most striking is Turbinia, Charles Parsons's revolutionary steam turbine ship. Turbinia has pride of place in the main gallery of the museum and the original plans are deposited with us, along with many other records relating to the revolutionary work of Charles Parsons. It is also possible to see one of Joseph Swan's original incandescent light bulbs in the museum - and then visit the archives to see some of his original design sketches.

Our central location in Newcastle means we are ideally placed for visitors by car, bus or train. There is a small car park immediately outside the

The Mauritania
© Tyne and Wear Archives

Sgt Peacock's Slice
© Tyne and Wear Archives

building although it can sometimes be very difficult to find a parking space, especially during school holidays. Newcastle Central train and Metro station is less than a ten-minute walk away and the new coach station is just across the road from us. If you are planning to stay in the area for a few days, there are numerous hotels to suit all budgets close by. (See Northumbria Tourist Board's website for latest prices and availability (www.ntb.org.uk)).

We are open Monday to Friday, 9 am until 5.15 pm and until 8.30 pm on a Tuesday. It is always advisable to book in advance especially to reserve a microfilm reader or to check on the availability of documents. At the time of going to press, we do not have a waiting list for microfilm readers and most users can visit on the day they wish.

When you visit us, you will find that we operate a service similar to most other Record Offices. You will need to sign our visitors' book and put your bags and personal possessions into a locker. And as we need to protect the documents in our care notes must be made in pencil. Eating and drinking is forbidden. It still comes as a great surprise to many users to discover that this includes sweets and chewing gum!

In the search room itself there is a self-service microfilm area with microfilm and microfiche readers, a reader-printer and detailed lists and indexes to help identify references and films. Many records commonly used for family history are microfilmed and available here (Church registers, census returns etc). We have a collection of genealogical CD-ROMs, three public access computers (one with access to the internet), trade directories and numerous reference aids. For further research into our collections, detailed catalogues and indexes to most collections are available. In most cases these are paper catalogues but some are also available to search electronically

in our database (now online as part of our website). It usually takes a few minutes only for a document to be produced once a request is made. To help with research, a comprehensive selection of reference books is available in our small search room library and ordnance survey maps of the area, for various dates and at different scales are also available. Details of our holdings for many well-used collections or subjects are summarised in our popular User Guide series. These guides are often a first point of reference when beginning research at Tyne and Wear Archives. Most types of record have an up-to-date user guide that can be obtained either direct from us or can be downloaded from our website. Each user guide has a brief introduction and a list of all the relevant documents with references.

Our collections cover every aspect of life Tyne and Wear between the 12th century and 21st centuries. Many visitors (over 70% in total) come in to research their family tree. Often people just 'pop in' because they are interested in where their grandmother was born or when their great grandfather was married. They then find themselves visiting every week for the next twenty years…hunting for that elusive grandmother who was born in Newcastle... There is a wealth of sources for family history at Tyne and Wear Archives. Some of the more popular are summarised below but please contact us if your ancestor(s) came from the area – we may be able to help you. Maritime history is also a popular research topic as researchers make use of our internationally important shipbuilding collections. Researchers range from academics studying naval architecture, to model enthusiasts creating scale replicas of ships, to retired sailors collecting photographs of ships they served on.

The microfilm area in the search room is used mainly by enthusiasts researching their family history. Although no original Church of England registers are deposited at Tyne and Wear Archives, we do hold microfilm copies of most registers, as well as many indexes, for churches in the Tyne and Wear area. Original registers, and other church records, for example, churchwarden's account books and tithe plans, for the area to the north of the Tyne originally part of Northumberland (now Newcastle and North Tyneside) are deposited at Northumberland Archives. Similarly, records for the area south of the Tyne originally part of County Durham (now Gateshead, South Tyneside and Sunderland) are deposited at Durham Record Office. Records of other church denominations are deposited with us. In most cases, microfilm copies are available but in others, original registers are produced. Registers for Roman Catholics, Methodists, Baptists, German Lutheran, Independent Evangelical, Swedenborgian, Unitarian, and United Reformed churches are available as are registers for Jehovah Witnesses and the Society of Friends. Full details are available either in our search room or on our website.

Over a number of years the records of the municipal cemeteries in Tyne and Wear were microfilmed and are now available in our search room. Coverage is almost complete and includes most cemeteries and crematoria in Gateshead, Newcastle, North Tyneside, South Tyneside and Sunderland.

Comprehensive census returns coverage for the Tyne and Wear area is available on either microfilm or microfiche. Original census returns are held at the Public Record Office in London. We hold copies of the returns for Tyne & Wear for 1841 - 1901 for the districts of Newcastle and North Tyneside (included as part of the county of Northumberland in the census returns) and Gateshead, South Tyneside and Sunderland (included as part of County Durham in the census returns). On some census the coverage overlaps slightly the Tyne & Wear border into areas of Northumberland and Durham - please check before your visit.Street indexes and some personal name indexes are also available. Internet access also provides access to the 1901 census website.

Guild records for Newcastle and Gateshead are deposited at Tyne and Wear Archives. All members of Newcastle guilds were Freemen elected to the Common Council. They monopolised the powers and offices of town government before 1835. The trade guilds of Gateshead were originally set-up to protect individuals from the power of the Newcastle Guilds across the river. The first Charter so granted was to the Dyers, Fullers, Locksmiths, Blacksmiths, Cutlers, Joiners and House Carpenters in 1595. Order and minute books contain information about the regulation of the companies and their members. When used with admission and apprenticeship books and lists of Freemen, these records can be invaluable to the family historian. Some guild records are microfilmed.

If you want to look at any of the documents described above you need to visit us in Blandford House. There is no charge to use our search room although a small charge is made if you want copies of documents. While we always welcome users to the search room, we know that not everyone can visit us in person. For this reason, we also offer a paid research service where an experienced member of staff will undertake a specific detailed research. This service is not restricted to family history enquiries – if we have relevant records we will research any aspect of the region's history. Recent non-genealogical research requests include the relationship between Newcastle and Arras after the Great War and the preferential treatment given to Czech companies relocating to the north east during the1930s. Up to three hours may be requested at any one time and the cost includes all

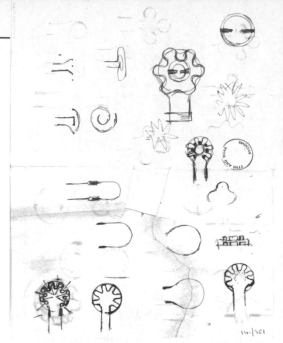
Joseph Swan's original design sketches

administrative, research, photocopying and postal charges. Latest prices and an application form are available from the Office or can be downloaded from our website.

Our website (www.thenortheast.com/archives) contains a great deal of helpful information. It is possible to download copies of all our user guides as well as forms to apply for photocopies and paid research. We have recently added a searchable online database that contains a number of catalogues to our collections. At present, it includes only a small percentage of catalogues, but it is still a useful starting point when investigating the collections we hold. However, it is important to remember to check our paper catalogues and indexes that have not yet been added to the system. It is also important to point out that the database does not include images of the documents. To see the actual document described in the database, you need to visit our search room.

It is difficult to summarise the holdings of such a large office in one short article. While some collections have enjoyed a passing mention, many have been ignored and while some lines of enquiry have been touched upon, many have been passed over completely. If you would like further information about any of our holdings or services, please contact us or visit our website. There's a whole lot more waiting for you!

Contact Details: Tyne and Wear Archive Service, Blandford House, Blandford Square Newcastle upon Tyne NE1 4JA
Tel: 0191 232 6789 x 22248 (this may change!)
Fax: 0191 230 2614
Email: twas@gateshead.gov.uk
Website:www.thenortheast.com/archives

A Royal Pardon
Jacqueline Cooper

Making connections could be said to lie at the heart of local and family history research. So often one document gives only one part of a story and needs to be linked to others for interpretation. The following example illustrates how a more rounded picture can be put together, by seeking out widely scattered repositories of information, as well as making use of that great aid to research, the internet and the goodwill generated among family historians.

In this case, a single sheet of paper set off a journey of historical discovery. This particular document, dated 1828, lies among the archives of Saffron Walden Museum in north-west Essex, and carries the authentic signature of King George IV on a royal pardon. Museums are normally thought of as places to find artifacts, rather than archives, but a 19th century foundation like that at Saffron Walden can possess a rich and diverse store of documentary ephemera which found its way there via various local worthies addicted to the collecting instinct.

On one side of the paper is the royal signature in brown ink, on the other a brief account of the offence pardoned. It concerned two young men, George Goodacre and Archibald Duprey or Dupree, who had been imprisoned after disturbing a congregation in a meeting house in Saffron Walden. There were no other documents with it, nor any explanation as to why they were pardoned, merely that 'certain circumstances' prevailed. Crimes are among the best recorded events, and the offence would surely turn up among the records of the local Sessions. The petty sessional minutes had a gap at precisely this point, but in any case it was serious enough to go to Quarter Sessions. On 15 April 1828, the men had appeared before the justices at Saffron Walden Court in the town hall, the Quarter Session minutes noting:

> George Goodacre true bill: indict for nuisance in disturbing a congregation of Protestants, plea not guilty, jury say guilty, fined £40 or commit till paid in common gaol; Archibald Duprey and James

> King: true bill Duprey, not found King; Duprey plea not guilty, jury say guilty, £40 or committed till paid in common gaol; Rebecca Burling, no bill; Henry Wisbey, no bill.

So this second source provided the information that Goodacre and Duprey were not alone – they were part of a small gang of young people making mayhem in the chapel, albeit that there was insufficient evidence to indict the others. It was frustrating that there were no indictments or depositions extant, as the latter in particular often give colourful local background. In this case, such detail can often be found in a local newspaper – indeed these are among the best sources for court cases, 19th century readers being no less enamoured of crime stories than we are today. Unfortunately there was no newspaper in Saffron Walden existing at this date, and a search of the county press did not turn up any reference.

A third possibility was that a contemporary

'Gentleman' John Player

might have written something in a diary or letter. In the case of Walden at this period, the most prolific recorder of events was 'Gentleman' John Player, a middle-aged and very religious worthy of ample time and means who had fingers in many pies and whose archives have survived in considerable numbers. As well as a brilliant museum, Saffron Walden also possesses a Victorian Studies Centre in the town library, with a large collection of antiquarian and archival material dating from its days as a Literary & Scientific Institute. It includes a volume of *Chronicles* written by John Player, who had a particular interest in law and order, and sure enough he expressed his outrage at the goings-on at the chapel:

Goodacre and Archibald Duprey were tried for interrupting public worship at Mrs. Webster's Meeting in Castle Street, and being found guilty were sentenced each to pay a fine of £40 and to be imprisoned till it be paid. his Lordship gave a manly exporation of the law on passing the sentence, which it is hoped will have much weight with the populace, great disturbance having been occasioned by the thoughtless and profane for some time past at the several places of worship in this town. The Grand Jury on this occasion threw out bills of indictment proffered for the like offence against Rebecca Burling, Henry Wisbey and James King who, there was little doubt, had more than once caused a disgraceful interruption at the time of divine service.

This third source expanded the information considerably. It revealed which chapel was involved, but also that other churches had suffered similar scandalous behaviour. It reflected a general feeling that those not indicted were just as guilty in effect. Player, as a dissenter, could not be a magistrate but did serve on the grand jury, and one can imagine him disagreeing with his fellow jurors on this point. A further new piece of information was that 'his Lordship', that is Lord Braybrooke, the aristocratic owner of nearby Audley End mansion, had made the effort to turn up to underline the seriousness of the case, and gave 'a manly exporation' to drive home the wickedness of interrupting Saffron divine worship. As if this were not enough, the two men were fined the huge sum of £40 (equivalent to almost two years wages for a labouring man), a fine that clearly they would be unable to pay. Hence the intention was to imprison them. I knew that a sentence on one of the 1795 food rioters in Saffron Walden had left him rotting in prison for five years until the fine was paid, so Goodacre and Duprey could have suffered the same, without the royal pardon.

Lord Braybrooke

A fourth source of information might occur among the archives of the chapel, Methodism being one of the best-documented denominations. I knew that Mrs Henrietta Webster had run her Wesleyan meeting house in Castle Street jointly with a Miss Charlotte Steigen Berger. The persecution could readily be attributed to the suspicion with which lady preachers were viewed at that time. From another book in the town library, a 19th century printed memoir on the pious life of Miss Berger, I found another reference to this same incident, and I later discovered that it had indeed become part of the folklore of Methodism, for it was repeated in an article in the *Methodist Recorder* in 1908.

This was not likely to go on in a place like Saffron Walden as it then was, without some opposition and persecution. But the bravery of the ladies appeared as much in the patience of their suffering and in their dignified remonstrance as in their fervent zeal... Inside the chapel... rough boys

Miss Berger

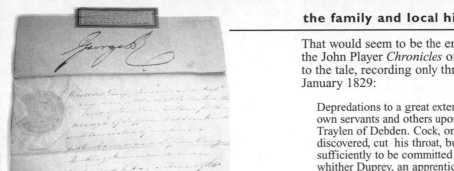

The Royal Pardon

behaved ludicrously, drunken men talked loudly and profanely and certain lewd fellows of the baser sort acted with scandalous indecency… certain of the ring leaders were prosecuted.

The good ladies had also suffered vandalism to trees and water butts and had stones thrown in their garden. The Wesleyans had not been in the town long and their preaching was supposed to calm down the disorderly poor, not make them worse, hence the severity of the sentence was to set an example and prevent further such incidents.

In spite of finding all this extra information about the offence, I had still not discovered on what 'certain circumstances' they were pardoned. As there is a large collection of pardon documents at the National Archives in Kew (formerly the PRO) I hoped to seek out a fifth source there. This took some tracking down, but in amongst Home Office indexed volumes there was the confirmation of the royal pardon on 20 September 1828, five months after they went to gaol:

> George Goodacre, Archibald Duprey, Free Pardon, George R:
> We in consideration of some circumstances humbly represented unto us are graciously pleased to extend Our Peace & Mercy unto them & to grant them Our Free Pardon for their said offence. Our will & pleasure therefore is that you give them the said George Goodacre & Archibald Duprey to be forthwith discharged out of custody… By command of Robert Peel.

The 'circumstances' have not revealed themselves, but one would guess that some local worthy had intervened to get them out of prison.

That would seem to be the end of the story, but the John Player *Chronicles* offered a further twist to the tale, recording only three months later in January 1829:

> Depredations to a great extent committed by his own servants and others upon the property of Mr Traylen of Debden. Cock, one of the men, on being discovered, cut his throat, but recovered sufficiently to be committed to Chelmsford, whither Duprey, an apprentice (see last year's Chronicles) had already been sent for like depredations. Apprehension of four confederates… In consequence of the confessions of the youths Rutherford and Dupree, four persons have been apprehended…

This time the Essex press (sourced at the British Library newspaper library in Colindale) did cover the story, since it came up two months later at the Lent Assize and from this it was clear that one of those apprehended was also Dupree's old partner in crime, George Goodacre. From this sixth source, I discovered that Dupree was not a deprived pauper driven to steal, but actually had a position working as an apprentice in a shop. Moreover Goodacre also had a trade of sorts, described as a 23-year-old hawker of books about the country, which presumably proved useful as a receiver of stolen property. He was transported for 14 years along with others – but not Dupree. Although he admitted he had supplied his master's property to others from the middle of 1826 onwards (actually covering the period in which he had committed the earlier offence), he was somehow acquitted.

Research is a time-consuming business, and with insufficient time to research further in the

National Archives, I thought I would try a seventh source of information, the excellent Australian archives on transportation. This is where the worldwide network of family historians comes in useful. Knowing that transportation is a topic of consuming interest in Australian genealogical circles, I posed a question on an internet discussion group, and was immediately overwhelmed with helpful responses, offering further information. Between them, the Australian genealogists discovered that George Goodacre, having been sentenced to 14 years transportation at Chelmsford, had been transported on the vessel 'Sarah'. He obtained his ticket of leave in 1839 and married another transportee, Margaret Cullen, obtaining a certification of freedom in 1843. They were married in Berrima, where Margaret died in 1858, and George in 1871. The ages do not quite add up, but it sounds like the same George.

Possibly the publication of this article may prompt further offerings, for no piece of historical research is ever finished (did George, for instance, behave himself once released after serving his time on the other side of the world?). But this does demonstrate how the use of many different sources in different places produces a far more comprehensive picture – and a means of cross-checking facts - than simply transcribing from one source, although there are always unanswered questions that may never be resolved. The discovery of the second case with the evidence that the depredations on the

Methodist (formerly Wesleyan) Chapel

shopkeeper had been going on for years also reflects that, whoever it was putting in a good word, they had persuaded the King to pardon a pair of rogues!

With thanks to Saffron Walden Museum, Saffron Walden Town Library Victorian Studies Centre and members of the Essex-UK Rootsweb list. Photograph of the Royal Pardon by courtesy of Saffron Walden Museum.
© Jacqueline Cooper 2003

Fulneck and The Moravians

Of interest to those whose forebears might have once been members of this sect – this article appeared in 'The Quiver' 1887.

In the histories of the smaller of the religious bodies there is often much of interest; and not the least is this true of the "Unitas Fratrum, or Church of the United Brethren." It has a past that is honourable, a present that is active, and surely a future of usefulness. It has had conferred upon it special privileges, has distinctive spheres of work, peculiar observances; and in its work, its systematic care for its members its zeal and its catholicity, it is in many respects a model Church. It maintains its weekly newspapers, its periodicals in several countries and languages, its almanack, its special histories, its own hymnal, its theological seminaries, and many schools, whilst its zeal for missions and its vast work therein are widely recognised. We need not glance back at the Church of Huss; but from the time of the awakening in some of the villages of Moravia in the beginning of the eighteenth century, we find the settlement of the '"Moravians" under Zinzendorf, at Herrnhut, in Saxony. Christian David led the band from the Moravian plains near the towns of Fulneck and New Tetschein in 1722, the first tree was felled for the building of Herrnhut, and two years later the foundation stone of a building was laid where "youths of rank should receive a Christian education." From thence spread the successors of the "Ancient Brethren" ; and with David Nitschman, Christian David, Tobias Leupold and Leonard Dober, began the series of missionary visits which have since that time continued to distinguish this " Missionary Church." Count Zinzendorf had been in England in 1737, but it is to Peter Bohler that the first society of Moravians in England is traceable (in 1738), the meetings being first held in the house of one of their members, and then in a chapel where Baxter had once preached, at No. 32, Fetter Lane, London. This address is still that of the " Moravian Church and Mission Agency" in London. We have now to do with the chief settlement of the Church of the United Brethren in England and our steps must be turned northwards.

August Gottlieb Spangenberg once a student at law in the University of Jena, then a propagator of the faith of the Brethren proceeded in April 1741, into Yorkshire, with two of his friends. They took charge there of some spiritually awakened people near Halifax, and formed several societies; but, later, they removed to a place then called Lamb's Hill, but renamed after the town of many memories in the Fatherland, Fulneck; and in the Moravian Almanack April 19th 1755, is given as the date of the establishment of the congregation.

The site was fixed upon by Count Zinzendorf. That establishment followed the recognition by the British Parliament of the Society as "an ancient Protestant Episcopal Church"; and it has been followed by the settlement of many other churches but still Fulneck remains the centre of the British Province of the Church of the United Brethren. It has the church with the largest congregation of the Brethren in Britain, and with the largest number of communicants; it has the largest schools; whilst around it are clustered many memories of this peculiar but honourable Church in England Fulneck is still, as ever, a retreat for the missionary and his kin, a nursery for the ministry and the headquarters of the Church.

In the heart of the home of the textile trades, between Leeds and Bradford, and close to the town of Pudsey, is this Moravian settlement of Fulneck. It is a quiet oasis, amidst a lusty, busy, and even turbulent life. Pudsey is a typical textile town; its people rough but honest and hearty its men wearing in the street the slop or "checkerbrat " proclaiming the calling, and its bonnie lasses still wearing the shawl for their only head-covering A few hundred yards from this place of warp and weft, of mills and looms, of oddly angled houses of grey stone and dark roofs, and in great contrast with it in most particulars is the settlement of the Unitas Fratrum . It is a large aggregation of buildings

the range extending to upwards of a mile in length -the main block is over a century old. There are the " Single Sisters' House," the "Widows' House " the house for time minister and the three large schoolrooms and chapel. Close thereto is the God's Acre of the Moravians, a pleasant slope of sward, with many flat gravestones, bearing usually a number a name and the year of death .The graves of the sexes seen divided; the grass grows thickly over and around at times obscuring the gravestone, and avenues of tall trees make music to serve as a monody.

Though the settlement has been made for more than a century there is still something distinctive about it and its people.It is not a trading village, though a few traders are there; it is a settlement where education is the aim and where that aim includes the training for the service of the Church in many lands. In the people who are seen too, there is a wide distinction from those in the villages whose chimneys may be seen from the terrace at Fulneck. There are "sisters" who are to be seen pacing along the front; there are "

adopted buy other denominations with much and marked success. The communion service amongst the Moravians has always been a strong bond of union and strikes a stranger as being solemn and impressive. The different congregations in each province all over the world, celebrate this on the same day throughout the year - every fourth Sunday-and a very large proportion of the communicant members almost invariably attend. Inthe bulk of the congregations the communion service is preceded by a short love-feast, preparatory to the sacrament and at the conclusion of the latter, during the singing of the closing hymn expressive of the bond of union, all present shake hands each with their neighbour.

brothers" resident, or " brothers" from a distance who are walking along to some of the separate homes of the place. At one time this distinctive character was apparent in the dress, each " choir" having its own recognised feature or colour; but in the English and American Provinces of the Church this has to a great extent become a thing of the past, although still in existence in the German Province.

It may not be out of place here to observe that although the educational establishments at Fulneck are the largest and most extensive in connection with the Church in England, there are some half a dozen or more other places where Moravian schools have long existed and flourished, the best-known being at Fairfield, near Manchester, and at Ockbrook, near Derby.

On " memorial days" and congregational anniversaries there are many thronging to the appointed place of meeting and now and again one of the dozen or so of bishops of the Church will give dignity to the occasion. The Moravian calendar has many memorial days in addition to those the Church Universal commemorates. Epiphany is in some places the memorial day for the mission work; there is the festival of all the " choirs," or spiritual unions; there is the " widows' festival," and that for the " single sisters;"the " festival of the elder girls," of the " elder boys," the " children's festival," that of the " single brethren," of the "widowers," and of the " married brethren and sisters; and at these and at the Sunday services the pealing of the great organ, the prescribed forms of prayer the chants and the hymns - all do much to stir up the devout mind amongst the Moravians.

In connection with the services, it is not a little singular to note how the old and well known meetings, formerly peculiar to the Moravian Church and including children's services, singing meetings and liturgies, have been taken up and

There is one observance that still survives in the Moravian Church — the use of the lot.. More than a century and a half ago, the history of the Unitas Fratrum tells us, the lot was " used only in the Conference of Elders under circumstances of perplexity; " no doubt in imitation of the method adopted by the eleven Apostles when by lot St Matthias was chosen as a successor to the traitor Judas. In 1731, the question of the union with the Lutheran Church was decided in the negative by the use of the lot; and in many exigencies it has been since used. In 1769 a Synod of the Church considered the question of its continued use, and the Brethren were agreed then that that means had been followed " with rich blessing and in many important matters." It was agreed on that " simple faith was necessary in the use of the lot." When Dober declined the office of General Warden, " his determination was sanctioned by lot," and it is the means of attaining the final decision in the election of bishops still.

In this country there are about two score Moravian congregations; in Germany and the United States there are larger numbers, and more churches and schools. The body is divided into three " provinces" —for the three nations. Over the whole is a supreme board of direction at Berthelsdorf, Herrnhut, Saxony ; the whole Unity of the Church is legislated for by the General Synod; which meet about every ten years, whilst the Provincial Synods meet for the separate provinces more frequently. The excutives of the Provincial Synods are the "Provincial Elders' Conferences", elected thereby. Below these latter conferences, again, are, in Britain, the "General Conferences of Elders" the different districts- -composed usually of "all persons having a spiritual office in the congregation" of the district — and intended to promote " inter-course and fellowship of work among the congregations, and for mutual counsel and help among the ministers." Again, and for the separate congregations, there are " Elders' Conferences," a committee for the management of temporal matters, and a congregational council. It may be added that The Moravian Almanack states that there are funds in the British Province, first to raise all 'ministers' salaries to the minimum of £100; a second to provide small pensions for invalided workers of both sexes; and others for training, education, chapel building, etc. Finally, there is a Church work of the Moravians which is peculiar. It is called the " Diaspora," or Home Mission Work of the German section of the Church. " It seeks not to make proselytes, or to draw members from other Protestant communities, but to excite and foster spiritual life by means additional to those provided by the established churches" of the Scandinavian, German, and other countries where it is carried on.

These, then, are some of the facts gathered, and the impressions received on a visit to Fulneck, the chief British settlement of this peculiar and honoured little Church. The life there goes on in even grooves; quietness and order reign in what may be called a little colony of those who are and are to be workers in spiritual and educational things, and who dwell in the midst of a population distinct in aim, in manner, and in custom.

J. W. S.

Electric Trams ~ Britain's lost transport system

Robert Blatchford

Albert Square, Manchester

The introduction of a horse drawn omnibus in 1824 at Pendleton, Salford by John Greenwood, a tollgate keeper, was the beginning of the use of 'buses' by the general public. These 'buses' ran between Pendleton and Market Street in Manchester. The service was very successful and by 1850 there were over 64 omnibuses serving central Manchester from outlying suburbs. The omnibus services sprang up in many major towns throughout the country. Amalgamations and mergers soon followed. America saw a rapid growth in the omnibus. By the 1870's tramways were being constructed but the limitations of horse power was obvious prompting the investigation of mechanical power. Steam tramways were developed but were not really suitable for urban use and cable tramways were successful for a time.

However the possibility of electric traction with the generation of electricity from a fixed point and supplying it to a live rail or overhead wire changed everything. The generation of electricity to running rails was unsuitable for streets. Overhead wires were the obvious solution and there followed the rapid introduction of electric trams in most major towns and cities.

Regulation of tramways was controlled by The Tramways Act 1870 and specifically forbid local authorities from running tramways themselves. An Act of Parliament in 1893 took away this restriction and local authorities actively began to operate services within their areas. In Manchester the Corporation act of 1897 granted the necessary powers for the authority to operate electric tram services. In June 1901 the service was officially opened and rapid expansion followed. By 1910 Manchester Corporation had a tramway network of over 100 miles and 582 operating vehicles and was making an annual profit of nearly £150,000. Tramcar depots were opened around the city and by the start of the First World War in 1914 Manchester had a fleet of 662 cars. The lack of maintenance through the war and inflation following it brought an increase in running costs. Competition from petrol powered buses had also had a detrimental effect. The service in Manchester continued to increase and by 1930 it covered 163 route miles and had over 1000 cars. The tramcars were beginning to show their age and several routes were replaced by motor buses also run by the Corporation. Capital expenditure was needed to improve the vehicles and the rail system. Road widening schemes also had a detrimental effect with routes being abandoned to motor buses. In 1937 the decision

Oxford Street, Manchester

Market Street, Manchester

were approaching the end of the line. Motorbuses were more flexible and could better serve the newly built housing estates. In 1934 a public meeting voted in favour of scrapping the trams. In November 1935 the final tram journey in York took place with Tram No1 being driven by the same JA Stewart (now an Inspector) who had driven the inaugural tram 25 years earlier.

Leicester Corporation operated electric trams from 1904 until 1949. Likewise Barrow in Furness Corporation authorised the construction of tramways in 1881 and electrification followed in 1903 with the first electric trams operating in 1904. The system expanded to cover the whole of the town and Walney Island with the Corporation purchasing the tramways in 1919. However the same decline followed as in other towns and cities. Barrow determined to close the service in 1930 with the last tram running in 1932 being replaced by buses.

Perhaps the most famous place associated with trams is Blackpool where it is claimed that the first electric tram ran in July 1885. The fleet consisted on 10 trams one of which gave demonstrations at The Science Museum in London. Apart from being the first tram to run in London, it achieved further notoriety in 1887 on its return to Blackpool when it became the first tramcar to be involved in a fatal accident. The development of the service in Blackpool mirrored the development in other parts of the

was taken to abandon the tramway system completely and this would be phased in over the following three years. The outbreak of war delayed the abandonment until peace was resumed. By 1945 the intention was to complete the abandonment by 1947 but this did not happen until 1949 because of problems in obtaining new buses. January 1949 finally saw the last tram in Manchester and brought to an end the third largest tramway system in the country.

The same scenario took place in many other towns and cities. Birmingham opened its first tramway in 1872 with the same rapid expansion over the following years. In 1922 trolleybuses began to replace trams on some routes starting a decline with gradual closures of routes over several years. In July 1953 over 70 years of tram operations came to an end in Birmingham.

In York the construction of an electric tramway was a major undertaking with the widening of many streets in this ancient city. The first electric tram was driven by Mr J A Stewart on 20th January 1910 from Fulford to the city centre. The system expanded over the years with the strengthening and rebuilding of some bridges and the introduction of new routes. However in York as in every other city and town by 1932 trams

Ramsden Square   Barrow-in-Furness

country. There were one or two setbacks. The groove in the rail was much wider than permitted by the Board of Trade allowing bicycle wheels to drop into the grooves. In addition the gauge (track width) was also wrong and the curves of the rails were too tight for the trams to negotiate. An expensive relay of the track was necessary. However visitors to the town soon made the service profitable. In 1902 the Promenade was widened and by 1905 it was the longest in Britain. At the same time the trams were given their own roadway running parallel with the foreshore and the road. This more than anything ensured the preservation of the system and prevented it from sharing the same demise as all other services.

Preservation of the vehicles was not a priority but the establishment of The National Tramway Museum at Crich Tramway Village, nr Matlock, Derbyshire, has ensured that future generations will be able to see a form of transport that existed for just over 70 years.

At Crich trams operate throughout the day in a reconstructed village with original facades of historic buildings out into the countryside. An exhibition hall brings to life the history of the tram and includes a recreation of the 1905 Tramways Exhibition. The Workshop Viewing Gallery allows visitors to watch ongoing restoration and repair work that is carried out each day.
Refreshments are available at The Red Lion or The Village Tea Rooms. However following my experience of using them in 2003 I would recommend you take your own picnic and drinks.

There is also a Museum library which houses a unique collection of books, pamphlets, reports and Acts of Parliament covering the history of British, North American, European and other foreign tramways.

In addition the Archive holds records of transport operators, including British Electric Traction, and those

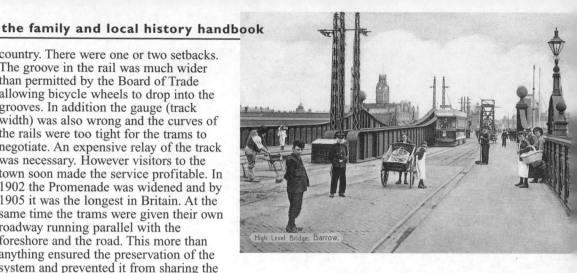

High Level Bridge, Barrow.

previously lodged with the Bus & Coach council, as well as the minutes of associations such as the Municipal Tramways and Transport Association and the Municipal Passenger Transport Association.

There is also an extensive journal and book collection containing descriptions of the world's tramway and light rail and information on the manufacturers of vehicles and equipment, transport law and planning so that the development of a town's transport can be studied in total. In addition The Photograph and Film Archive covers the tramway systems of Great Britain and the world. The collections include negatives and glass plates, prints and commercial postcards. The library is open all the year to visitors by prior appointment with the Librarian, Rosemary Thacker MA, ALA.

The National Tramway Museum, Crich Tramway Village, nr Matlock, Derbyshire, DE4 5DP. Telephone: 0870 75 TRAMS (87267)
Fax: 01773 85 23 26 Web: www.tramway.co.uk

The National Tram Museum, Crich

Estate and Related Records at the National Library of Wales

Eirionedd A. Baskerville
Editorial Officer - Department of Public Services
National Library of Wales

When information available in parish registers, bishops' transcripts and wills has been exhausted, genealogical researchers should turn their attention to the records of the manor and the estate. From the medieval period to the beginning of the twentieth century, large landed estates owned by the aristocracy and gentry were a prominent feature of the Welsh countryside, and much of the population lived and worked as tenants on these estates. Estate records are, therefore, an important source of information on tracing the history of an area and its inhabitants.

Records drawn up in the administration of an estate, such as rentals, surveys, title deeds (leases, mortgages, etc.) may enable you to discover names of owners and occupiers over several centuries. While the muniments of many large landed estates are likely to include good series of rentals and accumulations of title deeds, not all Welsh estates will be represented by long series of manorial records. The manorial system never came to full development in the counties of the medieval Principality, in west Wales, but the Marcher lordships generated a wealth of manorial records. However, notable amongst the series of manorial records held by the National Library of Wales are those for north Wales in the archives of the Chirk Castle and Wynnstay estates, and for mid-Wales in the Powis Castle archives. Amongst those of Badminton are manorial records for Chepstow, from 1568, Monmouth, from 1416, Porthgaseg, from 1262, Raglan, from 1364, Treleck, from 1508, and Usk, from 1517, while Bute includes manorials records from the fourteenth century for many manors in cos. Glamorgan and Monmouth, and Tredegar contains records of many Monmouthshire manors, those of the manor of Brecon and others in co. Brecon. A manorial database for Wales can be found on http://www2.hmc.gov.uk/mdr/mdr.htm.

In general terms, amongst the manorial documents are found the Court Leet rolls which give the names of the manorial officers and local jurors and details of cases brought to court, e.g. the scouring of ditches, straying of cattle and cases of assault, theft or trespass. Court Baron rolls deal with tenancy matters and property disputes, while extents and surveys contain descriptions of boundaries, valuations and names of tenants, their holdings and rents paid. Custumals contain names of all the tenants with details of the land which they held and particulars of rents, labour services and payments owed to the lord, while bailiffs' accounts list the income from rents and fines and expenditure on ploughing, repairs and replacing implements, and the names of incoming and outgoing tenants can be found in admittances and surrenders.

It must be remembered that not all estates were secular - prior to the dissolution of the monasteries in 1536 the Church was a powerful landowner. The Library's Wynnstay archive contains a group of early charters of Strata Marcella Abbey, while the Margam Abbey group of records in the Penrice and Margam collection is one of the fullest surviving British monastic archives. Crosswood Deeds and Documents 1184 is a translation of a charter of Rhys, Prince of Wales, and his sons, Griffith, Rhys and Meredith, granting and confirming to the Abbot of Strata Florida all the lands previously granted by the said prince and then held by the said abbey.

References to the acquisition of monastic estates by secular landowners can be found throughout the estate records held by the National Library, as shown in the following example from the schedule to the Crosswood collection:

1659-60 Mar 10 Indenture (counterpart) being a grant from John Vaughan of Trowscoed, co. Card. esq to Morgan Herbert of Havodychtrid, co. Card. esq of the tenement called Dol-dologe in the parish of Gwnnus and in the grange of Cwmystwith, co. Cardigan, being late parcel of the possessions of the dissolved monastery of Strata Florida, but reserving to the grantor the minerals thereunder, a perpetual yearly rent of £5 and suit at Pyran Mill

The records of the Welsh Church Commission held at the National Library of Wales also prove a fruitful field for researchers. Surveys were undertaken in the early 1940s, and contain much information on the history of manors: rentals, surveys, disputes over manorial rights, and especially foreshore rights around Bangor, going back to the 16th and 17th centuries. They also contain some tithe records which could provide valuable cross-references to the tithe material held at the Library. The Church in Wales schedules give reference to relevant records such as glebe terriers, surveys not only of glebe land but also of all buildings, including parsonages and church cottages.

The amount of land, and hence power and patronage, held by an estate in a parish or parishes was of supreme importance in determining the whole character of parishes. Title deeds will usually give a history of landowning and landholding, that is the acquisition of properties, the takeover of one estate by another, sometimes by purchase but usually through marriage. Lewis Owen (d. 1691) was responsible for the first substantial addition to the Peniarth estate, co. Merioneth, by marriage. In 1653 he married Jane, daughter of Richard Lloyd of Esclusham, Denbighshire, who eventually brought with her the Gelli Iorwerth estate in the parishes of Trawsfynydd and Llanddwywe. A further example is found in the Tredegar Papers:

109/9 1633, March 26
1. William Morgan of Therrowe, co. Brecon, esq;
2. Sir William Morgan of Tredegar, co. Mon., knight, and Thomas Morgan of Machen, esq., eldest son of the said Sir William Morgan, and Roweland Morgan, gent., another son of the said Sir William Morgan

Settlement made before the marriage of the said William Morgan and Elizabeth Morgan, one of the daughters of the said Sir William Morgan, and in consideration of sixteen pounds paid to the said William Morgan, touching the lordship of Keinsham alias Neither Keinsham with its appurtances in cos. Hereford and Radnor; the divided third part of the lordship of Lliswen with its appurtances in co. Brecon; the capital messuage called Therrowe with its appurtenances in the parishes of Glasbury and Lliswen, co. Brecon; other messuages and lands in the parishes of Lliswen; a messuage and lands called *the Gare* in the parishes of Glasbury, Lliswen, and Llandevalty, co. Brecon; lands, being parcel of the demesnes of the lordship of Brecon, called *Heneuske* in the parish of Llavayes *alias* Llanvary, *the Greene* in the same parish, *the Lake* in the parish of St John's; other lands in the parish of St John's including those called *Pedebagh, Henny, Plucklocke, St John's land*; lands called *Tyr y Piscoidwr* in Glintawy in the parish of Divynocke; lands at Tallemere, parcel of the lordship of Brecon; lands in the parish of Llanham Wokgh (sic); messuages and lands called *Tir blaen Carrand* and *Tir dan y Graig* in the parish of Vaynor; properties in the parish of Penderin; and messuages and lands called Tyr Carne *y Crochan, Tir Pant y Lloyne, Tir pulch y gelynen, Tyr Blaen Neath, Tir Aber Llia(?), tyr Kay yr Hendre, Tir Lloyn Bedo, Tir Nant David Croyn, Tir Maes David Gwyn, Tir Inys Willy and Tyr bulch Ryweddedw'th, all in the parish of Istradvelty, co. Brecon.*

Generally called conveyances but also known by various technical names, (e.g. feoffment, bargain and sales; leases and releases; final concords, and common recoveries), title deeds give the name, abode and occupation of parties with relationships,

Caerphilly Castle

names of witnesses, details of seals in early deeds, recital of earlier deeds affecting the property, names of farms and houses and references to all kinds of property - mills, chapels, schools and fisheries - together with foreshore rights. They are valuable sources of information for the growth and decline of the estate, the history of a particular house of farm, the distribution of local trades, the origins of schools or chapels, and family history.

However, estates are not only of relevance to rural communities; there were great urban landlords. It is a sobering thought that perhaps half the population of Wales today live within what was once the boundaries of the Bute and Tredegar estates in Monmouthshire and Glamorgan. By studying the rentals of these two estates you can virtually see before your very eyes the green fields being turned into streets. The same is true, to a lesser extent, of Aberystwyth (in the Crosswood, Nanteos and Gogerddan estates). Estates also held mineral deposits, and much of the early industrial history of Wales is to be found in the archives of landed families - Bute and Tredegar with coal and iron, Nanteos and Wynnstay with lead mines, the Chirk Castle archives with the early iron and coal industries of north east Wales, whilst the early industry of the Swansea area is reflected in the Badminton archives and the beginnings of its copper industry in the Vivian archives.

Estate accounts provide a wealth of information on the income of domestic and farm labourers. Servants, whether domestic or labourers were the most transient of the community, moving from household to household and from parish to parish, as is amply borne out by evidence in the estate accounts of the high turnover of staff.

Under estate management are found surveys which contain descriptions of land and buildings, names of tenants, fields and the rents payable and valuations, with details of land use and state of cultivation and content of buildings. In an age lacking precise statistics, the chief economic indicator of a rural society's fortune within estate archives are the rentals which give the names of tenants, their holdings, acreage and rents paid; they reflect periods of agricultural depression and boom. A study of the rentals of the Gogerddan estate, co. Cards., in 1756 and 1757, where little is noted in the column 'cash received' but where there are numerous entries in the arrears column, reveals that farmers were struggling in those years owing to disastrous harvests. However, the rental for the same estate in 1810, in the middle of the Napoleonic War, when demand for livestock and corn was exceptionally high, shows that cash received is equivalent to the rent demanded, apart from one entry of arrears of £3.

Estate ledgers include accounts and wages books containing details of indoor and outdoor labour, wages paid and the prices of goods and provisions. Household management records of the housekeeper or butler, including ledgers, bills and vouchers, accounts of servants' wages, provisions and domestic utensils and cellar books, are valuable sources of information for family life; education of children; changing trends in food; furniture, clothing and household goods; employment of servants; and prices, wages and costs of goods and provisions. In addition, family papers often contain pedigrees and genealogical notes.

In 1870 a list was published of estates which were either over 3000 acres in extent or carried an annual rental of over £3000 per annum. The Library holds records of 54 such estates totalling roughly about three-quarters of a million acres. If we add to this the archives of about 600 smaller estates then the figure must be nearly a million acres. Such a vast class of records is bound to contain information of immense value to the local historian.

Outstanding among the National Library of Wales' archives of landed families are those of Badminton, which contain records of the Welsh estates of the dukes of Beaufort, earlier of the earls of Worcester and William Herbert, first earl of Pembroke. These include records for the Breconshire lordships of Crickhowell, from 1382, and Tretower, from 1532, ministers' accounts for Monmouthshire lordships from 1387 and records of the Seignory of Gower and Kilvey from 1366 and for the borough and manor of Swansea, 1657-

1835, deeds for the 13th cent. and industrial records for the 16th cent. Brogyntyn contains estate records and family correspondence, 14th-20th cent., of the families of Owen of Brogyntyn, Wynne of Clenennau, Glyn and Ystumcegid, Maurice of Clenennau, Vaughan of Corsygedol, Longueville, Godolphin and Owen of Glasynys and Ormsby-Gore, barons Harlech, and others, whose estates lay mainly in cos Caernarfon, Flint, Merioneth, Montgomery and Salop. Chirk Castle was, from 1595, the estate of the Myddelton family, and the collection holds estate and family records relating mainly to co. Denbigh, while the Wynnstay Archive includes many legal manuscripts of 16th and 17th century, election papers, and manorial records.

A related category of archives is that which derives from solicitors' offices. Solicitors were often the election agents for the landed gentry, and records from the offices of Longueville & Co. of Oswestry, solicitors for many prominent north Wales families, Eaton Evans & Williams of Haverfordwest, and D. T. M. Jones of Carmarthen are notable examples.

Although the Land tax was introduced in 1692, few records have survived before 1780 when copies of the assessments began to be filed by the Clerk of the Peace. Land tax assessments contain the names of the owner and the occupier of the property, a description of the property (not always given and then often vague, e.g. 'house and land'), and details of the sum assessed. As well as the records of central government taxation, parochial rate assessment (church rate, poor rate, highway rate, etc.) also give details of occupiers of a property. You will be lucky, however, in Wales, to find a complete series of rate assessment books for a particular parish, even during the second half of the 19th c.

It is much easier to trace the history of a property if it formed part of a large estate.

A study of Quarter Sessions records can also prove rewarding. Most of these records have long since been transferred from the National Library of Wales to local County Record Offices. What remains at the Library is a quantity of stray records, often embedded in the archives of landed families (for example, the early Denbighshire Quarter Sessions records among the Chirk Castle archives) and a number of small deposits, including some of the few surviving Cardiganshire records. Amongst these are lists of freeholders to serve on juries.

The twentieth century has seen the demise or fragmentation of many landed estates in Wales, and the Library holds numerous sale catalogues which give details of the properties - farms, cottages, implements, etc.,- which were on sale. Thus, the documents relating to the life of an estate, from its birth, through its periods of growth occasioned by the accession of other properties or from mineral and industrial wealth, to its decline and final demise, can provide an invaluable source of information to the local and family historian who is prepared to delve into its records.

Researching the History of Houses
Eirionedd A. Baskerville
Editorial Officer - Department of Public Services
National Library of Wales

Researching the history of houses has become a very popular pastime recently, with television programmes promoting interest in the subject. However, tracing the history of individual properties can be a slow and painstaking process. The National Library of Wales holds a wealth of documentary sources but evidence earlier than the nineteenth century is, at best, uneven. After all, the records relating to a particular building were not written in order to assist present-day owners trace its past. The information available will often consist merely of names of individuals who owned or occupied the property at various times. Likewise, whereas the sources may contain evidence regarding the existence of a dwelling on a particular piece of land they will not, in most cases, enable the specific dating of the building or provide information on its original structure or details of subsequent alterations. Remember that a house could have been rebuilt on the same or an adjoining site without any change of name, and that houses were often renamed.

If you were a relevant newcomer to the subject it would be worthwhile beginning your research by asking some of the oldest inhabitants of the area if they know anything about the history of your house; they might be able to recount former inhabitants of your house and say whether it had ever been known by another name. The next step would be to consult the title deeds, which may be in your possession or held by your solicitor. Abstracts of title contain summaries of previous transactions and modern abstracts may take you back to the nineteenth century.

To build up a complete history of a property, it is best to combine documentary evidence with architectural evidence. The Welsh Assembly Government has a statutory responsibility for recording, protecting and helping to conserve historical buildings throughout Wales. If you think that your house is of special architectural or historical interest you might wish to consult the Library's copies of Lists of Buildings of Special Architectural or Historical Interest compiled by CADW.

Before delving into the primary sources of information you should search for any secondary sources. Have any books been written on the history of your area? Ceredigion, Pembrokeshire and Carmarthenshire historical houses and their families are well served by Francis Jones' volumes on the subject. There might be an article of interest to you in the Transactions and Historical Record Society Journal of your county. References in such publications could lead you directly to primary documentary sources.

Printed trade and local directories and guidebooks will often contain lists of principal private residents and tradesmen, giving their addresses and occupations. The earliest trade directory in the National Library of Wales is Pigots Trade Directory of 1822 which covers many of the principal towns in Wales. Printed electoral registers, introduced in 1832 and containing names and addresses of electors if you know where an ancestor lived. For example, the Library holds poll books for Pembrokeshire, 1765 and 1768, for Denbighshire, 1741, a list compiled, July 1852, of electors in the borough of Brecon, a register of Flintshire electors, 1833, and The Register of Persons entitled to vote at any election for members to serve in Parliament

for the county of Cardigan between the Thirtieth of November 1860 and the First of December 1861.

You are now in a position to enquire as to what documentary evidence does the National Library of Wales hold which will help you in your search? A good starting point is the map collection. The Library holds maps of all kinds – town maps, estate and farm maps. The Copyright Act of 1911 gave the Library the right to receive a copy of all commercially produced maps in Britain, this now extends to all those issued by the Ordnance Survey maps, on all scales. Maps at a medium scale (6ins to 1 mile) and the larger scale (25 ins to a mile) appeared in the late 19th century and the latter, in particular show all buildings, roads, fields, and streams. In addition, the substantial and important manuscript (i.e. hand drawn) maps of farms and estates in Wales date from around 1600 to the end of the 19th century. Most are linked to large estates, e.g. the Tredegar Park estate in Monmouthshire and Breconshire, and there are also bound volumes of estate maps as well as loose maps. These maps tell us much about the agriculture of the times, the names of landowners and tenants, and owners of plots of adjacent land, and, therefore, are a potential source of information for the 'house-hunter'.

If you are fairly certain that your house existed before the middle of the 19th century the appropriate parish tithe map and apportionment could yield valuable information. The Tithe Commutation Act of 1836 allowed the substitution of payment in kind. Tithe maps show most buildings in the parish, but towns and villages are treated with a varying degree of detail from parish to parish. Tithe maps were produced mainly between 1838 and 1854 and are often the earliest detailed maps available, although most of those for Wales were based on previous surveys and estate documents. The accompanying apportionment will give names of owners and occupiers of individual properties, the amount of tithe payable, acreages and often field names and details regarding land use. It is, therefore, an invaluable aid for those researching the history of houses. However, land freed from the tithe before the 1836 Act will not be included.

Enclosure maps and awards, although concerned with land rather than buildings, may show the existence or absence of a building on a plot of land. The Library holds various enclosure maps and awards, mainly 19th century but also some late 18th century, particularly for Cardiganshire, Montgomeryshire and Breconshire. For enclosure records you should also consult the indexes, particularly the index to schedules under the heading Land: Enclosure.

It is also worth consulting the Library's collections of photographs, prints and postcards as they also show buildings, especially those in towns and villages. During the 1850s photography became more accessible and professional photographers set up studios in towns and villages throughout Wales. One of the best collections at the Library is that of John Thomas, a photographer who travelled around Wales photographing his fellow countrymen and women, painstakingly recording streets, villages, quarrymen, factory workers and railway stations. The task of placing the John Thomas Collection on the Library's website is an ongoing project, and the work of the twentieth century photojournalist Geoff Charles is being made available in similar fashion.

It is much easier to trace the history of a property if it formed part of a large estate. If the owner, as named on the tithe apportionment, was a reasonable extensive landowner, estate records may exists at the National Library of Wales. Records drawn up in the administration of an estate, such as rentals, surveys, title deeds (leases, mortgages, etc.) may enable you to discover names of owners and occupiers over several generations, although estate records are likely to have survived in a systematic form only for the larger properties. Costumals contain names of all the tenants with details of the land which they held and particulars of rents, labour services, payments owed to the lord, while the names of incoming and outgoing tenants can be found in admittances and surrenders. Title deeds give the name, abode and occupation of parties with relationships, names of witnesses, details of seals in early deeds, recital of earlier deeds affecting the property, names of farms and houses and reference to all kinds of property. They are invaluable sources of information for the history of a particular house or farm. If your house was held by copyhold (i.e. if the title deeds are copies of the court roll of the manor) you will need to discover firstly the name of the manor to which the house belonged and secondly whether any records survive from that manor. A database containing information about Welsh manorial records is available on the internet (http://www2.hmc/gov/uk/Welsh_Manorial_Docu ments_Register.htm) and a volume, Welsh Manors and their Records, by Helen Watt has also been published by the National Library of Wales. To consult manorial documents (court rolls or books, rentals, surveys, accounts, etc.) before the 19th century you will need to be familiar with court hand and to have a rudimentary knowledge of medieval Latin.

Where surveys and estate maps exist for an estate (they rarely occur before the middle of the 18th century) they are a good place to begin. Rentals are often a relatively easy source to use, but it is difficult to make much use of title deeds if they have not been listed in detail. There is no index to individual properties apart form large houses described as 'capital messuages' in old title deeds. You should check, therefore, the references given in the topographical index under the appropriate parish and perhaps township. The references on the index cards are to pages in the typescript schedules. The card index to manuscript estate plans records properties alphabetically under the appropriate county and parish. In addition, many of the Library's schedules are now being made available on-line, and you should search the website to see whether there are references to your property or to the records of the estate to which your property belonged.

If the property formed part of an estate, printed sale particulars produced by auctioneers and estate agents may well yield valuable information. Although the earliest of the 5000+ sale catalogues are from the 1790s the majority date from the first half of the twentieth century. The Finance Act of 1911 force the large estates to pay death duties; consequently in the years following 1911 many of the landowners were forced to sell off portions of the estate to pay the death duty. Details of sales of individual properties may also appear in local newspapers. Marriage settlements among estate and family papers often contain a wealth of information on the houses, farms, mills and other properties which were the subject of the settlement and can, therefore, provide documentary evidence of the existence of a property.

Census returns are another source of information on properties in a district. They list the occupants(who may be tenants or owners) of each household, noting their age, occupations and, from 1851 onwards, relationship to the head of the household and parish of birth. Although you may experience some difficulty in locating your property on the returns, especially if it was in a built-up area, they can be invaluable sources for nineteenth century buildings. The Library holds microform copies of the census returns for the whole of Wales and some border parishes, 1841-1901, and the 1881 index for England and Wales on microfiche. In addition, some of the returns have been transcribed and indexed by enthusiastic individuals and societies who have generously made them available to the Library's researchers.

Other sources concerning owners/occupiers of properties include parish registers, especially the post-1837 registers. Some earlier parish baptism and burial registers include the name of the family abode, a detail which appears in most registers of the nonconformist denominations.

If you were successful in tracing your house on the tithe map and apportionment you should then be able to work backwards by consulting the records of central government taxation, especially the Land Tax records. Although introduced in 1692, few records have survived before 1780, when copies began to be filed by the Clerk of the Peace. Land Tax Assessments contain the names of the owner and occupier of the property, a description of the property (not always given and then often vague, e.g. house and land) and details of the sum assessed. Working back from the latest available Land Tax assessment may enable you to discover when a property first appeared on a particular site. Some Land Tax Assessments can

but also of all buildings, including parsonages and church cottages), dilapidation papers (details of the fabric of parsonages) and miscellaneous papers, deeds and documents.

In addition to the records of central government taxation, parochial rate assessment (church rate, poor rate, highway rate, etc) also give details of occupiers of properties. You will be lucky, however, in Wales to find a complete set of rate assessment books for a particular parish, even during the second half of the 19th century. A search of the files of parochial records in the catalogue room of the Library's South Reading Room will provide details on any parochial records held at the Library relating to your parish.

Furthermore, having discovered the names of occupiers of your property you should check the probate indexes at the Library to see whether any wills survive for those individuals. Wills, especially before the 18th century, are often accompanied y inventories of the goods of the deceased, some of which describe in detail the contents of each room and the value of each item. Thus they may well indicate, as few other documentary sources will do, the number of rooms in a building, its general layout and the state of its furnishings.

be found among the Library's collections of manuscripts and estate papers, for example in NLW MS 144-50 there are Land Tax Assessments for the Cwmtwrch area, 1817, while the Cefn Papers have a schedule of them for the hundred of Builth, 1826, and the Penpont Collection for various parishes in Breconshire, 1734-87. The collection of solicitors Roberts and Evans are an especially rich resources of LTAs for Cardiganshire. The Library has also purchased microfilm copies of the 1798 Land Tax Assessments for the Welsh counties (excluding Flintshire, which have been lost).
Should you succeed in tracing the history of your house as far back as the late 17th century you will need to consult hearth tax records (1662-89), most of which are held in the National Archives at Kew. However, the National Library of Wales does hold some hearth tax records, for example in the Tredegar Collection there is an account of the hearth tax paid by Thomas Morgan of Tredegar in 1680, and the 1670 hearth tax records for Cardiganshire are found in NLW facs 644.

If you house was in any way connected with the Church, some of the records of the four Welsh dioceses held at the Library may well contain information of value to you. The Church in Wales schedules give references to relevant records such as glebe terriers (surveys not only of glebe land

Information on tollhouses will be found among turnpike trust records, and those available at the Library are listed in the index to the Handlist of Manuscripts in the National Library of Wales and the Index to Schedules, under the subject headings Transport: Roads: Turnpike, or the Library's website.

In all there are many sources of information on individual properties at The National Library of Wales, but in order to find what you want you will need a lot of patience, and maybe a little luck.

In the Steps of Paddy Leary
~ Irish Ancestors in the USA and the Empire
Joe O'Neill

Any one with a nodding acquaintance of traditional Irish music knows that emigration is a recurring theme. Paddy Leary, who was 'off to Philadelphia in the morning,' is only one of those famed in song. And there are as many emigration destinations as there are songs.

The Irish never seem to stay in one place - one of the problems of tracing Irish ancestry. Emigration has been central to Irish life for hundreds of years. From the 17th century they went to the USA, where Ulster Protestants played a major role in opening up the west. Later, during the period of the British Empire's growth, Irishmen and women made their homes in every red section of the globe, especially Canada and Australia.

The greatest era of emigration was from the 1820s to the 1930s. Most of these emigrants were Catholics. In total four and a half million went to the USA, half a million to Canada and 350,000 to Australia and New Zealand.
The first hurdle was the fare. Steerage, or Third Class, as it became at the end of the 19th century, cost between £3 and£ 5 to the USA and between £15 and £20 to Australia for most of the 19th century. As late as 1880 the average weekly wage of a labourer was little more than £1. So the emigrant had to sell everything he owned. For most their single valuable possession was their land, hard to sell in times of agricultural depression.

Some did not have to rely entirely on their own resources. There were periods when those able to provide skills in short supply Craftsmen, farm labourers and domestic servants all benefited from assisted passages. Others got help from domestic organisations, such as poor law unions, trade unions and parishes which assisted worthy families to emigrate. This is invariably detailed in their records.

The British Board of Trade listed passengers at their port of departure but the pre-1890 records no longer exist. More promising are the lists compiled at ports of entry. To access these, however, it is vital to establish the dates and places of departure and arrival. Details of these records and others referred to are available in the National Archives leaflet, *Irish Genealogy (Overseas Records Information 9)* which may be downloaded from the PRO's website http://www.nationalarchives.gov.uk

Irish immigrants in the USA have many feted precursors. John F Kennedy and Ronald Reagan are just two of the eleven Presidents with Irish ancestry. Henry Ford, Jesse James, Davy Crockett, Edgar Allen Poe and Henry James all had Irish ancestors.

Tracing them is becoming easier and easier as new passenger lists for ships arriving in America are appearing all the time. Check the following as a starting point: the American Immigrant Ship Transcription Guild http://www.istg.rootsweb.com and the National Archives and Records Administration, USA - www.nara.gov

Another invaluable source is *Irish Passenger Lists, 1847-1871*. It itemises all sailing from Derry to America on ships on the *J & J Cooke Line* and the *McCorkell Line*. Compiled by Brian Mitchell of the Derry Genealogical Centre and published by Genealogical Publications Co.

Consulting the Emigration Agent

Inc., what makes it particularly useful is that it covers the years of the great famine. The Northern Ireland Public Records Office has a copy.

Many of the poorest emigrants chose Canada rather than the USA simply because for most of the 19th century passage to Canada was cheaper. Large numbers of those for whom America was the ultimate destination, like Henry Ford's ancestors, went first to Canada. One in five Canadians has some Irish blood, most of their ancestors having arrived through St. John, Halifax, Quebec and Toronto.

The arrival of Australian transportees in New South Wales from 1788 is better documented than that of those who arrived by other means. When transportation ended in June 1849 about 40,000 of the 162,000 sent from the British Isles were Irish. Many modern Australians like to claim convict stock and in fact about one million can do so with justification. The State Paper Office in Dublin Castle has details of transportees, including their crimes and sentences. Details are available on the National archives website.

A large influx of immigrants to New Zealand began only in the 1830s. Prior to that most immigrants came from Australia. At first emigrants sailed from Glasgow and Plymouth and it was only in 1859 that Liverpool became the major port of departure.

Forty per cent of South Africa's white population claim British ancestry. Their antecedents were a mixture of private and assisted passengers. In 1819 the British Government introduced the Cape Emigration Scheme, offering assisted passages to the area of Cape Colony around Clanwilliam. Within two years 2,000 Irish people took advantage of the scheme. When first diamonds and then gold were discovered in 1866, there was a surge of immigrants. All those who received help are listed in the *Assisted Immigrants* handbook, published by the Biographical and Genealogical Division of the Human Sciences Research Council in Pretoria.

Many of the Irish immigrants in South Africa came as soldiers. Ireland has a long tradition of military service in the British Army. The sons of the gentry traditionally became officers and the poor Irish found in the army a source of employment and escape from poverty. The first Irish regiment to arrive in South Africa were the 86 Foot, afterwards the Royal Irish Rifles, in 1796 and the 8 Light Dragoons, afterwards the King's Royal Irish Hussars. In total about 450,000 British soldiers fought in the Boer War (1899-02) and about 28,000 of them were Irish Connaught Rangers, Dublin Fusiliers, Royal Inniskillin Fusiliers, Royal Irish Fusiliers and Royal Irish Rifles.

For a century Liverpool was synonymous with emigration. Between 1830 and 1930, forty million people left Europe for North America and Australasia and most them passed through Liverpool. By 1830, 15,000 emigrants passed through each year. Emigrants were big business.

The main Liverpool-based shipping companies dealing in human cargo were *Cunard, White*

Star, National, Inman, Guion, Dominion, Anchor and *Allan*. After 1890 Southampton, Hamburg and Bremen challenged Liverpool=s dominance. The inter-war immigration restrictions stemmed what had once been a flood and by 1930 only a few thousand a year were emigrating via the Mersey.

Liverpool remains a source of information on emigration to the new world. The Merseyside Maritime Museum produces a whole range of invaluable leaflets as well as a history of the port's role in emigration. All the relevant information is available on the Archive's website.

Of the information leaflets available from the National Archives which relate to emigrants the best is number 7. Most of the documents on emigrants are housed at the Kew branch of the PRO. Details are available on the website but unfortunately there is no single index of the names of emigrants.

The National Archives' sources are organised into special categories, such as wrong-doers and service personnel, rather than ordinary working people. yet it is the National Archives that holds all the papers of government departments involved with pre-Partition Ireland.

The National Archives' Search Department contains a great deal of the relevant material. Among these volumes are the Home Office (HO11) 1787-1871, 21 volumes of Convict Transportation Registers. HO10 deals with convicts sent to New South Wales and Tasmania, which also lists free emigrants and people actually born in Australia. The Board of Trade records include Passenger Lists Outwards (BT27) listing those leaving the UK by sea. These records, however, are only for the period after 1890.

The good news is that civil records in the New World are generally fuller and better kept than those in the old. Apart from the sources discussed here there are all the usual sources found here and in Ireland such as parish registers.

The passenger arrival records in the National Archive, Washington DC are the most useful source for researching immigrant ancestors to the USA. The least they do in all cases is identify the country of origin of virtually every immigrant arriving in the USA since 1820 and given the patchy nature of Britain records for most of this period they are indispensable. Lists of those arriving in Philadelphia, Customs Passenger Lists (Baggage Lists) for 1800-1819,

are housed at the Temple University / Bolch Institute Centre for Immigration Research in Philadelphia.

Customs' Passenger Lists, which list every immigrant, are the result of a law of 1819. Under its terms the masters of ships carrying immigrants were required to furnish the age, sex, occupation, home country, eventual destination and date and circumstances of death, should this have happened during the voyage, on each passenger. These are housed in the National Archives, as Records of the US Customs Service, Record Group 36. Details are available on the website.

The Act was subsequently supplemented and the 1903 Act required details of each immigrant's race. The 1907 Act required the actual birthplace of each passenger and the name and address of the nearest relative in the old country.

Naturalization records help to establish whether your ancestors became naturalized US citizens. If so, the records contain details of the date and place of naturalization. These records are in the National Archives.

Copies of many states records are held by The Genealogical Society of Utah. For original records after 1906 the best hope is local federal courts or file No. G-641 of the Immigration and Naturalization Service, 425, 1 Street NW, Washington DC 20536, where a fee is charged. For naturalization from 1906 -1956 it is necessary to contact the office where the alien lived.

All census schedules from 1800 to 1900 and 1910 may be searched in the National Archives' copies however most of the returns for 1890 were destroyed.

Similar in scope to the census are the Mortality Schedules. They date from the 1850 census and give information on those who died during the census year. Three major holdings of the originals belong to the National Archives, the Mormon Church's Family History Library and the Daughters of the American revolution.

The world's largest collection of genealogical records is the main Church library, the Family History Library, in Utah. This Mormon library in the Wasatch Mountains, near Salt Lake City, has more British and Irish records than anything else. The next best thing to being in Salt Lake City is visiting one of the several chapels which have Family History Centres. Details are available on the web.

The International Genealogical Index (IGI) is especially valuable for those who cannot visit Utah. Most of the information relates to the period between the early 16th century and 1875. The information on the Index is culled from a range of sources including birth, christening and marriage records. The Mormons produce a useful workbook, *A Guide to the Research: the Genealogical Library of the Church of Jesus Christ of Latter Day Saints*. All local Family History Centres have information on all current holdings.

The 1851 Census is a good place to begin your search for Canadian ancestors. It is lodged in the Dominion's Public Archive. There is no better way to find your way around the Archive than by using its booklet, *Tracing Your Ancestors in Canada*, which also gives details of provincial archives.Because there was no legal requirement for captains to keep detailed passenger lists, information relating to the pre-1865 period is very sketchy. Information for the 1865 to 1908 period is more readily available and is housed in the Canadian Public archives. Generally this shows the passenger's name, age, occupation and intended destination. Information on more recent arrivals since 1908 is available from the Records of Entry Unit. The Irish-Canadian Cultural Association is committed to helping those searching for their ancestors. The good starting point is Angus Baxter's *In Search of Your Canadian Roots*, published by Genealogical Publications, Baltimore.

For those of you whose ancestors emigrated to Australia, the bad news is that there is no central record repository. Begin your search by looking at the National Archives of Australia website. Each state has its own records of arrivals. But to track down an individual you will need to know the name, port of entry, the name of the vessel and its date of arrival in Australia. Unfortunately the details of children were not recorded, other than as part of a family group. On the other hand, once you have traced the ancestor's point of arrival, you will find that Australian records are among the best in the world, a major reason for this beingthe large number of immigrants who arrived under some sort of official scheme.

For ancestors who arrived prior to civil registration, church records are invaluable. The earliest registers date from the 18th century and are stored at the various offices of the Registrar-General of te relevant states. Unfortunately, it was the Australian government's policy to destroy census material once the information they contain was extracted for statistical purposes. There are, however, some surviving sections of the early censuses.

The Australian system of civil registration is similar to the British though the documentation usually includes more information than their British and Irish counterparts.

The *New South Wales Government Gazette* give details of interest to the family historian such as land grants and probates. The Australian Society of Archivists issues *Our Heritage: A Directory to Archives and Manuscript Repositories in Australia*, which describes the principal holdings and their whereabouts. Another valuable guide is Nick Vine Hall's *Tracing Your Ancestors in Australia*, which includes a list of published family histories.

If you are tracing ancestors who emigrated to New Zealand between 1840 and 1850, your starting point is the records of the New Zealand Company. These are located in the New Zealand Archives. They include immigrants to Wellington, Nelson, New Plymouth and Otago. Information for the period 1853 to 1876 is held in the country's various provincial centres. The best way to track these down is through the National Archives of New Zealand.

All church records for all denominations are held by the parishes, which means that without some idea of where your ancestors settled, locating the appropriate records can be an arduous task. As with Australia, the government of New Zealand systematically destroyed the original census records, though a small number survived. The Militia Returns, however, contain details of all able-bodied men living in Wellington in the 1840s.

Unfortunately for the family historian the

registration of Europeans became compulsory only in 1848 and even then it covered only to births and deaths. From 1855 all marriages were registered. After 1876 death certificates contain a great deal of valuable information as they give details of the deceased's burial, birth place, parents' names and the mother's maiden name. Wills, guaranteed to be fascinating, are housed in the High Court which had jurisdiction over the home of the deceased.

If you trace an ancestor to South Africa, your first port of call should be the Human Sciences Research Council, Pretoria. The Division for Bibliographical and Genealogical Research has a wealth of useful information Each province has its own National Archive Depot. Among their most useful sources are the Deeds Registers, which record all titles to fixed property. All civil registration records are held by the Registry of Births, Marriages and Deaths, Pretoria.

In the absence of any surviving census returns, church and chapel returns become very important. Those kept by military chaplains are the oldest of the English registers and date from 1795. These are stored with the Bishop of Lincoln's records at the Guildhall, London. Records of baptisms, marriages and burials according to the rite of the Dutch Reformed Church for 1665 to 1778 are housed in the Dutch reformed Church Archives in Cape Town, Bloemfontein, Pietermoritzburg and Pretoria. The Master of the Supreme Court is responsible for registering and administering wills. His offices are in Cape Town, Bloemfontein, Pietermoritzburg, Grahamstown and Pretoria. These offices also hold the original wills.

When Paddy Leary left home he hoped one day to go back across the ocean. By tracing your Irish ancestors you are re-establishing their link with dear old Ireland.

Useful Contacts
The Maritime Archives and Library, Merseyside Maritime Museum, Albert Dock, Liverpool L3 4AQ.
The Family History Library, 35, North West Temple Street, Salt Lake City, Utah.
Dominions Public Archive, 395, Wellington Street, Ottawa, Ontario, K1A 0N3.
The National Archives website (archives.ca)
Records of Entry Unit, Canada Employment and Immigration Commission, Place du Portage, Phase IV, Hull, Quebec KA OJP.
Genealogical Publications Co. Inc., Baltimore
National Archives of Australia website (naa.gov.au)
New South Wales Government Gazette
Australian Society of Archivists, PO Box 83, O'Connor, AC 2601
The National Archives of New Zealand., PO Box 6162, Tc Aro, Wellington
Web: archives.govt.nz).
Registry of Births, Marriages and Deaths, the Ministry of Home Affairs, Pvt. Bag X 114, Pretoria 0001 South Africa

The Public Record Office of Northern Ireland
Valerie Adams

The Public Record Office of Northern Ireland (PRONI) is the only dedicated archive repository in Northern Ireland, providing an integrated archival service for the whole country. It receives not only public records (those created by government departments, courts, local authorities and non-departmental public bodies) but also private records from a wide range of sources - individuals, families, businesses, charities, churches, societies, landed estates, etc. This unique combination of private and public records and its extensive record holdings, amounting to over 35Km, makes PRONI the most important resource for anyone researching their family tree or their local area.

On PRONI's website you will find out how to make best use of the records. There is a 'Frequently Asked Questions' section, copies of all our leaflet series and details of our policies on preservation and copying. You will also find on the website the introductions to the major private archives and to the classes of records of the Ministry/Department of Education some of which will be of interest to the family historian if one your ancestors was in the teaching profession. Also on the website will be news of new developments that are taking place.

Public Records
There is a misconception that because of the fire in the Public Record Office of Ireland in Dublin in 1922 that there are no surviving public records before that date. In fact, there are many series of records that go back to the early 19th century and even into the 18th century in the case of the Grand Jury Presentment Books that will give the names of those who received money for the construction and repair of roads and bridges etc. The most popular for the family and local historian relating to the six counties of Northern Ireland are: the valuation records from the 1830s to the present; the tithe applotment books, 1823-37, giving details of landholders and the size of their holdings; copy wills from 1838-c.1900 and all original wills from 1900 to 1996; registers and

inspections observation books of c.1,600 national/public elementary/primary schools dating mainly from the 1870s; the grant-aid applications of the Commissioners of National Education which record the history and state of national schools from 1832 to 1889; the Ordnance Survey maps at various scales from 1831 to the present; the minutes, indoor and outdoor relief registers, etc of the Boards of Guardians who administered the workhouse system; the records, including admission registers, of lunatic asylums, some dating back to the mid-19th century (but these are subject to extended closure for 100 years).

Guides to the tithe applotment books, the large scale town plans, education records and probate records are available in PRONI.

Private Archives

It is not surprising that because so many of the public records for the island of Ireland have not survived then private archives have assumed a much greater importance for family and local history.

The most valuable are those of the great landed estates (many of which go back into the 17th and 18th centuries), of solicitors' firms, of railway companies, and of churches as well as family and personal papers and the working notes of antiquarians and genealogists who worked in the Public Record Office of Ireland prior to 1922 and who took copious notes from the records. Almost all the major estate archives are held in PRONI; descriptions of many of them can be found on the PRONI website. Among the more notable are: Downshire (Cos Down and Antrim); Antrim (Co Antrim); Abercorn (Co Tyrone); Belmore (Co Fermanagh); Gosford, Brownlow and Caledon (Co Armagh); and Drapers' Company (Co Londonderry). A comprehensive listing of all the estate records in PRONI will be found in the 'Guide to Landed Estates' available in PRONI, at the Local Studies Libraries of each Education and Library Board and in the PRONI outreach centres.

Church records are an invaluable source for the family historian, especially before civil registration of births and deaths began in 1864 and Protestant marriages in 1845 (Roman Catholic marriages began to be registered from 1864). Microfilm copies of almost all pre-1900 church records of the main denominations are available in the Self-Service Microfilm Room in PRONI. On the PRONI website you will find an index of reference numbers to many of these microfilmed church records but fuller details can be found in the 'Guide to Church Records', the most up to date version of which is available in PRONI.

Printed Sources

Street directories are often a neglected source of information for the family and local historian. PRONI holds a very comprehensive set of the Belfast and Ulster Street Directories from c.1840 to 1996 and of Thom's Directories from 1845 to 1958. Another useful source are the printed will calendars that give a brief summary of every will proved and of letters of administration taken out in the civil courts from 1858 to 1996; those from 1922 relate only to Northern Ireland.

Improvements to service

To improve the public service area the reception has just been refurbished with our Mission Statement now prominently displayed as well as photographs of the Chief Executive and of the Head of Public Services. Regular consultation with users is vital to identify where we need to improve and to get feedback from users on improvements implemented or planned. To this end we have set up a PRONI Users Forum that is representative of the full range of our customers and which will meet four times a year.

Forthcoming Developments

One of the largest projects (the 'eCATNI Project') that PRONI has ever embarked on and that is now underway is the retrospective conversion of all our catalogues which will eventually be accessible on the PRONI website. The project aims to create comprehensive, accurate and up-to-date electronic catalogues that can be accessed at the touch of a button. This will permit remote access to a rich archival heritage, opening up the opportunities for lifelong learning to a new and wider customer base and improving the efficiency and accessibility of PRONI's customer service.

PRONI Outreach Centres

PRONI has three outreach centres currently operating – at Armagh Ancestry in St Patrick's Trian in Armagh City, at Ballymena Museum and at the Harbour Museum in Londonderry. Each centre holds PRONI's computerised subject and placename indexes, its web pages, the touch-screen interactive video (which is an introduction to PRONI and the archives it holds) and a set of Guides to records and PRONI publications. This will enable the public who live at a distance from PRONI to access some of the finding aids and therefore to be better prepared before their actual visit to PRONI.

Self-Service Microfilm Room

In order to speed up access to the archives, the most popular sources on microfilm for the family and local historian are available in the specially equipped Self-Service Microfilm Room. There you can view microfilms of church records, the 1901 census for Northern Ireland, the copy will books, 1858-c.1900, the tithe applotment books, the civil birth indexes, 1864-1922, and the surviving fragments of the 1831-1851 census returns for some parishes in Cos Antrim, Fermanagh, Londonderry and Cavan.

Finding Aids

Besides our extensive catalogues which include virtual transcripts of important runs of estate correspondence, PRONI provides a range of finding aids: guides to different categories of records (eg women's history) and county guides; subject, place and personal name indexes (although the latter is by no means complete it is often a useful starting point if you do not know precisely where your ancestors came from); an extensive leaflet series on different types of records for family and local history and also leaflets on historical topics such as the Great Famine and the Belfast Blitz.

New Acquisitions of interest to the family historian

Among the diverse range of archives either recently

deposited or microfilmed and of most interest to the family historian are: abstracts of the 1851 census for Cromac Ward, Belfast; the records of Drum Parish Church, Co Monaghan, 1828-1879; additional records of Devenish Parish Church, Co Fermanagh, 1874-1939; records of St Bartholomew's Parish Church, Belfast, 1918-89; and additional records of Templepatrick Presbyterian Church, Co Antrim, 1933-2002.

On-line records

PRONI's first large scale digitisation project was completed in May - the indexing and scanning of nearly half a million signatures of those who signed the Ulster Covenant in 1912. The database is fully searchable and available on-line on PRONI's website. In their original format the signatures were virtually inaccessible but now you can not only search by name and place but you can actually view the original signatures. The next digitisation project, funded by the New Opportunities Fund, to be launched in September will provide on-line access to the late 18th and early 19th century freeholders' registers for Ulster. The registers record the names of those who were entitled to vote or who actually voted at elections. This new on-line resource will provide speedier access to a unique resource for family and local history at a period when there is a scarcity of documentary sources.

External Relations

PRONI staff are available to give talks and lectures about PRONI and the sources we hold to outside organisations, including family and local history societies. These can be delivered either on-site or off-site. Regular monthly series of talks on sources for tracing your family and local history are given in PRONI with occasional ones delivered elsewhere. These are open to everyone, especially if you have never been to PRONI before. PRONI's website will give details of forthcoming talks.

Facilities and Services

There is limited carparking within the PRONI site but space will be made available for those with a disability. Free off-street parking is available but you should park responsibly as residents do need to get in and out of their driveways.
Restaurant facilities are available on-site where you can purchase snacks, beverages and lunches. It is possible to purchase a late evening meal on Thursdays when the Office is open until 8.45 but you must order this in advance at lunchtime.

Visiting PRONI and Opening Times
PRONI is open to the public without appointment and research is free for those pursuing personal and educational research. However, users will need to obtain a reader's ticket at Reception and will require proof of identity to gain admission and to use the computerised document ordering system. No advance booking is required. Group visits are very welcome but must be booked in advance.

Mon - Wed and Fri 9.00 – 16.45
Thurs - 10.00 – 20.45

Last orders for documents -16.15 apart from Thursdays when it is 20.15

PRONI is closed annually for stocktaking during the last week in November and the first week in December and on public holidays (see the PRONI website for details as there are different public holidays in Northern Ireland).

While there are detailed catalogues, guides and leaflets available, staff are always available at the Help Desk in the Public Search Room to give advice or help to researchers.

How to get there

If you are coming by car, there is easy access from the motorways and you should exit at Balmoral. While there is limited on-site carparking you can park in the vicinity of Balmoral Avenue. However, those with a disability will be accommodated on-site. If you are coming by bus, Nos 71 and 59 from the City Centre will take you to Balmoral Avenue and it is then is a short walk from the bus stop. Alternatively, Balmoral railway station on the Lisburn Road is only a short distance from PRONI.

Public Record Office of Northern Ireland
66 Balmoral Avenue, Belfast BT9 6NY
Tel: 028 9025 5905   Fax: 028 9025 5999
E-mail: proni@dcalni.gov.uk
Web: http://www.proni.gov.uk

QUEEN'S BRIDGE, BELFAST.

From Athenry to Oz: A Convict in the Family?
Tracing ancestors transported from Ireland
Joe O'Neill

Most people's knowledge of transportation is confined to the lyrics of the Fields of Athenry, a song now popular with football fans the country over. The narrator, a transportee, is no ordinary criminal. He is driven to 'steal Trevelyan's corn' as the only means of saving his children from starvation.

Many successful Australians number Irish convicts among their ancestors. Among these is the renowned author and Booker Prize-winner, Thomas Kenneally, on whose work Schindler's List is based. He is proud of his rebel ancestors and maintains that far from being the dregs of society they were the most principled and courageous of men, who resisted injustice. They brought their value to Australia and bequeathed to their adopted country an idealism that has served it well.

It is easy to dismiss this as Irish sentimentality. Yet the evidence suggests he is typical of many condemned to exile. An 18th century observer noted that the Irish were by far the best of the criminals in Van Diemen's Land because "a man is vanished from Scotland for a great crime, from England for a small one, and from Ireland, for hardly no crime at all."

It is difficult to date the beginning of transportation as a penal policy. But it certainly predates the time when the first Europeans reached Australia. By then it was an established part of British colonial policy and the statutory punishment for a certain type of crime.

The Vagrancy Act of 1547 was the first of many laws whereby beggars 'could be banished out of this realm to wherever the government thinks fit.' The courts despatched the first victims of this policy to Virginia in 1607.

From 1615 felons might be condemned to labour in the East Indies or the American plantations. In 1649 Cromwell exiled the first group of Irishmen to Virginia, Barbados and Jamaica. Their crime, like that of so many who were to follow them, was political – they had risen in rebellion against the alien ' planters' who had displaced them from the land.

An Act of 1679 legalised what was already the common practice of pardoning criminals on condition they accepted transportation to the colonies. Henceforward, transportation became the government's response to a growing number of crimes and was prescribed for Quakers who refused to take oaths, dissenters and those who burnt hay ricks or barns by night.

But it was during the 18th century that transportation attained a central role in English criminal law. By the Transportation Act of 1718 it became an alternative to execution and as the number of capital offences increased year by year so did the number of transportees. Most went to the American colonies, all of which, except New England, accepted some convicts at some time. Between 1719 and 1772 about 30,000 were transported from Britain, about two-thirds going to Virginia and Maryland.

Of these between 7,000 and 8,000 were Irish. As there was no Poor Law in Ireland an Act of 1736 decreed that 'vagabonds wandering about demanding victuals' were liable to transportation for seven years.

But Britain's desire to be rid

Success - the last Convict Ship

Killard Ireland

local or county gaol until preparations were made for transmitting him or her to the port.

Transportees from the southern counties were lodged in the city gaol at Cork. Built over the old gate to the northern part of the city, its rotted walls were crammed to bursting. Those brought to Dublin were housed, along with other offenders, mostly in Newgate and Kilmainham gaols. Newgate, Dublin's city gaol, was under constant criticism from reformers because of its deplorable condition and the fact that all categories of offender were housed together. Kilmainham was Dublin's county gaol, with arrangements for convicts much the same as in Newgate, except that transportees were separated from debtors and petty offenders.

of troublesome subjects was seldom matched by the dependencies' enthusiasm to accept them. As early as the end of the 16th century the American colonists made clear their anger at being used as a dumping ground for Britain's undesirables. With the War of Independence in 1775 America was no longer available.

Before an alternative destination was found the government resorted to the hulks – rotting vessels moored on the Thames. As crime increased and conditions on the hulks deteriorated the impetus to resume transportation increased. Many of its advocates believed it was far more humane than incarceration.

It gave criminals the chance to reform and to make a valuable contribution to their host country. Once there they would have no choice but to develop habits of industry which would prevent them from relapsing to a life of crime. In the early years of transportation many opposed it not because they believed it was too harsh but because they feared it was not harsh enough and that it had little deterrent value.

The first convicts were shipped to Australia, Britain's newest colony, in 1787. Transportation to Australia was not formally abolished until 1868 but in practice it was effectively stopped in 1857, and had become increasingly unusual well before then.

The first shipload of convicts left Ireland for New South Wales at the beginning of April 1791. Between 1787 until the termination of the system in 1853, Australia received over 160,000 convicts, approximately 26,500 of whom sailed from Ireland.

When a transportation sentence was handed down, the convict was usually returned to the

From 1817 a holding prison, known as a depot, was provided in Cork to house the large numbers of convicts accumulating there. From 1836 a depot was provided in Dublin for female convicts and between the Great Famine and the opening of Mountjoy convict prison in 1850, temporary depots and Smithfield in Dublin and Spike Island in Cork harbour were used for men.

What manner of Irish people suffered this sentence?

They made up a high percentage of those transported from Britain – about a quarter of the total were Irish. Thirty thousand were men, three time the number of women. As well as those transported directly from Ireland another 6,000 Irishmen were transported from England.

About one in five came from Dublin. Seventy-five per cent were first offenders, people never before in trouble. One reason for this is that many of the convicted, about twenty per cent, were, like the first transportees, political offenders.

Most of the Irish criminal and transportation records disappeared in the flames that engulfed the Four Courts in 1922. Yet remaining records show crime was less common in Ireland than elsewhere in Britain. Irish country people were remarkably honest.

The most celebrated political transportees were the men of '98, the sixty Fenians sent to Western Australia in 1867 and the leaders of the 1848 rising – Smith O'Brien, John Mitchell, Thomas Meigher, Patrick O'Donohue, Terence McManus, Kevin O'Doherty and John Martin. Their writings in exile won much sympathy for the Irish people and their struggle for independence.

Many of those convicted towards the end of the 18th century received no trial, but were condemned because they were out after curfew or merely suspected of disloyalty. Akin to these were the 'social rebels', whose crime was to resist the landlord system that subjected them to intolerable hardship. Among these were the members of the various agrarian societies – the Whiteboys, the Peep-of-Day Boys, the Thrashers, the Rockites and Ribbonmen.

Even the British authorities accepted that these men were not ordinary criminals, acknowledging that social conditions drove them to desperate measures. A Select Committee of 1823 concluded that ' a large portion of the Irish peasantry live in a state of misery of which one can form no conception, not imagining that any human beings could exist in such wretchedness.' Conditions got no better for fifty years.

Many of the 'disturbances' that led to transportation resulted from evictions, when tenants, unable to pay their rent, were turned out onto the road and their homes demolished. Especially in the early decades of the 19th century, many of these unfortunates came from the troubled counties of Limerick and Tipperary.

After 1830 the 'tithe war' – opposition by poor Catholic peasants to the payment of taxes to the Protestant Church of Ireland – added to the rural unrest. In certain years, such as 1838, about sixty per cent of those transported were Ribbonmen.

The last large batch sent to Australia were 4,000 '*Famine criminals*,' despatched in September 1848. For most of these transportation meant a reprieve from starvation. In 1868, sixty-three Fenians, convicted in Ireland, but incarcerated in England, were transported from London. They arrived in Western Australia on 9 January 1868 on the Hougoumont, the last convict ship to sail from England to Australia.

Reading John Boyle's description of conditions on the Hougoumont, tells us why the twelve week voyage into exile levied such a high death toll. "The smells were … among the notable feature of life on board. The combination of animal and human excrement, foul water … the remains of old cargoes and the perpetually rotten wooden structure of the vessel herself must between them have produced a dreadful stench, unrelieved by any kind of ventilation system in the ship".

Fortunately for the family historian a rich store of those condemned to such conditions are held at the Irish National Archives. Most of these relate to New South Wales, the almost exclusive destination of Irish deportees. In 1837 one-third of the total population of the colony was composed of Irish Catholics, nineteen-twentieths of them convicts or emancipated convicts. The present State of Queensland was then part of New South Wales. To this day there is a concentration of Irish-Australians in New South Wales and Queensland.

But before searching those archives it is wise to consult some of the general accounts. *Bound for Australia* and *Criminal Ancestors* are particularly useful as they give transcripts and facsimiles of the many different types of document that you may wish to consult. Unfortunately, there is no single name

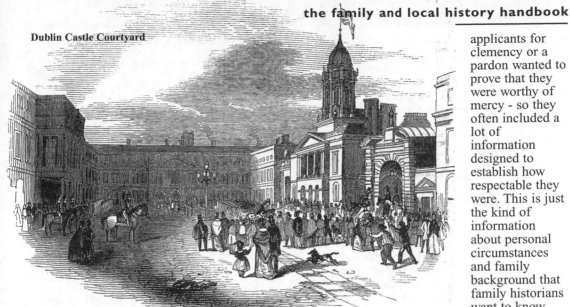

Dublin Castle Courtyard

applicants for clemency or a pardon wanted to prove that they were worthy of mercy - so they often included a lot of information designed to establish how respectable they were. This is just the kind of information about personal circumstances and family background that family historians want to know. However, you should bear in mind that the application is likely to paint a glowing picture of the convict and unlikely to include anything that reflects badly on him. Petitions for clemency are arranged in coded bundles so you will need to use the registers to identify the right one. The registers are arranged by the date of receipt of the petition. They date back to 1797 and include information about the response to the petition, so you can sometimes find out something useful about a convict even if the petition itself does not survive.

Reports and returns from the judges also make fascinating reading. They sometimes include an unofficial transcript of evidence (together with comments on the characters of both witnesses and juries) as well as memorials and petitions from friends and relatives of the accused. The judges' reports and their circuit letters are also indexed. Applications and reports are available at the PRO.

The National Archives of Ireland (NIA) holds a wide range of records relating to transportation of convicts from Ireland to Australia for the whole period, 1788 to 1868. In some cases the researcher may strike gold and find records of members of his convict's family transported as free settlers. In 1988, the Taoiseach presented microfilms of the most important of these records to the Government and People of Australia as a gift from the Government and People of Ireland. A computerised index to the records was prepared with the help of IBM and is available for use at various locations in Australia.

index of those transported to Australia. To locate a convict you will need to have a good idea of when he was tried and/or the date and ship in which he sailed to Australia. There are several ways of doing this.

Begin with the published censuses or musters of the penal colonies which often give the place of conviction and the date and ship of arrival in Australia. The names of those who arrived on the First and Second Fleets have also been published and are available in the PRO.

The microfiche index to the New South Wales Convict Indents and Ships, compiled by the Genealogical Society of Victoria, records the names and aliases of the convicts who arrived in New South Wales and Van Dieman's Land between 1788 and 1842. It also indexes ships recorded on the same documents. A CD-Rom copy of this is also available in the PRO Library.

If you look at the PRO's transportation registers you will find that convicts are not listed by name but by ship and date of departure. Once you have uncovered this information the registers will tell you where and when your convict was tried. It's at this stage you may be tempted to consult the trial record. This is invariably disappointing. Trial records don't normally contain transcripts of evidence or information about the age or family relationships of the accused. Information given about occupation and residence is rarely accurate.

An application for clemency is far more likely to provide valuable information about your convict. However, you should bear in mind that

This index to the transportation records of the NIA is available online. Unfortunately, the records from which the transportation database was compiled, transportation registers and petitions to government for pardon or commutation of sentence, are incomplete. The collection of convict petitions dates from the beginning of transportation from Ireland to Australia in 1791. But all the transportation registers compiled before 1836 were destroyed. Therefore, if the person you are researching was convicted before 1836, but was not the subject of a petition, he or she will not appear on this database.

It is impossible to underestimate the importance of Irish convicts to Australia's development . They and their children formed the majority of the population from the first settlement in 1788 to the 1820's. They formed the great labour force which laid the foundations of Australia prior to the Gold Rushes of the 1850's.

In return Australia gave them the chance of a better life far from the tyranny of landlords such as Trevelyan.

Selected Bibliography
D T Hawkings, *Bound for Australia* (Chichester, 1987)
D T Hawkings, *Criminal Ancestors, a guide to historical criminal records in England and Wales* (Sutton Publishing, revised edn 1996)
R Hughes, *The Fatal Shore: A History of Transportation*

of Convicts to Australia, 1781-1868 (London, 1987)

For an overview of UK records relating to prisoners transported to Australia, check the PRO's leaflet on 19th century criminals and transportation.
For records of transportation to Australia see *Transportation to Australia 1787-1868*
For records of transportation to America and the West Indies see *Transportation to America and the West Indies, 1615-1776*

Records relating to trials by Quarter Sessions court are now held by the relevant British county record office. Records of trials by an Assizes court are held by the PRO, Kew, London which has a handy leaflet on the subject. Few records have survived relating to trials in Ireland of convicts transported to Australia. Published Censuses/Musters of Early Australian Settlers (Including Convicts) Available from the PRO
C J Baxter, *Muster and lists of NSW and Norfolk Island, 1800-1802* (Sydney, 1988)
C J Baxter, *General Musters of NSW, Norfolk Island and Van Diemen's Land, 1811* (Sydney, 1987)
C J Baxter, *General muster and lands and stock muster of NSW, 1822*
N G Butlin, C W Cromwell and K L Suthern, *General Return of convicts in NSW 1837,* (Sydney, 1987)
P G Fidlon and R J Ryan ed, *The First Fleeters* (Sydney, 1981)
R J Ryan, *The Second Fleet Convicts* (Sydney, 1982)
M R Sainty and K A Johnson ed, *New South Wales: Census...November 1828* (Sydney, 1980)

For details of names of Irish ships, numbers embarked, numbers landed, dates, ports from which the vessels set out and their destinations, see Charles Bateson, *The Convict Ships* (Sydney,1974).

Websites:
The National Archives of Ireland on www.nationalarchives.ie/searchO1.html
Irish Convicts Transported to Australia on www.rootsweb.com/-fianna/oc/ozaz/pascontue.html
Claim a Convict on http:/users.bigpond.net.au/convicts
The International Centre for Convict Studies on http://iccs.arts.utas
The Society of Australian Genealogists on www.sag.org.au/assources/crime.htm
Convicts in the Family on www.homeaustarnet.com.au/wmr/convicts
The Public Records Office (Transportation) http://wwwpro.gov.uk/pathways/familyhistory/gallery5/prisoners.htm.

General Register Office for Scotland

Registration of births, deaths and marriages in Scotland

Registration of baptisms and proclamations of marriage was first enacted in Scotland by a Council of the Scottish clergy in 1551. The earliest recorded event - a baptism of 27 December 1553 - can be found in the register of baptisms and banns for Errol in Perthshire. Following the Reformation registration of births, deaths and marriages became the responsibility of the ministers and session clerks of the Church of Scotland. Standards of record-keeping varied greatly from parish to parish, however, and even from year to year. This together with evidence of the deterioration and loss of register volumes through neglect led to calls for the introduction of a compulsory and comprehensive civil registration system for Scotland. This came into being on 1 January 1855 with the establishment of the General Register Office for Scotland headed by the Registrar General and the setting up of 1027 registration districts. In 2003 registration districts number 285.

Records in the custody of the Registrar General

The main series of vital events records of interest to genealogists are held by the Registrar General at New Register House in Edinburgh. They are as follows:

Old parish registers (1553-1854):

the 3500 surviving register volumes (the OPRs) compiled by the Church of Scotland session clerks were transferred to the custody of the Registrar General after 1855. They record the births and baptisms; proclamations of banns and marriages; and deaths and burials in some 900 Scottish parishes. They are far from complete, however, and most entries contain relatively little information. Microfilm copies of these records are available world-wide and there are computerised and microfiche indexes to baptisms and marriages. A project to index the death and burial entries got under way in 1997 and is still ongoing.

Register of neglected entries (1801-1854): this register was compiled by the Registrar General and consists of births, deaths and marriages proved to have occurred in Scotland between 1801 and 1854 but which had not been recorded in the OPRs. These entries are included in the all-Scotland computerised indexes.

Statutory registers of births, deaths and marriages (from 1855): these registers are compiled by district registrars. They are despatched by the district examiners to New Register House at the end of each calendar year. Microfiche copies of the register pages are then made available in the New Register House search rooms. By the end of 2003 the microfiche copies will have been replaced by digital images.

Adopted children register (from 1930): persons adopted under orders made by the Scottish courts. The earliest entry is for a birth in October 1909.

Register of divorces (from 1984): records the names of the parties, the date and place of marriage, the date and place of divorce and details of any order made by the court regarding financial provision or custody of children. Prior to May 1984 a divorce would be recorded in the RCE (formerly the Register of Corrected Entries, now the Register of Corrections Etc), and a cross-reference would be added to the marriage entry.

Births, deaths and marriages occurring outside Scotland (The Minor Records): these relate to

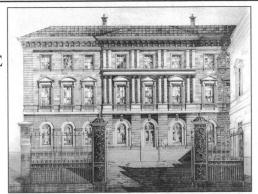

GENERAL REGISTER OFFICE FOR SCOTLAND
New Register House
Edinburgh EH1 3YT
Scotland, UK
Tel: 0131 334 0380
Fax: 0131 314 4400
Email: records@gro-scotland.gov.uk

New Register House is at the east end of Edinburgh's Princes Street, directly opposite the Balmoral Hotel, a few minutes' walk from the main Waverley railway station, the bus station and the airport bus stop. There is no space for car parking or for baggage storage. If informed in advance we can make arrangements for customers with disabilities.

Opening hours:- 09:00 to 16:30 Mondays to Fridays (except some Scottish public holidays)
We have 100 places available for self-service searching. Booking is free but there is a statutory fee for access.
For further information please phone 0131 314 4433.
If you would like us to search in our records for a specific event and sell you an extract (an officially certified copy of an entry) please post or fax details to the above address. A 24-hour priority service is available.
To find out more about our records and services see our Web-site at
http://www.gro-scotland.gov.uk

persons who are or were usually resident in Scotland.

Marine Register of Births and Deaths (from 1855)
Air Register (from 1948)
Service Records (from 1881)
War Registers for the Boer War (1899-1902) and the two World Wars
Consular returns (from 1914)
High Commissioners' returns (from 1964)
Foreign Marriages (from 1947)
Register of births, deaths and marriages in foreign countries (1860-1965)

Census records (from 1841): these are the enumerators' transcript books of the decennial census of the population of Scotland. They record the name, age, marital state, occupation and birthplace of every member of a household present on census night. Census records are closed for 100 years and only the schedules for the 1841 to 1901 censuses are open to the public.
To discover more details about the history of these records please see GROS's publication "Jock Tamson's Bairns: a history of the records of the General Register Office for Scotland" by Cecil Sinclair, ISBN 1 874451 591, 52 pages, cost GBP5.00 (USD8.00).
See http://www.gro-scotland.gov.uk for details of how to order.

Searching at New Register House
New Register House was opened in 1861 as a purpose-built repository for Scotland's civil registration records. Today it provides 100 search places and is open to the public from 09:00 to 16:30, Monday to Friday. Access to the indexes requires payment of a statutory fee which also allows self-service access to digital and microform copies of all the open records. The fee can be for a day, a week, four weeks, a quarter or a year. There are discount arrangements and a limited number of seats can be booked in advance. There is also provision for group evening visits.

Indexes to the statutory records (including overseas events), OPR baptism and marriage entries, and the 1881, 1891 and 1901 census records are available on computer, and most of these entries are now linked to digital images created as part of the DIGROS (Digitally Imaging the Genealogical Records of Scotland's people) project. For records not yet in digital form, there is self-service access to the statutory register pages on microfiche and the OPR and Census records on roll microfilm. It is also possible to order official extracts of any entry. The process of digitising the records is expected to be complete by the end of March 2004.

Online Access to the New Register House Indexes
The all-Scotland computerised indexes and images can also be accessed from local registration offices which have links to the New Register House system. Some local registration offices provide search room facilities with access to microfiche copies of the statutory registers for their area. The Family Records Centre in London has also been provided with online access (the "Scotlink"); while the indexes to birth records over 100 years old, marriage records over 75 years old and death records over 50 years old have been made available for searching over the Internet on the pay-per-view website 'Scotland's People'.

To find out more see the GROS website at **http://www.gro-scotland.gov.uk**.
Pay-per-view search website is **http://www.scotlandspeople.gov.uk**

The Scotland's People Internet Service
Martin Tyson General Register Office for Scotland

Since September 2002, *Scotland's People* has been giving access to indexes and digitised images of GROS's historical records on the Internet. It is a fully searchable pay-per-view website provided in partnership with Scotland Online, a well-known Internet provider with a particular interest in Scottish heritage (and replaces the successful *Scots Origins* website).

Scotlandspeople.gov.uk gives access to a uniquely comprehensive range of Scottish genealogical data. This includes:
Indexed digital images of the statutory registers of births for Scotland, 1855-1903
Indexed digital images of the statutory registers of marriages for Scotland, 1855-1928
Indexed digital images of the statutory registers of deaths for Scotland, 1855-1953
Indexed digital images of the 1891 and 1901 census returns for Scotland
Indexes to the 1881 census returns for Scotland
Indexes to the Old Parochial Registers of baptisms and proclamations/marriages for Scotland, 1553-1854

In addition, digital images of the Old Parochial Registers of baptisms, proclamations of banns/marriages and deaths, and of the 1841-1881 census returns will become available on scotlandspeople.gov.uk during 2004.

The various cut-off dates detailed above have been applied to the statutory registers to avoid raising concerns about browsing on the Internet among records relating to living people. An additional year of index data and images will be added at the beginning of each year, so 1904 birth data, 1929 marriage data, and 1954 death data will be available from January 2005.

Features
The site includes a number of free features, including a free surname search where the customer can see how many entries there are under their name on the indexes, a regularly updated feature on Famous Scots, giving access to data on the site regarding well-known figures in Scottish history, a place-name search, and news items.

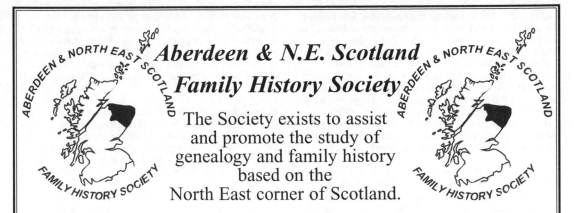

Registration

Customers need to register the first time they access the database. Once registered, customers only need to use their customername and password when they return to the site. It uses customer registration forms and order forms so that customers can request particular products, but does not handle credit- or debit-card details. This information is entered once customers have been directed to the Streamline secure payment gateway of the Royal Bank of Scotland Group, a major UK bank. Credit card or debit-card information, including account number, is not held by Scotland Online or GROS at any time.

It costs £6, payable by credit card, to access the index database. This gives 30 'page credits' and allows access for a period of 48 hours (starting from the time a credit card payment is authorised), however many times the customer logs on and off in that time. Further credits can be purchased. Customers can access any of the previous records they have downloaded, outside the 48-hour registration period. The site also offers a timeline feature to help customers keep track of the records they have found. Customers can also order hard copies from any of the previously viewed records without having to pay the £6 again.

Searching

Searching is straightforward, with soundex and wild card search options available. The customer can search across all the records on the database, or narrow their search by type of record, time period or geographical area. Each time a search is done, the number of records found is displayed; each record refers to a specific event, ie a particular birth/baptism,

marriage or death. When the customer decides to download these records to their PC, they are displayed in pages each containing a maximum of 25 records. Each page they choose to download costs 1 credit. The index page will indicate if a digital image of each record is available - if so, it can be accessed at the click of a mouse. To view a digital image costs 5 credits.

If a customer wishes to order an extract of any register entry found in the index, they can do this on-line, again making a credit card payment. The system automatically transfers the request to the General Register Office for Scotland to fulfil the order and mail the extract. A fixed fee of £10 is payable per extract.

You can access the records of Scotland's people at http://www.scotlandspeople.gov.uk

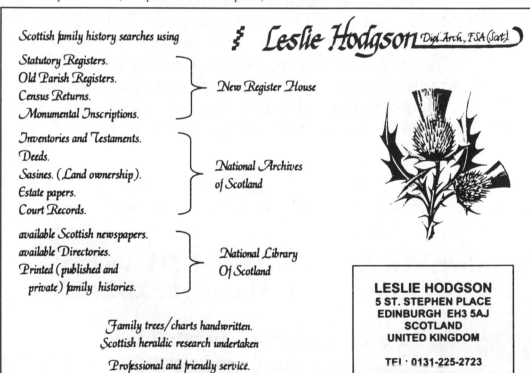

A Foothold on the Land
Exploring the records of Scottish landlord and tenant
Rosemary Bigwood

"My ancestor was just a labourer": "Sasines are not designed for genealogists": "Land records are a source of difficulty". These are the views one hears with regard to tackling records of landownership and land tenure and certainly in some respects they do present a challenge. The system is complex, the legal language daunting and the possible prospect of being faced not only with Old Scots handwriting before 1700, but also with a document in Latin may lead to instant abandonment of the quest. There are at the present time many opportunities for easy access to information on the web – the exchange of research done, the possibility of finding transcribed records, indexes – but this should not blind family historians to the enormous value of exploring for themselves some of the more "difficult" series of records. It is always surprising to find how many people from differing backgrounds were, in fact, involved in landholding. How, then, does the system of land tenure in Scotland work? What does one need to know to understand the contents? What are the records which will yield most information and where are they to be found? And is the labour worthwhile?

The system of landownership in Scotland
From ancient times, all land was deemed to belong to the Crown, who was termed the superior. The Crown granted lands to others – religious bodies (before the Reformation), individuals or bodies such as burghs – who were then known as vassals. In return for these grants of land the vassal originally usually paid in the form of military service (wardholding). Later,

lands were held for the payment of a feu either paid in kind as produce – grain or beasts – or later converted to an annual money payment. The vassal might sub-infeudate his property. He then became a subject superior, still acknowledging the Crown as his superior, but in turn demanding feu payments for his lands from his vassal. Lands held by the vassal or feuar could be sold (alienated), passed on to an heir. Lands might also be used as security for a loan (wadset) at which time the lender was seised in lands or a set rental from them. In this case the lands were conveyed under reversion, with the lands returning to the ownership of the borrower once the money was repaid.

The grant of land by a superior or subject-superior to his vassal was given by charter and the authorisation for the representatives of the superior to give sasine – (also known as infeftment) or legal possession was the precept. This was originally a separate document from the charter, but later incorporated in it. The superior's officers, known as bailies, were instructed to give "actual, real and corporal possession" of the lands by handing over a token of earth or stone, net and coble for a fishing or clap and happer for a mill, in presence of witnesses. As it was later realised that such tokens were not always convincing evidence of possession, the giving of sasine was accompanied by an instrument – a legal written recording of the event. This might be written by a lawyer – the notary public – and recorded in his protocol book but by the end of the sixteenth century the need for a more formal recording of sasines was recognised. In 1599 the first official register of sasines was introduced. Not all the registers of the seventeen districts into which Scotland was divided for this purpose have survived and due to protests that this registration was an "extortioun", the register was terminated. However, in 1617 an act was passed, bringing in a system of registration of sasines and reversions (wadsets) which continued with few changes until the nineteenth century. There was a General Register of Sasines covering the whole of Scotland (this was often used for those who were conveying property which spread over several districts), and also a Particular Register of Sasines for certain areas of

Perth

Scotland. This might include one county (such as Perthshire) or include several in a group (Roxburgh, Selkirk and Peebles, for example). The Royal Burghs were entitled to keep their own registers of sasines for property within the burgh. It is important to bear in mind that sasine registers were concerned with land ownership, not with tenancy.

Using and choosing the documents - Charters
In most cases, charters are not a first choice in genealogical research. In a charter, you will find out the name of the superior, to whom he granted lands (with a description of the lands) and on what terms – and occasionally there are names of previous holders of the lands – and the names of witnesses (who may be relatives). Most charters are written in Latin and often long. For those who held their lands from the Crown, however, the Register of the Great Seal (Registrum Magni Sigilli Scotorum – usually referred to as RMS) can be a mine of information. Abstracts of the charters have been published and indexed by person and place for the years 1314-1668 and they include details of an enormous number of Scottish families – both great landed proprietors and also many small lairds. It is often possible to trace a family through a number of generations in these charters. After 1668 things are not so easy: there are typed indexes to Great Seal charters but these only refer to the grantee and the lands involved – and there are no abstracts.

If you are lucky, there may be a surviving Signature for a crown charter dating between 1607 and 1847. As a preliminary stage in preparing a crown charter, a version of the charter was written in English. Not all have survived but there is a typed index in the National Archives of Scotland (NAS) in Edinburgh giving the name of the grantee and the lands concerned.

Charters – both concerning lands held by the crown or by subject superiors – may also form part of collections of family papers. Sometimes you may be lucky enough to find a reference in a particular inventory of muniments to a "progress of writs" which will list all the family charters (with dates and names of grantee), precepts and subsequent sasines. The NAS has a huge collection of family papers which are catalogued in their Gifts and Deposits series. Others may be found in local archives or libraries and many more are still held by the family concerned. These collections may have been catalogued in the National Register of Archives – the index can be accessed on the web site – www.hmc.gov.uk/nra/nra2.htm. Permissions for access to such documents has to be made through the National Archives of Scotland.

Sasines
Some of the earliest records of giving of sasine are in the notarial protocol books and this is where searches for sasines before the start of the registers in 1617 may have to be done. Some protocol books have been printed and indexed by the Scottish Record Society (there is a list in the NAS) but if not, then you would need to be both dedicated and skilled in reading Old Scots handwriting and very possibly Latin. After 1617, however, the change of ownership through inheritance, purchase or under a wadset, was recorded as a sasine recorded in either the General or Particular Register of Sasines or in a Burgh Register.

The good news is that from 1781 onwards there are printed Abridgements (in English), indexed both by person (all persons mentioned in the sasine, but not the witnesses) and place (except between 1830-1872). The abridgement volumes are arranged on a county basis and include sasines registered both in the Particular and General Registers. The Abridgements do not include the Burgh Registers of Sasines. The Abridgements and the indexes are in the NAS but some copies are available in local archives, and in libraries of the Church of Latter Day Saints microfilm copies can be consulted up to 1868.

The substance of the sasine is given in the abridgement and usually it will not be necessary to toil through the original document (a reference to the latter is given at the end of each abridgement) – though sometimes additional information will be found in the full text. It is, however, important to take a little time to understand what is going on in the transaction as it is not always easy to be certain who is getting the land, who is granting it and why. "Gets disposition" or "registers disposition" indicates that probably the person has bought land.

"Registers special or general service" or "under precept of clare constat" shows that this was a case of inheritance. Husbands often seised their wives in a liferent in some of their lands at the time of marriage and sasines may refer to several generations who have owned the same property, as well as passing on land to sons and daughters. A great many sasines were concerned with debt and the passing over of land as a security for a loan – or under reversion. Someone *getting* a bond and disposition for a certain sum of money "over" certain property is the person lending the money and being seised in property. Once the loan was paid off, another sasine was registered – a renunciation - whereby the lender renounced his right to the property which had secured the loan. Sometimes it may seem that several people own a property at the same time but this can usually be explained by getting to the bottom of what was happening. Either a debt was involved or a certain piece of land was divided into smaller sections.

Before 1781, consulting sasines does become more complicated. Indexes to the registers is sporadic. The General Register of Sasines is indexed from 1617-1720 and then there is a nasty gap till 1781: some of the Particular Registers are indexed in full over the period 1617-1780: some are indexed in part: some are unindexed. If there are no indexes, then one has to use minute books – not impossible but rather time-consuming unless a fairly exact date of registration is known.

One of the interesting aspects of the printed indexes is the evidence they offer as to how many classes of society are represented in the sasine registers. The index to the Lanarkshire register of sasines 1721-1780 includes references to plasterers, merchants, wig-makers, smiths, weavers and masons among others. A further advantage of the indexes is that on occasion it is possible to pick out several members of the same family and sometimes to more than one generation. Agnes Grainger, for example, is referred to as daughter of John Grainger, portioner of Flackfield in Lanarkshire, and spouse of Alexander Murray. We then find a mention of John Grainger, son of John Grainger, porter of Easter Flackfield and his spouse, Janet Marshall. The Burgh Registers of Sasines are mainly unindexed before the nineteenth century but as they are concerned with a limited locality, it is not difficult to go through the actual volumes over a series of years. Burgh sasines are usually in English and simpler in form.

What a sasine says
Legal documents tend to be long and sometimes repetitive but there are some ways of cutting through the verbiage. Which bits should one read with special care? In a sasine, the opening paragraph sets the scene with most of the characters named – the bailie who is acting for the granter or the granter himself: then the grantee or his agent, referred to as the attorney or procurator and thirdly the notary public who is the officiating lawyer. The description of the lands concerned will be given and an indication as to whether this is a matter of sale, inheritance or wadset. The second part of the proceedings is when the precept, which is the authority granted by the superior of the lands for infeftment to be given to the grantee, is read out. We learn the name of the superior, have a second reading of the lands concerned and the reason why they are changing hands (it should be noted particularly if it was on account of a precept of clare constat). The date of writing the precept is given (this is sometimes some years before the giving of sasine) and witnesses names are appended. (It is always worth noting names of witnesses as relatives of one or the other party may appear). Then the third part of the sasine records that the bailie gave sasine of the lands and "instruments" (legal writs) were recorded before witnesses – which should again be noted. If the writing is difficult, you may therefore have three shots at reading what is said, in the different sections. On the other hand, knowing the form of the sasine can mean that you do not have to read through the whole document and having got the main details from the first section, a quick check on the precept and the actual giving of sasine may be enough. The fact that Latin was used for many legal proceedings Scotland till the eighteenth century or later means that you are

likely to find sasines (except for the Burghs) written in Latin – especially in the seventeenth century.

Service of heirs

When an heir was seised in the lands of his forebear, this could only happen after he had proved that he was the rightful claimant. If the lands were held of a subject superior, then the latter would issue a precept of clare constat which the heir presented as his authority for infeftment and it is quoted in the sasine. Few separate precepts of clare constat exist, though occasionally they are found with other legal papers in the muniments of a family: in most cases you only find them in the form of a reference in the sasine. If, however, the lands were held of the Crown or if an heir wanted to make a special case for his right to inherit, then a retour (also known as Service of Heirs) may be recorded in Chancery. Chancery (by issuing a brieve) requested the relevant sheriff court to hold an inquest to examine the claims of the heir and the verdict was retoured to Chancery who then issued a precept. Sometimes, if the case was a dubious or difficult one, the papers relating to the hearing in the sheriff court may produce a lot of interesting additional evidence and in some of the sheriffdoms – Aberdeen, Banff, Berwick, Caithness among others - there are registers of retours listed in their repertories.

The Services of Heirs recorded in Chancery are easily accessible as summaries are printed and indexed in two series – the first covering the period 1544-1699 known as *Inquisitionum ad Capellam Regis Retornatarum Abbreviatio*: the second series covers the period 1700 to the present day and usually known as *Services of Heirs*. Both series have been put onto CD by the Scottish Genealogy Society.

Information given in retours is of great use to the family historian and it may be possible to trace the descent of a family through a number of generations just by working through this source. At the same time, however, one should remember that the early registers of retours are not complete and that retours recorded after 1700 concern only *some* of those who inherited land held of subject superiors, the majority receiving a precept of clare constat direct from that superior, which is very possibly not in the Chancery retours. Claims put forward in many recent genealogical writings highlighting the value of these records have failed to take account of what services of heirs were or were not included, which can be very misleading.

In most cases, the printed abstracts give all the information in the retour – the name of the deceased person, sometimes his or her date of death, the name of the heir, the relationship to the previous owner and the lands involved. If the descent is not direct - from father to son or daughter - then the full text of the retour (which will be in Latin) in the Chancery records should be consulted as it will usually provide full details of the descent – grandson to grandfather or nephew to uncle.

Tailzies

In 1685 a law was passed enabling landowners to lay down who was to inherit certain heritable property in the generations to come. The heirs named in order of priority may provide a great deal of information about the family, listing sons, daughters, cousins, nephews and even illegitimate children. In the case of female heirs, they often had to promise to keep the name of their father, though married, and to bear his arms. The register of tailzies is sometimes also useful in disproving claims of those who assert they are closely related to a particular family. The Register of Tailzies (in the NAS) commences in 1688 and is indexed up to 1938.

Owner or occupier?

Particularly in the case of the farming families, this is often a question which arises. Many prosperous farmers, in fact, rented their lands rather than owned them. The first clue may be found in references in various documents – Old Parish Registers, deeds, testaments: if someone is described as "of" a place, this denotes ownership but if a tenant, he or she will be noted as "in". From 1855 onwards the first place to look for information about ownership or tenancy is in the Valuation Rolls. From this date onwards (up to 1974) all lands and

The Clyde 1888

St Andrews 1740

property in Scotland were valued annually. The valuations are done by county and by parish within each county, with the burghs being listed separately. The name of the proprietor is given, then the name of the tenant and occupier (except those who paid rent of less than £4.00) and the value of the lands. Checking for property in large towns can be very difficult, particularly as numbering of houses in streets alters from time to time, but in the country districts, the valuation rolls are full of information. Valuations rolls are in the NAS and also local copies will be found in many larger libraries.

Before 1855, the indexes to persons and places for the registers of sasines may solve the problem of owner or occupier. If the family on whom research is being carried out is not listed in the index to persons, consult the index to places and look at an abridgment of a sasine concerning the place in which you are interested and see who owns it. An additional pay-off is that knowing the owner, you may be able to locate a deposit of family papers of the proprietor and find your ancestor mentioned as a tenant farmer. *Landownership in Scotland c. 1770* by Loretta Timperley (Scottish Record Society 1976) is a useful book as it lists the proprietors in each parish at this time – though the description of the lands they owned is not complete. The *First* and *Second Statistical Accounts of Scotland* (website – www.edina.ac.uk/cgi/Statacc.cgi) also indicate who were the chief heritors in each parish.

Tenants
Those who occupied the land – as distinct from owning it – fall into many categories –

prosperous farmers, small tenants, crofters, cottars who had a cottage for which they usually paid by work, and labourers, often moving from farm to farm every year. The major tenants might hold their land under formal leases – known as tacks – from the proprietor though many possessed their land without written formality. Tacks may be recorded in a register of deeds (Books of Council and Session, sheriff court deeds, burgh court register of deeds or deeds of a franchise court) or sometimes they are found in collections of family papers. A tack may tell you the conditions under which the tenant held his land – length of lease, improvements to be carried out etc. – but it is usually not very interesting. If there is a collection of family papers of the proprietor, there are often rentals which will document the possession of lands by tenants and show when they moved or whether a son took over on the death of his father. Some landowners, particularly in the second half of the eighteenth and nineteenth centuries, made surveys of their estates (Assynt, Sutherland, and Lochtayside for example) and these provide evidence not only of the names of the tenants and occupiers but also supply interesting details of land use. Inventories if taken at the time of death of a tenant often included full lists of all the farm stock (both crops and animals), implements and furnishings of the farm house. After the 1745 rebellion, a number of estates of Jacobites were forfeited and administered by the Crown for a number of years. The resulting records, known as the Forfeited Estate Papers (in the NAS among the Exchequer papers), contain a great deal of information about the people and their lifestyles in the rentals and reports of the factors, as well as in the correspondence.

Another source for information on local country life and on the people who lived in a particular area can sometimes be found in the records of the baron courts. Certain landowners (but by no means all) were given the right by the Crown to hold local courts within their lands, mainly concerned with the keeping of good neighbourhood, failures to pay rent or to manure the land, or theft and assault. Unfortunately, all too few of these baron court records have survived – but there are a number in the National Archives of Scotland and some have been printed.

Maps and Plans
These provide both information and a visual context to life on the land. A great many maps and plans have survived, particularly those forming part of family muniments or the result of court disputes. The National Library of Scotland Map Library in Edinburgh holds a wide range of maps of counties, town plans, military and marine charts, many of which can now be viewed on their web-site – www.nls.uk/collections/maps. The National Archives of Scotland has a huge collection of plans and local maps, and similar smaller holdings will also be found in district libraries and archives. Maps and plans may illustrate land use, document townships and farms which have now disappeared and some include names of both tenants and owners of lands.

Further Reading
Dictionary and Digest of the Law of Scotland by George Watson (various editions)
Formulary of Old Scots Legal Documents ed. Peter Gouldesbrough (Stair Society 1985)
Guide to the Archives of Scotland (Scottish Record Office & Stair Society 1996)
Early Maps of Scotland (2 vols.) (Royal Scottish Geographical Society 1973, 1983)
Exploring Scottish History 2nd ed. By Michael Cox (Scottish Library Association and others 1999)
Scottish Texts and Calendars – an Analytical Guide to Serial Publications by D. & W. Stevenson (SHS 1987

The National Burial Index for Scotland
David Webster

In parallel with the National Burial Index for England and Wales, the Scottish Association of Family History Societies (SAFHS) is involved in co-ordinating a similar project in Scotland.

The Scottish Old Parochial Registers (OPRs)
The OPRs are similar to the parish records in England and Wales, but there is a radical difference. This is that they were never as reliable in their keeping, and nor did they record the same amount of information as was recorded in England and Wales.

Apart from factors such as the schismatic nature of the main, presbyterian church in Scotland, an important factor leading to this situation was that there were never clear instructions as to the format and content, nor were standard blank registers made available. It was up to the minister or session clerk of the parish to decide on the information that he recorded, and on the format the OPR.

While the majority of the population belonged to the Established Church of Scotland there were significant breakaways throughout the history of the church, from its formation at the reformation. The earliest OPR dates back to 1553 in Errol in Perthshire, but the average starting date is the late 1600s to early 1700s, with some OPRs in the Western Isles not being started until the early 1800s.

While ministers of the Established Church of Scotland were supposed to record events relating to all those in their parish, there are relatively few OPR entries relating to members of other churches.

St Magus, Kirkwall

Sacraments of the Established Church of Scotland
The two important sacraments in the Established Church of Scotland were christening and marriages. Death did not rank as high! As is shown in the table below, just over 34% of the extant OPRs have no death or mortcloth records.

Where there are records these often give only a name and age, with only sometimes additional information, such as "relict of ...." (widow of ....), or "son of ......", allowing a genealogical link to be made.

Even worse, a substantial proportion of the OPR death records are not records of the death or burial itself, but the hiring out of the mortcloth, the cloth used to cover the coffin during the burial service and commitment. Where no charge was made for the hire, - it could be the case that heritor has supplied a mortcloth free of charge, - then there could be no record of a hire.

In the case of mortcloth hire records, the information can often be only a name and the amount charged, - there were quite often a number of different mortcloths of varying quality.

OPRs Containing Death/Mortcloth Records
The following table is based on the information given in Margaret Nikolic's "Genealogical Microform Holdings in Scottish Libraries", published in 1992 by Kirkcaldy District Libraries. This contains county maps showing the overall dates of Old Parochial Records held in Edinburgh as compiled and published by the Aberdeen and North East Scotland Family History Society (ANESFHS).

Statistics compiled from other similar sources may differ slightly in the resultant figures. The generally accepted figure of just over 900 parishes results from the amalgamation of parishes over the years, and the resulting situation in 1854. I've chosen to base my figures on OPRs that were for separate parishes at the time the burial/mortcloth records were made.

The table below shows all the Scottish counties, and the number of parishes in each of those counties that have no death/mortcloth records; the number of parishes that have

Hollyrood House

death/mortcloth records over a period of between 1 and 10 years; between 11 and 50 years; and so on, up to between 301 and 350 years, the sole entry in this category being the parish of Anstruther Wester in Fife which has records for the period of 1549 to 1854 with only 1819 missing. Note that the periods of years involved are quite often not continuous, i.e. it is not unusual for there to be a run of years in one century, followed by a gap, and then another run of years in a later century.

Unfortunately an OPR such as Anstruther Wester is exceptional as can be seen by the figures in the table. Not only are there 34.2% OPRs with no death/mortcloth records, but there are only 35.7% of OPRs where the death/mortcloth records stretch over a period of 51 or more years; with the equivalent figure for 101 years or more being a paltry 18.1% of OPRs.
Note the wide range of figures in terms of the proportion of OPRs in each county that have no death/mortcloth records, although such figures do not take account of the total numbers of records.

Some parishes have many records, other very few. To put this is perspective, according to the SAFHS project co-ordinator Jim Illingworth, there is one parish in Glasgow that has more records that the whole of 147 parishes in the NE (174,000).

NBI Scotland Progress
The Scottish NBI project was set up over 5 years ago. Participating family history societies were given a free hand in terms of deciding how they undertook the indexing. This has resulted in some societies giving the NBI project a lower priority than other projects, such as indexing the 1851 census.

The Scottish NBI will contain very basic data from the records of the Established Church of Scotland OPRs, - name, date of death/burial, parish, participating society.

Societies are recording more information (where it exists!) including abode, cause of death, relation details, etc.

As well as a possible eventual national CD, societies can publish their own data whenever it is ready. Publication of a CD is at least 2 years away according to the SAFHS NBI Project co-ordinator Jim Illingworth. SAFHS may decide to publish a CD once a significant proportion of the Scottish records have been indexed.

Number of Parishes with Total Number of Years in the OPRs Containing Death/Mortcloth Records

County	None	1-10	11-50	51-100	101-150	151-200	201-250	251-300	301-350	Total
Aberdeenshire	13 (15%)	14	22	17	10	7	2			85
Angus	10 (18%)	5	14	14	8	3	2			56
Argyll	47 (82%)	3	3	4						57
Ayrshire	15 (33%)	7	11	9	2	1				45
Banff	9 (41%)	3	3	2	5					22
Berwickshire	4 (12%)	2	11	10	5					32
Bute	7 (88%)		1							8
Caithness	6 (60%)	4								10
Clackmannanshire	0 (0%)	1	1	1	1					4
Dumfriesshire	12 (27%)	4	11	10	4	2	1			44
Dunbartonshire	12 (57%)	3	4	1	1					21
East Lothian	7 (28%)	5	2	6	4	1				25
Fife	7 (11%)	2	11	14	17	8	1		1	61
Inverness-shire	27 (73%)	4	4	1		1				37
Kincardine	3 (17%)	1	5	4	5					18
Kinross	0 (0%)		1	1	3	1				6
Kircudbrightshire	9 (31%)	1	12	6		1				29
Lanarkshire	10 (23%)		12	12	7	2				43
Midlothian	1 (3%..)	2	4	5	13	6	1			32
Moray	4 (22%)	1	9	3	1					18
Nairn	5 (83%)		1							6
Orkney	13 (48%)	1	7	4	1	1				27
Peebleshire	1 (6%)	1	2	5	3	4				16
Perthshire	22 (30%)	5	19	15	7	5				73
Renfrewshire	12 (57%)	3	4	1	1					21
Ross & Cromarty	29 (78%)	2	4	2						37
Roxburghshire	9 (27%)	5	5	8	6					33
Selkirkshire	2 (28%)		1	2	2					7
Shetland	7 (30%)	2	10	3	1					23
Stirlingshire	6 (25%)	4	4	5	4	1				24
Sutherland	12 (92%)		1							13
West Lothian	0 (0%)		2	4	4	2	1			13
Wigtonshire	8 (47%)	2	2	1	4					17
Totals	329	87	203	170	119	46	8	0	1	963
Percentage	34.2%	9.0%	21.1%	17.6%	12.4%	4.8%	0.8%		0.1%	100%

Fife FHS have completed the parishes in Fife, and have published the data. By the end of 2002 Aberdeen & North East Scotland FHS will publish their data for the counties of Moray, Banff, Aberdeen and Kincardine. Shetland FHS have completed the parishes of Shetland but there is no information on a publication date.

The Glasgow & West of Scotland FHS have a team of 35 transcribers, 16 inputters and 3 checkers working on the project in their area.

Work is progressing slowly in all other areas, except for Edinburgh and the Lothians where progress is at a standstill or not started. Some of the smaller societies have financial, membership and logistical constraints that limit the time that can be made available for this project.

Conclusions
Progress on the NBI Scotland project is slow, understandably so in terms of the relatively few parishes that have a significant number of records, and the paucity of genealogically useful information that the death/mortcloth records often contain. Some family history societies have or are about to publish their indexes, but a national CD is at least 2 years away.

Parliamentary Reports
Sources of Scottish Social History
Rosemary Bigwood

Royal Commissions and Select Committees
"What did you do when you were young?" is a question many children ask their parents but it illustrates the desire that all of us have who are interested in our family history. Food, clothing, housing, schools, travel, work – we want to be able both to understand and visualise conditions in the past. There are various contemporary accounts which may help – old newspapers, family papers, the statistical accounts written by the minister of each parish in the 1790's and 1840's, diaries or letters and kirk session minutes. One of the most fruitful sources of information about social conditions in past centuries, however, is to be found in parliamentary papers. From the end of the seventeenth century onwards, Parliament, in the formation of its statutes and process of government of the country, has sought information on a very wide range of subjects. On the one hand, Members of Parliament formed Select Committees who heard evidence and collected information relating to particular topics. Evidence would be heard, information assembled and the Committee might give in one report or a series at intervals over a number of years. On the other hand, there were the Royal Commissions, appointed to report back to the Crown or to a Minister. The Commissioners were outsiders – often specially chosen specialists - who again collected evidence and reported back. Their work might continue over several years before a report was prepared. Sometimes a Royal Commission became a permanent body – such as the Royal Commission on Historical Manuscripts – which reported periodically on their findings. Another series of parliamentary

papers was concerned with statistics and reports from various government departments and official bodies.

What the Commissions and Committees reported
There were few aspects of life which have not been studied by Parliament at some time, from the beginning of the eighteenth century onwards. Child employment, weavers' wages, emigration, cholera, education, salt duties, conditions of working in the mines, prisons, transport, the poor, agricultural workers or vaccination – these are just a few of the topics which have took up the time and attention of various Committees and Commissioners. The great value of the Commissions and reports of Select Committees lies not only in the reports but in the quoted evidence - the personal statements of what was seen and heard in various parts of Scotland, whether it concerned the conditions of the Highlanders in the crofting areas, the growing problems of the Paisley weavers or the lives of agricultural workers.

People of all classes of society were asked for their opinions and their original statements, in the words they used, have been preserved. These are of particular interest as the working classes – labourers, miners, crofters, the poor - so often

Parliament House and Square, Edinburgh

remain silent in history but here we have their personal testimonies. This evidence was balanced by the views of factors, ministers, landowners and professional people who often presented a differing picture. Particularly in the case of the Royal Commissions, the areas covered and the numbers of people interviewed were huge. The Royal Commission of 1884, led by Lord Napier, reporting on the crofting communities, held meetings in sixty one different locations and listened to what seven hundred and seventy five people had to say.

St Giles, Edinburgh

The range of persons asked for their views results in a many facetted picture of society, reflecting both class and politics and statements given have to be assessed against the possible vested interests of the person being interviewed. Mr. Kennedy, innkeeper and farmer at Poolewe, heard at the time of the Poor Law Enquiry of 1844, when asked for his opinion of the labouring population in the West Highlands, had little to say that was complimentary or sympathetic.

> "The people are very far from being well educated. Their ignorance leaves them lying dormant upon us. It is impossible, while they remain as they are, grovelling in their huts like so many pigs and neither seeing nor knowing anything better that they should improve their condition."

The factor for Mr. Stewart Mackenzie of Seaforth admitted that he scarcely ever turned his attention to the poor on his estates but left it to the kirk session and the minister. In general he thought that crofters had an abundance of food, each croft being sufficient to maintain a family. The schoolmaster at Lochs, however, drew a different picture - of wet houses, and lack of food, with shellfish often providing the only sustenance. In some cases, he added that the people were reduced to cooking grass to keep themselves alive. Another example of the subjective nature of evidence is given in 1884, in the Napier Commission, when the minister of Waternish, perhaps seeing a chance to get back at the Free Church, stated his view of the cause of poverty among the local people: "My opinion is that the people injure themselves by their giving to the Free Church collectors – this, too, very much helps to impoverish them". There

were, however, many others who gave a horrifying and sympathetic picture of the conditions around them in all parts of the country.

Class alignment and political affiliations were not the only aspects influencing the views held. The old might refer to the time of their youth with some nostalgia. One elderly man, interviewed in the Carse of Gowrie by the Commissioners on the Employment of Young Persons and Women in agriculture in 1867, looked back to the conditions of his earlier working life. "It was a hard place for men 30 years ago, but they do less work now and get more pay - £10 a year more nor we did and they're no better off. The men are no near so strong as they used to be with all their wages. They buy tea and white bread and fine clothes and dinna stick to the meal and the milk. They have ploughmen now would hardly have been sent to look after the cattle in my day. Some of their ploughmen can hardly toom their pokes."

The background information

In conjunction with evidence heard, there was often a mass of background documentation which contains much of interest to the social and economic historian. As part of the Napier Commission of 1884, each estate was expected to provide a record including the name of each crofter, the number of families living on each croft, the number of houses on the croft and total number of people: the rent and dues such as roadwork, the area of arable and pasture: numbers of cattle. This constituted an agricultural census of the areas concerned. Even this, however, might require some interpretation, as one of Lord Macdonald's factors on Skye complained that the crofters who supplied some of the information were not to be depended upon. It was in their interest to emphasize their poverty and he comments: "I thought the crofters were inclined to return fewer sheep than they have." The suspicion of the factor was evident, as the latter writes to the Commissioner: "A number of the crofters gave the returns unwillingly and some of them refused altogether." So much evidence was collected by the commissioners of the Napier Commission that some written and oral evidence was not added to the published report but has been retained in the National Archives of Scotland (AF50).

Many of the reports include lists of names which are of great interest to family historians. The names of all those who gave evidence are recorded and as part of the reports, there are many listings – rentals, names of workers on particular estates, lists of some of those who were forced to join the navy as part of the parish quota at the time of the Napoleonic wars. The parliamentary papers also contain an enormous amount of fascinating information not easily found elsewhere - the cost of building a decked fishing boat at the end of the eighteenth century, recipes for making soap, trade statistics, the diet provided for inmates of the poorhouse,

how to cure and pack herring, the allowances given to emigrants to New South Wales in 1848 and their medical comforts. (These included oatmeal, arrowroot, sago, preserved beef, lemon juice, sugar, port wine, sherry wine, stout, soap, preserved milk and brandy, rum and vinegar.) Plans of buildings are also sometimes submitted – such as those given in with the Board of Supervision Reports for Relief of the Poor in 1848 showing the model design of a poor house in a town, with boys' and girls' playgrounds, aged men and women's airing grounds, the school for children, provision for dissolute men and women, day rooms and even a post mortem examination room.

How to find the papers

Reprints of a great mass of parliamentary material were undertaken by the Irish University Press and some are available in university libraries and other main libraries throughout the world, either in printed form or on microfiche or microcard. In Scotland, the National Library of Scotland holds a complete set of printed material. This material, of course, covers not just Scotland but also England and many reports deal with both parts of the country, with only certain sections of national reports referring to Scotland. A useful guide in picking out Scottish material and revealing information buried in parliamentary papers is *Scotland in the Nineteenth Century – an Analytical Bibliography of Material Relating to Scotland in Parliamentary Papers 1800-1900* by J.A. Haythornthwaite (Scolar Press 1993). It is indexed by subject and gives a brief description of the subject of the report.

There are also a series of guides to British parliamentary papers which should be available in many larger libraries: *Hansard's Catalogue & Breviate of Parliamentary Papers 1696-1834* ed. P. & G. Ford (Irish University Press 1968) *Select List of Parliamentary Papers 1937-1899* ed. P. & G. Ford (Blackwell 1953) P. & G. Ford have also compiled breviates of parliamentary papers for the twentieth century.

Bibliographies in printed books on particular subjects – the linen industry, coal mining, Scottish fisheries or the poor, for example – will usually refer to relevant parliamentary papers.

The list below includes some – but by no means all – of the main reports concerning Scottish industry and social conditions mainly relating to the

Canongate Gaol, Edinburgh

nineteenth century.

Bibliography – Parliamentary Papers
Agriculture
    Reports from Select Committees – 1821 Vol.IX: 1822 Vol.V
    Reports of Select Committees – 1833 Vol.V: 1836 Vol.VIII pts. 1 and 2
    Employment of Children, Young Persons and Women in Agriculture – 4th Report of Commissioners 1870 Vol.XIII
    Preliminary Reports from Her Majesty's Commissioners on Agriculture 1882 Vols.XV and XVI and XVII
    Royal Commission on Agriculture (Scotland) 1895 Vol.XVII
Education
    Second Report from the Select Committee on Education of the Lower Orders 1818 Vol.IV
    Reports of the Commissioners on Religious Instruction, Scotland 1837- Vol.XXI to 1839 XXVI
    Report on State of Education in the Hebrides 1867 Vol. XXVI
    Report on Highland Schools 1884 Vol.XXVI
Emigration and Highland Distress
    Reports from Select Committee Inquiring into the Expediency of Encouraging
    Emigration from the United Kingdom 1826 Vol. IV: 1826-7 Vol.V
    Reports from the Select Committee Appointed to Inquire into the Condition of
    the Islands and Highlands of Scotland and into the Practicability of Affording
    the Proper Relief by Means of Emigration 1841 Vol.VI
    Report of Commissioners Inquiring into Administration of the Poor Laws in
    Scotland 1844 Vols. XX - XXVI
    Report of the Board of Supervision on Western Highlands and Islands of
    Scotland 1851 Vol. XXVI

Report of the Commissioners of Inquiry into the Condition of the Crofters and
Cottars in the Highlands and Islands of Scotland 1884 XXXII-XXXIX
Prisons
    Royal Burghs of Scotland – Report from Committee Respecting the Providing of Jails 1818 Vol.VI
    Report of Select Committee on Prisons 1826 Vol.V
Trade and Industry
    Select Committee on Present State of the Linen Trade in Great Britain and Ireland 1773 Vol.III
    Reports of the Committee on the State of the British Fisheries 1785, 1803 Vol.X
    First and Second Reports from the Select Committee Appointed to inquire into
    the Laws relating to the Salt Duties 1801 Vol.III
    Select Committee report on State of Children Employed in the Manufactories of the United Kingdom 1816 Vol.III
    Report from the Select Committee on Salt Duties 1818 Vol.V
    Report by Commissioners for the Herring Fishery 1821 Vol.XXI
    Select Committee on Hand Loom Weavers' Petitions 1834 Vol.X and 1835 Vol.XIII
    Assistant Commissioner's Reports from South of Scotland - a Return of Mills and Factories 1839 Vol. XLII, and East of Scotland 1839 Vol.XLII.
    Children's Employment Commission (Mines) Report 1842 Vol.XV
    Report by Commissioners on Herring Fishery 1870 Vol.XIV
    Fishing Boats (Scotland) Report 1849 Vol. LI
    Reports from Select Committee on Coal Mines – Inspectors' Reports (E. and W. Districts of Scotland) 1854-1876

Bridging The Genealogical Cultural Gap: Scotland to the USA?!

David W Webster B.Sc., FSA(Scot)

Introduction
The subject of culture gaps is always one that has fascinated me, but it is not until recently that I explored the situation from a genealogical point of view.

Addressing the situation in detail has been very enjoyable, leading to a conclusion that I had never considered in the first place.

Background
I have been fortunate through my business life to spend over 20 years travelling round the world, including most countries in Europe, plus India, the Far East (Japan, Taiwan, South Korea), N Africa and North America. This period included living and working in Sweden for 6 years.

The general subject of culture gaps between nations is one that has always fascinated me. This is not unusual for a Scot, as we share the situation with other countries such as Norway, Denmark, Finland and The Netherlands, among others, that we are a small country, - current population 5m in Scotland, - and have understood throughout our history that we need to be more outward looking in our philosophy than larger nations such as England and France in order to prosper as a nation.

That's not to say that there is not a significant proportion of Scots whom I define as "domestic" Scots, i.e. Scots who have not seriously travelled abroad - package tours don't count as the domestic culture is exported with the group, - more that there is a larger proportion of Scots than there are in other, larger nations who have at least a reasonable understanding of the reality and importance of culture gaps between nations.

Extending the above line of thought, - there are two other categories that I define, - "semi-international" Scots, - those who have travelled abroad extensively and have a good appreciation of culture gaps, - and "fully international" Scots, - those who have travelled abroad extensively,

and have also lived abroad for a period of years, so that they have developed an ability to look at their domestic national culture from the outside and appreciate that the values and solutions of other nations and cultures can be of equal value or better than the corresponding Scottish solutions.

It's my experience that this categorisation applies to many similar sized small nations.

In Sweden, there is a quite serious phenomenon that affects Swedes returning to their native land after several years of residence abroad, known as "reverse culture shock". This relates to the problems arising from being able to look back into Swedish culture from the outside and appreciate just how different Swedish culture is even from other European countries, along with the realisation that some at least of the basic values of Swedish culture are not unique solutions to various aspects of life, and that, sometimes, the solutions worked out by other countries may be better !

In my 6 years in Sweden I became deeply fluent in Swedish, to the extent that I can still switch to Swedish after only a couple of minutes. Beyond that, if I go back into a Swedish speaking environment for more than a couple of days, so that I switch to thinking in Swedish, I change character to a measurable extent, as it is a question not just of language but the surrounding culture and patterns of behaviour which influence and constrain my thoughts and actions.

Go to almost any country in the world outside the group to which there have been major emigrations of Scots and you will find that there are many Scots who have "gone native" to use the pejorative term. Again, this seems to happen more frequently to nationals from smaller nations as opposed to larger countries. I would argue that this is due in part at least to the greater willingness of Scots and

STANDING ON HIS DIGNITY

Shipping Agent. "ARE YOU A MECHANIC?

Intending Emigrant (justly indignant). "NO!—I'M A MACPHERSON!"

nationals of other similar, smaller nations to invest substantial time in understanding and appreciating the local and national culture concerned, as well as being prepared to adapt to the values involved.

What is a Culture Gap?
Simply put, the differences between the ways of life and patterns of thoughts and action between people of different nations, sometimes ethnic groups within nations, via their personal and national values, often evidenced by language.

There is rarely any problem in convincing someone that there is a large, and often very difficult to bridge culture gap between Japan and the nations of Western Europe and North America, because the gap is so large and evident.

But it is much more difficult to convince someone that the culture gaps that exist in Europe between many countries are real and can be significant.

The situation in Europe is complicated by various supra national groupings, i.e. France, part of Belgium, Luxembourg who share a common language; the Latin countries of Portugal, Spain and Italy who share the southern European Latin culture, although the Portuguese language is much closer to French than Spanish; the Nordic countries of Denmark, Norway, Sweden and Finland, although the Finnish language is totally unlike that of its Nordic neighbours (Finnish belongs to the Finno-Ugric group of languages, - its closest neighbour in linguistic terms being Hungarian, but the two languages split at least 2,000 years ago). In others words, shared history and geography also play a role that can spread across present day national boundaries.

In the other direction, there are culture gaps within countries, e.g. between the Flemish and French speakers in Belgium, between the Swedish (ca. 8%) and Finnish speakers in Finland, between the Basques and the rest of Spain, between the north and the south of Italy, and not least between the Scots and the English in the UK (and the Welsh and the Northern Irish would want to be mentioned as well!, - and then there's the culture gap between the North of England and the South-East.......).

In other words, culture gaps work at various levels, - national, regional within nations, and supra national, sometimes involving a common language, sometimes not. Coming at the situation from a different angle it might be better, perhaps, to talk about culture gaps between ethnic groups, which raises interesting questions as to whether there is an "United States of America" culture as such!, or rather a group of ethnic cultures that are still not fully melded together !!

I've been unable to determine if it was Winston Churchill or Oscar Wilde who made the comment about England and America - "two cultures separated by a common language". It's not just a question of jacket/coat, pavement/sidewalk, lift/elevator, boot/trunk, to list but a few of the different words used on either side of the Atlantic for everyday items, but goes well beyond that in terms of language and general attitudes to and way of life. In fact, it's incorrect to use those two terms, as it's not a question of England, but of the other parts of the United Kingdom of Great Britain and Northern Ireland, - Scotland, Wales, and Northern Ireland, and the many different parts of the United States of America and Canada, down to state and province level, although there are certain overall and basic cultural differences that are very easy to overlook because of the apparent commonality of the language.

At last I'm getting close to the title of this article !

Genealogical Research in Scotland
Whether or not you are Scottish, English, Welsh, Scotch-Irish, American, Canadian, Australian, New Zealander, etc., etc., genealogical research

A QUESTION OF TASTE.

Juvenis. "JOLLY DAY WE HAD LAST WEEK AT McFOGGARTY'S WEDDING! CAPITAL CHAMPAGNE E GAVE US, AND WE DID IT JUSTICE, I CAN TELL YOU——"
Senex (who prefers whiskey). "EH—H, MUN, IT'S A' VERA WEEL WEDDINS AT YE-ER TIME O' IFE. GIE ME A GUDE SOLID FUNERAL!"

and, particularly, Sweden. I could go on for a long time on this theme but that would be diverging from the subject of this article!

It is not just a question of learning about the geography and the history, but also developing an understanding of the society of the era being researched.

Take one simple example. In certain areas of Scotland in the 18th century, the rate of illegitimacy was very high. In fact, taken together with the amazingly short periods quite common between the date of marriage and the date of birth of the first child, it is not an exaggeration to state that the great majority of conceptions must have taken place outside marriage. The Established Church of Scotland did not approve of this situation and often severely punished those who were not married before the birth of the child, but often turned a blind eye to the fact that first pregnancies came to term in a much shorter time than later ones!, because this was the way that it had been for many centuries. Quite simply, before a man married he wanted to know if he and his intended bride could produce children.

In other words, while developing a knowledge of the geography and the history is very helpful, never mind enjoyable, the requirement goes beyond that in terms of there being substantial benefit in developing an understanding of the culture of the time, including an appreciation of regional differences as well, Highland/Lowland – the long-standing tensions over many centuries, West/East, etc.

Bridging The Genealogical Cultural Gap: Scotland to the USA ?!
My first approach to this postulate was on the basis of the need to understand the existence of culture gaps in terms of the undoubted gap that exists today between Scotland and the USA, but, regardless of the truth or otherwise of that understanding of that postulate, I have now moved on to a position where, however correct that need is in terms of modern day cultures, I

in the Scottish records is much more effective, never mind enjoyable, if the researcher appreciates the need to develop a knowledge of the associated geography and history of Scotland. Personally, in the last 15 years or so, I have learnt 10 times more than I previously knew concerning Scottish geography and history.

In addition, the Scottish diaspora has led to the need for me to develop a knowledge of the history and geography of the many countries to which Scots have emigrated over the centuries, - not just the obvious ones associated with the nationalities listed earlier in this section, but also South Africa, South East Asia, China, Japan - one of the founders of the modern day Japan was a Scot; - Sweden, Norway and Finland where the industrial revolution was greatly influenced by Scots, never mind the earlier Scottish influence in Denmark and Sweden, - in the Thirty Years War in the first half of the 17th century current research is producing the fact that upwards of 50,000 Scots served in the armies of Denmark and Sweden, - an amazing figure in the context of the total Scottish population at that time, variously estimated at between 800,000 and 1,000,000. Many of those Scottish mercenaries then settled in Denmark

would argue that the correct understanding of the postulate is the need to understand the culture of Scotland over the eras of interest, stretching back over the centuries.

What was it like to be a farm servant in Aberdeenshire or Angus in the 1800s?; what was it like to be a Covenanter in Ayrshire in the mid/late 1600s?; what was it like to be a miner, - coal, ironstone or shale in the mid/late 1800s?, - I've just carried out some research on a family in N Lanarkshire in that era in which the father, and four of his sons died in their late30s/40s/early 50s of causes that we would clearly understand today as pneumoconiosis and emphysema, i.e. a direct result of their employment as coal miners; and on, and on, and on !

Of course you can still trace Scottish family trees without a detailed understanding of such aspects of Scottish society, but it is amazing how often just some initial background research can help with a brick wall, or highlight the importance of a previously overlooked clue.

Over the past few years I've developed a parallel interest in matters military, especially as related to Scottish regiments which, simply put, have often been the bulwark of the British Army. On the modern day 100 mile or so road journey between Perth and Inverness on the A9, around half-way, you pass Ruthven Barracks, built in the early 1700s as part of the process to "control" the Highlands, - although it wasn't until the aftermath of the Battle of Culloden in 1746 that such "control" began to be achieved.

A question that has fascinated me for many years is what it was like to be a private soldier, part of an English or Scottish regiment (there were more Scots on the "English" side than there were on the "Scottish" side at Culloden) marching north from Perth in, say, 1730, to Inverness to be part of the garrisons at Fort George, Fort Augustus, Fort William and elsewhere. Two or three days march, presumably, from Perth to Ruthven Barracks and then at least the same to the destination, on the roads built by General Wade to "open up" the Highlands. Not surprisingly there are no such memoires written by a private soldier, but there are one or two written by NCOs that give a fascinating insight not just to the military situation but also the Highland society of the time.

In my opinion, however, in the specific context of genealogical research, the situation goes beyond the purely Scottish situation, in that a culture gap requires two cultures. In other words, the culture gap that needs to be bridged is that between the respective cultures of Scotland and the United States of America of 50, 100, 200 etc. years ago.

That, in turn, begs the question, of how many readers fully understand the culture of the USA of the immediate post-independence era and later eras, never mind the culture (cultures?) that existed prior to independence.

That is not a subject on which I would claim to be expert, so that I would welcome the opinions of those who are.

In other words, just as much research effort may be needed in North America in order to enable the culture of that society in the era of interest to be better understood.

Conclusions
In the context of efficient and enjoyable genealogical research, culture gaps need to be recognised and understood, not just in present day terms, and how that influences attitudes, but also in terms of the cultures of the era being researched.

The former is relatively easy to bridge and understand, but the latter can take substantial research in its own right before a sufficient understanding is reached, e.g. just what was it like for your Scottish ancestor to live in Scotland in, say, the early 1800s?, as well as when they emigrated to North America.

While this article has been written on the basis of the culture gap between N America and Scotland, I would argue that the postulate is valid in terms of any pair of cultures.

One very valuable lesson that I took away from NGS2002 in Milwaukee, was that emigration does not happen in a vacuum. In other words, there are always pressures that lead to emigration that need to be very carefully investigated and understood.

Sometimes, these are blatantly obvious, such as the Irish potato famine, or the various "Clearances" from Scotland, although these weren't always the simple situation based on the introduction of sheep, but a more complex situation based on that plus the breakdown of the traditional clan structure of Highland society with the clan chiefs losing interest in their clan members, - their "children" in classic Gaelic parlance. These pressures were often much more subtle and multi-factorial, - a good example here would be the re-emigration of the Ulster-Scots from Ulster to America, several generations after the initial move from Scotland to Ulster, or the French from Acadia.

In other words, the title of this article, - "Bridging The Genealogical Cultural Gap: Scotland to the USA ?!", - is now, in my opinion, only valid if restated as "The Necessity to Bridge The Genealogical Cultural Gaps Between Scotland and the USA in the 1700s for Effective Genealogical Research", ... or 1600s, 1800s, or 1900s, as appropriate !!!

Settling Up After Death
A look at Scottish testaments, dispositions and settlements
Rosemary Bigwood

Behind these rather forbidding legal terms lies a wealth of family information – intrigue, subterfuge, intimate details, feuds, fortunes and friendships - but getting behind the legal façade, locating the sources, understanding what is being said and what omitted, sometimes needs a little care.

Testaments
First of all – what is a testament? Things are different north and south of the Border: the term is often confused with the English words "probate" and "will" but under Scots law, a testament is a document concerning the confirmation of an executor. If the deceased person named their own executor, then on confirmation by the commissary court this was called a testament testamentar and the testament would probably also include a "latterwill" or "legacie" which were the personal wishes of the deceased with regard to the disposal of part of their moveable estate. If the person died intestate, then the commissary officers confirmed the appointment of an executor in what was known as a testament dative. The duty of the executor or executors was to take an inventory of the moveable goods – household possessions, farm crops or utensils, gold and silver but not land (until 1868) – and of all debts due to or by the deceased.

The commissary courts were originally the pre-Reformation consistorial courts of the Scottish bishops. They were abolished at the Reformation but almost immediately re-established as civil courts with responsibilities for confirming testaments and dealing with a range of other civil causes such as marriage, legitimacy, small debts and other local disputes. In 1823 the inferior commissary courts were abolished, the head court in Edinburgh also disappearing in 1836, and their work in

confirming testaments transferred to the sheriff courts.

The jurisdiction of each commissary court was based on the lands of the old bishoprics which is sometimes confusing as in various parts of the country the bishops held land in disparate portions. Edinburgh was the head court and there was an option for anyone to register a testament in either the head court or in the local court. As with so many series of Scottish records, the extent of the surviving registers varies. No register of testaments has survived for Aberdeen before 1715 due to a fire, the registers for Dumfries cover the period 1624-1827 (with some gaps) and Edinburgh testaments go back to 1569.

It is frustrating that only a small proportion of people left testaments but it is important to remember that persons of all classes of society are represented. For example, looking at a list of testaments recorded in Brechin Commissary Court up to 1800 shows that there were tenants, shoemakers, cottars, shipmasters, cordiners, indwellers, merchants, tailors and vintners – among others - and this is the situation found all over Scotland.

What can we learn about our ancestors in testaments?
The opening section of a testament will tell you whether the person died testate (testament testamentar) or intestate (testament dative) and the name of the executor. In some cases when the deceased died in debt, the executor, who wants to make his claims, may be termed "qua creditor" and is then usually unrelated, but often the executor is the surviving spouse, a child or children or near relative. The occupation and residence of the defunct may be stated and the date of death given (frustratingly left blank in

many cases). The death may have occurred a number of years before the registration of the testament.

The inventory of the moveable goods taken by the executor is then inserted – providing a fascinating insight into social life – farm stock (the horse is often lame, the beasts old – to keep down the value and resulting tax due to the commissary), crops (the valuation indicates the expected yield of grain sown), furniture (sometimes room by room), and even description of clothes owned. Then follows a list of the debts owed to and by the deceased, usually not of great genealogical interest though members of the family may be involved and a mention of duties owed to a named landlord may be useful.

The net value of the moveable estate was by law divided in certain proportions. If the deceased was survived by a spouse and child or children, then the estate was divided in three – one part to the spouse, one part among the children and one part "free" which, in cases of testacy, could be bequeathed according to the wishes of the deceased in the latterwill. If only a spouse or issue survived, then the value of the moveable goods were divided in two and if there were no survivors, then it was a case of "No division". In some testaments, the name or even existence of a spouse or children may not be indicated and it is only by looking at the "division" clause that you can divine that they survived. If the deceased had owned heritable property (land), then this would be inherited by the eldest son and he did not receive a share of the moveables. Sometimes, therefore, the name of this heir is omitted when all his younger siblings are listed.

Finally there is the formal confirmation by the commissary officer and usually the name of a cautioner who was responsible for seeing that the executor did his work properly. In the case of a testament testamentar, the latterwill is likely to be the most interesting part. It may name children and other relatives, list individual bequests and make arrangements for the future of the family. The most useful parts of the testament, therefore are the opening section, the note of the "division" and the latterwill if there is one.

After about 1823 (the date varies a little from area to area) the registers were kept in the sheriff courts and are listed in repertories in a section still called "Commissary Records" and titled "Inventories of Defuncts". You will still find people from a range of classes represented, but on the whole by the later eighteenth century onwards, the records are those of the professional classes, larger tenants and land owners.

The Inventories of Defuncts provide similar information to the testaments – confirmation of executors, an inventory and sometimes – in cases of testacy – the wills, dispositions or testamentary deeds as they are variously called - are quoted at the end. If they are not, then they may be registered in a separate section of the records of that sheriff court. A third possibility is that a note in the "Inventory" will state where the disposition was registered - in a register of deeds in a burgh court or sheriff court or in the Books of Council and Session.

These settlements, trust dispositions or wills are often very detailed documents. There may be bequests of money, references to family heirlooms, and jewellery left to members of the family. You may find references to previously unknown relations (such as illegitimate children for whom provision is now being made, while instructions for special financial care of certain individuals may indicate that either some were not capable of looking after themselves or that their way of life and profligacy was a source of suspicion. Light may also be thrown on business interests. Wills registered in a register of deeds might also concern the disposal of heritable property.

The Scottish Archive Network (SCAN)
Within the last year, searching the indexes of

testaments and inventories up to 1875 has been made very much easier – and this period is being extended to cover the years up to 1901. Previously, in the years before about 1823, it was necessary to find out within which commissary court the testament was likely to have been registered and then to search the printed indexes (published by the Scottish Record Society) for each court before consulting the registers in the National Archive of Scotland or a microfilmed copy of the registers elsewhere. After 1823, typed or printed indexes to Inventories of Defuncts for each sheriff court covered the period up to 1876 when the annual printed indexes to Confirmations begin, giving details of the appointment of executors, whether the person died intestate or testate and if the latter, in which court the will is registered. Now, the Scottish Archive Network (known as SCAN) provides on-line access to the indexes to the Registers of Testaments and to Inventories of Defuncts and these can be consulted, without payment, on the website *ScottishDocuments.com.* You can search the database by name, by place or by occupation over the whole period and for the whole of Scotland. It may enable you to pick up relatives of whom you did not know – the testaments of childless aunts and uncles sometimes produce a wealth of information if they have favoured their nieces and nephews. Testaments are also a valuable source of local history and it is now possible to study the inventories of all the bakers in Cupar, for example, or shoemakers in Haddington and study their social background through the inventories of their personal possessions. Having found a testament in which you are interested, you can downloaded the digital image on payment of a fee of £5 for each document. It is important to remember, however, that in cases of testacy after about 1823, unless the will is attached to the inventory, it cannot be downloaded through the SCAN site.

As with all good things, there are some problems. Scottish spelling is often individualistic and though the SCAN website provides some assistance in identifying alternative forms of a surname or placename, it is not foolproof and you may find it necessary to think carefully about possible variant spellings or consult the old printed indexes produced by the Scottish Record Society (these are available in many libraries and family history centres). Sadly, too, there is no cross-referencing between the maiden name and married name of a deceased married woman – information which is given in the printed indexes.

The other challenge may be in reading the testament. Before about 1700, the Old Scots hand was used and without practice, this can be very difficult to decipher. A study of the form of such documents – knowing which sections are likely to contain the most useful ancestral gems will shorten your task - and knowledge of the phrases used will be very helpful in providing a clue as to the handwriting. It is always worth going to a course in Old Scots handwriting if you are likely to be reading many pre-1700's documents. The SCAN website provides some useful guidance in dealing with old documents. *Scottish Handwriting 1500-1700* – a self-help pack produced by the Scottish Records Association and available from the National Archives of Scotland, is also useful for home study. Some professional genealogists offer a service in transcribing Old Scots documents – or in reading them and extracting the genealogical details, which is less time-consuming and cheaper.

Finding other sources - the Commissary Court

Ease of looking for testaments or wills through SCAN can induce "tunnel-vision" and it is important to remember that registers of testaments in the commissary courts, inventories of defuncts and registers of wills in the sheriff courts are not the only places where you will find testamentary material.

The commissary court records contain a rich hoard of genealogical information about the deaths of our ancestors. The registration of a testament was, in fact, only part of the whole legal process of "winding up" a person's estate. The first action taken by the commissary officers was to issue an edict ordering all those who wished to be appointed as executors to appear and be confirmed in this office. The edict was posted up on the door of the parish church and read aloud. The details given in it - name of the deceased person, often their occupation, place of residence and sometimes the date, and the name of the executor – are often as detailed as those given in a testament dative. In a great many cases, edicts have survived when no testament is extant. In the case of under-age children left by the deceased, the courts would raise curatorial edicts appointing curators or tutors who were almost always close relatives

The appointment of executors was not always an uncontested affair and the records of hearings given either in a process relating to the legal hearing of a case or in papers accompanying the edict may open windows on family matters – accusations of death-bed manipulations, feuds between half-brothers and sisters, and problems of second marriages. Processes may also give a

Glasgow Cathedral

web-site repertories) of the Archives. For those who are interested in Argyllshire, there is a *Calender of Testaments, Inventories, Commissary Processes and Other Records 1700-1825* available either in book form or on a disc.

Searching the commissary court records may take some time but the results are almost always rewarding and a great many deaths are documented which do not appear in the registers of testaments.

detailed account of contested inheritance, covering the claims of several generations.

The first responsibility of the executor was to take an inventory of the moveable goods of the deceased and many of these inventories will be found with the commissary court papers – not only as part of a testament but also as registers of inventories or sometimes as loose papers folded with the edicts. Claims for debts due to or by the defunct, and particularly accounts for funerals provide a fascinating insight into family affairs. Bills have often survived for the cost of coffin, mournings, grave-digging and most interesting – what was provided for the funeral feast. Petitions might concern cases of hardships – widows who needed to sell or auction their late husband's assets to provide money to maintain themselves, or requests to consult documents in the hands of officials, for example. The commissary courts were also recognised as competent to register deeds and therefore you may find dispositions and settlements recorded there.

There are manuscript inventories (arranged not alphabetically but by date), of the records of most of the commissary courts in the National Archives of Scotland and these help in accessing what is often a rather chaotic collection of papers, bound in bundles according to the various classes, more or less according to date. An indication of what is available in each commissary court is given in *Guide to the National Archives of Scotland* and of course in the paper repertories (and hopefully soon on the

Finding other sources – Registers of Deeds
In cases of testacy, a will in the form of a disposition, trust or settlement might be recorded in any court competent to register deeds. In a document of this kind, the person concerned could also make arrangements for the disposal of certain heritable property, as well as of moveable goods.

There were a number of courts which could register deeds – the Court of Session in its huge register of deeds known officially as the Books of Council and Session; the sheriff courts; the burgh courts; the commissary courts (both the head court of Edinburgh and the local commissary courts); and higher franchise courts – of regality, stewartry and bailiery (but not the baronies).

This choice can be daunting. How does one decide where to look? As a general rule, the Court of Session's register of deeds are a fruitful searching ground for dispositions and settlements of the landed gentry, of well-to-do merchants and professional people and sometimes of prosperous tenants. It is, however, dangerous to take too narrow a view, and particularly in the seventeenth century a wide range of classes of person are represented – mariners, weavers, vintners, maltmen, candlemakers or tailors, as well as portioners, landowners and merchants. The sheriff court registers of deeds represent the same groups of people but more particularly the merchant and professional classes and better-off tenants. The registers of deeds kept by the courts of the royal burghs dealt with those living within the particular bounds of the burgh and might concern craftsmen, and burgesses and other professional persons. Deeds registered by the courts of regality, stewartry and bailiery are again localised – but unfortunately very fragmentary. Access to a hearing in the commissary courts appears to have been possible to persons of all classes of society but few labourers, cottars or small tenants would have had enough to leave to make it worth registering a settlement.

Apart from the class of the deceased, the other deciding factor in selecting which series of records to search is ease of access. Is the register extant for the period of interest? Are there indexes? How long will it take to search unindexed deeds over a series of years? The

series of registers making up the Books of Council and Session is vast and up till 1812 there are several parallel series of deeds in each year. Indexing is intermittent, with a frustrating gap between 1716 and 1770 (except for 1750-52) and the information given in the indexes themselves varies. Only in some years is the nature of the deed given – whether it is a bond, protest, disposition, factory or settlement – a detail which makes it possible to pick out the documents likely to be of most value. Where there are no indexes, one has to resort to minute books which are very slow to search. The sheriff court registers of deeds, being more localised, are less bulky and therefore more accessible. Indexing is again variable, though most sheriff court registers of deeds are indexed in the nineteenth century. For the burgh court registers of deeds, there are few searching aids but it is not an impossible task to search through the actual registers for information. Very few of the records of the franchise courts have survived: *Guide to the National Archives of Scotland* gives a useful summary of what there is and where it is to be found.

Edinburgh Castle

Conclusions

The scope of choice may be daunting but for the enthusiastic and tenacious much valuable information may be found concerning the deaths of our ancestors in these records. Failure to find a testament in a pre-1823 register in the commissary court, for instance, does not mark the end of that road but the start of a research journey. It is always important to bear in mind what the alternative sources are, to evaluate the time it will take to search the records and to assess what may be found there in relation to the particular research being undertaken. The bibliography given below suggests some works which will be helpful as guides to these legal sources.

Further Reading
Formulary of Old Scots Legal Documents Peter Gouldesbrough (The Stair Society 1985)
Guide to the National Archives of Scotland Scottish Record Office (HMSO 1996)
Tracing Your Scottish Ancestors in the Scottish Record Office Cecil Sinclair (HMSO 1990)
Tracing Scottish Ancestors Rosemary Bigwood (Harper Collins 2001)
Argyll Commissary Court – a Calendar of Testaments, Inventories, Commissary Processes and other Records 1700-1825 Frank Bigwood (privately printed, available from F. Bigwood, Flat B, The Lodge, 2 East Road, North Berwick)
Bell's Dictionary and Digest of the Law of Scotland (various editions)
A Legal History of Scotland 6 vols. David M. Walker (Edinburgh 1988-2001)
A Students' Glossary of Scottish Legal Terms (W.Green & Son, Edinburgh)
Scottish Handwriting 1150-1650 Grant G. Simpson (various editions)
Scottish Handwriting 1500-1700 (Scottish Record Office)
Note: The Scottish Record Office is now known as the National Archives of Scotland.

Scottish Poor Law Records: An Invaluable Aid to the Genealogist
David W Webster FSA(Scot)

This article aims to introduce the reader to the very valuable genealogical information increasingly available via computerised indexes of the Scottish Poor Relief records by means of a brief description of the records themselves, including information on the geographic coverage, but primarily by means of case studies based on actual research.

The 1845 Poor Law Amendment (Scotland) Act set up a system of Parochial Boards in Scotland for the administration of Poor Relief in Scotland, taking over this function from the Established Church of Scotland. Increasing computerisation of extant Scottish Poor Relief records with searchable surname indexes provides a rich source of information for genealogists. Very often a greater degree of genealogical information can be obtained from this source than from statutory or census records.

It is not the purpose of this article to describe in full detail the legislation, its administration, etc. This has already been excellently done in Andrew Jackson's article "Glasgow Poor Law Records as a Source for Migration"[1].

The Poor Law Amendment Act 1845
Prior to 1845 administration of poor relief was a parish based matter handled by the Established Church of Scotland. Records of those granted relief can be often found in the extant Kirk Session records at Scottish Record Office and various local archives throughout Scotland.

The information provided in these Kirk Session records is most often just a name and date with, perhaps, an age and description of condition and cause of death, e.g. pauper, or widow, or, at best, "relict of John SMITH" (i.e. widow of John SMITH), but most often with little further information of value to the genealogical researcher.

In 1845 the Poor Law Amendment (Scotland) Act was passed. This followed the breakdown of the traditional church administered system due to the industrial revolution and its effect in large cities where trade cycles could lead to thousands becoming unemployed. Such conditions resulted form a prolonged depression in 1840-1843.

In addition, in 1843, the Established Church of Scotland suffered its worst schism - "The Disruption" - that led to around one-third of its ministers and congregations leaving the Church of Scotland to form the Free Church of Scotland. This in itself produced major problems in terms of administration of the existing poor relief system.

This situation led to the reform of the poor relief system through the new act, giving responsibility for the administration of Poor Relief to local Poor Relief Boards set up on a parish. These new Parochial Boards were normally set up and in operation ca. 1850. In some areas a number of parishes combined to set up a "combination" poorhouse, the records of which, if extant, can also be of value.

The information recorded by these poor relief authorities for every application was extensive, and can often be of great value to the genealogist.

Extent of surviving Poor Law Records
In the West of Scotland the Poor Relief records are extant for the Glasgow parishes of City, Barony and Govan, with over 300,000 entries indexed for the period ca. 1850 to 1900. It should be noted that this figure is inflated by around 30% due to double entries for married women. This Glasgow index is currently being extended to include the records up to 1910. The records for Ayrshire towns of Adrossan and Kilmarnock are also extant, and have been indexed.

These records comprise both the original application records as well as original indexes. The age and birthplace are always given where known. All known dependents are listed together with details of the applicant's marital history, as well as previous addresses, sometime stretching back over a period of years. Married women had their maiden name shown as a middle name, e.g. Jane Ross Webster means Mrs Jane Webster, maiden name Ross.

There is a 75 year closure period for these records, with no indexing having taken place for records after 1900, apart from the ongoing project to extend the index to 1910. Glasgow City Archives have a computer based searchable index of these records.

In Ayrshire Poor Law application records survive, and have been indexed, for Ardrossan (known as "little Dublin" in the 19th century due to the numbers of Irish immigrants!), and Kilmarnock. Again these indexes can be consulted in a computer based system, at Ayrshire Archives, Craigie, Ayr. The method of indexing these two sets of records has been to list every name mentioned in the original application, not just the applicant but also persons such as Ministers, parents, grandparents, inlaws, employers, etc. These databases consist of the first name and surname plus maiden name where relevant, whether Pauper or otherwise, age at the time of the application, and place of birth, together, of course, with the Poor Relief reference number.

Elsewhere in Ayrshire there are 19th century Poor Relief Records for Maybole Poorhouse (minute books), West Kilbride, Largs, Kilwinning, Kilburnie, Irvine, Girvan, Dundonald and Beith. For these parishes the records are mostly Registers of the Poor with only some full Records of

Applications, not always for the full period. The parish records for Mauchline, Sorn and Muirkirk have only recently been discovered and saved. As yet it is not clear what Poor Relief Records are involved.

Elsewhere in the West of Scotland records survive for Paisley, Clydebank, and for a few Lanarkshire parishes including Dalziel, which includes Motherwell and Cambusnethan. The latter have been indexed by local volunteers (a copy of the index for the whole of Lanarkshire is also held by Glasgow City Archives), as may also be the case with the Paisley records, held at Paisley Central Library and Museum.

For extant records distinction must be made between indexes and full application records. It is the latter that are likely to supply information of value to the genealogical researcher, with the former of doubtful value.

The extant records for Dunbartonshire are currently being indexed in a volunteer project with the support of Glasgow City Archives.

In the rest of Scotland the survival is patchy. For the cities of Edinburgh, Dundee and Aberdeen there is unfortunately nothing known of equivalent to the almost complete series of applications or general registers such as survive in Glasgow.

Elsewhere little appears to be widely known about extant poor relief records. Who knows, it may the case that there is a pleasant surprise awaiting genealogists in the form of forgotten volumes lying in the basement of a local authority somewhere, exactly as was the case in Glasgow, - without the intervention of the then city Archivist, Andrew Jackson, the Poor Law records discovered mouldering away in a basement would have been destroyed.

For areas not covered above the best first points of contact are the local family history societies and the archivist at the local libraries or local authorities.

If any readers have information of other extant records, I'd be grateful for the information, as I'm keen to establish information on other areas where these records survive.

Poor Law Relief Records - Details
The procedure for the

survive but where the original applications survive, the genealogical "vein" can be rich indeed.

The best way of demonstrating the value of the Poor Law records is to examine a couple of case studies.

CASE STUDY 1
Kerry Farmer was researching her Scottish greatgrandmother, Annie (Barbara) MCNEILL. Her New South Wales marriage certificate gave Annie's parents as David MCNEILL and Ann MCKENZIE. The birth of Annie Barbara MCNEILL was found easily in Saltcoats in 1873, but showing her parents as John MCNEILL and Ann MCKENZIE, married in Stevenston in 1861. This marriage certificate was then quickly located, showing Ann's parents, but only John (David) MCNEILL's mother's name,- Jessie MCNEILL. The inference was that John (David) was illegitimate, and further progress could be difficult on the male line.

Further work in the Stevenston and Ardossan 1851 censuses produced some intriguing clues, including the presence in the household of Ann MCKENZIE's parents of a "nephew" John ANDERSON, and a possible census entry for Jessie where the original entry for the surname of MCNAIL had been scored out and ANDERSON inserted.

It is possible at that stage that further work in the censuses might have produced a solution to the situation but the Ardrossan Poor Relief records then provided the following entry from an application in 1863.

"Jessie ANDERSON, (m.s. MCNEILL) Pauper, 45 yrs at date of application. Born Ardrossan, children: Mary 10 yrs, b Stevenston and Jessie 4 yrs b Green St, Saltcoats"

Note that this entry directly leads to the 1852/53 birth of Mary in Stevenston and the 1858/59 birth of Jessie in Saltcoats, for which there will be a statutory record. In addition, the age declared of 45 gives a probable year of birth for Jessie of ca. 1818 ("45" might be regarded as being suspiciously rounded !).

This poor law record led to the location of a marriage between Jessie MCNEIL and William ANDERSON in 1850, and their children William, Mary and Jessie, born between 1850 and 1858.

The presumption is that John (David) was a child of Jessie's before she married William ANDERSON. As John (David) took the surname ANDERSON, it is possible that William ANDERSON was his father, but it is equally likely that William ANDERSON was not his father and that John (David) only adopted the surname ANDERSON after his mother's marriage, a quite common practice, - it may never be possible to

granting of "relief" involved the applicant being interviewed at their home or, if of no fixed abode, then at the Poorhouse. The details of this interview were recorded by the interviewer. Very similar procedures are still in operation today in relation to the various UK Social Security benefits.

While some might consider it a matter of shame that an ancestor received poor relief, it should be remembered that the great majority of families in the UK since WWII have received support for their families, particularly children, in the form of various social security benefits, e.g. Child Benefit. While a proportion of 19th century Poor Relief applications were from the truly destitute, many other applications were from those who had large families, of which there were many more than in today's world of the "2.4 child family".

In the Glasgow records the largest group were the sick, as many as two-thirds of the applications, followed by married women with children, often claiming desertion, or women with illegitimate children. Other smaller groups are foundlings and deserted children, and those over 65.
The recorded details of the first, and, sometimes, subsequent interviews can form a "minibiography" and can sometimes solve a genealogical link not possible to solve via statutory, census, and other more widely available records. In the case of some records indexes only

prove this one way or another.

Further checks of the Ardrossan and district censuses have produced no other possible solution for the situation other than John (David) MCNEILL or ANDERSON being an illegitimate son of Jessie MCNEILL, "farmed out" to the MCKENZIE family. Without the information from the Poor Relief Application, however, it might well have been the case that the situation described would never have been discovered.

Subsequent research on the MCKENZIE line produced the following, highly informative Poor Law application record for one Isabella SIMPSON or MCKENZIE.
Page 198, item 261 ref Ardrossan Poor Applications C03/21

"1898, August 4th 3.30 P.M.
Date/Hour of Inspector's Visit   August 6th 12.10 PM
Applicant Isabella SIMPSON or MCKENZIE. 5 Princess St, Ardrossan, 2 up "Black" with daughter. Application made by "self".
Age: 60 yrs past Feb
Religion: Protestant
Names of Dependants or Children living with Applicant
Mary (28) b 26.6.70 Ardrossan Rd. Saltcoats. per Regt. Wife of Wm. BLACK. Yachtsman. 4 children.
Earnings 30/ in
summer. County of Birth: Hamilton St. Saltcoats
Condition: Widow married 18 Sept 1860 Dalry Cause of Disablement: Eczema of the Legs
Wholly or Partially Destitute: Partially
Names of Parents:
Daniel SIMPSON (Sailor)
Janet MIDDLETON (bo[th] dead)
Detail:
Husband was Gilbert MCKENZIE who was drowned with ship "Kirkconnell" in Penzance Bay, Nov. 1893, aged 58 yrs, b. Hill St., Saltcoats (Stevenston), son of Gilbert MCKENZIE, sailor, and Mary DOBBS, bo[th] dead.
Residence:
Prior to husband's death 31 Manse St, 2 yrs. 6 mos., prior 168 Glasgow St., Ardrossan 1 yr., prior Stevenston 2 mos., prior 30 Clelland St, Glasgow 7 yrs. After husband's death remained 31 Manse St., Saltcoats 6 mos., then 39 Vernon St. Saltcoats 2 yrs, then Harbour Pl. 2 yrs, then present house since May.
How disposed of by Inspector: Referred
How disposed of by Parish Council: 2/6 per week. Admit.
Date: 1898 August 4th, August 9th"

What more could one ask for, in terms of background information, and information such as could never be obtained from a statutory certificate!
Just consider for a moment the information that the above record provides

Age of Isabella, giving an approximate year of birth of 1818
The fact that her husband Gilbert McKenzie was dead in 1898
The names of the parents of Isabella McKenzie née

Simpson
The marriage of Isabella in 1860 to Gilbert McKenzie
Details, including age and place of birth, including the street, for Gilbert McKenzie
Details of the place and date of Gilbert's death
The names of the parents of Gilbert McKenzie
The name of Isabella and Gilbert's daughter Mary (with date and place of birth), together with the name of the daughter's husband, and the existence of 4 children
A wealth of information regarding addresses for Isabella

It's just possible, I suppose, that if there are extant records for a range of other sources such as newspapers, shipping records, etc., that a great deal of hard work might produce the equivalent information, but not from a single, easily accessible source.

CASE STUDY 2
Julia Kenny is researching a number of Glasgow families including that of Andrew WH[Y/I]TE b 17 July 1825 in Glasgow d 22 July 1893 in the City Poorhouse, married Christina ROBERTSON 19 June 1846 in Glasgow, children Robert b 1848, Mary b 1850, John b 1852, Andrew Henry b 1854, Christina b 1856, Elizabeth Ann b 1858, William b 1860, Frederick Whillimina (sic) b 1862, Janet b 1864, James b 1866, and Cecilia b 1868.

A check of the Glasgow Poor Law computer index and reference to the full entry produced the following.

"Application for Relief No. C8,893
Hour and Date of Application
11.40 am 12th Feby 1879
Name of Applicant:
Andrew WHITE
Residence: 22 Graeme St Graham's
Place of Birth: 37 Rottenrow (17th July 1825)
Hour and Date of Inspector's
Visit to Applicant's Home 9 am 13/2/79
Condition: Widr
Age: 54
Occupation: Labr
Average Value of Weekly Earnings, if any: blank
Wholly or Partially Disabled: [blank]
Religious Denomination: Prot
Disability: "Catarrh"
Names and Ages of Dependants
Wife: Christina ROBERTSON born
Vennel died 9 yrs ago in Kirk St Cton (i.e. Calton)
Parents: Robt WHITE, Carpet Weaver & Christina GILMOUR both dead
Other Information to enable Parochial Board to decide Case
Names of Children not Dependants, Earnings, &c.
Fredk Wm17 born the "Glen" Duke St Single Res: not known
Elizth 15 Single dom sevt   Res: not known
Robert 18 born Drygate Single residence not known
No of Previous Application, if any: First
Settlement: Glasgow if Birth proven
Remarks: No relatives or any reference in proof of birth place. Thinks he was baptised in the High Church.

There then follow just over 3 densely packed pages of information relating to Andrew WH[Y/I]TE's 14 subsequent reapplications for relief up to his death in 1893, with much information concerning his children, their occupations, together with wages and contributions made to the support of Andrew, details of wives and children, addresses, etc., etc. In short, a wealth of information that would take a considerable amount of effort to build up from other sources if it were ever possible to do so, with some of the information such as wages most unlikely to be found anywhere else.

There is a degree of conflict between some of the information supplied by Andrew WH[Y/I]TE between his various applications, but there is sufficient information overall in all the applications put together that makes it reasonably straightforward to determine the real facts. The extent to which Andrew was suffering from some form of dementia or just dissembling in order to improve his chances of being granted relief is impossible to know.

This case may be exceptional in terms of the extra and repeated information resulting from the large number of times that Andrew applied for and was granted relief, then leaving the Poorhouse at his own request, and then reapplying a few months later, but it does illustrate the tremendous amount of information that can be found, not only relating to the applicant but also their family.

As with the first case study, just consider for a moment the information provided by this Poor Law source

The address of Andrew WH[Y/I]TE in 1879
Place of birth of Andrew with the exact date
Marital condition at the time of this application, i.e. widower
Occupation and earnings
Name of deceased wife with place and year of her death
The names of the parents of Andrew WH[Y/I]TE
The names, ages, places of birth, and occupations of 3 children (the names of the other 8 children, and other associated information occur in the subsequent re-applications, including information on the spouses and children).

Where else could you expect to obtain all this information?

Conclusions
Where extant the Scottish poor relief records can provide a wealth of information, much of which may not be available elsewhere, and which can allow a "workaround" of dead ends encountered in research in other, more widely used sources.

Hopefully it will increasingly become the case that poor relief records not yet available on computerised indexes will become so over the next few years. It is also to be hoped that there may still be some pleasant surprises in the future in terms of the discovery of extant records, previously forgotten.

Research Project Suggestion
The potential value of the Scottish Poor Law records to genealogists is such that it is surely worthwhile considering a project covering all of

Scotland to locate and computer index such records. It is quite possible that valuable records are languishing forgotten in damp cellars, their condition deteriorating. The recent discovery of the Mauchline, Sorn and Muirkirk is one indication of this. Glasgow City Archives would be interested in co-operating with such a project.

Reference
1. "Glasgow Poor Law Records as a Source for Migration". Andrew Jackson. European Immigration into Scotland: Proceedings of the 4th Annual Conference of the Scottish Association of Family History Societies (SAFHS), Glasgow 1992, pp 41-52. (Reprint available from the Glasgow & West of Scotland Family History Society.)

Acknowledgements
Thanks are due to Kerry Farmer and to Julia Kenny for permission to quote from their research.

Sincere thanks are also due to Andrew Jackson of Glasgow City Archives not only for permission to make use of his article, referred to above, but also his most helpful comments on the draft article.

Above all else great thanks are also due to all the anonymous volunteers in the West of Scotland and elsewhere who have given up their time to carry out the computerisation of the poor law records - in particular, Jim Steel and his fellow volunteers, for their work on the Ardrossan records as well as Jim's personal help with the above research, without which this article would never have been written.

The Glasgow Police Museum
Alastair Dinsmor

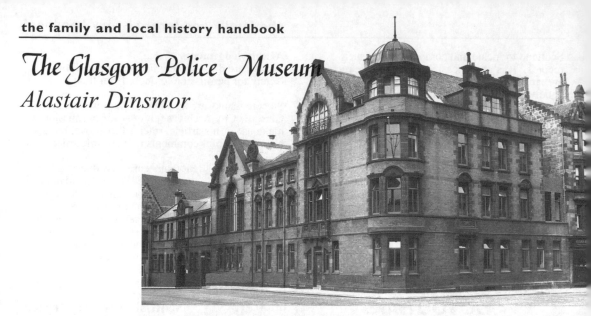

The Glasgow Police Museum was opened on 3 May 2002 by Glasgow's Lord Provost, Alex Mosson and Strathclyde's Chief Constable, William Rae. The opening was a culmination of almost two years of voluntary work by members of the Glasgow Police Heritage Society, who had raised the money from local businesses and organizations, converted the rooms and built the display cases.

The Museum is situated in the old C.I.D. offices of the former Central Police Office at 68 Turnbull Street, Glasgow, which had at one time been the headquarters of the City of Glasgow Police between 1906 and 1932. It is a historic building in every sense and is still the venue of the Central District Court, which still sits today, in much the same way as it has done since 1906. It is also a building that has seen many landmarks in the policing history of the City, the stories of which are illustrated around the walls of the Museum.

The principal theme of the Museum is the history of the oldest police force in the UK, the City of Glasgow Police. Many may raise their hands in horror and talk about Peel's Metropolitan Police of 1829 being the first, but like so many so-called 'family facts' that family historians have later found to be myths, so the myth of Peel has undeservedly found its way into the history books. There is no doubt that he was a great statesman, but his appetite for publicity in the newspapers of the day has been misinterpreted. His 'New Police' were only new to London and some other English cities and towns, and it is difficult to credit him with inventing something that was established in Glasgow at least 29 years before.

Visitors to the Glasgow Police Museum can read for themselves the history of the force laid out in clear text boards in the two historical display rooms, with many illustrations and photographs never displayed before.

Included are details of the early attempt by the city fathers to form a police force in 1779. This small force was disbanded in 1781 due to financial difficulties caused by their lack of power to levy a rate on the inhabitants.

Realising that they required an Act of Parliament to levy rates, the Council set up a committee in 1788 to make recommendations for the appointment of an 'Intendent of Police'. The recommendations in the committee's report of 10 December 1788 were radical and innovative, laying down the basic regulations for a preventative Police force, a far cry from the old city guard, and militia which had protected the city over many years.

The report recommended that the Council should appoint an 'Intendent of Police' and eight police officers in red uniforms. They would also wear numbered badges with the word 'Police' inscribed thereon. Their duties would include:
(a) patrolling the streets to prevent and detect crimes during the day, the evenings and at night.
(b) detecting house and shop breaking and theft by pocket picking.
(c) searching for stolen goods and detecting receivers of stolen goods.
(d) gathering information on crimes, convicted persons and the public houses they frequent, recording it in a book for the purpose.
(e) suppressing riots, squabbles, begging and singing songs.
(f) apprehending vagabonds, vagrants and disorderly persons.
(g) Controlling carts and carriages.
In February 1789, Intendent of Police Richard Marshall and his small force of eight police

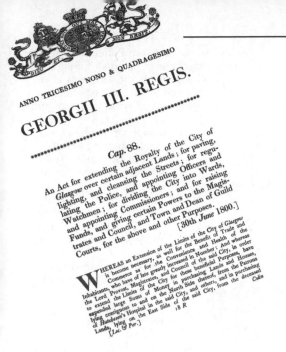

ANNO TRICESIMO NONO & QUADRAGESIMO

GEORGII III. REGIS.

Cap. 88.

An Act for extending the Royalty of the City of Glasgow over certain adjacent Lands; for paving, lighting, and cleansing the Streets; for regulating the Police, and appointing Officers and Watchmen; for dividing the City into Wards, and appointing Commissioners; and for raising Funds, and giving certain Powers to the Magistrates and Council, and Town and Dean of Guild Courts, for the above and other Purposes.

[30th June 1800.]

WHEREAS an Extension of the Limits of the City of Glasgow is become necessary, as well for the Benefit of Trade and Commerce as for the Convenience and Health of the Inhabitants, who have of late greatly increased in Number: And whereas the Lord Provost, Magistrates, and Council of the said City, in order to extend the Limits of the City for these beneficial Purposes, have expended large Sums of Money in purchasing Lands and Houses, lying contiguous to and on the North Side thereof, from the Patrons of Hutcheson's Hospital in the said City; and others, and in purchasing Lands lying on the East Side of the said City, from the deceased

18 R   Colin

[Loc. & Per.]

officers began patrolling the streets of Glasgow to prevent and detect crime. The struggle to get the Bill through Parliament would take eleven years, and in the meantime the small Glasgow Police force would again fail through lack of finance in 1790.

On 30 June 1800, the Glasgow Police Act received the Royal Assent of King George III (four weeks before the Thames River Police Act of 27 July 1800). They immediately set about re-establishing the police force and appointed John Stenhouse as Master of Police, three sergeants, six police officers and 68 watchmen to the force. This small force would grow with the City and serve it's citizens faithfully for 175 years through some of the most turbulent times in its history.

Criminal families anxious to escape the clutches of the new force moved to surrounding burghs. The burghs' answer to this problem was that they too established police forces and so the Gorbals Police (1805), Calton Police (1819) and Anderston Police (1824) were established. It is also interesting to note that before 1829, a total of twelve Scottish towns and cities had established police forces under Acts of Parliament.

Glasgow's first detective, Lieutenant Peter McKinlay, was appointed in 1819 and the Glasgow Criminal Department was created in 1821, over twenty years before the establishment of the famous Scotland Yard detectives. Throughout the 175 years of the force, Glasgow detectives were in constant

demand by other Scottish Police forces to assist them in investigating serious crimes and they frequently travelled to Europe and beyond while investigating serious crimes.

One particularly notable case was in October 1866, when a large number of forged banknotes were in circulation all over the West of Scotland. Superintendent McCall of the Glasgow Criminal Department took charge of the investigation and soon inormation was received that a photographer, John Henry Greatrex, had recently sold some printing equipment. The equipment was traced and it was confirmed that it had been used to make the forged notes.

Greatrex and one of his lady assistants, Jenny Weir, had left Glasgow and Detective Inspector Smith traced the couple to Southampton where they had boarded separate ships for America. On hearing this, Superintendent McCall immediately set off in pursuit.

On his arrival in New York he found the city teeming with refugees from the recent Civil War. He then thought of a trick to find Greatrex in the city. McCall put an advertisement in some newspapers for a female photographic assistant ending with the words "a Scotch girl preferred". Among the many replies was one from Jenny Weir.
Along with a New York detective, McCall went to her address and kept it under observation. Greatrex was quickly arrested and extradited to Glasgow.
In May 1867, Greatrex stood trial in Edinburgh High Court and was sentenced to 20 years penal servitude.

The case quickly established Superintendent McCall's reputation as a great detective and he was appointed Chief Constable of Glasgow three years later.

Another famous Glasgow detective of the late Victorian era was Archie Carmichael whose brilliant abilities, untiring energy and perseverance lead him to be known as 'Glasgow's Sherlock Holmes'. He joined the Glasgow Police in 1859 and in March 1869 he found his true vocation as a Detective Officer.

He served 30 of his 41 years service as a Detective and had a hand in every

Superintendent McCall

important case in that time and, like his fictional detective namesake, a book on his exploits, called 'Personal Adventures of a Detective' was published in 1892. Such was the high regard in which he was held that the rank of Detective Lieutenant was specially created for him. One of his famous cases was known as 'The Dynamitards', involved a scenario which, sadly, has been all too frequent in recent years.

In 1882, Irish sympathisers in Glasgow set up a secret organisation called the Ribbon Society, which, for political reasons, planned to blow up important public installations in Glasgow.

About 10pm on Saturday 20th January, 1883, the Tradeston Gas Works in Lilybank Street was the target of a bomb in a gasometer. Three people in the gasworks were injured. A second explosion destroyed a shed in Buchanan Street Railway Station, but no one was injured. Also about this time, an off-duty soldier was walking on the Possil Aquaduct carrying the Forth and Clyde Canal when he found a hatbox. There was a violent explosion and he received burns to his hands.

A similar case had occurred in Liverpool and the assistance of the Antwerp Police in Belgium was sought consignments of chemicals to Glasgow. Information was also received about the suspicious behavior of some Irishmen and on 31st August, 1883, nine men were arrested and were tried at Edinburgh High Court in December 1883. All were found guilty and sentenced to imprisonment. The City Council gave the Police officers specially struck medals and cash awards.

Archie Carmichael

The Edwardian era saw the introduction of police dogs to Glasgow. Following a number of serious burglaries in the west side of the city, the Glasgow Police purchased four Police dogs from a Major Richardson of Harrow, Essex, for the a total of £21. The dogs were specially bred Airedales and provided a means of searching large gardens for burglars and also protecting the police officers. Although widely used by the police in Germany, Belgium and France, this was the first time a British Police force had purchased dogs to aid their officers in combating crime.

With the onset of the First World War the majority of the Glasgow policemen who enlisted were posted to the Scots Guards. One such man was John McAulay, a constable in the Northern Division, who was awarded the Victoria Cross for his part in the Battle of Cambrai on 27 November, 1917. He had already won the Distinguished Conduct Medal at Ypres in July 1916. He was presented with his Victoria Cross by the King at Buckingham Palace in March, 1918. 'Jock' McAulay returned to Glasgow Police after the war and retired as an Inspector in 1946.

During the war, 748 Glasgow Policemen had enlisted. 173 were killed or reported missing. The Glasgow Police War Memorial embracing both World Wars is on display in the Museum.

With the 'troubles' in Ireland continuing into the 1920's, and Glasgow having a frequent ferry service to and from Belfast, it should not have come as a surprise to Glaswegians that some of their fellow citizens had strong links to the conflict. But the events that unfolded in the city on Wednesday 4 May 1921 were to become known as 'The Glasgow Outrage'.
On that fateful day, a prisoner who gave the

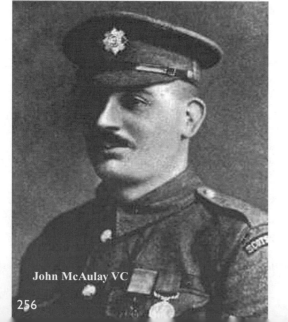

John McAulay VC

name of Frank Somers appeared at the Central Police Court, Turnbull Street, Glasgow, charged with the theft of a revolver and jail-breaking. He was to be remanded in custody in Duke Street Prison.

The Glasgow Police knew they had a prisoner of particular importance in the I.R.A. movement, so Detective Sergeant Stirton and Detective Constable Murdoch McDonald were armed with revolvers and took their place in the front of the prison-van alongside Inspector Johnstone and the van-driver, Constable Ross. Shortly before 12.30 pm, the prison-van with Somers left the Central Police Office in St. Andrew's Square and continued up High Street. When the prison van reached Rottenrow, a fusilade of shots rang out from thirteen armed I.R.A. men, killing Inspector Johnston. D.S. Stirton and D.C. McDonald jumped out of the van and started firing at the attackers.

Inspector Johnston

D.S. Stirton stood astride the body of Inspector Johnston, and continued firing until a bullet shattered his right wrist. D.C. McDonald fired at the attackers at the rear door of the van, but the door had withstood the attack. Inspector Johnston was taken to the nearby Royal Infirmary, where he was found to be dead.

Glasgow Police mounted searching operations in the east-end of the city where a large number of known I.R.A. sympathizers lived. Large quantities of firearms, ammunition and explosives were found and 34 persons arrested. Although 13 men were tried at Edinburgh High Court, none of them were convicted through lack of identification.

During the investigation Detective Superintendent Andrew Keith received a threatening letter from the I.R.A. Glasgow Brigade telling him to stop the operations among the Irish community. The original letter is on display in the Glasgow Police Museum.

Percy Joseph Sillitoe was appointed Chief Constable of Glasgow on 1 December 1931, and immediately set about reforming the force. Having served in the Police in Africa during the First World War, he returned to Britain in 1922. He had also been Chief Constable of Chesterfield, the East Riding of Yorkshire and Sheffield.

Shortly after taking over the reins of Glasgow Police, he held an open meeting of Glasgow Police officers in the City Halls and invited them to enter a prize competition for submitting the best plan to reorganize the city's police divisions. He also intimated that any of his senior officers with over thirty years service should retire, to make way for younger men.

He introduced the black and white chequered hat band onto the caps of the Glasgow Police in 1932, which became known as 'The Sillitoe Tartan', and has been adopted by police forces both in the rest of Britain and some forces across the World. He will be best remembered for his suppression of the Glasgow gangs, during which he utilised the experience he gained in Sheffield. In 1943 he resigned from the Glasgow Police to take over Kent Constabulary. He went on to become Director-General of MI5 in 1946.

Following the Second World War James Robertson, a 33 year old Constable in the Southern Division, was a beat officer in the Cumberland Street area of Glasgow. Although a family man, he had a relationship with a local

Chief Constable Percy Joseph Sillitoe

James Griffiths

woman, Catherine McCluskey.
Soon after midnight on 28 July, 1950, Catherine McCluskey's body was found on a country road on the outskirts of Glasgow. When Constable William Kevan, of the Traffic Department, examined the scene of the apparent 'road accident', he noticed that the vehicle tyre marks indicated that the vehicle had gone over the woman twice. The C.I.D. were called to the scene and Constable Kevin was able to convince them that the woman had been murdered.

Robertson's association with the woman was soon established and the vehicle he used to travel to work was impounded. It was found that the car had been stolen and fitted with false number plates. On examination, traces of the woman's hair were found on the underside of the vehicle.

James Robertson went on trial at the Glasgow High Court on 6 November, 1950. Found guilty of murder, he was executed at Barlinnie Prison on 16 December, 1950.

The year 1969 was a particularly tragic year for Glasgow Police when violent death would visit both a criminal and two police officers.

Following a murder of a woman in Ayrshire, it was suspected that a Rochdale-born man, James Griffiths, was implicated and enquiries revealed that he lived in an attic flat at 14 Holyrood Crescent, Glasgow. They did not suspect that he possessed firearms.

About 9.50am on Tuesday, 15 July, 1969, five

detectives went to Griffiths' flat and were met by a fusillade of shots. One detective fell wounded as the unarmed detectives retreated into the street. The area was quickly surrounded, but Griffiths managed to escape into nearby streets, but not before wounding six pedestrians. He also wounded a man and stole his car in Henderson Street.

After crashing the car, he entered the Round Toll Bar armed with two guns where he shot and killed a customer then calmly demanded a drink. He emerged from the bar, wounded two more pedestrians and stole a lorry. He drove into Kay Street, Springburn, where he abandoned the lorry and broke into a top-floor flat at No. 26.

Griffiths began firing indiscriminately from the windows of the flat and wounded a woman and child in an nearby children's playground. It was obvious something had to be done to stop Griffiths.

Chief Superintendent Malcolm Finlayson and Det. Sergeant Ian Smith, armed with revolvers, went up to the door of the flat. Mr. Finlayson managed to shoot Griffiths in his shoulder through the letterbox, but the bullet ricocheted off a bone and entered his heart. Griffiths died almost immediately. Both officers were awarded medals for their gallantry.

But 'the boot was on the other foot' in December 1969, when a series of robberies ended in murder.

Howard Wilson had joined Glasgow Police in 1958 but disillusioned, he resigned in 1967 and opened a greengrocery business. It got into financial difficulties and in July 1969, Wilson and two other men robbed a bank in Williamwood. Later, on 30 December 1969, Wilson, along with his two accomplices, also raided the Clydesdale Bank in Linwood, Renfrewshire. Their haul was £14,212 in notes and silver coins.

About 4.30pm that day, Inspector Andrew

Hyslop and Constable John Sellars were in a Police car in Allison Street, Glasgow . They were suspicious of Wilson and two men carrying suitcases into a flat at 51 Allison Street. Inspector Hyslop went to the nearby Southern Police Office and got the assistance of Detective Constables John Campbell and Angus McKenzie, and Constable Edward Barnett to search Wilson's flat.

During the search, Wilson pulled out a pistol and shot Inspector Hyslop in the face and neck paralysing him. Wilson then shot and killed Detective Constable McKenzie and P.C.Barnett.

Police Dog Handler 1911 .

Wilson then returned to Inspector Hyslop and was about to shoot him again when Detective Constable Campbell intervened. After a violent struggle, he managed to get the gun from Wilson and arrested him. Wilson pleaded guilty to the murders and robberies and was imprisoned for life. He was released in 2002 after 33 years imprisonment.

Detective Constable McKenzie and P.C. Barnett were posthumously awarded the Queen's Police Medal for Gallantry. Inspector Hyslop and Detective Constable Campbell both received the George Medal for their gallantry. Inspector Hyslop's medals are on display in the museum.

The Glasgow Police Museum takes the 175 years of history of the force up to 1975 when local government reorganization merged the city force with the surrounding county police forces to form Strathclyde Police.

Another feature of the Museum is the International Display, which illustrates the spread of policing throughout the World. Over 6000 items of Police uniforms, headgear and insignia adorn the display cases from every country of the World. This area is particularly popular with children who visit the Museum and delight is seeing the uniforms of a Canadian Mountie, New York Cop and many more.

From 1 April to 31 October each year, the Museum opens from 10am until 4.30pm each day, although the hours are 12 noon until 4.30pm on Sundays. During the Winter Season the Museum opens on Tuesdays and Sundays only. Admission is free.
Evening group visits can be arranged.

The Glasgow Police Museum website www.policemuseum.org.uk is very popular and provides interesting stories about the force and the people who served during the 175 years of the Glasgow Police.

The Museum does not have police registers or personnel records. However, with our experience in researching careers of Glasgow policemen, we can point family history researchers in the right direction, identify police uniforms from photographs and provide additional historical information where appropriate.

Alastair Dinsmor is Curator
of The Glasgow Police Museum

Police Records & Museums

International Police Association - British Section - Genealogy Group Thornholm Church Lane South Muskham Newark Nottinghamshire NG23 6EQ T: 01636 676997 E: ipagenuk@thornholm.freeserve.co.uk

National Police Officers' Roll of Honour Roll of Honour project Lancashire Contabulary Headquarters Hutton Preston Lancashire PR4 5SB

Police History Society 37 Greenhill Road Timperley Altrincham Cheshire WA15 7BG T: 0161-980-2188 E: alanhayhurst@greenhillroad.fsnet.co.uk W: www:policehistorysociety.co.uk Whilst the society is not primarily interested in family history and having no personal records of its own is unable to answer enquiries re individual officers. However members may contact each other via the Newsletter or ask for specific information which maybe available. shortly to have a 'notice board' on the website which may assist researchers, as well as links to many police-related sites

Berkshire

Thames Valley Police Museum Sulhamstead Nr Reading Berkshire RG7 4DX T: 0118 932 5748 F: 0118 932 5751 E: ken.wells@thamesvalley.police.uk W: www.thamesvalley.police.uk Thames Valley Police formed April 1968 from Berkshire, Oxfordshire, Oxford City and Reading Borough constabularies. Only records of officers are those who served in Reading Borough and Oxfordshire. Appointments only with Curator

Essex

Essex Police Museum Police Headquarters PO Box 2 Springfield Chelmsford Essex CM2 6DA T: 01245 491491-ext-50771 F: 01245 452456 The Museum only staffed on Tuesdays & Wednesdays. Open by appointment only.

Greater Manchester

The Greater Manchester Police Museum 57 Newton St Manchester Lancashire M1 1ES T: 0161 856 3287 T: 0161 856 3288 F: 0161 856 3286

Lancashire

The Greater Manchester Police Museum see Greater Manchester

London

Metropolitan Police Archives Room 517, Wellington House 67-73 Buckingham Gate London SW1E 6BE T: 020 7230 7186 E: margarter.bird@met.police.uk The Metropolitan Police do not hold any records. All records that have survived are in the National archives. Do not hold records for City of London Police or other police forces or constabularies. The Archives have some finding aids. SAE for information

Metropolitan Police Historical Museum c/o T.P.H.Q., Fin & res 4th Floor Victoria Embankment London SW1A 2JL T: (020) 8305-2824 T: (020) 8305-1676 F: (020) 8293-6692 Visits by appointment only . Metropolitan Police records including officers from 1829, Uniforms, police memorabilia. History of The Metropolitan Police

Oxfordshire

Thames Valley Police Museum see Berkshire

Tyne and Wear

North Eastern Police History Society Brinkburn Cottage 28 Brinkburn St High Barnes Sunderland SR4 7RG T: 0191-565-7215 E: harry.wynne@virgin.net W: http://nepolicehistory.homestead.com

Research into Family and Police History 52 Symons Avenue Eastwood Leigh on Sea Essex SS9 5QE T: 01702 522992 F: 01702 522992 E: fred@feather1.demon.co.uk

Surrey

Surrey Police Museum Mount browne Sandy Lane Guildford Surrey GU3 1HG T: 001483 482155 W: WWW: www.surreymuseums.org.uk/museums/Police.htm

Sussex

Royal Military Police Museum Roussillon Barracks Chichester Sussex PO19 6BL T: 01243 534225 F: 01243 534288 E: Museum @rhqrmp.freeserve.co.uk W: WWW:

www.rhqrmp.freeserve.co.uk Depicts Military Police history from Tudor times to present day

West Midlands

West Midlands Police Museum Sparkhill Police Station Stratford Rd Sparkhill Birmingham West Midlands B11 4EA T: 0121 626 7181 W: stvincent.ac.uk/Resourcews/WMidPol

Yorkshire – North

Ripon Workhouse - Museum of Poor Law Allhallowgate Ripon HG4 1LE T: 01765 690799

Yorkshire – South

Sheffield Police and Fire Museum 101-109 West Bar Sheffield South Yorkshire S3 8TP T: 0114 249 1999 W: WWW: www.hedgepig.freeserve.co.uk

Scotland

Glasgow Police Heritage Society and Glasgow Police Museum 68 St Andrews Square Glasgow G2 4JS T: 07788 532691 E: curator@policemuseum.org.uk W: WWW: www.policemusaeum.org.uk

Ireland

Garda Síochána Museum and archives The Records Tower Dublin Castle Dublin 2 Ireland T: +353 1 6719 597 W: WWW: www.geocities.com/CapitolHill/7900/museum.html

List of Current Police Forces

England and Wales - Avon and Somerset Constabulary, Bedfordshire Police, Cambridgeshire Constabulary, Cheshire Constabulary, City of London Police, Cleveland Constabulary, Cumbria Constabulary, Derbyshire Constabulary, Devon and Cornwall Constabulary, Dorset Police, Durham Constabulary, Dyfed-Powys Police, Essex Police, Gloucestershire Constabulary, Greater Manchester Police, Gwent Constabulary, Hampshire Constabulary, Hertfordshire Constabulary, Humberside Police, Kent County Constabulary, Lancashire Constabulary, Leicestershire Constabulary, Lincolnshire Police, Merseyside Police, Metropolitan Police, Norfolk Constabulary, North Wales Police - Heddlu Gogledd Cymru , North Yorkshire Police, Northamptonshire Police, Northumbria Police, Nottinghamshire Constabulary, South Wales Police - Heddlu de Cymru, South Yorkshire Police, Staffordshire Police, Suffolk Constabulary, Surrey Constabulary, Sussex Police, Thames Valley Police, Warwickshire Constabulary, West Mercia Police, West Midlands Police, West Yorkshire Police, Wiltshire Constabulary

Scotland - Central Scotland Police, Dumfries and Galloway Constabulary, Fife Constabulary, Grampian Police, Lothian and Borders Police, Northern Constabulary, Strathclyde Police, Tayside Police

Non Geographic Police Forces

British Transport Police, Ministry of Defence Police, UK Atomic Energy Constabulary, Port of Dover Police, The National Crime Squad

Ireland

Northern Ireland - Police Service of Northern Ireland (Royal Ulster Constabulary)

Southern Ireland - Garda Síochána

Channel Islands - Guernsey Police, States of Jersey Police

Isle of Man - Isle of Man Constabulary

Other Forces - Royal Military Police, Belfast Harbour Police, Mersey Tunnels Police, Port of Bristol Police, Port of Tilbury London Police, Royal Parks Constabulary, Port of Liverpool Police

Wildcards in Genealogical Research
David W Webster FSA(Scot)

In this context the concept of wildcards derives from card games such as poker or brag where it is common practice to decide before a game that, for instance, "twos are wild". In other words a two can take any value from two through to an ace.

In searching databases this concept has translated into the use of "?" to mean any single character, and "*" to mean any number of characters. Just to confuse the situation the PRO 1901 census index uses the underline character "_" as the equivalent of "?".

Wildcards and names
So what does this all mean in genealogy?

Note first, however, that 100 years or so ago, many people didn't care too much or weren't able to check the spelling of their name. Today, many people are adamant that there is only one correct spelling of their name.

My mother's youngest sister always adamantly maintained that their mother's maiden name was McLennan, spelt just like that and **no** other way. She wasn't too pleased to be shown on a number of statutory certificates, in both his own signature, as well as entries made by the registrar, that the name was variously spelt McLennan, MacLennan, McLenan, MacLenan, Maclennan, Mclenan, and one or two others, by her grandfather George McLennan.

People were also at the mercy of the ear of the recorder. Galbraith is a well known surname in Ayrshire. Now **I** know that it is spelt that way, as it was in letters one foot high above the eponymous baker's shop in Ayr. But in Yorkshire it has become Gilbraith, because that's the way that it is pronounced in an Ayrshire accent and heard by a Yorkshire ear !

McMillen is a well known Scottish surname, but involve a broad Ulster accent, and what results can be McMullan.

My favourite example relates to an entry in the 1851 census for Dalry in the north of Ayrshire. A family appears with the surname Araphady, not a surname that I can fit to anything recognisable, unless I imagine a broad southern Irish pronunciation of O'Rafferty heard by an Ayrshire ear unaccustomed to such accents. I can't prove it, but I defy anyone else to come up with an alternative explanation!

In other words, when searching our trees we need to be very aware of such possible spelling variations. While a Soundex system will go some way towards helping, the use of wildcards is of even greater help when searching computerised indexes such as are available at ScotlandsPeople, and it is very worthwhile the effort to learn how to use wildcards if you are not familiar with them.

Types of surname variants
Before we look further into wildcards, let's take a look at surname variants that commonly occur in Scotland.

1. Simple variants
 • The substitution of a single letter, e.g Wabster instead of Webster.
 • The addition of a letter at the end, e.g. Yorkstone instead of Yorkston, or Roberts instead of Robert.
 •The use of a double letter instead of a single letter, or vice versa, e.g. Morison and Morrison. • Or any combination or permutation of these types.

2. Complex variants, ranging from -
 • The deceptively simple but far from obvious elision of a letter or letters, e.g. Wason instead of Watson, or Yorson instead of Yorkston.
 • To the much more difficult Lindsay for McLintock, thought to be an Anglification of Maclintock.
But note that apparently similar spelling variants do not always have the same derivation, e.g.
 • Yorson can derive from either Yorkston or Yorson, a distinct Scottish surname in its own right.
 • Similarly with Scullion and variants and Scallon and variants.

The occurrence of a variant is always more likely to be due to the recorder, be that the registrar, census enumerator, session clerk, etc., thinking that they are hearing a name with which they are already familiar, or writing down a name with which they are unfamiliar as they hear it.

In the OPRs it's quite amazing the difference in spellings that can result from a change of the

minister or session clerk changes. A similar comment applies to census enumerators who were quite often schoolmasters. In both cases it was very common for the minister or schoolmaster to be from outside the area.

3. Surnames derived from Gaelic
Then that leaves us with Scottish surnames derived from the Gaelic
• The etymology of such names is a subject in its own right.• There is no significance in the difference between "Mc" and "Mac".
• The full range of variants is "Mc", "Mac", "M'", "Mhic", and "Vc", all of which mean "son of", sometimes "descendant of".
• Spelling variants can be even more difficult due to the original "complex" (to non-Gaelic speakers) Gaelic spellings, and the effect that different dialects had on pronunciation. Take MacLaverty which in the last couple of centuries turns up as MacLafferty, MacLardie, MacLardy, MacLarty, MacLevertry, MacLacharty. Do back even further and you will come across M'Clorty, M'Clairtick, M'Laertike, and more...............

4. T-Names
In the North East of Scotland there are a number of fishing villages in which there are very few surnames. In the 1920s in Gamrie a compilation of a roll of male voters found:

17 Nicols	19 Wisemans
26 Wests	68 Watts

This led, understandably, to the use of nicknames, or "to-names", sometimes just referred to as "t-" or "tee-names". While some of these were based on physical characteristics, others used the name of the fisherman's boat. The t-name was regularly used on a statutory certificate.

The above situation can have interesting consequences. When carrying out some research in Gamrie I came across the re-marriage of a widow who was shown as Jane Watt, formerly Watt, maiden surname Watt !

5. Patronymics
If your search takes you to Orkney or Shetland (Zetland) you will need to develop an understanding of patronymics, e.g. the first generation could be John Donaldson, his father Donald Ericson, his father in turn Eric Peterson, and so on........

The use of such patronymics in these northern island groups only died out completely in the first decade or so of the 20th century. Note that there is a little known OPR forenames index. Unfortunately this has not been computerised and is only on fiche. The best way to explain further the situation regarding wildcards is to use examples.

Simple Examples
Let's say that you are searching the surname ROBERTS. It's very common for such a name

that the "s" is missed out in the original records, or by a transcriber. The simple solution is to search for ROBERT?, which will return results for both ROBERT and ROBERTS, - the "?" can also mean no character.

Or take a very simple surname such as REID. Use RE?D and you will reliably find entries for REED and READ as well.

Using ROBERT* as the search term will produce results for ROBERT, ROBERTS, and ROBERTSON (as well as McROBERT[S] in LDS census indexes).

Note the generally used convention of square brackets to indicate a possible variation. This can be extended to ...[O/E]... to indicate the possibility of this letter being an "O" or "E" (for any readers familiar with Boolean logic this is the equivalent of an "XOR").

More Complex Examples
Let's say that you are looking for a surname where you know that the name starts with an "RE" and ends with a "D", then searching on the basis of RE*D will produce REDFORD, REYNARD, READHEAD, REDHEAD, REDMOND, REAID, REYNOLD and REIGHEAD as well as REID, REED, and READ. Note in this example the name REAID that may just be a very unusual variant of REID.

Normally wildcards can also be used in combination. A search for ROB*S* will produce ROBERTSON, ROBERSON, ROBINASON, ROBINS, ROBBINS, ROBINSON, ROBRTSON (probably a mis-transcription of ROBERTSON but who knows ?!), ROBSON and ROBISON.

"Mc" and "Mac" Surnames
In Scottish research wildcards are invaluable for dealing with these types of names. Incidentally, there is no difference in meaning or religious background in general between "Mc" and "Mac". Searching for M?cLA*N will produce McLAUGHLAN, McLACHLAN, McLAUCHLAN, McLACHLAN, McLANAN, and all the "Mac" variants as well.
Note that in this and all the examples above I'm only using the Scottish Lowlands disk of the LDS 1881 census to generate the variants. Try the same

Feed Me

search in the Highlands disk, as well as other LDS census indexes and other database indexes and you will come up with even more variants.

The golden rule is to use your imagination in terms of the use of wildcards.

Quite often you will be able to rule out some of the results, but you will be pleasantly surprised at the number of results thrown up that weren't at all obvious.

Shortly after writing this article IU came across the country and western (or is it blues) singer Reba McEntire. However obvious with hindsight that this may be a variant of McIntyre, it's not one that I would necessarily have thought of initially, but a properly designed wildcard search would pick it up.

Limitations on Wildcard Use
You will find that most surname database indexes will not allow you to use a leading wildcard, - for example "?OX" or "*OX" is not allowed. This is due to the computing power that such a search would require.

On the ScotlandsPeople website there must be two characters at the start of the search term for a surname,- for example "WE*" is allowed but "W*" is not.

Given Names and Wildcards
Practice varies from database to database. In ScotlandsPeople, the search system assumes that if you enter, for example, "J" in the given name field, that there is an implied wildcard. In other words the system assumes that you are searching

for "J*" and will present results for James, Jacob, John, Joseph, etc., etc. That doesn't mean that you can't also search on the basis of "JO*" so that you only pick up John, Jon, Jonathan, etc.

In the ScotlandsPeople search system note that searching for "J*" will pick up not only those entries where "J*" is the first name, but also those examples where it is the second name. In other words you would be given entries for John Robert as well as Robert John.

While wildcards in given names are useful for spelling variations, they are at least as important for picking up shortened versions, for example Jas., Wm., Chas., etc., etc., as many databases will record such entries exactly as they are shown, however clear it is that the name involved is, say, William, rather than Wm. Some databases, such as the LDS IGI site will return Wm when you searfch on William, but other databases will not.

Summary
I can only repeat the golden rule – use your imagination !

As well as consulting standard books on surnames to see what advice is given on spelling variations, you should experiment with wildcards in sources such as the various LDS and other census indexes. However much you consider that you have seen it all in terms of a particular surname I can guarantee you that you will come up with some possible variants that may well stop you in your tracks and put you on the road to solving the "disappearance" of great-uncle Harry.

No, it wasn't kidnapping by aliens in flying saucers, just the much more mundane situation in which a highly unusual spelling variant was written down that day by great-uncle Harry himself, the registrar, the census enumerator, or other official, or a later transcriber got it badly wrong ……

Of course, that's always assuming that great-uncle Harry didn't want to disappear for one or more legal or less than legal reasons and quite deliberately changed his name !!!……….

The Western Front Association, Registered Charity 298365 was founded to further interest in the period 1914-1918. Its main aim is to perpetuate the memory, courage and comradeship, of those, on all sides, who served their countries. It does not seek to glorify war, is non-political, and welcomes members of all ages.

Benefits of membership include:-
National and local meetings, where members can hear high quality lectures and meet with like minded people.

Publications Stand To! (an authoratitive journal of the period) and The Bulletin (our in house magazine) are sent to all members 3 times annually.

Members services including trench maps, a full range of commodities, and advice and help relating to historical and genealogical research.

For details of membership, please apply to
THE WESTERN FRONT ASSOCIATION
PO BOX 1914
KIDDERMINSTER WORCS. DY10 2WZ

http://www.westernfrontassociation.com

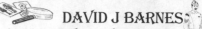

The Family and Local History Handbook
Local History Section
produced in collaboration with the

 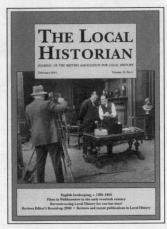 

Family and Local History
~ You can't have one without the other
Alan Crosby

I often give talks in this subject to organisations involved in both areas of research and I find that almost without exception people are excited by the challenge and the opportunities which linking these two themes can offer. It is in some ways obvious that the two subjects do go together, and are inextricably entwined. We cannot understand local communities - their origins, development and character - without giving the fullest possible attention to the people who made up those communities. After all, the farms and the fields, the streets and the houses, the industries and the churches, are all the product of untold human endeavour over the centuries. If we ignore the people we ignore the reason why, and that is absurd. Yet, at the same time, we cannot really understand the lives of individuals and the stories of families unless we consider their world, the environment they lived in and the lifestyles they enjoyed (or, maybe, didn't enjoy but rather suffered!).

How often, in researching your family history, have you wondered about what it was like for the people whose names, dates and brief historical record you have uncovered? What sort of housing did they live in, what clothes did they wear, what were their working conditions, what was the landscape which they knew from day to day and how did they fit into local society? Have you asked yourself why they moved from one place to another, what they felt about their fellow-citizens, how greater and lesser events impinged upon them, and what rituals and customs they encountered in birth, marriage and death. What sort of education was available to them - if any - and how did they tackle the burdens and oppressions of poverty, early and sudden death, natural disaster, illness and ill-health. What lightened their lives and what did they look forward to?

Local history can answer many such questions. It can set the lives of your forebears firmly in their proper context, helping to explain why they did what they did and what they met along life's path. All over the British Isles local history is a 'growth industry'. There are many hundreds of societies which are devoted to furthering the cause of local history - undertaking research, using original sources; holding lecture meetings and field visits; publishing the fruits of research and writing; campaigning for the extraordinarily rich heritage which is the legacy of the past and seeking to ensure its conservation and enhancement for future generations.

Local history is endlessly diverse, full of rewards and unexpected surprises, and something which is available and accessible to everybody. The British Association for Local History helps to further the cause of this fascinating and valuable subject. BALH promotes the study of, and interest in, our local heritage and history. All those who are interested in the history of the family will find that the study of local history can provide a much clearer and deeper understanding of where we came from and how it was in the past.

In collaboration with the British Association for Local History

Opocno, Czech Republic

Opočno. Partie ze zámeckého parku.

Other people's local history
Alan Crosby

Jurgów does not appear on most road maps. It is a small village in a landscape of remarkable beauty on the edge of the Tatra mountains 100 km south of Kraków. In a field near the centre of the village a cast-iron pillar about two feet high, shaped like an old-fashioned fire hydrant with the number 21 on its face, sticks up in the long grass. This oddity was erected about 120 years ago in the time of the Austro-Hungarian Empire, and it marks the old border between the kingdom of Hungary and the kingdom of Galicia (which was then an Austrian possession). Jurgów was part of Hungary, though ethnically it was (and still is) a mixture of Slovak, Polish and górale, the Polish name for the mountain people whose dialect and culture are distinct from those of all their neighbours. For centuries before that time Jurgów was part of Spis, a much fought-over, much disputed mountain duchy of uncertain status and allegiance. After 1918 the border, now separating the nation states of Poland and Czechoslovakia, shifted as the Poles pushed the frontier two kilometres further south. Henceforth the whole of Jurgów village lay in their territory and today if you go to the other end of the village, past the wooden huts which were until recently the summer dwellings of the shepherds, you find the border snaking through the woods, marked not by elegant cast iron pillars but by lumpy blocks of concrete.

What significance does the frontier have in such a place as this? Other people's local history is often so very different from ours. In Jurgów the ebbing and flowing of the tide of European history is

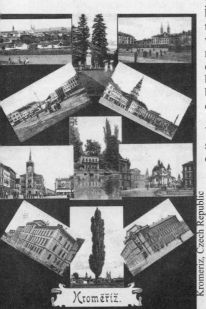

Kroměříž, Czech Republic

Kroměříž.

everywhere apparent. Much of its local history must be ascertained not in the equivalent of county record offices but in the papers of foreign ministries and interior ministries in Warsaw, Budapest, Vienna, Berlin, Moscow, Bratislava and Prague. Today you can have your picnic in Slovakia: only ten years ago it was Czechoslovak soil on which you ate your sheep's cheese and sausage. It makes the history of Much Binding in the Marsh seem somehow very simple, because there the framework is clear even if details need to be teased out. In Jurgów the framework itself - frontiers and national states – is evanescent and nebulous.

For the people of Jurgów, did these borders ever mean anything? Do they now? At the beautiful wooden church each Sunday the 9 o'clock mass is in Polish, the 11 o'clock in Slovak. Polish families have Slovak relatives. Slovak families live in Poland. They look both ways and they also look outwards to Warsaw, Germany and America. Boundaries are, to a considerable extent, no more than recently-drawn lines on a map, cutting across much older and deep-rooted patterns and identities.

Jurgów has a small and excellent folk museum and lovely wooden houses. People are very conscious of their heritage and proud of their identity. The little library has a display of old photographs of people seventy years ago, for whom the brilliantly-embroidered traditional costume was everyday wear. Pinned up, too, is a photocopy of a manuscript map of about 1900, written in Hungarian and showing the territory of Jurgów (in France it would be the pays) extending deep into what is now Slovakia. So the local history of this place is ambivalent. Remarkably, there are two published histories of the village (but is it remarkable? education and learning matter hugely here and twelve of the sons and daughters of Jurgów have academic doctorates). But one history is in Polish and written from a Polish perspective, the other in Slovak and written from the view of south of the border. The books might as well be about completely different places, so divergent are the stories they tell. In them a political and linguistic agenda is foremost. It was suggested to me that Jurgów really needs a local history written from the perspective of the community itself - not one which tries to pretend that the political and ethnic differences do not exist, for everybody knows they are there, but rather one which identifies and emphasises the common experience. Would that my command of either language was sufficient to embark upon that project, for the fieldwork would be truly delightful!

Local History News (November 2002)

THE LOCAL HISTORIAN
Journal of the British Association for Local History

Volume 29, appeared in February, May, August and December 1999, containing some 16 articles.
Once again, there was a considerable range in period, from the Anglo-Saxon (a study of sources for English beekeeping) to the almost contemporary (open-air schools in Birmingham, 1911-1970). Our contributors were representative of the wide variety of people who have an interest in local history, from the full-time teachers of the subject in further and higher education, to those who work as freelance researchers and writers; from retired professionals who have developed an interest in local history, to people who work in related fields, such as archivists and librarians. The geographical spread of contributions was restricted to the British Isles this year, although an article on the effects of the First World War on Scottish tourism did allow the author to mention the overseas destinations of Scottish travellers, and there was an Irish dimension in the discussion of the Irish in two London boroughs in 1851.

The nineteenth century still exercises a strong influence over the choice of research topics for local history, and this is reflected in two articles discussing aspects of enclosure (in Yorkshire and in Buckinghamshire), two making use of census material (the Irish in Hammersmith and Fulham, 1851; kinship ties in Sheffield, 1841–91), and another analysing retailing patterns (using Wolverhampton as a case study, and ranging in period from 1800 to 1950).

One very pleasing feature of the year was the use made of hitherto unrecognised forms of 'documentary' evidence. Scraps of clothing accompanying registration papers for foundlings led to a breakthrough in costume and textile history (infant fashion in the eighteenth century). An exploration and recording of those mysterious marks on the outside of letters, rather than the content of the letters themselves, gave an insight into postal routes and postal practice in Berkshire in the eighteenth century.
On a more traditional note, the potential of friendly society records for research was fully revealed, and we were challenged to think about the very nature and methodology of local history in an article which will probably continue to stir up debate well into the next year. The third Phillimore Lecture, published in November's issue, gave a masterly exposition of the current state of research and thinking into the patterns of trade and the role of towns in medieval England. We reviewed 27 books in some depth, and in his annual Round-up, the Reviews Editor surveyed some of the many publications issued to commemorate the 80th anniversary of the First World War.

www.thelocalhistorian.org
or details from BALHPO BOX 6549, Somersal Herbert, Ashbourne DE6 5WH

This book is essential reading for anybody who has written, is writing or might one day write local history. The earlier version of the book, *Writing Local History*, was first published in 1981 and became an instant classic. Now it has been totally rewritten, extended and updated so that local historians in the early 21st century, will have an even better reference book to help them produce work of the highest quality. David Dymond has spent most of a lifetime as a professional local historian, and he writes from that personal knowledge and experience. The contents of the book include an assessment of the present state of local history; the challenge of writing; choosing a subject; the search for sources; transcribing; analysing and assembling evidence; interpreting the evidence; writing techniques; the final draft; and numerous appendices which illustrate sample styles of local historians, show how to present information, and demonstrate good and bad practice in writing. It is, in short, an invaluable, stimulating and often entertaining exposition of how we should approach our subject.

180 pages   £12.00 (£10.00 for members)
from
BALH (P) PO BOX 6549, Somersal Herbert
Ashbourne DE6 5WH

Genuinely Authentic Imitation Replicas

Alan Crosby

What do we feel about the 'H-word'? I don't mean 'history' (a fine word in every sense) but rather that much more contentious, much more troublesome and much more recently-popular word, 'heritage'. Do we feel an instinctive reaction against anything so labelled. I know that nowadays I do, even though it was not so long ago that I was known to use this word in public without apparent shame. Thirty years ago, in my callow youth, I considered heritage to be a socially-acceptable term, one which could be used in polite company without a horrified silence falling upon the gathering, or in cynical company without provoking jeers of derision. But now it is a word which has (perhaps in a similar way to that erstwhile term of commendation, 'antiquarian') become unspeakable in the most literal sense. Now we have heritage bathroom suites, heritage duvet covers, heritage names for modern suburban houses, and heritage tablemats and thus we know that a once respectable word has fallen from grace in a dramatic fashion. To many people the very notion of heritage has come to mean not something which is true, genuine, authentic, real, cherishable, deep-rooted and permanent, but something which is fake, false, shallow, artificial and recent. 'Heritage' means new, in the pseudo-old style. It means 'too good to be true' and 'too new to be old'. It means that all the nastiness, dirtiness, scruffiness and roughness have been expunged. Heritage does not smell (except of the lavender and thyme in a heritage pillow for insomniacs); does not have disagreeable skin complaints; does not have rotten teeth; and does not die young of pitiful illness.

This tirade was provoked by reading an item in my local newspaper (I must say, with the fairness for which I am renowned, that it's become much better of late – more literate, more caustic and more sound in its views … that is, they coincide with mine more closely). This article was about a new 'village' [a.k.a. housing estate on a grand scale] which is being built midway between Preston and Chorley, on the vast site which was until recently one of Britain's largest Royal Ordnance factories, closed a few years ago in a 'downsizing' exercise by its privatised owners and now snapped up by property developers. Apart from a sixteenth century half-timbered manor house which miraculously survived marooned amid a sea of 1950s Cold War concrete, the entire site is being demolished, cleared and redeveloped in the vernacular styles favoured by our early 21st century developers. So far, I confess, so good.

One of the most important themes in the proposals was that the new village would be authentically 'Lancashire'. It would have instant heritage. Though appearances might deceive, I don't automatically quarrel even with this. I think that if architects and planners can escape from the 'little boxes made of ticky tacky' type of suburbia which fringes every town and city in the kingdom, all well and good. But I admit to finding it hard to believe my eyes when I read that the new village would include not only cobbled streets and terraced housing but also – prepare yourselves – a development of expensive apartments in a building which would be [though completely new and built from scratch] designed to look like a Victorian cotton mill which had been converted into apartments. What a strange world. In Lancashire, even now, we have numerous abandoned or disused cotton mills. There is a limit to the number of DIY warehouses, craft centres and small industrial units into which they can be converted. There are towns which desperately want some realistic and practical solution to the problem of what to do with these monumental, magnificent and marvellous buildings, redundant and purposeless but – quite often – Grade II* listed. But halfway between Preston and Chorley, in a place which has never had a cotton mill, a fake mill is to be built ready-converted into flats to produce the 'authentic' Lancashire feel. So it is, I suppose, early 1980s heritage which is being created … for that was when the conversion of industrial buildings into des. res. lofts and apartments began with a vengeance (and I say at once that that was and is a very good thing too) – but can't architects devise new buildings which are visually-appealing, practical for habitation, and appropriate to the context? I shake my wise old head at the folly of my fellow man and wonder whatever the heritage theme may produce next.

Local History News (February 2003)

THERE'S BEEN A TERRIBLE MISTAKE–THE IMPOVERISHED VICTORIAN ORPHAN WAS ONLY A FEATURE OF THE SHOW HOME….

HERITAGE – HOMES –

It really is good to talk

Alan Crosby

I wrote two years ago about my experiences talking to the Hell and District Local History Society. Now I must put the record straight and describe its opposite number, a society based in two small villages just north-east of Wigan. They will know which society I mean! It was, I think, one of the most enjoyable evenings I've ever spent in that idiosyncratic part of my existence which is concerned with 'giving talks'. I drove, on a February night, down the M61. The sky was brilliantly clear, though it was blowing a fierce gale. The myriad lights of the old milltowns on the Pennine foothills and of the stone-built farmhouses higher on the slopes were glittering and twinkling. These days you can see Lancashire in all its glory, because the smoke and the grime of mills and mines have long gone. Having been given admirably clear directions, I arrived at the church hall with no trouble (handily, it was next to the other local landmark, the pub … as befits an ex-pit village) and parked in a car park where the wind lashed the trees almost double – it is close to the summit of the highest hill for miles around, and the four winds blow with considerable vigour. At the corner of the car park I was met by the secretary who, gale-blasted but warmly-wrapped, had been waiting for me. She welcomed me and long before I'd gone into the building had asked if I would like a cup of tea. Very civilised and considerate. I would, it came instantly, and it was exactly right (fairly strong, very little milk, no sugar – useful information that if you ever ask me to talk to your society: I loathe milky tea).

And it got better. The hall was packed, with people who seemed anxious to hear what I said, and among the audience was an old acquaintance not seen for a good few years, with whom it was a pleasure to exchange news of goings-on and mutual friends. By a happy chance it was the evening on which the Great News had been broken to the eager world. I refer to the most important event of 2002, the granting of city status to the most excellent town of Preston. Several people, I felt most generously seeing that they live in a rival borough, congratulated me and my adopted place. Nobody expressed stupefaction or incredulity that Proud Preston should have been so honoured: all seemed, quite reasonably, to feel that it was an obvious and richly-deserved choice. The atmosphere was clearly propitious to a successful and entertaining evening. Then I looked down and … mirabile

dictu … the table in front of me was thickly piled with my own works! There were copies of my books (including one which belonged to the Society's library and which I was asked to sign). There were also several recent issues of The Local Historian and Local History News. And they were not there just for show, not spread out merely to flatter – though I am, I confess, susceptible to such gestures - for it emerged that my lament about the Hell and District Local History Society had been read aloud to a meeting the previous year. I was able to assure this entirely different Society, most warmly, that the article was not aimed at them or their ilk!

The room was warm, well-lit and comfortable, not so large that there were echoing draughty spaces, and not so small that people were sitting on each other's knees. I gave my talk (with fresh water in a clean glass helpfully provided) and the response was similarly rewarding: well-considered and informed questions, genuine interest, much evidence that the audience had listened, absorbed and thought about what I had to say. For my part, there was a real pleasure in sharing the subject and seeing and hearing the favourable response. I drove back feeling very content, because everything that I wanted had been achieved. A couple of weeks later came a delightful thank-you letter, expressing the general feeling that the evening had been much enjoyed and appreciated by the members of the Society, and hoping that I would come to visit again before long. I will, naturally, do so!

Local History News (November 2002)

It's for my Dad

Alan Crosby

Late night shopping in Warrington four weeks before Christmas. A strong icy wind whips the fresh smell of Persil across town from the Lever Brothers works at Bank Quay. In W.H. Smith, a table has been set up next to Gifts For Her and Gifts For Him. I confess that I wouldn't give Her any of them and hope that She won't give Me any of them either, but I am there to sign copies of my latest book, a history of the town which has just been published. The table is laden with copies of this impressive, superbly illustrated, meticulously researched and beautifully produced volume which, at £16.99, is a real bargain. 'Worth every penny', as I told a number of those who hovered round the table unable to make up their minds. As a veteran of quite a few signing campaigns I know the strategy. NEVER look people directly in the eye when they come into the shop. They turn away embarrassed. NEVER speak until they come near: don't call across 'Why don't you come and buy this brilliant book rather than that rubbish by Jeffrey Archer'. NEVER unscrew the top of the pen and lick lips in eager anticipation of another sale. NEVER appear bored, look at watch, twiddle thumbs ... ALWAYS seem to be a little busy – tidy a pile of books, make a note on a pad, leaf through the book as though you'd never seen it before. Appear relaxed. And when people do come near, never seem too pushy. If they don't want the book in the end, smile and imply that they've made the right decision, even though your royalties depend on them doing the opposite.

Most people were aware of the book already, having read about it in the local paper or seen the signs in the shop. They are curious to know how long it took – in this case, the work was spread over two and a half years – and whether it was difficult. That's always a hard one to answer – say 'yes' and you imply that you aren't a skilled researcher and writer, say 'no' and you are being boastful. My truthful reply was that the hardest part was cutting it down to 70,000 words: I suggested that ideally it would have been a three-volume set.

It's a great opportunity to observe another aspect of local history. We all want our books to succeed, but how many times in meetings with publishers have I been asked 'Who's going to buy this book'? Signing sessions are a way to find out. The person most likely to be on the receiving end is called 'Dad'. He doesn't do the buying – he's the one for whom the buying is done. People of all sorts and just about all ages have Dads, the victims who, all unknowing of their fate, are destined to receive the latest Crosby in gift-wrapping. Few, apparently, have Mums in a similar position, but of course Mums do the Christmas shopping. Few people declared that the History of Warrington was destined for themselves - not long before Christmas, it seems selfish to buy for oneself - but I warmed especially to two purchasers. One lady picked up a copy of the book and said that it was for Dad. Then she flicked through it more carefully and said 'No, on second thoughts I'll keep it for myself'. I expect Dad got socks. And a young man stared long and hard at the book on a rack near the tills [it was wall to wall Crosby], bought a magazine, went away, returned half an hour later with his girlfriend, picked up a copy of the book, and came hesitantly towards me. He had an earring and spiky hair. According to my reading of the situation he wasn't the usual type of local history purchaser, so I decided that he, too, must be the proud owner of a Dad. He was. Would I sign it? Of course, with great pleasure. But as he was moving away he said, 'I'm going to read it myself as well, it looks very good, I'm really interested in this sort of thing'. He had come out as a closet local historian, a subject which at his time in life conspicuously lacked the correct image ... but I wouldn't be at all surprised if in fifteen years time he isn't a leading light in the local history and archaeological society. Though maybe without the spiky hair!

Local History News February 2003

Bartholomew's Half-Inch Sheet 14
Alan Crosby

When I was a child living in Surrey we would visit my grandparents in Manchester once or twice a year. Sometimes we were picked up straight from school in the secondhand Ford Anglia - now so chic, thanks to Harry Potter, and ours was turquoise too - and drive up through the Midlands and Derbyshire. There were no motorways as yet, or at least they weren't in the right places, but given the fact that Dad once drove a Civil Service colleague from London to Manchester and the besuited companion had to get out of the car TO OPEN A GATE the delights of the motorway would not have been ours anyway. Indeed, using A-roads was for Dad a matter of shame. On a map he had drawn a straight line between our house and grandma's house, then transferred that alignment to his trusty set of Bartholomew's half-inch maps and simply followed any road, preferably yellow, that closely adhered to the line. So our journeys involved a string of for us very familiar names, which were highly unfamiliar to just about anybody else we knew. It was not an AA approved strip-map route, but one devised from careful study of those wonderful maps. He loved them and I love them still, for they taught me more about the geography and local history of these islands than any textbook ever did. Their layer colouring gave me an enduring three-dimensional sense of British topography, their county boundaries were an inspiration. Who could fail to be fascinated by the tortuous windings of the Worcestershire and Gloucestershire border past Broadway and Willersey and Weston sub Edge, though I now know that this was simple compared with the detached fragments which peppered the earlier editions of the sheet? And I always liked the bright blue, red and black covers proudly bearing the legend 'By appointment to the late King George V'. Why was he late if he had a Bartholomew's map to guide him?

The route to Manchester is engraved on my memory and I could drive it today without a map though it's almost forty years since we went that way. Sometimes I recite the place-names to myself … Twyford, Wargrave, Henley, Bix Bottom and Pishill (a combination greatly loved by my earthily-humoured father), Watlington and Wheatley, Stanton St John and Islip, Upper Heyford, Kenilworth (especially memorable for the deep ford on the main road beside the great castle), Stonebridge Roundabout, Lichfield, Yoxall, Ashbourne, Parsley Hay and Buxton, fabled town where my

paternal grandmother had lived, where Dad grew up, and for which he felt an intense longing all the rest of his days. Then down towards Manchester, as strings of streetlights lined the A6 and the names like a litany were chanted. Whaley Bridge, Disley, High Lane, Hazel Grove. By now, even in the long warm summer evenings, darkness would have fallen and sleep was probably upon us. Stockport, Heaton Norris, Levenshulme … those names are associated with heavy eyelids.

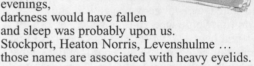

From my shelf I take down Bartholomew's Sheet 14 Oxford, the very copy on which I used to follow our route as I sat in the back of the car. It still has my pencil lines along the country roads. The map is badly frayed and falling apart on the folds (even the linen backing 'went' after serious use) but on it I can read the landscape of my childhood journeys, passing through what now seems a different world. There is no M40, the Oxford ring road is only half finished, Winston Churchill has not yet been buried at Bladon, steam trains still thunder along the old Great Central line from Aylesbury through Quainton Road and Calvert and Finmere and Helmdon, country branch lines thread the fawns and browns of the Cotswolds, Milton Keynes is a tiny village on an uncoloured lane near the little town of Bletchley, and the notion that one day I would be a student at that university city in the middle of the map is in nobody's imagination, for I am at junior school and on the back of the map I've just done my arithmetic in pencil. It is still there: $6/6 \times 7 = 45/6 - 7/6 = 38/0$. That's history too, and I even got it right!

Local History News (May 2003)

Country Church
Alan Crosby

Church
of
St Andrew
Storgursey

We visited Stogursey, in the forgotten flat country between the Quantock Hills and Bridgwater Bay. Stoke Courcy … a failed Norman borough, dusty and quiet. Very French: the erstwhile marketplace ought to have had a lively game of boules in progress, but this was Somerset, not Saumur. Down a scruffy lane, not tarted up for the photographers, and past the almshouses, malthouse, restored village pound, and mill (riotously overgrown with weeds even in April, but with the remnants of the great wheel and the dry course of the leat visible) is the enchanting and improbable cottage which in the seventeenth century was converted from the remains of the castle gatehouse. There is the complete circle of the moat, the rippling streams which feed it, the hummocky daisy-studded grass of the outer bailey, all fringed by the glorious red soil of Somerset (and plenty of sticky red mud too).

At the other end of the village street is the church of St. Andrew, painted a striking creamy-white, and very unEnglish when viewed past the burgage plots of the medieval borough. Its colouring draws attention to what is by anyone's criteria a remarkable building. Entering through the west door you at first might think 'Hmm, disappointing', for the nave – white plaster and regular pews – seems rather ordinary (fifteenth century, restored in the 1820s … though that itself is unusual). But then you notice the marvellous pristine beauty of the Norman arch in front of the crossing, fresh and crisp as when it was carved nine centuries ago, for this is an early medieval priory church and architecturally quite out of the ordinary. And moving closer, you see the other arches of the crossing, and the strange wide choir, all perfect and immaculate Norman work.

You investigate further. This is a proper English country church, so a range of literature is on sale - a short guide, a leaflet about the parish, and a substantial booklet giving plenty of information on the history of the building at only £3.50. Read on … observe … look around and see what the guidebook says and what it doesn't tell you. There is a superb collection of late seventeenth and eighteenth century monuments, with florid and laudatory inscriptions to the members of the Palmer family (MPs for the borough of Bridgwater, the city of Wells, the county of Somerset, devoted husbands, loving fathers, dedicated servants of the nation, incorruptible, admired, examples to others).

Many churches have such memorials, but how many have, in the most prominent place on the floor just in front of the altar, anything like the great stone slab which at Stogursey records that there 'lyeth the body of James Morgan … servant to Nathaniell Palmer esq. & Thomas Palmer esq. his son 39 years & behav'd himself with so great honesty & fidelity that his master caus'd this stone to be plac'd over him that his virtues might be remember'd after his death & his example recommended to Posterity'? James died in 1727 aged 54. He had gone to serve the Palmers at Fairfield when 15 and never left. A footnote engraved beneath this text tells us that buried there also is Elizabeth Griffin, another servant to the Palmers, who died in 1756 aged 78. The Palmers, those MPs and worthies, are commemorated in the side chapel, their servants in the most honoured place of all. The rest of the parish lie, in dignity but less prominence, not only below the masters but also below the servants of the great house. Thus perhaps is eighteenth century social stratification exemplified and immortalised.

Down in the nave stand the two great painted wooden boards, early nineteenth century in date, which were carried in parish processions by the members of the Stogursey Friendly Society. 'Speed The Plough', urges the painted motto of one, above a picture of the goddess Ceres amid the corn – a touch of incongruity in this Christian church, nice evidence of the way classical learning and inspiration slid into the corners of the land two hundred years ago. But the incongruity of this is a mere nothing compared with the strangest feature of all. The body of the oldest inhabitant of Stogursey is visible for all to see, on the floor of the north transept. To be strictly accurate, the oldest inhabitant is part of the floor, for he (or possibly she) is the complete fossil skeleton of an ichthyosaurus, 200 million years old, brought to the church after the Second World War set in a great slab of blue lias. A fascinating place – we drove away pondering on the idiosyncrasy and charm of the English country church, the social history which it tells, and the pleasure of discovery.

Local History News (August 2002)

Heritage Revisited
Alan Crosby

Sometime ago in *Local History News* I wrote about the misuse of the term 'heritage' and the strange tale of a fake cotton mill converted to flats in a new village in mid-Lancashire. The article produced a larger postbag than any other in the decade during which I've been writing these short items in Local History News. Clearly the H-word touches a very raw nerve in a very large number of people. Though the use of the word is recent, the condemnation of a spurious oldness is far from confined to our present age. Ivor Slocombe sent me a copy of a Punch cartoon from the 1930s, in which a landed-gentleman-cum-property-developer type and his architect stand in front of some half-erected 'rustic cottages' in a newly-built village.

A toothless yokel asks them if they need the services of a village idiot. Clearly, cynicism about property developers, as well as heritage, goes back many decades. Another reader, Derek West, noted that having visited the Tate Modern in Southwark (for which see the article by Stephen Murray in *The Local Historian* May 2003), and being familiar with the old Southwark, which was run-down and scruffy with a lot of warehouses, he went to an exhibition of photographs of the new Southwark. This showed that (as with my Lancashire pseudo-cotton mill) completely new imitation warehouses had been built in what the exhibition rather wittily called the 'faux warehouse' style.

I'M NONE TOO HAPPY WITH THE NEW COUPLE AT No 24. THEY HAVEN'T TUGGED THEIR FORELOCKS SINCE THEY MOVED IN

My own local example I had believed to be, if not unique, at least a remarkable example of the genre. But the Southwark examples have the benefit of a joky yet probably, before long, seriously accepted label. Early English ... Gothic Revival ... Art Deco ... Faux Warehouse. And even the local mid-Lancashire 'faux cotton mill' case was left far behind by an advertisement which appeared only a couple of weeks ago in the property supplement of the very same local newspaper. This described a new development some three miles up the road from

Oxford from Abingdon Road

the forthcoming imitation mill, and is I think even more extraordinary. It is a cluster of new houses, naturally all of them with en-suite everythings, which is 'designed to resemble converted farm buildings, including a mill, granary, farmhouse, haylofts, manor house and workers' cottages'. I relish the instant class distinctions which all this will involve. When the new residents move in, the occupants of the imitation manor house will of course shun the company of the poor humble folk living in the workers' cottages, while they in turn will regard with contempt the dregs of society living in the haylofts. The cash balance will matter for nothing: 'No Celia darling, absolutely not. We can't invite them for drinks, they live in the barn, what would Henry and Jennifer in the manor house think'? By the way, has anybody ever seen a bathroom, kitchen dining area and master bedroom in a hayloft? Will hay be included as a compulsory design element? I suppose that the supermarkets designed to look like half-timbered or tile-hung farmhouses and the DIY warehouses with Georgian columns are a more familiar example of this type of pastiche, but isn't it all going a little too far? And, looking at the design, I fail to recognise a single characteristic of the mid-Lancashire solid gritstone farm buildings. I might almost suspect,

doubtless unreasonably, that the elevations were dreamed up by some architect down in London from a picture of an East Anglian village.

Meanwhile, at Upper Heyford in Oxfordshire a different sort of heritage is being debated. The famous nuclear airbase, taken over by the US Air Force in 1950, was closed in 1994 and plans are afoot to build a new village on the site. Campaigners from the Oxfordshire Trust for Contemporary History, among others, argue that the base fully merits protection because it is the last surviving example of a Cold War airbase, where nine bombers loaded were warheads were kept on constant stand-by, ready to take off at three minutes' notice. That, they suggest, was a key phase in English history and deserves to be recognised. A sympathetic representative from English Heritage considered that 'the sheer scale and bare functionality of the structures can illustrate … in a way that no document can, the reality of the struggle against Soviet communism'. Now that is real heritage. I think, though it is certainly not beautiful or quaint. But how many years before we're being offered 'Nuclear Bunker' heritage homes, 'Warhead' bathroom suites, or 'Weapons of Mass Destruction' commemorative plates? Not many, I fear.

Local History News May 2003

The Amateur Historian and The Local Historian: some thoughts after fifty years

Alan Crosby

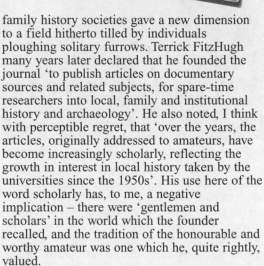

In August 2002 *The Local Historian* reached its fiftieth birthday, as good a moment as any to reflect on half a century of development, change and (dangerous word) progress. I had recently taken over as editor, following a line of distinguished predecessors who include two very well-known local historians, Lionel Munby and David Dymond. They, whose editorship together spanned 27 years from 1955, presided over an expansion from a small homespun publication to a substantial, authoritative and professional journal, a change which paralleled the development of the subject itself. In 1952 Terrick FitzHugh launched a new and experimental publication which he entitled *The Amateur Historian*. The title and the subject were both significant. Like many people in the past half-century (including me) Terrick FitzHugh came to local history from family history, though that term was rarely used in the early 1950s. The essentially amateur nature of the research involved in such pursuits was exemplified by the title of his new project, though he was himself a professional genealogical researcher and was later to be a founder member of the Association of Genealogists and Record Agents. The development of his thoughts was summed up when he wrote of local history that 'an ancestor's home town or village as it was in his lifetime is one context into which the family historian needs to set him', and this interlinking of the two areas of study remained central to his perception of both. In this Terrick FitzHugh was a pioneer, helping to give family history a more rounded and less elitist structure, and shifting its emphasis from the drawing-up of pedigrees and the mere collecting of facts towards the more three-dimensional approach which now characterises the work of many family historians. I fear that the other side of that coin, whereby the past should be populated by real human beings, is still not acknowledged by some local historians.

The early issues of the new journal were aimed at amateurs seeking to investigate in greater depth and to exploit the exciting range of new resources becoming available as county record offices were established, publishing and record societies expanded their activities, and local and family history societies gave a new dimension to a field hitherto tilled by individuals ploughing solitary furrows. Terrick FitzHugh many years later declared that he founded the journal 'to publish articles on documentary sources and related subjects, for spare-time researchers into local, family and institutional history and archaeology'. He also noted, I think with perceptible regret, that 'over the years, the articles, originally addressed to amateurs, have become increasingly scholarly, reflecting the growth in interest in local history taken by the universities since the 1950s'. His use here of the word scholarly has, to me, a negative implication – there were 'gentlemen and scholars' in the world which the founder recalled, and the tradition of the honourable and worthy amateur was one which he, quite rightly, valued.

In this article I consider the way in which local history as it is perceived and practiced has been reflected in the content of the journal. Until the end of the 1950s it drew its readership and its material to a substantial extent from the last generation of those antiquarian-historians so instrumental in moulding local and family history from the mid-nineteenth century onwards. This catchment determined its early character. Any reading of the first volume demonstrates the extraordinary diversity of the interests of these local historians half a century ago. Many of them were Victorian, born in the 1870s and 1880s, and their outlook on local history is redolent of that age. They wrote and asked (in politely-phrased, casually-interested queries) about everything and anything from the history of horseshoes, via inn signs and milestones, to maps, mills and medicines. Their interests were diverse, eclectic and, to a later generation, often dilettante and even eccentric. That world changed, beyond their recognition,

IT'S NOT ALL BAD NEWS—IN FIFTY YEARS YOU'LL BE A FREE MAN....

The standards of research and scholarship, quality of the text, and intellectual approach to the subject all bear the hallmarks of a vastly-improved education system and of the progress of local history itself.

We can readily enumerate some aspects of this progress: the employment of accurate referencing and other technical standards; the infinitely more extensive use of primary sources; serious attempts to provide comparison with other areas and periods; the notion of context for case-studies; and the clearer understanding of the significance of geographical variation and diversity. Not all regions or localities have the same experience and local history is not national history broken up into small chunks. Indeed, exactly the opposite could convincingly be proposed: much of national history is the small chunks of local history put together or aggregated. This lesson is one which has been widely-learned and the work of local historians is greatly improved as a result. I would argue, too, that the work of mainstream historians is also improved by the recognition of this reality, which gives a greater prominence to the local experience.

and local history was destined to expand, to become more inclusive (today's fashionable term) and to have different aspirations and ambitions. The notion of increased academic rigour emerged, with new methodologies and ideas about content borrowed or absorbed from mainstream history as well as from disciplines such as geography and archaeology. This was in part a response to the changing character of history itself. The older tradition of political and constitutional history had few points of close contact with other academic disciplines, but the newly-emergent realms of social history and economic history, coming into their own in the 1920s, had a more obvious relationship. History began to be pertinent to the lives and experiences not just of the elite groups, but of all people in the past.

By the early 1950s a full generation of historians had benefited from these new perspectives, and their work fed the evolving sub-discipline of local history. Good modern local history, with its new academic principles and frameworks, could now be contrasted with the older approach, for which antiquarian, a word once so proudly borne and loudly proclaimed, became the pejorative catch-all term of scathing abuse or contempt. The antiquarians fascinate me as individuals and their often underemphasised role in the evolving culture of history, heritage, and conservation is a subject of special interest in my own work, but I have no doubts about the dramatic improvement in the quality of local history in the fifty years since 'antiquarianism' waned. Indeed, I am struck by the way that articles submitted by 'amateur' local historians today are, almost without exception, incomparably better than those produced by the gentlemen-antiquarians (and indeed many of the professionals) of the past.

Another outstanding change evident during the first decade of *The Amateur Historian* was the fundamental revolution in the accessibility of sources. It is impossible to overstate the importance of this change, about which we are now so blasé. Without county record offices and the opportunities to use the primary sources relating to our localities, not only would local history as we know it scarcely be possible (as would family history in its modern sense) but many aspects of mainstream history would also be impossible. It is not usually acceptable for mainstream historians to acknowledge that much of their work is in fact local history, but the case studies of local circumstances used to illustrate general conclusions are legion. Most social and economic historians are, in reality and though they would deny it if challenged, local historians as well. Without access to local sources, who could write about nineteenth-century labour history? Could the economic and social structure of port towns be analysed without case studies of Merseyside or Tyneside? How could the growth of the English leisure industry be understood without reference to individual seaside resorts? Almost every aspect of social and economic history depends very heavily upon local sources and studies - the role of women in the eighteenth-century, the enclosure movement, monasticism and its economic and landscape significance … the list is endless and all of it involves an understanding of the local dimension. Local history often has a bad image among 'academic' historians. Some observers argue that the widespread use of terms such as 'community' or 'micro-history' is an attempt to conceal the reality – that many historians who do local history won't admit it in so many words.

Where would our history as a whole be without probate records, parish registers, local taxation returns, family and estate papers, business records, quarter sessions records, poor law papers, churchwardens' accounts, and all the other local archival resources which are now available to us all? Without county record offices some historians, with patrician connections and an entrée to the great houses, would be able to research on such records, and political and constitutional historians would get by using the PRO, but what of the rest? In the past seventy years we have been uniquely privileged to have had access to the documentary heritage of our country, and the growth of local history has been made possible primarily by this new opportunity. Nobody reading the first volume of *The Amateur Historian*, and seeing the uncertainty of approach and ignorance of sources which were the lot of the local historian fifty years ago, could fail to be impressed by our good fortune. By the mid-1960s the pages of *The Amateur Historian* were reflecting this new world. The research was more disciplined, structured and directed. The writing was less anecdotal and chatty, more focused and analytical. The length of articles grew rapidly. Instead of the early style - 'a little gentle observation on …' - the new way involved a contextual introduction, a descriptive middle, and an analytical end. The sense of opening the treasure chest was emphasised by the very large number of articles which talked of new sources to be exploited, introducing readers for the first time to archival material which now seems commonplace but was then seen with completely fresh eyes, wide open with excitement at the potential on offer: inventories, maps and plans, inquisitions post mortem, papers from the parish chest, and the records of coal companies and canals. Reading through these articles I am conscious time and again of the palpable sense of pioneering which prevailed at that time. It is sometimes a moving experience to read the words of people who were later famous (or, given that it is even now only forty years ago, still are famous!) when they wrote, sometimes hesitantly, of their ventures into archives new.

Winter 1944

As articles grew longer, fewer could be printed in each issue. 'Introductions to sources' and 'beginner's guides to new methodologies' started to influence the work being done. Courses multiplied and the proportion of substantial case-studies increased rapidly. Projects, dissertations and extended essays began to offer, as they still do, a rich source of articles for journals such as mine. Today, the great majority of articles are either case-studies, or present general findings through the medium of one or two detailed examples. It might be argued, though incorrectly in my view, that introductions and overviews are now unnecessary. If the subject were static (if no new sources appeared, no reassessments of existing sources took place, and no new interpretations and revisions of wider historical trends and processes ever happened) there would logically come a point at which all local history would simply be case-studies. But quite clearly, none of those circumstances actually applies. There are always new sources to be discovered, existing ones to be reworked, and new techniques and methods to be adopted. More importantly, history of any sort is always fluid, shifting and imprecise. There are always new perspectives, alternative explanations, and debates about themes and issues. It is always cumulative, never final. That is why history is so exciting – there are no certainties, no tedious predictabilities.

The problem for some readers was that these necessary and important changes, and the introduction of debate, reassessment and higher standards of research, began to reinforce the distinction between 'amateur' and 'professional', the former term being displayed in the original title of the journal, the latter a label for an entirely different realm. In the mid-1950s began a Great Debate which has continued on and off for forty years. What, the protagonists argued, should be the respective roles, approaches,

Covent Garden, London 1945

perspectives and (though they do not use this word) rights of the amateur and the professional in local history? Where is the frontier between the one kingdom and the other? And what of those who blur the boundaries between the two categories, the academically-trained non-professionals who have become so much more numerous with the proliferation of certificate and diploma courses, MAs and similar qualifications? In the 1960s, as universities expanded, higher education became available to unprecedented numbers of people and adult education to even more. The demarcation between amateur and professional, never clear, is now gone. In its place is a continuum of experience and aspiration which renders the divisions redundant.

Local history, in maturing and developing, acquired (as do all academic subjects) a theoretical dimension. To some today it has still not created enough of this framework of theory, to others it has developed too much. Some of us argue that it has therefore acquired just about the right level of principle and conceptual framework – enough to give it sound academic rigour, not so much as to divorce it from the realities of the world which it studies and the people, past and present, who are at the very heart of everything. One of the most heated debates carried on in the pages of the journal centred on definitions and boundaries. The seemingly-insoluble argument over the meaning of local, and the relationship between local, regional and national (with those sophisticated or semantic variants such as sub-regional and community) occupied much space, though with no conclusive result. It was exactly right that these debates should have been aired in The Local Historian, for undoubtedly the subject had hitherto lacked any intellectual framework. Debate can stimulate improvement and fresh perspectives, and these discussions surely did lead to the enhancement of much local history research and writing. It is possible that a sense

of true perspective was occasionally lacking – after all, to many people history itself is irrelevant and unimportant – and sometimes the debate seemed to destined to become a storm in a teacup. Indeed, by the early 1980s the 'boundaries' argument had largely subsided. The issues remained central to local history, but within our pages the controversy was quiescent. Maybe local history had reached another, less quarrelsome, phase … or were the doughty fighters of old were now less pugilistic, their hot blood cooled with age and time?

If you read, as I have, each article in more or less chronological progression, one conclusions to be drawn is that the subjects which local historians find interesting have changed. The role of fashion is powerful. In history departments of British universities today, some undergraduate courses, such as those on the Holocaust and Vietnam, are likely to be massively oversubscribed whereas, for example, medieval history is often much less popular. Local historians contributing to this journal seem to have had similarly changing preferences. Some subjects are conspicuous by their absence. In fifty years we have had almost nothing on theatre and drama, or their role in popular leisure and culture, though a few articles on film and cinema have appeared. There has been very little on music, song and dance, dialects, or regional and vernacular literature. Food and drink, so central to the lives of every human being and so deeply-rooted in local and regional culture, have been barely mentioned except, early on, in the context of breweries. Clothing and costume have received rather more coverage, especially in recent years but, given their centrality not only as 'what people wear' but also as dimensions to trades, crafts, and employment, the attention is less than might be expected. Other themes for which coverage is relatively limited include landscape history and architecture, transport history and the local impact of transport change, environmental history and the conservation movement [as contrasted with 'heritage']. Archaeology was intended by Terrick FitzHugh to be one of the main subjects covered by his journal, but since 1952 it has become a highly-specialised and scientific discipline in its own right, and now rarely appears in the pages of The Local Historian. Sometimes quite specific changes can be identified: in the 1960s and 1970s there was a good deal on vernacular architecture, whereas today this is quite rare. Subjects notably popular in the past decade or so include surnames (one of the most perennial of all topics), tourism and the resort towns, various perspectives on poverty and the Poor Law, the history of aspects of education, migration, military history in various guises including war

Rural Blacksmith's Shop 1946

acknowledge) the history of very recent times. Those on medieval themes or using medieval sources are unusual and almost always by, or guided by, 'professionals'. The sixteenth and seventeenth centuries are seemingly of relatively little interest to potential contributors, despite their popular appeal – the romantic glitter of 'Tudors and Stuarts' is not, apparently, matched by work on the local

memorials and, less expectedly, an abiding interest in the facets and divisions of religion.

The Amateur Historian was the first journal in the field, and inevitably others have appeared to parallel its role. Some have acquired a similarly authoritative and permanent place – I think, for example, of *Local Population Studies*, the key journal for anybody interested in demography and the sources available for research in this important area. *The Local History Magazine* is perhaps more publicly a competitor, but the two journals are very different in style, approach and the markets they serve: neither suffers from the existence of the other. There are also many specialised journals whose scope is limited to particular aspects of historical research and investigation. These are often based in mainstream history or related disciplines, but have much that is essential reading for any local historian whose work touches their themes – *Agricultural History Review*, the *Journal of Historical Geography* or the *Journal of Ecclesiastical History*, to name but a few of many dozens. Some, at least, of the apparent gaps in the coverage of *The Local Historian* can be explained by the existence of alternative outlets for publication.

A crucial change in the last thirty years has been immense growth in awareness of the history of the present. When the journal began in 1952 there were almost no articles on the later nineteenth century, let alone the twentieth. It is clear that for most local historians then, real history ended in about 1850. Today, in contrast, the majority of articles submitted for consideration deal with twentieth-century subjects and a good many embrace (or at least

dimension among our contributors. Why is this? One factor, no doubt, is that twentieth century sources present few technical problems for the researcher (though they impose numerous analytical and interpretational challenges), whereas palaeography, Latin, dialect and terminology, unfamiliar context and uncertain survival make pre-1800 material off-putting and alarming to many local historians. The twentieth century is probably (and wrongly) perceived as easy.

Thus, our own times predominate, and the influence of the new sub-divisions of mainstream history is also becoming clear. Gratifyingly, we have had a number of articles in recent years on the history of ethnic communities, with a pleasing range of subjects, including Somali seamen in the north-east, Indians in Leicester, and Jewish communities in inter-war Glasgow. There has also been a good range of material concerned with women's history or (I draw a deliberate distinction) the history of women. The history of wartime (and especially the Second World War) has produced a healthy crop of articles of late, reflecting its very high profile in wider historical circles and contemporary 'popular history' in the media. When our contributors emphasise that local history continues right up to the minute that you read this article, and add a 1990s dimension to their work, some readers are dismayed. It is, however, the perfect and unchallengeable counter-argument to those who suggest that local history is 'antiquarian'. If this journal can deal with IRA murals in the Bogside in the 1980s and 1990s, or with the Bankside power station up to its conversion into Tate Modern, the label antiquarian is manifestly inappropriate.

There is one other change, the impact of which is exceptional, that has transformed all aspects of our subject and will continue to do so. This is – inevitably perhaps – the technological revolution brought about by computers. In the late 1970s the first hesitant references to computing appeared in the journal, and by the mid-1980s these were a standard feature. It is impossible to overstate the significance of computers, and for many of us it is equally impossible to imagine how we would fare without them. David Dymond recalls how *The Local Historian* in the late 1970s was still typeset with hot metal, and he as editor had to cut up galley proofs and paste-up each issue by hand. This was more or less how a publication would have been prepared in 1882, and in essence in 1782 as well. In 2002 the text of *The Local Historian* is e-mailed to the *printe*r, and I change the details up to the last minute (sometimes beyond!), spellchecking and correlating and footnoting and referencing all at the touch of a button. I can check bibliographical details over the internet, draw maps and produce diagrams, scan in pictures and produce all manner of special fonts and fancy effects. Back in 1982 all that was but a dream or nightmare.

The computer has facilitated all sorts of changes to research and the gathering of data, as well as the analysis and assessment of material. The pages of *The Local Historian* include a growing number of articles in which computer analysis of data is central. By the mid-1990s the attention given to computing had been sharply reorientated. Twenty years ago articles tended to introduce the idea of the computer itself, but now of course that is 'understood' – it is the subtle and sophisticated methodology which is explained. Computers themselves are so commonplace that they require no explanation. However, the view that a computer is a means to an end, not the end in itself, has become more widespread. A recognition of their limitations as well as their potential is now acknowledged. Further, many local historians (like others in the field of history) have concluded that statistical analysis in their subject presents genuine problems, as well as exciting opportunities, because of imperfections in the data or because quantitative data is simply non-existent.

What does the future hold? *The Local Historian*, fifty years old and stronger than ever before, now has an established reputation. It must continue to reflect the realities of local history. The balance of articles will continue to be representative of what is being researched and written by amateurs, students on local courses, and professionals throughout the British Isles. Historical fashions will also change, the early twenty-first century will soon be 'new history', and some older subjects will regain their popularity. But what is certain, I think, is that local history itself is here to stay and that it will, with family history, its non-identical twin, represent a major leisure pursuit as well as an academic discipline. As I have argued elsewhere, this is a strength, not (as some would see it) a weakness, and the great advantage of *The Local Historian* will continue to be apparent: that it is a serious yet accessible, academic yet approachable, publication. Terrick FitzHugh's project of 1952 was a shot in the dark, but it hit the target. The journal, and now the organisation which is its parent, both flourish. To be its editor is a great pleasure. It is also a great privilege.

This is an edited version of an article which first appeared in *The Local Historian* Vol.32 No.3 August 2002

Last Judgement

Alan Crosby

Why is sin so enjoyable? You need not answer if you don't want to. I've just returned from leading a University of Liverpool Centre for Continuing Education study tour to south-west France (admirable courses of the highest possible quality) on the theme of pilgrimage and heresy. We visited sites associated with the routes to Santiago de Compostella and the Cathar heresies and discussed the importance of the buildings, art and sculpture, their topographical and geographical context, and the wider world in which they were created. At the glorious abbey of Conques, tucked away in a wooded gorge in northern Aveyron, we stood before the superb 12th century tympanum of The Last Judgement and thought about the scenes depicted. Christ sits in the centre, pure and virtuous, his right hand pointing upwards. Standing on his right are processions of those who made it to the celestial city, itself portrayed as a Romanesque arcade. They all have serene faces, lidded eyes, decorously folded hands and erect postures (apart from the detestable child saint Foye – she's impossibly virtuous - who is prostrate before a disembodied extra hand beckoning her towards Our Lord). So far, so good in every sense – artistically wonderful, spiritually perfect, behaviourally unchallenged.

Christ's left hand, however, points downwards. My students, worldly-wise persons of mature years and great sense of humour, turned with enthusiasm and eager anticipation in that direction. What does he point towards? Every juicy sin you can imagine! Monks cavort with bare-breasted women; gluttons are consumed by the flames of their passion; moneylenders are tortured by demons; poachers (who defied the 'natural' order of property ownership) are slaughtered; a figure representing spiritual laziness or theological laxity is trampled under foot by Satan while a toad (symbol of Black Magic) looks on; vain and supercilious kings and lords are led away to vile torment; a woman rides on a man's shoulders to show her dominance (also against the God-given order of this world). Satan, who looks unnervingly like a man who lives down our road (wild curly hair, round staring eyes and a rather jolly grin) is clearly having a great time. Who'd be Christ, all serene and bored, when such perpetual entertainment is going on around you? The students are in no doubt. Go left, young man (or woman) every time!

Four days later we are at Albi, with its overwhelming, slightly sinister cathedral, smooth towering walls of plain red brick, a military-religious fortress which conceals a riotous display of colour. Inside the west end is the immense late 15th century Last Judgement. Christ isn't there – a 17th century bishop chopped a doorway through the painting just where that guy in the white robes was sitting (extraordinary isn't it?). Beneath Christ's feet were the Seven Deadly Sins, but the cutting of the doorway means that there are now only four-and-a-half Deadly Sins, which makes life much easier. On the right of where Christ would be if he hadn't been unceremoniously removed are those dreary persons in long white robes suffering from heavenly ennui. A wide variety of human beings are sinking (some up to their waists) in a sort of thick brown cloud, as they struggle towards solid holy ground and Christ, but many others have already fallen through into the nether regions. There, it is party time. Some spectacularly scaly lizard-like demons are putting to good effect the lessons they learned from the Punishment Handbook. Sharp sticks are thrust down throats; clawed limbs lacerate white necks (the owners of the latter having understandably surprised expressions); little devils force feed gluttons; those who love luxury are squashed together in a cauldron under which the fire burns as a male demon

entrancing to the observer in 2003. We're bored with the good people, find the vacant faces of the virtuous merely tedious, yawn at the wholesome superiority of those who have gone upwards. But the gruesome, lascivious, luscious depiction of eternal damnation is captivating.

So are our minds different from those of our ancestors? Probably not. I think of the frescoes of the Last Judgement in the collegiate church of Santa Maria del' Assunta in San Gimignano. There the seven deadly sins are portrayed and in the centre Satan, a gigantic demented green and yellow monster, opens his huge toothy mouth and gobbles sinners, while between his outstretched legs other sinners are (how can I put this delicately) 'ejected' into the burning coals and torments of Hell. It was intended to terrify the viewer and to promote a sin-free way of life. But two things strike me in all of this. If I were a boy in 12th century Conques, 13th century San Gimignano, or 15th century Albi, my eyes would always be moving to Christ's left hand. Virtue? Boring! But the painting is a manual on how to sin! And what, I always wonder, was in the mind – and the personal track record – of the painters and sculptors who portrayed these sins with such sensationally exciting realism?

Local History News (August 2003)

with four horns, a large bust, wings and tail prods them viciously with a two-pronged fork; and fish eyes, medusa locks, arrow-ended tails, glittering scales and mad expressions proliferate. One of the demons looks like a 1970s high-on-drugs rock star, right down to the bleached blonde hair. Naturally, this is absolutely

Do You Know Hook Norton?
Sheila Terry
Chairman, Hook Norton Local History Group

Hook Norton is fortunate. Its main street is not a short cut to anywhere, thus leaving the village to remain itself.

That 'space' has quietly flourished since before the Norman Conquest with the emphasis, until after the Second World War, on agriculture. The farms are large now. Small brew houses have been replaced by the Hook Norton Brewery, where the beer is still made from spring water, hence its excellent flavour. Shop numbers – saddlers, cobblers, bakeries, butchers, etc. have dwindled to two sophisticated suppliers which cover most needs. Having a library (saved from closure by an active group supported by Norman Matthews, the County Councillor), a dentists, doctors and vets make public transport less vital and reinforces the atmosphere of independence which characterizes this village.

But Hook Norton no longer has its asylums; there were two, the expensive one in a fine house and the other humbler one, which was for the poor. Interestingly there were special cottages for those thought to be dangerous. The busy workhouse was

at the eastern end of the village.

Hook Norton cannot boast of any dramatic incidents. Its history, thank goodness, does not warrant one of those obtrusive brown signs. Nevertheless its history does reflect the social changes which took place in most rural areas throughout the country. Its first Anglo-Saxon name was Hocneratune, passing through various ramifications including Okenardtou to Hooking Norton in the 17th century. (I rather like that one. Perhaps it was turned into an exciting game – Poor Norton). William the Conqueror gave the manor to a Saxon with the splendid name of Wigod whose daughter married the powerful Norman knight, Robert d'Oily.

Although there was a Saxon church here, the 15th century tower with its eight pinnacles draws immediate attention, especially on Thursday evenings when the bell-ringers fill the sky with exuberant resonances. To leave St. Peters Church without referring to the superb Norman font would be sacrilegious. Its carvings are a mixture of pagan and Biblical symbols, with Aquarius and

Adam and Sagittarius and Eve, among others. Lodged in the church also is a pull-along pump wooden fire engine, last used by our volunteer fire fighters in 1896.

Hook Nortonians were noted as early as the 15th century for being 'borish' (sic) and 'offhand', and this independent-mindedness might be connected with having no Lord of the Manor (the d'Oilys had richer pickings elsewhere), and maybe contributed to the welcome given to non-conformists; among their buildings were a free and early Baptist Church, a strict Baptist Chapel, a Methodist Chapel (blown down by the 1985 storms), a Zionist Chapel and a Friends Meeting House. The Roman Catholic Church closed at the end of the last century.

The arrival of the railway coincided with the growth of Hook Norton's big industry, ironstone quarrying. This involved men with pickaxes, working throughout the light of the day, extracting lumps of ironstone from the earth, filling their 'trolleys' and pushing them along special tracks to the station to be loaded onto railway trucks. It was piece-work. They were paid two pence a trolley load. One old man whose father's farm bordered the quarry, said to me that as a child he would watch the men arrive for work walking normally. When they left, he said, some were so bent they could scarcely see where to drag their feet. It was terrible to see, he said.

To contrast this picture with the actual ones of the brewery builders at the same time is less depressing. Theirs too was hard physical, but much less painful labour, and their retention of satisfaction and dignity was apparent in them.

Mention has been made of the railway, the passenger line running from Banbury to Cheltenham (excursions to the seaside from Banbury in the summer, and yes, the train from Hook Norton did connect, and they ran on time), but the ironstone was taken to Swansea where the ore was extracted and exported. As it had grown with the railway so the ironstone profits declined

and died with it. Just a shed remains. The line was closed in 1962. Less than a century before hundreds of men had descended on Hook Norton, lodging locally or in primitive tents, to build viaducts over gigantic pillars before tackling the excavation of a long tunnel. It took four years – eight men were killed. The lanes must have been busier than then they are now. In 1964 it took four men four weeks to dismantle it. Those magnificent pillars still stand. For some inexplicable reason they are not listed.

Doubtless there were skirmishes here during the Civil War, close as the village is to Oxford and Banbury and Edgehill, and certainly monies and food and horses would have been commandeered, deserters and the injured possibly housed, but no records exist to tell us.

However, records do exist from the two World Wars. The death toll from the Great War is, not surprisingly, much higher than from the Second World War. After 1918 obvious social progress was made. Council houses were built, the villagers subscribed to and had erected the War Memorial Hall, which is still the base for many activities, from the monthly market, to cubs, keep fit classes and to both the local dramatic society performances and small touring companies, and to the flourishing film society. Electricity arrived to the better-off (they paid) in 1927, but mains water not until the 1950's.

Gradually the small farms have been absorbed and agriculture is no longer the largest source of work. The Brewery has that role. For more than a hundred years beer has been brewed in Hook Norton from its own spring water. Now a sophisticated business, brewing superb beer, with some deliveries still by dray, its tall Victorian edifice (building is too mundane a word) incongruous in this age of technology, it has its own museum full of beautiful and working machinery and offers informative brewery tours where the processes may be observed before sampling the results.

Clubs and societies abound in Hook Norton. Clubs

the Golden Jubilee?' Every person who had lived in Hook Norton when the Queen came to the throne, and ever since, was asked (with husband or wife) to a party held at the Brewery Visitor Centre. Coffee, sherry, then lunch. Wines, beer, then Jubilee cake and champagne with the loyal toast and entertainment between. No expense spared, as they say, nor energy!! Over eighty people attended or were collected, the oldest being 95. Over eighty people left, very happy.

The Group meets nowadays in the Brewery Visitor Centre at 7.30 p.m. on the first Tuesday of the month. The Clarkes, who own the brewery, offered the premises for our meetings. (The Clarkes are of that breed of employer who share good fortune with the place in which they live).

I now come on to that achievement of which this Group is most proud; our own local museum. Enthusiastically led by our indefatigable archivist/curator, Barbara Hicks, and given space in the Visitor Centre, all those records and log books and old photographs have a home; and artefacts – large and small – and all related to the people, places, works and industries mentioned in this article are on display. And, we are a real museum. To prove it, we had a Grand Opening with ribbon and scissors and Richard Munro to cut it. A glorious off-spring of our Local History Group.

So there's a taste of Hook Norton, which we all believe to be the best village in England. A place with its roots in its local people. It changes and, thank heavens, remains the same.

for the young, clubs for the old, clubs for the ages between, and clubs for all ages.

One of these clubs is Hook Norton Local History Group. The village described here is its inspiration. We have ten talks each season plus a couple of outings related usually to one of those talks. Subjects vary, say, from old manuscripts, to the map-makers, the Secret Army, bell-hanging, Saxon artefacts, Cotswold Churches – the list can go on. They might sound ordinary but they rarely are, and often provoke passionate interest and question times which have to be cut short. There are forty or so regular members and visitors attend also.

I'll pick out two highlights which without the co-operation of members and villagers alike would not have been possible and which were deeply satisfying, rewarding, successful and happy. The first was a decision to compile a Millenium Book. Almost every person, club, pub and place are in it. The second was the result of 'How do we celebrate

Lechlade Local History Society

Keith Newson describes the recording and conservation of an historic landscape beside the Upper Thames

The dry gravel terraces between the water-meadows of the River Thames and the Leach have been inhabited, cleared and cultivated for at least 4,000 years. Lechlade on Thames has had its local historians in the past 150 years, but the Historical Society was founded only in 1988. In that last decade of the 20th century the former Market Town was in yet another period of transition, and the expansion brought with it a fresh wave of interest in the history of the place. Those who had lived their lives in Lechlade joined with incomers buying houses on the new estates and others moving into the older, traditional Cotswold stone houses that had once formed the core of the market town. Members of this newly formed Society were aware that this was a community with a long independent history, now challenged by the rapid new growth of

nearby Swindon and its industries. They were eager to learn more about the landscape, the buildings, and the development of settlements on the banks of the Upper Thames.

At first the Committee and officers of the Society sought a wide range of speakers on a miscellany of topics that would interest – and entertain – members with many different interests in history, but it soon became clear that it was the history of of the place and its built environment and stories of the people who lived and worked there in the past, that brought those different interests together. Increasingly the programmes of monthly talks in the winter and summer visits to explore places within about 30 minutes' drive were all aimed at developing our understanding of local history and of the environment of the Upper Thames valley from pre-history through Roman, Saxon and Mediaeval times, into the eras of revolutions in agriculture, industry and transport, and up to the local impact of 20th century wars.

St Lawrence Church   LECHLADE.   Ha-Penny Bridge

Over the past two decades we have become more involved with research into social history and less concerned with political and military matters; we have sought to understand the effects of economic change on the lives of ordinary people living a long way from the centres of power. Three particular factors have recently influenced this process: a spate of local archaeological studies, an expanding demand from people (most of them only distantly connected with Lechlade) for information about a house or a family's history, and (thirdly) the potential of computer technology for holding archival material and making this easily accessible.

In and around Lechlade a number of green-field sites were released for new housing and many large new gravel pits were opened up in the 1970s, 80s and 90s. Fortunately the planning policies of that time put pressure on developers to call in professional archaeologists before they irreversibly disturbed the ancient landscape. As a direct result much evidence about the Iron Age, Romano-British and Saxon landscapes was revealed to us, and as a local History Society we received exciting reports of a large agricultural Roman villa and a wealthy West Saxon settlement and burial ground which had shared the same gravel terrace with our mediaeval market town. Our predecessors here must have related to the Thames and to the land-routes across the Cotswolds in much the same ways as the later inland port here did, at the height of the wool-trade, and again in the 17th, 18th and 19th centuries.

The rich grave-goods from the 6th-7th century Saxon cemetery, excavated in 1985, had national as well as local importance, and we realised that they were too valuable for our community to be able to hold securely in a local museum. But local people *did* take a proprietary interest in them, and the Society adopted a particularly fine brooch, studied with gems from distant places, as its logo (*above*). It seemed to symbolise the fact that, from the earliest times, this spot was a staging post, trading right down the Thames and across the Continent, even to the Middle East

Although we never claimed to be a "Family History" or "Genealogical Society", we soon found that local libraries and museums were directing more and more individual enquiries to us. No doubt many history societies have seen this growth in amateur investigations into personal history, and attribute this partly to the popularity of TV and radio programmes featuring archaeology and architecture, and perhaps also those involving antiques, period costumes, and various kinds of re-enact-ment of past events. For this reason, and because those doing historical research locally had more and more to show us and tell us, we found

we had to persuade someone to be our Archivist, an honorary post we created formally in 1995-6. Over the last 5 years of the century our Committee explored various ways of holding and cataloguing archival material, and making both documentary and photographic information accessible to this increasing number of enquirers. We concluded we needed some kind of resource room to hold relevant material, even if most of this has been copied or collated from much more valuable original sources or evidence. We were daunted by the responsibility (and costs) of running our own local museum, but intrigued by the potential of the new information technology that was rapidly becoming more affordable. In the end, we settled for a share in the attic of a cottage in the Market Place, which the St Lawrence P.C.C. was converting for church and community use, and for purchasing furniture to equip this room for archival storage, a lap-top computer, and a wider range of I.T. equipment that would allow us to hold and handle all kinds of archival material, including old maps and photographs, in digital format. To do this we applied for and received a Millennium "Awards for All" Lottery Grant.

We have found this an exciting process, from which some of us (mostly in retire-ment) have learned completely new skills. It has convinced us that I.T. offers an efficient and flexible method of holding and using historical evidence, not just to answer queries, but also to publish illustrated pamphlets and information sheets, and (ultimately) local history books. Time alone will tell us how easy it will be to hold archives in digital form for years or centuries to come, and how efficient we and our successors will be in keeping the databases up to date, and correct (in the light of newly discovered evidence).In our experience so far, the exploration of local history, whether by inviting in expert or knowledgeable speakers, visiting places of historical interest in our area, or collecting and researching documentary or pictorial material about the past, inevitably raises questions about conserving and protecting our local historical heritage. It has seemed to us that no other organisation, group or statutory body has quite the same responsibility as a local history society, when dealing with matters of restoration, re-

286

development, or indeed the improvement of amenities, in the context of a landscape containing buildings and features from previous centuries. The essential challenge is how to keep what is most precious from the past, for future generations, in the context of the economic and social demands of the present. As a Society, for some 13 years now, we have asked to be consulted on local planning matters that affect listed buildings, the local conservation area, and the traditional pattern of the landscape and the buildings in it.

As a mediaeval market town placed at the point where the highest navigable stretch of the Thames meets the ancient roads and pack-horse trails coming down from the Cotswold hills, Lechlade still depends, as it always has, on the people and goods passing through. The past and the future of the place are inextricably mixed with the River and

its banks. At this particular juncture, the opening up of the Thames Path and the Eastern part of the Cotswold Water Park, with a serious project to re-open navigation along the course of the former Thames and Severn Canal, all come together to make the community conscious of a heritage to be protected, cherished, and put to fresh use in the 21st century. We feel that it is our job to record what otherwise will be lost and forgotten, but equally it is our obligation to do what we can to persuade the planners and developers to save what they can of the unique character of the place and the landscape around it.

Keith Newson. After 15 years as Secretary of a local history group on the eastern side of the Cotswolds, Keith Newson wonders how far Lechlade History Society has developed any differently from similar groups elsewhere.

'The War Courts':the Stratford upon Avon Borough Tribunal 1916~1918
Philip Spinks

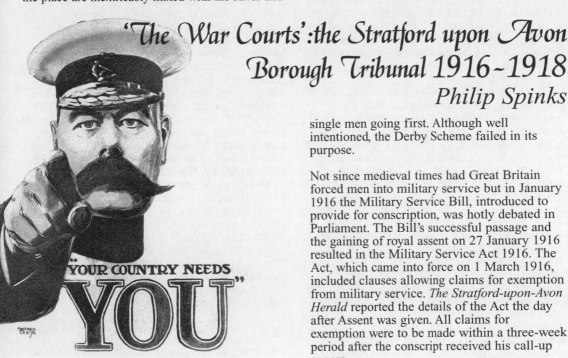

Although there had been an impressive stream of volunteers joining the Army in the first months of the First World War, the death and injury toll up to mid-1915 and the plans for offensives in 1916 meant that the British government was forced to consider other ways to fill the Army's ranks. In July 1915 a National Register was drawn up: all citizens, male and female, aged sixteen to sixty-five, were required to supply details of their age, sex, occupation and address. In October 1915 the earl of Derby introduced what became known as the Derby Scheme. This scheme encouraged all who were eligible for military service (all males aged between eighteen and thirty-nine) to attest their willingness to serve in the Army. They would be called up as, and if, necessary, with

single men going first. Although well intentioned, the Derby Scheme failed in its purpose.

Not since medieval times had Great Britain forced men into military service but in January 1916 the Military Service Bill, introduced to provide for conscription, was hotly debated in Parliament. The Bill's successful passage and the gaining of royal assent on 27 January 1916 resulted in the Military Service Act 1916. The Act, which came into force on 1 March 1916, included clauses allowing claims for exemption from military service. *The Stratford-upon-Avon Herald* reported the details of the Act the day after Assent was given. All claims for exemption were to be made within a three-week period after the conscript received his call-up papers.

The definition for grounds for appeal were summarised as 'Exemption in cases of hardship owing to financial, business or domestic obligations'. Claims for exemption on conscience grounds would also be allowed. Claims could be made by individuals or a sponsor, normally an employer. If the claimant could afford it, he was usually represented by a solicitor. The claims were to be heard, in the first instance, by local tribunals which were to be '[not] military, but civilian courts. They are to be filled by men who have local knowledge, and enjoy the confidence of their neighbours. Workmen are to represented upon them'. Because this was the first time such legislation had ever been passed, drafting to cover all eventualities must have been very difficult with even basic definitions open to ambiguity and speculation. What constituted a 'domestic obligation'? How special was 'special'? And what was 'hardship'? Such semantics had to be dealt with by tribunal members, and their patience at times was severely tested.

After considering the claim, a tribunal had a variety of ways in which they could dispose of the case: an absolute exemption, a conditional exemption (conditions being applied that the claimant performed particular functions during his exemption period), a temporary exemption (where the conscription date was delayed for a specified period ranging from one week to one year) or a refusal, whereby the claimant's call-up would proceed. Occasionally adjournments were ordered so that further information about the claim could be sought. Claims on the grounds of conscience could also result in a non-combatant exemption where the claimant would still have to join the Army but would serve in a support unit.

Stratford-upon-Avon was served by two local tribunals, one for the Borough and one for Stratford Rural District. This paper deals with the Borough tribunal, its formation and membership, its procedures and a brief analysis of cases which came before it. A small number of cases are described in detail to demonstrate examples of claims made. It is unfortunate that in 1921 the Ministry of Health (which inherited responsibility for these tribunals from the Ministry of National Service) ordered the destruction of all papers relating to them, with the exception of those from Middlesex and Midlothian which were to be retained as examples. Luckily, all the papers from the County Appeals Tribunal sitting at Warwick survived this order and are to be found today at the county record office. Moreover, the *Stratford-upon-Avon Herald* regularly reported the proceedings of the tribunals, giving full details of the claimants, their claims and the outcome of cases.

The Stratford-upon-Avon Borough Local Tribunal was formed and its members appointed at a meeting of the Borough Council on Tuesday 8 February 1916. During that meeting the clerk to the council, Robert Lunn, submitted a circular from the Local Government Board, dated 3 February 1916, detailing the action to be taken by local councils in setting up local tribunals under the Military Service Act, 1916. The Council agreed unanimously to appoint as tribunal members Alderman A.D. Flower (Mayor and Tribunal Chairman), Councillor F. Winter (Deputy Mayor and Deputy Tribunal Chairman), Councillor J.F. Burke, Alderman J. Metters and Mr F.J. Savage (member of the local Trade and Labour Council). Lunn would perform the duties

of clerk to the tribunal, a role similar to that of a justices' clerk in a magistrates' court, with authority to deal with non-contentious claims prior to tribunal sittings. All tribunals would have a military representative to act in the interests of the army, appointed by Parliamentary Recruiting Advisory Committees (the local committee was based in Rugby). He sat in an advisory capacity and was able to question the claimant but had no input into the tribunal's decision. He could also assent to non-contentious claims and worked closely with the clerk before tribunal hearings. These representatives sometimes served more than one tribunal: Major Bairnsfather, for example, a retired officer, also sat with the Alcester tribunal.

The decision of the Borough Council to appoint some of its own members to the tribunal may seem arbitrary and self seeking, but by doing so it was acting with the expediency required to have the tribunal in place and ready for the anticipated exemption claims. It also meant that the Borough Tribunal had, as a majority of its membership, elected representatives of the local population, albeit via a restricted franchise. In a sense, their position was therefore unique: elected people with a judicial function. The first sitting of the Stratford-upon-Avon Borough Local Tribunal took place at the Town Hall on Thursday 24 February 1916 at 5.00 p.m. Sittings continued to be held in the evening to ensure that the business and work of officials and claimants would be unaffected. In the tribunal's early days sittings took place on Thursdays, but they were switched to Wednesdays when it was discovered that Thursday sittings clashed with those of the County Appeals Tribunal. As some of the Borough Tribunal members were also magistrates, Wednesdays would be a very trying day indeed, since that was court day too.

BALH
Local History Award
Joint Winner 2002

The tribunal hearing of 16 March 1916 was attended by an insufficient number of members. Only three sat, attended by Robert Lunn and a Mr Talbot for the military. Winter suggested that the Borough Council should appoint two further members. Savage suggested a Labour man, but Winter referred the decision to the Borough Council. Accordingly, at its meeting on 11 April 1916, the Council made further appointments: Councillor G.W. Everard, Mr F. Cranmer and Mr. W. Hughes (replacing Metters who could not attend on a regular basis). Later in the year Alderman Flower suggested the appointment of Councillor Edward Fox to the tribunal, which was carried. Thus the Stratford-upon-Avon Borough Local Tribunal was established.

The members of the tribunal had a difficult task to perform and few could have envied them their

**Eager Young
Recruits for
Lord Kitchener's
New Army 1915**

job. Their decisions would not necessarily send men to the front line: the army would decide that. What they were deciding, using their own judgment and the evidence presented to them, was whether a man should serve at all. A poor decision could result in financial or business ruin for a claimant or severe hardship for his dependents. Their role was therefore often thankless and undoubtedly they made many enemies while dispensing justice among their neighbours and fellow townspeople, some of whom they would have known well. Nevertheless, however difficult their decisions, it was their responsibility to carry out the government policy of filling the army's ranks so that the war could be brought to a speedy end. They would also be required to balance the needs of the town of Stratford-upon-Avon against the military's demands.

Judging by the reports in the *Stratford-upon-Avon Herald*, the tribunal performed its duties impartially and 'without fear or favour', and on occasions when a member had an interest, his withdrawal from the hearing was conscientiously adhered to. Alderman Flower, the owner of Flower's Brewery, was the employer of many of the claimants appearing before the tribunal and always withdrew in such cases. When the Corporation applied for exemption for their only remaining carpenter (46-year-old Thomas Stanley) in 1918, Flower referred the case to the Stratford Rural District Tribunal, as three of the four Borough Tribunal members were also members of the Corporation. Tribunal hearings were held in public except (rare in Stratford's case) when the claimant asked for a private hearing. There are no reports to show that the viewing public was anything other than well-behaved at the Borough Tribunal. On the other hand, at the first sitting of the Stratford Rural District Tribunal at the boardroom of Arden House (the old workhouse), the chairman, Mr Couchman, declared that he 'deprecated the practice of canvassing Tribunal members prior to

hearings. A practice that is not proper and [is] useless'.

Although the tribunal members dealt with cases as equitably as they could, things did not always run smoothly. Over a six-month period, from November 1916 to May 1917, a number of altercations arose, all initiated by Cranmer, concerning claims of unfairness and double standards on the part of the tribunal and the military representatives. Later he complained about procedural irregularities and matters came to a head on 9 May when he again criticised the tribunal for applying double standards in its decision-making. Despite two separate public statements by the tribunal chairmen that each case was dealt with on its merits, Cranmer remained unconvinced: he left the meeting of 9 May, and did not sit on the tribunal again. If Cranmer's behaviour had proved an annoyance to the tribunal, the announcement at the sitting of 10 September 1916 that its clerk, Robert Lunn, had received his call-up papers, must have come as something of an embarrassment. Nevertheless, the military representative assented to Lunn's claim for exemption and the clerk received a conditional exemption. The condition was (presumably) that he was to continue to perform his duties as clerk to the tribunal.

One of the responsibilities of the military representatives was to provide substitute workers for employers whose work force had been seriously reduced. Some employers were not satisfied with these replacements and a committee of tribunal members was set up on 24 November 1916 to provide mediation. This committee comprised all tribunal members except Messrs Flower and Winter. By the second half of 1917 the sittings of the tribunal were becoming less regular. Some heard no claims at all, just applications from the military representatives for reviews of cases and requests for amendments to temporary exemptions. This was not because there was less demand for men to serve but rather that most of those eligible for conscription had already received their call-up and were either serving or had had their claims processed. Sittings therefore became fewer as time went on and on 9 October 1918 Lunn read to the tribunal a letter from the Local Government Board advocating the principle of amalgamation. The Board suggested a merger of tribunals across south-east Warwickshire to comprise six members from Stratford Borough, two from Brailes, two from Stratford Rural District and one from Farnborough. This was accepted but no such amalgamation took place as the war came to an end one month later.

In total, 809 claims were reported in the *Stratford-upon-Avon Herald*. Also reported were reviews and requests to appeal but these have not been included in the following analysis. Non-contentious claims, dealt with by the clerk and military representative, were not reported by the newspaper and are therefore also excluded. The workload of tribunals varied. It is known, for instance, that the Leeds tribunal dealt with an average of 120 cases daily (with about 50 per cent resulting in refusals). In comparison the Stratford Borough tribunal, with an average of 25 cases per weekly sitting, was very quiet though this is hardly surprising given the difference in populations. Claimants came from a wide range of occupations, including waggoners, wheelwrights, colporteurs, brewery workers, brewers' chemists, steam-plough drivers, coopers and gas works employees. A large proportion of claimants, were engaged in agricultural work (12.3 per cent) or the retail or retail supply sector (26.6 per cent). Skilled and unskilled men represented 23.2 per cent and 20 per cent respectively. Although there was a reduction in available manpower during the war, it would appear that trade in Stratford-upon-Avon did not suffer too greatly. Ages of claimants ranged from 18 to 51, with an annual average of 33.1 in 1916, 32.8 in 1917 and 41.9 in 1918 (following the increase in the upper age limit for conscripts to fifty).

Employers lodging a claim accounted for 43.5 per cent of cases, with individuals' claims making up the remainder. Claims for being in a reserved occupation were few (3.6 per cent), while domestic and financial reasons for a claim made up 11.4 per cent. The large numbers of claims for unfitness and invalidity (16.2 per cent) reflect both the general poor state of health of the nation at that time and the demand for older men in the war's later stages. Conscientious objection amounted to just 0.8 per cent of claims, all of which were on religious, rather than political or ethical grounds. The bulk of the claims, 63.6 per cent, were to do with business - either that trade would suffer or that an employee was indispensable.

With so little documentation surviving from the tribunals, it is difficult to determine whether or not the Borough tribunal was typical in the way it disposed of claims. Only 4.2 per cent of claimants received an absolute exemption and 12.2 per cent of claims were refused. Claimants granted conditional exemptions made up 23 per cent of the total and temporary exemptions 43 per cent. All remaining claims were either adjourned or withdrawn. When it is considered that two thirds of claimants received a conditional or temporary exemption, it would appear that the tribunal acted fairly, if not leniently.

The *Stratford-upon-Avon Herald* reported no obviously frivolous claims made to the tribunal. As might be expected, the majority of claims were made soon after conscription was introduced and men began receiving call-up papers. At the very first tribunal hearing C.H. Bullard, a Quaker living in Henley Street, claimed absolute exemption on the grounds of conscientious objection. He was granted a non-combatant exemption. His appeal to the County Appeals Tribunal was unsuccessful. His son recalled that 'the tribunals ... didn't give much in the way of exemption'. Forced into the Army, albeit as a non-combatant, Bullard refused to conform and was court-martialled and imprisoned.. Another conscientious objector did receive an absolute exemption: J. Ready, aged 40, an itinerant evangelist and colporteur. The case of A. L. Pearce demonstrates the administrative efficiency of the appeals process. His written claim for absolute exemption was entered on 21 February 1916. The military representative, Major Bairnsfather, disagreed, so the claim was processed on 26 February and heard on 2 March. Pearce received a three-month temporary exemption for him to put his business in order. On 9 March the military representative, this time Mr Talbot, appealed against Pearce's exemption. The appeal was heard on 23 March and the original exemption allowed to stand. In less than one month the whole claim and appeal process had been completed.

When, in January 1917, the employers of 28 year-old shoesmith, William Melburne, asked for an extension to a temporary exemption which he had received, they claimed he was indispensable to their business of supplying six hundred-weight of agricultural and military horseshoes per month, work considered to be of national importance. Captain Bros, the military representative, suggested that Melburne might be employed as a smith by the army. A conditional exemption was granted, but only on condition that the company, Messrs Hutchings and Co., produce six hundred-weight of shoes up to the end of February and nine hundred-weight monthly thereafter.

Evidence that the government was seeking to call-up as many men as possible is found in the case of two applicants who had previously volunteered for the army (one of them twice) but who had initially been rejected on medical grounds due to their stature. John Bone, aged 27, and Charles Guise were 4ft 11ins and 4ft 9ins tall respectively. Bone weighed just 94 pounds (an infantryman's fighting equipment weighed 66 pounds). On their call-up in 1916, both now claimed unfitness as grounds for exemption. Whether this was because their initial enthusiasm had waned (by that time the war had entered its third year with no end in sight) or because they resented such a demand after their earlier rejection may never be known: both, though, received exemptions. Arthur Fletcher, a 21 year-old painter and decorator, had only one eye but had been passed fit for military service. Although his claim on grounds of unfitness had been supported by Mr Savage, the tribunal decided that Fletcher should serve when it was brought to its attention that the military representative of the day, Mr Talbot, was blind in one eye but had served with the local volunteers. Military representatives were eager to get as many men as possible into the army's ranks and would go to some lengths to ensure that any claims for unfitness were authentic. James Henry Brooks, for example, a 36 year-old foreman cooper with a severe rupture, was sent to successive medical examinations locally and as far away as London.

A good deal of banter and badinage was exchanged during the hearings, some serious and cutting, some not. Mr Williams, the employer of  45 year-old Charles Marshall, a tailor, had suffered staff shortages due to the war and he claimed Marshall as indispensable. Mr Jackson, the military representative, commented that if the Germans got to England, Williams would not require Marshall, nor anyone else. Part of

Marshall's work was to make trousers and breeches for army officers and Williams declared: 'Officers can't fight without clothes!'. 'Can't they?' retorted Jackson. Marshall gained a three-month exemption. An example of a rather perplexing claim was that made by F.A. Southam. He was a 30 year-old widower employed as a labourer at Flower's Brewery. He had been passed fit for military service but claimed exemption on domestic grounds as he had two young children to care for. His case was adjourned for two weeks so that he could make arrangements for his children's welfare. When the case reopened on 28 March 1917 the fact came to light that Southam's younger child had died two months previously and Southam could give no explanation why he had not informed the tribunal of this at the earlier hearing. His claim was refused.

As a final case study, the brothers Frank and William Eborall of the Oddfellows Arms in Windsor Street appeared together at the tribunal on 17 May 1916. Frank wished to withdraw his claim for exemption and was willing to serve on condition that his brother was exempted. William, however, thought that, as he was single, he should go and that his brother should stay to run the public house and the small on-site brewery. Mr Everard acknowledged that is was 'refreshing to find two young men willing to serve' and asked, 'Can't they both go?'. It was decided that William would serve and that Frank would receive a conditional exemption so long as his brother remained in the army.

The last sitting of the Stratford-upon-Avon Borough Tribunal took place on 23 October 1918 and no reference to it subsequently appeared in the *Stratford-upon-Avon Herald*. Nor have any personal papers been identified that allude to the tribunal. Its members had performed their onerous duties conscientiously and, given the high proportion of various exemptions, with genuine humanity. It has not proved possible to follow through what happened to those who received temporary exemptions: some certainly went on to serve in the Army. Nevertheless, as well as providing men for the military, the tribunal had showed awareness for the interests of Stratford-upon-Avon and its people.

PHILIP SPINKS is a native of Stratford-upon-Avon. After service with the British and Omani armies, and a short spell as a stone conservator at the British Museum, he is now employed as an ambulance paramedic. He researched the Local Tribunals while on an Access to Higher Education course. He has always had an avid interest in history, and the local history of the Stratford area, and is currently a volunteer at the Shakespeare Birthplace Trust Records Office.
This article was first published in Warwickshire History (the journal of the Warwickshire Local History Society) vol.9 no.4 (Winter 2000-2001) and in The Local Historian vol.32 no.4 (November 2002).

The National Fairground Archive: its origins, development and holdings
Vanessa Toulmin

The National Fairground Archive (NFA) was formally inaugurated by the vice-chancellor of the University of Sheffield in November 1994, having been founded at a meeting in the University Library the previous June. However, the rationale behind such a collection came from a more personal experience, namely the death in 1991 of Arthur William Albert Francis, travelling showman, ex-boxer, painter and beloved uncle. The idea for an Archive arose from discussions with the Fairground Association of Great Britain (FAGB), which was increasingly receiving donations of photographic collections that had belonged to deceased members. Meanwhile I was researching for a doctorate at the University of Sheffield on the history of travelling showpeople. This began in 1993 but the research and methodology behind it started in 1991 when I returned to work on the family fair in Wales after the death of my uncle Arthur Francis. I realised that the wealth of history and stories that for so long had been a part of my life had gone. As a child in

Morecambe, the Winter Gardens fairground was my home, playground and schoolroom. Holidays were spent with my mother's sisters or brothers travelling on the family fair in Wales, East Anglia or Lancashire and it was to this tradition I returned in 1991. The death of an elderly relative often leaves one with a sense of regret at not listening or writing down the memories that only that person held or had experienced. My sense of loss propelled me into realising as a trained historian that there was no record or repository relating to any aspect of the tradition and culture that I had grown up with and which was also part of the social fabric of the United Kingdom. A further factor behind the formation of the Archive was the need to store the materials, photographs and items of information that had started to accumulate during my research on travelling showpeople. Storage was a problem, especially since the Showmen's Guild of Great Britain had loaned the entire set of World's Fair newspapers to my university to support my research. The issues of space, the

need to save or preserve a family heritage, and the wealth of material collected by the Fairground Association from its members, were the factors behind that meeting in the University Library.

At the original meeting, the collecting policy and mission statement was set out by the Fairground Association and the University Library. This was to preserve the history of travelling fairgrounds and allied entertainments (including circus, travelling theatre, popular entertainment, menageries and waxworks, for example). The new project was called the National Fairground Archive, the initials NFA standing not only for National Fairground Archive but also for the phrase No Fixed Abode often found on showmen's birth certificates! Nine years on the Archive is a unique collection of photographic, printed, manuscript and audio-visual material covering all aspects of the culture of travelling showpeople, their organisation as a community, their social history and everyday life, and the artefacts and machinery of fairgrounds. Henry Morley calls Bartholomew Fair 'the unwritten portion of the story of the people,' bound to the life of a nation by the ties of religion, trade and pleasure. The Archive therefore serves a dual purpose. Firstly, it collects and preserves the history of popular entertainment as found on travelling fairs in the United Kingdom and encompassing material of all types relating to the history of fairs and their role in the development of popular culture. Secondly, and more importantly, it serves as an archival repository for a community on wheels, the travelling showpeople who present these entertainments and have done for nearly two centuries. It is therefore a living archive, dedicated to preserving material relating to the lifestyle, tradition and culture of travelling showpeople in the United Kingdom and covers promotional, educational and social aspects of the fairground community.

Norm Cohen, one of the instigators of the transfer of the John Edwards Collection to the Southern Folklife Collection in 1989, wrote 'that hawking hotdogs dissipated manpower far too inefficiently, when trying to fundraise money for the collection'. Ironically, hawking hotdogs in the context of the NFA was one of the main reasons for its success in the acquisition of material. The Archive had decided that, unlike the doomed Fairground Heritage Trust, the collecting policy would be undertaken on a donation or loan system only and no money would be made available for the

acquisition of archival collections. The only exception was learning resources such as books, microfilms and digital catalogues. In return for the donation of the material the University Library would define a set of conditions tailored to the need of the individual collector, with as much (or as little) access as deemed acceptable by the donor. Within a few weeks of the original press release Graham Downie (the Chairman of the Fairground Association) and I travelled the length and breadth of the United Kingdom rescuing materials from cellars, belly trucks of living wagons, showmen's sheds and packing trucks. In addition to this I worked every weekend on the family fair in Lancashire, spinning candyfloss and hawking hotdogs to the general public. This gave further access to the community to collect material for the Archive as well as facilitating the fieldwork necessary for my doctoral study on travelling showpeople. Within three years we had collected over 30,000 photographs, 1,000 books and 10,000 items of ephemera, perhaps the most problematic being a tea chest lined with an 1888 poster from Whittington's Royal Menagerie. Since then the collections have gone from strength to strength, and the National Fairground Archive can today claim to be the leading repository of material relating to British fairs and the amusement industry. Collections range from a handful of Showmen's Year Books donated by a retired showman, to the Jack Leeson Collection, consisting of 12,000 images collected or taken by the late Jack Leeson and secured on long-term loan from his daughter.

Types of material held
Materials in the NFA now cover all main formats: printed books, photographs, posters, business records, autobiographical manuscripts and posters. The collections continue to grow, with some 80,000 images now in the photographic collection, in addition to audio and video material, journals and magazines, and nearly 4,000 monographs. It also includes a unique body of fairground ephemera (programmes, handbills, posters, charters, proclamations, plans and drawings). From Easter to October over 200 fairs are held weekly in the UK and the holdings provide a comprehensive record of these events from the 1890s to today, representing an important part of the cultural heritage of the nation. For example, over 2,000 images and associated documents relate to Nottingham Goose Fair alone, and a further 6,000 relate to fairs in the Midlands from the 1930s onwards. All types of fairs are covered, including charter and

prescriptive fairs such as Hull and Nottingham, wakes holidays in the North of England, mop and hiring fairs in the Midlands, and private business events attended by the showpeople in association with a local fete or gala.

The National Fairground Archive also contains materials from the Fair Organ Preservation Society, the Fairground Association of Great Britain, the Fairground Society, the Circus Friends Association, the Showmen's Guild of Great Britain and individual family collections. A substantial proportion of the photographs held in the Archive were taken by members of the Fairground Association, including the Ron Taylor, Jack Leeson, Stuart Johnson and George Tucker collections. All of these collections form part of the NFA digital database, which can be accessed in the Archive. The records are very detailed, in particular those taken by Jack Leeson, which consist of approximately 5,000 photographs and negatives taken by him and thirty notebooks with detailed lists of every fair visited and an elaborate system of cross-referencing which enables the researcher to match the photograph and Jack's account of the fair. Rowland Scott's photographic collection of 15,000 images has been catalogued through the Pilgrim Trust. It covers the north of England, and in particular Greater Manchester, Lancashire, Derbyshire and Yorkshire. Rowland worked as a bus conductor in Glossop and we are told that that he would often jump off a bus and leave his passengers waiting while he took a photograph of a visiting fair for his collection.

A strength of the Archive is the depth of material relating to fairground families. Three of the principal holdings comprise photographic material bequeathed by travelling showpeople. One is the Shufflebottom family material, donated by Margaret Bird, Florence Campbell and Maisie Smith, who were all members of the famous Wild West family. The photographic material dates from 1890 to the 1960s and covers three generations of the family shows, including the founder, Texas Bill Shufflebottom, a Buffalo Bill impersonator from Yorkshire who masqueraded as the great American showman. Within this collection can also be found Waddington family material including diaries, account books, receipts for living vans and other items relating to the day-to-day economics of travelling showpeople. One example is the diary of Abraham Waddington which records his daily life in 1916 in Hull, including accounts of Zeppelin raids and operating a blackout fair. The Archive also holds the extensive Smart Family

Archive, donated by Gary Smart, grandson of the celebrated Billy. This includes posters, programmes, letters and cine-film taken by the great man himself on his European travels.

Central to the collection is the newspaper and cuttings archive, which includes a complete run of the World's Fair newspaper which since its original publication in 1904 has become 'The means by which many showmen recruit labour and by which machines, stalls or caravans are bought and sold. Almost every aspect of the showman's business and personal life is catered for'. The World's Fair contains information ranging from the reporting of fairs in different regions and buying and selling equipment, via news of recent deaths and weddings, to grounds to let and the hiring of labour. The columns of advertising in the newspaper reflect the current popularity of particular rides or contemporary trends in prizes for fairground stalls. The advertising space in early issues is dominated by film companies, fairground suppliers, and makers of living vans and rides and is an important source of reference for identifying these early manufacturers. It is invaluable in illustrating the changes in the material culture of travelling people, not only in the workplace but also in the domestic environment. The World's Fair contains weekly reports of local fairs throughout the United Kingdom, including the types of amusements on show, the names of the showmen visiting the fair, and any local coverage of the event. This continues to the present day, with a minimum of eight pages in each issue being dedicated to such reports. For example, the World's Fair of 29 July 1911, reports, under the heading 'To Revive Town Fair - Old Time Carnival Project for Sunderland', 'the ambitious scheme of a committee at East Enders' in the town. It continues with a description of the fair before its abolition in 1868:

'To many members of the older generation the occasion recalls memories of the old fair which, abolished by Act of Parliament was held on the last time on the 13th and 14th of October, 1868. It was held twice a week - May and October. The whole length of the High Street within the then parish of Sunderland from Sans Street to Barracks Square, then known as the Town End, they lined on each side with stalls, where toys, sweetmeats, and other confections were sold. In Barrack Square itself the shows and roundabouts were set up, and the most popular showmen who attended year by year was the famous Billy Purvis. Children who had saved their Saturday day farthings for weeks before the fair, on the eve of the great event sang:

"To-moa'n's the fair,
W'll all be there
To see Billy Purvis's lily white hair
In ships wi'paper sails
Wooden horses wiv hairy tails."

The documentary holdings are constantly being updated with books and articles relating to fairs and showpeople. The Archive's collections of monographs and articles published from the 1700s onwards make it the UK's largest repository for printed material on the history of fairs. The periodicals section is equally comprehensive and full listings of magazines

and quarterlies, such as the Fairground Mercury, the Merry-Go-Round, Steaming, and Dutch fairground magazines such as Kermes can be found within the collection. The addition of circus periodicals has brought the number of individual titles held by the Archive to over 100, featuring journals from France, America, Germany, Australia and the Netherlands.

Circus material in the National Fairground Archive

When the Archive was officially inaugurated its aim was to collect and preserve the history of travelling fairgrounds and allied entertainments. The links with circus were important because they reflected the strong relationship between the travelling show families, and those who were connected to circus, such as the Shufflebottom and Scott families. Famous circus families such as the Smart family often started their show business activities on the fairground. With the donation of the Circus Friends' Association (CFA) library to the National Fairground Archive in 2002, this relationship can now be researched alongside other circus items in the main collection. The CFA library catalogue has now been published by the Circus Friends' Association and is available as a King Pole special issue (March 2003). The NFA's main catalogue also contains many items of interest to circus historians and enthusiasts, including not only photographic material but also handbills, programmes and posters. The impact of the great American showmen such as Buffalo Bill Cody and P.T. Barnum is well represented in the collection. Both the CFA library and the NFA book holdings include many notable items of interest, including three different programmes for Buffalo Bill's Wild West exhibition during its visits to the United Kingdom, handbills and brochures for Barnum's freak shows, and a souvenir coin or medal commemorating the visit of 'General' Tom Thumb to London in 1843. Posters relating to early freak show acts which appeared on the fairground and the circus are an important part of this material, such as an 1890 lithographic panoramic handbill from Barnum's Great Show. This and other items have been on loan at the Dusseldorf Film Museum in Germany where thousands of visitors have seen the exhibition. Printed pamphlets and illustrations relating to the history of circus performance are also well represented in the NFA. Items from the Illustrated London News, the Graphic and other nineteenth century newspapers and magazines have been repaired and are currently being catalogued. These include two wonderful four-page programmes from Astley's and Sanger's permanent circuses in London, dating from the 1860s. Steel engravings of circuses at Astley's Amphitheatre, the departure of 'Jumbo' from the London Zoo in 1882, and horsemanship at the Paris Hippodrome are just some of the items which reflect the international nature of circus and fairground history.

The modern and changing face of the fairground and circus is an important part of the NFA's collecting policy and recent posters from all the major circuses and fairs held in the United Kingdom are now finding their way into the Archive. This is due to the support of many of the enthusiasts who have sent examples from America and Germany as well as those that visit their local towns. During the next two years the NFA and its staff will be cataloguing and preserving this new material relating to circus, including the photographic collection of the late Hal Fisher, albums donated by Arthur Pedlar, and a recent donation of circus and fairground films from Noel Drewe. This large filmic record includes footage from the 1930s onwards, with film of Richard Shufflebottom's Wild West Show, Battersea Park and Brighton, the Mills and Smart circuses, and much more. It is hoped that during the tenth anniversary celebrations of the National Fairground Archive in 2004 much of this material will be displayed, exhibited and presented at the University to mark the occasion.

Ongoing projects

The staff are currently involved in four projects which, taken collectively, demonstrate the breadth and scope of the material held. Firstly, the Mitchell and Kenyon Project is a collaboration between the British Film Institute and the NFA to work on a three-year research programme sponsored by the Arts and Humanities Research Board. This is to examine, date and contextualise the 800-roll collection of non-fiction films commissioned by travelling showmen for screening at local venues including fairs across the Midlands, north of England and other localities between 1900 and 1909. The second project is a continuation of the NFA digital database in conjunction with the Health and Safety Executive (HSE) to examine the history, development and technology of adult riding machines on travelling fairs and theme parks. The principal indexing objective of the NFA digitised image catalogue is description of the actual content of the photograph. Approximately 50 per cent of our images feature adult riding machines. Classifying (and recognising) such machines is based upon

knowledge of their history and current development. Thirdly, the research director is co-curating an exhibition with Sheffield Museums Trust to be held at the Millennium Galleries in Sheffield and then to tour to Croydon and Edinburgh. Pleasure Land will be an exhibition celebrating popular tradition. It will explore the role of fairgrounds, circuses and sideshows in cultural experience from 1800 to the present day, featuring an enormous range of visually stunning material, selected from the very best of local, national and private collections. The fourth project is an international collaboration with the Museum Het Markiezenhof, Bergen op Zoom, Netherlands, the Museo Nazionale della Giostra e dello Spettacolo Popolare, Bergantino in Italy and Schaustellermuseum Essen in Germany. Funded by Culture 2000, the website will be a virtual exposition chronicling the history of travelling fairgrounds in Europe. Attention is given to the cultural importance of the fair as the cradle of the cinema, and its relationship to the circus, popular theatre and zoological gardens.

The development of the NFA digital collections

Although within the University it is used primarily as a teaching, learning and research resource, the NFA seeks to widen public understanding of travelling showpeople by creating greater access to what has historically been perceived as a closed community. Its remit is to preserve, conserve and make available the rich variety of material within the Archive to a wide spectrum of the public through multi-media, audio-visual, photographic and printed word forms. The most heavily used and requested category for research was the photographic collection. Because this was deemed to be most vulnerable in terms of security and conservation the practice of creating digital surrogates and accessing through a database was initiated. In 1998 the NFA received a grant of £88,000 from the Heritage Lottery Fund, to digitise and catalogue 30,000 photographs in the collection, while additional funding from the Pilgrim Trust has enabled a further 20,000 images to be placed on a searchable database within Special Collections. Recent awards from Culture 2000 and the Arts and Humanities Research Board will result in further material being made available on the NFA website with a proposed virtual museum with three European partners to be launched in September 2003.

• fairground enthusiasts - including the FAGB and the Fairground Society
• fairground community - Showmen's Guild of Great Britain and individual users
• media - television, radio and local and national newspapers.

Many of the published monographs on travelling fairs appear locally and copies are not usually held outside the area. Academic study on the history of travelling fairs is scarce, although some local historians have written on the subject – for example, Ned Williams, whose research on shows and fairs in the Black Country includes Pat Collins King of Showmen, Birmingham Onion Fair and Fairs and Circuses of the Black Country. Over 30 per cent of visitors use materials relevant to their particular local fair or show families. The Archive receives over 100 enquires a week and the website has an average of 6000 hits a month. This is expected to rise as additional material has recently been made available and there is a new policy of giving a monthly update of photographs and text in the form of an online newsletter.

The National Fairground Archive is open from Monday to Friday, 9.30 am to 1.00 pm and 2.00 pm to 4.30 pm. It is available to members of the public and academic researchers but appointments must be made in advance. The University Library is fully equipped with modern information technology, photocopying facilities and a photographic service, and these are all available to visitors to the collections. To find out more about the Archive, or to make arrangements to access the collections, please contact Dr Vanessa Toulmin, Research Director, National Fairground Archive, The University of Sheffield Library, Western Bank, Sheffield S10 2TN (tel: 0114 2227231; fax 0114 22 27290; e-mail fairground@sheffield.ac.uk; website: www.shef.ac.uk/nfa

The NFA website
(http://www.sheffield.ac.uk/uni/nfa) now provides over 100 pages of detailed information about the collections. Attracting enormous interest internationally, it is very heavily used, not only by academic researchers and fairground historians, but also by local historians wanting information pertaining to the show families who have visited their locality for over a hundred years. Links with collections housed in local archives and libraries will be further enhanced by the NFA regional database of photographs pertaining to the ten regional sections of the Showmen's Guild of Great Britain. This has been made possible by an award from the Pilgrim Trust who have funded the development of regional databases so that images relevant to Nottingham or Hull, for example, can be accessed in local libraries with a web portal of 1000 images acting as guide to the holdings in each locality.
The Archive can be visited in person or through the internet site. Since its inception the Archive has been consulted by a steady stream of visitors, and staff have handled requests from as far afield as Australia and North America. The main users of the resources in the NFA fall into the following categories:
• educational - particularly teachers and schoolchildren at primary and secondary level
• academic - at both research and undergraduate level
• general public - e.g. local history societies, Women's Institute, Rotary and PROBUS

VANESSA TOULMIN is the founder and research director of the National Fairground Archive. She is co-editor and founder of Living Pictures: The Journal of the Popular and Projected Image before 1914 and has published widely on all aspects of popular entertainment with a particular emphasis on early cinema on the fairground. Her publications include Hull Fair: An Illustrated History; A Fair Fight: An Illustrated Review of Boxing on the Fairgrounds; Visual Delights: Essays on the Popular and Projected Image in the Nineteenth Century; and Randall Williams King of Showmen.

This article was first published in The Local Historian vol.33 no.2 (May 2003).

History Societies & Organisations

Anglo-Zulu War Historical Society, Woodbury House, Woodchurch Road, Tenterden, TN30 7AE T: 01580-764189 W: www.web-marketing.co.uk/anglozuluwar

Association of Local History Tutors, 47 Ramsbury Drive, Earley, Reading, RG6 7RT T: 0118 926 4729

Battlefields Trust, 33 High Green, Brooke, Norwich, NR15 1HR T: 01508 558145 F: 01508 558145 E: BattlefieldTrust@aol.com W: www.battlefieldstrust.com

Black and Asian Studies Association, 28 Russell Square, London, WC1B 5DS T: (020) 7862 8844 E: marikas@sas.ac.uk

Brewery History Society, Manor Side East, Mill Lane, Byfleet, West Byfleet, KT14 7RS E: jsechiari@rmcbp.co.uk W: www.breweryhistory.com No information on publicans. Contact Pub History Society

British Association for Local History, PO Box 6549, Somersal Herbert, Ashbourne, DE6 5WH T: 01283 585947 F: 01722 413242 E: mail@balh.co.uk W: www.balh.co.uk

British Association of Paper Historians, 47 Ellesmere Road, Chiswick, London, W4 3EA E: baph@baph.freeserve.co.uk W: www.baph.freeserve.com Occupational/Genealogical Index Contact: Jean Stirk, Shode House, Ightham Kent TN15 9H

British Brick Society, 9 Bailey Close, High Wycombe, HP13 6QA T: 01494-520299 E: michael@mhammett.freeserve.co.uk W: www.britishbricksoc.free-online.co.uk www.tengula.freeserve.co.uk/acbmg/bt.htm.

British Records Association, 40 Northampton Road, London, EC1R 0HB T: (020) 7833 0428 F: (020) 7833 0416 E: britrecassoc@hotmail.com W: www.hmc.gov.uk/bra

British Records Society, Stone Barn Farm, Sutherland Road, Longsdon, ST9 9QD T: 01782 385446 E: carolyn@cs.keele.ac.uk britishrecordsociety@hotmail.com W: www.britishrecordsociety.org.uk

British Society for Sports History, Dept of Sports & Science, John Moore's University, Byrom Street, Liverpool, L3 3AF

Chapels Heritage Society - CAPEL, 2 Sandy Way, Wood Lane, Hawarden, CH5 3JJ T: 01244 531255

Chapels Society, 25 Park Chase, Wembley, HA9 8EQ T: 020 8903 2198 E: agworth296@hotmail.com No genealogical information.y

Coble and Keelboat Society, 19 Selwyn Avenue, Whitley Bay, NE25 9DH T: 0191 251 4412

Conference of Regional and Local Historians, The School of Humanities, Languages & Social Sciences, University of Wolverhampton, Dudley Campus, Castle View, Dudley, DY1 3HR T: 01902 321056 E: M.D.Wanklyn@wlv.ac.uk

Congregational History Circle, 160 Green Lane, Morden, SM4 6SR

Costume Society, St Paul's House, 8 Warwick Road, London, EC4P 4BN W: www.costumesociety.org.uk

Current Archaeology, 9 Nassington Road, London, NW3 2TX T: (020) 7435-7517 F: (020) 7916-2405 E: editor@archaeology.co.uk W: http://www.archaeology.co.uk CC accepted

Ecclesiastical History Society, 6 Gallows Hill, Saffron Walden, CB11 4DA

English Place Name Society, c/o School of English Studies, University of Nottingham, Nottingham, NG7 2RD T: 0115 951 5919 F: 0115 951 5924 E: janet.rudkin@nottingham.ac.uk W: www.nottingham.ac.uk/english/

Family and Community Historical Research Society, Fir Trees, 12 Fryer Close, Chesham, HP5 1RD W: www.fachrs.com

Family & Community Historical Society, 73 Derby Road, Cromford, Matlock, DE4 3RP W: www.fachrs.com

Friends Historical Society, c/o The Library, Friends House, 173-177 Euston Road, London, NW1 2BJ

Friends of War Memorials, 4 Lower Belgrave Street, London, SW1W 0LA T: (020) 7259-0403 F: (020) 7259-0296 E: fowm@eidosnet.co.uk W: http://www.war-memorials.com

Garden History Society, 70 Cowcross Street, London, EC1M 6EJ T: (020) 7608 2409 F: (020) 7490 2974 E: enquiries@gardenhistorysociety.org W: www.gardenhistorysociety.org

Glasgow Hebrew Burial Society, 222 Fenwick Rd, Griffnock, Glasgow, G46 6UE T: 0141 577 8226

Historical Association (Local History), 59A Kennington Park Road, London, SE11 4JH T: (020) 7735-3901 F: (020) 7582 4989 E: enquiry@history.org.uk W: http://www..history.org.uk

Historical Medical Equipment Society, 8 Albion Mews, Apsley, HP3 9QZ E: hmes@antiageing.freeserve.co.uk

Hugenot Society of Great Britain & Ireland, Hugenot Library University College, Gower Street, London, WC1E 6BT T: 020 7679 5199 E: s.massil@ucl.ac.uk W: (Library) www.ucl.ac.uk/ucl-info/divisions/library/huguenot.htm (Society) www.hugenotsociety.org.uk

Labour Heritage, 18 Ridge Road, Mitcham, CR4 2EY T: 020 8640 1814 F: 020 8640 1814,

Association of Local History Tutors, 47 Ramsbury Drive, Earley, Reading, RG6 7RT T: 0118 926 4729

Local Population Studies Society, School of Biological Sciences (Dr S Scott), University of Liverpool, Derby Building, Liverpool, L69 3GS

Mercia Cinema Society, 5 Arcadia Avenue, Chester le Street, DH3 3UH

Military Historical Society, Court Hill Farm, Potterne, Devizes, SN10 5PN T: 01980 615689 Daytime T: 01380 723371 Evenings F: 01980 618746

Oral History Society, British Library National Sound Archive, 96 Euston Road, London, NW1 2DB T: (020) 7412-7405 T: (020) 7412-7440 F: (020) 7412-7441 E: rob.perks@bl.uk W: www.oralhistory.org.uk

Police History Society, 37 Greenhill Road, Timperley, Altrincham, WA15 7BG T: 0161-980-2188 E: alanhayhurst@greenhillroad.fsnet.co.uk W:policehistorysociety.co.uk

Postal History Society, 60 Tachbrook Street, London, SW1V 2NA T: (020) 7821-6399 E: home@claireangier.co.uk

Pub History Society, 13 Grovewood, Sandycombe Road, Kew, Richmond, TW9 3NF T: (020) 8296-8794 E: sfowler@sfowler.force9.co.uk W: www.uk-history.co.uk/phs.htm

Richard III Society - Norfolk Group, 20 Rowington Road, Norwich, NR1 3RR

Royal Geographical Society (with IBG), 1 Kensington Gore, London, SW7 2AR T: 020 7291 3001 F: 020 7591 3001 W: www.rgs.org

Royal Photographic Society Historical Group, 7A Cotswold Road, Belmont, Sutton, SM2 5NG T: (020) 8643 2743

Royal Society, 6 - 9 Carlton House Terrace, London, SW1Y 5AG T: 020 7451 2606 F: 020 7930 2170 E: library@royalsoc.ac.uk W: www.royalsoc.ac.uk

Royal Society of Chemistry Library & Information Centre, Burlington House, Piccadilly, London, W1J 0BA T: (020) 7437 8656 F: (020) 7287 9798 E: library@rsc.org W: www.rsc.org

Society for Landscape Studies, School of Continuing Studies, Birmingham University, Edbaston, Birmingham, B15 2TT

Society for Nautical Research, Stowell House, New Pond Hill, Cross in Hand, Heathfield TN21 0LX

Society of Antiquaries, Burlington House, Piccadilly, London, W1J 0BE T: (020) 7479 7080 F: (020) 7287 6967 E: admin@sal.org.uk W: www.sal.org.uk

Society of Jewellery Historians, Department of Scientific Research, The British Museum, Great Russell Street, London, WC1B 3DG T: E: jewelleryhistorians@yahoo.co.uk

Strict Baptist Historical Society, 38 Frenchs Avenue, Dunstable, LU6 1BH T: 01582 602242 E: kdix@sbhs.freeserve.co.uk W: www.strictbaptisthistory.org.uk

Thoresby Society, 23 Clarendon Road, Leeds, LS2 9NZ T: 0113 245 7910 W: www.thoresby.org.uk

Unitarian Historical Society, 6 Ventnor Terrace, Edinburgh, EH9 2BL

United Kingdom Reminiscence Network, Age Exchange Reminiscence Centre, 11 Blackheath Village, London, SE3 9LA T: 020 83189 9105 E: age-exchange@lewisham.gov.uk

United Reformed Church History Society, Westminster College, Madingley Road, Cambridge, CB3 0AA T: 01223-741300 (NOT Wednesdays), Information on ministers of constituent churches not members

University of London Extra -Mural Society For Genealogy And History of The Family, 136 Lennard Road, Beckenham, BR3 1QT

Vernacular Architecture Group, Ashley, Willows Green, Chelmsford, CM3 1QD T: 01245 361408 W: www.vag.org.uk

Veterinary History Society, 608 Warwick Road, Solihull, B91 1AA

Victorian Military Society, PO Box 5837, Newbury, RG14 7FJ T: 01635 48628 E: vmsdan@msn.com W: www.vms.org.uk

Victorian Revival, Sugar Hill Farm, Knayton, Thirsk, YO7 4BP T: 01845 537827 F: 01845 537827 E: pamelagoult@hotmail.com

Victorian Society, 1 Priory Gardens, Bedford Park, London, W4 1TT T: (020) 8994 1019 F: (020) 8747 5899 E: admin@victorian-society.org.uk W: http://www.victorian-society.org.uk CC accepted

Voluntary Action History Society, National Centre for Volunteering, Regent's Wharf, 8 All Saints Street, London, N1 9RL T: (020) 7520 8900 F: (020) 7520 8910 E: instvolres.aol.com W: www.ivr.org.uk/vahs.htm

War Research Society, 27 Courtway Avenue, Birmingham, B14 4PP T: 0121 430 5348 F: 0121 436 7401 E: battletour@aol.com W: www.battlefieldtours.co.uk

Wesley Historical Society, 34 Spiceland Road, Northfield, Birmingham, B31 1NJ E: edgraham@tesco.net W: www.wesleyhistoricalsociety.org.uk

The Waterways Trust, The National Waterways Museum, Llanthony Warehouse, Gloucester Docks, Gloucester, GL1 2EH T: 01452 318053 F: 01452 318066 E: info@nwm.demon.co.uk W: www.nwm.org.uk

The West of England Costume Society, 4 Church Lane, Long Aston, Nr. Bristol, BS41 9LU T: 01275-543564 F: 01275-543564

Bedfordshire

Ampthill & District Archaeological and Local History, 14 Glebe Avenue, Flitwick, Bedford, MK45 1HS T: 01525 712778 E: petwood@waitrose.com W: www.museums.bedfordshire.gov.uk/localgroups/ampthill2/html

Ampthill & District Preservation Society, Seventh House, 43 Park Hill, Ampthill, MK45 2LP

Ampthill History Forum, 10 Mendham Way, Clophill, Bedford, MK45 4AL E: forum@ampthillhistory.co.uk W: www.ampthillhistory.co.uk

Bedfordshire Archaeological and Local History Society, 7 Lely Close, Bedford, MK41 7LS T: 01234 365095 W: www.museums.bedfordshire.gov.uk/localgroups

Bedfordshire Historical Record Society, 48 St Augustine's Road, Bedford, MK40 2ND T: 01234 309548 E: rsmart@ntlworld.com W: www.bedfordshirehrs.org.uk

Bedfordshire Local History Association, 29 George Street, Maulden, Bedford, MK45 2DF T: 1525633029

Biggleswade History Society, 6 Pine Close, Biggleswade, SG18 QEF

Caddington Local History Group, 98 Mancroft Road, Caddington, Nr. Luton, LUL 4EN W: www.caddhist.moonfruit.com

Carlton & Chellington Historical Society, 3 High Street, Carlton, MK43 7JX

Dunstable & District Local History Society, 7 Castle Close, Totternhoe, Dunstable, LU6 1QJ T: 01525 221963

Dunstable Historic and Heritage Studies, 184 West Street, Dunstable, LU6 1 NX T: 01582 609018

Harlington Heritage Trust, 2 Shepherds Close, Harlington, Near Dunstable, LU5 6NR

Knoll History Projext, 32 Ashburnham Road, Ampthill, MK45 2RH

Leighton-Linslade Heritage Display Society, 25 Rothschild Road, Linslade, Leighton Buzzard, LU7 7SY T:

Luton & District Historical Society, 22 Homerton Rd, Luton, LU3 2UL T: 01582 584367

Social History of Learning Disability Research Group, School of Health & Social Welfare, Open University, Milton Keynes, MK7 6AA

Toddington Historical Society, 21 Elm Grove, Toddington, Dunstable, LU5 6BJ W: www.museums.bedfordshire.gov.uk/local/toddington.htm

Wrestlingworth History Society, Wrestlingworth Memorial Hall, Church Lane, Wrestlingworth, SG19 2EJ

Berkshire

Berkshire Industrial Archaeological Group, 20 Auclum Close, Burghfield Common, Reading, RG7 DY

Berkshire Local History Association, 18 Foster Road, Abingdson, OX14 1YN E: secretary@blha.org.uk W: www.blha.org.uk

Berkshire Record Society, Berkshire Record Office, 9 Coley Avenue, Reading, RG1 6AF T: 0118-901-5130 F: 0118-901-5131 E: peter.durrant@reading.gov.uk

Bracknell & District Historical Society, 16 Harcourt Road, Bracknell, RG12 7JD T: 01344 640341

Brimpton Parish Research Association, Shortacre, Brimpton Common, Reading, RG7 4RY T: 0118 981 3649

Chiltern Heraldry Group, Magpie Cottage, Pondwood Lane, Shottesbrooke, SL6 3SS T: 0118 934 3698

Cox Green Local History Group, 29 Bissley Drive, Maidenhead, SL6 3UX T: 01628 823890

Datchet Village Society, 86 London Road, Datchet, SL3 9LQ T: 01753 542438 E: janet@datchet.com W: www.datchet.com

Eton Wick History Group, 47 Colenorton Crescent, Eton Wick, Windsor, SL4 6WW T: 01753 861674

Finchampstead History & Heritage Group, 134 Kiln Ride, California, Wokingham, RG40 3PB T: 0118 973 3005

Friends of Reading Museums, 15 Benyon Court, Bath Road, Reading, RG1 6HR T: 0118 958 0642

Friends of Wantage Vale & Downland Museum, 19 Church Street, Wantage, OX12 8BL T: 01235 771447,

Goring & Streatley Local History Society, 45 Springhill Road, Goring On Thames, Reading, RG8 OBY T: 01491 872625

Hare Hatch & Kiln Green Local History Group, Shinglebury, Tag Lane, Hare Hatch, Twyford, RG10 9ST T: 0118 940 2157 E: richard.lloyd@wargrave.net

Hedgerley Historical Society, Broad Oaks, Parish Lane, Farnham Common, Slough, SL2 3JW T: 01753 645682 E: brendakenw@tiscali.co.uk , **Heraldry Society,** PO Box 32, Maidenhead, SL6 3FD T: 0118-932-0210 F: 0118 932 0210 E: heraldry-society@cwcom.net

History of Reading Society, 5 Wilmington Close, Woodley, Reading, RG5 4LR T: 0118 961 8559 E: peterrussell7@hotmail.com

Hungerford Historical Association, 23 Fairview Road, Hungerford, RG170PB T: 01488 682932 E: mandm.martin@talk21.com W: www.hungerfordhistorical.org.uk

Maidenhead Archaeological & Historical Society, 70 Lambourne Drive, Maidenhead, SL6 3HG T: 01628 672196

Middle Thames Archaeological & Historical Society, 1 Saffron Close, Datchet, Slough, SL3 9DU T: 01753 543636

Mortimer Local History Group, 19 Victoria Road, Mortimer, RG7 3SH T: 0118 933 2819

Newbury & District Field Club, 4 Coombe Cottages, Coombe Road, Crompton, Newbury, RG20 6RG T: 01635 579076

Project Purley, 4 Allison Gardens, Purley on Thames, RG8 8DF T: 0118 942 2485

Sandhurst Historical Society, Beech Tree Cottage, Hancombe Road, Little Sandhurst, GU47 8NP T: 01344 777476 W: www.sandhurst-town.com/societies

Shinfield & District Local History Societies, Long Meadow, Part Lane, Swallowfield, RG7 1TB
Swallowfield Local History Society, Kimberley, Swallowfield, Reading, RG7 1QX T: 0118 988 3650
Thatcham Historical Society, 72 Northfield Road, Thatcham, RG18 3ES T: 01635 864820 W: www.thatchamhistoricalsociety.org.uk
Twyford & Ruscombe Local History Society, 26 Highfield Court, Waltham Road, Twyford, RG10 0AA T: 0118 934 0109
Wargrave Local History Society, 6 East View Close, Wargrave, RG10 8BJ T: 0118 940 3121 E: peter.delaney@talk21.com history@wargrave.net W: www.wargrave.net/history
Windsor Local History Publications Group, 256 Dedworth Road, Windsor, SL4 4JR T: 01753 864835 E: windlesora@hotmail.com
Wokingham History Group, 39 Howard Road, Wokingham, RG40 2BX T: 0118 978 8519
Alvechurch Historical Society, Bearhill House, Alvechurch, Birmingham, B48 7JX T: 0121 445 2222

Birmingham
Birmingham & District Local History Association, 112 Brandwood Road, Kings Heath, Birmingham, B14 6BX T: 0121-444-7470
Small Heath Local History Society, 381 St Benedicts Rd, Small Heath, Birmingham B10 9ND

Bristol
Alveston Local History Society, 6 Hazcl Gardens, Alveston, BS35 3RD T: 01454 43881 E: jc1932@alveston51.fsnet.co.uk
Avon Local History Association, 4 Dalkeith Avenue, Kingswood, Bristol, BS15 1HH T: 0117 967 1362
Bristol & Avon Archaeological Society, 3 Priory Avenue, Westbury on Trym, Bristol, BS9 4DA T: 0117 9620161 (evenings) W: http://www-digitalbristol.org/members/baas/
Bristol Records Society, Regional History Centre, Faculty of Humanities, University of the West of England, St Maththias Campus, Oldbury Court Road, Fishponds, Bristol, BS16 2JP T: 0117 344 4395 W: http://humanities.uwe.ac.uk/brs/index.htm
Congresbury History Group, Venusmead, 36 Venus Street, Congresbury, Bristol, BS49 5EZ T: 01934 834780 F: 01934 834780 E: rogerhards-venusmead@breathemail.net
Downend Local History Society, 141 Overndale Road, Downend, Bristol, B516 2RN
Whitchurch Local History Society, 62 Nailsea Park, Nailsea, Bristol, B519 1BB
Yatton Local History Society, 27 Henley Park, Yatton, Bristol, BS49 4JH T: 01934 832575

Buckinghamshire
Buckinghamshire Archaeological Society, County Museum, Church Street, Aylesbury, HP20 2QP T: 01269 678114
Buckinghamshire Record Society, Centre for Buckinghamshire Studies, County Hall, Aylesbury, HP20 1UU T: 01296 383013 F: 01296-382771 E: archives@buckscc.gov.uk W: www.buckscc.gov.uk/archives/publications/brs.stm
Chesham Bois One-Place Study, 70 Chestnut Lane, Amersham, HP6 6EH T: 01494 726103 E: cdjmills@hotmail.com
Chesham Society, 54 Church Street, Chesham, HP5 IHY
Chess Valley Archealogical & Historical Society, 16 Chapmans Crescent, Chesham, NP5 2QU T: 01494 772914
Lashbrook One-Place Study, 70 Chestnut Lane, Amersham, HP6 6EH T: 01494 726103 E: cdjmills@hotmail.com Covers Bradford, Talaton, Thornbury in Devon and Shiplake, Oxfordshire see also Lashbrook One-Name Study (Under Family History Societies)
Pitstone and Ivinghoe Museum Society, Vicarage Road, Pitstone, Leighton Buzzard, LU7 9EY T: 01296 668123 W: http://website.lineone.net/~pitstonemus, Pitstone Green Museum and Ford End Watermill

Princes Risborough Area Heritage Society, Martin's Close, 11 Wycombe Road, Princes Risborough, HP27 0EE T: 01844 343004 F: 01844 273142 E: sandymac@risboro35.freeserve.co.uk

Cambridgeshire
Cambridge Antiquarian Society, P0 Box 376, 96 Mill Lane, Impington, Cambridge , CB4 9HS T: 01223 502974 E: liz-allan@hotmail.com
Cambridge Group for History of Population and Social History, Sir William Hardy Building, Downing Place, Cambridge, CB2 3EN T: 01223 333181 F: 01223 333183 W: http://www-hpss.geog.cam.ac.uk

Cambridgeshire Archaeology , Castle Court, Shire Hall, Cambridge, CB3 0AP T: 01223 717312 F: 01223 362425 E: quentin.carroll@cambridgeshire.gov.uk W: http://edweb.camcnty.gov.uk/archaeology www.archaeology.freewire.co.uk
Cambridgeshire Local History Society, 1A Archers Close, Swaffham Bulbeck, Cambridge, CB5 0NG
Cambridgeshire Record Society, County Record Office, Shire Hall, Cambridge, CB3 0AP W: www.cambridgeshirehistory.com/societies/crs/index.html
Hemingfords Local History Society, Royal Oak Corner, Hemingford Abbots, Huntingdon, PE28 9AE T: 01480 463430 E: hemlocs@hotmail.com
Houghton & Wyton Local History Society, Church View, Chapel Lane, Houghton, Huntingdon, PE28 2AY T: 01480 469376 E: gerry.feake@one-name.org
Huntingdonshire Local History Society, 2 Croftfield Road, Godmanchester, PE29 2ED T: 01480 411202
Saffron Walden Historical Society, 9 High Street, Saffron Walden, CB10 1AT T:
Sawston Village History Society, 21 Westmoor Avenue, Sawston, Cambridge, CB2 4BU T: 01223 833475
Upwood & Raveley History Group, The Old Post Office, 71-73 High Street, Upwood, Huntingdon, PE17 1QE

Cheshire
Altrincham History Society, 10 Willoughby Close, Sale, M33 6PJ T: 0161 962 7658
Ashton & Sale History Society, Tralawney House, 78 School Road, Sale, M33 7XB T: 0161 9692795
Bowdon History Society, 5 Pinewood, Bowdon, Altrincham, WA14 3JQ T: 0161 928 8975
Cheshire Heraldry Society, 24 Malvern Close, Congleton, CW12 4PD
Cheshire Local History Association, Cheshire Record Office, Duke Street, Chester, CH1 1RL T: 01224 602559 F: 01244 603812 E: chairman@cheshirehistory.org.uk W: www.cheshirehistory.org.uk
Chester Archaeological Society, Grosvenor Museum, 27 Grosvenor Street, Chester, CH1 2DD T: 01244 402028 F: 01244 347522 E: p.carrington@chestercc.gov.uk W: http://www.chesterarchaeolsoc.org.uk
Christleton Local History Group, 25 Croft Close, Rowton, CH3 7QQ T: 01244 332410
Society of Cirplanologists, 26 Roe Cross Green, Mottram, Hyde, SK14 6LP T: 01457 763485
Congleton History Society, 48 Harvey Road Road, Congleton, CWI2 2DH T: 01260 278757 E: awill0909@aol.com
Department of History - University College Chester, Department of History, University College Chester, Cheveney Road, Chester, CH1 4BJ T: 01244 375444 F: 01244 314095 E: history@chester.ac.uk W: www.chester.ac.uk/history
Disley Local History Society, 5 Hilton Road, Disley, SK12 2JU T: 01663 763346 F: 01663 764910 E: chgris.makepeace@talk21.com
Historic Society of Lancashire & Cheshire, East Wing Flat, Arley Hall, Northwich, CW9 6NA T: 01565 777231
Lancashire & Cheshire Antiquarian Society, 59 Malmesbury Road, Cheadle Hulme, SK8 7QL T: 0161 439 7202 E: morris.garratt@lineone.net W: www.lancashirehistory.co.uk www.cheshirehistory.org.uk

Lawton History Group, 17 Brattswood drive, Church Lawton, Stoke on Trent, ST7 3EF T: 01270 873427 E: arthur@aburton83.freeserve.co.uk

Macclesfield Historical Society, 42 Tytherington Drive, Macclesfield, SK10 2HJ T: 01625 420250, SAE for all enquiries

Northwich & District Heritage Society, 13 Woodlands Road, Hartford, Northwich, CW8 1NS, Several publications available for Mid Cheshire area

Poynton Local History Society, 6 Easby Close, Poynton, SK12 1YG T:

South Cheshire Family History Society incorporating S E Cheshire Local Studies Group, PO Box 1990, Crewe, CW2 6FF T: W: www.scfhs.org.uk

Stockport Historical Society, 59 Malmesbury Road, Cheadle Hulme, Stockport, SK8 7QL T: 0161 439 7202

Weaverham History Society, Ashdown, Sandy Lane, Weaverham, Northwich, CW8 3PX T: 01606 852252 E: jg-davies@lineone.net

Wilmslow Historical Society, 4 Campden Way, Handforth, Wilmslow, SK9 3JA T: 01625 529381

Cleveland

Cleveland & Teesside Local History Society, 150 Oxford Road, Linthorpe, Middlesbrough, TS5 5EL,

Cornwall

Bodmin Local History Group, 1 Lanhydrock View, Bodmin, PL31 1BG T:

Cornwall Association of Local Historians, St Clement's Cottage, Coldrinnick Bac, Duloe, Liskeard, PL14 4QF T: 01503 220947 E: anne@coldrinnick.freeserve.co.uk

Cornwall Family History Society, 5 Victoria Square, Truro, TR1 2RS T: 01872-264044 E: secretary@cornwallfhs.com W: http://www.cornwallfhs.com Secretary/Administrator Mrs Frances Armstrong

Lighthouse Society of Great Britain, Gravesend Cottage, Gravesend, Torpoint, PL11 2LX E: k.trethewey@btinternet.com W: http://www.lsgb.co.uk Holds databases of lighthouses and their keepers.

Royal Institution of Cornwall, Courtney Library & Cornish History Research Centre, Royal Cornwall Museum, River Street, Truro, TR1 2SJ T: 01872 272205 E: RIC@royal-cornwall-museum.freeserve.co.uk W: www.cornwall-online.co.uk/ric

Cumbria

Ambleside Oral History Group, 1 High Busk, Ambleside, LA22 0AW T: 01539 431070 E: history@amblesideonline.co.uk W: www.aoghistory.f9.co.uk

Appleby Archaeology Group, Pear Tree Cottage, Kirkland Road, Skirwith, Penrith, CA10 1RL T: 01768 388318 E: martin@fellside-eden.freeserve.co.uk

Appleby In Westmorland Record Society, Kingstone House, Battlebarrow, Appleby-In-Westmorland, CA16 6XT T: 017683 52282 E: barry.mckay@britishlibrary.net

Caldbeck & District Local History Society, Whelpo House, Caldbeck, Wigton, CA7 8HQ T: 01697 478270

Cartmel Peninsula Local History Society, Fairfield, Cartmel, Grange Over Sands, LA11 6PY T: 015395 36503

Centre for North West Regional Studies, Fylde College, Lancaster University, Lancaster, LA1 4YF T: 01524 593770 F: 01524 594725 E: christine.wilkinson@lancaster.ac.uk W: www.lancs.ac.uk/users/cnwrs, cc accepted

Crosby Ravensworth Local History Society, Brookside, Crosby Ravensworth, Penrith, CA10 3JP T: 01931 715324 E: david@riskd.freeserve.co.uk

Cumberland and Westmorland Antiquarian and Archaeological Society, County Offices, Kendal, LA9 4RQ T: 01539 773431 F: 01539 773539 E: info@cwaas.org.uk W: www.cwaas.org.uk

Cumbria Amenity Trust Mining History Society, The Rise, Alston, CA9 3DB T: 01434 381903 W: www.catmhs.co.uk

Cumbria Industrial History Society, Coomara, Carleton, Carlisle, CA4 0BU T: 01228 537379 F: 01228 596986 E: gbrooksvet@tiscali.co.uk W: www.cumbria-industries.org.uk

Cumbrian Railways Association, Whin Rigg, 33 St Andrews Drive, Perton, Wolverhampton, WV6 7YL T: 01902 745472 W: www.cumbrian-rail.org

Dalton Local History Society, 15 Kirkstone Crescent, Barrow in Furness, LA14 4ND T: 01229 823558 E: davidhsd@aol.co.

Duddon Valley Local History Group, High Cross Bungalow, Broughton in Furness, LA20 6ES T: 01229 716196

Friends of Cumbria Archives, The Barn, Parsonby, Aspatria, Wigton, CA7 2DE T: 01697 320053 E: john@johnmary.freeserve.co.uk W: www.focasonline.org.uk

Friends of The Helena Thompson Museum, 24 Calva Brow, Workington, CA14 1DD T: 01900 603312

Holme & District Local History Society, The Croft, Tanpits Lane, Burton, Carnforth, LA6 1HZ T: 01524 782121

Keswick Historical Society, Windrush, Rogersfield, Keswick, CA12 4BN T: 01768 772771

Lorton and Derwent Fells Local History Society, Clouds Hill, Lorton, Cockermouth, CA13 9TX T: 01900 85259 E: michael@lorton.freeserve.co.uk

Matterdale Historical and Archaeological Society, The Knotts, Matterdale, Penrith, CA11 0LD T: 01768 482358

North Pennines Heritage Trust, Nenthead Mines Heritage Centre, Nenthead, Alston, CA9 3PD T: 01434 382037 F: 01434 382294 E: administration.office@virgin.net W: www.npht.com

Sedbergh & District History Society, c/o 72 Main Street, Sedbergh, LA10 5AD T: 015396 20504 E: history@sedbergh.org.uk

Shap Local History Society, The Hermitage, Shap, Penrith, CA10 3LY T: 01931 716671 E: liz@kbhshap.freeserve.co.uk

Solway History Society, 9 Longthwaite Crescent, Wigton, CA7 9JN T: 01697 344257 E: s.l.thornhill@talk21.com

Staveley and District History Society, Heather Cottage, Staveley, Kendal, LA8 9JE T: 01539 821194 E: Jpatdball@aol.com

Upper Eden History Society, Copthorne, Brough Sowerby, Kirkby Stephen, CA17 4EG T: 01768 341007 E: gowling@kencomp.net

Whitehaven Local History Society, Cumbria Record Office & local Studies Library, Scotch Street, Whitehaven, CA28 7BJ T: 01946 852920 F: 01946 852919 E: anne.dick@cumbriacc.gov.uk

The 68th (or Durham) Regiment of Light Infantry Display Team, 40 The Rowans, Orgill, Egremont, CA22 2HW T: 01946 820110 E: PhilMackie@aol.com W: www.68dli.com

Derbyshire

Allestree Local Studies Group, 30 Kingsley Road, Allestree, Derby, DE22 2JH

Arkwright Society, Cromford Mill, Mill Lane, Cromford, DE4 3RQ T: 01629 823256 F: 01629 823256 E: info@cromfordmill.co.uk W: www.cromfordmill.co.uk CC accepted not American Express

Chesterfield & District Local History Society, Melbourne House, 130 Station Road, Bimington, Chesterfield, S43 1LU T: 01246 620266

Derbyshire Archaeological Society, 2 The Watermeadows, Swarkestone, Derby, DE73 1JA T: 01332 704148 E: barbarafoster@talk21.com W: www.DerbyshireAS.org.uk

Derbyshire Local History Societies Network, Derbyshire Record Office, Libraries & Heritage Dept, County Hall, Matlock, DE4 3AG T: 01629-580000-ext-3520-1 F: 01629-57611 E: recordoffice@derbyshire.gov.uk W: www.derbyshire.gov.uk

Derbyshire Record Society, 57 New Road, Wingerworth, Chesterfield, S42 6UJ T: 01246 231024 E: neapen@aol.com W: www.merton.dircon.co.uk/drshome.htm

Holymoorside and District History Society, 12 Brook Close, Holymoorside, Chesterfield, S42 7HB T: 01246 566799 W: www.holymoorsidehistsoc.org.uk

Ilkeston & District Local History Society, 16 Rigley Avenue, Ilkeston, DE7 5LW

New Mills Local History Society, High Point, Cote Lane, Hayfield, High Peak, SK23 T: 01663-742814

Old Dronfield Soc 2 Gosforth Close, Dronfield, S18 INT

Nottinghamshire Industrial Archaeology Society, 18 Queens Avenue, Ilkeston, DE7 4DL T: 0115 932 2228

Pentrich Historical Society, c/o The Village Hall, Main Road, Pentrich, DE5 3RE E: mail@pentrich.org.uk W: www.pentrich.org

Devon

Chagford Local History Society, Footaway, Westcott, Chagford, Newton Abbott, TQ13 8JF T: 01647 433698 E: cjbaker@jetdash.freeserve.co.uk

Dulverton and District Civic Society, 39 jury Road, Dulverton, TA22 9EJ,

Holbeton Yealmpton Brixton Society, 32 Cherry Tree Drive, Brixton, Plymouth, PL8 2DD W: http://beehive.thisisplymouth.co.uk/hyb

Moretonhampstead History Society, School House, Moreton, Hampstead, TQ13 8NX

Newton Tracey & District Local History Society, Home Park, Lovacott , Newton Tracey, Barnstaple, EX31 3PY T: 01271 858451

Tavistock & District Local History Society, 18 Heather Close, Tavistock, PL19 9QS T: 01822 615211 E: linagelliott@aol.com

The Devon & Cornwall Record Society, 7 The Close, Exeter, EX1 1EZ T: 01392 274727 W: www.cs.ncl.ac.uk/genuki/DEV/DCRS

The Devon History Society, c/o 112 Topsham Road, Exeter, EX2 4RW T: 01803 613336 T: 01392 256686 F: 01392 256689

The Old Plymouth Society, 625 Budshead Road, Whitleigh, Plymouth, PL5 4DW

Thorverton & District History Society, Ferndale, Thorverton, Exeter, EX5 5NG T: 01392 860932

Wembury Amenity Society, 5 Cross Park Road, Wembury, Plymouth, PL9 OEU

Yelverton & District Local History Society, 4 The Coach House, Grenofen, Tavistock, PL19 9ES T: W: www.floyds.org.uk/ylhs

Dorset

Bournemouth Local Studies Group, 6 Sunningdale, Fairway Drive, Christchurch, BH23 1JY T: 01202 485903 E: mbhall@onetel.net.uk

Dorchester Association For Research into Local History, 7 Stokehouse Street, Poundbury, Dorchester, DT1 3GP

Dorset Natural History & Archaeological Society Dorset Record Society Dorset County Museum, High West Street, Dorchester, DT1 1XA T: 01305 262735 F: 01305 257180

Verwood Historical Society, 74 Lake Road, Verwood, BH31 6BX T: 01202 824175 E: trevorgilbert@hotmail.com W: www.geocities.com/verwood_historical

William Barnes Society, Pippins, 58 Mellstock Avenue, Dorchester, DT1 2BQ T: 01305 265358, William Barnes is primarily (but not exclusively) a Dorest Dialect Poet

Dorest - West

Bridport History Society, 22 Fox Close, Bradpole, Bridport, DT6 3JF T: 01308 456876 E: celia@cgulls.fsnet.co.uk

Durham

Elvet Local & Family History Groups, 37 Hallgarth Street, Durham, DH1 3AT T: 0191-386-4098 F: 0191-386-4098 E: Turnstone-Ventures@durham-city.freeserve.co.uk

Architectural & Archaeological Society of Durham & Northumberland, Broom Cottage, 29 Foundry Fielkds, Crook, DL15 9SY T: 01388 762620 E: belindaburke@aol.com

Durham County Local History Society, 21 St Mary's Close, Tudoe Village, Spennymoor, DL16 6LR T: 01388 816209 E: johnbanham@tiscali.co.uk W: www.durhamweb.org.uk/dclhs

Durham Victoria County History Trust, Redesdale, The Oval, North Crescent, Durham, DH1 4NE T: 0191 384 8305 W: www.durhampast.net

Lanchester Local History Society, 11 St Margaret's Drive, Tanfield Village, Stanley, DH9 9QW T: 01207-236634 E: jstl@supanet.com

Monkwearmouth Local History Group, 75 Escallond Drive, Dalton Heights, Seaham, SR7 8JZ

North-East England History Institute (NEEHI), Department of History University of Durham, 43 North Bailey, Durham, DH1 3EX T: 0191-374-2004 F: 0191-374-4754 E: m.a.mcallister@durham.ac.uk W: http://www.durham.ac.uk/neehi.history/homepage.htm

St John Ambulance History Group, 3 The Bower, Meadowside, Jarrow, NE32 4RS T: 0191 537 4252

Teesdale Heritage Group, Wesley Terrace, Middleton in Teesdale, Barnard Castle, DL12 0Q T: 01833 641104

The Derwentdale Local History Society, 36 Roger Street, Blackhill, Consett, DH8 5SX

Tow Law History Society, 27 Attleee Estate, Tow Law, DL13 4LG T: 01388-730056 E: RonaldStorey@btinternet.co.uk W: www.historysociety.org.uk

Wheatley Hill History Club, Broadmeadows, Durham Road, Wheatley Hill, DH6 3LJ T: 01429 820813, Mobile 0781 112387 E: wheathistory@onet.co.uk W: http://mypages.comcast.net/dcock104433/HISTORY/index.htm

The 68th (or Durham) Regiment of Light Infantry Display Team, 40 The Rowans, Orgill, Egremont, CA22 2HW T: 01946 820110 E: PhilMackie@aol.com W: www.68dli.com

Essex

Barking & District Historical Society, 449 Ripple Road, Barking, IG11 9RB T: 020 8594 7381 E: barkinghistorical@hotmail.com Covers the London Borough of Barking and Dagenham

Barking & District Historical Society, 16 North Road, Chadwell Heath, Romford, RM6 6XU E: barkinghistorical@hotmail.com Postal and Email enquiries only

Billericay Archaeological and Historical Society, 24 Belgrave Road, Billericay, CM12 1TX T: 01277 658989

Brentwood & District Historical Society, 51 Hartswood Rd, Brentwood, CM14 5AG T: 01277 221637

Burnham & District Local History & Archaeological Society, The Museum, The Quay, Burnham On Crouch, CM0 8AS

Colchester Archaeological Group, 172 Lexden Road, Colchester, CO3 4BZ T: 01206 575081 W: www.camulos.com//cag/cag.htm

Dunmow & District Historical and Literary Society, 18 The Poplars, Great Dunmow, CM6 2JA T: 01371 872496

Essex Archaeological & Historical Congress, 56 Armond Road, Witham, CM8 2HA T: 01376 516315 F: 01376 516315 E: essexahc@aol.com

Essex Historic Buildings Group, 12 Westfield Avenue, Chelmsford, CM1 1SF T: 01245 256102 F: 01371 830416 E: cakemp@hotmail.com

Essex Society for Archeaology & History, 2 Landview Gardens, Ongar, CM5 9EQ T: 1277363106 E: family@leachies.freeserve.co.uk W: www.leachies.freeserve.co.uk

Friends of Historic Essex, 11 Milligans Chase, Galleywood, Chelmsford, CM2 8QD T: 01245 436043 F: 01245 257365 E: geraldine.willden2@essexcc.gov.uk

Friends of The Hospital Chapel - Ilford, 174 Aldborough Road South, Seven Kings, Ilford, IG3 8HF T: (020) 8590 9972 F: (020) 8590 0366

Halstead & District Local History Society, Magnolia, 3 Monklands Court, Halstead, C09 1AB

(HEARS) Herts & Essex Architectural Research Society , 4 Nelmes Way, Hornchurch, RM11 2QZ T: 01708 473646 E: kpolrm11@aol.com

High Country History Group, Repentance Cottage, Drapers Corner, Greensted, Ongar, CM5 9LS T: 01277 364305 E: rob.brooks@virgin.net, Covers the rural area of S W Ongar being the parishes of Greensted, Stanford Rivers, Stapleford Tawney and Theydon Mount

Ingatestone and Fryerning Historical and Archaeological Society, 36 Pine Close, Ingatestone, CM4 9EG T: 01277 354001

Loughton & District Historical Society, 6 High Gables, Loughton, IG10 4EZ T: (020) 8508 4974

Maldon Society, 15 Regency Court, Heybridge, Maldon, CM9 4EJ

Nazeing History Workshop, 16 Shooters Drive, Nazeing, EN9 2QD T: 01992 893264 E: d_pracy@hotmail.com W: www.eppingforectmuseum.co.uk

Romford & District Historical Society, 67 Gelsthorpe Road, Collier Row, Romford, RM5 2LX T: 01708 728203 E: caroline@wiggins67.freeserve.co.uk

The Colne Smack Preservation Society, 76 New Street, Brightlingsea, CO7 0DD T: 01206 304768 W: www.colne-smack-preservation.rest.org.uk

Thurrock Heritage Forum, c/o Thurrock Museum, Orsett Road, Grays, RM17 5DX T: 01375 673828 E: enquiries@thurrockheritageforum.co.uk W: www.thurrockheritageforum.co.uk

Thurrock Local History Society, 13 Rosedale Road, Little Thurrock, Grays, RM17 6AD T: 01375 377746 E: tcvs.tc@gtnet.gov.uk

Waltham Abbey Historical Society, 28 Hanover Court, Quaker Lane, Waltham Abbey, EN9 1HR T: 01992 716830

Walthamstow Historical Society, 24 Nesta Road, Woodford Green, IG8 9RG T: (020) 8504 4156 F: (020) 8523 2399

Wanstead Historical Soc 28 Howard Road, Ilford, IG1 2EX

Witham History Group, 35 The Avenue, Witham, CM8 2DN T: 01376 512566

Woodford Historical Society, 2 Glen Rise, Woodford Green, IG8 0AW T:

Gloucestershire

Bristol and Gloucestershire Archaeological Society, 22 Beaumont Road, Gloucester, GL2 0EJ T: 01452 302610 E: david_j._h.smith@virgin.net W: http://www.bgas.org.uk

Campden & District Historical & Archaeological Society (CADWAS), The Old Police station, High Street, Chipping Campden, GL55 6HB T: 01386 848840 E: enquiries@chippingcampdenhistory.org.uk W: www.chippingcampdenhistory.org.uk

Charlton Kings Local History Society, 28 Chase Avenue, Charlton Kings, Cheltenham, GL52 6YU T: 01242 520492

Cheltenham Local History Society, 1 Turkdean Road, Cheltenham, GL51 6AP

Cirencester Archaeological and Historical Society, 8 Tower Street, Cirencester, GL7 1EF T: 01285 651516 F: 01285 651516 E: dviner@waitrose.com

Forest of Dean Local History Society, Patch Cottage, Oldcroft Green, Lydney, GL15 4NL T: 01594 563165 E: akearApatchcottage.freeserve.co.uk W: www.forestofdeanhistory.co.uk

Frenchay Tuckett Society and Local History Museum, 247 Frenchay Park Road, Frenchay, BS16 ILG T: 0117 956 9324 E: raybulmer@compuserve.com W: www.frenchay.org/museum.html

Friends of Gloucestershire Archives, 17 Estcourt Road, Gloucester, GL13LU T: 01452 528930 E: patricia.bath@talk21.com

Gloucestershire County Local History Committee, Gloucestershire RCC, Community House, 15 College Green, Gloucester, GL1 2LZ T: 01452 528491, Fax:, 01452-528493 E: glosrcc@grcc.org.uk

Lechlade History Society, The Gables, High Street, Lechlade, GL7 3AD T: 01367 252457 E: Gillkeithnewson.aol.com Archivist: Mrs Maureen Baxter Tel; 01367 252437

Leckhampton Local History Society, 202 Leckhampton Road, Leckhampton, Cheltenham, GL53 OHG W: www.geocities.com/llhsgl53

Moreton-In-Marsh & District Local History Society, Chapel Place, Longborough, Moreton-In-Marsh, GL56 OQR T: 01451 830531 W: www.moretonhistory.co.uk

Newent Local History Society, Arron, Ross Road, Newent, GL18 1BE T: 01531 821398

Painswick Local History Society, Canton House, New Street, Painswick, GL6 6XH T: 01452 812419

Stroud Civic Society, Blakeford House, Broad Street, Kings Stanley, Stonehouse, GL10 3PN T: 01453 822498

Stroud Local History Society, Stonehatch, Oakridge Lynch, Stroud, GL6 7NR T: 01285 760460 E: john@loosleyj.freeserve.co.uk

Swindon Village Society, 3 Swindon Hall, Swindon Village, Cheltenham, GL51 9QR T: 01242 521723

Tewkesbury Historical Society, 20 Moulder Road, Tewkesbury, GL20 8ED T: 01684 297871

Hampshire

Aldershot Historical and Archaeological Society, 10 Brockenhurst Road, Aldershot, GU11 3HH T: 01252 26589

Andover History and Archaeology Society, 140 Weyhill Road, Andover, SPlO 3BG T: 01264 324926 E: johnl.barrell@virgin.net

Basingstoke Archaeological and Historical Society, 57 Belvedere Gardens, Chineham, Basingstoke, RG21 T: 01256 356012

Bishops Waltham Museum Trust, 8 Folly Field, Bishop's Waltham, Southampton, S032 1EB T: 01489 894970

Bitterne Local History Society, Heritage Centre, 225 Peartree Avenue, Bitterne, Southampton T: (023) 80444837 F: (023) 80444837 E: sheaf@sheafrs.freeserve.co.uk W: www.bitterne.net

Botley & Curdridge Local History, 3 Mayfair Court, Botley, SO30 2GT

Fareham Local History Group, Wood End Lodge, Wood End, Wickham, Fareham, PO17 6JZ W: www.cix.co.uk/~catisfield/farehist.htm

Fleet & Crookham Local History Group, 33 Knoll Road, Fleet, GU51 4PT W: www.hants.gov.uk/fclhg

Fordingbridge Historical Society, 26 Lyster Road,, Manor Park, Fordingbridge, SP6 IQY T: 01425 655417

Hampshire Field Club and Archaeological Society, 8 Lynch Hill Park, Whitchurch, RG28 7NF T: 01256 893241 E: jhamdeveson@compuserve.com W: www.fieldclub.hants.org.uk/

Hampshire Field Club & Archaelogical Society (Local History Section), c/o Hampshire Record Office, Sussex Street, Winchester, SO23 8TH T:

Havant Museum, Havant Museum, 56 East Street, Havant, P09 1BS T: 023 9245 1155 F: 023 9249 8707 E: musmop@hants.gov.uk W: www.hants.gov.uk/museums, Also Friends of Havant Museum - Local History Section Local Studies Collection open Tuesday to Saturday 10.00.a.m. to 5.00.p.m.

Lymington & District Historical Society, Larks Lee, Coxhill Boldre, Near Lymington, 5041 8PS

Lyndhurst Historical Society - disbanded May 2003, Books and Documents handed into the New Forest Museum

Milford-on-Sea Historical Record Society, New House, New Road, Keyhaven, Lymington, S041 0TN

North East Hampshire Historical and Archaeological Society, 36 High View Road, Farnborough, GU14 7PT T: 01252-543023, E: nehhas@netscape.net W: www.hants.org.uk/nehhas

Parish Register Transcription Society, 50 Silvester Road, Waterlooville, PO8 5TL T: E: mail@prtsoc.org.uk W: www.prtsoc.org.uk

Porchester Society, Mount Cottage, Nelson Lane, Portchester, PO17 6AW T:

Somborne & District Society, Forge House, Winchester Road, Kings Somborne, Stockbridge, S020 6NY T: 01794 388742 E: w.hartley@ntlworld.com W: www.communigate.co.uk/hants/somsoc

South of England Costume Society , Bramley Cottage, 9 Vicarage Hill, Hartley Witney, Hook, RG27 8EH E: j.sanders@lineone.net

Southampton Local History Forum, Special Collections Library, Civic Centre, Southampton, England T: 023 8083 2462 F: 023 8022 6305 E: local.studies@southampton.gov.uk

Southern Counties Costume Society, 173 Abbotstone, Alresford, SO24 9TE T:

Stubbington & Hillhead History Society, 34 Anker Lane, Stubbington, Fareham, PO14 3HE T: 01329 664554

History of Thursley Society, 50 Wyke Lane, Ash, Aldershot, GU12 6EA E: norman.ratcliffe@ntlworld.com W: http://home.clara.net/old.norm/Thursley

West End Local History Society, 20 Orchards Way, West End, Southampton, S030 3FB T: 023 8057 5244 E: westendlhs@aol.com W: www.telbin.demon.co.uk/westendlhs, Museum at Old Fire Station, High Street, West End

Herefordshire

Eardisland Oral History Group, Eardisland, Leominster E: info@eardislandhistory.co.uk W: www.eardislandhistory.co.uk

Ewyas Harold & District WEA, c/o Hillside, Ewyas Harold, Hereford, HR2 0HA T: 01981 240529

Kington History Society, Kington Library, 64 Bridge Street, Kington, HR5 3BD T: 01544 230427 E: vee.harrison@virgin.net

Leominster Historical Society, Fircroft, Hereford Road, Leominster, HR6 8JU T: 01568 612874

Weobley & District Local History Society and Museum, Weobley Museum, Back Lane, Weobley, HR4 8SG T: 01544 340292

Hertfordshire

1st or Grenadier Foot Guards 1803 -1823 - Napoleonic Wars, 39 Chatterton, Letchworth, SG6 2JY T: 01462-670918 E: BJCham2809@aol.com W: http://members.aol.com/BJCham2809/homepage.html

Abbots Langley Local History Society, 19 High street, Abbots Langley, WD5 0AA E: allhs@btinternet.com W: http://www.allhs.btinternet.co.uk

Abbots Langley Local History Society, 159 Cottonmill Lane, St Albans, AL1 2EX

Baptist Historical Society, 60 Strathmore Avenue, Hitchin, SG5 1ST T: 01462-431816 T: 01462-442548 E: slcopson@dial.pipex.com W: www.baptisthistory.org.uk

Black Sheep Research (Machine Breakers, Rioters & Protesters), 4 Quills, Letchworth Garden City, SG6 2RJ T: 01462-483706 E: J_M_Chambers@compuserve.com

Braughing Local History Society, Pantiles, Braughing Friars, Ware, SG11 2NS

Codicote Local History Society, 34 Harkness Way, Hitchin, SG4 0QL T: 01462 622953

East Herts Archaeological Society, 1 Marsh Lane, Stanstead Abbots, Ware, SG12 8HH T: 01920 870664

Hertford Museum (Hertfordshire Regiment), 18 Bull Plain, Hertford, SG14 1DT T: 01992 552100 F: 01992 534797 E: enquiries@hertfordmuseum.org W: www.hertfordmuseum.org

Hertford & Ware Local History Society, 10 Hawthorn Close, Hertford, SG14 2DT

Hertfordshire Archaeological Trust, The Seed Warehouse, Maidenhead Yard, The Wash, Hertford, SG14 1PX T: 01992 558 170 F: 01992 553359 E: herts.archtrust@virgin.net W: www.hertfordshire-archaeological-trust.co.uk

Hertfordshire Association for Local History, c/o 64 Marshals Drive, St Albans, AL1 4RF T: 01727 856250 E: ClareEllis@compuserve.com

Hertfordshire Record Society, 119 Winton Drive, Croxley Green, Rickmansworth, WD3 3QS T: 01923-248581 E: info@hrsociety.org.uk W: www.hrsociety.org.uk

Hitchin Historical Society, c/o Hitchin Museum, Paynes Park, Hitchin, SG5 2EQ

Kings Langley Local History & Museum Society, Kings Langley Library, The Nap, Kings Langley, WD4 8ET T: 01923 263205 T: 01923 264109 E: frankdavies4@hotmail.com alan@penwardens.freeserve.co.uk W: www.kingslangley.org.uk

London Colney Local History Society, 51A St Annes Road, London Colney St. Albans, AL2 1PD

North Mymms Local History Society, 89 Peplins Way, Brookmans Park, Hatfield, AL9 7UT T: 01707 655970 W: www.brookmans.com

Potters Bar and District Historical Society, 9 Hill Rise, Potters Bar, EN6 2RX T: 01707 657586 E: johnscrivyer@aol.com

Rickmansworth Historical Society, 20 West Way, Rickmansworth, WD3 7EN T: 01923 774998 E: geoff@gmsaul.freeserve.co.uk

Royston & District Local History Society, 8 Chilcourt, Royston, SG8 9DD T: 01763 242677 E: david.allard@ntlworld.com W: www.royston.clara.net/localhistory

South West Hertfordshire Archaeological and Historical Society, 29 Horseshoe Lane, Garston, Watford, WD25 0LN T: 01923 672482

St. Albans & Herts Architectural & Archaeological Society, 24 Rose Walk, St Albans, AL4 9AF T: 01727 853204

The Harpenden & District Local History Society, The History Centre, 19 Arden Grove, Harpenden, AL5 4SJ T: 01582 713539

Welwyn Archaeological Society, The Old Rectory, 23 Mill Lane, Welwyn, AL6 9EU T: 01438 715300 F: 01438 715300 E: tony.rook@virgin.net

Welwyn & District Local History Society, 40 Hawbush Rise, Welwyn, AL6 9PP T: 01438 716415 E: p.jiggens-keen@virgin.net W: www.welwynhistory.org

Isle of Wight

Isle of Wight Natural History & Archaeological Society, Salisbury Gardens, Dudley Road, Ventnor, PO38 1EJ T: 01983 855385

Newchurch Parish History Society, 1 Mount Pleasant, Newport Road, Sandown, PO36 OLS

Roots Family & Parish History - Disbanded 2003, San Fernando, Burnt House Lane, Alverstone, Sandown, PO36 0HB T: 01983 403060 E: peters.sanfernando@tesco.net

St. Helens History Society, c/o The Castle, Duver Road, St Helens, Ryde, PO33 1XY T: 01983 872164

St Helens Historical Society, Gloddaeth, Westfield Road, St. Helens, Ryde , PO33 LUZ

Kent

Appledore Local History Society, 72 The Street, Appledore, Ashford, TN26 2AE T: 01233 758500 F: 01233 758500 E: trothfw@aol.com

Ashford Archaeological and Historical Society, Gablehook Farm, Bethersden, Ashford, TN26 3BQ T: 01233 820679,

Aylesford Society, 30 The Avenue, Greenacres, Aylesford, Maidstone, ME20 7LE

Bearsted & District Local History Society, 17 Mount Lane, Bearsted, Maidstone, ME14 4DD

Bexley Civic Society, 58 Palmeira Road, Bexleyheath, DA7 4UX

Bexley Historical Society, 36 Cowper Close, Welling, DAI6 2JT

Biddenden Local History Society, Willow Cottage, Smarden Road, Biddenden, Ashford, TN27 8JT

Brenchley & Matfield Local History Society, Ashendene, Tong Road, Brenchley, Tonbridge, TN12 7HT T: 01892 723476

Bridge & District History Soc, La Dacha, Patrixbourne Road, Bridge, Canterbury, CT4 5BL

Broadstairs Soc, 30 King Edward Avenue, Broadstairs, CT10 lPH T: 01843 603928 E: mike@termites.fsnet.co.uk

Bromley Borough Local History Soc, 62 Harvest Bank Road, West Wickham, BR4 9DJ T: 020 8462 5002

Canterbury Archaeology Soc, Dane Court, Adisham, Canterbury, CT3 3LA E: jeancrane@tiscali.co.uk

Charing & District Local History Soc, Old School House, Charing, Ashford, TN27 0LS

Chatham Historical Soc, 69 Ballens Road, Walderslade, Chatham, ME5 8NX T: 01634 865176

Council for Kentish Archaeology, 3 Westholme, Orpington, BR6 0AN F: information@the-cka.fsnet.co.uk W: www.the-cka.fsnet.co.uk

Cranbrook & District History Soc, 61 Wheatfield Way, Cranbrook, TN17 3NE

Crayford Manor House Historical and Archaeological Soc, 17 Swanton Road, Erith, DA8 1LP T: 01322 433480

Dartford History & Antiquarian Soc, 14 Devonshire Avenue, Dartford, DA1 3DW T: F: 01732 824741
Deal & Walmer Local History Soc, 7 Northcote Road, Deal, CT14 7BZ T:
Detling Society., 19 Hockers Lane, Detling, Maidstone, ME14 3JL T: 01622 737940 F: 01622 737408 E: johnowne@springfield19.freeserve.co.uk
Dover History Soc, 2 Courtland Drive, Kearsney, Dover, CT16 3BX T: 01304 824764
East Peckham Historical Soc, 13 Fell Mead, East Peckham, Tonbridge, TNI2 5EG
Edenbridge & District History Soc, 17 Grange Close, Edenbridge, TN8 5LT
Erith & Belvedere Local History Soc, 67 Merewood Road, Barnehurst, DA7 6PF
Farningham & Eynsford Local History Soc, Lavender Hill, Beesfield Lane, Farningham, Dartford, DA4 ODA
Faversham Soc, 10-13 Preston St, Faversham, ME13 8NS T: 01795 534542 F: 01795 533261 E: faversham@btinternet.com W: http://www.faversham.org. CC accepted. A detailed list of local Explosives Factory workers 1570-1934 to be published soon.
Fawkham & District Historical Soc, The Old Rectory, Valley Road, Fawkham, Longfield, DA3 8LX
Folkestone & District Local History Soc, 7 Shorncliffe Crescent, Folkestone
Friends of Lydd 106 Littlestone Rd New Romney TN28 8NH
Frittenden History Soc, Bobbyns, The Street, Frittenden, Cranbrook, TN17 2DG T: 01580 852459 F: 01580 852459
Gillingham & Rainham Local History Soc, 23 Sunningdale Road, Rainham, Gillingham, ME8 9EQ
Goudhurst & Kilndown Local History Soc, 2 Weavers Cottages, Church Road, Goudhurst, TN17 1BL
Gravesend Historical Soc, 58 Vicarage Lane, Chalk, Gravesend, DA12 4TE T: 01474 363998 W: www.ghs.org.uk Encompassess Northfleet and surrounding Parishes in 'The Gravesham Borough Council Area'
Great Chart Soc, Swan Lodge, The Street, Great Chart, Ashford, TN23 3AH
Hadlow History Soc, Spring House, Tonbridge Road, Hadlow, Tonbridge, TN11 0DZ T: 01732 850214 E: billanne@hadlow12.freeserve.co.uk
Halling Local History Soc, 58 Ladywood Road, Cuxton, Rochester, ME2 1EP T: 01634 716139
Hawkhurst Local History Soc, 17 Oakfield, Hawkhurst, Cranbrook, TN18 4JR T: 01580 752376 E: vcw@lessereagles.freeserve.co.uk
Headcorn Local History Soc, Cecil Way, 2 Forge Lane, Headcorn, TN27 9QQ T: 01622 890253 W: www.headcorn.org.uk
Herne Bay Historical Records Soc, c/o Herne Bay Museum, 12 William St, Herne Bay, CT6 5EJ
Higham Village History Group, Forge House, 84 Forge Lane, Higham, Rochester, ME3 7AH
Horton Kirby & South Darenth Local History Soc, Appledore, Rays Hill, Horton Kirby, Dartford, DA4 9DB T: 01322 862056
Hythe Civic Soc, 25 Napier Gardens, Hythe, CT2l 6DD
Isle of Thanet Historical Soc, 58 Epple Bay Avenue, Birchington on Sea
Kemsing Historical & Art Soc, 26 Dippers Close, Kemsing, Sevenoaks, TN15 6QD T: 01732 761774
Kent Archaeological Rescue Unit, Roman Painted House, New Street, Dover, CTI7 9AJ T: 01304 203279 T: 020 8462 4737 F: 020 8462 4737 W: www.the-cka.fsnet.co.uk
Kent History Federation, 14 Valliers Wood Road, Sidcup, DA15 8BG
Kent Mills Group, Windmill Cottage, Mill Lane, Willesborough, TN27 0QG
Kent Postal History Group, 27 Denbeigh Drive, Tonbridge, TN10 3PW
Lamberhurst L H S, 1 Tanyard Cotts, The Broadway, Lamberhurst, Tunbridge Wells, TN3 8DD
Lamorbey & Sidcup Local History Soc, 14 Valliers Wood Road, Sidcup, DA15 8BG
Legion of Frontiersmen of Commonwealth, 4 Edwards Road, Belvedere, DA17 5AL

Leigh and District History Soc, Elizabeths Cottage, The Green, Leigh, Tonbridge, TN11 8QW T: 01732 832459
Lewisham Local History Soc, 2 Bennett Park, Blackheath Village, London, SE3 9RB E: tom@trshepherd.fsnet.co.uk
Loose Area History Soc, 16 Bedgebury Close, Maidstone, ME14 5QY
Lyminge Historical Soc, Ash Grove, Canterbury Road, Etchinghill, Folkestone, CTI8 8DF
Maidstone Area Archaeological Group, 40 Bell Meadow, Maidstone, Kent ME15 9ND
Maidstone Historical Soc, 37 Bower Mount Road, Maidstone, ME16 8AX T: 01622 676472
Margate Civic Soc, 19 Lonsdale Avenue, Cliftonville, Margate, CT9 3BT
Meopham Historical Soc, Tamar, Wrotham Road, Meopham, DA13 0EX
Orpington History Soc, 42 Crossway, Petts Wood, Orpington, BR5 1PE
Otford & District History Soc, Thyme Bank, Coombe Road, Otford, Sevenoaks, TNI4 5RJ
Otham Soc, Tudor Cottage, Stoneacre Lawn, Otham, Maidstone, ME15 8RT
Paddock Wood History Soc, 19 The Greenways, Paddock Wood, Tonbridge, TNI2 6LS
Plaxtol Local History Group, Tebolds, High Street, Plaxtol, Sevenoaks, TN15 0QJ
Rainham Historical Soc, 52 Northumberland Avenue, Rainham, Gillingham, ME8 7JY
Ramsgate Soc, Mayfold, Park Road, Ramsgate, CT11 7QH
Ringwould History Soc, Back Street, Ringwould, Deal, CT14 8HL T: 01304 361030 T: 01304 380083 E: julie.m.rayner@talk21.com jeanwinn@beeb.net W: www.ringwould-village.org.uk
Romney Marsh Research Trust, 11 Caledon Terrace, Canterbury, CT1 3JS T: 01227 472490 E: s.m.sweetinburgh@kent.ac.uk W: www.kent.ac.uk/mts/rmrt/
Rye Local History Group, 107 Military Road, Rye, TN31 7NZ
Sandgate Soc, The Old Fire Station, 51 High Street, Sandgate, CT20 3AH
Sandwich Local History Soc, Clover Rise, 14 Stone Cross Lees, Sandwich, CT13 OBZ T: 01304 613476 E: frankandrews@FreeNet.co.uk
Sevenoaks Historical Soc, 122 Kippington Road, Sevenoaks, TN13 2LN E: wilkospin@beeb.net
Sheppey Local History Soc, 34 St Helens Road, Sheerness
Shoreham & District Historical Soc, The Coach House, Darenth Hulme, Shoreham, TNI4 7TU
Shorne Local History Group, 2 Calderwood, Gravesend, DAl2 4Q11
Sittingbourne Soc, 4 Stanhope Avenue, Sittingbourne, ME10 4TU T: 01795 473807 F: 01795 473807 E: mandbmoore@tinyonline.co.uk
Smarden Local History Soc, 7 Beult Meadow, Cage Lane, Smarden, TN27 8PZ T: 01233 770 856 F: 01233 770 856 E: franlester@fish.co.uk
Snodland Historical Soc, 214 Malling Road, Snodland, ME6 SEQ E: aa0060962@blueyonder.co.uk W: www.snodlandhistory.org.uk
St Margaret's Bay History Soc, Rock Mount, Salisbury Road, St Margarets Bay, Dover, CT15 6DL T: 01304 852236
Staplehurst Soc, Willow Cottage, Chapel Lane, Staplehurst, TN12 0AN T: 01580 891059 E: awcebd@mistral.co.uk
Tenterden & District Local History Soc, Little Brooms, Ox Lane, St Michaels, Tenterden, TN30 6NQ
Teston History Soc, Broad Halfpenny, Malling Road, Teston, Maidstone, ME18 SAN
Thanet Retired Teachers Association , 85 Percy Avenue, Kingsgate, Broadstairs, CT10 3LD
The Kent Archaeological Soc, Three Elms, Woodlands Lane, Shorne, Gravesend, DA12 3HH T: 01474 822280 E: secretary@kentarchaeology.org.uk W: www.kentarchaeology.org.uk
The Marden Soc, 6 Bramley Court, Marden, Tonbridge, TN12 9QN T: 01622 831904 W: www.marden.org.uk
Three Suttons Soc, Henikers, Henikers Lane, Sutton Valence, ME17 3EE T:

Tonbridge History Soc, 8 Woodview Crescent, Hildenborough, Tonbridge, TN11 9HD T: 01732 838698 E: s.broomfield@dial.pipex.com

Wateringbury Local History Soc, Vine House , 234 Tonbridge Road, Wateringbury, ME18 5NY

Weald History Group, Brook Farm, Long Barn Road, Weald, Sevenoaks

Wealden Buildings Study Group, 64 Pilgrims Way, East Otford, Sevenoaks, TN14 5QW

Whitstable History Soc, 83 Kingsdown Park, Tankerton, Whitstable

Wingham Local History Soc, 67 High Street, Wingham, Canterbury, CT3 1AA

Woodchurch Local History Soc, Woodesden, 24 Front Road, Woodclnurch, Ashford, TN26 3QE

Wrotham Historical Soc, Hillside House, Wrotham, TN15 7JH

Wye Historical Soc, I Upper Bridge Street, Wye, Ashford, TN2 5 SAW

Lancashire

Aspull and Haigh Historical Soc, 1 Tanpit Cottages, Winstanley, Wigan, WN3 6JY T: 01942 222769

Blackburn Civic Soc, 20 Tower Road, Blackburn, BB2 5LE T: 01254 201399

Burnley Historical Soc, 66 Langdale Road, Blackburn, BB2 5DW T: 01254 201162

Centre for North West Regional Studies, Fylde College, Lancaster University, Lancaster, LA1 4YF T: 01524 593770 F: 01524 594725 E: christine.wilkinson@lancaster.ac.uk W: www.lancs.ac.uk/users/cnwrs

Chadderton Historical Soc, 18 Moreton Street, Chadderton, 0L9 OLP T: 0161 652 3930 E: enid@chadderton-hs.freeuk.com W: http://www.chadderton-hs.freeuk.com

Ewecross History Soc, Gruskholme, Bentham, Lancaster, LA2 7AX T: 015242 61420

Fleetwood & District Historical Soc, 54 The Esplanade, Fleetwood, FY7 6QE

Friends of Smithills Hall Museum, Smithills Hall, Smithills Deane Road, Bolton, BL1 7NP

Garstang Historical & Archealogical Soc, 7 Rivermead Drive, Garstang, PR3 1JJ T: 01995 604913 E: marian.fish@btinternet.com

Holme & District Local History Soc, The Croft, Tanpits Lane, Burton, Carnforth, LA6 1HZ T: 01524 782121

Hyndburn Local History Soc, 20 Royds Avenue, Accrington, BB5 2LE T: 01254 235511

Lancashire & Cheshire Antiquarian Soc, 59 Malmesbury Road, Cheadle Hulme, SK8 7QL T: 0161 439 7202 E: morris.garratt@lineone.net W: www.lancashirehistory.co.uk www.cheshirehistory.org.uk

Lancashire Family History and Heraldry Soc, 2 The Straits, Union Road, Oswaldtwistle, BB5 3LU W: www.ifhhs.org.uk

Lancashire Local History Federation, 25 Trinity Court, Cleminson Street, Salford, M3 6DX E: secretary@lancashirehistory.co.uk W: www.lancashirehistory.co.uk

Lancashire Parish Register Soc, 135 Sandy Lane, Orford, Warrington, WA2 9JB E: tom_obrien@bigfoot.com W: http://www.genuki.org.uk/big/eng/LAN/lprs

Lancaster Military Heritage Group, 19 Middleton Road, Overton, Morecombe, LA3 1HB

Leyland Historical Soc, 172 Stanifield Lane, Farington, Leyland, Preston, PR5 2QT

Littleborough Historical and Archaeological Soc, 8 Springfield Avenue, Littleborough, LA15 9JR T: 01706 377685

Mourholme Local History Soc, 3 The Croft, Croftlands, Warton, Carnforth, LA5 9PY T: 01524 734110 E: nt.stobbs@virgin.net

Nelson Local History Soc, 5 Langholme Street, Nelson, BB9 ORW T: 01282 699475

North West Sound Archive, Old Steward's Office, Clitheroe Castle, Clitheroe, BB7 1AZ T: 01200-427897 E: nwsa@ed.lancscc.gov.uk W: www.lancashire.gov.uk/education/lifelong/recordindex

Saddleworth Historical Soc, 7 Slackcote, Delph, Oldham, OL3 5TW T: 01457 874530

Society for Name Studies in Britain & Ireland, 22 Peel Park Avenue, Clitheroe, BB7 1ET T: 01200-423771 F: 01200-423771

Urmston District Local History Soc, 78 Mount Drive, Urmston, Manchester, M41 9QA

Leicestershire

Desford & District Local History Group, Lindridge House, Lindridge Lane, Desford, LE9 9FD T: 01455 824514 E: jshepherd@freeuk.com

East Leake & District Local History Soc, 8 West Leake Road, East Leake, Loughborough, LE12 6LJ T: 01509 852390

Glenfield and Western Archaeological and Historical Group, 50 Chadwell Road, Leicester, LE3 6LF T: 1162873220

Great Bowden Historical Soc, 14 Langdon Road, Market Harborough, LE16 7EZ

Leicestershire Archaeological and Historical Soc, The Guildhall, Leicester, LE1 5FQ T: 0116 270 3031 E: alan@dovedale2.demon.co.uk W: www.le.ac.uk/archaeology/lahs/lahs.html

Sutton Bonington Local History Soc, 6 Charnwood Fields, Sutton Bonington, Loughborough, LE12 5NP T: 01509 673107

Vaughan Archaeological and Historical Soc, c/o Vaughan College, St Nicholas Circle, Leicester, LEl 4LB

Lincolnshire

Lincoln Record Soc, Lincoln Cathedral Library, The Cathedral, Lincoln, LN2 1PZ T: 01522 544544 E: librarian@lincolncathedral.com W: www.lincolncathedral.com

Long Bennington Local History Soc, Kirton House, Kirton Lane, Long Bennington, Newark, NG23 5DX T: 01400 281726

Society for Lincolnshire History & Archaeology, Jews' Court, Steep Hill, Lincoln, LN2 1LS T: 01522-521337 F: 01522 521337 E: slha@lincolnshirepast.org.uk W: www.lincolnshirepast.org.uk

Tennyson Soc, Central Library, Free School Lane, Lincoln, LN2 1EZ T: 01522-552862 F: 01522-552858 E: linnet@lincolnshire.gov.uk W: www.tennysonsociety.org.uk

Merseyside Archaeological Soc, 20 Osborne Road, Formby, Liverpool, L37 6AR T: 01704 871802

Acton History Group, 30 Highlands Avenue, London, W3 6EU T: (020) 8992 8698

London

Birkbeck College, Birkbeck College, Malet Street, London, WC1E 7HU T: (020) 7631 6633 F: (020) 7631 6688 E: info@bbk.ac.uk W: www.bbl.ac.uk

Brentford & Chiswick Local History Soc, 25 Hartington Road, London, W4 3TL

Brixton Soc, 82 Mayall Road, London, SE24 0PJ T: (020) 7207 0347 F: (020) 7207 0347 E: apiperbrix@aol.com W: www.brixtonsociety.org.uk

Centre for Metropolitan History, Institute of Historical Research, Senate House, Malet Street, London, WC1E 7HU T: (020) 7862 8790 F: (020) 7862 8793 E: olwen.myhill@sas.ac.uk W: www.history.ac.uk/cmh/cmh.main.html

Croydon Local Studies Forum, c/o Local Studies Library, Catherine Street, Croydon, CR9 1ET T:

Croydon Local Studies Forum, Flat 2, 30 Howard Road, South Norwood, London, SE25 5BY T: (020) 8654-6454

East London History Soc, 42 Campbell Road, Bow, London, E3 4DT T: 020 8980 5672 E: elhs@mernicks.com W: www.eastlondon.org.uk

Fulham And Hammersmith Historical Soceity, Flat 12, 43 Peterborough Road, Fulham, London, SW6 3BT T: (020) 7731 0363 E: mail@fhhs.org.uk W: www.fhhs.org.uk
Fulham & Hammersmith History Soc, 85 Rannoch Road, Hammersmith, London, W6 9SX
Hornsey Historical Soc, The Old Schoolhouse, 136 Tottenham Lane, London, N8 7EL T: (020) 8348 8429 W: www.hornseyhistorical.org.uk
London & Middlesex Archaeological Soc, Placements Office, University of North London, 62-66 Highbury Grove, London, N5 2AD
London Record Soc, c/o Institute of Historical Research, Senate House, Malet Street, London, WC1E 7HU T: (020) 7862-8798 F: (020) 7862 8793 E: heathercreaton@sas.ac.uk W: http://www.ihrininfo.ac.uk/cmh
Mill Hill Historical Soc, 41 Victoria Road, Mill Hill, London, NW7 4SA T: (020) 8959 7126
Newham History Soc, 52 Eastbourne Road, East Ham, London, E6 6AT T: (020) 8471 1171 W: www.pewsey.net/newhamhistory.htm
Paddington Waterways and Maida Vale Society (Local History), 19a Randolph Road, Maida Vale, London, W9 1AN T: 020 7289 0950
Royal Arsenal Woolwich Historical Soc, Main Guard House, Royal Arsenal Woolwich, Woolwich, London, SE18 6ST E: royalarsenal@talk21.com W: http://members.lycos.co.uk/RoyalArsenal
The Peckham Soc, 6 Everthorpe Road, Peckham, London, SE15 4DA T: (020) 8693 9412
The Vauxhall Soc 20 Albert Square, London, SW8 1BS
Walthamstow Historical Soc, 24 Nesta Road, Woodford Green, IG8 9RG T: (020) 8504 4156 F: (020) 8523 2399
Wandsworth Historical Soc, 31 Hill Court, Putney Hill, London, SW15 6BB, Covers the areas of Balham, Southfields, Tooting, Wandsworth, Roehampton, Earlsfield, Putney, Battersea
Willesden Local History Society (London Borough of Brent), 9 Benningfield Gardens, Berkhamstead, HP4 2GW T: 01442 878477, Covers the parishes of Cricklewood, Willesden, Kilburn, Park Royal, Harlesden, Neasden, Park Royal & Kensal Rise
Hendon & District Archaeological Soc, 13 Reynolds Close, London, NW11 7EA T: (020) 8458 1352 F: (020) 8731 9882 E: denis@netmatters.co.uk W: www.hadas.org.uk
Denton Local History Soc, 94 Edward Street, Denton, Manchester, M34 3BR
Stretford Local History Soc, 26 Sandy Lane, Stretford, Manchester, M32 9DA T: 0161 283 9434 E: mjdawson@cwcom.net W: www.stretfordlhs.cwc.net
Victorian Soc, 1 Priory Gardens, Bedford Park, London, W4 1TT T: (020) 8994 1019 F: (020) 8747 5899 E: admin@victorian-society.org.uk W: http://www.victorian-society.org.uk CC accepted

Merseyside
Birkdale & Ainsdale Historical Research Soc, 20 Blundell Drive, Birkdale, Southport, PR8 4RG W: www.harrop.co.uk/bandahrs
Friends of Williamson's Tunnels, 15-17 Chatham Place, Edge Hill, Liverpool, L7 3HD T: 0151 475 9833 F: 0151 475 9833 E: info@williamsontunnels.com W: www.williamsontunnels.com To ensure the preservation of the mysterious 19th century labyrinth under Liverpool and to further understanding of the life and times of its creator Joseph Williamson (1769 - 1840)
Historic Society of Lancashire & Cheshire see Cheshire
Liverpool Historical Soc, 46 Stanley Avenue, Rainford, WA11 8HU E: liverpoolhistsoc@merseymail.com W: www.liverpoolhistorysociety.merseyside.org
Maghull and Lydiate Local History Soc, 15 Brendale Avenue, Maghull, Liverpool, L31 7AX
Society of Cirplanologists, 26 Roe Cross Green, Mottram, Hyde, SK14 6LP T: 01457 7634857
Middlesex
Borough of Twickenham Local History Soc, 258 Hanworth Road, Hounslow, TW3 3TY E: pbarnfield@post.com

British Deaf History Soc, 288 Bedfont Lane, Feltham, TW14 9NU E: bdhs@iconic.demon.co.uk
Edmonton Hundred Historical Soc, Local History Unit, Southgate Town Hall, Green Lanes, London, N13 4XD T: (020) 8379 2724, Covers Tottenham, Wood Green, Palmers Green, Winchmore Hill, and Southgate (All London Postal Districts besides Enfield and Muken Hadley)
Honeslow Chronicle, 142 Guildford Avenue, Feltham, TW13 4E
Hounslow & District History Soc, 16 Orchard Avenue, Heston, TW5 0DU T: (020) 8570 4264
Middlesex Heraldry Soc, 4 Croftwell, Harpeden, AL5 1JG T: 01582 766372
Northwood & Eastcote Local History Soc, 3 Elbridge Close, Ruislip, HA4 7XA T: 01895 637134 W: www.rnelhs.flyer.co.uk
Pinner Local History Soc, 8 The Dell, Pinner, HA5 3EW T: (020) 8866 1918 E: mwg@pinnerlhs.freeserve.co.uk W: www.pinnerlhs.freeserve.co.uk/index.html
Ruislip Northwood & Eastcote Local History Soc, 3 Elmbridge Close, Ruislip, HA4 7XA T: 01895 637134 E: www.rnelhs.flyer.co.uk
Sunbury And Shepperton Local, 30 Lindsay drive, Shepperton, TW17 88JU T: 01932 226776 E: H.L.Brooking@eggconnect.net W: http://users.eggconnect.net/h.l.brooking/sslhs

Norfolk
Blakeney Area Historical Soc, 2 Wiveton Road, Blakeney, NR25 7NJ T: 01263 741063
Federation of Norfolk Historical and Archaeological Organisations, 14 Beck Lane, Horsham St Faith, Norwich, NR10 3LD
Feltwell (Historical and Archaeological) Soc, 16 High Street, Feltwell, Thetford, IP26 4AF T: 01842 828448 E: peterfeltwell@tinyworld.co.uk The Museum is at The Beck, Feltwell Open Tucsday & Saturday April to September 2.00.p.m. to 4.00.p.m.
Holt History Group 6 Kelling Close, Holt, NR23 6RU
Narborough Local History Soc, 101 Westfields, Narborough, Kings Lynn, PE32 ISY W: www.narboroughaerodrome.org.uk Narborough Aerodrome 1915-1919 ongoing research - Narborough Airfield Research group. Over 1000 names of Officers Men & Women who served at Narborough. 15 Military graves
Norfolk and Norwich Archaeological Soc, 30 Brettingham Avenue, Cringleford, Norwich, NR4 6XG T: 01603 455913
Norfolk Archaeological and Historical Research Group, 50 Cotman Road, Norwich, NR1 4AH T: 01603 435470
Norfolk Heraldry Soc, 26c Shotesham Road, Poringland, Norwich, NR14 7LG T: 01508 493832 F: 01508 493832 W: www.norfolkheraldry.co.uk
Norfolk Record Soc, 17 Christchurch Road, Norwich, NR2 2AE

Northamptonshire
Bozeat Historical and Archaeological Soc, 44 Mile Street, Bozeat, NN9 7NB T: 01933 663647
Brackley & District History Soc, 32 Church Lane, Evenley, Brackley, NN13 5SG T: 01280 703508
Higham Chichele Soc, 3 Bramley Close, Rushden, NN10 6RL
Houghtons & Brafield History, 5 Lodge Road, Little Houghton, NN7 IAE
Irchester Parish Historical Soc, 80 Northampton Road, Wellingborough, NN8 3HT T: 01933 274880 F: 01933 274888 W: www.irchester.org W: www.iphs.org.uk
Northamptonshire Assoc for Local History , 143 Clophill Road, Maulden, MK45 2AF E: enquiries@northants-history.org.uk W: www.northants-history.org.uk
Northamptonshire Record Soc, Wootton Park Hall, Northampton, NN4 8BQ T: 01604 762297
Oundle Historical Soc, 13 Lime Avenue, Oundle, Peterborough, PE8 4PT
Rushden & District History Soc, 25 Byron Crescent, Rushden, NN10 6BL E: rdhs.rushden@virgin.net W: www.rdhs.org.uk

Weedon Bec History Soc, 35 Oak Street, Weedon, Northampton, NN7 4RR

West Haddon Local History Group, Bramley House, 12 Guilsborough Road, West Haddon, NN6 7AD T:

Northumberland

Felton & Swarland Local History Soc, 23 Benlaw Grove, Felton, Morpeth, NE65 9NG T: 01670 787476 E: petercook@felton111.freeserve.co.uk W:

Hexham Local History Soc, Dilstone, Burswell Villas, Hexham, NE46 3LD T: 01434 603216

Morpeth Antiquarian Soc, 9 Eden Grove, Morpeth, NE61 2EN T: 01670 514792 E: hudson.c@virgin.net W: www.morpethnet.co.uk

Morpeth Nothumbrian Gathering, Westgate House, Dogger Bank, Morpeth, NE61 1RF

National Inventory of War Memorials (North East England), Bilsdale, Ulgham, Morpeth, NE61 3AR T: 01670 790465 E: gjb@bilsdale.freeserve.co.uk

Northumbrian Language Soc, Westgate House, Dogger Bank, Morpeth, NE61 1RE T: 01670 513308 E: kim@northumbriana.org.uk W: www.northumbriana.org.uk

Prudhoe & District Local History Soc, Prudhoe Community Enterprise Office, 82 Front Street, Prudhoe, NE42 5PU

Stannington Local History Soc, Glencar House, 1 Moor Lane, Stannington, Morpeth, NE61 6EA

The Ponteland Local History Soc, Woodlands, Prestwick Village, Ponteland, NE20 9TX T: 01661 824017 E: jmichaeltaylor@talk21.com W: www.ponthistsoc.freeuk.com

Nottinghamshire

Epperstone History Soc, Sunny Mead, Main Street, Epperstone, NG14 6AG

Basford & District Local History Soc, 44 Cherry Tree Close, Bucinsley, Nottingham, NG16 5BA T: 0115 927 2370

Beeston & District Local History Soc, 16 Cumberland Avenue, Beeston, NG9 4DH T: 0115 922 3008

Bingham & District Local History Soc, 56 Nottingham Road, Bingham, NG13 8AT T: 01949 875866

Bleasby Local History Soc, 5 Sycamore Lane, Bleasby, NG14 7GJ T: 01636 830094

Bulwell Historical Soc, 19 Woodland Avenue, Bulwell, Nottingham, NG6 9BY T: 0115 927 9519

Burton Joyce and Bulcote Local History Soc, 9 Carnarvon Drive, Burton Joyce, Nottingham, NG14 5ER T: 0115 931 3669

Caunton Local History Soc, Beech House, Caunton, Newark, NG23 6AF T: 01636 636564

Chinemarelian Soc, 3 Main Street, Kimberley, NG16 2NL T: 0115 945 9306, covers Kimberley

Cotgrave Local History Soc, 81 Owthorpe Road, Cotgrave, NG T: 0115 989 2115

Eastwood Historical Soc, 18 Park Crescent, Eastwood , NG16 3DU T: 01773 712080

Edwalton Local History Soc, 85 Tollerton Lane, Tollerton, Nottingham, NG12 4FS T: 0115 937 2391 F: 0115 986 1215 E: elviahugh@yahoo.co.uk

Edwinstowe Historical Soc, 12 Church Street, Edwinstowe, NG21 9QA T: 01623 824455

Farndon & District Local History Soc, 22 Brockton Avenue, Farndon, Newark, NG24 4TH T: 01636 610070

Flintham Soc, Flintham Museum, Inholms Road, Flintham, NG23 5LF T: 0163.6 525111 E: flintham.museum@lineone.net W: www.flintham-museum.org.uk

Gotham & District Local History Soc, 108A Leake Road, Gotham, NG11 0JN T: 0115 983 0494 F: 0115 983 0494

Hucknall Heritage Soc, 68 Papplewick Lane, Hucknall, Nottingham, NG15 8EF E: marion.williamson@ntlworld.com

Keyworth & District Local History Soc, Innisfree, Thelda Avenue, Keyworth, Nottingham, NG12 5HU T: 0115 937908 F: 0115 937908 E: info@keyworth-history.org.uk W: www.keyworth-history.org.uk

Lambley Historical Soc, 11 Steeles Way, Lambley, Nottingham, NG4 4QN T: 0115 931 2588

Lenton Local History Soc, 53 Arnesby Road, Lenton Gardens, Nottingham, NG7 2EA T: 0115 970 3891

Long Bennington Local History Soc, Kirton House, Kirton Lane, Long Bennington, Newark, NG23 5DX T: 01400 281726

Newark Archaeological & Local History Soc, 13 Main Street, Sutton on Trent, Newark, NG23 6PF T: 01636 821781 (Evenings) E: jill.campbell@ic24.net

North Muskham History Group, Roseacre, Village Lane, North Muskham, NG23 6ES T: 01636 705566

Nottingham Civic Soc, 57 Woodhedge Drive, Nottingham, NG3 6LW T: 0115 958 8247 F: 0115 958 8247 E: membership@nottinghamcivicsoc.org.uk

Nottingham Historical and Archaeological Soc, 9 Churchill Drive, Stapleford, Nottingham, NG9 8PE T: 0115 939 7140

Nottinghamshire Industrial Archaeology Soc, 18 Queens Avenue, Ilkeston, DE7 4DL T: 0115 932 2228

Nottinghamshire Local History Association, 128 Sandhill Street, Worksop, S80 1SY T: 01909 488878, Mobile: 07773887803 E: drossellis@aol.com

Nuthall & District Local History Soc, 14 Temple Drive, Nuthall, Nottingham, NG16 1BE T: 0115 927 1118 E: tony.horton@ntlworld.com

Old Mansfield Soc, 7 Barn Close, Mansfield, NG18 3JX T: 01623 654815 E: dcrut@yahoo.com W: www.old-mansfield.org.uk

Old Mansfield Woodhouse Soc, Burrwells, Newboundmill Lane, Pleasley, Mansfield, NG19 7QA T: 01623 810396

Old Warsop Soc, 1 Bracken Close, Market Warsop, NG20 0QQ

Pentagon Soc, Dellary, Mill Road, Elston, Newark, NG23 5NR T: 01636 525278, covers Elston, Shelton, Sibthorpe, East Stoke & Syerston CC accepted

Pleasley History Group, 8 Cambria Road, Pleasley, Mansfield, NG19 7RL T: 01623 810201

Radford Memories Project, 25 Manston Mews, Alfreton Road, Radford, Nottingham, NG7 3QY T: 0115 970 1256

Retford & District Historical & Archaeological Soc, Cambridge House, 36 Alma Road, Retford, DN22 6LW T: 7790212360 E: joan@granto.demon.co.uk

Ruddington Local History Soc, St Peter's Rooms, Church Street, Ruddington, Nottingham, NG11 6HA T: 0115 914 6645

Sherwood Archaeological Soc, 32 Mapperley Hall Drive, Nottingham, NG3 5EY T: 0115 960 3032 E: pjneale@aol.com

Shireoaks Local History Group, 22 Shireoaks Row, Shireoaks, Worksop, S81 8LP

Sneinton Environmental Soc, 248 Greenwood Road, Nottingham, NG3 7FY T: 0115 987 5035

Southwell & District Local History Soc, Fern Cottage, 70 Kirklington Road, Southwell, NG25 0AX T: 01636 812220

Stapleford & District Local History Soc, 25 Westerlands, Stapleford, Nottingham, NG9 7JE T: 0115 939 2573

Sutton Heritage Soc, 8 Sheepbridge Lane, Mansfield, NG18 5EA T: 01623 451179 E: lildawes@yahoo.co.uk

Sutton on Trent Local History Soc, 14 Grassthorpe Road, Sutton on Trent, Newark, NG23 6QD T: 01636 821228

Thoroton Society of Nottinghamshire, 59 Briar Gate, Long Eaton, Nottingham, NG10 4BQ T: 0115-972-6590 E: thoroton@keithgoodman.com W: www.thorotonsociety.org.uk

Tuxford Heritage Soc, 140 Lincoln Road, Tuxford, Newark, NG22 0HS

West Bridgford & District Local History Soc, 30 Repton Road, West Bridgford, NG2 7EJ T: 0115 923 3901

Whitwell Local History Group, 34 Shepherds Avenue, Worksop, S81 0JB E: wlhg@freeuk.com jandpwalker34@aol.com W: www.wlhg.freeuk.com

Wilford History Soc, 10 St Austell Drive, Wilford, Nottingham, NG11 7BP T: 0115 981 7061

Woodborough Local History Group, The Woodpatch, 19 Sunningdale Drive, Woodborough, NG14 6EQ T: 0115 965 3103 W: www.woodborough-heritage.org.uk

Worksop Archaeological & Local History Soc, 42 Dunstan Crescent, Worksop, S80 1AF T: 01909 477575

Oxfordshire

Abingdon Area Archaeological and Historical Soc, 4 Sutton Close, Abingdon, OX14 1ER T: 01235 529720 E: rainslie@hotmail.com W: www.aaahs.org.uk

Ashbury Local History Soc, Claremont , Asbury, Swindon, SN6 8LN E: marionlt@witrose.com

Banbury Historical Soc Banbury Museum, Spiceball Park Road, Banbury, OX16 2PQ T: 01295 672626

Blewbury Local History Group, Spring Cottage, Church Road, Blewbury, Didcot, OX11 9PY T: 01235 850427 E: aud@spcott.fsnet.co.uk

Bloxham Village History Group, 1 Hyde Grove, Bloxham, Banbury, OX15 4HZ T: 01295 720037

Chadlington Local History Soc, 5 Webbs Close, Chadlington, Chipping Nortro, OX7 3RA T: 01608 676116 E: kagewinter@aol.com

Charlbury Soc, 7 Park Street, Charlbury, OX7 3PS T: 01608 810390 E: charles.tyzack@btinternet.com

Chinnor Historical & Archealogical Soc, 4 Beech Road, Thame, OX9 2AL T: 01844 216538 E: kendmason@macunlimited.net

Chipping Norton History Soc, 9 Toy Lane, Chipping Norton, OX7 5FH T: 01608 642754

Cumnor and District History Soc, 4 Kenilworth Road, Cumnor, Nr Oxford, OX2 9QP T: 01865 862965 F: 01865 862965

Dorchester Historical Soc, 20 Watling Lane, Dorchester on Thames, Wallingford, OX10 7GJ T: 01865 340422 E: david.lucas1@which.net

Enstone Local History Circle, The Sheiling, Sibford Ferris, Banbury, OX15 5RG

Eynsham History Group, 11 Newland Street, Eynsham, OX29 4LB T: 01865 883141

Faringdon Archaeological & Historical Soc, 1 Orchard Hill, Faringdon, SN7 7EH T: 01367 240885 E: fdahs@bigfoot.com W: www.faringdon.org/hysoc

Finstock Local History Soc, 81 High Street, Finstock, OX7 3DA T: 01993 868965 E: jon@joncarpenter.co.uk

Hanney History Group, Willow Tree House, The Green, East Hanney, Wantage, OX12 0HQ T: 01238 68375 E: creason@EastHanney.demon.co.uk

Henley on Thames Archaeological and Historical Group, 52 Elizabeth Road, Henley on Thames, RG9 1RA T: 01491 578 530

Hook Norton Local History Group, Littlenook, Chapel Street, Hook Norton, OX15 5JT T: 01608 730355 E: sheila@littlenook.ndo.co.uk

Iffley Local History Soc, 4 Abberbury Avenue, Oxford, OX4 4EU T: 01865 779257

Kidlington and District Historical Soc, 18 Oak Drive, Kidlington, OX5 2HL T: 01865 373517 W: www.communigate.co.uk/oxford

Launton Historical Soc, Salamanca, Launton, OX26 5DQ T: 01869 253281 E: p_tucker@tesco.net

Lechlade History Soc, The Gables, High Street, Lechlade, GL7 3AD T: 01367 252457 E: Gillkeithnewson.aol.com Archivist: Mrs Maureen Baxter Tel; 01367 252437

Longworth Local History Soc, 7 Norwood Avenue, Southmoor, Abingdon, OX13 5AD T: 01865 820522 F: 01865 820522 E: keene@thematictrails.u-net.com W: www.kbsonline.org.uk http://freepages.history.rootsweb.com/~lhs1, Covers villages of Hinton Waldrist and Kingston Bagpuize with Southmoor

Marcham Soc, Prior's Corner, 2 Priory Lane, Marcham, Abingdon, OX13 6NY T: 01865 391439 E: e.dunford@btinternet.com

Over Norton History Group, Fountain Cottage, The Green, Over Norton, OX7 5PT T: 01608 641057

Oxfordshire Architectural and Historical Soc, 53 Radley Road, Abingdon, Oxford, OX14 3PN T: 01235 525960 E: tony@oahs.org.uk W: www.oahs.org.uk

Oxfordshire Local History Association, 12 Meadow View, Witney, OX28 6TY T: 01993 778345

Oxfordshire Record Soc, Bodleian Library, Oxford, OX1 3BG T: 01865 277164 E: srt@bodley.ox.ac.uk

Shrivenham Local History Soc, Ridgeway, Kings Lane, Loncot, Faringdon, SN7 7SS T: 01793 783083

Thame Historical Soc, 12 Park Terrace, Thame, OX9 3HZ T: 01844 212336 E: Csear58229@aol.com W: www.thamehistory.net

The Bartons History Group, 18 North Street, Middle Barton, OX7 7BJ T: 01869 347013 E: edbury@midbar18.freeserve,co,uk

Volunteer Corps of Frontiersmen, Archangels' Rest, 26 Dark Lane, Witney, OX8 5LE

Wallingford Historical and Archaeological Soc, Wallingford Museum, Flint House, 52a High Street, Wallingford, OX1O 0DB T: 01491 835065

Whitchurch: The Ancient Parish of Whitchurch Historical Soc, Ashdown, Duchess Close, Whitchurch on Thames, RG8 7EN

Witney & District Historical & Archaeological Soc, 16 Church Green, Witney, OX28 4AW T: 01993 703289 F: 01993 703281

Wolvercote Local History Soc, 18 Dovehouse Close, Upper Wolvercote, OX2 8BG

Wootton, Dry Sandford & District History Soc, 46 Church Lane, Dry Sandford, Abingdon, OX13 6JP T: 01865 390441

Wychwoods Local History Soc, Littlecott, Honeydale Farm, Shipton-Under-Wychwood, Chipping Norton, OX7 6BJ T: 01993 831023, Enquiry letters should be accompanied by an SAE or 2 IRCs if from abroad

Yarnton with Begbroke History Soc, 6 Quarry End, Begbroke, OX5 1SF

Rutland

Rutland Local History & Record Soc, c/o Rutland County Museum, Catmos Street, Oakham, LE15 6HW T: 01572 758440 F: 01572 757576 E: rutlandhistory@rutnet.co.uk W: www.rutnet.co.uk/rlhrs

Shropshire

Cleobury Mortimer Historical Soc, The Old Schoolhouse, Neen Savage, Cleobury Mortimer, Kidderminster, DY14 8JU T: 01299 270319 E: paddy@treves.freeserve.co.uk

Council for British Archaeology - West Midlands, c/o Rowley's House Museum, Barker Street, Shrewsbury, SY1 1QH T: 01743 361196 F: 01743 358411 E: mikestokes@shrewsbury-atcham.gov.uk W: www.shrewsburymuseums.com www.darwincountry.org

Field Studies Council, Head office, Preston Montford, Montford Bridge, Shrewsbury, SY4 1HW T: 01743 852100 F: 01743 852101 E: fsc.headoffice@ukonline.co.uk W: www.field-studies-council.org

Shropshire Archaeological and Historical Soc, Lower Wallop Farm, Westbury, Shrewsbury, SY5 9RT T: 01743 891215 T: 01743 891805 F: 01743 891805 E: walloparch@farming.co.uk W: www.shropshirearchaeology.com

Whitchurch History and Archaeology Group, Smallhythe, 26 Rosemary Lane, Whitchurch, SY13 1EG T: 01948 662120

Somerset

Axbridge Archaeological and Local History Soc, King John's Hunting Lodge, The Square, Axbridge, BS26 2AR T: 01934 732012

Bathford Soc, 36 Bathford Hill, Bathford, BA1 7SL

Bruton Museum Soc, The Dovecote Building, High Street, Bruton T: 01749 812851 W: www.southsomersetmuseum.org.uk

Castle Cary & District Museum & Preservation Soc, Woodville House, Woodcock Street, Castle Cary, BA7 7BJ T: 01963 3511122 T: 01963 350680 (Museum) Curator: Mrs P M Schiffer, Rosemary Cottage, Bailey Hill, Castle Cary BA7 7AD

Chard History Group, 17 Kinforde, Chard, TA20 1DT T: 01460 62722 E: carterw@globalnet.co.uk W: www.users.globalnet.co.uk/~carterw

Freshford & District Local History Soc, Quince Tree House, Pipehouse Lane, Freshford, Bath, BA2 7UH T: 01225 722339

Oakhill & Ashwick Local History Soc, Bramley Farm, Bath Road, Oakhill, BA3 5AF T: 01749 840 241

Somerset Archaeological & Natural History Soc, Taunton Castle, Taunton, TA1 4AD T: 01823 272429 F: 01823 272429 E: secretary@sanhs.freeserve.co.uk
Somerset Record Soc, Somerset Studies Library, Paul Street, Taunton, TA1 3XZ T: 01823-340300 F: 01823-340301
South East Somerset Archaeological and Historical Soc, Silverlands, Combe Hill, Templecombe, BA8 OLL T: 01963 371307 F: 01963 371307
South Petherton L H Group, Cobbetts Droveway, South Petherton, TAI3 5DA T: 01460 240252
South Petherton Local History, Crossbow, Hele Lane, South Petherton, TA13 5DY
Somerset - North
Nailsea & District Local History Soc, PO Box 1089, Nailsea, BS48 2YP

Staffordshire
Berkswich History Soc, 1 Greenfield Road, Stafford, ST17 OPU T: 01785 662401
Birmingham Canal Navigation Soc, 37 Chestnut Close, Handsacre, Rugeley, WS15 4TH
Landor Soc, 38 Fortescue Lane, Rugeley, WS15 2AE T: 01889 582709,
Lawton History Group, 17 Brattswood drive, Church Lawton, Stoke on Trent, ST7 3EF T: 01270 873427 E: arthur@aburton83.freeserve.co.uk
North Staffordshire Historians' Guild, 14 Berne Avenue, Newcastle under Lyme, ST5 2QJ
Ridware History Soc, 8 Waters Edge, Handsacre, Nr. Rugeley, WS15 7HP T: 01543 307456 E: davidandmonty@carefree.net
Stafford Historical & Civic Soc, 86 Bodmin Avenue, Weeping Cross, Stafford, ST17 OEQ T: 01785 612194 E: esj@supanet.com
Staffordshire Archaeological and Historical Soc, 6 Lawson Close, Aldridge, Walsall, WS9 0RX T: 01922 452230 E: sahs@britishlibrary.net W: www.sahs.uk.net

Suffolk
Framlingham & District Local History Soc, 28 Pembroke Road, Framlingham, IP13 9HA T: 01728 723214
Lowestoft Archaeological and Local History Soc, 1 Cranfield Close, Pakefield, Lowestoft, NR33 7EL T: 01502 586143
Suffolk Institute of Archaeology and History, Roots, Church Lane, Playford, Ipswich, IP6 9DS T: 01473-624556 E: brianseward@btinternet.com W: www.suffolkarch.org.uk
Suffolk Local History Council, Suffolk Community Resource Centre, 2 Wharfedale Road, Ipswich, IP1 4JP E: admin@suffolklocalhistorycouncil.org.uk W: www.suffolklocalhistorycouncil.org.uk

Surrey
Addlestone History Soc, 53 Liberty Lane, Addlestone, Weybridge, KT15 1NQ
Beddington & Carshalton Historical Soc, 57 Brambledown Road, Wallington, SM6 0TF
Beddington Carshalton & Wallington History Soc, 57 Brambledown Road, Wallington, SM6 0TF T: (020) 8647 8540
Bourne Soc, 54 Whyteleafe Road, Caterham, CR3 5EF T: 01883 349287 T: 01883 347143 F: 01883 341638 E: robert@friday-house.freeserve.co.uk W: www.bournesociety.org.uk Caterham, Chaldon, Chelsham, Chipstead, Coulsdon, Farleigh, Godstone, Kenley, Old Coulsdon, Parley, Sanderstead, Whyteleafe, Warlingham and Woldingham.
Carshalton Soc 43 Denmark Road, Carshalton, SM5 2JE
Centre for Local History Studies, Faculty of Human Sciences, Kingston University, Penrhyn Road, Kingston, KT1 2EE T: (020) 8547 7359 E: localhistory@kingston.ac.uk W: http://localhistory.kingston.ac.uk
Croydon Natural History & Scientific Society Ltd, 96a Brighton Road, South Croydon, CR2 6AD T: (020) 8688 4539 W: http://www.grieg51.freeserve.co.uk/cnhss

Domestic Buildings Research Group (Surrey), The Ridings, Lynx Hill, East Horsley, KT24 5AX T: 01483 283917
Dorking Local History Group, Dorking & District Museum, The Old Foundry, 62a West St, Dorking, RH4 1BS T: 01306 876591
Esher District Local History Soc, 45 Telegraph Lane, Claygate, KT10 0DT
Farnham and District Museum Soc, Tanyard House, 13a Bridge Square, Farnham, GU9 7QR
Friends of Public Record Office, The Public Record Office, Ruskin Avenue, Kew, Richmond, TW9 4DU T: (020) 8876 3444 ext 2226 E: friends-pro@pro.gov.uk W: www.pro.gov.uk/yourpro/friends.htm
Guildford Archaeology and Local History Group, 6 St Omer Road, Guildford, GU1 2DB T: 01483 532201 E: H.E.Davies@surrey.ac.uk
Hayward Memorial Local History Centre, The Guest House, Vicarage Road, Lingfield, RH7 6HA T: 01342 832058 F: 01342 832517
History of Thursley Soc, 50 Wyke Lane, Ash, Aldershot, GU12 6EA E: norman.ratcliffe@ntlworld.com W: http://home.clara.net/old.norm/Thursley
Leatherhead and District Local History Soc, Leatherhead Museum, 64 Church Street, Leatherhead, KT22 8DP T: 01372 386348, cc accepted
Nonsuch Antiquarian Soc, 17 Seymour Avenue, Ewell, KT17 2RP T: (020) 8393 0531 W: www.nonsuchas.org.uk
Puttenham & Wanborough History Soc, Brown Eaves, 116 The Street, Puttenham, Guildford, GU3 1AU
Richmond Local History Soc, 9 Bridge Road, St Margarets, Twickenham, TWI IRE
Send and Ripley History Soc, St Georges Farm House, Ripley, GU23 6AF T: 01483 222107 F: 01483 211832 E: slatford@johnone.freeserve.co.uk
Shere Gomshall & Peaslake Local History Soc, Twiga Lodge, Wonham Way, Gomshall, Guildford, GU5 9NZ T: 01483 202112 E: twiga@gomshall.freeserve.co.uk W: www.gomshall.freeserve.co.uk/sglshhp.htm
Surrey Archaeological Soc, Castle Arch, Guildford, GU1 3SX T: 01483 532454 E: surreyarch@compuserve.com W: www.ourworld.compuserve.com/homepages/surreyarch, Covers the Historic County of Surrey
Surrey Local History Council, Guildford Institute, University of Surrey, Ward Street, Guildford, GU1 4LII
Surrey Record Soc, c/o Surrey History Centre, 130 Goldsworth Rd, Woking, GU21 1ND T: 01483 594603
Walton On The Hill District Local History Soc, 5 Russell Close, Walton On The Hill, Tadworth, KT2O 7QH T: 01737 812013
Walton & Weybridge Local History Soc, 67 York Gardens, Walton on Thames, KT12 3EN
Westcott Local History Group, 6 Heath Rise, Westcott, Dorking, RH4 3NN T: 01306 882624 E: info@westcotthistory.org.uk W: www.westcotthistory.org.uk

Sussex
Danehill Parish Historical Soc, Butchers Barn, Freshfield Lane, Danehill, RH17 7HQ T: 01825 790292
Eastbourne Local History Soc, 12 Steeple Grange, 5 Mill Road, Eastbourne, BN21 2LY
Lewes Archaeological Group, Rosemary Cottage, High Street, Barcombe, near Lewes, BN8 5DM T: 01273 400878
Sussex Local History Forum, Anne of Cleves House, 52 Southover, High Street, Lewes, BN7 1JA
Sussex - East
Blackboys & District Historical Soc, 6 Palehouse Common, Framfield, Nr Uckfield, TN22 5QY
Brighton & Hove Archealogical Soc, 115 Braeside Avenue, Patcham, Brighton, BN1 8SQ T:
Eastbourne Natural History and Archaeological Soc, 11 Brown Jack Avenue, Polegate, BN26 5HN T: 01323 486014
Family & Community Historical Research Soc, 56 South Way, Lewes, BN7 1LY T: 01273 4/1897
Friends of East Sussex Record Office, The Maltings, Castle Precincts, Lewes, BN7 1YT T: 01273-482349 F: 01273-482341 W: www.esrole.fsnet.co.uk

Maresfield Historical Soc, Hockridge House, London Road, Maresfield, TN22 2EH T: 01825 765386
Mid Sussex Local History Group, Saddlers, Stud Farm Stables, Gainsborough Lane, Polegate, BN26 5HQ T: 01323 482215
Peacehaven & Telscombe Historical Soc, 2 The Compts, Peacehaven, BN1O 75Q T: 01273 588874 F: 01273 589881 E: paths@openlink.org W: www.history-peacehaven-telscombe.org.uk
Rye Local History Group, 107 Military Road, Rye, TN31 7NZ
Sussex Archaeological Society & Sussex Past, Barbican House, 169 High Street, Lewes, BN7 1YE T: 01273 405738 F: 01273 486990 E: library@sussexpast.co.uk W: sussexpast.co.uk
Sussex History Forum, Barbican House, 169 High Street, Lewes, BN7 1YE T: 01273-405736 F: 01273-486990 E: research@sussexpast.co.uk W: www.sussexpast.co.uk
Uckfield & District Preservation Soc, 89 Lashbrooks Road, Uckfield, TN22 2AZ
Warbleton & District History Group, Hillside Cottage, North Road, Bodle Street Green, Hailsham, BN27 4RG T: 01323 832339 E: junegeoff.hillside@tiscali.co.uk ,
Sussex - West
Beeding & Bramber Local History Soc, 19 Roman Road, Steyning, BN44 3FN T: 01903 814083
Billingshurst Local History Soc, 2 Cleve Way, Billingshurst, RH14 9RW T: 01403 782472 E: jane.lecluse@atkinsglobal.com
Bolney Local History Soc, Leacroft, The Street, Bolney, Haywards, RH17 5PG T: 01444 881550 E: constable@lespres.freeserve.co.uk
Chichester Local History Soc, 38 Ferndale Road, Chichester, P019 6QS
Horsham Museum Soc, Horsham Museum, 9 The Causeway, Horsham, RH12 1HE T: 01403 254959 E: museum@horsham.gov.uk
Midland Railway Soc, 4 Canal Road, Yapton, BN18 0HA T: 01243-553401 E: BeeFitch@aol.com W: www.derby.org/midland
The RH7 History Group, Bidbury House, Hollow Lane, East Grinstead, RH19 3PS
Steyning Soc, 30 St Cuthmans Road, Steyning, BN44 3RN
Sussex Record Soc, West Sussex Record Office, County Hall, Chichester, PO19 1RN T: 01243 753600 F: 01243-533959 E: peter.wilkinson@westsussex.gov.uk
The Angmering Soc, 45 Greenwood Drive, Angmering, BNI6 4JW T: 01903-775811 E: editor@angmeringsociety.org.uk W: www.angmeringsociety.org.uk
West Sussex Archives Soc, c/o West Sussex Record Office, West Sussex CountyCouncil County Hall, Chichester, P019 IRN T: 01243 753600 F: 01243 533959 E: records.office@westsussex.gov.uk W: www.westsussex.gov.uk/cs/ro/rohome.htm
Wivelsfield Historical Soc, Wychwood, Theobalds Road, Wivelsfield, Haywards Heath, RH15 0Sx T: 01444 236491

Tyne and Wear
Assoc of Northumberland Local History Societies, c/o The Black Gate, Castle Garth, Newcastle upon Tyne, NE1 1RQ T: 0191 257 3254
Cullercoats Local History Soc 33 St Georges Road, Cullercoats, North Shields, NE30 3JZ T: 0191 252 7042
North East Labour History Soc, Department of Historical & Critical Studies, University of Northumbria, Newcastle upon Tyne, NE1 8ST T: 0191-227-3193 F: 0191-227-4630 E: joan.hugman@unn.ac.uk
North Eastern Police History Soc, Brinkburn Cottage, 28 Brinkburn Street, High Barnes, Sunderland, SR4 7RG T: 0191-565-7215 E: harry.wynne@virgin.net W: http://nepolicehistory.homestead.com
Southwick History and Preservation Soc, 8 St Georges Terrace, Roker, Sunderland, SR6 9LX T: 0191 567 2438 T: 07833 787 481 E: pamela.tate@freedomnames.co.uk W: www.rootsweb.com/~engshps/index.htm

Sunderland Antiquarian Soc, 22 Ferndale Avenue, East Boldon, NE36 0TN T: 0191 536 1692
Association of Northumberland Local History Societies, c/o Centre for Lifelong Learning, King George VI Building, Newcastle upon Tyne University, Newcastle upon Tyne, NE1 7RU T: 0191 222 5680 T: 0191 222 7458
Society of Antiquaries of Newcastle upon Tyne, The Black Gate, Castle Garth, Newcastle upon Tyne, NE1 1RQ T: 0191 261 5390 E: admin@newcastle-antiquaries.org.uk W: www.newcastle-antiquaries.org.uk
South Hylton Local History Soc, 6 North View, South Hylton, Sunderland, SR4 0LH T: 0191 552 6587 T: 0191 534 4251 E: Douglas.Scrafton@aol.com W: www.shlhs.com
St John Ambulance History Group, 3 The Bower, Meadowside, Jarrow, NE32 4RS T: 0191 537 4252

Warwickshire
Kineton and District Local History Group, The Glebe House, Lighthorne Road, Kineton, CV35 0JL T: 01926 690298 F: 01926 690298 E: p.holdsworth@virgin.net
Warwickshire Local History Soc, 9 Willes Terrace, Leamington Spa, CV31 1DL T: 01926 429671

Watford
Watford and District Industrial History Soc, 79 Kingswood Road, Garston, Watford, WD25 0EF T: 01923 673253

West Midlands
Aldridge Local History Soc, 45 Erdington Road, Walsall, WS9 8UU
Barr & Aston Local History, 17 Booths Farm Road, Great Barr, Birmingham, 642 2NJ
Birmingham & District Local History Assoc, 112 Brandwood Road, Kings Heath, Birmingham, B14 6BX T: 0121-444-7470
Birmingham Heritage Forum, 95 Church Hill Road, Solihull, B91 3JH
Birmingham War Research Soc, 43 Norfolk Place, Kings Norton, Birmingham, B30 3LB T: 0121 459 9008 F: 0121 459 9008
Black Country Local History Consortium, Canal St, Tipton Rd, Dudley, DY1 4SQ T: 0121 522 9643 F: 0121 557 4242 E: info@bclm.co.uk W: www.bclm.co.uk
Black Country Soc, PO Box 71, Kingswinford, DY6 9YN
Local History Consortium, The Black Country Living Museum, Tipton Road, Dudley, DY1 4SQ T: 0121 557 9643
Local Studies Group of CILIP - Formerly the Library Assoc, 25 Bromford Gardens, Edgbaston, Birmingham, B15 3XD T: 0121 454 0935 F: 0121 454 7330 E: prthomaspdt@aol.com
Quinton Local History Soc, 15 Worlds End Avenue, Quinton, Birmingham, B32 1JF T: 0121-422-1792 F: 0121 422 1792 E: qlhs@bjtaylor.fsnet.co.uk W: www.qlhs.org.uk
Romsley & Hunnington History Soc, Port Erin, Green Lane, Chapmans Hill, Romsley, Halesowen, B62 0HB T: 01562 710295 E: ejhumphreys@mail.com
Smethwick Local Hist Soc, 47 Talbot Road, Smethwick, Warley, B66 4DX T: W: www.smethwicklocalhistory.co.uk
Small Heath Local History Soc, 381 St Benedicts Road, Small Heath, Birmingham, B10 9ND

Wiltshire
Amesbury Soc, 34 Countess Road, Amesbury, SP4 7AS T: 01980 623123
Ashbury Local History Soc, Claremont , Asbury, Swindon, SN6 8LN E: marionlt@witrose.com
Atworth History Group, 48D Post Office Lane, Atworth, Melksham, SN12 8JX T: 01225 702351 E: joan.cocozza@btinternet.com
Chiseldon Local History Group, 3 Norris Close, Chiseldon, SN4 0LW T: 01793 740432 E: DavidBailey22@aol.com
Devizes Local History Group, 9 Hartfield, Devizes, SN10 5JH T: 01380 727369
Highworth Historical Soc, 6 Copper Beeches, Highworth, Swindon, SN6 7BJ T: 01793 763863

Marshfield & District Local History Soc, Weir Cottage, Weir Lane, Marshfield, Chippenham, SN14 8NB T: 01225 891229

Melksham & District Historical Assoc, 13 Sandridge Road, Melksham, SN12 7BE T: 01225 703644

Mere Historical Soc, Bristow House, Castle Street, Mere, BA12 6JF T: 01747 860643

Mid Thorngate Soc, Yewcroft, Stoney Batter, West Tytherley, Salisbury, SP5 ILD T:

Pewsey Vale Local History Soc, 10 Holly Tree Walk, Pewsey, SN9 5DE T: 01672 562417 F: 01972 563924 E: westerberg@onetel.co.uk

Purton Historical Soc, 1 Church Street, Purton, SN5 4DS T: 01793 770331

Redlynch & District Local History Soc, Hawkstone, Church Hill, Redlynch, Salisbury, SP5 2PL E: pat.mill@btinternet.com

Salisbury Civic Soc, 4 Chestnut Close, Laverstock, Salisbury, SP1 1SL

Salisbury Local History Group, 67 St Edmunds Church Street, Salisbury, SP1 1EF T: 01722 338346

South Wiltshire Industrial Archaeology Soc, 34 Countess Road, Amesbury, SP4 7AS T: 01980 622092 E: goodhugh@btinternet.com

Swindon Soc, 4 Lakeside, Swindon, SN3 1QE T: 01793-521910

The Hatcher Soc, 11 Turner Close, Harnham, Salisbury, SP2 8NX

The Historical Association (West Wiltshire Branch), 24 Meadowfield, Bradford on Avon, BA15 1PL T: 01225 862722

Tisbury Local History Soc, Suzay House, Court Street, Tisbury, SP3 6NF

Trowbridge Civic Soc, 43 Victoria Road, Trowbridge, BA14 7LD

Warminster History Soc, 13 The Downlands, Warminster, BA12 0BD T: 01985 216022 F: 01985 846332

Wilton Historical Soc, 3 Wiley Terrace, North Street, Wilton, SP2 0HN T: 01722 742856

Wiltshire Archaeological and Natural History Soc, Wiltshire Heritage Library, 41 Long Street, Devizes, SN10 1NS T: 01380 727369 E: wanhs@wiltshireheritage.org.uk W: www.wiltshireheritage.org.uk

Wiltshire Archaeology & Natural History Soc, 41 Long Street, Devizes, SN1O 1NS T: 01380 727369 F: 01380 722150 E: wanhs@wiltshireheritage.org.uk

Wiltshire Buildings Record, Libraries and Heritage HQ, Bythesea Road, Trowbridge, BA14 8BS T: 01225 713740 E: dorothytreasure@wiltshire.gov.uk W: www.wiltshire.gov.uk

Wiltshire Local History Forum, Tanglewood, Laverstock Park, Salisbury, SP1 1QJ T: 01722 328922 F: 01722 501907 E: sarumjeh@aol.com

Wiltshire Record Soc, County Record Office, County Libraries Hq, Trowbridge, BA14 8BS T: 01225 713136 F: 01225 713515

Wootton Bassett Historical Soc, 20 The Broadway, Rodbourne Cheney, Swindon, SN25 3BT, Small local history Society with no genealogical information.

Wroughton History Group, 32 Kerrs Way, Wroughton, SN4 9EH T: 01793 635838

Worcestershire
Alcester & District Local History Soc, Applecross, Worcester Road, Inkberrow, Worcester, WR7 4ET E: cjjohnson@care4free.net

Bewdley Historical Research, 8 Ironside Close, Bewdley, DY12 2HX T: 01299 403582 E: angela.ironside@clara.co.uk**Dodderhill Parish History Project - Discovering Wychbol's Past,** 9 Laurelwood Close, Droitwich Spa, WR9 7SF

Droitwich History and Archaeology Soc, 45 Moreland Road, Droitwich Spa, WR9 8RN T: 01905-773420

Feckenham Forest History Soc, Lower Grinsty Farmhouse, Callow Hill, Redditch, B97 5PJ T: 01527 542063

Feckenham Parish, Worcestershire One Place Study, 33c Castle Street, Astwood Park, Worcester, B96 6DP E: benwright3@hotmail.com

Kidderminster District Archaeological and Historical Soc, 178 Birmingham Road, Kidderminster, DYlO 2SJ T: 01562 823530 W: www.communigate.co.uk/worcs/kidderminsterhistorysoc/index.phtml

Kidderminster & District Local History Soc, 39 Cardinal Drive, Kidderminster, DY104RZ E: kidderhist.soc@virgin.net W: www.communigate.co.uk/worcs/kidderminsterhistorysoc/index.phtml

Kidderminster Field Club, 7 Holmwood Avenue, Kidderminster, DYL 1 6DA

Open University History Soc, 111 Coleshill Drive, Chapel End, Nuneaton, CV10 0PG T: (024) 76397668

Pershore Heritage & History Soc, 6 Abbey Croft, Pershore, WR10 1JQ T: 01386 552482 E: kenmar.abcroft@virgin.net,

Wolverley & Cookley Historical Soc, 18/20 Caunsall Road, Cookley, Kidderminster, DYL 1 5YB or:The Elms, Drakelow Lane, Wolverley, Kidderminster, DY11 5RU T: 01562 850215, History of parishes of Wolverley & Cookley

Worcestershire Archaeological Service, Woodbury Hall, University College of Worcester, Henwick Grove, Worcester, WR2 6AJ T: 01905 855455 F: 01905 29054 E: archaeology@worcestershire.gov.uk W: http://www.worcestershire.gov.uk/archaeology

Worcestershire Archaeological Soc, The , 26 Albert Park Road, Malvern, WR14 1HN T: 01684 565190

Worcestershire Industrial Archealogy & Local History Soc, 99 Feckenham Road, Headless Cross, Redditch, B97 5AM

Worcestershire Local History Forum, 45 Moreland Road, Droitwich, WR9 8RN T: 01905-773420

Wythall History Soc, 64 Meadow Road, Wythall, Birmingham, B47 6EQ E: val@wythallhistory.co.uk W: www.wythallhistory.co.uk

Yorkshire
York Georgian Soc, King's Manor, York, YO1 7EW

Yorkshire Architectural & York Archaeological Soc, c/o Cromwell House, 13 Ogleforth, York, YO1 7FG W: www.homepages.tesco.net/~hugh.murray/yayas/,

Yorkshire Philosophical Soc, The Lodge, Museum Gardens, Museum Street, York, YO1 7DR T: 01904 656713 F: 01904 656713 E: yps@yorkphil.fsnet.co.uk W: www.yorec.org.uk

Yorkshire Vernacular Buildings Study Group, 18 Sycamore Terrace, Bootham, York, YO30 7DN T: 01904 652387 E: dave.crook@suleacy.freeserve.co.uk W: www.yvbsg.org.uk

Yorkshire - City of York
York Archaeological Trust, 13 Ogleforth, York, YO1 7FG T: 01904 663000 E: enquiries@yorkarchaeology.co.uk W: www.yorkarchaeology.co.uk

Yorkshire - East
East Riding Archaeological Soc, 455 Chanterland Avenue, Hull, HU5 4AY T: 01482 445232

East Yorkshire Local History Soc, 13 Oaktree Drive, Molescroft, Beverley, HU17 7BB

Yorkshire - North
Forest of Galtres Soc, c/o Crawford House, Long Street, Easingwold, York, YO61 3JB T: 01347 821685

Northallerton and District Local History Soc, 17 Thistle Close, Romanby Park, Northallerton, DL7 8FF T: 01609 771878

Poppleton History Soc, Russett House, The Green, Upper Poppleton, York, YO26 6DR T: 01904 798868 F: 01904 613330 E: susan.major@virgin.net W: www.poppleton.net/historysoc

Scarborough Archaeological and Historical Soc, 10 Westbourne Park, Scarborough, YO12 4AT T: 01723 354237 E: archaeology@scarborough.co.uk W: www.scarborough-heritage.org

Snape Local History Group, Lammas Cottage, Snape, Bedale, DL8 2TW T: 01677 470727 www.communigate.co.uk/ne/slhg/index.phtml

Stokesley Local History Study Group, Cropton Lodge, Belbrough Lane, Hutton Rudby, Yarm TS15 0HY Tel: 01642 700306 Email: christinemiller46@hotmail.com WWW: http://pride.webspace.co.uk/stokesley.htm

Upper Dales Family History Group Croft House, Newbiggin in Bishopdale, Nr Leyburn, DL8 3TD T: 01969 663738 E: glenys@bishopdale.demon.co.uk W: www.bishopdale.demon.co.uk

Upper Wharfedale Field Society (Local History Section), Brookfield, Hebden Hall Park, Grassington, Skipton, BD23 5DX T: 01756-752012

Upper Wharfedale Museum Society & Folk Museum, The Square, Grassington, BD23 5AU

Wensleydale Railway Assoc, WRA Membership Administration, PO Box 65, Northallerton, DL7 8YZ T: 01969 625182 (Railway Shop, Leyburn) W: www.wensleydalerailway.com

Yorkshire Dialect Soc, 51 Stepney Avenue, Scarborough, YO12 5BW

Yorkshire - South

Barnscan - The Barnsdale Local History Group, 23 Rushymoor Lane, Askern, Doncaster, DN6 0NH T: 01302 700083 E: barnscan@btinternet.com www.barnscan.btinternet.co.uk

Bentley with Arksey Heritage Soc, 45 Finkle Street, Bentley, Doncaster, DN5 0RP T:

Chapeltown & High Green Archives, The Grange, 4 Kirkstead Abbey Mews, Thorpe Hesley, Rotherham, S61 2UZ T: 0114 245 1235 E: bellamyted@aol.com W: www.chgarchives.co.uk

Doncaster Archaeological Society a Group of the Yorkshire Archaeological Soc, The Poplars, Long Plantation, Edenthorpe, Doncaster, DN3 2NL T: 01302 882840 E: d.j.croft@talk21.com

Friends of Barnsley Archives and Local Studies, 30 Southgate, Barnsley, S752QL E: hazel@snowie48.freeserve.co.uk

Grenoside & District Local History Group, 4 Stepping Lane, Grenoside, Sheffield, S35 8RA T: 0114 257 1929 T: 0114 245 6959 E: info@grenosidelocalhistory.co.uk W: www.grenosidelocalhistory.co.uk

Wombwell Heritage Group, 9 Queens Gardens, Wombwell, Barnsley, S73 0EE T: 01226 210648

The Yorkshire Buildings Preservation Trust, c/o Elmhirst & Maxton Solicitors, 17-19 Regent Street, Barnsley, S70 2HP

The Yorkshire Heraldry Soc, 35 Holmes Carr Road, West Bessacarr, Doncaster, DN4 7HJ T: 01302-539993,

Yorkshire - West

Beeston Local History Soc, 30 Sunnyview Avenue, Leeds, LS11 8QY T: 0113 271 7095, Beeston, Leeds not be confused with Beeston, Nottinghamshire

East Leeds Historical Soc, 10 Thornfield Drive, Cross Gates, Leeds, LS15 7LS, Also East Leeds Heritage Centre

Halifax Antiquarian Soc, 66 Grubb Lane, Gomersal, Cleckheaton, BD19 4BU T: 01274 865418

Kippax & District History Soc, 8 Hall Park Croft, Kippax, Leeds, LS25 7QF T: 0113 286 4785 E: mdlbrumwell@tinyworld.co.uk W: www.kippaxhistoricalsoc.leedsnet.org

Lowertown Old Burial Ground Trust, 16 South Close, Guisley, Leeds, LS20 8TD, Reg Charity 1003823 Lowertown Old Burial Ground is at Oxenhope, Keighley. The Trust has transcribed the Memorial Inscriptrions and hold some family trees.

Northern Society of Costume and Textiles, 43 Gledhow Lane, Leeds, LS8 1RT

Olicana Historical Soc, 54 Kings Road, Ilkley, LS29 9AT T: 01943 609206

Ossett & District Historical Soc, 29 Prospect Road, Ossett T: 01924 279449

Shipley Local History Soc, 68 Wycliffe Gardens, Shipley, BD18 3NH E: ian@slhs.abelgratis.co.uk

Wetherby & District Historical Soc, 73 Aire Road, Wetherby, LS22 7UE T: 01937 584875

Yorkshire Archaeological Society - Local History Study Section, Claremont, 23 Clarendon Road, Leeds, LS2 9NZ T: 0113-245-7910 F: 0113-244-1979

Wales

Pentyrch & District Local History Soc, 34 Castell Coch View, Tongwynlais, Cardiff, CF15 7LA

Carmarthenshire

Carmarthenshire Antiquarian Soc, Ty Picton, Llansteffan, SA33 5JG T: 01267 241 727 E: arfon.rees@btinternet.com

Gwendraeth Valley Hist Soc, 19 Grugos Avenue, Pontyberem, Llanelli, SA14 5AF

Ceredigion

Ceredigion Antiquarian Soc, Archives Department, Ceredigion County Council, Aberystwyth, SY23 T: 01970 633697 E: info@ceredigion.gov.uk

Friends of The Clwyd Archives, Bryn Gwyn, 2 Rhodea Anwyl, Rhuddlan, LL18 2SQ T: 01745 591676 F: 01745 591676 E: coppack@timyworld.co.uk

Conwy

Abergele Field Club and Historical Soc, Rhyd y Felin, 47 Bryn Twr, Abergele, LL22 8DD T: 01745 832497

Llandudno & District Historical Soc, Springfield, 97 Queen's Road, Llandudno, LL30 1TY T: 01492 876337,

Denbighshire

Flintshire Historical Soc, 69 Pen y Maes Avenue, Rhyl, LL18 4ED T: 01745 332220

Ruthin Local History Group, 27 Tan y Bryn, Llanbedr D.C., Ruthin, LL15 1AQ T: 01824 702632 F: 01824 702632 E: gwynnemorris@btinternet.com

Flintshire

Chapels Heritage Society - CAPEL, 2 Sandy Way, Wood Lane, Hawarden, CH5 3JJ T: 01244 531255

Llantrisant & District Local History Soc, Cerrig Llwyd, Lisvane Road, Lisvane, Cardiff, CF14 0SG T: 029 2075 6173 E: BDavies203@aol.com

Gwent

Ahertillery & District Museum, 5 Harcourt Terrace, Glandwr Street, Abertillery, NP3 ITS

Abertillery & District Museum Soc, The Metropole,

Market Street, Abertillery, NP13 1AH T: 01495 211140
Gwent Local History Council, 8 Pentonville, Newport, NP9 5XH T: 01633 213229 F: 01633 221812 E: byron.grubb@gavowales.org.uk
Newport Local History Soc, 72 Risca Road, Newport, NP20 4JA
Pontypool Local History Soc, 24 Longhouse Grove, Henllys, Cwmbran, NP44 6HQ T: 01633 865662,
Gwynedd
The Anglesey Antiquarian Society & Field Club, 1 Fronheulog, Sling, Tregarth, Bangor, LL57 4RD T: 01248 600083
Caernarvonshire Historical Soc, Gwynedd Archives, County offices, Caernarfon, LL555 1SH T: 01286 679088 E: caernarvonshirehistoricalsociety@btinternet.com W: www.caernarvonshirehistoricalsociety.btinternet.co.uk
Cymdeithas Hanes a Chofnodion Sir Feirionnydd Meirioneth Historicial and Record Soc, Archifdy Meirion Cae Penarlag, Dolgellau, LL40 2YB T: 01341 424444 F: 01341 424505,
Cymdeithas Hanes Beddgelert - Beddgelert History Soc, Creua, Llanfrothen, Penrhyndeudraeth, LL48 6SH T: 1766770534
Federation of History Societies in Caernarvonshire, 19 Lon Dinas, Cricieth, LL52 0EH T: 01766 522238,
Glamorgan
Glamorgan History Soc, 7 Gifford Close, Two Locks, NP44 7NX T: 01633 489725 (Evenings Only) E: rosemary_hewlett@yahoo.co.uk
Kenfig Soc, 6 Locks Lane, Porthcawl, CF36 3HY T: 01656 782351 E: terry.robbins@virgin.net W: www.kenfigsociety.supanet.com
Glamorgan - Mid
Merthyr Tydfil Historical Soc, Ronamar, Ashlea Drive, Twynyrodyn, Merthyr Tydfil, CF47 0NY T: 01685 385871,

Pembrokeshire
The Pembrokeshire Historical Soc, The Castle, Haeverford West, SA61 2EF T: 01348 873316,
Powys,
Radnorshire Soc, Pool House, Discoed, Presteigne, LD8 2NW E: sadie@cole.kc3ltd.co.uk
Wrexham
Denbighshire Historical Soc, 1 Green Park, Erddig, Wrexham, LL13 7YE

Scotland,
Scottish Local History Forum, 45 High Street, Linlithgow, EH54 6EW T: 01506 844649 F: 0131 260 6610 E: chantal.hamill@dial.pipex.com
Scottish Records Assoc, National Archives of Scotland, H M General Register House, Edinburgh, EH1 3YY T: 0141 287 2914 F: 0141 226 8452
Society of Antiquaries of Scotland, Royal Museum of Scotland, Chambers Street, Edinburgh, EH1 1JF T: 0131 247 4115 T: 0131 247 4133 and 0131 247 4145 F: 0131 247 4163 E: r.lancaster@nms.ac.uk W: www.socantscot.org,
Ayrshire
Ayrshire Federation of Historical Societies, 11 Chalmers Road, Ayr, KA7 2RQ
Maybole Historical Soc, 15F Campbell Court, Ayr, KA8 0SE T: 07776 445033 E: maybole@scotsfamilies.co.uk W: www.maybole.org,
Ayrshire - East , Stewarton Library, Cunningham Institute, Stewarton, KA3 5AB T: 01560 484385,
Dundee
Abertay Historical Soc, 27 Pitcairn Road, Downfield, Dundee, DD3 9EE T: 01382 858701 E: abertay@dmcsoft.com W: www.dcmsoft.com/abertay
Friends of Dundee City Archives, 21 City Square, Dundee, DD1 3BY T: 01382 434494 F: 01382 434666 E: richard.cullen@dundeecity.gov.uk W: http://www.dundeecity.gov.uk/archives,
Falkirk
Falkirk Local History Soc, 11 Neilson Street, Falkirk, FK1 5AQ

Glasgow
Glasgow Hebrew Burial Soc, 222 Fenwick Road, Griffnock, Glasgow, G46 6UE T: 0141 577 8226,
Midlothian
Monklands Heritage Soc, 141 Cromarty Road, Cairnhill, Airdrie, ML6 9RZ T: 01236 764192,
Perthshire, Dunning Parish Historical Soc, The Old Schoolhouse, Newtown-Of-Pitcairns, Dunning, Perth, PH2 0SL T: 01764 684448 W: www.dunning.uk.net,
Renfrewshire
Bridge of Weir History Soc, 41 Houston Road, Bridge Of Weir, PA11 3QR
Paisley Philosophical Institution, 14 Newton Avenue, Elderslie, PA5 9BE
Renfrewshire Local History Forum, 15 Victoria Crescent, Clarkston, Glasgow, G76 8BP T: 0141 644 2522 W: www.rlhf.info,
Stirlingshire, Drymen Library, The Square, Drymen, G63 0BL T: 01360 660751 E: drymenlibrary@stirling.gov.uk
West Lothian
Linlithgow Union Canal Soc, Manse Road Basin, Linlithgow, EH49 6AJ T: 01506-671215 E: info@lucs.org.uk W: www.lucs.org.uk
Scottish Local History Forum, 45 High Street, Linlithgow, EH54 6EW T: 01506 844649 F: 0131 260 6610 E: chantal.hamill@dial.pipex.com

Northern Ireland,
Federation for Ulster Local Studies, 18 May Street, Belfast, BT1 4NL T: (028) 90235254 F: (028) 9043 4086 E: fulsltd@aol.com W: www.ulsterlocalhistory.org, Umbrella group for almost 100 local societies in Ulster
Co Tyrone
Centre for Migration Studies, Ulster American Folk Park, Mellon Road, Castletown, Omagh, BT78 5QY T: 028 82 256315, 028 82 242241 E: uafp@iol.ie W: www.qub.ac.uk/cms/ www.folkpark.com
County Londonderry
Roe Valley Historical Soc, 36 Drumachose Park, Limavady, BT49 0NZ
Presbyterian Historical Society of Ireland, Church House, Fisherwick Place, Belfast, BT1 6DW T: (028) 9032 2284, Opening hours: Mon to Fri 10am to 12.30pm. Wed afternoons 1.30pm to 3.30pm

Isle of Man
Isle of Man Natural History & Antiquarian Soc, Ballacrye Stream Cottage, Ballaugh, IM7 5EB T: 01624-897306
Isle of Man Natural History & Local History Soc, Stream Cottage, Ballacrye, Ballaugh, IM7 5EB

Channel Islands
Societe Jersiaise, 7 Pier Road, St Helier, Jersey, 01534 730538 T: T: 01534 888262 E: societe@societe-jersiaise.org

Republic of Ireland
Federation of Local History Societies - Ireland, Rothe House, Kilkenny
Presbyterian Historical Society of Ireland, Church House, Fisherwick Place, Belfast, BT1 6DW T: (028) 9032 2284
Dublin
Raheny Heritage Soc, 68 Raheny Park, Raheny, Dublin 5 T: 01 831 4729 E: jussher@softhome.net
County Mayo
Mayo North Family Heritage Centre, Enniscoe, Castlehill, Ballina T: 00 44 096 31809 F: 00 44 096 31885 E: normayo@iol.ie W: www.mayo-ireland.ie/motm.htm,
South Mayo Family Research Centre, Main Street, Ballinrobe T: 353 92 41214 E: soumayo@iol.ie W: http:/mayo.irish-roots.net/

The Commonwealth War Graves Commission
Peter Francis
Commonwealth War Graves Commission

The Commonwealth War Graves Commission, was established by Royal Charter of 21 May 1917, the provisions of which were amended and extended by a Supplemental Charter of 8 June 1964. Its duties are to mark and maintain the graves of the forces of the Commonwealth who died during two world wars, to build and maintain memorials to the dead whose graves are unknown, and to keep records and registers. The cost is shared by the partner governments - those of Australia, Canada, India, New Zealand, South Africa and the United Kingdom - in proportions based upon the numbers of their graves.

The Commission is responsible for 1.7 million commemorations, with war graves at over 23,000 locations and in some 150 countries. The work is founded upon the principles that each of the dead should be commemorated individually by name either on the headstone on the grave or by an inscription on a memorial; that each of the headstones and memorials should be permanent; that the headstones should be uniform; and that no distinction should be made on account of military or civil rank, race or creed.

Today, the Commission's major concern is the maintenance of those graves, cemeteries and memorials, to the highest standards, in the face of exposure to the elements and the passage of time - to ensure that "Their Name Liveth For Evermore". In addition to the day to day horticultural and structural maintenance of the cemeteries and memorials, an enquiry service is on offer to the public, whereby the commemorative details for any Commonwealth casualty who died during either of the two world

The Tyne Cot Cemetery, Belgium

wars can be provided. Commemorative information for Commonwealth civilians who died as a result of enemy action during the Second World War is also available on a Roll of Honour numbering over 66,400 names.

Originally, casualty data was stored on card indexes in over 3,000 drawers. After the First World War, details were compiled into some 1,500 cemetery registers. All enquiries were handled by a wholly manual process until 1995. The work was carried out, as it had been for decades, by dedicated, knowledgeable staff, using large ledgers. The ledgers are organised by country, name of cemetery and alphabetically by surname. To overcome the challenge of an enquirer only knowing a casualty's surname and not the place of burial, there are large volumes of alphabetical lists, cross-referenced by code numbers to the appropriate cemetery register. In late autumn 1995 the Commission's vast resource of information was computerised, allowing for a more efficient service to be offered to the public. The information for each entry was broken down into searchable 'fields' - For example, Surname, Age, Regiment, Cemetery Name, Date of Death e.t.c.

Not only do the computerised records allow for better access to the casualty details and place of commemoration, it also allows the operator to trace single casualties more quickly, from less

The Menin Gate, Ypres

Thiepval Memorial

information, and offer services like casualty-listing reports. This has become increasingly important as the value of the database for educational purposes is recognised and enquiries become more complex. Some of the most popular criteria for casualty listings include a same surname search, a regimental search and a home town search. It is even possible to trace, for example, how many Captains were killed on the first day of the Battle of the Somme.

In line with this public access policy, the Commission took the initiative to use the Internet to further promote access to the records. In November 1998, to coincide with the eightieth anniversary of the Armistice that brought to an end the First World War, the Debt of Honour Register was launched. The Register, a search by surname database, is available to the public via the Commission's web site at www.cwgc.org. The database provides known details of the casualty as well as the name of the cemetery or memorial, directions on how to find it and the exact plot, row, grave or memorial panel reference to enable the enquirer to locate the place of burial or commemoration should they make a pilgrimage to the cemetery or memorial. A second page on the web site prints the casualty details in the form of a commemorative certificate for the enquirer.

The launch of the Debt of Honour Register on the Internet has been an incredible success - the site averages 500,000 hits a week. The Register has widened public knowledge and interest in commemoration, reunited families with

the records of their long-fallen loved ones, assisted the historian, researcher and the student and most importantly, proved a highly effective way of keeping the names of those the Commission commemorates alive in the hearts and minds of a new generation. Enhancements to the site since it was launched have reduced down time and increased the accessibility of the site still further. The Commission anticipates further enhancements to the site in the near future.

In 1926, the Commission's founder, Fabian Ware, said the cemeteries and memorials built and maintained by the Commonwealth War Graves Commission, 'will bear a message to future generations as long as the stone of which they are constructed endures.' With the launch of the Debt of Honour Register, names once kept alive only in stone are now readily available to be carried in the hearts and minds of a new generation. As we move further away from the two world wars the Commission will ensure the stone, the gardens, the records, the memory and the message endure - that 'Their Name Liveth for Evermore".

Further Information
The Commission welcomes enquiries from the public. We request that you supply the Commission's enquiries department with as much information as possible. This will enhance the chances of a positive trace.
A full list of the Commission's services and publications on offer to the public is available from:

The Records & Enquiries Section
The Commonwealth War Graves Commission
2 Marlow Road, Maidenhead, Berkshire, SL6 7DX
Tel: 01628 634221 Fax: 01628 771208

E-mail: casualty.enq@cwgc.org
Web Site: www.cwgc.org

The Tyne Cot Cemetery, Belgium

The Commonwealth War Graves Commission
Civilian Roll of Honour
Peter Francis
Commonwealth War Graves Commission

In 1938, the Imperial, now Commonwealth, War Graves Commission unveiled the Australian Memorial at Villers-Bretonneux. It was the last of the Great War memorials to be completed from the war that was to end all wars and yet within a year the Second World War had started and the Commission was called upon to prepare for a new harvest of death. This second catastrophe of the twentieth century was a very different conflict to the one that had taken place only twenty or so years previously. The war was one of quick movement - the German Blitzkrieg sweeping all before it and forcing the Commission to temporarily relinquish control of the cemeteries and memorials in occupied Europe.

With the conquest of mainland Europe complete, Hitler's forces concentrated their efforts on the invasion of the United Kingdom. In order to invade, Germany had first to achieve total air superiority and so began the Battle of Britain and the large-scale bombing of airfields, factories and later in an attempt to smash the morale of the British people, cities. Distinctions between soldiers and non-combatants were non-existent. The phrase Total War was coined to represent the fact that civilian populations as well as front line troops were now considered targets.

On 7 September 1940 the first major air raid on a British city was carried out by the Luftwaffe. The Commission's founder, Fabian Ware, witnessed first hand the deaths of women, children, firemen and air-raid wardens. This new and horrifying war was impacting on communities like never before. Surely, he reasoned, each casualty deserved a fitting commemoration? Soon London itself was a target of the Blitz. Ware decided to act and wrote to the Prime Minister, Winston Churchill, on 18 September, urging the commemoration of those civilians killed by enemy action. In his words, "The deliberate slaughter of civilians was creating a new category of normal war casualties. Theirs should be counted an equal sacrifice".

Churchill, who had so successfully argued for the Commission's principle of equality of treatment for the war dead while Chairman of the Commission during the parliamentary debates on commemoration of the early 1920s, had no objection. In fact, he believed that civilian deaths might well outnumber military casualties - fortunately, he was not proved correct.

In January 1941, the Commission began to keep records of all civilian deaths caused by enemy action and its Royal Charters were adjusted to give it the necessary powers to do so. The biggest single obstacle to this task was obtaining the names and addresses of those killed. The information provided by the authorities, like the Registrar General, was not always complete and often did not include the addresses of next of kin. In February 1941, to encourage a greater flow of information and further publicise the commemoration of civilians, Ware decided to make a tour of the hard-hit areas. During his tour he enlisted the help of mayors and local authorities and the information provided to the Commission greatly improved. In November 1941, he made a further appeal on national radio and in the press for help and the records began to take shape - the Commission already had over 18,000 individuals recorded.

However, Ware was not satisfied with the mere recording of names at the Commission's headquarters. As the Commission would have no responsibility for the graves of civilians, Ware suggested to the Dean of Westminster in January 1942 that the names should be inscribed on a Roll of Honour which might be placed in the Warrior's Chapel of the Abbey. "The symbolic significance of ...the admission of these civilian dead to the adjacency and companionship with the Unknown Soldier would...give a right inspiration." The Dean readily agreed.

In December 1942 the first typed lists, leather bound in three volumes, were deposited for safekeeping at Westminster. The volumes were not put on display until after the war because it was believed that if the extent of civilian casualties were known, it might damage the morale of the nation. It was not until 1956 that the completed volumes of the Civilian Roll of Honour were handed to the Dean of Westminster by the Duke of Gloucester. Today, there are six volumes with over 66,000 names recorded. In a fitting tribute to those commemorated, the books are still on display to the public at the Abbey. A new page of the Civilian Roll of Honour is turned every day and so unfolds 66,000 tragic stories - the sudden death of a pensioner aged one hundred or of an infant a few hours old, of 163 people killed in an instant when a V2 rocket fell on Woolworth's at New Cross, and of the 1,500 dead of Malta.

What information does the Civilian Roll of Honour have? The casualty details available include the person's name, age, date of death, last known address and the particulars of the next of kin. The entries are structured along the lines of the old Borough system and then alphabetically by surname. Just one moving example reads: Betty Francis, Civilian War Dead. Died 9 April 1941, Aged 2. Daughter of Emily and the late Tom Francis of Clevedon Road, Balasall Heath. County Borough of Birmingham. The civilian records, like the military records, are still updated to this day. Amendments made on the computerised system are later added to the leather bound volumes at the Abbey twice a year by a member of the Commission's records department. In this way, that 'equal sacrifice' is preserved for future generations.

For the family historian, all of this information is available from the Commission's enquiries department in Maidenhead and the Debt of Honour Register at www.cwgc.org The Civilian Roll of Honour is a highly moving tribute not only to the many innocents who had their lives brutally cut short by war but to the bravery of services like the Fire Brigade and Ambulance crews who risked their lives to save others. The Commonwealth War Graves Commission keeps faith with them all, ensuring that
Their Name Liveth For Evermore.

What's new at the Imperial War Museum

Sarah Paterson - Department of Printed Books

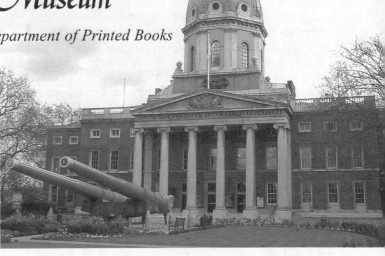

Many of you will already have read our previous articles relating to family history research at the Imperial War Museum, so rather than simply repeating them we thought it a much better idea to let you know what has been happening here and give you news about forthcoming developments.

Some of the catalogues for the different reference departments can now be found on the Museum's website at www.iwm.org.uk The three databases already available on Collections on-line are Documents, Film and Sound. Although no catalogue is ever one hundred per cent complete (new items are being acquired all the time and in many cases

older items may not yet have been catalogued on computer) this is a major achievement and is a boon for those wishing to prepare in advance of a visit, or for just seeing what is available.

The library catalogue is due to go on-line in April 2004 – this has been a major headache for us as the Department of Printed Books has its very own classification system that employs complex numerical codes and some verbal extensions, and these have all had to be rewritten into plain English. As this has involved converting over 75,000 records on top of our other duties, it is easy to see why we have had to curtail our family history activities this year! When the catalogue is on-line this will be an enormous aid in tracing what family members did during the First and Second World Wars. Many of the books we have are not unique and copies can be found elsewhere in the country, if you only know what you are looking for.

A website that has revolutionized Army genealogical research for the First World War is www.1914-1918.net This has all sorts of useful information about the British Army in the First World War, and provides orders of battle details that will enable you to trace the movements of different units, and work out which formations they would have served with and

under. With this information you will be able to use our on-line catalogue to great advantage, and either arrange to visit our reading room, or to get hold of other copies of the books through your local library service.

A couple of recently published titles that might help with genealogical research are Footprints on the sands of time: RAF Bomber Command prisoners-of-war in Germany, 1939-1945 by Oliver Clutton-Brock (London: Grub Street, 2003) and The Royal Corps of Signals: unit histories of the Corps (1920-2001) and its antecedents by Cliff Lord and Graham Watson (Solihull, West Midlands: Helion, 2003). The ISBNs are respectively 1-904010-35-0 and 1-874622-07-8.

Women and war, the Museum's new exhibition covering the range of the female experience opens on 15 October 2003 until 18 April 2004. We are expecting this to be very popular and have reprinted a couple of items in our collection to tie in with this. The story of British V.A.D. work in the Great War by Thekla Bowser was originally published circa 1917, and the 300 pages of text have been supplemented by an historical preface by Helen Pugh, British Red Cross Society Archivist, notes on how to trace Voluntary Aid Detachments in the First World War, and the text of a lecture delivered by the author in Birmingham in 1917. This would be an excellent starting point for finding out more about the experience of a VAD. We have also reprinted, in paperback form, Verses of a

V.A.D. and other war poems by Vera M Brittain, originally published in 1918. Women in uniform by Dorothea Collett Wadge has long been regarded as one of the very best sources on women in the services in the Second World War. Crammed full of photographs and detailed descriptions of the type of work undertaken by women, we have added an historical introduction by the author's nephew as well as a useful bibliography.

An amalgamation of our information sheets on Queen Mary's Army Auxiliary Corps and the Auxiliary Territorial Service appears on the following pages. The texts of our information sheets on the Women's Royal Naval Service and Voluntary Aid Detachments can be found on the Imperial War Museum website. The texts of our leaflets on the Army, Merchant Navy, Royal Navy, Royal Air Force and Prisoners of War can also be found on the website. Single copies of these leaflets can also be supplied to enquirers by post.

Four titles in our Tracing your family history series are currently available, covering the Army, Royal Air Force, Royal Navy and Merchant Navy. These sell for £5.50 each and are ideal introductions to the subject of tracing ancestors in each of these services from 1914 onwards, having been compiled in response to the many questions we get asked regularly. As well as providing information about where records can be found, they include information about the structure and organisation of the branch of service, medals, numbering, and suggestions for further research. Useful book titles, addresses and websites are also included.

If you wish to make an appointment to visit our Reading Room, or have a question you would like to ask (bearing in mind that we cannot embark on detailed research for you), please contact us in one of the following ways:
Telephone (enquiries): (020) 7416 5342
Post: Imperial War Museum, Department of Printed Books, Lambeth Road, London   SE1 6HZ
Email: books@iwm.org.uk
Website: www.iwm.org.u

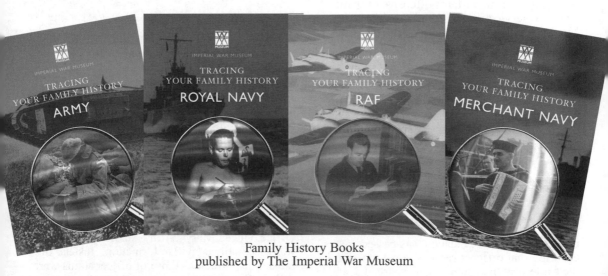

Family History Books
published by The Imperial War Museum

Women in the British Army – a brief history

Sarah Paterson
Department of Printed Books

The Women's Army Auxiliary Corps was established after a War Office investigation in December 1916 into the number of non-combatant tasks being performed by soldiers on the Lines of Communications in France. It was estimated that 12,000 men could be freed for service in the front line, and although women would not be suitable or strong enough to undertake all these jobs it was decided that they could make a significant contribution. The first party of 14 women arrived in France on 31 March 1917, and eventually 9,000 women were to serve there.

It was a continually evolving service with rules and regulations being formulated in response to experiences. The Women's Army Auxiliary Corps was formally established by Army Council Instruction 1069 of July 1917. On 9 April 1918, largely as a result of their sterling conduct during the German March offensive of that year, the service was renamed Queen Mary's Army Auxiliary Corps, with the Queen becoming Commander-in-Chief.

Queen Mary's Army Auxiliary Corps ceased to exist on 27 September 1921, but some 57,000 women had served with the unit, both at home and in France.

When war once again looked likely in the late 1930s, there was no question that women would have an important role to play. The Auxiliary Territorial Service was established on 9 September 1938, organised on the same lines as the Territorial Army. From April 1941 it was granted full military status, and in the following months, different legislation was passed ensuring that officers received a commission in the same way their male counterparts did, and that military discipline was enforced.

The ATS served in most theatres of war, as well as in locations such as Washington and the Caribbean. The variety of work also became much greater – as well as domestic and clerical trades, more technical work became available, and many women served with Anti-Aircraft Command, although they never (officially!) fired the guns.

Join now
A·T·S or W·A·A·F

Copyright Imperial War Museum

At its peak in June 1943, 210,308 officers and auxiliaries were serving with the ATS.

After the end of the war, it was decided that a small volunteer female force should be retained as part of the regular army, and on 1 February 1949 the Women's Royal Army Corps was established. This was disbanded in 1992, with many of its members being transferred to the Adjutant General's Corps, or elsewhere in the Army.

Service records
Although in uniform and working under the War Office, Queen Mary's Army Auxiliary Corps was essentially a civilian formation. Instead of ranks it had grades – those of officer status were called officials (unfortunately, no service records for officials have survived), other ranks were called members. Service records of members are held in Record Class WO 398 at the National Archives, Ruskin Avenue, Kew, Richmond, Surrey TW9 4DU (Tel: 020 8392 5200; Website: www.nationalarchives.gov.uk). The First World War Medal Roll may also provide useful information – the microfiche index for women's services can be found in WO

372, and the Medal Roll is in WO 329.

A useful information sheet on "Records of Women's Services, First World War" can be found on the PRO website at www.pro.gov.uk/leaflets/Riindex.asp A helpful publication is the third edition of Army Service Records of the First World War by William Spencer (Richmond, Surrey: Public Record Office, 2001).

Records for members of the Auxiliary Territorial Service and Women's Royal Army Corps are still held by the Ministry of Defence. These can be applied for by post from Army Personnel Centre, Historical Disclosures, Mailpoint 400, Kentigern House, 65 Brown Street, Glasgow G2 8EX. Initial contact can be made by telephone (0141 224 3030) or e-mail – please include your postal address (apc_historical_disclosures@dial.pipex.com). Records will be released to proven next of kin for a £25 fee, but there may be a lengthy wait for this service.

Casualty records
All those who died in service were entitled to an Imperial (later Commonwealth) War Graves Commission headstone (or, if there was no known grave, to have their name engraved on a Commission memorial). Details of their place of burial or commemoration are held by the Commonwealth War Graves Commission, 2 Marlow Road, Maidenhead, Berkshire SL6 7DX (Tel: 01628 634221; Website: www.cwgc.org). Their database Debt of Honour can be found on this website.

Details of the 8 officials who died in the First World War can be found in the publication Officers Died in the Great War (London: HMSO, 1919). Details of the 75 members who died can be found in the publication Soldiers Died in the Great War: Part 80 (London: HMSO, 1921). Both of these publications can be found on the CD-ROM of the latter title produced by Naval and Military Press. This can be viewed in our Reading Room.

The CD-ROM Army Roll of Honour: World War II produced by Naval and Military Press can be seen in our Reading Room, or may be available through other large reference libraries. This has details

of 717 members of the ATS who died during the Second World War.

Medal records
The First World War Medal Index at the Public Record Office, mentioned above, will provide details of campaign medals issued to members of the QMAAC. The only gallantry medal open to women during the First World War was the Military Medal. The Public Record Office has a nominal index of Military Medal award winners, and this provides details of the date it was notified in the London Gazette. Other decorations were also awarded, and some lists of these (and sometimes photographs) appear in the Women's Work Collection (see below).

Corps Collection
When the Women's Royal Army Corps Museum in Guildford closed down, the contents were passed to the National Army Museum, Royal Hospital Road, Chelsea, London SW3 4HT (Tel:

Copyright Imperial War Museum

EVERY FIT WOMAN CAN RELEASE A FIT MAN
JOIN THE
WOMEN'S ARMY AUXILIARY CORPS
TO-DAY
FOR WORK WITH THE FORCES EITHER AT HOME OR ABROAD
FOR ALL INFORMATION & ADVICE WRITE TO OR APPLY AT
NEAREST EMPLOYMENT EXCHANGE
OR LOCAL AGENCY
(THE ADDRESS CAN BE OBTAINED AT ANY POST OFFICE)

020 7730 0717; Website: www.national-army-museum.ac.uk) in 1993. An extensive collection of material relating to the QMAAC and ATS is held there, including photographs, personal papers (although no nominal rolls or listings of this nature). In order to visit the National Army Museum reading room it is necessary to have a reader's ticket – these can be applied for at the above address.

Further Reading
The Imperial War Museum has holdings relating to the QMAAC and ATS in all reference departments, and these can be visited by appointment. The Department of Printed Books has the books listed at the end of this information sheet, and an appointment can be made to view these in our Reading Room (Tel: 020 7416 5344), or alternatively, copies of these titles may be available through your local library's inter-library loan scheme. The Department also has an excellent reference source in the Women's Work Collection (only available on microfilm). This was compiled shortly after the end of the First World War, in order to record the female contribution. There is extensive material relating to the QMAAC and its origins and development and this can be found in ARMY 3/4 –7/12-15.

ATS CARRY THE MESSAGES

The motor cyclist messenger, roaring across country from Headquarters to scattered units is now an ATS girl

Copyright Imperial War Museum

The Women's Royal Army Corps Shelford Bidwell (London: Leo Cooper, 1977) [Famous Regiments Series]
Britain's other army: the story of the A.T.S. Eileen Bigland (London: Nicholson and Watson, 1946)
She walks in battledress: the day's work in the A.T.S. Anthony Cotterell (London: Christophers, 1942)
The Auxiliary Territorial Service compiled by Controller J M Cowper ([London]: War Office, 1949)
Women in khaki: the story of the British woman soldier Roy Terry (London: Columbus Books, 1988)
Service with the Army Chief Controller, Dame Helen Gwynne-Vaughan (London: Hutchinson, [1942])
Regulations for the Auxiliary Territorial Service 1941 War Office (London: HMSO, 1941)
Regulations for the Queen Mary's Army Auxiliary Corps War Office (London:pub [1918])
Women in uniform edited by D Collett Wadge (London: Sampson, Low, Marston, [1946]) [republished by the Department of Printed Books, Imperial War Museum]
We also hold a run of the *Old Comrades' Association Gazette* from July 1920 until March-April 1942 when it became the QMAAC and ATS Comrades Association Gazette. This continued until 1950 when it became *Lioness*. We have an almost complete run of this until 1995.

Some websites that might be helpful are listed below:
www.atsremembered.pwp.blueyonder.co.uk
www.wracassociation.i12.com/i12/
http://hometown.aol.co.uk/asummerof44/myhomep age/collection.html

Tracing Army Ancestry
Family History notes from the Imperial War Museum

The most important piece of information is the unit that an individual served with (it is a sad fact that those who died during the World Wars will be easier to trace than those who survived, and this information is readily obtainable from the **Commonwealth War Graves Commission**). The personal service record should be the starting point, but not all of these records for the First World War survived Second World War bombing. Records are located according to an individual's date of discharge.

The Imperial War Museum only covers the period from the First World War War onwards. Military history from 1485 to date is covered by the **National Army Museum, Royal Hospital Road, Chelsea, London SW3 4HT (Tel: 020 7730 0717 Website: http://www.national-army-museum.ac.uk)**. Pre-1914 service records are held at the **Public Record Office, Ruskin Avenue, Kew, Richmond, Surrey TW9 4DU (Tel: 020 8392 5200; Website: http://www.pro.gov.uk)**. The PRO also holds all surviving First World War service records for officers who left the Army before 1922. Surviving First World War Service records for other ranks who ceased service before 1920 are slowly being released to the PRO where they can be consulted on microfilm. It is hoped that this process will be complete by autumn 2002. The records of any First World War soldier who saw service after these cut-off dates or who rejoined the Army will still be held by the **Ministry of Defence, Army Records Centre, DR2B Bourne Avenue, Hayes, Middlesex UB3 1RF**. The publication *Army service records of the First World War* by William Spencer, 3rd edition, (Richmond, Surrey: PRO, 2001) is essential reading for those interested in the released First World War records, and *Army records for family historians* by Simon Fowler and William Spencer, 2nd edition, (Richmond, Surrey: PRO, 1998) will also prove helpful.

The **Army Records Centre** holds the records for those soldiers who served after 1920, and officers who served after 1922 until the mid 1990s (immediately after a soldier's discharge they are held by the **Army Personnel Centre** in Glasgow). The ARC will release records to proven next of kin for a £25 fee, but there may be a lengthy wait for this service.

The Brigade of Guards and Household Cavalry form an exception to this, and generally speaking retain their own records. The addresses to apply to for these are: **Regimental Headquarters Grenadier/Coldstream/Scots/Irish/Welsh Guards, Wellington Barracks, Birdcage Walk, London SW1E 6HQ** and **Household Cavalry Museum, Combermere Barracks, Windsor, Berkshire SL4 3DN**.

The careers of Army officers can be traced using the regular official publication *The Army List*, and the Department of Printed Books holds an almost complete set of these from 1914 to date.

Casualty Records

The **Commonwealth War Graves Commission, 2 Marlow Road, Maidenhead, Berkshire SL6 7DX (Tel: 01628 634221)** has details of all service personnel who died between the dates 4 August 1914-31 August 1921 and 3 September 1939-31 December 1947. The CWGC may charge a fee for postal enquiries, but the website containing their computerised database, *Debt of Honour* can be consulted at **http://www.cwgc.org**

Details about the burial places of soldiers who died outside the dates covered by the CWGC are held by the **Ministry of Defence, PS4 (A) (Cas/Comp), Building 43, Trenchard Lines, Upavon, Pewsey, Wiltshire SN9 6BE**. They also have some details relating to soldiers' wives or children who may have died outside the UK.

Sources held by Department of Printed Books include a complete set of the CWGC's memorial and cemetery registers and the 80 volume *Soldiers died in the Great War, 1914-19*. This was originally published in 1921 by HMSO but was republished by J B Hayward in 1989. It is also now available on a CD-ROM produced by Naval and Military Press. *Officers died in the Great War, 1914-19* is less detailed and has probably been superseded by *Officers who died in the service of British, Indian and East African Regiments and Corps, 1914-1919* by S D and D B Jarvis (Reading: Roberts Medals, 1993).

For the Second World War there is a computer coded roll of honour, which can be quite difficult to use in its present form. This is held by both the Department of Printed Books and the PRO, but Promenade Publications are in the process of publishing a ten volume set of this. Rolls of honour for other later conflicts are also held, and in addition the DPB has a large collection of published rolls of honour for localities, schools, institutions etc. Regimental histories and journals often contain rolls of honour.

The soldiers' own home area should not be forgotten when researching an individual's service - there may be local war memorial records, a local

account of war service may have been published, and contemporary local newspapers can prove very helpful. It is also possible that school, church or workplace records may still exist.

Medal Records

Campaign medals are those given to soldiers who are eligible for them because they were in a particular theatre of war within given dates. The PRO holds the First World War Medal Roll which provides a listing of all those who qualified for the 1914 Star, 1914/15 Star, British War Medal, Victory Medal, Territorial Force War Medal and/or the Silver War Badge. If a First World War record was destroyed some basic information about a soldier's service may be found in this.

Gallantry medals are those medals awarded for an especially heroic deed or action. Records for these are held at the PRO, but may not be very detailed. Notifications and citations (if published, which was not the case for awards such as the Military Medal and Mentions in Despatches) appeared in the official journal **London Gazette**. A complete set of this, and the all important indexes, is held at the PRO. The Department of Printed Books has some published listings of medal awards for decorations such as the Victoria Cross or Distinguished Conduct Medal. Usually you will need to go either to the official unit war diary (held at the PRO) or to a published unit history to see whether you can find out more about the action for which the decoration was awarded.

Regimental histories

The Department of Printed Books has an excellent collection of regimental histories. For those unable to visit our reading room (open 10am-5pm, Monday to Saturday), *A bibliography of regimental histories of the British Army* compiled by Arthur S White (London: London Stamp Exchange, 1988) provides details of published histories that may be available through your local library's inter-library loan scheme. Regimental journals and forces newspapers should not be overlooked.

A useful title for locating regimental museums (although these are very unlikely to hold information about individuals) is *A guide to military museums: and other places of military interest* by Terence and Shirley Wise (Knighton, Powys: Terence Wise, 1999).

We can also advise on the addresses of Old Comrades Associations. The internet has made it easier to establish contact with people who may have served in the Forces, or who may be conducting research similar to your own. The British Legion website at **www.britishlegion.org.uk** is a good place to start. Other websites of interest include The Western Front Association at **www.westernfront.co.uk** and Land Forces of Britain, the Empire and Commonwealth at **www.regiments.org/milhist/**

The Imperial War Museum does not hold any service records, official documentation or comprehensive listings of Prisoners of War, but it does have extensive material that will be helpful for providing information and understanding about their experience. This article should be read in conjunction with the relevant Imperial War Museum leaflet for the individual's branch of service – Army, Royal Air Force, Royal Navy or Merchant Marine.

The Department of Printed Books welcomes visitors by appointment (Monday to Saturday, from 10am to 5pm). Other reference departments in the Museum – Art, Documents, Exhibits and Firearms, Film and Video Archive, Photograph Archive, and the Sound Archive – may also be able to assist. Advance appointments are required.

R101 (G-FAAW) Airship Accident

David Barnes

The R100 and the R101 airships were built in England in the late 1920's, and were designed to fly to other parts of the British Empire and the Commonwealth - Canada, Egypt, India, perhaps even Australia. Nothing of this scale had ever been attempted before.

In 1930 one passenger was so confident in the proposed service that he had sent the Royal Airship Works £20,000 for one airship passage to New York in 1931. It was thought that the two airships, R100 and R101could earn useful revenue over 1931-1932 with commercial operations.

The R100 was designed by a private contract team headed by Sir Dennis Burney, with Barnes Wallis (later of 'Dambusters' fame) as his Chief Designer and Neville Shute Norway (Neville Shute, the author) as Chief Calculator and was designed on traditional lines. Making her maiden flight on 16 December 1929 from Howden to Cardington, she later successfully flew to Canada at the end of July 1930, returning to Cardington on 16 August 1930 after flying 57 hours 36 minutes

The R101was funded by the Government and although she was supposed to be an experimental aircraft, there was a lot of pressure to put her into active service. It had a different design team to the R100 and incorporated many innovations that had never been tried previously. The Cardington team were reaching towards the frontiers of technology and experienced a number of problems from the start. The framework, fabricated by Messrs Boulton & Paul of Norwich, was made of stainless steel and the power was supplied by five 600h.p. Beardmore Tornado diesel engines, two on each flank, the fifth centered at the rear, four engines drove forward, the fifth could only drive the ship astern. Weighing three tons, it was mainly dead weight, only used for a few minutes during landings and take-offs

Following R101's first static test, it was found that the amount of lift was unacceptable, the useful lift was only 35 tons, far below the 60 tons planned for. Measures were taken to remove all excess weight and the gas bags were expanded to their furthest limits. The ship was difficult to control and the extended gas cells rubbed against the metal framework causing leaks and constant patching of the calls
It was estimated that every hour the ship lost one ton of lift. The airship was not given a certificate of airworthiness.

In the Summer of 1930 a decision was made to split the framework and insert a further 45ft bay and gas bag, in order to gain extra lift. R101 had been 742 ft long but was now 777 ft long, with a volume of 5.5 million cubic feet. Basic repairs and reconstruction had been completed by 25 September 1930 and although a Permit to Fly was obtained over the telephone on 26 September 1930, bad weather delayed the test flight until the early morning 1 October 1930. The endurance flight after the modifications had taken place lasted 16 hours 51 minutes rather than the 48 hours originally contemplated and had not included any full-speed trials. However its flying qualities and reliability improved little, it was established that R101 was not a stable airship, tending to roll when on a horizontal flight and fly slightly nose-down on a vertical flight. In all eleven flights had taken place, prior to the final flight, and these had always been made in good weather.

The Labour Government's Secretary of State for Air, Lord Thompson, was eager to fly to India, some critics claimed that he had ambitions to become the next Viceroy. Equally it can be said that when the Treasury conditionally approved his ambitious plans for R102 and R103 , he was less and less prepared to accept opposition, however legitimate, as the deadline approached. Lord Thomson was

---

Original Schedule for R101 flight to Karachi:

Outward Times (approx. due to local conditions) .

Depart Cardington:	Midnight 26th September 1930 .
Arrive Ismalia:	After Sunset 28th September 1930 (refuel)
Depart Ismalia:	After Sunset 29th September 1930 .
Arrive Karachi:	Before Sunrise 1st October 1930 (refuel)

Return Times (approx. due to local conditions) .

Depart Karachi:	After Sunset 5th October 1930 .
Arrive Ismalia:	After Sunset 8th October 1930 (refuel)
Depart Ismalia:	Before Sunrise 9th October 1930.
Arrive Cardington:	After Sunset 11th October 1930 (refuel)

Duration: 15 days round trip   **Outward Journey**:5 days
Stop Over: 4 days   **Return Journey**: 6 Days

These large British ships were the first to adopt the use of the interior of the ship for it's passenger accommodation.
All meals for passengers and Officers were to be taken in the dining room which could seat up to 60 people.

Passengers and Officers Time	Crew Meal Times Time
Breakfast 07.30am - 09.30am	Breakfast 07.20am - 08.30am
Lunch 11.30am - 13.00pm	Lunch 11.20am - 12.30pm
Afternoon Tea 15.30pm - 16.30pm	Tea 15.30pm - 16.30pm
Dinner 19.30pm - 20.30pm	Supper 19.30pm - 20.30pm

The promenades showed off the views of the countryside and sea to the passenger's fullest advantage. Compared to the noisy smelly and tiring journey in an aeroplane of the period, the airships were seen as pure luxury, with service compared to that of the greatest ocean liners. The only contemporary airship that was running a passenger service was the German Zeppelin ZL127 - Graf Zeppelin, but that could only accommodate 20 passengers, situated in a stretched forward gondola beneath the hull of the ship.

Even though weight was the biggest issue with airships, crew and passengers could take up to 30lb's of kit/baggage as an allowance. On the R101's final flight the baggage and kit of some 54 people the average weight of baggage per person was 22lb's. Some of the other items included :
Fuel oil 25 tons
Water Ballast 5 tons
Rations 837lbs
500 gallons of drinking and bathing water
Silver painted 9 gallon Cask of Ale 70lbs
Carpet Roll 129lbs (flown over for the state dinner's at Karachi and Ismalia)
2 cases of Champagne 52lbs.

determined to make the prestigious flight to India as the start of a regular colonial airship service. With great political pressure on the project and despite the concerns of some of crew, a certificate of airworthiness was issued the R101 set off for India on 4 October 1930

The Certificate was prepared on October 2nd, to be handed over to the ship as soon as the AID were satisfied; it was issued on the recommendation of AMSR, based on a short letter from the designated Airworthiness Authority which said that, although they had not had time to draft a proper report and their calculations were based on very limited data, they were satisfied that lengthened R101 complied with the special requirements of the Airworthiness of Airships Panel.

It is quite clear that there was immense pressure on everyone concerned to cut corners to meet the deadline for departure. And it was purely for this reason that authority was granted to curtail the duration of the crucial test flight. So, one after another, all the checks and established practices were eroded and there was no one of independent standing or of sufficient authority to cry "halt and think a while" except for Sefton Brancker's informal submission to Lord Thomson, which was also dismissed.

As a comparison, the existing Imperial Airways service at that time took eight days ONE WAY and had 21 stops en-route. Travelling by Liner, the quickest sea route took four weeks!.

The Certificate of Airworthiness was only handed over to Flight Lieutenant H.C.Irwin, A.F.C. minutes before R101's departure from Cardington

The R101 was at the time the world's largest airship, 777 feet long and 132 feet in diameter. She had a gross lift of 165 tons (although most of this was required to lift the enormous metal structure of the airship).

Final Flight Route :
The first leg of the final flight route as planned by Atherstone was confirmed as follows :-

Bedford - London - Kent - leave coast over Hastings - North Paris - West to Rhone Valley - Toulouse - over the sea at Narbonne - across Mediterranean - Malta - Ismalia (Egypt)

The weather at Cardington was wet and gusty as the ship left in the evening and proceeded slowly southwards over the English countryside, carrying the Air Minister and his senior staff on what he hoped would be a dramatically successful journey to the Imperial Conference in India, due to start in a few days' time. Some engine trouble was soon experienced and as the R101 crossed the Channel she was tossed and buffeted by ever stronger gusts of wind. The Air Minister and his guests went to bed in their well-appointed cabins, and the ship ploughed on through the increasingly threatening weather. Visibility was reduced to nil, early next morning the watch was changed for the last time and the airship, travelling at about 1000 feet bucked in unintentional swoops, losing 200 – 300

open to the Germans (with the Graf Zeppelin and Hindenburg) and the Americans (with the Akron and Macon).

Crew Watch roster :
Airships had been operated by the Royal Naval Air Service during the First World War, and even after the war were run along the lines of Maritime service with ship watches set at along the similar lines of their naval colleagues.
An airship normally flew with a two-watch crew but on the outward journey a three watch crew was being carried so that the services of the third watch may be available on arrival at Karachi. When an airship was moored one watch was always on duty, a stand-by watch was in close attendance and undertakes maintenance duties during the day, and the third watch the (relief watch) is off-duty for 24 hours at a time.

The watches were split in duration as 4 hours for a "day" watch and reduced to 3 hours for a "night" watch :-

Watch Name	Time
Forenoon Watch	08.00 - 12.00noon
Afternoon Watch	12.00 noon - 16.00
Evening (Dog) Watch	16.00 - 20.00
1st Night Watch	20.00 - 23.00
Middle Watch	23.00 - 02.001st
Morning Watch	02.00 - 05.00
2nd Morning Watch	05.00 - 08.00

feet at a time. The crew were hardly able to correct these traumatic movements as within minutes the airship had struck a French hillside near Beauvais, at about 02.09 GMT on the morning of 5 October 1930, bursting into flames, killing 48 people, included two high ranking aviation officials. She had only been flying for just over seven hours.

No one has pinpointed why she crashed, though it is undoubtedly true that the over-weight, under-powered and unstable airship had just flown through some of the worst flying weather imaginable. The disaster shook the government's confidence in dirigibles, and ended British efforts to develop the lighter-then air aircraft for commercial use. The R100 was scrapped and all rigid airship development in Britain came to an end, leaving the field

Flight Log of the R101

Flight	Date	Departure	Arrival	Duration	Miles	Route
1	14 Oct 1929	11.17 am	16.57pm	5h 40min	108	Cardington –London and return
2	18 Oct 1929	08.12am	7.50pm	9hr 38min	210	Cardington – Midlands and return
3	1 Nov 1929	09.40am	16.55pm	7hr 15min	260	Cardington – Norfolk and return
4	2 Nov 1929- 3 Nov 1929	20.12pm	10.14am	14hr 2min	380	Cardington – South England and return
5	8 Nov 1929	13.47pm	16.51pm	3hr 4min	52	Cardington -Bedford and return
6	14 Nov 1929	13.34pm	16.43pm	3hr 9min	62	Cardington –Bedford and return
7	17 Nov 1929 - 18 Nov 1929	10.33am	17.14pm	30hr 41min	1,148	Cardington - Scotland Ireland - Midlands – Cardington
	30 Nov 1929 -23 June 1930					In Shed at Cardington for Winter (Alteration of gas bag, wiring etc)
8	26 Jun 1930	15.51pm	20.26pm	4hr 35 min	217	Cardington - Test Flight and return
9	27 Jun 1930	07.22am	19.50pm	12hr 33min	461	Cardington – Hendon and return
10	28 Jun 1930	07.25am	19.51pm	12hr 26min	435	Cardington – RAF Hendon Display and return
	29 Jun 1930 -1 Oct 1930					In shed at Cardington (Fitting of an extra 45 ft bay and gas bag)
11	1 Oct 1930 - 2 Oct 1930	15.36pm	08.27am	16hr 51min	637	Cardington - East of England - North Sea – Cardington
12	4 Oct 1930 - 5 Oct 1930	18.36pm	02.09am	7hr 33min	248	Cardington - India. Crashed near Beauvais, France

Total Flying time: 127 hours 20minutes
Miles Flown: 4,218
Total Passengers carried: 186

A Lavish floating hotel ....
The R101 was seen as a lavish floating hotel. The promenade decks and cabins, with hot air circulated for warmth were be seen as unique in the skies.

The Main Lounge
The 160ft x 30ft lounge with imitation palm trees was a colour scheme of white panels with gold inlay. The curtains on to the promenade deck were of fine Cambridge blue. The seating arrangements were of small tables, and the chairs were constructed of upholstered green cane wicker. At each side of the left hand side of the lounge were writing desks running along side the wall, on which paintings were hung. Three steps lead up to the deck. The curtains would be drawn closed at night in order to give those on the Promenade Deck a better view of the ground at night without the light pollution from the lounge. The cushions on the side chairs were inflated with air to assist in weight reduction.

The Dinning Room
The dining room was able to seat 50 people in one sitting. A "dumb waiter" hoisted the food up from the galley below to the dining room. There was also a fitted wireless set in the wall to provide music to diners whilst they ate.

The Promenade Decks
The promenade decks had deck chairs. The safety rail also had a foot rest. The design followed very traditional nautical designs and almost felt as if passengers were on the deck of a ship.
The promenade decks were on both sides of the lounge, and also ran along the side of the dining room. Even though early designs suggested that they both be interlinked, there was no door between the promenade decks in to each section. The original windows were made of glass but were removed and replaced by light weight cellon safety glass. A second set of windows and promenade ran along the corridor on the starboard side of the passenger accommodation near the sleeping quarters, however these windows were later removed in September of 1930 as part of the weight saving programme.

The Corridors
One of the two corridors leading from the lounge. A set of steps lead over a main ring girder and there was the staircase to the lower deck. To the right would have been the main washrooms for passengers. The walls were made of fine 2mm thick spruce cladding on main pillars and stretched doped double thickness cloth on the wall spaces. This was doped taught and pained white. The lines on the pillar inlays were painted gold, along with the edges to the cloth panels. There was a writing desk attached to the wall.

The Passenger Cabins
The sleeping arrangements were in the form of bunks. Even though they may seem spartan, the cabins were warmed by a heating vent driven from the main radiator which could be heated or cooled by being lowered out of the ship. Each cabin had a main "porthole" electric light was fitted to the wall with a small blind which would be drawn over it. This would continue with the "nautical" influence. A small reading light was also provided above each bunk. A small luggage stool would be provided for cabin bags. A small rug would be on the floor. Each cabin had a notice regarding the protocols of airship life, and details of summoning a steward etc.
Some 50 cabins were constructed in formations of singe, two and four berth arrangements.

Washroom facilities were available close by. These had aluminium sinks with long half length mirrors suspended on two wires in front of the basins. Toilets were on the lower deck.

Below Decks - Crew's Quarters
The crews sleeping quarters in the lower deck of the ship. The crew had a series of sets of sleeping accommodations and were comfortable compared to those of the Zeppelins whereby it was not uncommon for the crew to sleep in hammocks. The crew had a large mess hall for their private space. This contained a large table with bench seating. The lower deck also boasted the cargo hold whereby the luggage and stores could be hoisted up to the ship through the cargo hatch using the winch.

The Galley
All of the instruments were made of light aluminium. The galley was well fitted out with an all electric over, a vegetable steamer and ample space for the chef.

The Smoking Room
A unique example of design. The R101 was fitted with a smoking room on the lower deck able to seat some 24 people. The floor and ceiling were made of light asbestos with a thin sheet of metal on the floor. The walls were the same construction as the rest of the ship being made of cloth. The smoking room was not considered a hazard to the ship as all precautions had been taken with the materials in construction. This is where you could retire after dinner and enjoy a cigar and drinks.

Lower deck corridor.
The corridor from the nose of the ship to the passenger accommodation was constructed of a similar material to the corridors above in the upper deck. This meant that the passengers entering the ship would see a long white and gold "panelled" corridor to the lower deck accommodation, and a stair case up to the main cabins. The corridor had wooden doors on each side, to the crews quarters, the cargo room, the wireless room and galley, the smoking room and of course the toilets.

There were small windows in the lower deck corridor near the wireless room and the chart room. Lower windows were also in the crew room.

Uniform.
Dark blue uniform which had been recently approved for the Air Ministry Airship Crews, was to be worn on the flight probably as far as Egypt. At that stage it may be necessary to change into tropical kit, for which arrangements had been made. The blue uniform consists of a reefer pattern jacket with gold buttons in the case of the Officers and black for the men, peaked cap, and badge consisting of a circle surmounted by a crown in the centre of which are the words "R .101" and on the circle "R.A.W. Cardington". Similar badges were be worn on the khaki tropical kit .

It should be noted that the Crew of R.101, which consisted of five officers and 37 men, was entirely composed of civilian personnel, with the exception of two officers and one N.C.O. of the Royal Air Force, who are seconded for duty on Airships.

Notes on Officials and Officers
Wing Commander R.B.B Colmore, O.B.E, R.A.F
Director of Airship Development,
He was the Air Ministry Director under the Air
Member of Council for Supply and Research,
responsible for all airship activities. His directorate
was organised in five main divisions; research and
design; flying; organisation; construction and
maintenance ; and finance and administration. Each
of the first three divisions is in charge of an assistant
director; a works manager is responsible for the
fourth and a secretary and accountant for the last. The
Director had his headquarters at the Royal Airship
Works, Cardington, Bedford, where the airship R101
was designed and constructed and which was the
base for British airship operations. The trials of both
R100 and R101 were carried out at Cardington.

Wing Commander Colmore was born in Portsmouth
in 1887, was educated at Stubbington House, Fareham
and in H.M.S. "Britannia". He became a Sub-
Lieutenant in the Royal Navy in 1907 and was
promoted Lieutenant in 1909. He retired in 1911 and
on being mobilised at the outbreak of War became a
Lieutenant-Commander. He served with the
Armoured Car Division at Antwerp in 1914 and
commanded the Armoured Car Section employed at
Gallipoli in 1915. Later in 1915 he was Commanding
Officer in the first campaign against the Sensussi
tribes on the Egyptian borders.

He transferred to the Airship Section of the Royal
Naval Air Service in 1916 and after serving at the
airship station at Barrow became Commanding
Officer of the airship base at Mullion, Cornwall.
While holding this command he evolved a novel
scheme of dealing with the submarine menace by a
system of combined patrols of airship, seaplanes and
aeroplanes in conjunction with surface craft. This
method proved so successful that Lieut-Colonel
Colmore (as he became on formation of the Royal Air
Force) was appointed 1st Class Staff Officer, Aircraft
Operations, Plymouth, with a view to the same
principles being applied against submarines along the
whole British Coast. He was later posted as Chief
Staff Officer, Aircraft Operations, with Commander-
in-Chief, Grand Fleet, based at Dundee, but the war
ended, before the system could come in to general
operation.

After the War he was granted a permanent
commission as Squadron Leader, Royal Air Force,
and was attached as Staff Officer for Airships to the
Department of the Controller General of Civil
Aviation, Air Ministry. When it was decided in 1924
to proceed with the development of airships he was
appointed Deputy Director of Airship Development in
the Department of Air Member of Council for Supply
and Research and became Director at the beginning of
the present year. He is seconded from the Royal Air
Force for airship duty. He was on board R100 during
her Canadian flight in July and August 1930 and
represented the Air Ministry during her stay in
Canada.

Major G H Scott C.B.E, A.F.C Assistant Director of
Airship Development (Flying)
Born in 1888 at Catford, Kent and was educated at

Richmond School, Yorkshire, and at the Royal Naval
Engineering College, Keyham. From 1908 he was
engaged in general engineering until the outbreak of
War when he joined the Royal Naval Air Service.
After service at Farnborough, in H.M.A. 'Eta' and at
Kingsnorth, he proceeded in 1915 to the airship
station at Barrow and became captain of the Parseval
airship P.4. The following year he was appointed to
the command of the airship station at Anglesey and in
1917 became captain of R.9, the first British rigid
airship to fly, and was also appointed Experimental
officer, Airships, at Pulham airship base.
On the formation of the Royal Air Force he was given
the rank of Major. Towards the end of 1918 he was
chosen to command R.34 and was awarded the A.F.C.
for his work on airships. In 1919 he commanded R.34
on 1st flight from East Fortune, Scotland to the
United States and back to Pulham. For this he was
awarded a C.B.E. This was the first flight of any
aircraft to America and also the first outward and
homeward flight. He was demobilsed from the Royal
Air Force later in 1919.

In 1920 he was appointed to the technical staff of the
Royal Airship Works, Cardington. He is the inventor
of the Air Ministry system of airship mooring to a
tower, which is also employed in the United States. In
1924 he was appointed officer in Charge of Flying
and Training in the Airship Directorate and in January
1930 became Assistant Director (Flying). He visited
Canada in 1927 to advise the Canadian Government
on the selection of an airship base which resulted in
St. Hubert, Montreal being chosen and equipped.
Since the autumn of 1929 he has carried out extended
trials of the two British Airships R.101 and R.100,
which erre the largest airships in the world and
contain many novel features compared with previous
airship types. He took part in the Canadian Flight of
R.100 during July and August 1930 and was officer in
Charge of the Flight.

**Lieutenant-Colonel V.C. Richmond, O.B.E., B.Sc.,
A.R.C. F.R.A.S**. Assistant Director of Airship
Development (Technical)
Born in 1893 at Dalston, London, and was educated
at the Royal College of Science. London. He became
Engineer to Messrs. S. Pearson & Sons. for physical
and Structual problems in connection with dock
construction. In 1915 he joined the Royal Naval Air
Service and was engaged until the end of the War
principally on the construction of non-rigid airships.
In 1920 he went to Germany with the Inter-Allied
Commission of Control and during part of the time
was in charge of the Naval Sub-Commission for the
surrender of airships and seaplanes.
In 1921 he joined the Airship Research Department of
the Air Ministry and until 1923 was engaged on
research into problems connected with rigid airship
construction. From 1923 to 1924, during the cessation
of airship activity in this country, he was in charge of
the Material and Research Branch under the Director
of Research, Air Ministry and since 1923 also, has
been Lecturer in Airship Design and construction at
the Imperial College of Science. He joined the Royal
Airship Works in 1924 as Officer in Charge of Design
and Research, during which time the R.101 was
designed and constructed. In 1930 he was appointed
Assistant Director, Airship Development (Technical).

Flight Lieutenant H.C. Irwin, A.F.C., R.A.F., Captain of R.101

He was born in 1894 at Dundrum, Co. Cork, Ireland, and was educated at St. Andrew's College, Dublin. He joined the R.N.A.S. Airship Section in 1915 and from 1916 to 1917 was Captain of Non-Rigid airships S.S. Zero, Coastal and N.S. types in Home Waters and the East Mediterranean.

He commanded R.33 and R.36 in 1920 and from the following year to 1924 was performing R.A.F duty at Service Stations and Staff duties at the Air Ministry. In 1925 he was transferred to the Royal Airship Works, Cardington, and in 1926 again commanded R.33 when he carried out various experimental flights to gather technical data required in connection with the design of R.100 and R.101. From 1926 to 1928 he commanded the R.A.F. School of Balloon Training on Salisbury Plain and in 1929 was again transferred to the Royal Airship Works to take over command of R.101. He was a member of the British Olympic Athletic Team at Antwerp in 1920 and has repeatedly represented Ireland and the Royal Air Force in International and Inter-Service Athletic Contests. He was seconded for airship duty from the Royal Air Force.

Squadron Leader E.L. Johnston, A.F.C., O.B.E.,

Reserve of Air Force Officers, Navigator of R101
Born in Sunderland in 1891 and was educated at Tynemouth High School and the Marine School, South Shields. He is a qualified Master Mariner and originally served in the Royal Naval Reserve. He transferred to the R.N.A.S. (Airship Section) in 1916 and after commanding coastal type airships he later became Commanding Officer of Luce Bay airship station, in the South West of Scotland. On the formation of the Royal Air Force he was appointed Captain and later was promoted to the rank of Major. After the War he served in the navigation branch in the Air Ministry but later retired from the Royal Air Force. He was appointed to the Royal Airship Works, Cardington, in 1924 for navigational duties and was loaned for some time to Imperial Airways Ltd., in order to open up European aeroplane routes. In 1927 he was navigator to the Secretary of State for Air on the first Imperial Airways flight to India and back. He was navigator on R.100 as well as R.101 and in that capacity flew with the former on her voyage to Canada and return in July and August 1930. He is also an Air Ministry Examiner for Navigators licences. He recently organised the Guild of Air Pilots and Air Navigators of the British Empire and holds the Position of Deputy Master in that organisation.

Lieutenant-Commander N.G. Atherstone, A.F.C., R.N. (Retd.), First Officer R.101

He was born in 1894 at St. Petersburg; Russia, and was educated at Larchfield, Helensburgh, Winton House, Winchester, and Charterhouse. He joined the Royal Navy as a Cadet in 1913 and was appointed to H.M.S. "Highflyer" for training. On the outbreak of War he was appointed to H.M.S. "Gibraltar" and served with the 10th Cruiser Squadron, Grand Fleet and Destroyers until 1917 when he transferred to Airships, becoming Pilot of Non-Rigids SS. Zero, and N.S. types. In 1918 he was appointed 1st Officer of R.29 and was awarded the A.F.C.

He returned to the Royal Navy in 1919 and retired in 1920 becoming resident in Australia. He was promoted Lieutenant-Commander R.N.(Retd.) in 1926 and he returned to England in 1927 on being appointed to the Royal Airship Works, Cardington, for Airship duties. He was appointed First Officer R.101 in 1929.

Flying Officer M.H. Steff, R.A.F.,Second Officer

R.101 was born in 1896 at Luton, Beds. He joined the Navy in September, 1914 and served in H.M. S. "Inflexible" from 1915 onwards and was present at the battle of Jutland in 1916. He became a flight officer in the Kite Balloon section of the R.N.A.S. in the begining of 1918 and served in the Adriatic Barrage Kite Balloons in Italy. He took part in minesweeping operations in 1919 in the Aegean Sea, the Dardanelles and the Black Sea and in 1920 he was posted to the instructional staff of the School of Balloon Training in England where he served for four years. He proceeded in 1925 to the Royal Airship Works for Kite balloon experiments and was appointed 2nd Officer of R.101 in 1929. He has been loaned to R.100 for her Trial flights, as 2nd Officer, and in that capacity flew with her to Canada and back in July and August 1930. He is seconded from the Royal Air Force for airship duty.

Mr. M.A. Giblett, M.Sc., Meteorological Officer,

R101. He was born in 1894 at Englefield Green, Surrey, and was educated at the Universities of Reading and London, During the War he served as Meteorological Officer, Royal Engineers, in the North Russian Expeditionary Force, Archangel, and in 1919 loaned the Meteorological Office, Air Ministry, being in the Forecast Division until the beginning of 1925 except during 1921 when he was detached for duty during the trial flights of Airships R.80, R.36 and R.38. When an Airship Services Division was created in the Meteorological Office, Air Ministry, in 1925 he was

appointed Superintendent. He was a member of the Official Airship Mission which visited South Africa, Australia, New Zealand and India in 1927 to advise the Governments on the steps to be taken to provide the necessary ground organisation for airship operations. He has also organised the necessary meteorological services for airship flights to Canada and on the route to Egypt and India. He is on the Council of the Royal Meteorological Society and is Meteorological Secretary of Section A of the British Association. He flew in R.100 as Meteorological Officer on her trip to Canada and return in July and August 1930.

Squadron Leader F.M. Rope, R.A.F., Assistant to Assistant Director (Technical).
Born in 1888 at Shrewsbury and was educated at Shrewsbury School and Birmingham University where he took an engineering degree. He left the University in 1910 and until 1912 was an engineer to the British Electric Plant Co., Alloa. He then joined the Rio Tinto Co., London, Mining and Mechanical Engineers. From 1913 to 1914 he was employed on locomotive engineering by the Brighton Railway and from then to 1915 served in the same capacity with the Nigerian Government Railway, West Africa. He Joined the R.N.A.S. in 1915 serving at Capel and Kingsnorth Airship Stations where he subsequently became Staff Officer in the Director of Research Department.
From 1921 to 1924 he was Technical Staff Officer, R A.F, Iraq and was then appointed to the Royal Airship Works, Cardington. He is seconded to the Royal Airship Works from the Royal Air Force.

Mr. H.J. Leech, A.F.M., Foreman Engineer Royal Airship Works,
Born at Dudley, Worcestershire in 1890 and educated at Appleby. He served as an apprentice with the B.S.A. Co. on motor car manufacturing from 1906 to 1911 and was engaged in this l of engineering until 1916 when he joined the R.N.A.S .(Airship Section). He became an engineer on Non-Rigid Airships SS Zero, C.P. and C. Star types and the Parseval., and was an engineer on the S.R.1, an Italian Semi-Rigid, when she flew from Rome to England in 1918. He was demobilised in 1919 but rejoined. airships 1920 and was placed in charge of the Engine Shops at Pulham Airship Station. He remained there until 1924 when he was transferred to the Royal Airship Works, Cardington, and took charge of the Engine Shops where he has been engaged on test and research work and the development of the Diesel Oil Fuel Airship Engine

Fate of Passengers and Crew on board HMA R101 4/5 October 1930
Passengers
1. Brigadier-General, The Right Hen. Lord Thomson of Cardington (HM Secretary of State for Air) - Killed, body not identified.
2. Air Vice-Marshal Sir W. Sefton Brancker (Director of Civil Aviation)- Killed, body identified on return to London.
3. Major Percy Bishop (Chief Inspector AID)- Killed, body not identified.

4. Squadron Leader W Palstra RAAF (representing the Australian Government) - Killed, body not identified.
5. Squadron Leader W O'Neill (Deputy Director of Civil Aviation, India) - Killed, body identified on return to London.
6. Mr James Buck, Lord Thomson's valet - Killed, body identified on return to London.
Officials of the Royal Airship Works, Cardington
7. Wing Commander R.B.B. Colmore (DAD)- Killed, body identified on return to London.
8. Major G.H. Scott (ADAD Flying)- Killed, body not identified.
9. Lt.Col. V.C. Richmond (ADAD Technical)- Killed, body identified on return to London.
10. Squadron Leader EM. Rope (Assistant to DAD Technical) - Killed, body identified on return to London.
11. Mr Alexander Bushfield, AID - killed, identified on return to London.
12. Mr A.H. Leech, Foreman Engineer Cardington - survivor. Officers of R101

Officers
13. Flight Lieutenant H. Carmichael Irwin (Captain)- Killed, body identified on return to London.
14. Squadron Leader E.L. Johnston (Navigator)- Killed, body not identified.
15. Lt-Commander N.G. Atherstone (First Officer) - Killed, body identified on return to London.
16. Flying Officer M.H. Steff (Second Officer)- Killed, body not identified.
17. Mr M.A. Giblett (Chief Meteorological Officer) - Killed, body identified on return to London.

Petty Officers and Charge Hands

18. G.W. Hunt (Chief Coxswain) - Killed, body not identified.
19. W.R. Gent (Chief Engineer) - Killed, body identified on return to London.
20. G.W Short (Charge-Hand Engineer)- Killed, body not identified.
21. S.E. Scott (Charge-Hand Engineer) - Killed, body identified at Allonne.
22. T. Key (Charge-Hand Engineer)- Killed, body not identified.
23. S.T. Keeley (Chief Wireless Operator) - Killed, body not identified.
24. A.H. Savidge (Chief Steward) - Killed, body not identified.

R101 Crew members

25. Flight-Sergeant WA. Potter (Assistant Coxswain) - Killed, body identified at Allonne.
26. L.E Oughton (Assistant Coxswain) - Killed, body identified on return to London.
27. C.H. Mason (Assistant Coxswain) - Killed, body not identified.
28. M.G. Rampton (Assistant Coxswain)- killed, identified on return to London.
29. H.E. Ford (Assistant Coxswain)- Killed, body not identified.
30. P.A. Foster (Assistant Coxswain) - Killed, body not identified.
31. E.G. Rudd (Rigger) - Killed, body identified at Allonne.
32. C.E. Taylor (Rigger) - Killed, body identified on return to London.
33. A.W.J. Norcott (Rigger) - Killed, body not identified.
34. A.J. Richardson (Rigger)- Killed, body identified on return to London.
35. WG. Radcliffe (Rigger)- survived, but died at Beauvais on October 6th.
36. S. Church (Rigger)- survived, but died at Beauvais on October 8th.
37. R. Blake (Engineer)- Killed, body identified at Allonne.
38. C.A. Burton (Engineer)- Killed, body identified on return to London.
39. C.J. Fergusson (Engineer) - Killed, body not identified.
40. A.C. Hastings (Engineer) - Killed, body not identified.
41. W.H. King (Engineer) - Killed, body identified on return to London.
42. M.E Littlekitt (Engineer) No. 1 car - Killed, body not identified.
43. W Moule (Engineer) No. 2 car - Killed, body identified on return to London.
44. A.H. Watkins (Engineer) - Killed, body not identified.
45. A.V. Bell (Engineer) No. 5 car - survivor.
46. T.H. Binks (Engineer) No. 5 car - survivor.
47. A.J. Cook (Engineer) No. 4 car - survivor
48. V. Savory (Engineer) No. 3 car - survivor.
49. G.H. Atkins (Wireless Operator) - Killed, body identified on return to London.
50. E Elliott (Wireless Operator) - Killed, body identified on return to London.
51. A. Disley (Wireless Operator/Electrician) - survivor.
52. F Hodnett (aka J.Curran) (Assistant Steward) - Killed, body not identified.
53. E.A. Graham (Cook) - Killed, body not identified.
54. I W Megginson (Galley Boy) - killed, not identified.

The R101 Memorial can be found in the cemetery of St Mary's Church, Cardington, Bedfordshire which is detached from the actual church.

HERE LIES THE BODIES OF 48 OFFICERS AND MEN WHO PERISHED IN H.M. AIRSHIP R.101 AT BEAUVAIS, FRANCE OCT 5th 1930

Inside the church itself is the half-burned RAF ensign, recovered from the crash site

Although the victims of the R101 disaster were buried in one flower lined grave at St Mary's Churchyard at Cardington, tens of thousands of their countrymen paid homage at a lying-in-state at Westminster Hall, London, and others at a memorial service in St Paul's. From early morning to past midnight two seemingly endless streams of people walked reverently past the great catafalque bearing the 48 coffins. the Prince of Wales represented the King at the memorial service and a solemn procession through the streets of London, headed by a detachment of the Royal Air Force included Prime Ministers, ministers and representatives of the Dominions and India

A Memorial card was produced in remembrance of the British R101 airship which crashed in France with the loss of 48 lives including the Air Minister, Lord Thompson and the Air Vice Marshal, Sir Sefton Brancker.

This card is printed in black and silver, it's cover is decorated with a crucifix and flowers and bears the caption, *"Thy Will Be Done"*.
The inside shows an image of the R101 and the following text, *"The giant airship R101, which left Cardington at 7pm on Saturday, for India, crashed on a hill near Beauvais, France at 2.05 am and 48 of those on board - including Lord Thompson, Minister for Air, and Air Vice-Marshal Sir Sefton Brancker - were burned to death""*.

Opposite is the text, *"In sacred memory of The officers, crew and passengers of the British airship R101 which crashed in France on Sunday morning Oct. 5th 1930 with a loss of 48 lives including Lord Thompson, Air Minister and Sir Sefton Brancker, Air Vice Marshal. - May their souls rest in peace"*. Printed on the reverse is a list of all the men who perished.

The Court of Inquiry, chaired by Sir John Simon, *"to hold an investigation into the causes and circumstances of the accident which occurred on October 5th, 1930, near Beauvais in France, to the Airship R 101"*. Some 42 witness's, including the six survivors were examined before the hearing came to a close on 5 December 1930

Two of the statements are given below;

"Suddenly there was a terrific explosion. The front part of the ship burst instantly into flames. I was half-choked by the rush of gas and fumes backwards, and I owe my life - as do Binks and Bell - to the fact that when we hit the ground the water ballast tanks were released and drenched us.

We were convinced that our last hour had come. We shook hands and bade one another a last goodbye. A minute later everyone was fighting his way out . . We tore away the wreckage and were surprised when we staggered out and found ourselves safe except for our burns . . .
What was happening to Lord Thomson, Sir Sefton Branckner and the others in the forward part of the ship I cannot say. They may have been sleeping or not, but they were as far from me as if they were in another world . . .
It is hard to say from a technical point of view exactly what happened. I think that something went wrong with the steering gear and then a gas escape was created somewhere, but it is impossible for me to form an opinion . . ."

A.H. Leech, foreman engineer; one of the survivors

"I have little recollection of what preceded the impact, but I do remember that we had been losing altitude for some minutes before the crash . . . Simultaneously with the shattering crash flames seemed to appear from every quarter. As I hit the ground it seemed as if several houses collapsed on top of me, and I found that I was almost imprisoned amid an amazing network of duralumin, wires and furnishing fabrics from the vessel. Somehow or other I cleared the amazing tangle of wreckage and crawled out. I was dazed and burned, but I got through, and then, despite the roar of the flames and the minor explosions, I could hear my friend Bell shouting from one of the stern gondolas. I tried to make my way towards the rear of the blazing mountain, but the next thing I remember was collapsing into the arms of two men, one of whom spoke English . . ."

S. Church, rigger, who died three days after the crash from his injuries

The report was completed on 27 March 1931 and was subsequently published by His Majesty's Stationary Office in 1931. An abridged version of this report has been published by The Stationary Office in 1999
The Report of the Court of Inquiry stated : "It is impossible to avoid the conclusion that R101 would not have started for India on the evening of October 4th if it had not been that reasons of public policy were considered as making it

highly desirable for her to do so if she could." The Court of Inquiry Report contains no clear conclusion as to the airworthiness of R101 in the full operational sense of the word. Indeed, Major Phillip Teed, a former airshipman who, as a practising Barrister, represented the family of the Captain of R101 throughout the proceedings, wrote afterwards "There is no proof that the airship was airworthy in the operational sense when she left for India, while as regards gasbags and wiring, gas valves and vertical control there is evidence that she was defective. The distribution and method of release of water ballast was unsatisfactory."

Mr McWade, the A.I.D. Inspector-in-Charge at Cardington who had been over-ruled by his own Director, reaffirmed in Court that "padding" to the extent employed in R101 was not acceptable to him and asserted that if it had been left to him the airship would not have been granted a Certificate of Airworthiness. For her final trial flight before leaving for India, R101 was granted a temporary "Permit to Fly" and the Court went at considerable length into the investigation into her structural strength and what it called "the rather hurried circumstances" in which this Permit was secured

Further information
Documents on the R101 are held in The National Archives in Kew, under AIR 3,5,& 11. Photographs of the wreckage are under AIR5/1070
If you want to get information on the R100 and R101 airships should try the following books;
R101 The Airship Disaster 1930 - Report of the R101 Inquiry (The Stationary Office, Abridged Edition 1999)
Sir Peter Masefield; *To Ride the Storm* (William Kimber, London 1982) A most authoritative book on R101, and is full of technical details.
E A Johnston; *Airship Navigator* (Skyline, Stroud 1994) This is the result of a computer model investigation into why the crash occurred, and reaches different conclusions from Masefield. Johnston's father was the navigator on R101 and died on the ship.
Nevil Shute; *Slide Rule* (William Heinemann, London 1954). He was one of the R100's design team, and wrote a rather biased account of how good R100 compared with the badly designed R101
Ces Mowthorpe; *Battlebags - British Airships of the First World War*. One of the best illustrated books on British airships and includes notes on both the R100 and R101.
John G Fuller; *The Airmen who would not die* (Souvenir Press, London 1979) Disappearance of Capt Hinchliffe on an Atlantic flight in 1928 and psychic messages received by Eileen

Garrett, medium, regarding R101. Interesting background detail and story told from this unusual angle

Websites - Airship Heritage Trust - www.aht.ndirect.co.uk R101 www.rootsweb.com/~engbdf/ images/cardigtonr101.jpg

Crew of H.M.A. R101

Name	Age	Designation	Awards	Birthplace	Remarks
Atkins, G.K	30	W/T Operator		London	Joined Airship Service 1917, SS16, SSZ 37, SSZ 53, Coastal 3 & 5a, R101 and R100, R100 Canadian Flight
Bell, A.V.	31	Engineer		Fambridge Ferry,Essex	Joined Airship Service Nov 1919 R33 Joined Crew R101 July 1929 R33 Breakaway crew
Binks, J.H.	37	Engineer		Sheffield, Yorks	Joined Airship Service 1925, R33, Joined R101 Crew 06 Aug 1929
Blake, R	33	Engineer		Westminster, London	No previous flying experience. Joined crew R101 Oct 1929
Burton, C.A.	29	Engineer		Hull, Yorks.	No previous flying experience. Joined crew of R101 Oct 1929
Church, S.	25	Rigger		Cardington, Beds	No previous flying experience. Joined crew of R101 1929
Cook, A.J	.27	Engineer		Lambeth, London	No previous flying experience. Joined crew of R101 Oct 1929
Disley, A.	28	W/T Operator		Lancaster, Lancs	Joined Airship Service 04 March 1929, R101 and R100. R100 Canadian Flight
Fergusson, C.J.	36	Engineer		Gillingham, Kent	No previous flying experience. Joined crew of R101 Aug 1929
Ford, H.E.	27	Rigger		Kingsbridge, Devon	Balloons R.A.F from 27 April 1920 to 25 May 1929. Attached Cardington for construction of R37 and R33. Joined crew R101 1929
Foster, P.A.	28	Rigger		Bedford, Beds	No previous flying experience. Joined crew of R101 Oct 1929
Gent, W.R	53	1st Engineer	A.F.M.	Northampton	Joined Airship Service in 1915. Ships SS type, C.12, C Star 1, 14,A R29, R32, R34, R36, R33 Crew of R34 to U.S.A. and return, R.33 Breakaway crew
Graham, E.A.	28	Cook		Ranelagh, Co.Dublin	Previously employed on Ocean going vessels and Messrs Dudeney & Johnson Ltd. Bedford. Joined R101 Sept 1930
Hasting, A.C.	30	Engineer		East Ham, London	Joined Airship Service 1918, Ships R33, R80, R38. Joined R101 1929
Hodnett, F.	29	Assistant Steward		Youghal, Co Cork	Joined Airships 23 April 1930, Assistant Steward on R100 Canadian Flight
Hunt, G.F.	41	Chief Coswain & Bar	A.F.M.	Twyford Berks	Joined Airship Service in 1913. Ships "Beta" & Kite Balloons, Coxswain R29, R33, Joined R101 as Chief Coxswain, Aug 1929. R33 Breakaway crew

Crew of H.M.A. R101 (cont...)

Name	Age	Designation	Awards	Birthplace	Remarks
Keeley, S.T	35	Chief W/T Operator		Stufton, Diss, Norfolk	Joined Airship Service In 1924. R33, on bard when broke away. R101 and R100. R100 Canadian flight.
Key, T.A.A	35	Charge-Hand Engineer		Hastings, Sussex	Joined Airship Service 1915. Ships served on SS. SS8, SS19, and others, R36, R33 Joined R101 1929
King, W.H	.32	Engineer		Tonbridge, Kent	Served on Airships SSZ18, R29, R36, R33 Joining R101 in 1929. R33 Breakaway crew
Littlekit, M.F.	29	Engineer		Sherfield English Nr Romsey	No previous flying experience. Joined crew R101 July 1929
Mason, C.H.	33	Assistant Coxswain		Harringay, Middlesex	Joined Airship Service 1916. Ships SS and CP types No.9 2nd Coxswain of Parseval No.6. R33. Joined crew of R101 1929
Megginson, J. W	18	Galley Boy		York	No previous flying experience. Joined crew R101 Oct 1929
Moule, W.	30	Engineer		Wolverhampton	No previous flying experience. Joined crew R101 Oct 1929
Norcott A.W.J	29	Rigger		Royston, Herts	No previous flying experience. Joined crew R101 Oct 1929
Oughton, L.F.	29	Assistant Coxswain		St Pancras, London	Joined Airship Service 1919. Ships R24, R33, R36. Joined R101 1929
Potter, W.A.	32	Assistant Chief Coxswain	Mentioned in dispatches	Yoxford, Suffolk	Joined Airship Service 1915. Ships C.1, R9, R23, R31, Assistant Coxswain R33, Crew R33 Breakaway, Joined R101 Assistant Chief Coxswain in 1929
Radcliffe, W.G.	31	Rigger		Bedford, Beds	No previous flying experience. Joined crew R101 Oct 1929
Rampton, M.G.	31	Rigger		Binstead, Hants	Joined Airship Service 1915. Ships SS.22, Cox SS54 & others. R31, R32, R34, R9, R23, R36. Joined Crew R101 1929
Richardson, A.J.	29	Rigger		Wilstead, Beds	No previous flying experience Joined crew R101 Oct 1929
Rudd, E.G.	25	Rigger		Norwich, Norfolk	No previous flying Joined crew R101 Oct 1929
Savidge, A.H.	32	Chief Steward		Reading, Berks	Steward White Star, Cunard, Union Castle & Orient Lines. Joined Airships 1921, R36 R101 & R101. R100 Canadian Flight
Savory, V.	33	Engineer		London	No previous flying experience. Joined crew R101 Sept 1929
Scott, S.E.	40	Charge-Hand Engineer		Leicester	Joined Airship Service 1921. Ships R33 & R101 (July 1929) R33 breakaway crew
Short, G.W.	34	Charge-Hand Engineer		Maidenhead, Berks	Joined Airship Service July 1918. Ships C9 C2 SSZ R33, Joined crew R101 July 1929
Taylor, C.E.	33	Rigger		Wilstead, Beds	No previous flying experience. Joined crew R101 Oct 1929
Watson, G.	25	Engineer		Gillingham, Kent	No previous flying experience. Joined crew R101 May 1929

The RAF Witchford Display of Memorabilia
Barry Aldridge

The RAF Witchford Display of Memorabilia came into being through a series of strange events. In 1994 my Wife worked as a part time Custodian in Ely Museum in Cambridgeshire. At that time the museum was situated in the High Street. One Sunday afternoon a short Gentleman walked into the museum and asked my Wife what the museum had on RAF Witchford and Mepal airfields. Witchford airfield was situated two miles from Ely along the B 142, now A142 and RAF Mepal was six miles from Ely on the same road. So close were these two airfields that their landing circuits overlapped, also the last RAF building of Witchford while travelling towards Mepal, was only one mile away from the first RAF building of Mepal.

The Gentleman who had asked my Wife about the airfields was somewhat disappointed when told that the museum had no information or memorabilia of either airfield. The Gentleman introduced himself as Charlie Wembam, a former Rear Gunner with 115 Squadron based at RAF Witchford during late 1944 and early 1945. Charlie asked my Wife to convey his disgust to the Trustees of the museum for the lack of wartime memorabilia in the museum and especially the lack of any information on the two airfields, considering that 115 Squadron suffered the greatest losses in Bomber Command and 75 Squadron based at Mepal suffered the second most losses within the Command.

My Wife informed Charlie that I had several photographs of wartime Witchford which had been given to me by the Post Mistress of Witchford Post Office. Charlie showed great interest and asked if it was possible to meet me. My Wife said that I was at home and that if Charlie would like to make the short journey to our house she was sure I would love to talk to him. When Charlie arrived we talked all the afternoon about the airfield and I showed him the photographs I had. One photo caught his interest, it was a beautiful photo of a Lancaster landing at Witchford with Ely Cathedral in the background. My chance meeting with Charlie with whom I have been friends ever since, is probably what made me attend Ely Museums' AGM in August 1994. When the meeting reached the part of any other business, I had this sudden impulse (most unlike me) to stand up and ask 'What is the museum going to do for 1995 considering it is the commemoration year of the 50th anniversary of Victory in Europe and Japan.'

The Chairman of the museum said that nothing had been planned, to which I retorted. 'Well, that is disgusting, you had two airfields on your doorstep. Many local Men served with the Cambridgeshires and were captured at Singapore and suffered terribly at the hands of their captures, plus all that would have been going on in Ely and the surrounding villages, and you say you have nothing planned.' The Chairman thought quickly and said, 'Well, I think it is a good idea to put on an exhibition on the War years and you are just the man who would be ideal to organise it for us.' I had shot myself in the foot and could hardly back down and make myself look a fool, after causing such a fuss. The Chairman was a clever man.

So I took on the challenge and was very lucky in the fact that WWII was in living memory of so many people who wished to become involved in the War Years exhibition. The exhibition was intended to last for one month but so much material came in that it was decided to run the exhibition from May 1st to the end of November 1995. We also had a rota of ex servicemen from all the services who were always in attendance to answer the many questions put to them.

One day when I was at the museum I was approached by two visitors who were the Managing Director and a Director of a company called Grovemere Holdings, owners of a large part of the old Witchford airfield and now appropriately called The Lancaster Way Business Park. They asked what would happen to the information and memorabilia that was on display about the two airfields when the exhibition was over, and asked if it was possible for me to set up a small museum in the foyer of their main office block, if they made it possible. This was basically the start of the RAF Witchford Display of Memorabilia, which opened in Grovemeres foyer in 1996 and is now bursting at the seams of its confined area.

Another thing that Grovemere were of great help with along with another company called Amory Construction was the recovery of the wreckage of a MKII Bristol Hercules engines Lancaster Bomber, that was shot down in the early hours of April 19th 1944 when a German intruder ME4 10 joined the landing circuit over Witchford and claimed two aircraft and their crews. This incident was the largest loss of life in the Ely area during the war. The recovery of the wreckage took place on the weekend of August

Lancaster MkII LL667 Starboard Inner Engine
Recovered from depth of 16 feet close to the airfield

19th 1995 and one of the four engines recovered
in remarkable condition from 16 feet down is
centrepiece of our display along with many other
items also recovered at the time. The aim of the
Display of Memorabilia is to show in
photograph, story and artefact, the life of those
who served at Witchford and Mepal, not only
Airerew but all the trades and Personnel that
helped to keep these Bombers in the air night
after night.

The walls are full of stories of heroism and
tragedy all of which far from glorify war as some
people think but shows there are no winners in
war, only losers as the thousands of Military
grave yards throughout the world stand
testimony.

RAF Witchford like its near neighbour Mepal
was constructed and opened in a very short space
of time. Both airfields were started in 1941 and
ready for the RAF to take over in June 1944, a
remarkable feat considering the amount of work
involved.

In 1941 the village of Witchford with a
population of little over 400 saw the influx of
two and a half thousand workmen, a large
proportion of which were free state Irish. The
main contractors were Holland, Halam and Cubit
who before the war were house builders in the
London area. Huts were quickly erected to house
the workmen who at first were billeted with the
locals. The workmen got on well with the
villagers although some husbands were
concerned for the safety of their wives and

daughters after dark, but this was never a problem
unlike the massive amount of dust and mud that
was created during this massive project.

Site 1, the airfield itself was situated on the
outskirts of the village between Witchford and
Ely although the entrance was in the village.
The three runways were constructed from brick
rubble brought down from London by train to
nearby Stretham Station. The rubble came from
the buildings bombed by German aircraft. The
Domestic sites numbered 2 - 14 were dispersed
throughout the village.

The first squadron to arrive at Witchford on the
19thJuly 1943 was 196 who had been transferred
from Leconsfield in Yorkshire where they had
been flying Wellingtons. Now equipped with
MKIII Stirlings 196 took off on their first
operation from Witchford with three aircraft on
an operation to the Frisian Islands at 20.30 hrs on
27th August. Witchford was declared fully
operational on 2nd September.

513 Squadron was formed at Witchford on 15
September 1943 drawing men and Stirling
MKIII aircraft from 196 Squadron already on the
airfield and 75 Squadron who had taken
over RAF Mepal. 513 were disbanded on 21st
November without ever becoming operational.

196 Squadron also left Witchford on 21st
November for Leicester East to join 38 Group for
Glider towing. During their short stay at
Witchford they had lost eleven aircraft.
115 Squadron arrived at Witchford from Little
Snoring in Norfolk equipped with the
Lancaster MKII. They would stay at Witchford

for the rest of the war until they left for Gravely on 28th September 1945. 115 did share the airfield for a very short period with 195 Squadron which was formed from 115's C Flight on the 1 October 1944. 195 left Witchford for Wrattmg Common on 15th November 1944. 115 Squadron and 75 New Zealand Squadron at Mepal were in the thick of Bomber Command plans and 3 Groups operations throughout the war and both paid a heavy price in Men and Aircraft.

Many incidents took place at both airfields, a few amusing but most tragic. Of the amusing, a tale ex-115ers love to tell is when the squadron left Little Snoring on the night of the 26th,27th November to bomb Berlin, the fourteen aircraft taking part were to return to their new base at Witchford after the operation. Many of the crews knowing how large some of these airfield were decided to put their bikes on the aircraft rather than leave them behind. Hence the tale they loved to tell was, had they have been shot down and the Germans found the bikes among the wreckage, they would have thought that this was a new British idea for aircrew to bike home if they crash landed.

Of the sad. One particular incident which took place on the night of the 18th/19th April 1944 was when the squadron returned from what they had thought was an easy raid on the Marshalling Yards at Rouen in France. While the aircraft were circling over Witchford waiting for their tum to land a German ME410 joined the circuit and shot

down two aircraft with the loss of both crews.

At Mepal a 75 Squadron Stirling taking off on the 8th September 1943 swung violently to starboard and hit a petrol tanker before crashing into two Council houses at Park Road in the village of Sutton situated on the edge of the airfield. The occupant of one of the houses was killed and his wife injured. Thee of the crew were killed. A WAAF Officer, a Navigator on leave and a Fireman was also killed while trying to help with the rescue when the aircraft suddenly blew up.

Many stories like these with lots of photographs and memorabilia gives an insight into the history of these two Cambridgeshire airfields and the Men and Women who served there.

115 Squadron Memoria
Lancaster Way Business Park

The Royal Air Force 1918~19. V. Wheeler~Holohan
Introductory notes by David J Barnes

The following article was written shortly after the Royal Air Force came into existence. There have only been small changes made to the text that was originally printed in *The Boy's Own Annual* Vol XLI 1918-1919 and it retains the style of the period.

The illustrations have been taken from V. Wheeler-Holohan's original fold out illustration.

The original article is little known and difficult to obtain. I feel that it is of great historical value, since it covers the khaki uniform worn by the Royal Air Force between 1918-19, when the Royal Air Force also used Army style rank titles.

There is a mention in the article to a blue R.A.F. uniform, but this is not the 'R.A.F. blue' that we are familiar with now, but a much paler blue-grey colour. There is some suggestion that the cloth was originally destined for the Russian Imperial Cavalry, but it never left the United Kingdom due to the Russian Revolution.

In practical terms, as Officers had to buy their own uniform, former Royal Flying Corps and Royal Naval Air Service Officers, who transferred to the Royal Air Force on 1 April 1918 , were allowed to 'wear out' their old uniforms - so often photographs of the period show a variety of uniforms and mixtures of uniforms being worn.

The name of the author of the original article, V. Wheeler-Holohan may be familiar, he wrote the book '*Divisions and Other Signs*' , which was published in 1920. This book is widely regarded as an important reference work as it illustrates the signs for every British First World War Army Division, as well as those for Australia, Canada and New Zealand, and gives brief histories of the Divisions.

Reprints of the '*Divisions and Other Signs*' , By V. Whceler-Holohan 1920 are available for £7.95 plus post and packing from Ray Westlake - Military Books, 3 Llewellyn Walk, Malpas, Newport, Gwent, South Wales NP20 6LY (Telephone 01633 854135 Fax 01633 821860)

The Royal Air Force 1918-19
by V. Wheeler-Holohan
Originally printed in *The Boy's Own Annual* Vol XLI 1918-1919

On 1 April 1918, the " Royal Air Force" came into existence as a separate and distinct service, forming, with the Royal Navy and the Army, the third of Britain's fighting forces. The old Royal Naval Air Service and the Royal Flying Corps were amalgamated, and the men in both services placed upon the same footing. The reasons for this change are fairly well known — it is not our intention to offer any comment upon them.

It is enough to say that, in the few months which have elapsed since the birth of this new organisation it has rendered the most splendid service to the nation, and the British Airman, both as a fighter and an engineer, is in a position second to none.

There are no permanent commissions in the Royal Air Force at present. The following notes may give some idea of the qualifications necessary, and the training to be undergone, before a young fellow can serve as a pilot in the new arm.

To begin with, one must be "a natural British-born subject, and the son of natural British-born subjects." Not younger than 17 years and 11 months or older than 30 years, not over 6 feet 1 inch in height, or more than 13 stone in weight. The physical standard must be passed, and the eyesight must be very good - the medical test is stiff.

After applying to the nearest R.A.F. Reception Depot (there are depots in London, Bristol, Birmingham, Cardiff, Glasgow, Leeds, Liverpool, Newcastle, and Nottingham), the prospective candidate is granted an interview, and, if selected, is sent to an Acceptance Depot. He must realise that he will be subject to service anywhere, in any branch, and, if fit, may be sent up in aircraft of any description.

From the Acceptance Depot he is sent to an R.A.F. Cadet Brigade, and will be paid eighteen pence a day, with a messing allowance of one shilling a day. His kit, quarters, and rations are free. He will probably spend two months there. After this period of initial training he will be classed as either a " Flight Cadet " or a " Non-Commissioned Officer Cadet." It all depends upon his work and capability.

For a time, we will follow the career of one graded as a " Flight Cadet."

After his classification into Class " A," he receives an outfit allowance of £15. He then passes through a School of Aeronautics, which occupies about six weeks, and a School of Armament, which takes up another four weeks. He is then posted to a training squadron for flying, and will be graded for. pay as a "Flight Cadet" at 7s 6d., plus 4s a day "Flying Pay." He messes with the officers, but the extra 1s a day messing allowance is discontinued.

The next steps to pass are the "A and B Graduations," and safely through these, our Cadet becomes a Second Lieutenant and will draw 10s., with 4s. flying pay, per day. He is also given an extra £35 towards completing his kit. Then comes the "C Graduation," which confers the coveted "Wings " and increases the flying pay from 4s. to 8s a day. If, however, an officer is sent overseas before getting this qualification, he may be granted his wings in his new squadron. His way is then clear for promotion. The rates of pay of the various ranks are :

To return now to the fellow graded as a Non-Commissioned Officer Cadet. After the initial grading he goes through the same schools, and is also attached to a Training Squadron for flying. He is given the rank of sergeant, and draws 3s. 3d. per day with 1s. per day flying pay. His kit is a free issue. Once past the A and B graduations, he receives 6s. a day and the flying pay remains the same. When the third or " C " graduation is satisfactorily negotiated, he

Rates of Pay

Rank	Rate of pay	
Second-Lieutenant	10s. per day	Flying Pay, 8s. per day
Lieutenant	12s to 16s. per day	Flying Pay, 8s. per day
Captain	19s (rising to 20s.) per day	Flying Pay, 8s,per day
Major	32s consolidated	
Lieutenant-Colonel	40s consolidated	

On active service, further allowances are drawn.

The age limits " for the duration " are 18 to 41 ; for either of the latter periods 18 to 25. Men are enlisted who are skilled in certain trades, and the pay works out at—

Rank	Rate of pay	After 3 years' service	After 6 years' service
Third-class Air Mechanic	2s. per day-		
Second-class Air Mechanic	3s. per day	3s. 6d. per day	
First-class Air Mechanic	4s. per day	4s. 6d. per day	5s. per day
Corporal Mechanic	5s. per day	5s 6d per day	6s per day
Sergeant Mechanic	6s. per day	6s. 6d. per day	7s. per day
Chief Mechanic	7s. per day	8s. per day	9s. per day
Master Mechanic	11s. per day		
Chief Master Mechanic	12s. per day		

In the non-technical (or unskilled) branch, daily pay rates are —

Second-class Private	1s. 6d
First-class Private	1s. 8d
Corporal	2s. 4d
Sergeant	3s. 3d
Flight Sergeant	3s. 10d

There are no good-conduct badges with consequent pay. The scale of pensions has yet to be fixed, but it is certain that it will be as good as that granted to the Royal Navy and Army.

Royal Navy	Cuff insignia
Sub-Lieutenant	one ring
Lieutenant	two rings
Lieutenant-Commander	two and a half rings
Commander	three rings
Captain	four rings
Commodore	badge according to class
Rear Admiral	one broad and one ordinary ring
Vice Admiral	one broad and two ordinary rings
Admiral	one broad & three ordinary rings

Army	Shoulder strap insignia
Second-Lieutenant	one star
Lieutenant	two stars
Captain	three stars
Major	crown
Lieutenant-Colonel	crown and a star
Colonel	crown and two stars
Brigadier-General	crossed sword and baton
Major-General	crossed sword & baton & one star
Lieutenant-General	crossed sword & baton and crown
General	crossed sword & baton, crown, & star

Royal Air Force	Cuff insignia
Second-Lieutenant	no braid
Lieutenant	one ring
Captain	two rings
Major	two and a half ring
Lieutenant-Colonel	three rings
Colonel	four rings
Brigadier-General	one broad ring
Major-General	one broad and one ordinary ring
Lieutenant-General	one broad and two ordinary rings
General	one broad and three ordinary rings

in the service dress is khaki - very similar to that worn in the army, but with a light blue stripe running through the centre. The button is gilt, with the " Bird and Crown" device

The cap is of the Royal Navy type, with a khaki or blue crown, a black shiny leather peak and a black band, with the Royal Air Force badge - a bird surmounted by an Imperial crown with crossed palm leaves underneath. Captains and lieutenants wear two and one gold bars respectively on each side of the badge. All Field Officers (Majors, Lieutenant Colonels, and Colonels) wear a row of gold oak-leaves round the edge of the peak, while all general officers wear two rows of oak leaves on the peak.

The above list shows the insignia of the various ranks in the Royal Air Force, together with the corresponding rank in the other arms. It should be borne in mind that an officer in the Royal Navy takes precedence of an officer holding the corresponding rank in the Army or Royal Air Force, while the Army rank takes precedence of its corresponding rank in the new arm.

puts on the " Wings " and draws 4s. a day flying pay.

A man who joins the service as a mechanic enlists for—
  (a) The duration of the War;
  (&) Four years with the colours and four with the reserve ;or
  (c) Eight years with the colours and four with the reserve.

Boys between 15 and 17 are admitted (when vacancies occur) for long service, subject to certain conditions (i.e. consent of parents, &c.) being complied with.

Turning to the Uniform, for the present the ubiquitous khaki is the service dress. The real colour is a shade of light blue, very like the tint adopted by the French Army.

The officers' service-dress tunic is of the same pattern as that worn by officers of the Army, but it no longer has shoulder straps or collar badges, while a cloth belt with gilt buckle takes the place of the more familiar "Sam Browne" leather belt. The tie is black. A gilt metal 'Bird and Crown' is worn on each cuff by all commissioned ranks. The Braid around the cuffs denotes rank. In the blue dress the braid is gold,

It may be noted that the commissioned ranks are those of the Army, while the badges follow the Royal Navy fashion. The rings, however, are straight, and have no "Executive Curl."

First-class warrant officers wear the same kit as second lieutenants, with two exceptions. The gilt bird and crown are placed below each shoulder instead of on the cuffs, and no gold bars appear on the cap.

The service-dress tunic worn by all other ranks is the same as that worn by the rank and file in the Army, but without shoulder straps or belts. The buttons are of the same design as the officers, but are made of bronze. A bird worked in red silk is worn below the shoulder. The cap is similar to that of the officer, while the badge follows the petty officer, Royal Navy type, a bird being substituted for the anchor. Non-commissioned officers wear it embroidered in gold, air mechanics in red silk. When the light-blue uniform becomes universal for the rank and file, it will differ in one or two ways from the Service dress at present worn The caps will have light-blue crowns instead of khaki, warrant officers' being made of whipcord, other ranks' of serge. The first class W.O.'s badge will be the same as that of an officer, but made of gilt metal instead of gold wire. The badge worn by second class W.O.'s and N.C.O.'s will not be changed, but other ranks will wear it worked in light blue silk instead of the red silk as at present worn.

Warrant officers, flight sergeants and sergeants wear jackets with a turn down collar after the officers' pattern, gilt buttons, cloth belts, but pockets will be slit with a flap instead of attached like the officers'. Silver grey shirts and black ties will be worn instead of the officers - white collar and black tie
Other ranks will wear a light blue jacket with stand up collar, military patch breast pockets and cloth belts. Light blue silk Badges will take the place of the scarlet ones at present worn.

The rank badges of second class W.O.'s, N.C.O.'s. and first class air mechanics will not be changed, and will be worn in light blue. That of the first class W.O., however, will be altered from bird and crown to the Royal Arms, worked in light blue silk and worn below the elbow.

A crown on the cuff denotes a second-class warrant officer, a crown and three chevrons, a flight sergeant, three chevrons a sergeant and two chevrons a corporal. A first-class air mechanic wears a red single-bladed propeller under the bird, while the "hand and thunderbolt" denotes the wireless man

The pilot's badge, worn on the left breast, is the familiar "wings" of the Royal Flying Corps, the central monogram being R.A.F. instead of R.F.C. The observer's badge (a letter O with a single wing) has not been changed.

Medical officers may be recognised by their collar-badges, a bronze Caduceus of Mercury.

The Royal Air Force have four particular honours of their own.

The Distinguished Flying Cross for officers and warrant officers and the Distinguished Flying Medal for N.CO.s and men being awarded

"'for acts of gallantry when flying in active operations against the enemy."

The Air Force Cross for officers and warrant officers, and the Air Force Medal for other ranks, are given for acts of courage and devotion to duty when flying, although not in active operations against the enemy.

The design of the medal ribbons is unique, for the colours run horizontally instead of vertically. The two former ribbons are purple and white, the two latter red and white.

To a keen, high-spirited boy, the R.A.F. offers great opportunity for advancement. It will bring out all that is good in him, train his mind and his body. Dangerous work, it is true ; but the spice of danger gives most youngsters more zest to the work.

The flying man has faced and overcome the greatest difficulties— the careers of heroes like Ball, Bishop, and McCudden will always be remembered —- and the motto of the old R.F.C. is typical of the work of the Force -

PER ARDUA AD ASTRA
(Through difficulties to the stars)

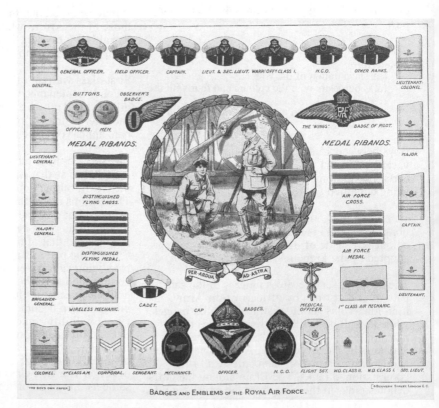

BADGES AND EMBLEMS OF THE ROYAL AIR FORCE.

The Royal Navy's Seagoing Reserves

Len Barnett

coastal defence: such as the River and Sea Fencibles in the late 1790s. Far from being a naval asset, even though made up of seamen they were protected from naval impressment: or indeed service in the army or militias.

With the inevitable massive run-down of the Royal Navy after the end of Napoleonic Wars manpower issues began to lose their importance. By the 1830s paper exercises, originally in the form of the 'Register of Seamen', were engaged in apparently to make forced recruitment more efficient. However, by this decade there were also advocates of schemes either of national service, or of seagoing naval reserves.

In the early 1850s another purely defensive reserve was introduced. Initially named the Naval Coast Volunteers, this was similar in nature to the fencibles. The Crimean War (1854-1856) showed up real weaknesses in naval manning. One immediate result was a reorganisation of the coast volunteers. Having by this time been given the title 'Royal' they were put under Admiralty control.

More importantly, through a Royal Commission, in 1859 the first elements of a Royal Naval Reserve came into being. Originally termed the 'Royal Naval Volunteers' this called for a maximum of 30,000 men who were good seamen, trained in gunnery and available for service onboard warships. Two years later, a reserve of officers was instituted. It is important to emphasise that the R.N.R. was exclusively drawn from professional

Outside limited areas of specialist expertise, with the passage of time since the two world wars and the decline of Britain as a maritime nation, naturally any knowledge of 'the Navy' that *may* once have generally existed in society has all but gone. So, for many people now researching their mariner forebears differentiation between the Royal Navy and those in merchant service can often be unclear, never mind between the R.N. and its reserves. That some reservists were merchant mariners, but others were not (though serving together in the same units) can give rise to confusion. This and other matters can be explained easily enough in the events leading to the two main reserves' formations.

Historical Background

While sea officers of the Monarch's (or Royal) Navy had held commissions or warrants from the requisite boards through to the nineteenth century, the 'people' of the lower-deck had theoretically at least, signed onto warships per voyage. They were recruited by a number of means, both voluntarily and through coercion. Saliently, skilled and experienced merchant mariners were required though. Not only were these men competent in the role of ship handling, merchantmen were very often armed for self-defence against enemy 'cruizers' and of course, pirates. Arguably, in the short to medium term pressed but trained seamen were of more use to commanders than volunteer landsmen. (See another of my articles within this publication entitled *Two Master Mariners in the Family - A Work in Progress* for some more information on this subject.) Even with modern research showing that life onboard men-o-war may not have been as bad as traditionally portrayed, retention rates often left much to be desired.

During the Revolutionary and Napoleonic Wars (1793-1815) Lord Nelson was apparently one of the first naval commanders to advocate a properly constituted naval reserve for seamen. Of course in times of dire emergency bodies had been raised for

Gun Drill

mariners: whether in mercantile service, or later from the fishing industry.

In spite of the original aims in the early decades, with very limited exceptions, the R.N.R. 'drilled' on shore. Until 1873 this was often alongside the R.N.C.V and subsequently with a successor reserve. The gunnery training left much to be desired. For most of the remaining century the reservists qualified in antique weapons - 'great guns', rifles and cutlasses.

With 'war scares' and increasingly large warship-building programmes from the 1890s onwards there were *some* improvements for the R.N.R. Though still less than the 30,000 originally envisioned, recruitment increased, partly through additions of new reserves of engineers and stoke-hold ratings, but also due to armed-merchant cruiser schemes fostered by the prestigious passenger liner companies.

In this era some of the reservists' complaints were addressed. Officers' commissions had been of such a limited and demeaning nature as to cause very real resentment. Improvements came about slowly. Also, through the Tyrone Committee of 1891 ratings received proper uniforms at last - not just caps and tallies.

However, it was not until wholesale naval reforms in the Edwardian era that the R.N.R. began to be taken at all seriously. Along with R.N. stiffening reservists were to man the reserve fleets, that is less up to date warships suitable for secondary duties, such as patrolling. Also, in 1910 the Trawler Section was formed - the genesis of the highly important minesweeping role that the R.N.R. was to become famous for.

At this point it is pertinent to bring in the Royal Naval Volunteer Reserve. Earlier in 1873, the Royal Naval Coast Volunteers had finally been disbanded. Through the efforts of a few well-placed individuals, in the same year the phoenix-like Royal Naval Artillery Volunteers appeared. Whilst the old R.N.C.V. had supposedly been drawn from professional seamen, the new

R.N.A.V. was not. For the larger urban divisions at least, these were effectively gentlemen's clubs and this tiny 'force' received the least support possible from the State. While cannonry and some other bits and pieces were supplied by the R.N., they were left to pay for everything else, including their drill-huts.

Having already received bad publicity through public arguments between divisions, the Tyrone Committee recommended its dissolution. Even if the Admiralty had no use in these amateur warriors, the War Office did. However, rather than suffer the perceived indignity of transfer to army control they chose instead to disperse.

'Naval' cruising clubs arose in their stead, with a National Resuscitation Committee to lobby in the appropriate places. In the aftermath of the Second Anglo-Boer War (1899-1902) came the Committee for Imperial Defence. An early product of its work was the Naval Forces Act of 1903. Through this a new naval reserve was formed: the Royal Naval Volunteer Reserve.

Unfortunately, the new reserve was similar to the old R.N.A.V. Standards were set deliberately low and the R.N. effectively had no use for this band in their war plans. All the old arguments between divisions resurfaced. However, they lobbied for functions and by the summer of 1914 a motor boat reserve was being considered.

Royal Marines had served aboard naval warships, in various roles, since the Corp's inception and with the Edwardian reorganisations a second body raised through the Naval Forces Act was the Royal Marine Reserve. This extended a scheme begun in 1895 and related to time-served men who had volunteered to be returned to service in war, for an annual retainer paid in peace. Incidentally, this was also the pattern adopted for the Royal Fleet Reserve, begun in 1901. In this latter case the reservists were past Royal Naval ratings.

In the days immediately leading to the Great War 1914-19 the reserves were called out as planned. The cruisers and armed-merchant cruisers patrolling the oceans were largely crewed by Royal Naval Reservists.

A great many other secondary, but essential, roles also required filling and the reserves met these. Of particular importance were those in the much-expanded Minesweeping Service and the Auxiliary Patrol. Intermingled, along with others such as retired regular naval officers, senior rates of the R.F.R. and even boy scouts, the officers and men of the R.N.R. and R.N.V.R. manned the sweepers and patrol-craft that had been civilian trawlers and drifters; steam-yachts on loan from magnates; and requisitioned assorted small craft including motor-boats and tugs.

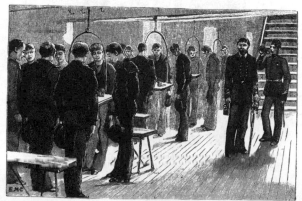

Mess Deck

Later in the war masters and mates of non-commissioned Mercantile Fleet Auxiliaries were given temporary commissions in the R.N.R. On completion of government service however, these officers had 28 days to return their commissions to the Admiralty!

Utilising professional expertise, in time mercantile mates and masters also became R.N.R. transport officers and salvage officers for instance. Often with other wider skills, such as enthusiasms for wireless or photography, those in R.N.V.R. uniforms filled an amazing multitude of tasks.

There was, of course, another group of reservists that had a very different war. Comprising R.N.R., R.N.V.R., R.F.R., R.M.R. and about a thousand 'Kitchener volunteers' to make up the numbers, they formed Churchill's famous Royal Naval Division. Deployed at Antwerp in October 1914 although ill-equipped and only half-trained, large numbers ended up interned in the Netherlands for the duration. Reformed the following year they were at Gallipoli, before service on the Western Front. In 1916 they were transferred to the army as the 63rd (Royal Naval) Division, though some past maritime links were retained, as can be seen in some copies of the *Yachting Monthly* magazine.

Similar to the Royal Navy, the naval reserves in the inter-war period were run down. During the Second World War naturally they were again heavily utilised. It is interesting to note that a significant proportion of naval aircrew were volunteer reservists. This can be seen in terms of the politics of air-warfare from 1918 onwards (when the Royal Air Force was formed out of the Royal Flying Corps and the Royal Naval Air Service).

In the 1950s the R.N.R. and the R.N.V.R. were amalgamated. Specialising in mine

countermeasures, while the old title Royal Naval Reserve was retained, its personnel are *not* now generally mariners by profession: so still has a similarity with the past R.N.V.R.

In spite of common dangers and close service, rivalries and prejudices are known to have continued. There were variations on a wardroom ditty that-while lighthearted, proves instructive. Apparently to the Royal Navy, the R.N.R. were sailors trying to be gentlemen; the R.N.V.R. were gentlemen trying to be sailors; and the R.N., of course, were both. However, the Merchant Service was said to have agreed with the R.N. about the R.N.R. and the R.N.V.R., but regarded the Royal Navy as neither sailors, nor gentlemen!

Concluding the historical profile are notes on uniforms. When first formed R.N.R. officers' uniforms were considerably different from those of the R.N. In particular, the pattern of the rings on their sleeves was of two narrow bands interwoven, with a large 'Star of David' as the loop. In the early twentieth century naval officers' uniforms were standardized, but R.N.R. officers' rank insignia remained in the old form until the 1950s, when replaced with the R.N. style but with the letter 'R' within the loop. R.N.V.R. officers inherited something of the old R.N.A.V. in that they had a single narrow band in a 'waved pattern' (hence the nickname 'wavy navy') with a large 'squared' loop. In both reserves arm of service colours (such as red for surgeons and purple for engineers) were worn as in the Royal Navy, though because of the complexity of R.N.R. 'rings' were shown slightly differently

There is an image on the index page of my website showing examples of these, at http://www.barnettresearch.freeserve.co.uk For midshipmen, those in the R.N.R. wore blue tabs and for the R.N.V.R. they were red.

H.M.S Agamemnon
Launched Woolwich 1852.
First battleship to be fitted
with a screw propeller.
The ship also had sails.

In the twentieth century reservist ratings generally wore the square and fore-and-aft rigs of the parent service as denoted for their rates. However there were exceptions, as in the trawler reserve early in the First World War. If uniform was actually worn at sea (and it is known that there were severe shortages in 1914) some ratings were only entitled to jerseys with the letter 'T' knitted in. Apparently there were also minor differences on early R.N.V.R. ratings' uniforms, one being a 'waved' pattern on the decorative 'tape' on their blue-jean collars.

The Records

Predominately the records discussed in this article will be service sheets of the R.N.R. and the R.N.V.R., as these are key to the study of individuals and therefore of interest to genealogists. Nevertheless, a few notes on the other reserves and documents may aid some readers.

The earlier reserves from fencibles through to artillery volunteers, though absorbing, were non-seagoing and therefore not central to this piece. Undoubtedly, records exist for these bodies, spread between national and county archives. Apparently the quality and quantity of these are variable.

As far as the author is aware there is virtually no surviving documentation separately dealing with men of the Royal Fleet Reserve. Instead, information can be found with that of the parent service: both administratively and operationally. This is also the case for the Royal Marines Reserve.

Royal Naval Reserve

The vast majority of documentation on this force is held as part of the National Archives, formerly the Public Records Office, Kew, Surrey. Officers' and ratings' service records were significantly different

Searchlight Drill

Spar Drill

and will be dealt with separately.

Excluding honourary commissions, R.N.R. officers' service sheets are to be found in three bodies of ledgers relating to formation in 1862 until 1920: designated as 'Admiralty' documents. With the exception of those recorded between the late 1890s and 1913, these are organised by date of officers' initial commissions (that can be determined from relevant editions of the *Navy List*) and show subsequent promotions, if relevant. Written up in specially formatted ledgers, the nineteenth century entries can be of considerable use as these give details of individuals' civilian sea time, as well as their drill periods. The information in those of the intermediary period is very strictly limited and gives no more than can usually be determined from the *Navy List*. For officers commissioned during the First World War, with the exception of civilian addresses apparently at the time of demobilisation, only details of naval service are recorded. Often highly abbreviated this can be less than clear to those not *au fait* with forms of naval administration. This is not helped as these were written up in longhand, the handwriting often scrawled. However, of considerable interest to researchers can be the short reports, made by superiors, on the capabilities (or otherwise) of these officers. Finding individual First World War entries can either be determined roughly by date of first commission, or by indexes.

Ratings' service sheets can be far more problematical. For reasons described by civil servants as modern 'archival practice' these have been classed, illogically and incorrectly in the opinion of this author, as Board of Trade records. As in the Royal Navy entries were made by service number. However, this is far more complex in the R.N.R. as service numbers changed with subsequent enrolments. Unfortunately, for those prior to 1914 no indexes have been released.

Nevertheless, if these numbers are known and they fall within the specimen registers of the several classes of reserve available, the level of information is comparable to that of officers and can be well worth the search. In 1914 a card system was introduced, with separate indexes. Theoretically these range through the First World War until amalgamation with the R.N.V.R. in the 1950s. However, this simply is not the case and the author has not seen any information entered later than 1937. There can be a *great* deal of information on these cards.

Royal Naval Volunteer Reserve
As with the R.N.R. the service records for this organisation are to be found at the National Archives, at Kew. These are all classed as 'Admiralty' documents, although I believe some of these records came via 'War Office' holdings and therefore, modern 'archival practice' cannot been followed in this particular case. In many respects they are similar to the R.N. and the R.N.R., but there are some differences that require space in explanation.

Officers' service sheets were written up in ledgers, in a form comparable to that of the R.N.R. Speedy location of relevant entries can be made by the (filmed) original card index system. As sometimes the case with R.N.R. officers, the nature of volunteer reservists' service means that great care must be kept when dealing with units mentioned. There are often references to documents raised in administrative bases that had exactly the same names as small vessels operating at sea. Reference to relevant copies of the *Navy List* can help, but operational records sometimes need to be viewed to resolve complexities.

As in the R.N. proper, volunteer reservist ratings' service sheets were recorded in ledgers, by official number. The relevant campaign medal rolls (at the National Archives, Kew) should be consulted in identifying individuals' service numbers. For some types of service, such as those in the R.N.D. and also the Shore Wireless Service, it may necessary to go via the Fleet Air Arm Museum (at the Royal Naval Air Station Yeovilton) for these though. It should also be noted that *some* R.N.V.R. ratings' official numbers were identical to those of the R.N.R. Additionally, there are some abbreviations, especially sub-ratings, that apparently do not follow normal naval patterns.
© Len Barnett 2003

Royal Navy & Royal Naval Volunteer Reserve Casualties in World War Two
David Barnes

British Naval Casualties in the course of the Second World War numbered nearly 51,000 killed and missing (Excluding Dominion Naval Losses and those of the Royal Marines), this total is some 20,000 more than those lost in the 1914-1918 war. The total losses of H.M Ships and craft of all sizes between 3 September 1939 to 31 August 1945 totals 3,282. It should also be mentioned that 4,786 Allied Merchant Ships were also lost through enemy action, over half belonged to the British Empire and some 490 were from Neutral Countries. Casualties to personnel on British Merchant vessel's totalled 29,180, with a further 814 casualties on fishing vessels

Although the Imperial War Museum is not the official repository for casualty records, the Department of Printed Books does hold copies of two important typescript listings: **Names of Officers who died during the period**

The Battle of Jutland 1916

© Robert Blatchford

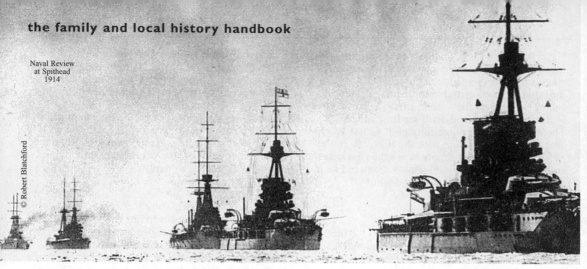

Naval Review
at Spithead
1914

© Robert Blatchford

beginning 3 September 1939 and ending 30 June 1948 and the **Register of Deaths (Naval Ratings), 3rd September 1939 to 30th June 1948**. These were copied from original sets held by the Royal Naval Museum, Portsmouth. Details of the servicemen are filed alphabetically by surname. The information given includes :- Port Division; Official Number (Other Ranks); Branch of Service; Ship or Unit; Date and Place of Birth; Cause, date and place of death, some Decorations are listed along with odd notes

The names of those lost at sea are recorded on six Naval Memorials that are looked after by the Commonwealth War Graves Commission, the first three are at the three Manning Ports.
Chatham - Naval Memorial (9,946 names)
Plymouth - Naval Memorial (15,575 names)
Portsmouth - Naval Memorial (14,787 names)
Lee-on-Solent - Fleet Air Arm Memorial (1,929 names)
Liverpool - Merchant Navy Memorial
 (1,390 names of men of Merchant Navy who died serving with the Royal Navy)
Lowestoft - Royal Naval Patrol Service Memorial (2,385 names)

The names recorded on these memorials were printed in Memorial Registers, though sadly these are no longer produced by the C.W.G.C., though occasionally some are sold through second hand book dealers etc.

If you know the name of a casualty, the Commonwealth War Graves Commission's Debt of Honour Database, http://www.cwgc.org/ can be searched for the place of burial or commemoration for all those who died in service during the period 1939-1947. As well as having information on the site of burial or place of commemoration, the Commonwealth War Graves Commission database has details of the date of death, usually the unit to which they were attached, and often details of their home town and next of kin are included.

Although there are a few rolls of honour for individual ships, it has previously been difficult to check for casualties on a particular ship on unit, without knowing all the names beforehand. This problem has now been resolved with the release of a fully searchable CD ROM, which is an Excel spreadsheet which has been compiled from the details recorded in CWGC Registers (now no longer available) and there are separate columns for the Service Number; Rank; Surname; First name(s) or initials; Honours and Awards; ship or unit; Branch of Service, Date of Death, Age, Family Details , Where Buried or Commemorated. It is possible to search for a specific unit name, or a surname or date of death for Royal Navy and Royal Naval Volunteer Reserve Casualties in World War Two. Deaths for the Royal Naval Reserve, Women's Royal Naval Service and Royal Marines are also available as a searchable spreadsheet on CD in a similar format. Data from these CD's are updatable if the files are saved to your own PC. These CD's are available via Ebay.com and from MM Publications of White Cottage, The Street, Ludgate, Newmarket, Suffolk, or by email fourfrontdata@hotmail.com

Currently casualty records of officers of the Royal Naval Reserve for the period 1939-1946 are to be found in the Board of Trade files BT 164, in the National Archives, and there is a 75 year restriction on deaths in the Royal Marines, though some references can be found in Admiralty files ADM 104, covering the period 1939-1948. *A Register of Royal Marine Deaths 1939-1945* was compiled by J A Good for the Royal Marine Museum, Southsea, Hampshire 1986-87, but this has been out of print for some time

Another book that is currently out of print, though may be available through specialist book dealers is the reprint of *British Vessels lost at sea 1939-45*, published by Patrick Stevens, Wellingborough, Northants 1988, which lists basic details about ships lost.

Twenty-one Years behind the Gun!
A Soldier in the Army of the East India Company

Peter Bailey   Secretary - Families in British India Society

It is conservatively thought that up to three million persons of British origin lived and served in India and south Asia during the 350 years of British presence there. A large number of us, therefore, have at least one ancestor who lived in that region, either for a brief period or even for their entire lives. The '*Families in British India Society*' is devoted to the establishment and recording of family history in India, Pakistan, Bangladesh, Burma,and Malaysia. A vast number of records are held at the British Library in the Oriental and India Office Collection (OIOC), and many of their records have been filmed and made available more widely by the Church of Jesus Christ of Latter Day Saints (LDS) at their Family History Centres.

Reflecting the needs of Empire, a very high proportion of the Britons who went to India were sent there as soldiers, either in the British Army or, earlier, in one of the three armies of the East India Company (EIC). The following narrative has been compiled almost exclusively from records and resources available at the OIOC and may be considered as reasonably typical of stories which may be compiled for soldiers of 'John Company' as the EIC was nick-named.

Peter Evers was a weaver. He had been born in Drogheda, Co. Louth, in Ireland, in 1804 and took up weaving virtually whilst still a boy. By the age of 22, he married Mary, but found it increasingly difficult to get sufficient work to provide an acceptable and steady income. Then the couple found that Mary was pregnant. Baby Mary was born in the December of 1826.

In that same month of December 1826, when the joy of their new baby was not matched by their circumstances, a recruiting party for the EIC visited Drogheda and persuaded Peter and Mary that by his joining the Company's army for eighteen years, not only could Peter be guaranteed a good steady income, he would receive an excellent pension for life at the end of his service. The recruiting serjeant would not, of course, have referred to the extremes of temperature or to the prevalence of disease in India but Peter and Mary were attracted enough to travel with him to Dublin where he could 'attest' for service in the Company's Artillery. Together with other recruits, Peter and Mary were embarked for the Company's principal Recruitment Depot at the Brompton Barracks at Chatham in Kent where they arrived in early 1827.

At Chatham, Peter was recorded as :

Name:	Peter Evers
Age:	22
Size:	5 ft 7^{1}/4 ins
Visage:	Round
Hair:	Black
Eyes:	Brown
Complexion:	Dark
Born:	St. Peter, Drogheda, Louth, Ireland
By whom enlisted:	Grange, Drogheda
Date of Attestation:	1 Jany 1827
Date of Enlistment:	3 Jany 1827
When Joined:	8 Feby 1827
Period of Service:	Unlimited

Occupation: Weaver
Remarks: Wife Mary, Child Mary 2 months

The Company permitted the recruitment of six percent of married soldiers whose wives and children would be permitted to accompany them to India. Peter was, evidently, one of these.

After three months of waiting and of basic training in Chatham, Peter and 249 of his colleagues were selected for embarkation in the Company's ship 'Minerva' to sail to Madras. On 11th of May 1827 they marched, together with Mary and fourteen other wives and their children, from Chatham to Gravesend, where they joined 'Minerva'. The next day she slowly manoeuvred downstream in the Thames estuary where she set sail for the three month voyage to Madras.

The ship's log records all aspects of the voyage, including three deaths and the receipt of a dozen lashes each by two of the Company recruits for the unauthorized taking of precious drinking water from their casks. 'Minerva' arrived in the Madras roads on August 23 1827 and the recruits were embarked at Fort St. George the following day. Those chosen for service in the Artillery were marched the 7 or 8 miles to the Madras Artillery Depot at St. Thomas' Mount, with the women and children trailing behind.

Following three months' training, Peter was classed as a 'Gunner' and assigned to one of the four companies in the first of the three Battalions of the Madras European Foot Artillery. His company was based at Bangalore, some 150 miles west of Madras. The march there would have taken up to two weeks in the gruelling sun and the teeming rains of the late monsoon period. The women and children either marched behind or, if available, would have travelled on a bullock cart designed particularly for carrying luggage. Having arrived in Bangalore, Peter and his small family were allocated married quarters, separate from his colleagues, who lived in the barracks allocated to the Artillery in this large garrison town.

In common with the great majority of his Irish colleagues - who comprised nearly 50 percent of the army - Peter was a Roman Catholic. Their religious needs were met by the priests of the French missionary church of St. Mary, which had been established several years before in Bangalore. However, pressure from these Irishmen caused the Company, in the 1830's, to fund the establishment of English-speaking Roman Catholic churches and chapels for its garrison towns in India. In Bangalore, St. Patrick's church was constructed in 1837 and the RC records of Christenings, Marriages and Burials commence from this date.

Peter and Mary produced a second daughter, Catherine, in 1829. Of course, Catherine was entered, with her mother and sister, onto the strength of the Battalion and Peter would receive an allowance for her from the army until she reached the age of 14 years.

In April 1830, the Madras Artillery underwent a minor change in structure and several gunners, based in Bangalore, were transferred from the 1st to the 2nd Battalion. Peter then found himself in 'A' Company, 2nd Battalion of the Madras European Foot Artillery.

Life at Bangalore, in common with that at most of the Company's garrisons, was complete with generally dull routine. When off duty, the troops were able to engage in a minimum of social activity, such as attending Company-run school lessons, a Company-run library, skittles, gardening and, rather unfortunately, drinking. Naturally, this last activity frequently led to drunkenness and conviction by court martial. No doubt, Mary kept him in order and Peter was, seemingly, never convicted! He was promoted to Bombardier in 1832.

In January 1834, after Peter had served seven years, the authorities in the Madras Presidency determined to displace the Rajah of the relatively small state of

Coorg, some 120 miles to the south-west of Bangalore. The Rajah had been accused of breaking a treaty with the Company by undue oppression of his subjects! Amongst the forces sent to overthrow the Rajah and his army was 'A' Company, 2nd Battalion, Madras Artillery - including Peter Evers. Following a short, sharp campaign the Company's forces prevailed. Coorg passed into the Company's hegemony and, with it, the state treasury. This entitled the participating soldiers to prize money and Peter received a sum of just over 46 rupees.

Following cessation of hostilities, Peter's Company returned to Bangalore, where it remained until 1837, although for some reason in 1836, he was sent on detachment to Trichinopoly.

At some time in late 1842, it appears that Peter and his family were sent to St. Thomas' Mount. At this time his daughter, Catherine, was approaching her fourteenth birthday, the age when she would cease to be provided with an allowance and food and lodging by the army. Peter therefore was anxious to find a husband for her. There was no shortage of soldiers looking for a wife in India and Peter did particularly well in identifying and selecting for her a 32-year old widower, Edward Evans, who was a Serjeant Instructor at the Artillery Depot at St. Thomas' Mount. This was a good match for Catherine since Edward went on to become a Conductor in the Madras Ordnance Department.

By the June of 1845, Peter would have served his full eighteen years in the Company's army. However, shortly before this, he accepted an offer to serve for three further years. This gained him an increase in pension from 9 pence to a shilling (12 pence) per day when he finally retired in 1848. In the intervening period he was transferred to the newly formed fourth battalion of Madras Artillery in 1845. He served with them as a Bombardier for his further three years until finally taking his pension in March of 1848. Initially, he decided to remain in India, possibly to be close to his daughter Catherine and the three grandchildren that she had produced by that time. However, after about a year, he decided to return to Ireland and to spend his retirement there. He sailed in the 'Vernon' for London in March of 1849.

Having arrived in London in the June of 1849, he collected his pension there before continuing to his birthplace in Drogheda, Co. Louth. Whilst in Europe, he collected his pension at one of the many designated offices spread throughout the British Isles, along with the many pensioners of the Queen's army. The closest was in Drogheda itself. However, in 1860, he moved to Newry in Co. Down and collected his pension there until he died. Sadly, his date of death is not recorded, and the pension records are missing from 1876 to 1882. He evidently died at some time within this period aged in his late seventies.

R. I. P.

Glider Pilot Regiment 24 February 1942~31 August 1957
A Short History
David Barnes

A Horsa Glide takes off

On 10 May 1940 some 78 German Army Engineers in ten DFS230 gliders captured the Belgian Eden Emael Fort, which covered the Albert Canal Bridge and three adjacent bridges in a skilfully planned and executed operation, in which their losses were only six killed and twenty wounded. This was the first recorded use of gliders in wartime. The Germans also successfully used Parachute troops on 26 April 1941 when they captured both ends of the Corinth Canal in Greece

On 21 June 1940, Winston Churchill issued an instruction to the War Office ordering the formation of 'a corps of at least five thousand parachutists and glide-borne troops'. An establishment was set up at the R.A.F. Station, Ringway, near Manchester and named the 'Central Landing School' and a call was put out for volunteers with pre-war experience in flying sailplanes, or those with an interest in parachuting. The General Staff, War Office and Air Ministry had been looking to raise a Glider borne to provide a means of getting heavy equipment and vehicles to the battle area and to assist the parachute troops. A Glider Training Squadron was formed at Ringway and a nation-wide search was launched, which produced a number of different types of sailplanes from private gliding clubs.

Attention for a service glider became focused on an eight seat glider (which later became known as the Hotspur), though such a small load for a major operation would have necessitated a massive glider force. However interest soon moved to a 25 seat glider, which became known as the Horsa. The prototype of this was test flown on 12 September 1941 and it went into production shortly afterwards. The Hotspur was manufactured, though it was used essentially for training purposes

A crashed Horsa Glider

In addition to the Gliding Training School, two other units were set up at Ringway; a Technical Development Unit and a Parachute School, and on 18 September 1940 the 'Central Landing School' was renamed the 'Central Landing Establishment.'

On 24 February 1942, the Army Air Corps was formed, at that time, comprising only the 1st Glider Pilot Regiment, but it was later joined by the Parachute Regiment when it was formed on August 1st 1942 and the Special Air Service (SAS), on April 1st 1944.
Lieut-Colonel John F Rock, Royal Engineers was appointed Commanding Officer of the 1st Glider Pilot Regiment with Major George J S Chatterton as Second-in-Command. Some forty trainee glider pilots were already assembled at No.16 Elementary Flying Training School. When Lieut-Colonel John Rock was killed on 8 October 1942, learning to fly a Hotspur glider, Chatterton took over command of the regiment, based at Tilshead, Salisbury Plain, where he put into practice his strict ideas about discipline, with the aid of two Warrant Officers from the Brigade of Guards.

Senior Officers in the Royal Air Force, on hearing that it was the Army's intention to train infantry corporals as glider pilots, ridiculed the idea. Air Marshal Sir Arthur Harris pointed out that landing an aircraft as large as a bomber, without power, required the highest level of skill.

All members of the Regiment were volunteers, mainly from many different Corps and Regiments of the British Army. Despite already being trained soldiers these men were put through a rigorous selection procedure. It was a daunting task to train them as pilots and to weld officers and men into an elite force capable of acting individually, or fighting as one, with Air Landed troops in the Airborne battle.

The first of the military gliders to fly, was the General Aircraft Hotspur, which was capable of carrying eight troops, but was soon superseded by the Airspeed Horsa , this could take twenty-eight fully equipped men, with alternative loads of, two Jeeps, one Jeep with a 75MM howitzer, one 25 pounder gun, or 7,130 lbs of freight.

Early in 1942 the General Aircraft Company produced the prototype of the Hamilcar, designed to carry a light tank or 17,500 Ibs of freight. The Horsa and the Hamilcar were used in operations, the Hotspur was confined to training duties.

The American Waco, the CG-4A, designated the Hadrian by the British, was also flown by the Regiment on some operations. It could carry 15 troops, or loads of, one Jeep, quarter ton truck, one 75mm howitzer or 3,800 lbs of freight.

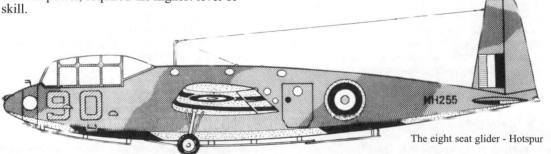
The eight seat glider - Hotspur

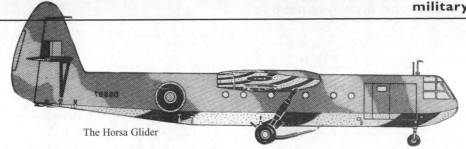

The Horsa Glider

Prospective Pilots received full flying training on De Havilland Tiger Moth and Miles Magister aircraft at No.16 Elementary Flying Training School (later No.21 Elementary Flying Training School at Booker, No.29 Elementary Flying Training School at Clyffe Pypard and No.3 Elementary Flying Training School at Shellingford). They then proceeded, as qualified power pilots, on to glider training, at either No.1 Glider Training School at Thame (later Croughton) or No.2 Glider Training School at Weston-on-Green, or No.3 Glider Training School at Stoke Orchard, then training on the Hotspur, at 101 Glider Operational Training Unit, Kidlington or 102 Glider Operational Training Unit, Shobdon. With the rank of Sergeant or Staff-Sergeant, the men would go on to No.21 Heavy Glider Conversion Unit at Shrewton or Brize Norton's satellite stations or No.22 Heavy Glider Conversion Unit at Fairford, flying the Horsa and Hamilcar.

The flying training continued hand in hand with an intensive military training programme. The aim of the Regiment, under its Commander, Brigadier George Chatterton, was to produce an elite force of 'Total Soldiers', able to fly any unit of the Army into action and to fight with them. The Regiment became so confident of its ability, that it took as its motto, 'Nothing is Impossible' and during its short life, achieved a very high degree of skill and efficiency, with some 172 Honours and Awards to its members.

The Glider Pilot Regiment was, at its peak, only 2,500 strong, it suffered 1301 casualties, including 551 pilots killed in action (more than one third its total strength of 1500). The Regiment's first operation was to send two gliders to land troops to attack the German 'heavy water' plant at Vermork, some 60 miles west of Oslo, Norway. Both gliders crashed and survivors were later executed by the Germans. Its next major operation was the invasion of Sicily from North Africa. However due to insufficient training between American tug crews and British glider pilots many gliders were released too early and 79 of the 143 gliders that took off, came down in the sea, with serious loss of life.

Gliders played an important part in the D-Day

Landings. Part of their operations was to seize two bridges over the River Orme and the Caen Canal, before the German troops had a chance to destroy them. Both bridges were taken intact by men of the Oxfordshire and Buckinghamshire Light Infantry, who were landed in five gliders alongside the bridges, and these men held out until relieved by men of the 5th Parachute Brigade. Commander of the Allied Air Forces on 'D' Day, Air Chief Marshal Sir Trafford Leigh-Mallory, described it as 'the airmanship feat of the war'.

Some 350 gliders were used in the Normandy invasion, with most reaching their assigned landing zones. The Divisional Commander, Major-General Richard Gale, wrote in his book 'The 6th Armoured Division in Normandy' 'There can be few bands of men to whom we can be more indebted that those of the Glider Pilot Regiment. The Regiment was decimated at Arnhem with 229 pilots killed, wounded or taken prisoner. Some 317 gliders on the first lift on 17 September 1944 reached the landing zone.

The Royal Air Force provided replacement pilots for the Rhine Operation where, after glider and military training, they also served with courage and distinction. The Glider Pilot Regiment lost 42 members, and the Royal Air Force lost 60 glider pilots during the Rhine Crossing, when some 440 Horsa and Hamilcar gliders were used

British Glider Operations:
Operation FRESHMAN Raid on heavy water plant at Vermork, Norway: 19-20 Nov 1942: 2 crews selected from 1st Battalion
Operation BEGGAR or TURKEY BUZZARD Ferrying of Horsas from UK to North Africa 1-28 Jun 1943: 1st Battalion
Operations LADBROKE and FUSTIAN Invasion of Sicily 9 - 14 Jul 1943: 1st Battalion
Operation OVERLORD (TONGA and MALLARD) 'D-Day': Invasion of France 6 Jun 1944: Both Wings (7 squadrons)
Operation DRAGOON:Invasion of the South of France 15 Aug 1944 : (Independent Squadron)
Operation MARKET: Airborne operation to capture the Rhine bridge at Arnhem 17-26 September 1944: Both Wings (7 Squadrons)
Operation VARSITY: Airborne operation for crossing of the Rhine 24 March 1945: (Both Wings (7 squadrons))

Battle Honours:

Normandy Landing	Pegasus Bridge
Merville Battery	Arnhem 1944
Rhine	Southern France
Europe 1944-45	
Landing in Sicily	Sicily 1943

The Glider Pilot Regiment was disbanded in 1957 and the remaining pilots were absorbed into the Army Air Corps

Further Reading
The History of the Glider Pilot Regiment, Claude Smith, Published by Leo Cooper, London 1992 - Deals with detailed history of the Regiment and

includes a Roll of Honour, List of Honours and Awards
Wot no Engines? Alan Cooper, Published by Woodfield Press, West Sussex 2002 - Deals with the RAF glider pilots brought in after the heavy losses of the Glider Pilot Regiment at Arnhem
Roll of Honour and Awards for The Glider Pilot Regiment 1942-1957 - Originally compiled in 1946 and revised in 1950, Revised versions prepared from 1982 onwards by The Museum of Army Flying with assistance from The Commonwealth War Graves Commission' records, Members of the Regiment and many other helpers and researchers 6th edition - Corrected to information as at 1st October 1995 Compiled by Major J.R. Cross AAC(Retd) Museum of Army Flying

Military Museums

Battlefields Trust see Museums - National
The Museum of The Adjutant General's Corps see Museums - Hampshire
Museum of Army Flying see Museums - Hampshire
Army Medical Services Museum see Museums - Hampshire
Army Physical Training Corps Museum see Museums - Hampshire
Commonwealth War Graves Commission see Museums - National
Coldstream Guards Record Office Wellington Barracks Birdcage Walk London SW1E 6HQ Access is by appointment made in advance. Search fee of £25.00 per search
Fleet Air Arm Museum Records Research Centre Box D61 RNAS Yeovilton Nr Ilchester BA22 8HT T: 01935-840565
Firepower - The Royal Artillery Museum see London
Grenadier Guards Record Office see Museums - National
Guards Museum see London
Imperial War Museum see Museums - National
IWM Film & Video Archive see Museums - National
Irish Guards Record Office Wellington Barracks Birdcage Walk London SW1E 6HQ E: bigbillaqq119@aol.com W: www.army.mod/ig~assoc
Ministry of Defence - Army Records Centre Defence Records 2 Bourne Avenue Hayes UB3 1RF F: 0181 573 9078 E: lhearn.defencerecords.hayes@gtnet.gov.uk
Museum of Defence Intelligence Chicksands Shefford SG17 5PR T: 01462 752340 F: 01462 752341
National Army Museum see London
National Army Museum Department of Archives (Photographs, Film & Sound) see Museums - National
Royal Air Force Museum see Museums - National
Royal Marines Museum see Museums - Hampshire
National Maritime Museum
Romney Road Greenwich London SE10 9NF T: (020) 8858-4422 F: (020) 8312-6632 W: www.nmm.ac.uk
Royal Military School of Music Museum see Museums - Middlesex
Royal Naval Museum see Museums - Hampshire
Royal Navy Submarine Museum see Museums - Hampshire
RHQ Scots Guards Archives Wellington Barracks Birdcage Walk London SW1E 6HQ E: sgarchives@dial.pipex.com
Welsh Guards Record Office Wellington Barracks Birdcage Walk London SW1E 6HQ T: 020 7414 3291 E: rhqwelshguards@milnet.uk.net Access is by appointment made in advance. Search fee of £25.00 per search
The Light Infantry Museum see Museums - Hampshire
Royal Military Police Museum see Museums - Sussex
England
Bedfordshire
Bedford Museum Bedfordshire Yeomanry
Bedfordshire and Hertfordshire Regimental Museum
Museum of Defence Intelligence
The Shuttleworth Collection see Museums - Bedfordshire
Buckinghamshire
Military Museum Trust Collection Old Gaol Museum Market Hill Buckingham MK18 13X T: 01280 823020 E: ian.beckett@luton.ac.uk
Berkshire
Commonwealth War Graves Commission see Museums National
R.E.M.E. Museum of Technology
Royal Berkshire Yeomanry Cavalry Museum
The Household Cavalry Museum see Museums - Berkshire
Wellington Exhibition see Museums - Berkshire

Cambridgeshire
Ely Museum see Museums - Cambridgeshire
RAF Witchford Display of Memorabilia see Museums - Cambridgeshire
Cheshire
Cheshire Military Museum
Deva Roman Experience
Griffin Trust
Miniature AFV Association (MAFVA)
Stockport Air Raid Shelters see Museums - Cheshire
Cleveland
HMS Trincomalee see Museums - Cleveland
Cornwall
Duke of Cornwall's Light Infantry Museum
Flambards Village and Cornwall Aircraft Park see Museums - Cornwall
Cumbria
Border Regiment & Kings Own Royal Border Regiment Museum see Museums - Cumbria
Senhouse Roman Museumsee Museums - Cumbria
Solway Aviation Museum see Museums - Cumbria
Derbyshire
Regimental Museum of the 9th/12th Royal Lancers see Museums - Derbyshire
Devon
Brixham Museumsee Museums - Devon
Museum of Barnstaple & North Devon incorporating Royal Devon Yeomanry Museumsee Museums - Devon
The Devonshire and Dorset Regiment (Archives) see Museums - Devon
Dorset
Bournemouth Aviation Museum see Museums - Dorset
Dorset Volunteers, Dorset Yeomanry Museum see Museums - Dorset
Royal Signals Museum see Museums - Dorset
Tank Museum see Museums - Dorset
The Keep Military Museum see Museums - Dorset
The Nothe Fort Museum of Coastal Defence see Museums - Dorset
Durham
The 68th (or Durham) Regiment of Light Infantry Display Team
Durham Light Infantry Museum see Museums - Durham
Essex
East Essex Aviation Society & Museum see Museums - Essex
Essex Regiment Museum see Museums - Essex
Essex Secret Bunker see Museums - Essex
Essex Volunteer Units see Museums - Essex
Essex Yeomanry Collection see Museums - Essex
Harwich Maritime Museum see Museums - Essex
Harwich Redoubt Fort see Museums - Essex
Kelvedon Hatch Secret Nuclear Bunker see Museums - Essex
Royal Gunpowder Mills see Museums - Essex
Gloucestershire
Jet Age Museum see Museums - Gloucestershire
Soldiers of Gloucestershire Museum see Museums - Gloucestershire
Wellington Aviation Museum see Museums - Gloucestershire
Hampshire
Action Stations see Museums - Hampshire
Airbourne Forces Museum see Museums - Hampshire
Aldershot Military Museum see Museums - Hampshire
Army Medical Services Museum see Museums - Hampshire

Army Physical Training Corps Museum see Museums - Hampshire

Broadlands see Museums - Hampshire

D-Day Museum and Overlord Museum see Museums - Hampshire

Explosion! The Museum of Naval Firepower see Museums - Hampshire

Historic Ships and The Naval Dockyard see Museums - Hampshire

HMS Victory see Museums - Hampshire

The Light Infantry Museum Peninsula Barracks Romsey Road Winchester SO23 8TS T: 01962 868550

Museum of Army Chaplaincy see Museums - Hampshire

Museum of Army Flying see Museums - Hampshire

Royal Hampshire Regimental Museum Serle's House Southgate Street Winchester SO23 9EG T: 01962 863658 F: 01962 888302 Closeduntil mid April 2004 for renovation. Archive service available via telephone and fax

Royal Marines Museum see Museums - Hampshire

Royal Naval Museum see Museums - Hampshire

Royal Navy Submarine Museum see Museums - Hampshire

Southampton Hall of Aviation see Museums - Hampshire

The Gurkha Museum see Museums - Hampshire

The King's Royal Hussars Museum (10th Royal Hussars PWO 11th Hussars PAO and The Royal Hussars PWO) see Museums - Hampshire

The Museum of The Adjutant General's Corps see Museums - Hampshire

The Royal Green Jackets Museum (Oxford and Bucks Light Infantry King's Royal Rifle Corps and The Rifle Brigade) see Museums - Hampshire

Royal Military Police Museum Roussillon Barracks Chichester PO19 6BL T: 01243 534225 F: 01243 534288 E: Museum @rhqrmp.freeserve.co.uk W: www.rhqrmp.freeserve.co.uk Depicts

Hertfordshire

De Havilland Heritage Centre inc The Mosquito Aircraft Museum see Museums - Hertfordshire

Hertford Museum (Hertfordshire Regiment) see Museums - Hertfordshire

Hertford Regiment Museum see Museums - Hertfordshire

Hull

4th Battalion East Yorkshire Regiment Collection see Museums - Hull

Isle of Wight

Needles Old Battery see Museums - Isle of Wight

Kent

Brenzett Aeronautical Museum see Museums - Kent

Buffs Regimental Museum see Museums - Kent

Dover Castle Dover CT16 1HU T: 01304 201628 W: www.english-heritage.org.uk

Fort Armherst see Museums - Kent

Fort Luton Museum see Museums - Kent

Gunpowder Chart Mills see Museums - Kent

Kent and Sharpshooters Yeomanry Museum see Museums - Kent

Kent Battle of Britain Museum see Museums - Kent

Lashenden Air Warfare Museum see Museums - Kent

Princess of Wales's Royal Regt & Queen's Regt Museum see Museums - Kent

Quebec House see Museums - Kent

RAF Manston History Museum see Museums - Kent

Rochester Cathedral Militia Museum see Museums - Kent

Roman Dover Tourist Centre see Museums - Kent

Roman Museum see Museums - Kent

Royal Engineers Library see Museums - Kent

Royal Engineers Museum of Military Engineering see Museums - Kent

Shoreham Aircraft Museum see Museums - Kent

Spitfire and Hurricane Memorial Building see Museums - Kent

St Margaret's Museum see Museums - Kent

The Buffs Regimental Museum see Museums - Kent

The Grand Shaft see Museums - Kent

The Historic Dockyard see Museums - Kent

The Queen's Own Royal West Kent Regiment Museum see Museums - Kent

The West Gate see Museums - Kent

Timeball Tower see Museums - Kent

Walmer Castle and Gardens see Museums - Kent

Lancashire

British in India Museum see Museums - Lancashire

East Lancashire Regiment see Museums - Lancashire

King's Own Royal Regimental Museum see Museums - Lancashire

Museum of Lancashire (Queen's Lancashire Regiment Duke of Lancaster's Own Yeomanry Lancashire Hussars 14th/20th King's Hussars) see Museums - Lancashire

Museum of the Manchester Regiment see Museums - Lancashire

Museum of the Queen's Lancashire Regiment (East South and Loyal (North Lancashire) Regiments, Lancashire Regiment (PWV) and The Queen's Lancashire Regiment see Museums - Lancashire

South Lancashire Regiment Prince of Wales Volunteers Museum see Museums - Lancashire

The Fusiliers Museum (Lancashire) see Museums - Lancashire

Leicestershire

Bosworth Battlefield Visitor Centre see Museums - Leicestershire

British Aviation Heritage see Museums - Leicestershire

Leicestershire Yeomanry, Leicestershire Tigers Museum see Museums - Leicestershire

Royal Leicestershire Regiment Museum Gallery see Museums - Leicestershire

Royal Leicestershire Regimental Gallery see Museums - Leicestershire

Lincolnshire

50 and 61 Suadrons' Museum see Museums - Lincolnshire

Battle of Britain Memorial Flight see Museums - Lincolnshire

Bomber County Aviation Museum see Museums - Lincolnshire

Cranwell Avation Heritage Centre see Museums - Lincolnshire

Lincolnshire Aviation Heritage Centre see Museums - Lincolnshire

Metheringham Airfield Visitor Centre see Museums - Lincolnshire

RAF Digby Ops Room Museum see Museums - Lincolnshire

Royal Lincolnshire Regiment Lincolnshire Yeomanry Museum see Museums - Lincolnshire

The Queen's Royal Lancers Regimental Museum (16th/5th and 17th/21st Lancers) see Museums - Lincolnshire

Thorpe Camp Visitor Centre see Museums - Lincolnshire

Liverpool

King's Regiment Collection see Museums - Liverpool

London

Berkshire and Westminster Dragoons Museum see Museums - London

Britain at War Experience see Museums - London

Coldstream Guards Record Office Wellington Barracks Birdcage Walk London SW1E 6HQ Access is by appointment made in advance. Search fee of £25.00 per search

Firepower - The Royal Artillery Museum see Museums - London

Fusiliers' London Volunteer Museum see Museums - London

Grenadier Guards Record Office see Museums - London

Guards Museum see Museums - London

Honourable Artillery Company see Museums - London

Imperial War Museum see Museums - London

Inns of Court and City Yeomanry Museum see Museums - London

Irish Guards Record Office Wellington Barracks Birdcage Walk London SW1E 6HQ E: bigbillaqq119@aol.com W: www.army.mod/ig~assoc For archives information contact Achivist in first instance Search fee of £25.00 per search

Ministry of Defence - Army Records Centre see Museums - London

James Clavell Library see Museums - London

London Irish Rifles Regimental Museum see Museums - London

London Scottish Regimental Museum see Museums - London

National Army Museum see Museums - London

National Army Museum Department of Archives (Photographs, Film & Sound) see Museums - London

Princess Louise's Kensington Regiment Museum see Museums - London

Royal Air Force Museum see Museums - London

The Royal Regiment of Fusiliers see Museums - London

RHQ Scots Guards Archives Wellington Barracks Birdcage Walk London SW1E 6HQ E: sgarchives@dial.pipex.com Access is by appointment made in advance. Search fee of £25.00 per search

The Association of Jewish Ex-Service Men and Women Military Museum see Museums - London

The Polish Institute and Sikorski Museum see Museums - London

Wellington Museum - Apsley House see Museums - London

Welsh Guards Record Office Wellington Barracks Birdcage Walk London SW1E 6HQ T: 020 7414 3291 E: rhqwelshguards@milnet.uk.net Access is by appointment made in advance. Search fee of £25.00 per search

Merseyside

Liverpool Scottish Regimental Museum see Museums - Merseyside

Middlesex

HQ No 11 (Fighter) Group Battle of Britain Operations Room see Museums - Middlesex

Ministry of Defence - Army Records Centre Defence Records 2 Bourne Avenue Hayes UB3 1RF F: 0181 573 9078 E: lhearn.defencerecords.hayes@gtnet.gov.uk

Royal Military School of Music Museum see Museums - Middlesex

Norfolk

Battlefields Trust see Museums - National

100th Bomb Group Memorial Museum see Museums - Norfolk

Air Defence Radar Museum see Museums - Norfolk

Cholmondeley Collection of Model Soldiers see Museums - Norfolk

City of Norwich Aviation Museum see Museums - Norfolk

Royal Norfolk Regimental Museum see Museums - Norfolk

The Muckleburgh Collection see Museums - Norfolk

Northamptonshire
Abington Museum and Museum of The Northamptonshire Regiment Abington Park Museum Abington NN1 5LW T: 01604 635412 F: 01604 238720 E: Museum s@northamton.gov.uk W: www.northampton.gov.uk/museums
Naseby Battle Museum Purlieu Farm Naseby Northampton NN6 7DD T: 01604 740241
Northumberland
A Soldier's Life 15th/19th The King's Royal Hussars
Northumberland Hussars and Light Dragoons see Museums - Northumberland
Chesterholm Museum see Museums - Northumberland
Chesters Roman Fort and Clayton Collection Museum see Museums - Northumberland
Corbridge Roman Site see Museums - Northumberland
Fusiliers Museum of Northumberland see Museums - Northumberland
Housteads Roman Fort Museum see Museums - Northumberland
King's Own Scottish Borderers Museum see Museums - Northumberland
Roman Army Museum see Museums - Northumberland
Nottinghamshire
Newark (Notts & Lincs) Air Museum see Museums - Nottinghamshire
Sherwood Foresters Museum and Archives see Museums - Nottinghamshire
Sherwood Foresters (Notts and Derby Regiment) Museum see Museums - Nottinghamshire
Oxfordshire
Edgehill Battle Museum see Museums - Oxfordshire
Oxfordshire and Buckinghamshire Light Infantry Regimental Museum see Museums - Oxfordshire
Shropshire
Cosford Royal Air Force Museum see Museums - Shropshire
Queen's Own Mercian Yeomanry Museum see Museums - Shropshire
Shropshire Regimental Museum (King's Shropshire Light Infantry, Shropshire Yeomanry) Shropshire Militia, Volunteers and TA see Museums - Shropshire
Somerset
Blake Museum see Museums - Somerset
Fleet Air Arm Museum see Museums - Somerset
Somerset Military Museum (Somerset Light Infantry, YeomanryMilitia and Volunteers) County Museum see Museums - Somerset
Staffordshire
Museum of The Staffordshire Regiment see Museums - Staffordshire
Museum of the Staffordshire Yeomanry see Museums - Staffordshire
The Potteries Museum & Art Gallery see Museums -Staffordshire
Suffolk
390th Bomb Group Memorial Air Museum see Museums - Suffolk
British Resistance Organisation Museum see Museums - Suffolk
Norfolk and Suffolk Aviation Museum - East Anglia's Aviation Heritage Centre see Museums - Suffolk
R.A.F. Regiment Museum see Museums - Suffolk
Royal Naval Patrol Association Museum see Museums - Suffolk
Suffolk Regiment Museum see Museums - Suffolk
Suffolk Regiment Museum -Museum closed to the public
Surrey
Queen's Royal Surrey Regiment Museum (Queen's Royal, East Surrey & Queen's Royal Surrey Regts) see Museums - Surrey
Regimental Museum Royal Logistic Corps see Museums - Surrey
Sandhurst Collection see Museums - Surrey
Staff College Museum see Museums - Surrey
Sussex
Sussex Combined Services Museum (Royal Sussex Regiment and Queen's Royal Irish Hussars) see Museums - Sussex
Tangmere Military Aviation Museum see Museums - Sussex
Sussex - East Newhaven Fort see Museums - Sussex East
Sussex Yeomanry Museum see Museums - Sussex
Tyne and Wear
101 (Northumbrian) Regiment Royal Artillery (Volunteers) Museum see Museums - Tyne & Wear
Military Vehicle Museum see Museums - Tyne & Wear
Arbeia Roman Fort and Museum see Museums - Tyne & Wear
North East Aircraft Museum see Museums - Tyne & Wear
Segedunum Roman Fort see Museums - Tyne & Wear
Warwickshire
Lunt Roman Fort see Museums - Warwickshire
Midland Air Museum see Museums - Warwickshire
Regimental Museum of The Queen's Own Hussars (The 3rd King's Own Hussars and 7th Queen's Own Hussars) see Museums - Warwickshire
The Royal Regiment of Fusiliers Museum (Royal Warwickshire) see Museums - Warwickshire

Warwickshire Yeomanry Museum see Museums - Warwickshire
Wellesborough Aviation Museum see Museums - Warwickshire
Wiltshire
RGBW (Salisbury) Museum see Museums - Wiltshire
Royal Wiltshire Yeomanry Museum see Museums - Wiltshire
The Infantry and Small Arms School Corps Weapons Collection see Museums - Wiltshire
Wirral
Historic Warships at Birkenhead see Museums - Wirral
Worcestershire
Commandery Civil War Museum see Museums - Worcestershire
The Museum of the Worcestershire Yeomanry Cavalry see Museums - Worcestershire
The Worcestershire Regiment Museum see Museums - Worcestershire
Worcestershire Regiment Archives (Worcestershire and Sherwood Forester's Regiment) see Museums - Worcestershire
Yorkshire – East
Museum of Army Transport see Museums - Yorkshire – East
Yorkshire – North
Eden Camp Museum see Museums - Yorkshire – North
Green Howards Regimental Museum see Museums - Yorkshire – North
Royal Dragoon Guards Military Museum (4th/7th Royal Dragoon Guards & 5th Royal Inniskilling Dragoon Guards) see Museums - Yorkshire – North
The Real Aeroplane Museum see Museums - Yorkshire – North
War Room & Motor House Collection see Museums - Yorkshire – North
Yorkshire Air Museum see Museums - Yorkshire – North
Yorkshire – South
Doncaster AeroVenture - The South Yorkshire Air Museum Aero Venture Lakeside Doncaster T: 01302 761616 F: 01302 316610
King's Own Yorkshire light infantry Regimental Gallery Doncaster Museum and Art Gallery Chequer Road Doncaster DN1 2AE T: 01302 734293 F: 01302 735409 E: Museum @doncaster.gov.uk W: www.doncaster.gov.uk/museums 51st (2nd Yorkshire, West Riding) the King's Own Light infantry regiment; 51st (2nd Yorkshire, West Riding) Regiment of Foot (Light Infantry); 51st (2nd Yorkshire, West Riding) Regiment of Foot; 51st Brudenell's Regiment of Foot; 53rd Napier's Regiment of Foot; 105th Madras (Light Infantry) regiment; 2nd Madras European Regiment (Light Infantry) (Honourable East India Company)
Regimental Museum 13th/18th Royal Hussars and The Light Dragoons Cannon Hall Cawthorne Barnsley S75 4AT T: 01226 790270
York and Lancaster Regimental Museum Library and Arts Centre Walker Place Rotherham S65 1JH T: 01709 823635 F: 01709 823631 E: karl.noble@rotherham.gov.uk W: www.rotherham.gov.uk
Yorkshire – West
Bankfield Museum & Gallery Boothtown Rd Halifax HX3 6HG 01422 354823 F: 01422 349020 E: bankfield-museum@calderdale.gov.uk W: www.calderdale.gov.uk Also holds Duke of Wellington's Regimental Museum
Duke of Wellington's Regimental Museum Bankfield Museum Akroyd Park Boothtown Road Halifax HX3 6HG T: 01422 354823 F: 01422 249020
Leeds Rifles Museum c/o 7 Wentworth Court Raistrick Brighouse HD6 3XD
Yorkshire – City of York
Kohima Museum c/o Legal Branch, HQ 2 Div, Imphal Barracks Fulford Road York YO10 4AU T: 01904 662086 01904 635212 F: 01904 662377 E: thekohimamuseum@hotmail.com A small collection of memorabilia donated by veterans of 2nd division who served in India and Burman 1942-1946

NORTHERN IRELAND
The Museum Of The Royal Irish Regiment St. Patricks Barracks Demesne Avenue Ballymena BT43 7BH T: (028) 2566 1386 (028) 2566 1383 F: (028) 2566 1378
Royal Irish Fusiliers Museum Sovereign's House Mall East Armagh BT61 9DL T: (028) 3752 2911 F: (028) 3752 2911 E: rylirfusilier@aol.com W: www.rirfus-museum.freeserve.co.uk
County Down The Somme Heritage Centre 233 Bangor Road Newtownards BT23 7PH T: 028 9182 3202 F: 028 9182 3214 E: sommeassociation@dnet.co.uk W: www.irishsoldier.org
Royal Inniskilling Fusiliers Regimental Museum The Castle Enniskillen BT74 7BB T: (028) 66323142 F: (028) 66320359
Royal Ulster Rifles Regimental Museum RHQ Royal Irish Regiment 5 Waring Street Belfast BT1 2EW T: (028) 90232086 F: (028) 9023 2086 E: rurmuseum@yahoo.co.uk W: www.rurmuseum.tripod.com
Ulster Aviation Heritage Centre Langford Lodge Airfield Belfast T: 028 9287 7030 028 9445 4444 E: emie@aimi.freeserve.co.uk W: www.d-n-a.net/users/dnetrAzQ

SCOTLAND
Aberdeenshire
Gordon Highlanders Museum see Museums - Aberdeenshire
Angus
Montrose Air Station Museum see Museums - Angus
Ayrshire
Ayrshire Yeomanry Museum see Museums - Ayrshire
West Lowland Fencibles see Museums - Ayrshire
Berwickshire
Coldstream Guards see Museums - Berwickshire
Dundee
HM Frigate Unicorn see Museums - Dundee
Fife
Edinburgh
Royal Scots Regimental Museum see Museums - Edinburgh
Fife and Forfar Yeomanry Museum see Museums - Fife
Glasgow
Kelvingrove Art Gallery and Museum see Museums - Glasgow
The Burrell Collection see Museums - Glasgow
Highland
Regimental Museum of The Highlanders (The Queen's Own Highlanders Collection) see Museums - Highland
Inverness-shire
Culloden Visitor Centre see Museums - Inverness-shire
Queen's Own Cameron Highlanderssee Museums - Inverness-shire
Queen's Own Highlanders (Seaforth & Camerons) Regimental Museum Archivessee Museums - Inverness-shire
Lanarkshire
The Cameronians (Scottish Rifles) Museum & Low Parks Museum see Museums - Lanarkshire
Orkney
Stromness Museum see Museums - Orkney
Perthshire
Atholl Highlanders see Museums - Perthshire
Regimental Museum and Archives of Black Watch see Museums - Perthshire
Scottish Horse Regimental Archives - Dunkeld Cathedral see Museums - Perthshire
Roxburghshire
Borders Museum of Arms see Museums -Roxburghshire
Stirlingshire
Regimental Museum Argyll and Sutherland Highlanders Roxburghshire see Museums -Stirlingshire
Strathclyde
Museum of The Royal Highland Fusilers (Royal Scots Fusilers and Highland Light Infantry) see Museums -Strathclyde

WALES
Cardiff
1st The Queen's Dragoon Guards Regimental Museum see Museums - Cardiff
Gwent
Roman Legionary Museum see Museums - Gwent
Gwynedd
Caernarfon Air World see Museums - Gwynedd
Llandudno Royal Artillery see Museums - Gwynedd
Segontium Roman Museum see Museums - Gwynedd
The Royal Welch Fusiliers Regimental Museum see Museums - Gwynedd
Monmouth
Nelson Museum see Museums - Monmouth
Monmouthshire Royal Engineers (Militia) see Museums - Monmouth
Pembrokeshire
Pembroke Yeomanry, Royal Pembroke Militia, Pembrokeshire Volunteers Museum see Museums - Pembrokeshire
Powys
Brecknock Militia see Museums - Powys
South Wales Borderers & Monmouthshire Regimental Museum of the Royal Regt of Wales (24th/41st Foot) see Museums - Powys

Isle of Man
Regimental Museum of the Manx Regiment The MacClellan Hall Tromode Road Douglas T: 01624 803146

Channel Islands
Guernsey
18th Century Loopholed Tower see Museums - Guernsey
Clarence Battery see Museums - Guernsey
Fort Grey Rocquaine Bay St Saviours
German Direction Finding Tower see Museums - Guernsey
German Underground Hospital see Museums - Guernsey
German Naval Signals Headquarters St Jacques
La Valette Underground Military Museum see Museums - Guernsey
German Occupation Museum see Museums - Guernsey
Royal Guernsey Militia and Royal Geurnsey Light Infantry see

Museums - Guernsey
Jersey
Elizabeth Castle - Jersey Militia see Museums - Jersey
German Underground Hospital see Museums - Jersey
La Hougue Bie see Museums - Jersey
Maritme Museum and Occupation Tapestry Gallery see Museums - Jersey
Noirmont Command Bunke see Museums - Jersey
St Peter's Bunker Museum of Wartime German Equipment and Occupation Relics see Museums - Jersey
The Channel Islands Military Museum see Museums - Jersey
Island Fortress Occupation Museum see Museums - Jersey
Sark
German Occupation Museum see Museums - Sark

BELGIUM
In Flanders Fields Museum Lakenhallen Grote Markt 34 Ieper B-8900 T: 00-32-(0)-57-22-85-84 F: 00-32-(0)-57-22-85-89 W: www.inflandersfields.be

BRING YOUR FAMILY TREE TO LIFE

with

FAMILY HISTORY
MONTHLY

Family History Monthly has been serving the needs of budding family historians and expert researchers since 1995. Every month we provide practical tips on how to trace your family tree and the background information to encourage you to dig deeper.

We make family history easy, with simple 'how to' guides, top tips for computer research, reviews of the best websites, and reports on what's new in the field.

Our expanded Family History Online section is second to none, with advice, walkthroughs, news and reviews from our team of expert writers.

We also feature:
- Comprehensive answers to your research problems
- Your family pictures and stories
- The latest family history news
- Reviews of the best books, websites, software and CDs
- The stories behind surnames

...And lots more

Family History Monthly is an essential tool for beginners and experts alike. We're here to help and inform.

To subscribe email janice.mayne@dpgsubs.co.uk, or call 0870 734 3030
Family History Monthly, Diamond Publishing, Unit 101, 140 Wales Farm Road, London W3 6UG
www.familyhistorymonthly.com

The Genealogical Services Directory

In association with

FAMILY HISTORY
MONTHLY

Family History Societies

All Family History & Genealogical Societies were circulated to confirm the information is correct and up to date. Some Societies did not respond (January 2004)

British Association for Local History PO Box 6549, Somersal Herbert, Ashbourne, Derbyshire, DE6 5WH Tel: 01283 585947 Fax: 01722 413242 Email: mail@balh.co.uk (Enquiries) W: www.balh.co.uk

East Anglian Group of Family History Societies 42 Crowhill, Godmanchester, Huntington, Cambridgeshire, PE29 2NR E: secretary@huntsfhs.org.uk W: www.huntsfhs.org.uk

Federation of Family History Societies, PO Box 2425, Coventry, CV5 6YX Tel: 070 41 492032 Fax: 070 41 492032 E: info@ffhs.org.uk W: www.ffhs.org.uk

Institute of Heraldic and Genealogical Studies 79 82 Northgate, Canterbury, Kent, CT1 1BA T: 01227 462618 Fax: 01227 765617 E: ihgs@ihgs.ac.uk W: www.ihgs.ac.uk

The North East Group of Family History Societies 11 Collins Street, Great Horton, Bradford, West Yorkshire, BD7 4HF, Group for Societies in North East of England. No individual members.

North West Group of FHS Family History Fairs see Lancashire

Society of Genealogists - Library, 14 Charterhouse Buildings, Goswell Road, London, EC1M 7BA T: 020-7251-8799 T: 020-7250-0291 Fax: 020-7250-1800 E: library@sog.org.uk - Sales at sales@sog.org.uk W: www.sog.org.uk

South West Group of Family History Societies see Somerset

Yorkshire Consortium of Family History Societies London Group see Yorkshire

England

Avon
Bristol & Avon Family History Society see Bristol
Sodbury Vale Family History Group see Bristol

Bedfordshire
Bedfordshire Family History Society P0 Box 214, Bedford, Bedfordshire, MK42 9RX E: bfhs@bfhs.org.uk W: www.bfhs.org.uk

Berkshire
Berkshire Family History Society Research Centre, Yeomanry House, 131 Castle Hill, Reading, Berkshire, RG1 7TJ T: 0118 966 3585 E: secretary@berksfhs.org.uk W: www.berksfhs.org.uk

Birmingham
Birmingham & Midland Society for Genealogy and Heraldry 2 Castle Croft, Oldbury, West Midlands, B68 9BQ T: 0121 429 9712 E: birmingham@terrymorter.fsnet.co.uk W: www.bmsgh.org

Bristol
Bristol & Avon Family History Society 60 Pound Road, Kingswood, Bristol, BS15 4QY T: 0117 967 7288 E: secretary@bafhs.org.uk W: www.bafhs.org.uk

Sodbury Vale Family History Group 36 Westcourt Drive, Oldland Common, Bristol, BS30 9RU T: 0117 932 4133 E: sladekf@supanet.com

Buckinghamshire
Buckinghamshire Family History Society PO Box 403, Aylesbury, Buckinghamshire, HP21 7GU E: secretary@bucksfhs.org.uk W: www.bucksfhs.org.uk CC accepted

Buckinghamshire Genealogical Society Varneys, Rudds Lane, Haddenham, Buckinghamshire, HP17 8JP T: 01844 291631 E: eve@varneys.demon.co.uk W: http://met.open.ac.uk/group/kaq/bgs.htm

Cambridgeshire
Cambridgeshire Family History Society 6 Chestnut Rise, Bar Hill, Cambridge, Cambridgeshire, CB3 8TF E: secretary@cfhs.org.uk W: www.cfhs.org.uk

Cambridge University H & G S, c/o Crossfield House, Dale Road, Stanton, Bury St Edmunds, Suffolk, IP31 2DY T: 01359 251050 Fax: 01359 251050 E: president@one-name.org W: www.cam.ac.uk/societies/cuhags/, Membership open to members of the University but non-members may be admitted at the discretion of the Executive Committee

Fenland Family History Society 70 Gorefield Road, Leverington, Cambridgeshire, PE13 5AT T: 01945 587723 E: peter.hunter3@btinternet.com W: Covers Fenland areas of Cambridgeshire, Lincolnshire and Norfolk

Huntingdonshire Family History Society 42 Crowhill, Godmanchester, Huntingdon, Cambridgeshire, PE29 2NR T: 01480 390476 E: secretary@huntsfhs.org.uk W: www.huntsfhs.org.uk

Peterborough & District Family History Society 33 Farleigh Fields, Orton Wistow, Peterborough, Cambridgeshire, PE2 6YB T: 01733 235956

Cheshire
Family History Society of Cheshire, 10 Dunns Lane, Ashton, Chester, Cheshire, CH3 8BU T: 01829 759089 E: info@fhsc.org.uk W: www.fhsc.org.uk

North Cheshire Family History Society 2 Denham Drive, Bramhall, Stockport, Cheshire, SK7 2AT T: 0161-439-9270 E: roger@demercado.demon.co.uk W: www.genuki.org.uk/big/eng/CHS/NorthChesFHS

South Cheshire Family History Society incorporating S E Cheshire Local Studies Group PO Box 1990, Crewe, Cheshire, CW2 6FF W: www.scfhs.org.uk

Cleveland
Cleveland Family History Society 1 Oxgang Close, Redcar, Cleveland, TS10 4ND T: 01642 486615 Fax: 01642 486615 W: www.clevelandfhs.org.uk

Cornwall
Cornwall Family History Society 5 Victoria Square, Truro, Cornwall, TR1 2RS T: 01872-264044 E: secretary@cornwallfhs.com W: www.cornwallfhs.com

Cornish Forefathers Society Credvill, Quakers Road, Perranwell, Truro, Cornwall, TR3 7PJ T: 0777 992 9361 (Mobile) E: forefathers@ukonline.co.uk W: www.cornish-forefathers.com

Fal Worldwide Family History Group 57 Huntersfield, South Tehidy, Camborne, Cornwall, TR14 0HW T: 01209-711557 Fax: 01209-711557 E: cfdell@clara.net W: http://beehive.thisiscornwall.co.uk/falwwfhg, Although our group is based in Cornwall only a few of our members have Cornish ancestry and are therefore researching our family history worldwide

Cumbria/Cumberland
Cumbria Family History Society Ulpha, 32 Granada Road, Denton, Manchester, M34 2LJ W: www.genuki.org.uk/big/eng/CUL/cumbFHS/membership.html The Society caters for those with interests in the old counties of Cumberland & Westmorland and those parts of Lancashire known as 'Lonsdale North of the Sands' Founded to help Cumbrians and those with Cumbrian Ancestors carry out their family history research in the area covered by the modern county of Cumbria

Furness Family History Society 64 Cowlarns Road, Hawcoat, Barrow-in-Furness, Cumbria, LA14 4HJ T: 01229-830942 E: julia.fairbairn@virgin.net W: www.members.aol.com/furnessfhs/fpw.htm

Derbyshire
Chesterfield & District Family History Society 16 Mill Crescent, Wingerworth, Chesterfield, Derbyshire, S42 6NN T: 01246 231900 E: cadfhs@aol.com

Derbyshire Family History Society Bridge Chapel House, St Mary's Bridge, Sowter Road, Derby, Derbyshire, DE1 3AT T: 01332 608101 W: www.dfhs.org.uk

Derbyshire Ancestral Research Group 86 High Street, Loscoe, Heanor, Derbyshire, DE75 7LF T: 01773-604916, Library is open on Wednesdays from 1030 to 1.30 Birchwood Chapel, Birchwood Lane, Somercoates, Nr Alfreton, Derbyshire Telephone first

Devon
Devon Family History Society PO Box 9, Exeter, Devon, EX2 6YP T: 01392 275917 E: members@devonfhs.org.uk W: www.deveonfhs.org.uk

Thorverton & District History Society Ferndale, Thorverton, Exeter, Devon, EX5 5NG T: 01392 860932

Dorset
Dorrset Family History Society Unit 40 Mannings Heath Works, 18 Mannings Heath Road, Parkstone, Poole, Dorset, BH12 4NJ T: 01202 736261 E: contact@dorsetfhs.freeserve.co.uk W: www.dfhs.freeserve.co.uk/index.html

Somerset & Dorset Family History Society see Somerset

Durham
Cleveland Family History Society see Cleveland

Elvet Local & Family History Groups, 37 Hallgarth Street, Durham, County Durham, DH1 3AT T: 0191-386-4098 Fax: 0191-386-4098 E: Turnstone-Ventures@durham-city.freeserve.co.uk

Newton Aycliffe Family History Society 4 Barnard Close, Woodham Village, Newton Aycliffe, County Durham, DL5 4SP T: 01325 315959 E: jtb2@totalise.com

Northumberland & Durham Family History Society see Northumberland

Essex
Essex Society for Family History, Research Centre, Essex Record Office, Wharf Road, Chelmsford, Essex CM2 6YT T: 01245 244670 E: secretary@esfh.org.uk W: www.esfh.org.uk

Waltham Forest Family History Society 49 Sky Peals Road, Woodford Green, Essex, IG8 9NE

Gloucestershire
Gloucestershire Family History Society 37 Barrington Drive, Hucclecote, Gloucester, Gloucestershire, GL3 3BT T: 01452 524344(RESOURCE CENTRE) T: 01452 535608 E: alexwood@blueyonder.co.uk W: www.gfhs.org.uk
Campden & District Family History Group 9 Wolds End, Chipping Campden, Gloucestershire, GL55 6JW T: 01386 840561 E: familyhistory@judithellis.org.uk
Bristol & Avon Family History Society see Bristol
Gloucestershire - South
Sodbury Vale Family History Group see Bristol

Hampshire
Hampshire Genealogical Society 198A Havant Road, Drayton, Portsmouth, Hampshire, PO6 2EH E: society@hgs-online.org.uk W: www.hgs-online.org.uk

Herefordshire
Herefordshire Family History Society 6 Birch Meadow, Gosmore Road, Clehonger, Hereford, Herefordshire, HR2 9RH T: 01981-250974 E: prosser_brian@hotmail.com W: www.rootsweb.com/~ukhfhs

Hertfordshire
Hertfordshire Family History Society 26 Vale Close, Harpenden, Hertfordshire, AL5 3LX E: secretary@hertsfhs.org.uk W: www.hertsfhs.org.uk
Royston & District Family History Society Baltana, London Road, Barkway, Royston, Hertfordshire, SG8 8EY T: 01763 848228 E: keith-curtis@lineone.net
Welwyn & District Local History Society 40 Hawbush Rise, Welwyn, Hertfordshire, AL6 9PP T: 01438 716415 E: p.jiggens-keen@virgin.net W: www.welwynhistory.org
Letchworth & District Family History Group 84 Kings Hedges, Hitchin, Hertfordshire, SG5 2QE
Codicote Local History Society 34 Harkness Way, Hitchin, Hertfordshire, SG4 0QL T: 01462 622953

Isle of Wight
Isle of Wight Family History Society Spindrift, 3 Milne Way, Newport, Isle of Wight, PO30 1YF T: 01983 524469 W: www.isle-of-wight-fhs.co.uk
Roots Family & Parish History - Disbanded 2003

Kent
Folkestone & District Family History Society 81 Wear Bay Road, Folkestone, Kent, CT19 6PR E: alisonfhs@aslan consultancy.freeserve.co.uk W: www.folkfhs.org.uk
Kent Family History Society Bullockstone Farm, Bullockstone Road, Herne Bay, Kent, CT6 7NL W: www.kfhs.org.uk Change of Secretary December 2001
North West Kent Family History Society 58 Clarendon Gardens, Dartford, Kent, DA2 6EZ E: secretary@nwkfhs.org.uk W: www.nwkfhs.org.uk Covers ancient parishes of Deptford, Greenwich Woolwich
Tunbridge Wells Family History Society The Old Cottage, Langton Road, Langton Green, Tunbridge Wells, Kent, TN3 0BA E: s.oxenbury@virgin.net W: www.tunwells fhs.co.uk
Woolwich & District Family History Society 54 Parkhill Road, Bexley, Kent, DA5 1HY E: FrEdnafhs@aol.com

Lancashire
Accrington Uncovered, 15 Christ Church Street, Accrington, Lancashire, BB5 2LZ T: 01254 398579 E: jhunt@christchurch92.freeserve.co.uk W: www.accringtonuncovered.co.uk
Bolton & District Family History Society 205 Crompton Way, Bolton, Lancashire, BL2 2RU T: 01204 525472 E: bolton@mlfhs.demon.co.uk W: www.mlfhs.demon.co.uk A branch of Manchester and Lancashire Family History Society
Lancaster Family History Group 116 Bowerham Road, Lancaster, Lancashire, LA1 4HL
Liverpool & S W Lancashire Family History Society 11 Bushbys Lane, Formby, Liverpool, L37 2DX W: www.liverpool genealogy.org.uk Society consists of eight groups: Liverpool, St Helens, Southport, Skelmersdale & Upholland, Warrington, Leigh, Widnes & special interest group Anglo Irish
Manchester and Lancashire Family History Society Clayton House, 59 Piccadilly, Manchester, M1 2AQ T: 0161 236 9750 Fax: 0161 237 3512 E: office@mlfhs.org.uk W: www.mlfhs.org.uk
North Meols Family History Society 9 The Paddock, Ainsdale, Southport, Lancashire, PR8 3PT T: 01704 578797 E: nadine@xplorasia.freeserve.co.uk W: www.users.zetnet.co.uk/nmfhs
North West Group of FHS Family History Fairs, North West Group of Family History Societies, 4 Lawrence Avenue, Simonstone, Burnley, Lancashire, BB12 7HX T: 01282 771999 E: ed@gull66.freeserve.co.uk
Oldham & District Family History Society Clayton House, 59 Piccadilly, Manchester, M1 2QA T: 0161 236 9750 Fax: 0161 237 3512 E: office@mlfhs.org.uk W: www.mlfhs.org.uk

Ormskirk & District Family History Society c/o Ormskirk College, Hants Lane, Ormskirk, Lancashire, L39 1PX T: 01695 578604 E: odfhs@skelmersdale.ac.uk W: www.odfhs.freeserve.co.uk
Wigan Family History Society 615 Wigan Road, Wigan, Lancashire, WN4 0BY W: www.ffhs.org.uk/members/wigan.htm

Leicestershire
Leicestershire & Rutland Family History Society 11 Spring Lane, Wymondham, Leicester, Leicestershire, LE14 2AY T: 01572 787331 E: secretary@lrfhs.org.uk W: www.lrfhs.org.uk CC accepted

Lincolnshire
Lincolnshire Family History Society 10 Windsor Avenue, Holbeach, Spalding, Lincolnshire, PE12 7AN E: chairman@lincolnshirefhs.org.uk W: www.lincolnshirefhs.org.uk
Isle of Axholme Family History Society Alwinton, 51 Mill Road, Crowle, Isle of Axholme, North Lincolnshire, DN17 4LW T: 01724 710578 E: secretary@axholme fhs.org.uk W: www.axholme fhs.org.uk www.linktop.demon.co.uk/axholme/

Liverpool
Liverpool & S W Lancashire FHS see Lancashire

London
East of London Family History Society 23 Louvaine Avenue, Wickford, Essex, SS12 0DP E: ean23@btopenworld.com W: www.eolfhs.rootsweb.com
Hillingdon Family History Society see Middlesex
London & North Middlesex FHS incorporating Westminster & Central Middlesex FHS 57 Belvedere Way, Kenton, Harrow, Middlesex, HA3 9XQ T: (020) 8204 5470 E: william.pyemont@virgin.net W: wwww.lnmfhs.dircon.co.uk
Society of Genealogists Library see National
Waltham Forest Family History Society 49 Sky Peals Road, Woodford Green, Essex, IG8 9NE
West Middlesex Family History Society see Middlesex

Manchester
Manchester and Lancashire FHS see Lancashire

Merseyside
Liverpool & S W Lancashire FHSty see Lancashire

Middlesex
Hillingdon Family History Society 20 Moreland Drive, Gerrards Cross, Buckinghamshire, SL9 8BB T: 01753 885602 E: gillmay@dial.pipex.com W: www.hfhs.co.uk
London & North Middlesex FHS incorporating Westminster & Central Middlesex FHS see London
West Middlesex FHS 241 Waldegrave Road, Twickenham, TW1 4SY T: 020 8892 5797 Fax: 020 8892 6662 E: secretary@west-middlesex fhs.org.uk W: www.west-middlesex fhs.org.uk

Norfolk
Norfolk Family History Society Headquarters, Library & Registered Office, Kirby Hall, 70 St Giles Street, Norwich, Norfolk, NR2 1LS T: 01603 763718 T: E: nfhs@paston.co.uk W: www.norfolkfhs.org.uk

Mid Norfolk Family History Society 47 Greengate, Swanton Morley, Dereham, Norfolk, NR20 4LX E: keasdown@aol.com W: http://www.uea.ac.uk/~s300/genuki/NFK/organisations/midnfhs

Northamptonshire
Northamptonshire Family History Society 17 Swyncombe Green, Hartwell, Northampton, Norrthamptonshire, NN7 2JA E: angela.malin@btinternet.com W: www.fugazi.demon.co.uk

Northumberland
Northumberland & Durham Family History Society 2nd Floor, Bolbec Hall, Westgate Road, Newcastle on Tyne, Tyne and Wear, NE1 1SE T: 0191 261 2159 W: www.ndfhs.org.uk Secretary Mrs Frances Norman, 23 Monkton Avenue, Simonside South Shields, Tyne & Wear, NE34 9RX.

Nottinghamshire
Nottinghamshire Family History Society 15 Holme Close, Woodborough, Nottingham, Nottinghamshire, NG14 6EX W: www..nottsfhs.org.uk
Mansfield & District Family History Society 15 Cranmer Grove, Mansfield, Nottinghamshire, NG19 7JR E: betty@flintham.freeserve.co.uk

Oxfordshire
Oxfordshire Family History Society 19 Mavor Close, Woodstock, Oxford, Oxfordshire, OX20 1YL T: 01993 812258 E: secretary@ofhs.org.uk W: www.ofhs.org.uk

Rutland
Leicestershire & Rutland Family History Society see Leicestershire

Shropshire
Shropshire Family History Society Redhillside, Ludlow Road, Church Stretton, Shropshire, SY6 6AD T: 01694 722949 E: secretary@sfhs.org.uk W: www.sfhs.org.uk
Cleobury Mortimer Historical Society The Old Schoolhouse, Neen Savage, Cleobury Mortimer, Kidderminster, Shropshire, DY14 8JU T: 01299 270319 E: paddy@treves.freeserve.co.uk

Somerset
Somerset & Dorset Family History Society PO Box 4502, Sherborne, Dorset, DH9 6YL T: 01935 389611 Fax: 01935 389611 E: society@sdfhs.org W: www.sdfhs.org
Weston Super Mare Family History Society 32 Marconi Close, Weston Super Mare, Somerset, BS23 3HH T: 01934 627053 E: kes.jack@virgin.co.uk
South West Group of Family History Societies, 32 Marconi Close, Weston Super Mare, Somerset, BS23 3HH T: 01934 627053
Sodbury Vale Family History Group see Bristol

Staffordshire
Ancestral Rescue Club, 19 Mansfield Close, Tamworth, Staffordshire, B79 7YE T: 01827 65322 E: ancestral@rescue.fsnet.co.uk W: www.rootsweb.com/~engarc/index.html
Audley & District Family History Society 20 Hillside Avenue, Endon, Stoke on Trent, Staffordshire, ST9 9HH E: famhist@audley.net
Birmingham & Midland Society for Genealogy and Heraldry see Birmingham
Burntwood Family History Group The Annexe, Green Lane Farm, Green Lane, Burntwood, Staffordshire, WS7 9HB E: gassor@ukonline.co.uk W: www.geocities.com/bfhg1986

Suffolk
Felixstowe Family History Society Drenagh, 7 Victoria Road, Felixstowe, Suffolk, IP11 7PT T: 01394 275631 Fax: 01394 275631 E: W: www.btinternet.com/~woodsbj/tths
Suffolk Family History Society Egg Hall Cottage, 14 Birch Street, Nayland, Colchester, Essex, CO6 4JA T: 01206 263116 W: www.genuki.org.uk/big/eng/SFK/Sfhs/Sfhs.htm

Surrey - East
East Surrey Family History Society PO Box 2506, Coulsdon, Surrey, CR5 3WF E: secretary@eastsurreyfhs.org.uk W: www.eastsurreyfhs.org.uk
Surrey - West
West Surrey Family History Society Deer Dell, Botany Hill, Sands, Farnham, Surrey, GU10 1LZ T: 01252 783485 E: secretary@wsfhs.org W: www.wsfhs.org

Sussex
Sussex Family History Group 40 Tandridge Park, Horsham, West Sussex, RG12 1SZ T: 01825 765561 E: secretary@sfhg.org.uk W: www.sfhg.org.uk Latest publications include Brighton Census Index 1851 Horsham Census index 1841 & 1851. Aim of the Group is to promote study of family history and preservatioin, transcription & publication of relevant documents & records.
Sussex - East
Family Roots Family History Society (Eastbourne & District), 94 Northbourne Road, Eastbourne, East Sussex, BN22 8QP E: sarahlslaughter@madasafish.com
Hastings & Rother Family History Society 73 Harley Shute Road, St Leonards on Sea, East Sussex, TN38 8BY T: 01424 436605 W: www.hrfhs.org.uk

Tyne and Wear
Northumberland & Durham Family History Society see Northumberland

Waltham Forest
Waltham Forest Family History Society see Essex

Warwickshire
Birmingham & Midland Society for Genealogy and Heraldry see Birmingham
Coventry Family History Society PO Box 2746, Coventry, Warwickshire, CV5 7YD T: (024) 7646 4256 E: enquiries@covfhs.org W: www.covfhs.org
Nuneaton & North Warwickshire Family History Society 14 Amos Avenue, Nuneaton, Warwickshire, CV10 7BD E: W: www.nnwfhs.org.uk
Rugby Family History Group Springfields, Rocherberie Way, Rugby, Warwickshire, CV22 6EG T: 01788 813957 E: j.chard@ntlworld.com W: www.rugbyfhg.co.uk
Warwickshire Family History Society 44 Abbotts Land, Coundon, Coventry, Warwickshire, CV1 4AZ E: n.wetton.@virgin.net W: www.wfhs.org.uk

Westmorland
Cumbria Family History Society

West Midlands
Birmingham & Midland Society for Genealogy and Heraldry see Birmingham
Sandwell FHS, 9 Leacroft Grove, Hill Top, West Bromwich, West Midlands, B71 2QP T: 0121 556 0731 E: a.hale@talk21.com

Wiltshire
Wiltshire Family History Society 10 Castle Lane, Devizes, Wiltshire, SN10 1HJ T: 01225 762648 E: society@wiltshirefhs.co.uk W: www.wiltshirefhs.co.uk
Worcestershire
Birmingham & Midland Society for Genealogy and Heraldry
Malvern Family History Group D'Haute Rive, 37 Tennyson Drive, St James' Park, Malvern, Worcestershire, WR14 2TQ T: 01684 561872 W: www.mfhg.org.uk
Yorkshire
Yorkshire Archaeological Society Family History Section, Claremont, 23 Clarendon Road, Leeds, LS2 9NZ W: www.users.globalnet.co.uk/~gdl/yasfhs.htm
Yorkshire Consortium of Family History Societies London Group 121 Layhams Road, West Wickham, Kent, BR4 9HE
Yorkshire - City of York
City of York & District Family History Society 140 Shipton Road, York, Yorkshire, YO30 5RU E: yorkfamilyhistory@btopenworld.com W: www.yorkfamilyhistory.org.ukResearch Room at The Study Centre, Community House, 10 Priory street, York YO1 6EZ T: 01904 652363
Yorkshire – East
Boothferry Family & Local History Group 17 Airmyn Avenue, Goole, Yorkshire, DN14 6PF E: howardrj@madasafish.com
City of York & District Family History Society see Yorkshire
East Yorkshire Family History Society 169 Beverley Road, Hessle, East Yorkshire, HU13 9AS E: secretary@eyfhs.org.uk W: www.eyfhs.org.uk Research Facilities at Room 21, Hull Business Centre, Guildhall Road, Hull, HU1 1BH (Tel: 01482 222262)
Yorkshire – North
City of York & District Family History Society see above
Cleveland Family History Society see Cleveland
Ripon Historical Society & Ripon, Harrogate & District Family History Group 16 Swinburne Close, Harrogate, North Yorkshire, HG1 3LX W: http://web.onetel.net.uk/~gdlawson/rh1.htm
Upper Dales Family History Group Croft House, Newbiggin in Bishopdale, Nr Leyburn, North Yorkshire, DL8 3TD T: 01969 663738 E: glenys@bishopdale.demon.co.uk W: www.bishopdale.demon.co.uk
Yorkshire – South
Barnsley Family History Society 58A High Street, Royston, Barnsley, South Yorkshire, S71 4RN E: secretary@barnsleyfhs.org.uk W: www.barnsleyfhs.co.uk
Doncaster & District Family History Society 'Marton House', 125 The Grove, Wheatley Hills, Doncaster, South Yorkshire, DN2 5SN T: 01302 367257 E: marton house@blueyonder.co.uk W: www.doncasterfhs.frccscrvc.co.uk
Grenoside & District Local History Group 4 Stepping Lane, Grenoside, Sheffield, South Yorkshire, S35 8RA T: 0114 257 1929 T: 0114 245 6959 (David Diver Chairman) E: info@grenosidelocalhistory.co.uk W: www.grenosidelocalhistory.co.uk Local and Family History Society
Sheffield & District Family History Society 5 Old Houses, Piccadilly Road, Chesterfield, Derbyshire, S41 0EH E: secretary@sheffieldfhs.org.uk W: www.sheffieldfhs.org.uk
Rotherham Family History Society 7 St Stephen's Road, Rotherham, South Yorkshire, S65 1PJ W: www.rotherhamfhs.f9.co.uk
Yorkshire – West
Bradford Family History Society 2 Leaventhorpe Grove, Thornton, Bradford, West Yorkshire, BD13 3BN E: DFlax@aol.com W: www.genuki.org.uk/big/eng/YKS/bfhs/
Boothferry Family & Local History Group see Yorkshire - East
Calderdale Family History Society incorporating Halifax & District, 61 Gleanings Avenue, Norton Tower, Halifax, West Yorkshire, HX2 0NU T: 01422 360756 W: www.users.globalnet.co.uk/~cfhs/
Huddersfield & District Family History Society 15 Huddersfield Road, Neltham, Huddersfield, West Yorkshire, HD9 4NJ T: 01484 852420 E: secretary@hdfhs.org.uk W: www.hdfhs.org.uk
Keighley & District Family History Society 2 The Hallows, Shann Park, Keighley, West Yorkshire, BD20 6HY T: 01535 672144
Morley & District Family History Group 19 Hawthorne Drive, Gildersome, Leeds, West yorkshire, LS27 7YJ W: www.morleyfhg.co.uk
Pontefract and District Family History Society 62 Wheatfield Avenue, Oakes, Huddersfield, West Yorkshire, HD3 4FR W: www.pontefract fhs.co.uk
Wharfedale Family History Group 1 West View Court, Yeadon, Leeds, West Yorkshire, LS19 7HX T: 0113 258 5597 T: 0113 250 7249 E: wfhg@yorksgen.org.uk W: www.wthg.org.uk http://web.onetel.net.uk/~gdlawson/wfhg1.htm

Wakefield & District Family History Society 32 Blenheim Road, Wakefield, West Yorkshire, WF1 3JZ T: 01924 373310 T: 01924 250882 (Membership Secretary) E: secretary@wdfhs.co.uk W: www.wdfhs.co.uk

Isle of Man
Isle of Man Family History Society Pear Tree Cottage, Llhergy Cripperty, Union Mills, Isle of Man, IM4 4NF T: 01624 622188 T: 01624 862088 W: www.isle-of-man.com/interests/genealogy/fhs

Channel Islands
Guernsey
Family History Section of La Société Guernesiaise, PO Box 314, Candie, St Peter Port, Guernsey, GY1 3TG
Jersey
Channel Islands Family History Society P0 Box 507, St Helier, Jersey, JE4 5TN E: cifhs@localdial.com W: www.user.itl.net/~glen/AbouttheChannelIslandsFHS.html

Wales
London Branch of the Welsh Family History Societies, 27 Princes Avenue, Carshalton Beeches, Surrey, SM5 4NZ E: regandpaddy@btinternet.com
Breconshire - see **Powys Family History Society**
Cardiganshire
Cardiganshire Family History Society Adran Casliadau, National library of Wales, Aberystwyth, Ceredigion, SY25 3BU W: www.cardiganshirefhs.org.uk www.cgnfhs.org.uk
Carmarthenshire
Dyfed Family History Society 12 Elder Grove, Llangunnor, Carmarthenshire, SA31 2LG T: 01267 232637 E: secretary@dyfedfhs.org.uk W: www.dyfed.org.uk
Ceredigion - see **Dyfed Family History Society**
Clwyd
Clwyd Family History Society The Laurels, Dolydd Road, Cefn Mawr, Wrexham, LL14 3NH T: 01978 822218 E: secretary@clwydfhs.org.uk W: www.clwydfhs.org.uk Covers the pre 1974 counties of Denbighshire and Flintshire
Denbighshire - see **Clwyd Family History Society**
Flintshire - see **Clwyd Family History Society**
Glamorgan
Glamorgan Family History Society 22 Parc y Bryn, Creigiau, Cardiff, Glamorgan, CF15 9SE E: secretary@glamfhs.org W: www.glamfhs.org, Glamorgan FHS covers the Old County of Glamorgan. Monthly meetings at all six branches. Extensive search facilities available to members. Quarterly journals
Gwent
Gwent Family History Society 11 Rosser Street, Wainfelin, Pontypool, Gwent, NP4 6EA E: secretary@gwentfhs.info W: www.gwentfhs.info
Gwynedd
Gwynedd Family History Society 36 Y Wern, Y Felinheli, Gwynedd, LL56 4TX T: 01248 670267 E: Gwynedd.Roots@tesco.net W: www.gwynedd.fsbusiness.co.uk
Monmouthshire - see **Gwent Family History Society**
Montgomeryshire
Montgomeryshire Genealogical Society Cambrian House, Brimmon Lane, Newtown, Powys, SY16 1BY T: 01686 624753 W: home.freeuk.net/montgensoc
Pembrokeshire - see **Dyfed Family History Society**
Powys
Powys Family History Society Waterloo Cottage, The Vineyards, Llandeilo Graban, Builth Wells, Powys, LD2 3SJ E: rspearson@breathemail.com W: www.rootsweb.com/~wlspfhs/faq/, Credit card facilities via secure server at GENfair for membership, services and publications
Radnorshire - see **Powys Family History Society**

Scotland
Scottish Genealogy Society 15 Victoria Terrace, Edinburgh, EH1 2JL T: 0131-220-3677 T: 0131-220-3677 E: info@scotsgenealogy.com W: www.scotsgenealogy.com
Aberdeen
Aberdeen & North East Scotland Family History Society 158 - 164 King Street, Aberdeen, AB24 5BD T: 01224 646323 T: 01224 639096 E: enquiries@anefhs.org.uk W: www.anesfhs.org.uk
Angus
Tay Valley Family History Society & Family History Research Centre see Dundee
Argyll - see **Glasgow & West of Scotland Family History Society**
Ayrshire
Alloway & Southern Ayrshire Family History Society c/o Alloway Public Library, Doonholm Road, Alloway, Ayr, Ayrshire, KA7 4QQ E: asafhs@mtcharlesayr.fsnet.co.uk
East Ayrshire Family History Society c/o Dick Institute, Elmbank Avenue, Kilmarnock, East Ayrshire, KA1 3BU E: enquiries@eastayrshirefhs.org.uk W: www.eastayrshirefhs.org.uk

Glasgow & West of Scotland Family History Society see Glasgow
Largs & North Ayrshire Family History Society Bogriggs Cottage, Carlung, West Kilbride, Ayrshire, KA23 9PS T: 01294 823690 W: www.freeyellow.com/members7/lnafhs/index.html
Troon @ Ayrshire Family History Society c/o M.E.R.C., Troon Public Library, South Beach, Troon, Ayrshire, KA10 6EF E: info@troonayrshirefhs.org.uk W: www.troonayrshirefhs.org.uk
South West Scotland Local/Family History Maybole Historical Society 15F Campbell Court, Ayr, Ayrshire, KA8 0SE T: 07776 445033 E: maybole@scotsfamilies.co.uk W: www.maybole.org Family History Room at Old Gala House, Galashiels.
Berwickshire / Borders
Borders Family History Society 2 Fellowhills, Ladykirk, TD15 1XN T: 01289 382060 E: hloughAukonline.co.uk
Bute - see Glasgow
Caithness
Caithness Family History Society Mill Cottage, Corsback, Dunnet, Caithness, KW1 48XQ E: a.e.lewis@btinternet.com W: www.caithnessfhs.org.uk
Central Scotland
Central Scotland Family History Society 11 Springbank Gardens, Dunblane, Perthshire, FK15 9JX T: 01786 823937 E: margaret.turner@tesco.net W: www.csfhs.org.uk
Dumfries
Dumfries & Galloway Family History Society Family History Research Centre, 9 Glasgow Street, Dumfries, DG2 9AF T: 01387-248093 E: shop@dgfhs.org.uk W: www.dgfhs.org.uk
Dunbartonshire - see Glasgow
Dundee
Tay Valley Family History Society & Family History Research Centre Family History Research Centre, 179–181 Princes Street, Dundee, DD4 6DQ T: 01382-461845 T: 01382 455532 E: tvfhs@tayvalleyfhs.org.uk W: www.tayvalleyfhs.org.uk
Edinburgh
Lothians Family History Society c/o Lasswade High School Centre, Eskdale Drive, Bonnyrigg, Midlothian, EH19 2LA T: 0131 660 1933 T: 0131 663 6634 E: lothiansfhs@hotmail.com W: www.lothiansfhs.org.uk
Scottish Genealogy Society 15 Victoria Terrace, Edinburgh, EH1 2JL T: 0131-220-3677 T: 0131-220-3677 E: info@scotsgenealogy.com W: www.scotsgenealogy.com
Fife
Fife Family History Society Glenmoriston, Duric Street, Leven, Fife, KY8 4HF T: 01333 425321 E: fife@ffhoc.freeserve.co.uk W: www.fifefhs.pwp.bluyonder.co.uk
Tay Valley Family History Society & Family History Research Centre
Glasgow
Glasgow & West of Scotland Family History Society Unit 5, 22 Mansfield Street, Partick, Glasgow, G11 5QP T: 0141-339-8303 W: www.gwsfhs.org.uk
Highland/Invernesshire
Highland Family History Society c/o Reference Room, Inverness Public Library, Farraline Park, Inverness, IV1 1NH
Kinross-shire - **Tay Valley Family History Society & Family History Research Centre**
Lanarkshire
Lanarkshire Family History Society Local History Lab, Motherwell Heritage Centre, 1 High Road, Motherwell, Lanarkshire, ML1 3HU
Lothian
Lothians Family History Society c/o Lasswade High School Centre, Eskdale Drive, Bonnyrigg, Midlothian, EH19 2LA T: 0131 660 1933 T: 0131 663 6634 E: lothiansfhs@hotmail.com W: www.lothiansfhs.org.uk
Midlothian - see Lothian
North East Scotland - see Aberdeen
Orkney
Orkney Family History Society Community Room, The Strynd, Kirkwall, Orkney, KW15 1HG T: 01856 761582 (Home) E: olaf.mooney@virgin.net W: www.orkneyfhs.co.uk
Peebleshire - see Borders Family History Society
Perthshire - see Tay Valley Family History Society
Refrewshire - Glasgow & West of Scotland Family History Society
Renfrewshire Family History Society c/o Museum and Art Galleries, High Street, Paisley, Renfrewshire, PA1 2BA W: www.renfrewshire.org.uk
Roxburghshire - see Borders Family History Society
Selkirkshire - see Borders Family History Society
Shetland
Shetland Family History Society 6 Hillhead, Lerwick, Shetland, ZE1 0EJ E: secretary@shetland-fhs.org.uk W: www.shetland-fhs.org.uk
Stirlingshire - see Central Scotland and Glasgow

Northern Ireland

Irish Heritage Association A.204 Portview, 310 Newtownards Road, Belfast, BT4 1HE T: (028) 90455325

North of Ireland Family History Society c/o Graduate School of Education, 69 University Street, Belfast, BT7 1HL E: R.Sibbett@tesco.net W: www.nifhs.org

Ulster Historical Foundation Balmoral Buildings, 12 College Square East, Belfast, BT1 6DD T: (028) 9033 2288, 028 9023 9885 E: enquiry@uhf.org.uk W: www.uhf.org.uk www.ancestryireland.com

Ireland

Council of Irish Genealogical Organisations, 186 Ashcroft, Raheny, Dublin 5

Ballinteer FHS, 29 The View, Woodpark, Ballinteer, Dundrum, Dublin, 16 T: 01-298-8082, Mobile: 086 8120463 E: ryanct@eircom.net Annual publication - 'Gateway to the Past' Membership 12.00

Cork Genealogical Society c/o 4 Evergreen Villas, Evergreen Road, Cork City, Co Cork T: 086 8198359 E: micaconl@eircon.ie W: http://homepage.eircon.net/~adcolemen

Flannery Clan / Clann Fhlannabhra, 81 Woodford Drive, Clondakin, Dublin, 22 E: oflannery@eircom.net W: www.flanneryclan.ie

Genealogical Society of Ireland, 11 Desmond Avenue, Dun Laoghaire, Co Dublin T: 353 1 284 2711 E: GenSocIreland@iol.ie W: www.gensocireland.org

Irish Ancestry Group Clayton House, 59 Piccadilly, Manchester, M1 2AQ T: 0161-236-9750 T: 0161-237-3512 E: office@mlfhs.org.uk W: www.mlfhs.org.uk A specialist group of Manchester and Lancashire Family History Society

Irish Family History Society P0 Box 36, Naas, Co Kildare E: ifhs@eircom.net W: http://homepage.eircom.net/~ifhs/

Wicklow County Genealogical Society 1 Summerhill, Wicklow Town, Co Wicklow

Irish Genealogical Research Society 18 Stratford Avenue, Rainham, Gillingham, Kent, ME8 0EP E: info@igrsoc.org W: www.igrsoc.org, **Raheny Heritage Society** 68 Raheny Park, Raheny, Dublin 5, Dublin T: 01 831 4729 E: jussher@softhome.net, Lists of individuals interests supplied on request to Hon Secretary with International Reply Coupo

Wexford Family History Society 24 Parklands, Wexford, Co Wexford T: 053-42273 E: murphyh@tinet.ie

Specialist Family History Societies

Ambleside Oral History Group 1 High Busk, Ambleside, Cumbria, LA22 0AW T: 01539 431070 E: history@amblesideonline.co.uk W: www.aoghistory.f9.co.uk

Anglo-French Family History Society 31 Collingwood Walk, Andover, Hampshire, SP10 1PU W: www.anglo-french-fhs.org

Anglo-German Family History Society 5 Oldbury Grove, Beaconsfield, Buckinghamshire, HP9 2AJ T: 01494 676812 E: gwendolinedavis@aol.com W: www.agfhs.org.uk www.art-science.com/agfhs

Anglo-Italian Family History Society 3 Calais Street, London, SE5 9LP T: 020 7274 7809 E: membership@anglo-italianfhs.org.uk W: www.anglo-italianfhs.org.uk

Anglo-Scottish Family History Society Clayton House, 59 Piccadilly, Manchester, M1 2AQ T: 0161 236 9750 T: 0161 237 3512 E: mlfhs.demon.co.uk A specialist group of Manchester and Lancashire Family History Society

Australian Society of the Lace Makers of Calais Inc, PO Box 946, Batemans Bay, New South Wales, 2536 T: 0244 718168 T: 0244 723421 E: carolynb@acr.net.au

British Ancestors in India Society 2 South Farm Avenue, Harthill, Sheffield, South Yorkshire, S26 7WY T: +44 (0) 1909 774416 T: +44 (0) 1909 774416 E: editorial@indiaman.com W: www.indiaman.com

British Association for Cemeteries in S.Asia, 76 1/2 Chartfield Avenue, London, SW15 6HQ T: (020) 8788-6953 W: www.bacsa.org.uk Records Cemeteries. Published over 40 surveys of cemeteries in Pakistan, India, Bangladesh, Burma, Malaysia, Indonesia, Thailand and Japan

Catholic Family History Society 45 Gates Green Road, West Wickham, Kent, BR4 9DE W: www.catholic-history.org.uk Regular meetings in London, Birmingham, Derwentside & South Lancashire

Cawdor Heritage Group Family & Local History Room, Nairn Museum, Viewfield Drive, Nairn, Nairnshire, IV12 4EE T: 01667 456791 T: 01667 455399 E: manager@nairnmuseum.freeserve.co.uk W: www.nairnmuseum.co.uk Information available on Nairnshire, census returns and Old Parish Registers

Chapels Heritage Society - CAPEL, 2 Sandy Way, Wood Lane, Hawarden, Flintshire, CH5 3JJ T: 01244 531255

Descendants of Convicts Group PO Box 12224, A'Beckett Street, Melbourne 3000, Victoria

Families in British India Society 51 Taylor's Ride, Leighton Buzzard, Bedfordshire, LU7 3JN E: lawrie.butler@talk21.com

Families in British India Society Sentosa, Godolphin Road, Weybridge, Surrey, KT13 0PT E: peter@bailey718.fsnet.co.uk W: www.fibis.org

Genealogical Society of Utah (UK), 185 Penns Lane, Sutton Coldfield, West Midlands, B76 1JU T: 0121 384 2028 T: 0121 384 9929

Heraldry Society PO Box 32, Maidenhead, Berkshire, SL6 3FD T: 0118-932-0210 T: 0118 932 0210 E: heraldry-society@cwcom.net

Historical Medical Equipment Society 8 Albion Mews, Apsley, Hertfordshire, HP3 9QZ E: hmes@antiageing.freeserve.co.uk

Hugenot & Walloon Research Association, Malmaison, Church St, Great Bedwyn, Wiltshire, SN8 3PE

International Police Association - British Section - Genealogy Group Thornholm, Church Lane, South Muskham, Newark, Nottinghamshire, NG23 6EQ T: 01636 676997 E: ipagenuk@thornholm.freeserve.co.uk

International Society for British Genealogy & Family History, P0 Box 3115, Salt Lake City, Utah, 84110-3115 T: 801 272 2178 W: www.homestart.com/isbgfh/

Irish Ancestry Group Clayton House, 59 Piccadilly, Manchester, M1 2AQ T: 0161-236-9750 T: 0161 237 3512 E: office@mlfhs.org.uk W: www.mlfhs.org.uk A specialist group of Manchester and Lancashire Family History Society

Irish Genealogical Research Society 18 Stratford Avenue, Rainham, Gillingham, Kent, ME8 0EP E: info@igrsoc.org W: www.igrsoc.org, The Society has a library of over four thousand books and two and a half thousand manuscripts

Jewish Genealogical Society of Great Britain, 48 Worcester Crescent, Woodford Green, Essex, IG8 0LU T: 020 8504 8013 E: pnking@onetel.net.uk W: www.jgsgb.org.uk

Lancashire Parish Register Society 135 Sandy Lane, Orford, Warrington, Lancashire, WA2 9JB E: tom_obrien@bigfoot.com W: www.genuki.org.uk/big/eng/LAN/lprs

Lighthouse Society of Great Britain, Gravesend Cottage, Gravesend, Torpoint, Cornwall, PL11 2LX E: k.trethewey@btinternet.com W: www.lsgb.co.uk Holds databases of lighthouses and their keepers. SAE required for enquiries

London & North Western Railway Society - Staff History Group 34 Falmouth Close, Nuneaton, Warwickshire, CV11 6GB T: 024 76 381090 T: 024 76 373577 E: nuneazon2000@aol.com W: www.progsol.co.uk/lnwr

North East England Family History Club, 5 Tree Court, Doxford Park, Sunderland, Tyne and Wear, SR3 2HR T: 0191-522-8344

Quaker Family History Society 1 Ormond Crescent, Hampton, Middlesex, TW12 2TJ E: info@qfhs.co.uk W: www.qfhs.co.uk

Railway Ancestors Family History Society Lundy, 31 Tennyson Road, Eastleigh, Hampshire, SO50 9FS T: (023) 8049 7465 T: (023) 8090 0923 Fax: (023) 8049 7465 E: jim@railwayancestors.org.uk W: www.railwayancestors.org.uk

Rolls Royce Family History Society 25 Gisburn Road, Barnoldswick, Colne, Lancashire, BB18 5HB T: 01282 815778 E: ken@ranson.org.uk

Romany & Traveller Family History Society 6 St James Walk, South Chailey, East Sussex, BN8 4BU W: http://website.lineone.net/~rtfhs

Scottish Association of Family History Societies, c/o 9 Glasgow Street, Dumdries, Dumfrieshire, DG2 9AF W: www.safhs.org.uk

Shap Local History Society The Hermitage, Shap, Penrith, Cumbria, CA10 3LY T: 01931 716671 E: liz@kbhshap.freeserve.co.uk

Society for Name Studies in Britain & Ireland, 22 Peel Park Avenue, Clitheroe, Lancashire, BB7 1ET T: 01200-423771 T: 01200-423771

Society of Brushmakers Descendants Family History Society 13 Ashworth Place, Church Langley, Essex, CM17 9PU T: 01279-629392 E: s.b.d@lineone.net W: www.brushmakers.com

Tennyson Society Central Library, Free School Lane, Lincoln, Lincolnshire, LN2 1EZ T: 01522-552862 T: 01522-552858 E: linnet@lincolnshire.gov.uk W: www.tennysonsociety.org.uk

The Clans of Ireland Ltd, 2 Westbourne Terrace, Quinsboro Road, Bray, County Wicklow, Ireland T: 01365-322353 E: theclansofireland@ireland.com

Victorian Military Society PO Box 5837, Newbury, Berkshire, RG14 7FJ T: 01635 48628 E: vmsdan@msn.com W: www.vms.org.uk The leading Society covering military history of all nations and races from 1837 to 1914

One Name Societies

Guild of One Name Studies, 14 Charterhouse Buildings, Goswell Road, London, EC1M 7BA T: 01293-411136 E: guild@one-name.org W: www.one-name.org

Alabaster Society No 1 Manor Farm Cottages, Bradenham, Thetford, Norfolk, IP25 7OE T: 01362-821243 F: Laraine_Hake@compuserve.com W: www.alabaster.org.uk

Alderson Family History Society 13 Spring Grove, Harrogate, North Yorkshire, HG1 2HS

Alderton Family, 16 Woodfield Dr, Gidea Park, Romford RM2 5DH

Allsop Family Group 86 High Street, Loscoe, Heanor, Derbyshire, DE75 7LF

Andy Punshon, 173 Derwent Road, Thatcham, Berkshire, RG79 3UP T: 01635 867448 E: apunshon@vodaphone-corporate.co.uk Researching the Punshon name in NE England and worldwide.

Armstrong Clan Association, Thyme, 7 Riverside Park, Hollows, Canonbie, Dumfriesshire, DG14 0UY T: 013873 71876 E: ted.armclan@aol.com W: www.armstrongclan.info

Badham One Name Society Woodlands Grange, Highwood, Uttoxeter, ST14 8JX E: gamebill@hotmail.com W: www.badham.org

Beresford Family Society 2 Malatia, 78 St Augustines Avenue, South Croydon, Surrey, CR2 6JH T: (020) 8686 3749 T: (020) 8681 3740 E: beresford@atlas.co.uk W: www.beresfordfamilysociety.org.uk

Birkbecks of Westmoreland and Others One Name Study, 330 Dereham Road, Norwich, Norfolk, NR2 4DL E: Seosimhin@btopenworld.com W: www.jgeoghegan.org.uk

Blanchard Family History Society 10 Stainers, Bishop Stortford, Hertfordshire, CM23 4GL W: www.blanshard.org

Bliss Family History Society Old Well Cottage, Washdyke Lane, Fulbeck, Lincolnshire, NG32 3LB T: 01400 279050 E: bliss@one-name.org W: www.members.aol.com/keithbliss/fhs/main.htm

Braund Society 12 Ranelagh Road, Lake, Sandown, Isle of Wight PO36 8NX E: braundsociety@fewiow.freeserve.co.uk

Brooking Family History Society 48 Regent Close, Edgbaston, Birmingham, West Midlands, B5 7PL T: 0121 249 1226 E: marylogan@blueyonder.co.uk W: www.brookingsociety.org.uk

Bunting Society 'Firgrove', Horseshoe Lane, Ash Vale, Surrey, GU12 5LL T: 01252-325644E: firgrove@compuserve.com W: http://freespace.virgin.net/teebee.axmeister/BuntingSociety.htm

Caraher Family History Society 142 Rexford Street, Sistersville, VA 26175

Cave Family History Society 45 Wisbech Road, Thorney, Peterborough, Cambridgeshire, PE6 0SA T: 01733 270881 E: hugh-cave@cave-fhs.org.uk W: www.cave-fhs.org.uk

Clan Davidson Association, Aisling, 67 Shore Road, Kircubbin, Newtownards, Co Down, BT22 2RP T: 028 427-38402 E: clan.davidson@virgin.net

Clan Gregor Society Administrative Office, 2 Braehead, Alloa, Clackmannanshire, FK10 2EW T: 01259 212076 T: 01259 720274 E: clangregor@sol.co.uk W: www.clangregor.com/macgregor

Cobbing Family History Society 89a Petherton Road, London, N5 2QT T: (020) 7226-2657, Covers Cobbing, Cobbin and other variations

Cory Society 3 Bourne Close, Thames Ditton, London, KT7 0EA W: www.corysociety.org.uk

Courtenay Society Powderham Castle, Kenton, Exeter, Devon, EX6 8JQ T: 01626-891554 T: 01626 891367 Fax: 01626 890729 E: courtenay@courtsoc.demon.co.uk W: www.courtenaysociety.org

Dalton Genealogical Society 11 Jordan Close, Leavesden, Watford, Hertfordshire, WD25 7AF T: 01923 661139 E: pam-lynam@lineone.net W: http://members.aol.com/daltongene/index.html

East Family History Soc 45 Wingrove Road, Ealing, London W5 3UP

Entwistle FH Association, 58 Earnsdale Road, Darwin, Lancashire, BB3 1HS W: www.entwistlefamily.org.uk

Family History Soc of Martin PO Box 9, Rosanna, Victoria, 3084

Family History Society of Martin (UK), 63 Higher Coombe Drive, Teignmouth, Devon, TQ14 9NL

Geoghegan/McGeoghegan One Name Study, 330 Dereham Road, Norwich, Norfolk, NR2 4DL E: josi@geoghegan18.fsnet.co.uk W: www.jgeoghegan.org.uk

Hamley, Hambly & Hamlyn F H Soc (International), 59 Eylewood Road, West Norwood, London, SE27 9LZ T: (020) 8670-0683 E: hamley@one-name.org W: www.hhh-fhs.com

Hards Family Society Venusmead, 36 Venus Street, Congresbury, Bristol, BS49 5EZ T: 01934 834780 T: 01934 834780 E: rogerhards-venusmead@breathemail.net W: www.hards.freewire.org.uk

Holdich Family History Society 19 Park Crescent, Elstree, Hertfordshire, WD6 3PT T: (020) 8953 7195 E: apogee.dtaylor@btopenworld.com

International Haskell Family Society 36 Hedley Davis Court, Cherry Orchard Lane, Salisbury, Wiltshire, SP2 7UE T: 01722 332873 T: 01722 410094 E: suzyflip@hotmail.com

International Relf Society Chatsworth House , Sutton Road, Somerton, Somerset, TA11 6QL T: 01458-274015 E: chris.relf@bucklebury.demon.co.uk

Kay Family Association UK 47 Moorway, Poulton le Flyde, Lancashire, FY6 6EX T: 01253 886171

Krans-Buckland Family Association, P0 Box 1025, North Highlands, California, 95660-1025 T: (916) 332 4359 E: jkbfa@worldnet.att.net

Leather Family History Society 134 Holbeck, Great Hollands, Bracknell, Berkshire, RG12 8XG T: 01344 425092 E: s.leather@ic.ac.uk

Lin(d)field One Name Group Southview, Maplehurst, Horsham, West Sussex, RH13 6QY T: 01403 864389 E: lindfield@one-name.org W: www.lindfield.force9.co.uk/long

Mackman Family History Society Chawton Cottage, 22a Long Ridge Lane, Nether Poppleton, York, North Yorkshire, YO26 6LX T: +44 (0)1904 781752 E: mackman@one-name.org

Mayhew Ancestory Research, 28 Windmill Road, West Croydon, Surrey, CR0 2XN

Morbey Family History Group 23 Cowper Crescent, Bengeo, Hertford, Hertfordshire, SG14 3DZ

Morgan Society of England & Wales, 11 Arden Drive, Dorridge, Solihull, West Midlands, B93 8LP T: 01564 774020 T: 01564 774020 E: morgansociety@tesco.net W: http://freepages.genealogy.rootsweb.com/~morgansociety http://homepages.tesco.net/n.morganpublications/morganpu.htm

Moxon Society

Moxon Family Research Trust, 1 Pine Tree Close, Cowes, Isle of wight, PO31 8DX T: 01983 296921 E: john.moxon@virgin.net W: www.moxon.org.uk

Offley Family Society 2 The Green, Codicote, Hitchin Hertfordshire SG4 8UR T: 01438 820006 E: jrrichards@onetel.net.uk W: http://homepages.ntlworld.com/kevin.offley/

Orton Family History Society 25a Longwood Avenue, Bingley, West Yorkshire, BD16 2RX E: derek@beckd.freeserve.co.uk W: www.redflag.co.uk/ortonfhs.htm

Palgrave Society Crossfield House, Dale Road, Stanton, Bury St Edmunds IP31 2DY T: 01359 251050 E: DerekPalgrave@btinternet.com W: www.ffhs.org.uk/members/palgrave.htm,

Penty Family Name Society Kymbelin, 30 Lych Way, Horsell Village, Surrey, GU21 4QG T: 01483 764904 E: pentytree@aol.com,

Percy-Piercy Family History Society 32 Ravensdale Avenue, North Finchley, London, N12 9HT T: 020 8446 0592 E: brian.piercy@which.net

Rix Family Alliance, 4 Acklam Close, Hedon, Hull, HU12 8NA W: www.rix-alliance.co.uk

Rose Family Society - disbanded 1st March 2002

Serman, Surman Family History Society 24 Monks Walk, Bridge Street, Evesham WR11 4SL T: 01386 49967 T: 01386 49967 E: design@johnsermon.demon.co.uk W: www.johnsermon.demon.co.uk,

Silverthorne Family Association, 1 Cambridge Close, Swindon, Wiltshire, SN3 1JQ T: 01793 537103

Society of Cornishes, 1 Maple Close, Tavistock, Devon, PL19 9LL T: 01822 614613 T: 01822 614613 E: cornish@one-name.org W: www.societyofcornishes.org

Sole Society 49 Kennel Ride, North Ascot, Berkshire, SL5 7NJ T: 01344 883700 E: info@sole.org.uk W: www.solesociety.freeserve.co.uk Interest in family names Sole, Saul, Sewell and Solly including spelling variations

Spencer Family, 1303 Azalea Lane, Dekalb, Illinois, 60115

Stendall & Variants One Name Study, PO Box 6417, Sutton in Ashfield, Nottinghamshire, NG17 3LE T: 01623 406870 W: www.genealogy-links.co.uk

Stockdill Family History Society 6 First Avenue, Garston, Watford, WD2 6PZ T: 01923-675292 E: roystock@compuserve.com W: http://ourworld.compuserve.com/homepages/roystock

Swinnerton Society 30 Coleridge Walk, London, NW11 6AT T: (020) 8458-3443 E: roger.swynnerton@whichnet

Talbot Research Organisation, 142 Albemarle Ave, Elson, Gosport PO12 4HY T: 023 92589785 E: mjh.talbot@tinyworld.cor.uk W: www.kiamara.demon.co.uk/index.html

The Goddard Association of Europe, 2 Lowergate Road, Huncoat, Accrington, Lancashire, BB5 6LN T: 01254-235135 E: johnc.goddard@virgin.net W: www.goddard-association.com

The Metcalfe Society 57 Westbourne Avenue, Hull, East Yorkshire, HU5 3HW T: 01482 342516 E: enquiries@metcalfe.org.uk W: www.metcalfe.org.uk

The Stockton Society The Leas, 28 North Road, Builth Wells, Powys, LD2 3BU T: 01982 551667 E: cestrienne@aol.com

Toseland Clan Society 40 Moresdale Lane, Seacroft, Leeds, West Yorkshire, LS14 5SY T: 0113 225 9954

Tyrrell Family History Society 16 The Crescent, Solihull, West Midlands, B91 7PE W: www.tyrrellfhs.org.uk

Watkins Family History Society PO Box 1698, Douglas, Georgia, 31534-1698 T: 912 383 0839 E: watkinsfhs@alltel.net buzzwatk@aol.com W: www.iinet.net.au/~davwat/wfhs/

Witheridge Family History Society 16 Haven Close, Dunster, Minehead, Somerset, TA24 6RW

AUSTRALIA

Australasian Federation of Family History Organisations (AFFHO)PO Box 3012, Weston Creek ACT 2611

Australian Institute of Genealogical Studies PO Box 359, Blackburn, Victoria 3130 E: info@aigs.org.au W: www.aigs.org.au

Society of Australian Genealogists Richmond Villa, 120 Kent Street, Observatory Hill, Sydney 2000 T: 61-02-92473953 Fax: 61-02-92414872 E: socgenes@ozemail.com.au

NEW SOUTH WALES

1788-1820 Pioneer Association PO Box 57, Croydon, New South Wales, 2132 T: (02)-9797-8107

Australian Society of the Lace Makers of Calais Inc
PO Box 946, Batemans Bay, New South Wales, 2536 T:
0244-718168, 0244-723421 E: carolynb@acr.net.au
Bega Valley Genealogical Society Inc
PO Box 19, Pambula, New South Wales, 2549
Berrima District Historical & Family History Society Inc
PO Box 851, Bowral, New South Wales, 2576
Blayney Shire Local & Family History Society Group Inc
c/o The Library, 48 Adelaide Street, Blayney, New South Wales, 2799
E: blayney.library@cww.octec.org.au
Botany Bay Family History Society Inc PO Box 1006, Sutherland,
New South Wales 1499 W: mypage.southernx.com.au/~bbfhs
Broken Hill Family History Group PO Box 779, 75 Pell Street,
Broken Hill, New South Wales, 2880 T: 08-80-881321
Burwood Drummoyne & District Family History Group
c/o Burwood Central Library, 4 Marmaduke Street, Burwood2134
Cape Banks Family History Society PO Box 67, Maroubra, New
South Wales, NSW 2035 E: hazelb@compassnet.com.au W:
www.ozemail.com.au/mhazelb/capebank
Capital Territory Historical & Genealogical Society of Canberra
GPO Box 585, Canberra, ACT 2601
Casino & District Family History Group Inc PO Box 586, Casino,
New South Wales, 2470 E: hughsie@nor.com W:
www.rootsweb/~nswcdfhg
Central Coast FHG Inc PO Box 4090 East Gosford NSW 2250
WWW: centralcoastfhs.org.au
Coffs Harbour Family History Society Inc
PO Box 2057, Coffs Harbour, New South Wales, 2450
Cowra FHG Inc PO Box 495, Cowra, New South Wales, 2794
Deniliquin Family History Group Inc PO Box 144, Multi Arts
Hall, Cressy Street, Deniliquin, New South Wales, 2710 T:
(03)-5881-3980 Fax: (03)-5881-1270
Dubbo & District FHS Inc PO Box 868 Dubbo NSW 2830
F H S of Singleton Inc PO Box 422, Singleton NSW 2330
Fellowship of First Fleeters First Fleet House, 105 Cathedral Street,
Woolloomooloo, New South Wales, 2000 T: (02)-9360-3988
Forbes Family History Group Inc PO Box 574, Forbes, New South
Wales, 2871 T: 0411-095311-(mobile)
Goulburn District Family History Society Inc
PO Box 611, Goulburn, New South Wales, 2580
Griffith Genealogical & Historical Society Inc
PO Box 270, Griffith, New South Wales, 2680
Gwydir Family History Society Inc
PO Box EM61, East Moree 2400 T: (02)-67549235-(President)
Hastings Valley Family History Group Inc
PO Box 1359, Port Macquarie, New South Wales, 2444
Hawkesbury FHG
C/o Hawkesbury City Council Library, Dight Street, Windsor, 2756
Hill End Family History Group Sarnia, Hill End 2850
Hornsbury Kuring-Gai FHS Inc PO Box 680, Hornsby, 2077
Illawarra FHG PO Box 1652 South Coast Mail Centre, Wollongong 2521
Inverell District FHG Inc PO Box 367, Inverells, 2360
Leeton Family History Society PO Box 475, Centre Point, Pine
Avenue, Leeton 2705 T: 02-6955-7199, 02-6953-2301
Little Forest Family History Research Group PO Box 87, 192
Little Forest Road, Milton , 2538 T: 02-4455-4780, 02-4456-4223 E:
cathyd@shoalhaven.net.au W:
www.shoalhaven.net.au/~cathyd/groups.html
Liverpool & District FHS PO Box 830, Liverpool NSW 2170
Maitland FH Circle No PO Box 247, Maitland, New South Wales
2320WWW: www.rootsweb.com/~ausmfhc
Manning Wallamba FHS c/o Greater Taree City Library, Pulteney
Street, Taree, New South Wales, 2430
Milton Ulladulla Genealogical Society Inc PO Box 619, Ulladulla,
New South Wales, 2539 T: 02-4455-4206
Nepean Family History Society PO Box 81, Emu Plains 2750 T:
(02)-47-353-798 E: istack@penrithcity.nsw.gov.au W:
www.penrithcity.nsw.gov.au/nfhs/nfhshome.htm
New South Wales Association of Family History Societies
PO Box 48, Waratah, New South Wales, 2298
Newcastle Family History Society PO Box 189, Adamstown, New
South Wales, 2289
Orange Family History Society PO Box 930, Orange, New South
Wales, 2800
Port Stephens-Tilligerry & Districts FHS PO Box 32, Tanilba Bay,
New South Wales, 2319
Richmond River Historical Society Inc PO Box 467, 165
Molesworth Street, Lismore2480 T: 02-6621-9993
Richmond-Tweed Family History Society PO Box 817, Ballina
2478 E: warmer@nor.com.au
Ryde District Historical Society Inc 770 Victoria Road, Ryde 2112
T: (02)-9807-7137
Scone & Upper Hunter Historical Society Inc PO Box 339,
Kingdon Street, Upper Hunter, Scone 2337 T: 02-654-51218
Shoalhaven Family History Society Inc PO Box 591, Nowra 2541
T: 02-44221253 Fax: 02-44212462 E: jmoorley@shoal.net.au
Snowy Mountains Family History Group PO Box 153, Cooma,
New South Wales, 2630

Wagga Wagga & District Family History Society Inc PO Box 307,
Wagga Wagga, New South Wales, 2650
Wingham FHGPO Box 72, Wingham, New South Wales, 2429
Young & District FHG Inc PO Box 586, Young 2594
Blue Mountains Family History Society
PO Box 97, Springwood, NSW, NSW 2777 Fax: 02-4751-2746
Dubbo & District Family History Society Inc
PO Box 868, Dubbo, NSW, 2830 T: 068-818635
Illawara Family History Group The Secretary, PO Box 1652, South
Coast Mail Centre, Wollongong, NSW, 2521 T: (02)-42622212 W:
www.magna.com.au/~vivienne/ifhg.htm
Lithgow & District Family History Society
PO Box 516, Lithgow, NSW, 2790
NORTHERN TERRITORY
Genealogical Society of the Northern Territory PO Box 37212,
Winnellie, Northern Territory, 0821 T: 08-898-17363
QUEENSLAND
Queensland Family History Society
PO Box 171, Indooroonilly, Brisbane, Oueensland, 4O68
Beaudesert Branch Genealogical Soc of Queensland Inc
PO Box 664, Beaudesert, Queensland, 4285
Bundaberg Genealocical association Inc
PO Box 103, Bundaberg, Queensland, 4670
Burdekin Contact Group Family Hist Assn of N Qld Inc
PO Box 393, Home Hill, Queensland, 4806
Caboolture FH Research Group Inc
PO Box 837, Caboolture, Queensland, 4510
Cairns & District Family History Society Inc
PO Box 5069, Cairns, Queensland, 4870 T: 07-40537113
Central Queensland Family History Asociation
PO Box 8423, Woolloongabba Queensland 4102
Charters Towers & Dalrymple F H Association Inc
PO Box 783, 54 Towers Street, Charters Towers, Queensland, 4820 T:
07-4787-2124
Cooroy Noosa Genealogical & Historical Research Group Inc PO
Box 792, Cooroy, Queensland 4563 E: info@genealogy-noosa.org.au
W: www.genealogy-noosa.org.au
Dalby FHS IncPO Box 962, Dalby, Queensland, 4405
Darling Downs Family History Society
PO Box 2229, Toowoomba, Queensland, 4350
Genealogical Society of Queensland Inc
PO Box 8423, Woolloongabba, Queensland, 4102
Gladstone Branch G.S.Q.
PO Box 1778, Gladstone, Queensland, 4680
Gold Coast & Albert Genealogical Society
PO Box 2763, Southport, Queensland, 4215
Gold Coast Family History Research Group
PO Box 1126, Southport, Gold Coast, Queensland, 4215
Goondiwindi & District Family History Society
PO Box 190, Goondiwindi, Queensland, 4390 T: 0746712156
Fax: 0746713019 E: pcz@bigpond.com
Gympie Ancestral Research Society Inc
PO Box 767, Gympie, Queensland, 4570
Ipswich Genealogical Society Inc.PO Box 323, 1st Floor, Ipswich
Campus Tafe, cnr. Limestone & Ellenborough Streets, Ipswich,
Queensland, 4305 T: (07)-3201-8770
Kingaroy Family History Centre
PO Box 629, James Street, Kingaroy, Queensland, 4610
Mackay Branch Genealogical Society of Queensland Inc
PO Box 882, Mackay, Queensland, 4740 T: (07)-49426266
Maryborough District Family History Society
PO Box 408, Maryborough, Queensland, 4650
Mount Isa FHS IncPO Box 1832, Mount Isa, Queensland, 4825 E:
krp8@+opend.com.au
North Brisbane Branch - Genealogical Soc of Queensland Inc
PO Box 353, Chermside South, Queensland, 4032
Queensland FHS Inc
PO Box 171, Indooroophilly, Queensland, 4068
Rockhampton Genealogical Society of Queensland Inc
PO Box 992, Rockhampton, Queensland, 4700
Roma & District Local & Family History Society
PO Box 877, Roma, Queensland, 4455
South Burnett Genealogical & Family History Society
PO Box 598, Kingaroy, Queensland, 4610
Southern Suburbs Branch - G.S.Q. Inc
PO Box 844, Mount Gravatt, Queensland, 4122
Sunshine Coast Historical & Genealogical Resource Centre Inc
PO Box 1051, Nambour, Queensland, 4560
Toowoomba Family History Centre c/o South Town Post Office,
South Street, Toowoomba, Queensland, 4350 T: 0746-355895
Townsville - Fam Hist Assoc of North Queensland Inc
PO Box 6120, Townsville M.C., Queensland, 4810
Whitsunday Branch - Genealogical Soc of Queensland Inc
PO Box 15, Prosperpine, Queensland, 4800
SOUTH AUSTRALIA
Fleirieu Peninsula FHG Inc Oarlunga Library, PO Box 411,
Noarlunga Centre South Australia 5168 E:
fleurpengroup@yahoo.co.uk W: www.rootsweb.com/~safpfhg

South Australian Genealogical & Heraldic SocietyGPO Box 592, Adelaide 5001 T: (08)-8272-4222 Fax: (08)-8272-4910 E: saghs@dove.net.au W: www.chariot.net.au/~saghs
South East FHG Inc PO Box 758, Millicent, South Australia, 5280
Southern Eyre Peninsula FHG
26 Cranston Street, Port Lincoln 5606
Whyalla FHG
PO Box 2190, Whyalla Norrie, South Australia, 5608
Yorke Peninsula Family History Group - 1st Branch SAGHS
PO Box 260, Kadina, South Australia, 5554
TASMANIA
Tasmanian FHS (Launceston Branch) PO Box 1290, Launceston, Tasmania 7250 Email; secretary@tasfhs.org W: www.tasfhs.org
Tasmanian FHS Inc PO Box 191, Launceston, Tasmania 7250 W: www.tasfhs.org
VICTORIA
Ararat Genealogical Society inc PO Box 361, Ararat, Victoria, 3377
Australian Institute of Genealogical Studies PO Box 339, Blackburn, Victoria, 3130 E: aigs@alphalink.com.all W: www.alphalink.com.au/~aigs/index.htm
Benalla & District Family History Group Inc PO Box 268, St Andrews Church Hall, Church Street, Benalla, Victoria, 3672 T: (03)-57-644258
Bendigo Regional Genealogical Society Inc
PO Box 1049, Bendigo, Victoria, 3552
Cobram Genealogical Group PO Box 75, Cobram, Victoria, 3643
East Gippsland Family History Group Inc
PO Box 1104, Bairnsdale, Victoria, 3875
Echuca/Moama Family History Group Inc
PO Box 707, Echuca, Victoria, 3564
Emerald Genealogy Group
62 Monbulk Road, Emerald, Victoria, 3782
Euroa Genealogical Group 43 Anderson Street, Euroa, Victoria, 3666
First Fleet Fellowship Victoria Inc Cnr Phayer & Barnet Streets, South Melbourne, Victoria, 3205
Geelong Family History Group Inc PO Box 1187, Geelong, 3220 E: flw@deakin.edu.au W: www.home.vicnet.net.au/wgfamhist/index.htm
Genealogical Society of Victoria Ancestor House, 179 Queen Street, Melbourne, Victoria, 3000 T: +61-3-9670-7033 Fax: +61-3-9670-4490 E: gsv@gsv.org.au W: www.gsv.org.au
Hamilton Family & Local History Group PO Box 816, Hamilton, Victoria, 3300 T: 61-3-55-724933 Fax: 61-3-55 724933 E: ham19.@mail.vicnet.net.au W: www.freenet.com.au/hamilton
Italian Historical Society 185 Faraday Street, Carlton 3053
Kerang & District Family History Group
PO Box 325, Kerang, Victoria, 3579
Mid Gippsland FHS Inc PO Box 767, Morwell, Victoria, 3840
Mildura & District Genealogical Society Inc
PO Box 2895, Mildura, Victoria, 3502
Narre Warren & District FHG PO Box 149, Narre Warren, Victoria, 3805 W: www.ozemail.com.au/~narre/fam-hist.html
Nathalia Genealogical Group Inc
R.M.B. 1003, Picola, Victoria, 3639
Port Genealogical Society of Victoria Inc
PO Box 1070, Warrambool, Victoria, 3280 E: joyceaustin@start.co.au
Sale & District Family History Group Inc
PO Box 773, Sale, Victoria, 3850
Stawell Biarri Group for Genealogy Inc
PO Box 417, Stawell, Victoria, 3380
Swam Hill Genealogical & Historical Society Inc
PO Box 1232, Swan Hill, Victoria, 3585
Toora & District FHG Inc PO Box 41, Toora, Victoria, 3962
Wangaratta Gen Soc Inc PO Box 683, Wangaratta, Victoria, 3676
West Gippsland Genealogical Society Inc PO Box 225, Old Shire Hall, Queen Street, Warragul, Victoria, 3820 T: 03-56252743 E: watts@dcsi.net.au W: www.vicnet.net.au/~wggs/
Wimmera Assoc for Genealogy PO Box 880, Horsham Victoria, 3402
Wodonga FHS Inc PO Box 289, Wodonga, Victoria, 3689
Yarram Genealogical Group Inc
PO Box 42, 161 Commercial Road, Yarram, Victoria, 3971
WESTERN AUSTRALIA
Australasian Federation of FH Orgs Inc 6/48 May Street, Bayswater, WA 6053 W: www.affho.org
Geraldton FHS PO Box 2502, Geralton 6531, Western Australia W: www.com.au/gol/genealogy/gfhs/gfhsmain.htm
Goldfields Branch West Australian Genealogical Society Inc
PO Box 1462, Kalgoorlie, Western Australia, 6430
Melville Family History Centre PO Box 108 (Rear of Church of Jesus Christ Latter Day Saints, 308 Preston Point Road, Attadale, Melville, Western Australia, 6156
Western Australia Genealogical Society Inc 6/48 May St Bayswater, WA 6053 T: 08-9271-4311 F: 08-9271-4311 E: wags@cleo.murdoch.edu.au W: www.cleo.murdoch.edu.au/~wags

NEW ZEALAND
Bishopdale Branch NZ Society of Genealogists Inc.
c/o 19a Resolution Place, Christchurch, 8005 T: 03 351 0625
Cromwell Family History Group
3 Porcell Court, Cromwell, 9191
Fairlie Genealogy Group
c/o 38 Gray Street, Fairlie, 8771
General Research Institute of New Zealand
PO Box 12531, Thorndon, Wellington, 6038
Hawkes Bay Branch NZ Society of Genealogists Inc.
P O Box 7375, Taradale, Hawkes Bay
Kapiti Branch NZ Society of Genealogists Inc.
P O Box 6, Paraparaumu, Kapiti Coast, 6450
Mercury Bay Branch NZ Society of Genealogists Inc.
31 Catherine Crescent, Whitianga, 2856 T: 0 7 866 2355
Morrinsville Branch NZ Society of Genealogists Inc.
1 David St., Morrinsville, 2251
N.Z. Fencible Society
P O Box 8415, Symonds Street, Auckland, 1003
New Zealand Family History Society
P O Box13,301, Armagh, Christchurch T: 03 352 4506 E: ranz@xtra.co.nz
New Zealand Family History Society Inc
PO Box 13301, Armagh, Christchurch E: ranz@extra.co.nz
New Zealand Society of Genealogists Inc
PO Box 8795, Symonds Street, AUCKLAND, 1035 T: 09-525—0625 Fax: 09-525-0620
Northern Wairoa Branch NZ Society of Genealogists Inc.
60 Gordon Street, Dargaville, 300
NZ Society of Genealogists Inc. - Alexandra Branch
21 Gregg Street, Alexandra, 9181
Palmerston North Genealogy Group
P O Box 1992, Palmerston North, 5301
Panmure Branch NZ Society of Genealogists Inc.
29 Mirrabooka Ave, Howick, Auckland, 1705
Papakura Branch NZ Society of Genealogists Inc.
P O Box 993, Papakura, Auckland
Polish Genealogical Society of New Zealand
Box 88, Urenui, Taranaki T: 06 754 4551 E: pgs.newzealand@clear.net.nz
Rotorua Branch NZ Society of Genealogists Inc.
17 Sophia Street, Rotorua, 3201 T: 0 7 347 9122
Scottish Interest Group NZ Society of Genealogists Inc.
P O Box 8164, Symonds Street, Auckland, 1003
South Canterbury Branch NZ Society of Genealogists Inc.
9 Burnett Street, Timaru, 8601
Tairua Branch NZ Society of Genealogists Inc.
c/o 10 Pepe Road, Tairua, 2853
Te Awamutu Branch NZ Society of Genealogists Inc.
Hairini, RD1, Te Awamutu, 2400
Te Puke Branch NZ Society of Genealogists Inc.
20 Valley Road, Te Puke, 3071
Waimate Branch NZ Society of Genealogists Inc.
4 Saul Shrives Place, Waimate, 8791
Wairarapa Branch NZ Society of Genealogists Inc.
34 Rugby Street, Masterton, 5901
Whakatane Branch NZ Society of Genealogists Inc.
P O Box 203, Whakatane, 3080
Whangamata Genealogy Group
116 Hetherington Road, Whangamata, 3062
Whangarei Branch NZ Society of Genealogists Inc.
P O Box 758, Whangarei, 115 T: 09 434 6508

SOUTH AFRICA
Genealogical Institute of South Africa 115 Banheok Road, Stellenbosch, Western Cape, South Africa T: 021-887-5070 E: GISA@RENET.SUN.AC.ZA
Genealogical Society of South Africa
Suite 143, Postnet X2600, Houghton, 2041, South Africa
Human Sciences Research Council Genealogy Information, HSRC Library & Information Service, Private Bag X41, Pretoria 0001, South Africa T: (012)-302-2636 Fax: (012)-302-2933 E: ig@legii.hsrc.ac.za
West Rand Family History Society
The Secretary, PO Box 760, Florida 1710, South Africa

ZIMBABWE
Heraldry & Genealogy Society of Zimbabwe
Harare Branch, 8 Renfrew Road, Eastlea, Harare, Zimbabwe

NORTH AMERICA
CANADA
ALBERTA
Alberta Family Histories Society
PO Box 30270, Station B, Calgary, Alberta, T2M 4P1

Alberta Genealogical Society (Edmonton Branch)
Room 116, Prince of Wales Armouries, 10440-108 Avenue,
Edmonton, Alberta, T5H 3Z9 T: (403)-424-4429
Fax: (403)-423-8980 E: agsedm@compusmart.ab.ca W:
www.compusmart.ab.ca/abgensoc/branches.html
Alberta Genealogical Society Drayton Valley Branch
PO Box 6358, Drayton Valley, Alberta, T7A 1R8 T: 403-542-2787 E:
c_or_c@telusplanet.net
Alberta Genealogical Society Fort McMurray Branch
PO Box 6253, Fort McMurray, Alberta, T9H 4W1
Alberta Gene Soc Grande Prairie & District Branch
PO Box 1257, Grande Prairie, Alberta, T8V 4Z1
Alberta Gen Society Medicine Hat & District Branch
PO Box 971, Medicine Hat, Alberta, T1A 7G8
Alberta Gen Society Red Deer & District Branch
PO Box 922, Red Deer, Alberta, T4N 5H3 E: evwes@telusplanet.net
Brooks & District Branch Alberta Genealogical Society
PO Box 1538, Brooks, Alberta, T1R 1C4
Ukrainian Genealogical & Historical Society of Canada
R.R.2, Cochrane, Alberta, T0L 0W0 T: (403)-932-6811
BRITISH COLUMBIA
British Columbia Genealogical Society
PO Box 88054, Lansdowne Mall, Richmond V6X 3T6
Campbell River Genealogy Club
PO Box 884, Campbell River, British Columbia, V9W 6Y4 E:
rcase@connected.bc.ca W: www.connected.bc.ca/~genealogy/
Comox Valley Family History Research Group
c/o Courtenay & District Museum & Archives, 360 Cliffe Street,
Courtenay, British Columbia, V9N 2H9
Kamloops Genealogical Society
Box 1162, Kamloops, British Columbia, V2C 6H3
Kelowna & District Genealogical Society
PO Box 501, Station A, Kelowna, British Columbia, V1Y 7P1 T:
1-250-763-7159 E: doug.ablett@bc.sympatico.ca
Nanaimo FHS PO Box 1027, Nanaimo, British Columbia, V9R 5Z2
Port Alberni Genealogy Club
Site 322, Comp. 6, R.R.3, Port Alberni V9Y 7L7
Powell River Gen Club PO Box 446, Powell RiverBC V8A 5C2
Prince George Genealogical Society
PO Box 1056, Prince George, British Columbia, V2L 4V2
Revelstoke Genealogy Group
PO Box 2613, Revelstoke, British Columbia, V0E 2S0
Shuswap Lake Genealogical Society
R.R.1, Site 4, Com 4, Sorrento, British Columbia, V0E 2W0
South Okanagan Genealogical Society
c/o Museum, 785 Main Street, Penticton V2A 5E3
Vernon & District FHS PO Box 1447, Vernon V1T 6N7
Victoria Gen Soc PO Box 45031, Mayfair Place, Victoria V8Z 7G9
MANITOBA
Canadian Federation of Gen & Family History Societies
227 Parkville Bay, Winnipeg, Manitoba, R2M 2J6 W:
www.geocities.com/athens/troy/2274/index.html
East European Genealogical Society
PO Box 2536, Winnipeg, Manitoba, R3C 4A7
La Societe Historique de Saint Boniface
220 Ave de la Cathedral, Saint Boniface, Manitoba, R2H 0H7
Manitoba Genealogical Society
Unit A, 1045 St James Street, Winnipeg, Manitoba, R3H 1BI
South West Branch of Manitoba Genealogical Society
53 Almond Crescent, Brandon, Manitoba, R7B 1A2 T: 204-728-2857
E: mla@access.tkm.mb.ca
Winnipeg Branch of Manitoba Genealogical Society
PO Box 1244, Winnipeg, Manitoba, R3C 2Y4
NEW BRUNSWICK
Centre d'Etudes Acadiennes
Universite de Moncton, Moncton, New Brunswick, E1A 3E9
New Brunswick Genealogical Society
PO Box 3235, Station B, Fredericton E3A 5G9
NEWFOUNDLAND & LABRADOR
Newfoundland & Labrador Genealogical Society
Colonial Building, Military Road, St John's A1C 2C9
NOVA SCOTIA
Archelaus Smith Historical Society
PO Box 291, Clarks Harbour, Nova Scotia, B0W 1P0 E:
timkins@atcon.com
Cape Breton Genealogical Society
PO Box 53, Sydney, Nova Scotia, B1P 6G9
Genealogical Association of Nova Scotia
PO Box 641, Station Central, Halifax, Nova Scotia, B3J 2T3
Queens County Historical Society
PO Box 1078, Liverpool, Nova Scotia, B0T 1K0
Shelburne County Genealogical Society
PO Box 248 Town Hall, 168 Water St, Shelburne B0T 1W0
ONTARIO
British Isles Family History Society of Greater Ottawa
Box 38026, Ottawa, K2C 1N0
Bruce & Grey Branch - Ontario Genealogical Society
PO Box 66, Owen Sound, Ontario, N4K 5P1

Bruce County Genealogical Society
PO Box 1083, Port Elgin, Ontario, N0H 2C0
Elgin County Branch Ontario Genealogical Society
PO Box 20060, St Thomas, Ontario, N5P 4H4
Essex County Branch Ontario Genealogical Society
PO Box 2, Station A, Windsor, Ontario, N9A 6J5
Haliburton Highlands Genealogy Group Box 834, Minden, Ontario
K0M2K0 tel; (705) 286-3154 Emai: hhggroup@hotmail.com
Halton-Peel Branch Ontario Genealogical Society PO Box 70030,
2441 Lakeshore Road West, Oakville, Ontario, L6L 6M9 E:
jwatt@ica.net W: www.hhpl.on.c9/sigs/ogshp/ogshp.htm
Hamilton Branch Ontario Genealogical Society
PO Box 904, LCD 1, Hamilton, Ontario, L8N 3P6
Huron County Branch Ontario Genealogical Society
PO Box 469, Goderich, Ontario, N7A 4C7
Jewish Genealogical Society of Canada
PO Box 446, Station A, Willowdale, Ontario, M2N 5T1 E:
henry_wellisch@tvo.org
Kawartha Branch Ontario Genealogical Society
PO Box 861, Peterborough, Ontario, K9J 7AZ
Kent County Branch Ontario Genealogical Society
PO Box 964, Chatham, Ontario, N7M 5L3
Kingston Branch Ontario Genealogical Society
PO Box 1394, Kingston, Ontario, K7L 5C6
Lambton County Branch Ontario Genealogical Society
PO Box 2857, Sarnia, Ontario, N7T 7W1
Lanark County Genealogical Society
PO Box 512, Perth, Ontario, K7H 3K4 E: gjbyron@magma.ca W:
www.globalgenealogy.com/LCGs
Marilyn Adams Genealogical Research Centre
PO Box 35, Ameliasburgh, Ontario, K0K 1A0 T: 613-967-6291
Niagara Peninsula Branch Ontario Genealogical Society
PO Box 2224, St Catharines, Ontario, L2R 7R8
Nipissing District Branch Ontario Genealogical Society
PO Box 93, North Bay, Ontario, P1B 8G8
Norfolk County Branch Ontario Genealogical Society
PO Box 145, Delhi, Ontario, N4B 2W9 E:
oxford.net/~mihaley/ogsnb/main.htm
Nor-West Genealogy & History Society
PO Box 35, Vermilion Bay, Ontario, P0V 2V0 T: 807-227-5293
Norwich & District Historical Society
C/o Archives, R.R. #3, Norwich, Ontario, N0J 1P0 T: (519)-863-3638
Ontario Genealogical Society
Suite 102, 40 Orchard View Boulevard, Toronto, Ontario, M4R 1B9
W: www.ogs.on.ca
Ontario Genealogical Society (Toronto Branch)
Box 513, Station Z, Toronto, Ontario, M4P 2GP
Ottawa Branch Ontario Genealogical Society
PO Box 8346, Ottawa, Ontario, K1G 3H8
Perth County Branch Ontario Genealogical Society
PO Box 9, Stratford, Ontario, N5A 6S8 T: 519-273-0399
Simcoe County Branch Ontario Genealogical Society
PO Box 892, Barrie, Ontario, L4M 4Y6
Sioux Lookout Genealogical Club
PO Box 1561, Sioux Lookout, Ontario, P8T 1C3
Societe Franco-Ontarienne DHistoire et de Genealogie
C.P.720, succursale B, Ottawa, Ontario, K1P 5P8
Stormont Dundas & Glengarry Genealogical Society
PO Box 1522, Cornwall, Ontario, K6H 5V5
Sudbury District Branch Ontario Genealogical Society
c/o Sudbury Public Library, 74 MacKenzie Street, Sudbury, Ontario,
P3C 4X8 T: (705)-674-9991 E: fredie@isys.ca
Thunder Bay District Branch Ontario Genealogical Soc
PO Box 10373, Thunder Bay, Ontario, P7B 6T8
Upper Ottawa Genealogical Group
PO Box 972, Pembroke, Ontario, K8A 7M5
Waterdown East Flamborough Heritage Society
PO Box 1044, Waterdown, Ontario, L0R 2H0 T: 905-689-4074
Waterloo-Wellington Branch Ontario Genealogical Soc 153
Frederick Street, Ste 102, Kitchener, Ontario, N2H 2M2 E:
lestrome@library.uwaterloo.ca
WWW: www.dos.iwaterloo.ca/~marj/genealogy/ww.html
West Elgin Genealogical & Historical Society
22552 Talbot Line, R.R.#3, Rodney, Ontario, N0L 2C0
Whitby - Oshawa Branch Ontario Genealogical Society
PO Box 174, Whitby, Ontario, L1N 5S1
QUEBEC
Brome County Historical Society
PO Box 690, 130 Lakeside, Knowlton, Quebec, J0E 1V0 T:
450-243-6782
Federation Quebecoise des Societies de Genealogie
C.P. 9454, Sainte Foy, Quebec, G1V 4B8
Les Patriotes Inc
105 Prince, Sorel, Quebec, J3P 4J9
Missisquoi Historical Society
PO Box 186, Stanbridge East, Quebec, J0J 2H0 T: (450)-248-3153 E:
sochm@globetrotter.com

Quebec Family History Society
PO Box 1026, Postal Station, Pointe Claire, Quebec, H9S 4H9
Societ de Genealogie de la Maurice et des Bois Francs
C.P. 901, Trois Rivieres, Quebec, G9A 5K2
Societe de Conservation du Patrimoine de St Fracois de la Riviere du Sud C P 306, 534 Boul St Francois Ouest, St Francois, Quebec, G0R 3A0
Societe de Genealogie de Drummondville
545 des Ecoles, Drummondville, Quebec, J2B 8P3
Societe de Genealogie de Quebec
C.P. 9066, Sainte Foy, Quebec, G1V 4A8
Societe de Genealogie des Laurentides
C.P. 131, 185 Rue Du Palais, St Jerome, Quebec, J7Z 5T7 T: (450)-438-8158
WWW: www.societe-genalogie-laurentides.gc.ca
Societe de Genealogie et d'Histoire de Chetford Mines
671 boul. Smith Sud, Thetford Mines, Quebec, G6G 1N1
Societe d'Histoire d'Amos
222 1ere Avenue Est, Amos, Quebec, J9T 1H3
Societe d'Histoire et d'Archeologie des Monts
C.P. 1192, 675 Chemin du Roy, Sainte Anne des Monts, Quebec, G0E 2G0
Societe d'Histoire et de Genealogie de Matane
145 Soucy, Matane, Quebec, G4W 2E1
Societe d'Histoire et de Genealogie de Riviere du Loup
300 rue St Pierre, Riviere du Loup, Quebec, G5R 3V3 T: (418)-867-4245 E: shgrd@icrdl.net W: www.icrdl.net/shgrdl/index.html
Societe d'Histoire et de Genealogie de Verdun
198 chemin de lAnce, Vaudreuil, Quebec, J7V 8P3
Societe d'histoire et de genealogie du Centre-du-Quebec
34-A, rue Laurier est, Victoriaville, Quebec, G6P 6P7 T: (819)-357-4029 Fax: (819)-357-9668
Email: geneatique@netscape.net W: www.geneatique.qc.ca
Societe d'Histoire et de Genealogie Maria Chapdeleine
1024 Place des Copains, C.P. 201, Dolbeau, Quebec, G8L 3N5
Societe d'Histoire et Genealogie de Salaberry de Valley Field
75 rue St Jean Baptiste, Valleyfield, Quebec, J6T 1Z6
Societe Genealogie d'Argenteuil
378 Principale, Lachute, Quebec, J8H 1Y2
Societe Genealogique Canadienne-Francaise
Case Postale 335, Place d Armes, Montreal, Quebec, H2Y 2H1
Societie de Genealogie de L'Outaouaid Inc
C.P. 2025, Succ. B , Hull, Quebec, J8X 3Z2
SASKATCHEWAN
Saskatchewan Genealogical Society 1870 Lorne Street, Regina, Saskatchewan S4P 3E1
Battleford's Branch S askatchewan Genealogical Society
8925 Gregory Drive, North Battleford, Saskatchewan, S9A 2W6
Central Butte Branch Saskatchewan Genealogical Society
P.O. Box 224, Central Butte, Saskatchewan, S0H 0T0
Grasslands Branch Saskatchewan Genealogical Society
P.O. Box 272, Mankota, Saskatchewan, S0H 2W0 T: 306-264-5149
Grenfell Branch Saskatchewan Genealogical Society
P.O. Box 61, Grenfell, Saskatchewan, S0G 2B0 T: (306)-697-3176
Moose Jaw Branch Saskatchewan Genealogical Society
1037 Henry Street, Moose Jaw, Saskatchewan, S6H 3H3
Pangman Branch Saskatchewan Genealogical Society
P.O. Box 23, Pangman, Saskatchewan, S0C 2C0
Radville Branch Saskatchewan Genealogical Society
P.O. Box 27, Radville, Saskatchewan, S0C 2G0
Regina Branch Saskatchewan Genealogical Society
95 Hammond Road, Regina, Saskatchewan, S4R 3C8
Saskatchewan Genealogical Society
1870 Lorne Street, Regina, Saskatchewan, S4P 3E1
South East Branch Saskatchewan Genealogical Society
P.O. Box 460, Carnduff, Saskatchewan, S0C 0S0
West Central Branch Saskatchewan Genealogical Society
P.O. Box 1147, Eston, Saskatchewan, S0L 1A0
Yorkton Branch Saskatchewan Genealogical Society
28 Dalewood Crescent, Yorkton, Saskatchewan, S3N 2P7
YUKON
Dawson City Museum & Historical Society
P.O. Box 303, Dawson City, Yukon, Y0B 1G0 T: 867-993-5291
Fax: 867-993-5839 E: dcmuseum@yknet.yk.ca

FAMILY HISTORY SOCIETIES - EUROPE
AUSTRIA
Heraldisch-Genealogische Gesellschaft 'Adler'
Universitatsstrasse 6, Wien, A-1096, Austria
BELGIUM
Cercle de Genealogie Juive de Belgique
74 Avenue Stalingrad, Bruxelles, B-1000, Belgium T: 32 0 2 512 19 63 Fax: 32 0 513 48 59 E: mjb<d.dratwa@mjb-jmb.org>
Federation des Associations de Famille
Bruyeres Marion 10, Biez, B-1390, Belgium
Federation Genealogique et Heraldique de Belgique
Avenue Parmentier 117, Bruxelles, B-1150, Belgium

Office Genealogique et Heraldique de Belgique
Avenue C Thielemans 93, Brussels, B-1150, Belgium
CROATIA
Croatian Genealogical Society
2527 San Carlos Ave, San Carlos, CA, 94070, USA
CZECHOSLOVAKIA
Czechoslovak Genealogical Society International
PO Box 16225, St Paul, MN, 55116-0225, USA
DENMARK
Danish Soc. for Local History
Colbjornsensvej 8, Naerum, DK-2850, Denmark
Sammenslutningen af Slaegtshistoriske Foreninger
Klostermarker 13, Aalborg, DK-9000, Denmark E: ulla@silkeborg.bib.dk
Society for Danish Genealogy & Biography
Grysgardsvej 2, Copenhagen NV, DK-2400, Denmark W: www.genealogi.dk
ESTONIA
Estonia Genealogical Society
Sopruse puiestec 214-88, Tallin, EE-0034, Estland
FINLAND
Genealogiska Samfundet i Finland
Fredsgatan 15 B, Helsingfors, SF-00170, Finland
Helsingfors Slaktforskare R.F.
Dragonvagen 10, Helsingfors, FIN-00330, Finland
FRANCE
Amicale des Familles d'alliance Canadiennne-Francaise
BP10, Les Ormes, 86220, France
Amities Genealogiques Bordelaises 2 rue Paul Bert, Bordeaux, Aquitaine, 33000, France T: 05 5644 8199 Fax: 05 5644 8199
Assoc. Genealogique et Historique des Yvelines Nord
Hotel de Ville, Meulan, 78250, France
Association Catalane de Genealogie
BP 1024, Perpignan Cedex, Languedoc Rousillon, 66101,
Association de la Bourgeoisie Ancienne Francaise
74 Avenue Kleber, Paris, 75116, France
Association Genealogique de la Charente
Archives Departementales, 24 avenue Gambctta, Angouleme, Poitou Charentes, 16000, France
Association Genealogique de l'Anjou
75 rue Bressigny, Angers, Pays de la Loire, 49100, France
Association Genealogique de l'Oise
BP 626, Compiegne Cedex, Picardie, 60206, France
Association Genealogique des Bouches-du-Rhone
BP 22, Marseilles Cedex, Provence Alpes Cote d'Azur, 1,
Association Genealogique des Hautes Alpes
Archives Departementales, route de Rambaud, Gap, Provence Alpes Cote d'Azur, 5000, France
Association Genealogique du Pas de Calais
BP 471, Arras Cedex, Nord-Pas de Calais, 62028
Association Genealogique du Pays de Bray
BP 62, Serqueux, Normandie, 76440 Fax: 02 3509 8756
Association Genealogique du Var
BP 1022, Toulon Cedex, Provence Alpes Cote d'Azur, 83051
Association Genealogique Flandre-Hainaut
BP493, Valenciennes Cedex, Nord-Pas de Calais, 59321
Association Recherches Genealogiques Historique d'Auvergne
Maison des Consuls, Place Poly, Clermont Ferrand, Auvergne, 63100
Bibliotheque Genealogique
3 Rue de Turbigo, Paris, 75001, France T: 01 4233 5821
Brive-Genealogie Maison des Associations, 11 place J M Dauaier, Brive, Limousin, 19100, France
Centre de Recherches Genealogiques Flandre-Artois
BP 76, Bailleul, Nord-Pas de Calais, 59270, France
Centre d'Entraide Genealogique de France 3 Rue de Turbigo, Paris, 75001, France T: 33 4041 9909 Fax: 33 4041 9963 E: cegf@usa.net W: www.mygale.org/04cabrigol/cegf/
Centre Departemental d'Histoire des Familles 5 place Saint Leger, Guebwiller, Alsace, 68500, France E: cdhf@telmat-net.fr W: web.telemat-net-fr~cdhf
Centre Entraide Genealogique Franche Comte
35 rue du Polygone, Besancon, Franche Comte, 25000
Centre Genealogique de la Marne
BP 20, Chalons-en-Champagne, Champagne Ardennes, 51005
Centre Genealogique de Savoie
BP1727, Chambery Cedex, Rhone Alpes, 73017, France
Centre Genealogique de Touraine
BP 5951, Tours Cedex, Centre, 37059, France
Centre Genealogique des Cotes d'Armor3bis rue Bel Orient, Saint Brieuc, Bretagne, 22000, France Fax: 02 9662 8900
Centre Genealogique des Landes
Societe de Borda, 27 rue de Cazarde, Dax, Aquitaine, 40100
Centre Genealogique des Pyrenees Atlantique
BP 1115, Pau Cedex, Aquitaine, 64011, France
Centre Genealogique du Perche 9 rue Ville Close, Bellame, Normandie, 61130, France T: 02 3383 3789
Centre Genealogique du Sud Ouest Hotel des Societes Savantes, 1 Place Bardineau, Bordeaux, Aquitaine, 33000, France

Centre Genealogique et Heraldique des Ardennes
Hotel de Ville, Charleville Mezieres, Champagne Ardennes, 8000
Centre Genealogique Protestant
54 rue des Saints-Peres, Paris, 75007, France
Cercle de Genealogie du Calvados Archives Departementales, 61 route de Lion-sur-Mer, Caen, Normandie, 14000, France
Cercle de Genealogie et d'Heraldique de Seine et Marne
BP 113, Melun Cedex, 77002, France
Cercle de Genealogie Juive (Jewish)
14 rue St Lazare, Paris, 75009, France T: 01 4023 0490 Fax: 01 4023 0490 E: cgjgeniefr@aol.com
Cercle d'Etudes Genealogiques et Heraldique d'Ile-de-France
46 Route de Croissy, Le Vesinet, 78110, France
Cercle d'Histoire et Genealogie du Perigord
2 rue Roletrou, Perigueux, Aquitaine, 24000, France
Cercle Genealogique Bull
rue Jean Jaures, BP 53, Les-Clayes-sous-Bois, 78340,
Cercle Genealogique d'Alsace
Archives du Bas-Rhin, 5 rue Fischart, Strasbourg, Alsace, 67000
Cercle Genealogique d'Aunis et Saintonge c/o Mr Provost, 10 ave de Metz, La Rochelle, Poitou Charentes, 17000, France
Cercle Genealogique de la Manche
BP 410, Cherbourg Cedex, Normandie, 50104, France
Cercle Genealogique de la Meurthe et Moselle
4 rue Emile Gentil, Briey, Lorraine, 54150, France
Cercle Genealogique de la Region de Belfort
c/o F Werlen, 4 ave Charles de Gaulle, Valdoie, Franche Comte, 90300
Cercle Genealogique de l'Eure Archives Departementales, 2 rue de Verdun, Evreux Cedex, Normandie, 27025, France
Cercle Genealogique de Saintonge
8 rue Mauny, Saintes, Poitou Charentes, 17100, France
Cercle Genealogique de Vaucluse
Ecole Sixte Isnard, 31 ter Avenue de la Trillade, Avignon, Provence Alpes Cote d'Azur, 84000, France
Cercle Genealogique des Deux-Sevres
26 rue de la Blauderie, Niort, Poitou Charentes, 79000, **Cercle Genealogique des P.T.T.** BP33, Paris Cedex 15, 75721, France
Cercle Genealogique d'Ille-et-Vilaine
6 rue Frederic Mistral, Rennes, Bretagne, 35200 T: 02 9953 6363
Cercle Genealogique du C.E. de la Caisse d'Epargne Ile de France-Paris 19 rue du Louvre, Paris, 75001, France
Cercle Genealogique du Finistere Salle Municipale, rue du Commandant Tissot, Brest, Bretagne, 29000 Fax: 02 9843 0176 E: cgf@eurobretagne.fr W: www.karolus.org/membres/cgf.htm
Cercle Genealogique du Haut-Berry place Martin Luther King, Bourges, Centre, 18000 F: 02 4821 0483 E: cgh-b@wanadoo.fr
Cercle Genealogique du Languedoc 18 rue de la Tannerie, Toulouse, Languedoc Rousillon, 31400, France T: 05 6226 1530
Cercle Genealogique du Loir-et-Cher
11 rue du Bourg Neuf, Blois, Centre, 41000 T: 02 5456 0711
Cercle Genealogique d'Yvetot et du Pays de Caux
Pavillion des Fetes, Yvetot, Normandie, 76190, France
Cercle Genealogique et Historique du Lot et Garonne
13 rue Etienne Marcel, Villeneuve sur Lot, Aquitaine, 47340
Cercle Genealogique Poitevin
22bis rue Arsene Orillard, Poitiiers, Poitou Charentes, 86000
Cercle Genealogique Rouen Seine-Maritime
Archives Departementales, Cours Clemenceau, Normandie, 76101
Cercle Genealogique Saone-et-Loire
115 rue des Cordiers, Macon, Bourgogne, 71000, France
Cercle Genealogique Vendeen Bat.H, 307bis, Cite de la Vigne aux Roses, La Roche-sur-Yon, Pays de la Loire, 85000, France
Cercle Genealogique Versailles et Yvelines Archives Departementales, 1 avenue de Paris, Versailles, 78000, France T: 01 3952 7239 Fax: 01 3952 7239
Cercle Geneologique du Rouergue Archives Departementales, 25 av Victor Hugo, Rodez, Midi-Pyrenees, 12000, France
Club Genealogique Air France CE Air France Roissy Exploitation, BP 10201, Roissy CDG Cedex, 95703, France Fax: 01 4864 3220
Club Genealogique Group IBM France CE IBM St Jean de Braye-Ste Marie, 50-56 ave Pierre Curie, St Jean de Braye Cedex, 45807, France
Confederation Internationale de Genealogie et d'Heraldique
Maison de la Genealogie, 3 rue Turbigo, Paris, F - 75001
Etudes Genealogique Drome-Ardeche
14 rue de la Manutention, Valence, Rhone Alpes, 26000
Federation Francaise de Genealogie 3 Rue de Turbigo, Paris, 75001, France T: 01 4013 0088 F: 01 4013 0089 W: www.karolus.org
France-Louisuane/Franco-Americanie Commission Retrouvailles, Centre CommercialeGatie, 80 avenue du Maine, Paris 75014 Fax: 01 4047 8321 W: www.noconnet.com:80/forms/cajunews.htm
Genealogie Algerie Maroc Tunisie Maison Marechal Alphonse, Juin 28 Av. de Tubingen, Aix en Provence, 13090, France
Genealogie Entraide Recherche en Cote d'Or
97 rue d'Estienne d'Orves, Clarmart, Bourgogne, 92140

Genealogie et Histoire de la Caraibe Pavillion 23, 12 avenue Charles de Gaulle, Le Pecq, Overseas, 78230, France E: ghcaraibe@aol.com W: //members.aol.com/ghcaraibe
Groupement Genealogique de la Region dy Nord
BP 62, Wambrechies, Nord-Pas de Calais, 59118, France
Groupement Genealogique du Havre et de Seine Maritime
BP 80, Le Havre Cedex, Normandie, 76050 T: 02 3522 7633
Institut Francophone de Genealogie et d'Histoire 5 rue de l'Aimable Nanette, le Gabut, La Rochelle, Overseas, 17000 T: 05 4641 9032 Fax: 05 4641 9032
Institut Genealogique de Bourgogne 237 rue Vendome, BP 7076, Lyon, Bourgogne, 69301
Loiret Genealogique BP 9, Orleans Cedex, Centre, 45016, France
Salon Genealogique de Vichy et du Centr48 Boulevard de Sichon, Vichy, Auvergne, 3200, France W: www.genea.com
Section Genealogique de l'Assoc. Artistique-Banque de France
2 rue Chabanais, Paris, 75002, France
Societe Genealogique du Bas-Berr Maison des Associations, 30 Espace Mendez France, Chateauroux, Centre, 36000, France
Societe Genealogique du Lyonnais
7 rue Major Martin, Lyon, Rhone Alpes, 69001, France
GERMANY
Arbeirkreis fur Familienforschung e.V Muhlentorturm, Muhlentortplatz 2, Lubeck, Schleswig-Holstein, D - 23552, Germany
Bayerischer Landesverein fur Familienkunde Ludwigstrasse 14/1, Munchen, Bayern, D-80539 E: blf@rusch.m.shuttle.de W: www.genealogy.com/gene/reg/BAY/BLF-d.html
Deutsche Zentalstelle fur Genealogie
Schongaver str. 1, Leipzig, D - 04329, Germany
Dusseldorfer Verein fur Familienkunde e.V Krummenweger Strasse 26, Ratingen, Nordrhein Westfalen, D - 40885, Germany
Herold - Verein fur Genealogie Heraldik und Reiwandte Wissen-Scahaften Archiv Str. 12-14, Berlin, D -14195, Germany
Niedersachsischer Gesellschaft fur Familienkunde e.V Stadtarchiv, Am Bokemahle 14 - 16, Hannover, Niedersachsen, D - 30171
Oldenburgische Gesellschaft fur Familienkunde
Lerigauweg 14, Oldenurg, Niedersachsen, D - 26131, Germany
Verein fur Familien-U. Wappenkunde in Wurttemberg und Baden
Postfach 105441, Stuttgart, Baden-Wuerttemberg, D - 70047, Germany
Westdeutsche Gesellschaft fur Familienkunde e.V Sitz Koln Unter Gottes Gnaden 34, Koln-Widdersdorf, Nordrhein Westfalen, D - 50859, Germany T: 49 221 50 48 88
Zentralstelle fur Personnen und Familiengeschichte
Birkenweg 13, Friedrichsdorf, D - 61381, Germany
GREECE
Heraldic-Genealogical Society of Greece
56 3rd Septemvriou Str., Athens, GR - 10433, Greece
HUNGARY
Historical Society of Hungary University of Eoetveos Lorand, Pesti Barnabas utca 1, Budapest, H - 1052, Hungary T: 267 0966
ICELAND
The Genealogical Society
P O Box 829, Reykjavick, 121, Iceland Fax: 354 1 679840
ITALY
Ancetres Italien 3 Rue de Turbigo, Paris, 75001, France T: 01 4664 2722 W: //members.aol.com/geneaita/
NETHERLANDS
Centraal Bureau voor Genealogie P O Box 11755, The Hague, NL - 2502 AT T: 070 315 0500 F: 070 347 8394 W: www.cbg.nl
Central Bureau Voor Genealogie PO Box 11755, 2502, The Hague, **Koninklijk Nederlandsch Genootschap voor Geslacht-en Wapen-Kunde**P O Box 85630, Den Haag, 2508 CH, Netherlands
Nederlandse Genealogische Vereniging Postbus 976, Amsterdam, NL - 1000 AZ, Netherlands E: info@ngu.nl W: www.ngu.nl
Stichting 'Genealogisch Centrum Zeeland'
Wijnaardstraat, Goes, 4416DA T: 0113 232 895
The Caledonian Society
Zuiderweg 50, Noordwolde, NL 8391 KH T: 0561 431580
NORWAY
Norsk Slektshistorik Forening Sentrum Postboks 59, Oslo, N - 0101, Norway T: 2242 2204 Fax: 2242 2204
POLAND
Polish Genealogical Society of America
984 N. Milwaukee Ave, Chicago, IL, 60622, USA
Polish Genealogical Society of New Zealand Box 88, Urenui, Taranaki, New Zealand T: 06 754 4551 E: pgs.newzealand@clear.net.nz
SLOVAKIA
Slovak GHS At Matica Slovenska
Novomeskeho, 32, 036 52 Martin, Slovakia
SPAIN
Asociacion de Diplomados en Genealogia y Nobilaria
Alcala 20, 2 Piso, Madrid, 28014 T: 34 522 3822 Fax: 34 532 6674
Asociacion de Ilidalgos a Fuer to de Espana
Aniceto Marinas 114, Madrid, 28008, Spain
Cercle Genealogic del Valles
Roca 29, 5 2, Sabadell, Barcelona, 8208, Spain

Circulo de Estudios Genealogicos Familiares
Prado 21, Ateneo de Madrid, Madrid, 28014, Spain
Instituto Aragones de Investigaciones Historiograficas
Madre Sacremento 33, 1', Zaragoza, 50004, Spain
Instituto de Estudios Heraldicos y Genealogicos de Extremadura
Lucio Cornelio Balbo 6, Caceres, 1004, Spain
Real Academia Matritense de Heraldica y Genealogia
Quintana 28, Madrid, 28008, Spain
Sociedad Toledana de Estudios Heraldicos y Genealogicos
Apartado de Correos No. 373, Toledo, Spain
Societat Catalana de Genealogia Heraldica Sigillografia
Vexillologia P O Box 2830, Barcelona, 8080, Spain
Societat Valenciana de Genealogia Heraldica Sigillografia
Vexillologia Les Tendes 22, Oliva, 46780, Spain

SWEDEN
Sveriges Slaktforskarforbund Box 30222, Stockholm, 104 25,
Sweden T: 08 695 0890 Fax: 08 695 0824 E:
genealog@genealogi.se
SWITZERLAND
Genealogical & Heraldry Association of Zurich
Dammbodenstrasse 1, Volketswil, CH-8604, Switzerland
Swiss Genealogical Society Eggstr 46, Oberengstringen, CH 8102,
Switzerland W: www.eye.ch/swissgen/SGFF.html
Swiss Society for Jewish Genealogy
P O Box 876, Zurich, CH-8021, Switzerland
Zentralstelle fur Genealogie Vogelaustrasse 34, CH-8953,
Switzerland Fax: 44 1 742 20 84 E: aicher@eyekon.ch

Family History Centres ~ The Church of Jesus Christ of The Latter Day Saints

Church of Jesus Christ of Latter Day Saints - North America Distribution Centre 1999 West 1700 South, Salt Lake City, Utah, 84104 United States of America
Church of Jesus Christ of Latter Day Saints - UK Distribution Centre 399 Garretts Green Lane, Birmingham, West Midlands, B33 0HU Tel: 0870-010-2051
Bedfordshire
St Albans Family History Centre London Road/Cutenhoe Road, Luton LU1 3NQ Tel: 01582-482234
Berkshire
Reading Family History Centre 280 The Meadway, Tilehurst, Reading RG3 4PF Tel: 0118-941 0211
Bristol
Bristol Family History Centre 721 Wells Road, Whitchurch, Bristol BS14 9HU Tel: 01275-838326
Cambridgeshire
Cambridgeshire Family History Centre 670 Cherry Hinton Road, Cambridge CB1 4DR Tel: 01223-247010
Peterborough Family History Centre Cottesmore Close off Atherstone Av, Netherton Estate
Peterborough PE3 9TP Tel: 01733-263374
Cleveland
Billingham Family History Centre The Linkway, Billingham TS23 3HG T: 01642-563162
Cornwall
Helston Family History Centre Clodgey Lane, Helston T: 01326-564503
Cumbria
Carlisle Family History Centre Langrigg Road, Morton Park, Carlisle CA2 5HT T: 01228-26767
Devon
Exeter Family History Centre Wonford Road Exeter T: 01392 250723
Plymouth Family History Centre Mannamead Road Plymouth PL3 5QJ T: 01752-668666
Dorset
Chickerell Family History Centre 396 Chickerell Road Chickerell Weymouth DT4 9TP T: 01305 787240
Poole Family History Centre 8 Mount Road Parkstone Poole BH14 0QW T: 01202-730646
Essex
Romford Family History Centre 64 Butts Green Road Hornchurch RM11 2JJ T: 01708-620727
Gloucestershire
Cheltenham Family History Centre Thirlestaine Road Cheltenham GL53 7AS T: 01242-523433
Forest of Dean Family History Centre Wynol's Hill Queensway Coleford T: 01594-542480
Yate Family History Centre Wellington Road Yate BS37 5UY T: 01454-323004
Hampshire
Portsmouth Family History Centre 82 Kingston Crescent Portsmouth PO2 8AQ T: (023) 92696243
Isle of Wight
Newport Family History Centre Chestnut Close Shide Road Newport PO30 1YE T: 01983-529643
Kent
Maidstone Family History Centre 76b London Road Maidstone ME16 0DR T: 01622-757811
Lancashire
Ashton Family History Centre Patterdale Road Ashton-under-Lyne OL7 T: 0161-330-1270
Blackpool Family History Centre Warren Drive Cleveleys Blackpool FY5 3TG T: 01253-858218
Chorley Family History Centre Preston Temple Chorley PR6 7EQ T: 01257 226147
Lancaster Family History Centre Ovangle Road Lancaster LA1 5HZ T: 01254-33571
Manchester Family History Centre Altrincham Road Wythenshawe Road Manchester M22 4BJ T: 0161-902-9279

Rawtenstall Family History Centre Haslingden Rawtenstall Rossendale BB4 6PU T: 01706 213460
Leicestershire
Leicestershire Family History Centre Wakerley Road Leicester LE5 4WD T: 0116-233-5544
Lincolnshire
Lincoln Family History Centre Skellingthorpe Road Lincoln LN6 0PB T: 01522-680117 Email: dann.family@diamond.co.uk
Lincolnshire - North East
Grimsby Family History Centre Linwood Avenue (NO LETTER BOX) Scartho Grimsby DN33 2NL T: 01472-828876
London
Hyde Park Family History Centre 64 - 68 Exhibition Road South Kensington London SW7 2PA T: (020) 789-8561
Wandsworth Family History Centre 149 Nightingale Lane Balham London SW12 T: (020) 8673-6741
Merseyside
Liverpool Family History Centre 4 Mill Bank Liverpool L13 0BW T: 0151-228-0433 Fax: 0151-252-0164
Middlesex
Staines Family History Centre 41 Kingston Road Staines TW14 0ND T: 01784-462627
Norfolk
Kings Lynn Family History Centre Reffley Lane Kings Lynn PE30 3EQ T: 01553-67000
Norwich Family History Centre 19 Greenways Eaton Norwich NR4 6PA T: 01603-452440
Northamptonshire
Northampton Family History Centre 137 Harlestone Road Duston Northampton NN5 6AA T: 01604-587630
Nottinghamshire
Mansfield Family History Centre Southridge Drive Mansfield NG18 4RJ T: 01623-26729
Nottingham Family History Centre Hempshill Lane Bulwell Nottingham NG6 8PA T: 0115-927-4194
Shropshire
Telford Family History Centre 72 Glebe Street Wellington
Somerset
Yeovil Family History Centre Forest Hill Yeovil BA20 2PH T: 01935 426817
South Yorkshire
Sheffield Family History Centre Wheel Lane Grenoside Sheffield S30 3RL T: 0114-245-3124
Staffordshire
Lichfield Family History Centre Purcell Avenue Lichfield WS14 9XA T: 01543-414843
Newcastle under Lyme Family History Centre PO Box 457 Newcastle under Lyme ST5 0TD T: 01782-620653 Fax: 01782-630178
Suffolk
Ipswich Family History Centre 42 Sidegate Lane West Ipswich IP4 3DB T: 01473-723182
Lowestoft Family History Centre 165 Yarmouth Road Lowestoft T: 01502-573851
Tyne and Wear
Sunderland Family History Centre Linden Road off Queen Alexandra Road Sunderland SR2 9BT T: 0191-528-5787
West Midlands
Coventry Family History Centre Riverside Close Whitley Coventry T: (024) 76301420
Harborne Family History Centre 38 Lordswood Road Harborne Birmingham B17 9QS T: 0121-427-9291
Sutton Coldfield Family History Centre 185 Penns Lane Sutton Coldfield Birmingham B76 1JU T: 0121-386-1690
Wednesfield Family History Centre Linthouse Lane Wednesfield Wolverhampton T: 01902-724097
Sussex – East
Crawley Family History Centre Old Horsham Road Crawley RH11 8PD T: 01293-516151

Sussex – West
Worthing Family History Centre Goring Street Worthing BN12 5AR
Wirral
Birkenhead Family History Centre Reservoir Road off Prenton Lane Prenton Birkenhead CH42 8LJ T: 0151 608 0157
Worcestershire
Redditch Family History Centre 321 Evesham Road Crabbs Cross Redditch B97 5JA T: 01527-550657
Yorkshire
Yorkshire - East
Hull Family History Centre 725 Holderness Road Kingston upon Hull HU4 7RT T: 01482-701439
Yorkshire – North
Scarborough Family History Centre Stepney Drive/Whitby Road Scarborough
Yorkshire – West
Huddersfield Family History Centre 12 Halifax Road Birchencliffe Huddersfield HD3 3BS T: 01484-454573
Leeds Family History Centre Vesper Road Leeds LS5 3QT T: 0113-258-5297
York
York Family History Centre West Bank Acomb York T: 01904-785128
Wales
Denbighshire
Rhyl Family History Centre Rhuddlan Road Rhyl
Glamorgan
Merthyr Tydfil Family History Centre Swansea Road Merthyr Tydfil CF 48 1NR T: 01685-722455
Glamorgan
Swansea Family History Centre Cockett Road Swansea SA2 0FH T: 01792-419520
South Glamorgan
Cardiff Family History Centre Heol y Deri Rhiwbina Cardiff CF4 6UH T: (029) 20620205
Isle of Man
Douglas Family History Centre Woodbourne Road Douglas IM2 3AP T: 01624-675834
Jersey
St Helier Family History Centre La Rue de la Vallee St Mary JE3 3DL T: 01534-82171

Scotland
Ayrshire
Kilmarnock Family History Centre Wahtriggs Road Kilmarnock KA1 3QY T: 01563-26560
Dumfrieshire
Dumfries Family History Centre 36 Edinburgh Road Albanybank Dumfries DG1 1JQ T: 01387-254865
Edinburgh
Edinburgh Family History Centre 30a Colinton Road Edinburgh EH4 3SN T: 0130-337-3049
Fife
Kirkcaldy Family History Centre Winifred Crescent Forth Park Kirkcaldy KY2 5SX T: 01592-640041
Glasgow
Glasgow Family History Centre 35 Julian Avenue Glasgow G12 0RB T: 0141-357-1024
Grampian
Aberdeen Family History Centre North Anderson Drive Aberdeen AB2 6DD T: 01224-692206
Highlands
Inverness Family History Centre 13 Ness Walk Inverness IV3 5SQ T: 01463-231220
Johnstone
Paisley Family History Centre Campbell Street Paisley PA5 8LD T: 01505-20886
Shetland
Lerwick Family History Centre Baila Croft Lerwick ZE1 0EY T: 01595-695732 Fax: 01950-431469
Tayside
Dundee Family History Centre 22 - 26 Bingham Terrace Dundee DD4 7HH T: 01382-451247
Northern Ireland
Belfast
Belfast Family History Centre 401 Holywood Road Belfast BT4 2GU T: (028) 90768250
Londonderry
Londonderry Family History Centre Racecourse Road Belmont Estate Londonderry T: Sun-only-(028) 71350179
Ireland
Co Dublin
Dublin Family History Centre The Willows Finglas Dublin 11 T: - 4625962

Libraries

National
Angus Library Regent's Park College, Pusey Street, Oxford, OX1 2LB T: 01865 288142 F: 01865 288121
Birmingham University Information Services - Special Collections, Main Library, University of Birmingham, Edgbaston, Birmingham, B15 2TT T: 0121 414 5838 F: 0121 471 4691 E: special-collections@bham.ac.uk W: www.is.bham.ac.uk
Bristol University Library - Special Collections, Tyndall Avenue, Bristol, BS8 1TJ T: 0117 928 8014 F: 0117 925 5334 E: library@bris.ac.uk W: www.bris.ac.uk/depts/library
British Genealogical Survey Library, Kingsley Dunham Centre, Keyworth, Nottingham, NG12 5GG T: 0115 939 3205 F: 0115 936 3200 E: info@bgs.ac.uk W: www.bgs.ac.uk
British Library, British Library Building, 96 Euston Road, London, NW1 2DB T: (020) 7412 7676 Bookings:Reader/admissions@bl.uk W: www.portico.bl.uk
British Library - Early Printed Collections, 96 Euston Road, London, NW1 2DB T: (020) 7412 7673 F: (020) 7412-7577 E: rare-books@bl.uk W: http://www.bl.uk
Cambridge University Library - Department of Manuscripts & University Archives see Cambridgeshire
House of Commons Library, House of Commons, 1 Derby Gate, London, SW1A 2DG T: (020) 7219-5545 F: (020) 7219-3921
Institute of Heraldic and Genealogical Studies seeKent
Jewish Studies Library, University College, Gower Street, London, WC1E 6BT T: (020) 7387 7050
National Gallery Library and Archive, Trafalgar Square, London, WC2N 5DN T: 020 7747 2542 F: 020 7753 8179 E: , iad@ng-london.org.uk W: www.nationalgallery.org.uk
National Maritime Museum, Romney Road, Greenwich, London, SE10 9NF T: (020) 8858-4422 F: (020) 8312-6632 W: http://www.nmm.ac.uk
National Maritime Museum - Caird Library, Park Row, Greenwich, London, SE10 9NF T: (020) 8312 6673 F: (020) 8312-6632 E: , ABuchanan@nmm.ac.uk W: http://www.nmm.ac.uk
Nuffield College Library, Oxford, OX1 1NF T: 01865 278550 F: 01865 278621 E: library-archives@nuf.ox.ac.uk W: www.nuff.ox.ac.uk/library/archives/archives-information.asp
Rhodes House Library, Bodleian Library, South Parks Road, Oxford, OX1 3RG T: 01865 270909 F: 01865 270912
Robinson Library seeTyne & wear

Royal Armouries, H.M Tower Of London, Tower Hill, London, EC3N 4AB T: (020) 7480 6358 ext 30 F: (020) 7481 2922 E: Bridgett.Clifford@armouries.org.uk W: www.armouries.org.uk
Royal Commonwealth Society Library, West Road, Cambridge, CB3 9DR T: 01223 333198 F: 01223 333160 E: tab@ula.cam.ac.uk W: www.lib.cam.ac.uk/MSS/
Royal Society of Chemistry Library & Information Centre, Burlington House, Piccadilly, London, W1J 0BA T: (020) 7437 8656 F: (020) 7287 9798 E: library@rsc.org W: www.rsc.org
Society of Antiquaries of London, Burlington House, Piccadilly, London, W1J 0BE T: 020 7479 7084 F: 020 7287 6967 E: library@sal.org.uk W: www.sal.org.uk
Society of Friends (Quakers) - Library (Ireland) see Ireland
Society of Genealogists - Library, 14 Charterhouse Buildings, Goswell Road, London, EC1M 7BA T: 020-7251-8799 T: 020-7250-0291 F: 020-7250-1800 E: library@sog.org.uk - Sales at sales@sog.org.uk W: www.sog.org.uk
Sussex University Library, Manuscript Collections, Falmer, Brighton, BN1 9QL T: 01273 606755 F: 01273 678441
The Kenneth Ritchie Wimbledon Library, The All England Lawn Tennis & Croquet Club, Church Road, Wimbledon, London, SW19 5AE T: (020) 8946 6131 F: (020) 8944 6497 W: www.wimbledon.org, Contains the world's finest collection of books and periodicals relating to lawn tennis
The Library & Museum of Freemasonry, Freemasons' Hall, 60 Great Queen Street, London, WC2B 5AZ T: (020) 7395 9257 W: www.grandlodge-england.org
The National Coal Mining Museum for England, Caphouse Colliery, New Road, Overton, Wakefield, WF4 4RH T: 01924 848806 F: 01924 840694 E: info@ncm.org.uk W: www.ncm.org.uk
Trinity College Library, Cambridge University, Trinity College, Cambridge, CB1 1TQ T: 01223 338488 F: 01223 338532 E: trin-lib@lists.cam.ac.uk W: http://rabbit.trin.cam.ac.uk
United Reformed Church History Society, Westminster College, Madingley Road, Cambridge, CB3 0AA T: 01223-741300 (NOT Wednesdays) Information on ministers of constituent churches not members
University of Wales Swansea Library seeGlamorgan-West
Victoria & Albert Museum - National Art Library, Cromwell Road, South Kensington, London, SW7 2RL T: (020) 7938 8313 F: (020) 7938 8461 W: www.nal.vam.ac.uk

Victoria & Albert Museum - National Art Library - Archive of Art & Design, Blythe House, 23 Blythe Road, London, W14 0QF T: (020) 7603 1514 F: (020) 7602 0980 E: archive@vam.ac.uk W: www.nal.vam.ac.uk

Specialist Records & Indexes

Berkshire Medical Heritage Centre, Level 4, Main Entrance, Royal Berkshire Hospital, London Road, Reading, RG1 5AN T: 0118 987 7298 W: www.bmhc.org

British Library Newspaper Library, Colindale Avenue, London, NW9 5HE T: 020-7412-7353 F: 020-7412-7379 E: newspaper@bl.uk W: www.bl/uk/collections/newspaper/ The National archive collections of British and Overseas newspapers as well as major collections of popular magazines. Open Mon to Sat 10am to 4.45pm. Readers must be over 18yrs of age and provide proof of identity bearing their signature.

British Library of Political and Economic Science, London School of Economics, 10 Portugal Street, London, WC2A 2HD T: 020 7955 7223 F: 020 7955 7454 E: info@lse.ac.uk W: www.lse.ac.uk

British Library Oriental and India Office Collections, 96 Euston Road, London, NW1 2DB T: (020) 7412-7873 F: (020) 7412-7641 E: oioc-enquiries@bl.uk W: www.bl.uk/collections/oriental

Catholic Central Library, Lancing Street, London, NW1 1ND T: (020) 7383-4333 F: (020) 7388-6675 E: librarian@catholic-library.demon.co.uk W: www.catholic-library.demon.co.uk

Department of Manuscripts and Special Collections, Hallward Library, Nottingham University, University Park, Nottingham, NG7 2RD T: 0115 951 4565 F: 0115 951 4558 E: mss-library@nottingham.ac.uk W: www.mss.library.nottingham.ac.uk

Dr Williams's Library, 14 Gordon Square, London, WC1H 0AR T: (020) 7387-3727 The collections of the library are primarily concerned with the history and theology of religious dissent or nonconformity, principally Unitarians and Congregationalists. The libary has few registers.The General Registers of Protestant Dissenters (so called Dr Williams's Library Registers) were surrendered to the Registrar General and are now at The Public Record Office (RG4/4666-4673)

Huguenot Library, University College, Gower Street, London, WC1E 6BT T: (020) 7679 7094 E: s.massilk@ucl.ac.uk W: www.ucl.ac.uk/ucl-info/divisions/library/hugenot.htm

John Rylands University Library see Manchester

Lambeth Palace Library, Lambeth Palace Road, London, SE1 7JU T: (020) 7898 1400 F: (020) 7928-7932 W: www.lambethpalacelibrary.org

Library of the Religious Society of Friends (Quakers), Friends House, 173 - 177 Euston Rd, London, NW1 2BJ T: 0207 663 1135 T: 0207 663 1001 E: library@quaker.org.uk W: www.quaker.org.uk/library Limited opening hours. Letter of introduction required. Please send SAE for details or enclose IRCs

Library of the Royal College of Surgeons of England, 35-43 Lincoln's Inn Fields, London, WC2A 3PN T: (020) 7869 6520 F: (020) 7405 4438, Email:, library@rseng.ac.uk W: www.rseng.ac.uk Research enquiries are not undertaken. Appointments required.

Lifelong Learning Service, Theodore Road, Port Talbot, SA13 1SP T: 01639-898581 F: 01639-899914, Email:, lls@neath-porttalbot.gov.uk W: www.neath-porttalbot.gov.uk

Liverpool University Special Collections & Archives, see Liverpool

Methodist Archives and Research Centre, John Rylands University Library, 150 Deansgate, Manchester, M3 3EH T: 0161 834 5343 F: 0161 834 5574

Methodist Evangelical Library 78a Chiltern Street, London, W1M 2HB

Library of Primitive Methodism, Englesea Brook Chapel and Museum, Englesea Brook, Crewe, Cheshire, CW2 5QW E: engleseabrook-methodist-museum@supanet.com W: www.engleseabrook-museum.org

Museum of the Order of St John, St John's Gate, St John's Lane, Clerkenwell, London, EC1M 4DA T: (020) 7253-6644 F: (020) 7336 0587 W: www.sja.org.uk/history

National Gallery Library and Archive Trafalgar Square, London, WC2N 5DN T: 020 7747 2542Fax: 020 7753 8179 E: iad@ng-london.org.uk W: www.nationalgallery.org.uk

National Maritime Museum - Caird Library, Park Row, Greenwich, London, SE10 9NF T: (020) 8312 6673 F: (020) 8312-6632, Email:, ABuchanan@nmm.ac.uk W: http://www.nmm.ac.uk

River & Rowing Museum, Rowing & River Museum, Mill Meadows, Henley on Thames, RG9 1BF T: 01491 415625 F: 01491 415601, Email:, museum@rrm.co.uk W: www..rrm.co.uk Thames linked families especially lock keepers , boat builders

Royal Institute of British Architects' Library, Manuscripts & archives Collection, 66 portland Place, London, W1N 4AD T: 020 7307 3615 F: 020 7631 1802

Royal Society of Chemistry Library & Information Centre, Burlington House, Piccadilly, London, W1J 0BA T: (020) 7437 8656 F: (020) 7287 9798 E: library@rsc.org W: www.rsc.org

School of Oriental and African Studies library, Thornhaugh Street, Russell Square, London, WC1H 0XG T: 020 7323 6112 F: 020 7636 2834, E: lib@soas.ac.uk W: www.soas.ac.uk/library/

Society of Antiquaries of London Burlington House, Piccadilly, London, W1J 0BE T: 020 7479 7084Fax: 020 7287 6967 E: library@sal.org.uk W: www.sal.org.uk

Society of Genealogists - Library see National

South Wales Miners' Library - University of Wales, Swansea, Hendrefoelan House, Gower Road, Swansea, SA2 7NB T: 01792-518603 F: 01792-518694, Email:, miners@swansea.ac.uk W: www.swan.ac.uk/lis/swml

The Science Museum Library, Imperial College Road, South Kensington, London, SW7 5NH T: 020 7938 8234 T: 020 7938 8218 F: 020 7938 9714

The Women's Library, Old Castle Street, London, E1 7NT T: (020) 7320-1189 F: (020) 7320-1188Email: fawcett@lgu.ac.uk W: W: http://www.lgu.ac.uk/fawcett

Thomas Plume Library see Essex

Trades Union Congress Library Collections - University of North London, 236 - 250 Holloway Road, London, N7 6PP F: 0171 753 3191Email: tuclib@unl.ac.uk W: www.unl.ac.uk/library/tuc

United Reformed Church History Society see National

Wellcome Library for the History and Understanding of Medicine : Contemporary Medical Archives Centre : Wellcome Library for the History of Medicine - Department of Western Manuscripts, 183 Euston Road, London, NW1 2BE T: (020) 7611-8582 F: (020) 7611 8369 E: library@wellcome.ac.uk W: www.wellcome.ac.uk/library Library catalogue is available through the internet: telnet://wihm.ucl.ac.uk

England

Bedfordshire

Bedford Central Library Harpur Street, Bedford, Bedfordshire, MK40 1PG T: 01234-350931Fax: 01234-342163 E: stephensonB@bedfordshire.gov.uk W: www.bedfordshire.gov.uk, 1901 census

Biggleswade Library Chestnut Avenue, Biggleswade, Bedfordshire, SG18 0LL T: 01767 312324 , 1901 census

Dunstable Library Vernon Place, Dunstable, Bedfordshire, LU5 4HA T: 01582 608441 , 1901 census

Leighton Buzzard Library Lake Street, Leighton Buzzard, Bedfordshire, LU7 1RX T: 01525 371788 , 1901 census

Local Studies Library Luton Central Library St George's Square, Luton, Bedfordshire, LU1 2NG T: 01582-547420 T: 01582-547421, F: 01582-547450 E: local.studies@luton.gov.uk W: www.luton.gov.uk, 1901 census

Berkshire

Ascot Heath Library Fernbank Road, North Ascot, Berkshire, SL5 8LA T: 01344 884030Fax: 01344 885472

Berkshire Medical Heritage Centre Level 4, Main Entrance, Royal Berkshire Hospital, London Road, Reading, Berkshire, RG1 5AN T: 0118 987 7298 W: www.bmhc.org

Binfield Library Benetfeld Road, Binfield, Berkshire, RG42 4HD T: 01344 306663Fax: 01344 486467

Bracknell Library - Local Studies Town Square, Bracknell, Berkshire, RG12 1BH T: 01344 352515Fax: 01344 411392

Crowthorne Library Lower Broadmoor Road, Crowthorne, Berkshire, RG45 7LA T: 01344 776431Fax: 01344 776431

Eton College, College Library Windsor, Berkshire, SL4 6DB T: 01753 671269 E: archivist@etoncollege.org.uk W: www.etoncollege.com Open by appointment 9.30.a.m. to 1.00.p.m. and 2.00.p.m. to 5.00.p.m. Monday to Friday

Newbury Reference Library Newbury Central Library The Wharf, Newbury, Berkshire, RG14 5AU T: 01635 519900Fax: 01635 519906 E: newburylib@westberks.gov.uk W: www.westberks.gov.uk

Reading Local Studies Library 3rd Floor, Central Library Abbey Square, Reading, Berkshire, RG1 3BQ T: 0118 901 5965Fax: 0118 901 5954 E: info@readinglibraries.org.uk W: www.readinglibraries.org.uk

Reading University Library University of Reading, Whiteknights PO Box 223, Reading, RG6 6AE T: 0118-931-8776Fax: 0118-931 6636 http://www.reading.ac.uk/

Royal Borough of Windsor and Maidenhead Local Studies Collections Maidenhead Library St Ives Road, Maidenhead, Berkshire, SL6 1QU T: 01628 796978Fax: 01628 796971 E: maidenhead.ref@rbwm.gov.uk W: www.rbwm.gov.uk, 1901 census. Open: Monday 9.30am - 5.00pm; Tuesday 9.30am - 8.00pm; Wednesday 9.30am - 5.00pm; Thursday 9.30am - 8.00pm; Friday 9.30am - 7.00pm; Saturday 9.30am - 4.00pm

Royal Borough of Windsor and Maidenhead Local Studies Collections Windsor Library Bachelors Acre, Windsor, Berkshire, SL4 1ER T: 01753 743941Fax: 01753 743942 E: windsor.library@rbwm.gov.uk W: www.rbwm.gov.uk, 1901 census. Open: Monday 9.30am - 5.00pm; Tuesday 9.30am - 8.00pm; Wednesday 2.00.pm - 5.00pm; Thursday 9.30am - 5.00pm; Friday 9.30am - 7.00pm; Saturday 9.30am - 3.00pm

Sandhurst Library The Broadway, Sandhurst, Berkshire, GU47 9BL T: 01252 870161Fax: 01252 878285

Slough Local Studies Library Top Floor, Slough Library High Street, Slough, Berkshire, SL1 1EA T: 01753 787511E: librarytop@sloughlibrary.org.uk W: www.sloughlibrary.org.uk

Whitegrove Library 5 County Lane, Warfield, Berkshire, RG42 3JP T: 01344 424211Fax: 01344 861233

Wokingham Library Local Studies The Library Denmark Street, Wokingham, Berkshire, RG40 2BB T: 0118 978 1368Fax: 0118 989 1214 E: libraries@wokingham.gov.uk W: www.wokingham.gov.uk/libraries

Birkenhead

Wirral Central Library Borough Road, Birkenhead, CH41 2XB T: 0151 652 6106 T: 0151 652 6107/8, F: 0151 653 7320 E: birkenhead.library@merseymail.com,

Birmingham

Birmingham Central Library - The Genealogist, Local Studies & History Service Floor 6, Central Library Chamberlain Square, Birmingham, West Midlands, B3 3HQ T: 0121 303 4549Fax: 0121 464 0993 E: local.studies.library@birmingham.gov.uk W: www.birmingham.gov.uk, 1901 census

Bolton

Central Library Civic Centre Le Mans Crescent, Bolton, BL1 1SE T: 01204-333185 ,

Bournemouth

Bournemouth Library see Hampshire

Bracknell Forest Borough

Ascot Heath Library see Berkshire

Binfield Library see Berkshire

Bracknell Library - Local Studies see Berkshire

Crowthorne Library see Berkshire

Sandhurst Library see Berkshire

Whitegrove Library see Berkshire, RG42 3JP

Brighton & Hove

Brighton & Hove Council Library Service see Sussex - East

Brighton Local Studies Library see Sussex - East

Bristol

Bristol Central Library Reference Section, College Green, Bristol, BS1 5TL T: 0117 903 7202 , 1901 census

Buckinghamshire

County Reference Library Walton Street, Aylesbury, Buckinghamshire, HP20 1UU T: 01296-382250Fax: 01296-382405

High Wycombe Reference Library Queen Victoria Road, High Wycombe, Buckinghamshire, HP11 1BD T: 01494-510241Fax: 01494-533086 E: lib-hiwref@buckscc.gov.uk W: www.buckscc.gov.uk, GRO Index England and Wales

Milton Keynes Reference Library 555 Silbury Boulevard, Milton Keynes, Buckinghamshire, MK9 3HL T: 01908 254160Fax: 01908 254088 E: mklocal@milton-keynes.gov.uk W: www.mkheritage.co.uk/mkl, 1901 census for Buckinghamshire

Cambridgeshire

The Cambridge Library Lion Yard Cambridge, Cambridgeshire, CB2 3QD

Cambridge University Library - Department of Manuscripts & University Archives West Road, Cambridge, Cambridgeshire, CB3 9DR T: 01223 333000 ext 33143 (Manuscripts) T: 01223 333000 ext 33148 (University Archives), F: 01223 333160 E: mss@ula.cam.ac.uk W: www.lib.cam.ac.uk/MSS/

Homerton College Library The New Library Hills Road, Cambridge, Cambridgeshire, CB2 2PH

Norris Library and Museum The Broadway, St Ives, Cambridgeshire, PE27 5BX T: 01480 497317, E: bob@norrismuseum.fsnet.co.uk,

Peterborough Local Studies Collection Central Library Broadway, Peterborough, PE1 1RX T: 01733 742700 01733 555277, libraries@peterborough.gov.uk W: www.peterborough.gov.uk, 1901 census

Cheshire

Alderley Edge Library Heys Lane, Alderley Edge, Cheshire, SK9 7JT T: 01625 584487Fax: 01625 584487, W: www.cheshire.gov.uk

Alsager Library Sandbach Road North, Alsager, Cheshire, ST7 2QH T: 01270 873552Fax: 01270 883093 E: alsager.infopoint@cheshire.gov.uk W: www.cheshire.gov.uk

Barnton Library Townfield Lane, Barnton, Cheshire, CW8 4LJ T: 01606 77343Fax: 01606 77343, W: www.cheshire.gov.uk

Bishops' High School Library Vaughans Lane, Chester, Cheshire, CH3 5XF T: 01244 313806Fax: 01244 320992, W: www.cheshire.gov.uk

Blacon Library Western Avenue, Blacon, Chester, Cheshire, CH1 5XF T: 01244 390628Fax: 01244 390628, W: www.cheshire.gov.uk

Bollington Library Palmerston Street, Bollington, Cheshire, SK10 5JX T: 01625 573058Fax: 01625 573058, W: www.cheshire.gov.uk

Chester Library Northgate Street, Chester, Cheshire, CH1 2EF T: 01244-312935Fax: 01244-315534 E: chester.infopoint@cheshire.gov.uk W: www.cheshire.gov.uk

Congleton Library Market Square, Congleton, Cheshire, CW12 1ET T: 01260 271141Fax: 01260 298774 E: congleton.infopoint@cheshire.gov.uk W: www.cheshire.gov.uk

Crewe Library Prince Albert Street, Crewe, Cheshire, CW1 2DH T: 01270 211123Fax: 01270 256952 E: crewe.infopoint@cheshire.gov.uk W: www.cheshire.gov.uk

Disley Library Off Buxton Old Road, Disley, Cheshire, SK12 2BB T: 01663 765635Fax: 01663 765635, W: www.cheshire.gov.uk

Ellesmere Port Library Civic Way, Ellesmere Port, South Wirral, Cheshire, L65 0BG T: 0151-355-8101Fax: 0151-355-6849 E: eport.infopoint@cheshire.gov.uk W: www.cheshire.gov.uk

Frodsham Library Rock Chapel, Main Street, Frodsham, Cheshire, WA6 7AN T: 01928 732775Fax: 01928 734214

Great Boughton Library Green Lane, Vicars Cross, Chester, Cheshire, CH3 5LB T: 01244 320709Fax: 01244 320709, W: www.cheshire.gov.uk

Halton Lea Library Halton Lea, Runcorn, Cheshire, WA7 2PF T: 01928-715351Fax: 01928-790221, W: www.cheshire.gov.uk

Handforth Library The Green, Wilmslow Road, Handforth, Cheshire, SK9 3ES T: 01625 528062Fax: 01625 524390, W: www.cheshire.gov.uk

Helsby Library Lower Robin Hood Lane, Helsby, Cheshire, WA5 0BW T: 01928 724659 W: www.cheshire.gov.uk

Holmes Chapel Library London Road, Holmes Chapel, Cheshire, CW4 7AP T: 01477 535126Fax: 01477 544193 E: homeschapel.infopoint@cheshire.gov.uk W: www.cheshire.gov.uk

Hoole Library 91 Hoole Road, Chester, Cheshire, England T: 01244 347401Fax: 01244 347401, W: www.cheshire.gov.uk

Hope Farm Library Bridge Meadow, Great Sutton, Cheshire, CH66 2LE T: 0151 355 8923 W: www.cheshire.gov.uk

Hurdsfield Library 7 Hurdsfield Green, Macclesfield, Cheshire, SK10 2RJ T: 01625 423788Fax: 01625 423788, W: www.cheshire.gov.uk

Knutsford Library Brook Street, Knutsford WA16 8BP T: 01565 632909 E: knutsford.infopoint@cheshire.gov.uk

Lache Library Lache Park Avenue, Chester, Cheshire, CH4 8HR T: 01244 683385 T: 01244 683385 W: www.cheshire.gov.uk

Little Sutton Library Chester Road, Little Sutton, Cheshire, CH66 1QQ T: 0151 339 3373Fax: 0151 339 3373, W: www.cheshire.gov.uk

Macclesfield Library 2 Jordongate, Macclesfield, Cheshire, SK10 1EE T: 01625-422512Fax: 01625-612818 E: macclesfield.infopoint@cheshire.gov.uk W: www.cheshire.gov.uk

Macclesfield Silk Museums Paradise Mill, Park Lane, Macclesfield, Cheshire, SK11 6TJ T: 01625 612045Fax: 01625 612048 E: silkmuseum@tiscali.co.uk W: www.silk-macclesfield.org, Reference library and archive. Museums cover the history of silk in macclesfield once the centre of the industry. Demonstartions of hand weaving, exhibitions and models. cc accepted

Malpas Library Bishop Herber High School, Malpas, Cheshire, SY14 8JD T: 01948 860571Fax: 01948 860962, W: www.cheshire.gov.uk

Middlewich Library Lewin Street, Middlewich, Cheshire, CW10 9AS T: 01606 832801Fax: 01606 833336, W: www.cheshire.gov.uk

Nantwich Library Beam Street, Nantwich, Cheshire, CW5 5LY T: 1270624867, F: 01270 610271 E: nantwich.infopoint@cheshire.gov.uk W: www.cheshire.gov.uk

Northwich Library Witton Street, Northwich, Cheshire, CW9 5DR T: 01606 44221Fax: 01606 48396 E: northwich.infopoint@cheshire.gov.uk W: www.cheshire.gov.uk

Poynton Library Park Lane, Poynton, Cheshire, SK12 1RB T: 01625 876257Fax: 01625 858027 E: poynton.infopoint@cheshire.gov.uk W: www.cheshire.gov.uk

Prestbury Library The Reading Room, Prestbury, Cheshire, SK10 4AD T: 01625 827501 W: www.cheshire.gov.uk

John Rylands University Library see Manchester

Sandbach Library The Common, Sandbach, Cheshire, CW11 1FJ T: 01270 762309Fax: 01270 759656 E: sandbach.infopoint@cheshire.gov.uk W: www.cheshire.gov.uk

Sandiway Library Mere Lane, Cuddington, Northwich, Cheshire, CW8 2NS T: 01606 888065Fax: 01606 883743, W: www.cheshire.gov.uk

Stockport Local Heritage Library Central Library Wellington Road South, Stockport, Cheshire, SK1 3RS T: 0161-474-4530Fax: 0161-474-7750 E: localheritrtage.library@stockport.gov.uk W: www.stockport.gov.uk

Tameside Local Studies Library Stalybridge Library Trinity Street, Stalybridge, Cheshire, SK15 2BN T: 0161-338-2708 T: 0161-338-3831 and 0161 303 7937Fax: 0161-303-8289 E: localstudies.library@mail.tameside.gov.uk W: www.tameside.gov.uk, 1901 census

Tarporley Library High School, Eaton Road, Tarporley, Cheshire, CW6 0BJ T: 01829 732558, F: 01829 733945, W: www.cheshire.gov.uk

Upton Library Wealstone Lane, Upton by Chester, Cheshire, CH2 1HB T: 01244 380053, F: 01244 377197, W: www.cheshire.gov.uk

Warrington Library & Local Studies Centre Museum Street, Warrington, Cheshire, WA1 1JB T: 01925 442890, F: 01925 411395 E: library@warrington.gov.uk W: www.warrington.gov.uk

Weaverham Library Russett Road, Weaverham, Northwich, Cheshire, CW8 3HY T: 01606 853359, F: 01606 853359, W: www.cheshire.gov.uk

Weston Library Heyes Hall, Weston, Macclesfield, Cheshire, SK11 8RL T: 01625 614008, F: 01625 614008 W: www.cheshire.gov.uk

Wharton Library Willow Square, Wharton, Winsford, Cheshire, CW7 3HP T: 01606 593883, F: 01606 593883, W: www.cheshire.gov.uk

Wilmslow Library South Drive, Wilmslow, Cheshire, SK9 1NW T: 01625 528977, F: 01625 548401 E: wilmslow.infopoint@cheshire.gov.uk W: www.cheshire.gov.uk

Winsford Library High Street, Winsford, Cheshire, CW7 2AS T: 01606 552065, F: 01606 861563 E: winsford.infopoint@cheshire.gov.uk W: www.cheshire.gov.uk

Cleveland

Hartlepool Central Library 124 York Road, Hartlepool, Cleveland, TS26 9DE T: 01429 263778 , 1901 census

Middlesbrough Libraries & Local Studies Centre Central Library Victoria Square, Middlesbrough, Cleveland, TS1 2AY T: 01642 729001 01642 729954, reference_library@middlesbrough.gov.uk W: www.middlesbrough.gov.uk, 1901 census. GRO index up to 2000

Stockton Reference Library Church Road, Stockton on Tees, Cleveland, TS18 1TU T: 01642-393994, F: 01642-393929 E: reference.library@stockton.bc.gov.uk W: www.stockton.bc.gov.uk 1901 census

Cornwall

The Cornwall Centre , Alma Place, Redruth, Cornwall, TR15 2AT T: 01209-216760, F: 01209-210283 E: cornishstudies@library.cornwall.gov.uk W: www.cornwall.gov.uk Cornwall Libraries main library of local studies material. Printed and published items about Cornwall incl books, pamphlets, journals, newspapers, maps, photographs etc. 1901 census

Royal Institution of Cornwall, Courtney Library & Cornish History Research Centre Royal Cornwall Museum, River Street, Truro, Cornwall, TR1 2SJ T: 01872 272205, F: 01872 240514 E: RIC@royal-cornwall-museum.freeserve.co.uk W: www.cornwall-online.co.uk/ric

County Durham

Darlington Local Studies Centre The Library Crown Street, Darlington, County Durham, DL1 1ND T: 01325-349630, F: 01325-381556 E: crown.street.library@darlington.gov.uk W: www.darlington.gov.uk 1901 census

Durham City Reference & Local Studies Library Durham Clayport Library Millennium Place, Durham, County Durham, DH1 1WA T: 0191-386-4003, F: 0191-386-0379 E: durhamcityref.lib@durham.gov.uk W: www.durham.gov.uk 1901 census

Durham Cultural Services, Library and Museums Department, County Hall, Durham, County Durham, DH1 5TY T: 0191 384 3777, F: 0191 384 1336 E: culture@durham.gov.uk W: www.durham.gov.uk

Durham University Library Archives and Special Collections, Palace Green Section, Palace Green, Durham, DH1 3RN T: 0191-374-3032, E: pg.library@durham.ac.uk W: www.durham.ac.uk

Cumbria, Carlisle Library 11 Globe Lane, Carlisle, Cumbria, CA3 8NX T: 01228-607310, F: 01228-607333 E: carlisle.library@cumbriacc.gov.uk W: www.cumbriacc.gov.uk 1901 census

Cumbria Record Office and Local Studies Library (Whitehaven) Scotch Street, Whitehaven, Cumbria, CA28 7BJ T: 01946-852920, F: 01946-852919 E: whitehaven.record.office@cumbriacc.gov.uk W: www.cumbria.gov.uk/archives

Cumbria Record Office & Local Studies Library 140 Duke St, Barrow in Furness, Cumbria, LA14 1XW T: 01229-894363, F: 01229-894371 E: barrow.record.office@cumbriacc.gov.uk W: www.cumbria.gov.uk/archives

Kendal Library Stricklandgate, Kendal, Cumbria, LA9 4PY T: 01539-773520, F: 01539-773530 E: kendal.library@cumbriacc.gov.uk W: www.cumbriacc.gov.uk

Penrith Library St Andrews Churchyard, Penrith, Cumbria, CA11 7YA T: 01768-242100, F: 01768-242101 E: penrith.library@dial.pipexcom W: www.cumbria.gov.uk

Workington Library Vulcans Lane, Workington, Cumbria, CA14 2ND T: 01900-325170, F: 01900-325181 E: workington.library@cumbriacc.gov.uk W: www.cumbriacc.gov.uk

Derbyshire

Chesterfield Local Studies Department Chesterfield Library New Beetwell Street, Chesterfield, Derbyshire, S40 1QN T: 01246-209292, F: 01246-209304 E: chesterfield.library@derbyshire.gov.uk 1901 census - North Derbyshire only on microfilm

Derby Local Studies Library 25b Irongate, Derby, Derbyshire, DE1 3GL T: 01332 255393, E: localstudies.library@derby.gov.uk W: www.derby.gov.uk/libraries/about/local_studies.htm, 1901 census

Matlock Local Studies Library County Hall, Smedley Street, Matlock, Derbyshire, DE4 3AG T: 01629-585579, F: 01629-585049 E: ruth.gordon@derbyshire.gov.uk W: www.derbyshire.gov.uk/librar/locstu.htm W: www.peaklandheritage.org.ukj W: www.picturethepast.org.uk CC Accepted. Full set GRO indexes

Devon

Exeter University Library Stocker Road, Exeter, Devon, EX4 4PT T: 01392 263870, F: 01392 263871 E: library@exeter.ac.uk W: www.library.exeter.ac.uk

Plymouth Local Studies Library Central Library Drake Circus, Plymouth PL4 8AL T: 01752 305909 E: localstudies@plymouth.gov.uk W: www.plymouth.gov.uk

Torquay Library Lymington Road, Torquay, Devon, TQ1 3DT T: 01803 208305 , 1901 census

West Country Studies Library Exeter Central Library Castle Street, Exeter, Devon, EX4 3PQ T: 01392 384216, F: 01392-384228 E: dlaw@devon-cc.gov.uk http://www.devon-cc.gov.uk/library/locstudy, 1901 census

Devon & Exeter Institution Library 7 The Close, Exeter, Devonshire, EX1 1EZ T: 01392 251017, F: 01392-263871 E: m.midgley@exeter.ac.uk W: www.ex.ac.uk/library/devonex.html

Dorset

Dorchester Reference Library Colliton Park, Dorchester, Dorset, DT1 1XJ T: 01305-224448, F: 01305-266120 1901 census

Dorset County Museum High West Street, Dorchester, Dorset, DT1 1XA T: 01305 262735, F: 01305 257180 E: dorsetcountymuseum@dor-mus.demon.co.uk W: www.dorsetcc.gov.uk

Poole Central Reference Library Dolphin Centre , Poole, Dorset, BH15 1QE T: 01202 262424 E: centrallibrary@poole.gov.uk W: www.poole.gov.uk The local studies collection deposited at The Waterfront Museum, Poole Some records at Dorset Record Office. Retains only general local history and national family history indexes

Weymouth Library, Great George St, Weymouth DT4 8NN T: 01305 762410 E: weymouthlibrary@dorsetcc.gov.uk

East Yorkshire

Bridlington Local Studies Library Bridlington Library King Street, Bridlington, East Yorkshire, YO15 2DF T: 01262 672917, F: 01262 670208 E: bridlingtonref.library@eastriding.gov.uk W: www.eastriding.gov.uk 1841 to 1901 Censuses for bridlington only

East Riding Heritage Library & Museum Sewerby Hall, Church Lane, Sewerby, Bridlington, East Yorkshire, YO15 1EA T: 01262-677874 T: 01262-674265, E: museum@pop3.poptel.org.uk W: www.bridlington.net/sew

Goole Local Studies Library Goole Library Carlisle Street, Goole, East Yorkshire, DN14 5DS T: 01405-762187, F: 01405-768329 E: goolref.library@eastriding.gov.uk W: www.eastriding.gov.uk

Essex

Central Reference Library - London Borough of Havering Reference Library St Edward's Way, Romford, Essex, RM1 3AR T: 01708 432393 T: 01708 432394Fax: 01708 432391 E: romfordlib2@rmplc.co.uk

Chelmsford Library PO Box 882, Market Road, Chelmsford, Essex, CM1 1LH T: 01245 492758, F: 01245 492536 E: answers.direct@essexcc.gov.uk W: www.essexcc.gov.uk 1901 census

Clacton Library Station Road, Clacton on Sea, Essex, CO15 1SF T: 01255 421207 , 1901 census

Colchester Central Library Trinity Square, Colchester, Essex, CO1 1JB T: 01206-245917, F: 01206-245901 E: jane.stanway@essexcc.gov.uk W: www.essexcc.gov.uk 1901 census

Harlow Library The High, Harlow, Essex, CM20 1HA T: 01279 413772 , 1901 census

Ilford Local Studies and Archives Central Library Clements Road, Ilford, Essex, IG1 1EA T: 020 8708 2417 , 1901 census

London Borough of Barking & Dagenham Local Studies Library Valence House Museum, Beacontree Avenue, Dagenham, Essex, RM8 3HT T: 020 8270 6896, F: 020 8270 6897 E: localstudies@bardaglea.org.uk W: www.barking-dagenham.gov.uk

Loughton Library Traps Hill, Loughton, Essex, IG10 1HD T: 020 8502 0181 , 1901 census

Redbridge Library Central Library Clements Road, Ilford, Essex, IG1 1EA T: (020) 8708-2417, F: (020) 8553 3299 E: Local.Studies@redbridge.gov.uk W: www.redbridge.gov.uk

Saffron Walden Library 2 King Street, Saffron Walden, Essex, CB10 1ES T: 01799 523178 , 1901 census

Southend Library Central Library Victoria Avenue, Southend on Sea, Essex, SS2 6EX T: 01702-612621, F: 01792-612652 and 01702 469241 E: library@southend.gov.uk W: www.southend.gov.uk/libraries/, Minicom 01702 600579

Thomas Plume Library Market Hill, Maldon, Essex, CM9 4PZ T: , No facilities for incoming telephone or fax messages

Valence House Museum, Valence House Museum, Becontree Avenue, Dagenham, Essex, RM8 3HT T: 020 8270 6866, F: 020 82706868, W: www.barking-dagenham.gov.uk Heritage service includes a local history museum, and archive section. A list of resources is available upon request. Archives of the Essex Parishes of Barking and Dagenham and the London Boroughs of the same names

Gloucestershire

Cheltenham Local Studies Centre Cheltenham Library Clarence Street, Cheltenham, Gloucestershire, GL50 3JT T: 01242-532678, F: 01242 532673

Gloucester Library, Arts & Museums County Library Quayside, Shire Hall, Gloucester, Gloucestershire, GL1 1HY T: 01452-425037, F: 01452-425042 E: clams@glosc.gov.uk http://www.gloscc.gov.uk

Gloucestershire County Library Brunswick Road, Gloucester, GL1 1HT T: 01452-426979, F: 01452-521468 E: clams@gloscc.gov.uk W: www.gloscc.gov.uk The Gloucester Collection at Gloucester Library is the largest local studies library in the County. Other libraries specialising in their particular areas are Cheltenham, Cinderford, Cirencester, Stow on the Wold, Stroud and Tewksbury 1901 census

Gloucestershire Family History Society 37 Barrington Drive, Hucclecote, Gloucester, Gloucestershire, GL3 3BT T: 01452 524344(RESOURCE CENTRE) T: 01452 535608Fax: 01452 615143 E: alexwood@blueyonder.co.uk W: www.gfhs.org.uk

Yate Library 44 West Walk, Yate, South Gloucestershire, BS37 4AX T: 01454 865661, F: 01454 865665 E: yate_library@southglos.gov.uk W: www.southglos.gov.uk

Gloucestershire – South
Thornbury Library St Mary Street, Thornbury, South Gloucestershire, BS35 2AA T: 01454-865655 E: thornbury.library@southglos.gov.uk W: www.southglos.gov.uk

Hammersmith
Hammersmith Central Library Shepherds Bush Road, London, W6 7AT T: 020 8753 3816, F: 020 8753 3815, W: www.lbhf.gov.uk

Hampshire
Aldershot Library 109 High Street, Aldershot, Hampshire, GU11 1DQ T: 01252 322456 ,

Andover Library Chantry Centre , Andover, Hampshire, SP10 1LT T: 01264 352807 E: clceand@hants.gov.uk W: www.hants.gov.uk

Basingstoke Library North Division Headquarters, 19 - 20 Westminster House, Potters Walk, Basingstoke, Hampshire, RG21 7LS T: 01256-473901, F: 01256-470666, W: www.hants.gov.uk

Bournemouth Library 22 The Triangle, Bournemouth, Hampshire, BH2 5RQ T: 01202 454817Fax: 01202 454830

Eastleigh Library The Swan Centre , Eastleigh, Hampshire, SO50 5SF T: 01703 612513 E: clweeas@hants.gov.uk W: www.hants.gov.uk

Fareham Library South Division Headquarters, Osborn Road, Fareham, Hampshire, PO16 7EN T: 01329-282715, F: 01329-221551 E: clsoref@hants.gov.uk W: www.hants.gov.uk

Farnborough Library Pinehurst, Farnborough, Hampshire, GU14 7JZ T: 01252 513838 E: clnoref@hants.gov.uk http://www.brit-a-r.demon.co.uk

Fleet Library 236 Fleet Road, Fleet, Hampshire, GU13 8BX T: 01252 614213 E: clnofle@hants.gov.uk W: www.hants.gov.uk

Gosport Library High Street, Gosport, Hampshire, PO12 1BT T: (023) 9252 3431 E: clsos@hants.gov.uk W: www.hants.gov.uk

Hampshire County Library West Division Headquarters, The Old School, Cannon Street, Lymington, Hampshire, SO41 9BR T: 01590-675767, F: 01590-672561 E: clwedhq@hants.gov.uk W: www.hants.gov.uk

Hampshire Local Studies Library Winchester Library Jewry Street, Winchester, Hampshire, SO23 8RX T: 01962 841408, F: 01962 841489 E: clceloc@hants.gov.uk W: www.hants.gov.uk/library, 1901 census

Lymington Library Cannon Street, Lymington, Hampshire, SO41 9BR T: 01590 673050 E: clwelym@hants.gov.uk W: www.hants.gov.uk

Portsmouth City Libraries Central Library Guildhall Square, Portsmouth, Hampshire, PO1 2DX T: (023) 9281 9311 X232 (Bookings) T: (023) 9281 9311 X234 (Enquiries)Fax: (023) 9283 9855 E: reference.library@portsmouthcc.gov.uk W: www.portsmouthcc.gov.uk 1901 census

Royal Marines Museum, Eastney, Southsea, Hampshire, PO4 9PX T: (023) 9281 9385-Exts-224Fax: (023) 9283 8420 E: matthewlittle@royalmarinesmuseum.co.uk W: www.royalmarinesmuseum.co.uk No charges for research other than material costs. Donations welcome. Visits by appointment Mon to Fri 10am to 4.30pm

Royal Naval Museum, H M Naval Base (PP66), Portsmouth, Hampshire, PO1 3NH T: (023) 9272 3795 (023) 9272 3942, W: www.royalnavalmuseum.org

Southampton City Libraries - Special Collections Southampton Reference Library Civic Centre , Southampton, Hampshire, SO14 7LW T: 023 8083 2205 023 8033 6305 E: local.studies@southampton.gov.uk W: www.southampton.gov.uk Special collections include information on Southampton and Hampshire, genealogy and maritime topics. 1901 census

Southampton University Library Highfield, Southampton, Hampshire, SO17 1BJ T: 023 8059 3724 T: 023 8059 2721, 023 8059 3007

Waterlooville Library The Precinct Waterlooville, Hampshire, PO7 7DT T: (023) 9225 4626 E: clsowvl@hants.gov.uk W: www.hants.gov.uk

Winchester Reference Library 81 North Walls, Winchester, Hampshire, SO23 8BY T: 01962-846059 01962-856615 E: clceref@hants.gov.uk W: www.hants.gov.uk

Herefordshire
Bromyard Library 34 Church Street, Bromyard, Herefordshire, HR7 4DP T: 01885 482657 , No Genealogical information held

Colwall Library Humphrey Walwyn Library Colwall, Malvern, Herefordshire, WR13 6QT T: 01684 540642 ,

Hereford Cathedral Archives & Library 5 College Cloisters, Cathedral Close, Hereford, Herefordshire, HR1 2NG T: 01432 374225 01432 374220 E: library@herefordcathedral.co.uk W: www.herefordcathedral.co.uk

Hereford Library Broad Street, Hereford, Herefordshire, HR4 9AU T: 01432-272456 01432-359668 E: herefordlibrary@herefordshire.gov.uk W: www.libraries.herefordshire.gov.uk The main local studies collection for the county of Herefordshire

Ledbury Library The Homend Ledbury, Herefordshire, HR8 1BT T: 01531 632133 ,

Leominster Library 8 Buttercross, Leominster, Herefordshire, HR6 8BN T: 01568-612384 01568-616025

Ross Library Cantilupe Road, Ross on Wye, Herefordshire, HR9 7AN T: 01989 567937 ,

Hertfordshire
Bushey Museum, Art Gallery and Local Studies Centre Rudolph Road, Bushey, Hertfordshire, WD23 3HW T: 020 8420 4057 020 8420 4923 E: busmt@bushey.org.uk W: www.busheymuseum.org, 1901 census for Bushey and Aldenham

Hertfordshire Archives and Local Studies County Hall, Pegs Lane, Hertford, Hertfordshire, SG13 8EJ T: 01438 737333 01923 471333 E: herts.direct@hertscc.gov.uk http://hertsdirect.org/hals, Hertfordshire Archives and Local Studies is comprised of the former Herts County Record Office and Herts Local Studies Library 1901 census

Welwyn Garden City Central Library Local Studies Section, Campus West, Welwyn Garden City, Hertfordshire, AL8 6AJ T: 01438 737333 01707 897 595

Hull
Brynmor Jones Library - University of Hull Cottingham Road, Hull, HU6 7RX T: 01482 465265 01482 466205 E: archives@acs.hull.ac.uk W: www.hull.ac.uk/lib W: www.hull.ac.uk/lib/archives

Hull Central Library Family and Local History Unit Central Library Albion Street, Kingston upon Hull, HU1 3TF T: 01482 616828 01482 616827 E: gareth@ukorigins.co.uk W: www.hullcc.gov.uk/genealogy/famhist.php, Free membership. Meets second Tuesday of every month 1901 census

Isle of Wight
Isle of Wight County Library Lord Louis Library Orchard Street, Newport, Isle of Wight, PO30 1LL T: 01983-823800 01983-825972 E: reflib@postmaster.co.uk W: www.iwight.com/thelibrary

Kent
Ashford Library Church Road, Asford, Kent, TN23 1QX T: 01233 620649 W: www.kent.gov.uk 1901 census

Broadstairs Library The Broadway, Broadstairs, Kent, CT10 2BS T: 01843-862994 W: www.kent.gov.uk

Canterbury Cathedral Library The Precincts, Canterbury, Kent, CT1 2EH T: 01227-865287 01227-865222 E: catlib@ukc.ac.uk W: www.canterbury-cathedral.org

Canterbury Library & Local Studies Collection 18 High Street, Canterbury, Kent, CT1 2JF T: 01227-463608 01227-768338, W: www.kent.gov.uk 1901 census

Dartford Central Library - Reference Department Market Street, Dartford, Kent, DA1 1EU T: 01322-221133 01322-278271, W: www.kent.gov.uk

Deal Library Broad Street, Deal, Kent, CT14 6ER T: 01304 374726 W: www.kent.gov.uk 1901 census

Dover Library Maison Dieu House, Biggin Street, Dover, Kent, CT16 1DW T: 01304 204241 01304 225914, W: www.kent.gov.uk 1901 census

Faversham Library Newton Road, Faversham, Kent, ME13 8DY T: 01759-532448 01795-591229, W: www.kent.gov.uk 1901 census

Folkestone Library & Local Heritage Studies 2 Grace Hill, Folkestone, Kent, CT20 1HD T: 01303-256710 01303-256710 E: janet.adamson@kent.gov.uk W: www.kent.gov.uk

Gillingham Library High Street, Gillingham, Kent, ME7 1BG T: 01634-281066 01634-855814 E: Gillingham.Library@medway.gov.uk W: www.medway.gov.uk

Gravesend Library Windmill Street, Gravesend, Kent, DA12 1BE T: 01474 352758 01474-320284, W: www.kent.gov.uk 1901 census

Greenhill Library Greenhill Road, Herne Bay, Kent, CT6 7PN T: 01227 374288 W: www.kent,gov.uk

Herne Bay Library 124 High Street, Herne Bay, Kent, CT6 5JY T: 01227-374896 01227-741582, W: www.kent.gov.uk

Institute of Heraldic and Genealogical Studies, 79 - 82 Northgate, Canterbury, Kent, CT1 1BA T: 01227 462618 01227 765617 E: ihgs@ihgs.ac.uk W: www.ihgs.ac.uk

London Borough of Bromley Local Studies Library Central Library High Street, Bromley, Kent, BR1 1EX T: 020 8460 9955 020 8313 9975 E: localstudies.library@bromley.gov.uk W: www.bromley.gov.uk 1901 census

Maidstone Reference Library St Faith's Street, Maidstone, Kent, ME14 1LH T: 01622 701943 W: www.kent.gov.uk 1901 census

Margate Library Local History Collection, Cecil Square, Margate, Kent, CT9 1RE T: 01843-223626 01843-293015, W: www.kent.gov.uk

Ramsgate Library and Museum, Guildford Lawn, Ramsgate, Kent, CT11 9QY T: 01843-593532 01843-852692, W: www.kent.gov.uk

Ramsgate Library Local Strudies Collection & Thanet Branch Archives Ramsgate Library Guildford Lawn, Ramsgate, Kent, CT11 9AY T: 01843-593532 W: www.kent.gov.uk Archives at this library moved to East Kent Archives CentreEnterprise Zone, Honeywood Road, Whitfield, Dover, Kent CT16 3EH. A Local Studies Collection will remain

Sevenoaks Library Buckhurst Lane, Sevenoaks, Kent, TN13 1LQ T: 01732-453118 01732-742682, W: www.kent.gov.uk 1901 census

Sheerness Library Russell Street, Sheerness, Kent, ME12 1PL T: 01795-662618 01795-583035, W: www.kent.gov.uk 1901 census

Sittingbourne Library Central Avenue, Sittingbourne, Kent, ME10 4AH T: 01795-476545 01795-428376, W: www.kent.gov.uk 1901 census

Sturry Library Chafy Crescent, Sturry, Canterbury, Kent, CT2 0BA T: 01227 711479 01227 710768, W: www.kent.gov.uk

Tonbridge Library Avenbury Avenue, Tonbridge, Kent, TN9 1TG T: 01732 352754 W: www.kent.gov.uk 1901 census

Tunbridge Wells Library Mount Pleasant, Tunbridge Wells, Kent, TN1 1NS T: 01892-522352 01892-514657, W: www.kent.gov.uk 1901 census

University of Kent at Canterbury Library Canterbury, Kent, CT2 7NU T: 01227 764000 01227 823984

Whitstable Library 31-33 Oxford Street, Whitstable, Kent, CT5 1DB T: 01227-273309 01227-771812

Kingston upon Hull
Hull Local Studies Library Central Library Albion Street, Kingston upon Hull, HU1 3TF T: 01482 210077 01482 616827 E: local.studies@hullcc.gov.uk http://www.hullcc.gov.uk/genealogy/

Lancashire
Bacup Library St James's Square, Bacup, Lancashire, OL13 9AH T: 01706 873324 , 1901 census

Barnoldswick Library Fernlea Avenue, Barnoldswick, Lancashire, BB18 5DW T: 01282-812147 1901 census

Blackburn Central Library Town Hall Street, Blackburn, Lancashire, BB2 1AG T: 01254 587920 01254 690539 E: reference.library@blackburn.gov.uk W: www.blackburn.gov.uk/library, 1901 census

Burnley Central & Local Studies Library Grimshaw Street, Burnley, Lancashire, BB11 2BD T: 01282-437115 01282 831682 E: burnley.reference@lcl.lancscc.gov.uk W: www.lancscc.gov.uk 1901 census

Bury Central Library - References and Information Services Bury Central Library Manchester Road, Bury, Lancashire, BL9 0DG T: 0161-253-5871 0161-253-5857 E: information@bury.gov.uk Bury.lib@bury.gov.uk W: www.bury.gov.uk/culture.htm, 1901 census

Chethams Library Long Millgate, Manchester, M3 1SB T: 0161 834 7961 0161 839 5797 E: librarian@chethams.org.uk W: www.chethams.org.uk

Chorley Central Library Union Street, Chorley , Lancashire, PR7 1EB T: 01257 277222 , 1901 census

Clitheroe Library Church Street, Clitheroe, Lancashire, BB7 2DG T: 01200 428788 , 1901 census

Colne Library Market Street, Colne, Lancashire, BB8 0AP T: 01282-871155 01282 865227 E: colne.reference@lcl.lancscc.gov.uk 1901 census

Haslingden Library Higher Deardengate, Haslingden, Rossendale, Lancashire, BB4 5QL T: 01706 215690 , 1901 census

Heywood Local Studies Library Heywood Library Church Street, Heywood, Lancashire, OL10 1LL T: 01706 360947 01706 368683 E:

Hyndburn Central Library St James Street, Accrington, Lancs, BB5 1NQ T: 01254-872385 01254 301066 E: accrington.localstudies@lcl.lancscc.gov.uk W: www.lancscc.gov.uk 1901 census

John Rylands University Library see Manchester
Lancashire Record Office Bow Lane, Preston, Lancashire, PR1 2RE T: 01772 263039 01772 263050 E: record.office@ed.lancscc.gov.uk W: www.lancashire.gov.uk/education/lifelong/recordindex.shtm, The Lancashire Local Studies Collection is now housed here 1901 census

Leigh Library Turnpike Centre Civic Centre , Leigh, Lancashire, WN7 1EB T: 01942-404559 01942 404567 E: heritage@wiganmbc.gov.uk W: www.wiganmbc.gov.uk 1901 census

Leyland Library Lancastergate, Leyland, Lancashire, PR25 2EX T: 01772 432804 01772 456549 E: leyland.library@lcl.lancscc.gov.uk W: www.lancashire.gov.uk/libraries, 1901 census

Morecambe Library Central Drive, Morecambe, Lancashire, LA4 5DL T: 01524 402110 , 1901 census - Lancaster District

Nelson Library Market Square, Nelson, Lancashire, BB9 7PU T: 01282 692511 01282 449584 E: nelson.reference@lcl.lancscc.gov.uk W: www.lancashire.gov.uk/libraries/

Oldham Local Studies and Archives 84 Union Street, Oldham, Lancashire, OL1 1DN T: 0161-911-4654 0161-911-4654 E: archives@oldham.gov.uk localstudies@oldham.gov.uk W: www.oldham.gov.uk/archives W: www.oldham.gov.uk/local_studies, 1901 census

Ormskirk Library Burscough Street, Ormskirk, Lancashire, L39 2EN T: 01695 573448 , 1901 census

Prestwich Library Longfield Centre , Prestwich, Lancashire, M25 1AY T: 0161 253 7214 T: 0161 253 7218, 0161 253 5372 E: Prestwich.lib@bury.gov.uk W: www.bury.gov.uk

Radcliffe Library Stand Lane, Radcliffe, Lancashire, M26 9WR T: 0161 253 7160 0161 253 7165 E: Radcliuffe.lib@bury.gov.uk W: www.bury.gov.uk

Ramsbottom Library Carr Street, Ramsbottom, Lancashire, BL0 9AE T: 01706 822484 01706 824638 E: Ramsbottom.lib@bury.gov.uk W: www.bury.gov.uk

Rawtenstall Library Haslingden Road, Rawtenstall, Rossendale, Lancashire, BB4 6QU T: 01706 227911 E: rawtenstall.reference@lcl.lancscc.gov.uk W: www.lancashire.gov.uk/libraries, 1901 census

Rochdale Local Studies Library Touchstones, The Esplanade, Rochdale, Lancashire, OL16 1AQ T: 01706 864915 01706 864944 E: localstudies@rochdale.gov.uk W: www.rochdale.gov.uk 1901 census. GRO Index 1837 - 1999

Salford Local History Library Peel Park, Salford, Lancashire, M5 4WU T: 0161 736 2649 01161 745 9490 E: salford.museums@salford/gov.uk W: www.salford.gov.uk

Salford Museum & Art Gallery, Peel Park, Salford, Lancashire, M5 4WU T: 0161 736 2649 E: Email: info@lifetimes.org.uk W: www.lifetimes.org.uk

Skelmersdale Central Library Southway, Skelmersdale, Lancashire, WN8 6NL T: 01695 720312 , 1901 census

St Anne's Library 254 Clifton Drive, St Anne's on Sea, Lancashire, FY8 1NR T: 01253 643900 , 1901 census

The Harris Reference Library Market Square, Preston, Lancashire, PR1 2PP T: 01772 404010 01772 555527 E: harris@airtime.co.uk 1901 census

Tameside Local Studies Library Stalybridge Library Trinity Street, Stalybridge, Cheshire, SK15 2BN T: 0161-338-2708 T: 0161-338-3831 and 0161 303 7937Fax: 0161-303-8289 E: localstudies.library@mail.tameside.gov.uk W: www.tameside.gov.uk 1901 census

Working Class Movement Library Jubilee House, 51 The Crescent, Salford, Lancashire, M5 4WX T: 0161 736 3601 0161-737 4115 E: enquiries2wcml.org.uk W: www.wcml.org.uk

Leeds
Brotherton Library see Yorkshire- West

Leicestershire
Hinckley Library Local Studies Collection Hinckley Library Lancaster Road, Hinckley, Leicestershire, LE10 0AT T: 01455-635106 01455-251385 E: hinckleylibrary@leics.gov.uk W: www.leics.gov.uk

Leicester Reference and Information Library Bishop Street, Leicester, Leicestershire, LE1 6AA T: 0116 299 5401 , 1901 census

Leicestershire Libraries & Information Service 929 - 931 Loughborough Road, Rothley, Leicestershire, LE7 7NH T: 0116 267 8023 0116 267 8039 E: skettle@leics.gov.uk W: www.leicestershire.gov.uk/libraries

Loughborough Library Local Studies Collection Granby Street, Loughborough, Leicestershire, LE11 3DZ T: 01509-238466 01509-212985 E: Jslater@leices.gov.uk W: www.leices.gov.uk/libraries, 1901 census

Market Harborough Library and Local Studies Collection Pen Lloyd Library Adam and Eve Street, Market Harborough, Leicestershire, LE16 7LT T: 01858-821272 01858-821265

Melton Mowbray Library Wilton Road, Melton Mowbray, Leicestershire, LE13 0UJ T: 01664 560161 01664 410199, W: www.leics.gov.uk

Southfields Library Reader Development Services, Saffron Lane, Leicester, Leicestershire, LE2 6QS

Lincolnshire
Boston Library County Hall Boston, Lincolnshire, PE21 6LX T: 01205 310010 ext 2874, 01205 357760

Gainsborough Library Cobden Street, Gainsborough, Lincolnshire, DN21 2NG T: 01427 614780 01427 810318 E: gainsborough.library@lincolnshire.gov.uk

Grantham Library Issac Newton Centre , Grantham, Lincolnshire, NG1 9LD T: 01476 591411 01476 592458

Lincoln Cathedral Library Lincoln Cathedral Library The Cathedral, Lincoln, Lincolnshire, LN2 1PZ England T: 01522-544544 01522-511307 E: librarian@lincolncathedral.com W: www.lincolncathedral.com

Lincolnshire County Library Local Studies Section, Lincoln Central Library Free School Lane, Lincoln, Lincolnshire, LN1 1EZ T: 01522-510800 01522-575011 E: lincoln.library@lincolnshire.gov.uk W: www.lincolnshire.gov.uk/library/services/family.htm, 1901 census

Stamford Library High Street, Stamford, Lincolnshire, PE9 2BB T: 01780 763442 01780 482518

Lincolnshire - North
Scunthorpe Central Library Carlton Street, Scunthorpe, North Lincolnshire, DN15 6TX T: 01724-860161 01724-859737 E: scunthorpe.ref@central-library.demon.co.uk W: www.nothlincs.gov.uk/library, 1901 census

Lincolnshire - North East
Grimsby Central Library Reference Department Central Library Town Hall Square, Great Grimsby, North East Lincolnshire, DN31 1HG T: 01472-323635 01472-323634 E: jennie.mooney@nelincs.gov.uk W: www.nelincs.gov.uk 1901 census. GRO indexes 1837-2001. 1901 census vouchers on sale
Liverpool
Liverpool Record Office & Local History Department Central Library William Brown Street, Liverpool, L3 8EW T: 0151 233 5817 0151-233 5886 E: recoffice.central.library@liverpool.gov.uk W: www.liverpool.gov.uk
Liverpool University Special Collections & Archives University of Liverpool Library PO Box 123, Liverpool, L69 3DA T: 0151-794-2696 0151-794-2081 W: www.sca.lib.liv.ac.uk/collections/index.html, The University holds the records of a number of charities, especially those which looked after children or encouraged emigration
London
Bancroft Library 277 Bancroft Road, London, E1 4DQ T: 020 8980 4366 , 1901 census
London Borough of Barking & Dagenham Local Studies Library see Essex
Bishopsgate Institute, Reference Librarian, 230 Bishopsgate, London, EC2M 4QH T: (020) 7392 9270 (020) 7392 9275 E: library@bishopsgate.org.uk W: www.bishopsgate.org.uk
Brent Community History Library & Archive 152 Olive Road, London, NW2 6UY T: (020) 8937 3541 (020) 8450 5211 E: archive@brent.gov.uk W: www.brent.gov.uk 1901 census
British Film Institute - Library & Film Archive 21 Stephen Street, London, W1T 1LN T: 020 7957 4824 W: www.bfi.org.uk
British Library see National
British Library - Early Printed Collections see National
British Library Newspaper Library see National
British Library of Political and Economic Science see National
British Library Oriental and India Office Collections see National
Catholic Central Library Lancing Street, London, NW1 1ND T: (020) 7383-4333 (020) 7388-6675 E: librarian@catholic-library.demon.co.uk W: www.catholic-library.demon.co.uk
Chelsea Public Library Old Town Hall, King's Road, London, SW3 5EZ T: (020) 7352-6056 T: (020) 7361-4158, (020) 7351 1294 Local Studies Collection on Royal Borough of Kensington & Chelsea south of Fulham Road
Dr Williams's Library see Special
Ealing Local History Centre Central Library 103 Broadway Centre Ealing, London, W5 5JY T: (020) 8567-3656-ext-37, (020) 8840-2351 E: localhistory@hotmail.com W: www.ealing.gov.uk/libraries, Closed Sundays & Mondays 1901 census
Fawcett Library London Guildhall University, Old Castle Street, London, E1 7NT T: (020) 7320-1189 (020) 7320-1188 E: fawcett@lgu.ac.uk W: http://www.lgu.ac.uk./fawcett
The Library & Museum of Freemasonry see National
Guildhall Library, Manuscripts Section Aldermanbury, London, EC2P 2EJ T: (020) 7332-1863 (020) 7600-3384 E: manuscripts.guildhall@corpoflondon.gov.uk http://ihr.sas.ac.uk/ihr/gh/, Opening hours Mon to Sat 9.30am to 4.45pm (last orders for manuscripts 4.30pm: on Sat no manuscripts produced bet 12noon and 2pm. Records: City of London parish records, probate records, City Livery companies, business records, Diocese of London, St Pauls Cathedral, etc. Prior booking unnecessary except some records on 24 hrs call/restricted 1901 census
Hammersmith Central Library Shepherds Bush Road, London, W6 7AT T: 020 8753 3816, F: 020 8753 3815, W: www.lbhf.gov.uk
Hounslow Library (Local Studies & Archives) Centrespace, Treaty Centre High Street, Hounslow, London, TW3 1ES T: 0845 456 2800 0845 456 2880, W: www.cip.com, 1901 census
House of Commons Library see National
Huguenot Library University College, Gower Street, London, WC1E 6BT T: (020) 7679 7094 E: s.massilk@ucl.ac.uk W: www.ucl.ac.uk/ucl-info/divisions/library/hugenot.htm
Imperial College Archives London University, Room 455 Sherfield Building, Imperial College, London, SW7 2AZ T: 020 7594 8850 020 7584 3763 E: archivist@ic.ac.uk W: www.lib.ic.ac.uk
James Clavell Library Royal Arsenal (West), Warren Lane, Woolwich, London, SE18 6ST T: 020 8312 7125 E: library@firepower.org.uk W: www.firepower.org.uk
Jewish Museum, The Sternberg Centre for Judaism, 80 East End Road, Finchley, London, N3 2SY T: 020 8349 1143 020 8343 2162 E: enquiries@jewishmuseum.org.uk W: www.jewishmuseum.org.uk
Jewish Studies Library see National
The Kenneth Ritchie Wimbledon Library see National
Lambeth Palace Library see Special
Library of the Religious Society of Friends (Quakers) see Special
Lewisham Local Studies & Archives, Lewisham Library 199 - 201 Lewisham High Street, Lewisham, London, SE13 6LG T: (020) 8297-0682 (020) 8297 1169 E: local.studies@lewisham.gov.uk W: www.lewisham.gov.uk Covering the Parishes of Lewisham, Lee & St Paul's, Deptford. Appointments advisable. 1901 census

Linnean Society of London Burlington House, Piccadilly, London, W1J 0BF T: 020 7437 4479 T: 020 7434 4470, 020 7287 9364 E: gina@linnean.org W: www.linnean.org
Local Studies Collection for Chiswick & Brentford Chiswick Public Library Dukes Avenue, Chiswick, London, W4 2AB T: (020) 8994-5295 (020) 8995-0016 and (020) 8742 7411, Restricted opening hours for local history room: please telephone before visiting
London Borough of Barnet, Archives & Local Studies Department Hendon Library The Burroughs, Hendon, London, NW4 3BQ T: (020) 8359-2876, (020) 8359-2885 E: hendon.library@barnet.gov.uk W: www.barnet.gov.uk
London Borough of Bromley Local Studies Library see Kent
Hertfordshire Archives and Local Studies, see Hertfordshire
London Borough of Camden Local Studies & Archive Centre Holborn Library 32 - 38 Theobalds Road, London, WC1X 8PA T: 020 7974 6342 020 7974 6284 E: localstudies@camden.gov.uk W: www.camden.gov.uk
L Borough of Croydon Library & Archives Service see Surrey
London Borough of Enfield Libraries, Southgate Town Hall, Green Lanes, Palmers Green, London, N13 4XD T: (020) 8379-2724
London Borough of Greenwich Heritage Centre Museum and Library Building 41 Royal Arsenal, Woolwich, London, SE18 6SP T: (020) 8858 4631 (020) 8293 4721 E: local.history@greenwich.gov.uk W: www.greenwich.gov.uk
Central Ref Library - London Borough of Havering see Essex
London Borough of Islington Finsbury Library 245 St John Street, London, EC1V 4NB T: (020) 7527 7994 (020) 7527 8821, W: www.islington.gov.uk/htm
London Borough of Islington History Centre Finsbury Library 245 St John Street, London, EC1V 4NB T: (020) 7527 7988 E: local.history@islington.gov.uk W: www.islington.gov.uk , Collection covers the LB of Islington. Material relating to (1) the former Metropolitan Borough of Islington; (2) the present London Borough of Islington and (3) the civil parish of St Mary, Islington (to 1900). The north and south part of the present London Borough of Islington - the former Metropolitan Borough of Finsbury and its predecessors, the former civil parishes of Clerkenwell and St Lukes, Finsbury. 1901 census. The Local History Service operates through an appointment system. Users must make an appointment, preferably by telephone. A postal enquiry service (SAE required) is available. A charge is made for extended research.
London Borough of Lambeth Archives Department Minet Library 52 Knatchbull Road, Lambeth, London, SE5 9QY T: (020) 7926 6076 (020) 7936 6080 E: lambetharchives@lambeth.gov.uk W: www.lambeth.gov.uk
London Borough of Newham Archives & Local Studies Library Stratford Library 3 The Grove, London, E15 1EL T: (020) 8430 6881 W: www.newham.gov.uk
London Borough of Waltham Forest Local Studies Library Vestry House Museum, Vestry Road, Walthamstow, London, E17 9NH T: (020) 8509 1917 E: Vestry.House@al.lbwf.gov.uk W: www.lbwf.gov.uk/vestry/vestry.htm
London Borough of Wandsworth Local Studies Local Studies Service, Battersea Library 265 Lavender Hill, London, SW11 1JB T: (020) 8871 7753 (020) 7978-4376 E: wandsworthmuseum@wandsworth.gov.uk W: www.wandsworth.gov.uk Open Tues & Wed 10am to 88pm, Fri 10am to 5pm, Sat 9am to 1pm - Research service offerred - £7.00 per half hour (the minimum fee) apointment advised to ensure archives, hard copy newspapers (if not microfilmed) and other items are available
Library of the Royal College of Surgeons of England see Special
London Hillingdon Borough Libraries, Central Library High Street, Uxbridge, Middlesex, UB8 1HD T: 01895 250702 01895 811164 E: clib@hillingdon.gov.uk W: www. hillingdon.gov.uk
London Metropolitan Archives, 40 Northampton Road, London, EC1R 0HB T: 020 7332 3820 T: Mini com 020 7278 8703, 020 7833 9136 E: ask.lma@ms.corpoflondon.gov.uk W: www.cityoflondon.gov.uk
London University - Institute of Advanced Studies Charles Clore House, 17 Russell Square, London, WC1B 5DR T: (020) 7637 1731 (020) 7637 8224 E: ials.lib@sas.ac.uk http://ials.sas.ac.uk
Manuscripts Room, Library Services, University College, Gower Street, London, WC1E 6BT T: (020) 7387 7050 020 7380 7727 E: mssrb@ucl.ac.uk W: www.ucl.ac.uk/library/special-coll/
Minet Library 52 Knatchbull Road, Lambeth, London, SE5 9QY T: (020) 7926 6076 (020) 7936 6080 E: lambetharchives@lambeth.gov.uk W: www.lambeth.gov.uk
Museum in Docklands Library & Archives Library & Archive, No 1 Warehouse, West India Quay, Hertsmere Road, London, E14 4AL T: (020) 7001 9825 (Librarian), (020) 7001 9801 E: bobaspinall@museumindocklands.org.uk W: www.museumindocklands.org.uk
Museum of London Library 150 London Wall, London, EC2Y 5IIN T: 020 7814 5588 020 7600 1058 E: info@museumoflondon.org.uk http://museumoflondon.org.uk
Museum of the Order of St John St John's Gate, St John's Lane, Clerkenwell, London, EC1M 4DA T: (020) 7253-6644 (020) 7336 0587, W: www.sja.org.uk/history

National Gallery Library and Archive see National
National Maritime Museum - Caird Library see National
Royal Armouries see National
Royal Borough of Kensington and Chelsea Libraries & Arts Service Central Library Phillimore Walk, Kensington, London, W8 7RX T: (020) 7361-3036 T: (020) 7361 3007, E: information.services@rbkc.gov.uk W: www.rbkc.gov.uk
Royal Botanic Gardens, Library & Archives, Kew, Richmond, Surrey, TW9 3AE T: 020 8332 5414 T: 020 8332 5417, 020 8332 5430 CC Accepted
Royal Society of Chemistry Library & Information Centre see Special
School of Oriental and African Studies Library see Special
Society of Antiquaries of London see Special
Society of Genealogists - Library National
Southwark Local Studies Library 211 Borough High Street, Southwark, London, SE1 1JA T: 0207-403-3507 0207-403-8633 E: local.studies.library@southwark.gov.uk W: www.southwark.gov.uk
Tower Hamlets Local History Library & Archives Bancroft Library 277 Bancroft Road, London, E1 4DQ T: (020) 8980 4366 Ext 129, (020) 8983 4510 E: localhistory@towerhamlets.gov.uk W: www.towerhamlets.gov.uk
Trades Union Congress Library Collections - University of North London see Special
Twickenham Library Twickenham Library Garfield Road, Twickenham, Middlesex, TW1 3JS T: (020) 8891-7271 (020) 8891-5934 E: twicklib@richmond.gov.uk W: www.richmond.gov.uk The Twickenham collection moved to Richmond Local Studies Library
United Reformed Church History Society see National
University of London (Library - Senate House) Palaeography Room, Senate House, Malet Street, London, WC1E 7HU T: (020) 7862 8475 020 7862 8480 E: library@hull.ac.uk W: www.ull.ac.uk
Victoria & Albert Museum - National Art Library see National
Victoria & Albert Museum - National Art Library - Archive of Art and Design see National
Wellcome Library - Contemporary Medical Archives Centre : **Wellcome Library for the History of Medicine - Department of Western Manuscripts : The Wellcome Trust : Wellcome Library for the History and Understanding of Medicine** see National
Westminster Abbey Library & Muniment Room Westminster Abbey, London, SW1P 3PA T: (020) 7222-5152-Ext-4830, (020) 7226-4827 E: library@westminster-abbey.org W: www.westminster-abbey.org
Westminster University Archives Information Systems & Library Services, 4-12 Little Titchfield Street, London, W1W 7UW T: 020 7911 5000 ext 2524, 020 7911 5894 E: archive@westminster.ac.uk W: www.wmin.ac.uk The archive is organisationally within the Library but is a separate entity. The University of Westminster Libraries do not have special collections relating to family and local history but the archive may be of interest to researchers
The Women's Library see Special
Luton BC
Local Studies Library Luton Central Library St George's Square, Luton, Bedfordshire, LU1 2NG T: 01582-547420 T: 01582-547421, F: 01582-547450 E: local.studies@luton.gov.uk W: www.luton.gov.uk 1901 census
Manchester
John Rylands University Library Special Collections Division, 150 Deansgate, Manchester, M3 3EH T: 0161-834-5343 0161-834-5343 E: spcoll72@fs1.li.man.ac.uk W: http://rylibweb.man.ac.uk Holdings include family muniment collections especially relating to Cheshire and major Non Conformist Archives Few genealogical records held except for family muniment collections, especially for Cheshire and Methodist Circuit plans, records, ministers
Manchester Archives & Local Studies, Manchester Central Library St Peter's Square, Manchester, M2 5PD T: 0161-234-1979 0161-234-1927 E: lsu@libraries.manchester.gov.uk W: www.manchester.gov.uk/libraries/index.htm, 1901 census
Methodist Archives and Research Centre John Rylands University Library 150 Deansgate, Manchester, M3 3EH T: 0161 834 5343 0161 834 5574
Medway
Medway Archives and Local Studies Centre , Civic Centre Strood, Rochester, Kent, ME2 4AU T: 01634-332714 01634-297060 E: archives@medway.gov.uk local.studies@medway.gov.uk W: www.medway.gov.uk 1901 census
Merseyside
Crosby Library (South Sefton Local History Unit), Crosby Road North, Waterloo, Liverpool, Merseyside, L22 0LQ T: 0151 257 6401 0151 934 5770 E: local-history.south@leisure.sefton.gov.uk W: www.sefton.gov.uk The Local History Units serve Sefton Borough Council area. The South Sefton Unit covers Bootle, Crosby, Maghull and other communities south of the River Alt. The North Sefton Unit covers Southport, Formby.
Huyton Central Library Huyton Library Civic Way, Huyton, Knowsley, Merseyside, L36 9GD T: 0151-443-3738 0151 443 3739 E: eileen.hume.dlcs@knowsley.gov.uk W: www.knowsley.gov.uk/leisure/libraries/huyton/index.html

Liverpool University Special Collections & Archives see Liverpool,
Southport Library (North Sefton Local History Unit), Lord Street, Southport, Merseyside, PR8 1DJ T: 0151 934 2119 0151 934 2115 E: local-history.north@leisure.sefton.gov.uk The Local History Units serve Sefton Borough Council area. The North Sefton Unit covers Southport, Formby. The South Sefton Unit covers Bootle, Crosby, Maghull and other communities south of the River Alt
St Helen's Local History & Archives Library Central Library, Gamble Institute, Victoria Square, St Helens, Merseyside, WA10 1DY T: 01744-456952 01744 20836 No research undertaken 1901 census
Middlesbrough
Middlesbrough Libraries & Local Studies Centre see Cleveland
Middlesex
London Borough of Harrow Local History Collection Civic Centre Library, PO Box 4, Station Road, Harrow, Middlesex, HA1 2UU T: 0208 424 1055 T: 0208 424 1056, 0181-424-1971 E: civiccentre.library@harrow.gov.uk W: www.harrow.gov.uk 1901 census
Hertfordshire Archives and Local Studies see Hertfordshire
Milton Keynes
Milton Keynes Reference Library see Buckinghamshire
Newcastle upon Tyne
Robinson Library see Tyne & Wear
Norfolk
Family History Shop & Library The Family History Shop, 51 Horns Lane, Norwich, Norfolk, NR1 1ER T: 01603 621152 E: jenlibrary@aol.com W: www.jenlibrary.u-net.com, Microfiche & 3.5" Disks. We have Parish & Non-conformist Registers (Norfolk,Suffolk & London), Census(1821 & 1831 Marylebone), Militia lists(Nfk, Sfk, Ldn, Sx, Ex,Ldn,Ireland, N'land) Census & Marriages Strays (Norfolk & Suffolk), Kelly's Upper Ten Thousand 1878; Kelly's Titled & Official Classes 1907, Harrod's 1872 Norfolk Directories. Norwich Gazette (contains a lot of London references) 1706 - 1712(m/fiche & Book) Norwich Mercury late 1700s (m/fiche) Licenced Victuallers Asylum Census. We also have a library with over 400 million names
Great Yarmouth Central Library Tolhouse Street, Great Yarmouth, Norfolk, NR30 2SH T: 01493-844551 T: 01493-842279, 01493-857628 E: yarmouth.lib@norfolk.gov.uk W: www.library.norfolk.gov.uk 1901 census
Heritage Centre, Norfolk and Norwich Millennium Library Millennium Plain, Norwich, Norfolk, NR2 1AW T: 01603 774740 01603-215258 E: norfolk.studies.lib@norfolk.gov.uk W: www.norfolk.gov.uk 1901 census
Kings Lynn Library London Road, King's Lynn, Norfolk, PE30 5EZ T: 01553-772568 T: 01553 761393, 01553-769832 E: kings.lynn.lib@norfolk.gov.uk W: www.norfolk.gov.uk 1901 census
Thetford Public Library Raymond Street, Thetford, Norfolk, IP24 2EA T: 01842-752048 01842-750125 E: thetford.lib@norfolk.gov.uk W: www.culture.norfolk.gov.uk 1901 census
Northumberland
Alnwick Library Green Batt, Alnwick, Northumberland, NE66 1TU T: 01665-602689 01665 604740, W: www.northumberland.gov.uk
Berwick upon Tweed Library Church Street, Berwick upon Tweed, Northumberland, TD15 1EE T: 01289-307320 01289-308299, W: www.northumberland.gov.uk
Blyth Library Bridge Street, Blyth, Northumberland, NE24 2DJ T: 01670-361352 W: www.northumberland.gov.uk
Border History Museum and Library Moothall, Hallgate, Hexham, Northumberland, NE46 3NH T: 01434-652349 01434-652425 E: museum@tynedale.gov.uk W: www.tynedale.gov.uk
Hexham Library Queens Hall, Beaumont Street, Hexham, Northumberland, NE46 3LS T: 01434 652474 01434-606043 E: cheane@northumberland.gov.uk W: www.northumberland.gov.uk
Nottinghamshire
Arnold Library Front Street, Arnold, Nottinghamshire, NG5 7EE T: 0115-920-2247 0115-967-3378, W: www.nottscc.gov.uk
Beeston Library Foster Avenue, Beeston, Nottinghamshire, NG9 1AE T: 0115-925-5168 0115-922-0841, W: www.nottscc.gov.uk
Eastwood Library Wellington Place, Eastwood, Nottinghamshire, NG16 3GB T: 01773-712209 W: www.nottscc.gov.uk
Mansfield Library Four Seasons Centre Westgate, Mansfield, Nottinghamshire, NG18 1NH T: 01623-627591 01623-629276 E: mansfield.library@nottscc.gov.uk W: www.nottscc.gov.uk
Newark Library Beaumont Gardens, Newark, Nottinghamshire, NG24 1UW T: 01636-703966 01636-610045, W: www.nottscc.gov.uk
Nottingham Central Library : Local Studies Centre Angel Row, Nottingham, Nottinghamshire, NG1 6HP T: 0115 915 2873 0115 915 2850 E: local-studies.library@nottinghamcity.gov.uk W: www.nottinghamcity.gov.uk/libraries
Retford Library Denman Library Churchgate, Retford, Nottinghamshire, DN22 6PE T: 01777-708724 01777-710020, W: www.nottscc.gov.uk
Southwell Minster Library Minster Office, Trebeck Hall, Bishop's Drive, Southwell NG25 0JP T: 01636-812649 E: mail@southwellminster.org.uk W: www.southwellminster.org.uk

Sutton in Ashfield Library Devonshire Mall, Sutton in Ashfield, Nottinghamshire, NG17 1BP T: 01623-556296 01623-551962, W: www.nottscc.gov.uk

University of Nottingham, Hallward Library University Park, Nottingham, NG7 2RD T: 0115-951-4514 0115-951-4558, W: www.nottingham.ac.uk/library/

Department of Manuscripts and Special Collections see Special

West Bridgford Library Bridgford Road, West Bridgford, Nottinghamshire, NG2 6AT T: 0115-981-6506 0115-981-3199, W: www.nottscc.gov.uk

Oxfordshire

Abingdon Library The Charter, Abingdon, Oxfordshire, OX14 3LY T: 01235-520374 01235 532643 E: abingdon_library@yahoo.com W: www.oxfordshire.gov.uk

Angus Library Regent's Park College, Pusey Street, Oxford, Oxfordshire, OX1 2LB T: 01865 288142 01865 288121

Banbury Library Marlborough Road, Banbury, Oxfordshire, OX16 8DF T: 01295-262282 01295-264331

Centre for Oxfordshire Studies Central Library Westgate, Oxford, Oxfordshire, OX1 1DJ T: 01865-815749 01865-810187 E: cos@oxfordshire.gov.uk W: www.oxfordshire.gov.uk

Henley Library Ravenscroft Road, Henley on Thames, Oxfordshire, RG9 2DH T: 01491-575278 01491-576187

Middle East Centre St Anthony's College, Pusey Street, Oxford, Oxfordshire, OX2 6JF T: 01865 284706 01865 311475

Nuffield College Library see National

Puysey House Library Pusey House, 61 St Giles, Oxford, Oxfordshire, OX1 1LZ T: 01865 278415 01865 278416 E: pusey.house@ic24.net,

River & Rowing Museum see National

Rhodes House Library see National

The Bodleian Library Broad Street, Oxford, Oxfordshire, OX1 3BG T: 01865 277000 01865 277182, W: www.bodley.ox.ac.uk The Bodleian is the largest of the libraries operated by Oxford University and includes the Old Library, the New Library and the Radcliffe Camera. In addition to the Central Bodleian, the library has 7 dependant libraries: The Indian Institute Library, The Bodleian Law Library, Rhodes House Library, the Radcliffe Science Library, The Bodleian Japanese Library, the Oriental Institute Library and the Philosophy Library

Wantage Library Stirlings Road, Wantage, Oxfordshire, OX12 7BB T: 01235 762291 01235 7700951

Witney Library Welch Way, Witney, Oxfordshire, OX8 7HH T: 01993-703659 01993-775993

Peterborough

Peterborough Local Studies Collection see Cambridgeshire

Redcar & Cleveland BC

Redcar Reference Library Coatham Road, Redcar, Cleveland, TS10 1RP T: 01642 489292 E: reference_library@redcar-cleveland.gov.uk

Rutland

Oakham Library Catmos Street, Oakham, Rutland, LE15 6HW T: 01572 722918 , 1901 census

Shropshire

Wrekin Local Studies Forum Madeley Library Russell Square, Telford, Shropshire, TF7 5BB T: 01952 586575 01952 587105 E: wlst@library.madeley.uk W: www.madeley.org.uk

Slough BC

Slough Local Studies Library see Berkshikre

Somerset

Bath Central Library 19 The Podium, Northgate Street, Bath, Somerset, BA1 5AN T: 01225 787400 1225787426 E: Bath_Library@bathnes.gov.uk W: www.bathnes.gov.uk 1901 census. GRO Index 1837 - 1950

Bristol University Library - Special Collections Tyndall Avenue, Bristol, BS8 1TJ T: 0117 928 8014 0117 925 5334 E: library@bris.ac.uk W: www.bris.ac.uk/depts/library

Nailsea Library Somerset Square, Nailsea, Somerset, BS19 2EX T: 01275-854583 01275-858373

Reference Library Binford Place, Bridgewater, Somerset, TA6 3LF T: 01278-450082 01278-451027 E: pcstoyle@somerset.gov.uk W: www.somerset.gov.uk

Reference Library Justice Lane, Frome, Somerset, BA11 1BA T: 01373-462215 01373-472003

Somerset Studies Library Paul Street, Taunton, Somerset, TA1 3XZ T: 01823-340300 01823-340301 E: somstud@somerset.gov.uk W: www.somerset.gov.uk/libraries

Weston Library The Boulevard, Weston Super Mare, Somerset, BS23 1PL T: 01934-636638 01934-413046 E: weston.library@n-somerset.gov.uk W: www.n-somerset.gov.uk 1901 census

Yeovil Library King George Street, Yeovil, Somerset, BA20 1PY T: 01935-421910 01935-431847 E: ransell@somerset.gov.uk W: www.somerset.gov.uk

Southampton

Southampton City Libraries - Special Collections see Hampshire

Staffordshire

Barton Library Dunstall Road, Barton under Needwood, Staffordshire, DE13 8AX T: 01283-713753 W: www.staffordshire.gov.uk

Biddulph Library Tunstall Road, Biddulph, Stoke on Trent, Staffordshire, ST8 6HH T: 01782-512103 W: www.staffordshire.gov.uk

Brewood Library Newport Street, Brewood, Staffordshire, ST19 9DT T: 01902-850087 W: www.staffordshire.gov.uk

Burton Library Burton Library Riverside, High Street, Burton on Trent, Staffordshire, DE14 1AH T: 01283-239556 01283-239571 E: burton.library@staffordshire.gov.uk W: www.staffordshire.gov.uk

Cannock Library Manor Avenue, Cannock WS11 1AA T: 01543-502019 01543-278509 E: cannock.library@staffordshire.gov.uk W: www.staffordshire.gov.uk

Cheslyn Hay Library , Cheslyn Hay, Walsall, Staffordshire, WS56 7AE T: 01922-413956 W: www.staffordshire.gov.uk

Codsall Library Histons Hill, Codsall, Staffordshire, WV8 1AA T: 01902-842764 W: www.staffordshire.gov.uk

Great Wyrley Library John's Lane, Great Wyrley, Walsall, WS6 6BY T: 01922-414632 W: www.staffordshire.gov.uk

Keele University Library , Keele, ST5 5BG T: 01782 583237 E: library@keele.ac.uk W: www.keele.ac.uk/library

Kinver Library Vicarage Drive, Kinver, Stourbridge, Staffordshire, DY7 6HJ T: 01384-872348 W: www.staffordshire.gov.uk

Leek Library Nicholson Institute, Stockwell Street, Leek, Staffordshire, ST13 6DW T: 01538-483210 01538-483216 E: leek.library@staffordshire.gov.uk W: www.staffordshire.gov.uk

Lichfield Library (Local Studies Section) Lichfield Library The Friary, Lichfield WS13 6QG T: 01543 510720 01543 510716

Newcastle Library Ironmarket, Newcastle under Lyme, ST5 1AT T: 01782-297310 E: newcastle.library@staffordshire.gov.uk W: www.staffordshire.gov.uk

Penkridge Library Bellbrock, Penkridge ST19 9DL T: 01785-712916 W: www.staffordshire.gov.uk

Perton Library Severn Drive, Perton WV6 7QU T: 01902-755794 01902-756123 E: perton.library@staffordshire.gov.uk W: www.staffordshire.gov.uk

Rugeley Library Anson Strect, Rugeley, Staffordshire, WS16 2BB T: 01889-583237 W: www.staffordshire.gov.uk

Staffordshire & Stoke on Trent Archive Service -Stoke on Trent City Archives Hanley Library Bethesda Street, Hanley, Stoke on Trent, Staffordshire, ST1 3RS T: 01782-238420 01782-238499 E: stoke.archives@stoke.gov.uk W: www.staffordshire.gov.uk/archives, 1901 census

Tamworth Library Corporation Street, Tamworth, Staffordshire, B79 7DN T: 01827-475645 01827-475658 E: tamworth.library@staffordshire.gov.uk W: www.staffordshire.gov.uk/locgov/county/cars/tamlib.htm, IGI (Derby, Leics, Notts, Shrops, Staffs, Warks, Worcs). Parish registers for Tamworth. Census for Tamworth and District, 1841 - 91. Street directories for Staffs and Warks.

Uttoxeter Library High Street, Uttoxeter, Staffordshire, ST14 7JQ T: 01889-256371 01889-256374, W: www.staffordshire.gov.uk

William Salt Library Eastgate Street, Stafford, Staffordshire, ST16 2LZ T: 01785-278372 01785-278414 E: william.salt.library@staffordshire.gov.uk W: www.staffordshire.gov.uk/archives/salt.htm

Wombourne Library Windmill Bank, Wombourne, Staffordshire, WV5 9JD T: 01902-892032 W: www.staffordshire.gov.uk

Stockport MBC

Local Heritage Library see Cheshire

Suffolk

Chantry Library Chantry Library Hawthorne Drive, Ipswich, Suffolk, IP2 0QY T: 01473 686117 ,

Surrey

Bourne Hall Library Bourne Hall, Spring Street, Ewell, Epsom, Surrey, KT17 1UF T: 020 8394 0372 020 8873 1603, W: www.surrey.gov.uk

Caterham Valley Library Caterham Valley Library Stafford Road, Caterham, Surrey, CR3 6JG T: 01883 343580 01883 330872, W: www.surrey.gov.uk

Cranleigh Library and Local History Centre High Street, Cranleigh, Surrey, GU6 8AE T: 01483 272413 01483 271327, W: www.surrey.gov.uk

London Borough of Croydon Library and Archives Service Central Library Katharine Street, Croydon, CR9 1ET T: (020) 8760-5400-ext-1112, (020) 8253-1012 E: localstudies@croydononline.org W: www.croydon.gov.uk/, 1901 census

London Borough of Lambeth Archives Department see Lambeth

Epsom and Ewell Local History Centre Bourne Hall, Spring Street, Ewell, Epsom, Surrey, KT17 1UF T: 020 8394 0372 020 8873 1603, W: www.surrey.gov.uk

Horley Library Horley Library Victoria Road, Horley, Surrey, RH6 7AG T: 01293 784141 01293 820084, W: www.surrey.gov.uk

Lingfield Library The Guest House, Vicarage Road, Lingfield, Surrey, RH7 6HA T: 01342 832058 01342 832517, W: www.surrey.gov.uk

London Borough of Merton Local Studies Centre Merton Civic Centre London Road, Morden, Surrey, SM4 5DX T: (020) 8545-3239 (020) 8545-4037 E: local.studies@merton.gov.uk W: www.merton.gov.uk/libraries

Minet Library see London

London Borough of Richmond upon Thames Local Studies Library Old Town Hall, Whittaker Avenue, Richmond upon Thames, Surrey, TW9 1TP T: (020) 8332 6820 (020) 8940 6899 E: localstudies@richmond.gov.uk W: www.richmond.gov.uk

Redhill Library Warwick Quadrant, Redhill, Surrey, RH1 1NN T: 01737 763332 01737 778020, W: www.surrey.gov.uk

Southwark Local Studies Library see London

Surrey History Centre and Archives Surrey History Centre 130 Goldsworth Road, Woking, Surrey, GU21 1ND T: 01483-594594 01483-594595 E: shs@surreycc.gov.uk W: www.surrey.gov.uk 1901 census

Surrey History Service Library Surrey History Centre 130 Goldsworth Road, Woking, Surrey, GU21 1ND T: 01483-594594 01483-594595 E: shs@surreycc.gov.uk W: www.surreycc.gov.uk 1901 census

Sutton Central Library St Nicholas Way, Sutton, Surrey, SM1 1EA T: (020) 8770 4745 (020) 8770 4777 E: sutton.information@sutton.gov.uk W: www.sutton.gov.uk

Sussex

Sussex University Library Manuscript Collections, Falmer, Brighton, Sussex, BN1 9QL T: 01273 606755 01273 678441

Sussex – West

Worthing Reference Library Worthing Library Richmond Road, Worthing, West Sussex, BN11 1HD T: 01903-212060 01903-821902 E: worthing.reference.library@westsussex.gov.uk W: www.westsussex.gov.uk Largest library in West Sussex and specialist centre for family history sources.

Sussex-East

Brighton & Hove Council Library Service Bibliographic Services, 44 St Annes Crescent, Lewes, East Sussex, BN17 1SQ T: 01273-481813 ,

Brighton Local Studies Library 155 Church Street, Brighton, East Sussex, BN1 1 UD T: 01273 296971, F: 01273 296962 E: brightonlibrary@pavilion.co.uk 1901 census

Hove Reference Library 182 - 186 Church Road, Hove, East Sussex, BN3 2EG T: 01273-296942 01273-296947 E: hovelibrary@brighton-hove.gov.uk W: www.brighton-hove.gov.uk

Tameside

Tameside Local Studies Library see Cheshire

Tyne and Wear

City Library & Arts Centre , 28 - 30 Fawcett Street, Sunderland, Tyne and Wear, BR1 1RE T: 0191-514235 0191-514-8444

North Shields Local Studies Centre Central Library Northumberland Square, North Shields, NE3O 1QU T: 0191-200-5424 0191 200 6118 E: eric.hollerton@northtyneside.gov.uk W: www.northtyneside.gov.uk/libraries.html

South Tyneside Central Library Prince George Street, South Shields, Tyne and Wear, NE33 2PE T: 0191-427-1818-Ext-7860, 0191-455-8085 E: reference.library@s-tyneside-mbc.gov.uk W: www.s-tyneside-mbc.gov.uk , 1901 census

Central Library Northumberland Square, North Shields, NE3O 1QU T: 0191-200-5424 0191-200-6118 E: local.studies@northtyneside.gov.uk W: www.northtyneside.gov.uk/libraries/index.htm

Gateshead Central Library & Local Studies Department Prince Consort Road, Gateshead, Tyne & Wear, NE8 4LN T: 0191 477 3478 0191 477 7454 E: a.lang@libarts.gatesheadmbc.gov.uk http://ris.niaa.org.uk.w W: www.gateshead.gov.uk/ls, 1901 census

Newcastle Local Studies Centre City Library Princess Square, Newcastle upon Tyne, NE99 1DX T: 0191 277 4116 E: local.studies@newcastle.gov.uk W: www.newcastle.gov.uk 1901 census

Robinson Library University of Newcastle upon Tyne, Newcastle Upon Tyne, Tyne & wear, NE2 4HQ T: 0191 222 7671 0191 222 6235 E: library@ncl.ac.uk http://www.ncl.ac.uk/library/

Warwickshire

Atherstone Library Long Street, Atherstone, Warwickshire, CV9 1AX T: 01827 712395 T: 01827 712034 & 01827 718373 - for requests, 01827 720285 E: atherstonelibrary@warwickshire.gov.uk W: www.warwickshire.gov.uk

Bedworth Library 18 High Street, Bedworth, Nuneaton, Warwickshire, CV12 8NF T: 024 7631 2267 024 7664 0429 E: bedworthlibrary@warwickshire.gov.uk W: www.warwickshire.gov.uk

Kenilworth Library Smalley Place, Kenilworth, Warwickshire, CV8 1QG T: 01926 852595 T: 01926 850708, 01926 864503 E: kenilworthlibrary@warwickshire.gov.uk W: www.warwickshire.gov.uk

Modern Records Centre University of Warwick Library Coventry, Warwickshire, CV4 7AL T: (024) 76524219 (024) 7652 4211 E: archives@warwick.ac.uk W: www.modernrecords.warwick.ac.uk

Nuneaton Library Church Street, Nuneaton, Warwickshire, CV11 4DR T: 024 7638 4027 T: 024 7634 7006, 024 7635 0125 (Megastream 6739) E: nuneatonlibrary@warwickshire.gov.uk W: www.warwickshire.gov.uk

Rugby Library Little ElborowStreet, Rugby, Warwickshire, CV21 3BZ T: 01788 533250 01788 533252 & Public Fax 01788 533267 E: rugbylibrary@warwickshire.gov.uk W: www.warwickshire.gov.uk

Shakespeare Birthplace Trust - Library Shakespeare Centre Library Henley Street, Stratford upon Avon, Warwickshire, CV37 6QW T: 01789-204016 T: 01789-201813, 01789-296083 E: library@shakespeare.org.uk W: www.shakespeare.org.uk 1901 census

Stratford on Avon Library 12 Henley Street, Stratford on Avon, Warwickshire, CV37 6PZ T: 01789 292209 T: 01789 296904 & 01926 476760 (Megastream), 01789 268554 & 01926 476774 (Megastream) E: stratfordlibrary@warwickshire.gov.uk W: www.warwickshire.gov.uk

Sutton Coldfield Library & Local Studies Centre 43 Lower Parade, Sutton Coldfield, Warwickshire, B72 1XX T: 0121-354-2274 T: 0121 464 0164, 0121 464 0173 E: sutton.coldfield.reference.lib@birmingham.gov.uk W: www.birmingham.gov.uk

Warwick Library - Warwickshire Local Collection (County Collection) Warwick Library Barrack Street, Warwick, Warwickshire, CV34 4TH T: 01926 412189 T: 01926 412488, 01926 412784 E: warwicklibrary@warwickshire.gov.uk W: www.warwickshire.gov.uk 1901 census

Warwickshire County Library Leamington Library Royal Pump Rooms, The Parade, Leamington Spa, Warwickshire, CV32 4AA T: 01926 742721 T: 01926 742722 & 01926 742720(Renewals), 01926 742749 (Staff) & 01926 742743 (Public Fax) E: leamingtonlibrary@warwickshire.gov.uk W: www.warwickshire.gov.uk

West Midlands

Birmingham University Information Services - Special Collections see National

Dudley Archives & Local History Service, Mount Pleasant Street, Coseley, Dudley, West Midlands, WV14 9JR T: 01384-812770 01384-812770 E: archives.pls@mbc.dudley.gov.uk W: www.dudley.gov.uk Family History Research Service (fee paying) available 1901 census

Coventry Local Studies Library Central Library Smithford Way, Coventry, West Midlands, CV1 1FY T: 012476 832336 02476 832440 E: covinfo@discover.co.uk W: www.coventry.gov.uk/accent.htm

MLA West Midlands: the Regional Council for Museums, Libraries and Archives see Worcestershire

Sandwell Community History & Archives Service Smethwick Library High Street, Smethwick, West Midlands, B66 1AB T: 0121 558 2561, 0121 555 6064

Sandwell Community Libraries Town Hall, High Street, West Bromwich, West Midlands, B70 8DX T: 0121-569-4909 0121-569-4907 E: dm025@viscount.org.uk

Solihull Heritage and Local Studies Service Solihull Central Library Homer Road, Solihull, West Midlands, B91 3RG T: 0121-704-6977 0121-704-6212 E: info@solihull.gov.uk W: www.solihull.gov.uk/wwwlib/#local

Walsall Local History Centre , Essex Street, Walsall, West Midlands, WS2 7AS T: 01922-721305 01922-634594 E: localhistorycentre@walsall.gov.uk W: www.walsall.gov.uk/culturalservices/library/welcome.htm, 1901 census

Wolverhampton Archives & Local Studies 42 - 50 Snow Hill, Wolverhampton, West Midlands, WV2 4AG T: 01902 552480 01902 552481 E: wolverhamptonarchives@dial.pipes.com W: www.wolverhampton.gov.uk/archives, 1901 census

Wigan MBC

Abram Library Vicarage Road, Abram, Wigan, Lancashire, WN2 5QX T: 1942866350

Ashton Library Wigan Road, Ashton in Makerfield, Wigan, Lancashire, WN2 9BH T: 01942 727119 ,

Aspull Library Oakfield Crescent, Aspull, Wigan, Lancashire, WN2 1XJ T: 01942 831303 ,

Atherton Library York Street, Atherton, Manchester, Lancashire, M46 9JH T: 01942 404817 T: 01942 4044816

Beech Hill Library Buckley Street West, Beech Hill, Wigan, WN6 7PQ

Golborne Library Tanners Lane, Golborne, Warrington, WA3 3AW T: 01942 777800 ,

Hindley Library Market Street, Hindley, Wigan, WN2 3AN T: 01942 255287 ,

Ince Library Smithy Green, Ince, Wigan, WN2 2AT T: 01942 255287 ,

Leigh Library Turnpike Centre Civic Square, Leigh, WN7 1EB T: 01942 404557 01942 404567

Marsh Green Library Harrow Road, Marsh Green, Wigan, WN5 0QL T: 01942 760041

Orrell Library Orrell Post, Orrell, Wigan, WN5 8LY T: 01942 705060 ,

Shevington Library Gathurst Lane, Shevington, Wigan, WN6 8HA T: 01257 252618

Standish Library Cross Street, Standish, Wigan, WN6 0HQ T: 01257 400496

Tyldesley Library Stanley Street, Tyldesley, Manchester, M29 8AH T: 01942 882504

Wigan Library College Avenue, Wigan, WN1 1NN T: 01942 827619 01942 827640
Wigan Metropolitan Borough Council - Leisure Services Department Information Unit, Station Road, Wigan WN1 1WA
Wiltshire
Salisbury Reference and Local Studies Library Market Place, Salisbury, Wiltshire, SP1 1BL T: 01722 411098 01722 413214, W: www.wiltshire.gov.uk
Swindon Borough Library Reference Library Regent Circus, Swindon, Wiltshire, SN1 1QG T: 01793 463240 01793 541319 E: reference.library@swindon.gov.uk W: www.swindon.gov.uk 1901 census
Swindon Local Studies Library Swindon Central Library Regent Circus, Swindon, Wiltshire, SN11QG T: 01793 463240 01793 541319 E: swindonref@swindon.gov.uk http://www.swindon.gov.uk
Wiltshire Archaeological and Natural History Society Wiltshire Heritage Library 41 Long Street, Devizes, Wiltshire, SN10 1NS T: 01380 727369 01380 722150 E: wanhs@wiltshireheritage.org.uk W: www.wiltshireheritage.org.uk
Wiltshire Buildings Record Libraries and Heritage HQ, Bythesea Road, Trowbridge, Wiltshire, BA14 8BS T: 01225 713740 E: dorothytreasure@wiltshire.gov.uk W: www.wiltshire.gov.uk
Wiltshire Heritage Museum Library Wiltshire Archaeological & Natural History Society, 41 Long Street, Devizes, Wiltshire, SN10 1NS T: 01380 727369 01380 722150 E: wanhs@wiltshireheritage.org.uk W: www.wiltshireheritage.org.uk Unique Wiltshire material for the Family and Local Historian including pedigrees, newspapers, poll books, maps, prints, photographs, postcards, sale catalogues. Photocopying and research facilities. Comprehensive indexes
Wiltshire Studies Library Trowbridge Reference Library Bythesea Road, Trowbridge, Wiltshire, BA14 8BS T: 01225-713732 T: 01225 713727, 01225-713715 E: libraryenquiries@wiltshire.gov.uk W: www.wiltshire.gov.uk
Worcestershire
Bewdley Museum Research Library Load Street, Bewdley, Worcestershire, DY12 2AE T: 01229-403573 E: museum@online.rednet.co.uk angela@bewdleyhistory.evesham.net W: www.bewdleymuseum.tripod.com, Research of Bewdley families and older properties in the town undertaken by Bewdley Historical research Group. Minimum donation £10. Local History room at Bewdley Museum open Wednesdays 9.30.a.m. to 12.30.p.m. (last enquiry 12 noon)
Bromsgrove Library Stratford Road, Bromsgrove, Worcestershire, B60 1AP T: 01527-575855 01527-575855, W: www.worcestershire.gov.uk
Evesham Library Oat Street, Evesham, Worcestershire, WR11 4PJ T: 01386-442291 01386-765855 E: eveshamlib@worcestershire.gov.uk W: www.worcestershire.gov.uk
Kidderminster Library Market Street, Kidderminster, Worcestershire, DY10 1AD T: 01562-824500 01562-827303 E: kidderminster@worcestershire.gov.uk W: www.worcestershire.gov.uk
Malvern Library Graham Road, Malvern, Worcestershire, WR14 2HU T: 01684-561223 01684-892999, W: www.worcestershire.gov.uk
MLA West Midlands: the Regional Council for Museums, Libraries and Archives 2nd Floor, Grosvenor House, 14 Bennetts Hill, Worcestershire, B2 5RS T: 01527 872258 01527 576960
Redditch Library 15 Market Place, Redditch, B98 8AR T: 01527-63291 01527 68571 E: redditchlibrary@worcestershire.gov.uk W: www.worcestershire.gov.uk
Worcester Library Foregate Street, Worcester, Worcestershire, WR1 1DT T: 01905 765312 01905 726664 E: worcesterlib@worcestershire.gov.uk W: www.worcestershire.gov.uk/libraries
Worcesterhire Library & History Centre History Centre Trinity Street, Worcester, Worcestershire, WR1 2PW T: 01905 765922 01905 765925 E: wlhc@worcestershire.gov.uk W: www.worcestershire.gov.uk/records
Yorkshire
York Minster Library York Minster Library & Archives, Dean's Park, York, YO1 2JQ T: 01904-625308 Library T: 01904-611118 Archives, 01904-611119 E: library@yorkminster.org W: www.yorkminster.org
Yorkshire Family History - Biographical Database York Minster Library & Archives, Dean's Park, York, Yorkshire, YO1 7JQ T: 01904-625308 Library T: 01904-611118 Archives, 01904-611119 E: library@yorkminster.org archives@yorkminster.org W: www.yorkminster.org
Yorkshire - City of York
City of York Libraries - Local History & Reference Collection York Central Library Library Square, Museum Street, York, YO1 7DS T: 01904-655631 01904-611025 E: reference.library@york.gov.uk http://www.york.gov.uk
Yorkshire – North
Catterick Garrison Library Gough Road, Catterick Garrison, North Yorkshire, DL9 3EL T: 01748 833543 W: www.northyorks.gov.uk or

Harrogate Reference Library Victoria Avenue, Harrogate, North Yorkshire, HG1 1EG T: 01423-502744 01423-523158, W: www.northyorks.gov.uk 1901 census
Malton Library St Michael's Street, Malton, North Yorkshire, YO17 7LJ T: 01653 692714 W: www.northyorks.gov.uk 1901 census
North Yorkshire County Libraries 21 Grammar School Lane, Northallerton, DL6 1DF T: 01609-776271 01609-780793 E: elizabeth.melrose@northyorks.gov.uk W: www.northyorks.gov.uk
Northallerton Reference Library 1 Thirsk Road, Northallerton, DL6 1PT T: 01609-776202 E: northallerton.libraryhq@northyorks.gov.uk W: www.northyorks.gov.uk 1901 census
Pickering Reference Library The Ropery, Pickering, YO18 8DY T: 01751-472185 W: www.northyorks.gov.uk
Richmond Library Queen's Road, Richmond DL10 4AE T: 01748 823120 W: www.northyorks.gov.uk 1901 census
Ripon Library The Arcade, Ripon HG4 1AG T: 01765 792926 W: www.northyorks.gov.uk 1901 census
Scarborough Reference Library Vernon Road, ScarboroughYO11 2NN T: 01723-364285 E: scarborough.library@northyorks.gov.uk W: www.northyorks.gov.uk 1901 census
Selby Reference Library 52 Micklegate, Selby YO8 4EQ T: 01757-702020 01757 705396, W: www.northyorks.gov.uk 1901 census
Skipton Reference Library High Street, Skipton BD23 1JX T: 01756-794726 01756-798056, W: www.northyorks.gov.uk
Whitby Library Windsor Terrace, Whitby, North Yorkshire, YO21 1ET T: 01947-602554 01947 820288 1901 census
Yorkshire – East
Beverley Local Studies Library Beverley Library Champney Road, Beverley, East Riding of Yorkshire, HU17 9BG T: 01482 392755, F: 01482 881861 E: beverleyref.library@eastriding.gov.uk W: www.eastriding.gov.uk 1841 to 1901 East Riding Census
Hull Central Library Family and Local History Unit see Hull
Yorkshire – South
Barnsley Archives and Local Studies Department Central Library Shambles Street, Barnsley, South Yorkshire, S70 2JF T: 01226-773950 T: 01226-773938, 01226-773955 E: Archives@barnsley.gov.uk librarian@barnsley.gov.uk W: www.barnsley.gov.uk 1901 census
Doncaster & District Family History Society 'Marton House', 125 The Grove, Wheatley Hills, Doncaster, South Yorkshire, DN2 5SN T: 01302 367257 E: marton-house@blueyonder.co.uk http://www.doncasterfhs.freeserve.co.uk
Doncaster Libraries - Local Studies Section Central Library Waterdale, Doncaster, South Yorkshire, DN1 3JE T: 01302-734307 01302 369749 E: reference.library@doncaster.gov.uk W: www.doncaster.gov.uk 1901 census
Rotherham Archives & Local Studies Central Library Walker Place, Rotherham, South Yorkshire, S65 1JH T: 01709-823616 E: archives@rotherham.gov.uk W: www.rotherham.gov.uk
Sheffield Central Library Surrey Street, Sheffield, South Yorkshire, S1 1XZ T: 0114 273 4711 0114 273 5009 E: sheffield.libraries@dial.pipex.com,
Sheffield University Library Special Collections & Library Archives, Western Bank, Sheffield, South Yorkshire, S10 2TN T: 0114 222 7230 0114 222 7290
Yorkshire – West
Batley Library Market Place, Batley, West Yorkshire, WF17 5DA T: 01924 326021 01924 326308 E: batley.library@kirklees.gov.uk W: www.kirklees.gov.uk
Bradford Local Studies Reference Library Central Library Prince's Way, Bradford, West Yorkshire, BD1 1NN T: 01274 433661 01274 753660 E: local.studies@bradford.gov.uk W: www.bradford.gov.uk 1901 census.
British Library , Boston Spa, Wetherby, West Yorkshire, LS23 7BY
British Library Acquisitions Unit - Monograph Ordering The British Library Boston Spa, Wetherby, West Yorkshire, LS23 7BQ T: 01937-546212
Calderdale Central Library Northgate House, Northgate, Halifax, West Yorkshire, HX11 1UN T: 1422392631 01422-349458, W: www.calderdale.gov.uk
Cleckheaton Library Whitcliffe Road, Cleckheaton, West Yorkshire, BD19 3DX T: 01274 335170
Dewsbury Library Dewsbury Retail Park, Railway Street, Dewsbury, West Yorkshire, WF12 8EQ T: 01924 325080 , 1901 census
Huddersfield Local History Library Huddersfield Library & Art Gallery, Princess Alexandra Walk, Huddersfield HD1 2SU T: 01484-221965 01484-221952 E: ref-library@geo2.poptel.org.uk http://www.kirkleesmc.gov.uk 1901 census
Keighley Reference Library North Street, Keighley BD21 3SX T: 01535-618215 E: keighleylibrary@bradford.gov.uk W: www.bradford.gov.uk
Leeds Local Studies Library Leeds Central Library Calverley Street, Leeds, West Yorkshire, LS1 3AB T: 0113 247 0290 E: local.studies@leeds.gov.uk W: www.leeds.gov.uk/library/services/ **Mirfield Library** East Thorpe Lodge, Mirfield, West Yorkshire, WF14 8AN T: 01924 326470 1901 census

The National Coal Mining Museum for England see National

Olicana Historical Society 54 Kings Road, Ilkley, West Yorkshire, LS29 9AT T: 01943 609206

Pontefract Library & Local Studies Centre Pontefract Library Shoemarket, Pontefract, West Yorkshire, WF8 1BD T: 01977-727692

Wakefield Metropolitan District Libraries & Information Services Castleford Library & Local Studies Dept, Carlton Street, Castleford, West Yorkshire, WF10 1BB T: 01977-722085

Wakefield Library Headquarters - Local Studies Department Balne Lane, Wakefield, West Yorkshire, WF2 0DQ T: 01924-302224 01924-302245 E: wakehist@hotmail.com W: www.wakefield.gov.uk 1901 census

Yorkshire Archaeological Society Claremont, 23 Clarendon Rd, Leeds, West Yorkshire, LS2 9NZ T: 0113-245-6342 T: 0113 245 7910, 0113-244-1979 E: j.heron@sheffield.ac.uk (Society business) yas@wyjs.org.uk (Library and Archives) W: www.yas.org.uk

Brotherton Library Department of Special Collections, Leeds University, Leeds, West Yorkshire, LS2 9JT T: 0113 233 55188 0113 233 5561 E: special-collections@library.leeds.ac.uk http://leeds.ac.uk/library/spcoll/

WALES

National Library of Wales Penglais, Aberystwyth, Ceredigion, SY23 3BU T: 01970 632800 T: 01970 632902 Marketing, 01970 615709 E: holi@llgc.org.uk http://www.llgc.org.uk

South Wales Miners' Library - University of Wales, Swansea Hendrefoelan House, Gower Road, Swansea, SA2 7NB T: 01792-518603 01792-518694 E: miners@swansea.ac.uk W: www.swan.ac.uk/lis/swml

University of Wales Swansea Library see Glamorgan - West

Blaenau Gwent

Ebbw Vale Library Ebbw Vale Library 21 Bethcar Street, Ebbw Vale, Gwent, NP23 6HH T: 01495-303069 01495-350547

Tredegar Library The Circle Tredegar, Gwent, NP2 3PS T: 01495-722687 01495-717018 Monmouthshire Census 1901, 1891, 1881 (microfiche) Wales and Vital records Index. Merthyr express 1909-1950 and South Wales Argus 1909-1950 (microfiche) .

Caerphilly

Bargoed Library The Square, Bargoed, Caerphilly, CF81 8QQ T: 01443-875548 01443-836057 E: 9e465@dial.pipex.com, 1901 census

Caerphilly Library HQ, Unit 7 Woodfieldside Business Park, Penmaen Road, Pontllanfraith, Blackwood, Caerphilly, NP12 2DG T: 01495 235584 01495 235567 E: cacl.libs@dial.pipex.com,

Cardiff

Cardiff Central Library (Local Studies Department) St Davids Link, Frederick Street, Cardiff, CF1 4DT T: (029) 2038 2116 (029) 2087 1599 E: p.sawyer@cardlib.gov.uk W: www.cardiff.gov.uk

Carmarthenshire

Carmarthen Library St Peters Street, Carmarthen, Carmarthenshire, SA31 1LN T: 01267-224822

Llanelli Public Library Vaughan Street, Lanelli, Carmarthenshire, SA15 3AS T: 01554-773538 01554 750125

Ceredigion

Aberystwyth Reference Library Corporation Street, Aberystwyth, Ceredigion, SY23 2BU T: 01970-617464 01970 625059 E: llyfrygell.library@ceredigion.gov.uk W: www.ceredigion.gov.uk/libraries

Flintshire

Flintshire Reference Library Headquarters County Hall Mold, Flintshire, CH7 6NW T: 01352 704411 01352 753662 E: libraries@flintshire.gov.uk W: www.flintshire.gov.uk

Glamorgan

Bridgend Library & Information Service Coed Parc, Park Street, Bridgend, Glamorgan, CF31 4BA T: 01656-767451 01656-645719 E: blis@bridgendlib.gov.uk W: www.bridgendlib.gov.uk

Dowlais Library Church Street, Dowlais, Merthyr Tydfil, Glamorgan, CF48 3HS T: 01985-723051

Merthyr Tydfil Central Library (Local Studies Department) Merthyr Library High Street, Merthyr Tydfil, Glamorgan, CF47 8AF T: 01685-723057 01685-722146 E: library@merthyr.gov.uk W: www.merthyr.gov.uk Specialises in the Borough of Merthyr Tydfil - all census returns 1841 - 1891 arranged by surname for the Borough

Glamorgan - Vale of

Barry Library King Square, Holton Road, Barry, Glamorgan, CF63 4RW T: 01446-735722 01446 734427

Glamorgan – West

Neath Central Library (Local Studies Department) 29 Victoria Gardens, Neath, Glamorgan, SA11 3BA T: 01639-620139 W: www.neath-porttalbot.gov.uk

Port Talbot Library 1st Floor Aberafan Shopping Centre Port Talbot, Glamorgan, SA13 1PB T: 01639-763490 W: www.neath-porttalbot.gov.uk

University of Wales Swansea Library Library & Information Centre Singleton Park, Swansea, SA2 8PP T: 01792 295021 01792 295851

Swansea Reference Library Alexandra Road, Swansea, SA1 5DX T: 01792-516753 01792 516759 E: central.library@swansea.gov.uk W: www.swansea.gov.uk

West Glamorgan Archive Service - Port Talbot Access Point Port Talbot Library 1st Floor, Aberavon Shopping Centre Port Talbot, West Glamorgan, SA13 1PB T: 01639 763430 W: www.swansea.gov.uk/archives, 1901 Census - West Glamorgan area

Rhondda Cynon Taff

Aberdare Library Green Street, Aberdare, Rhondda Cynon Taff, CF44 7AG T: 01685 880053 01685 881181 E: alun.r.prescott@rhondda-cynon-taff.gov.uk W: www.rhondda-cynon-taff.gov.uk/libraries/aberdare.htm, 1901 census

Pontypridd Library Library Road, Pontypridd, Rhondda Cynon Taff, CF37 2DY T: 01443-486850 01443 493258 E: hywel.w.matthews@rhondda-cynon-taff.gov.uk W: www.rhondda-cynon-taff.gov.uk/libraries/pontypri.htm

Treorchy Library Station Road, Treorchy, Glamorgan, CF42 6NN T: 01443-773204 01443-777407

Gwent

Abertillery Library Station Hill, Abertillery, Gwent, NP13 1TE T: 01495-212332 01495-320995

Gwynedd

Canolfan Llyfrgell Dolgellau Library FforddBala Dolgellau, Gwynedd, LL40 2YF T: 01341-422771 01341-423560, W: www.gwynedd.gov.uk

Llyfrgell Caernarfon, Lon Pafiliwn Caernafon, Gwynedd, LL55 1AS T: 01286-679465 01286-671137 E: library@gwynedd.gov.uk W: www.gwynedd.gov.uk

Merthyr Tydfil

Merthyr Tydfil Central Library (Local Studies Department) Merthyr Library High Street, Merthyr Tydfil, Glamorgan, CF47 8AF T: 01685-723057 01685-722146 E: library@merthyr.gov.uk W: www.merthyr.gov.uk Specialises in the Borough of Merthyr Tydfil - all census returns 1841 - 1891 arranged by surname for the Borough

Treharris Library Perrott Street, Treharris, Merthyr Tydfil, CF46 5ET T: 01443-410517 01443 410517

Monmoputhshire

Chepstow Library & Information Centre Manor Way, Chepstow, Monmoputhshire, NP16 5HZ T: 01291-635730 T: 01291-635731, 01291-635736 E: chepstowlibrary@monmouthshire.gov.uk W: www.monmouthshire.gov.uk/leisure/libraries

Neath Port Talbot

Lifelong Learning Service Theodore Road, Port Talbot, SA13 1SP T: 01639-898581 01639-899914 E: lls@neath-porttalbot.gov.uk W: www.neath-porttalbot.gov.uk

Newport

Newport Library & Information Service Newport Central Library John Frost Square, Newport, South Wales, NP20 1PA T: 01633-211376 01633-222615 E: reference.library@newport.gov.uk W: www.earl.org.uk/partners/newport/index.html, The Local Studies

Pembrokeshire

Pembrokeshire Libraries, The County Library Dew Street, Haverfordwest, Pembrokeshire, SA61 1SU T: 01437 775248 01437 769218 E: sandra.matthews@pembrokeshire.gov.uk W: www.pembrokeshire.gov.uk

Powys

Brecon Area Library Ship Street, Brecon, Powys, LD3 9AE T: 01874-623346 01874 622818 E: breclib@mail.powys.gov.uk W: www.powys.gov.uk 1901 census

Llandrindod Wells Library Cefnllys Lane, Llandrindod Wells, Powys, LD1 5LD T: 01597-826870 llandod.library@powys.gov.uk W: www.powys.gov.uk 1901 census

Newtown Area Library Park Lane, Newtown, Powys, SY16 1EJ T: 01686-626934 01686 624935 E: nlibrary@powys.gov.uk W: www.powys.gov.uk 1901 census

Wrexham CBC

Wrexham Library and Arts Centre , Rhosddu Road, Wrexham, LL11 1AU T: 01978-292622 01978-292611 E: joy.thomas@wrexham.gov.uk W: www.wrexham.gov.uk

SCOTLAND

National

Edinburgh University Library, Special Collections Department George Square, Edinburgh, EH8 9LJ T: 0131 650 3412 0131 650 6863 E: special.collections@ed.ac.uk W: www.lib.ed.ac.uk

Edinburgh University New College Library Mound Place, Edinburgh, EH1 2UL T: 0131 650 8957 0131 650 6579 E: New.College.Library@ed.ac.uk W: www.lib.ed.ac.uk

Glasgow University Library & Special Collections Department Hillhead Street, Glasgow, G12 8QE T: 0141 330 6767 0141 330 3793 E: library@lib.gla.ac.uk W: www.gla.ac.uk/library

National Library of Scotland George IV Bridge, Edinburgh, EH1 1EW T: 0131-226-4531 0131 622 4803 E: enquiries@nls.uk W: www.nls.uk Due to essential building works from Sept 1997 to March 1999 reading room services will be provided in the Causewayside building, 33 Salisbury Place, Edinburgh. EH9 1SL

National Monuments Record of Scotland Royal Commission on the Ancient & Historical Monuments of Scotland, John Sinclair House, 16 Bernard terrace, Edinburgh, EH8 9NX T: 0131 662 1456 0131 662 1477 or 0131 662 1499 E: nmrs@rcahms.gov.uk W: www.rcahms.gov.uk

National Museums of Scotland Library Royal Museum, Chambers Street, Edinburgh, EH1 1JF T: 0131 247 4137 0131 247 4311 E: library@nms.ac.uk W: www.nms.ac.uk Holds large collection of family histories, esp Scottish

National War Museum of Scotland Library The Castle, Museum Square, Edinburgh, EH1 1 2NG T: 0131 225 7534 Ext 2O4 T: 0131 225 3848 E: library@nms.ac.uk W: www.nms.ac.uk

Royal Botanic Garden, The Library 20a Inverleith Row, Edinburgh, EH3 5LR T: 0131 552 7171 0131 248 2901

Scottish Genealogy Society, 15 Victoria Terrace, Edinburgh, EH1 2JL T: 0131-220-3677 0131-220-3677 E: info@scotsgenealogy.com W: www.scotsgenealogy.com

St Andrews University Library - Special Collections Department North Street, St Andrews, Fife, KY16 9TR T: 01334 462339 E: speccoll@st-and.ac.uk http://specialcollections.st-and.ac.uk

Strathclyde University Archives McCance Building, 16 Richmond Street, Glasgow, G1 1XQ T: 0141 548 2397 0141 552 0775

Aberdeen

Aberdeen Central Library - Reference & Local Studies Rosemount Viaduct, Aberdeen, AB25 1GW T: 01224-652511 T: 01224 252512 F: 01224 624118 E: refloc@arts-rec.aberdeen.net.uk W: www.aberdeencity.gov.uk

University of Aberdeen DISS: Heritage Division Special Collections & Archives Kings College, Aberdeen, AB24 3SW T: 01224-272598 F: 01224-273891 E: speclib@abdn.ac.uk W: www.abdn.ac.uk/diss/heritage

Aberdeenshire Library & Information Service The Meadows Industrial Estate, Meldrum Meg Way, Oldmeldrum, AB51 0GN T: 01651-872707 T: 01651-871219/871220 F: 01651-872142 E: ALIS@aberdeenshire.gov.uk W: www.aberdeenshire.gov.uk

Angus

Angus Archives, Montrose Library 214 High Street, Montrose, DD10 8PH T: 01674-671415 F: 01674-671810 E: angus.archives@angus.govuk W: www.angus.gov.uk/history/history.htm, Family history research service. Archive holdings for Angus County, Arbroath, Brechin, Carnoustie, Forfar, Montrose, Monifieth, Kittiemuir.

Angus District, Montrose Library 214 High Street, Montrose, MO10 8PH T: 01674-673256

Dundee University Archives Tower Building, University of Dundee, Dundee, DD1 4HN T: 01382-344095 F: 01382 345523 E: archives@dundee.ac.uk W: www.dundee.ac.uk/archives/

Tay Valley FHS & Research Centre see Dundee,

Argyll

Argyll & Bute Council Library Service - Local Studies Highland Avenue, Sandbank, Dunoon, PA23 8PB T: 01369 703214 F: 01369 705797 E: eleanor.harris@argyll-bute.gov.uk W: www.argyll-bute.gov.uk Census 1841-1901 and OPR.

Argyll & Bute Library Service Library Headquarters, Highland Avenue, Sandbank, Dunoon, PA23 8PB T: 01369-703214 F: 1369705797 E: andyewan@abc-libraries.demon.co.uk W: www.argyll-bute.gov.uk

Campbeltown Library and Museum Hall St, Campbeltown, PA28 6BU T: 01586 552366 F: 01586 552938 E: mary.vanhelmond@argyll-bute.gov.uk W: www.argyle-bute.gov.uk/content/leisure/museums

Ayrshire

East Ayrshire Council District History Centre & Museum Baird Institute, 3 Lugar Street, Cumnock, KA18 1AD T: 01290-421701 F: 01290-421701 E: Baird.institute@east-ayrshire.gov.uk W: www.east-ayrshire.gov.uk

East Ayrshire Libraries Dick Institute, Elmbank Avenue, Kilmarnock, KA1 3BU T: 01563 554310 T: 01290 421701 F: 01563 554311 E: baird.institute@east-ayrshire.gov.uk W: www.east-ayrshire.gov.uk

North Ayrshire Libraries Library Headquarters, 39 - 41 Princes Street, Ardrossan, KA22 8BT T: 01294-469137 F: 01924-604236 E: reference@naclibhq.prestel.co.uk W: www.north-ayrshire.gov.uk

South Ayrshire Libraries Carnegie Library 12 Main Street, Ayr, KA8 8ED T: 01292-286385 T: 01292-611593 E: carnegie@south-ayrshire.gov.uk W: www.south-ayrshire.gov.uk

Ayrshire – East

East Ayrshire Libraries – Cumnock 25-27 Ayr Road, Cumnock, KA18 1EB T: 01290-422804, W: www.east-ayrshire.gov.uk

Auchinleck Library Community Centre, Well Road, Auchinleck, KA18 2LA T: 01290 422829, W: www.east-ayrshire.gov.uk

Bellfield Library 79 Whatriggs Road, Kilmarnock, KA1 3RB T: 01563 534266 E: libraries@east-ayrshire.gov.uk W: www.east-ayrshire.gov.uk

Bellsbank Library Primary School, Craiglea Crescent, Bellsbank, KA6 7UA T: 01292 551057 E: libraries@east-ayrshire.gov.uk W: www.east-ayrshire.gov.uk

Catrine Library A M Brown Institute, Catrine, KA5 6RT T: 01290 551717 E: libraries@east-ayrshire.gov.uk W: www.east-ayrshire.gov.uk

Crosshouse Library 11-13 Gatehead Road, Crosshouse, KA2 0HN T: 01563 573640 E: libraries@east-ayrshire.gov.uk W: www.east-ayrshire.gov.uk

Dalmellington Library Townhead, Dalmellington, KA6 7QZ T: 01292 550159 E: libraries@east-ayrshire.gov.uk W: www.east-ayrshire.gov.uk

Dalrymple Library Barbieston Road, Dalrymple, KA6 6DZ E: libraries@east-ayrshire.gov.uk W: www.east-ayrshire.gov.uk

Darvel Library Town Hall, West Main Street, Darvel, KA17 0AQ T: 01560 322754 E: libraries@east-ayrshire.gov.uk W: www.east-ayrshire.gov.uk

Drongan Library Mill O'Shield Road, Drongan, KA6 7AY T: 01292 591718 E: libraries@east-ayrshire.gov.uk W: www.east-ayrshire.gov.uk

Galston Library Henrietta Street, Galston, KA4 8HQ T: 01563 821994 E: libraries@east-ayrshire.gov.uk W: www.east-ayrshire.gov.uk

Hurlford Library Blair Road, Hurlford, KA1 5BN T: 01563 539899 E: libraries@east-ayrshire.gov.uk W: www.east-ayrshire.gov.uk

Kilmaurs Library Irvine Road, Kilmaurs, KA3 2RJ T: E: libraries@east-ayrshire.gov.uk W: www.east-ayrshire.gov.uk

Mauchline Library 2 The Cross, Mauchline, T: 01290 550824 E: libraries@east-ayrshire.gov.uk W: www.east-ayrshire.gov.uk

Muirkirk Library Burns Avenue, Muirkirk, KA18 3RH T: 01290 661505 E: libraries@east-ayrshire.gov.uk W: www.east-ayrshire.gov.uk

Netherthird Library Ryderston Drive, Netherthird, KA18 3AR T: 01290 423806 E: libraries@east-ayrshire.gov.uk W: www.east-ayrshire.gov.uk

New Cumnock Library Community Centre, The Castle, New Cumnock, KA18 4AH T: 01290 338710 E: libraries@east-ayrshire.gov.uk W: www.east-ayrshire.gov.uk

Newmilns Library Craigview Road, Newmilns, KA16 9DQ T: 01560 322890 E: libraries@east-ayrshire.gov.uk W: www.east-ayrshire.gov.uk

Ochiltree Library Main Street, Ochiltree, KA18 2PE T: 01290 700425 E: libraries@east-ayrshire.gov.uk W: www.east-ayrshire.gov.uk

Patna Library Doonside Avenue, Patna, KA6 7LX T: 01292 531538 E: libraries@east-ayrshire.gov.uk W: www.east-ayrshire.gov.uk

Clackmannanshire

Clackmannanshire Archives, Alloa Library 26/28 Drysdale Street, Alloa, FK10 1JL T: 01259-722262 F: 01259-219469 E: libraries@clacks.gov.uk W: www.clacksweb.org.uk/dyna/archives

Clackmannanshire Libraries, Alloa Library 26/28 Drysdale Street, Alloa, FK10 1JL T: 01259-722262 F: 01259-219469 E: clack.lib@mail.easynet.co.uk

Dumfrieshire

Ewart Library Ewart Library Catherine Street, Dumfries, DG1 1JB T: 01387 260285 T: 01387-252070 F: 01387-260294 E: ruth_airley@dumgal.gov.uk libsxi@dumgal gov.uk W. www.dumgal.gov.uk Fee paid research service availble

Dumbartonshire

Dumbarton Public Library Strathleven Place, Dumbarton, G82 1BD T: 01389-733273 F: 01389-738324 E: wdlibs@hotmail.com W: www.wdcweb.info

Dundee, Dundee Central Library The Wellgate, Dundee, DD1 1DB T: 01382-434377 F: 01382-434036 E: local.studies@dundeecity.gov.uk W: www.dundeecity.gov.uk/dcchtml/nrd/loc_stud.htm, Material held mainly Angus and Dundee

Tay Valley Family History Society & Family History Research Centre Family History Research Centre, 179–181 Princes Street, Dundee, DD4 6DQ T: 01382-461845 F: 01382 455532 E: tvfhs@tayvalleyfhs.org.uk W: www.tayvalleyfhs.org.uk

East Dunbarton

Bishopbriggs Library 170 Kirkintilloch Road, Bishopbriggs, G64 2LX T: 0141 772 4513 F: 0141 762 5363 W: www.eastdunbarton.gov.uk

Craighead Library , Milton of Campsie, G66 8Dl T: 01360 311925, W: www.eastdunbarton.gov.uk

Lennoxtown Library Main Street, Lennoxtown, G66 7HA T: 01360 311436 F: 01360 311436,

Lenzie Library 13 - 15 Alexandra Avenue, Lenzie, G66 5BG T: 0141 776 3021, W: www.eastdunbarton.gov.uk

Milgarvie Library Allander Road, Milngarvie, G62 8PN T: 0141 956 2776 F: 0141 956 2776 W: www.eastdunbarton.gov.uk

Westerton Library 82 Maxwell Avenue, Bearsden, G61 1NZ T: 0141 943 0780 F: 0141 943 0780,

East Dunbartonshire Local Record Offices and Reference Libraries William Patrick Library 2 West High Street, Kirkintilloch, G66 1AD T: 0141-776-8090 F: 0141-776-0408 E: libraries@eastdunbarton.gov.uk W: www.eastdunbarton.gov.uk

East Renfrewshire

Giffnock Library Station Road, Giffnock, Glasgow, G46 6JF T: 0141-577-4976 F: 0141-577-4978 E: devinem@eastrenfrewshire.co.uk W: www.eastrenfrewshire.co.uk

Edinburgh
Edinburgh Central Library Edinburgh Room, George IV Bridge, Edinburgh, EH1 1EG T: 0131-242 8030 F: 0131-242 8009 E: eclis@edinburgh.gov.uk W: www.edinburgh.gov.uk
Scottish Genealogy Society - Library see Scotland National
Falkirk
Falkirk Library Hope Street, Falkirk, FK1 5AU T: 01324 503605 F: 01324 503606 E: falkirk-library@falkirk-library.demon.co.uk W: www.falkirk.gov.uk Holds Local Studies Collection
Falkirk Museum History Research Centre Callendar House, Callendar Park, Falkirk, FK1 1YR T: 01324 503778 F: 01324 503771 E: ereid@falkirkmuseums.demon.co.ukcallandarhouse@falkirkmuseums .demon.co.uk W: www.falkirkmuseums.demon.co.uk Records held: Local Authority, business, personal and estate records, local organmisations, trade unions, over 28,000 photographs Falkirk District
Fife
Dunfermline Library - Local History Department Abbot Street, Dunfermline, KY12 7NL T: 01383-312994 F: 01383-312608 E: info@dunfermline.fifelib.net W: www.fife.gov.uk
Fife Council Central Area Libraries Central Library War Memorial Grounds, Kirkcaldy, KY1 1YG T: 01592-412878 F: 01592-412750 E: info@kirkcaldy.fifelib.net W: www.fife.gov.uk
Tay Valley FHS & Research Centre see Dundee
St Andrews Library Church Square, St Andrews, KY16 9NN T: 01334-412685 F: 01334 413029 E: info@standres.fiflib.net W: www.fife.gov.uk
St Andrews University Library North Street, St Andrews, KY16 9TR T: 01334-462281 F: 01334-462282 W: www.library.st-and.ac.uk
St Andrews University Library - Special Collections Department see Scotland National
Glasgow
Brookwood Library 166 Drymen Road, Bearsden, Glasgow, G61 3RJ T: 0141-942 6811 F: 0141 943 1119 W: www.eastdunbarton.gov.uk
Glasgow City Libraries & Archives Mitchell Library North Street, Glasgow, G3 7DN T: 0141 287 2937 F: 0141 287 2912 E: history_and_glasgow@gcl.glasgow.gov.uk W: www.glasgow.gov.uk/html/council/cindex.htm
Glasgow University Library & Special Collections Department Hillhead Street, Glasgow, G12 8QE T: 0141 330 6767 F: 0141 330 3793 E: library@lib.gla.ac.uk W: www.gla.ac.uk/library
Social Sciences Department - History & Glasgow Room The Mitchell Library North Street, Glasgow, G3 7DN T: 0141-227-2935 T: 0141-227-2937 & 0141-227-2938 F: 0141-227-2935 E: history-and-glasgow@cls.glasgow.gov.uk W: www.libarch.glasgow
Highland
North Highland Archive Wick Library Sinclair Terrace, Wick, KW1 5AB T: 01955 606432 F: 01955 603000
Isle of Barra
Castlebay Community Library Community School, Castlebay, HS95XD T: 01871-810471 F: 01871-810650
Isle of Benbecula
Community Library Sgoil Lionacleit, Liniclate, HS7 5PJ T: 01870-602211 F: 01870-602817
Isle of Lewis
Stornoway Library 19 Cromwell Street, Stornoway, HS1 2DA T: 01851 708631 F: 01851 708676/708677 E: dfowler@cne-siar.gov.uk
Kinross-shire
Perth & Kinross Libraries, A K Bell Library 2 - 8 York Place, Perth, PH2 8EP T: 01738-477062 F: 01738-477010 E: jaduncan@pkc.gov.uk W: www.pkc.gov.uk
Tay Valley Family History Society & Family History Research Centre see Dundee
Kirkcudbrightshire
Ewart Library Ewart Library Catherine Street, Dumfries, DG1 1JB T: 01387 260285 T: 01387-252070 F: 01387-260294 E: ruth_airley@dumgal.gov.uk libsxi@dumgal.gov.uk W: www.dumgal.gov.ukf, Fee paid research service availble
Lanarkshire
Airdrie Library Wellwynd, Airdrie, ML6 0AG T: 01236-763221 T: 01236-760937 F: 01236-766027 W: www.northlan.gov.uk/
Cumbernauld Central Library 8 Allander Walk, Cumbernauld, G67 1EE T: 01236-735964 F: 01236-458350 W: www.northlan.org.uk
Leadhills Miners' Library 15 Main Street, Leadhills, ML12 6XP T: 01659-74326 E: anne@leadshilllibrary.co.uk W: www.lowtherhills.fsnet.co.uk
Midlothian
Midlothian Archives and Local Studies Centre 2 Clerk Street, Loanhead, EH20 9DR T: 0131 271 3976 F: 0131 440 4635 E: local.studies@midlothian.gov.uk W: www.midlothian.gov.uk
Midlothian Libraries Local History Centre Midlothian Council Libraries Headquarters, 2 Clerk Street, Loanhead, EH20 9DR T: 0131-440-2210 F: 0131-440-4635 E: local.studies@midlothian.gov.uk W: www.earl.org.uk.partners/midlothian/index.html

Morayshire
Buckie Library Clunu Place, Buckie, AB56 1HB T: 01542-832121 F: 01542-835237 E: buckie.lib@techleis.moray.gov.uk W: www.moray.gov.uk
Forres Library Forres House, High Street, Forres, IV36 0BJ T: 01309-672834 F: 01309-675084 W: www.moray.gov.uk
Keith Library Union Street, Keith, AB55 5DP T: 01542-882223 F: 01542-882177 E: keithlibrary@techleis.moray.gov.uk W: www.moray.gov.uk
Moray Local Heritage Centre Grant Lodge, Cooper Park, Elgin, IV30 1HS T: 01343 562644 T: 01343 562645 F: 01343-549050 E: graeme.wilson@techleis.moray.gov.uk W: www.morray.org/heritage/roots.html, The Moray District Record Office has now been combined with the Local studies section at Grant Lodge, Cooper Park, Elgin to form the Local Heritage Centre.
North Lanarkshire
Kilsyth Library Burngreen, Kilsyth, G65 0HT T: 01236-823147 F: 01236-823147 W: www.northlan.org.uk
Motherwell Heritage Centre High Road, Motherwell, ML1 3HU T: 01698-251000 F: 01698-253433 E: heritage@mhc158.freeserve.co.uk W: www.northlan.org.uk
Shotts Library Benhar Road, Shotts, ML7 5EN T: 01501-821556, W: www.northlan.org.uk
Orkney
Orkney Library The Orkney Library Laing Street, Kirkwall, KWI5 1NW T: 01856-873166 F: 01856-875260 E: karen.walker@orkney.gov.uk W: www.orkney.gov.uk
Perthshire
Perth & Kinross Libraries, A K Bell Library 2 - 8 York Place, Perth, PH2 8EP T: 01738-477062 F: 01738-477010 E: jaduncan@pkc.gov.uk W: www.pkc.gov.uk
Tay Valley FHS & Research Centre see Dundee
Renfrewshire
Renfrewshire Council Library & Museum Services Central Library & Museum Complex, High Street, Paisley, PA1 2BB T: 0141-889-2350 F: 0141-887-6468 E: local_studies.library@renfrewshire.gov.uk W: www.renfrewshire.gov.uk
Watt Library 9 Union Street, Greenock, PA16 8JH T: 01475 715628 F: 01475 712339 E: library.watt@inverclyde.gov.uk W: www.inverclyde-libraries.info
Scottish Borders
Scottish Borders Archlve & Local History Centre Library Headquarters, St Mary's Mill, Selkirk, TD7 5EW T: 01750 20842 T: 01750 724903 F: 01750 22875 E: archives@scotborders.gov.uk W: www.scotborders.gov.uk/libraries
Shetland
Shetland Library Lower Hillhead, Lerwick, ZE1 0EL T: 01595-693868 F: 01595-694430 E: info@shetland-library.gov.uk W: www.shetland-library.gov.uk
Stirling
Bridge of Allan Library Fountain Road, Bridge of Allan, FK9 4AT T: 01786 833680 F: 01786 833680 W: www.stirling.gov.uk
Dunblane Library High Street, Dunbland, FK15 0ER T: 01786 823125 F: 01786 823125 E: dunblanelibrary@stirling.gov.uk W: www.stirling.gov.uk
St Ninians Library Mayfield Centre, St Ninians, FK7 0DB T: 01786 472069 E: stninlibrary@stirling.gov.uk W: www.stirling.gov.uk
Stirling Central Library Central Library Corn Exchange Road, Stirling, FK8 2HX T: 01786 432106 F: 01786 473094 E: centrallibrary@stirling.gov.uk W: www.stirling.gov.uk
West Lothian
West Lothian Council Libraries Connolly House, Hopefield Road, Blackburn, EH47 7HZ T: 01506-776331 F: 01506-776345 E: localhistory@westlothian.org.uk W: www.wlonline.org
Wigtownshire
Ewart Library see Dumfries

NORTHERN IRELAND
Belfast
Belfast Central Library Irish & Local Studies Dept, Royal Avenue, Belfast, BT1 1EA T: (028) 9024 3233 (028) 9033 2819 E: info@libraries.belfast-elb.gov.uk W: www.belb.org.uk
Belfast Linen Hall Library 17 Donegall Square North, Belfast, BT1 5GD T: (028) 90321707
County Antrim
Local Studies Service, Area Library HQ, Demesne Avenue, Ballymena, Co Antrim, BT43 7BG T: (028) 25 664121 (028) 256 46680 E: yvonne_hirst@hotmail.com W: www.neelb.org.uk
North Eastern Library Board & Local Studies Area Reference Library Demesne Avenue, Ballymena, Antrim, BT43 7BG T: (028) 25 6641212 (028) 256 46680 E: yvonne_hirt@hotmail.com W: www.neelb.org.uk
County Fermanagh
Enniskillen Library Halls Lane, Enniskillen, Co Fermanagh, BT1 3HP T: (028) 66322886 01365-324685 E: librarian@eknlib.demon.co.uk
County Londonderry

Central and Reference Library 35 Foyle Street, Londonderry, Co Londonderry, BT24 6AL T: (028) 71272300 01504-269084 E: trishaw@online.rednet.co.uk

Irish Room, Coleraine County Hall, Castlerock Road, Ballymena, County Londonderry, BT1 3HP T: (028) 705 1026 (028) 705 1247, W: www.neelb.org.uk

County Tyrone
Centre for Migration Studies, Ulster American Folk Park, Mellon Road, Castletown, Omagh, Co Tyrone, BT78 5QY T: 028 82 256315 028 82 242241 E: uafp@iol.ie W: www.qub.ac.uk/cms/

Omagh Library 1 Spillars Place, Omagh, Co Tyrone, BT78 1HL T: (028) 82244821 01662-246772 E: librarian@omahlib.demon.co.uk

County Down
South Eastern Library Board & Local Studies Library HQ, Windmill Hill, Ballynahinch, County Down, BT24 8DH T: (028) 9756 6400 (028) 9756 5072 E: ref@bhinchlibhq.demon.co.uk

South Antrim
South Eastern Library Board & Local Studies Library HQ, Windmill Hill, Ballynahinch, County Down, BT24 8DH T: (028) 9756 6400 (028) 9756 5072 E: ref@bhinchlibhq.demon.co.uk

IRELAND

National Library of Ireland, Kildare Street, Dublin, 2 T: 661-8811 676-6690 E: coflaherty@nli.ie,

Society of Friends (Quakers) - Historical Library Swanbrook House, Bloomfield Avenue, Dublin, 4 T: (01) 668-7157 , By 2001 will have completed computerisation of card index

Dublin
Dublin Public Libraries, Gilbert Library - Dublin & Irish Collections, 138 - 142 Pearse Street, Dublin, 2 T: 353 1 674 4800 353 1 674 4879 E: dublinpubliclibraries@dublincity.ie W: www.dublincity.ie

County Clare
Clare County Library The Manse, Harmony Row, Ennis, Co Clare T: 065-6821616 065-6842462 E: clarelib@iol.ie W: www.iol.ie/~clarelib

County Cork
Cork City Library Grand Parade, Cork, Co Cork T: 021-277110 021-275684 E: cork.city.library@indigo.ie W: www.corkcity.ie/
Mallow Heritage Centre , 27/28 Bank Place, Mallow, Co Cork T: 022-50302 W: www.corkcoco.com/

County Dublin
Dun Laoghaire Library Lower George's Street, Dun Laoghaire, Co Dublin T: 2801147 2846141 E: eprout@dlrcoco.ie W: www.dlrcoco.ie/library/lhistory.htm

County Kerry
Kerry County Library Genealogical Centre Cathedral Walk, Killarney, Co Kerry T: 353-0-64-359946

County Kildare
Kildare County Library , Newbridge, Co Kildare T: 045-431109 045-432490 W: www.kildare.ie/countycouncil/
Kildare Hertiage & Genealogy Kildare County Library Newbridge, Co Kildare T: 045 433602 045-432490 E: capinfo@iol.ie W: www.kildare.ie

County Mayo
Central Library , Castlebar, Co Mayo T: 094-24444 094-24774 E: cbarlib@iol.ie W: www.mayococo.ie

County Sligo
Sligo County Library Westward Town Centre Bridge Street, Sligo, Co Sligo T: 00-353-71-47190 00-353-71-46798 E: sligolib@iol.ie W: www.sligococo.ie/

County Tipperary
Tipperary County Library Local Studies Department Castle Avenue, Thurles, Co Tipperary T: 0504-21555 0504-23442 E: studies@tipplibs.iol.ie W: www.iol.ie/~TIPPLIBS

County Waterford
Waterford County Library Central Library Davitt's Quay, Dungarvan, Co Waterford T: 058 41231 058 54877 W: www.waterfordcoco.ie/

County Wexford
Enniscorthy Branch Library Lymington Road, Enniscorthy, Co Wexford T: 054-36055 W: www.wexford.ie/
New Ross Branch Library Barrack Lane, New Ross, Co Wexford T: 051-21877 W: www.wexford.ie/
Wexford Branch Library Teach Shionoid, Abbey Street, Wexford, Co Wexford T: 053-42211 053-21097 W: www.wexford.ie/

County Donegal
Donegal Local Studies Centre Central Library & Arts Centre Oliver Plunkett Road, Letterkenny, County Donegal T: 00353 74 24950 00353 74 24950 E: dgcolib@iol.ie W: www.donegal.ie/library

County Dublin
Ballyfermot Public Library Ballyfermot, Dublin, 10 T: W: www.dublincity.ie

County Limerick
Limerick City Library The Granary, Michael Street, Limerick, County Limerick T: 061-314668 061 411506 E: doyledolores@hotmail.com W: www.limerickcoco.ie/

Australia

ACT
National Library of Australia Canberra, 2600 T: 02 6262 1111 WWW: http://www.nla.gov.au
New South Wales
Mitchell Library Macquarie Street Sydney, 2000 T: 02 9230 1693 Fax: 02 9235 1687 E: slinfo@slsw.gov.au
State Library of New South Wales Macquarie Street Sydney, 2000 T: 02 9230 1414 F: 02 9223 3369 E: slinfo@slsw.gov.au
Queensland
State Library of Queensland PO Box 3488, Cnr Peel and Stanley Streets, South Brisbane, Brisbane, 4101 T: 07 3840 7775 Fax: 07 3840 7840 E: genie@slq.qld.gov.au WWW: http://www.slq.qld.gov.au/subgenie/htm
South Australia
South Australia State Library PO Box 419 Adelaide, 5001 T: (08) 8207 7235 F: (08) 8207 7247 E: famhist@slsa.sa.gov.au W: http://www.slsa.sa.gov.au/library/collres/famhist/
Victoria
State Library of Victoria 328 Swanston Street Walk Melbourne, 3000 T: 03 9669 9080 E: granth@newvenus.slv.vic.gov.au W: http://www.slv.vic.gov.au/slv/genealogy/index
Western Australia
State Library Alexander Library, Perth Cultural Centre Perth, 6000 T: 09 427 3111 F: 09 427 3256

New Zealand

Auckland Research Centre Auckland City Libraries PO Box 4138, 44 46 Lorne Street Auckland T: 64 9 377 0209 F: 64 9 307 7741 E: heritage@auckland library.govt.nz
National Library of New Zealand PO Box 1467 Thorndon, Wellington T: (0064)4 474 3030 F: (0064)4 474 3063 WWW: http://www.natlib.govt.nz
Alexander Turnbull Library PO Box 12 349 , Wellington, 6038 T: 04 474 3050 F: 04 474 3063

Canterbury Public Library PO Box 1466 , Christchurch T: 03 379 6914 F: 03 365 1751
Dunedin Public Libraries PO Box 5542, Moray Place Dunedin T: 03 474 3651 F: 03 474 3660 E: library@dcc.govt.nz
Fielding Public Library PO Box 264 , Fielding, 5600 T: 06 323 5373
Hamilton Public Library PO Box 933, Garden Place Hamilton, 2015 T: 07 838 6827 F: 07 838 6858
Hocken Library PO Box 56 , Dunedin T: 03 479 8873 Fax: 03 479 5078
Porirua Public Library PO Box 50218 , Porirua, 6215 T: 04 237 1541 F: 04 237 7320
Takapuna Public Library Private Bag 93508 , Takapuna, 1309 Tel: 09 486 8466 F: 09 486 8519
Wanganui District Library Private Bag 3005, Alexander Building, Queens Park, Wanganui, 5001 T: 06 345 8195 F: 06 345 5516 E: wap@wdl.govt.nz

South Africa

South African Library PO Box 496 , Cape Town, 8000 T: 021 246320 F: 021 244848

Canada

Alberta
Calgary Public Library 616 MacLeod Tr SE Calgary, T2G 2M2 T: 260 2785
Glenbow Library & Archives 130 9th Avenue SE Calgary, T2G 0P3 T: 403 268 4197 F: 403 232 6569
British Columbia
British Columbia Archives 865 Yates Street Victoria, V8V 1X4 T: 604 387 1952 F: 604 387 2072 E: rfrogner@maynard.bcars.gs.gov.bc.ca
Cloverdale Library 5642 176a Street Surrey, V3S 4G9 T: 604 576 1384 E: GenealogyResearch@city.surrey.bc.ca WWW: http://www.city.surrey.bc.ca/spl/
New Brunswick
Harriet Irving Library PO Box 7500 Fredericton, E3B 5H5 T: 506 453 4748 **Loyalist Collection & Reference Library** PO Box 7500 Fredericton, E3B 5H5 T: 506 453 4749
Newfoundland
Newfoundland Provincial Resource Library Arts and Cultural Centre, Allandale Road St Johns, A1B 3A3 T: 709 737 3955 E: genealog@publib.nf.ca W: http://www.publib.nf.ca
Ontario
National Library 395 Wellington Street Ottawa, K1A 0N4 Tel: 613 995 9481 F: 613 943 1112 Email:reference@nlc bnc.ca W: http://www.nlc bnc.ca
Toronto Reference Library 789 Yonge Street Toronto, M4W 2G8 T: 416 393 7155 **James Gibson Reference Library** 500 Glenridge Avenue St Catherines, L2S 3A1

Tel: 905 688 5550 F: 905 988 5490
Public Library PO Box 2700, Station LCD 1 Hamilton, L8N 4E4
Tel: 546 3408 E: speccol@hpl.hamilton.on.ca
Public Library 85 Queen Street North Kitchener, N2H 2H1
Tel: 519 743 0271 F: 519 570 1360
Public Library 305 Queens Avenue London, N6B 3L7
Tel: 519 661 4600 F: 519 663 5396
Public Library 301 Burnhamthorpe Road West Mississauga, L5B
3Y3 T: 905 615 3500 E: library.info@city.mississauga.on.ca
WWW: http://www.city.mississauga.on.ca/Library
Toronto Public Library North York (Central Library) Canadiana
Department, 5120 Yonge Street North York, M2N 5N9
Tel: 416 395 5623 W: http://www.tpl.tor.on.ca
Public Library 74 Mackenzie Street Sudbury, P3C 4X8
Tel: 01673 1155 F: 01673 9603

St Catharines Public Library 54 Church Street St Catharines, L2R
7K2 T: 905 688 6103 F: 905 688 2811 E:
scpublib@stcatharines.library.on.ca W:
http://www.stcatharines.library.on.ca
Quebec
Bibliotheque De Montreal 1210, Rue Sherbrooke East Street ,
Montreal, H2L 1L9 T: 514 872 1616 F: 514 872 4654
Email: daniel_olivier@ville.montreal.qc.ca
WWW: http://www.ville.montreal.qc.ca/biblio/pageacc.htm
Saskatchewan
Public Library PO Box 2311 Regina, S4P 3Z5 T: 306 777 6011
Fax: 306 352 5550 E: kaitken@rpl.sk.ca
Public Library 311   23rd Street East Saskatoon, S7K 0J6 T: 306
975 7555 F: 306 975 7542

This list is not exhaustive and we would be pleased to receive details of other cemeteries & crematoria to add to our future lists.

England
Avon
Bristol General Cemetery Co, East Lodge, Bath Rd, Arnos Vale,
Bristol, BS4 3EW T: 0117 971 3294
Canford Crematorium & Cemetery, Canford Lane, Westbury On
Trym, Bristol, BS9 3PQ T: 0117 903 8280 Fax: 0117 903 8287
Administration Office for: Canford Crematorium, Canford Cemetery,
Shirehampton Cemetery, Henbury Cemetery, Avonview Cemetery,
Brislington Cemetery, Ridgeway Park Cemetery
Cemetery of Holy Souls, Bath Rd, Bristol, BS4 3EW T: 0117 977 2386
Haycombe Crematorium & Cemetery, Whiteway Rd, Bath,
BA2 2RQ T: 01225 423682
South Bristol Crematorium & Cemetery, Bridgwater Rd, Bristol,
BS13 7AS T: 0117 963 4141
Westerleigh Crematorium, Westerleigh Rd, Westerleigh, Bristol,
BS37 8QP T: 0117 937 4619
Weston Super Mare Crematorium, Ebdon Rd, Worle, Weston-
Super-Mare, BS22 9NY T: 01934 511717
Bedfordshire
Norse Rd Crematorium 104 Norse Rd, Bedford, MK41 0RL
Tel: 01234 353701
Church Burial Ground, 26 Crawley Green Rd, Luton, LU2 0QX T:
01582 722874 T: 01582 721867 WWW: www.stmarysluton.org
Correspondence to; St Mary's Church, Church Street, Luton LU1 3JF
Dunstable Cemetery, West St, Dunstable, LU6 1PB T: 01582 662772
Kempston Cemetery, Cemetery Lodge, 2 Green End Rd, Kempston,
Bedford, MK43 8RJ T: 01234 851823
Luton Crematorium, The Vale, Butterfield Green Road, Stopsley,
Luton, LU2 8DD T: 01582 723700 T: 01582 723730
Luton General Cemetery, Rothesay Rd, Luton, LU1 1QX T: 01582 727480
Berkshire
Easthampstead Park Cemetry & Crematorium, Nine Mile Ride,
Wokingham, RG40 3DW T: 01344 420314
Henley Road Cemetery & Reading Crematorium, All Hallows
Road, Henley Road, Caversham, Reading, RG4 5LP
Tel: 0118 947 2433
Larges Lane Cemetery, Larges Lane, Bracknell, RG12 9AL
Tel: 01344 450665
Newbury Cemetery, Shaw Hill, Shaw Fields, Shaw, Newbury,
RG14 2EQ T: 01635 40096
Slough Cemetery & Crematorium, Stoke Rd, Slough, SL2 5AX T:
01753 523127 (Cemetery) Fax: 01753 520702 (Crematorium) E:
sloughcrem@hotmail.com WWW: www.slough.gov.uk
Bristol
South Bristol Crematorium and Cemetery, Bridgwater Road,
Bedminster Down, Bristol, BS13 7AS T: 0117 903 833
 Fax: 0117 903 8337 Administration Office for South Bristol Crematorium,
South Bristol Cemetery, Greenbank Cemetery
Buckinghamshire
Crownhill Crematorium, Dansteed Way, Crownhill, Milton Keynes,
T: 01908 568112
Chilterns Crematorium, Whielden Lane, Winchmore Hill,
Amersham, HP7 0ND T: 01494 724263
Cambridgeshire
American Military Cemetery, Madingley Rd, Coton, Cambridge,
CB3 7PH T: 01954 210350 Fax: 01954 211130 E:
Cambridge.Cemetery@ambc-er.org WWW: http://www.ambc.gov
Cambridge City Crematorium, Huntingdon Rd, Girton, Cambridge,
CB3 0JJ T: 01954 780681
City of Ely Council, Ely Cemetery, Beech Lane, Ely, CB7 4QZ T:
01353 669659
Marholm Crematorium, Mowbray Rd, Peterborough, PE6 7JE T:
01733 262639
Cheshire
Altrincham Cemetery, Hale Rd, Altrincham, WA14 2EW T: 0161
980 4441
Altrincham Crematorium, White House Lane, Dunham Massey,
Altrincham, WA14 5RH T: 0161 928 7771

Cemeteries & Crematoria

Chester Cemetries & Crematorium, Blacon Avenue, Blacon,
Chester, CH1 5BB T: 01244 372428
Dukinfield Crematorium, Hall Green Rd, Dukinfield, SK16 4EP T:
0161 330 1901
Macclesfield Cemetery, Cemetery Lodge, 87 Prestbury Rd,
Macclesfield, SK10 3BU T: 01625 422330
Middlewich Cemetery, 12 Chester Rd, Middlewich, CW10 9ET T:
01606 737101
Overleigh Rd Cemetery, The Lodge, Overleigh Rd, Chester,
CH4 7HW T: 01244 682529
Walton Lea Crematorium, Chester Rd, Higher Walton, Warrington,
WA4 6TB T: 01925 267731
Widnes Cemetery & Crematorium, Birchfield Rd, Widnes,
WA8 9EE T: 0151 471 7332
Cleveland
Teesside Crematorium, Acklam Rd, Middlesbrough, TS5 7HE T:
01642 817725 Fax: 01642 852424 E:
peter_gitsham@middlesbrough.gov.uk WWW:
www.middlesbrough.gov.uk Also contact address for: Acklam Cemetery,
Acklam Road, Middlesbrough; Linthorpe Cemetery, Burlam Road; Thorntree
Cemetery, Cargo Fleet Lane; Thorntree RC Cemetery, Cargo Fleet Lane; North
Ormesby Cemetery; St josephs Cemetery, Ormesby Road, Middlesbrough
Cornwall
Glynn Valley Crematorium, Turfdown Rd, Fletchers Bridge,
Bodmin, PL30 4AU T: 01208 73858
Penmount Crematorium, Penmount, Truro, TR4 9AA T:
01872 272871 Fax: 01872 223634 E: mail@penmount-
crematorium.org.uk W: www.penmount-crematorium.org.uk
County Durham
Birtley Cemetery & Crematorium, Windsor Rd, Birtley, Chester Le
Street, DH3 1PQ T: 0191 4102381
Chester Le Street Cemetery, Chester Le Street District Council
Civic Centre, Newcastle Rd, Chester Le Street, DH3 3UT T:
0191 3872117
Horden Parish Council, Horden Cemetery Lodge, Thorpe Rd,
Horden, Peterlee, SR8 4TP T: 0191 5863870
Mountsett Crematorium, Ewehurst Rd, Dipton, Stanley, DH9 0HN
T: 01207 570255
Murton Parish Council, Cemetery Lodge, Church Lane, Murton,
Seaham, SR7 9RD T: 0191 5263973
Newton Aycliffe Cemetery, Stephenson Way, Newton Aycliffe,
DL5 7DF T: 01325 312861
Princess Road Cemetery, Princess Rd, Seaham, SR7 7TD T:
0191 5812943
Trimdon Foundry Parish Council, Cemetary Lodge, Thornley Rd,
Trimdon Station, TS29 6NX T: 01429 880592
Trimdon Parish Council, Cemetery Lodge, Northside, Trimdon
Grange, Trimdon Station, TS29 6HN T: 01429 880538
Wear Valley District Council, Cemetery Lodge, South Church Rd,
Bishop Auckland, DL14 7NA T: 01388 603396
Cumbria
Carlisle Cemetery, Richardson St, Carlisle, CA2 6AL T:
01228 625310 Fax: 01228 625313 E: junec@carlisle-city.gov.uk
Penrith Cemetery, Beacon Edge, Penrith, CA11 7RZ T:
01768 862152
Wigton Burial Joint Committee, Cemetery House, Station Hill,
Wigton, CA7 9BN T: 016973 42442
Derbyshire
Bretby Crematorium, Geary Lane, Bretby, Burton-On-Trent,
DE15 0QE T: 01283 221505 Fax: 01283 224846 E:
bretby.crematorium@eaststaffsbc.gov.uk
WWW: www.eaststaffsbc.gov.uk CC accepted
Castle Donington Parish Council, Cemetery House, The Barroon,
Castle Donington, Derby, DE74 2PF T: 01332 810202
Chesterfield & District Joint Crematorium, Chesterfield Rd,
Brimington, Chesterfield, S43 1AU T: 01246 345888 Fax: 01246
345889
Clay Cross Cemetery, Cemetery Rd, Danesmoor, Chesterfield,
S45 9RL T: 01246 863225

Dronfield Cemetery, Cemetery Lodge, 42 Cemetery Rd, Dronfield, S18 1XY T: 01246 412373

Glossop Cemetery, Arundel House, Cemetery Rd, Glossop, SK13 7QG T: 01457 852269

Markeaton Crematorium, Markeaton Lane, Derby, DE22 4NH T: 01332 341012 Fax: 01332 331273

Melbourne Cemetery, Pack Horse Rd, Melbourne, Derby, DE73 1BZ T: 01332 863369

Shirebrook Town Council, Common Lane, Shirebrook, Mansfield, NG20 8PA T: 01623 742509

Devon

Drake Memorial Park Ltd The, Haye Rd, Plympton, Plymouth, PL7 1UQ T: 01752 337937

Exeter & Devon Crematorium, Topsham Rd, Exeter, EX2 6EU T: 01392 496333

Littleham Church Yard, Littleham Village, Littleham, Exmouth, EX8 2RQ T: 01395 225579

Mole Valley Green Burial Ground, Woodhouse Farm, Queens Nympton, South Molton, EX36 4JH T: 01769 574512 Fax: 01769 574512 E: woodhouse.org.farm@farming.co.uk

North Devon Crematorium, Old Torrington Rd, Barnstaple, EX31 3NW T: 01271 345431

Ford Park Cemetery Trust, Ford Park Rd, Plymouth, PL4 6NT T: 01752 665442 Fax: 01752 601177 E: trustees@ford-park-cemetery.org WWW: www.ford-park-cemetery.org

Tavistock Cemetery, Cemetery Office, Plymouth Rd, Tavistock, PL19 8BY T: 01822 612799 Fax: 01822 618300 E: tavistocktc@aol.com WWW: www.tavistock.gov.uk

Torquay Crematorium & Cemetery, Hele Rd, Torquay, TQ2 7QG T: 01803 327768

Dorset, Dorchester Cemetery Office, 31a Weymouth Avenue, Dorchester, DT1 2EN T: 01305 263900

Parkstone Cemetery, 134 Pottery Rd, Parkstone, Poole, BH14 8RD T: 01202 741104

Poole Cemetery, Dorchester Rd, Oakdale, Poole, BH15 3RZ T: 01202 741106

Poole Crematorium, Gravel Hill, Poole, BH17 9BQ T: 01202 602582

Sherborne Cemetery, Lenthay Rd, Sherborne, DT9 6AA T: 01935 812909

Weymouth Crematorium, Quibo Lane, Weymouth, DT4 0RR T: 01305 786984

Essex

Basildon & District Crematorium, Church Rd, Bowers Gifford, Basildon, SS13 2HG T: 01268 584411

Chadwell Heath Cemetery, Whalebone Lane, North Chadwell Heath, Romford, RM6 5QX T: 0181 590 3280

Chelmsford Crematorium, Writtle LaneChelmsford, CM1 3BL T: 01245 256946

Chigwell Cemetery, Frog Hall LaneChapman, Manor Rd, Chigwell, IG7 4JX T: 020 8501 4275 Fax: 020 8501 2045 E: chigwell@tesco.net, Earliest record - April 1973**Colchester Cemetery & Crematorium,** Mersea Rd, Colchester, CO2 8RU T: 01206 282950

Eastbrookend Cemetery, Dagenham Rd, Dagenham, RM10 7DR T: 01708 447451

Federation of Synagogues Burial Society, 416 Upminster Rd North, Rainham, RM13 9SB T: 01708 552825

Great Burstead Cemetery, Church St, Great Burstead, Billericay, CM11 2TR T: 01277 654334

Parndon Wood Crematorium and Cemetery, Parndon Wood Rd, Harlow, CM19 4SF T: 01279 446199 T: 01279 423800, E: chris.brown@harlow.gov.uk

Pitsea Cemetery, Church Rd, Pitsea, Basildon, SS13 2EZ T: 01268 552132

Romford Cemetery, Crow Lane, Romford, RM7 0EP T: 01708 740791

Sewardstone Road Cemetery, Sewardstone Rd, Waltham Abbey, EN9 1NX T: 01992 712525

South Essex Crematorium, Ockendon Rd, Corbets Tey, Upminster, RM14 2UY T: 01708 222188

Sutton Road Cemetery, The Lodge, Sutton Rd, Southend-On-Sea, SS2 5PX T: 01702 603907 Fax: 01702 603906 CC accepted**Weeley Crematorium,** Colchester Rd, Weeley, Clacton-On-Sea, CO16 9JP T: 01255 831108 Fax: 01255 831440 Also covers and is contact address for: Clacton Cemetery; Kirby Cross Cemetery; Dovercourt Cemetery; Walton on the Naze Cemetery

Wickford Cemetery, Park Drive, Wickford, SS12 9DH T: 01268 733335

Gloucestershire

Cheltenham Cemetery & Crematorium, Bouncers Lane, Cheltenham, GL52 5JT T: 01242 244245 Fax: 01242 263123 E: cemetery@cheltenham.gov.uk WWW: www.cheltenham.gov.uk

Coney Hill Crematorium, Coney Hill Rd, Gloucester, GL4 4PA T: 01452 523902

Forest of Dean Crematorium, Yew Tree Brake, Speech House Rd, Cinderford, GL14 3HU T: 01594 826624

Mile End Cemetery, Mile End, Coleford, GL16 7DB T: 01594 832848

Hampshire

Aldershot Crematorium, 48 Guildford Rd, Aldershot, GU12 4BP T: 01252 321653

Anns Hill Rd Cemetery, Anns Hill Rd, Gosport, PO12 3JX T: 023 9258 0181 Fax: 023 9251 3191 WWW: www.gosport.gov.uk

Basingstoke Crematorium, Manor Farm, Stockbridge Rd, North Waltham, Basingstoke, RG25 2BA T: 01256 398784

Magdalen Hill Cemetery, Magdalen Hill, Arlesesford Rd, Winchester, SO21 1HE T: 01962 854135

Portchester Crematorium, Upper Cornaway Lane, Portchester, Fareham, PO16 8NE T: 01329 822533

Portsmouth Cemeteries Office, Milton Rd, Southsea, PO4 8 T: 023 9273 2559

Southampton City Council, 6 Bugle St, Southampton, SO14 2AJ T: 01703 228609

Warblington Cemetery, Church Lane, Warblington, Havant, PO9 2TU T:

Worting Rd Cemetery, 105 Worting Rd, Basingstoke, RG21 8YZ T: 01256 321737

Herefordshire

Hereford Cemetery & Crematorium, Bereavement Services office, Westfaling Street, Hereford, HR4 0JE T: 01432 383200 Fax: 01432 383201

Hertfordshire

Vicarage Road Cemetery, Vicarage Road, Watford, WD18 0EJ T: 01923 672157 Fax: 01923 672157

Almonds Lane Cemetery, Almonds Lane, Stevenage, SG1 3RR T: 01438 350902

Bushey Jewish Cemetery, Little Bushey Lane, Bushey, Watford, WD2 3TP T: 0181 950 6299 One of the burial grounds maintained by the United Synagogue

Chorleywood Road Cemetery, Chorleywood Rd, Rickmansworth, WD3 4EH T: 01923 772646

Dacorum Borough Council, Woodwells Cemetery, Buncefield Lane, Hemel Hempstead, HP2 7HY T: 01442 252856

Harwood Park Crematorium Ltd, Watton Rd, Stevenage, SG2 8XT T: 01438 815555

Hatfield Road Cemetery, Hatfield Rd, St. Albans, AL1 4LU T: 01727 819362 Fax: 01727 819362 E: stalbans@cemeteries.freeserve.co.uk St Albans City & District Council administers three Cemeteries from Hatfield Road. The other two are situated London Road, St Albans and Westfield Road, Harpenden

North Watford Cemetery, North Western Avenue, Watford, WD25 0AW T: 01923 672157 Fax: 01923 672157

Tring Cemetery, Aylesbury Rd, Aylesbury, Tring, HP23 4DH T: 01442 822248

Vicarage Road Cemetery, Vicarage Rd, Watford, WD1 8EJ T: 01923 225147

Watton Rd Cemetery, Watton Rd, Ware, SG12 0AX T: 01920 463261

West Herts Crematorium, High Elms Lane, Watford, WD25 0JS T: 01923 673285 Fax: 01923 681318 E: postmaster@weshertscrem.org WWW: www.weshertscrem.org CC accepted

Western Synagogue Cemetery, Cheshunt Cemetery, Bulls Cross Ride, Waltham Cross, EN7 5HT T: 01992 717820

Weston Road Cemetery, Weston Rd, Stevenage, SG1 4DE T: 01438 367109

Woodcock Hill Cemetery, Lodge, Woodcock Hill, Harefield Rd, Rickmansworth, WD3 1PT T: 01923 775188

Isle Of Wight

Shanklin Cemetery, 1 Cemetery Rd, Lake Sandown, Sandown, PO36 9NN T: 01983 403743

Kent

Barham Crematorium, Canterbury Rd, Barham, Canterbury, CT4 6QU T: 01227 831351 Fax: 01227 830258

Beckenham Crematorium & Cemetery, Elmers End Rd, Beckenham, BR3 4TD T: 0208650 0322

Chartham Cemetery Lodge, Ashford Rd, Chartham, Canterbury, CT4 7NY T: 01227 738211 T: 01227 738211 Minicom, Fax: 01227 738211 All burial records computerised

Gravesham Borough Council, Old Rd West, Gravesend, DA11 0LS T: 01474 337491

Hawkinge Cemetery & Crematorium, Aerodrome Rd, Hawkinge, Folkestone, CT18 7AG T: 01303 892215

Kent & Sussex Crematorium, Benhall Mill Rd., Tunbridge Wells, TN2 5JH T: 01892 523894

Kent County Crematorium plc, Newcourt Wood, Charing, Ashford, TN27 0EB T: 01233 712443 Fax: 01233 713501

The Cremation Society, 2nd Floor Brecon House, 16/16a Albion Place, Maidstone, ME14 5DZ T: 01622 688292/3 Fax: 01622 686698 E: cremsoc@aol.com WWW: www.cremation.org.uk

Medway Crematorium, Robin Hood Lane, Blue Bell Hill, Chatham, ME5 9QU T: 01634 861639 Fax: 01634 671206 E: paul.edwards@medway.gov.uk CC accepted

Northfleet Cemetery, Springhead Rd, Northfleet, Gravesend, DA11 8HW T: 01474 533260

Snodland Cemetery, Cemetery Cottage, Cemetery Rd, Snodland, ME6 5DN T: 01634 240764

Thanet Crematorium, Manston Rd, Margate, CT9 4LY T: 01843 224492 Fax: 01843 292218 Also covers: Margate Cemetery, Kent; Ramsgate and St Lawrence Cemeteries

Vinters Park Crematorium, Bearstead Rd, Weavering, Maidstone, ME14 5LG T: 01622 738172 Fax: 01622 630560 CC accepted

Lancashire

Accrington Cemetery & Crematorium, Burnley Rd, Accrington, BB5 6HA T: 01254 232933 Fax: 01254 232933

Atherton Cemetery, Leigh Road, Atherton

Audenshaw Cemetery, Cemetery Rd, Audenshaw, Manchester, M34 5AH T: 0161 336 2675

Blackley Cemetery & Crematorium, Victoria Avenue, Manchester, M9 8 T: 0161 740 5359

Burnley Cemetery, Rossendale Rd, Burnley, BB11 5DD T: 01282 435411 Fax: 01282 458904 WWW: www.burnley.gov.uk

Carleton Crematorium, Stocks Lane, Carleton, Poulton-Le-Fylde, FY6 7QS T: 01253 882541

Central & North Manchester Synagogue Jewish Cemetery, Rainsough Brow, Prestwick, Manchester, M25 9XW T: 0161 773 2641**Central & North Manchester Synagogue Jewish Cemetery,** Rochdale Rd, Manchester, M9 6FQ T: 0161 740 2317

Chadderton Cemetery, Cemetery Lodge, Middleton Rd, Chadderton, Oldham, OL9 0JZ T: 0161 624 2301

Gidlow Cemetery, Gidlow Lane, Standish, Wigan, WN6 8RT T: 01257 424127

Greenacres Cemetery, Greenacres Rd, Oldham, OL4 3HT T: 0161 624 2294

Hindley Cemetery, Castle Hill Road Road, Ince, Wigan, WN3

Hollinwood Cemetery (incorporating Oldham Crematorium), Central Cemeteries Office, Roman Rd, Hollinwood, Oldham, OL8 3LU T: 0161 681 1312 Fax: 0161 683 5233 E: oper.cemeteries@oldham.gov.uk WWW: www.oldham.gov.uk The Central Cemeteries Office covers seven cemeteries and one crematorium: Hollinwood, Greenacres, Crompton, Royton, Lees, Chadderton and Failswoprth Cemeteries and Oldham Crematorium

Howe Bridge Crematorium, Crematorium Management Ltd, Lovers Lane, Atherton, Manchester, M46 0PZ T: 01942 870811

Howebridge Cemetery, Lovers Lane, Atherton

Ince in Makerfield Cemetery, Warrington Road, Lower Ince, Wigan

Leigh Cemetery, Manchester Rd, Leigh, WN7 2 T: 01942 671560 Fax: 01942 828877 WWW: www.wiganbc.gov.uk

Lower Ince Cemetery and Crematorium, Cemetery Road, Lower Ince, Wigan, WN3 4NH T: 01942 866455 Fax: 01942 828855 F: t.bassett@wiganmbc.gov.uk

Lytham Park Cemetery & Cremarotium, Regent Avenue, Lytham St. Annes, FY8 4AB T: 01253 735429 Fax: 01253 731903

Manchester Crematorium Ltd, Barlow Moor Rd, Manchester, M21 7GZ T: 0161 881 5269

Middleton New Cemetery, Boarshaw Rd, Middleton, Manchester, M24 6 T: 0161 655 3765

New Manchester Woodland Cemetery, City Rd, Ellenbrook, Worsley, Manchester, M28 1BD T: 0161 790 1300

Overdale Crematorium, Overdale Drive, Chorley New Rd, Heaton, Bolton, BL1 5BU T: 01204 840214

Padiham Public Cemetery, St. Johns Rd, Padiham, Burnley, BB12 7BN T: 01282 778139

Preston Cemetery, New Hall Lane, Preston, PR1 4SY T: 01772 794585 Fax: 01772 703857 E: m.birch@preston.gov.uk WWW: www.preston.gov.uk All burial records are available on microfilm at the Lancashire Record Office, Bow Lane, Preston as well as at the Cemetery Office

Preston Crematorium, Longridge Rd, Ribbleton, Preston, PR2 6RL T: 01772 792391 Fax: 01772 703857 E: m.birch@preston.gov.uk WWW: www.preston.gov.uk All records relating to Preston Crematorium are held at Preston Cemetery office, New Hall Lane, Preston PR1 4SY T: 01772 794585

Rochdale Cemetery, Bury Rd, Rochdale, OL11 4DG T: 01706 645219

Southern Cemetery, Barlow Moor Rd, Manchester, M21 7GL T: 0161 881 2208

St. Mary's Catholic Cemetery, Manchester Rd, Wardley, Manchester, M28 2UJ T: 0161 794 2194 E: cemeteries@salforddiocese.org

St Joseph's Cemetery, Moston Lane, Manchester, M40 9QL T: 0161 681 1582 E: cemeteries@salforddiocese.org

Tyldesley Cemetery, Hough Lane, Tyldesley

United Synagogue Burial Ground, Worsley Hill Farm, Phillips Park Rd, Whitefield, Manchester, M45 7ED T: 0161 766 2065

Wigan Council Cemeteries and Crematorium Section, 1 - 3 Worsley Terrace, Standishgate, Wigan, WN1 1XW T: 01942 828993 T: 01942 828994, Fax: 01942 828877 E: t.boussele@wiganmbc.gov.uk

Whitworth Cemetery, Edward St, Whitworth, Rochdale, OL16 2EJ T: 01706 217777

Westwood Cemetery, Westwood Lane, Lower Ince, Wigan,

Leicestershire

Cemetery Lodge, Thorpe Rd, Melton Mowbray, LE13 1SH T: 01664 562223

Loughborough Crematorium, Leicester Rd, Loughborough, LE11 2AF T: 01743 353046

Saffron Hill Cemetery, Stonesby Avenue, Leicester, LE2 6TY T: 0116 222 1049

Lincolnshire

Boston Crematorium, Cemeteries and Crematorium Office, Marian Rd, Boston, PE21 9HA T: 01205 364612 Fax: 01205 364612 E: martin.potts@boston.gov.ukW: www.boston.gov.uk Administers Boston Cemetery (1855), Fosdyke Cemetery (1952) and Boston Crematorium (1966)

Bourne Town Cemetery, South Rd, Bourne, PE10 9JB Tel: 01778 422796

Grantham Cemetery & Crematorium, Harrowby Rd, Grantham, NG31 9DT T: 01476 563083 T: 01476 590905 Fax: 01476 576228

Horncastle Cemetery, Boston Rd, Horncastle, LN9 6NF Tel: 01507 527118

Stamford Cemetery, Wichendom, Little Casterton Rd, Stamford, PE9 1BB T: 01780 762316

Tyler Landscapes, Newport Cemetery, Manor Rd, Newport, Lincoln, LN4 1RT T: 01522 525195

Lincolnshire - North East

Cleethorpes Cemetery, Beacon Avenue, Cleethorpes, DN35 8EQ T: 01472 324869 Fax: 01472 324870

North East Lincolnshire Council Crematorium & Cemeteries Department, Weelsby Avenue, Grimsby, DN32 0BA T: 01472 324869 Fax: 01472 324870

Lincolnshire - North

Woodlands Crematorium, Brumby Wood Lane, Scunthorpe, DN17 1SP T: 01724 280289 Fax: 01724 871235 E: crematorium@northlincs.gov.uk WWW: www.northlincs.gov.uk/environmentalhealth/cemetery.htm Central Office for holding documents for: Barton Upon Humber Cemetery, Brumby Cemetery, Crosby Cemetery, Brigg Cemetery, Scawby Cemetery, Winterton Cemetery and Woodlands Cemetery

London

Abney Park Cemetery, The South Lodgfe, Stoke Newington High St, Stoke Newington, London, N16 0LH T: 020 7275 7557 Fax: 020 7275 7557 E: abney-park@ges2.poptel.org.uk WWW: www.abney-park.org.uk

Brockley Ladywell Hithergreen & Grove Park Cemeteries, Verdant Lane, Catford, London SE6 1TP T: 0181 697 2555

Brompton Cemetery, Fulham Rd, London, SW10 9UG T: 0171 352 1201

Cemetery Management Ltd, The City of Westminster Office, 38 Uxbridge Rd, London, W7 3PP T: 0181 567 0913

Charlton Cemetery, Cemetery Lane, London, SE7 8DZ T: 0181 854 0235

Chingford Mount Cemetery London Borough of Waltham Forest, Old Church Rd, London, E4 6ST T: 020 8524 5030

City of London Cemetery & Crematorium, Aldersbrook Rd, London, E12 5DQ T: 0181 530 2151

Coroners Court, 8 Ladywell Rd, Lewisham, London, SE13 7UW T: 0208690 5138

East London Cemetery Co.Ltd, Grange Rd, London, E13 0HB Tel: 020 7476 5109 Fax: 020 7476 8338 E: enquiries@eastlondoncemetery.co.uk WWW: www.eastlondoncemetery.co.uk

Edmonton Cemetery, Church St, Edmonton, London, N9 9HP T: 0208360 2157

Eltham Cemetery & Crematorium, Crown Woods Way, Eltham, London, SE9 2RF T: 0181 850 2921 (Cemetery) Fax: 0181 850 7046 (Crematorium)

Gap Road Cemetery, Gap Rd, London, SW19 8JF T: 0208879 0701

Golders Green Crematorium, 62 Hoop Lane, London, NW11 7NL T: 0208455 2374

Greenwich Cemetery, Well Hall Rd, London SE9 6TZ T: 0181 856 8666

London Borough of Hackney Mortuary, Lower Clapton Rd, London, E5 8EQ T: 0181 985 2808

Hendon Cemetery & Crematorium, Holders Hill Rd, London, NW7 1NB T: 0181 346 0657

Highgate Cemetery, Swains Lane, London, N6 6PJ T: 0181 340 1834

Honor Oak Crematorium, Brenchley Gardens, London, SE23 3RB T: 020 7639 3121 Fax: 020 7732 3557 E: terry.connor@southwark.gov.uk

Islington Cemetery & Crematorium, High Rd, East Finchley, London, N2 9AG T: 0208883 1230

Kensal Green Cemetery, Harrow Road, London, W10 4RA T: 020 8969 0152 Fax: 020 8960 9744

L B S Cemeteries, Brenchley Gardens, London, SE23 3RD T: 020 7639 3121 Fax: 020 7732 3557 E: terry.connor@southwark.gov.uk

Lambeth Cemetery and Crematorium, Cemetery Lodge, Blackshaw Rd, Tooting, London, SW17 0BY T: 0181 672 1390

Lewisham Crematorium, Verdant Lane, London, SE6 1TP T: 0208698 4955

Liberal Jewish Cemetery, The Lodge, Pound Lane, London, NW10 2HG T: 0181 459 1635

Manor Park Cemetery Co.Ltd, Sebert Rd, Forest Gate, London, E7 0NP T: 020 8534 1486 Fax: 020 8519 1348 E: supt@manorpark15.fsbusiness.co.uk WWW: www.mpark.co.uk CC accepted Grave of John Cornwell VC

New Southgate Cemetery & Crematorium Ltd, 98 Brunswick Park Rd, London, N11 1JJ T: 0181 361 1713

Newham, London Borough of, High St South, London, E6 6ET T: 0181 472 9111

Plumstead Cemetery, Wickham Lane, London, SE2 0NS T: 0181 854 0785

Putney Vale Cemetery & Crematorium, Kingston Rd, London, SW15 3SB T: 0181 788 2113

South London Crematorium & Streatham Park Cemetery, Rowan Rd, London, SW16 5JG T: 0181 764 2255

St. Marylebone Crematorium, East End Rd, Finchley, London, N2 0RZ T: 0208343 2233

St. Pancras Cemetery (London Borough Of Camden), High Rd, East Finchley, London, N2 9AG T: 0181 883 1231

St. Patrick's Catholic Cemetery, Langthorne Rd, London, E11 4HL T: 0181 539 2451

St.Mary's Catholic Cemetery, Harrow Rd, London, NW10 5NU T: 0181 969 1145

Tottenham Park Cemetery, Montagu Rd, Edmonton, N18 2NF T: 0181 807 1617

United Synagogue, Beaconsfield Rd, Willesden, London, NW10 2JE T: 0208459 0394

West End Chesed V'Ameth Burial Society, 3 Rowan Rd, London, SW16 5JF T: 0181 764 1566

West Ham Cemetery, Cemetery Rd, London, E7 9DG T: 0208534 1566

West London Synagogue, Hoop Lane, London, NW11 7NJ T: 0208455 2569

West Norwood Cemetery & Crematorium, Norwood Rd, London, SE27 9AJ T: 0207926 7900

Woodgrange Park Cemetery, Romford Rd, London, E7 8AF T: 0181 472 3433

Woolwich Cemetery, Kings Highway, London, SE18 2BJ T: 0181 854 0740

Merseyside
Anfield Crematorium, Priory Rd, Anfield, Liverpool, L4 2SL T: 0151 263 3267

Southport Cemeteries & Crematoria, Southport Rd, Scarisbrick, Southport, PR8 5JQ T: 01704 533443

St. Helens Cemetery & Crematorium, Rainford Rd, Windle, St. Helens, WA10 6DF T: 01744 677406 Fax: 01744 677411

Thornton Garden Of Rest, Lydiate Lane, Thornton, Liverpool, L23 1TP T: 0151 924 5143

Middlesex
Adath Yisroel Synagogue & Burial Society, Carterhatch Lane, Enfield, EN1 4BG T: 0181 363 3384

Breakspear Crematorium, Breakspear Rd, Ruislip, HA4 7SJ T: 01895 632843 Fax: 01895 624209

Enfield Crematorium, Great Cambridge Rd, Enfield, EN1 4DS T: 0181 363 8324

Heston & Isleworth Borough Cemetry, 190 Powder Mill Lane, Twickenham, TW2 6EJ T: 0181 894 3830

South West Middlesex Crematorium, Hounslow Rd, Hanworth, Feltham, TW13 5JH T: 0208894 9001

Spelthorne Borough Council, Green Way, Sunbury-On-Thames, TW16 6NW T: 01932 780244

Norfolk
Colney Wood Memorial Park, Colney Hall, Watton Rd, Norwich, NR4 7TY T: 01603 811556

Mintlyn Crematorium, Lynn Rd, Bawsey, King's Lynn, PE32 1HB T: 01553 630533 Fax: 01553 630998 E: colin.houseman@west-norfolk.gov.uk WWW: www.west-norfolk.gov.uk

Norwich & Norfolk Crematoria - St. Faiths & Earlham, 75 Manor Rd, Horsham St. Faith, Norwich, NR10 3LF T: 01603 898264

Sprowston Cemetery, Church Lane, Sprowston, Norwich, NR7 8AU T: 01603 425354

North Tyneside - North Tyneside Metropolitan Borough Council
Earsdon Cemetery, Earsdon, Whitley Bay, NE25 9LR T: 0191 200 5861 0191 200 5860

Longbenton Cemetery, Longbenton, Newcastle Upon Tyne, NE12 8EY T: 0191 2661261

Whitley Bay Cemetery, Blyth Rd, Whitley Bay, NE26 4NH T: 0191 200 5861 Fax: 0191 200 5860

Northamptonshire
Counties Crematorium, Towcester Rd, Milton Malsor, Northampton, NN4 9RN T: 01604 858280

Dallington Cemetery, Harlstone Rd, Dallington, Northampton, NN5 7 T: 01604 751589

Northumberland
Alnwick Cemetary, Cemetery Lodge Office, South Rd, Alnwick, NE66 2PH T: 01665 602598 T: 01665 579272, Fax. 01665 579272 WWW: www.alnwicktown.com

Blyth Cemetery, Links Rd, Blyth, NE24 3PJ T: 01670 369623
Cowpen Cemetery, Cowpen Rd, Blyth, NE24 5SZ T: 01670 352107

Embleton Joint Burial Committee, Spitalford, Embleton, Alnwick, NE66 3DW T: 01665 576632

Haltwhistle & District Joint Burial Committee, Cemetery Lodge Haltwhistle, NE49 0LF T: 01434 320266 Fax: 01434 320266

Rothbury Cemetery, Cemetery Lodge, Whitton Rd Rothbury, Morpeth, NE65 7RX T: 01669 620451

Nottinghamshire
Bramcote Crematorium, Coventry Lane, Beeston, Nottingham, NG9 3GJ T: 0115 922 1837

Mansfield & District Crematorium, Derby Rd, Mansfield, NG18 5BJ T: 01623 621811

Northern Cemetery, Hempshill Lane, Bulwell, Nottingham, NG6 8PF T: 0115 915 3245 Fax: 0115 915 3246 E: alec.thomson@nottinghamcity.gov.uk WWW: www.nottinghamcity.gov.uk/bereavement Also covers: ~Basford Cemetery Npottingham Road, General Cemetery Waverley Street, Canning Circus and Church (Rock) Cemetery, Mansfield Road

Southern Cemetery & Crematoria, Wilford Hill, West Bridgford, Nottingham, NG2 7FE T: 0115 915 2340

Tithe Green Woodland Burial Ground, Salterford Lane, Calverton, Nottingham, NG14 6NZ T: 01623 882210

Oxfordshire
Oxford Crematorium Ltd, Bayswater Rd, Headington, Oxford, OX3 9RZ T: 01865 351255

Shropshire
Bridgnorth Cemetery, Mill St, Bridgnorth, WV15 5NG T: 01746 762386

Emstrey Crematorium, London Rd, Shrewsbury, SY2 6PS T: 01743 359883

Hadley Cemetery, 85 Hadley Park Rd, Hadley, Telford, TF1 4PY T: 01952 223418

Longden Road Cemetery, Longden Rd, Shrewsbury, SY3 7HS T: 01743 353046

Market Drayton Burial Committee, Cemetery Lodge, Cemetery Rd, Market Drayton, TF9 3BD T: 01630 652833

Oswestry Cemetery, Cemetery Lodge, Victoria Rd, Oswestry, SY11 2HU T: 01691 652013 Fax: 01691 652013 E: graham.lee2@btinternet.com

Whitchurch Joint Cemetery Board, The Cemetery Lodge, Mile Bank Rd, Whitchurch, SY13 4JY T: 01948 665477

Somerset
Burnham Area Burial Board, The Old Courthouse, Jaycroft Rd, Burnham-On-Sea, TA8 1LE T: 01278 795111

Chard Town Council, Holyrood Lace Mill, Hollyrood Street, Chard, TA20 12YA T: 01460 260370 Fax: 01460 260372

Minehead Cemetery, Porlock Rd, Woodcombe, Minehead, TA24 8RY T: 01643 705243

Sedgemoor District Council, The Cemetery, Quantock Rd, Bridgwater, TA6 7EJ T: 01278 423993

Taunton Deane Cemeteries & Crematorium, Wellington New Rd, Taunton, TA1 5NE T: 01823 284811 Fax: 01823 323152 W: www.tauntondeane.gov.uk/TDBCsites/crem

Wells Burial Joint Committee, 127 Portway, Wells, BA5 1LY T: 01749 672049

Yeovil Cemetery, Preston Rd, Yeovil, BA21 3AG T: 01935 423742
Yeovil Crematorium, Bunford Lane, Yeovil, BA20 2EJ T: 01935 476718

Staffordshire
Bretby Crematorium, Geary Lane, Bretby, Burton-On-Trent, DE15 0QE T: 01283 221505 Fax: 01283 224846 E: bretby.crematorium@eaststaffsbc.gov.uk WWW: www.eaststaffsbc.gov.uk CC accepted

Cannock Cemetery, Cemetery Lodge, 160 Pye Green Rd, Cannock, WS11 2SJ T: 01543 503176

Carmountside Cemetery and Crematorium Leek Rd, Milton, Stoke-On-Trent, ST2 7AB T: 01782 235050 Fax: 01782 235050 E: karendeaville@civic2.stoke.gov.uk

Leek Cemetery, Condlyffe Rd, Leek, ST13 5PP T: 01538 382616

Newcastle Cemetery, Lymewood Grove, Newcastle, ST5 2EH T: 01782 616379 Fax: 01782 630498 E: jeanette.hollins@newcastle-staffs.gov.uk

Newcastle Crematorium, Chatterley Close, Bradwell, Newcastle, ST5 8LE T: 01782 635498 Fax: 01782 710859

Stafford Crematorium, Tixall Rd, Stafford, ST18 0XZ T: 01785 242594

Stapenhill Cemetery, 38 Stapenhill Rd, Burton-On-Trent, DE15 9AE T: 01283 508572 Fax: 01283 566586 E: cemetery@eaststaffsbc.gov.uk WWW: www.eaststaffsbc.gov.uk

Stilecop Cemetary, Stilecop Rd, Rugeley, WS15 1ND T: 01889 577739

Uttoxeter Town Council, Cemetery Lodge, Stafford Rd, Uttoxeter ST14 8DS T: 01889 563374

Suffolk
Brinkley Woodland Cemetery, 147 All Saints Rd, Newmarket, CB8 8HH T: 01638 600693

Bury St. Edmunds Cemetery, 91 Kings Rd, Bury St. Edmunds, IP33 3DT T: 01284 754447

Hadleigh Town Council, Friars Rd, Hadleigh, Ipswich, IP7 6DF T: 01473 822034

Haverhill Cemetery, Withersfield Rd, Haverhill, CB9 9HF T: 01440 703810

Ipswich Cemetery & Crematorium, Cemetery Lane, Ipswich, IP4 2TQ T: 01473 433580 Fax: 01473 433588 E: carol.egerton@ipswich.gov.uk

Leiston Cemetery, Waterloo Avenue, Leiston, IP16 4EH T: 01728 831043

West Suffolk Crematorium, Risby, Bury St. Edmunds, IP28 6RR T: 01284 755118 Fax: 01284 755135

Surrey

American Cemetery, Cemetery Pales, Brookwood, Woking, GU24 0BL T: 01483 473237

Bandon Hill Cemetery Joint Committee, Plough Lane, Wallington, SM6 8JQ T: 0181 647 1024

Brookwood Cemetery, Cemetery Pales, Brookwood, Woking, GU24 0BL T: 01483 472222

Confederation of Burial Authorities, The Gate House, Kew Meadow Path, Richmond, TW9 4EN T: 0181 392 9487

Guildford Crematorium & Cemetaries, Broadwater, New Pond Rd, Goldaming, Godalming, GU7 3DB T: 01483 444711

Kingston Cemetary & Crematorium, Bonner Hill Rd, Kingston Upon Thames, KT1 3EZ T: 020 8546 4462 Fax: 020 8546 4463

London Road Cemetery, Figs Marsh, London Rd, Mitcham, CR4 3 T: 0208648 4115

Merton & Sutton Joint Cemetery, Garth Rd, Morden, SM4 4LL T: (020) 8337 4420 Fax: (020) 8337 4420

Mortlake Crematorium Board, Kew Meadow Path, Town Mead Rd, Richmond, TW9 4EN T: 0181 876 8056

Mount Cemetery, Weyside Rd, Guildford, GU1 1HZ T: 01483 561927

North East Surrey Crematorium Board, Lower Morden Lane, Morden, SM4 4NU T: 020 8337 4835 Fax: 020 8337 8745 E: nescb.crematorium@talk21.com WWW: www.nes-crematorium.org.uk Opened May 1958

Randalls Park Crematorium, Randalls Rd, Leatherhead, KT22 0AG T: 01372 373813

Redstone Cemetery, Philanthropic Rd, Redhill, RH1 4DN T: 01737 761592

Dorking Cemetery, Reigate Rd, Dorking, RH4 1QF T: 01306 879299 Fax: 01306 876821 E: carole.brough@mole-valley.gov.uk WWW: www.mole-valley.gov.uk Victorian Cemetery concecrated in 1855 (listed Grade II in 1999)

Richmond Cemeteries, London Borough of Richmond upon Thames, Sheen Rd, Richmond, TW10 5BJ T: 020 8876 4511 Fax: 020 8878 8118 E: cemeteries@richmond.gov.uk

Surbiton Cemetery, Lower Marsh Lane, Kingston Upon Thames, KT1 3BN T: 0208546 4463

Sutton & Cuddington Cemeteries, Alcorn Close, off Oldfields Road, Sutton, SM3 9PX T: 020 8644 9437 Fax: 020 8644 1373

The Godalming Joint Burial Committee, New Cemetery Lodge, Ockford Ridge, Godalming, GU7 2NP T: 01483 421559

Woking Crematorium, Hermitage Rd, Woking, GU21 8TJ T: 01483 472197 Oldest crematorium in the UK. Search fee payable

Sussex - East

Afterthoughts Grave Care, 16 Derwent Rd, Eastbourne BN20 7PH T: 01323 730029

Brighton Borough Mortuary, Lewes Rd, Brighton, BN2 3QB T: 01273 602345

Downs Crematorium, Bear Rd, Brighton, BN2 3PL T: 01273 601601

Eastbourne Cemeteries & Crematorium, Hide Hollow, Langney, Eastbourne, BN23 8AE T: 01323 766536 (Cemetery) Fax: 01323 761093 (Crematorium)

Woodvale Crematorium, Lewes Rd, Brighton, BN2 3QB T: 01273 604020

Sussex - West

Chichester Crematorium, Westhampnett Rd, Chichester, PO19 4UH T: 01243 787755

Midhurst Burial Authority, Cemetery Lodge, Carron Lane, Midhurst, GU29 9LF T: 01730 812758

Surrey & Sussex Crematorium, Balcombe Rd, Crawley, RH10 3NQ T: 01293 888930

Worthing Crematorium & Cemeteries, Horsham Rd, Findon, Worthing, BN14 0RG T: 01903 872678 Fax: 01903 872051 E: crematorium@worthing.gov.uk

Tyne And Wear

Byker & Heaton Cemetery, 18 Benton Rd, Heaton, Newcastle Upon Tyne, NE7 7DS T: 0191 2662017

Gateshead East Cemetery, Cemetery Rd, Gateshead, NE8 4HJ T: 0191 4771819

Heworth Cemetery, Sunderland Rd, Felling, Gateshead, NE10 0NT T: 0191 4697851

Preston Cemetery & Tynemouth Crematorium, Walton Avenue, North Shields, NE29 9NJ T: 0191 2005861

Saltwell Crematorium, Saltwell Road South, Gateshead, NE8 4TQ T: 0191 4910553

St. Andrews Cemetery, Lodges 1-2, Great North Rd, Jesmond, Newcastle Upon Tyne, NE2 3BU T: 0191 2810953

St. Johns & Elswick Cemetery, Elswick Rd, Newcastle Upon Tyne, NE4 8DL T: 0191 2734127

St. Nicholas Cemetery, Wingrove Avenue Back, Newcastle Upon Tyne, NE4 9AP T: 0191 2735112

Union Hall Cemetery, Union Hall Rd, Newcastle Upon Tyne, NE15 7JS T: 0191 2674398

West Road Cemetery, West Rd, Newcastle Upon Tyne, NE5 2JL T: 0191 2744737

Warwickshire

Mid-Warwickshire Crematorium & Cemeteries, Oakley Wood, Bishops Tachbrook, Leamington Spa, CV33 9QP T: 01926 651418

Nuneaton Cemetery, Oaston Rd, Nuneaton, CV11 6JZ T: 024 7637 6357 Fax: 024 7637 6485

Stratford-on-Avon Cemetery, Evesham Rd, Stratford-Upon-Avon, CV37 9AA T: 01789 292676

West Midlands

Robin Hood Cemetery and Crematorium, Sheetsbrook Road, Shirley, Solihull, B90 3NL T: 0121 744 1121 Fax: 0121 733 8674

Widney Manor Cemetery, Widney Manor Road, Bentley Heath, Solihull, B93 3LX T:

Birmingham Crematorium 1973, 389 Walsall Rd, Perry Barr, Birmingham, B42 2LR T: 0121 356 9476

Birmingham Hebrew Congregation Cemetery, The Ridgeway, Erdington, Birmingham, B23 7TD T: 0121 356 4615

Brandwood End Cemetery, Woodthorpe Rd, Kings Heath, Birmingham, B14 6EQ T: 0121 444 1328

Coventry Bereavement Services, The Cemeteries & Crematorium Office, Cannon Hill Rd, Canley, Coventry, CV4 7DF T: 01203 418055

Handsworth Cemetery, Oxhill Rd, Birmingham, B21 8JT T: 0121 554 0096

Lodge Hill Cemetery & Cremetorium, Weoley Park Rd, Birmingham, B29 5AA T: 0121 472 1575

Quinton Cemetery, Halesowen Rd, Halesowen, B62 9AF T: 0121 422 2023

Stourbridge Cemetry & Crematorium, South Rd, Stourbridge, DY8 3RQ T: 01384 813985

Streetly Cemetery & Crematorium, Walsall Metropolitan Borough Council - Bereavement Services Division, Little Hardwick Road, Aldridge, Walsall, WS9 0SG T: 0121 353 7228 Fax: 0121 353 6557 E: billingss@walsall.gov.uk Also administers: Bentley Cemetery (opened 1900), Wolverhampton Road West, Willenhall; Bloxwich Cemetery, Field Road, Bloxwich, Walsall (opened 1875), James Bridge Cemetery (opened 1857), Cemetery Road, Darlaston, Walsall; North Walsall Cemetery (opened 1996), Saddleworth Road, Bloxwixh, Ryecroft Cemetery (opened 1894), Coalpool Lane, Walsall; Steetley Cemetery & Crematorium (opened 1938/1984); Willenhall Lawn Cemetery (opened 1966); Wood Street Cemetery (opened prior to 1857), Willenhall

Sutton Coldfield Cemetery, Rectory Rd, Sutton Coldfield, B75 7RP T: 0121 378 0224

Sutton Coldfield Cremetorium, Tamworth Rd, Four Oaks, Sutton Coldfield, B75 6LG T: 0121 308 3812

West Bromwich Crematorium, Forge Lane, West Bromwich, B71 3SX T: 0121 588 2160

Willenhall Lawn Cemetery, Bentley Lane, Willenhall, WV12 4AE T: 01902 368621

Witton Cemetery, Moor Lane Witton, Birmingham, B6 7AE T: 0121 356 4363 Fax: 0121 331 1283 E: wittoncem@birmingham.gov.uk

Woodlands Cemetery and Crematorium, Birmingham Rd, Coleshill, Birmingham, B46 2ET T: 01675 464835

Wiltshire

Box Cemetery, Bath Road, Box, Corsham, SN13 8AA T: 01225 742476

The Cemetery Chippenham, London Road, Chippenham, SN15 3RD T: 01249 652728

Devizes & Roundway Joint Burial Committee, Cemetry Lodge, Rotherstone, Devizes, SN10 2DE T: 01380 722821

Salisbury Crematorium, Barrington Road, Salisbury, SP1 3JB T: 01722 333632

Swindon Crematorium Kingsdown, Swindon, SN25 6SG T: 01793 822259 Holds records for Radnor Street and Whitworth Road Cemeteries, Swindon

West Wiltshire Crematorium, Devizes Road, Semington, Trowbridge, BA14 7QH T: 01380 871101

Wirral

Landican Cemetery, Arrowe Park Rd, Birkenhead, CH49 5LW T: 0151 677 2361

Worcestershire

Pershore Cemetery, Defford Rd, Pershore, WR10 3BX T: 01386 552043

Redith Crematorium & Abbey Cemetery, Bordesley Lane, Redditch, B97 6RR T: 01527 62174

Westall Park Woodland Burial, Holberrow Green, Redditch, B96 6JY T: 01386 792806

Worcester Crematorium, Astwood Rd, Tintern Avenue, Worcester, WR3 8HA T: 01905 22633

Yorkshire - East
East Riding Crematorium Ltd, Octon Cross Rd, Langtoft, Driffield, YO25 3BL T: 01377 267604
East Riding of Yorkshire Council, Cemetery Lodge, Sewerby Rd, Bridlington, YO16 7DS T: 01262 672138
Goole Cemetery, Hook Rd, Goole, DN14 5LU T: 01405 762725
Yorkshire - North
Fulford New Cemetery, Cemetery Lodge, Fordlands Rd, Fulford, York, YO19 4QG T: 01904 633151
Mowthorpe Garden of Rest, Southwood Farm, Terrington, York, YO60 6QB T: 01653 648459 Fax: 01653 648225 E: robert@robertgoodwill.co.uk
Stonefall Cemetery & Cremetoria, Wetherby Rd, Harrogate, HG3 1DE T: 01423 883523
Waltonwrays Cemetery, The Gatehouse, Carlton Rd, Skipton, BD23 3BT T: 01756 793168
York Cemetery, Gate House, Cemetery Rd, York, YO10 5AF T: 01904 610578
Yorkshire - South
Barnsley Crematorium & Cemetery, Doncaster Rd, Ardsley, Barnsley, S71 5EH T: 01226 206053
City Road Cemetery, City Rd, Sheffield, S2 1GD T: 0114 239 6068
Ecclesfield Cemetery, Priory Lane, Ecclesfield, Sheffield, S35 9XZ T: 0114 239 6068 Fax: 0114 239 3757
Eckington Cemetery, Sheffield Rd, Eckington, Sheffield, S21 9FP T: 01246 432197
Grenoside Crematorium, 5 Skew Hill Lane, Grenoside, Sheffield, S35 8RZ T: 0114 245 3999
Handsworth Cemetery, 51 Orgreave Lane, Handsworth, Sheffield, S13 9NE T: 0114 254 0832
Hatfield Cemetery, Cemetery Rd, Hatfield, Doncaster, DN7 6LX T: 01302 840242
Mexborough Cemetery, Cemetery Rd, Mexborough, S64 9PN T: 01709 585184
Rose Hill Crematorium, Cantley Lane, Doncaster, DN4 6NE T: 01302 535191
Rotherham Cemeteries & Crematorium, Ridgeway East, Herringthorpe, Rotherham, S65 3NN T: 01709 850344
Sheffield Cemeteries, City Rd, Sheffield, S2 1GD T: 0114 253 0614
Stainforth Town Council, Cemetery Office, Church Rd, Stainforth, Doncaster, DN7 5AA T: 01302 845158
Yorkshire - West
Brighouse Cemetery, Cemetery Lodge, 132 Lightcliffe Rd, Brighouse, HD6 2HY T: 01484 715183
Cottingly Hall, Elland Rd, Leeds, LS11 0 T: 0113 271 6101
Dewsbury Moor Crematorium, Heckmondwike Rd, Dewsbury, WF13 3PL T: 01924 325180
Exley Lane Cemetery, Exley Lane, Elland, HX5 0SW T: 01422 372449
Killingbeck Cemetery, York Rd, Killingbeck, Leeds, LS14 6AB T: 0113 264 5247
Lawnswood Cemetery & Crematorium, Otley Rd, Adel, Leeds, LS16 6AH T: 0113 267 3188
Leeds Jewish Workers Co-Op Society, 717 Whitehall Rd, New Farnley, Leeds, LS12 6JL T: 0113 285 2521
Moorthorpe Cemetery, Barnsley Rd, Moorthorpe, Pontefract, WF9 2BP T: 01977 642433
Nab Wood Crematorium, Bingley Rd, Shipley, BD18 4BG T: 01274 584109 Fax: 01274 530419
Oakworth Crematorium, Wide Lane, Oakworth, Keighley, BD22 0RJ T: 01535 603162
Park Wood Crematorium, Park Rd, Elland, HX5 9HZ T: 01422 372293
Pontefract Crematorium, Wakefield Rd, Pontefract, WF8 4HA T: 01977 723455
Rawdon Crematorium, Leeds Rd, Rawdon, Leeds, LS19 6JP T: 0113 250 2904
Scholemoor Cemetery & Crematorium, Necropolis Rd, Bradford, BD7 2PS T: 01274 571313
Sowerby Bridge Cemetery, Sowerby New Rd, Sowerby Bridge, HX6 1LQ T: 01422 831193
United Hebrew Congregation Leeds, Jewish Cemetery, Gelderd Rd, Leeds, LS7 4BU T: 0113 263 8684
Wakefield Crematorium, Standbridge Lane, Crigglestone, Wakefield, WF4 3JA T: 01924 303380
Wetherby Cemetery, Sexton House, Hallfield Lane, Wetherby, LS22 6JQ T: 01937 582451

Wales
Bridgend
Coychurch Crematorium, Coychurch, Bridgend, CF35 6AB T: 01656 656605 Fax: 01656 668108
Clwyd
Golden Memorial Care, 5 Golden Grove, Rhyl, LL18 2RR T; 0800 9170201
Mold Town Cemetery, Cemetery Lodge, Alexandra Rd, Mold, CH7 1HJ T: 01352 753820

Wrexham Cemeteries & Crematorium Pentre Bychan, Wrexham, LL14 4EP T: 01978 840068
Wrexham Cemetery Lodge, Ruabon Rd, Wrexham, LL13 7NY T: 01978 263159
Conwy County
Colwyn Bay Crematorium, Bron y Nant, Dinerth Rd, Colwyn Bay, LL28 4YN T: 01492 544677
Dyfed
Aberystwyth Crematorium, Clarach Rd, Aberystwyth, SY23 3DG T: 01970 626942
Carmarthen Cemetery, Elim Rd, Carmarthen, SA31 1TX T: 01267 234134
Llanelli District Cemetery, Swansea Rd, Llanelli, SA15 3EX T: 01554 773710
Milford Haven Cemetery, The Cemetery Milford Haven, SA73 2RP T: 01646 693324
Gwent
Christchurch Cemetry Christchurch, Newport, NP18 1JJ T: 01633 277566
Ebbw Vale Cemetery & Crematorium, Waun-y-Pound Rd, Ebbw Vale, NP23 6LE T: 01495 302187
Gwent Crematorium, Treherbert Rd, Croesyceiliog, Cwmbran, NP44 2BZ T: 01633 482784 Opened 1960. Records mainly on computer. No search fees payable
Gwynedd, Bangor Crematorium, Llandygai Rd, Bangor, LL57 4HP T: 01248 370500
Mid Glamorgan
Cemetery Section, Monks St, Aberdare, CF44 7PA T: 01685 885345
Ferndale Cemetery, Cemetery Lodge, Highfield, Ferndale, CF43 4TD T: 01443 730321
Llwydcoed Crematorium Llwydcoed, Aberdare, CF44 0DJ T: 01685 874115 Fax: 01685 874115 E: enquiries@crematorium.org.uk WWW: www.crematorium.org.uk
Maesteg Cemetery, Cemetery Rd, Maesteg, CF34 0DN T: 01656 735485
Penrhys Cemetery, Cemetery Lodge, Penrhys Rd, Tylorstown, Ferndale, CF43 3PN T: 01443 730465
Trane Cemetery, Gilfach Rd, Tonyrefail, Porth, CF39 8HL T: 01443 670280 T: 01443 673991, Fax: 01443 676916
Treorchy Cemetery, The Lodge, Cemetery Rd, Treorchy, CF42 6TB T: 01443 772336
Ynysybwl Cemetery, Heol Y Plwyf, Ynysybwl, Pontypridd, CF37 3HU T: 01443 790159
South Glamorgan
Cardiff Crematorium and Thornhill Cemetery, Bereavement Services, Thornhill Road, Cardiff, CF14 9UA T: 029 2062 3294 Fax: 029 20692904 WWW: www.cardiff.gov.uk Opened 1953 Administered from: Bereavement Services, Thornhill Road, Llanishen, Cardiff CF14 9UA Tel 029 2062 3294 Fax 029 2069 2904 Also administers: Pantmawr Cemetery, Radyr Cemetery, Llanishen Cemetery, Llandaff Cemetery, Cathay Cemetery, Western Cemetery, Thornhill Cemetery and Cardiff (Thornhill) Crematorium
Cathays Cemetery, Fairoak Rd, Cathays, Cardiff, CF24 4PY T: 029 2062 3294 WWW: www.cardiff.gov.uk Opened 1859 Administered from: Bereavement Services, Thornhill Road, Llanishen, Cardiff CF14 9UA Tel 029 2062 3294 Fax 029 2069 2904
Western Cemetery, Cowbridge Road West, Ely, Cardiff, CF5 5TF T: 029 2059 3231 WWW: www.cardiff.gop.uk Opened 1936 - Administered from: Bereavement Services, Thornhill Road, Llanishen, Cardiff CF14 9UA Tel 029 2062 3294 Fax 029 2069 2904
West Glamorgan, Goytre Cemetery, Neath Port Talbot CBC, Abrafan House, Port Talbot, SA13 1PJ T: 01639 763415
Margam Crematorium, Longland Lane, Margam, Port Talbot, SA13 2PP T: 01639 883570
Oystermouth Cemetery, Newton Road, Oystermouth, Swansea, SA3 4GW T: 07980 721 559 First internment in 1883
Wrexham
Coedpoeth Cemetery, The Lodge, Cemetery Rd, Coedpoeth, LL11 3SP T: 01978 755617

Scotland
Aberdeenshire
Springbank Cemetery, Countesswells Rd, Springbank, Aberdeen, AB15 7YH T: 01224 317323
St. Peter's Cemetery, King St, Aberdeen, AB24 3BX T: 01224 638490
Trinity Cemetery, Erroll St, Aberdeen, AB24 5PP T: 01224 633747
Aberdeen Cemeteries, St Nicholas House, Broad Street, Aberdeen, AB10 1BX T: 01224 523 155
Aberdeenshire (except Aberdeen City) Cemeteries (North), 1 Church Street, Macduff, AB44 1UR T: 01261 813387
Angus
Barnhill Cemetery, 27 Strathmore St, Broughty Ferry, Dundee, DD5 2NY T: 01382 477139
Dundee Crematorium Ltd, Crematorium, Macalpine Rd, Dundee, DD3 8 T: 01382 825601
Park Grove Crematorium, Douglasmuir, Friocheim, Arbroath, DD11 4UN T: 01241 828959

Dundee City Cemeteries, Tayside House Dundee, DD1 3RA T: 01382 434 000 E: parks.burials@dundeecity.gov.uk

Angus (except Dundee City) Cemeteries, County Buildings, Market Street, Forfar, DD8 3WA T: 01307 461 460 Fax: 01307 466 220

Argyll

Argyll & Bute Council Cemeteries, Amenity Services, Kilmory, Lochgilphead, PA31 8RT T: 01546 604 360 Fax: 01546 604 208 E: alison.mcilroy@argyll-bute.gov.uk WWW: www.argyll-bute.gov.uk/couninfo/dev.htm

Ayrshire

Ardrossan Cemetery, Sorbie Rd, Ardrossan, KA22 8AQ T: 01294 463133

Dreghorn Cemetery, Station Rd, Dreghorn, Irvine, KA11 4AJ T: 01294 211101

Hawkhill Cemetery, Kilwinning Rd, Saltcoats, Stevenston, KA20 3DE T: 01294 465241

Holmsford Bridge Crematorium, Dreghorn, Irvine, KA11 4EF T: 01294 214720

Kilwinning Cemetery, Bridgend, Kilwinning, KA13 7LY T: 01294 552102

Largs Cemetery, Greenock Rd, Largs, KA30 8NG T: 01475 673149

Maybole Cemetery, Crosshill Rd, Maybole, KA19 7BN T: 01655 884852 Fax: 01655 889621 E: maybole.registrars@south-ayrshire.gov.uk Also contact for Crosshill, Dunure, Kirkmichael, Kirkoswald and Straiton Cemeteries

Newmilns Cemetery, Dalwhatswood Rd Newmilns, KA16 9LT T: 01560 320191

Prestwick Cemetery, Shaw Rd, Prestwick, KA9 2LP T: 01292 477759

Stewarton Cemetery, Dalry Rd, Stewarton, Kilmarnock, KA3 3DY T: 01560 482888

West Kilbride Cemetery, Hunterston Rd, West Kilbride, KA23 9EX T: 01294 822818

North Ayrshire Cemeteries, 43 Ardrossan Road, Saltcoats, KA21 5BS T: 01294 605 436 Fax: 01294 606 416 E: CemeteriesOffice@north-ayrshire.gov.uk Administers: Irvine Area Dreghorn Cemetery, Station Road, Dreghorn; Knadgerhill Cemetery, Knaderhill, Irvine; Kilwinning Cemetery, Glasgow Road, Kilwinning; Shewalton Cemetery, Ayr Road, Irvine; Old P

South Ayrshire Cemeteries, Masonhill Crematorium, By Ayr, KA6 6EN T: 01292 266 051 Fax: 01292 610 096

Banffshire

Moray Crematorium, Clochan, Buckie, AB56 5HQ T: 01542 850488

Berwickshire

Scottish Borders Council Cemeteries, Council Offices, 8 Newtown Street, Duns, TD11 3DT T: 01361 882 600

Bute

Arran and Cumbrae Cemeteries, 43 Ardrossan Road, Saltcoats, KA21 5BS T: 01294 605 436 Fax: 01294 606 416 E: CemeteriesOffice@north-ayrshire.gov.uk

Caithness

Caithness Cemeteries, Wick, Caithness, KW1 4AB T: 01955 607 737 Fax: 01955 606 376

Clackmannanshire

Alva Cemetery, The Glebe, Alva, FK12 5HR T: 01259 760354

Sunnyside Cemetery, Sunnyside Rd, Alloa, FK10 2AP T: 01259 723575

Tillicoultry Cemetery, Dollar Rd, Tillicoultry, FK13 6PF T: 01259 750216

Dumfrieshire

Dumfrieshire Cemeteries, Kirkbank, English Street, Dumfries, DG1 2HS T: 01387 260042 Fax: 01387 260188

Annan & Eskdale Cemeteries, Dumfries and Galloway Council, Dryfe Road, Lockerbie, DG11 2AP T: 01576 205 000

Dumbartonshire

Cardross Crematorium, Main Rd, Cardross, Dumbarton, G82 5HD T: 01389 841313

Dumbarton Cemetery, Stirling Rd, Dumbarton, G82 2PF Tel: 01389 762033

Vale Of Leven Cemetery, Overton Rd, Alexandria G83 0LJ Tel: 01389 752266

West Dumbartonshire Crematorium, North Dalnottar, Clydebank, G81 4SL T: 01389 874318

West Dumbartonshire Crematorium, Richmond Street, Clydebank, G81 1RF T: 01389 738709 Fax: 01389 738690 E: helen.murray@westdunbarton.gov.uk

East Dumbartonshire Cemeteries, Broomhill Industrial Estate, Kilsyth Road, Kirkintilloch, G66 1TF T: 0141 574 5549 Fax: 0141 574 5555 E: Alan-Copeland@EastDunbarton.gov.uk

West Dumbartonshire Cemeteries, Roseberry Place, Clydebank, G81 1TG T: 01389 738 709 Fax: 01389 733 493

Dumbartonshire - East Cadder Cemetery, Kirkintilloch Road, Bishopbriggs, Glasgow, G64 2QG T: 0141 772 1977 Fax: 0141 775 0696

Edinburgh

Edinburgh Crematorium Ltd, 3 Walker St, Edinburgh, Midlothian, EH3 7JY T: 0131 225 7227

Fife

Dunfermline Cemetery, Halbeath Rd, Dunfermline, KY12 7RA T: 01383 724899

Dunfermline Crematorium, Masterton Rd, Dunfermline, KY11 8QR T: 01383 724653

Kirkcaldy Crematorium, Rosemount Avenue, Dunnikier, Kirkcaldy, KY1 3PL T: 01592 260277 Fax: 01592 203438

Central Fife Cemeteries, Rosemount Avenue, Dunnikier, Kirkcaldy, KY1 3PL T: 01592 260 277 Fax: 01592 203 438

East Fife Cemeteries, St Catherine Street, Cupar, KY15 4TA T: 01334 412 818 Fax: 01334 412 896

East Fife Cemeteries, Masterton Road, Dunfermline, KY11 8QR T: 01383 724 653 Fax: 01383 738 636

Inverness-Shire

Inverness Crematorium, Kilvean Rd, Kilvean, Inverness, IV3 8JN T: 01463 717849 Fax: 01463 717850

Invernessshire Cemeteries, Fulton House, Gordon Square, Fort William, PH33 6XY T: 01397 707 008 Fax: 01397 707 009 Service restructuring in late 2002 transferred responsilility for all burial grounds in Lochaber area will be transferred to Highland Council, TEC Services, Carrs Corner, Fort William, PH33 6TQ

Badenoch & Strathspey Cemeteries, Ruthven Road, Kingussie, PH21 1EJ T: 01540 664 500 Fax: 01540 661 004

Inverness Cemeteries, Administration Office, Kilvean Cemetery, Kilvean Road, Inverness, IV3 8JN T: 01463 717849 Fax: 01463 717850 E: derek.allan@highland.gov.uk and fiona.morrison@highland.gov.uk WWW: www.highland.gov.uk

Highland Council Cemeteries, T.E.C. Services, Broom Place, Portree, Isle of Skye, IV51 9HF T: 01478 612717 Fax: 01478 612255

Isle Of Cumbrae, Millport Cemetery, Golf Rd, Millport, KA28 0HB T: 01475 530442

Kirkcudbright

Kirkcudbright Cemeteries, Daar Road, Kirkcubright, DG6 4JG Tel: 01557 330 291

Lanarkshire

Airbles Cemetery, Airbles Rd, Motherwell, ML1 3AW T: 01698 263986

Bedlay Cemetery, Bedlay Walk, Moodiesburn, Glasgow, G69 0QG T: 01236 872446

Bothwellpark Cemetery, New Edinburgh Rd, Bellshill, ML4 3HH T: 01698 748146

Cambusnethan Cemetery, Kirk Road, Wishaw, ML2 8NP T: 01698 384481

St. Patrick's Cemetery, Kings Drive, New Stevenston, Motherwell, ML1 4HY T: 01698 732938

Glasgow

Campsie Cemetery, High Church of Scotland, Main Street, Lennoxtown, Glasgow, G66 7DA T: 01360 311127

Cardonald Cemetery, 547 Mosspark Boulevard, Glasgow, G52 1SB T: 0141 882 1059

Daldowie Crematorium, Daldowie Estate, Uddingston, Glasgow, G71 7RU T: 0141 771 1004

Glasgow Crematorium, Western Necropolis, Tresta Rd, Glasgow, G23 5AA T: 0141 946 2895

Glebe Cemetery, Vicars Rd, Stonehouse, Larkhall, ML9 3EB T: 01698 793674

Glenduffhill Cemetery, 278 Hallhill Rd, Glasgow, G33 4RU T: 0141 771 2446

Kilsyth Parish Cemetery, Howe Rd, Kirklands, Glasgow, G65 0LA T: 01236 822144

Larkhall Cemetery, The Cemetery Lodge, Duke St, Larkhall, ML9 2AL T: 01698 883049

Old Aisle Cemetery, Old Aisle Rd, Kirkintilloch, Glasgow, G66 3HH T: 0141 776 2330

St. Conval's Cemetery, Glasgow Rd, Barrhead, Glasgow, G78 1TH T: 0141 881 1058

St. Peters Cemetery 1900 London Rd, Glasgow, G32 8RD T: 0141 778 1183

The Necropolis 50 Cathedral Square, Glasgow, G4 0UZ T: 0141 552 3145

Glasgow Cemeteries, 20 Trongate, Glasgow, G1 5ES T: 0141 287 3961 Fax: 0141 287 3960 inc crematoria Linn and Daldowie

North Lanarkshire Cemeteries

Old Edinburgh Road, Bellshill, ML4 3JS T: 01698 506 301 Fax: 01698 506 309

Lanarkshire - South

South Lanarkshire Cemeteries, Atholl House East Kilbride, G74 1LU T: 01355 806 980 Fax: 01355 806 983

Midlothian

Dean Cemetery, Dean Path, Edinburgh, EH4 3AT T: 0131 332 1496

Seafield Cemetery & Crematorium, Seafield Rd, Edinburgh, EH6 7LQ T: 0131 554 3496

Warriston Crematorium, 36 Warriston Rd, Edinburgh, EH7 4HW T: 0131 552 3020

Midlothian Council Cemeteries, Dundas Buildings, 62A Polton Street, Bonnyrigg, EH22 3YD T: 0131 561 5280 Fax: 0131 654 2797 E: nancy.newton@midlothian.gov.uk

City of Edinburgh Council Cemeteries, Howdenhall Road, Edinburgh, EH16 6TX T: 0131 664 4314 Fax: 0131 664 2031 Five private cemeteries in Edinburgh - council does not have access to their records

Lothian - West
West Lothian Cemeteries, County Buildings, High Street, Linlithgow, EH49 7EZ T: 01506 775 300 Fax: 01506 775 412
Moray
Morayshire Cemeteries, Cooper Park, Elgin, IV30 1HS T: 01343 544 475 Fax: 01343 549 050 E: graeme.wilson@moray.gov.uk WWW: www.moray.org/heritage/roots.html
Perthshire
Perth Crematorium, Crieff Rd, Perth, PH1 2PE T: 01738 625068 Fax: 01738 445977 E: dpmartin@pkc.gov.uk
Renfrewshire
Hawkhead Cemetery, 133 Hawkhead Rd, Paisley, PA2 7BE T: 0141 889 3472
Paisley Cemetery Co.Ltd, 46 Broomlands St, Paisley, PA1 2NP T: 0141 889 2260
Renfrewshire Cemeteries, Tweedie Halls, Ardlamont Square, Linwood, PA3 3DE T: 01505 322 135 Fax: 01505 322135
Cemeteries Division - Renfrewshire Council, Environmental Services Department, Cotton Street, South Building, Paisley, PA1 1BR T: 0141 840 3504 Fax: 0141 842 1179
Renfrew Cemeteries, 3 Longcroft Drive, Renfrew, PA4 8NF T: 0141 848 1450 Fax: 0141 886 2807
East Renfrewshire - including Neilston, Newton Mearns and Eaglesham Cemeteries, Rhuallan House, 1 Montgomery Drive, Giffnock, G46 6PY T: 0141 577 3913 Fax: 0141 577 3919 E: sandra.donnelly@eastrenfrewshire.gov.uk
Roxburghshire
Roxburghshire Environmental Health - Burials, High Street, Hawick, TD9 9EF T: 01450 375 991
Scottish Borders
Scottish Borders Council - Burials, Paton Street, Galashiels, TD1 3AS T: 01896 662739 Fax: 01896 750329
Scottish Borders Council Burial Grounds Department, Council Offices, Rosetta Road, Peebles, EH45 8HG T: 01721 726306 Fax: 01721 726304 E: p.allan@scot.borders.gov.uk
Shetland
Shetland Burial Ground Management Grantfield Lerwick, ZE1 0NT T: 01595 744 871 Fax: 01595 744869 E: jim.grant@sic.shetland.gov.uk WWW: www.users.zetnet.co.uk/eats-operations
Stirlingshire
Larbert Cemetery, 25 Muirhead Rd, Larbert, FK5 4HZ T: 01324 557867
Stirlingshire Cemeteries, Viewforth, Stirling, FK8 2ET T: 01786 442 559 Fax: 01786 442 558 E: mcbrier@stirling.gov.uk WWW: www.stirling.gov.uk
Falkirk Cemeteries and Crematorium, Dorrator Road, Camelon, Falkirk, FK2 7YJ T: 01324 503 654 Fax: 01324 503 651 E: billbauchope@falkirk.gov.uk
Wigtown
Wigtown Cemeteries, Dunbae House, Church Street, Stranraer, DG9 7JG T: 01776 888 405

Northern Ireland
County Antrim
Ballymena Cemetery, Cushendall Rd, Ballymena, BT43 6QE T: 01266 656026
Ballymoney Cemetery, 44 Knock Rd, Ballymoney, BT53 6LX T: 012656 66364
Blaris New Cemetery, 25 Blaris Rd, Lisburn, BT27 5RA T: 01846 607143
Carnmoney Cemetery, 10 Prince Charles Way, Newtownabbey, BT36 7LG T: 01232 832428
City Cemetery, 511 Falls Rd, Belfast, BT12 6DE T: 028 90323112
Greenland Cemetery, Upper Cairncastle Rd, Larne, BT40 2EG T: 01574 272543
Milltown Cemetery Office, 546 Falls Rd, Belfast, BT12 6EQ T: 01232 613972
County Armagh, Kernan Cemetery, Kernan Hill Rd, Portadown, Craigavon, BT63 5YB T: 028 38339059
Lurgan Cemetery, 57 Tandragee Rd, Lurgan, Craigavon, BT66 8TL T: 028 38342853
County Down
City of Belfast Crematorium, 129 Ballgowan Road, Crossacreevy, Belfast, BT5 7TZ T: 028 9044 8342 Fax: 028 9044 8579 E: crematorium@belfastcity.gov.uk WWW: www.belfastcrematorium.co.uk
Ballyvestry Cemetery, 6 Edgewater Millisle, Newtownards, BT23 5 T: 01247 882657
Banbridge Public Cemetery, Newry Rd, Banbridge, BT32 3NB T: 018206 62623
Bangor Cemetery, 62 Newtownards Rd, Bangor, BT20 4DN T: 028 91271909
Clandeboye Cemetery, 300 Old Belfast Rd, Bangor, BT19 1RH T: 028 91853246
Comber Cemetery, 31 Newtownards Rd, Comber, Newtownards, BT23 5AZ T: 01247 872529
Down District Council, Struell Cemetery, Old Course Rd, Downpatrick, BT30 8AQ T: 01396 613086
Down District Council - Lough Inch Cemetery, Lough Inch Cemetery, Riverside Rd, Ballynahinch, BT24 8JB T: 01238 562987
Kirkistown Cemetery, Main Rd, Portavogie, Newtownards, BT22 1EL T: 012477 71773
Movilla Cemetery, Movilla Rd, Newtownards, BT23 8EY T: 01247 812276
Redburn Cemetery, Old Holywood Rd, Holywood, BT18 9QH T: 01232 425547
Roselawn Cemetery, 127 Ballygowan Rd, Crossnacreevy, Belfast, BT5 7TZ T: 01232 448288
Whitechurch Cemetery, 19 Dunover Rd, Newtownards, BT22 2LE T: 012477 58659
County Londonderry
Altnagelvin Cemetery, Church Brae, Altnagelvin, Londonderry, BT47 3QG T: 01504 343351
City Cemetery, Lone Moor Rd, Londonderry, BT48 9LA T: 02871 362615 F: 02871 362085
County Tyrone
Greenhill Cemetery, Mountjoy Rd, Omagh, BT79 7BL T: 028 8224 4918
Westland Road Cemetery, Westland Rd, Cookstown, BT80 8BX T: 016487 66087

France
Russian Cemetery, Cimetiere Russe de Sainte Genevierve des Bois (Russian Cemetery), 8 Rue Léo Lagrange, 91700, Sainte Genevierve des Bois

Record Offices & Archives

NATIONAL

The National Archives Public Records Office Ruskin Avenue Kew Richmond Surrey TW9 4DU T: (020) 8392 5271 F: (020) 8392 5266 WWW: www.nas.gov.uk/

BBC Written Archives Centre see Berkshire

The Boat Museum & David Owen Waterways Archive South Pier Road Ellesmere Port Cheshire CH65 4FW T: 0151-355-5017 F: 0151-355-4079 E: boatmuseum@easynet.co.uk Records relating to the management, maintenance and operation of inland waterways in ngland, Scotland and Wales. Substantial Waterways library. Date range: late 17th century to 20th century. Information held on some boatmen and boatwomen.

Birmingham University Information Services - Special Collections see West Midlands

Black Cultural Archives 378 Coldharbour Lane London SW9 8LF T: (020) 7738 4591 F: (020) 7738 7168 E: info@99mbh.org.uk W: www.99mbh.org.uk

Bristol University Library - Special Collections see Somerset

British Airways Archives Trident House - Block E S583 London heathrow airport Hounslow Middlesex TW6 2JA

British Library Newspaper Library Colindale Avenue London NW9 5HE T: 020-7412-7353 F: 020-7412-7379 E: newspaper@bl.uk W: www.bl.uk/collections/newspaper/

British Library of Political and Economic Science London School of Economics 10 Portugal Street London WC2A 2HD T: 020 7955 7223 F: 020 7955 7454 E: info@lse.ac.uk W: www.lse.ac.uk

British Film Institute - Library & Film Archive 21 Stephen Street London W1T 1LN T: 020 7957 4824 W: www.bfi.org.uk

British Waterways Archives and The Waterways Trust Llanthony Warehouse Gloucester Docks Gloucester Gloucestershire GL1 2EJ T: 01452 318041 F: 01452 318076 E: roy.jamieson@britishwaterways.co.uk W: www.britishwaterways.org.uk Records relating to the management, maintenance and operation of inland waterways in England, Scotland and Wales for which British Waterways is the statutory undertaker. Date range: late 17th to 20th Centuries. NB The archive is NOT part of the National Waterways Museum. Opening Hours Mon-Fri 1000 to 1700 by prior appointment only.

Cambridge University Library - Department of Manuscripts & University Archives see Cambridgeshire

College of Arms Queen Victoria Street London EC4V 4BT T: (020) 7248-2762 F: (020) 7248-6448 E: enquiries@college-of-arms.gov.uk W: www.college-of-arms.gov.uk The College of Arms maintains the official registers of arms for England and Wales

Commonwealth War Graves Commission 2 Marlow Road Maidenhead Berkshire SL6 7DX T: 01628-634221 F: 01628-771208 E: General Enquiries: General.enq@cwgc.org Casualty & Cemetery Enquiries: casualty.enq@cwgc.org W: www.cwgc.org

Department of Manuscripts and Special Collections Hallward Library Nottingham University University Park Nottingham NG7 2RD T: 0115 951 4565 F: 0115 951 4558 E: mss-library@nottingham.ac.uk W: www.mss.library.nottingham.ac.uk

Family Records Centre 1 Myddleton Street London EC1R 1UW T: (020) 8392-5300 F: (020) 8392-5307 E: info@familyrecords.gov.uk W: www.familyrecords.gov.uk

Heritage Royal Mail Freeling House, Phoenix Place London WC1X 0DL T: (020) 7239 2570 T: (020) 7239 2561 - Libby Buckley F: (020) 7239 2576 E: heritage@royalmail.com W: www.royalmail.com/heritage The National Postal Museum formerly in King Edward Street, London closed in December 1998. The Philatelic collection is available to view by appointment at Heritage Royal Mail. Public record archives on all aspects of Royal Mail and postal history.

House of Lords Record Office - The Parliamentary Archives House of Lords London SW1A 0PW T: (020) 7219-3074 F: (020) 7219-2570 E: hlro@parliament.uk W: www.parliament.uk Holdings include protestation returns of 1642 and evidence of witnesses on private bills

Huguenot Library University College Gower Street London WC1E 6BT T: (020) 7679 7094 E: s.massilk@ucl.ac.uk W: www.ucl.ac.uk/ucl-info/divisions/library/hugenot.htm

Imperial War Museum - Department of Documents Department of Documents Lambeth Road London SE1 6HZ T: (020) 7416-5221/2/3/6 F: (020) 7416-5374 E: docs@iwm.org.uk W: www.iwm.org.uk

Imperial War Museum Film and Video Archive Lambeth Road London SE1 6HZ T: 020 7416 5291 E: W: www.iwm.org.uk/collections/film.htm

Institute of Heraldic and Genealogical Studies see Kent

Liverpool University Special Collections & Archives University of Liverpool Library PO Box 123 Liverpool L69 3DA T: 0151-794-2696 F: 0151-794-2081 W: www.sca.lib.liv.ac.uk/collections/index.html The University holds the records of a number of charities, especially those which looked after children or encouraged emigration

Labour History Archive and Study Centre People's History Museum 103 Princess Street Manchester M1 6DD T: 0161 228 7212 F: 0161 237 5965 E: archives@nmlhweb.org W: http://rylibweb.man.ac.uk

Lloyds Register of Shipping Information Services 71 Fenchurch Street London EC3M 4BS T: (020) 7423 2531 F: (020) 7423 2039 W: www.lr.org Personal callers only. Reserarch cannot be undertaken

National Gallery Library and Archive Trafalgar Square London WC2N 5DN T: 020 7747 2542 F: 020 7753 8179 E: iad@ng-london.org.uk W: www.nationalgallery.org.uk

National Monuments Record Enquiry and Research Services 55 Blandford Street London W1H 3AF T: 020 7208 8200 F: 020 7224 5333 W: www.english-heritage.org.uk/knowledge/nmr

National Museum of Photography, Film and Television Bradford West Yorkshire BD1 1NQ T: 01274-202030 F: 01274 -723155 W: www.nmpft.org.uk

National Portrait Gallery Heinz Archive & library 2 St. Martins Place London WC2H 0HE T: (020) 7306 0055 F: (020) 7306 0056 W: www.npg.org.uk

National Railway Museum Leeman Road York YO26 4XJ T: 01904 621261 F: 01904 611112 E: nrm@nmsi.ac.uk W: www.nrm.org.uk Does not hold Railway Company staff records generally at PRO and NAS. Does hold a good run of railway staff magazines which often contain information about named staff members especially if they were senior or killed/missing in action in both World Wars.

North West Sound Archive Old Steward's Office Clitheroe Castle Clitheroe Lancashire BB7 1AZ T: 01200-427897 F: 01200-427897 E: nwsa@ed.lancscc.gov.uk W: www.lancashire.gov.uk/education/lifelong/recordindex

Probate Service Probate Sub Registry, 1st Floor, Castle Chambers, Clifford Street York YO1 9RG T: 01904 666777 W: www.courtservice.gov.uk Designated Office for dealing with postal enquiries concerning probate records for the whole of England and Wales

Royal Air Force Museum - Department of Research & Information Services Grahame Park Way Hendon London NW9 5LL T: (020) 83584873 F: (020) 8200 1751 E: research@rafmuseum.org W: www.rafmuseum.org CC accepted

The Royal College of Physicians 11 St Andrews Place London NW1 4LE T: (020) 7935 1174 ext 312 F: (020) 7486 3729 E: info@rcplondon.ac.uk W: www.rcplondon.ac.uk Holds records relating to administration and members from 1518 to date

Royal College of Obstetricians and Gynaecologists College Archives 27 Sussex Place Regents Park London NW1 4RG T: 020 7772 6277 F: 020 7723 0575 E: archives@rcog.org.uk W: www.rcog.org.uk

Royal Commission on Historical Manuscripts Quality House Quality Court Chancery Lane London WC2A 1HP T: (020) 7242-1198 F: (020) 7831-3550 E: nra@hmc.gov.uk W: www.hmc.gov.uk Maintains the National Register of Archives and the Manorial Documents Register

Royal Society 6 - 9 Carlton House Terrace London SW1Y 5AG T: 020 7451 2606 F: 020 7930 2170 E: library@royalsoc.ac.uk W: www.royalsoc.ac.uk

John Rylands University Library Special Collections Division 150 Deansgate Manchester M3 3EH T: 0161-834-5343 F: 0161-834-5343 E: spcoll72@fs1.li.man.ac.uk W: http://rylibweb.man.ac.uk Holdings include family muniment collections especially relating to Cheshire and major Non Conformist Archives Few genealogical records held except for family muniment collections, especially for Cheshire and Methodist Circuit plans, records, ministers

School of Oriental and African Studies library Thornhaugh Street Russell Square London WC1H 0XG T: 020 7323 6112 F: 020 7636 2834 E: lib@soas.ac.uk W: www.soas.ac.uk/library/

Shakespeare Birthplace Trust - Records Office Henley Street Stratford Upon Avon Warwickshire CV37 6QW T: 01789 201816 T: 01789 204016 F: 01789 296083 E: records@sharespeare.org.uk W: www.shakespeare.org.uk 1901 census

Society of Antiquaries of London Burlington House Piccadilly London W1J 0BE T: 020 7479 7084 F: 020 7287 6967 E: library@sal.org.uk W: www.sal.org.uk

Society of Genealogists - Library 14 Charterhouse Buildings Goswell Road London EC1M 7BA T: 020-7251-8799 T: 020-7250-0291 F: 020-7250-1800 E: library@sog.org.uk - Sales at sales@sog.org.uk W: www.sog.org.uk

Tate Archive Collection Tate Britain Millbank London SW1P 4RG T: 020 7887 8831 F: 020 7887 8637 Tate Gallery, Millbank, London SW1P 4RG :Tate Modern, Bankside, London SE1 9TG

Tennyson Research Centre Central Library Free School Lane Lincoln Lincolnshire LN2 1EZ T: 01522-552862 F: 01522-552858 E: sue.gates@lincolnshire.gov.uk W: www.lincolnshire.gov.uk The collection concentrates on Alfred Lord Tennyson and his immediate family. Do not hold detailed genealogical information nor details of any other generations of the Tennysons

TRAP - Tracking Railway Archives Project Al Mafrak George Hill Road Broadstairs Kent CT10 3JT E: d.kelso@btinternet.com
United Reformed Church History Society Westminster College Madingley Road Cambridge CB3 0AA T: 01223-741300 (NOT Wednesdays) Information on ministers of constituent churches not members
Victoria & Albert Museum - National Art Library - Archive of Art and Design Blythe House 23 Blythe Road London W14 0QF T: (020) 7603 1514 F: (020) 7602 0980 E: archive@vam.ac.uk W: www.nal.vam.ac.uk
Wellcome Library for the History and Understanding of Medicine 183 Euston Road London NW1 2BE T: (020) 7611-8582 F: (020) 7611 8369 E: library@wellcome.ac.uk W: www.wellcome.ac.uk/library Library catalogue is available through the internet: http://library.wellcome.ac.uk

Specialist Records
Brewing
Bass Museum Horninglow Street Burton on Trent Staffordshire DE14 1YQ T: 0845 6000598 F: 01283 513509 W: www.bass-museum.com
Guinness Archive Park Royal Brewery London NW10 7RR
Southern Courage Archives Southern Accounting Centre PO Box 85 Counterslip Bristrol BS99 7BT
Whitbread Archives - Permanently Closed The Brewery Chiswell Street London EC1Y 4SD
The Archives of Worshipful Company of Brewers Brewers' Hall Aldermanbury Square London EC2V 7HR T: (020) 7606 1301
Young's & Co's Brewery Archives Ram Brewery High Street Wandsworth London SW18 4JD
Church Records
Church of England Record Centre 15 Galleywall Road South Bermondsey London SE16 3PB T: 020 7898 1030 F: 020 7898 1031 W: www.church-of-england.org
Church of Ireland Archives Representative Church Body Library Braemor Park Churchtown Dublin 14 Co Dublin T: 01-492-3979 F: 01-492-4770 E: library@ireland.anglican.org W: www.ireland.anglican.org/
Lambeth Palace Library Lambeth Palace Road London SE1 7JU T: (020) 7898 1400 F: (020) 7928-7932 W: www.lambethpalacelibrary.org
Presbyterian Historical Society of Ireland Church House Fisherwick Place Belfast BT1 6DW T: (028) 9032 2284
Scottish Catholic Archives Columba House 16 Drummond Place Edinburgh EH3 6PL T: 0131-5563661 W: www.scottishcatholicarchives.org Minimal parish registers are held - all have been copied and are available at The National archives of scotland
Methodist
Archives of the Independent Methodist Churches Independent Methodist Resource Centre Fleet Street Pemberton Wigan Lancashire WN5 0DS T: 01942 223526 01942 227768 E: archives@imcgb.org.uk W: www.imcgb.org.uk Visits by appointment. Normally open 10.00 to 17.00 Monday to friday
Evangelical Library 78a Chiltern Street London W1M 2HB
Methodist Archives and Research Centre John Rylands University Library 150 Deansgate Manchester M3 3EH T: 0161 834 5343 F: 0161 834 5574
Jewish
Aberdeen Synagogue 74 Dee Street Aberdeen AB11 6DS T: 01224 582135
Dundee Synagogue St Mary Place Dundee DD1 5RB
Edinburgh Synagogue 4 Salisbury Road Edinburgh EH16 5AB Scotland
Glasgow Jewish Representative Council 222 Fenwick Road Giffnock Glasgow G46 6UE T: 0141 577 8200 F: 0141 577 8202 E: jrepcouncil@aol.com W: www.j-scot.org/glasgow
Scottish Jewish Archives Centre Garnethill Synagogue 129 Hill Street Garnethill Glasgow G3 6UB T: 0141 332 4911 F: 0141 332 4911 E: archives@sjac.fsbusiness.co.uk W: www.sjac.org.uk
Quakers
Library of the Religious Society of Friends (Quakers) Friends House 173 - 177 Euston Rd London NW1 2BJ T: 0207 663 1135 T: 0207 663 1001 E: library@quaker.org.uk W: www.quaker.org.uk/library Limited opening hours. Letter of introduction required. Please send SAE for details or enclose IRCs
United Reformed Church History Society Westminster College Madingley Road Cambridge CB3 0AA T: 01223-741300 (NOT Wednesdays) Information on ministers of constituent churches not members
Gypsy
The Gypsy Collections University of Liverpool PO Box 229 Liverpool L69 3DA T: 0151 794 2696 F: 0151 794 2081 W: www.sca.lib.liv.ac.uk/collections/index.html The University holds the records of a number of charities, especially those which looked after children or encouraged emigration

The Robert Dawson Romany Collection Rural History Centre, University of Reading Whiteknights PO Box 229 Reading RG6 6AG T: 0118-931-8664 F: 0118-975-1264 E: j.s.creasey@reading.ac.uk W: www.ruralhistory.org/index.html Appointments required
The Romany Collections Brotherton Library Leeds University Leeds West Yorkshire LS2 9JT T: 0113 233 55188 F: 0113 233 5561 E: special-collections@library.leeds.ac.uk W: http://leeds.ac.uk/library/spcoll/
Masonic
The United Grand Lodge of England Freemasons' Hall 60 Great Queen Street London WC2B 5AZ T: (020) 7831 9811 W: www.grandlodge.org
Canonbury Masonic Research Centre Canonbury Tower London N1 2NQ W: www.canonbury.ac.uk
Grand Lodge of Ireland Freemasons' Hall 17 Molesworth Street Dublin 2 T: 00 353 01 6760 1337
Grand Lodge of Scotland Freemasons' Hall 96 George Street Edinburgh EH2 3DH T: 0131 225 5304
The Library & Museum of Freemasonry Freemasons' Hall 60 Great Queen Street London WC2B 5AZ T: (020) 7395 9257 W: www.grandlodge-england.org
Police
Metropolitan Police Archives Room 517, Wellington House 67-73 Buckingham Gate London SW1E 6BE T: 020 7230 7186 E: margarter.bird@met.police.uk The Metropolitan Police do not hold any records. All records that have survived are in the National archives. Do not hold records for City of London Police or other police forces or constabularies. The Archives have some finding aids. SAE for information
Thames Valley Police Museum Sulhamstead Nr Reading Berkshire RG7 4DX T: 0118 932 5748 F: 0118 932 5751 E: ken.wells@thamesvalley.police.uk W: www.thamesvalley.police.uk Thames Valley Police formed April 1968 from Berkshire, Oxfordshire, Oxford City and Reading Borough constabularies. Only records of officers are those who served in Reading Borough and Oxfordshire. Appointments only with Curator

England
Bedfordshire
Bedfordshire & Luton Archives & Record Service County Hall Cauldwell Street Bedford Bedfordshire MK42 9AP T: 01234-228833 T: 01234-228777 F: 01234-228854 E: archive@csd.bedfordshire.gov.uk W: www.bedfordshire.gov.uk 1901 census
Berkshire
BBC Written Archives Centre Caversham Park Reading Berkshire RG4 8TZ T: 0118 948 6281 F: 0118 946 1145 E: wac.enquiries@bbc.co.uk W: www.bbc.co.uk/thenandnow Access by appointment only. Brief enquiries can be answered by post or telephone
Berkshire Medical Heritage Centre Level 4, Main Entrance Royal Berkshire Hospital London Road Reading Berkshire RG1 5AN T: 0118 987 7298 W: www.bmhc.org
Berkshire Record Office 9 Coley Avenue Reading Berkshire RG1 6AF T: 0118-901-5132 F: 0118-901-5131 E: arch@reading.gov.uk W: www.reading.gov.uk/berkshirerecordoffice 1901 census
Eton College College Library Windsor Berkshire SL4 6DB T: 01753 671269 E: archivist@etoncollege.org.uk W: www.etoncollege.com Open by appointment 9.30.a.m. to 1.00.p.m. and 2.00.p.m. to 5.00.p.m. Monday to Friday
Museum of English Rural Life, Rural History Centre University of Reading Whiteknights PO Box 229 Reading RG6 6AG T: 0118-931-8664 F: 0118-975-1264 E: j.s.creasey@reading.ac.uk W: www.ruralhistory.org/index.html Appointments required
The Museum of Berkshire Aviation Trust Mohawk Way off Bader Way Woodley Reading Berkshire RG5 4UE T: 0118 944 8089 E: museumofberkshireaviation@fly.to http://fly.to/museumofberkshireaviation
West Berkshire Heritage Service - Newbury The Wharf Newbury Berkshire RG14 5AS T: 01635 30511 F: 01635 38535 E: heritage@westberks.gov.uk W: www.westberks.gov.uk/tourism
Bristol
Bristol Record Office B Bond Warehouse Smeaton Road Bristol BS1 6XN T: 0117-922-4224 F: 0117-922-4236 E: bro@bristol-city.gov.uk W: www.bristol-city.gov.uk/recordoffice 1901 census
British Empire & Commonwealth Museum Clock Tower Yard Temple Meads Bristol BS1 6QH T: 0117 925 4980 F: 0117 925 4983 E: staff@empiremuseum.co.uk W: www.empiremuseum.co.uk
Buckinghamshire
Buckinghamshire Record Office County Offices Walton Street Aylesbury Buckinghamshire HP20 1UU T: 01296 383013 F: 01296-382274 E: archives@buckscc.gov.uk W: www.buckscc.gov.uk/leisure/libraries/archives
Cambridgeshire
Cambridge University Library Department of Manuscripts & University Archives West Road Cambridge Cambridgeshire CB3 9DR T: 01223 333000 ext 33143 (Manuscripts) T: 01223 333000 ext 33148 (University Archives) F: 01223 333160 E: mss@ula.cam.ac.uk W: www.lib.cam.ac.uk/MSS/

Cambridgeshire Archive Service (Huntingdon) County Record Office Huntingdon Grammar School Walk Huntingdon Cambridgeshire PE29 3LF T: 01480-375842 F: 01480 375842 E: county.records.hunts@cambridgeshire.gov.uk W: www.cambridgeshire.gov.uk 1901 census

Cambridgeshire Archives Service County Record Office Shire Hall Castle Hill Cambridge Cambridgeshire CB3 0AP T: 01223 717281 F: 01223 717201 E: County.Records.Cambridge@cambridgeshire.gov.uk W: www.cambridgeshire.gov.uk/ 1901 census

Centre for Regional Studies Anglia Polytechnic University East Road Cambridge Cambridgeshire CB1 1PT T: 01223-363271 ext 2030 F: 01223-352973 E: t.kirby@anglia.ac.uk W: www.anglia.ac.uk APU also offers a course (BA Combined Honours) in family and Community History

Peterborough Local Studies Collection Central Library Broadway Peterborough PE1 1RX T: 01733 742700 F: 01733 555277 E: libraries@peterborough.gov.uk W: www.peterborough.gov.uk The telephone number may change in 2002 1901 census

Cheshire

Cheshire & Chester Archives & Local Studies Duke Street Chester Cheshire CH1 1RL T: 01244-602574 F: 01244-603812 E: recordoffice@cheshire.gov.uk W: www.cheshire.gov.uk/recoff/home.htm In April 2000 management of all original archives was transferred to Cheshire & Chester Archives & Local Studies, Duke Street, Chester. All archives must be consulted there. Secondary sources such as Chester Census, Cemetery Registers, Parish Records etc are also available at Chester History & Heritage, St Michael's Church 1901 census

Cheshire Military Museum The Castle Chester Cheshire CH1 2DN T: 01244 327617 Cheshire Yeomanry elements of 3rd Carabiniers and 5th Royal Inniskilling Dragoon Guards)

Chester History & Heritage St Michaels Church Bridge Street Row Chester Cheshire CH1 1NW T: 01244 402110 E: s.oswald.gov.uk W: www.chestercc.gov.uk/chestercc/htmls/heritage.htm

Macclesfield Silk Museums Paradise Mill Park Lane Macclesfield Cheshire SK11 6TJ T: 01625 612045 F: 01625 612048 E: silkmuseum@tiscali.co.uk W: www.silk-macclesfield.org Reference library and archive. Museums cover the history of silk in macclesfield once the centre of the industry. Demonstrations of hand weaving, exhibitions and models. cc accepted

Stockport Archive Service Central Library Wellington Road South Stockport Cheshire SK1 3RS T: 0161-474-4530 F: 0161-474-7750 E: localheritage.library@stockport.gov.uk W: www.stockport.gov.uk

Tameside Local Studies Library Stalybridge Library Trinity Street Stalybridge Cheshire SK15 2BN T: 0161-338-2708 T: 0161-338-3831 and 0161 303 7937 F: 0161-303-8289 E: localstudies.library@mail.tameside.gov.uk W: www.tameside.gov.uk 1901 census

The Boat Museum & David Owen Waterways Archive see National

Warrington Library & Local Studies Centre Museum Street Warrington Cheshire WA1 1JB T: 01925 442890 F: 01925 411395 E: library@warrington.gov.uk W: www.warrington.gov.uk

Cleveland

Tees Archaeology - The Archaeological Service for Teeside Sir William Gray Clarence Road Hartlepool TS24 8BT T: 01429 523455 F: 01429 523477 E: tees-archaeology@hartlepool.gov.uk W: www.hartlepool.gov.uk

Teesside Archives Exchange House 6 Marton Road Middlesbrough Cleveland TS1 1DB T: 01642-248321 F: 01642 248391 E: teesside_archives@middlesbrough.gov.uk W: www.middlesbrough.gov.uk 1901 census

Cornwall

Cable & Wireless Archive & Museum of Submarine Telegraphy Eastern House, Porthcurno Penzance Cornwall TR19 6JX T: 01736 810478 T: 01736 810811 F: 01736 810640 E: info@tunnels.demon.co.uk W: www.porthcurno.org.uk Housed in one of Porthcurno's former telegraph ststion buildings, and adjacent to the Museum of Submarine Telegraphy, the archive is a unique resource for learning about: the history of Porthcurno; cable communications linking Cornwall with the rest of the world; the company, and the people who have worked for it over the years.

Cornish-American Connection Murdoch House Cross Street Redruth Cornwall TR15 2BU T: 01209 216333 E: m.s.tangye@exeter.ac.uk W: www.ex.ac.uk/~cnfrench/ics/welcome.htm

Cornwall Record Office County Hall Truro Cornwall TRI 3AY T: 01872-323127 F: 01872-270340 E: cro@cornwall.gov.uk W: www.cornwall.gov.uk

Royal Institution of Cornwall, Courtney Library & Cornish History Research Centre Royal Cornwall Museum River Street Truro Cornwall TR1 2SJ T: 01872 272205 F: 01872 240514 E: RIC@royal-cornwall-museum.freeserve.co.uk W: www.cornwall-online.co.uk/ric

The Cornwall Centre Alma Place Redruth Cornwall TR15 2AT T: 01209-216760 F: 01209-210283 E: cornishstudies@library.cornwall.gov.uk W: www.cornwall.gov.uk Cornwall Libraries main library of local studies material. Printed and published items about Cornwall incl books, pamphlets, journals, newspapers, maps, photographs etc. 1901 census

Cumbria

Centre for North West Regional Studies Fylde College Lancaster University Lancaster Lancashire LA1 4YF T: 01524 593770 F: 01524 594725 E: christine.wilkinson@lancaster.ac.uk W: www.lancs.ac.uk/users/cnwrs cc accepted Oral History Archives; Elizabeth Roberts Archive: Penny Summerfield Archive

Cumbria Archive Service Cumbria Record Office The Castle Carlisle Cumbria CA3 8UR T: 01228-607285 T: 01228-607284 F: 01228-607270 E: carlisle.record.office@cumbriacc.gov.uk W: www.cumbriacc.gov.uk/archives

Cumbria Record Office County Offices Stricklandgate Kendal Cumbria LA9 4RQ T: 01539 773540 F: 01539 773538 E: kendal.record.office@cumbriacc.gov.uk W: www.cumbria.gov.uk/archives 1901 census

Cumbria Record Office and Local Studies Library (Whitehaven) Scotch Street Whitehaven Cumbria CA28 7BJ T: 01946-852920 F: 01946-852919 E: whitehaven.record.office@cumbriacc.gov.uk W: www.cumbria.gov.uk/archives

Cumbria Record Office & Local Studies Library 140 Duke St Barrow in Furness Cumbria LA14 1XW T: 01229-894363 F: 01229-894371 E: barrow.record.office@cumbriacc.gov.uk W: www.cumbria.gov.uk/archives

Ulverston Heritage Centre Lower Brook St Ulverston Cumbria LA12 7EE T: 01229 580820 F: 01229 580820 E: heritage@tower-house.demon.co.uk W: www.rootsweb.com/~ukuhc/

Derbyshire

Derby Local Studies Library 25b Irongate Derby Derbyshire DE1 3GL T: 01332 255393 E: localstudies.library@derby.gov.uk W: www.derby.gov.uk/libraries/about/local_studies.htm 1901 census

Derby Museum & Art Gallery The Strand Derby Derbyshire DE1 1BS T: 01332-716659 F: 01332-716670 W: www.derby.gov.uk/museums No archive material as such, but some local genealogical information available and numerous indices on local trades, etc eg clock makers, gunmakers, etc

Derbyshire Record Office County Hall Matlock Derbyshire DE4 3AG T: 01629-580000-ext-35207 F: 01629-57611 The Record Office for Derbyshire - City and County and the Diocese of Derby. The Record Office is located New Street, Matlock, Derbyshire DE4 3AG. The address at County Hall is for correspondence only. Fee paid family history search service available. 1901 census

Erewash Museum The Museum High Street Ilkeston Derbyshire DE7 5JA T: 0115 907 1141 F: 0115 907 1121 E: museum@erewash.gov.uk W: www.erewash.gov.uk

Devon

Beaford Photograph Archive Barnstaple Devon EX32 7EJ T: 01271 288611

Bill Douglas Centre for the History of Cinema and Popular Culture University of Exeter Queen's Building Queen's Drive Exeter Devon EX4 4QH T: 01392 264321 W: www.ex.ac.uk/bill.douglas

Devon Record Office Castle Street Exeter Devon EX4 3PU T: 01392 384253 F: 01392 384256 E: devrec@devon.gov.uk W: www.devon.gov.uk/dro/homepage.html

North Devon Record Office Tuly Street Barnstaple Devon EX31 1EL T: 01271 388607 T: 01271 388608 F: 01271 388608 E: ndevrec@devon.gov.uk W: www.devon.gov.uk/dro/homepage Open: Mon, Tues, Thurs & Fri 9.30 to 5pm; Wed 9.30 to 1pm; 2 Sats per month 9.30 to 4pm. Admission charges £2 per day

Plymouth & West Devon Record Office Unit 3 Clare Place Coxside Plymouth Devon PL4 0JW T: 01752-305940 E: pwdro@plymouth.gov.uk W: www.plymouth.gov.uk/star/archives.htm

South West Film and Television Archive Melville Building Royal William Yard Stonehouse Plymouth Devon PL1 3RP T: 01752 202650 W: www.tswfta.co.uk

The Devonshire and Dorset Regiment (Archives) RHQ, Devonshire and Dorset Regiment, Wyvern Barracks Barrack Road Exeter Devon EX2 6AR T: 01392 492436 F: 01392 492469

Dorset

Dorset Archives Service 9 Bridport Road Dorchester Dorset DT1 1RP T: 01305-250550 F: 01305-257184 E: dcc_archives@dorset-cc.gov.uk W: www.dorset-cc.gov.uk/archives Research service available. Search fee The service covers the areas served by Dorset County, Bournemouth Borough and the Borough of Poole. 1901 census

Poole Central Reference Library Dolphin Centre Poole Dorset BH15 1QE T: 01202 262424 F: 01202 262442 E: centrallibrary@poole.gov.uk W: www.poole.gov.uk The local studies collection was relocated to The Waterfront Museum, Poole Some records moved to Dorset Record Office. Retains only general local history and national family history indexes.

Waterfront Musuem and Local Studies Centre 4 High St Poole Dorset BH15 1BW T: 01202 683138 T: 01202 262600 F: 01202 660896 E: museums@poole.gov.uk mldavidw@poole.gov.uk W: www.poole.gov.uk 1901 census

Dorset – West
Bridport Museum Trust - Local History Centre The Coach House
Grundy Lane Bridport Dorset DT6 3RJ T: 01308 458703 F: 01308
458704 E: sh-bridportmus@btconnect.com Wide range of resources.
The service is free. Open Tues - Thurs 10.a.m. to 1.p.m. and 2.p.m. to
4.p.m. year round

Durham
Darlington Local Studies Centre The Library Crown Street
Darlington County Durham DL1 1ND T: 01325-349630 F: 01325-
381556 E: crown.street.library@darlington.gov.uk W:
www.darlington.gov.uk 1901 census
Durham County Record Office County Hall Durham County
Durham DH1 5UL T: 0191-383-3474 T: 0191-383-3253 F: 0191-383-
4500 E: record.office@durham.gov.uk W:
www.durham.gov.uk/recordoffice 1901 census
Durham University Library Archives and Special Collections
Palace Green Section Palace Green Durham DH1 3RN T: 0191-374-
3032 E: pg.library@durham.ac.uk W: www.durham.ac.uk

Essex
Central Reference Library - London Borough of Havering
Reference Library St Edward's Way Romford Essex RM1 3AR T:
01708 432393 T: 01708 432394 F: 01708 432391 E:
romfordlib2@rmplc.co.uk
Chelmsford Library PO Box 882 Market Road Chelmsford Essex
CM1 1LH T: 01245 492758 F: 01245 492536 E:
answers.direct@essexcc.gov.uk W: www.essexcc.gov.uk 1901 census
Essex Record Office Wharf Road Chelmsford Essex CM2 6YT T:
01245 244644 F: 01245 244655 E: ero.enquiry@essexcc.gov.uk
(General Enquiries) ero.search@essexcc.gov.uk (Search Service) W:
www.essexcc.gov.uk/ero 1901 census
Essex Record Office, Colchester & NE Essex Branch Stanwell
House Stanwell Street Colchester Essex CO2 7DL T: 01206-572099
F: 01206-574541 W: www.essexcc.gov.uk/ero
Essex Record Office, Southend Branch Central Library Victoria
Avenue Southend on Sea Essex SS2 6EX T: 01702-464278 F: 01702-
464253 W: www.essexcc.gov.uk 1901 census
London Borough of Barking & Dagenham Local Studies Library
Valence House Museum Beacontree Avenue Dagenham Essex RM8
3HT T: 020 8270 6896 F: 020 8270 6897 E:
localstudies@bardaglea.org.uk W: www.barking-dagenham.gov.uk
Redbridge Library Central Library Clements Road Ilford Essex IG1
1EA T: (020) 8708-2417 F: (020) 8553 3299 E:
Local.Studies@redbridge.gov.uk W: www.redbridge.gov.uk
Valence House Museum Valence House Museum Becontree Avenue
Dagenham Essex RM8 3HT T: 020 8270 6866 F: 020 82706868 W:
www.barking-dagenham.gov.uk Heritage service includes a local history
museum, and archive section. A list of resources is available upon request.
Archives of the Essex Parishes of Barking and Dagenham and the London
Boroughs of the same names

Gloucestershire
Gloucestershire Record Office Clarence Row Alvin Street
Gloucester GL1 3DW T: 01452-425295 F: 01452-426378 E:
records@gloscc.gov.uk W: www.gloscc.gov.uk Daily admission
charge £2 (£1.50 for over 60's.) I/d required 1901 census

Hampshire
Hampshire Local Studies Library Winchester Library Jewry Street
Winchester Hampshire SO23 8RX T: 01962 841408 F: 01962 841489
E: clceloc@hants.gov.uk W: www.hants.gov.uk/library 1901 census
Hampshire Record Office Sussex St Winchester Hampshire SO23
8TH T: 01962-846154 F: 01962-878681 E:
enquiries.archives@hants.gov.uk W: www.hants.gov.uk/record-office
Portsmouth City Libraries Central Library Guildhall Square
Portsmouth Hampshire PO1 2DX T: (023) 9281 9311 X232
(Bookings) T: (023) 9281 9311 X234 (Enquiries) F: (023) 9283 9855
E: reference.library@portsmouthcc.gov.uk W:
www.portsmouthcc.gov.uk 1901 census
Portsmouth City Museum and Record Office Museum Road
Portsmouth Hampshire PO1 2LJ T: (023) 92827261 F: (023)
92875276 E: Email: portmus@compuserve.com 1901 census
Portsmouth Roman Catholic Diocesan Archives St Edmund House
Edinburgh Road Portsmouth Hampshire PO1 3QA T: 023 9282 5430
F: 023 9287 2424 E: archive@portsmouth-dio.org.uk These are
private archives and arrangements to visit have to be agreed
beforehand.
Royal Marines Museum Eastney Southsea Hampshire PO4 9PX T:
(023) 9281 9385-Exts-224 F: (023) 9283 8420 E:
matthewlittle@royalmarinesmuseum.co.uk W:
www.royalmarinesmuseum.co.uk No charges for research other than
material costs. Donations welcome. Visits by appointment Mon to Fri
10am to 4.30pm
Southampton Archive Service Civic Centre Southampton Hants
SO14 7LY T: (023) 80832251 T: (023) 8022 3855 x 2251 F: (023)
80832156 E: city.archives@southampton.gov.uk W:
www.southampton.gov.uk

Southampton City Libraries - Special Collections Southampton
Reference Library Civic Centre Southampton Hampshire SO14 7LW
T: 023 8083 2205 F: 023 8033 6305 E:
local.studies@southampton.gov.uk W: www.southampton.gov.uk
Special collections include information on Southampton and
Hampshire, genealogy and maritime topics. 1901 census
Wessex Film and Sound Archive Hampshire Record Office Sussex
Street Winchester Hampshire SO23 8TH T: 01962 847742 W:
www.hants.gov.uk/record-office/film.html
Herefordshire
Hereford Cathedral Archives & Library 5 College Cloisters
Cathedral Close Hereford Herefordshire HR1 2NG T: 01432 374225
F: 01432 374220 E: library@herefordcathedral.co.uk W:
www.herefordcathedral.co.uk
Herefordshire Record Office The Old Barracks Harold Street
Hereford Herefordshire HR1 2QX T: 01432 260750 F: 01432 260066
E: shubbard@herefordshire.gov.uk W: www.herefordshire.gov.uk
1901 census

Hertfordshire
Ashwell Education Services 59 High Street Ashwell Baldock
Hertfordshire SG7 5NP T: 01462 742385 F: 01462 743024 E:
aes@ashwell-education-services.co.uk W: www.ashwell-education-
services.co.uk Research into the History and family histories of
ashwell and its people
Bushey Museum, Art Gallery and Local Studies Centre Rudolph
Road Bushey Hertfordshire WD23 3HW T: 020 8420 4057 F: 020
8420 4923 E: busmt@bushey.org.uk W: www.busheymuseum.org
1901 census for Bushey and aldenham
Hertfordshire Archives and Local Studies County Hall Pegs Lane
Hertford Hertfordshire SG13 8EJ T: 01438 737333 F: 01923 471333
E: herts.direct@hertscc.gov.uk http://hertsdirect.org/hals

Hull
Brynmor Jones Library - University of Hull Cottingham Road Hull
HU6 7RX T: 01482 465265 F: 01482 466205 E:
archives@acs.hull.ac.uk W: www.hull.ac.uk/lib W:
www.hull.ac.uk/lib/archives
Hull City Archives 79 Lowgate Kingston upon Hull HU1 1HN T:
01482-615102 T: 01482-615110 F: 01482-613051 E:
city.archives@hcc.gov.uk W: www.hullcc.gov.uk
Local History Unit Hull College Park Street Centre Hull HU2 8RR
T: 01482-598952 F: 01482 598989 E: historyunit@netscape.net W:
www.historyofhull.co.uk

Isle of Wight
Isle of Wight Record Office 26 Hillside Newport Isle of Wight PO30
2EB T: 01983-823820/1 F: 01983 823820 E:
record.office@iow.gov.uk W: www.iwight.com/library/default.asp
1901 census

Kent
Bexley Local Studies and Archive Centre Central Library Bourne
Townley Road Bexleyheath Kent DA6 7HJ T: (020) 8301 1545 F:
(020) 8303 7872 E: archives@bexleycouncil.freeserve.co.uk W:
www.bexley.gov.uk As well as being a designated local authority
record office the Local Studies Centre is Diocesan Record Office for
all the (C of E) Parishes within the Borough ie Rochester &
Southwark Dioceses 1901 census
Canterbury Cathedral Archives The Precincts Canterbury Kent
CT1 2EH T: 01227 865330 F: 1227865222 E: archives@canterbury-
cathedral.org W: www.canterbury-cathedral.org
Canterbury Library & Local Studies Collection 18 High Street
Canterbury Kent CT1 2JF T: 01227-463608 F: 01227-768338 W:
www.kent.gov.uk 1901 census
Centre for Kentish Studies / Kent County Archives Service
Sessions House County Hall Maidstone Kent ME141XQ T: 01622-
694363 F: 01622 694379 E: archives@kent.gov.uk W:
www.kent.gov.uk/e&l/artslib/ARCHIVES/archiveshome.htm 1901
census
East Kent Archives Centre Enterprise Zone Honeywood Road
Whitfield Dover Kent CT16 3EH T: 01304 829306 F: 01304 820783
E: eastkentarchives@kent.gov.uk W: www.kent.gov.uk 1901 census
Institute of Heraldic and Genealogical Studies 79 - 82 Northgate
Canterbury Kent CT1 1BA T: 01227 462618 F: 01227 765617 E:
ihgs@ihgs.ac.uk W: www.ihgs.ac.uk
London Borough of Bromley Local Studies Library Central
Library High Street Bromley Kent BR1 1EX T: 020 8460 9955 F:
020 8313 9975 E: localstudies.library@bromley.gov.uk W:
www.bromley.gov.uk 1901 census
Margate Library Local History Collection Cecil Square Margate
Kent CT9 1RE T: 01843-223626 F: 01843-293015 W:
www.kent.gov.uk
Pembroke Lodge Family History Centre and Museum 2-6 Station
Approach Birchington on Sea Kent CT7 9RD T: 01843-841649 E:
pattersonheritage@tesco.net Please address all mail to 4 Station
approach, Birchington on Sea Kent CT7 9RD. No fees Donations
welcome

Ramsgate Library Local Strudies Collection & Thanet Branch Archives Ramsgate Library Guildford Lawn Ramsgate Kent CT11 9AY T: 01843-593532 W: www.kent.gov.uk Archives at this library moved to East Kent Archives CentreEnterprise Zone, Honeywood Road, Whitfield, Dover, Kent CT16 3EH. A Local Studies Collection will remain

Sevenoaks Archives Office Central Library Buckhurst Lane Sevenoaks Kent TN13 1LQ T: 01732-453118 T: 01732-452384 F: 01732-742682

Lancashire

Blackburn Cathedral & Archives Cathedral Close Blackburn Lancashire BB1 5AA T: 01254 51491 F: 01254 689666 E: cathedral@blackburn.anglican.org W: www.blackburn.anglican.org

Blackburn Central Library Town Hall Street Blackburn Lancashire BB2 1AG T: 01254 587920 F: 01254 690539 E: reference.library@blackburn.gov.uk W: www.blackburn.gov.uk/library 1901 census

Bolton Archive & Local Studies Service Central Library, Civic Centre Le Mans Crescent Bolton Lancashire BL1 1SE T: 01204-332185 F: 01204 332225 E: archives.library@bolton.gov.uk W: www.bolton.gov.uk 1901 census

Bury Archive Service 1st Floor, Derby Hall Annexe Edwin Street off Crompton Street Bury Greater Manchester BL9 0AS T: 0161-797-6697 F: 0161 797 6697 Telephone before faxing E: archives@bury.gov.uk W: www.bury.gov.uk/culture.htm May be moving to new premises in 2002 check before visiting

Lancashire Record Office Bow Lane Preston Lancashire PR1 2RE T: 01772 263039 F: 01772 263050 E: record.office@ed.lancscc.gov.uk W: www.lancashire.gov.uk/education/lifelong/recordindex.shtm The Lancashire Local Studies Collection is now housed here 1901 census

North West Sound Archive Old Steward's Office Clitheroe Castle Clitheroe Lancashire BB7 1AZ T: 01200-427897 F: 01200-427897 E: nwsa@ed.lancscc.gov.uk W: www.lancashire.gov.uk/education/lifelong/recordindex

Oldham Local Studies and Archives 84 Union Street Oldham Lancashire OL1 1DN T: 0161-911-4654 F: 0161-911-4654 E: archives@oldham.gov.uk localstudies@oldham.gov.uk W: www.oldham.gov.uk/archives W: www.oldham.gov.uk/local_studies 1901 census

Rochdale Local Studies Library Touchstones The Esplanade Rochdale Lancashire OL16 1AQ T: 01706 864915 F: 01706 864944 E: localstudies@rochdale.gov.uk W: www.rochdale.gov.uk 1901 census. GRO Index 1837 - 1999

Salford City Archives Salford Archives Centre 658/662 Liverpool Rd Irlam Manchester M44 5AD T: 0161 775-5643

Salford Local History Library Peel Park Salford Lancashire M5 4WU T: 0161 736 2649 F: 01161 745 9490 E: salford.museums@salford/gov.uk W: www.salford.gov.uk

The Documentary Photography Archive - Manchester c/o 7 Towncroft Lane Bolton Lancashire BL1 5EW T: 0161 832 5284 T: 01204-840439 (Home) F: 01204-840439

Traceline PO Box 106 Southport Lancashire PR8 2HH T: 0151 471 4811 F: 01704-563354 E: traceline@ons.gov.uk W: www.ons.gov.uk To be put in touch with lost relatives and acquaintances. The ONS must be satisfied that contact would be in the best interests of the person being sought. Traceline uses the NHS Central Register. NHSCR does not officially operate under the name Traceline and adheres to other strict criteria

Trafford Local Studies Centre Public Library Tatton Road Sale M33 1YH T: 0161-912-3013 F: 0161-912-3019 E: traffordlocalstudies@hotmail.com The collection covers the former Lancashire and Cheshire towns of Stretford, Old Trafford, Urmston, Daveyhulme, Flixton, Altincham, Bowdon, Hale, Dunham Massey, Sale, Ashton-o-Mersey, Carrington, Partington, Warburton, etc. 1901 census

Wigan Heritage Service Town Hall Leigh Wigan Greater Manchester WN7 2DY T: 01942-404430 F: 01942-404425 E: heritage@wiganmbc.gov.uk W: www.wiganmbc.gov.uk Open by appointment: Mon, Tues, Thurs & Fri

Wigan Heritage Service Museum History Shop Library Street Wigan Greater Manchester WN1 1NU T: 01942 828020 F: 01942 827645 E: heritage@wiganmbc.gov.uk W: www.wiganmbc.gov.uk 1901 census

Leicestershire

East Midlands Oral History archive Centre for Urban History University of Leicester Leicester Leicestershire LE1 7RH T: 0116 252 5065 E: emoha@le.ac.uk W: www.le.ac.uk/emoha

Melton Mowbray Library Wilton Road Melton Mowbray Leicestershire LE13 0UJ T: 01664 560161 F: 01664 410199 W: www.leics.gov.uk

Record Office for Leicestershire, Leicester and Rutland Long Street Wigston Magna Leicestershire LE18 2AH T: 0116-257-1080 F: 0116-257-1120 E: recordoffice@leics.gov.uk W: www.leics.gov.uk

Lincolnshire

Lincolnshire Archives St Rumbold Street Lincoln Lincolnshire LN2 5AB T: 01522-526204 F: 01522-530047 E: archive@lincolnshire.gov.uk W: www.lincolnshire.gov.uk/archives 1901 census

Lincolnshire County Library Local Studies Section Lincoln Central Library Free School Lane Lincoln Lincolnshire LN1 1EZ T: 01522-510800 F: 01522-575011 E: lincoln.library@lincolnshire.gov.uk W: www.lincolnshire.gov.uk/library/services/family.htm 1901 census

North East Lincolnshire Archives Town Hall Town Hall Square Grimsby North East Lincolnshire DN31 1HX T: 01472-323585 F: 01472-323582 E: john.wilson@nelincs.gov.uk W: www.nelincs.gov.uk

Liverpool

Liverpool Record Office & Local History Department Central Library William Brown Street Liverpool L3 8EW T: 0151 233 5817 F: 0151-233 5886 E: recoffice.central.library@liverpool.gov.uk W: www.liverpool.gov.uk

London

Alexander Fleming Laboratory Museum / St Mary's NHS Trust Archives St Mary's Hospital Praed Street Paddington London W2 1NY T: (020) 7886 6528 F: (020) 7886 6739 E: kevin.brown@st-marys.nhs.uk W: www.st-marys.nhs.uk

Bank of England Archive Archive Section HO-SV The Bank of England Threadneedle Street London EC2R 8AH T: (020) 7601-5096 F: (020) 7601-4356 E: archive@bankofengland.co.uk W: www.bankofengland.co.uk

Bethlem Royal Hospital Archives and Museum Monks Orchard Road Beckenham Kent BR3 3BX T: (020) 8776 4307 T: (020) 8776 4053 F: (020) 8776 4045 E: museum@bethlem.freeserve.co.uk The archives of the Bethlem and Maudsley NHS Trust (the Bethlem Royal Hospital and the Maudsley Hospital). Records relating to individual patients are closed for 100 years. The museum does not contain material relating to genealogy or family history

Black Cultural Archives see National

Brent Community History Library & Archive 152 Olive Road London NW2 6UY T: (020) 8937 3541 F: (020) 8450 5211 E: archive@brent.gov.uk W: www.brent.gov.uk 1901 census

British Library Oriental and India Collections 197 Blackfriars Rd London SE1 8NG T: (020) 7412-7873 F: (020) 7412-7641 E: oioc-enquiries@bl.uk W: www.bl.uk/collections/oriental

British Library Western Manuscripts Collections 96 Euston Road London NW1 2DB T: (020) 7412-7513 F: (020) 7412-7745 E: mss@bl.uk W: www.bl.uk/ Note: can only respond to enquiries related to their own collections

British Red Cross Museum and Archives 9 Grosvenor Crescent London SW1X 7EJ T: (020) 7201 5153 F: (020) 7235 6456 E: enquiry@redcross.org.uk W: www.redcross.org.uk/museum&archives Open by appointment 10am to 4pm Monday to Friday.

Centre for Metropolitan History Institute of Historical Research Senate House Malet Street London WC1E 7HU T: (020) 7862 8790 F: (020) 7862 8793 E: olwen.myhill@sas.ac.uk W: www.history.ac.uk/cmh/cmh.main.html

Chelsea Public Library Old Town Hall King's Road London SW3 5EZ T: (020) 7352-6056 T: (020) 7361-4158 F: (020) 7351 1294 Local Studies Collection on Royal Borough of Kensington & Chelsea south of Fulham Road

City of Westminster Archives Centre 10 St Ann's Street London SW1P 2DE T: (020) 7641-5180 F: (020) 7641-5179 W: www.westminster.gov.uk Holds records for whole area covered by City of Westminster incl former Metropolitan Boroughs of Paddington and St Maryleborne. 1901 census

Corporation of London Records Office PO Box 270 Guildhall London EC2P 2EJ T: (020) 7332-1251 F: (020) 7710-8682 E: clro@corpoflondon.gov.uk W: www.cityoflondon.gov.uk/archives/clro

Deed Poll Records Section Room E 15 Royal Courts of Justice Strand London WC2A 2LL T: (020) 7947 6528 F: (020) 7947 6807

Documents Register Quality House Quality Court Chancery Lane London WC2A 1HP T: (020) 7242-1198 F: (020) 7831-3550 E: nra@hmc.gov.uk W: www.hmc.gov.uk

Dr Williams's Library 14 Gordon Square London WC1H 0AR T: (020) 7387-3727 E: enquiries@dwlib.co.uk

Ealing Local History Centre Central Library 103 Broadway Centre Ealing London W5 5JY T: (020) 8567-3656-ext-37 F: (020) 8840-2351 E: localhistory@hotmail.com W: www.ealing.gov.uk/libraries

Family Records Centre see National

Grenadier Guards Record Office Wellington Barracks Birdcage Walk London London SW1E 6HQ E: rhqgrengds@yahoo.co.uk Access is by appointment made in advance. Search fee of £25.00 per search

Guildhall Library, Manuscripts Sect Aldermanbury London EC2P 2EJ T: (020) 7332-1863 E: manuscripts.guildhall@corpoflondon.gov.uk http://ihr.sas.ac.uk/ihr/gh/ Records: City of London parish records, probate records, City Livery companies, business records, Diocese of London, St Pauls Cathedral, etc. Prior booking unnecessary except some records on 24 hrs call/restricted 1901 census

Hackney Archives Department 43 De Beauvoir Road London Borough of Hackney London N1 5SQ T: (020) 7241-2886 F: (020) 7241-6688 E: archives@hackney.gov.uk W: www.hackney.gov.uk/history/index.html Covers Hackney, Shoreditch & Stoke Newington

Heritage Royal Mail see National

Hillingdon Local Studies & Archives Central Library High Street Uxbridge London Middlesex UB8 1HD T: 01895 250702 F: 01895 811164 E: ccotton@hillingdon.gov.uk W: www.hillingdon.gov.uk/goto/libraries 1901 census

Hounslow Library (Local Studies & Archives) Centrespace, Treaty Centre High Street Hounslow London TW3 1ES T: 0845 456 2800 F: 0845 456 2880 W: www.cip.com 1901 census

Imperial College Archives London University Room 455 Sherfield Building Imperial College London SW7 2AZ T: 020 7594 8850 F: 020 7584 3763 E: archivist@ic.ac.uk W: www.lib.ic.ac.uk

Institute of Historical Research University of London Senate House Malet Street London WC1E 7HU T: (020) 7862 8740 F: 020 7436 2145 E: ihr@sas.ac.uk http://ihr.sas.ac.uk

King's College London Archives Kins College Strand London WC2R 2LS T: 020 7848 2015 T: 020 7848 2187 F: 020 7848 2760 E: archives@kcl.ac.uk W: www.kcl.ac.uk/depsta/iss/archives/top.htm includes Student records, staff records and hospital records for Kins College Hospital

L B of Hammersmith & Fulham Archives & Local History Centre The Lilla Huset 191 Talgarth Road London W6 8BJ T: 0208-741-5159 F: 0208-741-4882 W: www.lbhf.gov.uk 1901 census

Lewisham Local Studies & Archives Lewisham Library 199 - 201 Lewisham High Street Lewisham London SE13 6LG T: (020) 8297-0682 F: (020) 8297-1169 E: local.studies@lewisham.gov.uk W: www.lewisham.gov.uk Covering the Parishes of Lewisham, Lee & St Paul's, Deptford. Appointments advisable. 1901 census

Library of the Royal College of Surgeons of England 35-43 Lincoln's Inn Fields London WC2A 3PN T: (020) 7869 6520 F: (020) 7405 4438 E: library@rseng.ac.uk W: www.rseng.ac.uk Research enquiries are not undertaken. Appointments required.

Liddell Hart Centre for Military Archives King's College London Strand London WC2R 2LS T: 020 7848 2015 T: 020 7848 2187 F: 020 7848 2760 E: archives@kcl.ac.uk W: www.kcl.ac.uk/lhcma/top.htm

Linnean Society of London Burlington House Piccadilly London W1J 0BF T: 020 7437 4479 T: 020 7434 4470 F: 020 7287 9364 E: gina@linnean.org W: www.linnean.org

Local Studies Collection for Chiswick & Brentford Chiswick Public Library Dukes Avenue Chiswick London W4 2AB T: (020) 8994-5295 F: (020) 8995-0016 and (020) 8742 7411 Restricted opening hours for local history room: please telephone before visiting

London Borough of Barnet, Archives & Local Studies Department Hendon Library The Burroughs Hendon London NW4 3BQ T: (020) 8359-2876 F: (020) 8359-2885 E: hendon.library@barnet.gov.uk W: www.barnet.gov.uk

London Borough of Camden Local Studies & Archive Centre Holborn Library 32 - 38 Theobalds Road London WC1X 8PA T: 020 7974 6342 F: 020 7974 6284 E: localstudies@camden.gov.uk W: www.camden.gov.uk

London Borough of Croydon Library and Archives Service see Surrey

London Borough of Enfield Archives & Local History Unit Southgate Town Hall Green Lanes Palmers Green London N13 4XD T: (020) 8379-2724 F: (020) 8379 2761 The collections specifically relate to edmonton and Enfield (both formerly in Middlesex) 1901 census

London Borough of Greenwich Heritage Centre Museum and Library Building 41 Royal Arsenal Woolwich London SE18 6SP T: (020) 8858 4631 F: (020) 8293 4721 E: local.history@greenwich.gov.uk W: www.greenwich.gov.uk The library will be moving to a new Heritage Centre autumn 2002. Please contact the library for more details

London Borough of Haringey Archives Service Bruce Castle Museum Lordship Lane Tottenham London N17 8NU T: (020) 8808-8772 F: (020) 8808-4118 E: museum.services@haringey.gov.uk W: www.haringey.gov.uk

London Borough of Islington History Centre Finsbury library 245 St John Street London EC1V 4NB T: (020) 7527 7988 E: local.history@islington.gov.uk W: www.islington.gov.uk Collection covers the LB of Islington. Material relating to (1) the former Metropolitan Borough of Islington; (2) the present London Borough of Islington and (3) the civil parish of St Mary, Islington (to 1900). The north and south part of the present London Borough of Islington - the former Metropolitan Borough of Finsbury and its predecesors, the former civil parishes of Clerkenwell and St Lukes, Finsbury. 1901 census. The Local History Service operates through an appointment system. Users must make an appointment, preferably by telephone. A postal enquiry service (SAE required) is available. A charge is made for extended research.

London Borough of Lambeth Archives Department Minet Library 52 Knatchbull Road Lambeth London SE5 9QY T: (020) 7926 6076 F: (020) 7936 6080 E: lambetharchives@lambeth.gov.uk W: www.lambeth.gov.uk

London Borough of Newham Archives & Local Studies Library Stratford Library 3 The Grove London E15 1EL T: (020) 8430 6881 W: www.newham.gov.uk

London Borough of Wandsworth Local Studies Local Studies Service Battersea Library 265 Lavender Hill London SW11 1JB T: (020) 8871 7753 F: (020) 7978-4376 E: wandsworthmuseum@wandsworth.gov.uk W: www.wandsworth.gov.uk Open Tues & Wed 10am to 88pm, Fri 10am to 5pm, Sat 9am to 1pm - Research service offferred - £7.00 per half hour (the minimum fee) apointment advised to ensure archives, hard copy newspapers (not microfilmed) and other items are available

London Metropolitan Archives 40 Northampton Road London EC1R 0HB T: 020 7332 3820 T: Mini com 020 7278 8703 F: 020 7833 9136 E: ask.lma@ms.corpoflondon.gov.uk W: www.cityoflondon.gov.uk

London University - Institute of Advanced Studies Charles Clore House 17 Russell Square London WC1B 5DR T: (020) 7637 1731 F: (020) 7637 8224 E: ials.lib@sas.ac.uk http://ials.sas.ac.uk

London University - Institute of Education 20 Bedford Way London WC1H 0AL T: 020 7612 6063 F: 020 7612 6093 E: lib@ioe.ac.uk W: www.ioe.ac.uk/library/

Manorial Documents Register Quality House Quality Court Chancery Lane London WC2A 1HP T: (020) 7242-1198 F: (020) 7831-3550 E: nra@hmc.gov.uk W: www.hmc.gov.uk

Manuscripts Room Library Services University College Gower Street London WC1E 6BT T: (020) 7387 7050 F: 020 7380 7727 E: mssrb@ucl.ac.uk W: www.ucl.ac.uk/library/special-coll/

Museum of London Library 150 London Wall London EC2Y 5HN T: 020 7814 5588 F: 020 7600 1058 E: info@museumoflondon.org.uk http://museumoflondon.org.uk

Museum of the Order of St John St John's Gate St John's Lane Clerkenwell London EC1M 4DA T: (020) 7253-6644 F: (020) 7336 0587 W: www.sja.org.uk/history

Museum of the Royal Pharmaceutical Society Museum of the Royal Pharmaceutical Society 1 Lambeth High Street London SE1 7JN T: (020) 7572 2210 F: (020) 7572 2499 E: museum@rpsgb.org.uk W: www.rpsgb.org.uk CC accepted. Records of pharmacists from 1841 Research fee charged £20 per person or premises researched to Non members of the Society, £10 per person or premises researched for members(Genealogical Enquiries) Enquirers may visit and undertake research themselves by appointment only at a cost of £10.00 per day

National Army Museum Royal Hospital Road London London SW3 4HT T: (020) 7730-0717 F: (020) 7823-6573 E: info@national-army-museum.ac.uk W: www.national-army-museum.ac.uk incorporating Middlesex Regiment Museum & Buffs regiment Museum

National Army Museum Department of Archives (Photographs, Film & Sound) Royal Hospital Road London SW3 4HT T: (020) 7730-0717 F: (020) 7823-6573 E: info@national-army-museum.ac.uk W: www.national-army-museum.ac.uk

National Register of Archives Quality House Quality Court Chancery Lane London WC2A 1HP T: (020) 7242 1198 F: (020) 7831 3550 E: nra@hmc.gov.uk W: www.hmc.gov.uk The National Register of Archives (NRA) is maintained by the Historical Manuscripts Commission (HMC) as a central collecting point for information concerning the location of manuscript sources for British History, outside the Public RecordsHMS's Archives in Focus website (W: www.hmc.gov.uk/focus) provides an introduction to archives in the UK including guides to local and family history

Probate Principal Registry of the Family Division First Avenue House 42 - 49 High Holborn London WC1V 6NP T: (020) 7947 6939 F: (020) 7947 6946 W: www.courtservice.gov.uk Postal Searches: York Probate Sub Registry, Duncombe Place, York YO1 7EA

Royal Air Force Museum Grahame Park Way Hendon London NW9 5LL T: (020) 8205-2266 F: (020) 8200 1751 E: groupbusiness@refmuseum.org.uk W: www.rafmuseum.org.uk

Royal Borough of Kensington and Chelsea Libraries & Arts Service Central Library Phillimore Walk Kensington London W8 7RX T: (020) 7361-3036 T: (020) 7361 3007 E: information.services@rbkc.gov.uk W: www.rbkc.gov.uk

Royal Botanic Gardens Library & Archives Kew Richmond Surrey TW9 3AE T: 020 8332 5414 T: 020 8332 5417 F: 020 8332 5430 CC Accepted

Royal London Hospital Archives and Museum Royal London Hospital Newark Whitechapel London E1 1BB T: (020) 7377-7608 F: (020) 7377 7413 E: r.j.evans@mds.qmw.ac.uk W: www.bartsandthelondon.org.uk

Southwark Local Studies Library 211 Borough High Street Southwark London SE1 1JA T: 0207-403-3507 F: 0207-403-8633 E: local.studies.library@southwark.gov.uk W: www.southwark.gov.uk

St Bartholomew's Hospital Archives & Museum Archives and Museum West Smithfield London EC1A 7BE T: (020) 7601-8152 F: (020) 7606 4790 E: marion.rea@bartsandthelondon.nhs.uk W: www.brlcf.org.uk Visitors to use the archive by appointment only - Mon to Fri 9.30am to 5pm

The Galton Institute 19 Northfields Prospect London SW18 1PE

Tower Hamlets Local History Library & Archives Bancroft Library 277 Bancroft Road London E1 4DQ T: (020) 8980 4366 Ext 129 F: (020) 8983 4510 E: localhistory@towerhamlets.gov.uk W: www.towerhamlets.gov.uk

Twickenham Library Twickenham Library Garfield Road Twickenham Middlesex TW1 3JS T: (020) 8891-7271 F: (020) 8891-5934 E: twicklib@richmond.gov.uk W: www.richmond.gov.uk The Twickenham collection moved to Richmond Local Studies Library

University of London (Library - Senate House) Palaeography Room Senate House Malet Street London WC1E 7HU T: (020) 7862 8475 F: 020 7862 8480 E: library@ull.ac.uk W: www.ull.ac.uk

Waltham Forest Archives Vestry House Museum Vestry Road Walthamstow London E17 9NH T: (020) 8509 1917 E: vestry.house@al.lbwf.gov.uk W: www.lbwf.gov.uk/vestry/vestry.htm Visits by prior appointment only 1901 census

Westminster Abbey Library & Muniment Room Westminster Abbey London SW1P 3PA T: (020) 7222-5152-Ext-4830 F: (020) 7226-4827 E: library@westminster-abbey.org W: www.westminster-abbey.org

Westminster Diocesan Archives 16a Abingdon Road Kensington London W8 6AF T: (020) 7938-3580 This is the private archive of the Catholic Archbishop of Westminster and is not open to the public. Pre 1837 baptismal records have been transcribed and copies are with the Society of Genealogists. No registers earlier than 18th century. Appointments and enquiries through the Catholic FHS

Westminster University Archives Information Systems & Library Services 4-12 Little Titchfield Street London W1W 7UW T: 020 7911 5000 ext 2524 F: 020 7911 5894 E: archive@westminster.ac.uk W: www.wmin.ac.uk The archive is organisationally within the Library but is a separate entity. The University of Westminster Libraries do not have special collections relating to family and local history but the archive may be of interest to researchers

Manchester

Greater Manchester County Record Office 56 Marshall St New Cross Manchester Greater Manchester M4 5FU T: 0161-832-5284 F: 0161-839-3808 E: archives@gmcro.co.uk W: www.gmcro.co.uk

Manchester Archives & Local Studies Manchester Central Library St Peter's Square Manchester M2 5PD T: 0161-234-1979 F: 0161-234-1927 E: lsu@libraries.manchester.gov.uk W: www.manchester.gov.uk/libraries/index.htm 1901 census

Methodist Archives and Research Centre see Methodist

North West Film Archive Manchester Metropolitan University Minshull House 47-49 Chorlton Street Manchester M1 3EU T: 0161 247 3097 W: www.nwfa.mmu.ac.uk

Medway

Medway Archives and Local Studies Centre Civic Centre Strood Rochester Kent ME2 4AU T: 01634-332714 F: 01634-297060 E: archives@medway.gov.uk local.studies@medway.gov.uk W: www.medway.gov.uk 1901 census

Merseyside

Crosby Library (South Sefton Local History Unit) Crosby Road North Waterloo Liverpool Merseyside L22 0LQ T: 0151 257 6401 F: 0151 934 5770 E: local-history.south@leisure.sefton.gov.uk W: www.sefton.gov.uk The Local History Units serve Sefton Borough Council area. The South Sefton Unit covers Bootle, Crosby, Maghull and other communities south of the River Alt. The North Sefton Unit covers Southport, Formby.

Huyton Central Library Huyton Library Civic Way Huyton Knowsley Merseyside L36 9GD T: 0151-443-3738 F: 0151 443 3739 E: eileen.hume.dlcs@knowsley.gov.uk W: www.knowsley.gov.uk/leisure/libraries/huyton/index.html 1901 census

Merseyside Maritime Museum Maritime Archives and Library Albert Dock Liverpool Merseyside L3 4AQ T: 0151-478-4418 T: 0151 478 4424 F: 0151-478-4590 E: archives@nmgmarchives.demon.co.uk W: www.nmgm.org.uk

Southport Library (North Sefton Local History Unit) Lord Street Southport Merseyside PR8 1DJ T: 0151 934 2119 F: 0151 934 2115 E: local-history.north@leisure.sefton.gov.uk The Local History Units serve Sefton Borough Council area. The North Sefton Unit covers Southport, Formby. The South Sefton Unit covers Bootle, Crosby, Maghull and other communities south of the River Alt

St Helen's Local History & Archives Library Central Library, Gamble Institute Victoria Square St Helens Merseyside WA10 1DY T: 01744-456952 F: 01744 20836 No research undertaken 1901 census

Wirral Archives Service Wirral Museum, Birkenhead Town Hall Hamilton Street Birkenhead Merseyside CH41 5BR T: 0151-666 3903 F: 0151-666 3965 E: archives@wirral-libraries.net W: www.wirral-libraries.net/archives Open: Thursday & friday 10.00.a.m. to 5.00.p.m. Saturday: 10.00.a.m. to 1.00.p.m.

Middlesex

British Deaf History Society 288 Bedfont Lane Feltham Middlesex TW14 9NU E: bdhs@iconic.demon.co.uk

London Borough of Harrow Local History Collection Civic Centre Library, PO Box 4 Station Road Harrow Middlesex HA1 2UU T: 0208 424 1055 T: 0208 424 1056 F: 0208 424 1971 E: civiccentre.library@harrow.gov.uk W: www.harrow.gov.uk 1901 census

Norfolk

East Anglian Film Archive University of East Anglia Norwich Norfolk NR4 7TJ T: 01603 592664 W: www.uea.ac.uk/eafa

Kings Lynn Borough Archives The Old Gaol House Saturday Market Place Kings Lynn Norfolk PE30 5DQ T: 01553-774297 T: 01603 761349 F: 01603 761885 E: norfrec.nro@norfolk.gov.uk http://archives.norfolk.gov.uk

Norfolk Record Office Gildengate House Anglia Square Upper Green Lane Norwich Norfolk NR3 1AX T: 01603-761349 F: 01603-761885 E: norfrec.nro@norfolk.gov.uk W: www.norfolk.gov.uk

Northamptonshire

Northamptonshire Central Library Abington Street Northampton Northamptonshire NN1 2BA T: 01604-462040 F: 01604-462055 E: ns-centlib@northamptonshire.gov.uk W: www.northamptonshire.gov.uk Northamptonshire Studies Room collection includes census returns 1841 to 1891, name indexes to 1851 & 1881 census, Parish Registers on microfiche, I.G.I., trade and street directories, poll books, electoral registers for Northampton Borough, biographical indexes and newscuttings. GRO index 1837 - 1983 Free internet access to many family history websites

Northamptonshire Record Office Wootton Hall Park Northampton Northamptonshire NN4 8BQ T: 01604-762129 F: 01604 767562 E: archivist@nro.northamton.gov.uk W: www.nro.northamptonshire.gov.uk also holds Peterborough Diocesan Record Office

Northumberland

Berwick upon Tweed Record Office Council Offices Wallace Green Berwick-Upon-Tweed Northumberland TD15 1ED T: 01289 301865 T: 01289-330044-Ext-265 01289-330540 E: lb@berwick-upon-tweed.gov.uk W: www.swinhope.demon.co.uk/genuki/NBL/Northumberland RO/Berwick.html GRO indexes 1837-1940: Pre 1855 OPR Christening & Marriage inedxes for all Scottish counties Office open Wed & Thurs 9.30am to 1pm and 2pm to 5pm. Research service - £8 per half hour. 1901 census

Friends of Northumberland Archives 19 Rodsley Court Rothbury Northumberland NE65 7UY

Northumberland Archive Service Morpeth Records Centre The Kylins Loansdean Morpeth Northumberland NE61 2EQ T: 01670-504084 F: 01670-514815 E: archives@northumberland.gov.uk W: www.swinnhope.myby.co.uk/nro 1901 census

Nottinghamshire

Media Archive for Central England Institute of Film Studies University of Nottingham Nottingham Nottinghamshire NG7 2RD T: 0115 846 6448 W: www.nottingham.ac.uk/film/mace

Nottingham Catholic Diocese Nottingham Diocesan Archives Willson House Derby Road Nottingham Nottinghamshire NG1 5AW T: 0115 953 9803 F: 0115 953 9808 E: archives@nottinghamdiocese.org.uk W: www.nottinghamdiocese.org.uk

Nottingham Central Library : Local Studies Centre Angel Row Nottingham Nottinghamshire NG1 6HP T: 0115 915 2873 F: 0115 915 2850 E: local-studies.library@nottinghamcity.gov.uk W: www.nottinghamcity.gov.uk/libraries

Nottinghamshire Archives Castle Meadow Road Nottingham Nottinghamshire NG2 1AG T: 0115-950-4524 Admin T: 0115 958 1634 Enquiries F: 0115-941-3997 E: archives@nottscc.gov.uk W: www.nottscc.gov.uk/libraries/archives/index.htm 1901 census

Southwell Minster Library Minster Office, Trebeck Hall Bishop's Drive Southwell Nottinghamshire NG25 0JP T: 01636-812649 F: 01636 815904 E: mail@southwellminster.org.uk W: www.southwellminster.org.uk

Oxfordshire

Oxfordshire Archives St Luke's Church Temple Road Cowley Oxford Oxfordshire OX4 2EX T: 01865 398200 F: 01865 398201 E: archives@oxfordshire.gov.uk W: www.oxfordshire.gov.uk 1901 census

Peterborough

Peterborough Local Studies Collection Central Library Broadway Peterborough PE1 1RX T: 01733 742700 F: 01733 555277 E: libraries@peterborough.gov.uk W: www.peterborough.gov.uk The telephone number may change in 2002 1901 census

Rutland

Record Office for Leicestershire, Leicester and Rutland Long Street Wigston Magna Leicestershire LE18 2AH T: 0116-257-1080 F: 0116-257-1120 E: recordoffice@leics.gov.uk W: www.leics.gov.uk

Shropshire

Ironbridge Gorge Museum, Library & Archives The Wharfage Ironbridge Telford TF8 7AW T: 01952 432141 F: 01952 432237 E: library@ironbridge.org.uk W: www.ironbridge.org.uk

Shropshire Archives Castle Gates Shrewsbury Shropshire SY1 2AQ T: 01743 255350 F: 01743 255355 E: research@shropshire-cc.gov.uk W: www.shropshire-cc.gov.uk/research.nsf 1901 census

Wrekin Local Studies Forum Madeley Library Russell Square
Telford Shropshire TF7 5BB T: 01952 586575 F: 01952 587105 E:
wlst@library.madeley.uk W: www.madeley.org.uk

Somerset

Bath & North East Somerset Record Office Guildhall High St Bath
Somerset BA1 5AW T: 01225-477421 F: 01225-477439 E:
archives@bathnes.gov.uk

Bristol University Library - Special Collections Tyndall Avenue
Bristol BS8 1TJ T: 0117 928 8014 F: 0117 925 5334 E:
library@bris.ac.uk W: www.bris.ac.uk/depts/library

Somerset Archive & Record Service Somerset Record Office
Obridge Road Taunton Somerset TA2 7PU T: 01823-337600
Appointments T: 01823 278805 Enquiries F: 01823-325402 E:
archives@somerset.gov.uk W: www.somerset.gov.uk 1901 census

Staffordshire

Burton Archives Burton Library Riverside High Street Burton on
Trent Staffordshire DE14 1AH T: 01283-239556 F: 01283-239571 E:
burton.library@staffordshire.gov.uk W: www.staffordshire.gov.uk

Coal Miners Records Cannock Record Centre Old Mid-Cannock
(Closed) Colliery Site Rumer Hill Road Cannock Staffordshire WS11
3EX T: 01543-570666 F: 01543-578168 Employment and training
records held for ex mineworkers post 1917

Keele University Special Collections & Archives Keele
Staffordshire ST5 5BG T: 01782 583237 F: 01782 711553 E:
h.burton@keele.ac.uk W: www.keele.ac.uk/depts/li/specarc

Lichfield Record Office Lichfield Library The Friary Lichfield
Staffordshire WS13 6QG T: 01543 510720 F: 01543-510715 E:
lichfield.record.office@staffordshire.gov.uk W:
www.staffordshire.gov.uk/archives/ Advance booking required. Lichfield
Records Research Service. Covers all the holdings of the office, including
Lichfield Diocesan records such as wills including, bishop's transcripts and
marriage bonds for Staffordshire, Derbyshire, north east Warickshire and North
Shropshire

Staffordshire Record Office Eastgate Street Stafford Staffordshire
ST16 2LZ T: 01785 278373 (Bookings) T: 01785 278379 (Enquiries)
F: 01785 278384 E: staffordshire.record.office@staffordshire.co.uk
W: www.staffordshire.gov.uk/archives For research into all Staffordshire
records including parish and nonconformist registers, census and electoral
registers contact:Staffordshire Record Office, Eastgate Street, Stafford ST16 2LZ
Lichfield Records Research Service For research into all Lichfield Diocesan
records including will, bishop's transcripts and marriage bonds for Staffordshire,
Derbyshire, north east Warickshire and North Shropshire 1901 census

**Staffordshire & Stoke on Trent Archive Service -Stoke on Trent
City Archives** Hanley Library Bethesda Street Hanley Stoke on Trent
Staffordshire ST1 3RS T: 01782-238420 F: 01782-238499 E:
stoke.archives@stoke.gov.uk W: www.staffordshire.gov.uk/archives
1901 census

Tamworth Library Corporation Street Tamworth Staffordshire B79
7DN T: 01827-475645 F: 01827-475658 E:
tamworth.library@staffordshire.gov.uk W:
www.staffordshire.gov.uk/locgov/county/cars/tamlib.htm IGI (Derby,
Leics, Notts, Shrops, Staffs, Warks, Worcs). Parish registers for
Tamworth. Census for Tamworth and District, 1841 - 91. Street
directories for Staffs and Warks.

William Salt Library Eastgate Street Stafford Staffordshire ST16
2LZ T: 01785-278372 F: 01785-278414 E:
william.salt.library@staffordshire.gov.uk W:
www.staffordshire.gov.uk/archives/salt.htm

Suffolk

Suffolk Record Office - Bury St Edmunds Branch 77 Raingate
Street Bury St Edmunds Suffolk IP33 2AR T: 01284-352352 F:
01284-352355 E: bury.ro@libher.suffolkcc.gov.uk W:
www.suffolkcc.gov.uk/sro/ 1901 census

Suffolk Record Office Ipswich Branch Gatacre Road Ipswich
Suffolk IP1 2LQ T: 01473 584541 F: 01473 584533 E:
ipswich.ro@libher.suffolkcc.gov.uk W: www.suffolkcc.gov.uk/sro/
1901 census

Suffolk Record Office Lowestoft Branch Central Library Clapham
Road Lowestoft Suffolk NR32 1DR T: 01502-405357 F: 01502-
405350 E: lowestoft.ro@libher.suffolkcc.gov.uk. W:
www.suffolkcc.gov.uk/sro/ 1901 census

Suffolk Regiment Archives Suffolk Record Office 77 Raingate
Street Bury St Edmunds Suffolk IP33 2AR T: 01284-352352 F:
01284-352355 E: bury.ro@libher.suffolkcc.gov.uk W:
www.suffolkcc.gov.uk/sro/

Surrey

Cranleigh Library and Local History Centre High Street Cranleigh
Surrey GU6 8AE T: 01483 272413 F: 01483 271327 W:
www.surrey.gov.uk

Domestic Buildings Research Group (Surrey) The Ridings Lynx
Hill East Horsley Surrey KT24 5AX T: 01483 283917

Epsom and Ewell Local History Centre Bourne Hall Spring Street
Ewell Epsom Surrey KT17 1UF T: 020 8394 0372 F: 020 8873 1603
W: www.surrey.gov.uk

Horley Local History Centre Horley Library Victoria Road Horley
Surrey RH6 7AG T: 01293 784141 F: 01293 820084 W:
www.surrey.gov.uk

Kingston Museum & Heritage Service North Kingston Centre
Richmond Road Kingston upon Thames Surrey KT2 5PE T: (020)
8547-6738 F: (020) 8547-6747 E: local.history@rbk.kingston.gov.uk
W: www.kingston.gov.uk/museum/ Research service available £7.50
per half hour - max 3 hours

London Borough of Lambeth Archives Department see London

London Borough of Wandsworth Local Studies see London

London Borough of Merton Local Studies Centre Merton Civic
Centre London Road Morden Surrey SM4 5DX T: (020) 8545-3239
F: (020) 8545-4037 E: local.studies@merton.gov.uk W:
www.merton.gov.uk/libraries Open: Mon to Fri 9.30 to 7.00: Weds
9.30 to 1.00: Sats 9.30 to 5.00

London Borough of Croydon Library and Archives Service
Central Library Katharine Street Croydon CR9 1ET T: (020) 8760-
5400-ext-1112 F: (020) 8253-1012 E:
localstudies@croydononline.org W: www.croydon.gov.uk/

London Borough of Sutton Archives Central Library St Nicholas
Way Sutton Surrey SM1 1EA T: (020) 8770-4747 F: (020) 8770-4777
E: local.studies@sutton.gov.uk W: www.sutton.gov.uk

North Tandridge Local History Centre Caterham Valley Library
Stafford Road Caterham Surrey CR3 6JG T: 01883 343580 F: 01883
330872 W: www.surrey.gov.uk

Redhill Centre for Local and Family History Redhill Library
Warwick Quadrant Redhill Surrey RH1 1NN T: 01737 763332 F:
01737 778020 W: www.surrey.gov.uk

Surrey History Service Surrey History Centre 130
Goldsworth Road Woking Surrey GU21 1ND T: 01483-594594 F:
01483-594595 E: shs@surreycc.gov.uk W: www.surrey.gov.uk

Southwark Local Studies Library see London

Surrey History Service Library Surrey History Centre 130
Goldsworth Road Woking Surrey GU21 1ND T: 01483-594594 F:
01483-594595 E: shs@surreycc.gov.uk W: www.surreycc.gov.uk 1901
census

East Sussex Record Offic see Sussex - East

South East Film and Video Archive University of Brighton Grand
Parade Brighton Sussex BN2 2JY T: 01273 643213 W:
www.bton.ac.uk/sefva

Sussex

Sussex - East Brighton History Centre Brighton Museum and Art
Gallery Royal Pavilion Gardens Brighton East Sussex BN1 1EE T:
01273 296972 (Enquiries) T: 01273 296971 (Bookings) T: 01273
296962 E: localhistory@brighton-hove.gov.uk W:
www.citylibraries.info/localhistory 1901 census

Sussex - West West Sussex Record Office County Hall Chichester
West Sussex PO19 1RN T: 01243-753600 F: 01243-533959 E:
records.office@westsussex.gov.uk W: www.westsussex.gov.uk/ro/
1901 census

Worthing Reference Library Worthing Library Richmond Road
Worthing West Sussex BN11 1HD T: 01903-212060 F: 01903-821902
E: worthing.reference.library@westsussex.gov.uk W:
www.westsussex.gov.uk Largest library in West Sussex and specialist
centre for family history sources.

Tyne and Wear

Local Studies Centre Central Library Northumberland Square North
Shields NE3O 1QU T: 0191-200-5424 F: 0191 200 6118 E:
eric.hollerton@northtyneside.gov.uk W:
www.northtyneside.gov.uk/libraries.html

South Tyneside Central Library Prince George Street South Shields
Tyne and Wear NE33 2PE T: 0191-427-1818-Ext-7860 F: 0191-455-
8085 E: reference.library@s-tyneside-mbc.gov.uk W: www.s-
tyneside-mbc.gov.uk 1901 census

Gateshead Central Library & Local Studies Department Prince
Consort Road Gateshead Tyne & Wear NE8 4LN T: 0191 477 3478 F:
0191 477 7454 E: a.lang@libarts.gatesheadmbc.gov.uk W:
http://ris.niaa.org.uk W: www.gateshead.gov.uk/ls 1901 census

Newcastle Local Studies Centre City Library Princess Square
Newcastle upon Tyne NE99 1DX T: 0191 277 4116 F: 0191 277 4118
E: local.studies@newcastle.gov.uk W: www.newcastle.gov.uk 1901
census

Northumberland County Record Office Melton Park North
Gosforth Newcastle upon Tyne NE3 5QX T: 0191-236-2680 F: 0191-
217-0905 E: archives@northumberland.gov.uk W:
www.swinnhopc.myby.co.uk/nro 1901 census

Tyne & Wear Archives Service Blandford House Blandford Square
Newcastle upon Tyne Tyne and Wear NE1 4JA T: 0191-232-6789 F:
0191-230-2614 E: twas@dial.pipex.com W:
www.thenortheast.com/archives/ 1901 census

Warwickshire

Coventry City Archives Mandela House Bayley Lane Coventry West
Midlands CV1 5RG T: (024) 7683 2418 F: (024) 7683 2121 E:
coventryarchives@discover.co.uk W: www.theherbest.com

Modern Records Centre University of Warwick Library Coventry
Warwickshire CV4 7AL T: (024) 76524219 F: (024) 7652 4211 E:
archives@warwick.ac.uk W: www.modernrecords.warwick.ac.uk

Rugby School Archives Temple Reading Room Rugby School Barby Road Rugby Warwickshire CV22 5DW T: 01788 556227 F: 01788 556228 E: dhrm@rugby-school.warwks.sch.uk W: www.rugby-school.warwks.sch.uk

Sutton Coldfield Library & Local Studies Centre 43 Lower Parade Sutton Coldfield Warwickshire B72 1XX T: 0121-354-2274 T: 0121 464 0164 F: 0121 464 0173 E: sutton.coldfield.reference.lib@birmingham.gov.uk W: www.birmingham.gov.uk

Warwick County Record Office Priory Park Cape Road Warwick Warwickshire CV34 4JS T: 01926 738959 F: 1926738969 E: recordoffice@warwickshire.gov.uk W: www.warwickshire.gov.uk

West Midlands

Birmingham City Archives Floor 7, Central Library Chamberlain Square Birmingham West Midlands B3 3HQ T: 0121-303-4217 F: 0121-464 1176 E: archives@birmingham.gov.uk W: www.birmingham.gov.uk/libraries/archives/home.htm 1901 census

Birmingham Roman Catholic Archdiocesan Archives Cathedral House St Chad's Queensway Birmingham West Midlands B4 6EU T: 0121-236-2251 F: 0121 233 9299 E: archives@rc-birmingham.org W: www.rc-birmingham.org

Birmingham University Information Services - Special Collections Main Library University of Birmingham Edgbaston Birmingham West Midlands B15 2TT T: 0121 414 5838 F: 0121 471 4691 E: special-collections@bham.ac.uk W: www.is.bham.ac.uk

Dudley Archives & Local History Service Mount Pleasant Street Coseley Dudley West Midlands WV14 9JR T: 01384-812770 F: 01384-812770 E: archives.pls@mbc.dudley.gov.uk W: www.dudley.gov.uk Family History Research Service (fee paying) available 1901 census

Sandwell Community History & Archives Service Smethwick Library High Street Smethwick West Midlands B66 1AB T: 0121 558 2561 F: 0121 555 6064

Solihull Heritage and Local Studies service Solihull Central Library Homer Road Solihull West Midlands B91 3RG T: 0121-704-6977 F: 0121-704-6212 E: info@solihull.gov.uk W: www.solihull.gov.uk/wwwlib/#local

Walsall Local History Centre Essex Street Walsall West Midlands WS2 7AS T: 01922-721305 F: 01922-634594 E: localhistorycentre@walsall.gov.uk W: www.walsall.gov.uk/culturalservices/library/welcome.htm 1901 census

Wolverhampton Archives & Local Studies 42 - 50 Snow Hill Wolverhampton West Midlands WV2 4AG T: 01902 552480 F: 01902 552481 E: wolverhamptonarchives@dial.pipes.com W: www.wolverhampton.gov.uk/archives 1901 census

Wiltshire

Images of England Project National Monuments Records Centre Kemble Drive Swindon Wiltshire SN2 2GZ T: 01793 414779 W: www.imagesofengland.org.uk

Salisbury Reference and Local Studies Library Market Place Salisbury Wiltshire SP1 1BL T: 01722 411098 F: 01722 413214 W: www.wiltshire.gov.uk

Wiltshire and Swindon Record Office Libraries HQ Bythesea Road Trowbridge Wiltshire BA14 8BS T: 01225 713709 F: 01225-713515 E: wrso@wiltshire.gov.uk W: www.wiltshire.gov.uk 1901 census

Wiltshire Buildings Record Libraries and Heritage HQ Bythesea Road Trowbridge Wiltshire BA14 8BS T: 01225 713740 E: dorothytreasure@wiltshire.gov.uk W: www.wiltshire.gov.uk

Wiltshire Studies Library Trowbridge Reference Library Bythesea Road Trowbridge Wiltshire BA14 8BS T: 01225-713732 T: 01225 713727 F: 01225-713715 E: libraryenquiries@wiltshire.gov.uk W: www.wiltshire.gov.uk

Worcestershire

MLA West Midlands: the Regional Council for Museums, Libraries and archives 2nd Floor, Grosvenor House 14 Bennetts Hill Worcestershire B2 5RS T: 01527 872258 F: 01527 576960

St Helens Record Office - Worcestershire St Helens Record Office Fish Street Worcester Worcestershire WR1 2HN T: 01905-765922 F: 01905-765925 E: recordoffice@worcestershire.gov.uk W: www.worcestershire.gov.uk/records

Worcesterhire Library & History Centre History Centre Trinity Street Worcester Worcestershire WR1 2PW T: 01905 765922 F: 01905 765925 E: wlhc@worcestershire.gov.uk W: www.worcestershire.gov.uk/records For Family History Researchers 1901 census

Worcestershire Regimental Archives RHQ The Worcestershire & Sherwood Foresters Regiment Norton Barracks Worcester Worcestershire WR5 2PA T: 01905-354359 01905-353871 E: rhq_wfr@lineone.net W: www.wfrmuseum.org.uk Records of the Regiment and predecessors from1694, some bibliographical details

Yorkshire

Borthwick Institute of Historical Research St Anthony's Hall Peasholme Green York YO1 7PW T: 01904-642315 W: www.york.ac.uk/inst/bihr W: www.york.ac.uk/borthwick Appointment necessary to use Archives. Research Service Available

Yorkshire Family History - Biographical Database York Minster Library & Archives Dean's Park York Yorkshire YO1 7JQ T: 01904-625308 Library T: 01904-611118 Archives F: 01904-611119 E: library@yorkminster.org archives@yorkminster.org W: www.yorkminster.org

Yorkshire - City of York

City of York Libraries - Local History & Reference Collection York Central Library Library Square Museum Street York YO1 7DS T: 01904-655631 F: 01904-611025 E: reference.library@york.gov.uk W: www.york.gov.uk

York City Archives Exhibition Square Bootham York YO1 7EW T: 01904-551878/9 F: 01904-551877 E: archives@york.gov.uk W: www.york.gov.uk

Yorkshire – East

East Yorkshire Archives Service County Hall Champney Road Beverley East Yorkshire HU17 9BA T: 01482 392790 F: 01482 392791 E: archives.service@eastriding.gov.uk W: www.eastriding.gov.uk/learning Correspondence to County Hall, Champney Road, Beverley, HU17 9BA . Reading Room at The Chapel, Lord Roberts Road, Beverley HU17 9BQ T: 01482 392790 F: 01482 392791 Appointments necessary

Hull Central Library Family and Local History Unit Central Library Albion Street Kingston upon Hull HU1 3TF T: 01482 616828 F: 01482 616827 E: gareth@ukorigins.co.uk W: www.hullcc.gov.uk/genealogy/famhist.php Free membership. Meets second Tuesday of every month 1901 census

Yorkshire – North

Catterick Garrison Library Gough Road Catterick Garrison North Yorkshire DL9 3EL T: 01748 833543 W: www.northyorks.gov.uk Extensive collection of over 1350 military history books available for reference or loan. Open Mon 10.am to 12, 1pm to 5.30pm; Wed 10am to 12, 1pm to 5pm; Fri 10am to 12 noon.

North Yorkshire County Record Office County Hall Northallerton North Yorkshire DL7 8AF T: 01609-777585 W: www.northyorks.gov.uk

Royal Dragoon Guards Military Museum (4th/7th Royal Dragoon Guards & 5th Royal Inniskilling Dragoon Guards) 3A Tower Street York North Yorkshire YO1 9SB T: 01904-662790 T: 01904 662310 F: 01904 662310 E: rdgmuseum@onetel.net.uk W: www.rdg.co.uk co located with Prince of Wales' Own Regiment of Yorkshire Military Museum (West & East Yorkshire Regiments)

Whitby Pictorial Archives Trust Whitby Archives & Heritage Centre 17/18 Grape Lane Whitby North Yorkshire YO22 4BA T: 01947-600170 F: 01947 821833 E: info@whitbyarchives.freeserve.co.uk W: www.whitbyarchives.freeserve.co.uk

Yorkshire Film Archive York St John College Lord Mayor's Walk York North Yorkshire YO31 7EX T: 01904 716550 F: 01904 716552 E: yfa@yorksj.ac.uk

Yorkshire – South

Archives & Local Studies Central Library Walker Place Rotherham South Yorkshire S65 1JH T: 01709-823616 F: 01709-823650 E: archives@rotherham.gov.uk W: www.rotherham.gov.uk 1901 census

Barnsley Archives and Local Studies Department Central Library Shambles Street Barnsley South Yorkshire S70 2JF T: 01226-773950 T: 01226-773938 F: 01226-773955 E: Archives@barnsley.gov.uk librarian@barnsley.gov.uk W: www.barnsley.gov.uk 1901 census

Central Library Surrey Street Sheffield South Yorkshire S1 1XZ T: 0114 273 4711 F: 0114 273 5009 E: sheffield.libraries@dial.pipex.com

Doncaster Archives King Edward Road Balby Doncaster DN4 0NA T: 01302-859811 E: doncasterarchives@hotmail.com W: www.doncaster.gov.uk Diocesan Record Office for the Archdeaconry of Doncaster (Diocese of Sheffield) 1901 census

Sheffield Archives 52 Shoreham Street Sheffield South Yorkshire S1 4SP T: 0114-203-9395 F: 0114-203-9398 E: sheffield.archives@dial.pipex.com W: www.sheffield.gov.uk/in-your-area/libraries/archives W: www.familia.org.uk/services/england/sheffield.html Please include a postal address when contactinmg by Email 1901 census

Yorkshire – West

Bradford Archives West Yorkshire Archive Service 15 Canal Road Bradford West Yorkshire BD1 4AT T: 01274-731931 F: 01274-734013 E: bradford@wyjs.org.uk W: www.archives.wyjs.org.uk

John Goodchild Collection Local History Study Centre Below Central Library Drury Lane Wakefield West Yorkshire WF1 2DT T: 01924-298929 Primarily concerned with regional history; many tens of 000s of index cards, many tons of MSS, maps, illustrations. SAE essential for reply. No photocopying; use by prior appointment. All services free of charge, including lectures and guided walks and advice. 50 years experience in the field; no genealogical research undertaken

Local Studies Library Leeds Central Library Calverley Street Leeds West Yorkshire LS1 3AB T: 0113 247 8290 F: 0113 247 4882 E: local.studies@leeds.gov.uk W: www.leeds.gov.uk/library/services/loc_reso.html
National Museum of Photography, Film & Television see National
Wakefield Library Headquarters - Local Studies Department Balne Lane Wakefield West Yorkshire WF2 0DQ T: 01924-302224 F: 01924-302245 E: wakehist@hotmail.com W: www.wakefield.gov.uk 1901 census
West Yorkshire Archive Service
Wakefield & Headquarters Registry of Deeds Newstead Road Wakefield West Yorkshire WF1 2DE T: 01924-305980 F: 01924-305983 E: wakefield@wyjs.org.uk W: www.archives.wyjs.org.uk This Office hold county-wide records of the West Riding and West Yorkshire and records of Wakefield Metropolitan District. Appointment always required.
Kirklees Central Library Princess Alexandra Walk Huddersfield West Yorkshire HD1 2SU T: 01484-221966 F: 01484-518361 E: kirklees@wyjs.org.uk W: www.archives.wyjs.org.uk Appointment always required
Bradford 15 Canal Road Bradford West Yorkshire BDI 4AT T: 01274-731931 F: 01274-734013 E: bradford@wyjs.org.uk W: www.archives.wyjs.org.uk Appointment always required
Calderdale Central Library Northgate House Northgate Halifax West Yorkshire HX1 1UN T: 01422-392816 F: 01422-341083 E: calderdale@wyjs.org.uk W: www.archives.wyjs.org.uk Appointment always required
Leeds Chapeltown Road Sheepscar Leeds West Yorkshire LS7 3AP T: 0113-214-5814 F: 0113-214-5815 E: leeds@wyjs.org.uk W: www.archives.wyjs.org.uk Also at Yorkshire Archeaological Society, Claremont, 23 Clarendon Road, Leeds LS2 9NZ (0113-245-6362; fax 0113-244-1979)
Yorkshire Archaeological Society Claremont 23 Clarendon Rd Leeds West Yorkshire LS2 9NZ T: 0113-245-6342 T: 0113 245 7910 F: 0113-244-1979 E: j.heron@sheffield.ac.uk (Society business) yas@wyjs.org.uk (Library and Archives) W: www.yas.org.uk Opening Hours: Tues,Wed 2.00 to 8.30pm; Thurs, Fri 10.00 to 5.30; Sat 9.30 to 5.00 Appointment necessary for use of archival material.

Wales
National Monuments Record of Wales Royal Commission on the Ancient & Historical Monuments of Wales Crown Building Plas Crug Aberystwyth Ceredigion SY23 1NJ T: 01970-621200 F: 01970-627701 E: nmr.wales@rcahmw.org.uk W: www.rcahmw.org.uk
National Library of Wales Penglais Aberystwyth Ceredigion SY23 3BU T: 01970 632800 T: 01970 632902 Marketing F: 01970 615709 E: holi@llgc.org.uk W: www.llgc.org.uk
Department of Manuscripts Main Library, University of Wales College Road Bangor Gwynedd LL57 2DG T: 01248-382966 F: 01248-382979 E: iss04@bangor.ac.uk
National Monuments Record of Wales Royal Commission - Ancient & Historical Monuments of Wales Crown Building Plas Crug Aberystwyth SY23 1NJ T: 01970 621200 F: 01970 627701 E: nmr.wales@rchamw.org.uk W: www.rchamw.org.uk
Department of Manuscripts Main Library, University of Wales College Road Bangor Gwynedd LL57 2DG T: 01248-382966 F: 01248-382979 E: iss04@bangor.ac.uk
National Monuments Record of Wales Royal Commission on the Ancient & Historical Monuments of Wales Crown Building Plas Crug Aberystwyth Ceredigion SY23 1NJ 01970-621200 F: 01970-627701 E: nmr.wales@rcahmw.org.uk W: www.rcahmw.org.uk
National Monuments Record of Wales Royal Commission - Ancient & Historical Monuments Wales Crown Building Plas Crug Aberystwyth SY23 1NJ T: 01970 621200 F: 01970 627701 E: nmr.wales@rchamw.org.uk W: www.rchamw.org.uk

Anglesey
Anglesey County Archives Service Shirehall Glanhwfa Road Llangefni Anglesey LL77 7TW T: 01248-752080 W: www.anglesey.gov.uk 1901 census
Carmarthenshire
Carmarthenshire Archive Service Parc Myrddin Richmond Terrace Carmarthen Carmarthenshire SA31 1DS T: 01267 228232 F: 01267 228237 E: archives@carmarthenshire.gov.uk W: www.carmarthenshire.gov.uk
Ceredigion
Archifdy Ceredigion, Ceredigion Archives Swyddfa'r Sir, County Offices Glan y Mor, Marine Terrace Aberystwyth Ceredigion SY23 2DE T: 01970-633697 F: 01970 633663 E: archives@ceredigion.gov.uk W: www.ceredigion.gov.uk 1901 census
National Library of Wales Penglais Aberystwyth Ceredigion SY23 3BU T: 01970 632800 T: 01970 632902 Marketing F: 01970 615709 E: holi@llgc.org.uk W: www.llgc.org.uk
National Screen and Sound Archive of Wales Unit 1 Science Park Aberystwyth Ceredigion SY23 3AH T: 01970 626007 E. http://screenandsound.llgc.org.uk

Conwy
Conwy Archive Service Old Board school Lloyd Street Llandudno Conwy LL30 2YG T: 01492 860882 F: 01492 860882 E: archifau.archives@conwy.gov.uk W: www.conwy.gov.uk/archives 1841-1901 census, parish records, non-parochial records, school records, rate books, maps, newspapers, photographs
Denbighshire
Denbighshire Record Office 46 Clwyd Street Ruthin Denbighshire LL15 1HP T: 01824-708250 F: 01824-708258 E: archives@denbighshire.go.uk W: www.denbighshire.gov.uk Extensive refurbishment until early Summer 2002 - telephone before visiting
Flintshire
Flintshire Record Office The Old Rectory Rectory Lane Hawarden Flintshire CH5 3NR T: 01244-532364 F: 01244-538344 E: archives@flintshire.gov.uk W: www.flintshire.gov.uk
Glamorgan
Glamorgan Record Office Glamorgan Building King Edward VII Avenue Cathays Park Cardiff CF10 3NE T: (029) 2078 0282 F: (029) 2078 0284 E: GlamRO@cardiff.ac.uk W: www.glamro.gov.uk 1901 census
Neath Central Library (Local Studies Department) 29 Victoria Gardens Neath Glamorgan SA11 3BA T: 01639-620139 W: www.neath-porttalbot.gov.uk
Swansea Reference Library Alexandra Road Swansea SA1 5DX T: 01792-516753 F: 01792 516759 E: central.library@swansea.gov.uk W: www.swansea.gov.uk Extensive holdings of trade directories, local census returns, newspapers (partially indexed) 1901 census
Gwent
Blaenavon Ironworks Blaenavon Tourist information Office North Street Blaenavon Gwent NP4 9RQ T: 01495 792615 W: www.btinternet.com~blaenavon.ironworks/pages/genealogy.htm
Gwent Record Office County Hall Croesyceiliog Cwmbran Gwent NP44 2XH T: 01633-644886 F: 01633-648382 E: gwent.records@torfaen.gov.uk W: www.llgc.org.uk/cac
Gwynedd
Archifdy Meirion Archives Swyddfeydd y Cyngor Cae Penarlag Dolgellau Gwynedd LL40 2YB T: 01341-424444 F: 01341-424505 E: EinionWynThomas@gwynedd.gov.uk W: www.gwynedd.gov.uk/archives/
Caernarfon Area Record Office, Gwynedd Archives Caernarfon Area Record Office Victoria Dock Caernarfon Gwynedd LL55 1SH T: 01286-679095 F: 01286-679637 E: archifau@gwynedd.gov.uk W: www.gwynedd.gov.uk/adrannau/addysg/archifau 1901 census
Pembrokeshire
Pembrokeshire Libraries The County Library Dew Street Haverfordwest Pembrokeshire SA61 1SU T: 01437 775248 F: 01437 769218 E: sandra.matthews@pembrokeshire.gov.uk W: www.pembrokeshire.gov.uk The Local Studies Library covers people, places and events relating to the County of Pembrokeshire past and present. The Library also houses the Francis Green Genealogical Collection consisting of over 800 pedigree sheets and 35 volumes of information relating to the prominent families of Pembraokeshire, Cardiganshire and Carmarthenshire.
Pembrokeshire Record Office The Castle Haverfordwest Pembrokeshire SA61 2EF T: 01437-763707 F: 01437 768539 E: record.office@pembrokeshire.gov.uk W: www.pembrokeshire.gov.uk
Tenby Museum Tenby Museum & Art Gallery Castle Hill Tenby Pembrokeshire SA70 7BP T: 01834-842809 F: 01834-842809 E: tenbymuseum@hotmail.com W: www.tenbymuseum.free-online.co.uk Archives & Museum Mainly Tenby Town & immediate area. Search fee £5
Powys
Powys County Archives Office County Hall Llandrindod Wells Powys LD1 5LG T: 01597 826088 F: 01597 826087 E: archives@powys.gov.uk W: http://archives.powys.gov.uk 1901 census
Newport
Newport Library & Information Service Newport Central Library John Frost Square Newport South Wales NP20 1PA T: 01633-211376 F: 01633-222615 E: reference.library@newport.gov.uk W: www.earl.org.uk/partners/newport/index.html The Local Studies Collection contains information on all aspects of Monmouthshire and or Gwent. A fee paying postal research service is available, which uses the library's own resources.
West Glamorgan
West Glamorgan Archive Service County Hall Oystermouth Road Swansea West Glamorgan SA1 3SN T: 01792-636589 F: 01792-637130 E: archives@swansea.gov.uk W: www.swansea.gov.uk/archives 1901 census
West Glamorgan Archive Service - Neath Archives Access Point Neath Mechanics Institute Church Place Neath Glamorgan SA11 3BA T: 01639-620139 W: www.swansea.gov.uk/archives 1901 census
West Glamorgan Archive Service - Port Talbot Access Point Port Talbot Library 1st Floor, Aberavon Shopping Centre Port Talbot West Glamorgan SA13 1PB T: 01639 763430 W: www.swansea.gov.uk/archives 1901 Census - West Glamorgan area

Wrexham
Wrexham Local Studies and Archives Service A N Palmer Centre for Local Studies and archives Wrexham Museum, County Buildings Regent Street Wrexham LL11 1RB T: 01978-317976 F: 01978-317982 E: archives@wrexham.gov.uk W: www.wrexham.gov.uk/heritage 1901 census E: localstudies@wrexham.gov.uk

Isle of Man
Civil Registry Registries Building Deemster's Walk Bucks Road Douglas Isle of Man IM1 3AR T: 01624-687039 F: 01624-687004 E: civil@registry.gov.im
Isle of Man Public Record Office Unit 3 Spring Valley Industrial Estate Braddan Douglas Isle of Man IM2 2QR T: 01624 613383 F: 01624 613384
Manx National Heritage Library Douglas Isle of Man IM1 3LY T: 01624 648000 F: 01624 648001 E: enquiries@mnh.gov.im W: www.mnh.gov.im 1901 census

Guernsey
Guernsey Island Archives 29 Victoria Road St Peter Port Guernsey GY1 1HU T: 01481 724512 F: 01481 715814
Jersey
Jersey Archives Service - Jersey Heritage Trust Clarence Road St Helier Jersey JE2 4JY T: 01534 833303 F: 01534 833301 Do not hold genealogical sources but do have 30,000 registration cards for the population of the island 1940 - 1945 during the German occupation. 1901 census
Judicial Greffe Morier House Halkett Place St Helier Jersey JE1 1DD T: 01534-502300 F: 01534-502399/502390 E: jgreffe@super.net.uk W: www.jersey.gov.uk

SCOTLAND
National
General Register Office for Scotland New Register House Edinburgh EH1 3YT T: 0131-334-0380 T: Certificate Order 0131 314 4411 F: 0131-314-4400 E: records@gro-scotland.gov.uk W: www.gro-scotland.gov.uk A fully searchable index of Scottish birth and marriage records from 1553 to 1901 and death records from 1855 to 1926 can be accessed on the internet at W: www.origins.net
Scottish Genealogy Society & Library 15 Victoria Terrace Edinburgh EH1 2JL T: 0131-220-3677 F: 0131-220-3677 E: info@scotsgenealogy.com W: www.scotsgenealogy.com
National Archives of Scotland HM General Register House 2 Princes Street Edinburgh EH1 3YY T: 0131 535 1334 F: 0131 535 1328 E: enquiries@nas.gov.uk W: www.nas.gov.uk The Scottish Record Office holds the National Archives of Scotland
National Monuments Record of Scotland Royal Commission on the Ancient & Historical Monuments of Scotland John Sinclair House 16 Bernard Terrace Edinburgh EH8 9NX T: 0131 662 1456 F: 0131 662 1477 or 0131 662 1499 E: nmrs@rcahms.gov.uk W: www.rcahms.gov.uk Website gives access to the searchable database of NMRS Records - 'CANMORE'
National Library of Scotland - Department of Manuscripts National Library of Scotland George IV Bridge Edinburgh EH1 1EW T: 0131 466 2812 F: 0131 466 2811 E: mss@nls.uk W: www.nls.uk The division will answer general enquiries but cannot undertake detailed genealogical research
National Archives of Scotland - West Search Room West Register House Charlotte Square Edinburgh EH2 4DJ T: 0131-535-1413 F: 0131-535-1411 E: wsr@nas.gov.uk W: www.nas.gov.uk All correspondence to: National Archives of Scotland, HM General Register House, Edinburgh EH1 3YY
National Register of Archives (Scotland) H M General Register House 2 Princes Street Edinburgh EH1 3YY T: 0131 535 1405/1428 T: 0131 535 1430 E: nra@nas.gov.uk W: www.nas.gov.uk The papers mentioned on the Register are not held by the NRA(S) but are deposited elsewhere or remain in private hands. While the NRA staff are always happy to answer limited and specific POSTAL enquiries about the existence of papers relating to a particular individual or subject, they are unable to undertake research on belahf of enquirers. Once they have advised on possible sources it is then up to enquiriers either to carry out the research themselves or to engage a record agent to do so on their behalf. Where papers remain in private hands written applications for access should be made in the first instance to the NRA(S)
Glasgow University Library & Special Collections Department see Glasgow
Glasgow University Archive Services 13 Thurso Street Glasgow G11 6PE T: 0141 330 5515 F: 0141 330 4158 E: archives@archives.gla.ac.uk W: www.archives.gla.ac.uk
Scottish Brewing Archive 13 Thurso Street Glasgow G11 6PE T: 0141 330 2640 F: 0141 330 4158 E: sba@archives.gla.ac.uk W: www.archives.gla.ac.uk/sba/
Heriot-Watt University Archives see Edinburgh
St Andrews University Library - Special Collections Department see Fife
Strathclyde University Archives McCance Building 16 Richmond Street Glasgow G1 1XQ T: 0141 548 2397 F: 0141 552 0775

Aberdeen
Aberdeen City Archives Aberdeen City Council Town House Broad Street Aberdeen AB10 1AQ T: 01224-522513 F: 01224 638556 E: archives@legal.aberdeen.net.uk W: www.aberdeencity.gov.uk also covers Aberdeenshire
Aberdeen City Archives - Old Aberdeen House Branch Old Aberdeen House Dunbar Street Aberdeen AB24 1UE T: 01224-481775 F: 01224-495830 E: archives@legal.aberdeen.net.uk W: www.aberdeencity.gov.uk
Angus
Angus Archives Montrose Library 214 High Street Montrose Angus DD10 8PH T: 01674-671415 F: 01674-671810 E: angus.archives@angus.govuk W: www.angus.gov.uk/history/history.htm Family history research service. Archive holdings for Angus County, Arbroath, Brechin, Carnoustie, Forfar, Montrose, Monifieth, Kittiemuir.
Argyll
Argyll & Bute District Archives Manse Brae Lochgilphead Argyll PA31 8QU T: 01546 604120
Ayrshire
Ayrshire Archives Centre Craigie Estate Ayr Ayrshire KA8 0SS T: 01292-287584 F: 01292-284918 E: archives@south-ayshire.gov.uk W: www.south-ayrshire.gov.uk/archives/index.htm includes North Ayrshire, East Ayrshire and South Ayrshire.
East Ayrshire Council District History Centre & Museum Baird Institute 3 Lugar Street Cumnock Ayrshire KA18 1AD T: 01290-421701 F: 01290-421701 E: Baird.institute@east-ayrshire.gov.uk W: www.east-ayrshire.gov.uk
North Ayrshire Libraries Library Headquarters 39 - 41 Princes Street Ardrossan Ayrshire KA22 8BT T: 01294-469137 F: 01924-604236 E: reference@naclibhq.prestel.co.uk W: www.north-ayrshire.gov.uk
Clackmannanshire
Clackmannanshire Archives Alloa Library 26/28 Drysdale Street Alloa Clackmannanshire FK10 1JL T: 01259-722262 F: 01259-219469 E: libraries@clacks.gov.uk W: www.clacksweb.org.uk/dyna/archives
Dumfries & Galloway
Dumfries & Galloway Library and Archives Archive Centre 33 Burns Street Dumfries DG1 1PS T: 01387 269254 F: 01387 264126 E: libsxi@dumgal.gov.uk W: www.dumgal.gov.uk Open : Tues, Wed, Fri, 11am to 1pm, 2pm to 5pm and on Thurs 6pm to 9pm. Please book. Postal and consultation genealogical service available. Details on application.
Ewart Library Ewart Library Catherine Street Dumfries DG1 1JB T: 01387 260285 T: 01387-252070 F: 01387-260294 E: ruth_airley@dumgal.gov.uk W: www.dumgal.gov.ukf Fee paid research service availble
Dundee
Dundee City Archives 21 City Square (callers use 1 Shore Terrace) Dundee DD1 3BY T: 01382-434494 F: 01382-434666 E: archives@dundeecity.gov.uk W: www.dundeecity.gov.uk/archives.html
Dundee City Council - Genealogy Unit 89 Commercial Street Dundee DD1 2AF T: 01382-435222 F: 01382-435224 E: grant.law@dundeecity.gov.uk W: www.dundeecity.gov.uk/registrars
East Dunbartonshire
East Dunbartonshire Local Record Offices and Reference Libraries William Patrick Library 2 West High Street Kirkintilloch East Dunbartonshire G66 1AD T: 0141-776-8090 F: 0141-776-0408 E: libraries@eastdunbarton.gov.uk W: www.eastdunbarton.gov.uk
East Renfrewshire
East Renfrewshire Record Offices East Renfrewshire District Council Rouken Glen Road Glasgow East Renfrewshire G46 6JF T: 0141-577-4976
Edinburgh
Edinburgh City Archives City Chambers High St Edinburgh EH1 1YJ T: 0131-529-4616 F: 0131-529-4957
Heriot-Watt University Archives Coporate Communications Heriot-Watt university Edinburgh EH14 4AS T: 0131 451 3218 T: 0131 451 3219 & 0131 451 4140 F: 0131 451 3164 E: a.e.jones@hw.ac.uk W: www.hw.ac.uk/archive
Scottish Archive Network Thomas Thomson House 99 Bankhead Crossway North Edinburgh EH11 4DX T: 0131 242 5800 F: 0131 242 5801 E: enquiries@scan.org.uk W: www.scan.org.uk A lottery funded project to open up access to Scotland's archives. Providing access to scottish wills and many other genealogicalsources in scotland
Falkirk
Falkirk Library Hope Street Falkirk FK1 5AU T: 01324 503605 F: 01324 503606 E: falkirk-library@falkirk-library.demon.co.uk W: www.falkirk.gov.uk Holds Local Studies Collection
Falkirk Museum History Research Centre Callendar House Callendar Park Falkirk FK1 1YR T: 01324 503778 F: 01324 503771 E: callandarhouse@falkirkmuseums.demon.co.uk W: www.falkirkmuseums.demon.co.uk Records held: Local Authority, business, personal and estate records, local organmisations, trade unions, over 28,000 photographs Falkirk District

Fife
Fife Council Archive Centre Carleton House, Haig Business Park Balgonie Road Markinch Glenrothes Fife KY6 6AQ T: 01592 416504 E: andrew.dowsey@fife.gov.uk W: www.fifedirect.org.uk Open Mon to fri 9.00.a.m. to 5.00.p.m. by appointment
St Andrews University Library - Special Collections Department North Street St Andrews Fife KY16 9TR T: 01334 462339 F: 01334 462282 E: speccoll@st-and.ac.uk http://specialcollections.st-and.ac.uk
Glasgow
Scottish Screen Archive Scottish Screen 1 Bowmont Gardens Glasgow G12 9LR T: 0141 337 7400 W: www.scottishscreen.com
Glasgow City Archives Mitchell Library North Street Glasgow G3 7DN T: 0141-287-2913 F: 0141-226-8452 E: archives@cls.glasgow.gov.uk http://users.colloquium.co.uk/~glw_archives/src001.htm
Glasgow University Archive Services 13 Thurso Street Glasgow G11 6PE T: 0141 330 5515 F: 0141 330 4158 E: archives@archives.gla.ac.uk W: www.archives.gla.ac.uk
Glasgow University Library & Special Collections Department Hillhead Street Glasgow G12 8QE T: 0141 330 6767 F: 0141 330 3793 E: library@lib.gla.ac.uk W: www.gla.ac.uk/library
Royal College of Physicians and Surgeons of Glasgow 232 - 242 St Vincent Street Glasgow G2 5RJ T: 0141 221 6072 F: 0141 221 1804 E: library@rcpsglasg.ac.uk W: www.rcpsglasg.ac.uk
Strathclyde University Archives McCance Building 16 Richmond Street Glasgow G1 1XQ T: 0141 548 2397 F: 0141 552 0775
Highland
North Highland Archive Wick Library Sinclair Terrace Wick KW1 5AB T: 01955 606432 F: 01955 603000
Invernesshire
Highland Council Genealogy Centre Inverness Public Library Farraline Park Inverness IV1 1NH T: 01463-236463 : T: 01463 220193 ext 9 F: 01463 711128 E: genealogy@highland.gov.uk W: www.highland.gov.uk/publicservices/genealogy.htm
Isle of Lewis
Stornoway Record Office Town Hall 2 CromwellStreet Stornoway Isle of Lewis HS1 2BD T: 01851-709438 F: 01851 709438 E: emacdonald@cne-siar.gov.uk
Lanarkshire
South Lanarkshire Council Archives 30 Hawbank Road College Milton East Kilbride South Lanarkshire G74 5EX T: 01355 239193 F: 01355 242365
Midlothian
Midlothian Archives and Local Studies Centre 2 Clerk Street Loanhead Midlothian EH20 9DR T: 0131 271 3976 F: 0131 440 4635 E: local.studies@midlothian.gov.uk W: www.midlothian.gov.uk
Moray
Moray Local Heritage Centre Grant Lodge Cooper Park Elgin Moray IV30 1HS T: 01343 562644 T: 01343 562645 F: 01343-549050 E: graeme.wilson@techleis.moray.gov.uk W: www.morray.org/heritage/roots.html The Moray District Record Office has now been combined with the Local studies section at Grant Lodge, Cooper Park, Elgin to form the Local Heritage Centre.
North Lanarkshire
North Lanarkshire - Lenziemill Archives 10 Kelvin Road Cumbernauld North Lanarkshire G67 2BA T: 01236 737114 F: 01236 781762 W: www.northlan.gov.uk
Orkney
Orkney Archives The Orkney Library Laing Street Kirkwall Orkney KW15 1NW T: 01856-873166 F: 01856-875260 E: alison.fraser@orkney.gov.uk W: www.orkney.gov.uk Open Mon to Fri 9am to 1pm & 2pm to 4.45pm. Appointments preferred
Orkney Library The Orkney Library Laing Street Kirkwall Orkney KW15 1NW T: 01856-873166 F: 01856-875260 E: karen.walker@orkney.gov.uk W: www.orkney.gov.uk
Perthshire
Dunkeld Cathedral Chapter House Museum Dunkeld PH8 0AW T: 01350 728732 T: 01350 728971 W: www.dunkeldcathedral.org.uk contains Scottish Horse Regimental Archives
Perth and Kinross Council Archives A K Bell Library 2 - 8 York Place Perth Perthshire PH2 8EP T: 01738-477012 T: 01738 477022 F: 01738-477010 E: archives@pkc.gov.uk W: www.pkc.gov.uk/library/archive.htm
Scottish Horse Regimental Archives - Dunkeld Cathedral Dunkeld PH8 0AW T: 01350 727614 F: 01350 727614 Scottish Horse Regimental Museum closed 1999 - archives now held in Dunkeld Cathedral Chapter House Museum. View by prior appointment
Regimental Museum and Archives of Black Watch Balhousie Castle Hay Street Perth Perthshire PH1 5HR T: 0131 310 8530 F: 01738-643245 E: archives@theblackwatch.co.uk W: www.theblackwatch.co.uk
Renfrewshire
Renfrewshire Archives Central Library & Museum Complex High Street Paisley Renfrewshire PA1 2BB T: 0141-889 3350 F. 0141-887-6468 E. local_studies.library@renfrewshire.gov.uk W: www.renfrewshire.gov.uk

Scottish Borders
Scottish Borders Archive & Local History Centre Library Headquarters St Mary's Mill Selkirk Scottish Borders TD7 5EW T: 01750 20842 T: 01750 724903 F: 01750 22875 E: archives@scotborders.gov.uk W: www.scotborders.gov.uk/libraries
Shetland
Shetland Archives 44 King Harald St Lerwick Shetland ZE1 0EQ T: 01595-696247 F: 01595-696533 E: shetland.archives@zetnet.co.uk
Unst Heritage Centre Haroldswick Unst Shetland ZE2 9ED T: 01957 711528 T: 01957 711387 (Home)
Stirlingshire
Stirling Council Archives Unit 6 Burghmuir Industrial Estate Stirling FK7 7PY T: 01786-450745 F: 01786 473713 E: archive@stirling.gov.uk W: www.stirling.gov.uk Main holdings are local authority records, local church records, Justice of the Peace records, Customs and Excise and over 100 privately deposited records.
Strathclyde
Registrar of Births, Deaths and Marriages - Glasgow The Register Office 22 Park Circus Glasgow G3 6BE T: 0141 287 8350 F: 0141 287 8357 E: bill.craig@pas.glasgow.gov.uk
Tayside
Dundee University Archives Tower Building University of Dundee Dundee DD1 4HN T: 01382-344095 F: 01382 345523 E: archives@dundee.ac.uk W: www.dundee.ac.uk/archives/
West Lothian
West Lothian Council Archives - Archives & Records Management 7 Rutherford Square Brucefield Industrial Estate Livingston West Lothian EH54 9BU T: 01506 460 020 F: 01506 416 167

NORTHERN IRELAND
Belfast Family History & Cultural Heritage Centre 64 Wellington Place Belfast BT1 6GE T: (028) 9023 5392 F: (028) 9023 9885
General Register Office of Northern Ireland Oxford House 49 - 55 Chichester Street Belfast BT1 4HL T: (028) 90 252000 F: (028) 90 252120 E: gro.nisra@dfpni.gov.uk W: www.groni.gov.uk
Belfast Local Central Library Irish & Local Studies Dept Royal Avenue Belfast BT1 1EA T: (028) 9024 3233 F: (028) 9033 2819 E: info@libraries.belfast-elb.gov.uk W: www.belb.org.uk
Derry City Council Heritage & Museum Service Harbour Museum Harbour Square Derry Co Londonderry BT48 6AF T: (028) 7137 7331 F: (028) 7137 7633 The archives of Derry City Council are an invaluable source of information for the history of both the City and the Council from the early seventeeth century to the present day.
Banbridge Genealogy Services Gateway Tourist Information Centre 200 Newry Road Banbridge County Down BT32 3NB T: 028 4062 6369 F: 028 4062 3114 E: banbridge@nitic.net
Northern Ireland Film Commission 21 Ormeau Avenue Belfast BT2 8HD T: W: www.nifc.co.uk
Presbyterian Historical Society of Ireland Church House Fisherwick Place Belfast BT1 6DW T: (028) 9032 2284 Opening hours: Mon to Fri 10am to 12.30pm. Wed afternoons 1.30pm to 3.30pm
Public Record Office of Northern Ireland 66 Balmoral Avenue Belfast BT9 6NY T: (028) 9025 5905 F: (028) 9025 5999 E: proni@dcalni.gov.uk W: www.proni.nics.gov.uk Recent publications

IRELAND
Church of Ireland Archives see Church Records
Genealogical Office / Office of The Chief Herald Kildare Street Dublin 2 Co Dublin T: +353-1-6030 200 F: +353-1-6621 062 E: herald@nli.ie W: www.nli.ie
Grand Lodge of Ireland see Masonic
National Archives Bishop Street Dublin 8 T: 01-407-2300 F: 01-407-2333 E: mail@nationalarchives.ie W: www..nationalarchives.ie
Registrar General for Ireland Joyce House 8 - 11 Lombard Street East Dublin 2 T: Dublin-711000
Presbyterian Historical Society of Ireland see Church Records
County Donegal
Donegal Local Studies Centre Central Library & Arts Centre Oliver Plunkett Road Letterkenny County Donegal T: 00353 74 24950 F: 00353 74 24950 E: dgcolib@iol.ie W: www.donegal.ie/library
Donegal Ancestry Old Meeting House Back Lane Ramleton Letterkenny County Donegal T: 00353 74 51266 F: 00353 74 51702 E: donances@indigo.ie W: www.indigo.ie/~donances
Donegal County Council Archive Centre 3 Rivers Centre Lifford County Donegal T: + 00353 74 72490 F: + 00353 74 41367 E: nbrennan@donegalcoco.ie W: www.donegal.ie
Dublin
Dublin City Archives City Assembly House 58 South William Street Dublin 2 T: (01)-677-5877 F: (01)-677-5954
County Clare
Clare County Archives Clare County Council New Road Ennis Co Clare T: 065-28525 T: 065 21616 W: www.clare.ie
County Dublin
Dublin Heritage Group Ballyfermot Library Ballyfermot Road Ballyfermot Dublin 10 T: 6269324 F: E: dhgeneal@iol.ie

County Limerick Limerick City Library Local History Collection The Granary Michael Street Limerick T: +353 (0)61-314668 T: +353 (0)61-415799E: noneill@citylib.limerickcorp.ie W: www.limerickcorp.ie/librarymain.htm
Limerick Regional Archives Limerick Ancestry, The Granary Michael Street Limerick T: 061-415125 F: 061-312985 W: www.mayo-ireland.ie
County Mayo
Local Record Offices The Registration Office New Antrim Street Castlebar Co Mayo T: 094-23249 094 23249
County Waterford
Waterford Archives and Local Records St Joseph's Hospital Dungarvan Co Waterford T: 058-42199

AUSTRALIA
National Archives of Australia - Canberra PO Box 7425, Canberra Mail Centre, Canberra, ACT, 2610 T: 02-6212-3600 E: archives@naa.gov.au W: www.naa.gov.au
National Archives of Australia - Hobart 4 Rosny Hill Road, Rosny Park, Tasmania, 7018 T: 03-62-440101 F: 03-62-446834 E: reftas@naa.gov.auWWW: www.naa.gov.au
National Archives of Australia - Northern Territories Kelsey Crescent, Nightcliffe, NT, 810 T: 08-8948-4577
National Archives of Australia - Queensland 996 Wynnum Road, Cannon Hill, Queensland, 4170 T: 07-3249-4226 F: 07-3399-6589WWW: www.naa.gov.au
National Archives of Australia - South Australia 11 Derlanger Avenue, Collingwood, South Australia, 5081 T: 08-269-0100
National Archives of Australia - Sydney 120 Miller Road, Chester Hill, Sydney, New South Wales, 2162 T: 02-96450-100 F: 02-96450-108 E: refnsw@naa.gov.auWWW: www.naa.gov.uk
National Archives of Australia - Victoria PO Box 8005, Burwood Heights, Victoria, 3151 T: 03-9285-7900
National Archives of Australia - Western Australia 384 Berwick Street East, Victoria Park, Western Australia, 6101 T: 09-470-7500 F: 09-470-2787,
New South Wales - State Archives Office 2 Globe Street, Sydney, New South Wales, 2000 T: 02-9237-0254
Queensland State Archives PO Box 1397, Sunnybanks Hills, Brisbane, Queensland, 4109 T: 61-7-3875-8755 F: 61-7-3875-8764 E: qsa@ipd.pwh.qld.gov.auWWW: www.archives.qld.gov.au
South Australia State Archives PO Box 1056, Blair Athol West, South Australia, 5084 T: 08-8226-8000 F: 08-8226-8002,
Tasmania State Archives Archives Office of Tasmania, 77 Murray Street, Hobart, Tasmania, 7000 T: (03)-6233-7488 E: archives.tasmania@central.tased.edu.au W: www.tased.edu.au/archives
Victoria State Archives - Ballarat State Offices, Corner of Mair & Doveton Streets, Ballarat, Victoria, 3350 T: 03-5333-6611 F: 03-5333-6609,
Victoria State Archives - Laverton North 57 Cherry Lane, Laverton North, Victoria, 3028 T: 03-9360-9665 F: 03-9360-9685,
Victoria State Archives - Melbourne Level 2 Casselden Place, 2 Lonsdale Street, Melbourne, Victoria, 3000 T: 03-9285-7999 F: 03-9285-7953,
Western Australia - State Archives & Public Records Office Alexander Library, Perth Cultural Centre, Perth, Western Australia, 6000 T: 09-427-3360 F: 09-427-3256,

NEW ZEALAND
National Archives of New Zealand PO Box 10-050, 10 Mulgrave Street, Thorndon, Wellington, New Zealand T: 04-499-5595 E: national.archives@dia.govt.nz W: www.archives.dia.govt.nz

AFRICA
South Africa
Cape Town Archives Repository Private Bag X9025, Cape Town, 8000, South Africa T: 021-462-4050 F: 021-465-2960,
Dutch Reformed Church Archive PO Box 398, Bloemfontein, 9301, South Africa T: 051-448-9546,
Dutch Reformed Church Archive of O.F.S P O Box 398, Bloemfontein, 9301, RSA T: 051 448 9546,
Dutch Reformed Church Records Office PO Box 649, Pietermaritzburg, 3200 T: 0331-452279 F: 0331-452279,
Dutch Reformed Church Synod Records Office of Kwa Zulu-Natal P O Box 649, Pietermaritzburg , 3200, RSA T: 0331 452279 F: 0331 452279 E: ngntlargrief@alpha.futurenet.co.za,
Free State Archives Private Bag X20504, Bloemfontein, Free State, 9300, South Africa T: 051-522-6762 F: 051-522-6765
Free State Archives Repository Private Bag X20504, Bloemfontein, 9300, South Africa T: 051 522 6762 F: 051 522 6765,
National Archives - Pretoria Private Bag X236, Pretoria, 1, South Africa T: 323 5300
South Africa National Archives Private Bag X236, Pretoria, 1
South African Library - National Reference & Preservation P O Box 496, Cape Town, 8000, South Africa T: 021 246320 F: 021 244848 E: postmaster@salib.ac.za

NAMIBIA
National Archives of Namibia Private Bag, Windhoek, 13250, Namibia T: 061 293 4386 E: Renate@natarch.mec.gov.na W:

www.witbooi.natarch.mec.gov.na

ZIMBABWE
National Archives of Zimbabwe "Hiller Road, off Borrowdale Road", Gunhill, Harare, Zimbabwe T: 792741/3 F: 792398

EUROPE
BELGIUM
Archives de l'Etat a Liege 79 rue du Chera, Liege, B-4000, Belgium T: 04-252-0393 F: 04-229-3350 E: archives.liege@skynet.be
De Kerk van Jezus Christus van den Heiligen
Der Laaste Dagen, Kortrijkse Steenweg 1060, Sint-Deniss-Westrem, B-9051, Belgium T: 09-220-4316
Provinciebestuur Limburg Universititslaan 1, Afdeling 623 Archief, Hasselt, B-3500, Belgium
Rijks Archief te Brugge Academiestraat 14, Brugge, 8000, Belgium T: 050-33-7288 F: 050-33-7288 E: rijksarchief.brugge@skynet.be
Rijksarchief Kruibekesteenweg 39/1, Beveren, B-9210, Belgium T: 03-775-3839
Service de Centralisation des Etudes Genealogique et Demographiques Belgique Chaussee de Haecht 147, Brussels, B-1030, Belgium T: 02-374-1492
Staatsarchiv in Eupen Kaperberg 2-4, Eupen, B-4700, Belgium T: 087-55-4377
Stadsarchief te Veurne Grote Markt 29, Veurne, B-8630, Belgium T: 058-31-4115 F: 058-31-4554

CYPRUS
Cyprus Center of Medievalism & Heraldry P O Box 80711, Piraeus, 185 10, Greece T: 42-26-356

DENMARK
Association of Local History Archives P O Box 235, Enghavevej 2, Vejle, DK-7100, Denmark F: 45-7583-1801 W: www.lokalarkiver.dk
Cadastral Archives Rentemestervej 8, Copenhagen NV, DK-2400, Denmark F: 45-3587-5064 W: www.kms.min.dk
Danish Data Archive Islandsgade 10, Odense C, DK-5000, Denmark Fax: 45-6611-3060, W: www.dda.dk
Danish Emigration Archives P O Box 1731, Arkivstraede 1, Aalborg, DK-9100, Denmark T: 045 9931 4221 F: 45 9810 2248 E: bfl-kultur@aalbkom.dk W: www.cybercity.dk/users/ccc13656
Danish National Archives Rigsdagsgaarden 9, Copenhagen, DK-1218 T: 45-3392-3310 F: 45-3315-3239 W: www.sa.dk/ra/uk/uk.htm
Det Kongelige Bibliotek POB 2149, Copenhagen K, DK-1016 T: 045-3393-0111 F: 045-3393-2218
Frederiksberg Municipal Libraries Solbjergvej 21-25, Frederiksberg, DK-2000, Denmark T: 45-3833-3677, Web: www.fkb.dk
Kobenhavns Stadsarkiv Kobenhavns Radhus, Kobenhavn, DK01599, Denmark T: 3366-2374 F: 3366-7039
National Business Archives Vester Alle 12, Aarhus C, DK-8000, Denmark T: 45-8612-8533 E: mailbox@ea.sa.dk W: www.sa.dk/ea/engelsk.htm
Provincial Archives for Funen
Jernbanegade 36, Odense C, DK-5000, Denmark T: 6612-5885 F: 45-6614-7071 W: www.sa.dk/lao/default.htm
Provincial Archives for Nth Jutland Lille Sct. Hansgade 5, Viborg, DK-8800, Denmar T: 45-8662-1788 W: www.sa.dk/lav/default.htm
Provincial Archives for Southern Jutland Haderslevvej 45, Aabenraa, DK-6200, Denmark
Tel: 45-7462-5858 W: www.sa.dk/laa/default.htm
Provincial Archives for Zealand etc Jagtvej 10, Copenhagen, DK-2200, Denmark F: 45-3539-0535 W: www.sa.dk/lak.htm
Royal Library Christains Brygge 8, Copenhagen K, DK-1219, Denmark F: 45-3393-2219 W: www.kb.dk
State Library Universitetsparken, Aarhus C, DK-8000, Denmark Tel: 45-8946-2022 F: 45-8946-2130 W: www.sb.aau.dk/english

FINLAND
Institute of Migration Piispankatu 3, Turku, 20500Tel: 2-231-7536 Fax: 2-233-3460 E: jouni.kurkiasaaz@utu.fi
W: www.utu.fi/erill/instmigr/

FRANCE
Centre d'Accueil et de Recherche des Archives Nationales 60 rue des Francs Bourgeois, Paris Cedex, 75141, France T: 1-40-27-6000 F: 1-40-27-6628
Centre des Archives d'Outre-Mer 29 Chemin du Moulin de Testas, Aix-en-Provence, 13090
Service Historique de la Marine Chateau de Vincennes, Vincennes Cedex, 94304, France
Service Historique de l'Armee de l'Air Chateau de Vincennes, Vincennes Cedex, 94304, France
Service Historique de l'Armee de Terre BP 107, Armees, 481, France
Military (Army), Service Historique de L'Armee De Terre, Fort de Vincennes, Boite Postale 107 T: 01 4193 34 44 F: 01 41 93 38 90
Military (Navy), Service Historique De La Marine, Chateau de Vincennes, Boite Postale 2 T: 01 43 28 81 50 F: 01 43 28 31 60 E: shistorique@cedocar.fr

GERMANY

German Emigration Museum Inselstrasse 6, Bremerhaven, D-2850 T: 0471-49096

Historic Emigration Office Steinstr. 7, Hamburg, (D) 20095, Germany T: 4940-30- 51-282 F: 4940-300-51-220 E: ESROKAHEA@aol.com W: users.cybercity.dk/gccc13652/addr/ger_heo.htm

Research Centre Lower Saxons in the USA Postfach 2503, Oldenburg, D-2900, Germany T: 0441 798 2614 F: 0441-970-6180
Email: holtmann@hrzl.uni-oldenburg.de
W: www.uni-oldenburg.de/nausa

Zentralstelle fur Personen und Familiengeschichte Birkenweg 13, Friedrichsdorf, D-61381 T: 06172-78263 W: www.genealogy.com/gene/genealogy.html

GREECE

Cyprus Center of Medievalism & Heraldry P O Box 80711, Piraeus, 185 10, Greece T: 42-26-356

LIECHTENSTEIN

Major Archives Record Offices & Libraries Liechtenstein W: www.genealogy.com/gene/reg/CH/lichts.html

NETHERLANDS

Amsterdam Municipal Archives P O 51140, Amsterdam, 1007 EC
Brabant-Collectie Tilburg University Library, P O Box 90153, Warandelaan, Tilburg, NL-5000 LE, Netherlands T: 0031-134-662127
Gemeentelijke Archiefdienst Amersfoort P O Box 4000, Amersfoort, 3800 EA T: 033-4695017 F: 033-4695451
Het Utrechts Archief Alexander Numankade 199/201, Utrecht, 3572 KW, T: 030-286-6611 F: 030-286-6600 E: Utrecht@acl.archivel.nl
Rijksarchief in Drenthe P O Box 595, Assen, 9400 AN, Netherlands T: 0031-592-313523 F: 0031-592-314697 E: RADR@noord.bart.nl
W: obd-server.obd.nl/instel/enderarch/radz.htm
Rijksarchief in Overijssel Eikenstraat 20, Zwolle, 8021 WX, Netherlands T: 038-454-0722 F: 038-454-4506 E: RAO@euronet.nl W: www.obd.nl/instel/arch/rkarch.htm
Zealand Documentation CTR
P O Box 8004, Middelburg, 4330 EA, Netherlands

NORWAY

Norwegian Emigration Centre
Strandkaien 31, Stavanger, 4005, Norway T: 47-51-53-88-63
Email: detnu@telepost.no W: www.emigrationcenter.com

POLAND

Head Office Polish State Archives
Ul Dluga6 Skr, Poczt, Warsaw, 1005-00-950 F: 0-22-831-9222

RUSSIA

Moscow
Russian State Military Historical Archive 2, Baumanskaya 3, 107864, Moscow T: 7 (095) 261-20-70
St Petersburg
Russian State Historical Archive (RGIA), Naberejnaya 4 (English Embankment), 1900000 St Petersburg T: 7 (812) 315-54-35 , T: 7 (812) 311-09-26 F: 7 (812) 311-22-52

SPAIN

Archivo Historico National Serrano 115, Madrid, 28006 T: 261-8003-2618004
Instituucion Fernando el Catolico Plaza de Espagna 2, Zaragoza, 50071, Espagn T: 09-7628-8878 E: ifc@isendanet.es.mail

SWEDEN

Harnosand Provincial Archive Box 161, Harnosand, S-871 24, Sweden T: 611-835-00 E: landsarkivet@landsarkivet-harnosand.ra.se W: www.ra.se/hla
Goteborg Provincial Archive Box 19035, Goteborg, S-400 12, Sweden T: 31-778-6800
House of Emigrants Box 201, Vaxjo, S-351 04, Sweden T: 470-201-20 E: info@svenskaemigrantinstitulet.g.se
Kinship Centre Box 331, Karlstad, S-651 08, Sweden T: 54-107720
Lund Provincial Archive Arkivagen 1, Lund, S-220 02 T: 046-197000 F: 046-197070 E: landsarkivet@landsarkivet-lund.ra.se
Orebro Stadsarkiv Box 300, Orebro, S-701 35 T: 19-211075 F: 19-211050
Ostersund Provincial Archive Arkivvagen 1, Ostersund, S-831 31, Sweden T: 63-10-84-85 E: landsarkivet@landsarkivet-ostersund.ra.se W: www.ra.se/ola/
Stockholm City & Provincial Archives Box 22063, Stockholm, S-104 22 T: 8-508-283-00 F: 8-508-283-01
Swedish Military Archives Banergatan 64, Stockholm, S-115 88 T: 8-782-41-00
Swedish National Archives Box 12541, Stockholm, S-102 29, Sweden T: 8-737-63-50
Uppsala Provincial Archive Box 135, Uppsala, SE-751 04, Sweden T: 18-65-21-00
Vadstena Provincial Archive Box 126, Vadstena, 0-592 23, Sweden T: 143-130-30
Visby Provincial Archive Visborgsgatan 1, Visby, 621 57, Sweden T: 498-2129-55

SWITZERLAND

Achives de la Ville de Geneve Palais Eynard, 4 rue de la Croix-Rouge, Geneve 3, 1211 T: 22-418-2990 E: didier.grange@seg.ville-ge.ch
Archives Canonales Vaudoises rue de la Mouline 32, Chavannes-pres-Renens, CH 1022, Switzerland T: 021-316-37-11 F: 021-316-37-55
Archives de l'Ancien Eveche de Bale
10 rue des Annonciades, Porrentruy, CH-2900, Suisse
Geneva
Archives d'Etat, 1 Rue de l'Hotel de Ville, Case Postale 164, Geneve 3 T: 41 21 319 33 95 F: 41 21 319 33 65
Lausanne
Archives De La Ville De Lausanne, Rue de Maupas 47, Case Postale CH-1000 Lausanne 9 T: 41 21 624 43 55 F: 41 21 624 06 01
Staatsarchiv Appenzell Ausserhoden Obstmarkt, Regierungsgebaede, Herisau, CH-9100, T: 071-353-6111 E: Peter.Witschi@kk.ar.ch
Staatsarchiv des Kantons Basel-Landschaft Wiedenhubstrasse 35, Liestal, 4410 T: 061-921-44-40 E: baselland@lka.bl.ch W: www.baselland.ch
Staatsarchiv des Kantons Solothurn Bielstrasse 41, Solothurn, CH-4509, Switzerland T: 032-627-08-21 F: 032-622-34-87
Staatsarchiv Luzern Postfach 7853, Luzern, 6000 T: 41-41-2285365 E: archiv@staluzern.c W: www.staluzern.ch

UKRAINE

Odessa, Odessa State Archive, 18 Shukovskovo Street, Odessa 270001

NORTH AMERICA - CANADA
Archives & Special Collections
PO Box 7500, Fredericton, New Brunswick, E3B 5H5 T: 506-453-4748 F: 506-453-4595,
Archives Nationales PO Box 10450, Sainte Foy, Quebec, G1V 4N1 T: 418-643-8904 F: 418-646-0868
Glenbow Library & Archives 130-9th Avenue SE, Calgary, Alberta, T2G 0P3 T: 403-268-4197 F: 403-232-6569
Hudson's Bay Company Archives, 200 Vaughan Street, Winnipeg R3C 1T5 T: 204-945-4949 F: 204-948-3236 E: hbca@chc.gov.mb.ca W: http://www.gov.mb.ca/chc/archives/hbca/index.html
Loyalist Collection & Reference Department PO Box 7500, Fredericton, New Brunswick, E3B 5H5 T: 506-453-4749 F: 506-453-4596,
Manitoba Provincial Archives 200 Vaughan Street, Winnepeg, Manitoba, R3C 1T5 T: 204-945-4949 F: 204-948-3236,
National Archives of Canada 395 Wellington Street, Ottawa, Ontario, K1A 0N3 T: 613-996-7458 W: http://www.archives.ca,
New Brunswick Provincial Archives PO Box 6000, Fredericton, New Brunswick, E3B 5H1 T: 506-453-2122 E: provarch@gov.nb.ca W: www.gov.nb.ca/supply/archives
Newfoundland & Labrador Archives Colonial Building, Military Road, St Johns, Newfoundland, A1C 2C9 T: 709-729-0475 F: 709-729-0578,
Nova Scotia State Archives 6016 University Avenue, Halifax, Nova Scotia, B3H 1W4 T: 902-424-6060,
Ontario Archives Unit 300, 77 Grenville Street, Toronto, Ontario, M5S 1B3 T: 416-327-1582 E: reference@archives.gov.on.ca WWW: www.gov.on.ca/MCZCR/archives
Public Archives & Record Office PO Box 1000, Charlottetown, Prince Edward Island, C1A 7M4 T: 902-368-4290 F: 902-368-6327 E: archives@gov.pe.ca W: www.gov.pe.ca/educ/
Saskatchewan Archives Board - Regina 3303 Hillsdale Street, Regina, Saskatchewan, S4S 0A2 T: 306-787-4068 E: sabreg@sk.sympatico.ca W: www.gov.sk.ca/govt/archives
Saskatchewan Archives Board - Saskatchewa Room 91, Murray Building, University of Saskatchewan, 3 Campus Drive, Saskatoon, Saskatchewan, S7N 5A4 T: 306-933-5832 E: sabsktn@sk.sympatico.ca W: www.gov.sk.ca/govt/archives
Yarmouth County Museums & Archives 22 Collins Street, Yarmouth, Nova Scotia, B5A 3C8 T: (902)-742-5539 E: ycn0056@ycn.library.ns.ca W: www.ycn.library.ns.ca/museum/yarcomus.htm

UNITED STATES OF AMERICA
Alaska State Archives 141 Willoughby Avenue, Juneau, Alaska, 99801-1720, United States of America, T: 907-465-2270 E: sou@bham.lib.al.usarchives@educ.state.ak.us,
Arizona Department of Library Archives & Public Records State Capitol, 1700 West Washington, Phoenix, Arizona, 85007, United States of America, T: 602-542-3942
Arizona Historical Foundation Library Hayden Library, Arizona State Univeristy, Tempe, Arizona, 85287, United States of America, T: 602-966-8331
Arkansas History Commission OneCapitol Mall, Little Rock, Arkansas, 72201 T: 501-682-6900,
California State Archives Office of the Secretary of State, 1020 O Street, Sacramento, 95814 T: (916)-653-7715 E: archivesweb@ss.ca.gov W: www.ss.ca.gov/archives/archives.htm
Colorado State Archives Room 1b-20, 1313 Sherman Street, Denver, Colorado, 80203-2236, United States of America T: 303-866-2390,
Connecticut State Archives 231 Capitol Ave, Hartford 6106, T: 0860 757 6580 E: isref@cslib.org W: www. cslib.org
Daughters of the American Revolution Library 1776 D Street N W, Washington, District of Columbia, 20006-5392, United States of America, T: 202-879-3229,

District of Columbia Archives 1300 Naylor Court North West, Washington, District of Columbia, 20001-4225 T: 203-566-3690,

Family History Library of the Church of Jesus Christ of LDS 35 N West Temple Street, Salt Lake City, Utah, 84150, USA,

Georgia State Archives 330 Capital Avenue SE, Atlanta 30334-9002 T: 404-656-2350 W: http://www.state.ga.us/SOS/Archives/,

Hawaii State Library 478 South King Street, Honolulu, Hawaii, 96813

Indiana Archives Room117, 140 N Senate Avenue, Indianapolis, Indiana, 46204-2296 T: 317-232-3660 F: 317-233-1085,

Kansas State Historical Society - Archives 6425 SW Sixth Street, Topeka, Kansas, 66615-1099 T: 913-272-8681 F: 913-272-8682 E: reference@hspo.wpo.state.ks.us W: www.kshs.org

Maryland State Archives Hall of Records Building, 350 Rowe Boulevard, Annapolis, Maryland, 21401 T: 410-974-3914,

Missouri State Archives PO Box 778, Jefferson City, Missouri, 65102 T: 314-751-3280,

National Archives - California 100 Commodore Drive, San Bruno, California, 94066-2350

National Archives - Colorado PO Box 25307, Denver, Colorado, 80225-0307 T: 303-866-2390,

National Archives - Georgia 1557 St Joseph Avenue, East Point, Georgia, 30344, T: 404-763-7477 F: 404-763-7059 Web: www.nara.gov

National Archives - Illinois 7358 South Pulaski Road, Chicago, Illinois, 60629

National Archives - Massachusetts 380 Trapelo Road, Waltham, Massachusetts, 2154,

National Archives - Massachusetts 100 Dan Fox Drive, Pittsfield, Massachusetts, 01201-8230

National Archives - Missouri 2306 East Bannister Road, Kansas City, Missouri, 64131

National Archives - New York 201 Varick Street, New York, New York, 10014 - 4811

National Archives - Northwest Pacific Region 6125 Sand Point Way NE, Seattle, Washington, 98115 T: 206-524-6501 E: archives@seattle.nara.gov,

National Archives - Pennsylvania Rom 1350, 900 Market Street, Philadelphia, PA 19144,

National Archives - Texas Box 6216, 4900 Hemphill Road, Fort Worth, Texas, 76115

National Archives - Washington Pennsylvania Avenue, Washington, District of Colombia, 20408,

National Archives - Pacific Alaska Region 654 West 3rd Avenue, Anchorage, Alaska, 99501 - 2145 T: 011 1-907-271-2443 F: 011 1-907-271-2442 E: archives@alaska.nara.gov W: www.nara.gov/regional/anchorage.html

National Archives (Pacific Region) 1st Floor East, 24000 Avila Road, Orange County, Laguna Niguel, California, 92677 T: (949)-360-2641 F: (949)-360-2624 E: archives@laguna.nara.gov W: www.nara.gov/regional/laguna.html

Nevada State Archives Division of Archives & Records, 100 Stewart Street, Carson City, Nevada, 89710 T: 702-687-5210,

New Jersey State Archives PO Box 307, 185 West State Street, Trenton, New Jersey, 08625-0307 T: 609-292-6260,

New Mexico State Archives 1205 Camino carlos Rey, Sante Fe, New Mexico, 87501 T: (505)-827-7332 F: (505)-476-7909 E: cmartine@rain.state.nm.us W: www.state.nmus/cpr

Ohio State Archives 1982 Velma Avenue, Columbus, Ohio, 43211-2497 T: 614-297-2510,

Pennsylvania State Archives PO Box 1026, 3rd & Forster Streets, Harrisburg, Pennsylvania, 17108-1026 T: 717-783-3281,

South Carolina Department Archives & History 8301 Parklane Road, Columbia, South Carolina, 292223 T: 803-896-6100,

South Carolina State Archives PO Box 11669, 1430 Senate Street, Columbia, South Carolina, 29211-1669 T: 803-734-8577,

South Dakota Archives Cultural Heritage Center, 900 Governors Drive, Pierre, South Dakota, 57501-2217 T: 605-773-3804,

Tennessee State Library & Archives 403 7th Avenue North, Nashville, Tennessee, 37243-0312 T: 615-741-2764 E: reference@mail.state.tn.us W: www.state.tn.us/sos/statelib

Texas State Archives PO Box 12927, Austin, Texas, 78711-2927 T: 512-463-5463,

Vermont Public Records Division PO Drawer 33, U S Route 2, Middlesex, Montpelier, Vermont, 05633-7601 T: 802-828-3700 and 802-828-3286 F: 802-828-3710,

Vermont State Archives Redstone Building, 26 Terrace Street, Montpelier, Vermont, 05609-1103 T: 802-828-2308,

Virginia State Archives 11th Street at Capitol Square, Richmond, Virginia, 23219-3491 T: 804-786-8929,

West Virginia State Archives The Cultural Center, 1900 Kanawha Boulevard East, Charleston, West Virginia, 25305-0300 T: 304-558-0230,

Wisconsin State Archives 816 State Street, Madison 53706 T: 608-264-6460 F: 608-264-6742 E: archives.reference@ccmail.adp.wisc.edu W: www.wisc.edu/shs-archives

Wyoming State Archives Barrett State Office Building, 2301 Central Avenue, Cheyenne, Wyoming, 82002 T: 307-777-7826

Registrars of Births, Marriages & Deaths ~ England, Wales and Scotland

Following is a list of Superintendent Registrars of Births, Marriages and Deaths in alphabetical order by County. We have also included details of Registration Sub Districts. **Note:** Many of the Registration Officers listed here share Office accommodation with other parties. When using the addresses given they should be prefixed "Superintendent Registrar, Register Office ...." *We offer the following advice to help readers and Superintendent Registrars* The volume and page number references which are found on the microfiche and film indexes of the General Register Office must only be used when applying for certificates from the GRO. These reference numbers are not a reference to the filing system used at local register offices and do not assist Superintendent Registrars in any way to find the entry. The General Register Office hold the records for the whole of England and Wales and therefore have their own filing system, whereas the majority of register offices are still manually searching handwritten index books which is extremely time consuming. Most offices only became computerised in the early 1990s and do not hold records before this date on computer and will never have the staff time to backlog 150 years of records. Finally, many offices are only part time, some just open a few hours per week. Unlike the larger offices they do not have receptionists or staff employed specifically to assist people researching their family history, and have to devote the majority of their time to providing certificates urgently required for passport applications, marriage bookings and pension applications. Once the applicant has carried out their research fully using all the records and data widely available to them at no cost, they can apply to their local office with sufficient information for the Registrar to trace the entry within minutes instead of hours.

The General Register Office Trafalgar Road Birkdale Southport PR8 2HH T: 0870 243 7788 Fax: 01704 550013

England

Bath & North East Somerset The Register Office 12 Charlotte Street Bath BA1 2NF T: 01225 312032 Fax: 01225 334812

Bedfordshire
Ampthill Court House Woburn Street Ampthill MK45 2HX T: 01525-403430 Fax: 01525-841984 E: denmanm@csd.bedfordshire.gov.uk
Bedfordshire The Register Office Pilgrim House 20 Brickhill Drive Bedford MK41 7PZ T: 01234 290450 Fax: 01234 290454
Biggleswade The Register Office 142 London Road Biggleswade SG18 8EL T: 01767-312511 Fax: 01767-315033
Dunstable Grove House 76 High Street North Dunstable LU6 1NF T: 01582-660191 Fax: 01582-471004
Leighton Buzzard Bossard House West Street Leighton Buzzard LU7 7DA T: 01525-851486 Fax: 01525-381483
Berkshire
Wokingham The Old School Reading Road Wokingham RG41 1RJ T: 0118 978 2514 Fax: 0118 978 2813
Bracknell Forest Easthampstead House Town Square Bracknell RG12 1AQ T: 01344 352027 Fax: 01344 352010
Reading The Register Office Yeomanry House 131 Castle Hill Reading RG1 7TA T: 0118 901 5120 T: 0118 901 5194 Fax: 0118 951 0212

Slough Slough Register Office The Centre Farnham Road Slough SL1 4UT T: 01753 787601 Fax: 01753 787605
West Berkshire Peake House 112 Newtown Road Newbury RG14 7EB T: 01635 48133 Fax: 01635 524694
Windsor & Maidenhead Town Hall St Ives Road Maidenhead SL6 1RF T: 01628 796422 Fax: 01628 796625
Beverley (Beverley B Sub-district) The Council Offices Market Green Cottingham HU16 5QG T: 01482 393565 Fax: 01482 393567
Bexley LB Bexley Manor House The Green Sidcup DA14 6BW T: (020) 8300 4537 Fax: (020) 8308 4967
Birmingham MD Birmingham The Register Office 300 Broad Street Birmingham B1 2DE T: 0121 212 3421 Fax: 0121 303 1396
Blackburn with Darwen and (Darwen & Turton Sub-district) Town Hall Croft Street Darwen BB3 2RN T: 01254-702443
Bolton MD The Register Office Mere Hall Merehall Street Bolton BL1 2QT T: 01204 525165 Fax: 01204 525125
Bournemouth The Register Office 159 Old Christchurch Road Bournemouth BH1 1JS T: 01202 551668
Bradford MD The Register Office 22 Manor Row Bradford BD1 4QR T: 01274 752151 Fax: 01274 305139
Keighley Town Hall Bow Street Keighley BD21 3PA T: 01535 618060 Fax: 01535 618208
Brent LB Brent Town Hall Forty Lane Wembley HA9 9EZ T: (020) 8937 1010 Fax: (020) 8937 1021
Brighton and Hove Brighton Town Hall Bartholomews Brighton BN1 1JA T: 01273 292016 Fax: 01273 292019

Bromley LB Room S101, Bromley Civic Centre Stockwell Close Bromley BR1 3UH T: (020) 8313 4666 Fax: (020) 8313 4699
Buckinghamshire
Aylesbury Vale County Ofices Walton Street Aylesbury HP20 1XF T: 01296 382581 Fax: 01296 382675
Chiltern and South Bucks Transferred to Chiltern Hills RD wef November 1998
Chiltern Hills Wycombe Area Offices Easton Street High Wycombe HP11 1NH T: 01494 475200 T: 01494 475205 Fax: 01494 475040
Bury MD Town Hall Manchester Road Bury BL9 OSW T: 0161 253 6027 Fax: 0161 253 6028
Calderdale MD
Calderdale The Register Office 4 Carlton Street Halifax HX1 2AH T: 01422 353993 Fax: 01422 253370
Todmorden Municipal Offices Rise Lane Todmorden OL14 7AB T: 01706 814811 Ext 208 Fax: 01706 814811 Ext 208
Cambridgeshire
Cambridge Castle Lodge Shire Hall Castle Hill Cambridge CB3 0AP T: 01223 717401 Fax: 01223 717888 All churches on computer index from 1837 to date. For general searches please arrange in advance.
Ely Old School House 74 Market Street Ely CB7 4LS T: 01353 663824
Fenland The Old Vicarage Church Terrace Wisbech PE13 1BW T: 01945 467950 Fax: 01945 467950
Huntingdon Wykeham House Market Hill Huntingdon PE29 3NN T: 01480 375821 T: 01480 375822 Fax: 01480 375725
Peterborough The Lawns 33 Thorpe Road Peterborough PE3 6AB T: 01733 566323 Fax: 01733 566049
Camden LB Camden Register Office, Camden Town Hall Judd Street London WC1H 9JE T: (020) 7974 5600 T: (020) 7974 1900 Fax: (020) 7974 5792
Cheshire
Cheshire Central The Register Office Delamere House Chester Street CW1 2LL T: 01270 505106 Fax: 01270 505107
Cheshire East The Register Office Park Green Macclesfield SK11 6TW T: 01625 423463 Fax: 01625 619225
Chester West Goldsmith House Goss Street Chester CH1 2BG T: 01244 602668 Fax: 01244 602934
Halton The Register Office Heath Road Runcorn WA7 5TN T: 01928 576797 Fax: 01928 573616
Vale Royal Transferred to Cheshire Central wef April 1998
Warrington The Register Office Museum Street Warrington WA1 1JX T: 01925 442762 Fax: 01925 442739
Bristol The Register Office Quakers Friars Bristol BS1 3AR T: 0117 903 8888 Fax: 0117 903 8877
City of London The Register Office Finsbury Town Hall Roseberry Avenue EC1R 4QT T: (020) 7527 6347 T: (020) 7527 6357 Fax: (020) 7527 6308
Cornwall
Bodmin Lyndhurst 66 St Nicholas Street Bodmin PL31 1AG T: 01208 73677 Fax: 01208 73677
Camborne-Redruth The Register Office Roskear Camborne TR14 8DN T: 01209 612924 Fax: 01209 719956
Falmouth Berkeley House 12-14 Berkeley Vale Falmouth TR11 3PH T: 01326 312606 Fax: 01326 312606
Kerrier The Willows Church Street Helston TR13 8NJ T: 01326 562848 Fax: 01326 562848
Launceston 'Hendra' Dunheved Road Launceston PL15 9JG T: 01566 772464 Fax: 01566 772464
Liskeard 'Graylands' Dean Street Liskeard PL14 4AH T: 01579 343442 Fax: 01872 327554
Penzance The Register Office Alphington House Alverton Place Penzance TR18 4JJ T: 01736 330093 Fax: 01736 369666
St. Austell The Register Office 12 Carlyon Road St. Austell PL25 4LD T: 01726 68974 Fax: 01726 67048
St. Germans The Register Office Plougastel Drive St Germans Saltash PL12 6DL T: 01752 842624 Fax: 01752 848556
Stratton The Parkhouse Centre Ergue Gaberic Way Bude EX23 8LF T: 01288 353209 Fax: 01288 359968
Truro Dalvenie House New County Hall Truro TR1 3AY T: 01872 322241 Fax: 01872 323891
Coventry MD The Register Office Cheylesmore Manor House Manor House Drive CoventryCV1 2ND T: (024) 7683 3137 Fax: (024) 7683 3110
Croydon LB The Register Office Mint Walk Croydon CR10 1EA T: (020) 8760 5617 Fax: (020) 8760 5633
Cumbria
Cockermouth (Workington Sub-district) Hill Park Ramsay Brow Workington CA14 4TG T: 01900 325160 Fax: 01900 325161
Kendal (Kirkby Lonsdale Sub-district) 15 Market Square Kirkby Lonsdale Carnforth LA6 2AN T: 01524 271222
Kendal (Lakes Sub-district) Windermere Library Ellerthwaite Windermere LA23 2AJ T: 01539 462420
Penrith (Alston Sub-district) Alston Register Office Townhead Alston CA9 3SL T: 01434 381784 Fax: 01434 381784
Penrith (Appleby Sub-district) Shire Hall The Sands Appleby in Westmorland CA3 8DA T: 01768 352976

Barrow-in-Furness Nan Tait Centre Abbey Road Barrow-in-Furness LA14 1LG T: 01229 894510 Fax: 01229 894513
Carlisle The Register Office 23 Portland Square Carlisle CA1 1PE T: 01228 607432 Fax: 01228 607434
Cockermouth The Register Office Fairfield Station Road Cockermouth CA13 9PT T: 01900 325960 Fax: 01900 325962
Kendal The Register Office County Offices Kendal LA9 4RQ T: 01539 773567 Fax: 01539 773565
Millom The Millom Council Centre St Georges Road Millom LA18 4DD T: 01229 772357 Fax: 01229 773412
Penrith The Register Office Friargate Penrith CA11 7XR T: 01768 242120 Fax: 01768 242122
Ulverston Town Hall Queen Street Ulverston LA12 7AR T: 01229 894170 Fax: 01229 894172
Whitehaven College House Flatt Walks Whitehaven CA28 7RW T: 01946 852690 Fax: 01946 852673
Wigton Wigton Registry Office Station Road Wigton CA7 9AH T: 016973 66117 Fax: 016973 66118
Darlington The Register Office Central House Gladstone Street Darlington DL3 6JX T: 01325 346600 Fax: 01325 346605
Derby The Register Office 9 Traffic Street Derby DE1 2NL T: 01332 716030 T: 01332 716025 Fax: 01332 716021 This office holds all the South Derbyshire (formerly Swadlingcote and Gresley District) records
Derbyshire
Bakewell (Matlock Sub-district) The Register Office Firs Parade Matlock DE4 3AS T: 01629-582870
High Peak (Buxton Sub-district) The Registrar's Office Hardwick Square West Buxton SK17 6PX T: 01298 25075
High Peak (Chapel en le Frith Sub-district) The Town Hall Chapel en le Frith SK23 0HB T: 01298 813559
High Peak (Glossop Sub-district) 46-50 High Street West Glossop SK13 8BH T: 01457 852425
South Derbyshire The Register Office Traffic Street Derby DE1 2NL T: 01332 716020 T: 01332 716025 Fax: 01332 716021
Amber Valley The Register Office Market Place Ripley DE5 3BT T: 01773 841380 Fax: 01773 841382
Ashbourne Town Hall Market Place Ashbourne DE6 1ES T: 01335 300575 Fax: 01335 345252
Bakewell The Register Office Town Hall Bakewell DE45 1BW T: 01629 812261
Chesterfield The Register Office New Beetwell Street Chesterfield S40 1QJ T: 01246 234754 Fax: 01246 274493
Erewash The Register Office 87 Lord Haddon Road Ilkeston DE7 8AX T: 0115 932 1014 Fax: 0115 932 6450
High Peak Council Offices Hayfield Road Chapel-en-le-Frith SK23 0QJ T: 01663 750473
Devon
East Devon The Register Office Dowell Street Honiton EX14 1LZ T: 01404 42531 Fax: 01404 41475
Exeter 1 Lower Summerlands Heavitree Road Exeter EX1 2LL T: 01392 686260 Fax: 01392 686262
Holsworthy The Register Office 8 Fore Street Holsworthy EX22 6ED T: 01409-253262
Mid Devon The Great House 1 St Peter Street Tiverton EX16 6NY T: 01884 255255 Fax: 01884 258852
North Devon The Register Office Civic Centre Barnstaple EX31 1ED T: 01271 388456
Okehampton Transferred to West Devon wef July 1997
Plymouth The Register Office Lockyer Street Plymouth PL1 2QD T: 01752 268331 Fax: 01752 256046
South Hams Follaton House Plymouth road Totnes TQ9 5NE T: 01803 861234 Fax: 01803 868965
Teignbridge The Register Office 15 Devon Square Newton Abbot TQ12 2HN T: 01626 206341 T: 01626 206340 Fax: 01626 206346
Torbay The Register Office Oldway Mansion Paignton TQ3 2TU T: 01803 207130 Fax: 01803 525388
Torridge Council Offices Windmill Lane Northam Bideford EX39 1BY T: 01237 474978 Fax: 01237 473385
West Devon Town Council Offices Drake Road Tavistock PL19 0AU T: 01822 612137 Fax: 01822 618935
Doncaster and (Mexborough Sub-district) Council Offices Main Street Mexborough S64 9LU T: 01302 735705
Doncaster The Register Office Elmfield Park Doncaster DN1 2EB T: 01302 364922 Fax: 01302 364922
Dorset
East Dorset King George V Pavilion Peter Grant Way Ferndown BH22 9EN T: 01202 892325
North Dorset The Register Office Salisbury Road Blandford Forum DT11 7LN T: 01258 484096 Fax: 01258 484090 This is a part-time office with only 2 members of staff and no receptionist. All Blandford births and deaths from 1837 to 1974 are held at Poole Register Office
South and West Dorset The Guildhall St Edmund Street Weymouth DT4 8AS T: 01305 772611 Fax: 01305 771269
West Dorset The Register Office Mountfield Offices Rax Lane Bridport DT6 3JL T: 01308 456047
Dudley MD Priory Hall Priory Park Dudley DY1 4EU T: 01384 815373 Fax: 01384 815339

Stourbridge Crown Centre Crown Lane Stourbridge DY8 1YA T: 01384 815384 Fax: 01384 815397

Durham

Durham Central The Register Office 40 Old Elvet Durham DH1 3HN T: 0191 386 4077 Fax: 0191 383 9961

Durham Eastern Register Office York Road Acre Rigg Peterlee SR8 2DP T: 0191 586 6147 Fax: 0191 518 4607

Durham Northern The Register Office 7 Thorneyholme Terrace Stanley DH9 0BJ T: 01207 235849 Fax: 01207 235334

Durham Western Cockton House 35 Cockton Hill Road Bishop Auckland DL14 6HS T: 01388 607277 Fax: 01388 664388

Ealing LB Ealing Town Hall New Broadway Ealing W5 2BY T: (020) 8758 8946 Fax: (020) 8758 8722

East Riding of Yorkshire The Register Office Walkergate House Walkergate Beverley HU17 9BP T: 01482 393600 Fax: 01482 873414

East Sussex

Crowborough Beaconwood Beacon Road Crowborough TN6 1AR T: 01892 653803 Fax: 01892 669884

Eastbourne Town Hall Grove Road Eastbourne BN21 4UG T: 01323 415051 Fax: 01323 431386

Hastings & Rother The Register Office, Summerfields Bohemia Road Hastings TN34 1EX T: 01424 721722 Fax: 01424 465296

Lewes Southover Grange Southover Road Lewes BN7 1TP T: 01273 475916 Fax: 01273 488073

Enfield LB Public Offices Gentlemen's Row Enfield EN2 6PS T: (020) 8367 5757 Fax: (020) 8379 8562

Essex

Castle Point and Rochford Civic Centre Victoria Avenue Southend-on-Sea SS2 6ER T: 01702 343728 Fax: 01702 612610

Castle Point and Rochford (Sub-district) District Council Offices Hockley Road Rayleigh SS6 8EB T: 01268-776362 Fax: 01268-776362

Braintree John Ray House Bocking End Braintree CM7 9RW T: 01376 323462 Fax: 01376 342432

Brentwood The Register Office 1 Seven Arches Road Brentwood CM14 4JG T: 01277 233565 Fax: 01277 262712

Chelmsford The Register Office 17 Market Road Chelmsford CM1 1GF T: 01245 430700 Fax: 01245 430707

Colchester Stanwell House Stanwell Street Colchester CO2 7DL T: 01206 572926 Fax: 01206 540626

Epping Forest The Register Office St Johns Road Epping CM16 5DN T: 01992 572789 Fax: 01992 571236

Harlow Watergarden Offices College Square The High Harlow CM20 1AG T: 01279 427674 Fax: 01279 444594

Southend-on-Sea Civic Centre Victoria Avenue Southend-on-Sea SS2 6ER T: 01702 343728 Fax: 01702 612610 This office now covers Southend-on-Sea, Castle Point and Rochford Registration Districts.

Thurrock The Register Office 2 Quarry Hill Grays RM17 5BT T: 01375 375245 Fax: 01375 392649

Uttlesford Council Offices London Road Saffron Walden CB11 4ER T: 01799 510319 Fax: 01799 510332

Gateshead MD Civic Centre Regent Street Gateshead NE8 1HH T: 0191 433 3000 T: 0191 433 2000 Fax: 0191 477 9978

Gloucestershire

Cheltenham The Register Office St. Georges Road Cheltenham GL50 3EW T: 01242 532455 Fax: 01242 254600

Cirencester Old Memorial Hospital Sheep Street Cirencester GL7 1QW T: 01285 650455 Fax: 01285 640253

Gloucester Maitland House Spa Road Gloucester GL1 1UY T: 01452 425275 Fax: 01452 385385

North Cotswold North Cotswold Register Office High Street Moreton-in-Marsh GL56 0AZ T: 01608 651230 Fax: 01608 651226

Stroud The Register Office Parliament Street Stroud GL5 1DY T: 01453 766049 Fax: 01453 752961

Forest of Dean Belle Vue Centre 6 Belle Vue Road Cinderford GL14 2AB T: 01594 822113 Fax: 01594 826352

Greenwich LB The Register Office, Town Hall Wellington Street London SE18 6PW T: (020) 8854 8888 Fax: (020) 8317 5754

Hackney LB The Register Office, Town Hall Mare Street London E8 1EA T: (020) 8356 3376 Fax: (020) 8356 3552

Hammersmith & Fulham LB The Register Office Nigel Playfair Avenue London W6 9JY T: (020) 8748-3020 T: (020) 8576-5032 Fax: (020) 8748-6619

Hammersmith and Fulham Hammersmith & Fulham Register Office, Fulham Town Hall Harwood Road Fulham London SW6 1ET T: (020) 8576 5217 Fax: (020) 8753 2146

Hampshire

South East Hampshire (Fareham Sub-district) 4 - 8 Osborn Road South Fareham PO16 7DG T: 01329 280493

South East Hampshire (Gosport Sub-district) 3 Thorngate Way Gosport PO12 1DX T: (023) 9258 0629 Fax: (023) 9258 0629

South East Hampshire (Havant Sub-district) Fernglen Town Hall Road Havant PO9 1AN T: (023) 9248 2533 Fax: (023) 9248 2533

Winchester (Eastleigh Sub-district) 101 Leigh Road Eastleigh SO50 9DR T: (023) 8061 2058 Fax: (023) 8061 2058

Alton The Register Office 4 Queens Road Alton GU34 1HU T: 01420 85410

Andover Wessex Chambers South Street Andover SP10 2BN T: 01264 352943 T: 01264 352513 Fax: 01264 366849

Droxford Bank House Bank Street Bishop's Waltham SO32 1GP T: 01489 894044 Fax: 01489 892219

Hampshire North Register Office Goldings London Road Basingstoke RG21 4AN T: 01256 322188 Fax: 01256 350745

Kingsclere & Whitchurch Council Offices Swan Street Kingsclere, Nr Newbury RG15 8PM T: 01635-298714

New Forest Public Offices 65 Christchurch Road Ringwood BH24 1DH T: 01425 470150 Fax: 01425 471732

North-East Hampshire The Register Office 30 Grosvenor Road Aldershot GU11 3EB T: 01252 322066 Fax: 01252 338004

Petersfield The Old College College Street Petersfield GU31 4AG T: 01730 265372 Fax: 01730 261050

Romsey Hayter House Hayter Gardens Romsey SO51 7QU T: 01794 513846 Fax: 01794 830491

South-East Hampshire The Register Office 4-8 Osborn Road South Fareham PO16 7DG T: 01329 280493 Fax: 01329 823184

Winchester The Register Office Station Hill Winchester SO23 8TJ T: 01962 869608 T: 01962 869594 Fax: 01962 851912

Haringey LB The Register Office, Civic Centre High Road Wood Green London N22 4LE T: (020) 8489 2605 T: (020) 8489 2601 Fax: (020) 8489 2912

Harrow LB The Civic Centre Station Road Harrow HA1 2UX T: (020) 8424 1618 Fax: (020) 8424 1414

Hartlepool The Register Office Raby Road Hartlepool TS24 8AF T: 01429 236369 Fax: 01429 236373 E: registrar@hartlepool.gov.uk

Havering LB 'Langtons' Billet Lane Hornchurch RM11 1XL T: 01708 433481 T: 01708 433403 Fax: 01708 433413

Hendon Hendon see Barnet The Register Office 182 Burnt Oak Broadway, Edgware HA8 0AU T: (020) 8952-0876 T: (020) 8952-0024 Fax: (020) 8381-2346 Transferred to Barnet wef April 1999

Herefordshire

Bromsgrove The Register Office School Drive Bromsgrove B60 1AY T: 01527 578759 Fax: 01527 578750

Bromyard Council Offices 1 Rowberry Street Bromyard Hereford HR7 4DU T: 01432 260258 Fax: 01432 260259

Redditch The Register Office 29 Easmore Road Redditch B98 8ER T: 01527 60647 Fax: 01527 584561

Ledbury Town Council Offices Church Street Ledbury HR8 1DH T: 01531 632306

Hereford County Offices Bath Street Hereford HR1 2HQ T: 01432 260565 Fax: 01432 261720 Owing to the large number of sub-districts operational from 1837 to 1935 this office has a preference for genealogical enquiries by post rather than visits in person.

Kington The Register Office, Old Court House Market Hall Street Kington HR5 3DP T: 01544 230156 Fax: 01544 231385

Leominster The Register Office, The Old Priory Church Street Leominster HR6 8EQ T: 01568 610131 Fax: 01568 614954

Ross The Old Chapel Cantilupe Road Ross on Wye HR9 7AN T: 01989 562795 Fax: 01989 564869

Hertfordshire

Bishops Stortford The Register Office 2 Hockerill Street Bishops Stortford CM23 2DL T: 01279 652273 Fax: 01279 461492

Broxbourne Borough Offices Churchgate Cheshunt EN8 9XQ T: 01992 623107 Fax: 01992 627605

Dacorum The Bury Queensway Hemel Hemstead HP1 1HR T: 01442 228600 Fax: 01442 243974

Hatfield The Register Office 19b St Albans Road East Hatfield AL10 0NG T: 01707 283920 Fax: 01707 283924

Hertford & Ware County Hall Pegs Lane Hertford SG13 8DE T: 01992 555590 Fax: 01992 555493

Hitchen & Stevenage The Register Office Danesgate Stevenage SG1 1WW T: 01438 316579 Fax: 01438 357197

St Albans Hertfordshire House Civic Close St. Albans AL1 3JZ T: 01727 816806 Fax: 01727 816804

Watford The Register Office 36 Clarendon Road Watford WD1 1JP T: 01923 231302 Fax: 01923 246852

Hillingdon LB The Register Office Hillingdon Civic Centre Uxbridge UB8 1UW T: 01895 250418 Fax: 01895 250678

Hounslow LB The Register Office 88 Lampton Road Hounslow TW3 4DW T: (020) 8583 2090 T: (020) 8583 2086 Fax: (020) 8577 8798

Isle of Wight The Register Office, County Hall High Street Newport PO30 1UD T: 01983 823230 Fax: 01983 823227

Isles of Scilly The Register Office Town Hall St Marys TR21 0LW T: 01720 422537

Islington LB The Register Office, Finsbury Town Hall Roseberry Avenue London EC1R 4QT T: (020) 7527 6347 T: (020) 7527 6350 Fax: (020) 7527 6308

Kensington & Chelsea LB The Kensington & Chelsea Register Office Chelsea Old Town Hall Kings Road London SW3 5EE T: (020) 7361 4100 Fax: (020) 7361 4054

Kent The Archbishop's Palace Palace Gardens Mill Street Maidstone ME15 6YE T: 0845 678 5000 T: 01622 701922 Fax: 01622 663690

Kent - Medway Medway Medway Register Office, Ingleside 114 Maidstone Road Chatham ME4 6DJ T: 01634 844073 Fax: 01634 840165

Kingston-upon-Hull Hull Municipal Offices 181-191 George Street Kingston Upon Hull HU1 3BY T: 01482 615401 Fax: 01482 615411

Kingston-upon-Thames RB Kingston upon Thames The Register Office 35 Coombe Road Kingston upon Thames KT2 7BA T: (020) 8546 7993 Fax: (020) 8287 2888

Kirklees MD

Dewsbury The Register Office Wellington Street Dewsbury WF13 1LY T: 01924 324880 Fax: 01924 324882

Huddersfield Civic Centre 11 High Street Huddersfield HD1 2PL T: 01484 221030 Fax: 01484 221315

Knowsley MD District Council Offices High Street Prescot L34 3LH T: 0151 443 5210 Fax: 0151 443 5216

Lambeth MB The Register Office 357-361 Brixton Road Lambeth London SW9 7DA T: (020) 7926 9420 Fax: (020) 7926 9426

Lancashire

Fleetwood and Fylde The Register Office South King Street Blackpool FY1 4AX T: 01253 477177 Fax: 01253 477176

Fleetwood and Fylde (Fleetwood Sub-district) Fleetwood Central Library North Albert Street Fleetwood FY7 6AJ T: 01253 874580

Fleetwood and Fylde (Fylde Sub-district) The Library Clifton Street Lytham FY8 5ED T: 01253 737530

Hyndburn and Rossendale (Rossendale Sub-district) 1 Grange Street Rawtenstall Rossendale BB4 7RT T: 01706 215496

Lancaster (Garstang Sub-district) Old Posthouse Market Place Garstang PR3 1ZA T: 01995 601651 Fax: 01995 601651

Lancaster (Preesall Sub-district) The Over Wyre Medical Centre Pilling Lane Preesall FY6 0FA T: 01253 810722

Blackburn with Darwen The Register Office Jubilee Street Blackburn BB1 1EP T: 01254 587524 Fax: 01254 587538

Blackpool The Register Office South King Street Blackpool FY1 4AX T: 01253 477177 Fax: 01253 477176

Burnley and Pendle The Register Office 12 Nicholas Street Burnley BB11 2AQ T: 01282 436116 Fax: 01282 412221

Chorley The Register Office 16 St George's Street Chorley PR7 2AA T: 01257 263143 Fax: 01257 263808

Garstang

Hyndburn & Rossendale The Mechanics Institute Willow Street Accrington BB5 1LP T: 01254 871360 Fax: 01254 239391

Lancaster The Register Office 4 Queen Street Lancaster LA1 1RS T: 01524 65673 Fax: 01524 842285

Preston and South Ribble The Register Office PO Box 24 Bow Lane Preston PR1 8SE T: 01772 263800 T: 01772 263808 Fax: 01772 261012

Ribble Valley The Register Office Off Pimlico Road Clitheroe BB7 2BW T: 01200 425786 Fax: 01200 425786

West Lancashire Greetby Buildings Derby Street Ormskirk L39 2BS T: 01695 576009 Fax: 01695 585819

LB of Barking & Dagenham Arden House 198 Longbridge Road Barking IG11 8SY T: (020) 8270 4743 Fax: (020) 8270 4745

LB of Barnet The Register Office 182 Burnt Oak Broadway Edgware HA8 0AU T: (020) 8731 1100 Fax: (020) 8731 1111

Leeds MD Belgrave House Belgrave Street Leeds LS2 8DQ T: 0113 224 3604 T: 0113 247 6707 Fax: 0113 247 6708

Leicester The Register Office 5 Pocklington's Walk Leicester LE1 6BQ T: 0116 253 6326 Fax: 0116 253 3008

Leicestershire Leicestershire Register Office County Hall Glenfield Leicester LE3 8RN T: 0116 265 6585 Fax: 0116 265 6580 Covering Coalville, Loughborough, Market Harborough, Melton Mowbray, Hinckley, South Wigston

Lewisham LB The Register Office 368 Lewisham High Street London SE13 6LQ T: (020) 8690 2128 Fax: (020) 8314 1078

Lincolnshire The Register Office 4 Lindum Road Lincoln LN2 1NN T: 0845 330 1400 Fax: 01522 589524

Liverpool MD Liverpool Register Office The Cotton Exchange Old Hall Street Liverpool L3 9UF T: 0151 233 4972 Fax: 0151 233 4944

Luton The Register Office 6 George Street West Luton LU1 2BJ T: 01582 722603 Fax: 01582 429522

Manchester MD HeronHouse 47 Lloyd Street Manchester M2 5LE T: 0161 234 7878 Fax: 0161 234 7888 E: register-office@manchester.gov.uk

Merton LB Morden Park House, Morden Hall London Road Morden SM4 5QU T: (020) 8648 0414 Fax: (020) 8648 0433

Middlesbrough The Register Office Corporation Road Middlesbrough TS1 2DA T: 01642 262078 Fax: 01642 262091

Milton Keynes Bracknell House Aylesbury Street Bletchley MK2 2BE T: 01908 372101 Fax: 01908 645103

Newcastle-upon-Tyne MD Newcastle-upon-Tyne Civic Centre Barras Bridge Newcastle-upon-Tyne NE1 8PS T: 0191 232 8520 Fax: 0191 211 4970

Newham LB The Register Office, Passmore Edwards Building 207 Plashet Grove East Ham London E6 1BT T: (020) 8430 2000 T: (020) 8430 3616 Fax: (020) 8430 3127

Norfolk

North Walsham (Erpingham Sub-district) Council Offices North Lodge Park Overstrand Road Cromer NR27 0AH T: 01263 513078

North Walsham (Smallburgh Sub-district) 18 Kings Arms Street North Walsham NR28 9JX T: 01692 403075

Depwade Council Offices 11-12 Market Hill Diss IP22 3JX T: 01379 643915 Fax: 01379 643915

Downham The Register Office 15 Paradise Road Downham Market PE38 9HS T: 01366 388080 Fax: 01366 387105

East Dereham 59 High Street Dereham NR19 1DZ T: 01362 698021 Fax: 01362 698021

Fakenham The Register Office Fakenham Connect Oak Street Fakenham NR21 9SR T: 01328 850122 Fax: 01328 850150

Great Yarmouth 'Ferryside' High Road Southtown Great Yarmouth NR31 0PH T: 01493 662313 Fax: 01493 602107

King's Lynn St Margaret's House St Margaret's Place King's Lynn PE30 5DW T: 01553 669251 Fax: 01553 769942

North Walsham The Register Office 18 Kings Arms Street North Walsham NR28 9JX T: 01692 406220 Fax: 01692 406220

Norwich Churchman House 71 Bethel Street Norwich NR2 1NR T: 01603 767600 Fax: 01603 632677

Wayland Kings House Kings Street Thetford IP24 2AP T: 01842 766848 Fax: 01842 765996

North- East Lincolnshire The Register Office Town Hall Square Grimsby DN31 1HX T: 01472 324860 Fax: 01472 324867

North Lincolnshire Register Office 92 Oswald Road Scunthorpe DN15 7PA T: 01724 843915 Fax: 01724 872668

North Somerset The Register Office 41 The Boulevard Weston-super-Mare BS23 1PG T: 01934 627552 Fax: 01934 412014

North Tyneside MD Maritime Chambers 1 Howard Street North Shields NE30 1LZ T: 0191 200 6164

North Yorkshire Registration Service Bilton House 31 Park Parade Harrogate HG1 5AG T: 01423 506949 Fax: 01423 502105 Holds all historical records for the County of North Yorkshire (except the City of York)

Northamptonshire

Brackley Brackley Lodge High Street Brackley NN13 5BD T: 01280-702949

Corby The Old Stables Cottingham Road Corby NN17 1TD T: 01536 203141

Daventry Council Offices Lodge Road Daventry NN11 5AF T: 01327 302209 Fax: 01327 300011

Kettering The Register Office 75 London Road Kettering NN15 7PQ T: 01536 514792 Fax: 01536 526948

Northampton The Guildhall St Giles Square Northampton NN1 1DE T: 01604 745390 Fax: 01604 745399

Oundle and Thrapston The Old Courthouse 17 Mill Road Oundle Peterborough PE8 4BW T: 01832 273413

Towcester & Brackley Sunnybanks 55 Brackley Road Towcester NN12 6DH T: 01327 350774

Wellingborough Council Offices Swanspool House Wellingborough NN8 1BP T: 01933 231549

Northumberland

Northumberland Central Post Office Chambers Station Road Ashington NE63 8RJ T: 01670 812243 Fax: 01670 814255

Northumberland North First (Belford Sub-district) The Sheltered Housing Community Centre Stone Close Seahouses NE68 7YL T: 01289 307373

Northumberland North First (Berwick Sub-district) 5 Palace Street East Berwick on Tweed TD15 1HT T: 01289 307373

Northumberland North First (Wooler Sub-district) 33 Glendale Road Wooler NE71 6DN T: 01668 281656

Northumberland Central The Register Office 94 Newgate Street Morpeth NE61 1BU T: 01670 513232 Fax: 01670 519260

Northumberland North First The Register Office 5 Palace Street East Berwick upon Tweed TD15 1HT T: 01289 307373

Northumberland North Second The Register Office 6 Market Place Alnwick NE66 1HP T: 01665 602363 Fax: 01665 510079

Northumberland West Abbey Gate House Market Street Hexham NE46 3LX T: 01434 602355 T: 01434 602605 Fax: 01434 604957

Nottinghamshire

Basford (Beeston & Stapleford Sub-district) Register Office Marvin Road off Station Road Beeston NG9 2AP T: 0115-925-5530

Newark (Southwell Sub-district) North Muskham Prebend Church Street Southwell NG25 0HG T: 01636 814200

Basford The Register Office Highbury Road Bulwell NG6 9DA T: 0115 927 1294 Fax: 0115 977 1845

East Retford Notts County Council Offices Chancery Lane Retford DN22 6DG T: 01777 708631 Fax: 01777 860667

Mansfield Registry Office, Dale Close 100 Chesterfield Road South Mansfield NG19 7DN T: 01623 476564 Fax: 01623 636284

Newark County Offices Balderton Gate Newark NG24 1UW T: 01636 705455 Fax: 01636 679259

Nottingham The Register Office 50 Shakespeare Street Nottingham NG1 4FP T: 0115 947 5665 Fax: 0115 9415773

Rushcliffe The Hall Bridgford Road West Bridgford NG2 6AQ T: 0115 981 5307 Fax: 0115 969 6189

Worksop Queens Buildings Potter Street Worksop S80 2AH T: 01909 535534 Fax: 01909 501067

Basford (Carlton Sub-district) County Council Offices Carlton Square Carlton NG4 3BP T: 0115-961-9663

Basford (Eastwood Sub-district) Eastwood Health Clinic Nottingham Road Eastwood NG16 3GL T: 01773-712449

Oldham MD Metropolitan House Hobson Street Oldham OL1 1PY T: 0161 678 0137 Fax: 0161 911 3729

Oxfordshire The Register Office Tidmarsh Lane Oxford OX1 1NS T: 01865 816246 Fax: 01865 815632

Poole The Register Office Civic Centre Annexe Park Road Poole BH15 2RN T: 01202 633744 Fax: 01202 633725

Portsmouth The Register Office Milldam House Burnaby Road PO1 3AF T: (023) 9282 9041 T: (023) 9282 9042 Fax: (023) 9283 1996

Redbridge LB Queen Victoria House 794 Cranbrook Road Barkingside Ilford IG6 1JS T: (020) 8708 7160 Fax: (020) 8708 7161

Redcar and Cleveland The Register Office Westgate Guisborough TS14 6AP T: 01287 632564 Fax: 01287 630768

Richmond Upon Thames LB The Register Office 1 Spring Terrace Richmond TW9 1LW T: (020) 8940 2853 Fax: (020) 8940 8226

Rochdale MD Town Hall The Esplanade Rochdale OL16 1AB T: 01706 864779 Fax: 01706 864786

Rotherham MD Bailey House Rawmarsh Road Rotherham S60 1TX T: 01709 382121 Fax: 01709 375530

Rutland Catmose Oakham Rutland LE15 6JU T: 01572 758370 Fax: 01572 758371

Salford MD 'Kingslea' Barton Road Swinton M27 5WH T: 0161 909 6501 Fax: 0161 794 4797

Sandwell MD Highfields High Street Sandwell B70 8RJ T: 0121 569 2480 Fax: 0121 569 2473

Sefton MD

Sefton North Town Hall Corporation Street Southport PR8 1DA T: 01704 533133 Fax: 0151 934 2014

Sefton South Crosby Town Hall Great Georges Road Waterloo Liverpool L22 1RB T: 0151 934 3045 Fax: 0151 934 3056

Sheffield MD The Register Office Surrey Place Sheffield S1 1YA T: 0114 203 9423 Fax: 0114 203 9424

Shropshire

Ludlow (Craven Arms Sub-district) The Library School Road Craven Arms SY7 9PE T: 01588 673455

North Shropshire (Market Drayton Sub-district) Health Centre Cheshire Street Market Drayton TF9 3AA T: 01630 657119

North Shropshire (Whitchurch Sub-district) 29 St Mary's Street Whitchurch SY13 1RA T: 01948 660902

Bridgnorth The Register Office 12 West Castle Street Bridgnorth WV16 4AB T: 01746 762589 Fax: 01746 764270

Clun The Pines Colebatch Road Bishop's Castle SY9 5JY T: 01588 638588

Ludlow The Register Office Stone House Corve Street, Ludlow SY8 1DG T: 01584 813208 Fax: 01584 813122

North Shropshire Edinburgh House New Street Wem Shrewsbury SY4 5DB T: 01939 238418

Oswestry The Register Office Holbache Road Oswestry SY11 1AH T: 01691 652086

Shrewsbury The Register Office The Shirehall Abbey Foregate Shrewsbury SY2 6LY T: 01743 252925 Fax: 01743 252939

Telford and Wrekin The Beeches 29 Vineyard Road Wellinton Telford TF1 1HB T: 01952 248292 Fax: 01952 240976

Solihull MD

Solihull The Register Office Homer Road Solihull B91 3QZ T: 0121 704 6100 Fax: 0121 704 6123

Solihull North The Library Stephenson Drive Chelmsley Wood Birmingham B37 5TA T: 0121-788-4376 Fax: 0121 788 4379

Somerset

Mendip (Frome Sub-district) West Hill House West End Frome BA11 3AD T: 01373 462887

Mendip (Shepton Mallet Sub-district) The Register Office 19 Commercial Road Shepton Mallet BA4 5BU T: 01749 342268

Mendip (Wells Sub-district) Town Hall Market Place Wells BA5 2RB T: 01749 675355

Yeovil (Chard Sub-district) Holyrood Lace Mill Holyrood Street Chard TA20 2YA T: 01460 260472 Fax: 01460 66899

Mendip The Register Office 19b Commercial Road Shepton Mallet BA4 5BU T: 01749 343928 Fax: 01749 342324

Sedgemoor Morgan House Mount Street Bridgewater TA6 3ER T: 01278 422527 Fax: 01278 452670

Taunton Flook House Belvedere Road Taunton TA1 1BT T: 01823 282251 Fax: 01823 351173

West Somerset 2 Long Street Williton Taunton TA4 4QN T: 01984 633116

Yeovil Maltravers House Petters Way Yeovil BA20 1SP T: 01935 411230 Fax: 01935 413993

Yeovil (Wincanton Sub-district) Council Offices Churchfield Wincanton BA9 9AG T: 01963 435008 Fax: 01963 34182

South Gloucestershire Poole Court Poole Court Drive Yate BS37 5PT T: 01454 863140 Fax: 01454 863145

South Tyneside

Jarrow The Register Office Suffolk Street Jarrow NE32 5BJ T: 0191-489 7595 Fax: 0191 428 0931 District abolished 2001 - records transferred to South Tyneside

South Tyneside The Register Office 18 Barrington Street South Shields NE33 1AH T: 0191 455 3915 Fax: 0191 427 7564 Records from Jarrow on abolition 2001 transferred here

Southampton The Register Office 6A Bugle Street Southampton SO14 2LX T: (023) 8063 1422 Fax: (023) 8063 3431 Visa, Switch, etc are accepted. Marriage indexes are computerised from 1837 - 1900 and some others. Births and deaths computerised from 1988.

Southwark LB The Register Office 34 Peckham Road Southwark London SE5 8QA T: (020) 7525 7651 Fax: (020) 7525 7652

St Helens MD The Register Office Central Street St Helens WA10 1UJ T: 01744 23524 T: 01744 732012 Fax: 01744 23524

Staffordshire

Cannock Chase (Rugeley Sub-district) Council Offices Anson Street Rugeley WS15 2BH T: 01889 585322

East Staffordshire (Uttoxeter Sub-district) 63 High Street Uttoxeter ST14 7JQ3 T: 01889 562168 Fax: 01889 569935

Lichfield (Tamworth Sub-district) 26 Albert Road Tamworth B79 7JS T: 01827 62295 Fax: 01827 62295

Newcastle under Lyme (Kidsgrove Sub-district) The Town Hall Liverpool Road Kidsgrove Stoke on Trent ST7 4EH T: 01782 296734

Staffordshire Moorlands (Biddulph Sub-district) Town Hall High Streeet Biddulph ST8 6AR T: 01782 297939 Fax: 01782 297815

Staffordshire Moorlands (Cheadle & Alton Sub-district) Council Offices Leek Road Cheadle Stoke on Trent ST10 1JF T: 01538 752435 Fax: 01538 752435

Staffordshire Moorlands (Leek & Cheddleton Sub-district) The Register Office High Street Leek ST13 5EA T: 01538 373191 Fax: 01538 386985

Cannock Chase The Register Office 5 Victoria Street Cannock WS11 1AG T: 01543 512345 Fax: 01543 512347

East Staffordshire Rangemore House 22 Rangemore Street Burton-upon-Trent DE14 2ED T: 01283 538701 Fax: 01283 547338

Lichfield The Old Library Buildings Bird Street Lichfield WS13 6PN T: 01543 510771 Fax: 01543 510773

Newcastle-under-Lyme The Register Office 20 Sidmouth Avenue The Brampton Newcastle-under-Lyme ST5 0QN T: 01782 297581 Fax: 01782 297582 Wolstanton Registration District is split between Newcastle-under-Lyme and Stoke-on-Trent Register Offices.

South Staffordshire Civic Centre Gravel Hill Wombourne Wolverhampton WV5 9HA T: 01902 895829 Fax: 01902 326779

Stafford Eastgate House 79 Eastgate Street Stafford ST16 2NG T: 01785 277880 Fax: 01785 277884

Staffordshire Moorlands The Register Office High Street Leek ST13 5EA T: 01538 373166 Fax: 01538 386985

Stockport MD Town Hall - John Street Entrance Stockport SK1 3XE T: 0161 474 3399 Fax: 0161 474 3390

Stockton-on-Tees Nightingale House Balaclava Street Stockton-on-Tees TS18 2AL T: 01642 393156 Fax: 01642 393159

Stoke-on-Trent Town Hall Albion Street Hanley Stoke on Trent ST1 1QQ T: 01782 235260 Fax: 01782 235258

Suffolk

Bury St. Edmunds St. Margarets Shire Hall Bury St Edmunds IP33 1RX T: 01284 352373 Fax: 01284 352376

Deben Council Offices Melton Hill Woodbridge IP12 1AU T: 01394 444331 T: 01394 444682 Fax: 01394 383171

Gipping & Hartismere Milton House 3 Milton Road South Stowmarket IP14 1EZ T: 01449 612060 T: 01449 612054

Ipswich St Peter House, County Hall 16 Grimwade Street Ipswich IP4 1LP T: 01473 583050 Fax: 01473 584331

Sudbury The Register Office 14 Cornard Road Sudbury CO10 2XA T: 01787 372904

Waveney St Margarets House Gordon Road Lowestoft NR32 1JQ T: 01502 405325 Fax: 01502 508170

Sunderland MD Town Hall & Civic Centre PO Box 108 Sunderland SR2 7DN T: 0191 553 1760 Fax: 0191 553 1769

Surrey

North Surrey 'Rylston' 81 Oatlands Drive Weybridge KT13 9LN T: 01932 254360 Fax: 01932 227139

West Surrey Artington House Portsmouth Road Guildford GU2 4DZ T: 01483 562841 Fax: 01483 573232

East Surrey East Surrey Register Office The Mansion 70 Church Street Leatherhead KT22 8DA T: 01372 373668 Fax: 01372 376811 This Office now deals with all enquiries for the Reigate Office which closed in 2000

Sutton LB Russettings 25 Worcester Road Sutton Surrey SM2 6PR T: (020) 8770 6790 F: (020 8770 6772

Swindon 1st Floor, Aspen House Temple Street Swindon SN1 1SQ T: 01793 521734 Fax: 01793 433887

Tameside MD Town Hall King Street Dukinfield SK16 4LA T: 0161 330 1177 Fax: 0161 342 2625

Tower Hamlets LB The Register Office Bromley Public Hall Bow Road E3 3AA T: (020) 7364 7891 T: (020) 7364 7898 Fax: (020) 7364 7885 This office holds the records of the former RDS of Stepney, Whitechapel, Bethnal Green, Poplar Mile end of Old Town and St George in the East. Please note records of the former East London RD are held by Islington Register Office.

Trafford MD Town Hall Tatton Road Sale M33 1ZF T: 0161 912 3025 Fax: 0161 912 3031

Wakefield MD
Pontefract The Register Office Town Hall Pontefract WF8 1PG T: 01977 722670 Fax: 01977 722676
Wakefield The Register Office 71 Northgate Wakefield WF1 3BS T: 01924 302185 Fax: 01924 302186
Walsall M D Walsall The Register Office, Civic Centre Hatherton Road Walsall WS1 1TN T: 01922 652260 Fax: 01922 652262
Waltham Forest LB The Register Office 106 Grove Road Walthamstow E17 9BY T: (020) 8520 8617 Fax: (020) 8509 1388
Wandsworth LB The Register Office The Town Hall Wandsworth High Street SW18 2PU T: (020) 8871 6120 Fax: (020) 8871 8100
Warwickshire
Mid Warwickshire (Leamington Spa Sub-district) 1 Euston Square Leamington Spa CV32 4NE T: 01926 428807 Fax: 01926 339923
Mid Warwickshire (Southam Sub-district) The Grange Coventry Road Southam CV47 1QB T: 01926 812636
South Warwickshire (Alcester Sub-district) Globe House Priory Road Alcester B49 5DZ T: 01789 765441
South Warwickshire (Shipston on Stour Sub-district) Clark House West Street Shipston on Stour CV36 4HD T: 01608 662839
South Warwickshire (Stratford on Avon Sub-district) Register Office 7 Rother Street Stratford on Avon CV37 6LU T: 01789 293397 Fax: 01789 261423
Mid Warwickshire Pageant House 2 Jury Street Warwick CV34 4EW T: 01926 494269 Fax: 01926 496287
North Warwickshire Warwick House Ratcliffe Street Atherstone CV9 1JP T: 01827 713241 Fax: 01827 720467
Nuneaton and Bedworth Riversley Park Coton Road Nuneaton CV11 5HA T: (024) 7634 8944 T: (024) 7634 8948 Fax: (024) 7635 0988
Rugby The Register Office 5 Bloxam Place Rugby CV21 3DS T: 01788 571233 Fax: 01788 542024
South Warwickshire The Register Office 7 Rother Street Stratford-on-Avon CV37 6LU T: 01789 293711 Fax: 01789 261423
West Sussex
Crawley (Sub-district) County Buildings Northgate Avenue Crawley RH10 1XB T: 01293-514545 Fax: 01293-553832
Chichester Greyfriars 61 North Street Chichester PO19 1NB T: 01243 782307 Fax: 01243 773671
Crawley Town Hall The Boulevard Crawley RH10 1UZ T: 01293 438341 Fax: 01293 526454
Haywards Heath West Sussex County Council Offices Oaklands Road Haywards Heath RH16 1SU T: 01444 452157 Fax: 01444 410128
Horsham Town Hall Market Square Horsham RH12 1EU T: 01403 265368 Fax: 01403 217078
Worthing Centenary House Durrington Lane Worthing BN13 2QB T: 01903 839350 Fax: 01903 839356
Westminster LB The Register Office Westminster Council House Marylebone Road NW1 5PT T: (020) 7641 1161 Fax: (020) 7641 1246
Wigan MD Wigan & Leigh New Town Hall Library Street Wigan WN1 1NN T: 01942 705000 Fax: 01942 705013
Wiltshire
Chippenham The Register Office 4 Timber Street Chippenham SN15 3BZ T: 01249 654361 Fax: 01249 658850
Devizes & Marlborough The Beeches Bath Road Devizes SN10 2AL T: 01380 722162 Fax: 01380 728933
Marlborough The Register Office 1 The Green Marlborough SN8 1AL T: 01672-512483 From 5/10/98 Devizes and Marlborough Districts merged as one district and all records at Devizes.
Salisbury The Laburnums 50 Bedwin Street Salisbury SP1 3UW T: 01722 335340 Fax: 01722 326806
Trowbridge East Wing Block County Hall Trowbridge BA14 8EZ T: 01225 713000 Fax: 01225 713096
Warminster The Register Office 3 The Avenue Warminster BA12 9AB T: 01985 213435 Fax: 01985 217688
Wirral MD
Wallasey The Register Office Town Hall Wallasey L44 8ED T: 0151-691-8505 The Wallasey Register Office is now closed, having been amalgamated with Birkenhead Register Office. All records for Birkenhead and Wallasey (ie the whole of the Wirral peninsula) are now held at Birkenhead.
Wirral Town Hall Mortimer Street Birkenhead L41 5EU T: 0151 666 4096 Fax: 0151 666 3685 This office now holds the records formerly held at the Wallasey office, which has been closed and amalgamated with Birkenhead. Registration District now named "Wirral".
Wolverhampton Civic Centre St Peters Square Wolverhampton WV1 1RU T: 01902 554989 Fax: 01902 554987
Worcestershire
Droitwich Council Offices Ombersley Street East Droitwich WR9 8QX T: 01905 772280 Fax: 01905 776841
Evesham County Offices Swan Lane Evesham WR11 4TZ T: 01386 443945 Fax: 01386 448745
Kidderminster Council Offices Bewdley Road Kidderminster DY11 6RL T: 01562 829100 Fax: 01562 60192

Malvern Hatherton Lodge Avenue Road Malvern WR14 3AG T: 01684 573000 Fax: 01684 892378
Pershore Civic Centre Queen Elizabeth Drive Station Road Pershore WR10 1PT T: 01386 565610 Fax: 01386 553656
Tenbury Council Buildings Teme Street Tenbury Wells WR15 8AD T: 01584 810588 Fax: 01584 819733
Worcester The Register Office 29-30 Foregate Street Worcester WR1 1DS T: 01905 765350 Fax: 01905 765355
York The Register Office 56 Bootham York YO30 7DA T: 01904 654477 Fax: 01904 638090
Yorkshire – South
Barnsley Town Hall Church Street Barnsley S70 2TA T: 01226 773085 T: 01226 773080

Wales
Anglesey
Ynys Môn Shire Hall Glanhwfa Road Llangefni LL77 7TW T: 01248 752564
Blaenau Gwent
Blaenau Gwent (Abertilley Sub-district) Council Offices Mitre Street Abertilley NP3 1AE T: 01495-216082
Blaenau Gwent (Ebbw Vale & Tredegar Sub-district) The Grove Church Street Tredegar NP2 3DS T: 01495-72269
Bridgend County Borough Offices Sunnyside Bridgend CF31 4AR T: 01656 642391 Fax: 01656 667529
Caerphilly
Caerphilly (Bargoed Sub-district) Hanbury Square Bargoed CF8 8QQ T: 01443-875560 Fax: 01443-822535
Caerphilly (Islwyn Sub-district) Council Offices Pontllanfraith Blackwood NP2 2YW T: 01495 235188 Fax: 01495 235298
Caerphilly The Council Offices, Ystrad Fawr Caerphilly Road Ystrad Mynach Hengoed CF82 7SF T: 01443 863478 Fax: 01443 863385
Cardiff The Register Office 48 Park Place Cardiff CF10 3LU T: (029) 2087 1690 Fax: (029) 2087 1691
Carmarthenshire
Carmarthen Carmarthen Register Office Parc Myrddin Richmond Terrace Carmarthen SA31 1DS T: 01267 228210 Fax: 01267 228215
Llanelli County Council Offices Swansea Road Llanelli SA15 3DJ T: 01554 774088 Fax: 01554 749424
Ceredigion
Cardiganshire Central The Register Office 21 High Street Lampeter SA48 7BG T: 01570 422558 Fax: 01570 422558
Cardiganshire North Swyddfar Sir Marine Terrace Aberystwyth SY33 2DE T: 01970 633580
Cardiganshire South Glyncoed Chambers Priory Street Cardigan SA43 1BX T: 01239 612684 Fax: 01239 612684
Conwy
Colwyn (Sub-district) Bod Alaw Rivieres Avenue Colwyn Bay LL29 7DP T: 01492-530430
Aberconwy Muriau Buildings Rose Hill Street Conwy LL32 8LD T: 01492 592407
Colwyn New Clinic and Offices 67 Market Street Abergele LL22 7BP T: 01745 823976 Fax: 01745 823976
Public Protection Department - Conwy County Borough Council Civic Offices Colwyn Bay LL29 8AR T: 01492 575183 Fax: 01492 575204
Denbighshire
Denbighshire North Morfa Hall Church Street Rhyl LL18 3AA T: 01824 708368 Fax: 01745 361424
Denbighshire South The Register Office Station Road Ruthin LL15 1BS T: 01824 703782 Fax: 01824 704399
Flintshire
Flintshire East The Old Rectory Rectory Lane Hawarden CH5 3NN T: 01244 531512 Fax: 01244 534628
Flintshire West The Register Office Park Lane Holywell CH8 7UR T: 01352 711813 Fax: 01352 713292
Gwent
Blaenau Gwent The Grove Church Street Tredegar NP2 3DS T: 01495 722305
Gwynedd
Ardudwy Bryn Marian Church Street Blaenau Ffestiniog LL41 3HD T: 01766 830217
Bangor The Register Office Town Hall Bangor LL57 2RE T: 01248 362418
Caernarfon Swyddfa Arfon Pennrallt Caernarfon LL55 1BN T: 01286 682661
De Meirionndd Meirionnydd Area Office Office Cae Penarlag Dolgellau LL40 2YB T: 01341 424341
Dwyfor The Register Office 35 High Street Pwllheli LL53 5RT T: 01758 612546 Fax: 01758 701373
Penllyn Penllyn Register Office Fron Faire High Street Bala LL23 7AD T: 01678 521220 Fax: 01678 521243
Merthyr Tydfil The Register Office, Ground Floor Castle House Glebeland Street Merthyr Tydfil CF47 8AT T: 01685 723318 Fax: 01685 721849
Monmouthshire

Monmouth (Abergavenny Sub-district) Coed Glas Firs Road Abergavenny NP7 5LE T: 01873 735435

Monmouth (Chepstow Sub-district) High Trees Steep Street Chepstow NP6 6RL T: 01291 635725

Monmouth Coed Glas Firs Road Abergavenny NP7 5LE T: 01873 735435 Fax: 01837 735429

Neath Port Talbot The Register Office 119 London Road Neath Port Talbot SA11 1HL T: 01639 760020 Fax: 01639 760023

Newport The Register Office 8 Gold Tops Newport NP9 4PH T: 01633 265547 Fax: 01633 220913

Pembrokeshire

Haverfordwest The Register Office Tower Hill Haverfordwest SA61 1SS T: 01437 762579 Fax: 01437 779357

South Pembroke The Register Office East Back Pembroke SA71 4HL T: 01646 682432 Fax: 01646 621433

Powys

Mid Powys

Mid Powys (Builth Sub-district) The Strand hall Strand Street Builth Wells LD2 3AA T: 01982 552134

Mid Powys (Radnorshire West Sub-district) Register Office Powys County Hall Llandrindod Wells LD1 5LG T: 01597 826382

Newtown (Llanidloes Sub-district) Town Hall Llanidloes SY18 6BN T: 01686 412353

Welshpool & Llanfyllin (Llanfyllin Sub-district) Room 8 First Floor Powys County Council Area Offices Youth & Community Centre Llanfyllin SY22 5DB T: 01691 649027

Brecknock Neuadd Brycheiniog Cambrian Way Brecon LD3 7HR T: 01874 624334 Fax: 01874 625781

Hay The Borough Council Offices Broad Street Hay-on-Wye HR3 5BX T: 01497 821371 Fax: 01497 821540

Machynlleth The Register Office 11 Penrallt Street Machynlleth SY20 8AG T: 01654 702335 Fax: 01654 703742

Mid Powys Powys County Hall Llandrindod Wells LD1 5LG T: 01597 826386

Newtown Council Offices The Park Newtown SY16 2NZ T: 01686 627862

Radnorshire East The Register Office 2 Station Road Knighton LD7 1DU T: 01547 520758

Welshpool & Llanfyllliin Neuadd Maldwyn Severn Road Welshpool SY21 7AS T: 01938 552828 Ext 228 Fax: 01938 551233

Ystradgynlais County Council Offices Trawsffordd Ystradgynlais SA9 1B3 T: 01639 843104

Rhonda Cynon Taff

Rhondda Cynon Taf The Register Office Courthouse Street Pontypridd CF37 1LJ T: 01443 486869 Fax: 01443 406587

Pontypridd

Pontypridd (Cynon Valley Sub-district) The Annexe Rock Grounds Aberdare CF44 7AE T: 01685 871008

Pontypridd (Rhondda No 2 Sub-district) Crown Buildings 69 High Street Ferndale Rhondda CF43 4RR T: 01443 730369

Pontypridd (Rhondda No1 Sub-district) De Winton Field Tonypandy CF40 2NJ T: 01443 433163 Fax: 01443 441677

Swansea

Swansea The Swansea Register Office County Hall Swansea SA1 3SN T: 01792 636188 Fax: 01792 636909

Torfaen The Register Office Hanbury Road Pontypool NP4 6YG T: 01495 762937 Fax: 01495 769049

Vale of Glamorgan The Register Office 2-6 Holton Road Barry CF63 4RU T: 01446 709490 Fax: 01446 709502

Wrexham The Register Office 2 Grosvenor Road Wrexham LL11 1DL T: 01978 265786 Fax: 01978 262061

Isle of Man

Civil Registry Registries Building Deemster's Walk Bucks Road Douglas IM1 3AR T: 01624-687039 Fax: 01624-687004 E: civil@registry.gov.im

Channel Islands

Guernsey

Greffe Royal Court House St Peter Port GY1 2PB T: 01481 725277 Fax: 01481 715097

Jersey

Judicial Greffe Morier House Halkett Place St Helier JE1 1DD T: 01534-502300 Fax: 01534-502399/502390 E: jgreffe@super.net.uk W: www.jersey.gov.uk

General Register Office of Northern Ireland Oxford House 49 - 55 Chichester Street Belfast BT1 4HL Northern Ireland T: (028) 90 252000 Fax: (028) 90 252120 E: gro.nisra@dfpni.gov.uk W: www.groni.gov.uk

Scotland

Aberdeen St Nicholas House Upperkirkgate Aberdeen AB10 1EY T: 01224 522616 T: 01224 522033 (search Room) Fax: 01224 522616

Braemar Operating from Ballater Registrars Office Temporarily

Inverurie, Oldmeldrum, Skere and Echt Gordon House Blackhall Road Inverurie AB51 3WA T: 01467 620981 (Fax: 01467 628012 E: diane.minty@aberdeenshire.gov.uk incorporating Inverurie (319), Oldmeldrum(320) , Skere and Echt (323)

Maud County Offices Maud AB4 SND T: 01771 613667 Fax: 0771 613204

Peterhead Arbuthnot House Broad Street Peterhead AB42 1DA T: 01779 483244 Fax: 01779 483246 E: shirley.dickie@aberdeenshire.gov.uk

Strathdon Area Office School Road Alford AB33 8PY T: 01975 564811

Tarves Area Office Schoolhill Road Ellon AB41 9AN T: 01358 720295 Fax: 01358 726410 E: kathleen.stopani@aberdeenshire.gov.uk

Aberfeldy, Dull & Weem 1 Orchard Brae Kenmore Street Aberfeldy PH15 2BL T: 01887 829335 Fax: 01887 829335

Aberfoyle and Mentheith Aberfoyle Local Office Main Street Aberfoyle FK8 3UQ T: 01877 382986 Fax: 01877 382986

Aboyne and Torphins District Council Offices Bellwood Road Aboyne AB34 5HQ T: 01339 886109 Fax: 01339 86798 E: esther.halkett@aberdeenshire.gov.uk

Alford and Sauchen Council Office School Road Alford AB33 8PY T: 01975 652421 Fax: 01975 563286 E: anne.shaw@aberdeenshire.gov.uk in corporating Sauchen (327)

Angus Dundee City Council Genealogy Unit 89 Commercial Street Dundee DD1 2AF T: 01382 435222 Fax: 01382 435224 E: grant.law@dundeecity.gov.uk W: www.dundeecity.gov.uk/registrars

Arbroath The Register Office 69/71 High Street Arbroath DD11 1AN T: 01241 873752 Fax: 01241 874805 E: arbroath@angusregistrar.sol.co.uk

Ardgour The Register Office 9 Clovullin Ardgour by Fort William PH33 7AB T: 01855 841261

Argyle and Bute Rosneath Registration Office Easter Garth Rosneath by Helensburgh G84 0RF T: 1436831679 E: elsa.rossetter@eastergarth.co.uk W: www.eastergarth.co.uk

Dunoon Council Offices Hill Street Dunoon PA23 7AP T: 01369 704374 Fax: 01369 705948 E: ann.sadler@argyll bute.gov.uk

Lismore Baleveolan Isle of Lismore PA34 5UG T: 01631 760274

Campbeltown Council Office Dell Road Campbeltown PA28 6JG T: 01586 552366 Fax: 01586 552366 E: julie.mclellan@!argyll bute.gov.uk W: www.argyll bute.gove.uk

Kilbrandon and Kilchattan Dalanasaig Clachan Seil By Oban PA34 4TJ T: 01852 300380

Arrochar The Register Office 1 Cobbler View Arrochar G83 7AD T: 01301 702289

Assynt Post Office House Lochinver Lochinver by Lairg IV27 4JY T: 01571 844201

Auchinleck The Register Office 28 Well Road Auchlinleck Cummock KA18 2LA T: 01290 420582

Auchterarder The Ayton Hall 91 High Street Auchterarder PH3 11QD T: 01764 662155 Fax: 01764 662120

Aviemore Tremayne Dalfaber Road Aviemore PH22 1PU T: 01479 810694

Ayr Sandgate House 43 Sandgate Ayr KA7 1DA T: 01292 284988 Fax: 01292 885643 E: ayr.registrars@south ayrshire.gov.uk

Ballater An Creagan 5 Queens Road. Ballater AB35 5NJ T: 01339 755535 T: 01339 755284

Banchory Aberdeenshire Council The Square High Street Banchory AB3 1 T: 01330 822878 Fax: 01330 822243

Banff Seafield House 37 Castle Street Banff AB45 1FQ T: 01261 812001 T: 01261 813439 Direct Fax: 01261 818244

Barra Council Offices Castlebay Barra HS9 5XD T: 01871 810431

Barrhead Council Office 13 Lowndes Street Barrhead 078 2QX T: 0141 577 33551 Fax: 0141 577 3553

Beauly The Register Office 7 Viewfield Avenue Beauly 1V4 7BW T: 01463 782264

Bellshill The Register Office 20/22 Motherwell Road Bellshill ML4 1RB T: 01698 346780 Fax: 016989 346789 E: registrars bellshill@nothlan.gov.uk

Benbecula Council Offices Balivanich Benbecula South Uist HS7 5LA T: 01870 602425

Biggar The Register Office 4 Ross Square Biggar MLI2 EAT T: 01899 220997

Bishopbriggs Council Offices The Triangle Kirkintilloch Bishopbriggs G64 2TR T: 0141 578 8557 E: mary.neill@eastdunbarton.gov.uk

Black Isle Blacxk Isle Leisure Centre Deans Road Fortrose IV10 8TJ T: 01381 620797 Fax: 01381 621085 E: marion.phimister@highland.gov.uk

Blairgowrie Council Buildings 46 Leslie Street Blairgowrie PH10 6AW T: 01250 872051 Fax: 01250 876029

Bo'ness and Carriden Registration Office 15a Seaview Place Bo'ness EH51 0AJ T: 01506 778990

Boisdale Post Office House Daliburgh South Uist HS8 5SS T: 01878 700300

Bonar and Kincardine Post Office Bonar Bridge Ardgay IV24 3EA T: 01863 766219

Bonnybridge Operating from Denny T: 01324 504280

Brechin The Register Office 32 Panmure Street Brechin DD9 6AP T: 01356 622107

Bressay The Register Office No 2 Roadside Bressay Lerwick ZE2 9BL T: 01595 820356

Broadford The Register Office Fairwinds Broadford IV49 9AB T: 01471 822270

Buckie Town House West Cluny Place Buckie AB56 1UB T: 01542 832691 Fax: 01542 833384 E: Jill.addison@chief.moray.gov.uk

Bucksburn Nea Office 23 Inverurie Road. Bucksburn AB21 9LJ T: 01224 712866 Fax: 01224 716997

Carnoch Operating from Dingwall IV15 9QR T: 01349 863113

Carnoustie Council Chambers 26 High Street Carnoustie DD7 6AP T: 01241 853335/6 T: 01241 803112 Fax: 01241 857554

Castle Douglas District Council 5 Street Andrew Street Castle Douglas DG7 1DE T: 01557 330291

Castleton 10 Douglas Square Newcastleton TD9 0QD T: 01387 375606

Chryston The Register Office Lindsaybeg Road Muirhead Glasgow G69 9HW T: 0141 779 1714

Clackmannanshire Marshill House Marshill Alloa FK10 1AB T: 01259 723850 Fax: 01259 723850 E: registration@clacks.gov.uk W: www.clacksweb.org.uk

Clyne Brora Service Point Gower Street Brora KW9 6PD T: 01408 622644

Coalburn 'Pretoria 200 Coalburn Road Coalburn ML11 0LT T: 01555 820664

Coigach 29 Market Street Ullapool IV26 2XE T: 01854 612426

Coldstream 73 High Street Coldstream TD12 4AE T: 01890 883156

Coll The Register Office 9 Carnan Road Isle of Coll PA78 6TA T: 01879 230329

Colonsay & Oronsay Colonsay Service point Village Hall Colonsay PA61 7YW T: 01951 200263

Coupar Angus Union Bank Buildings Coupar Angus PH13 9AJ T: 01828 628395 Fax: 01828 627147 E: legalservices@wandlb.co.uk

Crawford Raggengill 45 Carlisle Road Crawford Biggar ML12 6TP T: 01864 502633

Crieff Crieff Area Office 32 James Square Crieff PH7 3EY T: 01764 657550 Fax: 01764 657559

Cumbernauld Fleming House Tryst Road Cumbernauld G67 1JW T: 01236 616390 Fax: 01236 616386

Dalbeattie Town Hall Buildings Water Street Dalbeattie DG5 4JX T: 01557 330291 Ext323

Dalmellington Dalmellington Area Centre 33 Main Street Street Dalmellington KA6 7QL T: 01292 552880 Fax: 01292 552 884

Dalry 42 Main Street Dalry Castle Douglas DG7 3UW T: 01644 430310

Delting Soibakkan Mossbank ZE2 9RB T: 01806 242209

Denny Carronbank House Carronbank Crescent Denny PK4 2DE T: 01324 504280

Dornoch The Register Office Cathedral Square Dornoch IV25 3SG T: 01862 812008

Douglas Post Office Ayr Road Douglas ML1 I OPU T: 01555 851227

Dumbarton 18 College Way Dumbarton G82 1LJ T: 01389 767515

Dumfries and Galloway

Thornhill Dumfreis and Galloway Council One Stop shop Manse Road Thornhill DG3 5DR T: 01848 330303

Dumfries Municipal Chambers Buccleuch Street Dumfries DO 1 2AD T: 01387 260000 Fax: 01387 269605 incorporating New Abbey (861)

Annan Council Offices 15 Ednay Street Annan DG12 6EF T: 01461 204914 Fax: 01461 206896

Gretna Registration Office Central Avenue Gretna DG16 5AQ T: 01461 337648 Fax: 01461 338459 E: gretnaonline@dumgal.gov.uk W: www.gretnaonline.net CC accepted

Kirkcudbright District Council Offices Daar Road Kirkcudbrigbt DG6 4JG T: 01557 330291 Ext 234 W: www.dumgal.gov.uk

Lockerbie Town Hall High Street Lockerbie DG11 2ES T: 01576 204267

Moffat Town Hall High Street Moffat DG10 9HF T: 01683 220536 Fax: 01683 221489 E: alisonQ@dumgal.gov.uk

Wigtown Area Council Sub office County Buildings Wigtown DG8 9HR T: 01988 402624 Fax: 01988 403201

Dunblane Municipal Buildings Dunblane FK15 0AG T: 01786 823300 Fax: 01786 823300 E: muirm@stirling.gov.uk

Dundee City Council Genealogy Unit 89 Commercial Street Dundee DD1 2AF T: 01382 435222 Fax: 01382 435224 E: grant.law@dundeecity.gov.uk W: www.dundeecity.gov.uk/registrars

Dundee The Register Office 89 Commercial Street Dundee DD1 2AO T: 01382 435222/3 Fax: 01382 435224 E: grant.law@dundesity.gov.uk W: www.dundeecity.gov.uk/registrars

Dunrossness Baptist Manse Dunrossness ZE2 93JB T: 01950 460792

Duns The Register Office 8 Newtown Street Duns TD11 3DT T: 01361 882600

Durness Service Point, Highlands of Scotland Tourist Board Sangomore Durness IV27 4PZ T: 01971 511368

East Ayrshire Catrine The Register Office 9 Co operative Avenue Catrine KA5 6SG T: 01290 551638

Darvel, Galston, Newmilns The Register Office 11 Cross Street Galston KA4 8AA T: 01563 820218

Kilmarnock Civic Centre John Dickie Street Kilmarnock KA1 1HW T: 01563 576695/6

East Kilbride Civic Centre Cornwall Street East Kilbride Glasgow G74 1AB T: 01355 806472 CC accepted

East Lothian Dunbar Town House 79/85 High Street Dunbar EH42 IER T: 01368 863434 Fax: 01368 865728 E: fwhite@eastlothian.gov.uk

Haddington The Register Office John Muir House Brewery Park Haddington EH41 3HA T: 01620 827308 Fax: 01620 827438 E: sforsyth@eastlothian.gov.uk

Eastwood and Mearns Eastwood and Mearns Council Offices Eastwood Park Roukenglen Road Giffnock G46 7JS T: 0141 638 7588

Eday and Pharay Eday and Pharay Redbanks Eday Orkney KW1 2AA T: 01857 622239

Edinburgh (India Buildings) 2 India Buildings Victoria Street Edinburgh EH1 2EX T: 0131 220 0349 Fax: 0131 220 0351 E: registrars.indiabuildings@edinburgh.gov.uk CC accepted

Edinburgh (Ratho) Operating from 2 India Buildings, Victoria Street, Edinburgh Ratho 0: 0131 220 0349 Fax: 0131 220 0351 E: registrars.indiabuildings@edinburgh.gov.uk CC accepted

Edinburgh (Currie) The Register Office 133 Lanark Road West Currie EH14 5NY T: 0131 449 5318

Edinburgh (Kirkliston) 19 Station Road Kirkliston EH29 9BB T: 0131 333 3210

Edinburgh (Leith) The Register Office 30 Ferry Road Edinburgh EH6 4AE T: 0131 554 8452

Edinburgh (Queensferry) Council Office 53 High Street South Queensferry EH30 9HN T: 0131 331 1590

Ellon Ellon Area Office Schoolhill Road Ellon AB41 9AA T: 01358 720295 Fax: 01358 726410 E: kathleen.stopani@aberdeenshire.gov.uk

Eyemouth Eyemouth Community Centre Albert Road Eyemouth TD14 5DE T: 01890 750690

Falkirk Falkirk Old Burgh Buildings Newmarket Street Falkirk FK1 IIE T: 01324 506580 Fax: 01324 506581

Fife (Auchterderran) The Register Office 145 Station Road Cardenden KY5 0BN T: 01592 414800 Fax: 01592 414848

Fife (Auchtermuchty) Local Office 15 High Street Auchtermuchty KY14 7AP T: 01337 828329 Fax: 01337 821166

Fife (Benarty) Benarty Local Office 6 Benarty Square Ballingry KY5 8NR T: 01592 414343 Fax: 01592 414363

Fife (Bucknaven) Local Office Municipal Buildings, College Streert Buckhaven KY8 1AB T: 01592 414444 Fax: 01592 414490

Fife (Cowdenbeath) The Register Office 123 High Street Cowdenbeath KY4 9QB T: 01383 313170 Fax: 01383 313190

Fife (Cupar) County Buildings St Catherine Street Cupar KY15 4TA T: 01334 412200

Fife (Dunfermline) The Register Office 34 Viewfield Terrace Dunfermline KY12 7HZ T: 01383 3 12121

Fife (East Neuk) Anstruther Local Office Ladywalk Anstruther KY10 3EX T: 01333 592110 Fax: 01333 592117

Fife (Glenrothes) Albany House Albany Gate Kingdom Centre Glenrothes KY7 5NP T: 01592 416570 Fax: 01592 416565 E: sophia.semple@fife.gov.uk

Fife (Inverkeithing) Civic Centre Queen Street Inverkeithing KY11 1PA T: 01383 313570 Fax: 01383 313585

(Fife) Kelty Kelty Local Services Sanjana Court 51 Main Street Kelty KY4 0AA T: 01383 839999

Fife (Kennoway) 6/7 Bishops Court Kennoway Fife KY8 5JW T: 01333 352635

Fife (Kirkcaldy) District Office Town House Kirkcaldy KY1 1XW T: 01592 412121 Fax: 01592 412123 E: jennifer.brymer@fife.gov.uk

Fife (Leven) Carberry House Scoonie Road Leven KY8 4JS T: 01333 592460

Fife (Lochgelly) Lochgelly Local Office Town House Hall Street Lochgelly KY5 9JN T: 01592 418180 Fax: 01592 418190 E: karen.henderson@fife.gov.uk

Fife (Newburgh) Tayside Institute 90 92 High Street Newburgh KY14 6DA T: 01337 883000

Fife (Newport on Tay) Blyth Hall Scott Street Newport On Tay DD6 8BJ T: 01382 542839

Fife (St Andrews) Area Office St Mary's Place St Andrews KY16 9UY T: 01334 412525 Fax: 01334 412650 E: jennifer.millar@fife.gov.uk

Fife (Tayport) Burgh Chambers Tayport DD6 9JY T: 01382 552544

Fife (West Fife) The Health Centre Chapel Street High Valleyfield Dunfermline KY12 8SJ T: 01383 880682

Forfar The Register Office 9 West High Street Forfar DD8 1BD T: 01307 464973 E: regforfar@angus.gov.uk

Forres 153 High Street Forres IV36 1DX T: 01309 694070

Fort Augustus Highland Council Service Point, Memorial Hall Oich Road Fort Augustus PH32 4DJ T: 01320 366733

Forth The Register Office 4 Cloglands Forth ML11 8ED T: 01535 811631

Fraserburgh The Register Office 14 Saltoun Square Fraserburgh AB43 5DB T: 01346 513281

Gairloch The Service Point Achtercairn Gairloch IV22 2BP T: 01445 712572 E: trudy.mackenzie@highland.gov.uk

Gairloch (South) The Service Point Achtercairn Gairloch IV22 2BP T: 01445 712572 Fax: 01445 712911 E: trudy.mackenzie@highland.gov.uk

Gigha 10 Ardminish Gigha PA41 7AB T: 01583 505249

Girthon and Anwoth Operating from Kirkcudbright DG6 4JG T: 01557 332534

Glasgow (Martha Street) The Register Office 1 Martha Street Glasgow G1 1JJ T: 0141 287 7677 Fax: 0141 287 7666

Glasgow (Park Circus) The Register Office 22 Park Circus Glasgow G3 6BE T: 0141 287 8350 Fax: 0141 225 8357

Golspie Council Offices Main Street Golspie KW10 6RB T: 01408 635200 Fax: 01408 633120 E: moira.macdonald@highland.gov.uk

Glasgow The Register Office 22 Park Circus Glasgow G3 6BE T: 0141 287 8350 Fax: 0141 287 8357 E: bill.craig@pas.glasgow.gov.uk

Grangemouth Municipal Chambers Bo'ness Road Grangemouth FK3 3AY T: 01324 504499

Hamilton (Blantyre) Local Office 45 John Street Blantyre G72 0JG T: 01698 527916 Fax: 01698 527923 CC accepted

Harris Council Offices Tarbert HS3 3DJ T: 01859 502367 Fax: 01859 502283

Hawick Council Offices 12 High Street Hawick TD9 9EF T: 01450 364710 Fax: 01450 364720

Helensburgh Scotcourt House 45 West princes Street Helensburgh G84 8BP T: 01436 658822 T: 01436 656600 Fax: 01436 658821

Helmsdale Operating from 12 Dunrobin StreetGower Street Brora KW9 6PD T: 01408 622644 Fax: 01408 622645

Highland Applecross Coire ringeal Applecross Strathcarron IV54 8LU T: 01520 744248

Area Repository Ross and Cromarty Council Offices Ferry Road Dingwall IV15 9QR T: 01349 863113 Fax: 01349 866164 E: alison.matheson@highland.gov.uk_anna.gallie@highland.gov.uk NOTE: All Statutory Registers (1855 1965) are held here for the following Districts:_Alness, Applecross, Avoch, Carnoch, Coigach, Contin, Cromarty, Dingwall, Edderton, Fearn, Fodderty, Gairloch, North Gairloch, South Glensheil, Killearnan, Kilmuir Easter Kiltearn, Kincardine, Kinlochluichart, Kintail, Knockbain, Lochalsh, Lochbroom, Lochcarron, Logie Easter Nigg, Resolis, Rosemarkie, Rosskeen, Shieldaig, Strathoykel, Tain, Tarbat, Urquart and Logie Wester Urray. All Ancestry Enquiries should be addressed to this Office. Records from 1965 to present at local Offices

Dingwall and Carnoch Council Offices Ferry Road Dingwall IV15 9QR T: 01349 863113 Fax: 01349 866164 E: alison.matheson@highland.gov.uk_anna.gallie@highland.gov.uk Area Repository for Ross and Cromarty

Dunvegan Tigh na Bruaich Dunvegan IV55 8WA T: 01470 521296 Fax: 01470 521519

Fort William and Ballachulish Tweeddale Buildings High Street Fort William PH33 6EU T: 01397 704583 Fax: 01397 702757 E: isobel.mackellaig@highland.gov.uk W: www.highland.gov.uk

Glenelg Taobh na Mara Na Mara Gleneig Kyle IV40 8JT T: 01599 522310 Only holds records from 1965

Grantown on Spey and Nethyridge Council Offices The Square Grantown On Spey PH26 3HF T: 01479 872539 Fax: 01479 872539 E: diane.brazier@highland.gov.uk

Inverness Registration Office Farraline Park Inverness IV1 1NH T: 01463 239792 Fax: 01463 712412 E: margaret.straube@highland.gov.uk W: www.highland.gov.uk

Kirkton and Tongue The Service Point Naver Teleservice Centre Bettyhill By Thurso KW14 7SS T: 01641 521242 Fax: 01641 521242 E: mary.cook@highland.gov.uk

Mallaig and Knoydart Sandholm Morar Mallaig PH40 4PA T: 01687 462592 Fax: 01687 462592

Rosskeen Invergordon Service Point 62 High St Invergordon IV18 0DH T: 01349 852472 Fax: 01349 853803

Tain 24 High Street Tain T: 01862 892122

Thurso, Strathy and Mey Library Buildings Davidsons Lane Thurso KW14 7AF T: 01847 892786 Fax: 1847894611 E: pauline.edmunds@highland.gov.uk

Wick Town Hall Bridge Street Wick KW1 4AN T: 01955 605713 Fax: 01955 605713 E: margaret.wood@highland.gov.uk

Thurso, Strathy and Mey District Office, Library Buildings Davidson's Lane Thurso KW14 7AF T: 01847 892786 Fax: 01847 894611 E: pauline.edmunds@highland.gov.uk Caithness Area Repository Genealogical Repository with on line access to GRO Scotland

Huntly The Register Office 25 Gordon Street Huntly AB54 5AN T: 01466 794488

Insch Marbert George Street Insch AB52 6JL T: 01464 820964

Inveraray Operating from Lochgilphead

Inverclyde The Register Office 40 West Stewart Street Greenock PA15 1YA T: 01475 714250 Fax: 01415 714253 E: maureen.bradley@inverclyde.gov.uk

Inveresk Brunton Hall Ladywell Way Musselburgh EH21 6AF T: 0131 665 3711

Irvine The Register Office 106 108 Bridgegate House Irvine KA12 8BD T: 01294 324988 Fax: 1294324984

Islay Council Office Jamieson Street Bowmore Islay PA43 7HL T: 01496 810332

Isle of Bute Council Office Mount Pleasant Road Rothesay PA20 9HH T: 01700 50331/501 Fax: 01700 504401

Isle of Lewis Carloway The Registry Knock Carloway HS2 9AU T: 01851 643264

Jedburgh Library Building Castlegate Jedburgh TD8 6AS T: 01835 863670 Fax: 01835 863670 E: aveitch@scotborders.gov.uk W: www.scotborders.gov.uk

Johnstone The Register Office 16 18 McDowall Street Johnstone PA5 8QL T: 01505 320012 T: 01505 331771 Fax: 01505 382130 W: www.renfrewshire.gov.uk

Jura Forestry Cottage Craighouse Jura PA60 7AY T: 01496 820326

Kelso Town House Kelso TD5 7HF T: 01573 225659 incorporates Gordon District

Kenmore Operating from Aberfeldy Acharn by Aberfeldy PH15 2HS T: 01887 829335

Kilbirnie, Beith and Dalry 19 School Wynd Kilbirnie KA25 7AY T: 01505 682416 Fax: 01505 684334 E: amcgurran@north ayrshire.gov.uk

Kilfinichen and Kilvickeon The Anchorage Fionnphort PA66 6BL T: 01681 700241

Killin 8 Lyon Villas Killin FK21 8TF T: 01567 820267

Kilwinning The Regsitrar's Office 32 Howgate Kilwinning KAI3 6EJ T: 01294 55226112 Fax: 01294 557787 E: mmccorquindale@north ayrshire.gov.uk

Kingussie Council Offices Ruthven Road Kingussie PH21 1EJ T: 01540 664529 Fax: 01540 661004 CC accepted

Kinlochbervie The Register Office 114 Inshegra Rhiconich Lairg IV27 4RH T: 01971 521388

Kinlochluichart The Old Manse Garve IV23 2PX T: 01997 414201

Kinross Kinross Area Office 21/25 High Street Kinross KY13 8AP T: 01577 867202 Fax: 01577 865352

Kirkconnell Nith Buildings Greystone Avenue Kelloholm Kirkconnel DG4 6RX T: 01659 67206 Fax: 01659 66052

Kirkintilloch and Lennoxtown Council Office 21 Southbank Road Kirkintilloch G66 1NH T: 0141 776 2109

Kirkmabreck The Bogue Creetowm Newton Stewart DG8 7JW T: 01671 820266

Kirriemuir 5 Bank Street Kirriemuir DD8 8BE T: 01575 572845

Lairg The Service Point Main Street Lairg IV27 4DB T: 01549 402588

Langholm Town Hall Langholm DG13 0JQ T: 01387 380255 Fax: 01387 81142

Larbert The Register Office 318 Main Street Stenhousemuir FK5 3BE T: 01324 503580 Fax: 01324 503581

Larkhall Council Office 55 Victoria Street Larkhall ML9 2BN T: 01698 882454/5

Latherton Post Office Latheron KW5 6DG T: 01593 741201

Laurencekirk Royal Bank Buildings Laurencekirk AB30 1AF T: 01561 377245 Fax: 01561 378020

Leadhills Operating from Lanark Temporarily Leadhills T: 01555 673220

Lerwick County Buildings Lerwick ZE1 0HD T: 01595 693535 Ext 368

Lesmahagow The Register Office 40/42 Abbeygreen Lesmahagow ML11 0DE T: 01555 893314

Loch Duich Operating from Hamilton House Kyle Of Lochalsh IV40 8BL T: 01599 534270

Lochalsh Hamilton House Plock Road Kyle IV40 8BL T: 01599 534270

Lochbroom and Coigach Locality Office 29 Market Street Ullapool 1V26 2XE T: 01854 612426 Fax: 01854 612717 E: doreen.macleod@highland.gov.uk

Lochcarron and Shieldaig Lochcarron Service Point Main Street Lochcarron IV54 8YB T: 01520 722241

Lochgilphead Dairiada House Lochnell Street Lochgilphead PA31 8ST T: 01546 604511

Lochgoilhead Dervaig Lettermay Lochgoilhead PA24 8AE T: 01301 703306

Lonforgan The Register Office 8 Norval Place Longforgan Dundee DD2 5ER T: 01382 360283

Mauchline The Register Office 2 The Cross Mauchline KA5 5DA T: 01290 550231 Fax: 01290 551991

Melrose Ormiston Institute Market Square Melrose TD6 9PN T: 01896 823114 Fax: 01896 823114

Mid and South Yell Schoolhouse Ulsta Yell ZE2 9BD T: 01957 722260

Midlothian The Register Office 2 4 Buccleuch Street Dalkeith EH22 IHA T: 0131 271 3281 T: 0131 271 3282 Fax: 0131 663 6842 E: dkregistrars@midlothian.gov.uk

Milnathort Rowallan 21 Church Street Milnathort KY13 7XH T: 01577 862536

Mochrum 13 South Street 85 Main Street Port William Newton Stewart DG8 9SH T: 01988 700741

Montrose The Register Office 51 John Street Montrose DD10 8LZ T: 01674 672351

Moray Council Elgin inc Tomintoul The Register Office 240 High Street Elgin IV30 1BA T: 01343 554600 Fax: 01343 554644

Morayshire Keith and Upper Speyside Area Office Mid Street Keith AE55 5BJ T: 01542 885525 Fax: 01542 885522 E: keith.registrar@chief.moray.gov.uk
Morvern The Register Office Dungrianach Lochaline Morvern PA34 5XW T: 01961 421662
Motherwell and Wishaw Civic Centre Windmillhill Street Motherwell ML1 1TW T: 01698 302206
Muckhart and Glendevon Operating from Alloa T: 01259 723850
Muirkirk 44 Main Street Muirkirk KA18 3RD T: 01290 661227
Nairn The Court House Nairn IV12 4AU T: 01667 458510
New Cumnock Town Hall The Castle New Cumnock KA18 4AN T: 01290 338214 Fax: 01290 338214
New Kilpatrick Council Office 38 Roman Road Bearsden G61 2SH T: 0141 942 2352/3
Newton Stewart Area McMillan Hall Dashwood Square Newton Stewart DG8 6EQ T: 01671 404187
North Ayrshire Isle of Arran District Council Office Lamlash KA27 8JY T: 01770 600338 Fax: 01770 600028 incorporates Lochranza (552)
Largs Moorburn 24 Greenock Road Largs KA30 8NE T: 01475 674521 Fax: 01475 687304 E: gmcginty@north ayrshire.gov.uk W: www.north ayrshire.gov.uk CC accepted_Also covers Cumbrae (551)
Saltcoats The Register Office 45 Ardrossan Road Saltcoats KA21 5BS T: 01294 463312 Fax: 01294 604868 E: j.kimmett@north ayrshire.gov.uk W: www.north ayrshire.gov.uk
West Kilbride Kirktonhall 1 Glen Road West Kilbride KA23 9BL T: 01294 823569 Fax: 01294 823569 E: westkilbrideregistrar@north ayrshire.gov.uk W: www.north ayrshire.gov.uk
Cumbrae Moorburn 24 Greenock Road Largs KA30 8NE T: 01475 674521 Fax: 01475 687304 E: gmcginty@north ayrshire.gov.uk W: www.north ayrshire.gov.uk CC accepted Also covers Largs
North Berwick The Register Office 2 Quality Street North Berwick EH39 4HW T: 01620 893957
North Lanarkshire Airdrie Area Registration Office 37 Alexander Street Airdrie ML6 0BA T: 01236 758080 Fax: 01236 758088 E: registrars airdrie@northlan.gov.uk
Coatbridge The Register Office 183 Main Street Coatbridge ML5 3HH T: 01236 812647 Fax: 01236 812643 E: registrars coatbridge@northlan.gov.uk W: www.northlan.gov.uk
Kilsyth Health Centre Burngreen Park Kilsyth G65 0HU T: 01236 826813
Shotts Council Ornee 106 Station Road Shotts ML7 8BH T: 01501 824740
North Ronaldsay Hooking North Ronaldsay KW17 2BE T: 01857 633257
North Uist Fairview Lochmaddy North Uist HS6 5AW T: 01876 500239
Oban Lorn House Albany Street Oban PA34 4AR T: 01631 567930 Fax: 01631 570379 E: emma.cummins@argyll bute.gov.uk
Old Cumnock Council Office Millbank 14 Lugar Street Cumnock KA18 1AB T: 01290 420666 Fax: 01290 426164
Old Kilpatrick Council Offices Rosebery Place Clydebank G81 1BL T: 01389 738770 Fax: 01389 738775
Oldmeldrum Gordon House Blackhall Road Inverurie AB51 3WA T: 01467 620981 T: 01467 628011 (Direct) Fax: 01467 628012 E: diane.minty@aberdeenshire.gov.uk incorporating Inverurie (319), Oldmeldrum(320) , Skere and Echt (323)
Orkney Birsay Sandveien Dounby Orkney KW15 2118 T: 01856 771226
Orphir The Bu Orphir Kirkwall KW17 2RD T: 01856 811319
Sanday The Register Office Hyndhover Sanday KW17 2BA T: 01857 600441 E: catharine@po,ona54.freeserve.co.uk
Firth & Stenness The Register Office Langbigging Stenness KWI6 3LB T: 01856 850320
Flotta Post Office Flotta Stromness KWI6 3NP T: 01856 701252
Harray New Breckan Harray KW17 2JR T: 01856 771233
Holm and Paplay The Register Office Netherbreck Holm KWI7 2RX T: 01856 781231
Hoy Laundry House Melsetter Longhope KWI6 3NZ T: 01856 791337
Kirkwall Council Offices School Place Kirkwall KW15 1NY T: 01856 873535 Fax: 01856 873319 E: chief.registrar@orkney.gov.uk W: www.orkney.gov.uk
Shapinsay The Register Office Girnigoe Shapinsay KWI7 2EB T: 01856 711256 E: jean@girnigoe.f9.co.uk W: www.visitorkney.com/accommodation/girnigoe
Stromness The Register Office Ferry Terminal Building Ferry Road Stromness KW16 3AE T: 01856 850854
Westray Myrtle Cottage Pierowall Westray KW17 2DH T: 01857 677278
Paisley Registration Office 1 Cotton Street Paisley PA1 1BU T: 0141 840 3388 Fax: 0141 840 3377 W: www.renfrewshire.gov.uk
Papa Westray Backaskaill Papa Westray KW17 2BU T: 01857 644221
Peebles Chambers Institute High Street. Peebles EH45 8AG T: 01721 723817 Fax: 01721 723817 E: showitt@scotborders.gov.uk
Penicuik and Glencorse The Registry Office 33 High Street Penicuik EH26 8HS T: 01968 672281 Fax: 01968 679547

Perth The Register Office 3 High Street Perth PH1 5JS T: 01738 475121 Fax: 01738 444133 Incorporates Dunkeld (388)
Perth & Kinross Blair Athol Operating from Pitlochry
Logierait Operating from Pitlochry
Pitlochry District Area Office 21 Atholl Road Pitlochry PH16 5BX T: 01796 472323 Fax: 01796 474226
Peterculter Lilydale 102 North Deeside Road Peterculter AB14 0QB T: 01224 732648 Fax: 01224 734637
Polmont and Muiravonside Council Offices Redding Road Brightons Falkirk FK2 0HG T: 01324 503990
Portree and Raasay Registrars Office King's House The Green Portree IV51 9BS T: 01478 613277 Fax: 01478 613277
Portsoy The Register Office 2 Main Street Portsoy AB45 2RT T: 01261 842510 Fax: 01261 842510
Prestonpans Aldhammer House High Street Prestonpans EH32 9SE T: 01875 810232 Fax: 01875 814921
Prestwick The Register Office 2 The Cross Prestwick KA9 1AJ T: 01292 671666
Rannoch and Foss Alltdruidhe Cottage Kinloch Rannoch Pitlochry PH17 2QJ T: 01882 632208
Renfrew Town Hall Renfrew PA4 8PF T: 0141 886 3589
Rousay, Egilsay and Wyre Braehead Rousay Kirkwall KW17 2PT T: 01856 821222
Rutherglen 1st Floor 169 Main Street Rutherglen G73 2HJ T: 0141 613 5330 Fax: 0141 613 5335 E: brenda.wilson@southlanarkshire.gov.uk
Sandness The Register Office 13 Melby Sandness ZE2 9PL T: 01595 870257
Sanquhar Council Offices 100 High Street Sanquhar DG4 6DZ T: 01659 50347
Scottish Borders Chirnside Operating from 8 Newton Street Duns TD11 3DT T: 01361 882600
Galashiels Library Buildings Lawyers Brac Galashiels TD1 3JQ T: 01896 752822
Lauder The Old Jail Mid Row Lauder TD2 6SZ T: 01578 722795
Scourie Operating from Assynt Lochinver IV27 4TD T: 01971 502425
Selkirk Municipal Buildings High Street Selkirk TD7 4JX T: 01750 23104
Shetland Burra Isles Roadside Hannavoe Lerwick ZE2 9LA T: 01595 859201
Fair Isle Field Fair Isle ZE2 9JU T: 01595 760224
Sandsting and Aitghsting The Register Office Modesty West Burrafirth Aithsting ZE2 9NT T: 01595 809428 Fax: 01595 809427
Fetlar Lower Toft Funzie Fetlar ZE2 9DJ T: 01957 733273
Foula Magdala Foula ZE2 9PN T: 01595 753236
Lunnasting Vidlin Farm Vidlin Shetland 7E2 9QB T: 01806 577204
Nesting Laxfirth Brettabister North Nesting ZE2 9PR T: 01595 694737
North Yell Breckon Cullivoe Yell ZE2 9DD T: 01957 744244 Fax: 01957 744352
Northmaven Uradell Eshaness ZEZ 9RS T: 01806 503362
Papa Stour North House Papa Stour ZE2 9PW T: 01595 873238
Sandwick The Register Office Yeldabreck Sandwick Stromness KWI6 3LP T: 01856 841596
Sandwick and Cunningsbur The Register Office Pytaslee Leebitton Sandwick ZE2 9HP T: 01950 431367 Fax: 01950 431367
Walls Victoria Cottage Walls Lerwick ZE2 9PD T: 01595 809478
Whalsay Conamore Brough Whalsay ZE2 9AL T: 01806 566544 CC accepted
Whalsay Skerries Fairview East Isle Skerries ZE2 9AR T: 01806 515224
Skere and Echt Gordon House Blackhall Road Inverurie AB51 3WA T: 01467 620981 T: 01467 628011 (Direct) Fax: 01467 628012 E: diane.minty@aberdeenshire.gov.uk incorporating Inverurie (319), Oldmeldrum(320) , Skere and Echt (323)
Slamannan Operating from Falkirk T: 01324 506580 Fax: 01324 50658!
Small Isles Kildonan House Isle of Eigg PH42 4RL T: 01687 482446
South Ayrshire Girvan, Barrhill, Barr, Dailly, Colmonell, Ballantrae Registration Office 22 Dalrymple Street Girvan KA26 9AE T: 01465 712894 Fax: 01465 715576 E: girvan.registrars@south ayrshire.gov.uk CC accepted
Maybole, Crosshill, Dunure, Kirkmichael, Kirkoswald, Straiton Council Office 64 High Street Maybole KAI9 7BZ T: 01655 884852 Fax: 01655 889621 E: maybole.registrars@south ayrshire.gov.uk
South Cowal Copeswood Auchenlochan High Rd Tighnabruaich PA21 2BE T: 01700 811601
South Lanarkshire Cambuslang Council Office 6 Glasgow Road Cambuslang G72 7BW T: 0141 641 8178 Fax: 0141 641 8542 E: registration@southlanarkshire.gov.uk W: www.southlanarkshire.gov.uk CC accepted
Carluke The Register Office 9 Kirkton Street Carluke MLB 4AJ T: 01555 772273 Fax: 01555 773721 E: catherine.watson@southlanarkshire.gov.uk
Hamilton The Register Office 21 Beckford Street Hamilton ML3 0BT T: 01698 454211 Fax: 01698 455746 E: jean lavelle@southlanarkshire.gov.uk CC accepted

Lanark The Register Office South Vennel Lanark ML11 7JT T: 01555 673220 T: 01555 673221 CC accepted

South Ronaldsay The Register Office West Cara Grimness South Ronaldsay KW17 2TH T: 01856 831509

Stirling Callander The Register Office 1 South Church Street Callander FK17 8BN T: 01877 330166

Stirling Municipal Buildings 8 10 Corn Exchange Road Stirling FK8 2HU T: 01786 432343 Fax: 01786 432056 E: registrar@stirling.gov.uk

Stonehaven, East Kincardine and Inverbervie Viewmount Arduthie Road Stonehaven AB39 2DQ T: 01569 768360 Fax: 01569 765455 Incorporates Inverbervie (343)

Stornoway and South Lochs Town Hall 2 Cromwell Street Stornoway HS1 2DB T: 01851 709438 Fax: 01851 709438 E: emacdonald@cne siar.gov.uk W: www.cne siar.gov.uk/w isles/registrars

Stranraer Area The Register Office, Council Offices Sun Street Stranraer DG9 7AB T: 01776 888439

Strathaven Royal Bank of Scotland Buildings 34 Common Green Strathaven ML10 6AQ T: 01357 520316

Strathclyde Glasgow The Register Office 22 Park Circus Glasgow G3 6BE T: 0141 287 8350 F: 0141 287 8357 E: bill.craig@pas.glasgow.gov.uk

Strathcur Crosshaig Strathcur PA27 8BY T: 01369 860316

Strathendrick Balfron Local Office 32 Buchanan Street Balfron G63 0TR T: 01360 40315 F: 01360 441254 E: phillips@stirling.gov.uk CC accepted

Stronsay The Register Office Strynie Stronsay Kirkwall KW17 2AR T: 01857 616239

Strontian Easgadail Longrigg Road Strontian Acharacle PH36 4HY T: 01967 402037

Tarbat The Bungalow Chaplehill Portmahomack Portmathom Tain IV20 1XJ T: 01862 871328

Tarbert Argyll House School Road Tarbert PA29 6UJ T: 01880 820374

Tarradale Service Point Office Seaforth Road Muir Of Ord IV6 7TA T: 01463 870201 F: 01463 871047 E: lorraine.ross@highland.gov.uk

Tayinloan Bridge House Tayinloan Tarbert PA29 6XG T: 01583 441239

Tingwall Vindas Laxfirth Tingwall ZE2 9SG T: 01595 840450

Tobermory County Buildings Breadalbanc Street Tobennory PA75 6PX T: 01688 302051

Tranent The Register Office 8 Civic Square Tranent EH33 1LH T: 01875 610278 F: 01875 615420

Troon Municipal Buildings 8 South Beach Troon KA10 6EF T: 01292 313555 F: 01292 318009

Turriff Towie House Manse Road Turiff AB53 7AY T: 01888 562427 F: 01888 568559 E: sheila.donald@aberdeenshire.gov.uk

Tyree The Register Office Crossapol PA77 6UP T: 01879 220349

Uig (Lewis) The Register Office 10 Valtos Uig Lewis HS2 9HR T: 01851 672213

Uig (Skye)(Inverness) The Register Office 3 Ellishadder Staffin Portree IV51 9JE T: 01410 562303 Records held are from 1967 to date. all previous records now held at Portree

Unst New Hoose Baltasound Unst ZE2 9DX T: 01957 11348

Vale of Leven The Register Office 77 Bank Street Alexandria G83 0LE T: 01389 608980 F: 01389 608982 E: tony.gallagher@west dunbarton.gov.uk

Wanlockhead Operating from Sanquhar T: 01659 74287

West Linton Council Office West Linton EH46 7ED T: 01968 660267

West Lothian (Bathgate) The Register Office 76 Mid Street Bathgate EH48 1QD T: 01506 776192 F: 01506 776194

West Lothian (East Calder) East Calder Library 200 Main Street East Calder EH53 0EJ T: 01506 884680 F: 01506 883944

West Lothian (Linlithgow) The Register Office High Street Linlithgow EH49 7EZ T: 01506 775373 F: 01506 775374 E: joyce.duncan@westlothian.gov.uk

West Lothian (Livingston) Lammermuir House Owen Square Avondale Livingston EH54 6PW T: 01506 775833 F: 01506 775834

West Lothian (Uphall) Strathbrock Partnership 189a West Main Street Broxburn EH52 5LH T: 01506 775509 F: 01506 773756 E: laura.clarke@westlothian.gov.uk

West Lothian (West Calder) The Register Office 24 26 Main Street West Calder EH55 8DR T: 01506 871874

West Lothian (Whitburn) The Register Office 5 East Main Street Whitburn EH47 0RA T: 01501 678005 F: 01506 678085 E: agnes.mcconnell@westlothian.gov.uk

Western Ardnamurchan Doirlinn House Kilchoan Acharacle PH36 4HY T: 01967 402037 F: 01967 402037

Whiteness and Weisdale Vista Whiteness ZE2 9LJ T: 01595 830332

Whithorn Area The Register Office 75 George Street Whithorn DG8 8NU T: 01988 500458 E: archietaylor@supanet.com

Registration Records in The Republic of Ireland

Oifig An Ard-Chlaraitheora (General Register Office) Joyce House, 8/11 Lombard Street East, Dublin, 2.

The General Register Office and Research Room are open Monday to Friday, (excluding public holidays) from 9.30 a.m. to 12.30 p.m. and from 2.15 p.m. to 4.30 p.m. for the purpose of searching the indexes to birth, death and marriage records

The following records are deposited in the General Register Office:-
1. Registers of all Births registered in the whole of Ireland from 1st January, 1864, to 31 December, 1921, and in Ireland (excluding the six north-eastern counties of Derry, Antrim, Down, Armagh, Fermanagh and Tyrone know as Northern Ireland) from that date.
2. Registers of all Deaths registered in the whole of Ireland from 1st January, 1864, to 31st December 1921, and in Ireland (excluding Northern Ireland) from that date.
3. Registers of all Marriages registered in the whole of Ireland from 1st April 1845, to 31st December 1863, except those celebrated by the Roman Catholic clergy.
4. Registers of all Marriages registered in the whole of Ireland from 1st January, 1864, to 31st December, 1921, and in Ireland (excluding Northern Ireland) from that date.
5. Registers of Births at Sea of children, one of whose parents was Irish, registered from 1st January, 1864, to 31st December, 1921. Register of Births at Sea of Children one of whose parents were born in the Republic of Ireland, registered after 1921.
6. Register of Deaths at Sea of Irish-born persons, registered from 1st January, 1864, to 31st December, 1921, and after 1921 of Irish born persons other than those born in Northern Ireland.
7. Registers of Births of children of Irish parents, certified by British Consuls abroad, from 1st January, 1864 to 31st December, 1921.
8. Registers of Deaths of Irish-born persons, certified by British Consuls abroad, from 1st January, 1864, to 31st December, 1921.
9. Register of Marriages celebrated in Dublin by the late Rev. J F G Schulze, Minister of the German Protestant Church, Poolbeg Street, Dublin, from 1806 to 1837, inclusive.
10. Registers under the Births, Deaths and Marriages (Army) Act,

1879.
11. Adopted Children Register – legal adoptions registered in the Republic of Ireland on or after 10th July, 1953. Note: Cost of certificates issued from the Adopted Children Register: £5.50 for full certificate: £3.50 for short certificate: £0.70 for certificate for Social Welfare purposes.
12. Birth and Death Registers under the Defence (Amendment) (No. 2) Act, 1960.
13. Registers of certain births and deaths occurring outside the State (The Births, Deaths and Marriages Registration Act, 1972, Sec. 4).
14. Register of Certain Lourdes Marriages (Marriages Act, 1972, Sec.2).
15. Registers of Stillbirths registered in Republic of Ireland from 1st January 1995 (certified copies available to parents only).

Reading Room Searches.
There are two types of searches available to the public.
A search for a maximum of 5 years or a general search for one day covering all years. Fees apply Photocopies may be purchased

Records for births, deaths and Catholic marriages commenced in 1864. Records for non-Catholic marriages date from 1845. Information prior to this (1864) may be available from parish records which are kept in the Genealogical Office in the National Library, Kildare Street, Dublin, 2. Records of births, deaths and marriages for Northern Ireland are only available up to 1921.

The indexes are complied on a yearly/quarterly basis in alphabetical order. Records for the years 1878 to 1903 and 1928 to 1965 are divided into four quarters ending March, June, September and December. Marriages are indexed under both the maiden name of the bride and the grooms surname, therefore, if you check under each name you find a cross reference which will indicate it is the correct entry relating to the marriage.

Museums

National

Battlefields Trust 33 High Green Brooke Norwich NR15 1HR T: 01508 558145 F: 01508 558145 E: BattlefieldTrust@aol.com WWW: www.battlefieldstrust.com

The Boat Museum & David Owen Waterways Archive see Cheshire

Black Cultural Archives 378 Coldharbour Lane London SW9 8LF T: (020) 7738 4591 F: (020) 7738 7168 E: info@99mbh.org.uk W: www.99mbh.org.uk

British Empire & Commonwealth Museum Clock Tower Yard Temple Meads Bristol BS1 6QH T: 0117 925 4980 0117 925 4983 E: staff@empiremuseum.co.uk W: www.empiremuseum.co.uk

British Museum The Secretariat Great Russell St London WC1B 3DG T: (020) 7323 8768 T: (020) 7323 8224 F: (020) 7323 8118 E: jwallace@thebritishmuseum.ac.uk W: www.thebritishmuseum.ac.uk

British Red Cross Museum and Archives 9 Grosvenor Crescent London SW1X 7EJ T: (020) 7201 5153 F: (020) 7235 6456 E: enquiry@redcross.org.uk W: www.redcross.org.uk/museum&archives Open by appointment 10am to 4pm Monday to Friday.

Commonwealth War Graves Commission 2 Marlow Road Maidenhead SL6 7DX T: 01628 634221 F: 01628 771208 W: www.cwgc.org

The Galleries of Justice Shire Hall High Pavement Lace Market Nottingham NG1 1HN T: 0115 952 0555 F: 0115 993 9828 E: info@galleriesofjustice.org.uk W: www.galleriesofjustice.org.uk

Imperial War Museum - Duxford Imperial War Museum The Airfield Duxford Cambridge CB2 4QR T: 01223 835 000 F: 01223 837 237 E: duxford@iwm.org.uk

Imperial War Museum Film & Video Archive Lambeth Rd London SE1 6HZ T: 020 7416 5291 W:www.iwm.org.uk/collections/film.htm

Labour History Archive and Study Centre People's History Museum 103 Princess Street Manchester M1 6DD T: 0161 228 7212 F: 0161 237 5965 E: archives@nmlhweb.org_lhasc@fs1.li.man.ac.uk WWW: http://rylibweb.man.ac.uk

The National Coal Mining Museum for England Caphouse Colliery New Road Overton Wakefield WF4 4RH T: 01924 848806 F: 01924 840694 E: info@ncm.org.uk W: www.ncm.org.uk

National Museum of Photography, Film and Television Bradford BD1 1NQ T: 01274-202030 F: 01274 -723155 W: www.nmpft.org.uk

National Gallery St. Vincent House 30 Orange St London WC2H 7HH T: (020) 7747 5950

Natural History Museum Cromwell Rd London SW7 5BD T: (020) 7938 9238 F: 020 7938 9290 W: www.nhm.ac.uk

National Portrait Gallery 2 St. Martins Place London WC2H 0HE T: (020) 7306 0055 F: (020) 7206 0058 W: www.npg.org.uk

National Railway Museum Leeman Road York YO26 4XJ T: 01904 621261 F: 01904 611112 E: nrm@nmsi.ac.uk W: www.nrm.org.uk

National Tramway Museum Crich Tramway Village Crich Matlock DE4 5DP T: 01773 852565 F: 01773 852326 E: info@tramway.co.uk W: www.tramway.co.uk cc accepted

The National Waterways Museum Llanthony Warehouse Gloucester Docks Gloucester GL1 2EH T: 01452 318054 F: 01452 318066 E: curatorial1@nwm.demon.co.uk W: www.nwm.demon.co.uk

Royal Armouries Armouries Dr Leeds LS10 1LT T: 0990 106666

Royal Armouries H.M Tower Of London Tower Hill London EC3N 4AB T: (020) 7480 6358 ext 30 F: (020) 7481 2922 E: Bridgett.Clifford@armouries.org.uk W: www.armouries.org.uk

The Science Museum Exhibition Rd London SW7 2DD T: 0870 8704868 E: sciencemuseum@nmsp.ac.uk

Victoria & Albert Museum Cromwell Rd London South Kensington SW7 2RL T: (020) 7942 2164 T: (020) 7638 8500 F: (020) 7942 2162 W: www.nal.vam.ac.uk

Bedfordshire

Bedford Museum Castle Lane Bedford MK40 3XD T: 01234 353323 F: 01234 273401 E: bmuseum@bedford.gov.uk W: www.bedfordmuseum.org

Bedfordshire Yeomanry Castle Lane Bedford MK40 3XD T: 01234 353323 F: 01234 273401 E: bmuseum@bedford.gov.uk W: www.bedfordmuseum.org

Bedfordshire and Hertfordshire Regimental Museum Luton Museum Wardown Park Luton LU2 7HA T: 01582 546722 F: 01582 546763 W: www.luton.gov.uk/enjoying/museums

Cecil Higgins Art Gallery Castle Close Castle Lane Bedford MK40 3RP T: 01234 211222 F: 01234 327149

Elstow Moot Hall Elstow Bedford MK42 9XT T: 01234 266889 E: wilemans@deed.bedfordshire.gov.uk W: www.bedfordshire.gov.uk

John Dony Field Centre Hancock Drive Bushmead Luton LU2 7SF T: 01582 486983

Luton Museum Service & Art Gallery Wardown Park Luton LU2 7HA T: 01582 546725 F: 01582-546763 E: adeye@luton.gov.uk

Museum of Defence Intelligence Chicksands Shefford SG17 5PR T: 01462 752340 F: 01462 752341

Shuttleworth Collection Old Warden Aerodrome Old Warden Biggleswade SG18 9ER T: 01767 627288 F: 01767 626229 E: collection@shuttleworth.org W: www.shuttleworth.org

Shuttleworth Veteran Aeroplane Society PO Box 42 Old Warden Aerodrome Biggleswade SG18 9UZ T: 01767 627398 E: svas@oldwarden.fsnet.co.uk

Station X - Bletchley Park Bletchley Park Trust The Mansion Bletchley Milton Keynes MK3 6EB T: 01908 640404 W: www.bletchleypark.org.uk

Berkshire

Blake's Lock Museum Gasworks Rd Reading RG1 3DS T: 0118 939 0918

Friends of Royal Borough Collection, Windsor 14 Park Avenue Wraysbury TW19 5ET T: 01784 482771

Maidenhead Heritage Centre 41 Nicholsons Centre Maidenhead SL6 1LL T: 01628 780555

Museum of English Rural Life, Rural History Centre University of Reading Whiteknights PO Box 229 Reading RG6 6AG T: 0118 931 8664 F: 0118 975 1264 E: j.s.creasey@reading.ac.uk W: www.ruralhistory.org/index.html Appointments required

R.E.M.E. Museum of Technology Isaac Newton Road Arborfield Reading RG2 9NJ T: 0118 976 3375 F: 0118 976 3375 E: reme-museum@gtnet.gov.uk W: www.rememuseum.org.uk

Royal Berkshire Yeomanry Cavalry Museum T A Centre Bolton Road Windsor SL4 3JG T: 01753 860600 F: 01753 854946

Royal Borough Museum (Windsor & Maidenhead) Tinkers Lane Windsor SL4 4LR T: 01628 796829 E: olivia.gooden@rbwm.gov.uk

Slough Museum 278-286 High St Slough SL1 1NB T: 01753 526422

The Household Cavalry Museum Combermere Barracks Windsor SL4 3DN T: 01753 755112 F: 01753 755161 Admission Free

The Museum of Berkshire Aviation Trust Mohawk Way Woodley Reading RG5 4UE T: 0118 944 8089 E: museumofberkshireaviation@fly.to WWW: http://fly.to/museumofberkshireaviation

The Museum of Reading Town Hall Blagrave Street Reading RG1 1QH T: 0118 939 9800 W: www.readingmuseum.org.uk

Wantage Vale & Downland Museum Church Street Wantage OX12 8BL T: 01235 771447

Wellington Exhibition Stratfield Saye House Reading RG7 2BT T: 01256 882882 F: 01256 882882 W: www.stratfield-saye.co.uk

West Berkshire Heritage Service - Newbury The Wharf Newbury RG14 5AS T: 01635 30511 F: 01635 38535 E: heritage@westberks.gov.uk W: www.westberks.gov.uk/tourism

West Berkshire Museum The Wharf Newbury RG14 5AS T: 01635 30511 F: 01635 38535 E: heritage@westberks.gov.uk W: www.westberks.gov.uk

Bristol

Ashton Court Visitor Centre Ashton Court Long Ashton Bristol BS41 8JN T: 0117 963 9174

Blaise Castle House Museum Henbury Bristol BS10 7QS T: 0117 903 9818 F: 0117 903 9820 E: general_museum@bristol-city.gov.uk W: www.bristol-city.gov.uk/museums

Bristol Industrial Museum Princes Wharf Wapping Road Bristol BS1 4RN T: 0117 925 1470

British Empire & Commonwealth Museum see National

City Museum & Art Gallery Queens Road Bristol BS8 1RL T: 0117 921 3571 F: 0117 922 2047 E: general_museum@bristol-city.gov.uk W: www.bristol-city.gov.uk/museums

Clevedon Story Heritage Centre Waterloo House 4 The Beach Clevedon BS21 7QU T: 01275 341196

Clifton Suspension Bridge Visitor Centre Bridge House Sion Place Bristol BS8 4AP T: 0117 974 4664 F: 0117 974 5255 E: visitinfo@clifton-suspension-bridge.org.uk W: www.clifton-suspension-bridge.org.uk

Georgian House 7 Great George St Bristol BS1 5RR T: 0117 921 1362

Harveys Wine Museum 12 Denmark St Bristol BS1 5DQ T: 0117 927 5036 E: alun.cox@adwev.com W: www.j-harvey.co.uk

Red Lodge Park Row Bristol BS1 5LJ T: 0117 921 1360 W: www.bristol-city.gov.uk/museums

SS Great Britain and Maritime Heritage Centre Wapping Wharf Gasferry Road Bristol BS1 6TY T: 0117 926 0680

Buckinghamshire

Amersham Local History Museum 49 High Street Amersham HP7 0DP T: 01494 725754 F: 01494 725754

Bletchley Park Trust The Mansion Bletchley Park Bletchley Milton Keynes MK3 6EB T: 01908 640404 F: 01908 274381 E: info@bletchleypark.org.uk WWW: www.bletchleypark.org.uk

Blue Max Wycombe Air Park Booker Marlow SL7 3DP T: 01494 449810

Buckinghamshire County Museum Church Street Aylesbury HP20 2QP T: 01296 331441 F: 01296 334884 E: museum@buckscc.gov.uk

Buckinghamshire Military Museum Trust Collection Old Gaol Museum Market Hill Buckingham MK18 13X T: 01280 823020 F: E: ian.beckett@luton.ac.uk

Chesham Town Museum Project Chesham Library Elgiva Lane Chesham HP5 2JD T: 01494 783183

Chiltern Open Air Museum Ltd Newland Park Gorelands Lane Chalfont St. Giles HP8 4AB T: 01494 871117 F: 01494 872774

Milton Keynes Museum Stacey Hill Farm Southern Way Wolverton Milton Keynes MK12 5EJ T: 01908 316222

Pitstone and Ivinghoe Museum Society Vicarage Road Pitstone Leighton Buzzard LU7 9EY T: 01296 668123 http://website.lineone.net/~pitstonemus Pitstone Green Museum and Ford End Watermill

Wycombe Museum Priory Avenue High Wycombe HP13 6PX T: 01494 421895 E: enquiries@wycombemuseum.demon.co.uk W: www.wycombe.gov.uk/museum

Cambridgeshire

Cambridge Brass Rubbing The Round Church Bridge St Cambridge CB2 1UB T: 01223 871621

Cambridge Museum of Technology Old Pumping Station Cheddars Lane Cambridge CB5 8LD T: 01223 368650

Cromwell Museum The Cromwell Museum Huntingdon T: 01480 375830 E: cromwellmuseum@cambridgeshire.gov.uk http://edweb.camcnty.gov.uk/cromwell

Cromwell Museum Grammar School Walk Huntingdon PE18 6LF T: 01480 375830 F: 01480 459563

Duxford Aviation Society Duxford Airfield Duxford Cambridge CB2 4QR T: 01223 835594

Duxford Displays Ltd Duxford Airfield Duxford Cambridge CB2 4QR T: 01223 836593

Ely Museum The Old Goal Market Street Ely CB7 4LS T: 01353-666655 E: elymuseum@freeuk.com W: www.ely.org.uk includes Cambridge Regiment displays

Farmland Museum Denny Abbey Ely Rd Waterbeach Cambridge CB5 9PQ T: 01223 860988 F: 01223 860988 E: f.m.denny@tesco.net W: www.dennyfarmlandmuseum.org.uk

Fenland & West Norfolk Aviation Museum Lynn Rd West Walton Wisbech PE14 7 T: 01945 584440

Folk Museum 2 - 3 Castle St Cambridge CB3 0AQ T: 01223 355159 E: info@folkmuseum.org.uk W: www.folkmuseum.org.uk

March & District Museum Society Museum High St March PE15 9JJ T: 01354 655300

Museum of Classical Archaeology Sidgwick Avenue Cambridge CB3 9DA T: 01223 335153 W: www.classics.cam.ac.uk/ark.html/

Nene Valley Railway Wansford Station Peterborough PE8 6LR T: 01780 782833 T: 01782 782855

Norris Library and Museum The Broadway St Ives PE27 5BX T: 01480 497317 E: bob@norrismuseum.fsnet.co.uk

Octavia Hill Birthplace Museum Trust 1 South Brink Place Wisbech PE13 1JE T: 01945 476358

Peterborough Museum & Art Gallery Priestgate Peterborough PE1 1LF T: 01733 343329 F: 01733 341928 E: museum@peterborough.gov.uk

Prickwillow Drainage Engine Museum Main St Prickwillow Ely CB7 4UN T: 01353 688360

RAF Witchford Display of Memorabilia Grovemere Building Lancaster Way Business Park Ely T: 01353 666666 T: 01353 664934

Railworld Museum - Nene Valley Railway Oundle Road Peterborough PE2 9NR T: 01733 344240 W: www.railworld.net

Ramsey Rural Museum The Woodyard Wood Lane Ramsey Huntingdon PE17 1XD T: 01487 815715

Sedgwick Museum University of Cambridge Downing St Cambridge CB2 3EQ T: 01223 333456 F: 01223 333450 E: mgd2@esc.cam.ac.uk

Soham Community History Museum PO Box 21 The Pavilion Fountain Lane Soham CB7 5PL T:

Wisbech and Fenland Museum Museum Square Wisbech PE13 1ES T: 01945-583817 F: 01945-589050 E: wisbechmuseum@beeb.net

Cheshire

Catalyst Gossage Building Mersey Road Widnes WA8 0DF T: 0151 420 1121

Cheshire Military Museum The Castle Chester CH1 2DN T: 01244 327617 Cheshire Yeomanry elements of 3rd Carabiniers and 5th Royal Inniskilling Dragoon Guards

Cheshire Military Museum The Castle Chester CH1 2DN T: 01244 327617 W: www.chester.cc.uk/militarymuseum

Chester Heritage Centre - closed August 2000 St. Michaels Church Bridge St Chester CH1 1NQ T: 01244 317948

Deva Roman Experience Pierpoint Lane off Bridge Street Chester CH1 2BJ T: 01244 343407 F: 01244 343407

Griffin Trust The Hangars West Road Hutton Park airfield Ellesmere Port CH65 1BQ T: 0151 350 2598 F: 0151 350 2598

Grosvenor Museum 27 Grosvenor St Chester CH1 2DD T: 01244 402008 F: 01244 347587 E: s.rogers@chestercc.gov.uk W: www.chestercc.gov.uk/heritage/museums

Hack Green Secret Nuclear Bunker PO Box 127 Nantwich CW5 8AQ T: 01270 623353 F: 01270 629218 E: coldwar@dial.pipex.com W: www.hackgreen.co.uk

Lion Salt Works Trust Ollershaw Lane Marston Northwich CW9 6ES T: 01606 41823 F: 01606 41823 E: afielding@lionsalt.demon.co.uk W: www.lionsaltworkstrust.co.uk

Macclesfield Museums Heritage Centre Roe St Macclesfield SK11 6UT T: 01625 613210 F: 01625 617880 E: postmaster@silk-macc.u-net.com

Macclesfield Silk Museums Paradise Mill Park Lane Macclesfield SK11 6TJ T: 01625 612045 F: 01625 612048 E: silkmuseum@tiscali.co.uk W: www.silk-macclesfield.org

Miniature AFV Association (MAFVA) 45 Balmoral Drive Holmes Chapel CW4 7JQ T: 01477 535373 F: 01477 535892 E: MAFVAHQ@aol.com W: www.mafva.com

Nantwich Museum Pillory St Nantwich CW5 5BQ T: 01270 627104

Norton Priory Museum Trust Ltd Tudor Road Manor Park Runcorn WA7 1SX T: 01928 569895 F: 01928 589743 E: info@nortonpriory.org W: www.nortonpriory.org

Stockport Air Raid Shelters 61 Chestergate Stockport SK1 1NG T: 0161 474 1942 F: 0161 474 1942

The Boat Museum & Waterways see National

Warrington Library, Museum & Archives Service 3 Museums Street Warrington WA1 1JB T: 01925 442733 T: 01925 442734 E: museum@warrington.gov.uk W: www.warrington.gov.uk/museum

West Park Museum Prestbury Rd Macclesfield SK10 3BJ T: 01625 619831

Cleveland

HMS Trincomalee Maritime Avenue Hartlepool Marina Hartlepool TS24 0XZ T: 01429 223193 F: 01429 864385 W: www.thisishartlepool.com

Captain Cook Birthplace Museum Stewart Park Marton Middlesbrough TS7 6AS T: 01642 311211 W: www.aboutbritain.com/CaptainCookBirthplaceMuseum

Captain Cook & Staithes Heritage Centre High St Staithes Saltburn-By-The-Sea TS13 5BQ T: 01947 841454

Dorman Musuem Linthorpe Rd Middlesbrough TS5 6LA T: 01642 813781 E: dormanmuseum@middlesbrough.gov.uk W: www.dormanmuseum.org.uk W: www.dormanmuseum.co.uk

Green Dragon Museum Theatre Yard High St Stockton-On-Tees TS18 1AT T: 01642 393938

Hartlepool Historic Quay Maritime Avenue Hartlepool Marina Hartlepool TS24 0XZ T: 01429 860077 F: 01429 860077 E: arts-museum@hartlepool.gov.uk W: www.thisishartlepool.com

Margrove Heritage Centre Margrove Park Boosbeck Saltburn-By-The-Sea TS12 3BZ T: 01287 610368 F: 01287 610368

Preston Hall Museum Yarm Road Stockton-On-Tees TS18 3RH T: 01642 781184

Stockton Museums Service Education, Leisure & Cultural Services, Po Box 228 Municipal Buildings Church Road Stockton on Tees TS18 1XE T: 01642 415382 F: 01642 393479 E: rachel.mason@stockton.gov.uk W: www.stockton.gov.uk

The Tom Leonard Mining Experience Deepdale Skinningrove Saltburn TS13 4AA T: 01287 642877

Cornwall

Automobilia The Old Mill Terras Rd St. Austell PL26 7RX T: 01726 823092

Bodmin Museum Mount Folly Bodmin PL31 2DB T: 01208 77067 F: 01208 79268

Cable & Wireless Archive & Museum of Submarine Telegraphy Eastern House, Porthcurno Penzance TR19 6JX T: 01736 810478 E: info@tunnels.demon.co.uk W: www.porthcurno.org.uk

Charlestown Shipwreck & Heritage Centre Quay Rd Charlestown St. Austell PL25 3NX T: 01726 69897 F: 01726 68025

Duke of Cornwall's Light Infantry Museum The Keep Bodmin PL31 1EG T: 01208 72810 F: 01208 72810 E: dclimis@talk21.com W: www.britrishlightinfantry.org.ca

Flambards Village and Cornwall Aircraft Park Flambards Village Theme Park Culdrose Manor Helston TR13 0GA T: 01326 573404 F: 01326 573344 E: info@flambards.co.uk W: www.flambards.co.uk

Helston Folk Museum Market Place Helston TR13 8TH T: 01326 564027 F: 01326 569714 E: enquiries@helstonmuseum.org.uk W: www.helstonmuseum.org.uk

John Betjeman Centre Southern Way Wadebridge PL27 7BX T: 01208 812392

Lanreath Farm & Folk Museum Lanreath Farm Near Looe PL13 2NX T: 01503 220321

Lawrence House Museum 9 Castle St Launceston PL15 8BA T: 01566 773277

Maritime Museum 19 Chapel Street Penzance TR18 4AF T: 01736 68890

Merlin's Cave Crystal Mineral & Fossil Museum & Shop Molesworth St Tintagel PL34 0BZ T: 01840 770023

National Maritime Museum (Falmouth, Cornwall) 48 Arwenack St Falmouth TR11 3SA T: 01326 313388

National Maritime Museum (Saltash, Cornwall) Cotehele Quay Cotehele Saltash PL12 6TA T: 01579 350830

Penryn Museum Town Hall Higher Market St Penryn TR10 8LT T: 01326 372158 F: 01326 373004

Penzance Maritime Museum 19 Chapel St Penzance TR18 4AW T: 01736 368890

Potter's Museum of Curiosity Jamaica Inn Courtyard Bolventor Launceston PL15 7TS T: 01566 86838 F: 01566 86838

Royal Cornwall Museum River St Truro TR1 2SJ T: 01872 272205

Mevagissey Museum Society Frazier Ho The Quay Mevagissey Cornwall PL26 6QU T: 01726 843568 T: 01726 844692 F: E: haycas02@yahoo.co.uk W: www.geocities.com/mevamus All correspondence to: "An Cala", 55 Lavorrick Orchards, Mevagissey, St Austell, Cornwall PL26 6TL

Trinity House National Lighthouse Centre Wharf Road Penzance TR18 4BN T: 01736 60077 F: 01736 64292

Cumbria

Aspects of Motoring Western Lakes Motor Museum The Maltings The Maltings Brewery Lane Cockermouth CA13 9ND T: 01900 824448

Birdoswald Roman Fort Gilsland Brampton CA6 7DD T: 01697 747602 F: 01697 747605

Border Regiment & Kings Own Royal Border Regiment Museum Queen Mary's Tower The Castle Carlisle CA3 8UR T: 01228 532774 F: 01228 521275 E: rhq@kingsownborder.demon.co.uk W: www.armymuseums.org.uk

Dove Cottage & The Wordsworth Museum Town End Grasmere Ambleside LA22 9SH T: 015394 35544

Friends of The Helena Thompson Museum 24 Calva Brow Workington CA14 1DD T: 01900 603312

Haig Colliery Mining Museum Solway Road Kells Whitehaven CA28 9BG T: 01946 599949 F: 01946 618796 W: www.haigpit.com

Keswick Museum & Art Gallery Station Rd Keswick CA12 4NF T: 017687 73263 F: 1768780390 E: hazel.davison@allerdale.gov.uk

Lakeland Motor Museum Holker Hall Cark In Cartmel Grange-Over-Sands LA11 7PL T: 015395 58509

Lakeside & Haverthwaite Railway Haverthwaite Station Ulverston LA12 8AL T: 01539 531594

Laurel & Hardy Museum 4c Upper Brook St Ulverston LA12 7BH T: 01229 582292

Maritime Museum 1 Senhouse Street Maryport CA15 6AB T: 01900 813738 F: 01900 819496

Maryport Steamship Museum Elizabeth Dock South Quay Maryport CA15 8AB T: 01900 815954

North Pennines Heritage Trust Nenthead Mines Heritage Centre Nenthead Alston CA9 3PD T: 01434 382037 F: 01434 382294 E: administration.office@virgin.net W: www.npht.com

Penrith Museum Middlegate Penrith CA11 7PT T: 01768 212228 F: 01768 867466 E: museum@eden.gov.uk

Roman Army Museum Carvoran House Greenhead Carlisle CA6 7JB T: 016977 47485 F:

Ruskin Museum Yewdale Rd Coniston LA21 8DU T: 015394 41164 F: 015394 41332 W: www.coniston.org.uk

Senhouse Roman Museum The Battery Sea Brows Maryport CA15 6JD T: 01900 816168 F: 01900 816168 E: romans@senhouse.freeserve.co.uk W: www.senhousemuseum.co.uk

Senhouse Roman Museum The Battery The Promenade Maryport CA15 6JD T: W: www.aboutbritain.com/SenhouseRomanMuseum.htm

Solway Aviation Museum Carlisle Airport Carlisle CA6 4NW T: 01228 573823

Solway Aviation Museum Aviation House Carlisle Airport Carlisle CA6 4NW T: 01227 573823 F: 01228 573517 E: info@solway-aviation-museum.org.uk W: www.solway-aviation-museum.org.uk

The Dock Museum North Rd Barrow-In-Furness LA14 2PW T: 01229 894444 E: docmuseum@barrowbc.gov.uk W: www.barrowtourism.co.uk

The Guildhall Museum Green Market Carlisle CA3 8JE T: 01228 819925

Tullie House Museum and Art Gallery Castle Street Carlisle CA3 8TP T: 01228-534781 F: 01228-810249

Ulverston Heritage Centre Lower Brook St Ulverston LA12 7EE T: 01229 580820 F: 01229 580820 E: heritage@tower-house.demon.co.uk W: www.rootsweb.com/~ukuhc/

William Creighton Mineral Museum & Gallery 2 Crown St Cockermouth CA13 0EJ T: 01900 828301 F: 01900 828001

Windermere Steamboat Museum Rayrigg Rd Windermere LA23 1BN T: 015394 45565 F: 1539448769 W: www.steamboat.co.uk

Derbyshire

Chesterfield Museum & Art Gallery St Mary's Gate Chesterfield S41 7TY T: 01246 345727 F: 01246 345720

Derby Industrial Museum Silk Mill Lane Derby DE1 3AR T: 01332 255308

Derby Industrial Museum Silk Mill Lane Off Full Street Derby DE1 3AF T: 01332 255308 F: 01332 716670 W: www.derby.gov.uk/museums

Derby Museum & Art Gallery The Strand Derby DE1 1BS T: 01332-716659 F: 01332-716670 W: www.derby.gov.uk/museums

Derwent Valley Visitor Centre Belper North Mill Bridge Foot Belper DE56 1YD T: 01773 880474

Donington Grandprix Collection Donington Park Castle Donington Derby DE74 2RP T: 01332 811027

Donington Park Racing Ltd Donington Park Castle Donnington Derby DE74 2RP T: 01332 814697

Elvaston Castle Estate Museum Elvaston Castle Country Park Borrowash Road Elvaston Derby DE72 3EP T: 01332 573799

Erewash Museum The Museum High Street Ilkeston DE7 5JA T: 0115 907 1141 F: 0115 907 1121 E: museum@erewash.gov.uk W: www.erewash.gov.uk

Eyam Museum Eyam S32 5QP T: 01433 631371 F: 01433 631371 E: johnbeck@classicfm.net W: www.eyam.org.uk

Glossop Heritage Centre Bank House Henry St Glossop SK13 8BW T: 01457 869176

High Peak Junction Workshop High Peak Junction Cromford Matlock DE4 5HN T: 01629 822831

High Peak Trail Middleton Top Rise End Middleton Matlock DE4 4LS T: 01629 823204

Midland Railway Centre Butterley Station Ripley DE5 3QZ T: 01773 570140

National Stone Centre Porter Lane Wirksworth Matlock DE4 4LS T: 01629 824833

Peak District Mining Museum The Pavilion South Parade Matlock Bath DE4 3NR T: 01629 583834 F: 01629 583834 E: mail@peakmines.co.uk W: www.peakmines.co.uk

Pickford's House Museum 41 Friar Gate Derby DE1 1DA T: 01332 255363 F: 01332 255277 W: www.derby.gov.uk/museums

Regimental Museum of the 9th/12th Royal Lancers Derby City Museum and Art Gallery The Strand Derby DE1 1BS T: 01332 716656 F: 01332 716670 E: angela.tarnowski@derby.gov.uk W: www.derby.gov.uk/museums

Devon

Allhallows Museum of Lace & Antiquities High St Honiton EX14 1PG T: 01404 44966 F: 01404 46591 E: dyateshoniton@msn.com W: www.honitonlace.com

Bill Douglas Centre for the History of Cinema and Popular Culture University of Exeter Queen's Building Queen's Drive Exeter EX4 4QH T: 01392 264321 W: www.ex.ac.uk/bill.douglas

Brixham Museum Bolton Cross Brixham TQ5 8LZ T: 01803 856267 E: mail@brixhamheritage.org.uk W: www.brixhamheritage.org.uk

Century of Playtime 30 Winner St Paignton TQ3 3BJ T: 01803 553850

Crownhill Fort Crownhill Fort Road Plymouth PL6 5BX T: 01752 793754 F: 01752 770065

Devon & Cornwall Constabulary Museum Middlemoor Exeter EX2 7HQ T: 01392 203025

Dunkeswell Memorial Museum Dunkeswell Airfield Dunkeswell Ind Est Dunkeswell Honiton EX14 0RA T: 01404 891943

Fairlynch Art Centre & Museum 27 Fore St Budleigh Salterton EX9 6NP T: 01395 442666

Finch Foundary Museum of Rural Industry Sticklepath Okehampton EX20 2NW T: 01837 840046

Ilfracombe Museum Wilder Rd Ilfracombe EX34 8AF T: 01271 863541 E: ilfracombe@devonmuseums.net W: www.devonmuseums.net

Museum of Barnstaple & North Devon incorporating Royal Devon Yeomanry Museum Peter A Boyd The Square Barnstaple EX32 8LN T: 01271 346 747 F: 01271 346407 E: admin@sal.org.uk

Newhall Visitor & Equestrian Centre Newhall Budlake Exeter EX5 3LW T: 01392 462453

Newton Abbot Town & Great Western Railway Museum 2A St. Pauls Rd Newton Abbot TQ12 2HP T: 01626 201121

North Devon Maritime Museum Odun House Odun Rd Appledore Bideford EX39 1PT T: 01237 422064 F: 01237 422064 W: www.devonmuseums.net/appledore

North Devon Museum Service St.Anne's Chapel Paternoster Row Barnstaple EX32 8LN T: 01271 378709

Otterton Mill Otterton Budleigh Salterton EX9 7HG T: 01395 568521 E: escape@ottertonmill.com W: www.ottertonmill.com

Park Pharmacy Trust Thorn Park Lodge Thorn Park Mannamead Plymouth PL3 4TF T: 01752 263501

Plymouth City Museum Drake Circus Plymouth PL4 8AJ T: 01752 304774 F: 01752 304775 E: plymouth.museum@plymouth.gov.uk W: www.plymouthmuseum.gov.uk W: www.cottoniancollection.org.uk

Royal Albert Memorial Museum Queen Street Exeter EX4 3RX T: 01392 265858

Seaton Tramway Harbour Road Seaton EX12 2NQ T: 01297 20375 F: 01297 625626 E: info@tram.co.uk W: www.tram.co.uk

Sidmouth Museum Hope Cottage Church St Sidmouth EX10 8LY T: 01395 516139

Teignmouth Museum 29 French St Teignmouth TQ14 8ST T: 01626 777041

The Dartmouth Museum The Butterwalk Dartmouth TQ6 9PZ T: 01803 832923

The Devonshire and Dorset Regiment (Archives) RHQ, Devonshire and Dorset Regiment, Wyvern Barracks Barrack Road Exeter EX2 6AR T: 01392 492436 F: 01392 492469

The Museum of Dartmoor Life West Street Okehampton EX20 1HQ T: 01837 52295 F: 01837 659330 E: dartmoormuseum@eclipse.co.uk W: www.museumofdartmoorlife.eclipse.co.uk

Dorset

Bournemouth Aviation Museum Hanger 600 Bournemouth International Airport Christchurch BH23 6SE T: 01202 580858 F: 01202 580858 E: admin@aviation-museum.co.uk_phil@philbc.freeserve.co.uk W: www.aviation-museum.co.uk

Bridport Harbour Museum West Bay Bridport DT6 4SA T: 01308 420997

Cavalcade of Costume Museum Lime Tree House The Plocks Blandford Forum DT11 7AA T: 01258 453006 W: www.cavalcadeofcostume.com

Christchurch Motor Museum Matchams Lane Hurn Christchurch BH23 6AW T: 01202 488100

Dinosaur Land Coombe St Lyme Regis DT7 3PY T: 01297 443541

Dorset County Museum High West Street Dorchester DT1 1XA T: 01305 262735 F: 01305 257180 E: dorsetcountymuseum@dor-mus.demon.co.uk W: www.dorsetcc.gov.uk

Dorset Volunteers, Dorset Yeomanry Museum Gillingham Museum Chantry Fields Gillingham SP8 4UA T: 01747 821119 W: www.brWebsites.com/gillingham.museum

Lyme Regis Philpot Museum Bridge St Lyme Regis DT7 3QA T: 01297 443370 E: info@lymeregismuseum.co.uk W: www.lymeregismuseum.co.uk

Nothe Fort Barrack Rd Weymouth DT4 8UF T: 01305 766626 F: 01305 766425 E: fortressweymouth@btconnect.com W: www.fortressweymouth.co.uk

Portland Museum Wakeham Portland DT5 1HS T: 01305 821804

Priest's House Museum 23-27 High St Wimborne BH21 1HR T: 01202 882533

Red House Museum & Gardens Quay Rd Christchurch BH23 1BU T: 01202 482860

Royal Signals Museum Blandford Camp Nr Blandford Forum DT11 8RH T: 01258-482248 T: 01258-482267 F: 01258 482084 W: www.royalsignalsarmy.org.uk/museum/

Russell-Cotes Art Gallery & Museum East Cliff Bournemouth BH1 3AA T: 01202 451858 F: 01202 451851 E: diane.edge@bournemouth.gov.uk W: www.russell-cotes.bournemouth.gov.uk

Shaftesbury Abbey Museum & Garden Park Walk Shaftesbury SP7 8JR T: 01747 852910

Shaftesbury Town Museum Gold Hill Shaftesbury SP7 8JW T: 01747 852157 Open Daily 10.30.a.m. to 4.30.p.m. Closed wednesdays. Admission charge Adults

Sherborne Museum Association Abbey Gate House Church Avenue Sherborne DT9 3BP T: 01935 812252

Tank Museum Bovington BH20 6JG T: 01929 405096 F: 01929 462410 E: librarian@tankmuseum.co.uk_davidw@tankmuseum.co.uk W: www.tankmuseum.co.uk

The Dinosaur Museum Icen Way Dorchester DT1 1EW T: 01305 269880 F: 01305 268885

The Keep Military Museum The Keep Bridport Road Dorchester DT1 1RN T: 01305 264066 F: 01305 250373 E: keep.museum@talk21.com W: www.keepmilitarymuseum.org CC accepted

Wareham Town Museum 5 East St Wareham BH20 4NS T: 01929 553448

Waterfront Musuem and Local Studies Centre 4 High St Poole BH15 1BW T: 01202 683138 T: 01202 262600 F: 01202 660896 E: museums@poole.gov.uk_mldavidw@poole.gov.uk W: www.poole.gov.uk 1901 census

Weymouth & Portland Museum Service The Esplanade Weymouth DT4 8ED T: 01305 765206

Weymouth Museum Brewers Quay, Hope Square, Weymouth DT4 8TR T: 01305 777622 E: admin@brewers-quay.co.uk W: www.brewers-quay.co.uk

West Bridport Museum Trust - Local History Centre The Coach House Grundy Lane Bridport DT6 3RJ T: 01308 458703 F: 01308 458704 E: sh-bridportmus@btconnect.com

Durham

The 68th (or Durham) Regiment of Light Infantry Display Team 40 The Rowans Orgill Egremont CA22 2HW T: 01946 820110 E: PhilMackie@aol.com W: www.68dli.com

The Bowes Museum Newgate Barnard Castle DL12 8NP T: 01833 690606 F: 01833 637163 E: info@bowesmuseum.org.uk W: www.bowesmuseum.org.uk

Darlington Railway Centre & Museum North Road Station Station Rd Darlington DL3 6ST T: 01325 460532

Darlington Railway Preservation Society Station Rd Hopetown Darlington DL3 6ST T: 01325 483606

Discovery Centre Grosvenor House 29 Market Place Bishop Auckland DL14 7NP T: 01388-662666 F: 01388-661941 E: west.durham@groundwork.org.uk

Durham Cultural Services Library and Museums Department County Hall Durham DH1 5TY T: 0191 384 3777 F: 0191 384 1336 E: culture@durham.gov.uk W: www.durham.gov.uk

Durham Heritage Centre St Mary le Bow North Bailey Durham DH1 5ET T: 0191-384-5589

Durham Light Infantry Museum Aykley Heads Durham DH1 5TU T: 0191-384-2214 F: 0191-386-1770 E: dli@durham.gov.uk W: www.durham.gov.uk/dli

Durham Mining Museum Easington Colliery Welfare Memorial Road Easington T: 07931 421709 W: www.dmm.org.uk

Fulling Mill Museum of Archaeology The Banks Durham T: 0191 374 3623

Killhope Lead Mining Centre Cowshill Weardale DL13 1AR T: 01388-537505 F: 01388-537617 E: killhope@durham.gov.uk W: www.durham.gov.uk/killhope/index.htm

Timothy Hackworth Victorian & Railway Museum Shildon DL4 1PQ T: 01388-777999 F: 01388-777999

Weardale Museum South View 2 Front Street Ireshopeburn DL13 1EY T: 01388-537417

Essex

Barleylands Farm Museum & Visitors Centre Barleylands Farm Billericay CM11 2UD T: 01268 282090

Battlesbridge Motorcycle Museum Muggeridge Farm Maltings Road Battlesbridge Wickford SS11 7RF T: 01268 560866

Castle Point Transport Museum Society 105 Point Rd Canvey Island SS8 7TJ T: 01268 684272

Chelmsford Museum Oaklands Park Moulsham Street Chelmsford CM2 9AQ T: 01245 615100 F: 01245 262428 E: oaklands@chelmsfordbc.gov.uk

East England Tank Museum Oak Business Park Wix Rd Beaumont Clacton-On-Sea CO16 0AT T: 01255 871119

East Essex Aviation Society & Museum Martello Tower Point Clear Clacton on Sea T: 01255 428020 T: 01206 323728

Epping Forest District Museum 39-41 Sun St Waltham Abbey EN9 1EL T: 01992 716882

Essex Police Museum Police Headquarters PO Box 2 Springfield Chelmsford CM2 6DA T: 01245 491491-ext-50771 F: 01245 452456

Essex Regiment Museum Oaklands Park Moulsham Street Chelmsford CM2 9AQ T: 01245 615101 F: 01245 262428 E: pompadour@chelsfordbc.gov.uk W: www.essexregimentmuseum.co.uk

Essex Secret Bunker Crown Building Shrublands Road Mistley CO11 1HS T: 01206 392271 (24 hour information line)

Essex Volunteer Units Colchester Museums 14 Ryegate Road Colchester CO1 1YG T: 01206 282935 F: 1206282925 E: tomhodgson@colchester.gov.uk Uniform, accessories, some ephemera

Essex Yeomanry Collection Springfield Lyons TA Centre Colchester Road Chelmsford CM2 5TA T: 01245 462298

Great Dunmow Maltings Museum The Maltings Mill Lane Great Dunmow CM6 1BG T: 01371 878979

Harwich Maritime Museum Low Lightouse Harbour Crescent Harwich T: 01255 503429 F: 01255 503429 E: theharwichsociety@quista.net W: www.harwich-society.com

Harwich Redoubt Fort Behind 29 Main Road Harwich T: 01255 503429 E: theharwichsociety@quista.net W: www.harwich-society.com

Hollytrees Museum High St Colchester CO1 1DN T: 01206 282940

Kelvedon Hatch Secret Nuclear Bunker Kelvedon Hall Lane Kelvedon Common Kelvedon Hatch Brentwood CM15 0LB T: 01277 364883 F: 01277 372562 E: bunker@japar.demon.co.uk W: www.japar.demon.co.uk Visitor Access via A128

Leigh Heritage Centre & Museum 13a High St Leigh-On-Sea SS9 2EN T: 01702 470834 E: palmtree@nothdell.demon.co.uk

Maldon District Museum 47 Mill Rd Maldon CM9 5HX T: 01621 842688

National Motorboat Museum Wattyler Country Park Pitsea Hall Lane Pitsea Basildon SS16 4UH T: 01268 550077 F: 01268 581903

Royal Gunpowder Mills Beaulieu Drive Powdermill Lane Waltham Abbey EN9 1JY T: 01992 767022 F: 01992 710341 E: info@royalgunpowder.co.uk W: www.royalgunpowder.co.uk

Saffron Walden Museum Museum Street Saffron Walden CB10 1JL T: 01799 510333 E: museum@uttlesford.gov.uk

Southend Central Museum Museum Victoria Avenue Southend-On-Sea SS2 6EW T: 01702 434449 F: 01702 349806

The Cater Museum 74 High St Billericay CM12 9BS T: 01277 622023

The Museum of Harlow Muskham Rd Harlow CM20 2LF T: 01279 4549569 F: 01279 626094 W: www.tmoh.org

Thurrock Museum Ossett Road Grays RM17 5DX

Valence House Museum Valence House Museum Becontree Avenue Dagenham RM8 3HT T: 020 8270 6866 F: 020 82706868 W: www.barking-dagenham.gov.uk

Gloucestershire

Campden & District Historical & Archaeological Society (CADWAS) The Old Police station High Street Chipping Campden GL55 6HB T: 01386 848840 E: enquiries@chippingcampdenhistory.org.uk W: www.chippingcampdenhistory.org.uD

Dean Heritage Centre Soudley Cinderford Forest of dean GL14 2UB T: 01594 822170 F: 01594 823711 E: deanmuse@btinternet.com

Frenchay Tuckett Society and Local History Museum 247 Frenchay Park Road Frenchay BS16 ILG T: 0117 956 9324 F: E: raybulmer@compuserve.com W: www.frenchay.org/museum.html

Gloucester City Museum & Art Gallery Brunswick Rd Gloucester GL1 1HP T: 01452 524131

Gloucester Folk Museum 99-103 Westgate St Gloucester GL1 2PG T: 01452 526467 F: 01452 330495 E: christopherm@glos-city.gov.uk

Holst Birthplace Museum 4 Clarence Rd Cheltenham GL52 2AY T: 01242 524846 F: 01242 580182

Jet Age Museum Hangar 7 Meteor Business Park Gloucestershire Airport Cheltenham Road East Gloucester GL2 9QY T: 01452 715100 W: www.aboutbritain.com/JetAgeMuseum.htm

John Moore Countryside Museum 42 Church St Tewkesbury GL20 5SN T: 01684 297174

Nature In Art Wallsworth Hall Tewkesbury Rd Twigworth Gloucester GL2 9PG T: 01452 731422 F: 01452 730937 E: rinart@globalnet.co.uk W: www.nature-in-art.org.uk

Regiments Of Gloucestershire Museum Gloucester Docks Gloucester GL1 2HE T: 01452 522682

Shambles Museum Church Street Newent GL18 1PP T: 01531 822144 Museum of Victorian Life

Soldiers of Gloucestershire Museum Gloucester Docks Commercial Road Gloucester GL1 2EH T: 01452 522682 F: 01452 311116

Soldiers of Gloucestershire Museum Custom House Gloucester Docks Gloucester GL1 2HE T: 01452 522682 F: 01452 31116 W: www.glosters.org.uk

The Great Western Railway Museum (Coleford) The Old Railway Station Railway Drive Coleford GL16 8RH T: 01594 833569 T: 01594 832032 F: 01594 832032

The Guild Of Handicraft Trust Silk Mill Sheep Street Chipping Campden GL55 6DS T: 01386 841417

The Jenner Museum Church Lane Berkeley GL13 9BH T: 01453 810631 F: 01453 811690 E: manager@jennermuseum.com W: www.jennermuseum.com

The National Waterways Museum see National

Wellington Aviation Museum Broadway Road Moreton in the Marsh GL56 0BG T: 01608 650323 W: www.wellingtonaviation.org Collection of Royal Air Force Treasures

Gloucestershire(TidenhamParish) Chepstow Museum Bridge St Chepstow NP16 5EZ T: 01291 625981 F: 01291 635005 E: chepstowmuseum@monmouthshire.gov.uk

Hampshire

Action Stations Boathouse No 6 HM Naval Base Portsmouth PO1 3LR T: 023 9286 1512

Airborne Forces Museum Browning Barracks Aldershot GU11 2BU T: 01252 349619 F: 0125 349203

Airbourne Forces Museum Browning Barracks Aldershot GU11 2BU T: 01252 349619 E: airbourneforcesmuseum@army.mod.uk.net

Aldershot Military Historical Trust Evelyn Woods Rd Aldershot GU11 2LG T: 01252 314598 F: 01252 342942

Aldershot Military Museum Queens Avenue Aldershot GU11 2LG T: 01252-314598 F: 01252-342942 E: musmim@hants.gov.uk W: www.hants.gov.uk/museum/aldershot

Andover Museum & Iron Age Museum 6 Church Close Andover SP10 1DP T: 01264 366283 F: 01264 339152 E: andover.museum@virgin.nbet_musmda@hants.gov.uk_musmad@hants.gov.uk W: www.hants.gov.uk/andoverm

Army Medical Services Museum Keogh Barracks Ash Vale Aldershot GU12 5RQ T: 01252 868612 F: 01252 868832 E: museum@keogh72.freeserve.co.uk Records the history of the army Mediacl Services which includes medical, veterinary, dental and nursing services CC accepted

Army Medical Services Museum Keogh Barracks Ash Vale Aldershot GU12 5RQ T: 01252 868612 F: 01252 868832 E: museum@keogh72.freeserve.co.uk

Army Physical Training Corps Museum ASPT Fox Line Queen's Avenue Aldershot GU11 2LB T: 01252 347168 F: 01252 340785 E: regtsec@aptc.org.uk W: www.aptc.org.uk

Balfour Museum of Hampshire Red Cross History Red Cross House Weeke Winchester SO22 5JD T: 01962 865174 F: 01962 869721

Bishops Waltham Museum Brookstreet Bishop's Waltham Southampton S032 1 T:

Bishops Waltham Museum Trust 8 Folly Field Bishop's Waltham Southampton S032 1EB T: 01489 894970

Broadlands Romsey SO51 9ZD T: 01794 505056 F: 01794 505040 E: admin@broadlands.net W: www.broadlands.net

D-Day Museum and Overlord Museum Clarence Esplanade Southsea PO5 3NT T: 023 9282 7261 F: 023 9282 7527

Dockyard Apprentice Exhibition Portsmouth Royal Dockyard 19 College Road HM Naval Base Portsmouth PO1 3LJ T:

Eastleigh Museum 25 High St Eastleigh SO50 5LF T: (023) 8064 3026 E: musmst@hants.gov.uk W: www.hants.gov.uk/museum/eastlmus/index.html

Eling Tide Mill Trust Ltd The Tollbridge Eling Hill Totton Southampton SO40 9HF T: (023) 80869575

Explosion! The Museum of Naval Firepower Priddy's Hard Gosport PO12 4LE T: 023 9258 6505 F: 023 9258 6282 E: info@explosion.org.uk W: www.explosion.org.uk

Gosport Museum Walpole Rd Gosport PO12 1NS T: (023) 9258 8035 F: (023) 9250 81951 E: musmie@hunts.gov.uk

Hampshire County Museums Service Chilcomb House Chilcomb Lane Winchester SO23 8RD T: 01962 846304

Havant Museum Havant Museum 56 East Street Havant P09 1BS T: 023 9245 1155 F: 023 9249 8707 E: musmop@hants.gov.uk W: www.hants.gov.uk/museums

Historic Ships and The Naval Dockyard HM Naval Base Portsmouth PO1 3LR T: 023 9286 1512 T: 023 9286 1533 W: www.flagship.org.uk

HMS Victory Victory Gate HM Naval Base Portsmouth PO1 3LR T: (023) 9277 8600 F: (023) 9277 8601 E: info@hmswarrior.org W: www.hmswarrior.org

HMS Warrior (1860) Victory Gate HM Naval Base Portsmouth PO1 3LR T: (023) 9277 8600 F: (023) 9277 8601 E: info@hmswarrior.org W: www.hmswarrior.org

Hollycombe Steam Collection Iron Hill Midhurst Rd Liphook GU30 7LP T: 01428 724900

Museum of Army Chaplaincy Amport House Nr Andover Andover SP11 8BG T: 01264 773144 x 4248 T: 01264 771042 E: rachdcurator@tiscali.co.uk

Museum of Army Flying Middle Wallop Stockbridge SO20 8DY T: 01980 674421 F: 01264 781694 E: daa@flying-museum.org.uk W: www.flying-museum.org.uk

New Forest Museum & Visitor Centre High St Lyndhurst SO43 7NY T: (023) 8028 3914 F: (020) 8028 4236 E: nfmuseum@lineone.net

Portsmouth City Museum and Record Office Museum Road Portsmouth PO1 2LJ T: (023) 92827261 F: (023) 92875276 E: portmus@compuserve.com 1901 census

Priddy's Hard Armament Museum Priory Rd Gosport PO12 4LE T: (023) 92502490

Rockbourne Roman Villa Rockbourne Fordingbridge SP6 3PG T: 01725 518541

Royal Armouries - Fort Nelson Fort Nelson Down End Roadd Fareham PO17 6AN T: 01329 233734 F: 01329 822092 E: enquiries@armouries.org.uk W: www.armouries.org.uk

Royal Marines Museum Eastney Southsea PO4 9PX T: (023) 9281 9385-Exts-224 F: (023) 9283 8420 E: matthewlittle@royalmarinesmuseum.co.uk W: www.royalmarinesmuseum.co.uk

Royal Naval Museum H M Naval Base (PP66) Portsmouth PO1 3NH T: (023) 9272 3795 F: (023) 9272 3942 W: www.royalnavalmuseum.org

Royal Navy Submarine Museum Haslar Jetty Road Gosport PO12 2AS T: (023) 92510354 F: (023) 9251 1349 E: admin@rnsubmus.co.uk W: www.rnsubmus.co.uk

Sammy Miller Motor Cycle Museum Bashley Manor Farm Bashley Cross Rd New Milton BH25 5SZ T: 01425 620777

Search 50 Clarence Rd Gosport PO12 1BU T: (023) 92501957

Southampton Hall of Aviation Albert Road South Southampton SO1 1FR T: 01703 635830

Southampton Maritime Museum Bugle St Southampton SO14 2AJ T: (023) 80223941

The Bear Museum 38 Dragon St Petersfield GU31 4JJ T: 01730 265108 E: judy@bearmuseum.freeserve.co.uk W: www.bearmuseum.co.uk

The Gurkha Museum Peninsula Barracks Romsey Road Winchester SO23 8TS T: 01962 842832 F: 01962 877597 E: curator@thegurkhamuseum.co.uk W: www.thegurkhamuseum.co.uk

The King's Royal Hussars Museum (10th Royal Hussars PWO 11th Hussars PAO and The Royal Hussars PWO) Peninsula Barracks Romsey Road Winchester SO23 8TS T: 01962 828540 F: 01962 828538 E: beresford@krhmuseum.freeserve.co.uk W: www.hants.gov.uk/leisure/museum/royalhus/index.html

The Light Infantry Museum Peninsula Barracks Romsey Road Winchester SO23 8TS T: 01962 868550

The Mary Rose Trust 1-10 College Road HM Naval Base Portsmouth PO1 3LX T: (023) 92750521

The Museum of The Adjutant General's Corps RHQ Adjutant General's Corps Worthy Down Winchester SO21 2RG T: 01962 887435 F: 01962 887690 E: agc.regtsec@virgin.net

The Royal Green Jackets Museum (Oxford and Bucks Light Infantry King's Royal Rifle Corps and The Rifle Brigade) Peninsula Barracks Romsey Road Winchester SO23 8TS T: 01962 828549 F: 01962 828500 E: museum@royalgreenjackets.co.uk W: www.royalgreenjackets.co.uk

The Willis Museum Of Basingstoke Town & Country Life Old Town Hall Market Place Basingstoke RG21 7QD T: 01256 465902 F: 01256 471455 E: willismuseum@hotmail.com W: www.hants.gov.uk/leisure/museums/willis/index.html

West End Local History Society 20 Orchards Way West End Southampton S030 3FB T: 023 8057 5244 E: westendlhs@aol.com W: www.telbin.demon.co.uk/westendlhs Museum at Old Fire Station, High Street, West End

Westbury Manor Museum West St Fareham PO16 0JJ T: 01329 824895 F: 01329 825917 W: www.hants.gov.uk/museum/westbury/

Whitchurch Silk Mill 28 Winchester St Whitchurch RG28 7AL T: 01256 892065

Winchester Museums Service 75 Hyde St Winchester SO23 7DW T: 01962 848269 F: 01962 848299 E: museums@winchester.gov.uk W: www.winchester.gov.uk/heritage/home.htm

Herefordshire

Churchill House Museum Venns Lane Hereford HR1 1DE T: 01432 260693 F: 01432 267409

Cider Museum & King Offa Distillery 21 Ryelands St Hereford HR4 0LW T: 01432 354207 F: 01432 341641 E: thompson@cidermuseum.co.uk W: www.cidermuseum.co.uk

Leominster Museum Etnam St Leominster HR6 8 T: 01568 615186 F:

The Judge's Lodging Broad St Presteigne LD8 2AD T: 01544 260650 F: 01544 260652 W: www.judgeslodging.org.uk

Teddy Bears of Bromyard 12 The Square Bromyard HR7 4BP T: 01885 488329

Waterworks Museum 86 Park Street Broomy Hill Hereford HR1 2RE T: 01432-356653

Weobley & District Local History Society and Museum Weobley Museum Back Lane Weobley HR4 8SG T: 01544 340292

Hertfordshire

Bushey Museum, Art Gallery and Local Studies Centre Rudolph Road Bushey WD23 3HW T: 020 8420 4057 F: 020 8420 4923 E: busmt@bushey.org.uk W: www.busheymuseum.org 1901 census for Bushcy and aldenham

De Havilland Heritage Centre inc The Mosquito Aircraft Museum PO Box 107 Salisbury Hall London Colney AL10 1EX T: 01727 822051 F: 01727 826400 W: www.hertsmuseums.org

First Garden City Heritage Museum 296 Norton Way South Letchworth Garden City SG6 1SU T: 01462 482710 F: 01462 486056 E: fgchm@letchworth.com

Hertford Museum (Hertfordshire Regiment) 18 Bull Plain Hertford SG14 1DT T: 01992 552100 F: 01992 534797 E: enquiries@hertfordmuseum.org W: www.hertfordmuseum.org

Hertford Regiment Museum Hertford Museum 18 Bull Plain Hertford SG14 1DT T: 01992 582686 F: 01992 534797

Hitchin British Schools 41-42 Queen St Hitchin SG4 9TS T: 01462 420144 F: 01462 420144 E: brsch@britishschools.freeserve.co.uk W: www.hitchinbritishschools.org.uk

Hitchin Museum Paynes Park Hitchin SG5 1EQ T: 01462 434476 F: 01462 431316 W: www.nndc.gov.uk

Kingsbury Water Mill Museum St. Michaels Street St. Albans AL3 4SJ T: 01727 853502

Letchworth Museum & Art Gallery Broadway Letchworth Garden City SG6 3PF T: 01462 685647 F: 01462 481879 E: l.museum@north-herts.gov.uk W: www.north-herts.gov.uk

Mill Green Museum & Mill Mill Green Hatfield AL9 5PD T: 01707 271362 F: 01707 272511

Rhodes Memorial Museum & Commonwealth Centre South Rd Bishop's Stortford CM23 3JG T: 01279 651746 F: 01279 467171 E: rhodesmuseum@freeuk.com W: www.hertsmuseums.org.uk

Royston & District Museum 5 Lower King St Royston SG8 5AL T: 01763 242587

Stondon Transport Museum Station Road Lower Stondon SG16 6JN T: 01462 850339 F: 01462 850824 E: info@transportmuseum.co.uk W: www.transportmuseum.co.uk

The De Havilland Aircraft Museum Trust P.O Box 107 Salisbury Hall London Colney St. Albans AL2 1EX T: 01727 822051

The Environmental Awareness Trust 23 High St Wheathampstead St. Albans AL4 8BB T: 01582 834580

The Forge Museum High St Much Hadham SG10 6BS T: 01279 843301

Verulamium Museum St. Michaels St St. Albans AL3 4SW T: 01727 751810 T: 01727 751824 F: 01727 836282 E: d.thorold.stalbans.gov.uk

Walter Rothschild Zoological Museum Akeman St Tring HP23 6AP T: (020) 7942 6156 F: (020) 7942 6150 E: ornlib@nhm.ac.uk W: www.nhm.ac.uk

Ware Museum Priory Lodge 89 High St Ware SG12 9AD T: 01920 487848

Watford Museum 194 High St Watford WD1 2DT T: 01923 232297

Welwyn Hatfield Museum Service Welwyn Roman Baths By-Pass-Road Welwyn AL6 0 T: 01438 716096

Hull

4th Battalion East Yorkshire Regiment Collection Kingston upon Hull City Museums Wilberforce House 23-25 High Street Kingston upon Hull HU1 T: 01482 613902 F: 01482 613710

Ferens Art Gallery Kingston upon Hull City Museums Queen Victoria Square Kingston upon Hull HU1 3RA T: 01482 613902 F: 01482 613710

Wilberforce House Kingston upon Hull City Museums 23-25 High Street Kingston upon Hull HU1 T: 01482 613902 F: 01482 613710

Isle Of Wight

Bembridge Maritime Museum & Shipwreck Centre Providence House Sherborne St Bembridge PO35 5SB T: 01983 872223

Calbourne Water Mill Calbourne Mill Newport PO30 4JN T: 01983 531227

Carisbroke Castle Newport PO30 1XL W: www.english-heritage.org.uk

Carisbrooke Castle Museum Carisbrooke Castle Newport PO30 1XY T: 01983 523112 F: 01983 532126 E: carismus@lineone.net

East Cowes Heritage Centre 8 Clarence Rd East Cowes PO32 6EP T: 01983 280310

Guildhall Museum Newport High St Newport PO30 1TY T: 01983 823366 F: 01983 823841 E: rachel.silverson@iow.gov.uk W: www.iwight.com

Natural History Centre High St Godshill Ventnor PO38 3HZ T: 01983 840333

Needles Old Battery West High Down Totland Bay PO39 0JH T: 01983 754772 F: 01983 7596978

The Classic Boat Museum Seaclose Wharf Town Quay Newport PO30 2EF T: 01983 533493 F: 01983 533505 E: ebmiow@fsmail.net

The Island Aeroplane Company Ltd Embassy Way Sandown Airport Sandown PO36 9PJ T: 01983 404448 F: 01983 404448

The Lilliput Museum of Antique Dolls & Toys High St Brading Sandown PO36 0DJ T: 01983 407231 E: lilliput.museum@btconnect.com W: www.lilliputmuseum.co.uk

Ventnor Heritage Museum 11 Spring Hill Ventnor PO38 1PE T: 01983 855407

Kent

Brenzett Aeronautical Museum Ivychurch Road Brenzett Romney Marsh TN29 0EE T: 01233 627911 W: www.aboutbritain.com/renzettAeronauticalMuseum

Buffs Regimental Museum The Royal Museum & Art Gallery 18 High Street Canterbury CT1 2RA T: 01227-452747 F: 01227-455047 E: museum@canterbury.gov.uk W: www.canterbury-museums.co.uk

Canterbury Roman Museum Butchery Lane Canterbury CT1 2JR T: 01227 785575 F:

Chartwell House Chartwell Westerham TN16 1PS T: 01732 866368 F: 01732 868193 E: chartwell@nationaltrust.org.uk W: www.nationaltrust.org.uk Home of Sir Winston Churchill from 1924 until his death in 1965

Chatham Dockyard Historical Society Museum Cottage Row Barrack Rd Chatham Dockyard Chatham ME4 4TZ T: 01634 844897(museum)

Cobham Hall Cobham DA12 3BL T: 01474 823371 F: 01474 822995 and 01474 824171

Dickens House Museum 2 Victoria Parade Broadstairs CT10 1QS T: 01843 861232 T: 01843 862853

Dolphin Sailing Barge Museum Crown Quay Lane Sittingbourne ME10 3SN T: 01795 423215

Dover Castle Dover CT16 1HU T: 01304 211067

Dover Museum Market Square Dover CT16 1PB T: 01304 201066 F: 01304 241186 E: museum@dover.gov.uk W: www.dovermuseum.co.uk

Dover Transport Museum Old Park Barracks Whitfield Dover CT16 2HQ T: 01304 822409 F:

Fleur De Lis Heritage Centre 13 Preston Street Faversham ME13 8NS T: 01795 534542 F: 01795 533261 E: faversham@btinternet.com W: www.faversham.org

Fort Armherst Dock Road Chatham ME4 4UB T: 01634 847747 W: www.fortamhurst.org.uk

Fort Luton Museum Magpie Hall Road Chatham ME4 5XJ T: 01634 813969

Guildhall Museum Guildhall Museum High Street Rochester ME1 1PY T: 01634 848717 F: 01634 832919 E: guildhall@medway.gov.uk W: www.medway.gov.uk

Guildhall Museum Rochester High St Rochester ME1 1PY T: 01634 848717 From 22/7/00 museum only responsible for the museum and Brook Pumping Station

Gunpowder Chart Mills Off Stonebridge Way Faversham ME13 7SE T: 01795 534542 F: 01795 533261 E: faversham@btinternet.com W: www.faversham.org

Herne Bay Museum Centre 12 William St Herne Bay CT6 5EJ T: 01227 367368 F: 01227 742560 E: museum@canterbury.gov.uk W: www.hernebay-museum.co.uk

Kent and Sharpshooters Yeomanry Museum Hever Castle Edenbridge TN8 7DB T: 020 8688 2138

Kent Battle of Britain Museum Aerodrome Rd Hawkinge Folkestone CT18 7AG T: 01303 893140

Lashenden Air Warfare Museum Headcorn Aerodrome Headcorn Nr Ashford TN27 9HX T: 01622 890226 F: 01622 890876

Maidstone Museum & Art Gallery St. Faith St Maidstone ME14 1LH T: 01622 754497

Margate Old Town Hall Museum Old Town Hall Market Place Margate CT9 1ER T: 01843 231213

Masonic Library & Museum St. Peters Place Canterbury CT1 2DA T: 01227 785625

Minster Abbey Gatehouse Museum Union Rd Minster On Sea Sheerness ME12 2HW T: 01795 872303

Minster Museum Craft & Animal Centre Bedlam Court Lane Minster Ramsgate CT12 4HQ T: 01843 822312

Museum of Kent Life Cobtree Lock Lane Sandling Maidstone ME14 3AU T: 01622 763936 F: 01622 662024 E: enquiries@museum-kentlife.co.uk W: www.museum-kentlife.co.uk

Pembroke Lodge Family History Centre and Museum 2-6 Station Approach Birchington on Sea CT7 9RD T: 01843-841649 E: pattersonheritage@tesco.net Please address all mail to 4 Station approach, Birchington on Sea Kent CT7 9RD.

Penshurst Place & Gardens Penshursts Tonbridge TN11 8DG T: 01892 870307 F: 01892 870866 E: enuiries@penshurstplace.com W: www.penshurstplace.com

Powell-Cotton Museum, Quex House and Gardens Quex Park Birchington CT7 0T: 01843 842168 F: 01843 846661 E: powell-cotton.museum@virgin.net W: www.powell-cottonmuseum.co.uk

Princess of Wales's Royal Regt & Queen's Regt Museum Howe Barracks Canterbury CT1 1JY T: 01227-818056 F: 01227-818057 Covers Infantry Regiements of Surrey, Kent, Sussex, Hampshire and Middlesex

Quebec House Quebec Square Westerham TN16 1TD T: 01892 890651 F: 01892 890110

RAF Manston History Museum The Airfield Manston Road Ramsgate CT11 5DF T: 01843 825224 E: museum@rafmanston.fsnet.co.uk W: www.rafmuseum.fsnet.co.uk

Ramsgate Maritime Museum Clock House Pier Yard Royal Harbour Ramsgate CT11 8LS T: 01843 587765 F: 01843 582359 E: museum@ekmt.fsnet.co.uk W: www.ekmt.fsnet.co.uk

Ramsgate Maritime Museum The Clock House Pier Yard Royal Harbour Ramsgate CT11 8LS T: 01843 570622 F: 01843 582359 E: museum@ekmt.fsnet.co.uk W: www.ekmt.fsnet.co.uk

Rochester Cathedral Militia Museum Guildhall Museum High Street Rochester ME1 1PY T: 01634 848717 F: 01634 832919 E: guildhall@medway.gov.uk

Roman Dover Tourist Centre Painted House New street Dover CT17 9AJ T: 01304 203279

Roman Museum Butchery Lane Canterbury CT1 2JR T: 01227 785575 W: www.aboutbritain.com/CanterburyRomanMuseum

Romney Toy & Model Museum New Romney Station Romney TN28 8PL T: 01797 362353

Royal Engineers Library Brompton Barracks Chatham ME4 4UX T: 01634 822416 F: 01634 822419

Royal Engineers Museum of Military Engineering Prince Arthur Road Gillingham ME4 4UG T: 01634 822839 F: 01634 822371 E: remuseum.rhgre@gtnet.gov.uk W: www.army.mod.uk/armymuseums

Royal Museum & Art Gallery 18 High St Canterbury CT1 2RA T: 01227 452747

Sheerness Heritage Centre 10 Rose St Sheerness ME12 1AJ T: 01795 663317

Shoreham Aircraft Museum High Street Shoreham Sevenoaks TN14 7TB T: 01959 524416 W: www.s-a-m.freeserve.co.uk

Spitfire and Hurricane Memorial Building The Airfield Manston Road Ramsgate CT11 5DF T: 01843 821940 F: 01843 821940 W: www.spitfire-museum.com

St Margaret's Museum Beach Road St Margaret's Bay Dover CT15 6DZ T: 01304 852764

Tenterden Museum Station Rd Tenterden TN30 6HN T: 01580 764310 F: 01580 766648

The Buffs Regimental Museum The Royal Museum 18 High Street Canterbury CT1 2JE T: 01227 452747 F: 01227 455047

The C.M Booth Collection Of Historic Vehicles 63-67 High St Rolvenden Cranbrook TN17 4LP T: 01580 241234

The Charles Dickens Centre Eastgate House High St Rochester ME1 1EW T: 01634 844176

The Grand Shaft Snargate Street Dover CT16 7 T: 01304 201066

The Historic Dockyard Chatham ME4 4TZ T: 01634 823800 F: 01634 823801 E: info@chdt.org.uk W: www.chdt.org.uk

The Queen's Own Royal West Kent Regiment Museum Maidstone Museum and Art Gallery St Faith's Street Maidstone ME14 1LH T: 01622 602842 F: 01622 685022 E: simonlace@maidstone.gov.uk

The Romney, Hythe & Dymchurch Railway New Romney Station Romney TN28 8PL T: 01797 362353

The West Gate St Peters Street Canterbury T: 01227 452747 F: 1227455047

Timeball Tower Victoria Parade Deal CT14 7BP T: 01304 360897

Victoriana Museum Deal Town Hall High St Deal CT14 6BB T: 01304 380546

Walmer Castle and Gardens Kingsdown Road Walmer Deal CT14 7LJ T: 01304 364288 W: www.english-heritage.org.uk

Watts Charity Poor Travellers House 97 High St Rochester ME1 1LX T: 01634 845609

Whitstable Museum & Gallery 5a Oxford St Whitstable CT5 1DB T: 01227 276998 W: www.whitstable-museum.co.uk

Lancashire

Blackburn Museum and Art Gallery Museum Street Blackburn BB1 7AJ T: 01254 667130 F: 01254 685541 E: paul.flintoff@blackburn.gov.uk W: www.blackburnworld.com

Bolton Museum & Art Gallery Le Mans Crescent Bolton BL1 1SE T: 01204 332190 F: 01204 332241 E: bolwg@gn.apc.org

British in India Museum Newton Street Colne BB8 0JJ T: 01282 870215 T: 01282 613129 F: 01282 870215

Duke of Lancaster's Own Yeomanry Stanley St Preston PR1 4AT T: 01772 264074

East Lancashire Railway Bolton Street Station Bolton Street Bury BL9 0EY T: 0161 764 7790 F: 0161 763 4408 E: admin@east-lancs-rly.co.uk W: www.east-lancs-rly.co.uk

East Lancashire Regiment Towneley Hall Burnley BB11 3RQ T: 1282424213 F: 01282 436138 E: towneleyhall@burnley.gov.uk W: www.towneleyhall.org.uk

Ellenroad Trust Ltd Ellenroad Engine House Elizabethan Way Milnrow Rochdale OL16 4LG T: 01706 881952 E: ellenroad@aol.com W: http:\\ellenroad.homepage.com

Fleetwood Museum Queens Terrace Fleetwood FY7 6BT T: 01253 876621 F: 01253 878088 E: fleetwood.museum@mus.lancscc.gov.uk W: www.nettingthebay.org.uk

Gawthorpe Hall Habergham Drive Padiham Burnley BB12 8UA T: 01282 771004 F: 01282 770178 E: gawthorpehall@museumsoflancs.org.uk W: www.museumsoflancs.org.uk

Hall I'Th' Wood Museum Hall I Th' Wood Tonge Moor Bolton BL1 8UA T: 01204 301159

Heaton Park Tramway (Transport Museum) Tram Depot Heaton Park Prestwich Manchester M25 2SW T: 0161 740 1919

Helmshore Textile Museums Holcombe Road Helmshore Rossendale BB4 4NP T: 01706 226459 F: 01706 218554

Heritage Trust for the North West within Pendle Heritage Centre Colne Rd Barrowford Nelson BB9 6JQ T: 01282 661704

Judge's Lodgings Museum Church St Lancaster LA1 1LP T: 01524 32808

King's Own Royal Regimental Museum The City Museum Market Square Lancaster LA1 1HT T: 01524 64637 F: Fax: 01524 841692 E: kingsownmuseum@iname.com

Kippers Cats 51 Bridge St Ramsbottom Bury BL0 9AD T: 01706 822133

Lancaster City Museum Market Square Lancaster LA1 1HT T: 01524 64637 F: 01524 841692 E: awhite@lancaster.gov.uk

Lancaster Maritime Museum Custom House St George's Quay Lancaster LA1 1RB T: 01524 64637 F: 01524 841692

Lytham Heritage Group 2 Henry St Lytham St. Annes FY8 5LE T: 01253 730767

Manchester Museum University of Manchester Oxford Rd Manchester M13 9PL T: 0161 275 2634

Manchester Museum Education Service University of Manchester Oxford Rd Manchester M13 9PL T: 0161 275 2630 F: 0161 275 2676 E: education@man.ac.uk W: http://museum.man.ac.uk

Museum of Lancashire Stanley Street Preston Lancashire PR1 4YP T: 01772-264079 E: museum@lancs.co.uk

Museum of Lancashire (Queen's Lancashire Regiment Duke of Lancaster's Own Yeomanry Lancashire Hussars 14th/20th King's Hussars) Stanley Street Preston PR1 4YP T: 01772 534075 F: 01772 534079 Credit Cards accepted

Museum of the Manchester Regiment Ashton Town Hall Market Place Ashton-u-Lyne OL6 6DL T: 0161 342 3078 E: museum.manchester@nxcorp1.tameside.gov.uk W: www.tameside.gov.uk

Museum of the Queen's Lancashire Regiment (East South and Loyal (North Lancashire) Regiments, Lancashire Regiment (PWV) and The Queen's Lancashire Regiment Fulwood Barracks Preston PR2 8AA T: 01772 260362 F: 01772 260583 E: rhq.qlr@talk21.com Including associated Volunteer, TA and Militia Units

North West Sound Archive Old Steward's Office Clitheroe Castle Clitheroe BB7 1AZ T: 01200-427897 F: 01200-427897 E: nwsa@ed.lancscc.gov.uk W: www.lancashire.gov.uk/education/lifelong/recordindon

Oldham Museum Greaves St Oldham OL1 1T: 0161 911 4657

Ordsall Hall Museum Taylorson St Salford M5 3HT T: 0161 872 0251

Pendle Heritage Centre Park Hill Colne Rd Barrowford Nelson BB9 6JQ T: 01282 661702 F: 01282 611718

Portland Basin Museum Portland Place Ashton-Under-Lyne OL7 0QA T: 0161 343 2878

Queen St Mill Harle Syke Queen St Briercliffe Burnley BB10 2HX T: 01282 459996

Rawtenstall Museum Whitaker Park Haslingden Road Rawtenstall T: 01706 244682 F: 01706 250037

Ribchester Museum of Roman Antiquities Riverside Ribchester Preston PR3 3XS T: 01254 878261 W: www.aboutbritain.com/Ribchester Roman Museum.htm

Ribchester Roman Museum Riverside Ribchester Preston PR3 3XS T: 01254 878261 T: 01772 264080

Rochdale Museum Service The Arts & Heritage Centre The Esplanade Rochdale OL16 1AQ T: 01706 641085

Rochdale Pioneers Museum Toad Lane Rochdale OL12 0NU T: 01706 524920

Saddleworth Museum & Art Gallery High St Uppermill Oldham OL3 6HS T: 01457 874093 F: 01457 870336

Salford Museum & Art Gallery Peel Park Salford M5 4WU T: 0161 736 2649 E: info@lifetimes.org.uk W: www.lifetimes.org.uk

Slaidburn Heritage Centre 25 Church St Slaidburn Clitheroe BB7 3ER T: 01200 446161 F: 01200 446161 E: slaidburn.heritage@htnw.co.uk W: www.htnw.co.uk_slaidburn.org.uk

Smithills Hall Museum Smithills Hall Dean Road Bolton BL1 7NP T: 01204 841265

South Lancashire Regiment Prince of Wales Volunteers Museum Peninsula Barracks Warrington

The British in India Museum Newtown Street Colne T: 01282 613129 0976 665320 F: 01282 870215 Open April to september Wednesday & Saturdays 2pm to 5pm

The Fusiliers Museum (Lancashire) Wellington Barracks Bolton Road Bury BL8 2PL T: 0161 764 2208

The Greater Manchester Police Museum 57 Newton St Manchester M1 1ES T: 0161 856 3287 0161 856 3288 F: 0161 856 3286

The Museum of Science and Industry In Manchester Liverpool Rd Castlefield Manchester M3 4JP T: 0161 832 2244 0161 832 1830 (24 hour info line) F: 0161 833 2184 E: marketing@msim.org.uk W: www.msim.org.uk

The Rochdale Pioneers' Museum 31 Toad Lane Rochdale T: 01706-524920

Weaver's Cottage Bacup Road Rawtenstall T: 01706 229937 01706 226459 E: rossendale_leisure@compuserve.com

Weavers Cottage Heritage Centre Weavers Cottage Bacup Rd Rawtenstall Rossendale BB4 7NW T: 01706 229828 F: 01706 210915

Whitworth Museum North Street Whitworth T: 01706 343231 01706 853655 E: rossendale_leisure@compuserve.com

Leicestershire

New Walk Museum New Walk Museum 53 New Walk Leicester LE1 7AE T: 0116 247 3220 E: hide001@leicester.gov.uk W: www.leicestermuseums.co.uk

Abbey Pumping Station Corporation Rd Abbey Lane Leicester LE4 5PX T: 0116 299 5111 F: 0116 299 5125 W: www.leicestermuseums.ac.uk

Ashby De La Zouch Museum North St Ashby-De-La-Zouch LE65 1HU T: 01530 560090

Belgrave Hall & Gardens Church Rd Belgrave Leicester LE4 5PE T: 0116 266 6590 F: 0116 261 3063 E: marte001@leicester.gov.uk W: www.leicestermuseums.org.uk

Bellfoundry Museum Freehold St Loughborough LE11 1AR T: 01509 233414

Bosworth Battlefield Visitor Centre Sutton Cheney Market Bosworth Nuneaton CV13 0AD T: 01455 290429 T: 0116 265 6961 (Rosemary Mills) F: 01455 292841 E: bosworth@leics.gov.uk W: www.leics.gov.uk

British Aviation Heritage Bruntingthorpe Aerodrome Bruntingthorpe Lutterworth LE17 5QH T: 0116 221 8426 E: Banmuseums@hotmail.com W: www.jetman.dircon.co.uk/brunty

Charnwood Museum Granby St Loughborough LE11 3DU T: 01509 233754 F: 01509 268140 W: www.leics.gov.uk/museums/musinliecs.htm#charnwood

Foxton Canal Museum Middle Lock Gumley Rd Foxton Market Harborough LE16 7RA T: 0116 279 2657

Harborough Museum Council Offices Adam and Eve Street Market Harborough LE16 7AG T: 01858 821085 F: 01509 268140 E: museums@leics.gov.uk W: www.leics.gov.uk/museums/musinliecs.htm#harborough

Hinckley & District Museum Ltd Framework Knitters Cottage Lower Bond St Hinckley LE10 1QU T: 01455 251218

Jewry Wall Museum St. Nicholas Circle Leicester LE1 4LB T: 0116 247 3021

Leicester City Museum & Art Gallery 53 New Walk Leicester LE1 7EA T: 0116 255 4100

Leicester Gas Museum - Closed Aylestone Rd Leicester LE2 7LF T: 0116 250 3190 F: Archive material transferred to The National Gas Archive.

Leicestershire Ecology Centre Holly Hayes Environmental Resources Centre 216 Birstall Rd Birstall Leicester LE4 4DG T: 0116 267 1950 F: 0116 267 7112 E: dlott@leics.gov.uk

Leicestershire Yeomanry, Leicestershire Tigers Museum Loughborough War Memorial Queen's Park Loughborough T: 01509 263370

Melton Carnegie Museum Thorpe End Melton Mowbray LE13 1RB T: 01664 569946 F: 01664 569946 E: museums@leics.gov.uk W: www.liecs.gov.uk/museums/#melton

Royal Leicestershire Regiment Museum Gallery New Walk Museum New Walk Leicester LE1 7FA T: 0116 2470403 closed for refurbishment to 2005 Postal enquiries: Newarke Houses Museum, The Newarke, Leicester LE2 7BY

Royal Leicestershire Regimental Gallery New Walk Museum 53 New Walk Leicester LE1 7AE T: 0116 247 3220 F: E: hide001@leicester.gov.uk W: www.leicestermuseums.co.uk

Snibston Discovery Park Ashby Rd Coalville LE67 3LN T: 01530 510851 F: 01530 813301 E: museums@leics.gov.uk W: www.leics.gov.uk/museums/musinliecs.htm#snibston

The Guildhall Guildhall Lane Leicester LE1 5FQ T: 0116 253 2569

The Manor House Manor Rd Donington Le Heath Coalville LE67 2FW T: 01530 831259 F: 01530 831259 E: museums@leics.gov.uk W: www.leics.gov.uk/museums/musinliecs.htm#manor

Lincolnshire

50 and 61 Suadrons' Museum The Lawn Union Road Lincoln

Alford Civic Trust Manor House Museum West Street Alford LN13 9DJ T: 01507 463073 Closed Sept 2003 to 2005 for refurbishment.

Ayscoughfee Hall Museum & Gardens Churchgate Spalding PE11 2RA T: 01775 725468 F: 01775 762715

Battle of Britain Memorial Flight Visitor Centre R.A.F Coningsby Coningsby Lincoln LN4 4SY T: 01526 344041 F: 01526 342330 E: bbmf@lincolnshire.gov.uk W: www.lincolnshire.gov.uk/bbmt

Bomber County Aviation Museum Ex RAF Hemswell Hemswell cliff Gainsborough T: 01724 855410 T: 01482 215859

Boston Guildhall Museum South Street Boston PE21 6HT T: 01205 365954 E: heritage@originalboston.freeserve.co.uk

Church Farm Museum Church Rd South Skegness PE25 2HF T: 01754 766658 F: 01754 898243 E: wifff@lincolnshire.gov.uk

Cranwell Avation Heritage Centre Heath Farm North Rauceby Near Cranwell Sleaford NG34 8QR T: 01529 488490 F: 01529 488490

Gainsborough Old Hall Parnell St Gainsborough DN21 2NB T: 01427 612669

Gordon Boswell Romany Museum Hawthorns Clay Lake Spalding PE12 6BL T: 01775 710599

Grantham Museum St. Peters Hill Grantham NG31 6PY T: 01476 568783 F: 01476 592457

Lincolnshire Aviation Heritage Centre East Kirkby Airfield East Kirkby Spilsby PE23 4DE T: 01790 763207 F: 01790 763207 E: enquiries@lincsaviation.co.uk W: www.lincsaviation.co.uk cc accepted

Lincs Vintage Vehicle Society Whisby Rd North Hykeham Lincoln LN6 3QT T: 01522 500566

Louth Naturalists Antiquarian & Literary Society 4 Broadbank Louth LN11 0EQ T: 01507 601211

Metheringham Airfield Visitor Centre Westmoor Farm Martin Moor Metheringham LN4 3BO T: 01526 378270 F: 01526 378604 E: foma-lincs@hotmail.com

Museum of Lincolnshire Life Old Barracks Burton Road Lincoln LN1 3LY T: 01522-528448 F: 01522-521264 E: lincolnshirelife_museum@lincolnshire.gov.uk W: www.lincolnshire.gov.uk/museumoflincolnshirelife

National Fishing Heritage Centre Alexander Dock Great Grimsby DN31 1UZ T: 01472-323345 W: www.nelincs.gov.uk

RAF Digby Ops Room Museum RAF Digby Scopwick Lincoln LN4 3LH T: 01526 327503 W: www.airops.freeserve.co.uk

Royal Lincolnshire Regiment Lincolnshire Yeomanry Museum Old Barracks Burton Road Lincoln LN1 3LY T: 01522-528448 F: 01522-521264 E: finchj@lincolnshire.gov.uk

The Incredibly Fantastic Old Toy Show 26 Westgate Lincoln LN1 3BD T: 01522 520534

The Queen's Royal Lancers Regimental Museum (16th/5th and 17th/21st Lancers) Belvoir Castle nr Grantham NG32 1PD T: 0115 957 3295 F: 0115 957 3195

Thorpe Camp Visitor Centre Tattersall Thorpe Lincoln LN T: 01205 361334 E: mjhodgson@lancfile.demon.co.uk W: www.thorpecamp.org.uk

Lincolnshire – North

Baysgarth House Museum Caistor Rd Barton-Upon-Humber DN18 6AH T: 01652 632318

Immingham Museum Immingham Resorce Centre Margaret St Immingham DN40 1LE T: 01469 577066

North Lincolnshire Museum Oswald Rd Scunthorpe DN15 7BD T: 01724 843533 E: David.Williams@northlincs.gov.uk W: www.northlincs.gov.uk\museums

Liverpool

King's Regiment Collection Museum of Liverpool Life Pier Head Liverpool L3 1PZ T: 0151-478-4062 Collection of 8th Kings Liverpool Regiment 1685 to 1958 & the Kings Regt 1958 to date.
Liverpool Maritime Museum William Brown Street Liverpool L3 8EN T: 0151-2070001

London

Alexander Fleming Laboratory Museum / St Mary's NHS Trust Archives St Mary's Hospital Praed Street Paddington London W2 1NY T: (020) 7886 6528 F: (020) 7886 6739 E: kevin.brown@st-marys.nhs.uk W: www.st-marys.nhs.uk
Bank of England Archive Archive Section HO-SV The Bank of England Threadneedle Street London EC2R 8AH T: (020) 7601-5096 F: (020) 7601-4356 E: archive@bankofengland.co.uk W: www.bankofengland.co.uk
Berkshire and Westminster Dragoons Museum Cavalry House, Duke of York's Headquarters Kings Road Chelsea London SW3 4SC T: 020 7414 5233
Bethlem Royal Hospital Archives and Museum Monks Orchard Road Beckenham BR3 3BX T: (020) 8776 4307 T: (020) 8776 4053 F: (020) 8776 4045 E: museum@bethlem.freeserve.co.uk
Bethnal Green Museum of Childhood Cambridge Heath Rd London E2 9PA T: (020) 8980 2415 F: (020) 8983 5225 E: k.bines@vam.ac.uk
Black Cultural Archives see National
Britain at War Experience Winston Churchill 64-66 Tooley Street London Bridge London SE1 2TF T: 020 7403 3171 F: 020 7403 5104 E: britainatwar@dial.pipex.com W: www.britainatwar.co.uk
British Dental Association Museum (MUSEUM CLOSED) 64 Wimpole Street London W1M 8AL T: (020) 7935-0875-ext-209
British Museum see National
British Red Cross Museum and Archives see National
Cabinet War Rooms Clive Steps King Charles Street SW1A 2AQ T: (020) 7930 6961 E: cwr@iwm.org.uk W: www.iwm.org.uk
Church Farmhouse Museum Greyhound Hill Hendon NW4 4JR T: (020) 8203 0130 F: (020) 8359 2666 W: www.earl.org.uk/partners/barnet/churchf.htm
Crystal Palace Museum Anerley Hill London SE19 T: 020 8676 0700
Cutty Sark King William Walk London SE10 9HT T: (020) 8858 2698 F: (020) 8858 6976 E: info@cuttysark.org.uk W: www.cuttysark.org.uk Postal address:2 Greenwich Church Street London SE10 9BG
Design Museum Butlers Wharf 28 Shad Thames London SE1 2YD T: (020) 7940 8791 T: (020) 7403 6933 F: (020) 7378 6540 E: enquiries@designmuseum.org.uk W: www.designmuseum.org
Dickens House Museum 48 Doughty St London WC1N 2LF T: (020) 7405 2127 E: DHmuseum@rmplc.co.uk W: www.dickensmuseum.com
Doctor Johnson's House 17 Gough Square London EC4A 3DE T: (020) 7353 3745
Firepower - The Royal Artillery Museum Royal Arsenal Woolwich London SE18 6ST T: (020) 8855 7755 E: info@firepower.org.uk W: www.firepower.org.uk
Florence Nightingale Museum 2 Lambeth Palace Road London SE1 7EW T: (020) 7620-0374 F: (020) 7928-1760 E: curator@florence-nightingale.co.uk W: www.florence-nightingale.co.uk
Freud Museum 20 Maresfield Gardens London NW3 5SX T: (020) 735-2002 T: (020) 735-5167 F: (020) 431 5452 E: freud@gn.apc.org W: www.freud.org.uk
Fusiliers' London Volunteer Museum 213 Balham High Road London SW17 7BQ T: 020 8672 1168
Geffrye Museum Kingsland Rd London E2 8EA T: (020) 7739 9893 F: (020) 7729 5647 E: info@geffrye-museum.org.uk W: www.geffrye-museum.org.uk CC Accepted
Golden Hinde Living History Museum St. Mary Overie Dock Cathedral St SE1 9DE T: 08700 118700 F: 020 7407 5908 E: info@goldenhinde.co.uk W: www.goldenhinde.co.uk
Grange Museum of Community History The Grange Neasden Lane Neasden London NW10 1QB T: (020) 8452 8311 T: (020) 8937 3600 F: (020) 8208 4233
Grenadier Guards Record Office Wellington Barracks Birdcage Walk London SW1E 6HQ E: rhqgrengds@yahoo.co.uk Access is by appointment made in advance. Search fee of £25.00 per search
Guards Museum Wellington Barracks Birdcage Walk London SW1E 6HQ T: (020) 7414 3271/3428 F: (020) 7414 3429
Gunnersbury Park Museum Gunnersbury Park Popes Lane W3 8LQ T: (020) 8992 1612 F: (020) 8752 0686 E: gp-museum@cip.org.uk
H.M.S. Belfast Morgans Lane Tooley Street London SE1 2JH T: (020) 7940 6300 F: (020) 7403 0719 W: www.iwm.org.uk
Hackney Museum Service Parkside Library Victoria Park Rd London E9 7JL T: (020) 8986 6914 E: hmuseum@hackney.gov.uk W: www.hackney.gov.uk/hackneymuseum
Handel House Museum 25 Brook Street London W1K 4HB T: (020) 7495 1685 T: (020) 7495 1759 E: mail@handelhouse.org W: www.handelhouse.org

Hogarth's House Hogarth Lane Chiswick London W4 2QN T: (020) 8994 6757
Honourable Artillery Company Armoury House City Road London EC1Y 2BQ T: 020 7382 1537 F: 020 7382 1538 E: hac@hac.org.uk W: www.hac.org.uk
Horniman Museum 100 London Rd Forest Hill London SE23 3PQ T: (020) 8699 1872 F: (020) 8291 5506 E: enquiries@horniman.co.uk W: www.horniman.co.uk
House Mill River Lea Tidal Mill Trust , Three Mills Island Three Mill Lane Bromley by Bow London E3 3DU T: (020) 8980-4626
Imperial War Museum Lambeth Road London SE1 6HZ T: (020) 7416-5000 T: (020) 7416 5348 F: (020) 7416 5374 (020) 7416 5246 E: books@iwm.org.uk W: www.iwm.org.uk
Imperial War Museum Film and Video Archive see National
Inns of Court and City Yeomanry Museum 10 Stone buildings Lincoln's Inn London WC2A 3TG T: 020 7405 8112 Open Mon to Fri 1000 - 1600 by appointment only
Island History Trust St. Matthias Old Church Woodstock Terrace Poplar High St London E14 0AE T: (020) 7987 6041
Islington Museum Foyer Gallery Town Hall Upper St N1 2UD T: (020) 7354 9442
James Clavell Library Royal Arsenal (West) Warren Lane Woolwich London SE18 6ST T: 020 8312 7125 E: library@firepower.org.uk W: www.firepower.org.uk
Jewish Museum The Sternberg Centre for Judaism 80 East End Road Finchley London N3 2SY T: 020 8349 1143 F: 020 8343 2162 E: enquiries@jewishmuseum.org.uk W: www.jewishmuseum.org.uk
Keats House Museum Wentworth Place Keats Grove NW3 2RR T: (020) 7435 2062
Kensington Palace State Apartments Kensington Palace London W8 4PX T: (020) 7937 9561
Leighton House Museum 12 Holland Park Rd London W14 8LZ T: 020 7602 3316 F: 020 7371 2467 E: museums@rbkc.gov.uk W: www.rbkc.gov.uk/leightonhousemuseum
Library of the Royal College of Surgeons of England 35-43 Lincoln's Inn Fields London WC2A 3PN T: (020) 7869 6520 F: (020) 7405 4438 E: library@rseng.ac.uk W: www.rseng.ac.uk Research enquiries are not undertaken. Appointments required.
Livesey Museum for Children 682 Old Kent Rd London SE15 1JF T: (020) 7639 5604 F: (020) 7277 5384 E: livesley.museum@southwark.gov.uk
Lloyds Nelson Collection Lloyds of London Lime Street London EC3M 7HA T: 020 7327 6260 F: 020 7327 6400
London Borough of Greenwich Heritage Centre Museum and Library Building 41 Royal Arsenal Woolwich London SE18 6SP T: (020) 8858 4631 F: (020) 8293 4721 E: local.history@greenwich.gov.uk W: www.greenwich.gov.uk
London Canal Museum 12-13 New Wharf Rd London N1 9RT T: (020) 7713 0836 W: www.charitynet.org/~LCanalMus/
London Fire Brigade Museum 94a Southwark Bridge Rd London SE1 0EG T: (020) 7587 2894 F: (020) 7587 2878 E: esther.mann@london-fire.gov.uk
London Gas Museum Twelvetrees Crescent London E3 3JH T: (020) 7538 4982 Closed. Exhibits in storage John Doran Gas Museum 0116 250 3190 or National Gas Archive 0161 777 7193
London Irish Rifles Regimental Museum Duke of York's Headquarters Kings Road Chelsea London SW3 4SA
London Scottish Regimental Museum RHQ 95 Horseferry Road London SW1P 2DX T: 020 7233 7909 E: smallpipes@aol.com
London Toy & Model Museum 21-23 Craven Hill London W2 3EN T: (020) 7706 8000
London Transport Museum Covent Garden Piazza London WC2E 7BB T: (020) 7379 6344 F: (020) 7565 7250 E: contact@ltmuseum.co.uk W: www.ltmuseum.co.uk
Mander & Mitchenson Theatre Collection c/o Salvation Army Headquarters PO BOx 249 101 Queen Victoria Street London EC49 4EP T: (020) 7236 0182 F: (020) 7236 0184
Markfield Beam Engine & Museum Markfield Rd London N15 4RB T: (020) 8800 7061 T: 01763 287 331 E: alan@mbeam.org W: www.mbeam.org
Metropolitan Police Historical Museum c/o T.P.H.Q., Fin & res 4th Floor Victoria Embankment London SW1A 2JL T: (020) 8305-2824 T: (020) 8305-1676 F: (020) 8293-6692
Museum in Docklands Library & Archives Library & Archive No 1 Warehouse, West India Quay Hertsmere Road London E14 4AL T: (020) 7001 9825 (Librarian) F: (020) 7001 9801 E: bobaspinall@museumindocklands.org.uk W: www.museumindocklands.org.uk
Museum of London London Wall London EC2Y 5HN T: F: 0171-600-1058 E: info@museumoflondon.org.uk
Museum of the Order of St John St John's Gate St John's Lane Clerkenwell London EC1M 4DA T: (020) 7253-6644 F: (020) 7336 0587 W: www.sja.org.uk/stjohn
Museum of the Royal Pharmaceutical Society Museum of the Royal Pharmaceutical Society 1 Lambeth High Street London SE1 7JN T: (020) 7572 2210E: museum@rpsgb.org.uk W: www.rpsgb.org.uk

Museums Association 42 Clerkenwell Close London EC1R 0PA T: (020) 7250 1789 F: (020) 7250 1929

National Army Museum Royal Hospital Road London SW3 4HT T: (020) 7730-0717 F: (020) 7823-6573 E: info@national-army-museum.ac.uk W: www.national-army-museum.ac.uk incorporating Middlesex Regiment Museum & Buffs regiment Museum

National Army Museum Department of Archives (Photographs, Film & Sound) Royal Hospital Road London SW3 4HT T: (020) 7730-0717 F: (020) 7823-6573 E: info@national-army-museum.ac.uk W: www.national-army-museum.ac.uk

National Gallery see National

National Portrait Gallery see National

Newham Museum Service The Old Town Hall 29 The Broadway Stratford E15 4BQ T: (020) 8534 2274

North Woolwich Old Station Musuem Pier Rd North Woolwich London E16 2JJ T: (020) 7474 7244

Percival David Foundation of Chinese Art 53 Gordon Square London WC1H 0PD T: (020) 7387 3909 F: (020) 7383 5163

Petrie Museum of Egyptian Archaeology University College London Gower St WC1E 6BT T: (020) 7504 2884 F: (020) 7679 2886 E: petrie.museum@ucl.ac.uk

Pitshanger Manor & Gallery Mattock Lane London W5 5EQ T: (020) 8567 1227 F: (020) 8567 0595 E: pitshanger@ealing.gov.uk

Polish Institute & Sikorski Museum 20 Princes Gate London SW7 1PT T: (020) 7589 9249

Pollock's Toy Museum 1 Scala St London W1P 1LT T: (020) 7636 3452

Princess Louise's Kensington Regiment Museum Duke of York's Headquarters Kings Road Chelsea London SW3 4RX T:

Pump House Educational Museum Lavender Pond & Nature Park Lavender Rd Rotherhithe SE16 1DZ T: (020) 7231 2976

Ragged School Museum Trust 46-50 Copperfield Rd London E3 4RR T: (020) 8980 6405 F: (020) 89833481 W: www.ics-london.co.uk/rsm

Royal Air Force Museum Grahame Park Way Hendon London NW9 5LL T: (020) 8205-2266 F: (020) 8200 1751 E: groupbusiness@refmuseum.org.uk W: www.rafmuseum.org.uk

Royal Armouries see National

Royal London Hospital Archives and Museum Royal London Hospital Newark Whitechapel London E1 1BB T: (020) 7377-7608 F: (020) 7377 7413 E: r.j.evans@mds.qmw.ac.uk W: www.bartsandthelondon.org

Royal Observatory Greenwich Romney Road Greenwich London SE10 9NF T: (020) 8858-4422 F: (020) 8312-6632 W. www.nmm.ac.uk

Sam Uriah Morris Society 136a Lower Clapton Rd London E5 0QJ T: (020) 8985 6449

Sir John Soane's Museum 13 Lincolns Inn Fields London WC2A 3BP T: (020) 7430 0175 F: (020) 7831 3957 W: www.soane.org

St Bartholomew's Hospital Archives & Museum Archives and Museum West Smithfield London EC1A 7BE T: (020) 7601-8152 F: (020) 7606 4790 E: marion.rea@bartsandthelondon.nhs.uk W: www.brlcf.org.uk

The Association of Jewish Ex-Service Men and Women Military Museum AJEX House East Bank Stamford London N16 5RT T: 020 8800 2844 020 8802 7610 F: 020 8880 1117 W: www.ajex.org.uk

The Clink Prison Museum 1 Clink St London SE1 9DG T: (020) 7403 6515 F:

The Fan Museum 12 Crooms Hill London SE10 8ER T: (020) 8858 7879 F: (020) 8293 1889 E: admin@fan-museum.org W: WWW: www.fan-museum.org

The Iveagh Bequest Kenwood House Hampstead Lane London NW3 7JR T: (020) 8348 1286

The Museum of Women's Art 3rd Floor 11 Northburgh St London EC1V 0AN T: (020) 7251 4881

The Natural History Museum Cromwell Road London SW7 5BD T: (020) 7942 5000 W: www.nhm.ac.uk

The Old Operating Theatre Museum & Herb Garret 9a St. Thomas's St London SE1 9RY T: (020) 7955 4791 F: (020) 7378 8383 E: curator@thegarret.org.uk W: www.the garret.org.uk

The Polish Institute and Sikorski Museum 20 Princes Gate London SW7 1QA T: 020 7589 9249 F:

The Royal Regiment of Fusiliers H M Tower of London London EC3N 4AB T: (020) 7488 5610 F: (020) 7481 1093

The Science Museum see National

The Sherlock Holmes Museum 221b Baker St London NW1 6XE T: (020) 7935 8866 F: (020) 7738 1269 E: sherlock@easynet.co.uk W: www.sherlock-holmes.co.uk

The Wellcome Trust 183 Euston Rd London NW1 2BE T: (020) 7611 8888 F: (020) 7611 8545 E: infoserv@wellcome.ac.uk W: www.wellcome.ac.uk

Theatre Museum Russell Street Convent Garden London WC2 T: 020 7943 4700 E: info@theatremuseum.org W: www.theatremuseum.org

Valence House Museum see Essex

Vestry House Museum Vestry Road Walthamstow London E17 9NH T: (020) 8509-1917 E: vestry.house@al.lbwf.gov.uk W: WWW: www.lbwf.gov.uk/vestry/vestry.htm 1901 census

Veterinary Museum Royal Vetinerary College Royal College Street London NW1 0TU T: (020) 768-5165 T: (020) 768-5166 F: (020) 7468 5162 E: Email: fhouston@rvc.ac.uk W: WWW: www.rvc.uk

Victoria & Albert Museum see National

Wallace Collection Hertford House Manchester Square London W1V 3BN T: 020 7563 9500 F: 020 7224 2155 E: enquiries@wallacecollection.org W: www.wallacecollection.org

Wellington Museum - Apsley House Apsley House 149 Piccadilly Hyde Park Corner London W1J 7NT T: 020 7499 5676 F: 020 7493 6576 W: www.apsleyhouse.org.uk

Westminster Abbey Museum Westminster Abbey Deans Yard SW1P 3PA T: (020) 7233 0019

Wimbledon Lawn Tennis Museum The All England Lawn Tennis & Croquet Club Church Road Wimbledon London SW19 5AE T: (020) 8946 6131 F: (020) 8944 6497 E: museum@aeltc.com W: www.wimbledon.org/museum CC accepted

Wimbledon Museum of Local History 22 Ridgeway London SW19 4QN T: (020) 8296 9914

Manchester

Manchester Jewish Museum 190 Cheetham Hill Road Manchester M8 8LW T: 0161 834 9879 F: 0161 834 9801 E: info@machesterjewishmuseum.com W: www.machesterjewishmuseum.com

Manchester Museum of Science and Industry Liverpool Road Castlefield Manchester M3 4FP T: 0161 832 2244 F: 0161 833 1471 E: n.forder@msim.org.uk W: www.msim.org.uk

Wigan Heritage Service Museum History Shop Library Street Wigan WN1 1NU T: 01942 828020 F: 01942 827645 E: heritage@wiganmbc.gov.uk W: www.wiganmbc.gov.uk 1901 census

Merseyside

Beatle Story Ltd Britannia Vaults Albert Dock Liverpool L3 4AA T: 0151 709 1963 F: 0151 708 0039

Botanic Gardens Museum Churchtown Southport PR9 7NB T: 01704 227547 F: 01704 224112

Liverpool Scottish Regimental Museum 15 Rydal Bank Lower Bebington Wirral L23 2SH T: 0151 645 5717 E: ilriley@liverpoolscottish.org.uk W: www.liverpoolscottish.org.uk

Merseyside Maritime Museum Maritime Archives and Library Albert Dock Liverpool L3 4AQ T: 0151-478-4418 T: 0151 478 4424 F: 0151-478-4590 E: archives@nmgmarchives.demon.co.uk W: www.nmgm.org.uk

National Museums & Galleries on Merseyside 127 Dale St Liverpool L2 2JH T: 0151 207 0001

Prescot Museum 34 Church St Prescot L34 3LA T: 0151 430 7787

Shore Road Pumping Station Shore Rd Birkenhead CH41 1AG T: 0151 650 1182

Western Approaches 1 Rumford St Liverpool L2 8SZ T: 0151 227 2008 F: 0151 236 6913

Middlesex

Forty Hall Museum Forty Hill Enfield EN2 9HA T: (020) 8363 8196

Harrow Museum & Heritage Centre Headstone Manor Pinner View Harrow HA2 6PX T: 020 8861 2626

HQ No 11 (Fighter) Group Battle of Britain Operations Room RAF Uxbridge Uxbridge UB10 0RZ T: 01895 815400 F: 01895 815666

Kew Bridge Steam Museum Green Dragon Lane Brentford TW8 0EN T: (020) 8568 4757 F: (020) 8569 9978 E: info@kbsm.org W: www.kbsm.org

Royal Military School of Music Museum Kneller Hall Twickenham TW2 7DU T: 020 8744 8652 F: 020 8898 7906 E: rmsm.kellerhall@btinternet.com

The Musical Museum 368 High St Brentford TW8 0BD T: (020) 8560 8108

Norfolk

Battlefields Trust see National

100 Bomb Group Memorial Museum Common Rd Dickleburgh Diss IP21 4PH T: 01379 740708

100th Bomb Group Memorial Museum Common Road Dickleburgh Diss IP21 4PH T: 01379 740708 Correspondence address: 41 Vancouver Avenue, Kings Lynn, Norfolk PE30 5RD

Air Defence Radar Museum RAF Neatishead Norwich NR12 8YB T: 01692 633309 F: 01692 633214 E: curator@radarmuseum.co.uk W: www.radarmuseum.co.uk

Bressingham Steam & Gardens Bressingham Diss IP22 2AB T: 01379 687386 T: 01379 687382 (24 hour info line) F: 01379 688085

Bure Valley Railway Norwich Road Aylsham NR11 6BW T: 01263 733858

Castle Museum Castle Hill Norwich NR1 3JU T: 01603 493624

Cholmondeley Collection of Model Soldiers Houghton Hall Houghton Kings Lynn PE31 6UE T: 01485 528569 F: 01485 528167 E: administrator@houghtonhall.com W: www.houghtonhall.com

City of Norwich Aviation Museum Hosham St Faith Norwich NR10 3JF T: 01603 893080 F: 01692 633214

City of Norwich Aviation Museum Ltd Old Norwich Rd Horsham St. Faith Norwich NR10 3JF T: 01603 893080

Diss Museum The Market Place Diss IP22 3JT T: 01379 650618

EcoTech Swaffham PE37 7HT T: 01760 726100 F: 01760 726109 E: info@ecotech.rmplc.co.uk W: www.ecotech.org.uk

Elizabethan House Museum 4 South Quay Great Yarmouth NR30 2QH T: 01493 855746

Feltwell (Historical and Archaeological) Society 16 High Street Feltwell Thetford IP26 4AF T: 01842 828448 E: peterfeltwell@tinyworld.co.uk The Museum is at The Beck, Feltwell

Glandford Shell Museum Church House Glandford Holt NR25 7JR T: 01263 740081

Iceni Village & Museums Cockley Cley Swaffham PE37 8AG T: 01760 721339

Inspire Hands On Science Centre Coslany St Norwich NR3 3DJ T: 01603 612612

Lynn Museum Old Market St King's Lynn PE30 1NL T: 01553 775001 F: 01553 775001 W: www.norfolk.gov.uk/tourism/museums

Maritime Museum for East Anglia 25 Marine Parade Great Yarmouth NR30 2EN T: 01493 842267

Norfolk Motorcycle Museum Station Yard Norwich Rd North Walsham NR28 0DS T: 01692 406266

Norfolk Rural Life Museum & Union Farm Beach House Gressenhall East Dereham NR20 4DR T: 01362 860563 F: 01362 860563 E: frances.collinson.mus@norfolk.gov.uk W: www.norfolk.gov.uk

Royal Norfolk Regimental Museum Shirehall Market Avenue Norwich NR1 3JQ T: 01603 493649 F: 01603 765651 E: regimental.museum@central.norfolk.gov.uk W: www..norfolk.gov.uk

Sheringham Museum Station Rd Sheringham NR26 8RE T: 01263 821871

Shirehall Museum Common Place Walsingham NR22 6BP T: 01328 820510 F: 01328 820098 E: walsinghammuseum@farmline.com

The Air Defence Battle Command & Control Museum Neatishead Norwich NR12 8YB T: 01692 633309

The Muckleburgh Collection Weybourne Holt NR25 7EG T: 01263 588210 F: 01263 588425 E: info@muckleburgh.co.uk W: www.muckleburgh.co.uk

The North Norfolk Railway The Station Sheringham NR26 8RA T: 01263 822045 F: 01263 823794 W: www.nnrailway.co.uk

Northamptonshire

Abington Museum and Museum of The Northamptonshire Regiment Abington Park Museum Abington NN1 5LW T: 01604 635412 F: 01604 238720 E: museums@northampton.gov.uk W: www.northampton.gov.uk/museums

Canal Museum Stoke Bruerne Towcester NN12 7SE T: 01604 862229

Naseby Battle Museum Purlieu Farm Naseby Northampton NN6 7DD T: 01604 740241

National Dragonfly Museum Ashton Mill Ashton Peterborough PE8 5LB T: 01832 272427 E: ndmashton@aol.com WWW: natdragonflymuseum.org.uk

Northampton Iron Stone Railway Trust Hunsbury Hill Country Park Hunsbury Hill Rd West Hunsbury Northampton NN4 9UW T: 01604 702031 T: 01604 757481 ; 01908 376821 E: bnile98131@aol.com_raf968y@aol.com

Northampton & Lamport Railway Preservation Society Pitsford & Brampton Station Pitsford Road Chapel Brampton Northampton NN6 8BA T: 01604 820327

Rushden Historical Transport Society The Station Station Approach Rushden NN10 0AW T: 01933 318988

Wellingborough Heritage Centre Croyland Hall Burystead Place Wellingborough NN8 1AH T: 01933 276838

Northumberland

A Soldier's Life 15th/19th The King's Royal Hussars Northumberland Hussars and Light Dragoons Discovery Museum Blandford Square Newcastle-upon-Tyne NE1 4JA T: 0191 232 6789 F: 0191 230 2614 E: ralph.thompson@twmuseums.org.uk

Berwick Borough Museum The Barracks The Parade Berwick-Upon-Tweed TD15 1DG T: 01289 330933

Bewick Studios Mickley Square Mickley Stocksfield NE43 7BL T: 01661 844055

Border History Museum and Library Moothall Hallgate Hexham NE46 3NH T: 01434-652349 F: 01434-652425 E: museum@tynedale.gov.uk W: www.tynedale.gov.uk

Chesterholm Museum Vindolanda Trust Bardon Mill Hexham NE47 7JN T: 01434 344 277 F: 01434 344060 E: info@vindolanda.com W: www.vindolanda.com

Chesters Roman Fort and Clayton Collection Museum Vindolanda Trust Chollerford Humshaugh Hexham NE46 4EP T: 01434 681 379 E: info@vindolanda.com W: www.vindolanda.com

Corbridge Roman Site Corbridge NE45 5NT T: 01434 632349 W: www.english-heritage.org.uk

Fusiliers Museum of Northumberland The Abbot's Tower Alnwick Castle Alnwick NE66 1NG T: 01665-602151 F: 01665-603320 E: fusmusnorthld@btinternet.com

Housteads Roman Fort Museum Haydon Bridge Hexham NE47 6NN T: 01434 344363

King's Own Scottish Borderers Museum The Barracks The Parade Berwick upon Tweed TD15 1DG T: 01289 307426 W: www.kosb.co.uk

Marine Life Centre & Fishing Museum 8 Main St Seahouses NE68 7RG T: 01665 721257

North East Mills Group Blackfriars Monk Street Newcastle upon Tyne NE1 4XN T: 0191 232 9279 F: 0191 230 1474 E: nect@lineone.net W: //welcome.to/North.East.Mill.Group

Roman Army Museum Carvoran Greenhead CA6 7JB T: 01697 747485 F: 01697 747487 E: info@vindolanda.com W: www.vindolanda.com

The Heritage Centre Station Yard Woodburn Road Bellingham Hexham NE48 2DF T: 01434 220050 E: bell.heritage@btopenworld.com W: www.bellingham-heritage.org.uk

The Vindolanda Trust Chesterholm Museum Bardon Mill Hexham NE47 7JN T: 01434 344277 F: 01434 344 060 E: info@vindolanda.com W: www.vindolanda.com

Tynedale Council Museums Department of Leisure & tourism Prospect House Hexham NE46 3NH T: 01461 652351

Nottinghamshire

D.H Lawrence Heritage Durban House Heritage Centre Mansfield Rd Eastwood Nottingham NG16 3DZ T: 01773 717353

Flintham Museum & Flintham Society Flintham Museum Inholms Road Flintham NG23 5LF T: 0163.6 525111 E: flintham.museum@lineone.net W: www.flintham-museum.org.uk

Greens Mill & Science Musuem Windmill Lane Sneinton Nottingham NG2 4QB T: 0115 915 6878

Harley Gallery Welbeck Worksop S80 3LW T: 01909 501700

Mansfield Museum & Art Gallery Leeming Street Mansfield NG18 1NG T: 01623-463088 F: 01623-412922

Millgate Museum of Folk Life 48 Millgate Newark NG24 4TS T: 01636 655730 F: 01636 655735 E: museums@newark-sherwood.gov.uk W: www.newark-sherwood.gov.uk

Natural History and Industrial Musuem Wollaton Hall Wollaton Park Nottingham NG8 2AE T: 0115 915 3910 F: 0115 915 3941

Newark Museum Appletongate Newark NG24 1JY T: 01636 655740 F: 01636 655745 E: museums@nsdc.info W: www.newark-sherwooddc.gov.uk

Newark (Notts & Lincs) Air Museum The Airfield Winthorpe Newark NG24 2NY T: 01636 707170 E: mail@newarkair.lineone.net W: www.newarkairmuseum.co.uk

Newark Town Treasures and Art Gallery The Town Hall Market Place Newark NG24 1DU T: 01636 680333 F: 01636 680350 E: post@newark.gov.uk W: www.newarktowntreasures.co.uk

Newstead Abbey Museum Newstead Abbey Park Ravenshead Nottingham NG15 8NA T: 01623 455900 F: 01623 455904 E: sally@newsteadabbey.org.uk W: www.newsteadabbey.org.uk

Nottingham Castle Museum & Art Gallery Castle Rd Nottingham NG1 6EL T: 0115 915 3700 F: 0115 915653

Ruddington Framework Knitters' Museum Chapel St Ruddington Nottingham NG11 6HE T: 0115 984 6914 F: 0115 984 1174 W: www.rfkm.org

Ruddington Village Museum St. Peters Rooms Church St Ruddington Nottingham NG11 6HD Tel: 0115 914 6645

Sherwood Foresters Museum & Archives RHQ WFR, Foresters House Chetwynd Barracks Chilwell Nottingham NG9 5HA Tel: 0115 946 5415 F: 0115 946 9853 E: curator@wfrmuseum.org.uk W: www.wfrmuseum.org.uk

Sherwood Foresters (Notts and Derby Regiment) Museum The Castle Nottingham NG1 6EL Tel: 0115 946 5415 F: 0115 946 9853 E: rhqwfr-nottm@lineone.net W: www.wfrmuseum.org.uk Address for enquiries: RHQ WFR, Foresters House, Chetwynd Barracks, Chilwell, Nottingham NG9 5HA

The Museum of Nottingham Lace 3-5 High Pavement The Lace Marke t Nottingham NG1 1HF Tel: 0115 989 7365 F: 0115 989 7301 E: info@nottinghamlace.org W: www.nottinghamlace.org

Whaley Thorn Heritage & Environment Centre Portland Terrace Langwith Mansfield NG20 9HA Tel: 01623 742525

Oxfordshire

Abingdon Museum County Hall Market Place Abingdon OX14 3HG Tel: 01235 523703 F: 01235 536814

Ashmolean Museum University of Oxford Beaumont Street Oxford OX1 2PH Tel: 01865 278000

Chipping Norton Museum 4 High Street Chipping Norton OX7 5AD Tel: Email: museum@cn2001.fsnet.co.uk

Edgehill Battle Museum The Estate Yard Farnborough Hall Farnborough Banbury OX17 1DU Tel: 01926 332213 **Great Western Society Ltd** Didcot Railway Centre Station Rd Didcot OX11 7NJ Tel: 01235 817200

Oxfordshire and Buckinghamshire Light Infantry Regimental Museum Slade Park Headington Oxford OX3 7JL Tel: 01865 780128

Pitt Rivers Museum University Of Oxford South Parks Rd Oxford OX1 3PP Tel: 01865 270927 F: 01865 270943 E: prm@prm.ox.ac.uk W: www.prm.ox.ac.uk

River & Rowing Museum Rowing & River MuseumMill MeadowsHenley on ThamesRG9 1BF Tel: 01491 415625 F: 01491 415601 E: museum@rrm.co.uk W: www..rrm.co.uk

The Oxfordshire Museum Fletchers House Park St Woodstock OX20 1SN Tel: 01993 811456 T: 01993 814104 F: 01933 813239 E: oxon.museum@oxfordshire.gov.uk

Vale & Downland Museum 19 Church St WantageOX12 8BL Tel: 01235 771447 E: museum@wantage.com

Wallingford Museum Flint House High StWallingfordOX10 0DB Tel: 01491 835065

Witney & District Museum Gloucester Court MewsHigh StWitneyOX8 6LX Tel: 01993 775915 E: janecavell@aol.com

Rutland

Rutland County Museum Catmose StreetOakhamLE15 6HW Tel: 01572-723654 F: 01572-757576 W: www.rutnet.co.uk

Rutland Railway Museum Iron Ore Mine SidingsAshwell RdCottesmoreOakhamLE15 7BX Tel: 01572 813203

Shropshire

Acton Scott Historic Working Farm Wenlock LodgeActon ScottChurch StrettonSY6 6QN Tel: 01694 781306

Blists Hill Open Air Museum Ironbridge Gorge Museum Trust Ltd Legges Way Madeley TelfordTF7 5DU Tel: 01952 586063Fax: 01952 588016

Coalport China Museum Ironbridge Gorge Museum Trust Ltd High St Coalport Telford TF8 7AW Tel: 01952 580650

Cosford Royal Air Force Museum Cosford ShifnalTF11 8UP Tel: 01902 376200 E: cosford@rafmuseum.org W: www.rafmuseum.org

Ironbridge Gorge Museum , Library & Archives The WharfageIronbridgeTelfordTF8 7AW Tel: 01952 432141 F: 01952 432237 E: library@ironbridge.org.uk W: www.ironbridge.org.uk

Museum Of The River Visitor Centre Ironbridge Gorge Museum Trust LtdThe WharfageIronbridgeTF8 7AW Tel: 01952 432405

Jackfield Tile Museum Ironbridge Gorge Museum Trust LtdJackfieldTelfordTF8 7AW Tel: 01952 882030

Ludlow Museum Castle StLudlowSY8 1AS Tel: 01584 875384

Midland Motor Museum Stanmore HallStourbridge RdStanmoreBridgnorthWV15 6DT Tel: 01746 762992

Museum Of Iron Ironbridge Gorge Museum Trust LtdCoach RdCoalbrookdaleTelfordTF8 7EZ Tel: 01952 433418

Oswestry Transport Museum Oswald RdOswestrySY11 1RE Tel: 01691 671749 Email:lignetts@enterprise.netWWW: www.cambrian-railways-soc.co.uk

Queen's Own Mercian Yeomanry Museum Bridgeman House Cavan Drive, Cemetery Road DawleyTelfordTF4 2BQ Tel: 01952 632930 F: 01952 632924

Rosehill House Ironbridge Gorge Museum Trust LtdTelfordTF8 7AW Tel: 01952 432141Fax: 01952 432237

Rowley's House Museum Barker StreetShrewsburySY1 1QH Tel: 01743 361196 F: 01743 358411

Shropshire Regimental Museum (King's Shropshire Light Infantry, Shropshire Yeomanry) Shropshire Militia, Volunteers and TA The Castle Shrewsbury SY1 2AT Tel: 01743 358516 T: 01743 262292 F: 01743 270023 E: shropshire@zoom.co.uk W: www.shropshireregimental.co.uk

Somerset

Abbey Barn - Somerset Rural Life Museum Abbey Barn Chilkwell St Glastonbury BA6 8DB Tel: 01458 831197Fax: 01458 834684 Email:county-museum@somerset.gov.ukWWW: www.somerset.gov.uk/museums

Admiral Blake Museum Bridgwater HouseKing SquareBridgwaterTA6 3AR Tel: 01278 435399 F: 01278 444076 E: Museum s@sedgemoor.gov.uk

American Museum Claverton ManorBathBA2 7BD Tel: 01225 460503 T: 01225 463538 F: 01225 480726

Bakelite Museum Orchard MillBridge St WillitonTauntonTA4 4NS Tel: 01984 632133

Bath Postal Museum 8 Broad StBathBA1 5LJ Tel: 01225 460333 F: 01225 460333 E: a.swindells@virgin.net W: www.bathpostalmuseum.org

Bath Royal Literary & Scientific Institution16-18 Queen SquareBathBA1 2HN Tel: 01225 312084

Blake Museum Blake StreetBridgwaterTA6 3NB Tel: 01278 456127 F: 01278 456127 E: Museum s@sedgemoor.gov.uk W: www.sedgemoor.gov.uk

Blazes Fire Museum Sandhill ParkBishops LydeardTauntonTA4 3DE Tel: 01823 433964

Bruton Museum Society The Dovecote Building High StreetBruton Tel: 01749 812851 W: www.southsomersetmuseum.org.uk

Chard & District Museum Godworthy HouseHigh StChardTA20 1QB Tel: 01460 65091Contact: 17 Cedric Close, Chard, Somerset TA20 1NR Tel: 01460 64017

Fleet Air Arm Museum R.N.A.S Yeovilton Yeovil BA22 8HT Tel: 01935 840565

Fleet Air Arm Museum Records Research Centre Box D61RNAS YeoviltonNr IlchesterBA22 8HT Tel: 01935-840565

Glastonbury Lake Village Museum The Tribunal 9 High St Glastonbury BA6 9DP Tel: 01458 832949

Holburne Museum of Art Great Pulteney St Bath BA2 4DB Tel: 01225 466669 W: www.bath.ac.uk/holbourne

Lambretta Scooter Museum 77 Alfred St Weston-Super-Mare BS23 1PP Tel: 01934 614614 F: 01934 620120 E: lambretta@wsparts.force.net

Museum of Bath at Work Camden Works Julian Road Bath BA1 2RH Tel: 01225 318348 F: 01225 318348 E: mobaw@hotmail.com W: www.bath-at-work.org.uk

Museum of South Somerset HenfordYeovil Tel: 01935 424774 F: 01935 424774 E: heritage.services@southsomerset.gov.uksouthsomersetmuseums.org.uk

No.1 Royal Crescent 1 Royal Crescent Bath BA1 2LR Tel: 01225 428126 Fax:01225 481850 Email:no1@bptrust.demon.co.ukWWW: www.bath-preservation-trust.org.uk

North Somerset Museum Service Burlington St Weston-Super-MareBS23 1PR Tel: 01934 621028 F: 01934 612526 E: Museum .service@n-somerset.gov.uk W: www.n-somerset.gov.uk

Radstock, Midsomer Norton & District Museum Waterloo RoadRadstockBathBA3 3ER Tel: 01761 437722 E: radstockmuseum@ukonline.co.uk W: www.radstockmuseum.co.uk

Roman Baths Museum Abbey ChurchyardBathBA1 1LZ Tel: 01225 477773 F: 01225 477243

Somerset County Museum Service Taunton CastleTauntonTA1 4AA Tel: 01823 320200

Somerset & Dorset Railway Trust Washford StationWashfordWatchetTA23 0PP Tel: 01984 640869 T: 01308 424630 E: info@sdrt.org W: www.sdrt.org

Somerset Military Museum (Somerset Light Infantry, Yeomanry Militia and Volunteers) County Museum** The County Museum Taunton CastleTauntonTA1 4AA Tel: 01823 333434 F: 01823 351639 E: info@sommilmuseum.org.uk W: www.sommilmuseum.org.uk

The Building of Bath Museum The Countess of Huntingdon's ChapelThe VineyardsBathBA1 5NA Tel: 01225 333 895 F: 01225 445 473 E: admin@bobm.freeserve.co.uk W: www.bath-preservation-trust.org.uk

The Haynes Motor Museum Castle Cary RdSparkfordYeovilBA22 7LH Tel: 01963 440804Fax: 01963 441004 Email:mike@gmpwin.demon.co.ukWWW: www.haynesmotormuseum.co.uk

The Helicopter Museum The HeliportLocking Moor RoadWeston-Super-MareBS24 8PP Tel: 01934 635227Fax: 01934 645230 E: office@helimuseum.fsnet.co.uk W: www.helicoptermuseum.co.uk

The Jane Austen Centre40 Gay StreetBathBA1 2NT Tel: 01225 443000 E: info@janeausten.co.uk

The John Judkyn Memorial Garden ThorpeFreshfordBathBA3 6BX Tel: 01225 723312

The Museum Of East Asian Art12 Bennett StBathBA1 2QL Tel: 01225 464640Fax: 01225 461718 Email:museum@east-asian-art.freeserve.co.ukWWW: www.east-asian-art.co.uk

The South West Museum s Council Hestercombe HouseCheddon FitzpaineTauntonTA2 8LQ Tel: 01823 259696 F: 01823 413114 E: robinbourne@swmuseums.co.uk

Wells Museum 8 Cathedral GreenWellsBA5 2UE Tel: 01749 673477

West Somerset Museum The Old SchoolAllerfordMineheadTA24 8HN Tel: 01643 862529

William Herschel Museum 19 New King StBathBA1 2BL Tel: 01225 311342

Staffordshire

Bass Museum Horninglow Street Burton on TrentDE14 1YQ Tel: 0845 6000598 F: 01283 513509 W: www.bass-museum.com

Borough Museum & Art Gallery Brampton ParkNewcastleST5 0QP Tel: 01782 619705

Clay Mills Pumping Engines Trust Ltd Sewage Treatment WorksMeadow LaneStrettonBurton-On-TrentDE13 0DB Tel: 01283 509929

Etruria Industrial Museum Lower Bedford StEtruriaStoke-On-TrentST4 7AF Tel: 01782 233144Fax:01782 233144 E: etruria@swift.co.uk W: www.stoke.gov.uk/museums

Gladstone Pottery Museum Uttoxeter RdLongtonStoke-On-TrentST3 1PQ Tel: 01782 319232Fax: 01782 598640

Hanley Museum & Art Gallery Bethesda StHanleyStoke-On-TrentST1 3DW Tel: 01782 232323

Museum of The Staffordshire Regiment Whittington BarracksLichfieldWS14 9PY Tel: 0121 311 3240 T: 0121 311 3229 F: 0121 311 3205 E: Museum @rhqstaffords.fsnet.co.uk

Museum of the Staffordshire Yeomanry The Ancient High HouseGreengate StreetStaffordST16 2HS Tel: 01785 619130

Samuel Johnson Birthplace Museum Breadmarket StLichfieldWS13 6LG Tel: 01543 264972 W: www.lichfield.gov.uk

The Potteries Museum & Art Gallery Bethesda StreetHanleyStoke-On-TrentST1 3DE Tel: 01782 232323 Tel: 01782 232515 (minicom) F: 01782 232500 Email:museums@stoke.gov.ukWWW: www.stoke.gov.uk/museums

Uttoxeter Heritage Centre34-36 Carter StUttoxeterST14 8EU Tel: 01889 567176Fax:01889 568426

Suffolk

390th Bomb Group Memorial Air Museum Parham AirfieldParhamFramlington Tel: 01743 711275 F: 01728 621373
British Resistance Organisation Museum Parham AirfieldParhamFramlingham Tel: 01743 711275 F: 01728 621373 E: bretwar@supanet W: www.auxunit.org.uk
Christchurch Mansion & Wolsey Art Gallery Christchurch ParkSoane StIpswichIP4 2BE Tel: 01473 253246
Dunwich Museum St. James's StreetDunwichSaxmundhamIP17 3DT Tel: 01728 648796
East Anglia Transport Museum Chapel RdCarlton ColvilleLowestoftNR33 8BL Tel: 01502 518459
Felixstowe Museum Landguards FortFelixstoweIP11 8TW Tel: 01394 674355
Gainsborough House Society Gainsborough StSudburyCO10 2EU Tel: 01787 372958Fax: 01787 376991 Email:mail@gainsborough.orgWWW: www.gainsborough.org
HMS Ganges Museum Victory HouseShotley Point MarinaIpswichIP9 1QJ Tel: 01473 684749
International Sailing Craft Association Maritime Museum Caldecott RdOulton BroadLowestoftNR32 3PH Tel: 01502 585606 F: 01502 589014 E: admin@isca-maritimemuseum.org
Ipswich Museum & Exhibition Gallery High StIpswichIP1 3QH Tel: 01473 213761
Ipswich Transport Museum Ltd Old Trolley Bus DepotCobham RdIpswichIP3 9JD Tel: 01473 715666
Long Shop Steam Museum Main StLeistonIP16 4ES Tel: 01728 832189Fax: 01728 832189 W: www.suffolkcc.gov.uk/libraries_and_heritage/sro/garrett/index.html
Lowestoft Museum Broad HouseNicholas Everitt ParkOulton BroadLowestoftNR33 9JR Tel: 01502 511457 T: 01502 511795 F: 01502 513795
Maritime Museum Sparrows Nest The Museum Whapload RdLowestoftNR32 1XG Tel: 01502 561963
Mid Suffolk Light Railway Brockford StationWetheringsettStowmarketIP14 5PW Tel: 01449 766899
Mildenhall and District Museum 6 King Street Mildenhall Bury St Edmunds IP28 7EX Tel: 01638 716970 T: 01638 713835
Norfolk and Suffolk Aviation Museum Buckeroo Way The Street Flixton Bungay NR35 1NZ Tel: 01986 896644 E: nsam.flixton@virgin.net W: www.aviationmuseum.net
R.A.F. Regiment Museum Home of The RAF RegimentR A F HoningtonBury St EdmundsIP31 1EE Tel: 01359 269561 ext 7824 F: 01359 269561 ext 7440
Rougham Tower Association Rougham Estate OfficeRoughamBury St. EdmundsIP30 9LZ Tel: 01359 271471 F: 01359 271555 E: bplsto@aol.com
Royal Naval Patrol Association Museum Sparrows NestLowestoftNR32 1XG Tel: 01502 586250 F: 01502 586250
Suffolk Regiment Museum The Keep, Gibraltar BarracksOut Risbygate StreetBury St EdmundsIP33 3RN The Museum is closed pending relocation
Suffolk Regiment Museum -Museum closed to the public Suffolk Record Office77 Raingate StreetBury St EdmundsIP33 2AR Tel: 01284-352352 F: 01284-352355 E: bury.ro@libher.suffolkcc.gov.ukhttp:// W: www.suffolkcc.gov.uk/sro/
The National Horseracing Museum 99 High St NewmarketCB8 8JH Tel: 01638 667333
West Stow Country Park & Anglo-Saxon Village Icklingham Rd West Stow Buet St Edmunds IP28 6HG Tel: 01284 728718

Surrey

Bourne Hall Museum Bourne HallSpring StEwellEpsomKT17 1UF Tel: (020) 8394 1734 W: www.epsom.townpage.co.uk
Chertsey Museum The Cedars33 Windsor StChertseyKT16 8AT Tel: 01932 565764Fax: 01932 571118 Email:enquiries@chertseymuseum.org.uk
Dorking & District Museum Dorking & District Museum The Old Foundry62a West StDorkingRH4 1BS T: 01306 876591
East Surrey Museum 1 Stafford RdCaterhamCR3 6JG Tel: 01883 340275
Elmbridge Museum Church StWeybridgeKT13 8DE Tel: 01932 843573 F: 01932 846552 E: info@elm-mus.datanet.co.uk W: www.surrey-online.co.uk/elm-mus
Godalming Museum 109a High StGodalmingGU7 1AQ Tel: 01483 426510Fax: 01483 869495 Email:musaeum@goldaming.ndo.co.uk
Guildford Museum Castle ArchQuarry StGuildfordGU1 3SX Tel: 01483 444750 E: Museum @remote.guildford.gov.uk
Haslemere Educational Museum 78 High StHaslemereGU27 2LA Tel: 01428 642112Fax: 01428 645234 E: haslemere_museum@compuserve.com
Kingston Museum & Heritage Service North Kingston CentreRichmond RoadKingston upon ThamesKT2 5PE Tel: (020) 8547-6738 F: (020) 8547-6747 E: local.history@rbk.kingston.gov.uk W: www.kingston.gov.uk/museum/

Kingston Upon Thames Museum North Kingston CentreRichmond RoadNew MaldenKT3 3UQ Tel: 020 8547 67381901 census
Merton Heritage Centre The CannonsMadeira RdMitchamCR4 4HD Tel: (020) 8640 9387
Queen's Royal Surrey Regiment Museum (Queen's Royal, East Surrey & Queen's Royal Surrey Regiments) Clandon ParkWest ClandonGuildfordGU4 7RQ Tel: 01483 223419 E: queenssurreys@caree4free.net W: www.surrey-online.co.uk/queenssurreys_www.queensroyalsurreys.org.uk
Regimental Museum Royal Logistic Corps Princess Royal Barracks Deepcut Camberley GU16 6RW Tel: 01252 833371 E: query@rlcmuseum.freeserve.co.uk W: www.army-rlc.co.uk/museum
Reigate Priory Museum Reigate PrioryBell StReigateRH2 7RL Tel: 01737 222550
Rural Life Centre Old Kiln Museum The ReedsTilfordFarnhamGU10 2DL Tel: 01252 795571Fax: 01252 795571 Email:rural.life@argonet.co.uk
Sandhurst Collection Royal Military Academy SandhurstCamberleyGU15 4PQ Tel: 01276 412489 F: 1276421595
Staff College Museum Old Staff College BuildingCamberleyGU15 4NP Tel: 01276 41271901276 412602
Wandle Industrial Museum Vestry Hall AnnexLondon RdMitchamCR4 3UD Tel: (020) 8648 0127 W: www.wandle.org
Woking Museum & Arts & Craft Centre The GalleriesChobham RdWoking GU21 1JF Tel: 01483 725517 F: 01483 725501 E: the.galleries@dial.pipex.com

Sussex

Brighton Fishing Museum 201 Kings RoadArchesBrightonBN1 1NB Tel: 01273-723064 F: 01273-723064
Museum of The Royal National Lifeboat Institution King Edward Parade Eastbourne BN Tel: 01323 730717
Royal Military Police Museum Roussillon Barracks Chichester PO19 6BL Tel: 01243 534225 F: 01243 534288 E: Museum @rhqrmp.freeserve.co.uk W: www.rhqrmp.freeserve.co.uk
Sussex Combined Services Museum (Royal Sussex Regiment and Queen's Royal Irish Hussars) Redoubt Fortress Royal Parade Eastbourne BN22 7AQ Tel: 01323 410300
Tangmere Military Aviation Museum Tangmere Chichester PO20 2ES Tel: 01243 775223 F: 01243 789490 E: admin@tangmere-museum.org.uk W: www.tangmere-museum.org.uk

Sussex – East
Sussex Yeomanry Museum 198 Dyke Road Brighton BN1 5AS Tel: **Anne of Cleves House Museum** 52 SouthoverHigh StLewesBN7 1JA Tel: 01273 474610
Battle Museum Langton Memorial Hall High StBattleTN33 0AQ Tel: 01424 775955
Bexhill Museum Egerton Rd Bexhill-On-SeaTN39 3HL Tel: 01424 787950 E: Museum @rother.gov.uk W: www.1066country.com
Bexhill Museum of Costume & Social History Assoc Manor Gardens Upper Sea Rd Bexhill-On-Sea TN40 1RL Tel: 01424 210045
BN1 Visual Arts Project Brighton Media Centre 9-12 Middle St BrightonBN1 1AL Tel: 01273 384242
Booth Musuem 194 Dyke Rd BrightonBN1 5AA Tel: 01273 292777 F: 01273 292778 E: boothmus@pavilion.co.uk
Dave Clarke Prop Shop Long BarnCross In HandHeathfieldTN21 0TP Tel: 01435 863800
Ditchling Museum Church Lane DitchlingHassocksBN6 8TB Tel: 01273 844744 F: 01273 844744 E: info@ditchling-museum.com
Eastbourne Heritage Centre2 Carlisle RdEastbourneBN21 4BT Tel: 01323 411189 T: 01323 721825
Filching Manor Motor Museum Filching ManorJevington RdPolegateBN26 5QA Tel: 01323 487838
Fishermans Museum Rock A Nore RdHastingsTN34 3DW Tel: 01424 461446
Hastings Museum & Art Gallery Johns PlaceBohemia RdHastingsTN34 1ET Tel: 01424 781155Fax: 01424 781155 E: Museum @hastings.gov.uk W: www.hmag.org.uk
Hove Musuem & Art Gallery19 New Church RdHoveBN3 4AB Tel: 01273 290200Fax: 01273 292827 Email:abigail.thomas@brighton-hove.gov.ukWWW: www.brighton-hove.gov.uk
How We Lived Then Museum of Shops20 Cornfield Terrace EastbourneBN21 4NS Tel: 01323 737143
Michelham Priory Upper Dicker Hailsham BN27 3QS Tel:
Newhaven Fort Fort Rd Newhaven BN9 9DL Tel: 01273 517622 F: 01273 512059 E: ian.everest@newhavenfort.org.uk W: www.newhavenfort.org.uk
Newhaven Local & Maritime Museum Garden Paradise Avis WayNewhavenBN9 0DH Tel: 01273 612530
Preston Manor Musuem Preston DroveBrightonBN1 6SD Tel: 01273 292770 F: 01273 292771
Rye Castle Museum East StRyeTN31 7JY Tel: 01797 226728
Seaford Museum of Local History Martello Tower The Esplanade SeafordBN25 1NP Tel: 01323 898222 E: Museum seaford@tinyonline.co.uk W: www.seaforedmuseum.org

The Engineerium The Droveway Nevill Rd Hove BN3 7QA Tel: 01273 554070 Email:info@britishengineerium.com
Wish Tower Puppet Museum Tower 73 King Edwards Parade Eastbourne BN21 4BY Tel: 01323 411620 E: puppet.workshop@virgin.net W: www.puppets.co.uk

Sussex - West
Amberley Working Museum Station Rd Amberley ArundelBN18 9LT Tel: 01798 831370 F: 1798831831 E: office@amberleymuseum.co.uk W: www.amberleymuseum.co.uk3
Chichester District Museum 29 Little LondonChichesterPO19 1PB Tel: 01243 784683 F: 01243 776766 E: Email: chichmus@breathemail.net
Fishbourne Roman Palace Roman WaySalthill RdFishbourneChichesterPO19 3QR Tel: 01243 785859 F: 01243 539266 E: adminfish@sussexpast.co.uk W: www.sussexpast.co.uk
Horsham Museum 9 The Causeway Horsham RH12 1HE Tel: 01403-254959 F: 01403 217581 E: Museum @horsham.gov.uk
Marlipins Museum High StShoreham-By-Sea BN43 5DA Tel: 01273 46299401323 441279 F: 01323 844030 E: smermich@sussexpast.co.uk W: www.sussexpast.co.uk
Petworth Cottage Museum 346 High StPetworthGU28 0AU Tel: 01798 342100 W: www.sussexlive.co.uk
The Mechanical Music & Doll Collection Church RdPortfieldChichesterPO19 4HN Tel: 01243 372646
Weald & Downland Open Air Museum SingletonChichesterPO18 0EU Tel: 01243-811363 F: 01243-811475 E: wealddown@mistral.co.uk W: www.wealddown.co.uk

Tyne and Wear
101 (Northumbrian) Regiment Royal Artillery (Volunteers) Museum Napier ArmouryGatesheadNE8 4HX Tel: 0191 239 6130 F: 0191 239 6132
Military Vehicle Museum Exhibition Park PavilionNewcastle upon TyneNE2 4PZ Tel: 0191 281 7222
Arbeia Roman Fort Baring Rd South ShieldsNE33 2BB Tel: 0191 4561369 F: 0191 4276862 E: liz.elliott@tyne-wear-museums.org.uk
Arbeia Roman Fort and Museum Baring StreetSouth ShieldsNE33 2BB Tel: 0191 456 1369 F: 0191 427 6862 E: lis.elliott@rwmuseums.org.uk W: www.aboutbritain.com/ArbeiaRomanFort.htm
Bede's World Museum Church BankJarrowNE32 3DY Tel: 0191 4892106
Castle Keep Castle GarthSt. Nicholas StNewcastle Upon TyneNE1 1RE Tel: 0191 2327938
Hancock Museum Barras BridgeNewcastle Upon TyneNE2 4PT Tel: 0191 2227418 F: 0191 2226753 E: hancock.museum@ncl.ac.uk
Military Vehicles Museum Exhibition Park PavilionNewcastle Upon TyneNE2 4PZ Tel: 0191 2817222 E: miltmuseum@aol.com W: www.military-museum.org.uk
Newburn Motor Museum Townfield Gardens Newburn Newcastle Upon Tyne NE15 8PY Tel: 0191 2642977
North East Aircraft Museum Old Washington Road Sunderland SR5 3HZ Tel: 0191 519 0662
Ryhope Engines Trust Pumping Station Stockton Rd Ryhope Sunderland SR2 0ND Tel: 0191 5210235 W: www.g3wte.demon.co.uk
Segedunum Roman Fort, Baths and Museum WallsendNE Tel: 0191 236 9347 F: 0191 295 5858 E: segesunum@twmuseums.org.uk W: www.twmuseums.org.ukI
South Shields Museum & Art Gallery Ocean RoadSouth ShieldsNE33 2JA Tel: 0191-456-8740 F: 0191 456 7850
Stephenson Railway Museum Middle Engine LaneNorth ShieldsNE29 8DX Tel: 0191 200 7146 F: 0191 200 7146
Sunderland Maritime Heritage1st Floor Office, North East SideSouth DockPort of SunderlandSunderlandSR1 2EE Tel: 0191 510 2055 F: 0191 510 2055 E: info@sunderlandMH.fsnet.co.uk W: www.sunderlandmaritimeheritage.com
Sunderland Museum & Art Gallery and Monkwearmouth Station Museum Borough RoadSunderlandSR1 1PP Tel: 0191 565 0723 F: 0191 565 0713 E: martin.routledge@tyne-wear-museums.org.uk
The Bowes Railway Co Ltd Springwell RdSpringwell VillageGatesheadNE9 7QJ Tel: 0191 4161847 T: 0191 4193349 E: alison_gibson77@hotmail.com W: www.bowesrailway.co.uk

Warwickshire
Leamington Spa Art Gallery & Musuem Royal Pump Rooms The Parade Leamington Spa CV32 4AA Tel: 01926 742700 E:prooms@warcickdc.gov.ukW: www.royal-pump-rooms.co.uk
Lunt Roman Fort Coventry Road Baginton Coventry Tel: 024 7683 2381
Midland Air Museum Coventry Airport Baginton CV8 3AZ Tel: 01203 301033 W: www.discover.co.uk/~mam/
Nuneaton Museum & Art Gallery Riversley Park NuneatonCV11 5TU Tel: (024) 76376473
Regimental Museum of The Queen's Own Hussars (The 3rd King's Own Hussars and 7th Queen's Own Hussars) The Lord Leycester Hospita l High StreetWarwickCV34 4EW Tel: 01926 492035 F: 01926 492035 E: trooper@qohm.fsnet.co.uk

Shakespeare Birthplace Trust - Museum Henley Street Stratford upon AvonCV37 6QW Tel: 01789-204016 F: 01789 296083 E: Museum s@shakespeare.org.uk
The Royal Regiment of Fusiliers Museum (Royal Warwickshire) St. John's HouseWarwick CV34 4NF Tel: 01926 491653
Warwick Castle WarwickCV34 4QU Tel: 01926-406600 F: 01926 401692 W: www.warwick-castle.co.uk
Warwick Doll Museum Okens HouseCastle StWarwickCV34 4BP Tel: 01926 495546
Warwickshire Market Hall Museum Market PlaceWarwickCV34 4SA Tel: 01926 412500 F: 01926 419840 E: Museum @warwickshire.gov.uk W: www.warwickshire.gov.uk/museumcc accepted
Warwickshire Yeomanry Museum The Court HouseJury StreetWarwick CV34 4EW Tel: 01926 492212 F: 01926 494837 E: wtc.admin@btclick.com
Wellesborough Aviation Museum Control Tower EntranceWellesboroughWarwickCV34 4EW Tel:

West Midlands
Aston Manor-Road Transport Museum Ltd208-216 Witton LaneBirminghamB6 6QE Tel: 0121 322 2298
Bantock House & Park Bantock Park,Finchfield RdWolverhamptonWV3 9LQ Tel: 01902 552195 F: 01902 552196
Birmingham & Midland Museum Of Transport Chapel LaneWythallB47 6JX Tel: 01564 826471 E: enquiries@bammot.org.uk W: www.bammot.org.uk
Birmingham Museum & Art Gallery Chamberlain SquareBirminghamB3 3DH Tel: 0121 235 2834 F: 0121 303 1394 W: www.birmingham.gov.uk/bmag
Birmingham Railway Museum Ltd670 Warwick RdTyseleyBirminghamB11 2HL Tel: 0121 707 4696
Black Country Living Museum Canal StTipton RdDudleyDY1 4SQ Tel: 0121 522 9643 F: 0121 557 4242 E: info@bclm.co.uk W: www.bclm.co.uk
Blakesley Hall Blakesley Rd Yardley Birmingham B25 8RN Tel: 0121 783 2193
Dudley Museum & Art Gallerey St James's Road Dudley DY1
Haden Hall & Haden Hill House Haden Hill Park Barrs Road Cradley Heath B64 7JX Tel: 01384 569444
Herbert Art Gallery & Museum Jordan Well Coventry CV1 5QP Tel: 024 76832381
Midland Air Museum Coventry AirportCoventry RdBagintonCoventryCV8 3AZ Tel: (024) 76301033
Museum of theJewellery Quarter75-79 Vyse St Hockley BirminghamB18 6HA Tel: 0121 554 3598Fax: 0121 554 9700
Oak House Museum Oak Rd West Bromwich B70 8HJ Tel: 0121 553 0759
Selly Manor Museum Maple Rd Birmingham B30 2AE Tel: 0121 472 0199
The Lock Museum 55 New RdWillenhallWV13 2DA Tel: 01902 634542 F: 01902 634542http://members.tripod.co.uk/lock_museum/
Walsall Leather Museum Littleton St West WalsallWS2 8EN Tel: 01922 721153 E: leather.museum@walsall.gov.uk
West Midlands Police Museum Sparkhill Police Station Stratford Rd Sparkhill Birmingham B11 4EA Tel: 0121 626 7181
Whitlocks End Farm Bills Lane Shirley Solihull B90 2PL Tel: 0121 745 4891

Wiltshire
Alexander Keiller Museum High St Avebury Marlborough SN8 1RF Tel: 01672 539250 E: avebury@nationaltrust.org.uk
Atwell-Wilson Motor Museum Trust Stockley Lane Calne SN11 0 Tel: 01249 813119
Lydiard House Lydiard Park Lydiard Tregoze Swindon SN5 9PA Tel: 01793 770401
RGBW (Salisbury) Museum The Wardrobe 58 The Close Salisbury SP1 2EX Tel: 01722 419419 W: www.thewardrobe.org.uk
Royal Wiltshire Yeomanry Museum A (RWY) Sqn Royal Yeomanry Church Place Swindon SN1 5EH Tel: 01793 523865 F: 01793 529350 E: arwsqn@hotmail.com
Salisbury & South Wiltshire Museum The King's House 65 The Close SalisburySP1 2EN Tel: 01722 332151 F: 01722 325611 E: Museum @salisburymuseum.freeserve.co.uk
Sevington Victorian School Sevington Grittleton ChippenhamSN14 7LD Tel: 01249 783070
Steam: Museum of the Great Western Railway Kemble Drive SwindonSN2 2TA Tel: 01793 466646 F: 01793 466614 E: tbryan@swindon.gov.uk
The Infantry and Small Arms School Corps Weapons Collection HQ SASCHQ Infantry Warminster Training CentreWarminsterBA12 0DJ Tel: 01985 222487
The Science Museum Wroughton Wroughton Swindon SN4 9NS Tel: 01793 814466 E: enquiries.wroughton@nmsi.ac.uk W: www.sciencemuseum.org.uk/wroughton
Wiltshire Heritage Museum Library Wiltshire Archaeological & Natural HS 41 Long Street DevizesSN10 1NS Tel: 01380 727369 E: wanhs@wiltshireheritage.org.uk W: www.wiltshireheritage.org.uk

Yelde Hall Museum Market Place Chippenham SN15 3HL Tel: 01249 651488

WirralHistoric Warships at Birkenhead East Float Dock Dock Road Birkenhead L41 1DJ Tel: 0151 6501573 E: manager@warships.freeserve.co.uk W: www.warships.freeserve.co.uk

Worcestershire
Almonry Museum Abbey Gate Evesham WR11 4BG Tel: 01386 446944 W www.almonry.ndo.co.uk

Avoncroft Museum of Historic Buildings Redditch RdStoke HeathBromsgroveB60 4JR Tel: 01527 831363 T: 01527 831886 E: Avoncroft1@compuserve.com W: www.avoncroft.org.uk

Bewdley Museum Research Library Load StreetBewdleyDY12 2AE Tel: 01229-403573 E: Museum @online.rednet.co.uk_angela@bewdleyhistory.evesham.net W: www.bewdleymuseum.tripod.com

Kidderminster Railway Museum Station DriveKidderminsterDY10 1QX Tel: 01562 825316

Malvern Museum Priory GatehouseAbbey RoadMalvernWR14 3ES Tel: 01684 567811

MLA West Midlands Regional Council for Museums Libraries & Archive 2nd Floor Grosvenor House14 Bennetts HillB2 5RS Tel: 01527 872258 F: 01527 576960

Museum of Worcester Porcelain The Royal Porcelain Works Severn Street WorcesterWR1 2NETel:Email: rwgeneral@royal-worcester.co.uk

The Almonry Heritage Centre Abbey GateEveshamWR11 4BG Tel: 01385 446944 E: tic@almonry W: www.almonry.ndo.co.uk

The Commandery Civil War Museum SidburyWorcesterWR1 2HU Tel: 01905 361821 E: thecommandery@cityofworcester.gov.uk W: www.worcestercitymuseums.org.uk

The Elgar Birthplace Museum Crown East LaneLower BroadheathWorcesterWR2 6RH Tel: 01905 333224Fax: 01905 333224WWW: www.elgarfoundation.org

The Mueseum of Local Life Tudor HouseFriar StreetWorcesterWR1 2NA Tel: 01905 722349 W: www.worcestercitymuseums.org.uk

The Museum of the Worcestershire Yeomanry Cavalry Worcester City Museum & Art GalleryForegate StWorcesterWR1 1DT Tel: 01905 25371Fax:01905 616979 E: tbridges@cityofworcester.gov.uk W: www.worcestercitymuseums.org.uk

The Worcestershire Regiment Museum Worcester City Museum & Art GalleryForegate StreetWorcesterWR1 1DT Tel: 01905-25371 Museum T: 01905 354359 Office F: 01905-616979 Museum 01905 353871 Office E: rhq_wfr@lineone.net Postal Address: The Curator, The Worcestershire Regimental Museum Trust, RHQ WFR, Norton Barracks, Worcester WR5 2PA

Worcestershire City Museum and Art Gallery Foregate StreetWorcesterWR1 1DT Tel: 01905 25371 F: 01905 616979 E: artgalleryandmuseum@cityofworcester.gov.uk W: www.worcestercitymuseums.org.uk

Worcestershire County Museum Hartlebury CastleHartleburyDY11 7XZ Tel: 01229-250416 F: 01299-251890 E: Museum @worcestershire.gov.ukhttp:// W: www.worcestershire.gov.uk/museum

Worcestershire Regiment Archives (Worcestershireand Sherwood Forester's Regiment)RHQ WFR Norton BarracksWorcesterWR5 2PA Tel: 01905 354359 F: 01905 353871 E: rhg_wfr@lineone.net

Yorkshire – East
Museum of Army Transport FlemingateBeverleyHU17 0NG Tel: 01482 860445 F: 01482 872767

East Riding Heritage Library & Museum Sewerby HallChurch LaneSewerbyBridlingtonYO15 1EA Tel: 01262-677874 T: 01262-674265 E: Museum @pop3.poptel.org.uk W: www.bridlington.net/sew

The Hornsea Museum Burns Farm11 NewbeginHornseaHU18 1AB Tel: 01964 533 443WWW: www.hornseamuseum.comVictorian farmhouse Museum .

Withernsea Lighthouse Museum Hull RdWithernseaHU19 2DY Tel: 01964 614834

Yorkshire – North
Eden Camp Museum MaltonYO17 6RT Tel: 01653 697777 F: 01653 698243 E: admin@edencamp.co.ukhttp:// W: www.edencamp.co.uk

Green Howards Regimental Museum Trinity Church SquareRichmondDL10 4QN Tel: 01748-822133 F: 01748-826561 Story of the Green Howards (Alexandra, Princess of Wales's Own Yorkshire Regiment from 1688 to date)

Royal Dragoon Guards Military Museum (4th/7th Royal Dragoon Guards& 5th Royal Inniskilling Dragoon Guards)3A Tower StreetYorkYO1 9SB Tel: 01904-662790 T: 01904 662310 F: 01904 662310 E: rdgmuseum@onetel.net.uk W: www.rdg.co.uk Also Prince of Wales' Own Regt of Yorkshire Military Museum (West & East Yorkshire Regiments)

The Real Aeroplane Museum The Aerodrome Breighton Selby YO8 7DH Tel: 01757 289065 F: 01977 519340

Upper Wharfedale Museum Society & Folk Museum The SquareGrassingtonBD23 5AU

War Room and Motor House Collection30 Park ParadeHarrogateHG1 5AG Tel: 01423 500704

Yorkshire Air Museum Halifax WayElvingtonYorkYO41 4AU Tel: 01904 608595 E: Museum @yorkshireairmuseum.co.uk W: www.yorkshireairmuseum.co.uk Canada Branch, (Doug Sample CD), 470 Petit Street, St Laurent, Quebec Canada. H4N 2H6

Aysgarth Falls Carriage Museum Yore Mill Asgarth FallsLeyburnDL8 3SR Tel: 01969 663399

Beck Isle Museum of Rural Life PickeringYO18 8DU Tel: 01751 473653

Captain Cook Memorial Museum Grape Lane Whitby YO22 4BA T: 01947 601900 E: captcookmuseumwhitby@ukgateway.net W: www.cookmuseumwhitby.co.uk

Captain Cook Schoolroom Museum 10 High Street Great Ayton TS9 7HB T: 01642 723358

Dales Countryside Museum Station Yard Burtersett Rd Hawes DL8 3NT T: 01969 667494 F: 01969 667165 E: dcm@yorkshiredales.org.uk

Life In Miniature 8 Sandgate Whitby YO22 4DB T: 01947 601478

Malton Museum The Old Town Hall Market Place Malton YO17 7LP T: 01653 695136

Micklegate Bar Museum Micklegate York YO1 6JX T: 01904 634436

Nidderdale Museum Council Offices King Street Pateley Bridge HG3 5LE T: 01423-711225

Old Courthouse Museum Castle Yard Knaresborough T: 01423 556188 F: 01423 556130 W: www.harrogate.gov.uk/museums

Richard III Museum Monk Bar York YO1 2LH T: 01904 634191 W: www.richardiiimuseum.co.uk

Richmondshire Museum Ryder's Wynd Richmond DL10 4JA T: 01748 825611 Contact by letter only - queries dealt with by volunteer staff as soon as possible

Ripon Museum Trust Ripon Prison & Police Museum St Marygate Ripon HG4 1LX T: 01765-690799 E: ralph.lindley@which.net

Rotunda Museum Vernon Rd Scarborough YO11 2NN T: 01723 374839

Royal Pump Room Museum Crown Place Harrogate T: 01423 556188 F: 01423 556130 E: lg12@harrogate.gov.uk W: www.harrogate.gov.uk

Ryedale Folk Museum Hutton le Hole YO62 6UA T: 01751 417367 E: library@dbc-lib.demon.co.uk

The Forbidden Corner Tupgill Park Estate Coverham Middleham Leyburn DL8 4TJ T: 01969 640638 T: 01969 640687

The North Yorkshire Moors Railway Pickering Station Pickering YO18 7AJ T: 01751 472508 E: info@northyorkshiremoorsrailway.com W: www.northyorkshiremoorsrailway.com

The World of James Herriott 23 Kirkgate Thirsk YO7 1PL T: 01845 524234 F: 01845 525333 E: anne.keville@hambleton.gov.uk W: www.hambleton.gov.uk

Whitby Lifeboat Museum Pier Rd Whitby YO21 3PU T: 01947 602001

Whitby Museum Pannett Park Whitby YO21 1RE T: 01947 602908 F: 01947 897638 (Telephone first) E: graham@durain.demon.co.uk W: www.durain.demon.co.uk

Yorkshire – South
Abbeydale Industrial Hamlet Abbeydale Road South Sheffield S7 2 T: 0114 236 7731

Bishops' House Norton Lees Lane Sheffield S8 9BE T: 0114 278 2600 W: www.sheffieldgalleries.org.uk

Bishops House Museum Meersbrook Park Nortin Lees Lane Sheffield S8 9BE T: 0114 255 7701

Cannon Hall Museum Cannon Hall Cawthorne Barnsley S75 4AT T: 01226 790270

Clifton Park Museum Clifton Lane Rotherham S65 2AA T: 01709 823635 E: guy.kilminster@rotherham.gov.uk W: www.rotherham.gov.uk

Fire Museum (Sheffield) Peter House 101-109 West Bar Sheffield S3 8PT T: 0114 249 1999 F: 0114 249 1999 W: www.hedgepig.freeserve.co.uk

Kelham Island Museum Alma St Kelham Island Sheffield S3 8RY T: 0114 272 2106

Magna Sheffield Road Templeborough Rotherham S60 1DX T: 01709 720002 F: 01709 820092 E: info@magnatrust.co.uk W: www.magnatrust.org.uk

Sheffield Police and Fire Museum 101-109 West Bar Sheffield S3 8PT T: 0114 249 1999 W: www.hedgepig.freeserve.co.uk

Sandtoft Transport Centre Ltd Belton Rd Sandtoft Doncaster DN8 5SX T: 01724 711391

Sheffield City Museum Weston Park Sheffield S10 2TP T: 0114 278 2600 W: www.sheffieldgalleries.org.uk

Yorkshire – West
Manor House Art Gallery & Museum Castle Yard Castle Hill Ilkley LS29 9D T: 01943 600066

Middleton Railway The Station Moor Road Hunslet Leeds LS10 2JQ T: 0113 271 0320 E: howhill@globalnet.co.uk w W: www.personal.leeds.ac.uk/mph6mip/mrt/mrt.htm

National Museum of Photography, Film & Television see National Royal Armouries see National

Shibden Hall Lister Rd Shibden Halifax HX3 6AG T: 01422 352246 E: shibden.hall@calderdale.gov.uk W: www.calderdale.gov.uk

Skopos Motor Museum Alexandra Mills Alexandra Rd Batley WF17 6JA T: 01924 444423

Temple Newsham House Temple Newsham Road off Selby Road Leeds LS15 0AE T: 0113 264 7321

Thackray Medical Museum Beckett Street Leeds LS9 7LN T: 0113-244-4343 F: 0113-247-0219 E: info@thackraymuseum.org W: www.thackraymuseum.org

The Colour Museum 1 Providence Street Bradford BD1 2PW T: 01274 390955 F: 01274 392888 E: Museum s@sdc.org.uk W: www.sdc.org.uk

Thwaite Mills Watermill Thwaite Lane Stourton Leeds LS10 1RP T: 0113 249 6453

Vintage Carriages Trust Station Yard Ingrow Keighley BD21 1DB T: 01535 680425 F: 01535 610796 E: admin@vintagecarriagestrust.org W: www.vintagecarriagestrust.org

Wakefield Museum Wood St Wakefield WF1 2EW T: 01924 305351 F: 01924 305353 E: cjohnstone@wakefield.gov.uk W: www.wakefield.gov.uk/culture

Yorkshire & Humberside Museum s Council Farnley Hall Hall Lane Leeds LS12 5HA T: 0113 263 8909

Yorkshire – York

Archaeoligical Resource Centre St Saviourgate York YO1 8NN T: 01904 654324 F: 01904 627097 E: enquiries.ar.yat@yorkarch.demon.co.uk W: www.jorvik-viking-centre.co.uk

Bar Convent 17 Blossom Street York YO24 1AQ T: 01904 643238 F: 01904 631792 E: info@bar-convent.org.uk W: www.bar-convent.org.uk

York Castle Museum The Eye of York York YO1 9RY T: 01904 687687 F: 01904 671078 W: www.yorkcastlemuseum.org.uk/

Yorkshire Museum Museum Gardens York YO1 7FR T: 01904 629745 F: 01904 651221 W: www.york.gov.uk

WALES
Anglesey

Beaumaris Gaol Museum Bunkers Hill Beaumaris LL58 8EP T: 01248 810921 T: 01248 724444 01248 750282 E: beaumariscourtand gaol@anglesey.gov.uk

The Maritime Museum Beach Rd Newry Beach Holyhead LL65 1YD T: 01407 769745 E: cave@holyhead85.freeserve.co.uk

Caernarfon

Welsh Slate Museum Padarn Country Park Llanberis Gwynedd LL55 4TY T: 01286 870630 F: 01286 871906 E: wsmpost@btconnect.com W: WWW: www.nmgw.ac.uk

Cardiff

1st The Queen's Dragoon Guards Regimental Museum Cardiff Castle Cardiff CF10 2RB T: (029) 2022 2253 T: (029) 2078 1271 F: (029) 2078 1384 E: clivejmorris@lineone.net W: WWW: www.qdg.org.uk

Cardiff Castle Castle Street Cardiff CF1 2RB T: (029) 20822083 F: (029) 2023 1417 E: cardiffcastle@cardiff.gov.uk

Museum of Welsh Life St Fagans Cardiff CF5 6XB T: (029) 2057 3500 F: (029) 2057 3490 E: post@nmgw.ac.uk W: WWW: www.nmgw.ac.uk/mwl/

Techniquest Stuart St Cardiff CF10 5BW T: (029) 20475475

Carmarthenshire

Parc Howard Museum & Art Gallery Mansion House Parc Howard Llanelli SA15 3LJ T: 01554 772029

Ceredigion

Cardigan Heritage Centre Teifi Wharf Castle St Cardigan SA43 3AA T: 01239 614404

Ceredigion Museum Coliseum Terrace Rd Aberystwyth SY23 2AQ T: 01970 633088 F: 01970 633084 E: Museum @ceredigion.gov.uk W: WWW: www.ceridigion.gov.uk

Mid-Wales Mining Museum Ltd Llywernog Silver Mine Ponterwyd Aberystwyth SY23 3AB T: 01970 890620

Mid-Wales Mining Museum - Silver River Mines Ltd Llywernog Mine Ponterwyd Aberystwyth SY23 3AB T: 01970 890620 F: 01545 570823 E: silverrivermine@aol.com W: www.silverminetours.co.uk

Conwy

Great Orme Tramway Tramffordd Y Gogarth Goprsaf Victoria Church Walks Llandudno LL30 1AZ T: 01492 575350 E: enq@greatormetramway.com W: www.greatormetramway.com

Sir Henry Jones Museum Y Cwm Llangernyw Abergele LL22 8PR T: 01492 575371 T: 01754 860661 E: info@sirhenryjones-museums.org W: www.sirhenryjones-museums.org

Denbighshire

Cae Dai Trust Cae Dai Lawnt Denbigh LL16 4SU T: 01745 812107 T: 01745 817004

Llangollen Motor Museum Pentrefelin Llangollen LL20 8EE T: 01978 860324

Dyfed

Kidwelly Industrial Museum Broadford Kidwelly SA17 4UF T: 01554 891078

Pembrokeshire Motor Museum Keeston Hill Haverfordwest SA62 6EH T: 01437 710950

Wilson Museum of Narberth Market Square Narberth SA67 7AX T: 01834 861719

Glamorgan Brecon Mountain Railway Pant Station Merthyr Tydfil CF48 2UP T: 01685 722988 E: enquiries@breconmountainrailway.co.uk W: www.breconmountainrailway.co.uk

Gwent

Abergavenny Museum The Castle Castle St Abergavenny NP7 5EE T: 01873 854282

Big Pit Mining Museum Blaenavon Torfaen NP4 9XP T: 01495-790311

Castle & Regimental Museum Monmouth Castle Monmouth NP25 3BS T: 01600 772175 E: curator@monmouthshirecastlemuseum.org.uk W: www.monmouthshirecastlemuseum.org.uk

Drenewydd Museum 26-27 Lower Row Bute Town Tredegar NP22 5QH T: 01685 843039 E: morgac1@caerphilly.gov.uk

Newport Museum & Art Gallery John Frost Square Newport NP20 1PA T: 01633-840064 F: 01633 222615 E: Museum @newport.gov.uk

Pillgwenlly Heritage Community Project within Baptist Chapel Alexandra Rd Newport NP20 2JE T: 01633 244893

Roman Legionary Museum High St Caerleon Newport NP18 1AE T: 01633 423134

Roman Legionary Museum High Street Caerleon NP6 1AE T: 01633 423134 W: www.nmgw.ac.uk

Valley Inheritance Park Buildings Pontypool Torfaen NP4 6JH T: 01495-752036 F: 01495-752043

Gwynedd

Bala Lake Railway Rheilfford Llyn Tegid The Station Yr Orsaf Llanuwchllyn LL23 7DD T: 01678 540666 F: 01678 540535 W: www.bala-lake-railway.co.uk

Betws-y-Coed Motor Museum Museum Cottage Betws-Y-Coed LL24 0AH T: 01690 710760

Caernarfon Air World Caernarfon Airport Dinas Dinlle Caernarfon LL54 5TP

Gwynedd Museum s Service Victoria Dock Caernarvon LL55 1SH T: 01286 679098 F: 01286 679637 E: amgueddflydd-museums@gwynedd.gov.uk

Llanberis Lake Railway Rheilffordd Llyn Padarn Llanberis LL55 4TY T: 01286 870549 F: 01286 870549 E: info@lake-railway.co.uk W: www.lake-railway.co.uk

Llandudno & Conwy Valley Railway Society Welsh Slate Museum Llanberis T: 01492 874590

Llandudno Royal Artillery Llandudno Museum 17-19 Gloddaeth Street Llandudno LL30 2DD T: 01492 876517

Lloyd George Museum Llanstumdwy Criccieth LL52 0SH T: 01766 522071 W: www.gwynedd.gov.uk/adrannau/addysg/amgueddfeydd/english/lg_1.htm

Porthmadog Maritime Museum Oakley Wharf 1 The Harbour Porthmadog LL49 9LU T: 01766 513736

Segontium Roman Museum Beddgelert Rd Caernarfon LL55 2LN T: 01286 675625 F: 01286 678416 W: www.nmgw.ac.uk

Snowdon Mountain Railway Llanberis LL55 4TY T: 0870 4580033 F: 01286 872518 E: info@snowdonrailway.co.uk W: www.snowdonrailway.co.uk

Teapot Museum 25 Castle St Conwy LL32 8AY T: 01492 596533

The Royal Welch Fusiliers Regimental Museum The Queen's Tower The Castle Caernarfon LL55 2AY T: 01286 673362 F: 01286 677042 E: rwfusiliers@callnetuk.com W: www.rwfmuseum.org.uk

Welsh Highland Railway Tremadog Road Porthmadog LL49 9DY T: 01766 513402 W: www.whr.co.uk

Welsh Slate Museum Llanberis LL55 4TY T: 01286 870630 F: 01286 871906 E: slate@nmgw.ac.uk W: www.nmgw.ac.uk

Home Front Experience New Street Llandudno LL30 2YF T: 01492 871032 W: www.homefront-enterprises.co.uk

Mid Glamorgan

Cyfartha Castle Museum Cyfartha Park Brecon Road Merthyr Tydfil CF47 8RE T: 01685 723112 T: 01685 723112

Joseph Parrys Cottage 4 Chapel Row Merthyr Tydfil CF48 1BN T: 01685 383704

Pontypridd Historical & Cultural Centre Bridge St Pontypridd CF37 4PE T: 01443 409512 F: 01443 485565

Ynysfach Iron Heritage Centre Merthyr Tydfil Heritage Trust Ynysfach Rd Merthyr Tydfil CF48 1AG T: 01685 721858

Monmouth Nelson Museum & Local History Centre Priory St Monmouth NP5 3XA T: 01600 710630 E: nelsonmuseum@monmouthshire.gov.uk

Chepstow Museum Bridge St Chepstow NP16 5EZ T: 01291 625981 E: chepstowmuseum@monmouthshire.gov.uk

Monmouthshire Royal Engineers (Militia) Castle and Regimental Museum The Castle Monmouth NP25 3BS T: 01600-712935 E: curator@monmouthcastlemuseum.org.uk W: www.monmouthcastlemuseum.org.uk
Monmouthshire Usk Rural Life Museum The Malt Barn New Market Street Usk NP15 1AU T: 01291-673777 E: uskrurallife.museum@virgin.net W: www.uskmuseum.members.easyspace.com
Pembrokeshire
Haverfordwest Town Museum Castle St Haverfordwest SA61 2EF T: 01437 763087 W: www.haverfordwest-town-museum.org.uk
Milford Haven Museum Old Customs House The Docks Milford Haven SA73 3AF T: 01646 694496
Pembroke Yeomanry, Royal Pembroke Militia, Pembrokeshire Volunteers Museum Scolton Manor Museum Spittal Haverfordwest SA62 5QL T: 01437 731328 F: 01437 731743
Pembrokeshire Service Castle Gallery Castle St Haverfordwest SA61 2EF T: 01437 775246 F: 01437 769218
Tenby Museum Tenby Museum & Art Gallery Castle Hill Tenby SA70 7BP T: 01834-842809 F: 01834-842809 E: tenbymuseum@hotmail.com W: www.tenbymuseum.free-online.co.uk Archives & Museum Mainly Tenby Town & immediate area. Search fee £5
Powys
Brecknock Militia Howell Harris Museum Coleg Trefeca Brecon LD3 0PP T: 01874 711423 F: 01874 711423 E: post@trefeca.org.uk W: www.trefeca.org.uk
Llanidloes Museum Town Hall Great Oak Street Llanidloes SY18 6BN T: 01686 413777 W: http://powysmuseums.powys.gov.uk
Powysland Museum The Canal Wharf Welshpool SY21 7AQ T: 01938 554656 W: http://powysmuseums.powys.gov.uk Local Museum with display on Montgomeryshire Yeomanry Cavalry
Powysland Museum & Montgomery Canal Centre Canal Yard Welshpool SY21 7AQ T: 01938 554656 F: 01938 554656
Radnorshire Museum Temple St Llandrindod Wells LD1 5DL T: 01597 824513 E: radnorshire.museum@powys.gov.uk
South Wales Borderers & Monmouthshire Regimental Museum of the Royal Regt of Wales (24th/41st Foot) The Barracks Brecon LD3 7EB T: 01874 613310 F: 01874 613275 E: swb@rrw.org.uk W: www.rrw.org.uk
The Judge's Lodging Broad St Presteigne LD8 2AD T: 01544 260650 F: 01544 260652 W: www.judgeslodging.org.uk
Water Folk Canal Centre Old Store House Llanfrynach Brecon LD3 7LJ T: 01874 665382
South Glamorgan
National Museum & Galleries of Wales Cathays Park Cardiff CF10 3NP T: (029) 20397951 F: (029) 2057 3389
Welch Regiment Museum of Royal Regiment of Wales The Black & Barbican Towers Cardiff Castle And Grounds Cardiff CF10 3RB T: 029 2022 9367 E: welch@rrw.org.uk_john.dart@rrw.org.uk W: www.rrw.org.uk
West Glamorgan
Cefn Cocd Colliery Museum Blaenant Colliery Crynant Neath SA10 8SE T: 01639 750556
Glynn Vivian Art Gallery Alexandra Rd Swansea SA1 5DZ T: 01792 655006 F: 01792 651713 E: glynn.vivian.gallery@business.ntl.com W: www.sawnsea.gov.uk
Neath Museum The Gwyn Hall Orchard Street Neath SA11 1DT T: 01639 645726 F: 01639 645726 Open Tuesday to Saturday 10.00.a.m. to 4.00.p.m. Admission free
Wrexham
Wrexham County Borough Museum County Buildings Regent Street Wrexham LL11 1RB T: 01978-317970 F: 01978-317982 E: Museum @wrexham.gov.uk W: www.wrexham.gov.uk/heritage

SCOTLAND
Royal Museum & Museum of Scotland Chambers St Edinburgh EH1 1JF T: 0131 247 4115 T: 0131-225-7534 W: www.nms.ac.uk
National War Museum of Scotland The Castle Museum Square Edinburgh EH1 2NG T: 0131 225 7534 F: 0131 225 3848 E: library@nms.ac.uk W: www.nms.ac.uk/war
Aberdeenshire
Aberdeen Maritime Museum 52-56 Shiprow Aberdeen AB11 5BY T: 01224 337700 E: johne@arts-recreation.aberdeen.net.uk W: www.aagm.co.uk
Alford Heritage Centre Alford & Donside Heritage Association Mart Road Alford AB33 8BZ T: 019755 62906
Arbuthnot Museum St. Peter St Peterhead AB42 1DA T: 01779 477778 F: 01771 622884
Fraserburgh Heritage Society Heritage Centre Quarry Rd Fraserburgh AB43 9DT T: 01346 512888 W: www.fraserburghheritage.com Open 1st April to 31st October
Gordon Highlanders Museum St Lukes Viewfield Road Aberdeen AB15 7XH T: 01224 311200 F: 01224 319323 E: Museum @gordonhighlanders.com W: www.gordonhighlanders.com
Grampian Transport Museum Alford AB33 8AE T: 019755-62292
Hamilton T.B Northfield Farm New Pitsligo Fraserburgh AB43 6PX T: 01771 653504

Provost Skene's House Guestrow Aberdeen AB10 1AS T: 01224 641086
The Museum of Scottish Lighthouses Kinnaird Head Fraserburgh AB43 9DU T: 01346-511022 F: 01346-511033 E: enquiries@lighthousemuseum.demon.co.uk
Angus
Arbroath Museum Signal Tower Ladyloan Arbroath DD11 1PY T: 01241 875598 F: 01241 439263 E: signal.tower@angsu.gov.uk W: www.angus.gov.uk/history
Glenesk Folk Museum The Retreat Glenesk Brechin DD9 7YT T: 01356 670254 E: retreat@angusglens.co.uk W: www.angusglens.co.uk
Montrose Air Station Museum Waldron Road Montrose DD10 9BB T: 01674 673107 T: 01674 674210 F: 01674 674210 E: info@RAFmontrose.org.uk W: www.RAFmontrose.org.uk
The Meffan Institute 20 High St. West Forfar DD8 1BB T: 01307 464123 F: 01307 468451 E: the.meffan@angus.gov.uk
Argyll
Campbeltown Heritage Centre Big Kiln Witchburn Rd Campbeltown PA28 6JU T: 01586 551400
Campbeltown Library and Museum Hall St Campbeltown PA28 6BU T: 01586 552366 F: 01586 552938 E: mary.vanhelmond@argyll-bute.gov.uk W: www.argyle-bute.gov.uk/content/leisure/museums
Castle House Museum Castle Gardens Argyll St Dunoon PA23 7HH T: 01369 701422 E: info@castlehousemuseum.org.uk W: www.castlehousemuseum.org.uk
Kilmartin House Trust Kilmartin House Kilmartin Lochgilphead PA31 8RQ T: 01546 510278 F: 01546 510330 E: Museum @kilmartin.org W: www.kilmartin.org
Ayrshire
Ayrshire Yeomanry Museum Rozelle House Monument Road Alloway by Ayr KA7 4NQ T: 01292 445400 (Museum)
Dalgarven Mill Dalry Rd Dalgarven Kilwinning KA13 6PL T: 01294 552448
East Ayrshire Council District History Centre & Museum Baird Institute 3 Lugar Street Cumnock KA18 1AD T: 01290-421701 F: 01290-421701 E: Baird.institute@east-ayrshire.gov.uk W: www.east-ayrshire.gov.uk
Glasgow Vennel Museum 10 Glasgow Vennel Irvine KA12 0BD T: 01294 275059
Irvine Burns Club & Burgh Museum 28 Eglinton St Irvine KA12 8AS T: 01294 274511
McKechnie Institute Dalrymple St Girvan KA26 9AE T: 01465 713643 E: mkigir@ukgateway.net
North Ayrshire Museum Manse St Saltcoats KA21 5AA T: 01294 464174 F: 01294 464174 E: namuseum@globalnet.co.uk
Rozelle House Rozelle Park Ayr KA7 4NQ T: 01292 445447
The Largs Museum Kirkgate House Manse Court Largs KA30 8AW T: 01475 687081
The Scottish Maritime Museum Gottries Road Irvine KA12 3QE T: 01294 278283 F: 1294313211 E: jgrant5313@aol.com
West Lowland Fencibles Culzean Castle Maybole KA19 8LE T: 01655 884455 F: 01655 884503 E: culzean@nts.org.uk W: www.culzeancastle.net
Banffshire
The Buckie Drifter Maritime Heritage Centre Freuchny Rd Buckie AB56 1TT T: 01542 834646
Berwickshire Coldstream Guards Coldstream Museum 13 Market Square Coldstream TD12 4BD T: 01890 882630
The Jim Clark Room 44 Newtown St Duns TD11 3DT T: 01361 883960
Caithness
Clangunn Heritage Centre & Museum Old Parish Kirk Latheron KW5 6DL T: 01593 741700
Dunbeath Preservation Trust Old School Dunbeath KW6 6EG T: 01593 731233 F: 01593 731233 E: info@dunbeath-heritage.org.uk W: www.dunbeath-heritage.org.uk
The Last House John O'Groats Wick KW1 4YR T: 01955 611250
Dumfrieshire
Robert Burns House Burns Street Dumfries DG1 2PS T: 01387 255297
Dumfries Museum & Camera Obscura The Observatory Dumfries DG2 7SW T: 01387 253374 F: 01387 265081 E: info@dumgal.gov.uk W: www.dumfriesmuseum.demon.co.uk
Ellisland Trust Ellisland Farm Dumfries DG2 0RP T: 01387 740426
Gretna Museum & Tourist Services Headless Cross Gretna Green DG16 5EA T: 01461 338441 F: 01461 338442 E: info@gretnagreen.com W: www.gretnagreen.com
John Paul Jones Birthplace Museum Arbigland Kirkbean Dumfries DG2 8BQ T: 01387 880613 W: www.jpj.demon.co.uk
Old Bridge House Museum Old Bridge House Mill Rd Dumfries DG2 7BE T: 01387 256904 W: www.dumfriesmuseum.demon.co.uk
Robert Burns Centre Mill Road Dumfries DG2 7BE T: 01387 264808 F: 01387 264808 E: dumfreis.museum@dumgal.gov.uk W: www.dumgal.gov.uk/museums

Sanquhar Tolbooth Museum High St Sanquhar DG4 6BL T: 01659 50186

Savings Banks Museum Ruthwell Dumfries DG1 4NN T: 01387 870640 E: tsbmuseum@btinternet.com

Shambellie House Museum of Costume New Abbey Dumfries DG2 8HQ T: 01387 850375 F: 01387 850461 E: info@nms.ac.uk W: www.nms.ac.uk

Dundee

Dundee Heritage Trust Verdant Works West Henderson's Wynd Dundee DD1 5BT T: 01382-225282 F: 01382-221612 E: info@dundeeheritage.sol.co.uk W: www.verdant-works.co.uk

HM Frigate Unicorn Victoria Dock Dundee DD1 3JA T: 01382 200893 T: 01382 200900 F: 01382 200923 E: frigateunicorn@hotmail.com W: www.frigateunicorn.org

Royal Research Ship Discovery Discovery point Discovery Quay Dundee DD1 4XA T: 01382 201245 F: 01382 225891 E: info@dundeeheritage.sol.co.uk W: www.rrs-discovery.co.uk

East Lothian

Dunbar Museum High St Dunbar EH42 1ER T: 01368 863734

John Muir House Museum 126-128 High St Dunbar EH42 1JJ T: 01368 862585

Myreton Motor Museum Aberlady EH32 0PZ T: 01875 870288 T: 07947 066 666 F: 01368 860199

North Berwick Museum School Rd North Berwick EH39 4JU T: 01620 895457

Edinburgh

Heritage Projects (Edinburgh) Ltd Castlehill Royal Mile Midlothian EH1 2NE T: 0131 225 7575

Museum of Edinburgh Huntly House 142 Canongate Edinburgh EH8 8DD T: 0131 529 4143 F: 0131 557 3346 W: www.cac.org.uk

Royal Scots Regimental Museum The Castle Edinburgh EH1 2YT T: 0131-310-5014 F: 0131-310-5019 E: rhqroyalscots@edinburghcastle.fsnet.co.uk W: www.theroyalscots.co.uk

Royal Yatch Britannia & Visitor Centre Ocean Drive Leith Edinburgh EH6 6JJ T: 0131 555 5566 T: 0131 555 W: www.royalyachtbritannia.co.uk

Scottish Museum Council County House 20-22 Torphichen Street Edinburgh EH3 8JB T: 0131 229 7465 F: 0131 229 2728 E: inform@scottish.museums.org.uk W: www.scottish.museums.org.uk

The Real Mary King's Close 2 Warriston's Close Writers' Court Edinburgh EH1 1PG T: 08702 430160 W: www.realmarykingsclose.com

Falkirk

Falkirk Museum History Research Centre Callendar House Callendar Park Falkirk FK1 1YR T: 01324 503778 F: 01324 503771 E: ereid@falkirkmuseums.demon.co.uk W: www.falkirkmuseums.demon.co.uk R

Fife

Andrew Carnegie Birthplace Museum Moodie St Dunfermline KY12 7PL T: 01383 724302

Dunfermline Museum Viewfield Dunfermline KY12 7HY T: 01383 313838 F: 01383 313837 Enquiries can be made at this address for: Inverkeithing Museum , Pittencrief House Museum & St Margaret's Cave

Fife and Forfar Yeomanry Museum Yeomanry House Castlebrook Road Cupar KY15 4BL T: 01334 656155 F: 01334 652354

Inverkeithing Museum The Friary Queen St Inverkeithing KY11 1 T: 01383 313595

John McDouall Stuart Museum Rectory Lane Dysart Kirkcaldy KY1 2TP T: 01592 653118

Kirkcaldy Museum and Art Gallery War Memorial Gardens Kirkcaldy KY1 1YG T: 01592 412860 F: 01592 412870

Methil Heritage Centre 272 High St Methil Leven KY8 3EQ T: 01333 422100

Pittencrieff House Museum Pittencrieff Park Dunfermline KY12 8QH T: 01383 722935

Scotland's Secret Bunker Underground Nuclear Command Centre Crown Buildings (Near St Andrews) KY16 8QH T: 01333-310301

Scottish Fisheries Museum St. Ayles Harbourhead Anstruther KY10 3AB T: 01333 310628 F: 01333 310628 E: andrew@scottish-fisheries-museum.org W: www.scottish-fisheries-museum.org

The Fife Folk Museum High St Ceres Cupar KY15 5NF T: 01334 828180

Verdant Works - A Working Jute mill West Henderson's Wynd Dundee DD1 5BT T: 01382-225282 F: 01382-221612 E: info@dundeeheritage.sol.co.uk W: www.verdantworks.co.uk

Glasgow

Fossil Grove Victoria Park Glasgow G14 1BN T: 0141 287 2000 W: www.glasgowmuseums.com

Glasgow Museum of Transport 1 Burnhouse Road Glasgow G3 8DP T: 0141 287 2720 W: www.glasgowmuseums.com

Glasgow Police Museum 68 St Andrews Square Glasgow G2 4JS T: 07788 532691 E: curator@policemuseum.org.uk W: www.policemusaeum.org.uk

Heatherbank Museum Glasgow Caledonian University Cowcaddens Road Glasgow G4 0BA T: 0141 331 8637 F: 0141 331 3005 E: A.Ramage@gcla.ac.uk W: www.lib.gcal.ac.uk/heatherbank

Kelvingrove Art Gallery and Museum Kelvingrove Glasgow G3 8AG T: 0141 287 2699 F: 0141 287 2690 W: www.cis.glasgow.gov.uk The Gallery and Museum closed on 29 June 2003 for 3 years for refurbishment

Martyrs School Parson street Glasgow G4 0PX T: 0141 552 2356 F: 0141 552 2356 W: www.glasgowmuseums.com

McLellan Galleries 270 Sauchiehall Street Glasgow G2 3EH T: 0141 565 4100 F: 0141 565 4111 W: www.glasgowmuseums.com

Museum of Piping The Piping Centre 30-34 McPhater Street Cowcaddens Glasgow T: 0141-353-0220

Open Museum 161 Woodhead Road South Nitshill Industrial Estate Glasgow G53 7NN T: 0141 552 2356 F: 0141 552 2356 W: www.glasgowmuseums.com

Pollok House Pollok Country Park 2060 Pollokshaws Road Glasgow G43 1AT T: 0141 616 6410 F: 0141 616 6521 W: www.cis.glasgow.gov.uk

Provand's Lordship 3 Castle Street Glasgow G4 0RB T: 0141 552 8819 F: 0141 552 4744 W: www.glasgowmuseums.com

Scotland Street School Museum 225 Scotland St Glasgow G5 8QB T: 0141 287 0500 F: 0141 287 0515 W: www.glasgowmuseums.com Scotland Street School

St Mungo Museum of Religious Life and Art 2 Castle Street Glasgow G4 0RH T: 0141 553 2557 F: 0141 552 4744 W: www.glasgowmuseums.com

The Burrell Collection Pollok Country Park 2060 Pollokshaws Road Glasgow G43 1AT T: 0141 287 2550 F: 0141 287 2597 W: www.glasgowmuseums.com

The Hunterian Museum Glasgow University Glasgow G12 8QQ T: 0141 330 3711 F: 0141 330 3617 E: e.smith@admin.gla.ac.uk

The Lighthouse 11 Mitchell Lane Glasgow G1 3NU T: 0141 221 6362 F: 0141 221 6395 E: enquiries@thelighthouse.co.uk W: www.thelighthouse.co.uk

Inverness-shire – Highland

Regimental Museum of The Highlanders (The Queen's Own Highlanders Collection) Fort George IV2 7TD T: 01463 224380 E: rhqthehighlanders@btopenworld.com

Clan Cameron Museum Achnacarry Spean Bridge PH34 4EJ T: 01397 712090 E: Museum @achnarcarry.fsnet.co.uk W: www.clan-cameron.org

Culloden Visitor Centre Culloden Moor Inverness IV2 5EU T: 01463 790607 F: 01463 794294 E: dsmyth@nts.org.uk W: www.nts.org.uk

Highland Folk Museum Duke St Kingussie PH21 1JG T: 01540 661307 F: 01540 661631 E: rachel.chisholm@highland.gov.uk

Highland Folk Museum Aultlarie Croft Kingussie Rd Newtonmore PH20 1AY T: 01540 673551 E: highland.folk@highland.gov.uk W: www.highlandfolf.com

Highland Railway Museum 5 Druimlon Drumnadrochit Inverness IV63 6TY T: 01456 450527

Inverness Museum & Art Gallery Castle Wynd Inverness IV2 3ED T: 01463 237114

Mallaig Heritage Centre Station Rd Mallaig PH41 4PY T: 01687 462085 E: curator@mallaigheritage.org.uk W: www.mallaigheritage.org.uk

Queen's Own Cameron Highlanders Fort George Arderseir Inverness IV1 2TD T: 01667 462777 Fort George is owned by Historic Scotland

The Clansman Centre Canalside Fort Augustus PH32 4AU T: 01320 366444

West Highland Museum Cameron Square Fort William PH33 6AJ T: 01397 702169 F: 01397 701927 E: info@westhighlandmuseum.org.uk W: www.westhighlandmuseum.org.uk

Queen's Own Highlanders (Seaforth & Camerons) Regimental Museum Archives Fort George Ardersier Inverness IV1 7TD T: 01463-224380

Isle Of Arran

Arran Heritage Museum Rosaburn House Brodick KA27 8DP T: 01770 302636

Isle Of Islay

Finlaggan Trust The Cottage Ballygrant PA45 7QL T: 01496 840644 F: 01496 810856 E: lynmags@aol.com W: www.islay.com

Isle Of Mull

The Columba Centre Fionnphort Isle Of Mull PA66 6BN T: 01681 700660

Isle Of North Uist

Taigh Chearsabhagh Trust Taigh Chearsabhagh Lochmaddy HS6 5AE T: 01876 500293 E: taighchearsabhagh@zetnet.co.uk W: www.taighchearsabhagh.org.uk

Isle Of South Uist

Kildonan Museum Kildonan Lochboisdale HS8 5RZ T: 01878 710343

Kirkcudbrightshire
The Stewartry Museum St Mary Street Kirkcudbright DG6 4AQ T:
01557 331643 F: 01557 331643 E: david@dumgal.gov.uk W:
www.dumgal.gov.uk/museums Information service for family and
local history research for Kirkcudbrightshire
Lanarkshire
Auld Kirk Musuem The Cross Kirkintilloch Glasgow G66 1 T:
0141 578 014
Biggar Museum Trust Moat Park Kirkstyle Biggar ML12 6DT T:
01899 221050
Discover Carmichael Visitors Centre Warrenhill Farm Warrenhill
Road Thankerton Biggar ML12 6PF T: 01899 308169
Greenhill Covenanters House Museum Kirkstyle Biggar ML12
6DT T: 01899 221572
Heritage Engineering 22 Carmyle Avenue Glasgow G32 8HJ T:
0141 763 0007
Hunter House Maxwellton Rd East Kilbride Glasgow G74 3LW T:
01355 261261
John Hastie Museum Threestanes Road Strathaven ML10 6EB T:
01357 521257
Lanark Museum 7West Port Lanark ML11 9HD T: 01555 666680
E: paularchibald@hotmail.com W: www.biggar-
net.co.uk/lanarkmuseum
Low Parks Museum 129 Muir St Hamilton ML3 6BJ T: 01698
283981 T: 01698 328232 F: 01698 328232
New Lanark Conservation Trust Visitors Centre Mill No 3 New
Lanark Mills Lanark ML11 9DB T: 01555 661345 F: 01555 665738
E: visit@newlanark.org W: www.newlanark.org
**The Cameronians (Scottish Rifles) Museum & Low Parks
Museum** c/o Low Parks Museum 129 Muir Street Hamilton ML3
6BJ T: 01698 452163 T: 01698 328232 F: 01698 328412
The People's Palace Glasgow Green Glasgow G40 1AT T: 0141
554 0223 F: 0141 550 0897 W: www.glasgowmuseums.com The
story of the people and city of Glasgow from 1750 to present.
admission free
Weavers' Cottages Museum 23-25 Wellwynd Airdrie ML6 0BN T:
01236 747712
Midlothian
History of Education Centre East London St Edinburgh EH7 4BW
T: 0131 556 4224
Lauriston Castle 2a Cramond Rd South Edinburgh EH4 5QD T:
0131 336 2060
Newhaven Heritage Museum 24 Pier Place Edinburgh EH6 4LP T:
0131 551 4165 F: 0131 557 3346 W: www.cac.org.uk
Scottish Mining Museum Trust Lady Victoria Colliery
Newtongrange Dalkeith EH22 4QN T: 0131 663 7519 F: 0131 654
1618 E: enwuiries@scottishminingmuseum.com W:
www.scottishminingmuseum.com
Midlothian
Scots Dragoon Guards Museum Shop The Castle Edinburgh EH1
2YT T: 0131 220 4387
Morayshire
Elgin Museum 1 High St Elgin IV30 1EQ T: 01343 543675 F:
01343 543675 curator@elginmuseum.demon.co.uk W:
www.elginmuseum.demon.co.uk
Falconer Museum Tolbooth St Forres IV36 1PH T: 01309 673701
F: 01309 675863 alasdair.joyce@techleis.moray.gov.uk W:
www.moray.gov.uk
Grantown Museum & Heritage Trust Burnfield House Burnfield
Avenue Grantown-On-Spey PH26 3HH T: 01479 872478 F: 01479
872478 Molly.Duckett@btinternet.com W: www.grantown-on-
spey.co.uk
Lossiemouth Fisheries Museum Pitgaveny St Lossiemouth IV31
6TW T: 01343 813772
Nairnshire
Nairn Museum Viewfield House King St Nairn IV12 4EE T: 01667
456791
Orkney
Orkney Farm & Folk Museum Corrigall Farm Museum Harray
KW17 2LQ T: 01856 771411
Orkney Farm & Folk Museum Kirbister Farm Birsay KW17 2LR
T: 01856 771268
Orkney Fossil & Vintage Centre Viewforth Burray KW17 2SY T:
01856 731255
Orkney Museum Tankerness House Broad Street Kirkwall KW15
1DH T: 01856-873191 F: 01856 871560
Orkney Wireless Museum Kiln Corner Kirkwall KW15 1LB T:
01856-871400
Scapa Flow Visitor Centre Lyness Stromness KW16 3NT T: 01856
791300 W: www.scapaflow.co.uk
Stromness Museum 52 Alfred Street Stromness T: 01856 850025 F:
01856 871560
Perthshire
Atholl Country Collection The Old School Blair Atholl PH18 5SP
T: 01796-481232 E: r.cam@virgin.net
Atholl Highlanders Blair Castle Blair Atholl PH18 5TL T: 01796
481207 E: office@blair-castle.co.uk W: www.blair-castle.co.uk

Clan Donnachaidh (Robertson) Museum Clan Donnachaidh
Centre Bruar Pitlochry PH18 5TW T: 01796-483338 E:
clandonnachaidh@compuserve.com
Clan Menzies Museum Castle Menzies Weem by Aberfeldy PH15
2JD T: 01887-820982
Dunkeld Cathedral Chapter House Museum Dunkeld PH8 0AW
T: 01350 728732 T: 01350 728971 W: www.dunkeldcathedral.org.uk
contains Scottish Horse Regimental Archives
The Hamilton Toy Collection 111 Main St Callander FK17 8BQ T:
01877 330004
Meigle Museum Dundee Rd Meigle Blairgowrie PH12 8SB T:
01828 640612
Regimental Museum and Archives of Black Watch Balhousie
Castle Hay Street Perth PH1 5HR T: 0131 310 8530 F: 01738-
643245 E: archives@theblackwatch.co.uk W:
www.theblackwatch.co.uk
Scottish Horse Regimental Archives - Dunkeld Cathedral
Dunkeld PH8 0AW T: 01350 727614 F: 01350 727614 Scottish
Horse Regimental Museum closed 1999 - archives now held in
Dunkeld Cathedral Chapter House Museum View by prior
appointment
Renfrewshire
Mclean Museum & Art Gallery 15 Kelly St Greenock PA16 8JX
T: 01475 715624
Old Paisley Society George Place Paisley PA1 2HZ T: 0141 889
1708
Paisley Museum Paisley Museum & Art Galleries High Street
Paisley PA1 2BA T: 0141-889-3151
Ross-Shire
Dingwall Museum Trust Town Hall High St Dingwall IV15 9RY T:
01349 865366
Highland Museum of Childhood The Old Station Strathpeffer IV14
9DH T: 01997 421031 E: info@hmoc.freeserve.co.uk W:
www.hmoc.freeserve.co.uk
Tain & District Museum Tain Through Time Tower Street Tain
IV19 1DY T: 01862 894089 F: 01862 894089 E:
info@tainmuseum.edmon.co.uk
Tain Through Time Tower St Tain IV19 1DY T: 01862 894089
The Groam House Museum High St Rosemarkie Fortrose IV10
8UF T: 01381 620961
Ullapool Museum & Visitor Centre 7 & 8 West Argyle St Ullapool
IV26 2TY T: 01854 612987 E: ulmuseum@waverider.co.uk
Roxburghshire
Borders Museum of Arms Henderson's Knowe Teviot Hawick TD9
0LF T: 01450 850237
Hawick Museum & Scott Gallery Wilton Lodge Park Hawick TD9
7JL T: 01450 373457 F: 01450 378506 E:
hawickmuseum@hotmail.com
Jedburgh Castle Jail Museum Castlegate Jedburgh TD8 6BD T:
01835 863254 F: 01835 864750
Mary Queen of Scots House and Visitor Centre Queens St
Jedburgh TD8 6EN T: 01835 863331 F: 01835 893331 E:
hawickmuseum@hotmail.com fionacolton@hotmail.com
Selkirkshire
Halliwells House Museum Halliwells Close Market Place Selkirk
TD7 4BL T: 01750 20096 F: 01750 23282 E: Museum
s@scotborders.gov.uk
Shetland
Fetlar Interpretive Centre Beach Of Houbie Fetlar ZE2 9DJ T:
01957 733206 E: fic@zetnet.co.uk W: www.zetnet.co.uk/sigs/centre/
Old Haa Museum Burravoe Yell Shetland ZE2 9AY T: 01957
722339
Shetland Museum Lower Hillhead Lerwick ZE1 0EL T: 01595
695057 E: shetland.museum@zetnet.co.uk W: www.shetland-
museum.org.uk
Tangwick Haa Museum Tangwick Eshaness Shetland ZE2 9RS T:
01806 503389
The Shetland Textile Working Museum Weisdale Mill Weisdale
Shetland ZE2 9LW T: 01595 830419
Stirlingshire
Stirling Smith Art Gallery & Museum Dumbarton Road Stirling
FK8 2RQ T: 01786 471917 F: 01786 449523 E: Museum
@smithartgallery.demon.co.uk
Regimental Museum Argyll and Sutherland Highlanders Stirling
Castle Stirling FK8 1EH T: 01786 475165 F: 01786 446038
Stranraer
Stranraer Museum 55 George Street Stranraer DG9 7JP T: 01776
705088 F: 01776 705835 E: JohnPic@dumgal.gov.uk W:
www.dumgal.gov.uk
Strathclyde
**Museum of The Royal Highland Fusiliers (Royal Scots Fusiliers
and Highland Light Infantry)** 518 Sauchiehall Street Glasgow G2
3LW T: 0141 332 0961 F: 0141 353 1493 W: www.rhf.org.uk
Sutherland
Strathnaver Museum Bettyhill KW14 7SS T: 01641 521 418 E:
strathnavermuseum@ukonline.co.uk W:
www.aboutbritain.com/StrathnaverMuseum.htm W:
www.strathnaver.org

...useum & Art Gallery Perth Museum & Art Gallery
... Street Perth PH1 5LB T: 01738-632488 F: 01738 443505 E:
...n @pkc.gov.uk W: www.pkc.gov.uk/ah
...othian Almond Valley Heritage Trust Livingston Mill Farm
...d Livingston EH54 7AR T: 01506 414957
...othian Bennie Museum Mansefield St Bathgate EH48 4HU
...6 634944 W: www.benniemuseum.homestead.co.uk
...l Museum Kinneil Estate Bo'Ness EH51 0AY T: 01506
...0
...nsferry Museum 53 High St South Queensferry EH30 9HP T:
...331 5545 W: www.cac.org.uk
...Linlithgow Story Annet House 143 High St Linlithgow EH49
...T: 01506 670677 F: 011506 670677 E:
...iries@linlithgowstory.fsnet.co.uk W: www.linlithgowstory.org.uk
...townshire
...lor's Farm Tradition, Barraer Newton Stewart DG8 6QQ T:
...71 404890 E: jtaylor@bosinternet.com

...ORTHERN IRELAND
...rmagh County Museum The Mall East Armagh BT61 9BE T:
(028) 37523070 F: (028) 37522631 E: acm.um@nics.gov.uk W:
www.magni.org.uk
Ballymoney Museum & Heritage Centre 33 Charlotte St
Ballymoney BT53 6AY T: (028) 2762280
Fermanagh County Museum Enniskillen Castle Castle Barracks
Enniskillen BT74 7HL T: 028 66 32 5000 F: 028 66 32 73 42 E:
castle@fermanagh.gov.uk
Friends of the Ulster Museum 12 Malone Road Belfast BT9 5BN
T: (028) 90681606
Garvagh Museum 142 Main St Garvagh Coleraine BT51 5AE T:
(028) 295 58216 T: (028) 295 58188 F: (028) 295 58993 E:
jclyde@garvaghhigh.garvagh.ni.sch.uk
Down County Museum The Mall Downpatrick BT30 6AH T: (028)
44615218
Downpatrick Railway Museum Railway Station Market St
Downpatrick BT30 6LZ T: (028) 44615779
Foyle Valley Railway Museum Foyle Rd Londonderry BT48 6SQ
T: (028) 71265234
NI Museum s Council 66 Donegall Pass Belfast BT7 1BU T: (028)
90550215 F: (028) 9055 0216 W: www.nimc.co.uk
Odyssey Science Centre Project Office Project Office NMGNI
Botanic Gardens Belfast BT9 5AB T: (028) 90682100
Roslea Heritage Centre Church St Roslea Enniskillen BT74 7DW
T: (028) 67751750
Royal Inniskilling Fusiliers Regimental Museum The Castle
Enniskillen BT74 7BB T: (028) 66323142 F: (028) 66320359
Royal Irish Fusilers Museum Sovereign's House Mall East Armagh
BT61 9DL T: (028) 3752 2911 F: (028) 3752 2911 E:
rylirfusilier@aol.com W: www.rirfus-museum.freeserve.co.uk
The Museum Of The Royal Irish Regiment St. Patricks Barracks
Demesne Avenue Ballymena BT43 7BH T: (028) 2566 1386 T: (028)
2566 1383 F: (028) 2566 1378
Royal Ulster Rifles Regimental Museum RHQ Royal Irish
Regiment 5 Waring Street Belfast BT1 2EW T: (028) 90232086 F:
(028) 9023 2086 E: rurmuseum@yahoo.co.uk W: W:
www.rurmuseum.tripod.com
The Somme Heritage Centre 233 Bangor Rd Newtownards BT23
7PH T: (028) 9182 3202 F: (028) 9182 3214 E:
sommeassociation@dnet.co.uk W: www.irishsoldier.org
Ulster American Folk Park Project Team Belfast 4 The Mount
Albert Bridge Rd Belfast BT5 4NA T: (028) 90452250
Ulster Aviation Heritage Centre Langford Lodge Airfield Belfast T:
028 9267 7030 T: 028 9445 4444 E: emie@aimi.freeserve.co.uk W:
www.d-n-a.net/users/dnetrAzQ
Ulster American Folk Park Centre for Migration Studies Mellon Rd
Castletown Omagh BT78 5QY T: (028) 8225 6315 F: 028 8224 2241
E: uafp@iol.ie W: www.folkpark,com_ W: www.qub.ac.uk/cms/
The Ulster History Park Cullion Lislap BT79 7SU T: (028) 8164
8188 F: (028) 8164 8011 E: uhp@omagh.gov.uk W:
www.omagh.gov.uk/historypark.htm
Ulster Museum Botanic Gardens Botanic Gardens Stranmillis
Road Belfast BT9 5AB T: (028) 90381251

IRELAND
Irish Jewish Museum 3 - 4 Walworth Road South Circular Road
Dublin 8 Ireland T: 453-1797
Dublin Civic Museum 58 South William Street Dublin 2 Ireland T:
679-4260 677 5954

IISLES OF SCILLY
Isles of Scilly Museum Church Street St Mary's Isles of Scilly TR21
0JT T: 01720-422337
Valhalla Museum Tresco Abbey Tresco Isle of Scilly TR24 0QH T:
01720 422849 F: 01720 422106 W:
www.tresco.co.uk/gard/f_gard.htm

CHANNEL ISLANDS
Alderney
The Alderney Society Museum Alderney GY9 3TG T: 01481
823222
Guernsey
18th Century Loopholed Tower PO Box 23 St Peter Port Guernsey
GY1 3AN Located at Rousse headland, Vale, Guernsey
Clarence Battery Fort George St Peter Port Guernsey
Fort Grey Rocquaine Bay St Saviours Guernsey
German Direction Finding Tower PO Box 23 St Peter Port
Guernsey GY1 3AN Tower at Plienmont Headland, Torteval,
Guernsey
German Military Underground Hospital La Vassalerie Road St
Andrew's Guernsey T: 01481 239100
German Naval Signals Headquarters St Jacques Guernsey
German Occupation Museum Les Houards Forest Guernsey GY8
0BG T: 01481 328205 W:
www.aboutbritain.com/OccupationMuseum.htm
La Valette Underground Military Museum St Peter Port Guernsey
T: 01481 722300
Royal Guernsey Militia and Royal Geurnsey Light Infantry Castle
Comet St Peter Port Guernsey T: 01481 726518 T: 01481 721657 F:
01481 715177 W: www.museum.guernsey.net/castle.htm
Jersey
Elizabeth Castle - Jersey Militia St Aubin's Bay St Helier Jersey T:
01534 633300 F: 01534 633301
German Underground Hospital Meadowbank St Lawrence Jersey
T: 01534 863442
Island Fortress Occupation Museum 9 Esplanade St Helier T:
01534 633300 F: 01534 633301
La Hougue Bie Grouville Jersey T: 01534 633300 F: 01534 633301
Maritme Museum and Occupation Tapestry Gallery New North
Quay St Helier Jersey T: 01534 811043 F: 01534 874099 E:
marketing@jerseyheritagetrust.org W: www.jerseyheritagetrust.org
Mont Orgueil Castle Gorey St Martin Jersey T: 01534 633300 F:
01534 633301
Noirmont Command Bunker Noirmont Point St Brelade Jersey T:
01534 482089
**St Peter's Bunker Museum of Wartime German Equipment and
Occupation Relics** La Petite Rue De L'eglise St Peter Jersey JE3
7AF T: 01534 723136
The Channel Islands Military Museum The Five Mile Road St
Ouen Jersey T: 01534 23136
Sark
German Occupation Museum Rue Lucas Sark Sark T: 01481
832564 F: 01481 832135

CANADA
Manitoba
Manitoba Museum of Man and Nature 190 Rupert Avenue
Winnipeg Manitoba R3B 0N2 Canada W:
www.manitobamuseum.mb.ca

SOUTH AFRICA
Kafframan Museum PO Box 1434 King William's Town 5600 T:
0430-24506 F: 0433-21569 E: stephani@hubertd.ry.ac.2a
Huguenot Memorial Museum PO Box 37 Franschoek Western
Cape 7690 T: 021-876-2532
Kaffrarian Museum P O Box 1434 King Williamstown 5600 T:
0433 24506
Huguenot Museum P O Box 37 Franschhoek Western Cape 7690 T:
021 876 2532

UNITED STATES OF AMERICA
Arizona
Arizona Historical Society Pioneer Museum , The PO Box 1968
2340 North Fort Valley Rd Flagstaff Arizona 86002 T: 602-774-6272
Phoenix Museum of History PO Box 926 1002 West Van Buren
Street Phoenix Arizona 85001 T: 602-253-2734
Nevada
Museum Division of Museum s & History 700 Twin Lakes Drive Las
Vegas Nevada 89107 T: 702-486-5205

Disclaimer
The Editor and Publishers of The Family & Local History Handbook make every effort to verify all information published. Nearly every organisation in this handbook has been contacted and asked to confirm that our information is correct. We provided reply paid envelopes and are grateful to those organisations who took the time to reply. We must express our disappointment that there were some organisations who did not reply. We cannot accept responsibilty for any errors or omissions or for any losses that may arise.

Advertisers are expected to provide a high standard of service to our readers. If there is a failure to provide such a service the Editor and Publishers reserve the right to refuse to accept advertising in future editions.

The Editor and Publishers cannot be held responsible for the errors, omissions or non performance by advertisers. Where an advertiser's performance falls below an acceptable level readers are asked to notify the Publisher in writing.

The views and opinions expressed in each of the articles are those of the author and do not necessarily reflect the opinions of the Editor.

Email and Internet or Web Addresses
Email and Web addresses shown in this book have been notified to us by the Organisation or advertiser. Unlike a normal postal address these addresses are subject to frequent change. In the case of businesses Email forwarding and Website transfer are usually provided by links to the original address. This does not always happen and the only solution is to use the various search engines available on the internet.

Browsers and Search engines will accept an address beginning with either http:// or www

Index to Advertisers

About the Editor and Publisher

Robert Blatchford LL.B (Hons)

s a law graduate of The University of Hull, England and has been involved in genealogy for several years. He is a member of The Society of Genealogists as well as Cleveland, The City of York, Devon, Dyfed, Glamorgan, Somerset & Dorset and Gwent Family History Societies. A member of The British Association for Local History and The Poppleton History Society. He is a former Chairman of The City of York Family History Society and former Vice Chairman of the North East Group of Family History Societies. He has undertaken research in the United Kingdom & Australia. He has undertaken research in England, Wales, Scotland, Belgium and France as well as in Ireland, Australia and the United States.

Published by
Robert Blatchford Publishing Ltd
33 Nursery Road, Nether Poppleton YORK, YO26 6NN England

E Mail: sales@genealogical.co.uk
WWW: www.genealogical.co.uk

The Genealogical Services Directory
1st Edition Published 1997
2nd Edition Published January 1998 (Revised & Reprinted April 1998)
3rd Edition Published January 1999
4th Edition Published January 2000

The Family & Local History Handbook
5th Edition Published January 2001   ISBN 0 9530297 4 3
6th Edition Published February 2002   ISBN 0 9530297 5 1
7th Edition Published February 2003   ISBN 0 9530297 6 X
8th Edition Published March 2004   ISBN 0 9530297 7 8
© 2004 Robert Blatchford

ISSN 1368-9150   ISBN 0 9530297 7 8

Printed by
AWP
9 Advance Workshops, Wild Street, Dukinfield SK16 4DL